Foundations of Contemporary Interpretation

Six Volumes In One

Foundations of Contemporary Interpretation

Six Volumes in One

V. Philips Long

Tremper Longman III

Richard A. Muller

Vern S. Poythress

Moisés Silva

Moisés Silva, General Editor

ZondervanPublishingHouse
Grand Rapids, Michigan

A Division of HarperCollins*Publishers*

Foundations of Contemporary Interpretation
Copyright © 1996 by The Zondervan Corporation

Has the Church Misread the Bible?
Copyright © 1987 by Moisés Silva

Literary Approaches to Biblical Interpretation
Copyright © 1987 by Tremper Longman III

God, Language and Scripture
Copyright © 1990 by Moisés Silva

The Art of Biblical History
Copyright © 1994 by V. Philips Long

Science and Hermeneutics
Copyright © 1988 by Vern S. Poythress

The Study of Theology
Copyright © 1991 by Richard A. Muller

Requests for information should be addressed to:

▦ ZondervanPublishingHouse
Grand Rapids, Michigan 49530

Library of Congress Cataloging-in-Publication Data

Silva, Moisés.
    Foundations of contemporary interpretation /Moisés Silva...[et. al.]
      p.   cm.
    Includes bibliographical references and indexes.
    Contents: Has the church misread the Bible?/ Moisés Silva — Literary approaches to biblical
interpretation / Tremper Longman III — God, language, and Scripture / Moisés Silva — The art of
biblical history / V. Philips Long — Science and hermeneutics / Vern S. Poythress — The study of
theology / Richard A. Muller — Indexes.
    ISBN 0–310–20828–9 (alk. paper)
    1. Bible—Hermeneutics. 2. Hermeneutics—Religious aspects—Christianity. I. Silva, Moisés.
BS476.F675 1996
220.6'01-dc 20   96–13830
                                                    CIP

Interior design by Sue Vandenberg Koppenol

Printed in the United States of America

96 97 98 99 00 01 02 03 /❖ DH/ 10 9 8 7 6 5 4 3 2 1

Contents

THE STUDY OF THEOLOGY
Richard A. Muller

Abbreviations

AARTT	American Academy of Religion Texts and Translations
AB	Anchor Bible
AnBib	Analecta biblica
ANF	*The Ante-Nicene Fathers*
ANRW	*Anstieg und Niedergang der römischen Welt*
BGBH	Beitrag zur Geschichte der biblischen Hermeneutik
Bib	*Biblica*
BJRL	*Bulletin of the John Rylands Library*
BJS	Brown Judaic Studies
BRE	Biblioteca románica española
BSac	*Bibliotheca sacra*
BT	*Bible Translator*
BTB	*Biblical Theology Bulletin*
CHB	*The Cambridge History of the Bible*
CBQ	*Catholic Biblical Quarterly*
CGNT	Cambridge Greek Testament Commentaries
CTL	Cambridge Textbooks in Linguistics
EI	*Eretz Israel*
FCI	Foundations of Contemporary Interpretation
FOTL	*Forms of the Old Testament Literature*, Eerdmans
GKC	Gesenius-Kautzsch-Cowley, *Hebrew Grammar*
GNT	Grundrisse zum Neuen Testament
HAC	*Hermeneutics, Authority, and Canon*
HIB	*Hermeneutics, Inerrancy, and the Bible*
Hth	*History and Theory*
HTR	*Harvard Theological Review*
ICBI	International Council for Biblical Inerrancy
IDB	*The Interpreter's Dictionary of the Bible*
Int	*Interpretation*
ISBE	*The International Standard Bible Encyclopedia (rev. ed.)*
JBL	*Journal of Biblical Literature*
JETS	*Journal of the Evangelical Theological Society*
JHI	*Journal of the History of Ideas*
JQRS	*Jewish Quarterly Review Supplement*
JSNT	*Journal for the Study of the New Testament*
JSOT	*Journal for the Study of the Old Testament*
JSOTS/ JSOTSS	Journal for the Study of the Old Testament Supplement Series

JTS	*Journal of Theological Studies*
LTCS	*Linguistics: The Cambridge Survey* (ed. Newmeyer, 1988)
MSU	Mitteilungen der Septuaginta-Unternehmens
NICNT	New International Commentary on the New Testament
NPNF	*The Nicene and Post-Nicene Fathers*
NTS	*New Testament Studies*
Proof	*Prooftexts: A Journal of Jewish Literary History*
PTS	Patristische Texte und Studien
RGG	*Die Religion in Geschichte und Gegenwart*
SBLDS	Society of Biblical Literature Dissertation Series
SBLMS	Society of Biblical Literature Monograph Series
SBLSS	Society of Biblical Literature Semeia Studies
SBS	Stuttgarter Bibelstudien
SBT	Studies in Biblical Theology
ScotBEv	*Scottish Bulletin of Evangelical Theology*
SJOT	*Scandinavian Journal of the Old Testament*
SJT	*Scottish Journal of Theology*
Them	*Themelios*
TrinJ	*Trinity Journal*
TynB	*Tyndale Bulletin*
VT	*Vetus Testamentum*
VTSup	Supplements to *Vetus Testamentum*
WBC	Word Biblical Commentaries
WEC	Wycliffe Exegetical Commentary
WTJ	*Westminster Theological Journal*
WUNT	Wissenschaftliche Untersuchungen zum Neuen Testament
ZAW	*Zeitschrift für die alttestamentliche Wissenschaft*

HAS
THE CHURCH
MISREAD
THE BIBLE?

*The History of Interpretation
in the Light of Current Issues*

Moisés Silva

Dedicated to the Memory of My Revered Teacher
EDWARD J. YOUNG
erudite scholar and humble believer,
whose hermeneutics reflected no conflict
between devotion to the Scriptures
and regard for the intellect

Contents

Preface

*T*he first chapter of this book serves as an introduction to the series *Foundations of Contemporary Interpretation* as a whole. It is therefore unnecessary here to describe its purpose in detail.

It may be useful, however, to point out that all of the contributors, committed as they are to the divine authority of Scripture, assume from the start that a right relationship with its divine author is the most fundamental prerequisite for proper biblical interpretation. The point needs to be stressed here precisely because the series itself does not attempt to develop that truth. This volume and those that follow it are addressed primarily to readers who share such a commitment with the authors.

The problem is that this theological conviction, while essential for a true understanding of Scripture, does not by itself guarantee that we will interpret Scripture aright. We have become increasingly aware that the interpretation of *any* document is fraught with many and serious difficulties. What, then, are those principles that concern *general* hermeneutics? And how do those principles bear on our understanding of the Bible?

A satisfactory response to these questions requires the concerted effort of scholars who are willing to move beyond the narrow confines of exegesis as such. Indeed, one is hard-pressed to think of an academic discipline that does not have something substantive to contribute to our concerns. Each volume in the present series addresses one discipline that seems distinctly promising in aiding the work of biblical exegesis.

Our main audience consists of seminary students who have at least an initial acquaintance with theological scholarship and who are willing to ask the hard questions, even when simple answers are nowhere to be found. As seminarians prepare to take positions of leadership in ecclesiastical and academic settings, this important period in their theological formation must develop in them a genuine appreciation of the foundational problems faced by biblical exegetes. Perhaps our efforts will aid today's students to provide some of the answers we ourselves have failed to give them.

The series is intended, however, to reach a broader readership as well. On the one hand, each contributor seeks to make the material clear and accessible to lay Christians who see the need to be fully informed in this important field of hermeneutics. On the other hand, the volumes are carefully documented in the footnotes so that advanced students and scholars can pursue special points of interest in the literature.

The reader should note that the term *hermeneutics* is used here in its traditional sense, namely, the study of those principles that should guide our work of interpretation. This decision, however, is not meant to prejudge the question whether biblical hermeneutics should concern itself with the present significance of a text (and not only with its original meaning). On the contrary, this issue will occupy us repeatedly in the course of the series.

The more recent term *hermeneutic,* though often used to describe a specific approach to interpretation (as in "the new hermeneutic"), is rather vague. We shall avoid this term except in certain contexts in which a contrast with *hermeneutics* is necessary. Unless otherwise specified, no distinction is intended between the terms *presupposition* and *preunderstanding*—much less by the use of such pairs of words as *interpretive/interpretative* (the first of which, though sometimes ridiculed, has a noble pedigree reaching back to at least the eighteenth century), *method/methodology, synonymy/synonymity,* etc. On stylistic questions of this sort, the authors follow their own preferences.

The present series is launched with the conviction, not only that the Christian church faces a grave challenge, but also that God, who has not left his people alone, will surely guide them to a full knowledge of his truth.

one

TODAY'S HERMENEUTICAL CHALLENGE

*T*he radio speaker that Sunday morning was a successful minister in one of the major Protestant denominations. His text was Acts 5. His topic was "power." He spoke eloquently of the many ways in which most of us misuse our authority. Parents abuse their children by their negativism. Government leaders show insensitivity to the pains of those in need. We destroy by our criticism when we should build up with our praise.

As he approached the last part of his radio message, the preacher finally came to his text. In the narrative of Acts he found a dramatic example of the misuse of power. Ananias and Sapphira, weak Christians who had just given in to their temptations, were in need of reassurance and upbuilding. The apostle Peter, in an ugly display of arrogance, abused his authority and denounced their conduct with awful threats. Terror consumed each of them in turn, and they died on the spot under Peter's unbearable invective.

Most readers of this book will no doubt shake their heads in unbelief at such an example of biblical interpretation. But how can we account for it? This preacher was not an ignoramus but a very well-educated minister serving a sophisticated middle-class parish in a Philadelphia suburb. The exegetical tools he was given during his theological training were probably not significantly different from those of most other seminarians. Most disturbing of all, the very *process* going on in his mind as he arrived at an interpretation of Acts 5 was basically the same process all of us use—not only in interpreting Scripture but also in our understanding of a social conversation, the morning paper, or the evening news.

The history of the Christian church, like the history of society generally, has been characterized by repeated conflicts regarding the interpretation of evidence. Precisely because Christians place enormous significance on the Bible, disagreements regarding *biblical* evidence can have serious consequences.

In our day, however, "the hermeneutical issue" has surfaced with a vengeance. Only a generation ago, conservative Christians enjoyed a sense of unity in their interpretation of the Bible. They knew, of course, that differences existed among various denominations and that some of these differences touched on matters of considerable importance, such as the meaning and practice of baptism, the proper understanding of sanctification, expectations regarding the end times, and so on. Relatively few people, however, seemed to appreciate the implications of this state of affairs; and no one was arguing that Evangelicals were faced with a hermeneutical crisis.

There must be some way to account for that period of innocence. Perhaps it is simply that a conservative Methodist could listen to a conservative Baptist and agree with 99 percent of what he or she heard. A sermon on the parable of the Prodigal Son would sound basically the same, whether it came from a Pentecostal evangelist or from a Presbyterian theologian. With so much obvious agreement, who would stop to worry about differences in interpretation?

But things have changed. As many have pointed out, one can no longer assume that an individual who professes an evangelical faith will hold "the party line" on key social and ethical issues such as capital punishment, abortion, nuclear armament, divorce, premarital sex, or homosexuality.

> Contemporary evangelicals are finding it difficult to achieve anything like a consensus on each succeeding theological topic they address. Moreover, they seem stymied in any effort toward unity, unable to agree on a collective interpretive strategy for moving beyond their current impasse. . . . If evangelicals cannot discover a way to move more effectively toward theological consensus, can they still maintain in good conscience their claim to Biblical authority as a hallmark?[1]

Gone are the days when one could predict where a biblical scholar would come down on the date of the Exodus, the authorship of Isaiah, and comparable critical questions. As if to dramatize the depth of the hermeneutical disarray, conservatives could not even agree on how to handle the publication, in 1982, of a commentary by a prominent evangelical scholar who argued that many events related in the Gospel of Matthew are not to be interpreted as fully historical.[2]

Already in the late 1970s, members of the International Council for Biblical Inerrancy recognized the need to address hermeneutical principles if their claims for biblical authority were to mean anything and, as a result, held the ICBI Summit II in 1982. Sixteen papers, covering a wide range of topics in the area of hermeneutics, were presented and discussed at this meeting and then published in a hefty volume.[3] The participants represented the

---

[1]Robert K. Johnston, *Evangelicals at an Impasse: Biblical Authority in Practice* (Atlanta: John Knox, 1979), pp. 147 and 7.

[2]Robert H. Gundry, *Matthew: A Commentary on His Literary and Theological Art* (Grand Rapids: Eerdmans, 1982). For a summary of the controversy, which led to Gundry's resignation from the Evangelical Theological Society, see *Christianity Today* 28:2 (Feb. 3, 1984): 36–38.

[3]Earl D. Radmacher and Robert D. Preus, eds., *Hermeneutics, Inerrancy, and the Bible* (Grand Rapids: Zondervan, 1984), hereafter *HIB*. Note, incidentally, Elliott Johnson's comment: "In a sense, evangelicals have lived with an interpretational truce" (p. 409).

conservative wing of Evangelicalism and thus from the start agreed on some very basic issues. Moreover, they reached the necessary consensus to produce a significant document, "The Chicago Statement on Biblical Hermeneutics."

And yet all was not well. A reviewer of *HIB* commented,

> I was left with a nagging question: if, as the participants affirm, the meaning in each biblical text is "single, definite and fixed" and applies to all cultural contexts, and the Holy Spirit alone enables believers to apply the scripture to their lives, to what purpose are these nine hundred pages of argument?[4]

Although this objection reveals a failure to grasp the intent of the participants, the Chicago Statement nevertheless makes biblical interpretation sound easier than it often is. The very discussions at the summit show that the participants, when dealing with a number of crucial interpretive issues, found oneness of mind to be a very distant hope indeed.[5]

One attempt to deal with this hermeneutical crisis has been to argue that the doctrine of inerrancy *entails* certain interpretive positions. In the face of turmoil, this approach is very tempting because it appears to eliminate, with one stroke, a variety of undesirable viewpoints.

Such a move, however, has desperation written all over it, and it undermines the very task of interpretation. The truth of scriptural authority does not automatically tell us what a given passage means: it does assure us that, once we have correctly identified the biblical teaching (in other words, proper interpretation is assumed), that teaching may be trusted unequivocally.[6] At any rate, the very events that have led to the present crisis show rather clearly—unpleasant as this may sound—that a sincere and intelligent commitment to the classical doctrine of biblical inerrancy in no way guarantees that an individual will adopt expected interpretations.

One could argue that the present impasse is the result of accumulated hermeneutical assumptions, unspoken and even unconscious. And it is probably no accident that similar tensions have surfaced in other fields, including literary criticism and science. *Foundations of Contemporary Interpretation* is an attempt to make a positive contribution to this general problem by drawing on a variety of disciplines. We hope thereby to focus on the debate at its most fundamental level. This level is not that of "special hermeneutics" (the specific principles one must keep in mind when interpreting prophecy, parables, etc.), nor is it a question of determining whether a particular critical tool (form criticism, redaction criticism, etc.) is legitimate. Rather we are concerned with the basic processes that affect our understanding of everything we see, hear, or read.

---

[4]C. S. Rodd, *Book List* (n.p.: Society for Old Testament Study, 1986), p. 94.

[5]See esp. chaps. 2, 4, and 7, dealing respectively with historical problems, normativeness, and authorial intention. Other evangelical scholars, though themselves clearly committed to inerrancy, from time to time express dissatisfaction with some aspects of ICBI; see D. A. Carson and John D. Woodbridge, eds., *Hermeneutics, Authority, and Canon* (Grand Rapids: Zondervan, 1986), hereafter *HAC*, pp. 7, 64–69. As the following material will make clear, however, the current "hermeneutical crisis" affects others besides Evangelicals. Fundamental interpretive questions are being debated across the various fields of biblical scholarship, conservative and liberal alike.

[6]I have treated this matter in greater detail in my inaugural lecture, "Old Princeton, Westminster, and Inerrancy," forthcoming in *WTJ* 50 (1988).

Scholars have traditionally used the term *general hermeneutics* to identify our topic, and the most successful writers in this field have cast their net widely in their attempt to identify those elements that characterize the sane interpretation of any document.[7] This task has been made more difficult by the explosion of knowledge in the twentieth century. The present series seeks to introduce the student to those areas that seem to provide the most relevant points of contact with biblical interpretation. I survey here six of these areas.

PHILOSOPHY

One of the most remarkable developments in the history of philosophy took place at the beginning of this century, when a number of leading British thinkers, disenchanted with much of current philosophical reflection, concluded that the real business of philosophy was not to build speculative systems but simply to analyze the way language is used. This apparently modest goal led to an almost complete reorientation of the way "one does philosophy" in Britain and America. *Analytical Philosophy,* whatever its weaknesses, has had some salutary effects, especially through its emphasis on the study of linguistic data.[8]

Across the English Channel, to be sure, it was pretty much business as usual. And yet even in the Continent, philosophers were showing increasing interest in the phenomenon of language. In their case, it was a matter of pursuing questions that have plagued philosophers even before Socrates decided to make a nuisance of himself. More to the point, some nineteenth-century idealists had expended considerable effort seeking to develop an encompassing (and speculative) philosophy of language. This interest forms part of the background for the development of certain movements, particularly existentialism, that have had great impact on the course taken by European philosophers in the twentieth century.[9]

This idealist tradition is vulnerable to some powerful criticisms, yet within the context of that tradition some of the most crucial questions about hermeneutics have arisen. Such thinkers as Martin Heidegger, for example, have forced us to take seriously the role that *preunderstanding* plays in the process of interpretation.[10] None of us is able to approach new data with a blank mind, and so our attempts to understand new information consist largely of adjusting our prior "framework of understanding"—integrating the new into the old.

---

[7]See the old classic by Milton S. Terry, *Biblical Interpretation: A Treatise on the Interpretation of the Old and New Testaments,* rev. ed. (New York: Easton & Maines, 1890), p. 17. Friedrich Schleiermacher is usually regarded as the first scholar to insist that biblical hermeneutics must be part of a general theory of understanding.

[8]Particularly striking is the way modern linguists, though starting from quite different perspectives and interested in "purely scientific" endeavors, have developed formulations that coincide significantly with those of Anglo-Saxon philosophers. See M. Silva, *Biblical Words and Their Meaning: An Introduction to Lexical Semantics* (Grand Rapids: Zondervan, 1983), p. 106n.

[9]For a brief but useful description of Continental views on language, see Kenneth Hamilton, *Words and the Word* (Grand Rapids: Eerdmans, 1971), pp. 28–36.

[10]The views of Heidegger are treated, among other works, in Richard E. Palmer, *Hermeneutics: Interpretation Theory in Schleiermacher, Dilthey, Heidegger, and Gadamer* (Evanston: Northwestern University Press, 1969), and in Anthony C. Thiselton, *The Two Horizons: New Testament Hermeneutics and Philosophical Description* (Grand Rapids: Eerdmans, 1980).

These ideas have immediate consequences for the way we interpret the Bible and do theology. The common insistence that we should approach the text without any prior ideas regarding its meaning becomes almost irrelevant. And the standard advice given to theological students to study the text before consulting commentaries, or to determine its meaning before considering its application, appears self-defeating. Perhaps we are unable to find out what a passage meant to its original audience except by way of our own situation!

Could it be that it is impossible to shed our presuppositions precisely because it is they that mediate understanding? If so, do we drown in our subjectivity and abandon the goal of objective exegesis? Is every interpretive effort destined to be relativized by the reality of our situation?

One can hardly think of a more fundamental set of questions to ask. These questions will not go away, and adequate answers require careful and patient reflection. One of the volumes in this series will seek to clarify the nature of the problem and suggest responsible approaches toward a solution.

LITERARY CRITICISM

Philosophical discussions about meaning are quickly taken up by literary critics—understandably so, since their livelihood depends on their ability to say something about what a literary piece "means." In their own way, however, critics have contributed significantly to the present skepticism.

A few generations ago, it seemed obvious to all that a student of literature was supposed to determine the intention of the original author of a piece. Great effort was therefore expended on discovering as much as possible about the author, the circumstances in which the piece was written, and so forth. But then a reaction developed among a number of scholars who argued that the literary piece itself had an existence quite independent of its author. The meaning of the composition, therefore, could not be tied to the author's intention. New questions were being posed, particularly with regard to the ambiguity that is so characteristic of poetry.

> Instead of asking "Does the text mean this or that?" with a "Tea or coffee?" intonation, implying that only one answer can be chosen, critics began to ask "Can the text mean this or that?" with a "Cigarettes or liquor?" intonation, seeing a text as a bag of mysteries not advertised on the surface. (There is some debate whether the author knows what he has packed.) To take an example, in Marvell's lines:
>
> > *Meanwhile the mind, from pleasure less,*
> > *Withdraws into its happiness*
>
> should we understand that the mind is less because of pleasure or that because of pleasure the mind withdraws? The answer now was to be "Both—and what else can you find?"[11]

When some of the philosophical currents discussed previously join forces with this approach to literature, the results can be unnerving. Some years back E. D. Hirsch

---

[11]G. W. Turner, *Stylistics* (Baltimore: Penguin, 1973), pp. 100–101. Turner further remarks, "If intention is not to be the criterion for understanding a poem, should a poet read reviews of his own poetry to find out what it means? If he disagrees with a consensus of critics, who is right?" (p. 148).

mounted a valiant attack on these forces by presenting a fresh argument that supported the importance of an author's intent. He has truly been a voice crying in the wilderness, however, and the current scholarly orthodoxy views him as something of an anomaly. He has found, to be sure, a very receptive audience among evangelical theologians, although enthusiasm for his argument seems to be declining.[12]

At any rate, it is worthwhile noting here that the classic formulations of the doctrine of inerrancy placed considerable emphasis on the need to ascertain the intention, or purpose, of the biblical author. Surely one cannot attribute infallibility to arbitrary and haphazard inferences from a biblical passage—one must know what the writer "really meant." In one of the fundamental papers expounding the evangelical view of inspiration, Hodge and Warfield assumed that the primary question to be asked was that of the biblical author's "professed or implied purpose." They asserted: "Exegesis must be historical as well as grammatical, and must always seek the meaning *intended,* not any meaning that can be tortured out of a passage."[13]

In view of this connection between the doctrine of infallibility and the need to determine the biblical writer's intended meaning, one can see that recent developments in literary criticism have clear implications for biblical authority. Some contemporary voices have in fact argued (rather naïvely, it seems to me) that Evangelicals ought to stop wasting their time fussing over inerrancy: after all, these critics claim, any appeal to an author's intent is passé!

But there is more. In recent years a growing number of biblical scholars have argued for the need to use the tools and methods of literary criticism in the interpretation of the Bible. A thriving section in the Society of Biblical Literature, for example, is devoted to rhetorical criticism, which attempts to understand biblical material as carefully composed literary works.

The extent to which the Bible may or may not be viewed as a work of art has long been a matter of debate, with no less a literary critic than C. S. Lewis arguing that, because of its sacred character, Scripture

> does not invite, it excludes or repels, the merely aesthetic approach. You can read it as literature only by a *tour de force.* You are cutting the wood against the grain, using the tool for a purpose it was not intended to serve. It demands incessantly to be taken on its own terms: it will not continue to give literary delight very long except to those who go for it for something quite different.[14]

Any person's view on this question will depend largely on how the expression *work of art* is understood, but no reasonable person is likely to deny that, at least in some sense, the biblical books are literature and therefore patient of literary study. Again, different scholars

---

[12]E. D. Hirsch, Jr., *Validity in Interpretation* (New Haven: Yale University Press, 1967). Though critical of Hirsch in some important respects, Charles Altieri takes seriously and reformulates some elements of his work; see Altieri, *Act and Quality: A Theory of Literary Meaning and Humanistic Understanding* (Amherst: University of Massachusetts Press, 1981), chap. 3, esp. pp. 143–59. Hirsch is referred to frequently in *HIB.* On the other hand, note the qualifications expressed by Vern S. Poythress in "Analysing a Biblical Text: Some Important Linguistic Distinctions," *SJT* 32 (1979): 113–37.

[13]A. A. Hodge and B. B. Warfield, *Inspiration* (Grand Rapids: Baker, 1979; orig. 1881), pp. 42–43. On the problems associated with such terms as *purpose* and *intention,* see my article "Old Princeton, Westminster, and Inerrancy."

[14]C. S. Lewis, *The Literary Impact of the Authorised Version* (London: University of London, 1950), p. 25.

will view specific approaches, such as that of structuralism, with varying degrees of sympathy, but all will recognize that literary sensitivity is a significant aid to the appreciation of the Bible.

The question becomes truly problematic, however, in the attempt to relate literature and history. Earlier biblical scholarship (both liberal and conservative) is often criticized for paying too much attention to the historicity of biblical stories. If conservative scholars wonder what may have motivated a biblical character to act in a particular way, they are chastised for focusing on the historical event rather than on the literary skills of the biblical author. If liberal scholars ridicule a conservative reading of some historical portion, they too are criticized for missing the point. In other words, we are told that asking historical kinds of questions is basically irrelevant. One proponent of this point of view suggests that "the new literary criticism may be described as inherently ahistorical." He further comments: "Consideration of the Bible as literature is itself the beginning and end of scholarly endeavor. The Bible is taken first and finally as a literary object."[15]

In view of this wide range of complicated and intimidating questions, one of the most demanding volumes in our series will be devoted to literary approaches in the interpretation of the Scriptures.

LINGUISTICS

Some years back, while visiting an evangelical seminary, I was having lunch with several students, and the conversation turned, as it so often does, to the question of whether learning the biblical languages is really necessary. One of the students, who gave every indication of being highly motivated, raised the issue in a particularly interesting way. "I can appreciate," he said, "the value and importance of learning Greek. There are many passages in the New Testament in which the author's meaning becomes clearer by paying attention to the precise nuances and distinctions he's using. But I don't find that's the case with Hebrew. One spends a lot of time and effort on Hebrew but there seems to be very little pay-off."

No doubt many other students have felt the same way (to judge by the number of ministers that do not keep up their Hebrew). In one sense we may agree with this student's evaluation. Relative to the Old Testament, the New Testament contains much more material of an expressly theological character. Jesus' debates with his opponents, for example, and Paul's polemical writings often require a kind of attention to details that may be unnecessary, or even inappropriate, when studying Old Testament narrative or poetry.

To put it differently, much of the Old Testament consists of material written in a somewhat expansive style, in which repetition and stylistic variations play a prominent role; in such a case, meaning is conveyed by the impact of large sections as a whole and seldom by the precise force of individual words and sentences. In a passage such as Galatians 3, however, a great deal of conceptual richness is concentrated within brief sections; as a result, one is frequently faced by conflicting interpretations of individual clauses.

But the student to whom I was speaking did not really have in mind differences in content and style. The very fact that Hebrew is Hebrew, he seemed to think, makes it less susceptible to exegetical richness. My response to him was not that he had failed

[15]D. Robertson, "Literature, the Bible as," *IDB Supplementary Volume,* pp. 547–51, esp. p. 548.

to appreciate the special nuances of Hebrew words and syntax; rather, I argued that he was probably misusing his Greek.

In the interest of encouraging students to learn their Greek well, many teachers and writers have unwittingly created an unrealistic picture of how language works. A large number of people, for example, perceive Greek as perhaps the richest and most precise language that has ever been used, and it is taken for granted that Greek writers must have exploited semantic nuances, subtle tense distinctions, and syntactic variations to express their meaning in the fullest and clearest fashion possible.

Part of the problem is that in the nineteenth century the leading philologists shared an exaggerated high opinion of the classical languages.[16] Since Greek culture and literature had undoubtedly reached levels of greatness, it was assumed that a similar greatness must be attributed to the linguistic medium, that is, to the very *form* of communication. Understandably, Christians deduced that God must have chosen Greek as the medium to communicate the gospel because it was the "best" language available. With regard to the New Testament too, therefore, there was a tendency to confuse the value of the message with that of the medium. The following quotation is only one of many typical assessments:

> The Greek language is the beautiful flower, the elegant jewel, the most finished masterpiece of Indo-Germanic thought. . . . Its syntax is organized on the most perfect system. . . . [With the coming of the gospel] the Greek language had now to perform a work for which it had providentially been preparing, and yet one which it had never yet attempted, namely, to convey the divine revelation to mankind. [As a result the language was] employed by the Spirit of God, and transformed and transfigured, yes, glorified, with a light and sacredness that the classic literature never possessed.[17]

In the early decades of this century, however, a radically new conception of language began to develop. One important contributing factor in this change was the discovery and careful study of numerous "primitive" languages that proved to be every bit as complicated as Greek. The system of five or more cases found in the classical languages cannot hold a candle, for example, to the numerous morphological distinctions that exist in the Bantu tongues. And if the verbal system of Greek seems involved, what is one to say of Basque?

Moreover, it is now clear that the number of vocabulary items—and the consequent potential for semantic distinctions—in a language is a function of the interests and needs of a particular society, not a quality inherent in the language itself. Certainly the lexicon of contemporary English exceeds by many times what was available in Ancient Greek. And in spite of frequent warnings that linguistic corruptions have set English on a course of self-destruction, it is arguable that the morphological and syntactic simplicity into which English has evolved has resulted in a more flexible, efficient, and enduring system of communication.[18]

---

[16]According to Edward Sapir, most nineteenth-century "linguistic theorists themselves spoke languages of a certain type, of which the most fully developed varieties were the Latin and Greek that they had learned in their childhood. It was not difficult for them to be persuaded that these familiar languages represented the 'highest' development that speech had yet attained and that all other types were but steps on the way to this beloved 'inflective' type" (*Language: An Introduction to the Study of Speech* [New York: Harcourt, Brace & World, 1949; orig. 1921], p. 123).

[17]Charles A. Briggs, *General Introduction to the Study of Holy Scripture*, rev. ed. (Grand Rapids: Baker, 1970; orig. 1900), pp. 64, 67, 70–71.

[18]See Otto Jespersen, *Language: Its Nature, Development, and Origin* (New York: Norton, 1964; orig. 1921), pp. 332–34.

Be that as it may, the modern study of language (general linguistics) affects quite directly the way we interpret ancient texts like the Bible. The value of studying the biblical languages does not reside in its potential for displaying exegetical razzle-dazzle. In fact, striking interpretations that lean too heavily, sometimes exclusively, on subtle grammatical distinctions are seldom worth considering. On the other hand, genuine familiarity with Greek (and Hebrew!) develops sensitivity and maturity in the interpreter and allows his or her decisions to be built on a much broader base of information. More often than not, the fruit of language learning is intangible: it remains in the background, providing the right perspective for responsible exegesis.

Linguistics, however, does more than alter our attitude to the study of the biblical languages. It formulates principles and provides techniques for the analysis of written and oral communication. One volume in this series will summarize those areas of modern linguistics that appear most relevant for the development of biblical hermeneutics.

HISTORY

Still another volume in this series will be devoted to a very important set of questions arising from the fact that the biblical books were written within the context of an ancient culture. As we noted in our discussion of literary criticism, some scholars would argue that concern over history has been detrimental to biblical interpretation—that asking the question "What really happened?" has distracted us from the more important issue, "What is the *text* really saying?"

There clearly is a measure of truth in that criticism. Many of us are tempted to speculate about historical questions that are not at all addressed by the text (e.g., where did Cain get his wife? did Paul know that the earth is not flat?), and so we fall into the danger of missing the thrust of the passage itself. As usually formulated, however, the criticism implies a facile dichotomy between history and literature, and most biblical scholars would insist that the historical approach must continue to hold some sort of priority in the interpretive task. We should not infer that all of these scholars have high regard for the trustworthiness of the biblical narratives. Unfortunately, a good many specialists have concluded that significant portions of the Bible have little or no factual basis. And while the mainstream of biblical scholarship does not show nearly the degree of skepticism that was common a couple of generations ago, *some* skepticism is regarded as essential to the historical method.[19] As a result, a growing number of conservative scholars are becoming hesitant to apply the doctrine of infallibility to all the historical claims of Scripture.

The hermeneutical implications are obvious. Does a narrative passage in the Old Testament *mean* what it appears to be saying? If it does, according to some scholars, one still needs to decide whether the story is *factual* or not, whether the biblical author was accurate or in error. The other approach—that of some literary critics—argues that the

---

[19]Part of the reason for skepticism, of course, is that historians in all fields are expected to judge the reliability of their sources; see Marc Bloch, *The Historian's Craft* (New York: Knopf, 1963), chap. 3, "Historical Criticism," the most substantial chapter in the book, devoted to developing an informed skepticism. But biblical scholars, more often than not, find it necessary to make the point that the Bible cannot be trusted implicitly; see, for example, W. G. Kümmel, *The New Testament: The History of the Investigation of Its Problems* (Nashville: Abingdon, 1972), esp. p. 30, where the author, after praising the sixteenth-century Reformer M. Flacius, proceeds to condemn his approach as unhistorical on the grounds that Flacius did not allow for contradictions in Scripture.

passage does *not* mean what it appears to be saying, that the historical question is more or less irrelevant for determining the meaning of the passage.

To further complicate this discussion, one must consider the character of ancient historiography. Quite apart from the "literature versus history" debate, it is clear that contemporary historians produce works that differ in some important respects from ancient historical sources. What with quotation marks, square brackets, ellipsis points, footnotes, and so on, modern readers expect a measure of precision that was unknown to the ancients.

But just how great are the differences between the two types of history writing? And to what extent do differences in literary genre affect our answer to this question? Most evangelical scholars recognize that the discourses in the Book of Job, whatever their historical basis, reflect a certain measure of literary creativity. Not many, however, are ready to concede that the Book of Jonah relates a fictional story. Fewer still would agree that the gospel writers embellished their narratives with made-up stories about the life of Christ. Unfortunately, little has been done to formulate the criteria for determining whether a passage is intended to be taken as factual.

As if these questions were not enough, one must also face broader philosophical concerns that relate to all history writing, whether ancient or modern. Is it possible, as a number of prominent thinkers argue, that in principle *no narrative* can give an objective account of the past?[20] Must we admit that we are effectively cut off from the past? Only a minority of writers in the field accept these extreme conclusions, but the debate has forced a reconsideration of fundamental assumptions, many of which are directly relevant to the interpretive task.

In spite of all these obstacles to the historical interpretation of Scripture, historical research will continue to play a central role in the study of the Bible. But how is that role to be defined? It could be argued that, if our understanding of the Bible depends on extrabiblical data (from archaeology, for example), the believer becomes a slave to scholarly research and analysis.

Evangelicals, however, have seldom been shy to make use of archaeological discoveries; if anything, they may have been too quick to press such data into apologetic service. Some indeed would claim that conservatives tend to be unfairly selective of the material they use for their purposes. In any case, there must be some methodological boundary lines in the use (positive or negative) of extrabiblical material; more effort must be expended in formulating what those limits should be.

Of particular significance is the task of historical reconstruction. Quite often historical reconstruction implies a rejection of large portions of the biblical narrative. This inference is of course unnecessary. Any attempt to fill in historical details not explicitly stated in Scripture, such as the date of Jesus' birth or the length of his ministry, are exercises in historical reconstruction. Whenever conservatives seek to reconcile two biblical accounts that differ from each other (e.g., the nativity accounts in Matthew and Luke), they are involved in reconstructing history.[21]

---

[20]Well known in this connection is Jack W. Meiland, *Scepticism and Historical Knowledge* (New York: Random House, 1965). For a recent and very clear discussion of the issue, see R. F. Atkinson, *Knowledge and Explanation in History: An Introduction to the Philosophy of History* (Ithaca: Cornell University Press, 1978), chap. 2.

[21]I have made this point in "The Place of Historical Reconstruction in New Testament Criticism," in *HAC*, pp. 109–33.

Why, then, is there such wide disagreement between liberals and conservatives in this field? Does a commitment to the proposition that the Bible teaches no errors automatically place some limits on our historical investigation or analysis? If so, what precisely are those limits? Is it possible that we have merely *assumed,* but have not demonstrated, what those limits should be?

In addition to historical analysis and archaeological research, the student of ancient culture needs to pay attention to other disciplines that help to place literary documents in their proper context. Cultural anthropology, for example, has a great deal to contribute, even though biblical scholars seldom make use of it. More recently a number of researchers have placed much emphasis on sociological interpretations of the biblical books, a type of analysis that is certain to become more common in the near future.[22]

This proliferation of methods and materials makes it all the more urgent that the study of ancient culture be done within a framework that is hermeneutically coherent. The haphazard and undisciplined use of data that has characterized much biblical exegesis in the past needs to be challenged and corrected.

SCIENCE

Scientific work too involves both the collection and the *interpretation* of data. If we speak of a certain "hermeneutic" intrinsic to the scientific method, can biblical interpreters learn anything from it? The difficulties and uncertainties that attend the interpretation of literary, linguistic, and historical data may appear to us to be absent from scientific analysis. We generally think of the "hard sciences" as enjoying a measure of precision and certainty not attainable by the humanities. We realize, to be sure, that scientists sometimes formulate highly debatable theories, but we assume that such theories can and should be clearly distinguished from the facts. Thus Evangelicals often argue, and with some reason, that there is no conflict between science (i.e., "facts") and the Bible, that the conflict arises when certain modern theories are treated as scientific facts. In drawing a sharp—and, as we shall see, naïve—dichotomy between fact and theory, the Evangelical is hardly alone. This approach is common and popular, even among many scientists.

In the course of the present century, however, researchers have become increasingly aware of the extent to which the observer affects the identification of the data. Werner Heisenberg's well-known uncertainty principle has been popularized frequently enough to make most of us, even if quite innocent of subatomic physics, a little more skeptical than we used to be.

But the problem is more serious. Every *description* of data necessarily involves a measure of interpretation, that is, a theoretical framework that makes the description meaningful. What persuades an individual scientist, or a community of scientists, to prefer one such theoretical framework rather than another one (e.g., a Copernican view of our planetary system rather than the Ptolemaic universe)? "The facts," we might respond. But which facts? And how many of them?

---

[22]See the clear descriptions by Robert R. Wilson, *Sociological Approaches to the Old Testament* (Philadelphia: Fortress, 1984), and Derek Tidball, *The Social Context of the New Testament: A Sociological Analysis* (Grand Rapids: Zondervan, 1984).

Attempting to answer questions of this sort, Thomas S. Kuhn, more than two decades ago, proposed to study the way scientific revolutions come about.[23] His analysis provoked a revolution of its own, and writers in a wide variety of disciplines have since devoted a great deal of attention to the issues he has formulated. For Kuhn, all scientific theories, even those universally accepted, are basically *paradigms,* or models, that attempt to account for as much data as possible. No theory satisfactorily explains all of the data; one always encounters *anomalies,* facts that refuse to fit the theory. Much sixteenth-century resistance to the Copernican view, for example, cannot be explained as mere dogmatism; significant pockets of the scientific community refused to give up the Ptolemaic theory, though old and shaky, for the sake of a new interpretation that could *not* explain all the facts either.

In the course of his discussion, Kuhn makes many provocative suggestions, challenging long-established ideas regarding the role of scientific discovery. He has produced some fiercely loyal followers and not a few determined opponents who charge him, among other things, with espousing a dangerous form of relativism.[24] However we may respond to Kuhn's own analysis, he clearly has raised the most fundamental questions faced by the philosophy of science—indeed, by any discipline that occupies itself with the interpretation of data.

Not surprisingly, a number of theologians and exegetes have sought to appropriate these insights in their attempt to determine why different scholars or groups of scholars reach different interpretations of biblical passages. Can we understand hermeneutical changes as "paradigm shifts" of some sort? Are exegetical problems mere "anomalies" to be adjusted to the general theory? What is the connection between these discussions in the scientific community and current philosophical concerns with "preunderstanding"? And how do these concerns fit into the broader (and older) debate of whether theology itself may be regarded as a science? We may be sure that paying attention to problems in the philosophy of science will be of considerable aid in clarifying the role of biblical hermeneutics.

THEOLOGY

We have noticed, time and again in our brief survey so far, the recurrence of a basic question: What is the role of our preunderstanding in the process of interpretation? The question must now be raised once more in connection with the very discipline of which biblical exegesis is a part. Surely no one comes to the biblical text without certain *theological* presuppositions. How do those presuppositions affect our exegesis of that text?

Special attention needs to be given to the relationship between biblical exegesis and the other theological disciplines, such as biblical theology, historical and systematic theology, church history, and practical theology. The term *theological encyclopedia,* though not very common nowadays, conveniently focuses on the various elements that constitute an appropriate theological curriculum.[25] Is there a coherent logic to the traditional

---

[23]Thomas S. Kuhn, *The Structure of Scientific Revolutions,* 2d ed. (Chicago: University of Chicago Press, 1970; 1st ed. 1960).

[24]The various facets of the debate can be gleaned from several collections of articles, such as Gary Gutting, ed., *Paradigms and Revolutions: Appraisals and Applications of Thomas Kuhn's Philosophy of Science* (Notre Dame: University of Notre Dame Press, 1980).

[25]One of the most important works in this field is Abraham Kuyper, *Encyclopaedie der heilige godgeleerdheid,* 2d ed., 3 vols. (Kampen: J. H. Kok, 1908–9), part of the first edition of which was translated into English

theological encyclopedia? Can we adequately formulate how the various disciplines affect hermeneutical decisions?

A common way of expressing the relationship between the various parts of the theological encyclopedia is to view biblical criticism (including the biblical languages, historical backgrounds, literary questions, etc.) as foundational. Biblical exegesis—the detailed historico-grammatical analysis of discrete passages—builds on that foundation. The next step is biblical theology, which attempts a measure of synthesis by focusing on the distinctive teaching of individual writers (e.g., Pauline theology) or of well-defined historical periods (e.g., postexilic theology). This approach pays considerable attention to the issues of historical development and theological diversity, asking, for example, whether there is a *single* New Testament theology.

A more ambitious task is that of synthesizing the teaching of Scripture as a whole. This project is the goal of systematic theology, which requires careful attention to the development of dogma in the history of the church as well as familiarity with current cultural and philosophical concerns. Finally, there is the whole range of questions associated with practical theology: how does one communicate to present-day lay people the results of these prior disciplines? how do we present the gospel to unbelievers of various backgrounds? how does the church give expression to its faith in worship?

Anyone familiar with seminary curricula realizes that no school follows this pattern in strict sequence—as though a seminarian had to wait until the very last term to take courses in practical theology! Moreover, even apart from pragmatic academic considerations, there are substantive reasons for not following a "logical" sequence of courses. The truth is that one cannot really practice, say, biblical exegesis without taking into account the concerns of systematic theology; similarly, it would be artificial to suggest that we must not or cannot address the problems posed by practical ministry until we have fully explored the area of biblical theology.

It may appear logical to require an unbiased exegesis of all the biblical passages that touch on the nature of Christ before formulating a comprehensive christology. The problem is, however, that our exegesis is always influenced by any ideas that we may consciously or unconsciously hold regarding Christ. And even if we could avoid being influenced by those ideas, we should not do so, for they provide the means to process and understand the new information that we may gather from the text. We should keep in mind that the church has made great advances in scriptural knowledge, and it would be tragic if we were to ignore all of that understanding in our own study. It is actually an illusion to think that we can somehow skip over those centuries and face the teaching of Scripture directly, with a blank mind and without the counsel of those who have gone before us.

The reader may sense something of a paradox here. Our formulation of a theological doctrine depends on the text of Scripture, yet our understanding of that text depends on our prior doctrinal knowledge. This interconnection is an aspect of the so-called hermeneutical circle, a principle that is generally accepted by scholars, though in practice one finds a good deal of resistance to it.

---

as *Encyclopedia of Sacred Theology: Its Principles* (New York: Scribner, 1898). A recent treatment of this topic, quite distant from Kuyper's concerns, is Edward Farley, *Theologia: The Fragmentation and Unity of Theological Education* (Philadelphia: Fortress, 1983).

Many biblical scholars, for example, are deeply suspicious of systematic theology. A person who has a strong theological bent of mind is suspected of being unable to exegete the biblical text without prejudice. Indeed, to judge by comments often made at professional meetings, one might infer that the best training for biblical interpretation is to be as ignorant as possible of systematic theology. H. A. W. Meyer, the nineteenth-century scholar who could be viewed as the father of scientific commentaries, put it this way:

> The area of dogmatics and philosophy is to remain off limits for a commentary. For to ascertain the meaning the author intended to convey by his words impartially and historicogrammatically—that is the duty of the exegete. How the meaning so ascertained stands in relation to the teachings of philosophy, to what extent it agrees with the dogmas of the church or with the views of its theologians, in what way the dogmatician is to make use of it in the interest of his science—to the exegete as an exegete, all that is a matter of no concern.[26]

But no one can escape theological prejudice of one sort or another—even if it takes the form of approaching the text in an untheological fashion! And a scholar who has a keen and well-defined sense of what his or her theological commitments are may be in a better position to keep those commitments from distorting the text.

What is true of systematic theology is also true of practical theology. The needs of the pastor in the pulpit ought not to be set aside when doing biblical exegesis. One used to hear with some frequency that the exegete should be concerned only with what the text meant to the biblical writer and the original readers and that only after determining this meaning can we ask how the text applies to us today.[27]

Of course, we must be very careful not to read into the text present-day concerns that are not really there, but it is proper and even necessary to approach the Bible with a strong awareness of our needs. The problems faced in the gospel ministry often alert us to truths in Scripture that might otherwise remain veiled to us. Proper exegesis consists largely of asking the right questions from the text, and the life of the church can provide us with those very questions.

But there is even more. To interpret the biblical text (or any other text, for that matter) involves a *contextual shift*. Even when I seek merely to express what Paul meant, for example, I am constrained to do so in *my* situation: with English rather than Greek, with modern rather than ancient idioms, with Western nuances rather than Middle Eastern thought forms. In other words, all forms of interpretation necessarily include a measure of *contextualization*.[28] This point is a little frightening because it appears to relativize Scripture. On the contrary, it should remind us of the relativity of our interpretation, because we are weak, limited, ignorant, and sinful. God's truth remains sure, while our perception of that truth may need to change.

Still, one must ask whether there are any limits to be drawn. The contemporary debate over contextualization has the potential for serious divisiveness in the church.

---

[26]Quoted in Kümmel, *New Testament*, p. 111.

[27]See in this connection the famous article by Krister Stendahl, "Biblical Theology, Contemporary," *IDB* 1:418–32, esp. pp. 419–20, where he stresses how significant it was for the history of biblical criticism when the question about the meaning of the text was split into two tenses—what did/does the text mean?

[28]See the useful discussion by Harvie M. Conn in his inaugural address, "The Missionary Task of Theology: A Love/Hate Relationship?" *WTJ* 45 (1983): 1–21, esp. pp. 18–21; more extensively in *Eternal Word and Changing Worlds: Theology, Anthropology, and Mission in Trialogue* (Grand Rapids: Zondervan, 1984), chap. 6.

Must we accept the possibility that our evangelical theology is the product of sixteenth-century thought forms and that we should be open to a distinctively African theology, for example, in which indigenous religious concepts replace Christian doctrines as we know them? What is to keep believers in foreign lands from abandoning the signs of baptism and the Lord's Supper and putting pagan customs in their place on the grounds that they are interpreting the biblical data in the light of their own context?

These questions and many others are raised by the very fact that biblical hermeneutics must take place within the framework of the broad theological task that has been given to the church. It is therefore fitting that the final volume of the series be devoted to this fundamental issue.

To return now to our original illustration, perhaps we can see a little more clearly why a knowledgeable preacher can arrive at an interpretation of Acts 5 that most of us find bizarre. There is no need to assume that this man was ignorant, nor even that he deliberately twisted the Scriptures for his purposes. As already suggested, the basic process by which he reached his conclusion was not essentially different from the way we normally interpret whatever we read. As we all do, this speaker had identified a particular need in the church and used a specific framework, or preunderstanding, to make sense of the biblical text.

Does this analysis mean that there can be no certainty in interpretation? One grave danger in surveying hermeneutical problems as we have just done is that of exaggerating the obstacles involved in reading a text. We need to remind ourselves that, in spite of all the difficulties we have looked at, men and women go on in their daily lives, clearly understanding most of what they read and hear. (When was the last time we argued with our friends about how to interpret the front-page story in the newspaper?)

Interpretive problems do increase, of course, when we seek to understand documents produced in earlier times and written in different languages. In the case of Scripture, the very attention that has been devoted to its interpretation has led to a very large number of exegetical suggestions. Moreover, the significance of biblical teaching for our lives makes us particularly sensitive to interpretive disagreements. It is worthwhile repeating that our interpretations, just because they are *our* interpretations, may reflect our weaknesses and sin. This fact, however, does not affect the objective certainty of God's revelation, since the truth of Scripture is independent of anyone's ability to comprehend it or willingness to receive it.

Someone may object that biblical truth is worthless to us if we cannot be sure that we have understood it. At this point we must emphasize the role of the Holy Spirit in the believer's response to divine revelation. When John tells us in his first epistle that we do not need teachers to instruct us because the Spirit anoints us with his instruction, we are thereby assured that God has not left us to our own devices in our response to revelation (1 John 2:27). Similarly, Paul states a fundamental thesis in 1 Corinthians 2:11–16 when he insists that the things of God can be understood only by those who are spiritual, that is, people who have received God's Spirit, who alone understands the things of God.

Of course, the apostles do not suggest that the Spirit guarantees the infallibility of our interpretation whenever some exegetical question is raised. Users of this series on hermeneutics ought therefore to recognize that our devoting several volumes to modern problems of interpretation does not reflect any doubt concerning the effectiveness of the Spirit's work in the believer as he or she reads the Scriptures. Our concern, rather, is to acknowledge and build upon a corresponding truth—that believers are neither perfect nor omniscient and that their desire to *grow* in the grace and knowledge of our Lord Jesus Christ must be matched by a willingness to work hard at removing whatever obstacles impede that growth.

two

OBSTACLES IN THE STUDY OF THEHISTORY OF INTERPRETATION

B efore we can launch into the various disciplines outlined in the previous chapter, preliminary attention must be given to the historical roots of biblical interpretation. It
must be made clear from the outset, however, that I do not intend to provide in this
volume a full-blown history of biblical hermeneutics.[1] The usual chronological approach
is convenient, and for certain purposes, pedagogically effective. Unfortunately, surveys of
this type lead to a somewhat atomistic, item-by-item description that fails to uncover some
of the more interesting and suggestive connections.

Moreover, we need to avoid the antiquarian's approach to this history—as though the
concerns of ancient and medieval interpreters were oddities to be observed and then set aside.
The truth is that no aspect of the current hermeneutical crisis developed spontaneously
without any prior connections. The problems *we* face can be dealt with satisfactorily only
if we recognize that they are not altogether new, that many of the old controversies (silly
though they may look to us) are not substantially different from those that divide contemporary readers of the Bible.

---

[1]The most influential work in English has been Frederic W. Farrar, *History of Interpretation* (New York:
Dutton, 1886), impressive and learned—but also very misleading, as we shall see. A recent and popular
description is Robert M. Grant, *A Short History of the Interpretation of the Bible,* 2d ed. with additional material by David Tracy (Philadelphia: Fortress, 1984). Most Bible dictionaries contain useful surveys. See especially *IDB* 2:718–24 (K. Grobel) and pp. 436–56 in the *Supplementary Volume* (multiauthor). D. P. Fuller,
ISBE 2:863–74, emphasizes developments in the twentieth century. A highly regarded survey in the Continent is G. Ebeling, "Hermeneutik," *RGG* 3:242–62.

Of particular importance is the popular assumption that the Christian church, through most of its history, has misread the Bible. Did an invalid hermeneutics reign among interpreters while crucial theological issues were being decided? Before we can address this fundamental question, it may be useful to review briefly the common perception of the history of biblical interpretation.

THE USUAL CONCEPTION

A typical survey of the church's interpretation of the Bible might take this form:

The origins of biblical interpretation are to be found within Judaism, which provided the context for different approaches. First, among sectarians, such as the people of the Dead Sea Scrolls, biblical interpretation had a marked eschatological note. Passage after passage in the Old Testament was understood as referring to the end times, which were in the process of being fulfilled in the context of the Qumran community.

Second, among the rabbis, whose approach developed into mainstream Judaism, exegesis consisted of mechanical and artificial rules that paid virtually no attention to the context of the biblical passages. In the more extreme cases, such as the methods of Akiba, an irrational literalism and obsession with trivial details led to wholesale distortions of the Scriptures.

Third, in the Jewish Hellenistic world, particularly Alexandria, Greek allegorical methods used in the interpretation of Homeric legends were applied to the Bible. Best known among Jewish allegorizers is Philo, who rejected literalism on the grounds that it led to blasphemous and even immoral interpretations. For him, biblical narratives, if interpreted literally, were at best irrelevant: we must discover the underlying meaning of these passages, which usually corresponds to the best in Greek philosophy.

In contrast to these approaches, the New Testament shows a remarkably balanced method of interpretation. There may be a very few examples of allegorization (perhaps Gal. 4:21–31 and Heb. 7:1–10), but even these passages are rather moderate in comparison with Philo. Again, some rabbinic rules of interpretation seem to be reflected in various New Testament passages, but apostolic exegesis shows considerable respect for the Old Testament context. And while one must recognize that the apostles, like the Qumran community, used an eschatological hermeneutics, their approach was built upon a distinctively christological foundation.

As we move to the postapostolic period, the picture changes dramatically. Since the Qumran community had been destroyed in A.D. 70, its peculiar exegesis was basically unknown in the Christian church. Moreover, rabbinic methods had little impact on the Gentile church, partly because very few Christians were familiar with Hebrew and partly because anti-Jewish feelings prevented any significant communication (there were of course some important exceptions, such as Origen and Jerome, but even they did not adopt rabbinic exegesis).

Allegorical exegesis, however, was something else. Since Philo had written in Greek, his works were accessible to the Gentile church. Moreover, Christians were faced with the need to confront Greek culture, and Philo appeared to provide a way of doing so in an intellectually responsible way. Origen in particular made the allegorical method a central feature of his exegesis and his theology, and his influence was to be felt for many centuries.

To be sure, important Christian leaders such as Tertullian rejected any attempt to mix the gospel with Greek philosophy. And in Antioch an exegetical approach was developed during the fourth century that was self-consciously opposed to Origen and that could be described as "grammatico-historical," if only in a limited way. (Important representatives of this school were John Chrysostom and Theodore of

Mopsuestia.) As a whole, however, the allegorical interpretation was adopted by the church and hardly anything of exegetical value was produced during the Middle Ages.

Fortunately, the Reformation came along. Thanks in part to the Renaissance, which resurrected an interest in linguistic and historical investigation, the Reformers attacked the allegorical method as a major source of the many evils that had developed in the church. Many new commentaries, particularly those of John Calvin, inaugurated a new epoch in the interpretation of Scripture.

These advances were to some extent nullified by seventeenth-century orthodox theologians who reintroduced a scholastic mentality, but the eighteenth-century Enlightenment finally brought in a truly scientific approach to the interpretation of the Bible. While some scholars took matters to an extreme and their rationalism was damaging to the Christian faith, by and large the grammatico-historical method of exegesis established itself firmly during the nineteenth century and continues to be used in our day.

So much for the usual description. Depending on the theological stance of the person reporting this history, some aspects and details may differ here and there, particularly in the evaluation of post-Enlightenment scholarship. Generally speaking, however, our brief survey reflects rather accurately the usual understanding of the church's interpretation of the Scriptures. Unfortunately, there are some serious problems with this understanding.

OBJECTIONS

In the first place, our survey did not go back far enough, since it paid no attention to the earliest stage of biblical interpretation, namely, the Old Testament itself. The books of the Old Testament were written over a very long period of time, and it would be surprising if the later books made no use of the earlier ones. No one has denied that various kinds of references of this sort exist, but only recently have scholars focused on this issue with a view to drawing hermeneutical inferences.[2]

This field of study presents us with a few problems, not the least of which is the uncertainty we face when trying to establish the relative date of some of the documents. In certain cases—particularly the date of the Pentateuch—disagreement among scholars creates a serious obstacle, but we still have a number of clear instances in which later Old Testament writers have used, expanded, or otherwise applied earlier passages.

We might take, for instance, Jacob's prophecy that the scepter would not depart from Judah before *šlh* should come (Gen. 49:10). Is that Hebrew word the proper name *Shiloh,* as some translations have it? Or should we render the clause as the NIV does, "until he comes to whom it belongs"? In favor of the latter option is an apparent reference to this prophecy by Ezekiel, who predicts the removal of the crown from the prince of Israel and adds: "It will not be restored until he comes to whom it rightfully belongs; to him I will give it" (Ezek. 21:27).

One can find many other passages that almost surely depend on earlier material. An especially fruitful example is the way 1–2 Chronicles retells the historical material found in the Books of Samuel and Kings.[3] Even in such clear instances, however, it is seldom

---

[2]See esp. Michael A. Fishbane, *Biblical Interpretation in Ancient Israel* (Oxford: Clarendon, 1985), for the most thorough treatment of this question. Much briefer but also helpful is James L. Kugel and Rowan A. Greer, *Early Biblical Interpretation* (Library of Early Christianity; Philadelphia: Westminster, 1986), pt. 1.

[3]See the study by Raymond B. Dillard, "The Chronicler's Solomon," *WTJ* 43 (1980–81): 289–300

easy to identify a particular principle or technique that we can readily apply to our own exegetical efforts. Much work remains to be done in this area.

A second problem with the usual approach to the history of interpretation is the strongly negative note with which the subject is treated. Farrar's famous *History* is little more than a compilation of errors. Already in the preface he warns us about "the apparently negative character of much that is here dwelt upon," and in the first chapter he states his thesis thus:

> The task before us is in some respects a melancholy one. We shall pass in swift review many centuries of exegesis, and shall be compelled to see that they were, in the main, centuries during which the interpretation of Scripture has been dominated by unproven theories, and overladen by untenable results. We shall see that these theories have often been affiliated to each other, and augmented at each stage by the superaddition of fresh theories no less mistaken. Exegesis has often darkened the true meaning of Scripture, not evolved or elucidated it.

Near the end of that first chapter he tells us that "the misinterpretation of Scripture must be reckoned among the gravest calamities of Christendom." Much of the blame goes to the Septuagint, whose "intentional variations may be counted by scores, and their unintentional errors by hundreds; and alike their errors and their variations were in a multitude of instances accepted by Christian interpreters as the infallible word of God."[4] Although Farrar has some complimentary words here and there (particularly with reference to the Antiochenes and the Reformers), one is hard-pressed to find much in that history that would help us in our exegetical work—except possibly to avoid a multitude of errors.

Apart from the general negativism of the standard approaches, it is important to point out the particular areas that come under heavy attack. One of the main objects of derision is rabbinic exegesis. Here is Farrar's opinion of the Talmud:

> But it may be said, without fear of refutation, that, apart from a few moral applications and ritual inferences in matters absolutely unimportant, for every one text on which it throws the smallest glimmer of light, there are hundreds which it inexcusably perverts and misapplies. . . . [Hillel's rule known as Gezerah Shawa] furnished an excuse for masses of the most absurd conclusions. . . . Hillel was personally a noble Rabbi; yet by his seven rules he became the founder of Talmudism, with all its pettiness, its perversion of the letter of the Scripture which it professed to worship, and its ignorance of the spirit, of which no breath seemed to breathe over its valley of dry bones.[5]

Farrar believes that Christian exegesis, fortunately, did not share the particular perversions of the rabbis, but his introduction to patristic interpretation is not encouraging either:

> The history of exegesis thus far has been in great measure a history of aberrations. If we turn to the Fathers with the hope that now at last we shall enter the region of unimpeachable methods and certain applications, we shall be disappointed. . . . [Though admittedly one can find much that is valuable in the Fathers,] their exege-

---

[4]Farrar, *History*, pp. xi, xviii, 8–9, 39, 122. A similar attitude can be found in Samuel Davidson, *Sacred Hermeneutics: Developed and Applied* (Edinburgh: T. Clark, 1843), esp. p. 187. Grant, *Short History*, is better, but even he has some unnecessarily harsh remarks about Barnabas, Justin, and Protestant orthodoxy (pp. 41, 45, 97).

[5]Ibid., pp. 10, 20, 22; see also pp. 50 and 88.

sis in the proper sense of the word needs complete revision both in its principles and in its details.[6]

The main culprit behind patristic misinterpretation is of course Origen of Alexandria, who gave respectability to Philo's allegorical method. With regard to Philo's approach, Farrar had already stated: "It must be said quite plainly and without the least circumlocution that it is absolutely baseless. . . . his exegesis is radically false. It darkens what is simple and fails to explain what is obscure." Origen was hardly successful in improving upon Philo. What Origen regarded as exegetical "proofs" were nothing "but the after-thoughts devised in support of an unexamined tradition. They could not have had a particle of validity for any logical or independent mind."[7]

In addition to rabbinic exegesis and the allegorical method, a third object of Farrar's criticism is medieval scholasticism. We should note that, during the past few decades, specialists have developed a much more positive appreciation of the Middle Ages than was the case in Farrar's generation. Nowadays many scholars are ready to argue, for example, that "the medieval hermeneutical tradition . . . can be characterized as an authentic attempt to establish the *sensus literalis* of Scripture as its principal meaning, and to give it a theologically normative role in the formation of Christian theology."[8] In Farrar's opinion, on the other hand, the Schoolmen were "paralysed by vicious methods, traditional errors, and foregone conclusions," while their exegesis was "radically defective—defective in fundamental principles, and rife on every page of it with all sorts of erroneous details."[9]

Behind all of this invective is Farrar's conviction that, first, many of these errors are still to be found "here and there, unexorcised, in modern commentaries," and, second, that the main cause of these old exegetical perversions is the theory of "verbal dictation."[10] Farrar's own view of inspiration, incidentally, helps explain why he does not feel threatened by the miserable failure of the church in interpreting the Bible. In his opinion, inspiration assures only that the message of salvation, broadly understood, is preserved in Scripture: "the Bible

---

[6]Ibid., p. 162; on p. 165 he describes their interpretation as consisting of "a chaos" of diverse elements. David C. Steinmetz is probably correct when he views Farrar's book as "a triumph of what the late Sir Herbert Butterfield of Cambridge called 'Whig' historiography. Farrar admires about the past precisely those elements in it most like the present and regards the present, indeed, as the inevitable culmination of all that was best in the past" ("John Calvin on Isaiah 6: A Problem in the History of Exegesis," *Int* 36 [1982]: p. 169).

[7]Ibid., pp. 153, 191. Farrar concludes that the very foundations of Origen's "exegetic system are built upon the sand" (p. 201). Even St. Augustine, for all his greatness, made little advance in interpretive method. For Farrar, Augustine's exegesis "is marked by the most glaring defects. Almost as many specimens of prolix puerility and arbitrary perversion can be adduced from his pages as from those of his least gifted predecessors" (p. 236).

[8]James Samuel Preus, *From Shadow to Promise: Old Testament Interpretation from Augustine to Young Luther* (Cambridge, Mass.: Harvard University Press, Belknap, 1969), p. 3. For a renewed appreciation of medieval exegesis, we are largely indebted to Beryl Smalley's work, particularly *The Study of the Bible in the Middle Ages,* 2d ed. (Oxford: Blackwell, 1952).

[9]Farrar, *History,* pp. 267, 302.

[10]Ibid., pp. xii, xx, 190, 283, 430, etc. Farrar shows considerable confusion in dealing with this matter, as can be seen particularly in the footnotes on p. xx. In the first place, he equates "verbal dictation" with the doctrine of infallibility. Moreover, he refers with apparent approval to Tholuck's claim that this view is no earlier than the seventeenth century—even though such a claim blatantly contradicts his repeated attribution of that doctrine to many early historical figures, such as Philo, the rabbis, Athenagoras, Tertullian, and Origen (see pp. 148, 152, 162, 171, 177, 190).

is not so much a revelation as the *record* of revelation, and the inmost and most essential truths which it contains have happily been placed above the reach of Exegesis to injure."[11]

TOWARD A POSITIVE EVALUATION

Whatever we may think of Farrar's doctrine of Scripture, it is difficult to accept the thoroughgoing negativism with which he recounts the history of interpretation. After all, the individuals he discusses were believers seeking to make sense of God's Word, with a view to obeying the divine will. Are we to suppose that their efforts were, with the rarest of exceptions, virtually fruitless? Must we really think that, prior to the development of modern exegesis, the church lacked the Spirit's guidance?

Farrar appears to suggest that only two options are available to us: Either we accept modern exegetical methods and reject a good 95 percent of pre-eighteenth-century biblical interpretation, or else we condemn ourselves to adopting countless errors. Perhaps, however, we can be genuinely critical of shortcomings on the part of the Fathers and still learn something more positive than how to avoid their errors. Surely, it is conceivable that their failures may have been counterbalanced by other factors that can help us to formulate a valid hermeneutical approach. David C. Steinmetz comments that the answer to Farrar is not to point out examples of "modern" exegesis in the Middle Ages (or howlers in modern times): "The principal value of precritical exegesis is that it is not modern exegesis; it is alien, strange, sometimes even, from our perspective, comic and fantastical."[12]

In any case, we can hardly claim to have developed a satisfactory approach *if our exegesis is in essence incompatible with the way God's people have read the Scriptures throughout the centuries.* A genuine effort must be made to view the history of interpretation in a more positive light than is usually done. The reason why this is so necessary is not difficult to understand. Most believers even today lack the specialized skills that characterize modern "scientific" exegesis. Since they therefore read the Scriptures in a "nonscientific" way, they are basically in the same position as earlier Christians who lived in a prescientific period.

Moreover, one may argue that scholarly exegesis, though it rightly uses highly specialized methods, fails to provide proper guidance if it disregards the simple or instinctive response to Scripture on the part of lay readers. It may indeed appear impossible for modern biblical scholarship to discover any relationship between the historical method and the quasi-allegorical approach that is standard fare among lay Christians. The failure to confront this dilemma head-on, however, can only lead to an unbearable divorce between scholarly work and common piety.

There is, in addition to these concerns, a profound intellectual problem with the usual negative analysis. Take the case of Origen. It is agreed on all sides that Origen was one of the brightest luminaries in his day—not only within the Christian community, but even in the context of the whole cultural scene in the third century. How, then, does one account for his constructing a hermeneutical system that draws bitter scorn from moderns?

Origen's allegorical method was not some peripheral concern that we might disregard as an uncharacteristic quirk. Quite the contrary, it belonged at the center of his theological

---

[11]Ibid., p. xiv; cf. also p. 303.
[12]Steinmetz, "John Calvin," p. 170.

thinking. If, as Farrar claimed, his exegetical proofs had no "particle of validity for any logical or independent mind," are we not compelled to conclude that Origen's mind was neither logical nor independent? And is not that conclusion clear evidence that we have failed to solve, or maybe even to identify, the problem?

If my own experience as a seminarian was at all typical, most students find Origen a difficult, distant, unhelpful personality. One can find many objectionable elements in his writings and few that appear genuinely constructive. The more one reflects on the subsequent history of interpretation, however, the more one becomes aware of the significance of Origen's thought. He anticipated virtually every substantive hermeneutical debate in the history of the church, including some that have persisted to this day. It would no doubt be an exaggeration to say that the history of biblical interpretation consists of a series of footnotes to Origen, but there is enough truth in that remark to make us sit up and take notice. Accordingly, the chapters that follow pay a great deal of attention to Origen's writings. Even if we decide to reject his answers, it is impossible to avoid his questions.

Now what Origen's questions most clearly reveal is that the task of biblical interpretation seems to pull the believer in several different directions. I propose in this volume to study the history of interpretation precisely in that light. My thesis is simply that this history is characterized by the church's appreciation, sometimes implicit rather than consciously formulated, that we face a series of difficult "tensions" in our reading of Scripture:[13]

- The Bible is divine, yet it has come to us in human form.
- The commands of God are absolute, yet the historical context of the writings appears to relativize certain elements.
- The divine message must be clear, yet many passages seem ambiguous.
- We are dependent only on the Spirit for instruction, yet scholarship is surely necessary.
- The Scriptures seem to presuppose a literal and historical reading, yet we are also confronted by the figurative and nonhistorical (e.g., the parables).
- Proper interpretation requires the interpreter's personal freedom, yet some degree of external, corporate authority appears imperative.
- The objectivity of the biblical message is essential, yet our presuppositions seem to inject a degree of subjectivity into the interpretive process.

The attempt to hold these seeming polarities in tension is the principle that brings unity to the great diversity of problems surrounding the history of biblical interpretation. It may well be that the one great aim in our own interpretation of Scripture must be that of resisting the temptation to eliminate the tensions, to emphasize certain features of the Bible at the expense of others.

---

[13]I use quotation marks here to alert the reader to a certain ambiguity in the word *tension*. I am using the term not in any sophisticated fashion but in a simple, popular sense. As we seek to understand the Scriptures, we sometimes feel as though contradictory responses are expected of us. Besides such feelings, we also may experience intellectual frustration. But the believer knows well that these difficulties arise from our own ignorance and sin.

DIVINE OR HUMAN?

The first item listed above—the Bible as both divine and human—constitutes the most basic question of all. Strictly speaking, it is not so much a hermeneutical question as it is one of theology, even though, as we shall see in the course of our discussions, one can hardly divorce doctrine from interpretation. Since the present book is not intended to serve as a text for Christian theology, I consider here only briefly the doctrine of biblical inspiration.[14]

But treat it we must, for the relationship between the divine and human elements of Scripture directly affects how we handle every other item on the list. I do not say, of course, that our view of the character of Scripture automatically determines whether we will, for example, take prophetic passages in a literal or nonliteral way. Nevertheless, it is hardly possible to formulate a coherent set of hermeneutical principles unless one takes fully into account how those principles relate to the essential nature of the documents being interpreted.

Origen's most important theological work, *On First Principles*, consists of four books, the last of which is devoted to principles of biblical interpretation. Not surprisingly, the first chapter of that book deals with inspiration, and Origen intends to establish the divine character of Scripture as the foundation for hermeneutics. Origen develops his argument by appealing to fulfilled prophecy, the success of the apostles, and other types of evidence. As he approaches the end of the chapter, he writes:

> Now when we thus briefly demonstrate the divine nature of Jesus and use the words spoken in prophecy about him, we demonstrate at the same time that the writings which prophesy about him are divinely inspired and that the words which announce his sojourning here and his teaching were spoken with all power and authority and that this is the reason why they have prevailed over the elect people taken from among the nations.[15]

Origen also appeals to the reader's subjective response: "And he who approaches the prophetic words with care and attention will feel from his very reading a trace of their divine inspiration and will be convinced by his own feelings that the words which are believed by us to be from God are not the compositions of men." He realizes, of course, that not everyone who reads the Bible acknowledges it as divine, and so in section 7 he draws an analogy based on the failure of many people to detect God's existence through the works of providence:

> But just as providence is not abolished because of our ignorance, at least not for those who have once rightly believed in it, so neither is the divine character of scripture, which extends through all of it, abolished because our weakness cannot discern in every sentence the hidden splendour of its teachings, concealed under a poor and humble style.[16]

---

[14]In addition to Hodge and Warfield, *Inspiration,* note the important articles by Warfield brought together in *The Inspiration and Authority of the Bible,* ed. Samuel G. Craig (Philadelphia: Presbyterian & Reformed, 1948), esp. chaps. 2–4. One of the most recent and learned discussions, particularly valuable in addressing contemporary objections to Evangelicalism, is Carl F. H. Henry, God, Revelation, and Authority, 6 vols. (Waco, Tex.: Word, 1976–83), esp. vol. 4, chap. 6.

[15]Origen, *Origen on First Principles,* trans. G. W. Butterworth (New York: Harper & Row, 1966; orig. 1936) 4. 1. 6, p. 264.

[16]Ibid., 4. 1. 7, pp. 265, 267.

The very last clause just quoted, we may note, entails a recognition that there is *more* to be said about Scripture than that it is divine. The human character of Scripture does not concern Origen at this point (in fact, he nowhere deliberately reflects on the implications of that fact with the same thoroughness he displays in treating the Bible's divine character). As a result, he may appear to disregard or even ignore it. We have already seen his comment that the biblical writings "are not the compositions of men." In section 4. 2. 2 he identifies himself with "those who believe that the sacred books *are not the works of men,* but that they were composed and have come down to us as a result of the inspiration of the Holy Spirit."[17] It would be easy to multiply quotations from Origen's extensive writings that suggest he viewed the Scriptures as exclusively divine.

The very nature of his scholarly labors, however, belies such a conclusion. His concern with textual and philological details makes sense only on the assumption that he recognized the important role played by language and other human factors.[18] Our discussion in subsequent chapters should make clear that Origen's primary concern with what *God* says in Scripture does not necessarily preclude a commitment to find out what its human authors meant.

At any rate, we must acknowledge that heavy emphasis on the divine character of Scripture has characterized most of the history of interpretation. One reason for this emphasis, of course, is simply that some of the human features of the Bible are patent and undeniable: it was written by real-life historical individuals rather than appearing from nowhere, it was written in human languages rather than in some unknown angelic tongue, and so on. In other words, the church has not had to deal with people who deny, at least in any conscious or explicit form, the fact that there is a human side to the Scriptures, whereas it has had to respond to many who deny their divine origin.

One must admit, however, that in actual practice Origen and most of the interpreters who followed him in the ancient and medieval periods tended to disregard the human (and therefore historical) aspects of the text because of their commitment to its divine character. This tendency led to many interpretive errors, such as the full-scale development of allegorical exegesis, which usually focused on the divine meaning "behind" the human words, a matter that we consider in chapter 3.

The Renaissance witnessed a renewed interest in the historical character of ancient writings, including the Bible. Its effect on the Reformers, particularly Calvin, was direct. It must not be thought that the Reformers downplayed the divine origin of Scripture; their concern with the "plain" meaning of the Bible (that is, the meaning intended by the *human* author, as that sense can be plainly determined by the literary and historical context) did not entail a change in their view of inspiration. Significantly, Calvin at times so stressed the divine character of Scripture that he, like Origen, appeared to deny its humanity: "not the word of the apostles but of God himself; not a voice born on earth but

---

[17]Ibid. 4. 2. 2, p. 272, my emphasis.

[18]How this recognition affected Origen's practice of interpretation may be illustrated from the preface to *On First Principles.* Answering an objection based on a passage from *The Teaching of Peter* (a writing that Origen did not accept as inspired, though he granted its inspiration for the sake of the argument), he stated: "And the words must be understood in the sense intended by the author of that writing" (section 8 of the preface, p. 5). We are not concerned here primarily with Origen's critical labors, the best known of which was the Hexapla. It may be worth pointing out, however, that he saw such works, not as ends in themselves, but as the first steps in understanding the *divine* message.

one descended from heaven."[19] Although the arguments he used to defend the doctrine of inspiration marked a substantive advance over previous discussions, they have much in common with those of Origen. Calvin's commitment to the "paradox" that the Bible is both divine and human is no doubt a major reason why moderns can appeal to some of his statements as evidence that he did not believe in verbal inspiration, while other comments make absolutely no sense unless he did.[20]

Without denying the distinctiveness of the Reformers' contribution, then, we do well to remember their basic sense of continuity with earlier centuries, at least with respect to the divine character of Scripture. The Reformation, of course, also retained the medieval concern for application, though it sought to bind application to the clear meaning of the text.

The rise of the critical method, on the other hand, marked a radical change in the way students of the Bible approached the text. To begin with, there was a tendency to view exegesis as an end in itself. And for the first time in the history of the church, scholars who professed some form of Christian commitment argued that the Bible was to be understood just like any other book. In a sense, of course, the best exegetes had always attempted to interpret the Bible in this way, that is, according to the normal rules of language, paying attention to logic, literary conventions, historical data, and so on.

Now, however, interpreters argued that the Bible must be subjected to the same kind of full-blown *criticism* that one might apply to any human writing, even if the analysis leads to a negative assessment of its value at any point.[21] Proponents of this method did not agree with each other concerning whether the Bible could still be regarded as divine (and if so, in what sense), but they did agree that such a factor could not play a role in its interpretation. The whole conception of biblical authority, therefore, if not blatantly abandoned, was drastically altered: an individual's reason first had to make a judgment regarding the validity of a biblical statement or injunction before one could believe it.

The development of biblical hermeneutics during the past two centuries cannot possibly be separated from the application of critical tools to the biblical text. This factor raises a series of major problems. In the first place, the interpretation of the Bible now appears to require expertise in a number of highly specialized subdisciplines. Does this qualification put the Scriptures out of the reach of most believers? Can we possibly claim that the Bible is *clear*? (We consider this issue in chapter 4.)

Second, we are faced with a new and most difficult dilemma. On the one hand, many of the critical tools used by modern scholarship are patently consistent with a high view of scriptural authority; that is, scholars with strong evangelical convictions can plainly make

---

[19]John Calvin, *Institutes of the Christian Religion,* ed. John T. McNeill, trans. Ford Lewis Battles (Library of Christian Classics 20; Philadelphia: Westminster, 1967) 4. 11. 1, p. 1213. See section 1. 6–8 for his defense of inspiration.

[20]In my opinion, one can hardly doubt that Calvin's view of the authority of Scripture corresponds in all essential respects to that of Warfield. See John Murray, *Calvin on Scripture and Divine Sovereignty* (Philadelphia: Presbyterian & Reformed, 1960), esp. chap. 1. The apparent inconsistency of expression is more remarkable in Jerome; see Farrar, *History,* pp. 230–31.

[21]More accurately, it was claimed that critical exegesis should not consist in value judgments. The eighteenth-century scholar K. A. G. Keil, for example, argued that proper biblical interpretation could not ask whether the text is right or wrong. This restriction, however, meant that one must disregard inspiration (see Kümmel, *New Testament,* p. 108; cf. p. 110 on L. I. Ruckert). In other words, the divine element was excluded, and with it the possibility that the Scriptures were always reliable.

use of, say, textual criticism without compromising their view of biblical inspiration. On the other hand, most of these tools have taken shape in the context of blatant unbelief. The point here is not merely that some unbelievers have had a hand in their development but that such a development assumed, in the very nature of the case, that the Scriptures must be fallible. Are these tools therefore inherently "tainted," whether we realize it or not, and therefore unusable by anyone committed to the full authority of the Bible? Some conservative Christians would answer this question affirmatively. For that matter, liberal scholars often accuse Evangelicals of inconsistency in holding on to inerrancy while making use of critical tools.

> Troeltsch poured scorn on those of his contemporaries who attacked the historical method as a manifestation of unbelief while employing something like it to vindicate the truth of their own views. The method, he claimed, did not grow from an abstract theory, nor could one ignore the cumulative significance of its extraordinary results. "Whoever lends it a finger must give it a hand." Nor could the critical method be regarded as a neutral thing. It could not be appropriated by the church with only a bit of patchwork here and there on the seamless garment of belief. "Once the historical method is applied to the Biblical science and church history," he wrote, "it is a leaven that alters everything and, finally, bursts apart the entire structure of theological methods employed until the present."[22]

Third, and most directly relevant to our present concerns, it is now claimed that a full acceptance of the critical method, with its assumption of biblical fallibility, is the only approach that does justice to the humanity of Scripture. Ironically, conservatives become the theological felons, charged with a form of *docetism,* an ancient heresy that denied the true humanity of Christ.

The analogy between Scripture and the twofold nature of Christ, though very popular in some circles, suffers from some deep ambiguities.[23] Even if it did not, however, one wonders how the charge of docetism contributes to the discussion, other than by affecting the objectivity of the debate through the "slur" factor. Strangely, I have never heard anyone accused of *Arianism* in his or her view of Scripture, though it could be argued that, once we abandon the doctrine of infallibility, there is no meaningful way in which we can speak of the divine character of the Bible.

The last point can best be illustrated by referring to a World Council of Churches study report on biblical authority presented in 1971. Heavily influenced by Karl Barth's theology, the members of the committee were reluctant to base the authority of Scripture on the notion of inspiration, and so they pointed rather to "the experience in which the message of the Bible proves itself authoritative." To their credit, they went on to ask the embarrassing question:

[22]Van Austin Harvey, *The Historian and the Believer: The Morality of Historical Knowledge and Christian Belief* (New York: Macmillan, 1966), p. 5. From a somewhat different angle, James Barr has been particularly anxious to show that Evangelicals have a very equivocal approach to scholarship. See his *Fundamentalism* (London: SCM, 1977), esp. chap. 5. Barr observes, "The deservedly high reputation of some conservative scholarship rests to a large extent on the degree to which it fails to be conservative in the sense that the conservative evangelical public desiderate" (p. 128).

[23]For a perceptive discussion, see G. C. Berkouwer, *Holy Scripture* (Studies in Dogmatics; Grand Rapids: Eerdmans, 1975), chap. 7. See also D. A. Carson, "Recent Developments in the Doctrine of Scripture," in *HAC,* pp. 5–48, esp. his criticism of Bruce Vawter on pp. 26–28.

> If the assertion that the Bible is inspired is a conclusion drawn from actual encounter with God through the Bible, the question arises as to why this should only be true of the Bible.... Indeed, why should we not also speak of inspiration in the case of today's preaching which can also lead to an encounter with God and thus prove itself inspired in the same way as happens with the Bible?

It would certainly be difficult to think of a more fundamental question than that of the uniqueness of scriptural authority. The fact that this notion had lost all meaning for the committee may be inferred from their remarkable response: "Obviously a clearer explanation is required as to whether and in what sense God has bound Himself through the Spirit to the Bible in its entirety."[24] To paraphrase: We have no idea in what way the Bible is unique.

The position taken in this book is that error is not inherent to humanity—it may be true that to err is human, but it is most certainly untrue that to be human is to err! A human being can (and often does) utter sentences that contain no errors or falsehoods (e.g., "Hitler is dead" or, under the appropriate circumstances, "I saw my mother yesterday"). Accordingly, we do not jeopardize the humanity of Scripture if we say that all it affirms is true. At the same time, we may readily acknowledge that an evangelical view of Scripture has led many to downplay its human character—if not in theory, certainly in the practice of interpretation.

As with Calvin, our attempt to affirm both the divine and human sides of Scripture will almost inevitably lead to statements that appear inconsistent. This problem only reminds us of our finiteness. But the alternative would be to deny one or the other element, which we dare not do.

---

[24]Ellen Flesseman-van Leer, ed., *The Bible: Its Authority and Interpretation in the Ecumenical Movement* (Faith and Order Paper 99; Geneva: World Council of Churches, 1980), pp. 54–55.

three
LITERAL
OR FIGURATIVE?

T he concept of figurative language can encompass a rather wide variety of phenomena. Consider the following examples of biblical interpretation:

1. The promise that "new wine will drip from the mountains" (Amos 9:13) is a figure
    of speech indicating the abundance of divine blessings at the end time.
2. When the Bible speaks of God's "eyes" or his "mouth," we are not to deduce that
    God has a body; human qualities are being attributed to him so that we may better
    understand the biblical message.
3. Isaac was a historical character, but in Galatians 4:21–31 Paul views him as a type
    of those who are born by the Spirit of God.
4. The statement "Out of Egypt I called my son" (Hos. 11:1) refers to the people of Israel,
    but Matthew sees in it a fuller meaning that applies to Jesus' childhood (Matt. 2:15).
5. The Old Testament prophecies regarding the restoration of Israel should be under-
    stood in a spiritual sense, referring to the Christian church.
6. The story of Jonah is probably not historical: it should be viewed as a parable intend-
    ed to teach a lesson.
7. Jesus' changing the water to wine at the wedding in Cana (John 2:1–11) symbol-
    izes the need for those who are weak like water to be changed and become stead-
    fast like wine.

The first of these examples is a simple case of *metaphor*; the second is a special type
of metaphor known as *anthropomorphism*. With the third example we meet an interpretive method known as *typology*, the view that certain historical characters or events in

some way prefigure others corresponding to them in a later period. These three instances of interpretation are not normally disputed among biblical students.

The others are more controversial. Number 4 expresses a concept known as *sensus plenior,* which indicates that an Old Testament writer, for example, may be quite unaware of a deeper meaning found in his own writing. The fifth, an instance of so-called *spiritualizing,* divides some important segments of Christianity. We may refer to number 6 as an instance of *dehistoricizing* interpretation, while the last example illustrates *allegorizing.*

In this chapter I use the term *figurative* in a very broad sense to include all of these approaches. It may appear at first blush that I am thereby mixing apples and oranges. Was not the typological method, for example, developed in conscious opposition to allegorizing?[1] The answer to this type of question is that all of the approaches listed above share one fundamental feature: they recognize that, at certain points in the biblical text, there appears to be "something more" than is immediately apparent. This phenomenon is not peculiar to Scripture. In the reading of any text, one is always in danger of interpreting statements in a "woodenly literal" fashion.

It may help to clarify our problem if we describe two approaches that seem to represent extreme opposites: Aquila's literalistic translation of the Old Testament into Greek and Origen's full-blown allegorical method. Moderns routinely caricature Aquila and Origen as exemplifying puerile and nearly irrational methods of exegesis.

Seminary teachers have learned that they can get a quick laugh in Hebrew class by informing their sophisticated students that Aquila translated the particle *'et* in Genesis 1:1 (where it simply signals the direct object) as though it were the preposition meaning "with." And what respectable church history professor has allowed Origen and his "wild" interpretations to escape unscathed?[2] Surely Aquila and Origen are viewed as two great examples of how *not* to exegete. Their hermeneutical approaches are thought to represent the worst that prescientific, ancient exegesis had to offer.

This analysis is much too simple, however. As pointed out in chapter 2, Origen's intellectual gifts were second to none. Does it make sense that he would build his theological system on a method of exegesis that is so patently illogical? Similarly, it is apparent that Aquila was no fool, that his strange renderings reflect not ignorance of the

---

[1] I refer here to the Antiochene school, with which we shall deal below. We may note at this point Hans W. Frei, *The Eclipse of Biblical Narrative: A Study in Nineteenth Century Hermeneutics* (New Haven: Yale University Press, 1974). On p. 2 he identifies typology as figuration, yet at the same time as "a natural extension of literal interpretation. It was literalism at the level of the whole biblical story and thus of the depiction of the whole of historical reality. Figuration was at once a literary and a historical procedure." Later on, however, as a result of changes in the way scholars viewed narrative, "figural sense came to be something like the opposite of literal sense" (p. 7). More to the point, the ancients did not see a clear distinction between allegory and typology. Augustine, *On Christian Doctrine* 3. 11 (*NPNF* 2:561) identifies "allegorical or enigmatical" as "the kind of expression properly called *figurative.*" Wolfgang A. Bienert, «*Allegoria*» *und* «*Anagoge*» *bei Didymus dem Blinden von Alexandria* (PTS 13; Berlin: W. de Gruyter, 1972), pp. 42–43, argues that, both in the Greek church and in the Latin church, *allegoria* could refer to either allegorical or typological exegesis. On the varied uses of *tropikos* ("figurative"), see Theodoret de Cyr, *Commentaire sur Isaïe,* 3 vols., ed. and trans. Jean-Noel Guinot (Sources chrétiennes 276, 295, 315; Paris: Cerf, 1980–84), 1:70–71.

[2] For an entertaining list of insults, see Henri de Lubac, *Histoire et Esprit: L'intelligence de l'Écriture d'après Origène* (Théologie 16; Paris: Aubier, 1950), pp. 13ff.

Hebrew language but rather a self-conscious approach to a method of interpretation closely related to that of Rabbi Akiba.

At the very least, we need to attempt an explanation for this anomaly. What led intelligent people to develop such methods and to consider them important? That question needs to be answered before we can dismiss their approaches as having absolutely no value for us. As Wiles puts it, we can hardly sit in judgment of Origen, since "the fundamental problem remains unsolved."[3]

Another reason why this whole issue is not a simple one is that neither of the two approaches is used exclusively by underprivileged ancients and uneducated modern believers. For example, the difficult question concerning whether Bible translations (or translations of any text, for that matter) should be "literal" has not been satisfactorily resolved.[4] It is all very well to point to the results of modern linguistics and its demonstration that literal translations are not necessarily accurate. On that basis, translations that follow the principle of "formal correspondence" (e.g., the NASB) are ridiculed as more or less obscurantist and unscientific. Critics will then suggest that literalistic translators are ignorant of modern linguistics or that their view of verbal inspiration disqualifies them from proper translation work.

Now one must admit that a "dynamic equivalence," rather than "formal correspondence," approach to translation is more likely to transmit the main point of a text clearly and reliably to the reader. It is also undeniable, however, that the former approach, no less than the latter, entails almost inevitably the loss of certain aspects of meaning. For this reason, some classical scholars lament the modernized translations of Homer. One of them has argued that "the translator has to aim not at assimilating 'otherness' into English, but in moving English into some kind of 'otherness.' He has to let his own language be powerfully affected by another one."[5]

The view that a translation ought to preserve not only the content but also the form of the original has the support of a few modern and knowledgeable writers. Perhaps the most striking example is Hölderlin, the nineteenth-century German poet who attempted to translate, in a most literal way, several difficult Greek writers, including Pindar. The results appear bizarre, but the project had a carefully defined logic and cannot be simply dismissed as irrational. Indeed, as highly respected a figure as George Steiner argues eloquently for the validity of this approach:

> Charged as it is with stylistic genius and interpretative audacity, Hölderlin's art of translation always derives from literalism, almost, in fact, from a literalism not only of the single word but of the letter. . . . Paradoxically, therefore, the most exalted vision we know

---

[3]M. F. Wiles, "Origen as Biblical Scholar," *CHB* 1:454–89, esp. p. 488.

[4]To make matters worse, it is not even clear how a "literal translation" can be identified. See in particular James Barr, *Typology of Literalism in Ancient Biblical Translations* (MSU 15; Göttingen: Vandenhoeck & Ruprecht, 1979). For a more recent attempt to clarify the issues, see E. Tov and B. G. Wright, "Computer-Assisted Study of the Criteria for Assessing the Literalness of Translation Units in the LXX," *Textus* 12 (1985): 149–87.

[5]William Arrowsmith, professor of classics at Johns Hopkins University, as reported in *Chronicle of Higher Education* 20:4 (March 1980): 1. Soon after the complete NEB was released, I heard a radio program in England devoted to its evaluation. Some literary critics strongly objected to the way this new version avoided literal translations of transparent Hebrew idioms in the Psalms. Not only did this approach insult the intelligence of modern readers, they claimed, but it also reduced Hebrew poetry to banality.

of the nature of translation derives precisely from the programme of literalism, of word-for-word metaphrase which traditional theory has regarded as most puerile.[6]

I am not concerned at this point with evaluating the merits of the various approaches to biblical translation; another volume in the present series will consider that issue. For our purposes in this chapter we need only appreciate the fact that a literal method of interpretation, as exemplified in the translation of Aquila, is not merely the relic of a primitive era. One can find cultured, post-Enlightenment scholars, including a few who understand the contribution of modern general linguistics, who stand in the broad hermeneutical tradition to which Aquila belongs.

If these facts appear disconcerting, note that we can also draw surprising parallels at the other end of the hermeneutical spectrum, namely, with respect to the allegorical approach associated with Origen's work (see below, pp. 49–50). It may be useful to point out, incidentally, that the opposition between these two approaches is only apparent, since "literal" and "figurative" often operate at different conceptual levels.[7] Indeed, one can say that these two methods achieve the same end: getting "behind" the text with a view to discovering meanings that are not obvious to the casual reader. For the moment, however, it will be useful to focus on the differences between the two methods and to keep in mind that, at least in the interpretation of numerous specific passages, they do in fact represent polar opposites.

THE PUZZLE OF HISTORICAL EXEGESIS

We would not be exaggerating greatly if we described the progress of biblical exegesis as the gradual abandonment of allegorical interpretation. One can point to some important moments in the history of the church that have aided this progress. As early as the fourth century, we find in Antiochene exegesis a fairly systematic program aimed at debunking the more objectionable features of Origen's approach. The twelfth-century intellectual renaissance saw, in the work of such writers as Peter the Chanter, significant shifts away from a predominant concern with the figurative sense of Scripture. And of greater importance in the theological arena was the attack on allegorical exegesis mounted by the Protestant Reformers.

Only after the eighteenth-century Enlightenment, however, did "scientific," grammatico-historical exegesis come into its own. By the time that Farrar wrote his *History of Interpretation* (1886), it was clear that the allegorical method had completely lost respectability in the scholarly establishment. One could no longer expect such a method to shed any light on the meaning of the text. One now had to pay exclusive attention to the text's historical meaning, that is, the meaning intended by the biblical author.

---

[6]George Steiner, *After Babel: Aspects of Language and Translation* (London: Oxford University Press, 1975), pp. 322–33, esp. p. 333.

[7]This factor may help to explain the apparent blurring of the distinctions from time to time. For example, we find it surprising to be told that "the great defect of medieval exegesis" was not so much its obsession with allegory but "an excess of literalism, or even more, an excess of historicism" (Don Jean Leclercq, "From Gregory the Great to St. Bernard," *CHB* 2:195). Perhaps related to this question is the argument by N. R. M. de Lange, *Origen and the Jews: Studies in Jewish-Christian Relations in Third Century Palestine* (Cambridge: Cambridge University Press, 1976), p. 110, that one can detect similarities between Origen and Akiba.

This description, however, leaves out a series of interesting and suggestive bits of information. It is simplistic, for example, to view Origen and the Antiochenes as representing two opposite approaches more or less exclusive of each other.[8] As we shall see, Origen used and defended literal interpretation on a number of occasions. Moreover, certain exegetical features that we would quickly dismiss as in some sense "allegorical" were consciously adopted as legitimate by the Antiochene exegetes. A striking example is one of John Chrysostom's homilies on the Gospel of John. Dealing with the wedding at Cana, he comments:

> At that time, therefore, Jesus made wine from water, and both then and now He does not cease changing wills that are weak and inconstant. There are men who are no different from water: cold and weak and inconstant. Accordingly, let us bring to the Lord those who are thus disposed, so as to cause their will to change and become like wine, so that it no longer is inconstant, but steadfast, and they become a cause of rejoicing both for themselves and for others.[9]

And Theodoret, whose historical commentaries are highly regarded, has this to say about Isaac's reference to the dew from heaven and the fatness of the earth (Gen. 27:39):

> These things according to the obvious superficial sense of the letter denote grace from above and abundance of blessings from the earth; but according to the higher interpretation they depict the *divinity* of the Lord Christ by means of the expression *dew*; and by the fatness of the earth, his *humanity* received from us.[10]

We are also puzzled to find that, in the Middle Ages, a renewed appreciation for the *sensus literalis* did not mean an abandonment of allegorical exegesis. Modern students find it difficult to develop sympathy for the intellectual work of medieval scholars, partly because one can easily find examples of overly subtle or trivial reasoning that appears to discredit scholastic thinking.

We have all had our laughs hearing about the serious attention paid by Schoolmen to such questions as whether men at the resurrection will recover all the fingernail clippings they lost during their lives, whether several angels can simultaneously occupy the same physical space, and so on. A good case can be made, however, for the thesis that the development of the scientific method was directly dependent on the kinds of debates refined during the scholastic period.[11]

More relevant for us is the recent work on medieval exegesis. We now realize, for example, that Hugh of St. Victor, by carefully differentiating the literal sense from the

---

[8]Perhaps the clearest and most helpful brief comparison between the Alexandrian and Antiochene schools is to be found in chap. 2 of D. S. Wallace-Hadrill, *Christian Antioch: A Study of Early Christian Thought in the East* (Cambridge: Cambridge University Press, 1982). Pp. 33–35 show the high degree of variability among the Antiochenes themselves; Theodore of Mopsuestia was the most extreme in emphasizing historical exegesis.

[9]John Chrysostom, *Commentary on Saint John the Apostle and Evangelist: Homilies 1–47,* trans. T. A. Goggin (Fathers of the Church 33; Washington, D.C.: Catholic University of America Press, 1957), p. 219. Note also on p. 310 the ending of his otherwise very historical explanation of John 4:1–12.

[10]Quoted in Davidson, *Sacred Hermeneutics,* p. 143. Even Theodore of Mopsuestia, for all his relentless attack on allegorical interpretation, occasionally allowed himself some freedom, as in his exposition of Psalm 45. See Dimitri Z. Zaharopoulos, "Theodore of Mopsuestia's Critical Methods in Old Testament Study" (Ph.D. diss., Boston University, 1964), pp. 192–93; see pp. 228–30 for Theodore's views on prophecy.

[11]Christopher Dawson, *Religion and the Rise of Western Culture* (Garden City, N.Y.: Doubleday, 1958; orig. 1950), pp. 17–22, 189–91.

allegorical and the tropological, "enormously increased the dignity of the historical sense. . . . The importance of the letter is constantly stressed."[12]

Such a notable flourishing of grammatical exegesis meant that many Schoolmen could no longer be satisfied with the effort to resolve contradictions by appealing to allegorical meaning. "Sometimes the contradiction appears to lie between two literal meanings. It was above all in dealing with such cases that the twelfth century interpreters made their new contribution" by paying careful attention to the nature of language, lexical usage, rhetorical questions, and so on.[13]

This concern for historical exegesis, however, did not suspend the need for allegorical interpretation. And the resulting tension is seen most clearly in the work of Rupert of Deutz (d. ca. 1129), for whom

> the letter gives instruction in holiness, but the mystical sense is a demonstration or prophecy of something far higher. Everywhere in Rupert's exegesis we can feel his consciousness of this lively tension between the literal and the spiritual senses, as he looks for the "incorporeal and invisible" which is to come and which is foreshadowed by the "corporeal and visible" deeds done in the past. The literal sense is a veil over the beauties which Grace reveals, and which a man must search for in the mirror of his sense-impressions.[14]

Although one might think otherwise, the Reformation did not fully resolve the basic tension. The view that the Protestant Reformers broke with the allegorical method and argued passionately for the *sensus literalis* is of course accurate. It is also accurate to point out that John Calvin in particular translated this concern into practice. Calvin's commentaries are an extraordinary testimony to sober, historical exegesis at a time when the dominant approach was motivated by other concerns.[15]

On the other hand, the challenge of figurative exegesis did not go away. Luther, for example, was somewhat inconsistent in the application of his principle; moreover, he acknowledged, on the basis of Galatians 4:21–31, that allegories may be used as pretty ornaments.[16] Calvin is more consistent in his use of the grammatico-historical method (see

---

[12]Smalley, *Study of the Bible,* p. 89; cf. also the quotations she gives on subsequent pages. Hugh's disciple, Andrew, went as far as to interpret Isaiah 53 without reference to Christ (p. 185). A good sampling of Hugh's work may be found in James J. Megivern, *Official Catholic Teachings: Biblical Interpretation* (Wilmington, N.C.: McGrath, 1978), pp. 161–66.

[13]G. R. Evans, *The Language and Logic of the Bible: The Earlier Middle Ages* (Cambridge: Cambridge University Press, 1984), p. 143. See especially her discussion of Peter the Chanter (pp. 146–63).

[14]Ibid., p. 15.

[15]See Hans-Joachim Kraus, "Calvin's Exegetical Principles," *Int* 31 (1977): 8–18, esp. the principle of lucid brevity, p. 12. For greater detail, Richard C. Gamble, "*Brevitas et facilitas:* Toward an Understanding of Calvin's Hermeneutic," *WTJ* 47 (1985): 1–17. Calvin, incidentally, thought very highly of Chrysostom and sought to emulate him. See John R. Walchenbach, "John Calvin as Biblical Commentator: An Investigation into Calvin's Use of John Chrysostom as an Exegetical Source" (Ph.D. diss., University of Pittsburgh, 1974). More specialized is Alexandre Ganoczy and Klaus Müller, *Calvins handschriftliche Annotationen zu Chrysostomus: Ein Beitrag zur Hermeneutik Calvins* (Veröffentlichungen des Instituts für europäische Geschichte Mainz 102; Wiesbaden: F. Steiner, 1981); see pp. 28–31 on the question of literal meaning.

[16]See Farrar, *History,* p. 328. According to A. Skevington Wood, Luther recognized a Spirit-given sense as "a new interpretation, which is then the new literal sense" (*Luther's Principles of Biblical Interpretation* [London: Tyndale, 1960], p. 32). Wood considers that "in his recognition of a *sensus plenior* he was perhaps nearer to Origen then he knew."

his commentary on Gal. 4:22), yet at one point he remarks that God's promise to Abraham, according to Paul, "is to be fulfilled, *not only allegorically* but literally, for Abraham's physical offspring."[17] And as is well known, differences among the Reformers concerning figurative language in the Bible came to a head in the debates regarding the significance of the Lord's Supper.[18]

But the greatest puzzle of all is that twentieth-century scholars have raised anew the question whether we need to be bound in our interpretation by the historical intent of the biblical author! These modern scholars, to be sure, are not calling us back to practice Origenistic allegorizing, but the nature of the contemporary debate makes clear that we are not facing simple black-and-white choices.

Since contemporary figures are, strictly speaking, beyond the scope of a history of interpretation, we need not discuss them here. I mention only the work of Paul Ricoeur, a philosopher with broad interests who has paid special attention to the problems of biblical hermeneutics. His emphasis on what he calls the "reservoir of meaning" attached to all literary texts is by no means unique or extravagant.[19] Rather, it represents a more general reaction to certain literary theories (and to the common methods of biblical scholarship) that place primary or exclusive emphasis on historical interpretation. The question "What did the author mean?" is now regarded as still valid but largely uninteresting. The literary text, we are told, lives on long after its author is dead, and so the ideas that later readers associate with that text can and must be viewed as part of its meaning.

The point of view just described is the source of considerable debate, but broad segments of modern scholarship regard it as plausible and even respectable. What needs to be noted here is that biblical scholarship, after triumphantly demonstrating that grammatico-historical exegesis is all that really matters, is being pressed on various sides to acknowledge that maybe there is something "behind" or "around" the text (at any rate, distinct from the original author's intent) that should be regarded as part of its meaning. And for all the significant differences between an Origen and a Ricoeur, it is precisely this feature that was earlier thought to be completely unacceptable in the allegorical method.

UNDERSTANDING ORIGEN

We find, then, a curious ambiguity throughout the history of literal interpretation. Origen can hardly be blamed for this state of affairs—he simply managed to pose the

---

[17]Calvin, *Institutes* 4. 16. 15 (p. 1337, my emphasis). In section 3. 4. 5 he rebuts a scholastic allegory of the raising of Lazarus by offering his own allegory. Although Calvin seems to propose this allegory partly tongue-in-cheek, the passage is suggestive. See also T. H. L. Parker, *Calvin's New Testament Commentaries* (Grand Rapids: Eerdmans, 1971), pp. 63–38, esp. p. 66.

[18]See J. Pelikan, *Reformation of Church and Dogma (1300–1700)* (The Christian Tradition 4; Chicago: University of Chicago Press, 1984), pp. 193–95. The seriousness of the problem is brought out by Roland H. Bainton, "The Bible in the Reformation," *CHB* 3.1–37, esp. pp. 29–30: with regard to the commandment against images, Carlstadt insisted on the literal meaning while Luther on the spiritual, yet the tables were completely reversed when they discussed the words "this is my body."

[19]See Paul Ricoeur, *Essays on Biblical Interpretation* (Philadelphia: Fortress, 1980), esp. pp. 49–57 for his discussion of allegorical and similar approaches. Note also David C. Steinmetz, "The Superiority of Pre-Critical Exegesis," *Ex Auditi* 1 (1985): 74–82 (orig. in *Theology Today* 37 [1980]: 27–38), esp. p. 82: "The medieval theory of levels of meaning in the biblical text, with all its undoubted defects, flourished because it is true, while the modern theory of a single meaning, with all its demonstrable virtues, is false."

hermeneutical problem in a particularly forceful way. Perhaps he can also help us to find a way to its solution.

For Origen, literal meanings are indeed important. In his most basic theological work, *On First Principles,* he stresses the fact that most of the narrative material in Scripture is historical. Somewhat condescendingly, it is true, Origen explains that the literal meaning is useful for simple believers, the implication being that truly mature Christians will be able to see beyond the literal.[20]

But other passages make it plain that he sincerely viewed the literal meaning as important. Origen's interpretation of Psalm 37, for example, "is presented as exegesis of the original historical sense, and not as exegesis of another and higher content behind the historical. The allegorical meaning is itself to be found within the historical sense of the text."[21] Again, when he addresses an accusation by Celsus that the story of Lot and his two daughters in Genesis 19 is iniquitous, Origen criticizes Celsus for not paying attention to the ordinary sense of the passage. Indeed, Origen regards it as a mark of the Bible's superiority over pagan writers that the literal meaning of Scripture is morally commendable.[22]

As one begins to appreciate the character of Origen's debate with Celsus, a remarkable fact emerges. Among the Greeks, divine inspiration and allegorical meaning were often seen as coordinate, especially in the case of Homer. As a result, Origen was obliged to formulate his views of biblical interpretation in response to two quite different lines of attack. On the one hand, some people objected that Christians resorted to strained allegorizing to save themselves from embarrassment. On the other hand, an inability to interpret the Bible allegorically might be understood as evidence that the Bible was not inspired.

It is fascinating, therefore, to see Origen downplaying allegorical interpretation by asserting the truth, goodness, and value of the Bible's literal meaning (over against pagan myths, which can *only* be interpreted allegorically). At the same time, Origen devotes much of books 4 and 5 in *Contra Celsum* justifying the allegorical method; after all, the skill of allegorical interpretation is regarded by both Celsus and Origen as a sign of intelligence.[23]

We would be quite wrong, however, to think that Origen defended the allegorical method simply to win points with his intellectual contemporaries. Quite the contrary, he viewed the method as having basic theological significance. In the first place, he argued that the unbelief of the Jews could be traced to their insistence that the prophecies be interpreted literally.[24] We may want to respond, of course, that the application of the Old Testament prophecies to Christ is something quite different from allegorical interpretation. But it is important for us to understand that Origen himself did not see a substantial difference between the two approaches.

The question whether Old Testament prophecies should be interpreted literally is a fascinating problem that has surfaced repeatedly throughout church history. In the Middle

---

[20]Origen, *On First Principles* 4. 3. 4; 4. 2. 5 (pp. 294–96, 278).

[21]Karen Jo Torjesen, *Hermeneutical Procedure and Theological Method in Origen's Exegesis* (PTS 28; Berlin: W. de Gruyter, 1986), p. 23.

[22]Origen, *Contra Celsum* 4. 45 and 1. 17–18 (*ANF* 4:518 and 403), referred to by Dan G. McCartney, "Literal and Allegorical Interpretation in Origen's *Contra Celsum,*" *WTJ* 48 (1986): 281–301, esp. pp. 288–89. For other examples, see R. P. C. Hanson, *Allegory and Event: A Study of the Sources and Significance of Origen's Interpretation of Scripture* (London: SCM, 1959), p. 238. Note also Wiles, "Origen," pp. 470–74.

[23]McCartney, "Literal and Allegorical," pp. 292–93.

[24]Origen, *On First Principles* 4. 2. 1, p. 270.

Ages, for example, scholars devoted considerable attention to the precise classification of the various senses of Scripture, and messianic prophecies created a special difficulty.

> The Jews had been accused of interpreting Scripture "according to the letter", instead of according to the life-giving spirit. Was their interpretation of Old Testament prophecy to be called "the literal sense" of the prophecy, while the christological interpretation went under the heading "spiritual or allegorical"? This division seemed to clash with the received teaching that the literal sense was true and basic.[25]

Moreover, we should appreciate the substantive parallel between Origen's controversy with the Jews and modern debates touching on whether the Old Testament prophecies regarding the future of Israel will be interpreted literally. In one of the most popular premillennialist books at the turn of the last century, the story is told of a Jew who asked a Christian minister whether he took literally Gabriel's promise that Mary's son would reign over Jacob (Luke 1:32–33). The minister responded that the prophecy referred to Christ's spiritual reign over the church, to which the Jew replied: "Then . . . neither do I believe literally the words preceding, which say that this Son of David should be born of a virgin; but take them to be merely a figurative manner of describing the remarkable character for purity of him who is the subject of the prophecy."[26]

Second, Origen was convinced that to interpret everything literally would necessarily lead to blasphemy or contradiction. This sentiment has been shared by many other believers.[27] Particularly significant is the experience of Augustine, who for a time struggled with what he felt were offensive elements in the Old Testament. Finally, he heard with delight Ambrose's emphasis on 2 Corinthians 3:6 ("the letter kills, but the Spirit gives life"): "drawing aside the mystic veil, he spiritually laid open that which, accepted to the 'letter,' seemed to teach perverse doctrines."[28]

Here again, Origen and most ancients apparently failed to appreciate that what we may call a "straightforward" reading of the text—that is, one that is sensitive to simple figures of speech used by the biblical author—is more than adequate to avoid the problems he feared.[29] In some respects, however, the difference between Origen and many

---

[25]Beryl Smalley, "The Bible in the Medieval Schools," *CHB* 2:197–220, esp. p. 214. Cf. also Erwin I. J. Rosenthal, "The Study of the Bible in Medieval Judaism," ibid., pp. 252–79, esp. pp. 256, 268. Esra Shereshevsky's wonderful book *Rashi: The Man and His World* (New York: Sepher-Hermon, 1982) devotes chap. 5 to this general question.

[26]W. E. Blackstone, *Jesus Is Coming* (New York: Revell, 1898), pp. 20–21.

[27]On Jerome, see H. F. D. Sparks, "Jerome as Biblical Scholar," *CHB* 1:510–41, esp. p. 538: "To take some passages in the Old Testament literally would be either absurd or unedifying: Hosea cannot possibly be taken literally (for 'God commands nothing except what is honourable'); while to interpret Revelation literally would be to reduce it to the level of a purely Jewish tract." Similarly, the Reformed theologian Francis Turretin, *The Doctrine of Scripture*, trans. J. W. Beardslee III (Grand Rapids: Baker, 1981), p. 208.

[28]Augustine, *Confessions* 6. 4 (*NPNF*, 1st ser., 1:92). See also *On Christian Doctrine* 3. 5 (*NPNF* 2:559). Among many works devoted to Augustine's views, see Charles J. Costello, *St. Augustine's Doctrine on the Inspiration and Canonicity of Scripture* (Washington, D.C.: Catholic University of America, 1930), pp. 45–56, which focus on the issue of historicity. Gerhard Strauss, *Schriftgebrauch, Schriftauslegung, und Schriftbeweis bei Augustin* (BGBH 1; Tübingen: J. C. B. Mohr, 1959), esp. chaps. 3–4, which amount to a (difficult) commentary on *On Christian Doctrine*. Clearer and more comprehensive is Belford D. Jackson, "Semantics and Hermeneutics in Saint Augustine's *De doctrina Christiana*" (Ph.D. diss., Yale University, 1967), esp. pp. 171–87, which emphasize Augustine's theory of signs. More recently, Bertrand de Margerie has devoted volume 3 of *Introduction à l'histoire de l'exégèse* (Paris: Cerf: 1980–83) to Augustine; note pp. 98–100, which bring Ricoeur into the picture.

[29]Perhaps only Theodore of Mopsuestia clearly and explicitly included metaphorical meaning as part of the literal meaning. See Alexander Kerrigan, *St. Cyril of Alexandria: Interpreter of the Old Testament* (AnBib 2; Rome: Pontificio Istituto Biblico, 1952), pp. 51–56; note also p. 58 on Jerome and p. 86 on Cyril.

modern interpreters is often one of degree, that is, of where the line is drawn between figurative and nonfigurative interpretation. There is little if any substantive difference, for example, between the way that Origen or a modern scholar would argue that the Bible uses anthropomorphisms to speak of God.

Third, Origen was convinced that the New Testament itself, by using allegory, establishes the validity of the method. In this connection he can appeal to 1 Corinthians 9:9–10; 10:1–4; Galatians 4:21–31; and even Ephesians 5:31–32.[30] In particular, his homilies on Exodus (section 5. 1) deal with Paul's use of the Old Testament narrative in 1 Corinthians 10:

> You observe how greatly the sense Paul gives us differs from the narrative of the text. . . . Does it not seem right to keep a rule of this kind, as given to us, by observing a like standard in other cases? or, as some desire, are we to desert what the great and noble Apostle has told us and turn again to Jewish fables?[31]

His use of these passages makes it plain that one of our main difficulties is that of definition. We must return to the question of choosing the criteria that help us to establish what counts as allegorical interpretation.

Fourth, Origen stresses that part of the divine aim is to veil the truth. Origen is not as emphatic on this point as his predecessor Clement of Alexandria, but he does bring it up in some important passages.[32] At the very beginning of *On First Principles,* he states that the whole church believes that there is a secret meaning in the Bible that is hidden from the majority. Obviously this comment raises the larger question whether the Bible ought to be regarded as clear or obscure, the topic of chapter 4.

One aspect of this question, however, requires discussion here, and we may view it as a fifth point, namely, Origen's conception of human weaknesses in spiritual understanding. For Origen himself, this consideration afforded a means of distinguishing between immature and mature believers: the latter, through their skill in allegorical interpretation, show that they have the key to knowledge.[33] Whether consciously or not, Origen tends therefore to identify spiritual maturity with intellectual prowess.

On the other hand, once we relate human weakness to the allegorical method, a more positive development of the concept becomes possible. Indeed, "the whole of medieval exegesis is founded" on the assumption that we can understand God only dimly and that therefore he adapts his word to our damaged mental faculty.[34] An important exponent of this concept was Gregory the Great, whose writings played a foundational role in the development of medieval theology. In his view, those embarrassing features of the Bible that appear like banalities should be understood as evidences of God's mercy, for they show his willingness to speak in a way we can understand.

What appears strange, defective, or false is not really a fault in Scripture, but one in us. Paradoxically, biblical difficulties become aids for us. "Each obscure or tortuous

---

[30]See Origen, *Contra Celsum* 4. 49 (ANF 4:520) and On First Principles 4. 2. 6, p. 280.

[31]Quoted in R. B. Tollinton, *Selections from the Commentaries and Homilies of Origen* (London: SPCK, 1929), pp. 72–74.

[32]Origen, *On First Principles* 4. 2. 8; 4. 3. 1, 11 (pp. 284, 288, 305). From a different perspective, note Augustine's remark: "Some of the expressions are so obscure as to shroud the meaning in the thickest darkness. And I do not doubt that all this was *divinely arranged* for the purpose of subduing pride by toil and of preventing a feeling of satiety in the intellect, which generally holds in small esteem what is discovered without difficulty" (*On Christian Doctrine* 2. 6. 7, quoted by Gerald Bonner, "Augustine as Biblical Scholar," *CHB* 1:547).

[33]Origen, *On First Principles* 4. 1. 7; 4. 2. 3 (pp. 267–68, 274–75).

[34]Evans, *Language and Logic,* p. 1.

narrative, each ambiguity or contradiction, meets an obscurity or twist or confusion in human thinking and is thus more, not less, intelligible to man's clouded sinful mind.[35]

ALLEGORY AND PRACTICAL APPLICATION

It should be clear by now that the allegorical method was not an isolated quirk among early Christians. They did not adopt it arbitrarily or unthinkingly but viewed it rather as one of the foundation stones in a large theological and intellectual edifice.

But there is more to say about the method. Quite apart from broad theological commitments, allegorical interpretations are very difficult to avoid for a believer who wishes to apply the truth of Scripture to his or her life. One already senses this concern in the writings of Philo, who argued that there was no real point in reading about Abraham's journeys unless they refer to spiritual journeys in which we too participate.[36]

Similarly, Origen believed that the spiritual sense contains universal significance and shows "how the hearer or reader participates in" the history of salvation. Indeed, "For Origen it is most of all the 'usefulness' . . . of Scripture which inspiration through the Holy Spirit guarantees."[37]

But Origen was hardly peculiar in this respect. The purpose of all the Fathers in studying Scripture was "purely practical, and we do not understand their exegesis until we understand this."[38] Augustine himself provides a good illustration. In *On Christian Doctrine* 3. 10 (*NPNF* 2:560), after he has condemned interpretations that take literally that which is figurative ("a miserable slavery"), he also warns of taking the literal in a figurative way. How, then, does one differentiate between the two? "And the way is certainly as follows: Whatever then is in the word of God that cannot, when taken literally, be referred either to purity of life or soundness of doctrine, you may set down as figurative." As this subsequent discussion makes clear, Augustine has in mind here the command to love God and neighbor. This practical concern has become for him a basic hermeneutical principle that allows allegorizing.[39]

---

[35]Ibid., p. 3. See also Evans's work *The Thought of Gregory the Great* (Cambridge: Cambridge University Press, 1986), p. 95.

[36]Samuel Sandmel, *Philo of Alexandria: An Introduction* (New York: Oxford University Press, 1979), p. 25. On Philo's exegesis, see the important contribution by B. L. Mack, "Philo Judaeus and Exegetical Traditions in Alexandria," *ANRW* 2. 25. 2, pp. 227–71. For greater detail, see Irmgard Christiansen, *Die Technik der allegorischen Auslegungswissenschaft bei Philon von Alexandrien* (BGBH 7; Tübingen: J. C. B. Mohr, 1969). Several essays on biblical interpretation are included in Yehoshua Amir, Die hellenistische Gestalt des Judentums bei Philon von Alexandrien (Forschungen zum jüdisch-christlichen Dialog 5; Neukirchen-Vluyn: Neukirchener, 1983); note esp. "Rabbinischer Midrasch und philonische Allegorese," pp. 107–18.

[37]Torjesen, *Hermeneutical Procedure*, pp. 68–69, 124. On p. 126, Torjesen points out that this usefulness of Scripture is inherent in the meaning of the text; therefore, a distinction must be made between Origen's view and the modern understanding about application. On pp. 25–26, she remarks that, since Origen is intensely interested in the situation of the hearer, his exegesis of the original situation of the psalmist already includes its significance for the hearer, so that in this case there is no need for a separate task of allegorical exegesis. On the general question, note Jaroslav Pelikan, *The Emergence of the Catholic Tradition (100–600)* (The Christian Tradition 1; Chicago: University of Chicago Press, 1971), pp. 60–62. A negative aspect is pointed out by Hanson: while Origen's exegesis of Jeremiah 13:12 is admirable in many respects, "his interpretation is vitiated by his reliance on a faulty translation and his determination to extort some immediately edifying meaning from the passage" (*Allegory*, p. 179).

[38]R. P. C. Hanson, "Biblical Exegesis in the Early Church," *CHB* 1:412–53.

[39]See Jackson, "Semantics," pp. 79–86, and Preus, *Shadow*, p. 13.

Medieval scholars were no different. Smalley asks why the historical approach of the Antiochenes was neglected in the Middle Ages. "The answer must be that our Latin student preferred the Alexandrian method to the Antiochene. The former satisfied a paramount emotional need and corresponded to a world outlook while the latter struck him as cold and irrelevant."[40] Indeed, they might well have put it this way: "What value is there in the Bible if all you can do is state what the text says?" In the mind of the Schoolmen, there was no significant difference between applying the text and allegorizing. And we need to admit that *in practice* there is often very little difference.

Perhaps two modern examples will shed light on this problem. C. S. Lewis was a twentieth-century believer, far removed in time and culture from the likes of Origen. Moreover, Lewis was not a backwoods fundamentalist but a highly respected literary scholar. Toward the end of his popular little book *Reflections on the Psalms*, Lewis addresses the perplexing problem of the imprecatory psalms. Here is his personal solution to that problem:

> Of the cursing Psalms I suppose most of us make our own moral allegories. . . . We know the proper object of utter hostility—wickedness, especially our own. From this point of view I can use even the horrible passage in [Psalm] 137 about dashing the Babylonian babies against the stones. I know things in the inner world which are like babies; the infantile beginnings of small indulgences, small resentments, which may one day become dipsomania or settled hatred, but which woo us and wheedle us with special pleadings and seem so tiny, so helpless that in resisting them we feel we are being cruel to animals. They begin whimpering to us "I don't ask much, but", or "I had at least hoped", or "you owe yourself *some* consideration". Against all such pretty infants (the dears have such winning ways) the advice of the Psalm is the best. Knock the little bastards' brains out. And "blessed" is he who can, for it's easier said than done.[41]

My other example is a contemporary preacher I know who combines in a marvelous way theological soundness, academic achievement, and eloquence. Not too long ago I heard him preach a superb sermon on the raising of Lazarus. He had obviously done his exegetical homework, and up to the last five or ten minutes, he kept close to his text and communicated to the congregation, clearly and vigorously, the theological significance of John 11. In his church, however, there is great emphasis on the need to be practical and to apply the text as explicitly as possible to the audience, most of whom are believers. As he addressed the question "What does this mean to you?" he began to relate the raising of Lazarus to the believer's sanctification. There is of course nothing theologically wrong with viewing resurrection as a picture of sanctification (see Rom. 6:1–4). It seems fairly clear, however, that the idea was far removed from John's mind as he penned the eleventh chapter of his gospel. This preacher was therefore obligated to use the text allegorically, stating that, when Jesus orders that the grave clothes be removed from Lazarus, he is ordering us to remove the sins from our lives.[42]

---

[40]Smalley, *Study of the Bible*, p. 19.
[41]C. S. Lewis, *Reflections on the Psalms* (New York: Harcourt Brace Jovanovich, 1958), p. 136.
[42]Interestingly, Frei views application as something like an extension of typology, which is figural interpretation (*Eclipse,* p. 3). If a preacher is very concerned about direct application but does not wish to resort to allegorizing, the result is often a different sermon altogether, as happens not infrequently in Puritan works and quite characteristically in Chrysostom's homilies.

It is unnecessary to point out that every hour of every day thousands of Christians allegorize the Scriptures as they seek to find spiritual guidance. Moreover, many of the most effective preachers the Christian church has seen made consistent use of this approach. Charles Spurgeon, the nineteenth-century Baptist preacher whose powerful sermons exerted a tremendous influence week by week throughout the Christian world, is one of the clearest examples.

None of this makes the method right, and it certainly would be wrong-headed to suggest that allegorical interpretation be rehabilitated in modern scholarship. On the other hand, we can hardly justify developing a hermeneutical approach that works in splendid isolation from the way believers usually read the Scriptures. And the force of this consideration is pressed upon us when we realize that the method played a significant role in the shaping of Christian theology.[43]

Without attempting in our brief space to solve this difficult problem, we may take note of two or three relevant points. In the first place, the allegorical or "free" use of Scripture has much in common with the way literature in general is often handled. Numerous public speakers, especially if they are well read, will pepper their discourses with allusions to literary themes or actual quotations, even though the original context had little or nothing to do with the contemporary concerns to which they are being applied. In other words, there is a stylistic or emotional force about such a use of literature that appears to justify it (at least one never hears objections to this practice, so long as it does not show up in a proper commentary on the works themselves).

Similarly, we all know ministers who, when preaching on a particular topic, will ignore passages that address that topic directly and choose for their text a passage that does not. Certainly it is much more exciting for the congregation to hear an eloquent sermon on a passage that they had no idea meant what the preacher is taking it to mean than to listen through a careful exposition of what a passage plainly says!

In short, much allegorical exposition arises from the need for rhetorical effect. Unfortunately, to the extent that the congregation learns thereby to look for "hidden meanings" in the text, to that extent the text is either subjected to greater distortions or else it is removed from the common believer who is unable to produce exegetical surprises.

In the second place, allegorizing is difficult to resist because the believer, quite naturally, expects the Word of God to say and do more than is immediately apparent. Clearly, it is not simply the literary power of allegory that appeals to a Christian congregation. Our commitment to the divine inspiration of Scripture raises certain expectations in our minds as to what we are likely to find in it.

This approach to Scripture is especially prominent in the Pietist tradition. The eighteenth-century theologian J. J. Rambach, for example, stressed the Spirit's work both in the inspiration of Scripture and in the believer's reading. This view, as Frei puts it,

> demands that one be able to discern a spiritual sense above the ordinary grammatical and logical senses in at least some of the sacred words. Moreover, the spiritual sense of such individual words lends them an expanded force or emphasis, so that they

---

[43]For a particularly interesting example, see Jaroslav Pelikan, "The 'Spiritual Sense' of Scripture: The Exegetical Basis for St. Basil's Doctrine of the Holy Spirit," in *Basil of Caesarea: Christian, Humanist, Ascetic. A Sixteen-Hundredth Anniversary Symposium,* 2 vols., ed. P. J. Fedwick (Toronto: Pontifical Institute of Medieval Studies, 1981) 1:337–60.

have as much meaning and resonance attributed to them as they can possibly bear. "Emphasis" becomes a technical term. It stands for a doctrine or a way of seeing a meaning of scriptural words quite beyond what they appear to have in ordinary usage or in their immediate context.[44]

In a very important sense, we are quite right to assume that there is more to a passage than its obvious meaning, for our conception of the unity of the Bible requires us to assess specific portions in the light of the whole tenor of Scripture. We could argue, for example, that, when a preacher sees the doctrine of Christian sanctification taught in John 11, he is merely exploiting certain associations that are made explicit elsewhere. It would be better, of course, if the minister makes clear that the passage in question does not address sanctification directly, but there is nothing inherently wrong in his reminding the congregation that the Scriptures do in fact use the figure of resurrection to shed light on the doctrine of sanctification. Interestingly, Origen himself justified the use of allegory on the grounds that he was concerned to grasp the *entire* meaning of the biblical material.[45] This matter will come up again in chapter 4.

Wallace-Hadrill provides a marvelous illustration of the way in which cross-fertilization between passages can take place on the basis of belief in the unity of Scripture. Psalm 110:7 says, "He will drink from a brook beside the way; therefore he will lift up his head." Eusebius finds that, by referring to Psalm 123:4, he can link together the two Psalm references with Matthew 26:4; Philippians 2:8; and Ephesians 1:20. On the basis of Psalm 123:4, "the brook" must mean

> the time of temptations: *our soul hath passed through the brook, yea, our soul hath passed through the deep waters.* He therefore drinks in the brook, it says, that cup evidently of which He darkly spoke at the time of His passion, when He said: *Father, if it be possible let this cup pass from Me....* It was, then, by drinking this cup that He lifted up His head, as the apostle also says, for when He was *obedient to the Father unto death, even the death of the Cross, therefore,* he says, *God hath highly exalted Him,* raising Him from the dead.[46]

TOWARD A DEFINITION OF ALLEGORY

I have so far used the term *allegory* rather loosely—deliberately so, since we need to appreciate fully the fact that, in the mind of Origen and many others, virtually any type of figurative interpretation could be described as allegorical. The terminological problem is a serious one, since even today the argument is sometimes heard that Paul believed in the allegorical method—after all, did he not use the term *allēgoreō* in Galatians 4:24? We can hardly assume, however, that the meaning we associate with the English term corresponds exactly with that of the cognate Greek verb. One could just as easily argue, on the basis of the term *paroxysmos* in Acts 15:39, that Paul and Barnabas suffered physical convulsions over the question of whether Mark should accompany them.

A comparison between Paul's use of the Abraham-Hagar story in Galatians and Philo's allegorical treatment of that incident makes clear that the differences between the two approaches are much more significant than the similarities.[47] The fourth-century

---

[44]Frei, *Eclipse*, p. 38.
[45]Origen, *On First Principles* 4. 3. 5, pp. 296–97.
[46]D. S. Wallace-Hadrill, *Eusebius of Caesarea* (London: A. R. Mowbray, 1960), p. 93.
[47]See J. B. Lightfoot, *The Epistle of St. Paul to the Galatians* (Grand Rapids: Zondervan, 1962; orig. 1865), pp. 198–200.

exegetes from Antioch appreciated the fact that, whatever else Paul intended by his reference to Genesis, he continued to affirm the narrative's historicity. In their attack upon Origen's allegorical method, therefore, they properly focused on Origen's tendency (not as pronounced as Philo's, to be sure) to downplay the historical character of Old Testament narratives.[48]

The Antiochenes themselves, of course, would not have denied the metaphorical character of many biblical passages. Moreover, they would have insisted that there is a higher, or spiritual, meaning (that is, a messianic reference) to the Old Testament prophecies. They used the term *theōria* to describe their position, a matter that will concern us again in chapter 5. Origen regarded such interpretations as instances of allegorizing, but the Antiochenes were correct in identifying the historical issue as a distinguishing feature that separated Paul's approach from Origen's. In their view, Paul was using *typology* in Galatians 4:21–31, that is, an interpretation that affirms the historicity of the narrative and then attempts to discover a theological significance in it; this deeper meaning, though perhaps not obvious on the face of the narrative, is closely tied to the literal meaning.[49]

One can see why some scholars have objected to the distinction between allegory and typology. From one perspective one can argue that

> both allegory and *theōria* speak about the same anagogical dynamic Origen so eloquently described: the biblical text leads the reader upward into spiritual truths that are not immediately obvious and that provide a fuller understanding of God's economy of salvation. . . . The fact remains that in acknowledging the divine author of Scripture both sides sought deeper meaning and hidden treasures of revelation in the sacred text.[50]

We must admit that, as long as the allegorical method is perceived primarily as the attempt to look for a "deeper" or "higher" or "spiritual" meaning in the text, then the difference between it and typology seems trivial or even artificial. On the other hand, if we narrow the meaning of *allegorical* so that it describes a playing down or even a rejection of historicity, then the distinction becomes valid, useful, and important.

The qualification then needs to be made, however, that in this sense Origen himself did not adopt a full-blown allegorical approach. As we have seen, he sometimes defended the plain and historical meaning of narratives rather forcefully. Moreover, one may infer that he believed there should be a connection between such a meaning and the

---

[48]See Hanson, *Allegory*, p. 52 and chap. 10. Critics of Origen have seldom been fair in failing to recognize Origen's relatively high regard for historicity, in contrast to Philo's customary approach.

[49]For a summary of the interpretations of Chrysostom, Theodore, and Theodoret, see Robert J. Kepple, "An Analysis of the Antiochene Exegesis of Galatians 4:24–26," *WTJ* 39 (1976–77): 239–49. Modern formulations have refined the concept of typology. One of the most helpful brief discussions is R. T. France, *Jesus and the Old Testament: His Application of Old Testament Passages to Himself and His Mission* (Grand Rapids: Baker, 1982; orig. 1971), pp. 38–43.

[50]Karlfried Froehlich, trans. and ed., *Biblical Interpretation in the Early Church* (Sources of Early Christian Thought; Philadelphia: Fortress, 1984), pp. 20, 22. This volume includes an excellent translation of Theodore of Mopsuestia's commentary on Galatians 4:21–31, a basic source for our understanding of the controversy. The eighteenth-century skeptic Anthony Collins, incidentally, argued that "the meaningfulness of the biblical author's language must . . . be governed by the same criteria that govern the meaning of any proposition," yet this principle is "inapplicable to typological or allegorical or any other than literal meaning"; in short, nonliteral interpretation "results in rules that are completely arbitrary because they violate the natural use of language" (Frei, *Eclipse*, p. 82). For a more recent objection to the distinction between allegory and typology, see Paul K. Jewett, "Concerning the Allegorical Interpretation of Scripture," *WTJ* 17 (1954–55): 1–20.

meanings arrived at through allegory (though we may wonder whether he really put this theory to practice with any consistency).

True, Origen denied the historicity of certain passages that, in his opinion, would be dishonoring to God if taken literally. In these cases, however, Origen would have probably argued that the biblical writers themselves did not intend the material to be taken literally.[51] We need to appreciate the fundamental difference between (1) the view that a biblical narrative, while intended as historical, should be more or less dehistoricized in favor of an allegorical interpretation, and (2) the view that the original point itself of a biblical passage is not historical.

Evangelicals recognize that the parables of Jesus, for example, are not necessarily historical but rather are fictional stories told for illustrative purposes. Many conservative scholars believe that the discourses in the Book of Job, whatever historical basis they may have, are not intended to be taken as transcriptions of what was said but represent a certain amount of creative stylization for purposes of dramatic effect.

In a recent and controversial commentary, the highly respected evangelical scholar R. H. Gundry has argued that Matthew wrote his gospel to present a semihistorical, dramatized account of the life of Christ. One of many arguments Gundry used to support his position is that a literal, historical rendering of Matthew creates unbearable tensions between this gospel and the others—tensions that cannot be solved by a simple appeal to harmonization.

> Bending over backward for harmonizations results in falling flat on the ground. Furthermore, harmonizations often become so complicated that they are not only unbelievable, but also . . . damaging to the clarity of Scripture. They actually subvert scriptural authority by implicitly denying the plain meaning of the text.[52]

The parallels between this approach and Origen's are unmistakable. In both cases, we may want to respond that the narratives in question seem to present themselves as historical and that we would therefore need very compelling arguments to interpret them otherwise. I wish to point out, however, that the question of the allegorical method has not at all been raised in connection with Gundry's commentary; the reason is, of course, that Gundry has used a grammatico-historical approach to reach his conclusions. In a less obvious sense, however, Origen was following the same approach. He shows sensitivity to the importance of the author's intention, and that sensitivity we usually understand as the exact opposite of the allegorical method. In short, we cannot dismiss Origen's ideas on the grounds that he was merely allegorizing.

So much for the question of historicity. There are other ways, however, in which we may wish to restrict the meaning of *allegorical*. For example, for Philo the allegorical method was part of an involved *philosophical system*; similarly, there is a tendency in Origen's work to interpret biblical material as an expression of Christian Alexandrian philosophy. "The great

---

[51]Wiles comments: "How could the declared despiser of the 'letter' of scripture also hold that inspiration applied to every jot and tittle of the scriptural record? The answer lies in the fact that when Origen insists that every jot and tittle is inspired, he means every jot and tittle of the intended meaning. The minutest detail is important, but it is the detail spiritually understood that counts" ("Origen," p. 475).

[52]Gundry, *Matthew,* p. 626.

value of allegory to those who practiced it was the way in which it made possible a theologically unified interpretation of the Bible as a whole."[53]

It would be self-delusion, however, to think that the absence of allegory guarantees protection against extrabiblical forms of thought. Theodore of Mopsuestia used the concept of historical development to unify biblical teaching. He introduced other concepts, however, not always consciously. "Like the allegorists, he may think that he has found the categories he needs from within scripture itself, when in fact he deceives himself in so thinking."[54]

A third aspect that helps us restrict the scope of what allegorical exegesis entails is that of *arbitrariness*. While doubtless neither Philo nor Origen would have accepted such a characterization of their approach, very frequently it is impossible to detect any necessary connection between the text and the meaning ascribed to it by Alexandrian allegorizers. Medieval scholars, to be sure, made a valiant effort to formulate guidelines and boundaries, but one cannot say that they succeeded. The most powerful argument against the allegorical method is that it seems to allow for no controls. In effect, anyone can see any meaning he or she wishes to see in any passage.[55]

Finally, we may define the method as requiring the presence of an *elite* group of interpreters—spiritual, mature believers who alone are given the key to the deeper meaning of Scripture. This feature of allegory is in some respects the most disagreeable one, and it leads very naturally into the subject of chapter 4.

But we must first summarize our findings. A rigorous definition of the allegorical method emphasizes its dehistoricizing, philosophizing, arbitrary, and elitist aspects. It is easy to prove that one can find no evidence of such a method in the New Testament. But we do an injustice to Origen and to most subsequent so-called allegorizers if we fail to note that they perceived their method as a broad approach to Scripture, one that was sensitive to the Bible's many figurative expressions, prophetic announcements, and suggestive associations. Note, for example, how Jeremiah 3:1 alludes to the law regarding divorce in Deuteronomy 24:1–4, but not in order to say anything about literal divorce. Rather the prophet uses it to introduce the Lord's judgment: "But you have lived as a prostitute with many lovers—would you now return to me?"[56]

Perhaps we can still learn from the great commentator J. B. Lightfoot, who can hardly be accused of using anything but the most sober grammatico-historical methods:

> The power of allegory has been differently felt in different ages, as it is differently felt at any one time by diverse nations. Analogy, allegory, metaphor—by what boundaries are these separated the one from the other? What is true or false, correct or incorrect, as an analogy or an allegory? What argumentative force must be assigned to

---

[53]M. F. Wiles, "Theodore of Mopsuestia as Representative of the Antiochene School," *CHB* 1:508.

[54]Ibid., p. 509.

[55]Hanson reflects on the use of Proverbs 8:22 by various theologians in the early church: "It is indicative of the weakness of the exegetical principles adopted by the Fathers that these four writers, living in different times and in different places, could confidently quote exactly the same text in order to support four quite different Christological theories" ("Biblical Exegesis," p. 441). On p. 450, Hanson speaks of the method as "a technique for emancipating the exegete from bondage to the text." For a harsher (too harsh, I think) judgment of Origen's method, see Hanson, *Allegory,* pp. 245, 371. Note the discussion above concerning the Reformers' inconsistent use of literal versus figurative interpretation (p. 66).

[56]See Fishbane, *Biblical Interpretation,* pp. 308–11.

either? We should at least be prepared with an answer to these questions, before we venture to sit in judgment on any individual case.[57]

Common believers routinely exploit these aspects, sometimes with damaging effects; they need to learn from professional exegetes how to develop historical and textual sensitivity. For their part, exegetes need to consider whether their work should reflect, to some extent, those qualities that believers give expression to when they read the Scriptures with little more than their faith. The answers are not easy to come by, but scholars and pastors can hardly afford to ignore the questions.

[57]Lightfoot, *Galatians*, p. 200.

four

CLEAR

OR OBSCURE?

REFORMATION DOCTRINE AND THE CONTEMPORARY CHALLENGE

It is no exaggeration to say that the sixteenth-century Reformation was, at bottom, a hermeneutical revolution. Luther's meeting with Cardinal Cajetan at Augsburg in 1518 developed into a discussion of *Unigenitus* (a papal bull published in 1343), which asserted the notion of a treasury of merits. In response Luther wrote a statement in which he refused "to discard so many important clear proofs of Scripture on account of a single ambiguous and obscure decretal of a Pope who is a mere human being." Not surprisingly, Cajetan objected that *someone* has to interpret the Bible and that the Pope is supreme in this area. Interpretation, however, had been a crucial element in Luther's "individual struggle for spiritual existence." He therefore unambiguously denied the Pope's supreme authority and proceeded to make his hermeneutical concerns a key element in the religious conflict that followed.[1]

The connection between this chapter and the previous one is very close. The main contribution of the Protestant Reformers to biblical hermeneutics is their insistence on *the plain meaning* of Scripture. Their concern, however, focused specifically on the need to rescue the Bible from the allegorical method. We see this element strikingly expressed in many of Luther's remarks: "The Holy Spirit is the plainest writer and speaker in heaven and earth and therefore His words cannot have more than one, and that the very simplest sense, which we call the literal, ordinary, natural sense."[2] He can refer to allegories as dirt and scum that lead to idle speculations; indeed, for Luther, all heresies arise from neglecting the simple words of Scripture.[3]

As we have already noted, the contrast between the Reformers and the medieval scholastics should not be exaggerated. Not only had medieval scholarship made notable advances in historical and grammatical exegesis; it is also true that the Reformers' disapproval

---

[1]A. Skevington Wood, *Luther's Principles of Biblical Interpretation* (London: Tyndale, 1960), pp. 5–6.
[2]*Works of Martin Luther* (Philadelphia: Holman, 1930) 3:350.
[3]Frederic W. Farrar, *History of Interpretation* (New York: Dutton, 1886), pp. 327–28.

of allegory was not always consistent. Still, it is quite accurate to describe the Reformers as opponents of the allegorical method.

My concern in this chapter, however, is to identify their reason for that opposition. Up to the time of the Reformation, the Bible was perceived by most people as a fundamentally obscure book. The common folk could not be expected to understand it, and so they were discouraged from reading it.[4] Indeed the Bible was not even available in a language they could understand. They were almost completely dependent on the authoritative interpretation of the church.

But suppose the Bible is not to be allegorized. Suppose each passage has, not several meanings, but one, simple, literal meaning. In that case, all Christians may be encouraged to read the Bible. The Scriptures should be translated into the common tongue. Each believer has a right to private interpretation. Luther in particular was very insistent on these points, and he expended tremendous energy on his most enduring work, the translation of the Bible into German.

The very fact that a *translation* was needed, however, raises certain problems for the view that the Scriptures are easily accessible to common Christians. If a Christian is unable to read the Bible in its original languages, then he or she is dependent on knowledgeable individuals to analyze the biblical text, understand its meaning, and express it clearly in the language of the reader. For this reason and others, many Christians feel that the doctrine of the clarity of Scripture has become more and more difficult to defend.

In the first place, the tremendous advances in specialized knowledge during the past century are sufficient to intimidate even the brashest among us. We could point to numerous interpretations of Scripture that have been proved wrong by recent advances. Does not that fact raise serious questions about the measure of certainty we can claim to have for our present opinions? What is true more generally seems also to be true of the interpretation of Scripture: the more we know, the more conscious we are of our ignorance.

In the second place, to say that the Scriptures are clear seems to fly in the face of the realities of contemporary church life. As pointed out in chapter 1, even those who share significant areas of doctrinal agreement find themselves at odds in the interpretation of important biblical passages—passages dealing with baptism and the Lord's Supper, passages that address the question of violence, and passages that have relevance for serious ethical problems such as war, capital punishment, and abortion. If those who are wholeheartedly devoted to the authority of Scripture cannot agree on such questions, has the doctrine of the clarity of Scripture become meaningless?

In the third place, there appears to be a new sensitivity to the significance of corporate authority in the church. The Reformers' emphasis on the right of private interpretation was often balanced by a recognition that no Christian is an island but is part of the body of Christ. Modern Evangelicalism, however, afraid of the abuse of church authority and influenced by a strong sense of individualism, has not always appreciated

---

[4]This statement is an overgeneralization and has been disputed, esp. by H. Rost, *Die Bibel im Mittelalter: Beiträge zur Geschichte und Bibliographie der Bibel* (Augsburg: Kommissions-Verlag M. Seitz, 1939). Moreover, Smalley points out that the revival of popular preaching in the twelfth century led to the use of allegory for the specific purpose of instructing the laity (*Study of the Bible*, p. 244). It can hardly be denied, however, that the authorities discouraged private Bible reading and that the problem became worse by the eve of the Reformation.

the need for Christians to submit their understanding of Scripture to the judgment of the established church.

Yet things seem to be changing. One detects a strong sense of humility among a growing number of believers. Without succumbing to the opposite danger of compromising their convictions, many Christians show a genuine desire to submit to the wisdom and counsel of their elders in the faith. Though this development is a wholesome one, does it not challenge our conviction that the meaning of the Scriptures is plain and readily accessible to the common reader?

ERASMUS VERSUS LUTHER

These questions are all serious, but they are not really new. Without minimizing the distinctive pressures that characterize modern Christianity, we need to appreciate how much help we can receive from Christians in earlier ages. Already in the fourth century, for example, John Chrysostom had recognized the need for both affirming and qualifying this notion of the clarity of Scripture: in his words, *panta ta anankaia dēla,* "all the things that are necessary are plain."[5] Even Origen, though not so explicitly, was making the same point when he argued that virtually all Christians understand what he believed to be one of the most fundamental doctrines: the spiritual significance of the law.[6]

A qualification of this sort may seem to leave the door open for abuse: could not someone define *necessary* and *fundamental* in such a way that vast portions of the Bible remain inaccessible to believers? Indeed one could, but we need to remember that such abuses are possible whenever we seek to be careful and responsible in our formulation of doctrine. Any attempt we make to avoid simplistic answers by clarifying and qualifying our statements runs the risk of being misunderstood and misapplied. It is important to note, however, that the Reformers themselves—tempted though they must have been to overstate their position in the face of controversy—defined their doctrine of biblical clarity, or perspicuity, by focusing on the foundational truths of Scripture.

Particularly instructive in this regard is Luther, since no one was more forceful in affirming that the meaning of the Bible is plain and accessible to all. Perhaps the most revealing discussion is found in his famous essay *On the Bondage of the Will,* in which he responded to a series of criticisms Erasmus had made some time earlier.[7] Erasmus, in the preface to his work *On the Freedom of the Will,* had objected to Luther's statements on human freedom because this subject, he felt, was a very obscure one:

> For there are some secret places in the Holy Scriptures into which God has not wished us to penetrate more deeply and, if we try to do so, then the deeper we go, the darker and darker it becomes, by which means we are led to acknowledge the unsearchable majesty of the divine wisdom, and the weakness of the human mind.[8]

Echoing Chrysostom's remark about the things that are "necessary," Erasmus argues that just a few things are "needful to know" about the doctrine of free choice and that it

---

[5]See Farrar, *History,* p. 329n. (I have not been able to verify Farrar's vague reference.)

[6]Origen, *On First Principles* 2. 7. 2, p. 117.

[7]See E. G. Rupp et al., eds., *Luther and Erasmus: Free Will and Salvation* (Library of Christian Classics 17; Philadelphia: Westminster, 1969).

[8]Ibid., p. 38.

is irreverent to "rush into those things which are hidden, not to say superfluous." Then follows an important statement that could be interpreted as an affirmation of the clarity of Scripture on those matters that are truly significant:

> There are some things which God has willed that we should contemplate, as we venerate himself, in mystic silence; and, moreover, there are many passages in the sacred volumes about which many commentators have made guesses, but no one has finally cleared up their obscurity: as the distinction between the divine persons, the conjunction of the divine and human nature in Christ, the unforgivable sin; yet there are other things which God has willed to be *most plainly evident,* and such are the precepts for the good life. This is the Word of God, which is not to be bought in the highest heaven, nor in distant lands overseas, but it is close at hand, in our mouth and in our heart. These truths must be learned by all, but the rest are more properly committed to God, and it is more religious to worship them, being unknown, than to discuss them, being insoluble.[9]

Finally, he argues that certain topics, even if they can be understood, should not be discussed in the presence of the "untutored multitude," who might find them offensive and damaging.

As we might expect, Luther contests Erasmus's claim in the strongest of terms:

> But that in Scripture there are some things abstruse, and everything is not plain—this is an idea put about by the ungodly Sophists, with whose lips you also speak here, Erasmus; but they have never produced, nor can they produce, a single article to prove this mad notion of theirs. Yet with such a phantasmagoria Satan has frightened men away from reading the Sacred Writ, and has made Holy Scripture contemptible, in order to enable the plagues he has bred from philosophy to prevail in the Church.[10]

More important for our present purposes, however, is Luther's recognition that there *are* indeed certain kinds of obscurities in Scripture that require (as his words certainly imply) scholarly research:

> I admit, of course, that there are many texts in the Scriptures that are obscure and abstruse, not because of the majesty of their subject matter, but because of our ignorance of their vocabulary and grammar; but these texts in no way hinder a knowledge of the subject matter of Scripture.

Luther defines "subject matter" as "the supreme mystery brought to light, namely, that Christ the Son of God has been made man, that God is three and one, that Christ has suffered for us and is to reign eternally." Having thus defined the focus of his concern, Luther goes on:

> The subject matter of the Scriptures, therefore, is all quite accessible, even though some texts are still obscure owing to our ignorance of their terms. Truly it is stupid and impious, when we know that the subject matter of Scripture has all been placed in the clearest light, to call it obscure on account of a few obscure words. If the words are obscure in one place, yet they are plain in another; and it is one and the same theme, published quite openly to the whole world, which in the Scriptures is sometimes expressed in plain words, and sometimes *lies as yet hidden* in obscure words.[11]

---

[9]Ibid., pp. 39–40, my emphasis.
[10]Ibid., p. 110.
[11]Ibid., pp. 110–11 (my emphasis). Cf. Origen's remark: "If some time, as you read the Scripture, you stumble over a thought, good in reality yet a stone of stumbling and a rock of offence, lay the blame on yourself. For you must not give up the hope that this stone of stumbling and this rock of offence do possess meaning" (from Homily 39 on Jeremiah, quoted in Tollinton, *Selections,* pp. 49–50).

His conviction that difficult passages are made clear by others (a point that will occupy us again shortly) echoes Augustine's teaching:

> Accordingly the Holy Spirit has, with admirable wisdom and care for our welfare, so arranged the Holy Scriptures as by the plainer passages to satisfy our hunger, and by the more obscure to stimulate our appetite. For almost nothing is dug out of those obscure passages which may not be found set forth in the plainest language elsewhere.[12]

One could argue that Erasmus and Luther were not really at odds on the question of the clarity of Scripture: they both affirmed such a doctrine with regard to its essential message. They did differ, however, on how one defines that message; moreover, the tone and basic thrust in Erasmus's essay naturally lead one to distrust the ability of the common believer to understand the Bible. Luther's most fundamental concerns were diametrically opposed to that tendency.[13]

THE NEED FOR QUALIFICATIONS

We must remember, however, that Luther did not for a moment deny the limitations of the interpreter's knowledge. For one thing, Christians differ in their level of maturity; indeed, extensive ministry in the church is almost a prerequisite for correct interpretation:

> No-one can understand the Bucolics of Virgil who has not been a herdsman for five years; nor his Georgics unless he has labored for five years in the fields. In order to understand aright the epistles of Cicero a man must have been full twenty years in the public service of a great state. No one need fancy he has tasted Holy Scripture who has not ruled the churches for a hundred years with prophets, like Elijah and Elisha, with John the Baptist, Christ and the apostles.[14]

More to the point, the clarity of Scripture does not at all preclude the need for specialists who seek to bridge the gap that separates us from the languages and cultures of the biblical writers. Luther himself was a man of broad erudition and of fine philological skills. He could argue that "to expound Scripture, to interpret it rightly and to fight against those people who quote wrongly . . . cannot be done without knowledge of the languages."[15] The energies he expended on his translation of the Bible are the clearest testimonial to his conviction that the common folk did, in an important sense, depend on the expertise of scholars.

---

[12]Augustine, *On Christian Doctrine* 2.6 (*NPNF* 2:537). On the notion of Scripture as its own best interpreter, see further below (pp. 103–4).

[13]These comments are too simple; I have ignored other complicating factors in the debate that are not directly relevant to our purpose. It should also be noticed that, if Erasmus and Luther did indeed differ in their identification of the essential message of Scripture, that factor itself could be used as an objection against the clarity of Scripture: if the Bible is so clear, why could not Luther and Erasmus agree on its fundamental subject matter? Luther's likely response to this question may be inferred from the subsequent discussion.

[14]Wood, *Luther's Principles,* p. 16. This quotation comes from a note written by Luther two days before his death; cf. P. Stuhlmacher, *Vom Verstehen des Neuen Testaments: Eine Hermeneutik* (GNT Ergänzungsreihe 6; Göttingen: Vandenhoeck & Ruprecht, 1979), p. 98.

[15]Wood, *Luther's Principles,* p. 29. Wood notes Luther's attention to detail: on one occasion Luther and two of his helpers spent four days translating three lines in the Book of Job (ibid.).

In any case, it would be a misunderstanding of the Reformers to interpret their emphasis on the perspicuity of Scripture in such a way as to make biblical scholarship unnecessary or unimportant. Developments in the various relevant disciplines during the last century or two heighten our sense of dependence on the careful work of scholars, yet at the same time such developments ought to increase our confidence that the Bible is not a locked mystery box but an accessible book that continues to open up its truths to those willing to search them out.

The essence of the Protestant position is captured well by the Westminster Confession of Faith (1647). The first chapter of that document contains a full statement regarding the character of Scripture, and paragraph 7 addresses directly the doctrine of perspicuity:

> All things in Scripture are not alike plain in themselves, nor alike clear unto all; yet those things which are necessary to be known, believed, and observed for salvation, are so clearly propounded, and opened in some place of Scripture or other, that not only the learned, but the unlearned, in a due use of the ordinary means, may attain unto a sufficient understanding of them.

Here the confession achieves a remarkable balance in its formulation. The emphasis falls heavily on the clarity of the biblical message, but the framers have been careful to qualify the doctrine in several ways: (1) not every part of Scripture is equally clear; (2) the matters in view are those that are necessary for salvation; (3) readers of the Bible must be willing to make use of "ordinary means"—personal study, fellowship with other believers, attention to the preaching of the Word; and (4) the interpreter's understanding will not be complete but will certainly be "sufficient" for the purpose stated.

One should notice, incidentally, the phrase "nor alike clear unto all." This qualification reminds us of the relative obscurity to be found in the minds of individual readers, a topic that occupies a prominent place in Luther's work. Luther was well aware that to acknowledge incidental obscurities in the text of Scripture did not fully address the problem raised by Erasmus. Accordingly, Luther goes on to deal with an additional factor.

> It is true that for many people much remains abstruse; but this is not due to the obscurity of Scripture, but to the blindness or indolence of those who will not take the trouble to look at the very clearest truth. [Here he quotes 2 Cor. 3:15 and 4:3–4.] . . . Let miserable men, therefore, stop imputing with blasphemous perversity the darkness and obscurity of their hearts to the wholly clear Scriptures of God.

As he comes to the end of this discussion, Luther summarizes his doctrine by pointing out that there are two kinds of clarity and two kinds of obscurity:

> one external and pertaining to the ministry of the Word, the other located in the understanding of the heart. If you speak of the internal clarity, no man perceives one iota of what is in the Scriptures unless he has the Spirit of God. . . . For the Spirit is required for the understanding of Scripture, both as a whole and in any part of it. If, on the other hand, you speak of the external clarity, nothing at all is left obscure or ambiguous, but everything there is in the Scriptures has been brought out by the Word into the most definite light, and published to all the world.[16]

[16]Rupp, *Luther and Erasmus*, pp. 111–12; cf. Ralph A. Bohlmann, *Principles of Biblical Interpretation in the Lutheran Confessions,* rev. ed. (St. Louis: Concordia, 1983), pp. 53–63.

HUMAN DARKNESS AND THE SPIRIT'S LIGHT

Luther's emphasis on the darkness of the human heart is nothing new, of course. We saw how significant this principle was in the medieval development of allegorical interpretation. It may be useful, moreover, to remind ourselves of Origen's conception that part of the divine aim was to conceal truth. We should not be too quick to condemn Origen, since he could have easily appealed to several important passages of Scripture in support of his view.

For example, even if we allow for some degree of literary hyperbole in Isaiah 6:9–10, we cannot do justice to that passage unless we recognize that at least one aspect of Isaiah's mission was to darken the hearts of many Israelites.

> Go and tell this people:
> "Be ever hearing, but never understanding;
>   be ever seeing, but never perceiving."
> Make the heart of this people calloused;
>   make their ears dull
>   and close their eyes.
> Otherwise they might see with their eyes,
>   hear with their ears,
>   understand with their hearts,
> and turn and be healed.

This passage clearly speaks of divine retribution against those who have set themselves against the God of Israel. The point is developed from a different angle in 8:14–15, where the Lord describes himself, not only as a "sanctuary" (to believers), but also as

> a stone that causes men to stumble
>   and a rock that makes them fall.
> And for the people of Jerusalem he will be
>   a trap and a snare.
> Many of them will stumble;
>   they will fall and be broken,
>   they will be snared and captured.

These portions of Scripture became very important to the apostles as they sought to understand Israel's rejection of the gospel message. Jesus himself had appealed to Isaiah 6 in connection with his practice of speaking in parables. The relevant passage is Mark 4:10–12, one that itself has become quite a stone of stumbling to modern scholars, who think it is absurd to take Jesus' words in their apparent meaning. After all, parables are intended to illustrate and clarify a message! Why would our Lord say anything that was actually designed to keep people from understanding?[17]

In truth, however, Jesus' message had the same two-edged function as Isaiah's ministry: a blessing to believers and a curse to God's enemies. The elderly Simeon, as he held the baby Jesus in his arms, declared that Jesus was "destined to cause the falling and rising of many in Israel" (Luke 2:34). The apostle Paul described his message as a fragrance of life, the aroma of Christ for salvation, but he acknowledged that, to those who are perishing, it is "the smell

---

[17]According to C. F. D. Moule, it would be "perversely literalistic" to suggest "that parables are used *in order to* exclude" (*The Birth of the New Testament*, 3d rev. ed. [New York: Harper & Row, 1982], pp. 116–17).

of death" (2 Cor. 2:14–16). Not surprisingly, both Paul and Peter quote Isaiah 8:14 as they deal with the difficult problem of seeing many reject the message of the gospel (Rom. 9:32–33; 1 Peter 2:4–8; it should be noted that both of these passages have a very strong predestinarian motif).[18]

It was unfortunate that Origen should make the factor of God's concealing truth so basic in his hermeneutical system, but we dare not forget the principle altogether. Even those who have responded in faith to the divine message continue to be sinners. The corruption of sin will always affect our understanding of Scripture to a greater or lesser extent; part of our responsibility, therefore, is to learn to depend more and more on the illumination of the Holy Spirit.

We need to be careful, of course, not to use this blessing to justify our prejudices and laziness. The guidance of the Spirit does not preclude our making use of "the ordinary means" that the Westminster Confession refers to. Moreover, we need to appreciate that the passages that stress the role of the Spirit in interpreting God's message (one thinks primarily of 1 Cor. 2:6–14) do not focus on difficult exegetical details but precisely on those matters that are needful for salvation. Quite properly, therefore, the Westminster Confession reminds us: "Nevertheless, we acknowledge the inward illumination of the Spirit of God to be necessary *for the saving understanding* of such things as are revealed in the Word" (1. 6; my emphasis).

This factor helps us to deal with a troublesome matter: does it make sense to use commentaries written by unbelieving scholars? Why should we depend on the judgment of those whose hearts have not been enlightened by the ministry of the Spirit? The usual answer is that many of the issues modern commentators deal with do not directly affect Christian doctrine. Such a response, by itself, is not wholly satisfactory, yet there is enough truth in it to serve our present purposes. Even a heart deeply antagonistic to the gospel does not lead a scholar to identify a noun as a verb. Leaning on the expertise of scholars who have specialized interests should be regarded as one more instance of using "ordinary means" in the study of Scripture.

This perspective can help us make sense of a frequently cited verse that is both reassuring and puzzling: "As for you, the anointing you received from him remains in you, and you do not need anyone to teach you" (1 John 2:27). Some Christians tend to absolutize this statement and to resist the notion that scholarly work is helpful and important. They forget, of course, that they cannot even read the Bible without depending on the scholarly work that has made Bible translations possible. *Someone* had to learn Greek and Hebrew; *someone* had to study ancient culture; *someone* had to develop expertise in transferring the message of the original to clear, forceful English—all of which had to happen before modern American believers could claim that they need no one to teach them about the Bible!

THE ROLE OF SCHOLARSHIP

We do indeed need help not at all because the Scriptures are inherently obscure but because we are far removed from the biblical writers in time and culture. Even a document written carefully in clearly formulated English, such as the Declaration of Independence, can *appear* obscure two hundred years later. The very opening phrase, "When

---

[18]On the use of "stone" passages in the New Testament, see esp. Barnabas Lindars, *New Testament Apologetic: The Doctrinal Significance of the Old Testament Quotations* (London: SCM, 1961), pp. 169–86.

in the course of human events. . . ," will be partially lost to a modern reader who does not realize that the word *course* carried some strong philosophical nuances in the eighteenth century.[19] What shall we say, then, about a document written not two hundred but two thousand years ago? not in English but in very different languages? not in America but in the Mediterranean world?

The history of biblical interpretation during the past century or two—whatever objectionable features it has had—must be understood primarily as an attempt to bridge this massive linguistic and cultural gap between us and the original text. The development of highly specialized critical tools may appear to create a wall between the simple believer and the Bible, but in effect it facilitates bringing the two together. Not all scholars, of course, view their work in this way—and many who do often fail to meet such a goal. Furthermore, modern critical approaches should not be viewed naïvely as completely neutral with respect to the question of faith.[20] A believing scholar must bring any hermeneutical approach (even those developed by evangelical scholars!) under the searching light of Scripture itself.

In spite of such qualifications, we can state unequivocally that modern biblical scholarship has helped to open up the meaning of innumerable passages of Scripture, sometimes in very dramatic ways. The discovery and analysis of the Egyptian papyri, for example, has increased our understanding of New Testament Greek almost beyond reckoning. The development of Old Testament form criticism, though it has spun many questionable and radical theories, has made it possible for us to uncover the significance of various kinds of literary genres within the Hebrew Bible.[21] And so on and on.

We dare not confuse, therefore, the peculiar and often harmful proposals of radical scholars with the actual advances of biblical scholarship as a whole. Someone committed to the authority of Scripture and convinced that those proposals must be rejected can still recognize the enormous contribution of modern scholarship to the understanding of the Bible.[22]

If we think that nowadays we face more exegetical problems than earlier generations did, the reason is precisely that we know more about the Bible and therefore have a greater awareness of our ignorance. Two hundred years ago, Bible readers only thought that they understood many passages that now we have doubts about. Paradoxically, our

[19]Gary Wills, *Inventing America: Jefferson's Declaration of Independence* (Garden City, N.Y.: Doubleday, 1978), p. 93 and chap. 8.

[20]Cf. Troeltsch's views mentioned above in chap. 2. The most significant contribution to this fundamental question is the controversial thesis of the "twofold division of science," propounded by Abraham Kuyper (*Encyclopedia,* pp. 150–82). Though in many respects believing and unbelieving science have the same character, argued Kuyper, they move in different directions because of their different starting points (p. 155). Cornelius Van Til has insisted on the same point in many of his writings; see *A Christian Theory of Knowledge* (n.p.: Presbyterian and Reformed, 1969), pp. 21–22 and passim. For an attempt to develop the implications of this thesis, see Gary North, ed., *Foundations of Christian Scholarship: Essays in the Van Til Perspective* (Vallecito, Calif.: Ross House, 1976).

[21]In addition to the well-known research of A. Deissmann, J. H. Moulton, and others at the beginning of the century, see the recent work by G. H. R. Horsley, *New Documents Illustrating Early Christianity* (North Ryde, N.S.W.: Macquarie University, 1981–). See also Tremper Longman III, "Form Criticism, Recent Developments in Genre Theory, and the Evangelical," *WTJ* 47 (1985): 46–67.

[22]It is ironic that wrong-headed and obnoxious theories very often sensitize responsible scholars to valid questions that would otherwise not have occurred to them. See my article "The Place of Historical Reconstruction in New Testament Criticism," pp. 122–33.

subjective sense of the clarity of Scripture seems diminished at the same time that we have *greater objective evidence* regarding the clear meaning of the Bible. To recognize this fact is to remind ourselves that we cannot confuse what Luther called the external and internal aspects of the doctrine of scriptural perspicuity. We dare not attribute to Scripture the limitations of our minds and hearts.

Even more to the point, however, is our need to appreciate that all of the advances in modern scholarship—and all of the new questions raised by it—do not affect the basic outlines of Christian theology. Many individual scholars, of course, reject the great doctrines of the Reformation on the basis of modern philosophical commitments.[23] But changes in our understanding of individual passages of Scripture do not require or even suggest that we alter the essence of the Christian message.

Referring again to the Westminster Confession of Faith, perhaps the most comprehensive theological statement arising from the Reformation, we may ask: Is there any chapter in that document that needs revision because we now conclude that, say, the Song of Solomon was written, not as an allegory, but as a description of human love? Is there even a paragraph that must now be excised because of advances in textual criticism or philology? The answer is a definitive and unequivocal no.

Neither this document nor any other theological confession is perfect; we must recognize that Christians have grown in their understanding of Scripture and may indeed wish to revise certain aspects of any doctrinal statement. But all of the increased knowledge and sophistication of the modern era does not suggest for a moment that previous generations of Christians misunderstood the gospel message.

THE WHOLE COUNSEL OF GOD

The reason for such stability in the face of dramatic advancement is that the great teachings of Scripture are not dependent on the interpretation of any particular verse in isolation from others. Though Christians sometimes rely heavily on certain proof texts, the church has come to understand the divine message by developing sensitivity to the *consistent* teaching of the Bible *as a whole*.

The believer is thus not at all a slave to scholarly pronouncements. Believers may express puzzlement and even distress upon hearing a new interpretation of some favorite text, but they will usually adjust to it if they can eventually see how it fits their understanding of Scripture as a whole. What they will not tolerate—and rightly so—is an interpretation that obviously conflicts with the consistent tenor of the biblical teaching. In the most fundamental sense, believers need no one to teach them (1 John 2:27), and the most imposing scholarship will not intimidate them.

A most interesting sidelight to this discussion is the fact that even Origen justified his hermeneutical program along lines similar to those we have been considering. At one point, after acknowledging the validity of the literal meaning, he argued that we have the need and responsibility, not merely to grasp the sense of any given passage, but to assimilate the *entire*

---

[23]In particular, many scholars have adopted a thoroughgoing naturalism. Useful surveys documenting the development of biblical scholarship during the past two centuries are the essays by W. Neil and A. Richardson in *CHB* 3:238–338. For greater detail on the development of British views on Scripture, see the highly regarded work by H. G. Reventlow, *The Authority of the Bible and the Rise of the Modern World* (Philadelphia: Fortress, 1984).

meaning of Scripture.[24] Origen did not expand on this idea, and perhaps we should not make too much of it, but he apparently maintained a strong sense of the importance of contextual interpretation. Because of the unity of the Bible, the whole of Scripture constitutes the context to any one passage, and Christians who are spiritually mature may be expected to draw all the threads together. We make a serious mistake if we do not see this process as an essential aspect of allegorical interpretation. And what was true of Origen was certainly true of the Fathers in general:

> They knew what was their aim in handling scripture. It was not to produce an entirely consistent system of doctrine which would somehow fit in every little detail of the Bible, nor was it to set up a biblical literalism which would treat the Bible as one treats a railway timetable. It was to discover, and to preach and teach, the burden, the purport, the drift, the central message of the Bible.[25]

A corresponding principle vigorously formulated at the time of the Reformation is that Scripture is its best interpreter. We earlier noticed that Luther appealed to this notion in response to the charge that there are obscurities in the Bible ("If the words are obscure in one place, yet they are plain in another"). As early as the second century, Irenaeus articulated this principle when he argued against certain gnostic views:

> For no question can be solved by means of another which itself waits solution; nor, in the opinion of those possessed of sense, can an ambiguity be explained by means of another ambiguity, or enigmas by means of another greater enigma, but things of such character receive their solution from those which are manifest, and consistent, and clear.[26]

Oddly, Farrar objects to the idea that "Scripture interprets itself, a rule which exegetically considered has no meaning."[27] Quite the opposite, this rule is the most fundamental hermeneutical principle when dealing with any piece of literature; it is, in effect, the principle of contextual interpretation. Anyone who views God as the author of Scripture can hardly afford to ignore it.

CHURCH AND TRADITION

One final problem requires our attention in this chapter—the question that we raised earlier concerning submissiveness to the teaching of the church. How does the

---

[24]Origen, *On First Principles* 4. 3. 5, pp. 296–97. Wiles asked, from a somewhat different perspective, what criteria controlled a method as flexible as that of allegory: "An important part of the answer to that question is Origen's conviction that scripture must always be consistent with itself, that the real meaning of every passage will be part of the truth of the one Christian faith" ("Origen," pp. 479–80).

[25]Hanson, "Biblical Exegesis," p. 452. On the same issue, see Michael Andrew Fahey, *Cyprian and the Bible: A Study in Third-Century Exegesis* (BGBH 9; Tübingen: J. C. B. Mohr, 1971), p. 473. The great Charles Spurgeon, in spite of his questionable use of certain texts as the basis for his sermons, was kept from distorting the biblical message through his impressive familiarity with the overall teaching of Scripture.

[26]Irenaeus, *Against Heresies* 2. 10. 1 (*ANF* 1:370); cf. de Margerie, *Introduction* 1:70, who also refers to 2. 10. 2 and 3. 27. 1 and to Salvator Herrera, *Saint Irénée de Lyon exégète* (Paris: A. Savieta, 1920), pp. 120ff. Origen also held to this principle; see Hanson, *Allegory,* p. 180.

[27]Farrar, *History,* p. 332, n. 1. He does observe, however, that the watchword *analogia fidei* is a wise one insofar as it forbids us "to isolate and distort any one passage into authoritative contradiction to the whole tenor of Scripture" (p. 333). Cf. the positive treatment in Bohlmann, *Principles,* chap. 6.

clarity of Scripture relate to this question? Should we depend on the church to teach us about the Scripture?

For that matter, what is the role of tradition? The Protestant Reformation is usually characterized as a massive break with tradition. There is a very important element of truth in that characterization, but here again a crucial caveat is necessary. The Reformers opposed the authority of tradition and of the church, but *only insofar as this authority usurped the authority of Scripture.* They never rejected the value of the church's exegetical tradition when it was used in submission to the Scriptures.

> Luther could not have been the exegete he was without the help of the church's tradition. The tradition gave him a footing on which he could and did move and shift, but which he never lost. But this was so because he believed that under this footing was the foundation of the Scriptures themselves, which he, as an expositor of the Scriptures and also as a son of the church, was to receive gratefully. . . . Luther knew the difference between gratitude and idolatry in the reception of the church's heritage. In this sense he advanced the audacious claim that by his exposition of the Scriptures he was a most loyal defender of the tradition, and that the idolatrous traditionalism of his opponents could mean the eventual destruction both of Scripture and of tradition.[28]

Consider in this regard John Calvin's development. Calvin had no peer in the sixteenth century as an expositor of Scripture, but he was under no illusion that he could somehow skip a millennium and a half of exegetical tradition and approach the Bible free from the influence of the past. The first edition of his *Institutes of the Christian Religion* appeared in 1536, when Calvin was only in his twenties. Enlarged editions appeared in 1539 and 1541 and more significant alterations beginning in 1543, but the work did not reach its final form until 1559. During these two decades Calvin was immersed in biblical exposition and preaching. "As his understanding of the Bible broadened and deepened, so the subject matter of the Bible demanded ever new understanding in its interrelations within itself, in its relations with secular philosophy, in its *interpretation by previous commentators.*"[29]

This last point is most important, for Calvin also spent considerable time studying the major theologians of the church. Indeed, beginning with the 1543 edition, there were "vastly increased" references to the Fathers, including Augustine, Ambrose, Cyprian, Theodoret, and others.[30] Calvin's position was well thought out:

> Insofar as possible, we should hold to the work of earlier exegetes. The Reformer saw himself as bound by and indebted to the exegetical tradition of the church, above all the early church, especially Augustine. He was unwilling to give up the consensus of interpretation.[31]

---

[28]Jaroslav Pelikan, *Luther the Expositor: Introduction to the Reformer's Exegetical Writings* (companion vol. to *Luther's Works*; St. Louis: Concordia, 1959), p. 88.
[29]T. H. L. Parker, *John Calvin: A Biography* (Philadelphia: Westminster, 1975), p. 132, my emphasis.
[30]Ibid., p. 106.
[31]Kraus, "Calvin's Exegetical Principles," p. 11. Note also Peter Stuhlmacher, *Historical Criticism and Theological Interpretation of Scripture: Toward a Hermeneutics of Consent* (Philadelphia: Fortress, 1977), pp. 34–35.

It is clear, then, that the Reformation marked a break with the *abuse* of tradition but not with the tradition itself. This fact tells us a great deal about the Reformers' sense of corporate identity with the Christian church as a whole. It would not have occurred to them to interpret the Scripture as autonomous individuals. On the contrary, they were most forceful in their interpretations when they were convinced that they were giving expression to the truth *given to the church.*

Unfortunately, some would have us believe that the genius of the Reformation was a breaking loose from authority in general and that post-Enlightenment biblical critics, in their radical abandonment of church guidance and scriptural authority, were really giving more consistent expression to the fundamental principle of the Reformation.[32] Disturbing too is the fact that even conservative scholars in our day sometimes give much higher priority to individualism than to corporate responsibility. The idea of pursuing truth "wherever it may lead us" becomes a pious but misconceived motto, for truth rarely if ever manifests itself in isolation.

No doubt there are cases when a scholar hits on an idea whose time has not come, and the fact that the church is not immediately convinced of its validity is no reason to abandon it altogether. On the other hand, new theories and strange interpretations have been suggested by the thousands, most of them never to be propounded again. The humble believer who, innocent of historical and critical methods, cannot see how these interpretations fit in with the church's understanding of the truth may thereby show greater perception of the meaning of Scripture. In a paradoxical way, the clarity of Scripture thus proves triumphant over the misguided attempts of human wisdom, and Jesus' prayer finds a new application: "I praise you, Father, Lord of heaven and earth, because you have hidden these things from the wise and learned, and revealed them to little children. Yes, Father, for this was your good pleasure" (Matt. 11:25–26).

---

[32]Troeltsch's thesis clearly implies this view; note Harvey, *Historian and Believer,* pp. 3–9.

f i v e

RELATIVE

OR ABSOLUTE?

The fact that we encounter a variety of difficulties in our efforts to understand the Bible can be troubling to believers. If biblical interpretation is a *human* and therefore fallible activity, can any such interpretation be trustworthy? A related, but distinct, question has been raised in modern times by writers who doubt whether "objective" interpretation is at all possible. Strongly influenced by a Kantian world view, they argue that our perception of the world is basically determined by our subjective preconceptions. In a very important sense, according to this viewpoint, the past is really lost to us; therefore, we do not merely interpret past events and statements—we recreate them in our image. This way of thinking, if applied consistently, would certainly do away with the usual approach to biblical interpretation.

One other problem involves the claim that, not only our interpretation, but the biblical text itself must be viewed as relative. Such an objection cannot simply be ignored. Though we accept the divine origin and therefore absolute authority of the Scriptures, it is still true that the divine message is couched in human language and that it addresses specific historical and cultural situations, some of which have changed considerably in the course of time. Even the most conservative Christians recognize that at least some commands of Scripture cannot or need not be applied literally in our day, though there is plenty of disagreement as to which belong in this category (footwashing? length of women's hair? eating pork? muzzling the ox while it treads?). Does this fact relativize the Bible and compromise its absolute authority?

These questions bring us to the modern debate over _contextualization_.[1] This term has become suspect in the minds of many Christians because it is sometimes used to justify far-reaching changes in the proclamation of the gospel. Some have suggested, for

---

[1]This topic is more properly treated in the last volume of the series. I deal with it here only as it affects the general question of cultural relativity. For some preliminary bibliography, see the articles by J. Robertson McQuilkin and David J. Hesselgrave in *HIB*, pp. 219–40 and 693–738. Note also Ramesh P.

example, that, since Muslims have a very negative view of baptism (due to historical associations), a proper contextualizing of the gospel in Islamic culture may require replacing this rite with some other.

It would be a mistake, however, to jettison the basic concept of contextualization simply because it has been abused. The fact is that every attempt we make at understanding the Bible (or any other ancient document) necessarily involves transferring a particular text from one historical context to another. When contemporary Christians read a portion of Scripture (already partially contextualized by the English version!), they can make sense of it only from the context of their own knowledge and experience.

The question, therefore, is not *whether* we should contextualize, for we all do it, but rather, *how* to do it without compromising the integrity of the Bible. Does the history of interpretation give us any help here?

INTERPRETATION IN ISRAEL AND JUDAISM

We should remind ourselves that the history of biblical interpretation begins with the biblical writings themselves; not surprisingly, therefore, we find examples of contextualization within the pages of Scripture. One particularly beautiful instance is the way Psalm 16 appears to use Numbers 18:20, "Then the LORD said to Aaron, 'You shall have no inheritance in their land, nor own any portion among them; I am your portion and your inheritance among the sons of Israel'" (NASB; Deut. 18:1–2 speaks similarly of the Levites in general). It has been suggested, with some plausibility, that Psalm 16 was written by David at a time when he was forced to leave the Promised Land. Because the worship of the God of Israel was tied so closely to the inheritance of that land, abandoning one meant abandoning the other (cf. David's words in 1 Sam. 26:19). Whether or not Psalm 16 has this actual setting, David clearly had learned a profound lesson. He would not abandon the God of Israel. He could appropriate God's promise to the Levites: "The LORD is the portion of my inheritance and my cup; Thou dost support my lot. The lines have fallen to me in pleasant places; indeed, my heritage is beautiful to me" (Ps. 16:5–6 NASB).

Some may object that, strictly speaking, this example is not so much one of biblical interpretation as one of *application*.[2] The point here is of the greatest importance. The classic grammatico-historical method of interpretation insists precisely that a clear-cut distinction be maintained between exegesis (the biblical author's intended meaning at the time of writing) and application (the meaning, or significance, to the reader now). That distinction lies at the basis of virtually every interpretive advance made in the past couple of centuries, and we dare not undermine it.

Unfortunately, this is the very point at issue in the contemporary debate: is it really possible to exegete a text without appropriating it into the present? Note the fundamental difference between this question and the godly concern to apply Scripture to our daily

---

Richard, "Methodological Proposals for Scripture Relevance," *BSac* 143 (1986): 14–23, 123–33, 205–17. At the center of the debate has been the work by Charles H. Kraft, *Christianity and Culture: A Study in Dynamic Biblical Theologizing in Cross-Cultural Perspective* (Maryknoll, N.Y.: Orbis, 1979).

[2]In criticism of appeals to *sensus plenior*, for example, Walter C. Kaiser, Jr., speaks of those who confuse "the necessary work of the Holy Spirit in illumination, application, and personally applying a text with the original scope and content of that text in the singular act of revelation to the writer" (*The Uses of the Old Testament in the New Testament* [Chicago: Moody, 1985], p. 28).

lives. All believers recognize that exegesis should not remain merely an intellectual and antiquarian task: it ought to bear fruit in the present. The contemporary claim, however, is not that exegesis *ought* to be applied but that, in the very nature of the case, it is always applied, that we fool ourselves if we think we can formulate a biblical writer's meaning apart from the significance his writing has for us.

Interestingly, recent attempts to identify the character of Jewish exegesis, or *midrash,* focus precisely on the people's need to *actualize* the revealed Word of God.[3] Once again, we could point out many examples of this approach from within the Old Testament itself, such as Isaiah's use of the Exodus motif, the Chronicler's rewriting of the Samuel–Kings narrative, and so on.

Of special interest is the development of biblical interpretation during the intertestamental period, for the Jewish people were faced with the need to understand afresh the requirements of the law in view of their new cultural situation. An intense desire to obey that law in all its concreteness led to a growing body of interpretive tradition, the so-called Oral Law, which in course of time achieved its own authoritative status. Jesus spoke of these "traditions of the elders" as objectionable teachings of men that had the effect of annulling the word of God. Our Lord, of course, rebuked the Pharisees not for seeking to understand and apply the Scriptures but for allowing human interpretations—that is, their contextualizations—to be placed on a par with the divine revelation. The consequence of their hermeneutics was often to violate the commands of God.[4]

A separatist Jewish group, the community at Qumran, affords another notable example of how the Bible could be actualized. In their case the dominant concept was eschatological, a conviction that they were living in the last days, that many biblical passages were being fulfilled in their midst, and that they themselves would be God's instrument for the consummation of history. Their famous Habakkuk commentary, for instance, consists of running short citations from that prophet, followed usually by the term *pishro* ("its interpretation [is]"), which introduces their explanation of the text. Invariably, the explanation involves the identification of the biblical statements with people and events somehow related to the Qumran community. A typical case is their commentary on Habakkuk 2:17 ("The violence you have done to Lebanon will overwhelm you, and your destruction of animals [or "livestock"] will terrify you"):

> [The interpretation of the passage (*pishro*)] concerns the Wicked Priest [an enemy of the Qumran community], by heaping upon him the same recompense which he heaped upon the poor—for "Lebanon" is the Council of the Community; and the "livestock" are the simple of Judah the Law Doer—for God will condemn him to destruction, in as much as he plotted to destroy the poor.[5]

---

[3]Particularly influential has been an article by R. Bloch, "Midrash," reprinted in *Approaches to Judaism: Theory and Practice,* ed. W. S. Green (Brown Judaic Studies 1; Missoula, Mont.: Scholars Press, 1978), pp. 29–50. Warnings against the ambiguity of the term are commonplace. Helpful in this regard is Gary Porton, "Defining Midrash," in *The Ancient Study of Judaism,* 2 vols., ed. J. Neusner (n.p.: Ktav, 1981) 1:5–92; see also "Bibliography on Midrash" by Lee Haas on pp. 93–103. Worthy of special note is the literate study by Barry W. Holtz, "Midrash," in *Back to the Sources: Reading the Classic Jewish Texts,* ed. B. W. Holtz (New York: Summit Books, 1984), pp. 177–211.

[4]Note especially Mark 7:1–13. See my article "The Place of Historical Reconstruction," pp. 112–21.

[5]W. H. Brownlee, *The Midrash Pesher of Habakkuk* (SBLMS 24; Missoula, Mont.: Scholars Press, 1979), p. 196. Brownlee translates *pesher* as "the prophetic fulfillment." Note also F. F. Bruce, "Biblical Exposition at Qumran," in *Gospel Perspectives,* vol. 4, *Studies in Midrash and Historiography,* ed. R. T. France

This exegetical method has come to be known as *pesher*-interpretation.

Students of the New Testament will recognize a certain parallel between the concerns of the Qumranites and the teaching of Jesus and his apostles. When the Dead Sea Scrolls were discovered, some writers raised the possibility that the New Testament message was in some way dependent on the Qumran tradition. That suggestion has long since been discredited, but some of the parallels continue to be illuminating. Our Lord's proclamation that the kingdom of heaven was at hand, the many references in the Gospels to the fulfillment of prophecy, Paul's allusion to the revelation of the long-hidden "mystery" (Col. 1:26–27; cf. 1 Cor. 2:7–10), and various other statements (e.g., 1 Cor. 10:11; Heb. 1:2; 9:26) make clear that the New Testament writers approached the Old Testament from an eschatological perspective.

THE RIDDLE OF MESSIANIC PROPHECY

Our discussion so far may raise a new question: Is the interpretation of prophecy by the New Testament writers another instance of "contextualization"? This is a most difficult problem. A positive answer might suggest that Old Testament prophecies were not truly predictive, while a negative answer implies that those prophecies had little or no relevance for the original recipients.

For example, Isaiah's prophecy that the virgin would conceive and give birth to Immanuel (7:14) may be taken as purely predictive of Jesus' birth. But many scholars object that such a use of that verse wrenches the statement out of its historical and literary context; that is, the Immanuel prophecy sounds in its setting like something to be fulfilled in the very near future. But emphasis on this historical aspect could easily lead us to take Matthew's quotation (1:22–23) as a mere application of an ancient event to the birth of Jesus, and Evangelicals understandably tend to react strongly against such an approach. Unfortunately, it is very easy to overreact, and as a result the original context of the prophecy is often overlooked.

To complicate matters further, we need to consider whether the prophet himself would have been conscious of the explicitly messianic character of his statements. Conservatives have often handled this question by appealing to the divine origin of those prophecies. In other words, perhaps the prophets sometimes did not really know that they were predicting certain messianic events, but God did know, and this knowledge is revealed in the New Testament.

Other conservatives would argue, however, that this way of looking at the problem is fundamentally unsound—that the only way to find out what God means in Scripture is to identify what the *human writers* themselves meant. Any ad hoc appeal to God's intention (as distinguishable from the biblical writers' intention) in effect undermines grammatico-historical exegesis, which is the only sound method of understanding the Bible.[6]

---

and D. Wenham (Sheffield: JSOT, 1983), pp. 77–98, and G. J. Brooke, *Exegesis at Qumran: 4QFlorilegium in Its Jewish Context* (JSOT Supp. 29; Sheffield: JSOT, 1985).

[6]Note Daniel P. Fuller, "Interpretation, History of," *ISBE* 2:863–74, esp. the end of the article. Particularly forceful in expressing this point of view is Walter C. Kaiser; see his *Uses*, pp. 17–22, in which he deals in detail with 1 Peter 1:10–12. On p. 71 he appeals to the Antiochene concept of *theōria*, a matter that will occupy us presently. Darrell L. Bock has attempted a classification of viewpoints on this question; see his "Evangelicals and the Use of the Old Testament in the New," *BSac* 142 (1985): 209–23, 306–19. By far the best treatment of the relation between the divine and the human elements in biblical interpretation

The relation between this topic and that of allegorical interpretation is obvious, since the messianic interpretation of prophecy appears to see something "extra" in the text. Moreover, as we have noted, the allegorical method was motivated by the need for relevance, while in this chapter we are considering the use of Old Testament passages by later individuals who wished to actualize those texts.

Christians have for centuries been exercised about the messianic predictions in the Old Testament. Theodore of Mopsuestia, reacting to the Alexandrian approach, minimized this element. Though he did believe that Old Testament prophecies were predictive, he argued that they were normally fulfilled within the Old Testament period itself. In such a view, one finds in the New Testament use of those passages

> free and coherent accommodations of the original texts to analogous settings in the Christian revelation. The Old Testament texts, he held, lent themselves to this use because of their "hyperbolical" imagery and blessings, rich in metaphorical meaning, and phraseological symbolism.[7]

Centuries later, medieval interpreters, influenced by the Jewish emphasis on literal exegesis, could not always account for the messianic element. As distinguished a scholar as Andrew of St. Victor could actually read Isaiah 53 without reference to Christ![8] Even Calvin, for that matter, could not avoid being affected by this trend: Farrar proudly points to Calvin's interpretation of messianic Psalms as a genuine anticipation of the "modern" method.[9]

Opponents of Christianity have often focused on this problem. The eighteenth-century skeptic Anthony Collins argued that there were only two options available to Christians: literal or nonliteral interpretation. If the literal method is accepted, one thereby falsifies the New Testament use of the Old Testament. If one accepts a nonliteral approach, then any interpretation is possible, and the whole operation becomes meaningless.[10]

How can we respond to these challenges? Is it possible to do full justice to the original setting of the messianic prophecies without compromising their predictive element? One important item on the agenda of evangelical biblical scholarship is to demonstrate that the answer is yes.

To begin with, we need to remind ourselves that early Christian interpreters did not sharply distinguish between the meaning intended by the human author and that intended by God. In the Antiochene concept of *theōria,* the prophet's (but also the interpreter's)

---

is Vern S. Poythress, "Divine Meaning of Scripture," *WTJ* 48 (1986): 241–79. For an interesting contrast between two opposing ways of handling the Psalms, see the articles by Bruce K. Waltke and Walter C. Kaiser, Jr., in *Tradition and Testament: Essays in Honor of Charles Lee Feinberg,* ed. John S. Feinberg and Paul D. Feinberg (Chicago: Moody, 1981), pp. 3–37.

[7]Zaharopoulos, "Theodore of Mopsuestia's Critical Methods," p. 228. On p. 230 he states that even typological interpretation "is almost completely absent" in Theodore's system.

[8]Smalley, *Study of the Bible,* p. 165.

[9]Farrar, *History,* pp. 346–47, 472. It should be obvious by now that the hermeneutical problem of the Old Testament—underlined by the use that the New Testament writers make of it—is the central and foundational interpretive issue that the church has had to wrestle with throughout the centuries. The point comes out clearly in the brief article by J. N. S. Alexander, "Interpretation of Scripture in the Ante-Nicene Period," *Int* 12 (1958): 272–80.

[10]Frei, *Eclipse,* p. 70.

"vision" encompasses more than what is immediately evident.[11] But even Eusebius, who was very capable of Origenistic allegorizing, would have agreed.

> The definition of the literal sense as the sense intended by the author, independent-
> ly of the nature of its object, and the spiritual sense as the one intended by the Holy
> Ghost, but of which the prophet was unconscious, is inapplicable to the exegesis of
> Eusebius, and obviously of all the Fathers of the early centuries. Such dichotomy of
> the Biblical sense was unknown to them.[12]

Moreover, we should consider the possibility that fulfilled prophecy and contextualization (or application?) are not mutually exclusive ideas. One can hardly deny that the original audience that heard the Immanuel prophecies would have naturally assumed some kind of fulfillment within their lifetime (specifically, the coming of the Assyrians before the child was to grow up; see Isa. 7:16–17 and cf. 8:6–8). These same hearers, however, must surely have been impressed by the increasing greatness ascribed to this figure in the subsequent prophecies (9:1–7; 11:1–16). Without ignoring the historical situation of the original hearers, God was certainly stretching their horizons, that is, awakening them to the fact that the prophecies ultimately transcended their limited perspective.

The fact that the New Testament writers make no reference to the original situation when they quote these and other prophecies does not imply that they would have denied their historical significance. If this is correct, then it would be appropriate to say that they were contextualizing those passages to the new situation created by the coming of Christ. On the other hand, it would be a blatant fallacy to deduce that the apostles did not regard the prophecies as straightforward, supernatural predictions. In other words, there is no evidence that the early Christians made a sharp distinction between the fulfillment of prophecy and the actualizing of Scripture.

The point may be illustrated from Isaiah 52:15, "For what [nations and kings] were not told, they will see, and what they have not heard, they will understand." This statement is part of the prophecy regarding the Suffering Servant, itself part of a series of passages regarding a "servant" that seems at times identified with the prophet himself, at other times with the nation of Israel as a whole, and at still other times with the Messiah to come (cf. 42:14; 44:1; 49:3–6). It cannot be doubted that the New Testament writers saw these prophecies fulfilled in the coming of Jesus Christ, yet Paul has no misgivings about applying Isaiah 52:15 *to his own ministry* among the Gentiles (Rom. 15:20–21).[13]

---

[11]For a clear discussion of this approach and how it compares with the Alexandrian method, note Raymond E. Brown, *The Sensus Plenior of Scripture* (Baltimore: St. Mary's University, 1955), pp. 45–51. A helpful summary of the modern discussion may be found in de Margerie, *Introduction* 1:188–213. For a translation of the relevant passages in Diodore of Tarsus, see Froehlich, *Biblical Interpretation,* pp. 82–94.

[12]Carmel Sant, *The Old Testament Interpretation of Eusebius of Caesarea: The Manifold Sense of Holy Scripture* (Malta: Royal University of Malta, 1967), p. 119. For the Fathers, he continues, the literal and spiritual senses refer to two "orders of reality forming one object of the prophetic vision, hence both of them were intended and expressed by the writer." See also Wallace-Hadrill, *Eusebius,* pp. 83, 96–97; Kerrigan, *Cyril,* p. 234.

[13]Paul "acted in the spirit of the prediction that Christ should be preached where He had not been known. . . . There is, however, no objection to considering this passage as merely an expression, in borrowed language, of the apostle's own ideas" (Charles Hodge, *Commentary on the Epistle to the Romans* [Grand Rapids: Eerdmans, 1964; orig. 1886], p. 441). See also my article, "The New Testament Use of the Old Testament: Text-Form and Authority," in *Scripture and Truth,* ed. D. A. Carson and J. D. Woodbridge (Grand Rapids: Zondervan, 1983), pp. 147–65, esp. p. 158.

ANCIENT COMMANDS IN A MODERN WORLD

Even more clearly than for prophecy, the significance of numerous other passages of Scripture shifted from their original setting as later circumstances themselves changed.[14] It is a logical equivocation, however, to say that this concept "relativizes" the Bible so as to deprive it of its authority. The divine authority of Scripture comes to human beings in their concrete situations, which of course are susceptible to change. The absoluteness of God's commands would not be preserved but rather would be compromised if those commands were so general and vague that they applied equally to all situations.

Consider, for example, the sacrificial system. All believers recognize that the atoning work of Christ makes the Jewish sacrifices unnecessary. We agree that the various commands concerning animal sacrifices are not *applicable* today—that is, in the sense that they are not to be obeyed literally (although certainly they contain lessons that we can apply to our lives today). Does that fact suggest that the sacrificial laws did not have absolute divine authority? Of course they had such authority, unless we define *absolute* so as to preclude changes of any kind.

We may say that the situation (or context) created by the coming of Christ alters the way we, as part of this new situation, interpret the sacrificial system. We do not merely *apply* it differently, as would be argued by those who draw a sharp distinction between meaning (intended by the original author) and significance, or application. Rather, it would be accurate to say that we *interpret* that system differently; that is, we recognize now, in a way that could not have been recognized by the original audience, the essentially temporary character of those sacrifices.

In a very important sense, then, we contextualize the biblical passages in question without relativizing them in a way that undermines their authority. Quite the contrary, we thereby affirm that authority. If, on the other hand, we insisted that the sacrifices must be continued (as the recipients of the Epistle to the Hebrews appear to have argued), then we would indeed be violating the Word of God, which teaches us to look rather at the realities of which the Levitical system was but a shadow (Heb. 7:11–12; 9:8–12; 10:1).

This example, I admit, is rather simple, since the New Testament gives us explicit information regarding the temporary character of the sacrifices. Matters become a little more complicated when we consider the civil laws God imposed upon the nation of Israel; not surprisingly, Christians have failed to reach perfect agreement regarding their relevance. While we can find extreme positions on both sides of the issue, however, there seems to be a general (though ill-defined) consensus that the relevance of each of those laws should be considered individually.

In other words, rather than automatically dismissing or enforcing the Jewish civil laws, we should evaluate them within the framework of the teaching of Scripture as a whole. Generally speaking, then, believers recognize that some commands of Scripture, even if they are not explicitly superseded by subsequent biblical revelation, may have had a temporary or otherwise restricted significance. Conversely, we may feel obligated to act in certain ways not explicitly commanded in Scripture or to condemn certain modern practices not

---

[14]In addition to the bibliographical items mentioned in n. 1 above, see Harvey M. Conn, *Eternal Word and Changing Worlds*, esp. chaps. 5 and 8, and his article "Normativity, Relevance and Relativity," TSF Bulletin 10 (1987): 24–33.

at all mentioned by the biblical writers on the grounds that our new context calls us to a fresh interpretation of the biblical message.

Unfortunately, these ideas are very easily subject to abuse, and some "progressive" Christians find in them a way to justify questionable practices, such as homosexuality. After all—so goes the argument—the church's view of slavery has changed dramatically in modern times. Is it not possible that other ethical standards may also represent so much cultural baggage?[15]

We need not overreact to this line of argument by rejecting the principles mentioned earlier. The proper response is rather to insist on the priority of grammatico-historical exegesis. It is here that the distinction between meaning and significance (though not to be absolutized itself) assumes crucial importance. We can hardly expect to contextualize a biblical passage in a responsible way unless we have first identified accurately its significance in the original context.

It is worthwhile remembering that some practitioners of allegory in earlier centuries believed that allegorical interpretations should be tied in some way to the literal meaning of the text. How much more reason, then, for us who reject the allegorical method to make very sure that our attempts at reinterpreting the biblical text in the light of our modern context arise from a true appreciation of the original meaning. And this is just another way of saying that, in spite of contemporary claims to the contrary, emphasis on authorial intention must remain a major priority in biblical exegesis.

KANT AND BIBLICAL INTERPRETATION

We conclude, then, that our commitment to the divine authority of Scripture is not at all compromised by the recognition that shifting contexts often lead to a reinterpretation of the text. But what about the claim that our interpretive efforts themselves are engulfed by a cloud of subjectivity? In other words, even if we conclude that the Scriptures possess an enduring objective authority, is that objectivity perhaps unattainable by human beings?

In this case, the essential relativity of the *interpreter* supposedly prevents us from understanding the text. This particular objection is distinctively modern in character; in fact, it has been only during the past decade or two that the question has played a prominent role in biblical hermeneutics. (Even now the majority of biblical scholars basically ignore it in their actual exegetical work, though they may pay lip service to it in introductory comments and footnotes.)

Understandably, the history of interpretation gives us little direct help on this matter. Throughout the centuries it has been assumed without a second thought that our perception of data corresponds exactly with objective reality: if I see green grass, then it *must* really be green, and it must be grass! Now what is true of the scientific observer must surely be true as well of someone interpreting literature, though it might be recognized that in this case there is more room for ambiguity and misunderstanding.

---

[15]Numerous works exploring the relevance of biblical ethics for our day have appeared in recent years. I have found none of them satisfying. A representative book that asks the tough questions within an evangelical framework is Richard Longenecker, *New Testament Social Ethics for Today* (Grand Rapids: Eerdmans, 1984). John Murray, *Principles of Conduct: Aspects of Biblical Ethics* (Grand Rapids: Eerdmans, 1957), appears too traditional to many contemporary readers, but they ignore this wise book to their peril.

Biblical interpreters in earlier centuries have of course been conscious of the role played by personal bias, but they have simply taken for granted that such a bias can be overcome. It certainly would not have occurred to them that in the very nature of the case we are incapable of grasping objective reality. Consequently, one searches in vain through their writings for interpretive methods or exegetical insights that might help us solve our contemporary dilemma.

On the other hand, it must not be thought that today's concern arose out of nowhere in the middle of the twentieth century. We can identify certain problems in the history of philosophy, even in the ancient period, that lie at its root. By common consent, however, it is with Immanuel Kant that we reach a watershed, a genuine turning point between modern thought and everything that preceded it. The effect of Kant's contribution was so broad and so fundamental in character that no intellectual discipline could escape its impact—not even biblical interpretation, though relatively few exegetes were conscious of what was happening.

We cannot describe Kantian philosophy within the confines of this little volume. We should remember, however, that Kant was deeply preoccupied with the unbearable tension that the Enlightenment had created between science and religion. (This issue was, of course, the old philosophical problem of reason versus faith, in new dress.) His own solution to the problem was to divorce the two.

Such a divorce involved a certain circumscribing of the roles performed by both. Religion, for example, must recognize its limitations: the basic tenets of faith cannot be proved by theoretical reason. But science is also restricted: observers never see things as they are in themselves, since the mind is no mere receptacle molded by physical sensations but rather is an active organ that brings order to the chaotic stream of data it confronts. In a very important sense, therefore, we may say that the world that is known to us is a world created by our own ordering of sensations.[16]

To be sure, most scientists went about their work as though nothing had happened, but the seed had been sown for some fundamental changes in scientific outlook. Certainly, some of the most significant questions debated in twentieth-century philosophy of science concern the relativity of scientific thought. And if questions of this sort are being raised concerning a field that deals with highly "objective" experimentation, what are we to say about the more "subjective" tasks of literary interpretation? (Volume 3 in the present series explores some of these issues in more detail.)

What interests us for the moment is the effect of Kantian thought on nineteenth-century biblical interpretation. Kant himself, interestingly, reflected on this subject and suggested that we should approach the Bible in a way that sounds very much like a revival of allegorical interpretation.

---

[16]In his *Critique of Pure Reason*, Kant had intended "to solve all the problems of metaphysics, and incidentally to save the absoluteness of science and the essential truth of religion. What had the book really done? It had destroyed the naïve world of science, and limited it, if not in degree, certainly in scope,—and to a world confessedly of mere surface and appearance, beyond which it could issue only in farcical 'antinomies'; so science was 'saved'! The most eloquent and incisive portions of the book had argued that the objects of faith—a free and immortal soul, a benevolent creator—could never be proved by reason; so religion was 'saved'! No wonder the priests of Germany protested madly against this salvation, and revenged themselves by calling their dogs Immanuel Kant" (Will Durant, *The Story of Philosophy: The Lives and Opinions of the Greater Philosophers* [New York: Pocket Library, 1954; orig. 1926], pp. 274–75).

What may be required of the *art* of biblical *interpretation* . . . is . . . that the interpreter make clear to himself whether his statement should be understood as *authentic* or *doctrinal*. In the first case the interpretation must be literally (philologically) appropriate to the meaning of the author; in the second case, however, the writer has the freedom to write into the text (philosophically) that meaning which it has in exegesis, from a moral, practical point of view. . . . Therefore only the *doctrinal* interpretation, which does not need to know (empirically) what kind of meaning the holy author may have connected with his words, but rather what kind of doctrine the reason . . . can . . . read into the text of the Bible, only such a doctrinal interpretation is the sole evangelical, biblical method of teaching the people in true, inner, and universal religion.[17]

Even more blatant is the conclusion reached by a notable liberal New Testament scholar, Hans Windisch:

I claim for myself the privilege . . . of modernizing the assumedly historical Jesus for practical use, i.e. to work out a figure which is similar to the Jesus of Herrmann's theology. I am fully aware that I am reading subjective interpretations into what is historically provable and filling out gaps of scholarly research according to practical needs.[18]

FROM SCHLEIERMACHER TO BULTMANN

More systematic approaches to biblical hermeneutics on the basis of a post-Kantian world view were developed by several scholars. The so-called father of modern theology, Friedrich Schleiermacher, devoted considerable attention to this problem, and his writings are regarded as fundamental for the present discussion. Prior to his work, the discipline of biblical hermeneutics had not been carefully integrated into a general framework of human understanding. "An effective hermeneutics could only emerge in a mind which combined virtuosity of philological interpretation with genuine philosophic capacity. A man with such a mind was Schleiermacher."[19]

Of particular concern to us is his appreciation of the role played by the interpreter's presuppositions. Schleiermacher did not—as Windisch did many years later—use this principle to justify arbitrary exegesis. He recognized, however, the significance of the "hermeneutical circle" and sought to incorporate it into a total hermeneutics.

The understanding of a given statement is always based on something prior, of two sorts—a preliminary knowledge of human beings, a preliminary knowledge of the subject matter. . . .

Complete knowledge always involves an apparent circle, that each part can be understood only out of the whole to which it belongs, and vice versa. All

[17]James M. Robinson's translation in his introduction to the reprint of Albert Schweitzer's *The Quest of the Historical Jesus* (New York: Macmillan, 1968), p. xvii.

[18]Ibid.

[19]From an influential article on "The Development of Hermeneutics," published in 1901 by W. Dilthey. The quotation is taken from *W. Dilthey: Selected Writings,* ed. and trans. H. P. Rickman (Cambridge: Cambridge University Press, 1976), p. 255. On the history of nineteenth- and twentieth-century hermeneutics, see esp. Stuhlmacher, *Vom Verstehen,* pp. 102–205, but note Richard B. Gaffin, Jr.'s caveats in his review, *WTJ* 43 (1980–81): 164–68. A more recent and very interesting analysis is that of Klaus Berger, *Exegese und Philosophie* (SBS 123/124; Stuttgart: Katholisches Bibelwerk, 1986).

knowledge which is scientific must be constructed in this way. . . . Thus it follows . . . that a text can never be understood right away.[20]

Toward the end of the nineteenth century, W. Dilthey, though interested primarily in the social sciences, made an important contribution to the analysis of human understanding and interpretation. Much of his own work was devoted to the role of the historian, a role that he believed required an actual experience of the past events being described. His notion of *Nacherleben,* which he viewed as the most important level of historical understanding, can be defined as

> a mode of re-experiencing which is to be understood as a re-creation (*Nachbildung*) of an expressed meaning rather than as a psychologistically conceived re-production (*Abbildung*). The creative understanding involved in *Nacherleben* is a function of the historian's imagination.[21]

From a somewhat different perspective, the British philosopher R. G. Collingwood took up this theme and emphasized the view that "the past is never a given fact which [the historian] can apprehend empirically by perception." Moreover, he "does not know the past by simply believing a witness"; in fact,

> he is aware that what he does to his so-called authorities is not to believe them but to criticize them. If then the historian has no direct or empirical knowledge of his facts, and no transmitted or testimoniary knowledge of them, what kind of knowledge has he: in other words, what must the historian do in order that he may know them?
> My historical review of the idea of history has resulted in the emergence of an answer to this question: namely, that *the historian must re-enact the past in his own mind.*[22]

Though Collingwood does not in this context appeal to Kant, the reader must perceive that these words could only have been written in a post-Kantian world. We need to reflect on the modern conception of historiography because biblical interpretation impinges repeatedly on the evaluation of historical narratives in Scripture. These related concerns come together in Rudolf Bultmann's coherent approach to hermeneutics.

As is well known, Bultmann had very little regard for the historical trustworthiness of biblical narrative, particularly the Gospels, and he appealed to the modern discussions

---

[20]F. D. E. Schleiermacher, *Hermeneutics: The Handwritten Manuscripts,* ed. H. Kimmerle, trans. J. Forstman (AARTT 1; Missoula, Mont.: Scholars Press, 1977), pp. 59 and 113; see also aphorisms 120–22 on pp. 59–60 and the discussion on pp. 115–16. Note the clear description by Rudolf A. Makkreel, *Dilthey: Philosopher of the Human Studies* (Princeton: Princeton University Press, 1975), pp. 264–66, on Schleiermacher's architectonic approach. For a somewhat tendentious treatment, see Palmer, Hermeneutics, pp. 84–97. Schleiermacher's application of his hermeneutical principle to theological construction was problematic, however: "Schleiermacher's contention that 'it is a most precarious procedure to quote Scripture passages in a dogmatic treatise and, besides, in itself quite inadequate' (*Glaubenslehre,* I, 30) was only a pretext to justify the unscriptural method of deriving the theological truths from his reason, or the 'pious self-consciousness'" (Theodore Mueller, *Christian Dogmatics: A Handbook of Doctrinal Theology for Pastors, Teachers, and Laymen* [St. Louis: Concordia, 1934], pp. 93–94).

[21]Makkreel, *Dilthey,* p. 361. Makkreel, however, denies that "Dilthey supports a subjective, relativistic conception of philosophy" (pp. 6–7).

[22]R. G. Collingwood, *The Idea of History* (London: Oxford University Press, 1946), p. 282; my emphasis. He includes, incidentally, a perceptive analysis of Kant's view of history on pp. 93–104. On Collingwood's view of the historian's autonomy, see Royce G. Gruenler's comments in *HIB,* p. 580, building on the analysis of Cornelius Van Til.

regarding philosophy of history in support of his general approach.[23] Also distinctive in his work is a great emphasis on the fact that we cannot do exegesis without presuppositions. In his view it is valid, and even inevitable, for a "modern" person to read the Bible from a naturalistic perspective, that is, with the assumption that God does not break into history. Since biblical narrative is full of supernatural motifs, modern interpreters are obliged to bring their preunderstanding to bear on the text, to strip the narrative from first-century myths, and to reclothe it with other myths (such as existentialist concepts) that make sense to modern culture.

While Bultmann himself did not take the next step of arguing that our subjectivity eliminates objective reality, we can see clearly how such a conclusion could and would be drawn by subsequent writers. We find, then, a fairly direct line from the Kantian dichotomy to the recent claim that biblical interpretation can have no objective significance at all. Part of our response must be to challenge the Kantian world view. The Bible itself knows nothing of a faith that requires some kind of compartmentalization so that scientific inquiry can proceed unhindered; nor does it allow us to think of reason as an entity that should leave religious commitment alone.

We also should note that no thinker seems willing to push the principle of subjectivity to its ultimate conclusion. Kant himself, for example, while he argued that we do not really know the nature of objects by themselves, added that "our mode of perceiving" those objects is shared by all human beings.[24] Brought in as if through a back door, Kant's qualification salvages a very significant element of objectivity in scientific endeavor. Similarly, some of the most outspoken critics of objective interpretation themselves write with a marvelous assurance that their own words have a clear objective meaning that can be perceived by all their readers!

The solution to this problem is ultimately theological. John Calvin approached it brilliantly when he began his *Institutes* by raising the question of the knowledge of God. There are indeed many obstacles to our understanding of God and his message—our finitude, our corruption, and, yes, our relativity. But God himself is not circumscribed by

---

[23]See Palmer, *Hermeneutics,* pp. 51–52. Bultmann's most important essays on this general subject have been brought together in *Bibel und Hermeneutik,* vol. 3 of *Gesammelte und nachgelassene Werke,* ed. H. Beintker et al. (Göttingen: Vandenhoeck & Ruprecht, 1971); note esp. the 1956 article "Gotteswort und Menschenwort in der Bibel: Eine Untersuchung zu theologischer Grundfragen der Hermeneutik," pp. 138–89. His best-known article on hermeneutics was originally published in 1957 and translated as "Is Exegesis Without Presuppositions Possible?" This article is accessible in Rudolf Bultmann, *Existence and Faith: Shorter Writings of Rudolf Bultmann,* ed. Schubert M. Ogden (Cleveland: World, 1960), pp. 281–96.

[24]"We have intended, then, to say, that all our intuition is nothing but the representation of phenomena; that the things which we intuite, are not in themselves the same as our representations of them in intuition, nor are their relations in themselves so constituted as they appear to us; and that if we take away the subject, or even only the subjective constitution of our senses in general, then not only the nature and relations of objects in space and time, but even space and time themselves disappear; and that these, as phenomena, cannot exist in themselves, but only in us. What may be the nature of objects considered as things in themselves and without reference to the receptivity of our sensibility is quite unknown to us. We know nothing more than our own mode of perceiving them, which is peculiar to us, and which, though not of necessity pertaining to every animated being, is so to the whole human race" (Immanuel Kant, *Critique of Pure Reason,* trans. J. M. D. Meiklejohn, rev. ed. [New York: Colonian Press, 1898], p. 35).

any such limitation. He who created us knows how to speak to us. He who formed our minds knows how to reach them. The task of biblical interpretation is not an autonomous human endeavor but a response to God's command. And with God's command comes the power to fulfill that command. We therefore pray with Augustine, "Give what you command and command whatever you wish."[25]

25Augustine, *Confessions*, 10. 29 *("Da quot iubes et iube quod vis")*.

Epilogue

This book does not properly have a conclusion. We have sought only to identify and clarify the nature of the great hermeneutical task. Augustine's prayer, however, marks out the lines along which our solutions must be traced.

Consider the questions raised in the first chapter. The many disagreements that Christians discover in their reading of Scripture witness to the difficulties that face us in the work of biblical interpretation. We are now in a better position to appreciate what gives rise to different interpretations. A recent writer has argued that the real hermeneutical constraints "are provided by the interpreters" rather than the text and that "within very wide limits texts can be made compatible with interpretations." He adds, "Since it is a precondition of interpreting that what we interpret must be at least partially consistent and contain or indicate beliefs that we can share, we cannot . . . understand interpretations that challenge all our beliefs."[1]

The power of our hermeneutical predispositions makes growth a slow and often painful, *but not impossible,* process. Augustine's prayer teaches us that God is hardly a spectator from a distance, wondering how we will solve our problems. God is truly at work in the hearts of his people, causing us to grow together in unity unto the full measure of Christ (Eph. 4:11–16).

While the history of the Christian church contains many instances of discord, we cannot allow that fact to obscure the remarkable unity of understanding that has characterized God's people throughout the centuries. Precisely when one considers the numerous difficulties involved in reading an ancient document such as the Bible, touching as it does on many highly controversial issues, the great wonder is that the church has survived at all.

The history of biblical interpretation may be discouraging at times, but it also ought to reassure us that God has not left us alone. The evidence is plentiful that his Spirit has slowly guided believers to a fuller and increasingly clearer understanding of the divine revelation. And is not this progress sufficient grounds for assurance that he will continue to work in our hearts and minds as we devote ourselves to the study of his Word? The day will surely come when we will know fully, even as we are fully known (1 Cor. 13:12).

---

[1] Laurent Stern, "Hermeneutics and Intellectual History," *JHI* 46 (1985): 287–96, esp. pp. 293, 296.

For Further Reading

A complete list of works cited may be found in the index of modern authors and titles. In this section I have selected contributions in English that should prove especially helpful as introductions to historical periods or to important figures. Most of them include bibliographical references to specialized articles and monographs.

Brief but substantive surveys of the history of interpretation may be found in the standard biblical encyclopedias. Note esp. K. Grobel, "Interpretation, History and Principles of," *IDB* 2:718–24, updated by several authors in the supplementary volume, pp. 436–56. Also useful is Daniel P. Fuller, "Interpretation, History of," *ISBE* 2:863–74. The most successful popularization is Robert M. Grant, *A Short History of the Interpretation of the Bible,* 2d ed. with additional material by David Tracy (Philadelphia: Fortress, 1984). Somewhat tendentious, but for that very reason instructive, is Peter Stuhlmacher, *Historical Criticism and Theological Interpretation of Scripture: Toward a Hermeneutics of Consent* (Philadelphia: Fortress, 1977).

Comprehensive histories of biblical interpretation are rare. There is nothing in English to replace the old work by Frederic W. Farrar, *History of Interpretation* (New York: E. P. Dutton, 1886), although Raymond E. Brown, *The Sensus Plenior of Scripture* (Baltimore: St. Mary's University, 1955), updates some important aspects. Fortunately, *The Cambridge History of the Bible,* ed. P. R. Ackroyd et al., 3 vols. (Cambridge: Cambridge University Press, 1963–70), while it does not provide a running narrative, covers all major areas clearly and competently. Histories of Christian theology usually touch on our subject; pride of place goes to Jaroslav Pelikan's magnificent achievement, *The Christian Tradition,* 5 vols. (Chicago: University of Chicago Press, 1971–). For a good selection of primary literature see James J. Megivern, *Official Catholic Teachings: Biblical Interpretation* (Wilmington, N.C.: McGrath, 1978).

Hermeneutics during the biblical period itself is treated most thoroughly by Michael A. Fishbane, *Biblical Interpretation in Ancient Israel* (Oxford: Clarendon, 1985), though his views on many specific texts are highly debatable. An excellent introduction may be found in part 1 of James L. Kugel and Rowan A. Greer, *Early Biblical Interpretation* (Library of Early Christianity [Philadelphia: Westminster, 1986]). The New Testament use of the Old Testament is a subject that would require a special bibliography; two useful surveys are the highly regarded conservative treatment by R. Longenecker, *Biblical Exegesis in the Apostolic Period* (Grand Rapids: Eerdmans, 1975), and a more recent work by A. T. Hanson, *The Living Utterances of God: The New Testament Exegesis of the Old* (London: Darton, Longman and Todd, 1983).

With reference to literature outside of the canonical Scriptures, note the following clear surveys: Samuel Sandmel, *Philo of Alexandria: An Introduction* (New York: Oxford University Press, 1979), esp. chap. 3; F. F. Bruce, *Biblical Exegesis in the Qumran Texts* (Grand Rapids: Eerdmans, 1959); G. W. E. Nickelsburg, *Jewish Literature between the*

Bible and the Mishnah: An Historical and Literary Introduction (Philadelphia: Fortress, 1981), esp. chap. 7; and M. Mielziner, *Introduction to the Talmud,* 5th ed. (New York: Bloch, 1968), esp. pp. 117–87.

For studies of biblical interpretation in the ancient church we depend primarily on specialized works such as Alexander Kerrigan, *St. Cyril of Alexandria: Interpreter of the Old Testament* (AnBib 2 [Rome: Pontificio Istituto Biblico, 1952]), and Michael Andrew Fahey, *Cyprian and the Bible: A Study in Third-Century Exegesis* (BGBH 9 [Tübingen: J. C. B. Mohr, 1971]). More broadly conceived is the influential treatment by R. P. C. Hanson, *Allegory and Event: A Study of the Sources and Significance of Origen's Interpretation of Scripture* (London: SCM, 1959). Perhaps the best introduction to the methods of the Antiochene school is chap. 2 of D. S. Wallace-Hadrill, *Christian Antioch: A Study of Early Christian Thought in the East* (Cambridge: Cambridge University Press, 1982). Readings in the primary literature can be found in Karlfried Froehlich (trans. and ed.), *Biblical Interpretation in the Early Church* (Sources of Early Christian Thought [Philadelphia: Fortress, 1984]).

The medieval period has received good attention, especially in the work of Beryl Smalley, *The Study of the Bible in the Middle Ages,* 2d ed. (Oxford: Blackwell, 1952). Note also G. R. Evans, *The Language and Logic of the Bible,* 2 vols. (Cambridge: Cambridge University Press, 1984–86), as well as James Samuel Preus, *From Shadow to Promise: Old Testament Interpretation from Augustine to Young Luther* (Cambridge, Mass.: Belkamp, 1969). For a very helpful presentation of medieval Jewish hermeneutics, see Esra Shereshevsky, *Rashi: The Man and His World* (New York: Sepher-Hermon, 1982), esp. chap. 5.

Although we are lacking an adequate synthesis of Reformation hermeneutics, much can be gained from Ralph A. Bohlmann, *Principles of Biblical Interpretation in the Lutheran Confessions,* rev. ed. (St. Louis: Concordia, 1983). Otherwise, we depend on individual studies. A. Skevington Wood, *Luther's Principles of Biblical Interpretation* (London: Tyndale, 1960), is a brief but suggestive study. More detailed are Jaroslav Pelikan, *Luther the Expositor: Introduction to the Reformer's Exegetical Writings* (companion volume to *Luther's Works* [St. Louis: Concordia, 1959]), and Heinrich Bornkamm, *Luther and the Old Testament* (Philadelphia: Fortress, 1969). The best works on Calvin are T. H. L. Parker's two volumes: *Calvin's New Testament Commentaries* (Grand Rapids: Eerdmans, 1971) and *Calvin's Old Testament Commentaries* (Edinburgh: T. & T. Clark, 1986).

The development of modern critical methods is capably covered by W. G. Kümmel, *The New Testament: The History of the Investigation of Its Problems* (Nashville: Abingdon, 1972), which includes substantial excerpts from the scholars discussed in the text; S. Neill, *The Interpretation of the New Testament, 1861–1961* (London: Oxford University Press, 1964); and Emil G. Kraeling, *The Old Testament Since the Reformation* (London: Lutterworth, 1955). A briefer and more narrowly focused discussion is Edgar Krentz, *The Historical-Critical Method* (Guides to Biblical Scholarship [Philadelphia: Fortress, 1975]). For an in-depth and insightful treatment of one important subject, see Hans W. Frei, *The Eclipse of Biblical Narrative: A Study in Nineteenth Century Hermeneutics* (New Haven and London: Yale University Press, 1974). For the twentieth-century philosophical developments, see esp. Richard E. Palmer, *Hermeneutics: Interpretation Theory in Schleiermacher, Dilthey, Heidegger, and Gadamer* (Evanston: Northwestern University Press, 1969).

LITERARY
APPROACHES
TO BIBLICAL
INTERPRETATION

Tremper Longman III

To my wife, Alice,
and our three children,
Tremper IV, Timothy, and Andrew

Contents

Editor's Preface

*A*mong the various academic disciplines, literary criticism would appear to have the greatest potential for shedding light on the task of biblical hermeneutics. For a variety of reasons, however, biblical scholarship has until recently paid little attention to this field. In particular, conservative exegetes have, not without reason, feared that the use of literary criticism leads to a downplaying or even the denial of the historical worth of Scripture.

It is all the more gratifying, therefore, that, for the present series, we have been able to secure the services of a young scholar whose work blends an intelligent commitment to the authority of the Bible with an impressive expertise in contemporary literary theories. Professor Longman's doctoral research into a specialized area of Akkadian literature led him to examine in considerable detail competing approaches to literary criticism. He has since continued to pursue an interdisciplinary approach to biblical exegesis. For example, with a view to gaining a deeper understanding of the field, he participated, under a 1984 grant from the National Endowment for the Humanities, in a semiotics seminar at Princeton University directed by the eminent scholar Michael Shapiro.

The author has nurtured a special interest in biblical poetry, as reflected in a 1982 article in *Biblica* on the thorny question of Hebrew meter, a more popular work entitled *How to Read the Psalms,* and several other projects. Clearly, Professor Longman's work is not merely theoretical, and his commitment to wrestle with the details of the biblical text shows through in the present volume.

I am delighted to be able to introduce this volume in the *Foundations of Contemporary Interpretation* as a substantive and significant contribution to the task of biblical hermeneutics. Readers with little prior knowledge of modern literary theories will appreciate the clarity with which the field is described in this book. Students of literature, on the other hand, will be particularly grateful for a work that identifies, with commendable balance, the points of contact between literary criticism and biblical interpretation. Without ignoring the difficult questions, Professor Longman has pointed the way for a responsible "reading strategy" in Bible study.

Moisés Silva

Acknowledgments

My interest in the interaction between literary studies and ancient literature began during graduate work at Yale University. My dissertation focused on a particular literary genre in Akkadian, and I had occasion to examine contemporary theory to see what literary scholars were saying on the subject. In this effort I received much good guidance from my adviser W. W. Hallo. This initial contact with literary studies led me to continue my studies in the intersection between literary theory and ancient literature.

I soon came in contact with the vast secondary literature on the subject of literary approaches to the study of the Bible. As I discovered, there was both much of value and also much to discard in this literature. I trust that the present volume will aid the student and scholar in getting a foothold in this subdiscipline and will answer questions for ministers and laypeople who may have wanted more information about the literary approach to the Bible.

I thank my colleague Moisés Silva for guidance and criticism during the writing of this book. I am grateful also to other associates at Westminster Theological Seminary and elsewhere for their thoughtful advice and assistance on the manuscript: Raymond Dillard, Vern Poythress, Bruce Waltke, Alan Groves, Samuel Logan, Douglas Green, Steven McKenzie, V. Phillips Long, and Richard Whitekettle.

Unless noted otherwise, I use the New International Version in Scripture quotations. In poetic analyses, however, I have rearranged some of the poetic structure. I frequently depart from the NIV in chapter 7. Chapter 2 was presented in an earlier form as a lecture to the Institute of Biblical Research and then published as "The Literary Approach to the Study of the Old Testament: Promise and Pitfalls" in *JETS* 28 (1985): 385–98. It is used by permission of the editor.

My final thanks go to my wife and three sons, who are a source of love and encouragement to me.

Introduction

A weekend seminar on marriage takes place at a local church. A well-known Christian counselor has flown in to instruct the young couples about relationships. During the afternoon session on sexuality, the counselor begins by reading Song of Songs 1:2–4:

> Let him kiss me with the kisses of his mouth—
> for your love is more delightful than wine.
> Pleasing is the fragrance of your perfumes;
> your name is like perfume poured out.
> No wonder the maidens love you!
> Take me away with you—let us hurry!
> The king has brought me into his chambers.

Most modern students of the Bible would feel few qualms about applying this Scripture passage to human sexual relationships. A century ago, however, such an application of the Song of Songs would have aroused much uneasiness, and five hundred years ago a preacher might be dismissed from the church or worse if he taught that the book was a collection of poems about human love rather than an allegory of the relationship between Christ and the church.

A reflective reader of the Psalms begins Psalm 2:

> Why do the nations rage
> and the peoples plot in vain?
> The kings of the earth take their stand
> and the rulers gather together
> against the LORD
> and against his Anointed One.
> "Let us break their chains," they say,
> "and throw off their fetters."

While studying this passage, the reader observes much repetition between the lines. How should such repetition be taken? Are the parallel lines saying the same thing, using different words? Are they perhaps not really repeating at all? Are there both repetition and progression in the lines?

Finally, the following verses strike quite a different tone:

> And I saw a beast coming out of the sea. He had ten horns and seven heads, with ten crowns on his horns, and on each head a blasphemous name. The beast I saw resembled a leopard, but had feet like those of a bear and a mouth like a that of a lion. (Rev. 13:1–2)

How should this passage be interpreted? Is it a *literal* description of a future event? Or is it *figurative*?

Such questions, at least in part, are *literary* questions and are of major importance to the correct interpretation of Scripture. The reading from the Song of Songs raises the question of genre identification (see chapter 4). Psalm 2 raises the important question of poetic parallelism. Each of the three possible readings considered above has at some point in church history been adopted as the correct way to read the poetic line (see chapter 6). Finally, the description in Revelation of the beast rising from the sea reminds us not to ignore the possibility of metaphorical language.

I intend in this book to survey the literary nature of the Bible and to acquaint the reader with the research that is being carried out on the Bible by literary scholars. Such research is both theoretical and practical. Theorists ask questions about the nature of literary language. How does a literary text communicate to a reader? What does it communicate? Is the goal of interpretation to determine the intention of the author, or does the reader shape the meaning of the text? Or should we forget about the author and the reader and concentrate on the text alone? What is a genre? Does genre even exist? How do prose and poetry differ? Does truly literal language exist, or is all language metaphorical? On the other hand, literary research may be practical—that is, applicable to actual texts. What is the genre of Ecclesiastes? Are repetitions in the patriarchal narratives signs of multiple sources, or do they reflect conventions of ancient Hebrew storytelling?

The theory of literary criticism and its practice are, of course, not isolated from one another. One must have a theory of genre before asking about the genre of a particular text. At the same time, one must work with particular texts and see similarities between them before formulating a theory of genre. Nevertheless, such a division between theory and application is useful and underlies the two-part division of this book.

Various schools of thought have arisen in the field of secular literary theory, and it is not surprising that these differences are reflected in biblical studies. In the secondary literature we frequently encounter titles that begin "A Semiotic Approach to" or "A Structuralist Understanding of "; even the word *deconstruction* has been creeping into the literature. Technical terminology peppers the pages of contemporary journal articles—narratology, *signifié,* binary opposition, *langue/parole,* actant. The first chapter serves as a guide to the interaction between secular literary theory and biblical studies and attempts to bring some order out of the chaos of the many different approaches.

Chapter 2 then analyzes and evaluates the trends of modern literary criticism, particularly as applied to biblical studies. The pitfalls and promises of a literary approach for biblical studies will be highlighted. Certainly the most urgent of the potential pitfalls is the relationship between literature and history. Can the Bible, particularly if it is literature, make meaningful historical statements? In other words, does the Bible contain history or story? Conservative as well as traditional critical scholars have assumed that the Bible intends to make statements about history. (They disagree, however, about the accuracy of the history.) On the other hand, many advocates of literary criticism agree with D. Robertson that "nothing depends on the truth or falsity of [the Bible's] historical claims."[1]

The third chapter closes this first part with a brief summary of the method I advocate in this book. I seek an approach that is low on jargon and high on results in exegesis.

The practice of literary criticism is the focus of part 2. What tools, methods, and insights have been developed from the literary approach that are particularly helpful in

---

[1] D. Robertson, "Literature, the Bible as," *IDB* Supplementary Volume, p. 548.

understanding specific texts? Chapter 4 concerns prose narrative, and chapter 6 deals with poetry. Chapters 5 and 7 provide examples of the analysis of prose and poetry respectively. A short epilogue closes the discussion.

To use terminology popularized by Jonathan Culler, I seek to make readers conversant with the "enabling conventions" of prose and poetry and thus to encourage competence in reading biblical literature.[2] As we will see, writings are not created out of whole cloth but, rather, use the familiar forms of previous writings in order to communicate with the reader. The writer sends signals to the reader in order to instruct him or her regarding how to understand the message.

To learn the conventions of Old and New Testament literature is to take steps toward becoming a competent interpreter. When Culler speaks of competency in literature, he treats literature like language and borrows from linguistics. When a student becomes competent in a foreign language, it does not mean that he or she knows every word of, say, German, and can translate at sight any sentence encountered. It means rather that the student knows the basic rules of syntax and how to use a dictionary. Literature is similar to syntax and the interpretation of sentences, in that to know the rules is the first step toward understanding any particular text.

From many different quarters the claim is going out that biblical studies are undergoing a paradigm shift.[3] The literary approach is heralded as an innovation in interpretation and not simply another tool comparable to source, form, or redaction criticism. Indeed some of the more radical proponents of the approach downplay traditional approaches: "Literary critics in general do not believe it is necessary to use the traditional disciplines of biblical research or to employ the findings of those disciplines."[4] A good example of this attitude is found in the work of M. Weiss, who contrasts his "total interpretation" with traditional critical methods, in particular form criticism.[5] Believing that history is important to the critical understanding of a text, traditional critics have been increasingly opposed to the views of literary critics, who may be characterized as ahistorical in their approach.[6] As a result of these objections, it is common to find literary critics who acknowledge that the traditional methods are still important. This admission, however, often goes no further than lip service.

The center of the claim that literary criticism is an entirely new approach to interpretation (and also the point of disagreement with traditional approaches) is the contention that biblical texts should be studied as wholes. This view of literary criticism contrasts with the approach of form criticism, for example, because the latter emphasizes the division of a text into its constituent parts.

The following examples will demonstrate the genuine difference in mind-set between traditional criticism and literary criticism. A traditional critic discerns different sources that

---

[2] J. Culler, *Structuralist Poetics* (Ithaca: Cornell, 1975), pp. 113–60.

[3] J. D. Crossan, "'Ruth Amid the Alien Corn': Perspectives and Methods in Contemporary Biblical Criticism," in *The Biblical Mosaic*, ed. R. Polzin and E. Rothman (Philadelphia: Fortress, 1982), p. 199; see also M. Fishbane, "Recent Work on Biblical Narrative," *Prooftexts* 1 (1981): 99.

[4] Robertson, "Literature," p. 548.

[5] M. Weiss, *The Bible from Within: The Method of Total Interpretation* (Jerusalem: Magnes, 1984), pp. 1–46.

[6] The tension between traditional critics and literary critics has been mapped out in part by S. A. Geller, "Through Windows and Mirrors into the Bible: History, Literature, and Language in the Study of Text," in *A Sense of Text* (JQRS, 1982): 3–40.

were brought together to constitute the Joseph narrative. Doublets are taken as evidence of a composite text. E. A. Speiser's comments on Genesis 37 are representative:

> The narrative is broken up into two originally independent versions. One of these (J) used the name Israel, featured Judah as Joseph's protector, and identified the Ishmaelites as the traders who bought Joseph from his brothers. The other (E) spoke of Jacob as the father and named Reuben as Joseph's friend; the slave traders in that version were Midianites who discovered Joseph by accident and sold him in Egypt to Potiphar.[7]

For Speiser, two stories similar in details and structure signal two different sources. For the literary critic, on the other hand, the issue of sources is irrelevant. There may or may not be different sources; the important matter is the shape of the text as it is before us. Narrative style, not a conflation of sources, explains the doublets. (The approach displays a family resemblance with canonical criticism.)[8]

Such an approach to Genesis 37 may be found in Adele Berlin's helpful book *Poetics and Interpretation of Biblical Narrative*. She sets her analysis over against traditional source criticism and concludes, "On the basis of plot and discourse, the present text is a unified product. . . . To be sure, there are gaps, inconsistencies, retellings, and changes in vocabulary in biblical narrative, but these can be viewed as part of a literary technique and are not necessarily signs of different sources."[9]

The flood story also illustrates the emphasis of traditional criticism on discovering sources rather than interpreting whole texts. Scholars often divide Genesis 6:5–8:22 into two sources, P and a second source usually identified as J. The tendency of traditional criticism is to highlight apparent discrepancies and to attribute repetition to different sources.[10]

G. J. Wenham, on the other hand, examined this text as a whole and discovered that the flood account was very carefully and tightly structured. He was able to identify the structure as a chiasm (see chapter 7). His conclusion was that "Genesis vi–ix is a carefully composed piece of literature, which is more coherent than usually admitted. . . . The Genesis flood story is a coherent narrative within the conventions of Hebrew story-telling."[11]

Up to this point we have been speaking of literary approaches or literary criticism. This terminology is appropriate because it makes explicit the connection with nonbiblical literary criticism. As with other approaches, notably the sociological approach, literary criticism is highly interdisciplinary.[12] While biblical studies has had contact with secular literary studies for centuries (see chapter 1), until recently there has been only sporadic interaction. Within the last two decades biblical studies has become much more conscious of the need to understand and employ the concepts and tools of literary analysis. Biblical scholars have turned to literary study for help (Polzin, Detweiler, Crossan, Via, etc.), and an increasing number of literary scholars have turned to the Bible as an object

---

[7]E. A. Speiser, *Genesis* (Anchor Bible 1; Garden City, N.Y.: Doubleday, 1964), pp. 293–94.

[8]J. Barton, *Reading the Old Testament* (Philadelphia: Westminster, 1984), pp. 77–88.

[9]A. Berlin, *Poetics and Interpretation of Biblical Narrative* (Sheffield: Almond, 1983), p. 121.

[10]See, for instance, G. von Rad, *Genesis* (Philadelphia: Westminster, 1972), pp. 119–21; Speiser, *Genesis*, pp. 54–56.

[11]G. J. Wenham, "The Coherence of the Flood Narrative," *VT* 28 (1978): 337, 347.

[12]For a good introduction to the sociological method, see R. R. Wilson, *Sociological Approaches to the Old Testament* (Philadelphia: Fortress, 1984).

of study (Alter, Kermode, Ryken, Frye). Such interests have led to the rise of the literary approach in biblical studies, most commonly referred to as literary criticism.

The terminology may lead to confusion. The term *literary criticism* already has a specialized meaning in biblical studies, wherein it most commonly refers to source criticism. Due to the possibility of confusion, some have advocated the use of the term *aesthetic criticism* to describe the literary approach. Others desire to broaden the scope of *rhetorical criticism,* though it usually refers only to matters of style. Both terms, however, are too narrow for our purposes. In the literary approach, we are interested in more than the study of beauty and people's response to it. We are interested in more than the study of style, or those "artistic means (in a text) for achieving effects upon the reader or audience."[13] In the final analysis, *literary criticism,* in spite of ambiguity and possible confusion, is the best term to describe the type of analysis outlined in this book. Before going further, however, it is necessary to answer a few basic questions. What is literature? What is the literary approach? Is the Bible literature?

Some scholars and even more laypeople understandably object to the idea of a literary approach. It appears to reduce the Scriptures to the level of the classics or, worse than that, to equate the Bible with imaginative or fictional writing. Many are acquainted with a literary approach through high-school courses entitled "The Bible as Literature." Such a title connotes a supposedly neutral or nonreligious approach to the text, thus making it a "safe" course for state-supported schools. In short, the literary approach appears to reduce the Bible to something less than it is.

Scholars from many different theological stripes may be cited warning us against the dangers implicit in such an approach:

> There is something artificial in the idea of "the Bible as 'literature.'" Or rather, it can be artificial and contrary to the perception of both most believers and most unbelievers. (K. Stendahl)

> Those who talk of reading the Bible "as literature" sometimes mean, I think, reading it without attending to the main thing it is about. (C. S. Lewis)

> Whoever turns a gospel of Christ into a novel has wounded my heart. (J. G. Herder)

> The persons who enjoy these writings solely because of their literary merit are essentially parasites; and we know that parasites, when they become too numerous, are pests. I could easily fulminate for a whole hour against the men of letters who have gone into ecstasies over "the Bible as literature." (T. S. Eliot)[14]

The danger of reducing the Bible to the level of a good story without grounding in actual events and without impact in the real world is a real danger. The issue is simply what it means to "treat the Bible as literature."

The question "What is literature?" is not an easy one. Many answers have been proposed. Some have suggested that everything in print is literature.[15] Most scholars, however, argue that literature is a subset of written texts. According to the popular textbook

[13] M. H. Abrams, *A Glossary of Literary Terms,* 4th ed. (New York: Holt, Rinehart & Winston, 1981), p. 160.

[14] K. Stendahl, "The Bible as a Classic and the Bible as Holy Scripture," *JBL* 103 (1984): 6; C. S. Lewis, *Reflections on the Psalms* (Glasgow: Collins, 1961), p. 10; J. G. Herder, quoted in F. Kermode, *The Genesis of Secrecy* (Cambridge: Harvard University Press, 1979), p. 120; T. S. Eliot, *Essays, Ancient and Modern* (London, 1936), p. 95.

Theory of Literature, "The term 'literature' seems best if we limit it to the art of literature, that is, to imaginative literature. . . . We recognize 'fictionality,' 'invention,' or 'imagination' as the distinguishing trait of literature."[16] The full implications of adopting a similar view of the Bible will be discussed in chapter 2. For now, however, it is necessary simply to state that a literary approach to the study of Scriptures does not imply, as some might think, a belief that the Bible as a whole is story, not history, or that it speaks of another world and not the real world of time and space.

A literary approach to the Bible is possible because its texts are obviously self-conscious about form. Artful verbal expression is frequently encountered in the Old and New Testaments.[17] This attention to the verbal texture makes the Bible at least in great part amenable to a literary approach. C. S. Lewis qualifies his negative assessment (quoted above) about a literary approach by saying, "But there is a saner sense in which the Bible, since it is after all literature, cannot properly be read except as literature; and the different parts of it as the different sorts of literature they are."[18] Northrup Frye has well stated, "The Bible is as literary as it can well be without actually being literature."[19] Of course, the Bible is not uniformly literary. Poetry as a whole is certainly a more self-conscious use of language than prose, though Robert Alter (see chapter 4) has forcefully demonstrated that prose is artful in its composition.[20] A second problem inherent in the proposed approach to the Scriptures as literature is the vagueness of the phrase "artful verbal expression." What is literariness? Literary language is frequently defined by contrast with everyday language, but Di Girolamo and others have shown the immense difficulties of precision in such distinctions, and McKnight's position that texts are literary only when they are read as literature is not helpful.[21]

Nonetheless, such careful distinctions are not necessary to demonstrate the self-consciousness of biblical language. The descriptions of story structures and poetic devices are enough to show that literary concepts and tools are useful in the exegesis of biblical texts. Such descriptions will be given in chapters 4 and 6.

We begin now in part 1 by reviewing some aspects of the theory behind the literary approach to the Bible. Such a study will prepare the way for the analysis of seven specific texts in part 2.

---

[16]R. Wellek and A. Warren, *Theory of Literature,* 3d ed. (New York: Harcourt Brace Jovanovich, 1977), pp. 22, 26.

[17]Berlin, *Poetics and Interpretation,* esp. chap. 6, "The Art of Biblical Narrative."

[18]Lewis, *Psalms,* p. 10.

[19]N. Frye, *The Great Code* (London: Ark, 1982), p. 62.

[20]R. Alter, *The Art of Biblical Narrative* (New York: Basic Books, 1981), pp. 3–22.

[21]Di Girolamo, *Critical Theory,* pp. 13–20; E. McKnight, *The Bible and the Reader: An Introduction to Literary Criticism* (Philadelphia: Fortress, 1985), pp. 9–11.

SECTION ONE: THEORY

one

A HISTORICAL SURVEY

A literary approach to the study of the Bible is both a new and an old phenomenon. In the past two decades unprecedented attention has been directed to the literary qualities of the text. In the glare of the present explosion of interest, however, we must not lose sight of the long prehistory of literary approaches. The present chapter surveys the history of the interrelationship of biblical and literary studies. The early history is lightly treated, not to denigrate its importance, but by choice our focus is the different contemporary manifestations of the literary approach. It is appropriate to emphasize the recent past, given the current fascination of the biblical scholar for the literary approach.

The chapter is not exhaustive but serves as a beginning guide to the use of literary concepts and tools in the field of biblical studies. The concentration in the historical survey will clearly be on the second half of the twentieth century. Pre-twentieth-century schools and figures chosen for comment are cited as high points or representatives.

PRECURSORS TO THE LITERARY APPROACH

Patristic Interpretation

Many of the early church fathers were educated in classical rhetoric and poetics. As a result, they frequently applied the principles of literature that they learned in school to the study of the Scriptures. They often compared biblical stories and poems with ones familiar to them in classical literature. The result was, from a modern perspective, a distortion of understanding and evaluation of the biblical texts. Jerome, for example, scanned

Hebrew poems and described their poetic form in labels developed for Greek and Latin poetry.[1] Kugel quotes Jerome as saying:

> What is more musical than the Psalter? which, in the manner of our Flaccus or of the Greek Pindar, now flows in iambs, now rings with Alcaics, swells to a Sapphic measure or moves along with a half-foot? What is fairer than the hymns of Deuteronomy or Isaiah? What is more solemn than Solomon, what more polished than Job? All of which books, as Josephus and Origen write, flow in the original in hexameter and pentameter verses.[2]

Augustine too compared biblical stories with classical stories and found the former rough and clumsy in their form when compared with the latter. In his *Confessions* (Book 3:5) we find the following telling comment:

> So I made up my mind to examine the holy Scriptures and see what kind of books they were. I discovered something that was at once beyond the understanding of the proud and hidden from the eyes of children. Its gait was humble, but the heights it reached were sublime.... When I first looked into the Scriptures ... they seemed quite unworthy of comparison with the stately prose of Cicero.[3]

Augustine thought that the Bible had a low literary quality, which for him represented a test of faith and humility. The intellectual must be willing to accept the idea that the Bible is inferior literature and must still believe the message. Other fathers of the church attempted to prove that the Bible was actually superior to pagan literature in its form as well as in its content.

Of course, the flaw inherent in the Fathers' literary approach to the Bible is that they judged the text by standards developed for the analysis of a foreign literature. The imposition of alien values on the biblical text is a pitfall that continues to the present day (see chapter 2). The positive aspect of the Fathers' approach is that they recognized the literary qualities of the biblical stories, an awareness that gradually diminished as the content of the Scriptures was abstracted into various theological systems.

Robert Lowth and the Study of Hebrew Poetry

Poetry is so obviously literary, in the sense of artful and conventional, that it was subjected to literary analysis long before prose. Robert Lowth, who was a professor of English at Oxford in the late eighteenth century, wrote a landmark analysis of the workings of Hebrew poetry, particularly parallelism.[4] By categorizing parallelism, discussing meter, and describing other poetic devices, Lowth approached part of the Bible as a literary text. He was, in essence, describing the conventions that shaped the writing of the Psalms, Isaiah, and other poetic texts. Lowth's results, though eventually receiving considerable modification, aided in the correct reading of the poetry of the Old Testament.

Work on understanding the conventions and devices of Hebrew poetry has continued unabated ever since. Primarily, scholars have further refined Lowth's categories of

---

[1]J. Kugel, *The Idea of Biblical Poetry* (New Haven: Yale University Press, 1981), pp. 149–56.
[2]Ibid., p. 152.
[3]Quoted in ibid., pp. 159–60.
[4]R. Lowth, *Lectures on the Sacred Poetry of the Hebrews* (London: T. Tegg & Son, 1835; orig. 1753); cf. A. Baker, "Parallelism: England's Contribution to Biblical Studies," *CBQ* 35 (1973): 429–40.

parallelism and have suggested various schemes for describing meter. Interesting work has also been done in the area of grammatical parallelism and in the delineation of other secondary devices (see chapter 6).

Hermann Gunkel

In reading the most recent research on the literary method, one would be surprised to find Hermann Gunkel's name in a list of representative early developers of the literary approach. Indeed, in the eyes of some, Gunkel is the archenemy of a literary approach.[5] With his interest in discovering the individual forms and their setting in life, the emphasis was on individual texts outside of their canonical context and on a sociological rather than a literary explanation of their origins.

A definite gulf exists between Gunkel and contemporary aesthetic critics, but we should still recognize that Gunkel developed his understanding of form criticism in an interdisciplinary context. His use of the concepts of genre (*Gattung*), form (*Form*), and setting in life (*Sitz im Leben*) are heavily informed by literary and sociological theories of his day.[6] Indeed one of the difficulties with biblical form criticism as traditionally practiced is not that it is aliterary in its understanding of genre but that it adopts a neoclassical concept of genre that was obsolete even in Gunkel's day.[7] In any case, Gunkel advanced a literary approach to the study of Scripture by focusing attention on the all-important issue of identifying the genre of a text in the process of interpretation.

James Muilenburg and Rhetorical Criticism

James Muilenburg delivered his presidential address to the Society of Biblical Literature in 1968, an event that has since become a touchstone for holistic and literary approaches to the study of the Bible.[8] The title, "Form Criticism and Beyond," is instructive because, while appreciating the strengths of form criticism, he felt it was time to move beyond the impasse that had resulted from concentrating on individual pericopes within texts. He was concerned as well with the emphasis that form criticism placed on the "typical and representative" to the exclusion of "individual, personal, and unique features." On the positive side, he recognized that the Old Testament had a high literary quality and promoted the study of style. His work has since stimulated many other studies connected with the style of Hebrew poetry and prose.

The preceding survey is very schematic. It completely ignores some major figures of the past, particularly the medieval period and also of this century (Norden, König, and Alonso-Schökel, for instance). Nonetheless, it is now clear that the modern literary approach has a long history in the field of biblical interpretation, even if it has never before reached the current level of activity.

---

[5]For instance, Weiss, *The Bible from Within*.

[6]G. Tucker, *Form Criticism of the Old Testament* (Philadelphia: Fortress, 1971), pp. 4–5; and M. J. Buss, "The Study of Forms," in *Old Testament Form Criticism*, ed. J. H. Mayes (San Antonio: Trinity University Press, 1974), p. 50.

[7]Neo-classical genre theory is a nineteenth-century phenomenon that held a rigid view of genres as pure and hierarchical; see G. N. G. Orsini, "Genres," in *The Princeton Encyclopedia of Poetry and Poetics* (Princeton: Princeton University Press, 1974), p. 308.

[8]J. Muilenburg, "Form Criticism and Beyond," *JBL* 88 (1969): 1–18.

As we now turn to the modern period of literary study of the Bible, there are many ways in which we could proceed. One possible approach is chronological and charts the different dominant schools of thought in secular literary study and then gives examples concerning how each school of thought has exerted an influence on biblical studies. To proceed in such a way, one would begin with New Criticism, then consider structuralism and semiotics, and finally conclude with deconstruction. Other influential minority positions could then be discussed, particularly reader-response, archetypal, Marxist, and feminist literary criticism.

Biblical studies, however, does not follow the chronological pattern of secular theory. Some researchers in Bible write in a New Critical mode long after New Criticism has passed away as a major school in literary theory. Others adopt more traditional modes of literary criticism, even in this age of deconstruction. In reality, of course, this diversity reflects the situation in literary theory. Deconstruction may be the avant-garde movement today, but many in literary theory either blithely or studiously avoid it in order to continue in traditional, perhaps even pre-New Critical, modes of interpretation.[9] Instead of a diachronic survey of literary theory, then, I employ a synchronic analysis.

Each school of thought concentrates attention on one element of what might be called the act of literary communication. A literary text may be seen as a message of one sort or another addressed by an author to a reader. The communication itself takes place in a certain social and temporal context, which may be called the universe. These relations may be diagramed as follows: [10]

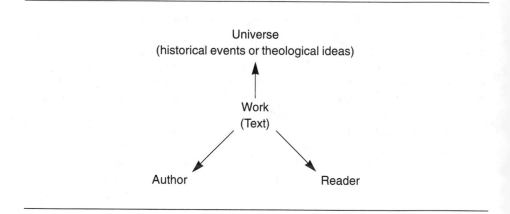

Theorists of the traditional school believe that we should interpret the meaning of a piece of literature by concentrating on the author. Others focus on the text, and still others focus on the reader. I discuss the various schools of literary theory under their respective focuses—author-centered, text-centered, and reader-centered. The main principles of

[9]Some believe, however, that deconstruction is already somewhat passé, evidence for which they see in an article by C. Campbell, "The Tyranny of the Yale Critics," *New York Times Magazine,* Feb. 9, 1986.
[10]M. H. Abrams, *The Mirror and the Lamp* (New York: Oxford University Press, 1953), pp. 3–29; and J. Barton, "Classifying Biblical Criticism," *JSOT* 29 (1984): 19–35.

each school of literary study will be examined, followed by specific examples of the influence each has exercised on biblical studies.

AUTHOR-CENTERED THEORIES

Literary Studies

Modern literary criticism has rejected the author as the major element in the interpretive process. Since the advent of New Criticism in the 1940s until the present, theorists have proclaimed the death of the author, granting authors no privileged insight into their own work. This trend, of course, is a complete reversal of the traditional approach to interpretation as it was known in the first half of the century.

Traditional Criticism

Traditional criticism before 1940 took great interest in the author. The key to interpretation was thought to lie in a knowledge of the activities and thought life of the author as he or she was writing a poem or narrative. The interpreter desired to discover the author's intentional meaning. Sandra Bermann describes the attitude of traditional criticism in the following illustrative way: "If we read histories, biographies, and Keats' own letters with enough scholarly patience and skill, we could be confident of 'getting the poem right,' 'understanding it,' 'interpreting its truth.'"[11] It is pivotal to know, for example, that Keats wrote his sonnet "Bright Star," with its themes of love and death, as he was caring for his brother Tom, who was dying of tuberculosis (and infecting John), and also that he was sobered by the reality of death in his passion for Fanny. This background knowledge, it was thought, provided the key to the interpretation of "Bright Star," with its lines such as the following: "I have two luxuries to brood over in my walks, your Loveliness and the hour of my death. O that I could have possession of them both in the same minute."

There are powerful arguments against such approaches. How is it possible to reconstruct an author's intention in a literary work, since he or she may not even have been conscious of it? The poet often is his or her own worst interpreter. How can we get back into the mind of the poet? The latter is a problem obviously heightened in the study of an ancient text.

As discussed below, the New Critics of the forties and fifties moved away from authorial intent, a view formalized by Wimsatt and Beardsley in their description of the "intentional fallacy" and their concomitant focus on the text alone in their own interpretive strategy.[12] The intentional fallacy may be defined as a view that:

> claimed that whether the author has expressly stated what his intention was in writing a poem, or whether it is merely inferred from what we know about his life and opinions, his intention is irrelevant to the literary critic, because meaning and value reside within the text of the finished, free-standing, and public work of literature itself.[13]

Certainly the argument of the intentional fallacy has some measure of validity. Traditional critics spent so much time discussing the life and habits of authors that they lost

---

[11]S. Bermann, "Revolution in Literary Criticism," *Princeton Alumni Weekly,* Nov. 21, 1984, p. 10.

[12]W. K. Wimsatt and M. Beardsley, "The Intentional Fallacy," reprinted in *The Verbal Icon: Studies in the Meaning of Poetry* (University Press of Kentucky, 1954), pp. 3–18. Some leading New Critics softened their view on intention later.

[13]Abrams, *Glossary,* p. 83.

sight of the text before them. The New Critics did a great service, as we will see, in direct-ing attention to the text itself in the interpretive process.

E. D. Hirsch

It is dangerous, however, to move completely away from any consideration of authorial intention, which is the decided direction of contemporary literary theory. E. D. Hirsch is an important contemporary advocate for the importance of the author.[14] Hirsch maintains that to lose sight of the author's intention in writing a text will result in the loss of any established meaning of a text. The author's intention provides a kind of anchor in the sea of interpretive relativity. For Hirsch, the meaning of a text is to be identified with the author's intended purpose. He is aware of all of the methodological difficulties asso-ciated with his position, notably the problem of recovering with certainty an author's purpose. After all, authors are usually not very explicit in literary works.

Hirsch's approach is interesting in that he approaches the author's meaning through a study of the text itself, particularly its genre. In other words, he infers the author's mean-ing primarily through a careful study of the text in relationship to other closely related texts. This move is important and approaches the balanced view that I advocate in chap-ter 3 below. Furthermore, Hirsch does not completely ignore the role of the reader in interpretation. He does not accept certain reader-response theories that argue that read-ers create meaning. Nevertheless, he does recognize that different readers will draw out different implications from the same text. He makes a distinction at this point between "meaning" and "significance." We have already seen that meaning is to be related to the author's intention. "Significance" of a literary work refers to the application that readers draw on the basis of their own background and interests.

Biblical Studies

While much of importance separates them, both critical and evangelical interpre-tation traditionally have focused on the author. The former has developed critical tools to enable the interpreter to go behind the final form of the text to its original setting, and the latter spends much energy on fixing and describing the time period in which the author wrote. If the author is known by name, then biographical information is utilized in interpretation.

Historical-Critical Method

Traditional criticism, also referred to as the historical-critical method, is usually contrasted with a literary approach. As pointed out in the introduction, historical critics and literary critics often define their positions as conflicting with each other. On anoth-er level, however, traditional criticism is a type of literary approach. It bears some resem-blance to pre-New Critical approaches that seek the meaning of a text in the light of a knowledge of the author and the author's background. In biblical studies this orienta-tion manifests itself in the concern to interpret a text in the light of its *original* setting.

The difference between traditional literary theory and traditional biblical criticism against contemporary forms of both is the difference between a diachronic and a syn-

[14]E. D. Hirsch, Jr., *Validity in Interpretation* (New Haven: Yale University Press, 1967); and idem, *The Aims of Interpretation* (Chicago: University of Chicago Press, 1976).

chronic approach. Roughly speaking a diachronic approach to literature examines the historical development of literature and is concerned with changes over time. On the other hand, a synchronic approach concentrates on one stage (usually the final form of the text), regardless of its prehistory.

Traditional critics developed tools for the study of the biblical text that were intended to recover the history of the text's development. They wanted to recover the original text and its setting. Explicitly or implicitly, these critics made the assumption that the meaning resides in its origin and has been distorted by its use in later forms. The tools most commonly associated with traditional criticism are source, form, and redaction criticism. Much could be written about each of these approaches, but for the purposes of this chapter, brief descriptions will be given. The interested reader may refer to the secondary literature cited in the footnotes.

No one has ever doubted that biblical authors utilized sources in the composition of certain books.[15] The author/editor of the books of Kings actually cites certain documents. At the end of the nineteenth century, however, hypothetical sources became the object of intense scrutiny. Source criticism of the Pentateuch came into its own primarily under the influence of Julius Wellhausen.[16] Since that time, the main impetus in Pentateuchal studies has been the delineation, description, and dating of the various preexisting sources that make up the Torah. Source criticism is not restricted to the Pentateuch, but it began in earnest in this portion of Scripture. Use of different divine names, doublets, and other types of repetition and supposed contradictions are some of the criteria used to distinguish one source from another. The result of the study of sources is to move away from the final form of the text to its prehistory. The method is thus diachronic. Furthermore, it fragments the final form of the text into a number of sources. Both of these tendencies are resisted by modern literary approaches to the study of the Bible. It is not surprising that the modern tendency in Pentateuchal studies is to move away from source analysis.[17]

Form criticism developed partly in reaction to source criticism, though it does not necessarily conflict with it.[18] As formulated by Gunkel and others, form criticism too is a diachronic method, seeking to discover the *original* form and setting of a particular biblical passage. The implicit assumption is that the key to the meaning of a passage is located in its original use and not in its final (distorted) form. Form criticism studies a text in the light of other texts that are similar in terms of structure, content, language, and so forth. Gunkel argued that each form had one and only one setting and that that setting was a sociological one. Sigmund Mowinckel, a student of Gunkel's, argued, for instance, that the Psalms for the most part found their original home in an annual enthronement festival.

---

[15]Barton, *Reading the Old Testament*, pp. 1–29; N. Habel, *Literary Criticism of the Old Testament* (Philadelphia: Fortress, 1971); R. E. Clements, *One Hundred Years of Old Testament Interpretation* (Philadelphia: Westminster, 1976).

[16]J. Wellhausen, *Geschichte Israels I* (Marburg, 1878); 2d ed., *Prolegomena zur Geschichte Israels* (1883; Eng. trans., *Prolegomena to the History of Israel,* 1885). See now J. Rogerson, *Old Testament Criticism in the Nineteenth Century: England and Germany* (Philadelphia: Fortress, 1985).

[17]I. M. Kikawada and A. Quinn, *Before Abraham Was: The Unity of Genesis 1–11* (Nashville: Abingdon, 1985).

[18]Barton, *Reading the Old Testament,* pp. 30–44; Tucker, *Form Criticism;* for a more detailed discussion and fuller bibliography, see my "Form Criticism, Recent Developments in Genre Theory and the Evangelical," *WTJ* 47 (1985): 46–67.

The next logical step is redaction criticism.[19] Once again it is partly a reaction against its past—in this case, form criticism. Form criticism tended to fragment a text. The concern was to *isolate* a passage from its context in the biblical text and study it in the light of its prehistory. Redaction criticism deals with the shape of the final form. What principles were active in the bringing together of these isolated forms? This approach usually tries to identify the theological concerns of the redactor, or editor, the so-called *Tendenz*. Redaction criticism is obviously helpful in the study of the Gospels or Kings and Chronicles, where the same events are being presented two or more times. It becomes much more tentative where there is no parallel text to serve as a control. Redaction criticism is a step beyond both source and form criticism in looking for the hand that drew the text into its final form. With redaction criticism we are moving closer to what we recognize as contemporary literary criticism with its interest on the final form of the text.

These brief descriptions of source, form, and redaction criticism show a contrast with the agenda of modern literary approaches. The difference may be summarized as the difference between a diachronic and a synchronic approach. The diachronic approach asks questions that are extrinsic to the text itself: Who is the author? What are the author's characteristics? What is the historical background of the text? and so forth. Implicitly or explicitly, the interpretive key is thought to lie outside of the text itself in its origin or background. These questions still arise in literary theory, but the approach to literature that they imply is now recognized as obsolete or problematic. Advocates of a literary approach tend to reject, ignore, or seriously modify these tools of historical criticism. Recently, however, there have been attempts at synthesis.[20]

Traditional Evangelical Approaches

Evangelicals, for the most part, have also assumed that the meaning of a text resides in the author's intention and the historical background. The *historical*-grammatical approach to interpretation has emphasized the need to study the Bible in the light of its historical origin. Of course, the major difference with traditional critical approaches is that the text has been identified with its canonical form, the final form of the text. A recent, lucid defense of identifying the meaning of a text with the author's intention is that of Walter Kaiser. Kaiser applied the theory of E. D. Hirsch to the situation of biblical exegesis and boldly stated, "The *author's* intended meaning is what a text means."[21]

TEXT-CENTERED THEORIES

Literary Studies

Extreme cases of the traditional approach studied everything but the work of literature itself. The reaction came in the 1940s and continues until the present day. Critics have shifted dramatically from a study of the origin and development of a piece of literature to a study of the text itself. Since text-oriented theories focus on the poem or prose narrative, they are collectively referred to as an objective theory of interpretation

---

[19]Barton, *Reading the Old Testament,* pp. 45–76; J. A. Wharton, "Redaction Criticism, Old Testament," *IDB,* Supplementary Volume, 729–32.

[20]V. Philips Long, "The Reign and Rejection of King Saul" (Ph.D. diss., Cambridge University, 1987).

[21]W. Kaiser, *Toward an Exegetical Theology* (Grand Rapids: Baker, 1981), p. 33.

as opposed to a mimetic or expressive theory.[22] Two major schools of thought will be presented at this point: New Criticism and structuralism.

New Criticism

New Criticism describes a general trend in literary theory that dominated thinking in the 1940s and 1950s. While many differences of opinion existed among the various scholars identified with this school of thought, they were united on the major points discussed below. Cleanth Brooks, Robert Penn Warren, and W. K. Wimsatt in the United States and F. R. Leavis in Britain are a few of the prominent scholars usually associated with New Criticism. The roots of the movement, however, may be traced to the thought of T. S. Eliot, I. A. Richards, and W. Empson. The name may be traced to the title of John Crowe Ransom's book *The New Criticism,* published in 1941. Many of the concerns of this predominantly Anglo-American school are shared by Russian formalism, but discussion of this latter school will be delayed until later, since there is a direct connection with structuralism.

The primary tenet of New Criticism may be expressed positively and negatively: the literary work is self-sufficient; the author's intention and background are unimportant to the critic. New Critics speak of the literary text as an artifact or verbal icon. Both of these metaphors express the self-sufficiency of the literary work. Such critics require (indeed must restrict themselves to) only the text and do not use outside, or extrinsic, information in its interpretation. The self-sufficiency of the literary text implies the denial of the author. The author does not speak from a position of privilege or special insight into his or her own text. Here, New Criticism parts company with traditional interpretation, not only of the first part of this century, but since the Enlightenment.

The self-sufficiency of the text further implies the necessity for a close reading of the text. If meaning resides in the text itself, it may be discovered only through careful analysis. Such close reading analyzes the complex interrelationships within the work itself. The study of poetic ambiguity (in the sense of multiple meaning), tension, irony, and paradox are examples of the literary concerns of New Critical scholars.

In the late 1950s New Criticism faded as the dominant force in literary studies.[23] Until that time the ideas associated with New Criticism were widespread, being taught even on the high-school level. It is not surprising, therefore, that its influence was felt on biblical studies as well. M. Weiss, for example, explicitly states and applies the principles of New Criticism to the interpretation of the biblical text.[24] Weiss cites various New Critical theories to justify his rejection of external approaches to the meaning of a passage of Scripture and to read the text "closely." He is concerned with the interpretation of the whole poem as it stands, thus the name *total interpretation* for his approach. His book begins with studies of texts on the word and phrase levels. He continues with an analysis of sentences and sequences of sentences and then concludes with research on structure and whole texts. The outline of his book illustrates his twin concerns with close reading and with the text as a whole.

---

[22]For this terminology, see Barton, "Classifying."
[23]F. Lentricchia, *After the New Criticism* (London: Methuen, 1980), p. 4.
[24]Weiss, *The Bible from Within.*

The "Sheffield school" and those more or less associated with it (mostly through the *Journal for the Study of the Old Testament*) have in the past adopted many of New Criticism's insights into biblical exegesis. Good examples may be cited in D. Gunn's stimulating studies of the Saul and David materials.[25] See also A. Berlin's work.[26]

J. Barton has advanced the provocative thesis that B. Childs's "canonical method" is formally related to New Criticism.[27] Childs himself, Barton concedes, distances himself from any literary justification for his approach. Nonetheless, Childs's treatment of biblical texts as self-sufficient and as understood within a literary tradition (canon) bears a close relationship to the principles of New Criticism.

Structuralism

New Criticism has had a relatively minor impact on biblical studies. In contrast, structuralism is of major importance in contemporary research on the Old and New Testaments. Structuralism describes a broad movement that affects many disciplines. Linguistics, anthropology, law, philosophy, and sociology are just a few, though perhaps the most discussed, of the fields of study in which an application of structural thinking may be found. Structuralism is broad in a second sense as well. Vastly different approaches are placed under the structuralist umbrella. As Poythress has stated, "Structuralism is more a diverse collection of methods, paradigms and personal preferences than it is a 'system,' a theory or a well formulated thesis."[28] Most important, perhaps, structuralism is broad in that it claims to be, "not a method of inquiry, but a general theory about human culture."[29]

By necessity then, our brief description of structuralism will be simplistic. After a short history of the development of structuralism, the main principles will be displayed and discussed. The structuralism presented here might be called the conservative version, associated with the early R. Barthes and the summarizing work of J. Culler.

History of development. The linguist Ferdinand de Saussure turned the attention of his field to the sign nature of language. He is commonly credited as the father of structuralism, though a lesser-known precursor is Charles S. Peirce. Saussure, whose major work is really the posthumous compilation of his lecture notes, proposed a series of distinctions that set the stage for modern studies.[30] His most famous division is between *langue* and *parole*. The former may be defined as "a system, an institution, a set of interpersonal rules and norms."[31] The latter refers to actual sentences used in writing or speaking. The second distinction identifies the two aspects of a sign, particularly the linguistic sign: the *signifier* and the *signified*. The signifier refers to the word, or acoustical image, while the signified pertains to the concept evoked by the signifier. Consider the word

---

[25]D. Gunn, *The Story of King David: Genre and Interpretation* (*JSOT* Supp. 6; Sheffield: JSOT, 1978); idem, *The Fate of King Saul: An Interpretation of a Biblical Story* (*JSOT* Supp. 14; Sheffield: JSOT, 1980).

[26]Berlin, *Poetics and Interpretation.*

[27]Barton, *Reading the Old Testament,* pp. 140–57.

[28]V. S. Poythress, "Structuralism and Biblical Studies," *JETS* 21 (1978): 221.

[29]Barton, *Reading the Old Testament,* p. 112.

[30]F. de Saussure, *Course in General Linguistics,* ed. C. Bally and A. Sechehaye (New York: McGraw-Hill, 1959).

[31]Culler, *Structuralist Poetics,* p. 8.

dog. The combination of the letters themselves, or, better, the phonemes represented by the letters, are the signifier. The concept (not the object, since the dog may be a nonexistent, metaphorical dog) evoked by the signifier is an animal of a certain species. The relationship between the signifier and the signified is *arbitrary* in that there is no inherent, predetermined relationship between the acoustical image and the concept. This fact may be demonstrated easily by noting the different words used in various languages to refer to the animal English speakers call *dog*.

A third distinction places syntagmatic analysis over against paradigmatic analysis. This distinction is illustrated most simply on the level of the sentence. In *the man saw the wolf*, a syntagmatic approach would analyze the five words in the sentence in their relationships to each other. A paradigmatic analysis, on the other hand, examines each slot in the sentence: *the man / saw / the wolf*. As McKnight states it: "Paradigmatic relationships of a word are those which may replace it in a sentence without making the sentence unacceptable."[32] These words are related as a group, and the use of any one will call into mind the others. For instance, *saw* could be replaced by *observed, espied,* or the like. This third Saussurian distinction is particularly important in differentiating the variation between Propp's and Lévi-Strauss's method of studying narrative (see below).

Meanwhile in Moscow and later in Prague, literary scholars (as a group labeled Russian formalists) were exploring avenues that eventually led to common concerns and approaches with European and American structuralists.[33] Indeed, the connection is embodied in one prominent practitioner of structuralism, Roman Jakobson. Jakobson was involved with the Moscow Linguistic Circle (founded in 1915), moved to Prague when the Moscow group was suppressed by the Soviets, and eventually ended up in New York, where he influenced the anthropologist Claude Lévi-Strauss. A second major figure of Russian formalism whose work provided a direct influence on the development of structuralist approaches to narrative is V. Propp.

Structuralism as a major school of literary criticism really began only in the 1960s. H. Felperin would date the coming of age of literary structuralism to 1966, the year in which Roland Barthes published *Critique et vérité*.[34] Here, Barthes proclaimed the importance of what he called the "science of literature," which is concerned not with the interpretation of particular works but with the "conditions of meaning." He and others such as Todorov desired to describe a "grammar" of literature.

Major principles. A major impetus for the development of structuralism in the area of literary criticism was the desire to be "scientific," to raise literary studies from the realm of the subjective to the objective—that is, to provide literature with a method of analysis that could be demonstrated and repeated. As R. C. Culley summarized it, structuralists "are seeking a method which is scientific in the sense that they are striving for a rigorous statement and an exacting analytical model."[35] More recent structuralist studies do not take such a radically scientific approach.[36]

---

[32]McKnight, *The Bible and the Reader,* p. 7.

[33]F. Jameson, *The Prison-House of Language* (Princeton: Princeton University Press, 1972), pp. 43–98; most recently, McKnight, *The Bible and the Reader,* pp. 16–19.

[34]H. Felperin, *Beyond Deconstruction* (Oxford: Clarendon, 1985), p. 74.

[35]R. C. Culley, "Exploring New Directions," in *The Hebrew Bible and Its Modern Interpreters*, ed. D. A. Knight and G. M. Tucker (Philadelphia: Fortress, 1985), p. 174.

[36]R. Polzin, *Biblical Structuralism* (Philadelphia: Fortress, 1977), esp. chap. 1, "What Is Structuralism?"

Structuralism developed from linguistics. In particular, the development traces to Saussure's insight into the nature of the sign in linguistics. Another common name for this field is semiotics (from the Greek word for *sign*). Words are perhaps the clearest examples of Saussure's thought as he discussed the workings of signs. Structuralism as a whole may be defined as the extension of the linguistic metaphor to other semiotic systems. Literature is considered by structuralists to be a "second-order semiotic system," in that literary texts are constructed from language. Literature and literary texts are, therefore, capable of structuralist analysis.

The analogy between linguistics and literature leads to insights into the nature of literature. The two most important ideas for our purposes are literary competence and literature as systemic. The conception of literary competence may be traced back to Saussure's foundational distinction between *langue* and *parole*, or abstract rules and actual utterances. Speakers of a language do not have a complete or explicit knowledge of all the rules. These rules are "tacitly shared by members of a speech community."[37] The internalization of *langue* permits the understanding of any particular utterance. When studying a second language, for instance, the student learns the rules of morphology and syntax, memorizes basic vocabulary, and thus becomes competent in that language. Noam Chomsky popularized the notions of *competence,* which describes the mastery of the basic rules of a language, and *performance,* which concerns the production of actual sentences.[38]

Early structuralist critics extended this linguistic notion to literature. One becomes competent in a literary tradition or literature in general by learning the syntax, or rules, of narrative. Deep underlying structures may be discerned that cut across literature as a whole. Another way of describing these rules is to call them *conventions.*

Structuralists and their interpreters often illustrate these ideas by using game analogies. American football, for example, is played by a set of rules that are not too difficult to assimilate or internalize, but unless they are learned, one cannot play the game or even follow it. To become competent in football entails learning the rules and conventions of the game (i.e., a forward pass is permissible, a lineman may not go downfield on a pass play, etc.).

Literary conventions are numerous and depend on the type of literature being analyzed. Indeed, genre is a way of describing a convention of literature. The interpreter needs to distinguish between prose and poetry, novel and lyric, etc. Such an approach to literature leads to the suppression of both the author and the reader in structuralist thought. As Culler describes it: "The [structuralist] concepts of *écriture* and *lecture* have been brought to the fore so as to divert attention from the author as source and the work as object and focus it instead on two correlated networks of convention: writing as an institution and reading as an activity."[39]

To put it perhaps in extreme form, writers are not seen as original contributors to their work but as users of previous devices. Their work is a conglomeration of previous works. Since, by necessity, only established literary conventions can be used, the meaning of the work is found in the convention rather than the intention of the author. The common use of literary conventions describes the structuralist notion *intertextuality.*

---

[37]Abrams, *Glossary,* p. 95.
[38]Culler, *Structuralist Poetics,* p. 9.
[39]Ibid., p. 131.

According to Julia Kristeva, "Every text takes shape as a mosaic of citations, every text is the absorption and transformation of other texts. The notion of intertextuality comes to take the place of the notion of intersubjectivity."[40] The reader meets the same fate. The competent reader has assimilated the conventions. He or she brings nothing to the interpretation of the text besides an explicit and implicit knowledge of how literature "works." In short, the meaning of a text resides in the conventional code, which has a public meaning, not in the author's intention or in the reader's preunderstanding. Reading is a "rule-governed process."[41] According to Robert Scholes, both readers and authors are "divided psyches traversed by codes."[42]

Besides the idea of literary competence, the notion of *literature as systemic* represents a second insight provided by the structuralist analogy between linguistics and literature. The division between the conventional nature of literature and literature as a system is artificial. The system of literature is composed of the various conventions. Once again it is helpful to begin with an illustration from linguistics. Phonemes, words, and sentences have no inherent meaning. Meaning is communicated by way of contrast within a closed system. For instance, the forms *pat* and *bat* are phonologically distinguished by the difference between *p* and *b*, which is a difference between voicelessness and voice. But *p* and *b* have meaning only in the system of English phonemes and particularly in contrast to one another. On the level of the distinctive feature, we notice *binarism,* another characteristic feature of structuralism. Structuralists "look for functional oppositions in whatever material they are studying."[43] According to Barton, structuralists

> tend to argue that all structures within which meaning can be generated, whether they be linguistic, social or aesthetic, can be analyzed in terms of pairs of opposites. . . .
> To be able to say what meaning is to be attached to an utterance, a gesture or an object, we need to know what it is not, as well as what it is: to know from what range of possibilities it has been selected, and what was excluded when it was chosen.[44]

Rigorous structuralists argue that, like computers, the human brain perceives and processes data according to the principle of binarism.

Structuralist approaches to prose narrative. Structuralism has emphasized prose narrative over against poetry. Structuralist study of plot and character in prose stories has had a major impact on the analysis of biblical texts. I thus describe briefly the development of structuralist thinking in this area, followed by the application of structuralism to the parable of the Good Samaritan.

I restrict my survey of structuralist approaches to prose narrative to its beginnings with V. Propp and the later refinements of A. J. Greimas. To be complete, one would need to examine the later insights of R. Barthes (in his work *S/Z*), T. Todorov, and others. Space will not permit such a survey.[45] In any case, the majority of biblical studies that adopt a structuralist perspective are theoretically dependent on Propp and Greimas.

---

[40]*Semiotikè: Recherches pour une sémanalyse* (Seuil, Paris, 1969), p. 146. Quoted in Culler, *Structuralist Poetics,* p. 9.
[41]Ibid., p. 241.
[42]R. Scholes, *Semiotics and Interpretation* (New Haven: Yale University Press, 1982), p. 14.
[43]Culler, *Structuralist Poetics,* p. 14.
[44]Barton, *Reading the Old Testament,* p. 111.
[45]See the summary (with bibliography) of McKnight, *The Bible and the Reader,* pp. 49–58.

Propp's *Morphology of the Folktale* deserves to be noted as one of the major contributions of Russian formalism.[46] Propp wrote a "morphology" or "poetics" of the folktale. He analyzed the folktale as consisting of two elements: roles and functions. In examining approximately a hundred Russian tales, he concluded that there was a structure to be discerned under the surface of the text. This insight led him to describe a finite number of roles and functions that surface in actual tales in different guises.

According to Propp there are seven roles, or "spheres of actions": the villain, the donor, the helper, the sought-for person and her father, the dispatcher, the hero, and the false hero. Specific characters may fill more than one of these roles in a particular folktale, but these categories exhaust the possibilities for characters.

Propp defines a function as "an act of a character, defined from the point of view of its significance for the course of the action."[47] There are thirty-one functions, according to Propp, and while not all functions occur in any one text, they always occur in the same sequence. By way of illustration, I list here the first five of Propp's functions:

1. A member of a family leaves home (*absentation*).
2. An *interdiction* is addressed to the hero.
3. There is a *violation* of the interdiction.
4. The villain makes an attempt at *reconnaissance*.
5. The villain receives information about his victim (*delivery*).

Greimas builds on Propp's analysis and refines it so that it is more manageable.[48] The refinement takes a decided turn under the influence of Lévi-Strauss.[49] Propp's analysis may be categorized as a syntagmatic approach that follows the linear sequence of the story. Lévi-Strauss adopts a paradigmatic stance that departs from the order of the story as given and probes the structure through the analysis of "schemata" that "exist simultaneously, superimposed on one another on planes with different levels of abstraction."[50] He is best known for his description of the oppositional character of Propp's "spheres of action." He refers to these spheres as *actants* and charts the relationship between them in a tale in the following way:

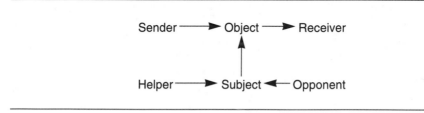

---

[46]V. Propp, *Morphology of the Folktale*, 2d ed., trans. L. A. Wagner (Austin: University of Texas Press, 1968).

[47]Ibid., p. 21.

[48]A. J. Greimas, *Structural Semantics: An Attempt at a Method*, trans. D. McDowell et al. (Lincoln: University of Nebraska Press, 1984).

[49]Cf. McKnight, *The Bible and the Reader*, pp. 53–54; R. Scheiffer, "Introduction" to Greimas, *Structural Semantics*.

[50]McKnight, *The Bible and the Reader*, p. 52.

The opposition in the tale occurs between the subject and the object, the sender versus the receiver, and the helper versus the opponent. By setting Propp's functions in binary opposition, Lévi-Strauss also reduces their number to twenty.

Biblical Studies

As mentioned, biblical scholars most frequently appeal to the work of Greimas to provide the theoretical basis for their structuralist study of the Bible. These scholars have particularly used his actantial model, which is only a part or one level of his analysis. Scheiffer has noted:

> Most commentators on Greimas . . . have taken Greimas's *actantial* analysis as the central feature of his semantics of discourse, and while this is not incorrect, it has the tendency to make the technique of actantial analysis the pinnacle of Greimas's pyramid rather than to position it as a structure which both crowns and supports its neighboring structures in a kind of geodesic dome.[51]

Greimas and other structuralist writers—as well as their commentators—are often unclear in their theoretical expression. Scholes finds that Greimas is "frequently crabbed and cryptic."[52] The result is that biblical scholars are at odds concerning the correct application of his theory to particular texts. More basic disagreement occurs regarding the value of structural analysis for the exegetical task.

These issues may be most clearly observed by referring to the essays of Patte, Crespy, Crossan, and Tannehill in *Semeia* (1974), which focus on the analysis of the parable of the Good Samaritan. Each attempts to apply Greimas's model to the parable and comes up with strikingly different results. I discuss Patte's analysis here, since it perhaps most accurately applies Greimas's model to the text.

Patte's structuralist analysis of the parable of the Good Samaritan (Luke 10:30–35) acknowledges Greimas's three structural levels—deep, superficial (intermediate), and surface—but Patte really treats only the middle level of narrative structure. Furthermore, he divides this middle level of analysis into two types: semiotic and semantic, with the strong emphasis on the latter.

The semantic narrative structure is in turn divided into "six hierarchically distinct elements" by Patte, following Greimas. They are "sequence, syntagm, utterance, actantial model, function, and actant."[53] Each of these items is briefly explained by Patte and situated in his overall method.

Patte begins his analysis of the parable by separating the sequences, which he does by analyzing the disjunctional functions (the "movements and encounters of actors") within the parable. This analysis uncovers eight sequences in the text of the parable, which transform themselves somehow (no explanation is given) into seven *lexie*.

Patte applies the actantial model of Greimas to each of the *lexie* (unlike Crossan, who develops it for the text as a whole). Since in this section I can give little more than a taste of this type of analysis, I discuss here only the model for *lexie* 6: "and bound up his wounds, pouring on oil and wine; then he set him on his own beast and brought him

---

[51]Scheiffer, "Introduction," p. xli.
[52]Quoted in J. D. Crossan, "Comments on the Article of Daniel Patte," *Semeia* 2 (1974): 121.
[53]D. Patte, "Narrative and Structure and the Good Samaritan," *Semeia* 2 (1974): 121.

to an inn, and took care of him. And the next day he took out two denarii and gave them to the innkeepers. . . ." (vv. 34–35 RSV).

Applying Greimas's actantial model to this text, we note that the sender is unknown; the object is the injured man's "status as subject," that is, his recovery; and the receiver is therefore the injured man. The subject, or hero, according to Propp's terminology, is the Samaritan; the opponents are the robbers (even though they are not mentioned in this *lexie*, Patte carries them over); and the helpers include the oil, wine, donkey, money, and innkeeper.

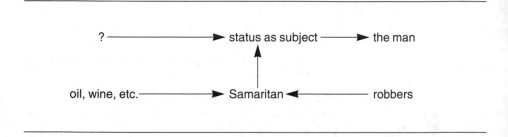

Such, in brief, is the type of analysis Patte and others use for biblical exegesis. He states that such an analysis serves the function of "reducing the narrative to its basic elements," which "clarifies what 'happens' in the text."[54] Both Crossan and Patte, however, believe that the importance of such studies really is found elsewhere in a "complete and systematic investigation of the forms and genres of the New Testament."[55] This claim has yet to be demonstrated. Perhaps, as Culley in his rather reserved praise of structuralism puts it, "Real insights are gained into the phenomenon of literature."[56] Nevertheless, its high level of complexity, its almost esoteric terminology, and its (thus far) very limited help toward understanding the text (which for many structuralists is not even a concern) have and likely will prevent the vast majority of biblical scholars from actively participating in the endeavor.

READER-CENTERED THEORIES

Literary Studies

So far we have surveyed theories that have placed the locus of meaning in the author and in the text. In addition, a number of recent approaches concentrate on the reader's role in the production of meaning.

Anyone who has worked with a number of students on a literary text knows that it is possible to obtain as many interpretations of the text as there are students in the class. Different readers will interpret the same text sometimes similarly, sometimes in vastly different ways. If meaning is not inherent in the author's intention or in the text itself, how are we to evaluate these different interpretations? One response is to say that they

---

[54]Ibid., p. 3.
[55]Crossan, "Comments on the Article," p. 122.
[56]Culley, "Exploring," p. 177.

are all equally valid. Meaning resides in the reader, not in the text. The reader creates the meaning of the text.

Many reader-response theories, however, are more limited, holding that the reader *in interaction with the text* produces meaning. According to E. V. McKnight:

> The relationship between reader as subject (acting upon the text) and the reader as object (being acted upon by the text), however, is not seen as an opposition but as two sides of the same coin. It is only as the reader is subject of text and language that the reader becomes object. It is as the reader becomes object that the fullness of the reader's needs and desires as subject are met.[57]

In this view, readers are not free to do what they will with the text but are constrained by the text in their interpretation.

Who is the reader according to these theories? Differences abound. Some refer to any reader; others have in mind a "superreader," "informed reader," "ideal reader," or, in structuralist terms, the completely competent reader.[58] We do not need to solve these problems. We simply recognize that certain theorists concentrate on the reader's role in the process of interpretation.

Biblical Studies

Thus far few biblical scholars have argued for an exclusively reader-response approach to exegesis. Scholars, however, are increasingly recognizing the role of the reader in interpretation. For instance, Anthony Thiselton describes the act of interpretation as a bridging of two horizons: that of the text and that of the reader. Significantly, he does not call for a complete divestment of the reader's preunderstanding as one encounters the text.[59]

The most frequent appeal to reader-response theory in biblical studies comes from those who might be called "ideological readers." Here I refer to those who read the Scriptures with a definite, usually political, agenda. The two most prominent types of ideological readers today are liberation theologians and feminist scholars.

Liberation theologians read the text, attending primarily to what they perceive are the needs of their contemporary society, doing so in the light of the modern political philosophy of Marxism.[60] Such a reading will bring certain elements of the text into prominence, in particular, those texts concerning the liberation of the oppressed. The Exodus, which is certainly a major biblical theme, takes on even larger proportions in the writings of theologians of liberation.

There are many differences among biblical scholars who operate under the rubric of feminism.[61] Some wish simply to explore the characters, books, and themes that are relevant to the situation of the modern woman. Studies of female characters, such as the wives of David, are an example. Others want to read the whole text from a female perspective to

---

[57]McKnight, *The Bible and the Reader,* p. 128.

[58]R. M. Fowler, "Who Is 'the Reader' in Reader Response Criticism," *Semeia* 31 (1985): 5–23.

[59]A. Thiselton, *The Two Horizons: New Testament Hermeneutics and Philosophical Description* (Grand Rapids: Eerdmans, 1980).

[60]I include here not only those scholars who *recognize* that they are reader-response critics but some who would assert that they are text oriented (e.g., N. Gottwald, *The Tribes of Yahweh* [Maryknoll: Orbis, 1979]).

[61]See the collected studies and bibliographies in *JSOT* 22 (1982).

see what difference it makes for the implied reader to be a woman. Still others wish to read the Bible as women in order to "explode the myth of patriarchy"—that is, to show the innate prejudice of the Scriptures against women and to expose the Bible as a tool of oppression. They are united in the sense that they approach the text with an agenda. Many utilize reader-response theory for their theoretical justification.

While extreme forms of liberation theology and feminism must be rejected and caution must be taken regarding all forms of ideological reading on the grounds that distortion is possible or even likely, much may nevertheless be learned from these perspectives. These readers bring out themes of Scripture that are commonly passed over by most readers of the Bible—concern for the poor, the role of women, and so forth.

We must remember that *no one* can approach the biblical text objectively or with a completely open mind. Indeed, such an approach to the text would be undesirable. Everyone comes to the text with questions and an agenda. One's attitude, however, should be one of openness toward change.

Consideration of the need for openness leads to a brief comment on contextualization.[62] Evangelical theologians and biblical scholars are becoming increasingly sensitive to the fact that each reader approaches the Scriptures with certain cultural and personal questions and assumptions.[63] We are not neutral and objective as we approach the text. We come at it from different perspectives. This preunderstanding will influence our interpretation of Scripture. The issue is not one of incorrect interpretation but of our giving prominence to certain parts of the text and not to others. We might read, say, the Song of Songs as a single man or woman and then some time later as a young married person and find that our attention is drawn to different aspects of the text.

Christian thinkers recognize this phenomenon as existing also between cultures. A Christian from Egypt, one from the United States, and one from China will each come to the text with different questions and needs. The Scriptures are the same for each. The preunderstanding of the interpreter encounters the text and *must* conform to it. Contextualization implies not that the interpreter creates meaning but simply that the interpretation of the biblical text involves its application to the respective contemporary situations.

DECONSTRUCTION

Literary Studies

The cutting edge of literary studies in the mid-1980s is deconstruction.[64] It is the "new wave" from France. Like the previous imports (existentialism, structuralism), deconstruction has brought strong reactions, both positive and negative, from English and American scholars.

I discuss deconstruction at the end of this survey of literary theory, not simply because it is the most prominent of recent approaches. Each of the other theories emphasizes one of the elements of the act of literary communication: author, text, or reader. Deconstruction, on the contrary, questions the grounds of all these approaches. Culler,

---

[62]See H. Conn, *Eternal Word and Changing Worlds* (Grand Rapids: Zondervan, 1984).

[63]See Thiselton, *The Two Horizons*.

[64]There are already indications, however, that the deconstruction school is no longer avant-garde. D. Tracy, *Plurality and Ambiguity* (San Francisco: Harper and Row, 1987), is a post-deconstructionist statement in hermeneutics.

in his insightful analysis comments, "It demonstrates the difficulties of any theory that would define meaning in a univocal way: as what an author intends, what conventions determine, what a reader experiences."[65] Deconstruction, therefore, stands outside of the pattern of the other theories and is treated separately.

As with New Criticism and structuralism, it must be said that deconstruction is "[not a] method, system, or settled body of ideas."[66] This caveat takes on special force since, as will be seen below, deconstruction is constantly in danger of taking itself too seriously and thus becoming another text-centered theory.

Deconstruction is most closely associated with Jacques Derrida. His first major writings appeared in 1967, but his major influence came in the 1970s and continues in the 1980s. Derrida is part philosopher and part literary critic, but his impact has occurred in the latter field, though in his hands the division between these two disciplines becomes quite fluid. Derrida, indeed, attacks the Western philosophical tradition that subordinates writing to speaking. Since at least Plato, speech has been thought to bear a closer relationship to pure thought than does writing. Writing removes communication a step further from authorial presence. Derrida argues that this attitude, which underlies Western philosophy, demonstrates a stubborn belief in *presence*. Ultimately, such a belief is grounded in what he calls "a transcendental signified," which Abrams describes as "an absolute foundation, outside the play of language itself, which is adequate to 'center' (that is, to anchor and organize) the linguistic system in such a way as to fix the particular meaning of a spoken or written discourse within that system."[67]

Derrida argues instead for the priority of writing over speech. He believes that writing is a clearer illustration of what characterizes all language acts: the slippage between sign and referent, signifier and signified. Derrida's extreme language skepticism calls into question the act of literary communication. Characteristic of Derrida is an analysis of pivotal philosophers such as Plato, Rousseau, Saussure, Lévi-Strauss, and Austin. He exposes their *logocentricism* (belief in a "metaphysics of presence"), which is implied in their fundamental *phonocentricism* (priority of speech over writing). He probes the text of these philosophers until he uncovers an *aporia* (a basic contradiction), which usually involves the philosopher's use of metaphor or some other rhetorical device. Metaphor is key in this regard because it displays the slippage between sign and referent. Its use by the philosopher demonstrates, contra the philosophers, that the truth claims of philosophy are no different from those of fiction.

The fundamental force behind Derrida's writing is his heightening the distance between signifier and signified. Here he threatens the possibility of literary communication. He begins with Saussure's premise that a sign has no inherent meaning but finds meaning only in distinction to other elements in the semiotic system. Meaning is thus a function not of presence but of absence. Derrida's concept of *différance* is helpful here. (The *a* in *différance* shows that the word is a neologism, constructed from two different French words, one meaning " to differ," the other "to defer.") The meaning of a linguistic or literary sign is based on its difference in comparison with other signs and as such

---

[65]J. Culler, *On Deconstruction: Theory and Criticism After Structuralism* (London: Routledge & Kegan Paul, 1982), p. 131.
[66]C. Norris, *Deconstruction: Theory and Practice* (London: Methuen, 1982), p. 1.
[67]Abrams, *Glossary,* p. 38.

is always deferred, or delayed. With deconstruction one enters the "endless labyrinth."[68] Meaning is never established; the pun becomes the favored interpretive device.

The main bastion of American deconstruction has been at Yale. G. Hartman, H. Bloom, P. DeMan, and J. Hillis Miller, though different from Derrida and from each other, have been identified as his most able representatives.[69] Some advocates for deconstruction have expressed fear that deconstruction may be threatened by its routine use in the study of texts. They fear that some scholars are applying Derrida's style of analysis to texts mechanically, which may signal its demise.

At present, however, deconstruction is alive and well and is threatened seriously only by Marxist or political interpreters. Marxist interpreters disdain deconstruction, since it removes literature and the critic from any meaningful interaction with the world. Derrida's motto "there is nothing outside of the text" irritates them. The clash between this-worldly and no-worldly interpretation will continue into the next decade.

Michael Edwards provides brief, but tantalizing, comments on deconstruction from a Christian perspective.[70] Instead of criticizing Derrida, he points out the fundamental insight into the nature of language that Derrida provides. Edwards does not gainsay Derrida's fundamental atheism but points out that like most non-Christian philosophers, Derrida builds on an essentially true insight. Edwards claims that Derrida is right to point out the extreme difficulties in communication. There are fissures or breaks between words and their referents. Derrida attributes this slippage to an absence of the "transcendental signified" (i.e., God), Edwards to the Fall.

Biblical Studies

Presently there are few signs of Derridean influence on biblical studies. We have observed, however, that every major school of thought has eventually influenced biblical studies, and there is no reason to doubt that deconstruction will follow suit.

To say that no influence has been registered would be incorrect. *Semeia* 23 (1982) is entitled *Derrida and Biblical Studies.* Furthermore, the New Testament scholar John Dominic Crossan has been active in bringing Derrida's thought to bear on issues of interpretation. This influence is most readily seen in his book *Cliffs of Fall: Paradox and Polyvalence in the Parables of Jesus* (1980), in which he analyzes the parables from a Derridean perspective. He finds that the metaphoricity of the parable has a "void of meaning at its core. . . . it can mean so many things and generate so many differing interpretations because it has no fixed, univocal or absolute meaning to begin with."[71] Instead of searching for the meaning of the parable, he *plays* (a favorite metaphor of deconstructive method) with the words of the text.

Perhaps the most explicit deconstructive study of Old Testament texts is found in Peter Miscall's *The Workings of Old Testament Narrative.* He devotes the bulk of his book to a close reading of Genesis 12 and 1 Samuel 16–22. For Miscall, such a reading reveals

---

[68]Lentricchia, *After the New Criticism,* p. 166.

[69]See V. B. Leitch, *Deconstructive Criticism: An Advanced Introduction* (New York: Columbia University Press, 1983), and more popularly, Campbell, "Tyranny."

[70]M. Edwards, *Towards a Christian Poetics* (London: Macmillan, 1984).

[71]J. D. Crossan, *Cliffs of Falls* (New York: Seabury, 1980), pp. 9–10; see also G. Aichele, Jr., *The Limits of Story* (Philadelphia: Fortress, 1985).

information that is insufficient for arriving at a single meaning. "There is, at the same time, too little and too much of the narrative, too few and too many details, and this gives rise to the many, and frequently contradictory, interpretations of and conjectures about OT narrative."[72] He concludes that to attempt to pin down a single meaning of the text is misguided and argues that most exegetical issues are undecidable: "The reading encounters ambiguity, equivocation, opposed meanings and cannot decide for or establish one or the other; the reading cannot stop, it cannot control or limit the text."[73]

In his analysis of the David and Goliath story, for example, Miscall concentrates on both the concrete details of the text as well as the gaps, for instance, information not given in the text about a character's motivation. By such an analysis of the text of 1 Samuel 17, Miscall claims that

> David's character is undecidable. The text permits us to regard David as a pious and innocent young shepherd going to battle the Philistine because of the latter's defiance of the Lord and as a cunning and ambitious young warrior who is aware of the effects that his defeat of Goliath will have on the assembled army.[74]

In the postscript Miscall explicitly connects his readings with a deconstructive approach to the text. He points out instances he finds of aporia, of inherent contradictions in the text. He argues that the type of ambiguity he thus demonstrates is the result of the nature of literary communication (the slippage of signifier and signified) and that the Bible, like other works of literature, always deconstructs itself.

[72]P. D. Miscall, *The Workings of Old Testament Narrative* (Philadelphia Fortress, 1983), p. 1.
[73]Ibid., p. 2.
[74]Ibid., p. 73.

two
AN APPRAISAL
OF THE LITERARY
APPROACH

*H*aving reviewed the history of the literary study of the Bible, we may now proceed to evaluation.[1] What are the disadvantages or even dangers of a literary approach, and can they be avoided? Are there benefits to be gained by analyzing the biblical text from this perspective?

PITFALLS

The Different Literary Approaches Are Contradictory

The first difficulty with the literary approach is that the field of secular literary theory and the related discipline of linguistics are divided among themselves. There is much infighting about the basic questions of literature and interpretation as a number of different schools of thought seek domination in the field. The biblical scholar faces a dilemma at this point. Students of the Bible find it difficult enough to keep abreast of their own field without keeping current with a second one. The usual result is that biblical scholars follow one particular school of thought or else one particularly prominent thinker as their guide to a literary approach. Because of the natural desire to seem current or avant-garde, the most current theory is commonly adopted.

Francis Schaeffer described the lag that occurs between biblical studies and the rest of the disciplines.[2] A new philosophical approach that comes on the scene influences art,

---

[1] This chapter was published in an earlier form as "The Literary Approach to the Study of the Old Testament: Pitfalls and Promise," *JETS* 28 (1985): 385–98.

[2] F. A. Schaeffer, *The God Who Is There* (Downers Grove, Ill.: InterVarsity, 1968), pp. 13–84.

literary theory, sociology, music, and then finally biblical studies. This process may be observed in the case of Derrida's deconstruction. It gained prominence in the late 1960s and early 1970s and just now is making an impact on biblical studies.

My concern is that the hard-and-fast school divisions in literary theory are imported into biblical studies with little methodological reflection. Every major movement in literary theory of the past forty years is mirrored in the work of biblical scholars: New Criticism (Weiss, Childs); Northrup Frye's archetypal approach to literature (Frye himself, Ryken); phenomenology (Detweiler, Ricoeur); structuralist (Jobling, Polzin, Patte); Marxism (Gottwald, liberation theologians); feminism (Trible, Reuther, Fiorenza); deconstruction (Crossan, Miscall).

The apologist must analyze the deep philosophical roots of each of these schools of thought. Students of the Bible and biblical scholars working on method, however, can recognize positive, though perhaps distorted, insights that each of these schools provides. I thus agree with John Barton, who has said that "all of the methods . . . have something in them, but none of them is the 'correct method.'" In his view, our methods are best seen as "codification of intuitions about the text which may occur to intelligent readers."[3]

Among the many positive contributions that may be gleaned from each of these schools of thought we could include the New Critical insight that we must focus our interpretation on the text rather than on the author's background; the structuralist attention to literary conventions; and the emphasis of feminism and Marxism on the themes of sexual and economic justice. Even deconstruction may give us an insight into the effect of the Fall on language, namely, the schism between signifier and signified.[4]

Notice that in each case the secular theory leads to a new imbalance. New Criticism rightly attacked certain cases of appealing to the author's intention for the meaning of a text, but it went too far in restricting the interpreter to the text alone, the text as artifact, leaving both author and reader out of the picture. Marxist and feminist readings distort the text by insisting that their themes are the only interpretive grids. And deconstructionists use their insight into the slippage between sign and object to attack theology or any type of literary communication.

The literary approach thus easily and often falls into the application of one particular (and usually current) literary theory to the biblical text. Biblical scholars, however, except in a very few exceptional cases, are not experts in a second field and therefore fall prey to the current theoretical fashion. The best approach in such a situation is an eclectic one. The Christian interpreter must reject any methodological insights that fundamentally conflict with basic Christian convictions but can, because of common grace, glean helpful insights from all fields of scholarship.

Literary Theory Is Often Obscurantist

The second pitfall is related to the first: literary theory is often obscurantist. Each school of thought develops its own in-language. Actant, *signifié,* narratology, interpretant, *différance,* and aporia are only a few among the many esoteric terms of the field. An illustration of the type of obscurantism to which I am referring is found in the structuralist

---

[3]Barton, *Reading the Old Testament,* p. 5.
[4]Edwards, *Towards a Christian Perspective,* pp. 217–37.

analysis of the Book of Job by Robert Polzin. Following the method of the famous anthropologist Claude Lévi-Strauss, Polzin summarizes the message of the book of Job with the following math-like formula:[5]

$$F_x(a) : F_y(b) \cong F_x(b) : F_{a-1(y)}$$

While we need not argue against technical terminology, neither must we glory in it. When new technical terms are introduced into scholarly discussion, they must be carefully defined, a precaution that most theoretical discussions seem to ignore.

The solution is not to throw out the literary approach but rather to seek clarity of expression. It is interesting that the two books that have had the biggest impact on biblical scholarship in the area of literary approach are Robert Alter's *The Art of Biblical Narrative* and James Kugel's *The Idea of Biblical Poetry*. Each one uses little technical jargon and gives much straightforward help in the explication of texts.

The Theory May Impose Western Concepts on Ancient Literature

The next danger is that of imposing modern Western concepts and categories on an ancient Semitic literature. If done, according to some critics of the literary approach, it could lead to a radical distortion of the text. On the surface of it, the danger appears real. Modern literary theory develops its concepts from its encounter with modern literature. Propp and Greimas developed their theories of the structure of folk tales by analyzing Russian stories.[6] This schema has been applied to biblical stories by many, notably Roland Barthes.[7] Theories of Hebrew metrics are usually based on systems employed in other modern poetic traditions. The oral basis of much of biblical literature is supposedly uncovered by means of comparisons with classical and Yugoslavian oral literature.[8]

Such a list could be lengthened considerably and apparently manifests an insensitivity toward what Anthony Thiselton calls the two horizons of the act of interpretation.[9] The ancient text comes from a culture far removed in time and space from that of the modern interpreter. This distance must be taken into account in our interpretation or else the exegesis will be distorted by reading modern values and presuppositions into the ancient text.

James Kugel is the harshest critic of the literary method from this perspective. He expresses his reservations theoretically in an article entitled "On the Bible and Literary Criticism" and practically in his justly acclaimed *Idea of Biblical Poetry*.[10] In the latter work he

---

[5]Polzin, *Biblical Structuralism*, p. 75.

[6]Propp, *Morphology of the Folktale* and Greimas, *Structural Semantics*.

[7]R. Barthes, "La lutte avec l'ange: Analyse textuelle de Genèse 32.23–33," in *Analyse structurale et exégèse biblique,* pp. 27–40.

[8]F. M. Cross, "Prose and Poetry in the Mythic and Epic Texts from Ugarit," *HTR* 67 (1974): 1–15; see A. B. Lord, *The Singer of Tales* (Cambridge: Harvard University Press, 1964).

[9]Thiselton, *The Two Horizons*.

[10]J. Kugel, "On the Bible and Literary Criticism," *Prooftexts* 1 (1981): 99–104; idem, *The Idea of Biblical Poetry*.

points out that biblical Hebrew has no word for "poetry." Thus, Kugel comments, "to speak of 'poetry' at all in the Bible will be in some measure to impose a concept foreign to the biblical world."[11] He also rightly points out that no single characteristic or group of characteristics can differentiate prose from poetry in the Hebrew Bible. Parallelism in fact occurs also in prose, and poetic meter does not exist. Instead of using the designation *poetry* to describe a distinct genre in the Old Testament, Kugel prefers to speak of "high style."

While one may agree with Kugel to a large extent, Kugel goes too far in rejecting the generic term *poetry*. If one reads a psalm and then a chapter of Numbers, one immediately notices a difference. On one level we can contrast the short, terse lines of the psalm with the lengthy lines of Numbers. There is also a heightening of certain rhetorical devices in the psalm that normally would not be found in the same magnitude in the Numbers section. In the psalm we encounter parallelism, metaphors, less restriction on the syntax, and so forth. In this relatively greater terseness and heightened use of rhetorical devices, we see a literary phenomenon that is related to our own distinction between poetry and prose. Kugel of course recognizes most of these differences but still hesitates to name the psalm poetic. His hesitation stems from the fear of distorting biblical materials by imposing foreign literary constructs on them.

On another level, not discussed by Kugel, the two passages differ in their relative deviance from common speech. Numbers is closer to common speech patterns than the psalms passage. In any literary tradition, poetry is characterized by its being further removed from common, everyday speech than is prose. The difference between prose and poetry is relative, and we must not downplay the obvious literary artifice in the prose sections of Scripture. But the difference is substantial enough to be called a generic distinction, and our modern categories of prose and poetry are the closest to the phenomenon we discover in the Bible.

I have struggled with this issue, particularly in the area of genre theory, as I worked on fifteen Akkadian texts that I described as fictional autobiographies. Since many would not date the beginning of autobiography until Rousseau in the eighteenth century, I needed to justify my genre identification.[12] We know that there is not universal generic similarity. New genres develop; old ones die out.[13] In addition, certain cultures use some genres and neglect others. For example, in the ancient world there is nothing comparable to the modern novel. In the same way, twentieth-century American literature contains few if any omens. Nevertheless, though a culture-free genre system does not exist, the native literary classification of each culture (or lack of such classification, as in the case of the distinction between prose and poetry in Hebrew) need not be adopted uncritically in order to identify the genres of that culture.

The separation of etic and emic approaches to literature deals with these cultural determinants in literary classification.[14] The emic describes native designations and

---

[11]Kugel, *The Idea of Biblical Poetry*, p. 69.

[12]T. Longman III, *Fictional Akkadian Autobiography* (Winona Lake, Ind.: Eisenbrauns, forthcoming).

[13]A. Fowler, "The Life and Death of Literary Forms," *New Literary History* 2 (1970–71): 199–216.

[14]K. Pike, *Language in Relation to a Unified Theory of Human Behavior* (The Hague: Mouton, 1967), chap. 2; and V. S. Poythress, "Analysing a Biblical Text: Some Important Linguistic Distinctions," *SJT* 32 (1979): 113–37. The emic/etic distinction was first proposed in linguistics, where it was used to distinguish native understanding of language from the analysis of a language by linguists or other outsiders. Pike was the first to generalize the distinction into a principle that could be used in the study of any aspect of culture. Poythress further refined the concept. For the tendency of taking linguistic categories and apply-

classification of literature. This approach has the advantage of giving the researcher insight into the native consciousness of a particular text and also the relationship between that text and others bearing the same designation. The etic view of literature imposes a non-native grid or classification scheme not necessarily defined in their language. While there is always the danger of distorting understanding of the texts by imposing foreign standards on them, it must be pointed out that Israelite scribes were not concerned with a precise and self-conscious generic classification of their literature. Both were innovations of the Greeks. While the biblical authors identified song (*šîr*), proverb (*māšāl*), and other speech forms, which provide helpful keys to research, they are predictably not systematic or rigorous in their categorization.

Secular Theory Eliminates the Author

The next pitfall is the danger of moving completely away from any concept of authorial intent and determinant meaning of a text. As we noted in chapter 1, secular theory since the advent of New Criticism in the middle of this century has united in its denial of any significance for the author. Traditional criticism before that point displayed considerable interest in the author and his or her background. The emphasis now has been redirected. Literature is an act of communication that may be described as a dynamic between poet, poem, and audience, or between author, text, and reader. Attention has been drawn by New Criticism and structuralism primarily to the text, and by reader-response theories (including those of Iser and Fish, feminism, and Marxism) to the reader and the reader's constitutive participation in the formation of meaning in the literary act.

One major voice has dissented from this trend. E. D. Hirsch posits an author-centered interpretive method that seeks to arrive at the author's intent.[15] This approach, Hirsch believes, provides an anchor of determinant meaning in the sea of relativity introduced by other theories. Although Hirsch's views have not been widely accepted by his fellow literary theorists, his emphasis provides a needed counterbalance to the trends in secular theory.

I comment further on this fourth pitfall when I discuss below the promises of the literary approach. Somewhat paradoxically, while there is danger in moving away from authorial intent, there is also benefit in the fact that the literary approach focuses our attention more on the text than on the author during the act of interpretation.

Contemporary Theory Denies Referential Function to Literature

The last pitfall is the most significant. Along with the move away from the author in contemporary theory, one can also note the tendency to deny or to limit severely any referential function to literature. "The poet affirmeth nothing," states Philip Sidney. Frank Lentricchia's masterful *After the New Criticism* follows the history of literary theory for the last forty years, using the theme of the denial of any external reference for literature. Literature in this view represents not an insight into the world but rather a limitless semiotic play.

---

ing them to other disciplines, see J. Culler, *The Pursuit of Signs* (Ithaca: Cornell University Press, 1981), pp. 27–29.

[15]See chapter 1, "Author-centered Theories."

Perhaps this modern tendency goes back to Saussure's theory of the sign. In his view, there is no natural connection between the signifier and the signified. The relationship between the two is arbitrary, or conventional. For Saussure, the fact that different languages have different words for the horse, for example, indicates that the relationship is arbitrary and determined by custom. Also note that, according to Saussure and the semiotic tradition that emanates from his writings, the sign does not point to an object in reality. The sign unites an acoustical image with a concept, rather than a word with a thing.[16] (The word sign might point to a nonexistent or metaphorical horse.)

In any case the rupture between the literary and the referential is an axiom of modern literary theory. As one might expect, recognition of the literary characteristics of the Bible has led scholars to equate the Bible and literature, with the corollary that the Bible as a literary text does not refer outside of itself and, in particular, makes no reference to history. This position leads on the part of some to a complete or substantial denial of a historical approach to the text, which most often takes the form of denying or denigrating traditional historical-critical methods. Source and form criticism particularly are attacked. The following quotations represent the views of some who adopt the literary approach.

> Above all, we must keep in mind that narrative is a *form of representation*. Abraham in Genesis is not a real person any more than the painting of an apple is real fruit.

> Once the unity of the story is experienced, one is able to participate in the world of the story. Although the author of the Gospel of Mark certainly used sources rooted in the historical events surrounding the life of Jesus, the final text is a literary creation with an autonomous integrity, just as Leonardo's portrait of the Mona Lisa exists independently as a vision of life apart from any resemblance or nonresemblance to the person who posed for it or as a play of Shakespeare has integrity apart from reference to the historical characters depicted there. Thus, Mark's narrative contains a closed and self-sufficient world with its own integrity. . . . When viewed as a literary achievement the statements in Mark's narrative, rather than being a representation of historical events, refer to the people, places, and events *in the story.*

> As long as readers require the gospel to be a window to the ministry of Jesus before they will see truth in it, accepting the gospel will mean believing that the story it tells corresponds exactly to what actually happened during Jesus' ministry. When the gospel is viewed as a mirror, though of course not a mirror in which we see only ourselves, its meaning can be found on this side of it, that is, between text and reader, in the experience of reading the text, and belief in the gospel can mean openness to the ways it calls readers to interact with it, with life, and with their own world. . . . The real issue is whether "his story" can be true if it is not history.[17]

For these authors, the truth of "his story" is independent of any historical information.

Similar evaluation may be seen in the hermeneutics of Hans Frei, who pinpoints the major error in both traditional critical and conservative exegesis in the loss of the understanding that biblical narrative is history-like and not true history with an ostensive, or external, reference.[18] Alter's brilliant analysis of Old Testament narrative is

---

[16]F. Lentricchia, *After the New Criticism,* p. 118.

[17]Berlin, *Poetics and Interpretation,* p. 13; D. Rhoads and D. Michie, *Mark as Story: The Introduction to the Narrative of a Gospel* (Philadelphia: Fortress, 1982), pp. 3–4; R. A. Culpepper, *Anatomy of the Fourth Gospel* (Philadelphia: Fortress, 1983), pp. 236–37.

[18]H. Frei, *The Eclipse of Biblical Narrative* (New Haven: Yale University Press, 1974).

coupled with the assumption that the nature of the narrative is "historicized fiction," or fictional history.[19]

The result of this approach is a turning away from historical investigation of the text as impossible or irrelevant. The traditional methods of historical criticism are abandoned or radically modified or given secondary consideration. Concern to discover the original *Sitz im Leben* or to discuss the tradition history of a text languishes among this new breed of scholar. This attitude understandably concerns traditional critical scholarship, so that we find among recent articles ones like Leander Keck's "Will the Historical-Critical Method Survive?"[20] While evangelicals might in some respects be glad to see the end of historical criticism, they, along with historical critics, have a high stake in the question of history.

According to Wellek and Warren in their *Theory of Literature,* the distinguishing characteristics of literature are fictionality, invention, and imagination. To identify Genesis simply as a work of literature is thus to move it out of the realm of history. This characterizes some, if not much, of the literary approach to the study of the Old Testament.

Frye's comment, quoted above in the introduction, suggests an alternative approach: "The Bible is as literary as it can well be without actually being literature."[21] We thus may consider Genesis, for example, more than simply literature. On the one hand, Genesis is not reducible to a work of fiction. On the other hand, we must apply a literary approach because it possesses literary qualities.

Another distinguishing characteristic of literature is its self-conscious structure and expression. In Russian formalist terms, language is *foregrounded*. As the framework hypothesis has pointed out, there is literary artifice in the parallelism between the first three days of creation and the last three.[22] Similarly, literary craft is displayed in the symmetrical structures of the Flood story, in the Babel story, or moving beyond Genesis, in the Solomon narrative.[23]

The point is that we do not have so-called objective, neutral, or unshaped reporting of events. (As many have pointed out, there is no such thing as a brute fact; an uninterpreted historical report is inconceivable.) Genesis is clearly not attempting to report events dispassionately. Rather it contains proclamation, which shapes the history to differing degrees. The biblical narrators are concerned not only to tell us facts but also to guide our perspective and responses to those events.

Old Testament prose narrative may thus be described as selective, structured, emphasized, and interpreted stories. The author/narrator controls the way in which we view the events. Here we can see how plot analysis, narrator studies, character studies, point-of-view analysis, and suspense-creating devices may be helpful, though definitely partial, approaches toward the understanding of a text.

The question of historical truth boils down to the question of who ultimately is guiding us in our interpretation of these events. If we look ultimately to human authors,

---

[19]Alter, *The Art of Biblical Narrative.*

[20]Leander Keck, "Will the Historical-Critical Method Survive?" in *Orientation by Disorientation,* ed. R. A. Spencer (Pittsburgh: Pickwick, 1980), pp. 115–27.

[21]Frye, *The Great Code,* p. 62.

[22]See among others, M. G. Kline, "Because It Had Not Rained," *WTJ* 20 (1958): 146–57.

[23]Wenham, "The Coherence"; J. P. Fokkelmann, *Narrative Art in Genesis* (Assen: van Gorcum, 1975), pp. 11ff.; R. B. Dillard, "The Literary Structure of the Chronicler's Solomon Narrative," *JSOT* 30 (1984): 85–93.

then literary art may be deceptive. If we look to God, then we cannot have deception. A literary analysis of a historical book is thus not incompatible with a high view of the historicity of the text, including the view that affirms the inerrancy and infallibility of Scripture in the area of history. (I do not want to give the mistaken impression that all of Scripture is historical in nature. The generic intention of each book and each section needs to be analyzed before attributing a historical reference to the book.)

We should note that some scholars argue that literature is an act of communication between the writer and the reader, an act that functions in more than one way. Besides a poetic function, the text may also have a referential function, according to Roman Jakobson's communication model of literary discourse.[24] Of course, the poetic function may become so dominant that the referential function ceases to exist, so that truly "the poet affirmeth nothing." The opposite pole is reached when there is a concerted effort to rid the text of self-referential language (i.e., metaphor), an impossible goal, as it is in scientific discourse. The biblical text for the most part is somewhere in between.

PROMISES

While there are potential pitfalls in pursuing a literary approach to biblical interpretation, we see that they are avoidable. Positively, though, what value is there in a literary approach? I have hinted at answers a number of times: while not to be reduced to literature pure and simple, the Bible is nonetheless amenable to literary analysis. Indeed, some of the most illuminating work done on the Bible in the past decade has been from a literary point of view, often done by literary scholars. Biblical scholars, particularly traditional critics, do not always make the most sensitive readers as C. S. Lewis once complained:

> Whatever these men may be as Biblical critics, I distrust them as critics. They seem to me to lack literary judgment, to be imperceptive about the very quality of the texts they are reading. . . . These men ask me to believe they can read between the lines of the old texts; the evidence is their obvious inability to read (in any sense worth discussing) the lines themselves. They claim to see fern-seed and can't see an elephant ten yards away in broad daylight.[25]

A literary approach, however, offers promise in three general areas.

Literary Theory Reveals the Conventions of Biblical Literature

A literary approach assists us in understanding the conventions of biblical storytelling. Alter has observed that

> every culture, even every era in a particular culture, develops distinctive and sometimes intricate codes for telling its stories, involving everything from narrative point of view, procedures of description and characterization, the management of dialogue, to the ordering of time and the organization of plot.[26]

The literary text is an act of communication from writer to reader. The text is the message. For it to communicate, the sender and receiver have to speak the same language.

---

[24]Cf. N. R. Petersen, *Literary Criticism for New Testament Critics* (Philadelphia: Fortress, 1978), pp. 33ff.

[25]C. S. Lewis, *Fern-seed and Elephants* (Glasgow: Collins, 1975), pp. 106, 111.

[26]R. Alter, "A Response to Critics," *JSOT* 27 (1983): 113–17.

The writer, through the use of conventional forms, sends signals to the readers to tell them how they are to take the message. We all know the generic signals in English (e.g., "once upon a time," "a novel by . . ."); we recognize poetry by all the white spaces on the page.

A literary approach explores and makes explicit the conventions of biblical literature in order to understand the message it intends to carry. It is significant to discover that Deuteronomy is in the form of a treaty, that the narrator shapes the reader's response to the characters of a text in different ways, and that repetition is not necessarily a sign of multiple sources but a literary device.

Now in ordinary reading we recognize much of this information automatically. We passively let the narrator shape our interpretation of the event being reported to us, we make an unconscious genre identification, and so forth. As interpreters of a text, however, it is important to make these conventions explicit, even more so with the Bible, since it is an ancient text and the conventions employed are often not ones we are used to.

A Literary Approach Stresses Whole Texts

Evangelicals commonly tend to atomize the text and to focus attention on a word or a few verses. Traditional critical scholarship displays the same tendency for a different reason, not believing that the whole text is original. The literary approach asks the question of the force of the whole. For this reason many evangelical scholars have seen the literary approach serving an apologetic function. If it can be shown that the Joseph narrative, the Flood narrative, the rise of the monarchy section (1 Sam. 8–12), and the Book of Judges are all examples of literary wholes, then we apparently have little use for source criticism.[27]

Literary Theory Focuses on the Reading Process

Work in literary criticism helps us to understand the reading process. I described above the act of literary communication as the author sending a message (text) to the reader. In the act of interpretation our focus must be on the text. As Geoffrey Strickland has said, "All that we say or think about a particular utterance or piece of writing presupposes an assumption on our part, correct or otherwise, concerning the intention of the speaker or writer."[28] But we must also recognize the role of readers and their predisposition as they approach the text. While not advocating the view of some reader-response theorists that readers actually create the meaning of the text—rather, the text imposes restrictions on possible interpretations—we must recognize that the readers' background and their interests will lead them to attend to certain parts of the Bible's message more than other parts.

In this connection we must consider the relevance of contextualization and multiperspectival approaches to the text. We also must mention here the value of what might be called ideological readers, even when they are unbalanced. Feminists and liberation theologians, for example, read the Bible with colored glasses, which often leads to distortion, but such readers do bring out important issues and themes that other, less interested, readers miss. My basic point here is that reading involves the interaction of the

[27]Wenham, "The Coherence"; L. Eslinger, "Viewpoints and Point of View in I Samuel 8–12," *JSOT* 26 (1983): 61–76; D. W. Gooding, "The Composition of the Book of Judges," *EI* 16 (1982): 70–79.
[28]G. Strickland, *Structuralism or Criticism? Thoughts on How We Read* (Cambridge: Cambridge University Press, 1981), p. 36.

writer with the reader through the text, so that any theory that concentrates on one of the three to the exclusion of the others may be distorted.[29]

More could be said about the promise and benefits of a literary approach. In the final analysis, however, the proof is the illuminating exegesis that this approach has led to. I refer to such insightful analyses as those of R. Alter, C. Conroy, A. Berlin, R. A. Culpepper, D. Gunn, and others listed in the section on further reading at the end of the book. Following a review of basic principles in chapter 3, I turn in part 2 to a discussion of several specific examples.

---

[29]After completing this chapter, I had occasion to read the helpful introductory book by L. Ryken, *Windows to the World* (Grand Rapids: Zondervan, 1985), which also adopts what I consider to be a balanced view of the dynamics of reading.

three
BASIC
PRINCIPLES

Thus far we have surveyed the history of literary approaches to the study of the Bible and have analyzed their positive and negative features. Along the way we have pointed to a positive program for literary readings of biblical texts. Before applying literary insights to particular prose and poetry texts, however, it will be advantageous to summarize and explicate more fully some of the major theoretical premises upon which the studies in part 2 are based. I consider, then, the act of literary communication and several functions of biblical literature.

THE ACT OF LITERARY COMMUNICATION

Communication involves a message that a sender directs toward a receiver. Different media may be used to send a message. A message may be (1) oral in face-to-face conversation, a phone call, or a radio show; (2) sent by signals of one sort or another; or (3) written. Literature is a subset of this third type of communication between a sender and receiver.

In the act of literary communication, the sender may be referred to as the author or the poet. The message is the text or literary work, and the receiver is the reader, the critic, or the audience. We have already observed that the various schools of thought concerning the interpretation of literary texts may be distinguished on the basis of which aspect of the act of literary communication (if any) they emphasize. Traditional interpretation emphasizes the author and his or her background; New Criticism and structuralism focus on the text; reader-response theory concentrates on the reader; and deconstruction questions the very idea of communication through literature.

While it is dangerous to generalize, we could suggest that this proliferation of approaches is the result of loss of faith in the act of literary communication. Since it is impossible to be absolutely certain and completely exhaustive about the meaning of a particular text, scholars have often abandoned the notion of determinant meaning in literature.

Such a loss of faith is unnecessary if we realize that our interpretations of any text, and biblical literature in particular, are partial, hypothetical, probable, and contextualized. Said positively, our interpretations may never be dogmatic, because the texts are rich in meaning, the mind of God (the final author) is ultimately unfathomable, and, recognizing that interpretation necessarily includes application, the situations that readers confront are various.

Many of our interpretations will be highly probable to the point of being nearly certain, but we must always retain a certain level of humility in our interpretations because of our inability to read the mind of the author of a text. Such an understanding of the interpretive process not only allows us to regain faith in the interpretive process but permits us to understand why there are legitimate differences of interpretation between readers. The position advocated in this book is that the biblical authors communicated to readers through texts. By way of summary and explication, I briefly review each of the elements of the communicative process.

Author

If literature is an act of communication, then meaning resides in the intention of the author. The author has encoded a message for the readers. Interpretation then has as its goal the recovery of the author's purpose in writing. The difficulties involved in such a position have been recognized in chapter 2. The hypothetical and probable nature of interpretation enters the picture because we cannot read minds and thus cannot be absolutely certain that we have recovered the correct meaning of a text. This fact should not lead us to throw up our hands in despair. As the next section indicates, there are constraints imposed on the meaning that an interpreter may impute to the author. The view that the author is the locus of the meaning of a text provides theoretical stability to interpretation. Our interpretation is correct insofar as it conforms to the meaning intended by the author.

When speaking of the author in the Bible, a number of questions arise that cannot be fully discussed here. One issue involves the composition of various books of the Bible and the issue of the use of sources and the levels of redaction. Here I use "author" to refer most pointedly to the final shaper of a canonical book. When I read Chronicles, I am interested in the intention of the author/redactor of that book and not in the intention of the author/redactor of his sources (say, the canonical Deuteronomic History). In other words, I am interested in how and for what purpose the final author uses his source.

A second issue concerning the intention of the author is the relationship between the human author and the divine author. God is the ultimate author of the Scriptures, so it must be said that final meaning resides in His intention. Of course, He condescended to reveal His message to the biblical authors, who did not write in a trance but had conscious intentions of their own. But it is wrong to equate fully the intention of God with that of the human author. For instance, the application in the New Testament of an Old Testament text frequently exceeds the obvious meaning intended by the author of the latter.[1]

---

[1] Kaiser, *Toward an Exegetical Theology*, pp. 108–14, in his legitimate concern to restrain eisegetical tendencies inherent in *sensus plenior* and other readings that appeal to God's ultimate authorship,

Before going on to the next closely related topic, I mention the importance of background studies. The study of the historical context of an author is helpful, since it places constraints on interpretation and helps to elucidate the meaning of a text. About the author Nahum, for example, we know only that he came from Elkosh, a town that we cannot now locate. But we do know that he lived and ministered in the seventh century B.C. To understand his message, it helps to understand the political, military, and religious situation in that part of the world at that time.

Text

The author sends à message, which is the text. In the case of biblical literature, the author is known only through the text. The intention of the author is hypothetically reconstructed through interaction with the text. Later we will see that this reconstructed author is the "implied" author. Interpretation thus calls for a close reading of the text. It calls for an acquaintance with the conventions and strategies of communication that guided the composition of the text.

I have noted Alter's comment that each culture or time period has its own conventions of literary communication. The primary task of the reader/critic is to recover these conventions and to learn their intended effect on the reader. Since the Bible did not come to us with an explicit analysis of its literary forms, we are frequently left to infer those conventions from our interaction with the text and must use etic rather than emic categories. Chapters 4 and 6 will discuss these conventions for prose and poetry respectively.

Reader

From the standpoint of the reader we recognize that our readings are partial and contextualized. Application is part of the exegetical task. It is unwise and indeed impossible for readers to divest themselves completely of personal interests and concerns while reading. Indeed the Scriptures encourage readers to come to the text with their wholehearted commitment and needs. E. D. Hirsch and W. Kaiser wish to separate textual meaning from application, or significance. Although such a view may be fine in theory, it is impossible to implement fully in reality.

It is appropriate to make some distinctions when referring to the reader of the text. One may speak of the original reader, the later reader, and the implied reader. Traditional interpretation has concentrated on the original audience. How was the Gospel of Mark received by its first readers? This type of question is important and helps us to understand the ancient conventions of writing and the original intention of the author. The later reader refers to the history of interpretation and contemporary interpretations. The implied reader is a New Critical category and distinguishes the actual original readers from the

---

swings the pendulum too far in the other direction by denying that there is any difference between the human and divine intention of a particular passage of Scripture. This position further manifests itself in Kaiser's unwillingness to read Old Testament texts in the light of further New Testament revelation. Kaiser infers (p. 111) that true revelation must involve a complete and full disclosure on the part of God. In the light of 1 Peter 1:10–12, however, it is clear that the prophets wrote better than they knew (contra Kaiser). Since the reality of the New Testament relates to the shadows of the Old Testament, at some stage of their reading of the Old Testament, Christians appropriately avail themselves of that clearer revelation.

readers addressed in the text itself.[2] The Book of Nahum once again provides a good example. The original readers of Nahum's prophecy were the inhabitants of Judah who were living under the vassalage of Assyria. The later readers include all subsequent commentators, including ourselves. The implied readers, then, were the Assyrians (though it is extremely unlikely that any Assyrian actually read it). Nahum addresses his prophecy to them, using taunt and satire.

In conclusion, literature is an act of communication between author and reader through a text. These three aspects of literature are interlocking and may not be abstracted from one another. Proper interpretation does not neglect any of the three.

FUNCTIONS OF BIBLICAL LITERATURE

As discussed in chapter 2, literary critics of the Bible all too frequently reduce the meaning of the biblical text to an aesthetic meaning. Literature, they say, does not refer outside of itself to external reality. Other scholars restrict the meaning of the biblical texts to their historical references.

Such positions result from a misunderstanding of the functions of literature in general and biblical literature in particular. The Bible is multifunctional. When viewed as an act of verbal communication from a sender to a receiver, the message of the text may be described as having many different purposes. With M. Sternberg, we may say, "Like all social discourse, biblical narrative is oriented to an addressee and regulated by a purpose or a set of purposes involving the addressee"; and with R. Jakobson, "Language must be investigated in all the variety of its functions."[3] While not intending to be exhaustive, I discuss here six major functions of biblical literature: historical, theological, doxological, didactic, aesthetic, and entertainment. Although I have isolated these functions from one another for the purpose of analysis, in the text they are all intertwined. Also, it is important to remember that the Bible contains a variety of literary types that vary in terms of the dominance of one or more of these functions.

Historical

As argued above, the Bible intends to impart historical information to its readers, primarily concerning the acts of God for and among His people. What I am calling the historical function of biblical literature may roughly be equated with what Jakobson terms the referential function of language.[4] Though most scholars today would not agree, I believe that this purpose is dominant in most biblical literature. The other functions are subsidiary in that they depend on the historical function.

In his recent volume on the poetics of biblical narrative, Sternberg provides a stimulating discussion of the historical function of biblical literature. He rightly points out that, ultimately, "nothing on the surface . . . infallibly marks off the two genres [fiction and

---

[2]G. Prince, "Introduction to the Study of the Narratee," in *Reader-Response Criticism*, ed. J. P. Tompkins (Baltimore: Johns Hopkins University Press, 1980), pp. 6–25.

[3]M. Sternberg, *The Poetics of Biblical Narrative* (Bloomington: Indiana University Press, 1985), p. 1; R. Jakobson, "Metalanguage as a Linguistic Problem," in *The Framework of Language* (Michigan Studies in the Humanities 1; Ann Arbor: University of Michigan, Department of Slavic Languages and Literatures, 1980), p. 81.

[4]Jakobson, "Metalanguage," p. 82.

history]." Nonetheless, he persuasively concludes that "the narrative is historiographic, inevitably so considering its teleology and incredibly so considering its time and environment. Everything points in this direction."[5] Sternberg's point stands whether the history is true or not. Biblical narrative, for the most part, *intends* to impart historical information.

Theological

The second function is closely related to the first. The Bible is not historical in a positivist, neutral sense; rather, it has a message to convey. What I am here calling theological, Sternberg labels ideological and Jakobson refers to as the emotive or expressive function of language. Jakobson describes the emotive function of language as that which "aims a direct expression of the speaker's attitude toward what he is speaking about."[6] The biblical storyteller as well as the biblical poet attributes the great events that happen in Israel to God. It intends to interpret that history in the light of the reality of God and His interaction with the world.

Doxological

Closely related to the theological function is the doxological purpose of the biblical text, a function that we could describe as partly theological and partly didactic. In short, the biblical authors intend to offer praise to God and to encourage the community to praise Him in response to the historical and theological truths that the text presents. Often this call to praise is implicit; at other times it is explicit (e.g., Exod. 15; Judg. 5).

Didactic

Biblical stories are often structured in order to shape the reader's ethical behavior. Jakobson similarly speaks of the connative function of language, which has its "orientation toward the addressee" and "finds its purest grammatical expression in the vocative and imperative."[7] Genesis 39, the story of Joseph and Potiphar's wife, is an excellent illustration. In this chapter Joseph is a virtual embodiment of the many proverbs that explicitly teach that young men should resist the advances of the strange or adulterous woman. A proper response to the story of Genesis 39 includes a chaste character on the part of the reader.

Aesthetic

In this book I concentrate particularly on the aesthetic function, but it is only one of many. Jakobson refers to the poetic function of all verbal communication as that function that is "set toward the message."[8] In other words, it concerns verbal self-reference. The aesthetic nature of the biblical text is observed in its self-consciousness about structure and language—about how the message is conveyed. It is seen in the indirection of the message (above also called distanciation). As Ryken comments specifically on the Gospels, "Instances from the life of Jesus such as these suggest a literary [or aesthetic]

---

[5]Sternberg, *The Poetics,* p. 30.
[6]Jakobson, "Metalanguage," p. 82.
[7]Ibid., p. 83.
[8]Ibid., p. 84.

approach to truth that frequently avoids direct propositional statement and embodies truth in distinctly literary forms."[9]

Entertainment

Biblical texts are shaped in a compelling way. They are enjoyable to read. This function is best seen in connection with the aesthetic function of the text.

It is essential to keep in mind the multifaceted nature of biblical literature. The danger of reducing the Bible to one or two functions is that it radically distorts the message as it comes from the ultimate sender (God) to us as its present receivers. The thrust of this book, however, is on the aesthetic function. Overall, then, my presentation is a partial analysis that must be supplemented by other forms of study.

[9]L. Ryken, *How to Read the Bible as Literature* (Grand Rapids: Zondervan, 1984), p. 9.

four

THE ANALYSIS
OF PROSE PASSAGES

*I*n this chapter I examine the nature of Hebrew narrative. Earlier we observed that all literature is conventional and that conventions differ, depending on time period and place of origin. It is of interest, therefore, to ask what characterizes Hebrew narrative. The following is not an exhaustive description of Hebrew prose but a beginning one intended to stimulate thought about particular passages. Neither is the following intended to be a step-by-step approach to the analysis of a passage from an aesthetic perspective. The concepts discussed here would be abused if applied in a mechanical fashion to biblical texts. In chapter 5, I analyze two prose sections of the Bible, 1 Kings 22:1–38 and Acts 10:1–11:18.

The reader must remember that a literary analysis is a partial analysis. It is best taken as an aspect of the historical-grammatical approach to the text; indeed, as L. Ryken points out, it is a "logical extension" of it.[1] A literary analysis will both highlight aspects of the passage that were previously unnoticed and also throw new light on the text as it is viewed from this different perspective.

The analysis of prose narrative will be presented under three subheadings. They are genre, the dynamics of narrative, and style. However, first prose narrative itself needs definition. Prose is best defined in contrast with poetry. Indeed, prose is often defined as nonpoetry—that is, as all discourse that does not display the traits of poetry. Since poetry awaits description in chapter 6, I must delay any adequate definition of prose until

---

[1]Ryken, *The Bible as Literature,* p. 12.

that time. Prose, though, is closer to ordinary speech than poetry and is structured by paragraphs rather than by lines and stanzas.

The adjective *narrative* distinguishes the prose under discussion as a special kind. Narration "suggests a communication process in which the narrative as message is transmitted by addresser to addressee" and emphasizes that there is a "succession of events." I tend to use the term synonymously with *story* though I am aware that there are differences.[2]

GENRE

I begin with genre for three reasons. First, the concept of genre describes the text as a whole.[3] Second, genre is, at least in part, an extrinsic analysis in that generic identification necessarily appeals to other texts. Third, genre, while treated in this chapter that concentrates on prose, is equally important in interpreting poetic passages.

What I here label genre analysis bears a close resemblance to form criticism. The major difference is that form criticism is a diachronic analysis, whereas genre analysis is synchronic, concerned to identify the type of literature, not its prehistory.

What Is a Genre?

The simplest definition of *genre* in literature is "a group of texts that bear one or more traits in common with each other." In the act of reading, as we have seen, a transaction takes place between the author and the reader, a transaction that is a form of communication.[4] An adage instructs us that "the individual is ineffable."[5] That is, something that is totally unprecedented is incommunicable. In literary terms, a text that bears no similarities of structure, content, or the like with anything previously written cannot be understood by a reader.

Readers approach a text with certain expectations that arise as soon as they begin reading it and that are grounded in their previous reading. When they start to read a text, they make a conscious or unconscious genre identification, which involves further expectations concerning what is to come. Texts may trigger generic expectations in different ways. We pick up *The Hobbit* by J. R. R. Tolkien and read:

> In a hole in the ground there lived a hobbit. Not a nasty, dirty, wet hole, filled with the ends of worms and an oozy smell, nor yet a dry, bare, sandy hole with nothing in it to sit down on or to eat: it was a hobbit-hole, and that means comfort.[6]

Already certain expectations are formed in our minds. Since there are no such creatures as hobbits in the real world, we know we are moving in the realm of fiction, even fantasy. Indeed the cover of the version I have before me describes *The Hobbit* as "the enchanting prelude to 'The Lord of the Rings.'" This description strengthens our generic suspicions. Furthermore, if we have read the libretto to Richard Wagner's *Ring Cycle* or another story that uses the ring-of-power motif, additional expectations will be evoked in our minds.

---

[2]S. Rimmon-Kenan, *Narrative Fiction* (London: Methuen, 1983), pp. 2, 15.

[3]I use *genre* in this book to refer to a work as a whole and *form* to refer to a unit within a whole text.

[4]For more background on this approach and others, see K. Hempfer, *Gattungstheorie* (Munich: W. Funk, 1973). For a more detailed exposition of genre, consult Longman, "Form Criticism."

[5]See Buss, "The Study of Forms," p. 32; and R. Pascal, *Design and Truth in Autobiography* (Cambridge: Harvard University Press, 1960), p. 2.

[6]J. R. R. Tolkien, *The Hobbit* (New York: Ballantine, 1966), p. 15.

Not only is genre recognizable in the expectations of the reader, but it also directs authors as they compose the text. It shapes or coerces writers so that their compositions can be grasped and communicated to the reader.[7]

Genre theorists have offered a number of metaphors or models to describe genre. Chief among these theorists, R. Wellek and A. Warren speak of genre as an institution, similar to the state, university, or church.[8] An individual joins an institution, follows its rules and regulations in the main, but may opt to fight for change in either a subtle or radical manner. Moreover, an author may choose to play with the usual elements of a genre simply for satiric or other effects. A second metaphor is the legal contract. An author sets up an agreement with the readers concerning how the text should be read. T. Todorov imagines genre to be a code with the author as the encoder and the reader as the decoder.[9] Another metaphor enters genre theory via philosophy, specifically language philosophy. E. D. Hirsch draws on L. Wittgenstein's analogy of the sentence as a game. Just as a sentence is a game, so too is genre. In games there are rules, which shape the play of the game. His game analogy is apt, since language (syntax, diction, etc.) and genre also have rules that govern their successful operation.[10] These metaphors illuminate genre in three ways: genre explains the possibility of communication in a literary transaction; genres rest upon expectations that arise in readers when they confront a text; and authors can be coerced in composition to conform to genre expectations.

Fluid Concept of Genre

In the nineteenth century, genre theorists believed that genres were rigid and pure. Literary texts, it was felt, could be pigeonholed into their respective generic categories, and the genres themselves could be arranged into hierarchies. Gunkel imported this unfortunate understanding of genre into biblical studies, though such a neoclassical position was already obsolete in his own day.[11] According to Gunkel, a particular text had one genre with a corresponding setting in life. Furthermore, so-called mixed genres (*Mischgattungen*) were considered late and corrupt.

In fact, such a position can be neither theoretically nor practically justified. Genre exists at all levels of generality. Genre, as stated above, refers to a class of texts united by the sharing of similarities, and thus it involves a generalization or abstraction from particular texts. It is, therefore, possible to speak of a broad genre of many texts with few traits in common, or of a narrow genre of as few as two texts that are identical in many ways. With Todorov, we thus speak of genres on a scale that ranges from one, in that all

---

[7]G. Dillon, *Constructing Texts: Elements of a Theory of Composition and Style* (Bloomington: Indiana University Press, 1981); Wellek and Warren, *Theory of Literature,* p. 226; and D. Kambouchner, "The Theory of Accidents," *Glyph* 7 (1980): 149–75.

[8]Wellek and Warren, *Theory of Literature,* p. 226.

[9]T. Todorov, *The Fantastic: A Structural Approach to a Literary Genre,* trans. R. Howard, with introduction by R. Scholes (Ithaca: Cornell University Press, 1974); cf. J. Culler, *The Pursuit of Signs* (Ithaca: Cornell University Press, 1981), pp. 11–12, 37.

[10]Hirsch, *Validity in Interpretation,* pp. 68–71; M. E. Amsler, "Literary Theory and the Genres of Middle English Literature," *Genre* 13 (1980): 389–90.

[11]See Tucker, *Form Criticism,* pp. 4–5; and Buss, "The Study of Forms," p. 50.

literature constitutes a single genre, to the maximum, that is where each text constitutes its own genre.[12] Such a notion of genre suggests that genres are not rigid categories.[13]

The fluidity of genre designations can be demonstrated by considering Psalm 98, a poem that may be classified in a variety of different genres, depending on the level of abstraction from the text itself.[14] It may be classified very broadly as a poem and have a few general similarities with other texts that we call poetry. On the other extreme, Psalm 98 may be classified narrowly in a genre with only Psalm 96. Psalm 96 is virtually identical to Psalm 98, with the exception that the former includes a diatribe against idol worship. Between these two extremes are a variety of other potential classifications for Psalm 98. Moving from broad to narrow, Psalm 98 may be treated as a poem, a cultic hymn, a hymn concerning God's kingship, a divine-warrior victory psalm, and finally as most closely related to Psalm 96. One of the benefits of such a fluid approach to genre is that it demands that the exegete attend as closely to the peculiarities of the texts as to its similarities.

How to Classify a Text

Difficulty arises because texts do not identify themselves. Indeed, genre identification is a good example of the emic/etic problem raised in chapter 2. We do not have many native, or emic genre labels, so we must create etic categories that, while admittedly not found in the ancient materials, describe what we have in the text.

The only way to identify the genre of a text properly is to read it in the context of other, particularly biblical, literature and to note similarities between texts. Genre classification is a form of the hermeneutical circle in that it involves constant interaction between the particular text and the generalizing genre. The individual text can be grasped only through a knowledge of the whole. In short, genres can be elucidated only from the texts themselves.

Part of the confusion surrounding the identification of texts that cohere into a genre originates in unclarity concerning the kind of similarities among texts that signal that they belong to the same genre. Gunkel felt that a text could be generically classified according to three criteria: the mood and thought(s) of the text, the linguistic forms (grammar and vocabulary), and the social setting.[15]

This list is too restrictive. The best approach is to accept similarities between texts on many levels as evidence of generic identity. These similarities can be divided into inner form and outer form.[16] The outer form of a text includes the structure of the text and the meter (or its lack) in the speech rhythm. The inner form refers to the nonformal aspects of the texts—the mood, setting, function, narrative voice, and content. We can classify Psalm 98, for example, with Psalms 18, 47, 68, 93, and 96 as a single genre on the basis of the following characteristics:

[12]Hempfer, *Gattungstheorie*, p. 137.
[13]The Wittgensteinian concepts of "blurred edges" or "fuzzy concepts" are appropriate to describe the overlapping that does occur between genres; see Amsler, "Literary Theory," p. 390.
[14]For a more complete treatment, see my "Psalm 98: A Divine Warrior Hymn," *JETS* 27 (1984): 267–74.
[15]H. Gunkel, *The Psalms* (Philadelphia: Fortress, 1967); Buss, "The Study of Forms," p. 1.
[16]Wellek and Warren, *Theory of Literature*, pp. 231–34.

Outer Form	Inner Form
Poetic Style (parallelism, imagery, etc.)	Kingship theme (content)
	Praise (mood)
	Divine-warrior hymn (function)

Why Consider Genre?

Consciously or unconsciously, genre identification triggers what I have earlier called expectations on the part of the reader. Indeed it triggers a whole reading strategy. Consider the second stanza of Psalm 1:

> *Not so the wicked!*
> > *They are like chaff*
> > *that the wind blows away.*
> *Therefore the wicked will not stand in the judgment,*
> > *nor sinners in the assembly of the righteous.*

For various reasons, our interpretive strategy takes these lines as poetry. We expect the use of images and so forth (see chap. 6).

In another passage we read, "In the twelfth year of Ahaz king of Judah, Hoshea son of Elah became king of Israel in Samaria, and he reigned nine years" (2 Kings 17:1). Our immediate reaction is that this sentence is historical narrative, and we recognize that the author intends to communicate historical or chronological information.

We might have the same initial reaction to the following words of Jesus: "Two men went up to the temple to pray, one a Pharisee and the other a tax collector" (Luke 18:10). These words however, are preceded by "Jesus told this parable." Here we have an explicit generic signal that triggers a reading strategy that is significantly different from the one we adopt for the 2 Kings 17 passage. Jesus' story is fictional. More specifically, it is didactic fiction—that is, it intends to impart a moral to the hearer or reader.

N. Frye discusses insightfully a second value of generic criticism:

> The purpose of criticism by genres is not so much to classify as to clarify . . . traditions and affinities, thereby bringing out a large number of literary relationships that would not be noticed as long as there were no context established for them.[17]

In other words, the very practice of examining a collection of generically related texts will result in the illumination of each individual text. This result is particularly true of individual texts that are themselves difficult to understand but that may be elucidated by comparing them with clearer examples in the same genre.

Since the psalms are a collection of individual and separate texts, they have no normal literary context. More benefit may be gained by studying a psalm in the context of

---

[17]N. Frye, *Anatomy of Criticism* (Princeton: Princeton University Press, 1957), pp. 247–48.

its genres than by examining the immediately preceding and following psalms. It is more fruitful, for example, to study Psalm 30 in the context of other thanksgiving hymns rather than in comparison with Psalms 29 and 31. For most other texts, insight is gained by studying both the immediate literary context and its generic context. For instance, Nahum 3:1–3 must be studied in its literary context (as occurring between two metaphorical taunts, 2:11–13 and 3:4–6). As a second essential step in understanding Nahum 3:1–3, the exegete must also compare and contrast it with all other occurrences of *hôy* oracles in the prophets and the historical books.

One frequently observed problem of the study of genre is its generalizing tendency. It concentrates on what is general or similar between texts, rather than on the uniqueness of each one. This imbalance is not inherent in the method, and indeed a genre analysis may be used to highlight the particular aspects of a psalm, since they will stand out in the context of the similarities of the texts.

For different reasons, then, it is important to discover the genre(s) of a text. By prompting a reading strategy and ruling out false expectations and standards of judgment of a text, genre classification represents an entrée to the meaning of the text.

THE DYNAMICS OF NARRATIVE

Up to this point, I have described the act of literary communication as involving three parts: author, text, and reader. The picture becomes more complex as we examine the story closely. The author does not make his or her presence known explicitly, and the reader is not referred to in the text. Critics interested in the working of literary narrative have made some important and helpful distinctions. They describe the interaction between author and audience using six terms:

Author→Implied Author→Narrator→Narratee→Implied Reader→Reader

---

I discuss in this section these terms and others that are important for describing narrative.[18]

Author/Reader

These terms require little explanation, since they are the most familiar to us. The author is the man or woman who actually composes the text, and the readers are those who actually read it. Of the six parts of the act of literary communication, the author and the reader are the only ones outside of the narrative itself.

Problems confront the biblical scholar at this point, however. It is likely that sources were used in the composition of certain biblical books, and it is possible that other books underwent some sort of editorial revision. Should we speak of one author, many authors, or even many editors?

---

[18]For a discussion and further bibliography, consult Culpepper, *Anatomy,* pp. 6ff.

For the purposes of literary analysis, this question is relatively unimportant. I do not deny that diachronic analysis may have its place, but for the purposes of a literary analysis, the question is at least momentarily set aside.

The question of the reader is also complicated, particularly in the study of an ancient text. Readers of biblical texts span centuries. One of the goals of traditional historical-grammatical exegesis is to answer the question, how did the *original* readers understand the passage? This question is valid and must be answered. Twentieth-century men and women, however, are readers too. We are distanced from the text in a way that the original readers were not. That is, we come with different questions and also have lost touch with some of the conventions of biblical literature. I therefore propose separating *reader* into original reader and contemporary reader. The goal of the contemporary reader is to understand the text by means of its ancient conventions, but such a reader approaches the text through a new grid of questions that are evoked by the situation of modern society and culture (see chap. 3).

Implied Author/Implied Reader

The distinction between, on the one hand, the implied author and implied reader and, on the other hand, the actual author and actual reader is a difficult one to express. Sometimes, it must be admitted, it is of little practical import to the analysis of a biblical text. The distinction is a real one, though. The implied author is the textual manifestation of the real author. Rimmon-Kenan states the matter very clearly: "The implied author is the governing consciousness of the work as a whole, the source of the norms embodied in the work."[19] *The implied author is the author as he or she would be constructed, based on inference from the text.* The work may contain and advocate beliefs and opinions that the real author does not actually hold. Although the distinction is theoretically valid, it becomes academic in many or most biblical books because our sole knowledge of the author is reconstructed from the text. In cases in which the narrator provides the structure to the whole and carries the author's viewpoint, the implied author is related to the narrator.

As one might expect, the implied reader, on analogy with the implied author, is not a real but an imaginary figure. S. Chatman provides a helpful description of the implied reader: "The *implied reader*—not the flesh-and-bones you or I sitting in our living rooms reading the book, but the audience presupposed by the narrative itself."[20]

Narrator/Narratee

Perhaps the most fruitful of the above three pairs for narrative analysis is the narrator/narratee. Both narrator and narratee are rhetorical devices and are often explicit in the text, though they both may take different forms from text to text. In general, the narrator is the one who tells the story and the narratee is the one who hears it. The narrator is most obviously seen when he or she is a character (for instance, Serenus Zeitblom in

---

[19]Rimmon-Kenan, *Narrative Fiction*, p. 86. The concept of implied author was to my knowledge first developed by W. Booth, *The Rhetoric of Fiction* (Chicago: University of Chicago Press, 1961), pp. 71–76, 211–21.

[20]S. Chatman, *Story and Discourse* (Ithaca: Cornell University Press, 1978), pp. 149–50.

Doctor Faustus, by Thomas Mann) but is no less true when the narrator is not a character and is unnamed (the narrator of *Jude the Obscure,* by Thomas Hardy).

A description of the role of the narrator in a story is closely related to the issue of point of view, a topic I discuss in the next section. The narrator plays a pivotal role in shaping the reaction of the reader to the passage he or she is reading. The narrator achieves this response in a variety of ways, from presenting and withholding information from the reader to explicit commentary.

Narratives may be divided into first- and third-person narratives. In the former, the narrator is usually a character in the story and, as a result, presents a limited point of view. Third-person narrative refers to all the characters impersonally, and in this mode the narrator may display omniscience and omnipresence. Note that most narrative in the Bible is third-person omniscient narrative (the exceptions include part of Nehemiah, Qohelet's "autobiography" in Ecclesiastes, and the "we" passages in Acts). Rhoads and Michie, for example, describe such a narrator and point of view in the Gospel of Mark:

> The narrator does not figure in the events of the story; speaks in the third person; is not bound by time or space in the telling of the story; is an implied invisible presence in every scene, capable of being anywhere to "recount" the action; displays full omniscience by narrating the thoughts, feelings, or sensory experiences of many characters; often turns from the story to give direct "asides" to the reader, explaining a custom or translating a word or commenting on the story; and narrates the story from one overarching ideological point of view.[21]

This summary describes the bulk of biblical narrative. The voice of the narrator is often the authoritative guide in the story, directing the reader in his or her analysis and response to the events and characters of the story.

It has been pointed out that readers react to a third-person omniscient narrator with an unconscious submissiveness. Rhoads and Michie note, "When the narrator is omniscient and invisible, readers tend to be unaware of the narrator's biases, values, and conceptual view of the world."[22] The choice of such a powerfully persuasive literary device fits in with the Bible's concern to proclaim an authoritative message.

The narratee, simply, is the person or group addressed by the narrator.[23] The narratee may or may not be a character in the text. In the Gospel of Luke, for instance, the narratee is Theophilus. An interesting book to which to apply the concept of the narratee is Nahum. The original readers were no doubt Judeans. The implied readers were faithful Judeans who desired the destruction of Nineveh. The narratee, however, is the Ninevites. It is doubtful whether the Ninevites ever read the book, but the narrator (and here narrator, implied author, and real author are impossible to distinguish) addresses the book to the Ninevites.

Point of View

The analogy with film is helpful toward understanding point of view in literature. In a film, the eye of the camera grants perspective as it moves from place to place,

---

[21]Rhoads and Michie, *Mark as Story,* p. 36.
[22]Ibid., p. 39.
[23]Prince, "Introduction," pp. 7–25.

coming in for a close-up here and then panning to another shot. The camera guides and limits the audience's insight.

As mentioned, point of view in literature is closely bound with the narrator. He is the one who mediates perspective on the characters and the events of the story. He guides readers in their interpretation of those characters and events and, through his manipulation of the point of view, draws readers into the story. Literary scholars have proposed different approaches to the description and categorization of point of view in narrative. The most fruitful is that of Boris Uspensky, who distinguishes five different "planes" of point of view: spatial, temporal, phraseological, psychological, and ideological.[24] Four of these planes are clearly important for the literary analysis of biblical texts.

Spatial. If the narrator is identified with a particular character, then quite often the narrator is localized. Otherwise, the narrator may be omnipresent, jumping from scene to scene, present where a character could not be. The latter is found far more frequently in biblical literature. In Joshua 5:13–15, the narrator is present with Joshua as he confronts the commander of the army of the Lord. In 2 Samuel 11, the narrator is with David as he is walking alone on his roof and notices Bathsheba.

Temporal. This term refers to the temporal limitation (or lack of it) imposed on the narrator. Is the narrator confined to telling the story as it unfolds—that is, as he witnesses it? Or possibly is the narrator telling the story at a later period of time and thus has information concerning the conclusion of a chain of events? Or is the narrator able to transcend time? In the Book of Esther, the narrator is third person and is omnipresent and omniscient, but temporally he does not anticipate the future, following the events as they unfold. This feature certainly enhances the suspense of the story.

Psychological. Does the narrator report the thoughts and emotions of the characters? Can he penetrate their inner life? If so, then the narrator is omniscient, providing information to which no character has access.

Ideological. The final category is the most interesting. Ideological point of view concerns evaluation by the narrator. In this plane the narrator guides the readers' interpretation of events.

The message of a prose narrative in Scripture may be better understood by closely questioning the text concerning the narrator and his point of view. The four aspects considered in this section provide a useful categorization of point of view.

Character

Some readers may hesitate at this point. Should we treat David, Solomon, Ezra, Esther, Jonah—even Jesus—as characters? Such a move appears to equate biblical personages with King Arthur, Billy Budd, Felix Holt, or Captain Ahab and thus to reduce them to fictional beings.

Indeed some advocates of the literary approach do so and rejoice that they have skirted the historical issue. In my view, however, to analyze David as a literary character in a text is not to deny that he was a historical king or that the events reported in the books of Samuel and Kings are accurate. We must admit, however, that we have a selective

---

[24]B. Uspensky, _A Poetics of Composition_ (Berkeley: University of California Press, 1973). Note the stimulating application of Uspensky's work to biblical literature in Berlin, _Poetics and Interpretation_, pp. 55–56.

account of the life of David and can agree that there is value in taking a close look at how the text portrays David and others. In other words, we must recognize that our accounts are shaped—that is, we have in the Bible selective, emphasized, and interpreted accounts of historical events.

We do not get a full report of the events of the life of Jesus, as John explicitly admits for his gospel: "Jesus did many other things as well. If every one of them were written down, I suppose that even the whole world would not have room for the books that would be written" (21:25). The immediately preceding verse indicates that the selective nature of his account did not impinge on its truthfulness: "This is the disciple who testifies to these things and who wrote them down. We know that his testimony is true" (v. 24).

The essential point is that a literary, in this case a characterological, analysis is partial. Although the focus of such research is not on the historical dimension of the text, still this dimension must in no way be ignored or rejected. Otherwise we would be trifling with the text and not taking seriously its original purpose.

The modern interpreter must understand the conventional means of characterization in Hebrew narrative. In the first place, the Bible rarely describes its characters.[25] We do not have any extensive physical or psychological descriptions of biblical characters. If such a detail is given, it is usually of great importance in the story. We are told at an appropriate place that Saul was "a head taller than any of the others" (1 Sam. 9:2), that Bathsheba was "very beautiful" (2 Sam. 11:2), that Ehud was left-handed (Judg. 3:15), and that Samson was strong and had long hair (Judg. 13–16). But such comments are isolated, of significance to the rest of the story.

This feature is strikingly different from nineteenth-century English authors, who describe their characters explicitly and with painstaking detail. Note the description of Denner, a rather minor character, in the opening of George Eliot's *Felix Holt*:

> Denner had still strong eyes of that shortsighted kind which see through the narrowest chink between the eyelashes. The physical contrast between the tall, eagle-faced, dark-eyed lady, and the little peering waiting-woman, who had been round-featured and of pale mealy complexion from her youth up, had doubtless had a strong influence in determining Denner's feeling towards her mistress.[26]

Furthermore, we are rarely given motives for the behavior of biblical characters. In Genesis 22 we are not told what Abraham is feeling or how he rationalized God's command to sacrifice Isaac. What was going through Gideon's mind when he made the golden ephod (Judg. 8:25–27)? The narrator's judgment is not totally lacking in biblical stories, but it is rare.

Alter's careful study of biblical characterization deserves lengthy quotation:

> Now, in reliable third-person narrations, such as in the Bible, there is a scale of means, in ascending order of explicitness and certainty, for conveying information about the motives, the attitudes, the moral nature of characters. Character can be revealed through the report of actions; through appearance, gestures, posture, costume; through one character's comments on another; through direct speech by the character; through

---

[25]This fact has been noticed in modern times at least since E. Auerbach's well-known judgment that biblical stories are "fraught with background" (*Mimesis* [Princeton: Princeton University Press, 1953], p. 12). R. Alter, A. Berlin, and M. Sternberg are among the most notable commentators on this phenomenon of biblical style.

[26]G. Eliot, *Felix Holt* (New York: Penguin, 1972), p. 102.

inward speech, either summarized or quoted as interior monologue; or through statements by the narrator about the attitudes and intentions of the personages, which may
come either as flat assertions or motivated explanations.[27]

Such characterization has significant consequences for interpretation. It means that we
generally have only indirect description of characters and motivations for their actions.
The interpreter must sometimes read between the lines to round out the picture (see
below on gapping). Without indulging in wholesale speculation and eisegesis, the reader must make inferences from the text about characters and in fact is encouraged to do
so by the text.

In Bruce Waltke's illuminating study of the Cain and Abel story (Gen. 4), he applies
some of Alter's insights into the nature of biblical characterization.[28] The question over the
rejection of Cain's sacrifice has plagued readers of the Bible for centuries. Was Cain's sacrifice unacceptable because it was not a bloody sacrifice? Or was it rejected because it
was not offered in faith? The enigma of Cain's sacrifice has arisen because of the silence
of the Old Testament text concerning Cain's motives for bringing his sacrifice and God's
motives for rejecting it. The text introduces Cain and Abel very abruptly and tells only
briefly the story leading up to Abel's murder.

Waltke points to indirect indications within the text that help solve the problem.
Generally speaking, the passage becomes clearer once it is realized that the text contrasts
Cain and Abel's actions. Alter highlights character contrast as a favorite device of Hebrew
narrative. Waltke notices two important differences in terms of the sacrifice that each
brother brought. The narrator mentions that Abel brought the "firstborn" of the flock,
whereas Cain's sacrifice from the "fruits of the soil" is not specified as the equivalent of
"firstfruits." Abel offered the "fat," which is the best part of the animal, whereas Cain's
sacrifice is not qualified in any equivalent way. Waltke's conclusion seems warranted:
"Abel's sacrifice is characterized as the best of its class and . . . Cain's is not. The point
seems to be that Abel's sacrifice represents heartfelt worship; Cain's represents unacceptable tokenism."[29]

Biblical literary critics find it useful to make distinctions between round and flat characters and what have been called agents. Berlin defines this threefold categorization and
provides examples, particularly from the David narrative.[30] A round (or full-fledged) character has many traits. A round character appears complex, less predictable, and therefore
more real. A flat character has only one trait and seems one-dimensional. An agent, finally, has no personality to speak of and simply moves the story along. Examples of these
three character types will be given in the next chapter.

Plot

Plot and character are closely related and may be separated only for purposes of
analysis. Henry James related the two elements by asking, "What is character but the

---

[27]Alter, *The Art of Biblical Narrative,* pp. 116–17.
[28]B. Waltke, "Was Cain's Offering Rejected by God Because It Was Not a Blood Sacrifice?" *WTJ* 48
(1986): 363–72.
[29]Ibid., p. 369.
[30]Berlin, *Poetics and Interpretation,* pp. 23–33.

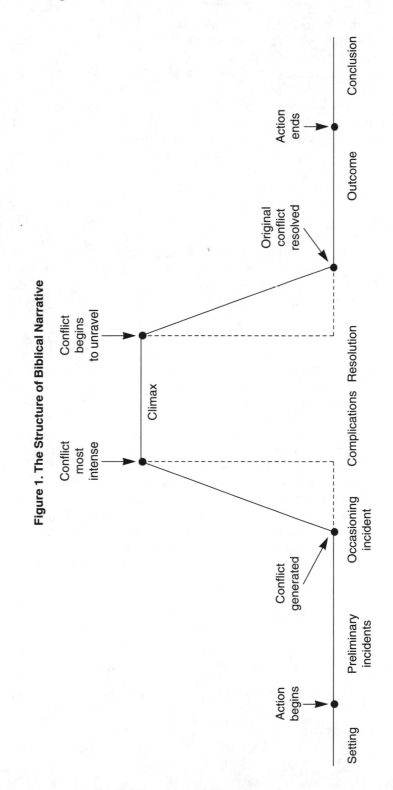

Figure 1. The Structure of Biblical Narrative

determination of incident? What is incident but the illustration of character?"[31] The debates over whether plot or character is prior seem ill-founded, since they are interdependent and equally important.

Descriptions of the dynamics of plot differ in detail between literary critics. The first and simplest is Aristotle's; he describes a plot as having a beginning, middle, and end.[32] P. Brooks defines plot in the following helpful way: "Plot is the principle of interconnectedness and intention which we cannot do without in moving through the discrete elements—incidents, episodes, actions—of a narrative."[33]

Poythress provides a more sophisticated analysis of narrative, which may be represented graphically as in figure 1.[34] The analyses of the next chapter will apply this model of plot description to particular passages.

As a general rule, plot is thrust forward by conflict. The conflict generates interest in its resolution. The beginning of a story, with its introduction of conflict, thus pushes us through the middle toward the end, when conflict is resolved.[35]

One other helpful distinction in the analysis of a story's plot is that between *fabula* and *sjužet*. "*Fabula* is defined as the order of events referred to by the narrative, whereas *sjužet* is the order of events presented in the narrative discourse."[36] This distinction provides a tool for the analysis of dischronologized narrative in the Bible.

Setting

Setting is also related to plot and character. The characters live and act, with the setting providing the background. The setting provides the physical location of the action, sometimes adds atmosphere, and at other times supports the message of the passage.

The settings of literary texts are sometimes real places, sometimes imaginary, sometimes a mixture. *Typee,* by Herman Melville, is set on a South Seas island; *The Hobbit* in the fictitious Middle Earth. Boccaccio's *Decameron* is a complex of numerous short stories, set in many different locales, but the frame of the story is set in Florence, Italy, in A.D. 1349. The setting of *The Decameron* contributes to the atmosphere of the story, since that place at that time was subject to the ravages of a horrible plague.

Setting is an important aspect of the biblical story. Again, to focus on setting is not to denigrate the historical basis of the story. A clear example of the importance of setting in the interpretation of the biblical text is the Sermon on the Mount. An interesting point here is the variation in setting between the accounts in Matthew and in Luke. In Luke the sermon is delivered on a level place (Luke 6:17); in Matthew Jesus is on a mountainside (Matt. 5:1). Harmonization is possible between the two accounts, but the question must be asked, Why does Matthew choose to report the sermon as taking place on a mountain? The answer comes as we recognize that Matthew repeatedly draws analogies

---

[31]Quoted in Chatman, *Story and Discourse*, pp. 112–13.

[32]K. A. Telford, *Aristotle's Poetics: Translation and Analysis* (South Bend, Ind.: Gateway Editions, 1961), p. 15.

[33]P. Brooks, *Reading for the Plot: Design and Intention in Narrative* (New York: Vintage Books, 1984), p. 5.

[34]I am indebted to L. Newell for bringing this model to my attention. The model itself is the work of V. Poythress, based on the work of J. Beekman, "The Semantic Structure of Written Communication" (Dallas: Summer Institute of Linguistics, unpublished paper).

[35]For a more sophisticated statement of this view of plot, see Brooks's discussion of "narrative desire" (*Reading for the Plot,* pp. 37–61).

[36]Ibid., p. 12.

between the life of Jesus and the Exodus, wilderness wanderings, and conquest of the Old Testament. In Matthew's account, after Jesus returns from forty days in the wilderness, he ascends the mountain where he talks about the law of God. Who can miss it? Jesus' preaching on the law on the mount is related to Moses' receiving the law on Mount Sinai.

STYLE

The third major subdivision of our analysis of prose narrative is style. We could examine style from a variety of levels. For instance, each individual writer has his or her own particular way of writing. In this chapter, however, we are concerned with a miscellany of items that characterize biblical style as a whole. Once again, the purpose is not to be exhaustive, but suggestive.

Many definitions of style have been proposed, but that of Leech and Short is clear and helpful, though couched in terms of individual style: "Every writer necessarily makes choices of expression, and it is in these choices, in his 'way of putting things,' that style resides. . . . Every analysis of style . . . is an attempt to find the artistic principles underlying a writer's choice of language."[37]

Repetition

Repetition is particularly noticeable in Old Testament narrative. Repetition in poetry has long been observed and categorized (see chapter 6). Prose too is repetitive. The scholarly reaction to repetition in prose, however, has usually been to defend source analysis. According to traditional biblical criticism, literary redundancy, either exact or more frequently partial, arises as the result of the merging of separate documents with one another. Advocates of a literary approach, on the other hand, are open to explaining repetition as a feature of Hebrew narrative style. Instead of weeding out redundancies, scholars thus pay close attention to the way in which repetitions function in the text.

Alter provides a kind of typology of repetitions in the Hebrew Bible.[38] He identified five types of repetitions: *Leitwort,* motif, theme, sequence of actions, and type-scene. Leitwort and type-scene are two types of repetition that are characteristic of the Bible and deserve special comment here.

Leitwort: In certain texts a particular word or words have prominence by virtue of frequent and strategic use. For instance, in 2 Samuel 7, which describes the establishment of a covenant between David and the Lord, the word *house* (*bayit*) takes on special significance. David wished to build a house (temple) for the Lord, especially since he has just built a house (palace) for himself. God does not permit David to do so; however, God will build a house (dynasty) for David. Identifying such words helps the exegete discover the structure and emphasis in a passage of Scripture.

Type-scene: Alter develops this term to describe texts that are similar in content and structure, or "an episode occurring at a portentous moment in the career of the hero which is composed of a fixed sequence of motifs."[39] J. G. Williams has studied the type-scene of barren women who give birth to boys who become biblical heroes.[40]

---

[37]G. N. Leech and M. H. Short, *Style in Fiction* (London: Longman, 1981), pp. 19, 74.
[38]Alter, *The Art of Biblical Narrative,* pp. 95–113.
[39]Ibid., p. 96.
[40]J. G. Williams, "The Beautiful and the Barren: Conventions in Biblical Type-Scenes," *JSOT* 17 (1980): 107–19.

There is a growing tendency in biblical scholarship to accept repetitions in biblical narrative as part of the text and not to excise them as indications of conflated texts. Indeed a close reading of passages to detect variation between doublets brings additional insight to the understanding of a passage. Particular sensitivity should be directed toward the minute variations that occur between generally repetitious lines.

Omission

Another stylistic characteristic of biblical texts, almost the opposite of repetition, is omission. The study of omission has received concentrated attention in recent secondary literature on prose narrative and has also been labeled "gapping" or "narrative reticence." Much of Meir Sternberg's work accentuates the major importance of gapping in Hebrew storytelling. He speaks of a "system of gaps" that constitutes a literary (biblical) work.[41]

Quite simply, a gap is an unstated piece of information that is essential to the understanding of a story, for instance, an unstated motive (see above under "Character"). Why did Uriah not sleep with his wife when he was called home from the front lines by David? Did he suspect David's plan, or was he observing certain holy-war provisions that included not sleeping with a woman before a battle? Uriah himself states the latter, but is he telling David his true motive? Motives are not the only omissions in the stories of the Bible. We are also left wondering about causes, purposes, and so forth. On many occasions we would be happier if the biblical narrator would have been explicit in terms of moral evaluation of some actions and characters.

The phenomenon of gaps in the biblical story is an important one for readers to recognize, although some scholars have overemphasized it. We observed above how a scholar such as the deconstructionist Miscall can exploit gaps to introduce a fundamental and unresolvable "undecidability" to texts. While we must reckon with intentional ambiguity, a close reading of the text will allow the reader to close the gap correctly.

The phenomenon of gapping may be explained partly as a function of the necessary selectivity of the story. Since some of the omissions are seemingly crucial to the proper understanding of a text, gapping plays other roles. Sternberg has correctly identified a second major function in that gaps involve the reader by raising "narrative interest: curiosity, suspense, surprise."[42]

Irony

Irony, like metaphor (see chapter 6), is a focus of recent discussion in literary criticism. Both irony and metaphor are figures of speech in that they "cannot be understood without rejecting what they seem to say."[43] Also, many exaggerated claims have been made about both of these figures, including the premises that all good literature is ironic or metaphorical. Since irony is frequently encountered in literature, including biblical literature, sensitive readers of the Scriptures must be able to recognize and interpret it.

The most lucid and helpful discussion of irony to be found today is that of Wayne Booth, upon whose work I am primarily dependent. Booth makes an important distinction between stable irony and unstable irony, of which only the former appears in the

---

[41]Sternberg, *The Poetics*, p. 186.
[42]Ibid., p. 259.
[43]W. Booth, *The Rhetoric of Irony* (Chicago: University of Chicago Press, 1974), p. 1.

Bible. Booth describes stable irony as sharing four characteristics. First, it is *intended* by the author. The ironic author asserts "something in order to have it rejected as false."[44] Of course, this view involves a hypothesis about an unstated intention of the author, but Booth points out that stable ironies are almost always easily recognized as such. Then stable irony is *covert.* The implied author and narrator are silent about the ironic nature of a statement or passage. Ironies are "intended to be reconstructed with meanings different from those on the surface."[45] Third, biblical ironies are *stable* in that there is a limit to how deeply they displace the surface meaning of the text. Finally, such ironies are limited in terms of scope, treating only a certain part of the text as ironic. In Booth's terms they are *local,* or *finite.*

Following his definition of stable irony, Booth neatly describes how the sensitive reader reacts as he or she encounters an ironic statement or passage. He summarizes "Four Steps of Reconstruction." The first step involves the necessary rejection of the surface, or plain, meaning of a text, which might arise because of a direct signal from the author, a patently false position being proclaimed as truth, "conflicts of fact within the work," or some other signal. All of these devices may be summed up as the belief that "if the author did not intend irony, it would be odd, or outlandish, or inept, or stupid of him to do things in this way."[46] Then, after rejecting the literal meaning of a passage, the possibility that the author was careless must be taken into account. This attitude involves, third, a hypothesis concerning the author's "knowledge or belief." Finally, a new meaning is chosen.

Irony has long been recognized as a literary device in the Bible. Indeed one of the first monographs written from a distinctively literary perspective was the book *Irony in the Old Testament.*[47] Recent work has concentrated on the fourth Gospel, with many beneficial results.[48] Irony is a particularly effective device to demolish self-satisfied and proud positions and peoples by exposing their blindness. The smug Pharisees and religious leaders of Israel are shown to be oblivious to the obvious by the use of irony throughout the gospel. The most striking and significant irony is their execution of Jesus with the intention of ridding the world of His influence. His death brought the church to life; indeed through death, life triumphs.

Dialogue

The last element of biblical style to be discussed here is the role of dialogue in biblical storytelling. Dialogue plays a major part in the narrative of the Bible, and the recent secondary literature includes some helpful descriptions of it. The work of Alter and Berlin is particularly insightful; much that follows is dependent on them.[49]

---

[44]D. C. Muecke, *Irony and the Ironic* (Critical Idiom 13; London: Methuen, 1970), p. 56.

[45]Booth, *The Rhetoric of Irony,* p. 6.

[46]Ibid., pp. 61, 52–53.

[47]E. M. Good, *Irony in the Old Testament* (Sheffield: Almond, 1981; orig. Philadelphia: Westminster, 1965).

[48]Culpepper, *Anatomy,* pp. 165–80; see also P. Duke, *Irony in the Fourth Gospel* (Atlanta: John Knox, 1985).

[49]Alter, *The Art of Biblical Narrative,* pp. 63–87; Berlin, *Poetics and Interpretation,* pp. 64–72.

In reading stories in the Bible, one quickly recognizes the high proportion of dialogue to narrative. In 1 Samuel 20, for instance, dialogue between David and Jonathan begins and ends the chapter, while a dialogue between Jonathan and Saul is found in the center. The narrative in this chapter functions to change the setting (e.g., vv. 24–25) or to provide "a bridge between much larger units of direct speech."[50]

In this brief section, only a few general characteristics of the conventions governing the presentation and function of dialogue may be given. Illustrations will come in the next chapter. As Alter has emphasized, dialogue almost invariably occurs between two characters, rarely three or more. One or both of the characters may be a group speaking as one person or actually speaking through a spokesman (1 Kings 12). The two characters engaged in dialogue are often contrasted with one another. Their styles of speech differ and serve to characterize a biblical personality. In his analysis of Genesis 25, Alter contrasts "Esau's inarticulate outbursts over against Jacob's calculated legalisms."[51] In general, the frequent use of dialogue in biblical narrative effects a strong measure of realism and vividness. With Berlin, it is possible to say, "Direct speech . . . is the most dramatic way of conveying the characters' internal psychological and ideological points of view."[52]

---

[50]Alter, *The Art of Biblical Narrative*, p. 65.
[51]Ibid., p. 72.
[52]Berlin, *Poetics and Interpretation*, p. 64.

five
EXAMPLES
OF PROSE
ANALYSIS

Having examined in general how to approach a prose narrative in the Bible, we now apply our study to two particular narratives. I consider here the account of King Ahab's demise and the record of the Gentiles' entrance into the early church.[1]

1 KINGS 22:1–38: GOD ENDS AHAB'S REIGN

I have chosen this particular story partly because literary theorists are naturally attracted to passages from Genesis and Samuel and have produced far fewer studies that are based on texts found in Kings or Chronicles. More positively, the story of Micaiah and Ahab is a stirring and self-contained plot. Of course, it is part of the larger Ahab narrative, which means that, by the time we come to 1 Kings 22, Ahab is a prominent figure. Another advantage of taking one of our examples from the Book of Kings is that we can compare it with the parallel story in the Book of Chronicles (2 Chron. 18). As we do so, we will see how close certain aspects of aesthetic criticism are to redaction criticism, particularly while identifying the point of view of the narrator in each version.

As mentioned before, all of the separate elements that we identified in the dynamics of prose narrative are actually interrelated. The descriptions of narrator, point of view, and the other dynamics of story are separated only for pedagogical reasons. Indeed the overlap between the various elements will be apparent from the start.

---

[1]A previous literary analysis of 1 Kings 22 is by D. Robertson, "Micaiah ben Imlah: A Literary View," in *The Biblical Mosaic: Changing Perspectives,* ed. R. M. Polzin and E. Rothman (Philadelphia: Fortress, 1982), pp. 139–46. I found Robertson's work very unhelpful.

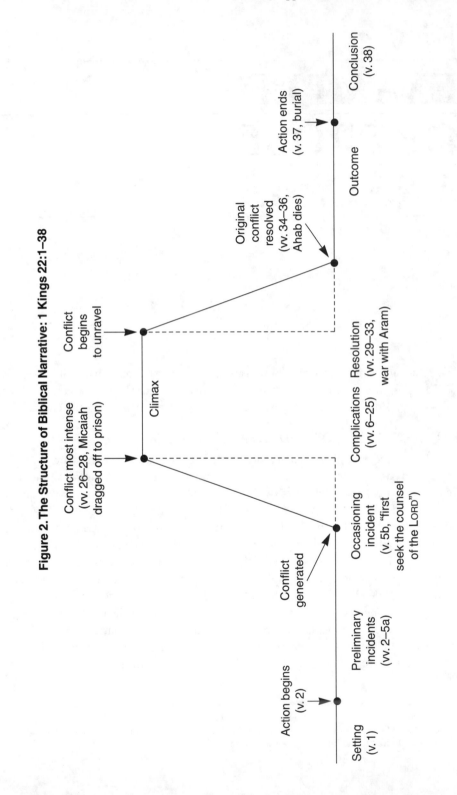

Figure 2. The Structure of Biblical Narrative: 1 Kings 22:1–38

Plot

Rather than giving a traditional plot summary that would simply paraphrase the sequence of events as they appear in the story, I use the plot line as presented above. (See fig. 2.) The account in Chronicles differs at the beginning and the end; the middle remains essentially the same. Nonetheless, the variation has important implications for the interpretation of the story. Chronicles focuses on Jehoshaphat rather than Ahab. Moreover, the Judean king's culpability is greatly heightened in Chronicles.

The plot may be traced by means of the conflict between characters in the story. This function of plot is not unusual. As Ryken aptly points out, "The essence of plot is a central conflict or set of conflicts moving toward a resolution."[2] At least three clashes occur in 1 Kings 22. The first is the war between Israel and Aram, the conflict that provides the setting for the other two and for all the action that takes place. The second conflict is between Micaiah and Zedekiah, the latter representing all of the false prophets and the former representing Yahweh's chosen messenger. The third and most important conflict is between Ahab and Micaiah. Ahab, as in the earlier narratives concerning his reign, represents the apostate people of God. Micaiah represents Yahweh. Indeed the conflict between Ahab and Micaiah is ultimately a conflict between the king of Israel and God Himself.

The narrative tension increases once Jehoshaphat requests that Ahab obtain a holy-war oracle. The Judean king persists until they hear an authentic word of the Lord from Micaiah. The tension escalates dramatically as the kings ignore the oracle and prepare for war. Ahab fights the oracle to the utmost by entering the battle in disguise and without his royal regalia and by inducing Jehoshaphat, who is likely a lesser treaty partner, to attract the attention of the enemy.

The plot finds its resolution as the arrow finds its target in the gaps of Ahab's armor and he eventually dies. The conflict between Ahab and God is thus the only one that finds explicit resolution in the story. The narrator is not concerned to inform us about the outcome of the struggle with Aram. Furthermore, we infer from events that Micaiah won the conflict with Zedekiah, though we hear nothing from the true prophet after he is dragged off to prison.

Genre

Genre, as argued above, is a fluid concept. First Kings 22 could thus be classified as a number of different genres from narrow to broad. Briefly, the narrative that focuses on Ahab and Micaiah may broadly be called *didactic history*. As a matter of fact, most of Kings and most, if not all, of the historical books in the Old Testament may be so labeled. First Kings 22 is didactic in two ways. First, it fits into the overall purpose of the Deuteronomic History to explain why Israel is now in exile. Second, it teaches the reader to avoid evil behavior (defined here as fleeing from Yahweh's law and will) as it is embodied in Ahab.

More specifically, however, 1 Kings 22 is a *prophetic story* or *prophetic history*. In other words, it is one of many episodes that center on the ministry of a prophet. In this case, the plot revolves around conflicting prophetic words and may be called a *prophetic*

---

[2]Ryken, *The Bible as Literature,* p. 40.

contest story, bearing a relationship to other texts in which prophets present conflicting oracles or represent different deities (chaps. 13, 18, etc.).[3]

Narrator

We come to know the narrator in 1 Kings 22 not only from his intrusive comments but also from his management of the dialogue. Nevertheless, he guides our attitudes toward the events and the characters of the story primarily through his explicit comments. The narrator is unnamed and not a character. He speaks of all the characters in the third person. His intrusive comments come at the beginning and end of scenes. Otherwise he permits the characters to speak for themselves. The narrator is omnipresent. He is a presence hovering in the king's council chambers (1 Kings 22:3), in the gate in Samaria (vv. 10–12), and in the Aramean camp (vv. 31–33). He is also with the messenger who summons Micaiah (v. 13).

The narrator is omniscient. However, during the first part and middle part of the plot, the narrator does not demonstrate his omniscience. He functions more like a tape recorder present on the scene in order to pick up conversations. There is even a minimum of interpretive comments in this center part of the story. Indeed evidence that exposes the omniscience of the narrator in this story is slight. But it surfaces at a crucial spot in the narrative. From some English translations of verse 32, it might be inferred that the narrator is reading the minds of the chariot commanders. For instance, the NIV translates the main verb of the verse "they thought." The verb (from *ʾāmar*), however, is better translated "they said" and therefore does not presuppose omniscience on the part of the narrator. The narrator's omniscience, though restrained, becomes manifest only in verse 34 in the comment that the arrow that killed Ahab was drawn at random. This comment assumes knowledge on the part of the narrator of the thought processes of the archer.

Ideological viewpoint provides an intersection between literary criticism and redaction criticism. Since the narrator is the literary device by which readers are guided in their interpretation of the events of the story, the analysis of the ideology of the narrator leads to a determination of the theological *Tendenz* of the passage, one of the goals of redaction criticism.

In the Kings version of the story, we find explicit ideological commentary by the narrator in verses 37–38. These two verses highlight the moral of the story that the prophetic word of judgment against Ahab has been fulfilled. In Chronicles Ahab is really a minor character (see below). The narrator is not concerned about the king of Israel; rather, he concentrates on Jehoshaphat. The narrator thus omits the explicit commentary on Ahab at the end of the story and substitutes a speech by Jehu, a prophet, which draws the moral. In brief, the moral is that Jehoshaphat has sinned because he was drawn into evil through a treaty alliance with the northern kingdom. Nonetheless, Jehoshaphat also receives qualified praise for his interest in cultic purity.

---

[3]For other views on the genre of this story, see S. J. DeVries, *Prophet Against Prophet: The Role of the Micaiah Narrative (I Kings 22) in the Development of Early Prophetic Tradition* (Grand Rapids: Eerdmans, 1978); idem, *I Kings* (Word 12; Waco, Tex.: Word, 1985), pp. 265–72; B. O. Long, *I Kings, with an Introduction to Historical Literature* (FOTL 9; Grand Rapids; Eerdmans, 1984), pp. 230–40.

Characterization

In this Ahab story, perhaps surprisingly, no character is presented as a psychologically complex person. They all appear as single- or double-trait characters or as agents who have no traits but simply carry the plot along.

Ahab. The obvious possible exception to this generalization about characterization is Ahab. He is introduced as a character as early as 1 Kings 16:28. There is more textual material on him than any other king except David and Solomon. As the reader proceeds, however, he or she may be surprised at how little the narrator reveals about Ahab or his motivations, beyond the fact that he is evil. Of course, the demonstration of his evil nature is most important for the moral of the story.

The one minor exception to this description of Ahab's characterization comes in the story of Naboth's vineyard (1 Kings 21). In this story we read of a man who is petty and inadequate—one who must be prodded by his even more wicked wife to get the land that he desires. At the end of the chapter he listens to the judgment of Elijah and repents, and the judgment is mollified. But only in this chapter does the figure of Ahab have depth.

In chapter 22 Ahab is presented again as consistently evil. He must be urged by Jehoshaphat to seek a holy-war oracle. He must be compelled a second time to seek a legitimate Yahweh prophet to do it. His attitude toward the Yahweh prophet is bad from the beginning, and he concludes by ignoring his oracle. He asks for the truth from the prophet, receives it, and then ignores the message. He even has recounted before him the prophet's report of events in the divine council and rejects it. He has the prophet cast into prison. He tries to falsify the oracle by disguising Jehoshaphat in his royal robes and entering battle dressed as a regular warrior.

One of the interesting aspects of the presentation of Ahab in chapter 22 is that he is nowhere named. Some critical scholars have argued on this basis that the narrative (or part of it) may have originally been about a different king.[4] That view misses the point. As Berlin argues, the narrator's attitude toward a character is frequently highlighted by the way he names the characters.[5] It is noticeable that Ahab, who is clearly the focus of concern in this narrative, is never mentioned by name but is always referred to as "the king of Israel." Jehoshaphat is named frequently, but never Ahab. This omission is all the more peculiar because it is clear in this context who he is.

We unfortunately cannot be dogmatic in interpreting the significance of the omission of Ahab's name from the text. It is possible that the narrator felt such disgust that he could not bring himself to name Ahab. On the other hand, the narrator may be emphasizing Ahab's position as "king of Israel" to highlight his culpability. The king should have acted as covenant mediator, but he actually perverted the covenant relationship.

In Chronicles the dramatic difference is that Ahab is a new character introduced for the first time in the narrative. His role, of course, concludes with his death at the end of the story. The interest of this narrative centers on Jehoshaphat. The focus of the camera has shifted to Jehoshaphat, and Ahab is mentioned only because of his connection with Jehoshaphat. Notice also that in Chronicles Ahab is identified by name, but only at the beginning in a section significantly modified from the account in 1 Kings.

---

[4]DeVries, *I Kings,* pp. 265ff.
[5]Berlin, *Poetics and Interpretation,* pp. 87–91.

In conclusion, Ahab, in the Micaiah story in particular and even in the entire section concerning his reign (1 Kings 16:29–22:40), is not a well-rounded figure. The narrator does not expose Ahab's thoughts or feelings. We also lack explanation for his behavior, since the narrative is generally silent concerning motivation. He usually disobeys the prophets, but when he occasionally obeys them, we hear no explanation for his change of heart from the narrator. His character may be summarized by stating simply that he is evil.

Jehoshaphat. Character is often displayed through contrast.[6] We get a partial contrast between Ahab and Jehoshaphat in Kings and in Chronicles. I begin with an analysis of Jehoshaphat's role in the Kings story, though we should note that the Chronicles version is more interested in Jehoshaphat. The contrast with Ahab is found initially in Jehoshaphat's persistent request that a Yahweh prophet be consulted before engaging in battle with the Arameans. Ahab is content with his four hundred court prophets, but Jehoshaphat urges him to bring Micaiah onto the scene. Jehoshaphat appears concerned to seek the will of Yahweh, in spite of Ahab's disinterest.

Even in Kings, however, the contrast between the two kings is not absolute. The second verse indicates that Jehoshaphat went down to Ahab without any mention of a summons. Perhaps there was a summons, but the narrator chose not to mention it and, accordingly, leaves the impression that the initiative was on Jehoshaphat's part. Second, when Ahab asks Jehoshaphat to support him against Ramoth Gilead, the latter's response is immediately affirmative. Only afterward does Jehoshaphat request a holy-war inquiry. Furthermore, after Jehoshaphat hears his requested Yahweh oracle, his response is quite surprising. He simply ignores it and goes to battle with Ahab.

The narrator provides no motivation for Jehoshaphat's actions. The lack of explicit motivation (which is one form of gapping) is typical of Old Testament narrative. The reader is left to infer the motivations. In the light of the oracle and its historical outcome, it is clear that the narrator views Jehoshaphat in a negative light.

In Chronicles this negative assessment of Jehoshaphat's actions increases dramatically. Whereas in Kings Jehoshaphat is introduced for the first time in connection with Ahab, in Chronicles he has been brought on the scene a chapter earlier. Second Chronicles 17 shows Jehoshaphat to be faithful in his early years, and as a result of his obedience, God blesses him with prosperity, which results in honor and wealth.

Jehoshaphat's wealth and honor are reemphasized at the beginning of the Micaiah story (2 Chron. 18:1a), followed by the statement that Jehoshaphat was related to Ahab by marriage and treaty. The effect of mentioning Jehoshaphat's wealth immediately before his treaty with the northern kingdom is significant. God granted Jehoshaphat wealth; he did not need a treaty with Ahab! Seen in this light, the conjunction (*waw*) that unites the two sentences of 18:1 should be translated "but" and not "and." The reference to Jehoshaphat's unnecessary treaty alliance at the beginning of the narrative shapes the reader's attitude against Jehoshaphat.

Furthermore, the reshaped introduction to the Micaiah story presents Jehoshaphat as an equal or near-equal with Ahab, which heightens the Judean king's culpability. When Jehoshaphat first arrives, the Chronicles narrator informs the reader about the

---

[6]Alter, *The Art of Biblical Narrative,* pp. 72–74, discusses this feature, in reference particularly to dialogue.

royal reception he receives. In short, Ahab wines and dines Jehoshaphat, presumably with the intention of persuading (not commanding) him to enter the war as his ally.

This interpretation of the Chronicler's modified introduction is confirmed by his changed conclusion. The report of an encounter between Jehoshaphat and Jehu ben Hanani (2 Chron. 19:1–3) replaces the evaluation of the death of Ahab by the King's narrator. Jehu explicitly condemns Jehoshaphat's treaty connections with Ahab.

Micaiah. The narrator never comments on Micaiah. He is presented exclusively through dialogue. Ahab's speech represents one perspective or point of view. The narrator places Micaiah in a good light by showing Ahab speaking badly of him. Ahab selects him immediately as a true prophet, the kind that Jehoshaphat wants, but he also maligns him.

The narrator gives Micaiah more depth than the other characters, which is shown in his speech before Ahab. When the messenger counsels Micaiah to conform his oracle to that of the other four hundred prophets, Micaiah rejects his suggestions immediately, saying that he must speak the word of God. Surprisingly, his initial speech before Ahab affirms Ahab's battle plans. The context makes it clear, however, that Micaiah spoke with ironic intent (see the discussion of irony in chap. 4), something Ahab realized without hesitation. When commanded to tell the truth, Micaiah delivers a judgment oracle. The effect of the irony is to heap more blame on Ahab. The initial, ironic prophecy evokes a command from Ahab to "tell the truth." When Ahab hears the truth, he recognizes it as such but blatantly rejects it.

Alter has commented on the narrator's ability to shape character by contrast, often by contrast in speech style and length. The only lengthy, smooth speech in the whole narrative is delivered by Micaiah as he gives God's sentence of judgment. This speech contrasts with all of the short, choppy speeches elsewhere in the story.

In the contrast drawn between Micaiah and Zedekiah and between Micaiah and Ahab, it is noteworthy to observe who has the last word. In both cases, Micaiah points to the future sure fulfillment of his prophetic word (1 Kings 22:25, 28). Nonetheless, there is no real interest in Micaiah as a developed character. For one thing, we do not learn of his fate. We are left with the strong impression that he was released after the oracle came true, but it is not reported because the narrator felt that it was unimportant.

Agents in the Micaiah narrative. Most of the other characters in the story are agents. They are given no character traits to speak of and are important only for the progress of the plot. Ahab's officials (1 Kings 22:3), his messenger (v. 13), the four hundred (v. 6), the king of Aram and his thirty-two chariot commanders (v. 31), and, most significantly, the anonymous archer (v. 34) are among those in this category.

ACTS 10:1–11:18: THE GENTILES COME INTO THE CHURCH

My New Testament example of prose analysis also comes from a book that has received less treatment from a literary perspective than other narrative portions. Most attention has been given to the Gospels, while Acts and Revelation, the other two major works of prose in the New Testament, have been relatively ignored. The epistles of the New Testament involve a whole different set of literary questions.[7]

---

[7] N. R. Petersen raises two methodological points in his book *Rediscovering Paul: Philemon and the Sociology of Paul's Narrative World* (Philadelphia: Fortress, 1985). He demonstrates that Paul's letters are amenable to a literary approach, since behind the letters are stories. Second, he shows how a literary analysis intersects with a sociological analysis.

Plot and Setting

The story in Acts 10:1–11:18 centers on the conversion of Cornelius, his relatives, and close friends. The broader story continues at least until Acts 15, when the implications of Gentile inclusion in the church and specifically Paul's ministry to the Gentiles is dealt with, but our attention will be restricted initially to a consideration of the story surrounding the conversion of Cornelius.

The shape of the plot is somewhat different from what we observed in the Micaiah story. Here we have a story with four episodes and two narrative climaxes. The four episodes are distinguished by a shift in setting. For the most part the *fabula* and the *sjužet* (see "Plot" in chapter 4) are the same. That is, the story is told in a fairly straightforward manner, which parallels the way in which Peter later narrates these amazing events to his brethren in Jerusalem ("Peter began and explained everything to them precisely as it had happened" [Acts 11:4]).

The first episode (10:1–8) is located in Caesarea in the home of a certain Gentile named Cornelius. The story opens by describing Cornelius as a Gentile and as "devout and God-fearing." The opening incident involves a vision that comes to Cornelius while he is in prayer. An angel, whom Cornelius addresses as "Lord," appears before him and instructs him to send for Peter, who is in Joppa.

The second episode (10:9–23a) shifts to Joppa and to Peter. There is also a time shift, since the introduction to this episode mentions that it is already the next day and the messengers who have been sent by Cornelius are nearing their destination. Peter too receives a vision. The vision confuses him because it strikes at the heart of his previous conceptions of how God relates to men and women. The vision is repeated three times, and each time Peter is exhorted to eat unclean food that is lowered from heaven in a sheet. As Peter attempts to understand the meaning of the vision, he is approached by the three men, who ask Peter to go to Caesarea with them. Peter takes the first step of faith and allows the three men to stay in his house as his guests.

The third episode (10:23b–48) shifts the setting back to the house of Cornelius. Peter significantly moves from his own Jewish household into a Gentile household, an act that goes against his previous conception of what God expected of him (vv. 28–29).

In this third episode the visions of the first two are brought together and the result is further clarification of the will of God. Cornelius narrates to Peter (our first instance of narrative flashback and repetition) the message that he had received from God four days earlier. Cornelius realizes that God has brought Peter to him for a purpose, and he stands ready to hear what Peter has to say on behalf of the Lord.

At this point the implications of the vision become clear to Peter, and he delivers the longest speech in the narrative, asserting that God accepts the Gentiles. As he speaks, Cornelius and his party manifest the gifts of the Spirit, and Peter and the other Jewish believers who were with him feel compelled to baptize them.

The first major portion of the plot surrounds the conversion of Cornelius and his household and centers on a conflict. The conflict is between Peter's theological prejudice and God's intention to include the Gentiles. The occasioning incident of the plot, then, is first of all the vision to Cornelius, but even more clearly Peter's vision, which raises a conflict in his mind that cries out for resolution. The climax of the story comes in Peter's moment of recognition that the Gentiles are recipients of the promise.

The story does not conclude here, however. Peter's personal conflict has found resolution, but now the conflict takes on a broader complexion as the rest of the church hears about this event. Peter goes to Jerusalem to explain himself in the fourth episode of the story (11:1–18). The conflict is now between Peter and the leaders of the church in Jerusalem. The occasioning incident comes when Peter is charged, "You went into the house of uncircumcised men and ate with them" (v. 3).

Peter then responds by narrating the story of his vision. The importance of the vision is highlighted by its being narrated in full a second time (11:5–10). He also recounts the vision of Cornelius, with a notable addition. The apostle reports that God told Cornelius that Peter "will bring you a message through which you and all your household will be saved" (v. 14). After Peter fully explained his actions, the leaders were satisfied and believed that God had indeed given the promise of salvation to the Gentiles. The plot thus again finds an ending in resolution of conflict.

The plot, which as we have argued has an independent unity, is significantly framed by other stories. Peter had been the main focus of Acts until chapter 8, when Saul/Paul is introduced. Paul, of course, is the main character of the rest of the book. The Paul narrative, however, is interrupted briefly with a second Peter narrative that begins in 9:32 and narrates two miracles that Peter performed. Clearly one of Luke's purposes in narrating these miracles before the Cornelius incident is to heighten our confidence in Peter's ministry. The story that immediately follows the Cornelius story also serves to validate the ministry of Peter to Cornelius as it describes the conversion of more Gentiles, a happening that is endorsed by Barnabas, an emissary from the Jerusalem church (11:19–30).

Even more broadly, the story of Peter and Cornelius fits very significantly into the story of the Book of Acts. One of the major functions of that story is to validate Paul's ministry to the Gentiles. As W. R. Long observes, "It is of extreme importance for Luke to show that it was through the ritually sensitive, law abiding Peter that the command to evangelize a Gentile came."[8]

The story takes place over time in three locales. Cornelius is in Caesarea, at this time the capital of Palestine. Significantly, the city is predominantly Gentile. It is a likely place for a Roman centurion to reside. Joppa, being a seaport, was likely a somewhat cosmopolitan town, but the Jewish population there was large. It is significant that Peter went to Cornelius in Caesarea rather than the latter's traveling to Joppa. That Peter was willing to make the trip shows that God was already breaking down the barriers between Jews and Gentiles in Christ (cf. 10:28). The third locale in the Cornelius narrative is Jerusalem. Peter goes there as the conversion of Cornelius moves from a matter of private conscience to that of the entire church. It is expected that Jerusalem be the locale of such a major institutional issue, for in both Luke and Acts "Jerusalem clearly emerges as the geographical locus of authority."[9]

Genre

As with the Micaiah narrative, it is impossible to give a full discussion of the genre of Acts 10:1–11:18 in the brief compass of this chapter. It is an issue of considerable

---

[8]W. R. Long, "The Trial of Paul in the Book of Acts: Historical, Literary, and Theological Considerations" (Ph.D. diss., Brown University, 1982), p. 293; see also D. P. Moessner, "'The Christ Must Suffer': New Light on the Jesus—Peter, Stephen, Paul Parallels in Luke-Acts," *NTS* 28 (1986): 220–56.

[9]E. S. Nelson, "Paul's First Missionary Journey as Paradigm: A Literary-Critical Assessment of Acts 13–14" (Ph.D. diss., Boston University, 1982), p. 72.

debate, and also, with our understanding of the fluid nature of genre, we know that it is not simply a matter of identifying a single, right genre.

The issue of the genre of this story is, of course, related to or even the same as the question of the genre of Acts as a whole. The debate usually concerns whether Acts is history or romance (or, better, historical fiction). One could conceivably point to certain indications within the text to argue in favor of the author's historical intention. I have in mind such things as details concerning characters that are of no special relevance to the plot. For instance, the narrator informs the reader that Peter was staying with Simon in Joppa but adds the fact that Simon was a tanner and that his house was by the sea. Cornelius is identified as an officer in the Italian Regiment. Furthermore, the narrative is given a close chronology. The time of day of Cornelius's prayer is given (10:3), as is the time of Peter's prayer (v. 9).

These incidental details in the story certainly give the impression that the author is concerned to impart historical information. Of course, a skeptic could point out that historical fiction also has such realism effects. However, remembering that the subject of the story is of decided importance for the practice of the early church in that it is citing a precedent for the inclusion of the Gentiles into the church, we see that the author clearly intends his reader to believe that the story took place in history.

Nonetheless, as with Old Testament historiography, it would be a disservice to the text to identify the genre as mere history. Once again we have *didactic* or *theological history*. Perhaps even better, since I am persuaded that Acts serves to justify Paul's ministry to the Gentiles, *apologetic history.*

Characterization

In our discussion of plot we have already touched on the characters. My summary here will accordingly be brief.

Cornelius. The introduction of Cornelius marks the beginning of the narrative. The narrator provides a description of him that, by virtue of its length alone, signals that he is an important character. He is initially presented with an emphasis on the fact that he is a Gentile. His name is a good Roman name. He is a centurion in the Roman army and lives in a predominantly Gentile city. The other emphasis that the narrator relates to the reader is that Cornelius is a kindhearted and religious man (10:2). The narrator's assessment of the centurion's personality is confirmed later by his messengers (v. 22).

Here is a man, then, who clearly is non-Jewish but religious. His heart is in the right place, but he is also somewhat confused. The latter point is illustrated when he first encounters Peter, and he does not know the proper way to relate to him (10:26). God is about to set him straight.

Peter. The other major figure in the story is of course Peter, and as so often happens in biblical texts, there is a contrast. Whereas Cornelius is clearly a Gentile, Peter is obviously a Jew. He is fastidious about Jewish customs, including the provisions that the Jew should stay separate from Gentiles and that they should not eat certain foods. It has long been recognized that these two customs are related. That is, the division between clean and unclean foods represents a similar division in humankind between the clean (Jew) and the unclean (Gentile).

Peter was consistent in his practice of such Jewish customs, which is heightened in the narrative by the fact that God must three times repeat the vision of the sheet lowering from heaven. Even after the vision, Peter has not understood what God has said. Peter's slowness in responding to the revelation of God also provides a contrast with Cornelius, who earlier had immediately responded to God's instruction.

Minor characters. Only one other character is named in the narrative—Simon the tanner. His significance has been mentioned above as injecting an atmosphere of realism into the narrative. Perhaps too his occupation is cited because tanning implies work with dead animals, which would lead to ritual uncleanness. Of even greater importance to the story, however, are four different groups.

The first group is *Cornelius's messengers.* One might ask why they were necessary; God could have told Peter to go to Cornelius's house through his vision. However, the nature of the vision went against everything Peter had previously believed, and the messengers function as a kind of external confirmation of what God had spoken through the vision. Then, we have *Peter's associates.* The text mentions six men who accompanied Peter to Cornelius's house (10:23; 11:12). They serve as witnesses on Peter's behalf to the work that God performed, for they too observed the work of the Holy Spirit. Third, *Cornelius's family and friends* were also saved (10:24, 44). Cornelius was not just an anomaly. Finally, the *apostles and brothers in Jerusalem* criticize and then affirm Peter's actions with Cornelius. Their role emphasizes the fact that Peter is not acting autonomously but that the inclusion of the Gentiles has the approval of the heart of the institutional church.

The Lord/the angel/the Spirit. Of course, the real mover of the narrative is God Himself. He is the one who appears to Cornelius and to Peter and effectively brings them together. The Spirit too is the one who saved the Gentiles and demonstrated to the Jewish believers that Gentiles were also included.

Narrator and Point of View

Once again, this subject interlocks with our previous discussion. Plot, characterization, and the point of view of the narrator are all dependent on one another. The type of third-person narration that we observe in the Cornelius story has already been discussed in conjunction with the Micaiah narrative. Such third-person omniscient narration is the norm in biblical storytelling.

The Cornelius story is narrated in full by an unnamed, omniscient, omnipresent narrator. Through his portrayal of the people and events involved in this story, he guides our reaction and forms our evaluation of it. He makes us, as readers, react positively to Cornelius. We also struggle with Peter and recognize that the inclusion of Cornelius into the household of faith was not an easy decision for Peter to make. We also learn through the narrator that Peter's decision was not quickly accepted by the church authorities in Jerusalem. All in all, we are thereby led to conclude that the right, and not the easy, decision has been made. God has indeed acted to bring the Gentiles into the church. To deny this conclusion is to deny God himself.

six

THE ANALYSIS
OF POETIC
PASSAGES

A surprising amount of the Bible is poetic. Poetry is primarily found in the Old Testament, though there are occasional poetic portions in the New Testament (e.g., Phil. 2:6–11). Within the Old Testament, poetic verse is concentrated in the Psalms and the so-called wisdom books (Song of Songs, Ecclesiastes, Proverbs, and Job). We must not forget, though, that the prophets also wrote energetic verse. Indeed, poetry is the predominant style of the prophets. Ancient poems are encountered in the Pentateuch (Gen. 49; Exod. 15; Deut. 32–33) as well as the historical books (Judg. 5; 2 Sam. 22). Poetry makes up about one-third of the whole Bible and would alone constitute a book the size of the whole New Testament.

Since the conventions that are associated with biblical poetry are foreign to us, poetry presents a number of questions to the modern reader. The poetry of the Bible is unlike its prose and also unlike modern poetry. We must therefore inquire into the workings of poetry in order to guide our reading of the biblical text.

Many exciting insights have been gained recently toward the understanding of biblical poetry. J. Kugel, followed by R. Alter, has modified our approach to semantic parallelism.[1] A. Berlin has recently carried the discussion into the area of grammatical parallelism, and M. O'Connor's learned tome anticipated this interest in the nonsemantic aspects of parallelism.[2] The workings of imagery, particularly metaphor, have received much attention in

---

[1]Kugel, *The Idea of Biblical Poetry*; R. Alter, *The Art of Biblical Poetry* (New York: Basic Books, 1985).
[2]A. Berlin, *The Dynamics of Biblical Parallelism* (Bloomington: Indiana University Press, 1985); M. O'Connor, *Hebrew Verse Structure* (Winona Lake, Ind.: Eisenbrauns, 1980).

both secular and biblical interpretation.[3] A new consensus on meter is merging, which, though negative, serves to move research beyond an impasse that has hindered our understanding of Hebrew poetry for centuries.[4]

DEFINITION OF POETRY

In the past, poetry has been distinguished from prose in the Bible by the presence of one or more key traits. Parallelism often has been cited as the poetic device *par excellence*. Many poems, however, demonstrate weak or even no parallelism, while parallelism is found in prose portions of Scripture as well. Meter also has been taken as a defining characteristic of poetry, on analogy with classical and most English poetic traditions. Nonetheless, no system of meter has been definitively uncovered in the Bible.

These facts have led Kugel to reject the presence of poetry in the Bible.[5] This position is overstated, however, because the difference between prose and poetry in the Bible is gradated or fluid, which is to be expected, since all generic distinctions are fluid and not absolute or rigid.

Poetry may be defined over against prose by reference to ordinary speech. Prose represents a certain departure from normal speech patterns and poetry a further departure. Poetry is a more self-consciously structured language. It is self-referring in the sense that increased attention is given to how something is said as well as to what is said. In this manner, poetry is characterized by a higher level of literary artifice than prose. Poetry may best be defined, then, through a description of the various conventions or devices encountered in the poems themselves. Prose is the relative absence of these devices. Instead of characterizing prose and poetry as discrete literary forms, we may better represent them as poles on a continuum, as in the following diagram:

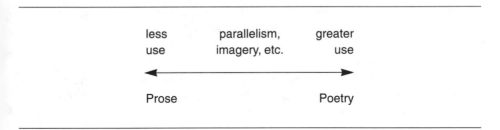

The rest of this chapter will be devoted to an exposition of the major literary conventions that cluster in Hebrew poetry: terseness, parallelism, and imagery. Space does not permit explanation of occasional poetic devices, for which I refer the reader to W. G. E. Watson's excellent handbook.[6]

---

[3]G. B. Caird, *The Language and Imagery of the Bible* (Philadelphia: Westminster, 1980); P. Ricoeur, *The Rule of Metaphor* (Toronto: University of Toronto Press, 1977); T. Hawkes, *Metaphor* (London: Methuen, 1972); Sheldon Sacks, ed., *On Metaphor* (Chicago: University of Chicago Press, 1978); M. Black, *Models and Metaphors* (Ithaca: Cornell University Press, 1962).

[4]T. Longman, III, "A Critique of Two Recent Metrical Systems," *Bib* 63 (1982): 230–54.

[5]Kugel, *The Idea of Biblical Poetry,* pp. 59–95.

[6]W. G. E. Watson, *Classical Hebrew Poetry* (*JSOT* 26; Sheffield: JSOT, 1984). For a more popular treatment, see my *How to Read the Psalms* (Downers Grove, Ill.: InterVarsity, 1988).

PRIMARY FEATURES OF POETRY

Terseness

The most neglected feature of Hebrew poetry is also one of its most common and distinctive traits: the lines of Hebrew poetry are terse; they are short and to the point. By comparison, lines are much longer in prose, which one can easily see by opening a typical English translation of the Old Testament to a poetic passage and looking at the layout of the poem on the page. Poetry is easily recognized because the lines are short.

Prose passages are composed of sentences that are grouped into paragraphs. Poetic passages, on the other hand, may be analyzed as consisting of clauses (or cola) that often are bound together into lines by semantic or grammatical repetition. Two cola so bound are labeled a bicolon; three, a tricolon; and so forth. Furthermore, the sentences of a prose passage vary in terms of length. Cola of poetic passages tend to be equal in length.

A device that intensifies the terseness of the poetic line in Hebrew is *ellipsis*. Frequently a noun but more commonly a verb occurs in the first colon of a line but has no parallel in the second colon. The verb in the first colon is understood in the second colon, for instance, in Psalm 33:12:

> Blessed is the nation whose God is the LORD,
>   the people he chose for his inheritance.

The opening word *blessed* is missing from the second colon, but to make sense of the line we must supply the word. Such ellipsis is quite common in biblical poetry.

A further aspect of the terseness of biblical verse is the lack of conjunctions and particles. The conjunctions *and, but, or* and the temporal markers *then, when, afterward* are rare in poetry. Logical markers such as *therefore* and *thus,* as well as the causal marker *because* occur infrequently. Since conjunctions function to guide the reader in his or her interpretation of the temporal or logical relationships between statements, their lack introduces an element of intentional ambiguity into the text.

Parallelism

While terseness is usually omitted in studies of Hebrew poetry, parallelism is often identified as the single major poetic device. Indeed, parallelism for all practical purposes frequently is equated with poetry. J. Kugel, however, has shown the fallacy of taking parallelism as the key to the definition of poetry.[7] On the one hand, he shows that many poems have either no parallelism or a very weak form of it. The first few lines of Jeremiah's complaint in chapter 12 show little parallelism except in the last two cola:

> You are always righteous, O LORD,
>   when I bring a case before you.
> Yet I would speak with you about your justice:
>   Why does the way of the wicked prosper?
>   Why do all the faithless live at ease?

Furthermore, it has long been recognized that prose passages often show a symmetry that can be described as parallelistic. Kugel provides the following example from Genesis 21:1:

---

[7]Kugel, *The Idea of Biblical Poetry.*

> And the LORD remembered Sarah as he had said
>   and the LORD did for Sarah as he had spoken.[8]

Nonetheless, parallelism, while not the defining characteristic of poetry, is certainly one of its major ornamental devices. Repetition abounds within lines (internal parallelism) and between the lines (external parallelism) of a typical Old Testament poem. The parallelism operates on both semantic and grammatical levels.

Semantic Parallelism. Jeremiah 30:12–14 provides clear examples of semantic parallelism in Hebrew poetry:

> "Your wound is incurable,
>   your injury beyond healing.
> There is no one to plead your cause,
>   no remedy for your sore,
>   no healing for you.
> All your allies have forgotten you;
>   they care nothing for you."

In the first two cola, "wound" and "injury" are close in meaning, as are "incurable" and "beyond healing." These parallel words lead the reader to meditate on one colon in the light of the other. In other words, repetition exhibits the coherence between two cola.

The obvious repetition that appears between cola in a parallel line has led to an overevaluation of the similarity between the lines. As a result, parallelism has even been described as two cola that express the same meaning twice, using two different sets of words. Such a definition of parallelism is extremely misleading, for it causes the reader to gloss over the progression from one colon to another. While cola show similarity with one another, there are also intentional divergences, differences of meaning to which attention must be given.

Once again, Kugel has been the scholar who has brought this important point to light. In traditional approaches to parallelism the first colon (A) of a parallel line is *equal* in meaning to the second colon (B).[9] Kugel, on the other hand, argues that the thought of the second colon always progresses in some way beyond the first, in his formulation, "A—what's more, B."

The beginning of Psalm 72 contains two parallel lines that are bicola:

> Endow the king with your justice, O God,
>   the royal son with your righteousness.
> He will judge your people in righteousness,
>   your afflicted ones with justice.

We may observe both similarity and difference between the cola in these lines. The imperative verb "endow" is elided from the second colon of the first line but is understood there. The object of the verb is "king" in the first colon but is expanded in the second as

---

[8]Ibid., p. 59.

[9]The traditional view is based on the work of R. Lowth, who lived in the eighteenth century and whose main insights into the workings of Hebrew poetry are found in his *Sacred Poetry of the Hebrews*. He is also well known for his tripartite division of semantic parallelism into synonymous, antithetic, and synthetic. For a critique of this typology of parallelism, consult Kugel, *The Idea of Biblical Poetry,* and my *How to Read the Psalms*.

"royal son." There is some ambiguity between two interpretations of "son," but in either case the second colon progresses beyond the thought of the first. Either the royal son is equated with the king (that is, he is God's son [see 2 Sam. 7:14]), or the phrase refers to the king's son, the heir. In the latter case, the progression of thought is obvious, since it refers to a second individual. In the former reading, the reference becomes more personal by highlighting the divine sonship of the king.

Psalm 37 begins with the following two lines:

> Do not fret because of evil men
>   or be envious of those who do wrong;
> for like the grass they will soon wither,
>   like green plants they will soon die away.

Once again we see illustrated the principle that the second colon develops the thought expressed in the first. The similarity between the cola in both of the lines leads the reader to consider them together, to meditate on how they relate, and to note how the second line reinforces the thought of the first.

The first line is brought together most forcefully by the parallel between "evil men" and "those who do wrong." Some progression may be observed in that the latter expression further defines the former. The progression is clearer with the verbs. The psalmist insists that the hearer/reader not worry about the evil men. More specifically, however, the reader is admonished not to be jealous. In this context, "envy" is more specific than "fret." One might fret for a variety of reasons (fear being the most obvious); in the second line, however, envy is singled out.

The second parallel line is grammatically subordinate to the first. Once again the progression is obvious between the verbs. In the first colon, the plants "wither." This thought is intensified in the second colon in that the plants "die."

In summary, semantic parallelism is frequently an ornament of biblical poetry. A verse often combines two similar, yet subtly divergent, cola. The second element of the verse always carries forward the thought of the first.

Grammatical parallelism. Our discussion has centered so far on semantic parallelism, for two reasons: (1) only recently have scholars seriously applied themselves to study grammatical parallelism, and (2) grammatical parallelism is not as directly relevant to the meaning of a poem. I mention grammatical parallelism here because, like semantic parallelism, it is another method writers used to relate cola to each other. The grammatical similarity between two cola in a bicolon will cause the reader to read them closely together, and subtle variations between the cola in terms of syntax add interest to the line. In short, it is another factor that leads us to describe the poetic line as exhibiting both coherence and variance, similarity and dissimilarity, symmetry and asymmetry.

Grammatical parallelism simply describes the relationship between the syntax and morphology of cola in a poetic line. Scholarly analysis of grammatical parallelism can be technical. I discuss here one well-presented view, that of T. Collins, as an example.[10]

Collins's basic premise is borrowed from transformational grammar, which postulates a finite number of basic sentences (deep structure) that generate an infinite number of actual sentences (surface structure). Simply put, Collins describes four basic sentences

---

[10]T. Collins, *Line-Forms in Hebrew Poetry* (Rome: Biblical Institute Press, 1978).

of Hebrew, defined by the grammatical units that they contain: (1) subject and verb; (2) subject, verb, and modifier; (3) subject, verb, and object; and (4) subject, verb, object, and modifier. The next step in his analysis involves the description and application of four "general line types." These types define the relations of basic sentences to one another: (1) lines that have one basic sentence; (2) lines that occur with two identical basic sentences; (3) lines that contain two similar basic sentences, with the second one only partially repeating the first syntactically; and (4) lines that have two completely different basic sentences.

Contrary to Collins's position, grammatical parallelism is not the key to the definition of poetry. The categories are too loose, and it is hard to imagine any line in the Bible, poetry or prose, as incapable of analysis by them. On the positive side, however, the analysis of the syntactic shape of poetical lines yields a picture of coherence and variation or similarity and dissimilarity that is like what we have in semantic parallelism. A. Berlin has written recently on the grammatical aspect of parallelism from this basic starting point:

> The grammatical aspect of parallelism—grammatical equivalence and/or contrast—is one of the fundamental aspects of biblical parallelism. There is almost always some degree of grammatical correspondence between parallel lines, and in many cases it is the basic structuring device of the parallelism—the feature that creates the perception of parallelism.[11]

One of the differences between prose and poetry is the free variation in syntax of the latter. Frequently, the syntactic shape within a poetic line will be the same but with subtle differences. The similar aspects of the cola in a line have the effect that readers will take the two cola as one unit, but the dissimilarity reminds them that the second colon is not a similar statement but a furtherance or sharpening of the first.[12]

The following is a simple syntactic analysis of Deuteronomy 32:1 (V = verb; S = subject; M = modifier; O = object).

Listen, O heavens, and I will speak;
V   S   M
hear, O earth, the words of my mouth.
V   S   O

In this first bicolon we observe a close syntactic parallelism between the first two elements of the cola, but then variation in the third section. Instead of a verb clause (acting as a modifier) in third position, the poet places a direct object in the second colon. Such variation breaks the monotony of repetition and lends interest to the line.

More subtle variations may also be seen in the Hebrew original of this simple bicolon. For instance, there is morphological variation between the verbs in the two cola[13] The first verb is causative (*hiphil*) and masculine, while the second verb is not causative (*qal*) and is feminine. Such variations help gain the attention of the Hebrew reader. The line on one level has the potential for being rather monotonous. Both "listen" and "hear"

[11]Berlin, *The Dynamics*, p. 31.
[12]The term *sharpening* was apparently introduced into the description of parallelism by Kugel, *The Idea of Biblical Poetry*, pp. 11–12.
[13]For the distinction within grammatical parallelism between syntactic and morphological parallelism, consult Berlin, *The Dynamics*, pp. 32–63.

and "heaven" and "earth" are frequently occurring word pairs.[14] The subtle variations of syntax and morphology that we just noticed add a level of sophistication to the line.

The next two bicola (Deut. 32:2) show a similar grammatical parallelism (PP = prepositional phrase).

Let my teaching fall like rain
        S   V   PP
and my words descend like dew,
        S   V   PP
like showers on new grass,
    PP   PP
like abundant rain on tender plants.
      PP   PP

These two bicola contain more similarities than the line from verse 1. Nonetheless, one may still observe subtle morphological differences. The masculine verb in the first colon, for instance, is answered by a feminine verb in the second.

These two examples of grammatical parallels illustrate lines that are relatively high in similarity. Many lines, particularly from later time periods (eighth century B.C. and after), show much less similarity of structure. Overall, it may be said without hesitation that Hebrew poetry shows more freedom in syntax (word order) than prose. Such freedom allows the subtle variations between cola that we observe. Syntactic variation is thus another element of language play that characterizes Hebrew verse.

Imagery

Imagery occurs in prose as well as in poetry. Since its use is intensified and heightened in poetry, however, and since it is one of the chief characteristics of poetic language, I have reserved discussion until this chapter. A literary image is a sensation evoked in the mind of the reader by the language of a text. As C. Day Lewis states in an often-quoted definition, "It is a picture made out of words."[15] Or as N. Friedman asserts:

> *Imagery* refers to images produced in the mind by language, whose words and statements may refer either to experiences which could produce physical perceptions were the reader actually to have those experiences, or to the sense-impressions themselves.[16]

The type of imagery that is our concern is virtually identical with *figurative language*. Unlike literal language, figurative language does not mean what it seems to mean on the surface. We may heartily agree with T. Hawkes when he observes that "all language, by the nature of its 'transferring' relation to 'reality' . . . is fundamentally metaphorical."[17] Perhaps what we call literal language is composed of dead (in the sense of forgotten)

---

[14]For a near-exhaustive study of word pairs, see Y. Avishur, *Stylistic Studies of Word-pairs in Biblical and Ancient Semitic Literature* (Kevelaer: Butzon & Bercker, 1984).

[15]Quoted in N. Friedman, "Imagery," in the *Princeton Encyclopedia of Poetry and Poetics*, ed. A. Preminger (Princeton: Princeton University Press, 1965), p. 363.

[16]Ibid.

[17]Hawkes, *Metaphor,* p. 60.

metaphors.[18] Nonetheless, a practical distinction may be made between literal and figurative language.

The scope of this book does not permit a detailed listing of the many different kinds of images encountered in literature in general and the Bible in particular. A major division may be suggested between imagery that functions on the basis of association or contiguity and that which functions on the basis of similarity.

Similarity. Images based on similarity are the most common in the Bible. In order to describe a person, object, or event, the poet will explicitly or implicitly compare the item with something or someone else that is similar in some way but that is also different. The difference between the two causes the reader to recognize the presence of an image and stimulates him or her to search for the similarity within the difference that the image conceals.

Many different types of image are based on the principle of similarity (personification, allegory, symbol, etc.), but the most common is metaphor, with its explicit correlate, simile. I concentrate here on metaphor. (Indeed it might plausibly be argued that all of the others are really a subtype of the master figure, metaphor.) A metaphor is an image based on similarity within difference. In Song of Songs 2:1, the beloved describes herself: "I am a rose of Sharon, a lily of the valleys." This sentence is absurd if interpreted literally. The differences shock us into realizing that this verse is imagery. The beloved is not describing herself as having one long green leg capped by a red or white head. The reader intuitively and meditatively must consider the similarity between the woman and the flowers by means of a process of elimination. This process will result in some vagueness of interpretation, but vagueness is an inherent characteristic of figurative language. Among the possible intended similarities between the woman in the Song of Songs and the flowers are beauty and pleasant smell.

Students of metaphor have subdivided different types. One of the most productive typologies of metaphor is that presented by G. B. Caird. He explains that metaphor may be broken down into "four points of comparison."[19] The first is *perceptual* metaphor and is based on one of the senses. The most common is visual, but this kind has often been overemphasized to the extent that some wrongly think that all metaphors are to be visualized. For instance, the sense of smell may be the important point of comparison in a metaphor. Psalm 141:2 compares the psalmist's prayer with the sweet smell of incense. Though a simile, Ecclesiastes 7:6 illustrates a comparison based on sound: "Like the crackling of thorns under the pot, so is the laughter of fools." Taste is in the center of the comparison in Song of Songs 7:2: "Your navel is a rounded goblet that never lacks blended wine." Of course, metaphors may evoke a plurality of senses.

Caird defines *pragmatic* metaphor as a comparison in which "we compare the activity or result of one thing with that of another." Isaiah 10:5 is a good example: "Woe to the Assyrian, the rod of my anger." The rod, which is an instrument of punishment, is compared with Assyria, a nation that God used to punish the rebellious northern kingdom.

The other two types of comparison are less frequent in the Scriptures than the first two. *Synesthetic* comparison may be seen as a subtype of perceptual in that it is "the use

[18]G. Lakoff and M. Johnson, *Metaphors We Live By* (Chicago: University of Chicago Press, 1980).

[19]For the definitions and examples considered in this section, see Caird, *Language and Imagery*, pp. 145ff.

in connexion with one of the senses of terms which are proper to another" (Psalm 55:21: "His speech is smooth as butter").

Affective comparisons are "those in which the feel or value, the effect or impression of one thing is compared with that of another." Speaking to the king of Assyria concerning the certain downfall of his nation, Nahum says, "Nothing can heal your wound; your injury is fatal" (Nah. 3:19).

Images of Association. Perhaps the two most well-known figures of speech based on the principle of association as opposed to similarity are *metonymy* and *synecdoche*. The former has been defined as "the substitution of one word for another word closely associated with it."[20] For instance, in Psalm 45:6, God's throne stands for his kingship. Synecdoche, on the other hand, is when a part stands for the whole. For instance, references to God's "right hand" and "holy arm" are synecdochic for God himself.

The Function of Imagery. Imagery, like poetic language in general, lacks the precision of most literal language. The meaning of a metaphor, we have seen above, is located in the similarity between two things that are also different. The similarity is unstated or hidden, and the reader must meditate on the metaphor to arrive at its interpretation. The result is lack of precision.

Imagery compensates for the lack of precision by its increase in vividness. Images are frequently clear and memorable. The simile of God as a drunk waking up from a long slumber (Ps. 78:65) is vivid and hard to forget because it is so striking. Images also speak directly to the heart. They are emotionally charged and often induce us to action of some sort or another. The image of God as shepherd as particularly expressed in Psalm 23 speaks to our heart and will as well as to our minds in a way that is impossible to paraphrase in prose.

Images also serve to bring our attention to old truths in new ways. Technically, this function of imagery and literature in general has been called distanciation or defamiliarization. For instance, the people of Israel may have become calloused to the prophet's message of coming judgment as a result of their sins, so Hosea preaches the old message of judgment through a series of gripping images in 13:3:

> *Therefore they will be like the morning mist,*
> * like the early dew that disappears,*
> * like chaff swirling from a threshing floor,*
> * like smoke escaping through a window.*

Jesus frequently taught by parables, a type of extended metaphor. He used parables to communicate ethical or theological principles.

Meter

Meter is common in the poetic traditions best known to us. Greek, Roman, English, and American poems, with some exceptions, have metrical structures. The modern student virtually equates poetic expression with meter. Scholars have thus long assumed that Hebrew poetry is metrical. The issue, then, has been not whether biblical poetry is metrical but what kind of meter it displays.

---

[20]Ryken, *The Bible as Literature*, p. 101.

Meter is best defined in relationship to rhythm. Rhythm is the unsystematic alternation of stressed and unstressed syllables. Prose and everyday speech are rhythmical. Meter differs from rhythm by being both regular and predictable. In other words, meter has a pattern. According to the literary critic P. Fussel, "Meter is what results when the natural rhythmical movements of colloquial speech are heightened, organized, and regulated so that pattern—which means repetition—emerges from the relative phonetic haphazard of ordinary utterance."[21]

Fussel also shows how meter generates meaning. Meter is not simply an ornament of language. He distinguishes three functions of meter. First, it triggers a reading strategy. Meter gives language an artificial air that signals to the reader that the text is poetry. Fussel likens the function of meter in literature to that of the picture frame around the painting of a landscape. The frame borders and separates the landscape from reality. Second, meter sets up a regular, repeated pattern. A departure from that pattern thus lends emphasis to the variant word or phrase. Finally, certain metrical patterns are sometimes associated with certain ideas or moods. Fussel cites the limerick as an example of a metrical form that is connected with a light-hearted mood. In biblical texts scholars have attempted to identify a certain metrical form (3-2 in an accentual schema) with laments, the so-called *qinah*.[22]

With reference to biblical poems, it can be said that, if the metrical pattern of Hebrew poems could be discerned, researchers would have a reliable tool to use in determining the original text of a poem. Indeed, for years scholars have been citing "metrical reasons" for the addition or omission of words and phrases from the poems. The critical apparatus of modern Hebrew texts is littered with the notation *metri causa* to justify textual emendations. Furthermore, if a metrical pattern could be discovered, it would be useful toward the discovery of the structure of the poems.

With all this benefit in discerning meter, it is disappointing to learn that no consensus has been reached on the metrical structure of biblical poetry. A great many systems have been proposed, but not one has won general acceptance. The two most popular approaches to meter are the older accentual meter and the newer syllable-counting meter.

The accentual approach to meter highlights the long syllables of words according to Masoretic accents. In the Masoretic accentual system, each word, regardless of its length, receives one stress (except for proclitics joined by the hyphen *maqqef*). In Hebrew the accent is usually on the last syllable. There is, however, great diversity in the way that the various practitioners of accentual meter apply their method. Such differences have to do partly with the use of different ancient traditions of accentuation as well as the subjectivity of assigning accents.

Syllable counting reckons the meter of Hebrew poems in analogy with the metrical systems of the French alexandrine and Japanese poetry.[23] As one reads biblical poetry, one is struck by the near equal length of cola. Often two cola of a line that are in parallel have an equal or very nearly equal number of syllables. Advocates of the

---

[21]P. Fussel, Jr., *Poetic Meter and Poetic Form* (New York: Random House, 1965), p. 5.

[22]See, for example, W. R. Garr, "The Qinah: A Study of Poetic Meter, Syntax, and Style," ZAW 95 (1983): 54–74.

[23]The most extensive description of the syllable-counting approach to meter is in D. Stuart, *Studies in Early Hebrew Meter* (Missoula, Mont.: Scholars, 1976).

syllable-counting approach to meter take this fact as evidence that the number of syllables is associated with the metrical pattern.

While these and other metrical schemas are popular and often encountered in commentaries, the tendency of scholars today is to be skeptical of meter. Some maintain that
the changes in the language have been such that we cannot detect the meter; others
believe that there is no such thing as meter in Hebrew poetry. There is no certain way to
decide whether meter is simply unknowable or nonexistent, but the result for practical
exegesis is the same in either case. At this point, meter plays simply no role in the exegesis of Hebrew poetry. Looking primarily at the poetic features of parallelism and
imagery, we turn now to consider five specific examples of biblical poetry.

seven

EXAMPLES
OF POETIC
ANALYSIS

I have selected parts of five poems for analysis to illustrate the poetic conventions described in chapter 6. The first is from the Torah (Exod. 15:1–5); the second, from wisdom literature (Song of Songs 5:10–16). The third selection is a short section of a psalm (51:3–6), while the fourth is an example of prophetic poetry (Mic. 4:2–5). The last example comes from the New Testament (Luke 1:46–55). These analyses are partial and suggestive. I point out primarily only the main conventions of biblical poetry—grammatical and semantic parallelism and imagery (terseness is self-evident).[1]

EXODUS 15:1–5: THE LORD IS A WARRIOR

Exodus 15 is, by general consent, one of the oldest poems in the Bible. As a hymn that praises the redemptive power of God, it is also one of the most memorable. The historical context of the Song of the Sea, as Exodus 15 is also called, is well known. The Israelites just narrowly escaped an angry Pharaoh and his troops. Moses and the Israelites have witnessed God's miraculous intervention, which resulted in their salvation and the judgment of their oppressors.

The poem opens:

I will sing to the LORD, for he is highly exalted.
He has thrown horse and its rider into the sea.

---

[1]In this chapter, some of the poetic structure does not follow the NIV but has been rearranged to express more clearly the structure of the original text.

English translations of these two lines often divide them into four cola in order to keep all of the song's cola roughly even in terms of length. Most of the bicola and tricola in Exodus 15 are indeed of very nearly equal length. Nevertheless there are a few long lines, often the initial line or two of a poem. They set the tone for the remainder of the hymn. Such is the function of the two long lines that begin Exodus 15.

The first clear bicolon follows:

> The LORD is my strength and song;
> He has become my salvation.

The second colon parallels the first colon in that the poet adds "salvation" as a third way in which the Lord relates to him. The sense of the line is that God is *x* and *y* to me; in addition, he is also *z* to me. The B colon sharpens the A colon in a second way as well. B is a climatic statement, explaining that the Lord is my strength and song because He is my salvation.

In the Hebrew, each colon in this line has six syllables. There are fewer words in the second colon, but the longer word for "salvation" replaces the two short words for "strength" and "song."

Equal syllable length is not a rigid rule in biblical poetry, which the next bicolon illustrates:

> He is my God, and I will praise him.
> My father's God, and I will exalt him.

In Hebrew, the first colon here has seven syllables, and the second has ten. This line is especially unusual in that the second colon is longer than the first. Nonetheless, the second colon functions normally in that it sharpens and carries forward the meaning of the A colon. The association of these two cola is also clear in their grammatical parallelism. First of all, ellipsis unites the two. A full reading of the B colon would begin, "He is (*zeh*) my father's God. . . ." Second, both cola begin with a noun phrase and an explicit mention of God, followed by a verbal clause. Both of the verbs are imperfect first-person singular with *waw* consecutive and also end with a third-person masculine suffix. These syntactic and morphological similarities bind the cola together and lead the reader to meditate on both cola in relationship with one another. Not only is He my God; He is also my father's God. Not only will I praise Him; I will also exalt Him. Both halves of the second line heighten the thought of the first.

The shortest line in the first five verses is also the most important:

> The LORD is a warrior;
> the LORD is his name.

This line explicitly states what the rest of poem describes and implies: God is a powerful warrior, or man of war. This metaphor informs the whole poem and also reverberates through Scripture from beginning to end. Here the image is stated tersely with a powerful effect upon the reader. God is identified as a warrior by way of praise and in reaction to His great redemptive act at the Red Sea.

The relationship between the two cola is not totally clear. Is it saying, "The Lord is a warrior—you heard right, the Lord"? Or perhaps Moses draws attention to the significance of the name Yahweh as it was explained to him at the burning bush (Exod. 3). "The Lord is a warrior—why are you surprised? He is, after all, the one who said, 'I am who I am.'"

The song then returns to meditate specifically on the great deed of God at the Red Sea. It is interesting that the first colon of this long line is similar in both meaning and syntax to the second opening monocolon (see above):

> *He has cast the chariots of Pharaoh and his army into the Red Sea.*
> *The choicest of his officers are drowned in the Red Sea.*

The meaning of these two long cola draw them into one line. Each colon is a similar reflection on a single event but is expressed in two different ways with a resultant progression. The intensification that the second colon provides is achieved primarily through stating the consequence of the action of the first colon. In other words, the chariots and armies of Pharaoh are cast into the sea *with the result* that they drowned.

The closing line of this opening section of the Song of the Sea is also a bicolon:

> *The deeps covered them;*
> *they went down into the depths like a stone.*

In a normal prose passage only one of these clauses would be necessary. The addition of the second colon serves to make the thought more vivid, especially since it includes a simile.

We can thus observe many of the conventions of Hebrew parallelism in this short section from a very early poem. I have reserved discussion of imagery to this point. While in some of the other examples in this chapter we encounter a number of local images (see especially the Song of Songs example), here we have a major metaphor that permeates the whole text but is expressed concisely in one line:

> *The LORD is a warrior;*
> *the LORD is his name.*

The metaphor is that drawn between God and a soldier. God has just won a great victory over a powerful human army. Moses therefore likens Him to a mighty soldier. The image is best labeled an affective metaphor, since the comparison is between the type of victory that a human soldier or army can provide and the one that God has just won over Egypt. The divine warrior is a pervasive image in the Scriptures. It is explicit from this point in biblical history until the time when Jesus Christ will return to wage war against the powers of evil (Rev. 19:11–21).[2]

SONG OF SONGS 5:10–16: THE BELOVED'S PRAISE TO HER LOVER

The Song of Solomon is a collection of loosely associated psalms extolling human love.[3] A common type of song encountered in the book is the hymn in which the man extols the physical beauty of the woman or vice versa. This particular subgenre of love poem has been labeled the *wasf*,[4] a name derived from a similar literary form in modern Arabic love poetry. The *wasf* is a metaphorical description of the body of the man or the woman that normally begins at the head and works down (4:1–7; 6:4–7; cf. the reverse

---

[2]T. Longman III, "The Divine Warrior: The New Testament Use of an Old Testament Motif," *WTJ* 44 (1982): 290–307, with relevant bibliography.

[3]M. Falk, *Love Lyrics from the Bible: A Translation and Literary Study of the Song of Songs* (Sheffield: Almond, 1982).

[4]M. Pope, *Song of Songs* (Anchor Bible 7C; Garden City, N.Y.: Doubleday, 1977), pp. 55–56.

order in 7:1–9). Of the four occurrences in the Song of Songs, the present example is the only one in which the woman describes the man.

The poem begins with a bicolon that commends the man's overall attractiveness.

> *My lover is radiant and ruddy,*
> *conspicuous among ten thousand.*

The first colon calls the lover "radiant" and "ruddy"; the second line further specifies his attributes as uncommon, that is, "conspicuous among ten thousand."[5] In this way, the second colon sharpens the first. In Kugel's terms, "My lover is radiant and ruddy—what's more, he is conspicuous among ten thousand!"

The following lines each describe one part of the man's physical appearance and vividly praise his beauty through a metaphor or a simile. This poem treats ten different parts of the man's body. The first line is a monocolon that compares the lover's head to "purest gold." We have already heard that he is ruddy, so the metaphor probably does not refer to the color of his complexion, say, to his golden tan. The primary point of contact is found in the high value of "pure gold." In other words, she prizes her lover above all else.

The second line is a bicolon that focuses on one aspect of the man's head, namely, his hair. "His hair is luxuriant," the woman lovingly says; even more (second colon), it is "black as a raven." The second colon thus adds a further loving description of the man's hair. The first line is literal language; the second is figurative, highlighting the deep blackness of the man's hair. The movement from literal to figurative is a pattern that Alter has noted as being common in biblical poetry.[6]

The next verse (v. 12) is a complex line that describes the man's eyes. The longer first line makes the parallelism unbalanced, and the metaphor is mixed.

> *His eyes are like doves by the water streams,*
> *washed in milk,*
> *mounted like jewels.*

Translations will often break the first colon into two to preserve a similar colon length. There are no substantive poetic reasons for the break, however, only the presumption that all lines must by definition be of near-equal length. We have seen this tendency in Hebrew poetry, but it is not a hard-and-fast rule.

The first colon gives an initial description of the man's eyes, followed by cola that give two further specifications. We need to be especially sensitive to cultural differences as we interpret the meaning of metaphors and other comparisons, including the images in these songs praising physical beauty. Cultures differ in their perception of what makes a body beautiful. Also, metaphorical expressions of that beauty change through time and from culture to culture. In Song of Songs 4:4, for instance, the woman's neck is likened to "the tower of David." Such a compliment would be greeted with contempt by most modern women, even if David's tower were culturally contextualized to a modern equivalent (e.g., the Empire State Building).

---

[5]In the following discussion I am much indebted to the philological work done by Pope in his *Song of Songs*, pp. 531–50.

[6]Alter, *The Art of Biblical Poetry*, p. 21.

The water streams of the simile refer to the moistness of the eyes as does the participle "washed" that begins the second colon. The point of comparison between doves and eyes is a little difficult, though not unique (see 4:1). Some scholars argue—improbably, I believe—that the man's eyes are compared with the eyes of the dove. Perhaps the delicateness of this bird, or more likely its color, is the point of the comparison. The pupils are likened to the sparkle and preciousness of jewels in the third colon, while in the second the poet captures the whiteness of the eyes with the reference to milk. One is tempted to carry the thought further by saying that the purity of milk suggests the additional dimension of purity or sincerity of character. As modern interpreters, however, we do not know whether milk carried that connotation at the time the Song of Songs was written.

While the previous parallel lines have been grounded on visual comparisons, the next two (v. 13) primarily appeal to the sense of smell. Both cheeks and lips are likened to highly fragrant substances.

The following three lines (vv. 14–15a) drop below the head and deal with the man's limbs and torso (arms, loins, and legs). Here the parallelism is again additive in the sense that the first colon provides one point of description, and the second adds a further specific description. The comparison is once again perceptual, in these cases both visual and tactile. The man's body is compared with beautiful, precious, and hardened substances.

The poem concludes (vv. 15b–16) with a second general description of the lover's overall appearance, followed by a description of his mouth. The mouth comes last in the description, an effective sequence since the woman obviously desires to kiss the man. The point of comparison is appropriately grounded in the sense of taste. His mouth is sweetness itself.

The semantic parallelism is supported by grammatical parallelism. There is both unity and diversity between the lines. In this text the basically similar syntactic pattern between the poetic lines is particularly striking. The first line invariably begins with a noun and suffix. After the initial first-person pronominal suffix on "my love" (v. 10), the pronoun is always "his." After the body part is named, it is then characterized by a noun phrase. The second colon of each of the lines begins with a participle. The participial clause is then completed by either a direct object or a prepositional phrase. Nonetheless, it is astounding that ten participial clauses are found in this short section. The only exceptions are the two monocola (vv. 11a and 16a) that lack any second colon and the description of the eyes (v. 12), which has two participial phrases.

The effect of such syntactic repetition might be monotonous, except that there is a significant amount of morphological variation. Considering only the participles that are the focus of repetition in the passage, we may observe variation between different types of participles including *qal* passive participles (vv. 10b, 16b), *qal* active participles that are feminine plural (vv. 11b, 12b, 12c, 13c), *pual* participles (vv. 14a, 14b, 15a), and a *piel* participle (v. 13b).

PSALM 51:3–6: A CONFESSION OF SIN

Psalm 51 is one of the best-known psalms in the Bible. Modern readers readily identify with its profound confession of sin and its appeal to God for forgiveness. The historical title situates the origin of the poem in the life of David, specifically after he is confronted by Nathan about his sin with Bathsheba (2 Sam. 12). The psalm surely played an important role in the life of the formal worship of God beyond this historical setting—and still does.

Formally, the psalm as a whole may be identified as a lament. Such psalms frequently begin with an invocation to the Lord and an appeal to Him for help. Laments may be subdivided further into those that contain a confession of sin and those that have a proclamation of innocence.[7] Psalm 51 fits into the former category. I have chosen the section containing the psalmist's confession of sin as an example of psalmic poetry.

The section begins:

> *For my transgressions I know;*
> *and my sin is before me continually.*

The parallelism between the two cola is firmly based on the common word pair "transgressions" and "sin." Variation occurs in the remainder of the cola. In colon A the psalmist admits awareness of his fault; in colon B, this thought is heightened by adding the temporal dimension. He is aware of his fault *all the time.*

In the next bicolon the psalmist shows that he is aware not only of his sin but of the fact that his sin is an affront to God himself:

> *Against you, you only, I have sinned;*
> *that which is evil in your eyes I have done.*

I have preserved the word order of the Hebrew in order to demonstrate the fact that poetic syntax is often quite different from the norm (which is defined according to the regular word order of prose). In the second colon the word order is direct object, prepositional phrase, and verb. This sequence is quite convoluted over against the typical prose pattern of verb, direct object, and prepositional phrase.

In the next poetic line the two verbs and the two prepositional phrases are clearly parallel to one another, even to the extent that both verbs are *qal,* imperfect, second-person singular.

> *So that you are righteous in your ways;*
> *you are pure in your judgments.*

In addition, both of the prepositional phrases begin with the preposition *b[c].* The intensification, however, that takes place between the two cola is that of a general statement leading to a specific one. Colon A asserts that the Lord is totally righteous in all that He does (the sense of the metaphor "way"), while the second colon focuses on God's judgments and declares that they are "pure."

Turning back to an assessment of himself, the psalmist confesses:

> *Indeed in sin I was brought to birth;*
> *and in sin my mother conceived me.*

The verse clearly indicates that the psalmist knows that he has been a sinner since his very beginning. The progress of meaning between the two cola is impossible to miss here. He

---

[7]See E. Gerstenberger, "Psalms," in *Old Testament Form Criticism* (San Antonio: Trinity University Press, 1974), p. 206.

admits to being a sinner at the time of his birth, and then he goes further in the second colon by confessing that his association with sin extends to the time of his conception.

He concludes:

Indeed truth you desire in the dark places;
and in the secret places you teach me wisdom.

Once again there is an obvious parallelism between the cola, with an additional binding by ending the first colon with a prepositional phrase that is both grammatically and semantically parallel with the opening prepositional phrase in colon B. The clearest progression may be seen in the verbs: in the first colon we have the desire of God stated, while in the second we learn that He is the one who teaches wisdom.

MICAH 4:2–5: THE FUTURE GLORY OF ZION

I have chosen a salvation oracle from Micah 4 as an example of prophetic poetry. A study of the whole oracle would require an analysis of the first verse, but I concentrate here on only the four verses that occur after the prose statement "many nations will come and say" (v. 2a).

The Book of Micah is an anthology of oracles that have a definite structure, but it is unnecessary to situate Micah 4 fully before we look at its poetic devices. It is of interest to observe, however, that this oracle that speaks of the future glorification of Zion follows immediately a particularly hard-hitting judgment oracle directed against Zion ("Zion will be plowed like a field" [3:12]).

The parallelism of this oracle is clear, being composed of ten neatly delineated bicola. The repetition in both meaning and grammar causes us to group them into separate bicola, while the subtle and not-so-subtle variations between the cola of a line develop the thought.

The opening line is a classic bicolon:

Come, let us go up to the mountain of the LORD;
to the God of Jacob's house.

The two lines are bound by ellipsis and by the repetition of the two prepositional phrases that begin with "to" (*'el*). The second line advances the meaning of the first by making the reference more specific. After all, the house of the Lord—the temple, of course—is located on His mountain, Zion. The nations wish to go to God's mountain to visit the temple. The variation in divine names is interesting. "Yahweh" in colon A is God's personal, covenant name, and "God of Jacob" identifies God as the one whom the patriarch worshiped. It is unwise to read too much into the variation. Certainly, in this case, the variation is partly for reasons of aesthetics. "God of Jacob" is a much longer phrase than "Yahweh," and so the prophet reaches for near-equal length of lines by supplying the long name for God in the second colon, which is missing the compound verb.

The next line is composed of two short cola that are nearly equal in length:

He will teach us his ways;
we will go in his paths.

The two clauses have a similar word order that binds them together. It is not obvious in the English translation, but both cola begin with a verb and then end with a prepositional phrase (the first colon is *midderākāw*, literally, "from his ways"). The other binding feature is the nearly synonymous meaning of "ways" (or "roads") and "paths." The second colon, though, obviously advances the thought of the first and is not simply saying the same thing twice. The relationship is one that often occurs in parallelism. Specifically, the second line shows the result of the action expressed in the first line. "He will teach us his ways" *with the result that* "we will go in his paths." Of course, "ways" and "paths" are a common metaphor in the Old Testament for guidance.

The next line contains two cola that are nearly synonymous. I have preserved the word order of the Hebrew and have shown the grammatical functions in order to expose the chiastic binding within the line.

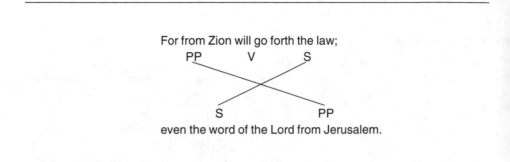

A chiasm is a crossing structure that may occur within a poetic line (occasionally also in prose), between two poetic lines, and even in much more elaborate structures. This line opens in colon A and closes in B with a prepositional phrase ("from"), and in the middle of the line the subjects appear ("the law" and "the word of the Lord"). This example is not simple chiasm because the verb that is elided in the second clause occurs in the middle of the first. While nearly synonymous, the second colon expands the thought of the first. "The law" (*tôrâh*) likely refers here to the first five books of Moses, while "the word of the Lord" may have a broader reference, perhaps including the prophets. Zion, of course, is the mountain of the Lord, located in Jerusalem. Jerusalem, the parallel to Zion, is the broader geographical area.

The next line is the longest one in the oracle, and the second colon is uncharacteristically longer than the first:

> He will judge between many peoples;
> he will settle quarrels for strong nations far away.

There is a clear parallelism here with the two verbs and the two prepositional phrases near in meaning to each other. The second line is longer because of the addition of modifiers. These modifiers (*ʿaṣumîm*, "strong"; *ʿad-rāḥôq*, "far away") provide more information to the thought of the first colon and in this way make the second colon more specific.

One of the most famous lines in Micah occurs next:

> They will beat their swords into plowshares;
> their spears into pruning hooks.

Once again the verb is elided in this verse. The two objects are both weapons, and the two prepositional phrases both mention agricultural implements. The mention of two weapons rather than one strengthens the impression that *all* weapons of war will be transformed into tools for the cultivation of the land, changing from tools of destruction into tools for cultivation.

The next line is not as clearly parallel as the immediately preceding examples:

Nation will not lift up sword against nation;
they will not even teach war.

Though there is not the kind of one-to-one relationship between words in this line, cola A and B are clearly related, and we may observe the typical intensification of thought that takes place between the cola. Not only will nations avoid active warfare (colon A); they will not even prepare for it (colon B).

The next line continues the theme of peace:

A man will sit under his vine,
and under his fig tree without fear.

The image evoked here is that of a man resting under a tree. It is a picture of peace and prosperity (see 1 Kings 4:25). The second colon both repeats the thought of the first and makes explicit that this resting is done devoid of fear.

A causal clause follows, and it is emphasized by being a monocolon in the middle of a number of bicola: "for the Lord of Hosts has spoken."

The concluding and climactic line is what has been traditionally described as an antithetical parallelism, a line that has two cola with contrasting perspective on the same idea:

For all the nations will walk in the name of their god;
we will walk in the name of the LORD our God forever and ever.

LUKE 1:46–55: THE MAGNIFICAT

The New Testament contains comparatively little poetry.[8] No single book is totally or even primarily poetic. We encounter only occasional, brief pieces of verse. Though rare, New Testament poetry is usually quite significant in its content. For example, the opening of the Gospel of Luke presents us with three important poems, the Magnificat of Mary (Luke 1:46–55), the Benedictus of Zechariah (vv. 68–79), and the Nunc Dimittis of Simeon (2:29–32). Paul occasionally interrupts the flow of his letters with an appropriate poetic hymn of praise (Phil. 2:6–11; Col. 1:15–20), and the Book of Revelation records poetic prayers and praise (e.g., 15:3–4).[9]

I analyze here the Magnificat.[10] Mary is visiting Elizabeth, the mother-to-be of John the Baptist, and in response to Elizabeth's greeting, Mary breaks out in a hymn of praise that bears close similarity to many hymns in the Old Testament, particularly to Hannah's song in 1 Samuel 2:1–10. The Magnificat is similar to Old Testament poems in both content and form. For instance, it displays the same type of parallelism that we have observed in various Old Testament passages.

---

[8]I thank my student Andrew Hwang for providing me with insights and bibliography on New Testament poetry in conjunction with a paper that he wrote on Philippians 2:6–11.

[9]See S. M. Baugh, "The Poetic Form of Col. 1:15–20," *WTJ* 47 (1985): 227–44.

[10]For previous analyses, see R. C. Tannehill, "The Magnificat as Poem," *JBL* 93 (1974): 263–75; and K. Bailey, "The Song of Mary," *Near East School of Theology Theological Review* 2 (1979): 29–35.

The opening line is an unmistakable bicolon:

My soul praises the Lord
my spirit exults in God, my Savior.

Here both syntax and semantics are parallel. In terms of grammar, both lines begin with a verb, continue with the subject (both followed by the first-person possessive), and then conclude with a direct object (colon A) or a prepositional phrase (colon B). Furthermore, the second line affirms and progresses beyond the thought of the first. It frequently has been noted that it is out of keeping with the conventions of parallelism to contrast "soul" and "spirit" as two separate entities within a person. On the other hand, B does not just repeat A. Leon Morris has indicated that "exult" in the second colon is a much more intense word than "praise"; in the Greek, the verbs also differ in tense.[11] Furthermore, Mary's expansion of "Lord" into "God, my Savior" both identifies one specific function of the Lord and also personalizes the reference.

The parallelism loosens in the immediately following lines. A rough connection may be posited between the next three clauses by virtue of their each being a causal clause. Like all hymns the Magnificat provides reasons for the praise offered to the Lord. In the Psalms such reasons are normally introduced by the causal "for" (*kî*). In these three clauses the English "for" translates *hoti* (first and third clauses) and *gar* (second clause).

For he has been mindful of the humble state of his servant,
for from now on all generations will call me blessed,
for the Mighty One has done great things for me.

The next two lines also are loose in their parallelism. Each meditates on a different attribute of God:

His name is holy
His mercy extends to those who fear him from generation to generation.

The next few lines delight in various actions that God has performed. The first colon gives a general description of those actions, followed by two that speak of His casting down the proud and the powerful. The third colon is antithetically parallel with the fourth, which contrasts God's humbling of the powerful with His exalting of the weak.

He has performed mighty deeds with his arm;
   he has scattered those who are proud in their inmost thoughts.
He has brought down rulers from their thrones,
   but has lifted the humble.

The next bicolon continues the thought of the last two cola and is in a chiastic relationship with them:

He has filled the hungry with good things
but has sent the rich away empty.

The last action of God is stated in verses 54–55:

---

[11]L. Morris, *The Gospel According to St. Luke* (Tyndale Commentary 3; Grand Rapids: Eerdmans, 1974), p. 76. The difference in verbs may reflect the common deviation between perfect and imperfect (*qtl/yqtl*) in Semitic poetry; see R. Buth, "Hebrew Poetic Tenses and the Magnificat," *JSNT* 21 (1984): 67–83.

> *He has helped his servant Israel, remembering to be merciful,*
> > *just as he said to our fathers,*
> > *to Abraham and to his descendants forever.*

The last two cola are obviously related to one another by ellipsis and by the fact that the second line specifies the thought of the first.

Epilogue

The literary approach is, as we have seen, not really a method alongside of other methods such as genre analysis or editorial analysis. Moreover, it is certainly not a paradigm shift, as some have claimed. Rather it is one perspective among many by which an interpreter views a text. Because the literary approach is one perspective among others, we must resist the suggestion by contemporary literary theory that we deny or downplay historical reference of the biblical text in the face of its literary artifice. The Bible as literature *or* history is a false dichotomy. It is both and much more.

The literary approach, however, highlights an extremely important function of biblical revelation. As we have had occasion to observe many times, the Bible is more like literature than nonliterature. For the most part, we encounter stories and poems in the Bible, not systematic theology, pure historical report, or journalism. Why does the Bible have this form? Why did not God reveal to us His mighty acts in history in the form of a *Cambridge Ancient History*? Or why is the Bible not in the form of a systematic theology?

The ultimate answer to such questions rests in God's wisdom. We can discern, however, two positive functions of the literary form of the Bible. The first falls under the rubric of defamiliarization or distanciation. These two labels identify a concept discussed by Russian formalists, who describe the function of art as "the renewal of perception, the seeing of the world suddenly in a new light, in a new and unforeseen way."[1] To cast truth in the form of a story leads the hearer or reader to pay closer attention to it, to be shocked to reconsider what otherwise might easily become a truism. A proverb is a good, focused example. Which communicates more powerfully, the simple imperative "speak righteously" or "the mouth of the righteous brings forth wisdom, but a perverse tongue will be cut out" (Prov. 10:31)? Which speaks more vividly, the bare command "love your neighbor as yourself!" or the story of the Good Samaritan (Luke 10:25–35)?

Second, literature appeals to the whole person. By its very nature, literature appeals not only to the intellect but also to one's will and emotions to a greater extent than, say, the Westminster Confession of Faith or Charles Hodge's *Systematic Theology*. We know and experience the power of stories and poems as children. Many, if not most, adults take less time to listen to well-told stories and striking poems.

We have recognized a tendency among some scholars to reduce the Bible to literature and to deny history. Other scholars, particularly those of us whose doctrine of Scripture is conservative, must resist the temptation to ignore the literary aspect of divine revelation by reducing the Scripture to history and theology. I have intended in this book to stimulate all of us to a more balanced reading of the Bible.

---

[1]Jameson, *The Prison-House of Language,* p. 52.

For Further Reading

A complete list of works cited may be found in the index of authors and titles. In this section I have selected contributions in English that should prove especially helpful as introductions to the major topics covered in this book.

A classic introduction to literary criticism is R. Wellek and A. Warren, *Theory of Literature,* 3d ed. (New York: Harcourt Brace Jovanovich, 1977). Balanced approaches to the study of prose literature may be found in W. Booth, *The Rhetoric of Fiction* (Chicago: University of Chicago Press, 1961); S. Chatman, *Story and Discourse* (Ithaca: Cornell University Press, 1978); and S. Rimmon-Kenan, *Narrative Fiction* (London: Methuen, 1983). A topically oriented handbook to literary criticism is M. H. Abrams, *A Glossary of Literary Terms,* 4th ed. (New York: Holt, Rinehart and Winston, 1981).

F. Lentricchia, *After the New Criticism* (London: Methuen, 1980) provides the best critical history of recent literary theory. For an excellent treatment of structuralism, consult J. Culler, *Structuralist Poetics* (Ithaca: Cornell University, 1975). For deconstruction, see J. Culler, *On Deconstruction: Theory and Criticism After Structuralism* (London: Routledge & Kegan Paul, 1982); and C. Norris, *Deconstruction: Theory and Practice* (London: Methuen, 1982).

Recently, literary critics have turned their attention to the Bible. The most notable example is R. Alter in his two books *The Art of Biblical Narrative* (New York: Basic Books, 1981) and *The Art of Biblical Poetry* (New York: Basic Books, 1985). M. Sternberg is an Israeli literary critic who has recently concentrated his skills on the Hebrew Bible. His book *The Poetics of Biblical Narrative* (Bloomington: Indiana University Press, 1985) is well worth reading, though it is verbose. F. Kermode deals with New Testament narrative in *The Genesis of Secrecy* (Cambridge, Mass.: Harvard University Press, 1979). Mention should also be made of two literary critics who hold to a conservative view of the Bible: C. S. Lewis, *Reflections on the Psalms* (Glasgow: Collins, 1961), and L. Ryken, *How to Read the Bible as Literature* (Grand Rapids: Zondervan, 1984) and *Windows to the World* (Grand Rapids: Zondervan, 1985).

Occasionally, biblical scholars analyze the use of literary theory in biblical studies. The most informative and well written is J. Barton, *Reading the Old Testament* (Philadelphia: Westminster, 1984).

Biblical scholars have produced a number of stimulating and well-written studies of particular sections of the Bible. It is in these studies that we find the best argument in favor of the literary approach to the Bible. Nonetheless, the reader must beware of the implicit or, occasionally, explicit denial of the historical function of the text. Good examples of the analysis of biblical prose include A. Berlin, *Poetics and Interpretation of Biblical Narrative* (Sheffield: Almond, 1983); C. Conroy, *Absalom Absalom! Narrative and Language in II Sam 13–20* (Rome: Biblical Institute Press, 1978); R. A. Culpepper, *Anatomy of the Fourth Gospel* (Philadelphia: Fortress, 1983); D. Gunn,

The Story of King David: Genre and Interpretation (*JSOT* Supp. 6; Sheffield: JSOT, 1978); idem., *The Fate of King Saul: An Interpretation of a Biblical Story* (*JSOT* Supp. 14; Sheffield: JSOT, 1980); and D. Rhoads and D. Michie, *Mark as Story: The Introduction to the Narrative as Gospel* (Philadelphia: Fortress, 1982).

Biblical scholars have made dramatic progress in reading biblical poetry within the last decade. The single most important book is J. Kugel, *The Idea of Biblical Poetry* (New Haven: Yale University Press, 1981). Alter's book on poetry mentioned above follows in Kugel's footsteps and provides some illuminating readings of particular biblical poems. A. Berlin, *The Dynamics of Biblical Parallelism* (Bloomington: Indiana University Press, 1985) is for those interested in the grammatical aspects of parallelism. W. G. E. Watson, *Classical Hebrew Poetry* (*JSOT* Supp. 26; Sheffield: JSOT, 1984) is a comprehensive handbook of biblical poetics.

GOD, LANGUAGE AND SCRIPTURE

Reading the Bible in the Light of General Linguistics

Moisés Silva

A Tía Mecha

Contents

Preface

One of the purposes of this book is to provide guidance in the use of the biblical languages. Unlike the other volumes in the Foundations of Contemporary Interpretation series, therefore, this one assumes some acquaintance with Greek and Hebrew. I should emphasize, however, that there is very little technical material here. Indeed, in the process of writing the book I found myself simplifying the subject matter more and more. Actual Greek and Hebrew scripts are used rarely, and the transliteration of Hebrew follows a very broad system (for example, no distinction is made on the basis of vowel "length"). Readers with any experience in consulting Bible commentaries should have little trouble following the argument even if they have not had formal training in the languages. (For the benefit of advanced readers, I have provided abundant bibliographical information in the footnotes.)

I have greatly enjoyed this opportunity to put down on paper ideas that had been brewing for more than two decades. Several generations of students, both at Westmont College and at Westminster Theological Seminary, have helped me develop those ideas. I am indebted to Richard J. Erickson (Fuller Theological Seminary) for serving as the formal reader of the manuscript. John Lübbe, Raymond B. Dillard, J. Alan Groves, and Vern S. Poythress, who also read a draft of the book, offered valuable suggestions and encouragement. I am also grateful to the administration and board of Westminster for granting me a study leave that made possible the production of the manuscript.

INTRODUCTION

*I*t is approximately the year 2790. The most powerful nation on earth occupies a large territory in Central Africa, and its citizens speak Swahili. The United States and other English-speaking countries have long ceased to exist, and much of the literature prior to 2012 (the year of the Great Conflagration) is not extant. Some archaeologists digging in the western regions of North America discover a short but well-preserved text that can confidently be dated to the last quarter of the twentieth century. It reads thus:

> Marilyn, tired of her glamorous image, embarked on a new project. She would now cultivate her mind, sharpen her verbal skills, pay attention to standards of etiquette. Most important of all, she would devote herself to charitable causes. Accordingly, she offered her services at the local hospital, which needed volunteers to cheer up terminal patients, many of whom had been in considerable pain for a long time. The weeks flew by. One day she was sitting at the cafeteria when her supervisor approached her and said: "I didn't see you yesterday. What were you doing?" "I painted my apartment; it was my day off," she responded.

The archaeologists know just enough English to realize that this fragment is a major literary find that deserves closer inspection, so they rush the piece to one of the finest philologists in their home country. This scholar dedicates his next sabbatical to a thorough study of the text and decides to publish an exegetical commentary on it, as follows:

> We are unable to determine whether this text is an excerpt from a novel or from a historical biography. Almost surely, however, it was produced in a religious context, as is evident from the use of such words as *devoted, offered, charitable*. In any case, this passage illustrates the literary power of twentieth-century English, a language full of wonderful metaphors. The verb *embarked* calls to mind an ocean liner leaving

for an adventuresome cruise, while *cultivate* possibly alerts the reader to Marilyn's botanical interests. In those days North Americans compared time to a bird—probably the eagle—that flies.

The author of this piece, moreover, makes clever use of word associations. For example, the term *glamorous* is etymologically related to *grammar*, a concept no doubt reflected in the comment about Marilyn's "verbal skills." Consider also the subtleties implied by the statement that "her supervisor approached her." The verb *approach* has a rich usage. It may indicate a similar appearance or condition (*this painting approaches the quality of a Picasso*); it may have a sexual innuendo (*the rapist approached his victim*); it may reflect subservience (*he approached his boss for a raise*). The cognate noun can be used in contexts of engineering (e.g., access to a bridge), sports (of a golf stroke following the drive from the tee), and even war (a trench that protects troops besieging a fortress).

Society in the twentieth century is greatly illumined by this text. The word *patient* (from *patience,* meaning "endurance") indicates that sick people then underwent a great deal of suffering: they *endured* not only the affliction of their physical illness, but also the mediocre skills of their medical doctors, and even (to judge from other contemporary documents) the burden of increasing financial costs.

A few syntactical notes may be of interest to language students. The preposition *of* had different uses: causal (*tired of*), superlative (*most important of all*), and partitive (*many of whom*). The simple past tense had several aoristic functions: *embarked* clearly implies determination, while *offered* suggests Marilyn's once-for-all, definitive intention. Quite noticeable is the tense variation at the end of the text. The supervisor in his question uses the imperfect tense, "were doing," perhaps suggesting monotony, slowness, or even laziness. Offended, Marilyn retorts with a punctiliar and emphatic aorist, "I painted."

Readers of Bible commentaries, as well as listeners of sermons, will recognize that my caricature is only mildly outrageous. What is wrong with such a commentary? It is not precisely that the "facts" are wrong (though even these are expressed in a way that misleads the reader). Nor is it sufficient to say that our imaginary scholar has taken things too far. There is a more fundamental error here: a misconception of how language normally works.

Our familiarity with the English language helps us see quite clearly that any "exegesis" such as the one I have just made up is, in the first place, an *overinterpretation* of the passage. Except perhaps in certain poetic contexts, we do not use words and grammatical functions as suggested by those comments. Of course, none of us—not even the finest scholar—can acquire the same familiarity with biblical Hebrew and New Testament Greek that we have with our native, living tongue. Consequently, it is a little easier to read alien concepts into an ancient text and sound quite scholarly as we do it. And if the text in question was written by a great classical author, we are even more readily disposed to assume that it contains great richness of meaning.

The problem intensifies when we deal with Scripture. Surely an inspired text must be full of meaning: we can hardly think that so much as a single word in the Bible is insignificant or dispensable. True enough. But we must never forget that God has spoken to us in the language of the people. Much of what passes for biblical interpretation, whether in books or sermons, implies that God has used an artificial, coded, or even esoteric language. Ironically, not a few examples of "grammatico-historical exegesis" suggest that the Bible is as distant from common believers as it was assumed by the proponents of the allegorical method. We must recall this basic principle: the richness and divine origin of the biblical *message* are not compromised by the naturalness and simplicity of the *form* in which God has chosen to communicate to us.

In addition to overinterpreting the passage, however, our whimsical commentary above is deficient at a more important level: it contributes virtually nothing to the reader's understanding of what the passage actually says! A simple translation into twenty-eighth-century Swahili would have conveyed far more accurately and efficiently the point of the text. Similarly, clear English versions of the Bible communicate to the modern reader the main (and therefore most important) point of any passage without recourse to obscure points of grammar.

Preachers who make appeals to "the original" may in some cases help their readers obtain a better insight into Scripture. More often than not, however, such appeals serve one of two functions: (1) they merely furnish illustrations to heighten interest so that hearers *think* they have a better understanding of the passage (cf. the comment on *embark* above); (2) they provide the occasion to make a point that has little to do with the passage (cf. the comment on *patient*).

In a Christian newspaper addressed specifically to preachers, the author of a column entitled "Gems from the Greek New Testament" focused on the noun *analysis* in 2 Timothy 4:6 ("the time of my *departure* is at hand"):

> The word which Paul chose to express his departure . . . from which our word *analysis* originates, is very unique and picturesque. . . . The beauty of this word is seen in the words from which it is formed: *ana* and *lusis*. The root of this word, *lusis*, was used extensively as a legal term to designate release from a binding obligation. An illustration of this is found in the release from a loan in a document dated 101 A.D. [The author proceeds to describe and quote the document.] As this example clearly illustrates, *lusis* indicates the release from a binding contract because the obligations of that contract were fulfilled. Another example of this meaning is found in the New Testament. In dealing with marriage, Paul writes, "Art thou bound to a wife? seek not to be loosed," *lusis* (I Cor. 7:27). Again, the idea expressed is the release from a legal obligation.
>
> The preposition *ana*, which is attached to *lusis*, expresses the basic meaning of up. Even when it is attached to a word written in composition, it retains the idea of the direction up. . . . Examine this word within the context of Paul's usage. Paul was viewing his death as a release upward from his binding contract. The contract was the work which he was called to do. Furthermore, he was entitled to this release because he had fulfilled the obligations of the contract. . . . What a beautiful way to view death! The release from our binding, contractual obligations to God as a child of God. Most of us look forward to the day when the mortgage on our house is paid off. Should not we also look forward to the day when God releases us from our obligation to Him through death?[1]

---

[1] This material appeared in *Pulpit Helps* 10, no. 12 (Sept. 1985): 1. One could just as easily focus on another meaning of the noun *solution* and argue that Paul has in mind the final resolution of all our earthly problems. The figurative meaning "to depart" for the cognate verb, *analyō*, probably arose from the nautical usage, "loose from moorings, weigh anchor." Someone may want to suggest that perhaps what Paul really intended was the picturesque notion of "sailing into the sunset"! Neither of these two suggestions is less probable than the meaning "release upward from a binding contract."

Certain kinds of commentaries often fall into the same trap. But even the better ones may convey, by their excessive attention to linguistic detail, a false impression of the nature of language and thus fail to explain what the biblical author was actually seeking to communicate. I am not suggesting, of course, that detailed linguistic analysis of a text is in itself harmful or irrelevant. Indeed, much of this book is devoted to helping readers in that very task. But every facet of interpretation must be kept in proper perspective, and the more we know about the nature of language, the more likely we are to "handle correctly the word of God" (2 Tim. 2:15).

Unfortunately, language is one of those fields of study—like psychology—where experts abound. The reason is simple. All of us are continually exposed to human behavior (our own no less than that of others), of which language is one form. Inevitably, and often unconsciously, we form judgments about behavior on the basis of our daily experience.

The cynics among my readers may well be thinking, "Yes, and the narrower the scope of that experience, the more dogmatic are those judgments likely to be!" Naturally, if we notice a certain type of behavior more than once (or only once, for that matter), we do tend to generalize, to infer a rule or principle from that observation. It seldom occurs to us that, even if we have led an unusually rich life, our casual personal observations represent but a *minuscule* ("statistically insignificant") sample of a *haphazard* cross-section of human society.

But personal experience is a very powerful emotional factor that will stand up against reams of contrary evidence, as anyone who has tried to debunk "old wives' tales" must have found out. And the phenomenon of language, for some reason or another, can elicit very profound emotions indeed. People who write books on language, therefore, must be singularly ingenuous or have very little regard for their longevity. In either case, they deserve pity.

Also to be pitied, of course, are people who write books on biblical interpretation—perhaps the only subject that draws an even more passionate response than linguistic judgments. And so I have gleefully decided to write a book on the significance of language for biblical interpretation. Only if I have succeeded in drawing out your deepest sympathy, my reader, do I invite you to read on.

Just as responsible psychologists seek to avoid the shortcomings of personal observation by means of intensive and systematic research, usually supplemented by independent work done in the broader community of scholars, so it is with linguists. I use the term *linguist* not in its popular sense, "someone who knows many languages" (the more precise, though admittedly cacophonous, term *polyglot* better fills that slot), but in the professional sense. A linguist is not necessarily proficient in many languages, though a wide familiarity with linguistic groups certainly helps.[2]

The discipline of linguistics is often referred to as *modern linguistics* to indicate its relatively recent development. This fact may seem surprising, since language study can be traced back to the ancient world, but here precisely lies an important clue to what linguists do. While many of the ancient concerns still come under the purview of linguistics, a series of distinctive emphases set the modern discipline apart from the earlier periods. Another clue lies in the label *linguistic science*: it was not until the last decades of the nineteenth century

---

[2]It is even conceivable (though in practice not very likely) that someone who has difficulties acquiring fluency in a foreign language could become fairly competent in various forms of linguistic research.

that linguists were prepared to make claims of a scientific character (though there are some significant differences between twentieth-century linguists and even their immediate predecessors, as we will see).

Most helpful of all, however, is the term *general linguistics* (more or less synonymous with *modern linguistics*). In contrast to scholars who devote their lives to the study of a specific language, such as French grammar and literature, linguists pay primary attention to the understanding of languages generally. They too may, of course, have a special interest in French, but they will probably have gained some expertise in at least one language family not closely related to French. They will use their knowledge of a specific language to enhance their understanding of *language* as such; conversely, they may apply that general understanding to the study of a specific tongue.

What all this means for us is that the systematic data accumulated by linguists over many years can correct our personal, hit-or-miss impressions. God has in his wisdom spoken to us in the Bible through human languages (Hebrew, Aramaic, and Greek). If we ignore the character of human language, we will likely misunderstand Scripture. All languages make heavy use of imagery, for example. Forget that fact, and you will decide that David was not a person but a lamb ("The Lord is my shepherd"). But not every feature of language is so immediately obvious. This is where linguistics comes in.

two
BIBLICAL
PERSPECTIVES
ON LANGUAGE

*B*efore seeking to apply linguistic principles to biblical hermeneutics, we must attend to a major question: What does the Bible itself have to say about language? Surely anyone committed to the authority of Scripture will want an answer. After all, we cannot expect to solve differences of opinion about details without a broad, coherent framework. In other words, we require a foundational, conceptual context if we hope to evaluate linguistic theories and methods responsibly. But such a framework or meaningful context is beyond our reach unless we take God's revelation into account.[1]

Moreover, the need for reflection on this issue is magnified by some apparent conflicts between the Bible and modern linguistics. What are the origins of human language? How did linguistic variation develop? Is oral communication of greater significance than

---

[1]Not every Christian will agree with such an approach. My own views on this question have been influenced by Abraham Kuyper's discussion in a chapter entitled "The Twofold Development of Science," in *Principles of Sacred Theology* (Grand Rapids: Eerdmans, 1954; orig. 1898), § 48–51. Cf. also Cornelius Van Til, *A Christian Theory of Knowledge* (Phillipsburg, N. J.: Presbyterian and Reformed, 1969), pp. 36–37: "The facts of the universe in general may either be regarded in the light of the system of truth presented in Scripture or they may be seen in the light of some other system of truth that men think they possess. . . . In every discussion about every fact, therefore, it is the two principles, that of the believer in Scripture and that of the non-Christian, that stand over against one another. Both principles are totalitarian. Both claim all the facts. It is in the light of this point that the relation of the Bible as the infallible Word of God to the 'facts' of science and history must finally be understood." I hasten to add, however, that even Christians who belong to a different theological tradition have more and more acknowledged the importance of subjecting every area of knowledge to the truths of Scripture. Witness in particular the growing number of Christian colleges that have sought to integrate their curriculum on the basis of the evangelical faith.

written literature? Is there such a thing as a standard of linguistic "correctness"? It may well be, of course, that the Bible will not give us the kind of information we are looking for. Certainly we should not expect the Scriptures to provide a complete and well-defined philosophical framework for every intellectual discipline. On the other hand, the effort must be made to discover whether God has revealed basic principles that are applicable to our understanding of what language is and how it works.

LANGUAGE AND CREATION

In fact, Scripture has a great deal to say on the subject. We no sooner begin reading in Genesis than we are faced by the statement that "God said . . . ." It is a startling expression, since God does not have a physical body—and even if he did, why should speech have anything to do with the creation of the world? The ancient rabbis were not far from the truth when they suggested that this form of expression was intended to emphasize God's power: "The artist—he can make nothing at all except by hard work; but the Holy One, blessed be He—He makes things by the mere breath of a word."[2] God does not need to plan and prepare, to organize a labor force, to toil for an extended period of time. God needs only to utter the word, and it is done: "Let them praise the name of the Lord, for he commanded and they were created" (Ps. 148:5).

We may wish to reflect further, however, on why this particular expression was used. Why not represent God as simply waving his hand, for example? Surely it is to call attention not only to God's power but specifically the power that is attached to his *word*. From the very beginning of the biblical narrative the power of God's word is impressed on the reader. The theme will recur often and at critical junctures in the succeeding biblical revelation. Moreover, it has often been noted that just as God exercises his divine sovereignty by his speaking (and by his naming [Gen. 1:5, 8]), so also Adam is represented as fulfilling God's mandate by naming the animals (Gen. 2:20). The connection between divine and human speech calls for careful thought, since it is part of the larger question about the creation of man, male and female, as the image of God. What is this image?

The extensive and heated theological debates that have arisen in answer to that question can be rather intimidating. Much of the discussion has been vitiated, however, by the tendency to phrase the question thus: What is the image of God *in* man? The Scriptures do not use that precise expression.[3] This concern may appear trivial or hair-splitting, yet

---

[2]*Midrash Tehillim* 18:26, from William G. Braude, trans., *The Midrash on Psalms*, 2 vols. (Yale Judaica Series 13; New Haven: Yale University Press, 1959), 1:257. In both Jewish and Samaritan thought, incidentally, one finds an association between the divine name, *YHWH,* and the creative word, *yehi,* "let there be." See Jarl E. Fossum, *The Name of God and the Angel of the Lord: Samaritan and Jewish Concepts of Intermediation and the Origin of Gnosticism* (WUNT 36; Tübingen: J. C. B. Mohr, 1985), pp. 76–84.

[3]I am indebted to my former teacher Norman Shepherd for help in clarifying this issue. (The subsequent comments on anthropomorphism also owe much to his lectures.) Claus Westermann, in *Genesis 1–11: A Commentary* (Minneapolis: Augsburg, 1984), p. 157, makes the valid point that the passage is concerned with "the nature of the act of creation which enables an event to take place between God and humans"; he creates a false dichotomy, however, when he deduces that the text is *not* concerned with the nature of human beings. A recent and helpful work on this topic is Philip Edgcumbe Hughes, *The True Image: The Origin and Destiny of Man in Christ* (Grand Rapids: Eerdmans and Leicester: Inter-Varsity, 1989), especially chaps. 1–2; note also the comprehensive volume by G. C. Berkouwer, *Man as the Image of God* (Grand Rapids: Eerdmans, 1962), and the fine article by D. J. A. Clines, "The Image of God in Man," *Tyndale Bulletin* 19 (1968): 53–103. For the history of interpretation see A.-G. Hamman, *L' homme, image de Dieu. Essai d'une anthropologie chrétienne dans l'église des cinq premiers siècles* (Relais-études 2; Paris: Desclée,

the failure to ask the right question can be very misleading. As long as students try to identify the image of God *in* human beings, they will look for some entity (the soul? the spirit?) or quality (immortality? ability to worship?). But the text of Genesis does not encourage us to look for some specific item. Man *as a whole*, male and female, is described as being made in God's image.

It is perhaps an exaggeration, but not by much, to say that *every* aspect of human beings is a reflection of the divine image. More to the point, the total complex of those aspects is what constitutes the image. Our emotions, to be sure, have been corrupted by sin, but even such "negative" features as anger and jealousy derive originally from holy divine qualities. And although God does not possess a physical body, our bodies too reflect certain aspects of who God is.

> *Take heed, you senseless ones among the people;*
> *   you fools, when will you become wise?*
> *Does he who implanted the ear not hear?*
> *Does he who formed the eye not see?*

These rhetorical questions from Psalm 94:8–9 are striking in several respects. At the very least, they throw light on biblical *anthropomorphisms* (figurative descriptions that attribute human characteristics to God). The notion that God thereby accommodates to our imperfect human understanding contains an element of truth, to be sure, but perhaps we are approaching the issue from the wrong end. Our use of this term reflects our human-centered perspective. Indeed, it is not altogether far-fetched to say that descriptions of what *we* are and do should be termed "theomorphisms"![4] In other words, it is not as though God looks at our existence and searches for some quality that will illustrate in simple language who God is. Rather, our human qualities are themselves but a reflection of God's person and attributes. And so the tables must be turned. With regard to God's speech in particular, the real question is not "How can God speak (since he does not have a body)?" but "How can *we* speak?" The answer to this is: We are made in the image of a God who speaks.[5]

We conclude, then, that when Genesis tells us that God created Adam and Eve "in his own image," the focus is not on some specific quality but on human beings in their totality. We can hardly refrain from asking, however, whether certain human characteristics, more than others, are indicative of this truth. After all, animals too have eyes and ears. Just how are we different from animals? Many legitimate answers could be given, such as in our ability to walk erect, to use tools, to commune with God. But if we are interested in what the author of Genesis had in mind, we should inquire whether the context gives us any clues.

1987), and Gunnlaugur A. Jónsson, *The Image of God: Genesis 1:26–28 in a Century of Old Testament Research* (CB OT Series 26; [Lund:] Almqvists & Wiksell International, 1988).

[4]This term can be misleading, however, especially if it suggests that the humanlike descriptions of God should be taken literally rather than metaphorically. Hughes rightly argues against this conception (*The True Image*, p. 12).

[5]This line of thought, incidentally, can and should be carried in other directions. For example, Geerhardus Vos argued persuasively that Jesus' parables, insofar as they appeal to nature, should not be considered mere illustrations used because they are convenient and simple to understand. Rather, we may say that spiritual truths are built into the very structure of the world God has created. See Vos' *Biblical Theology: Old and New Testaments* (Grand Rapids: Eerdmans, 1948), p. 380.

Indeed it does, for Genesis 1:26 explicitly connects the concept of image with that of dominion: "Let us make man in our image, in our likeness, *and let them rule* . . . ." We probably should not infer, as some have done, that image simply equals dominion. The connection between the two concepts appears to be rather that the one serves as the basis for the other.[6] God made Adam and Eve like him and so they are able to exercise dominion over the earth. Of course, insofar as they do exercise that dominion they may be regarded as vice-regents under God, so that their ruling function too derives from, *and is like,* God's reign over his creation. Just as God created the world (chap. 1), so Adam tills the land (2:15). Thus one clear respect in which human beings are different from animals is that humans cultivate the ground. And agriculture may certainly be viewed as but one specific expression of a much broader set of activities (all work in general, cultural functions, etc.) that reflect the rule of Adam and Eve and their descendants.

But there is more. As indicated earlier, Genesis 1–2 focuses on one specific analogy between God and Adam: both of them speak and both use speech to exercise rule. The biblical text, then, encourages us to view language as a distinctive human quality, as a particularly clear manifestation of the divine image. The fact is that we talk . . . and talk and talk incessantly. And as we look around at creation we find that we are the only ones that do![7]

Not surprisingly, scholars from a wide variety of perspectives have commented on the uniqueness of language. Ray Past, for example, remarks that "whatever the theologians may have to say, the most *obvious* thing distinguishing men and women from what we like to call lower forms of life is *speech.*" The well-known sociobiologist Edward O. Wilson, from a non-Christian, evolutionist perspective, argues as follows: "All of man's unique social behavior pivots on his use of language, which is itself unique. . . . The development of human speech represents a quantum jump in evolution comparable to the assembly of

---

[6]Cf. Franz Delitzsch, *A New Commentary on Genesis,* 2 vols. (Edinburgh: T. & T. Clark, 1899), 1:100: the rule promised is not a reference to the content of the image "but its consequence, or, as Frank thinks it better to express it . . . not its nature, but the manifestation of that nature." This interpretation can be supported, though not conclusively proved, from the grammar: the word and translates the so-called "weak waw," which is often used after cohortatives to indicate purpose. Cf. Gordon J. Wenham, Genesis 1–15 (WBC 1; Waco, Tex.: Word, 1987), p. 4, with reference to GKC §109f. Note also S. R. Driver, *A Treatise on the Use of the Tenses in Hebrew,* 3d ed. (Oxford: Clarendon, 1969; orig. 1912), chap. 5, and most recently Bruce K. Waltke and M. O'Connor, *An Introduction to Biblical Hebrew Syntax* (Winona Lake, Ind.: Eisenbrauns, 1990) §39.2.5.

[7]This is not to deny that communication of one sort or another goes on among animals. Nor do I wish to contest the claim that chimpanzees, for example, can be taught to use some elementary forms of communication that resemble human language. But the most successful experiments to date serve, if anything, to emphasize the enormous difference between the "language" of the most intelligent animals—even after extensive training—and the linguistic competence of even a three-year old human being. Note the fine synthesis by Richard A. Demers, "Linguistics and Animal Communication," *LTCS* 3:314–35, especially p. 333: "Recent research has certainly shown that the primates have communication systems which are more elaborate than was assumed earlier. What all nonhuman communication systems lack, however, is the unboundedness in scope that is the central feature of human language. The structural properties of the cotton-top tamarin's . . . appear to be similar to the lower levels of the structural properties of human language. . . . At the level of both word and phrase, however, human language achieves an openness and productivity totally beyond the capability of any nonhuman communication system." (For a more positive, but still cautious, evaluation in the same volume, see William Orr Dingwall, "The Evolution of Human Communicative Behavior," *LTCS* 3:274–313, especially pp. 289–90.) At any rate, the main and rather simple point that I wish to make is that speech is obviously *not* something that characterizes the animal world.

the eucaryotic cell." And Noam Chomsky, arguably the most influential linguist of our generation, puts it this way: "When we study human language, we are approaching what some might call the 'human essence,' the distinctive qualities of mind that are, so far as we know, unique to man."[8]

Chomsky's remark, in particular, calls attention to the highly debated issue concerning the relation between language and thought. Is thought possible without language? The answer, of course, depends largely on how we define thought. No doubt in some sense even dogs and cats "think," if all we have in view is a set of mental processes (such as recognition) related to the animals' behavior. Again, we may want to argue that babies, before they learn to speak, engage in some form of thought.

Normally, however, we use the term *thought* to indicate a rational capacity characteristic of older children and adults—and this kind of thinking always appears to function alongside language. (Deafness and muteness, incidentally, do not prevent the development of linguistic skills. Sign language, for example, is indeed a language.) The question whether thought is possible without language is theoretically interesting, but it has little practical relevance. As far as we can tell, all of the thinking that in fact goes on is inextricably tied to linguistic competence.

Adam's naming the animals, therefore, is not a mere historical curiosity, nor does it reflect some kind of primitive mythology. The point is that Adam cannot rule the earth unless he understands it, that his understanding is bound to the need for ordering what he sees, and that such ordering takes place through language.[9] While we should avoid extreme claims, such as the view that we create the world with our language,[10] most of us underestimate the power of language to bring order to our minds. The toddler's constant "What is that?" is more than childish curiosity. Similarly, the amateur collector of butterflies and the lover of classical music—indeed anyone interested in anything—will feel that they have failed to master their field unless they have names for everything.

In sum, the biblical narrative presents human language not precisely as a gift created by God for Adam but as a powerful attribute that is (1) intrinsic to God's own being and activity, (2) clear evidence of the fact that Adam and Eve were distinctive creatures made in God's image, and (3) inseparable from the mandate to Adam and Eve to rule creation.

---

[8]Ray Past, *Language as a Lively Art* (Dubuque, Iowa: William C. Brown, 1970), p. 1. Edward O. Wilson, *Sociobiology: The New Synthesis* (Cambridge, Mass.: Belknap, 1975), pp. 555–56. Noam Chomsky, *Language and Mind,* enlarged ed. (New York: Harcourt Brace Jovanovich, 1972), p. 1.

[9]For the view that naming in the Bible is little more than an act of discernment, see George W. Ramsey, "Is Name-Giving an Act of Domination in Genesis 2:23 and Elsewhere?" *CBQ* 50 (1988): 24–35. Much of Ramsey's material is valuable, but are we to say that God's own naming (1:5, 8) simply reflects God's discernment?

[10]It is often difficult to determine whether writers who make those claims are using only figurative expressions. At least some of them appear to mean what they say quite literally (and certainly the Kantian doctrine of reason is no mere metaphor). Linguists, psychologists, anthropologists, and philosophers continue to debate to what extent our thought is bound by our language. Although we can hardly doubt that our language *predisposes* us to think in certain ways, no one has been able to prove that we are unable to overcome the resultant limitations. For an up-to-date and insightful survey of the debate on linguistic determinism/relativity, see Jane H. Hill, "Language, Culture, and World View," *LTCS* 4:14–36.

LANGUAGE AND SIN

The entrance of sin into the world immediately affected the role for which Adam and Eve were created. They continued to bear the image of their Creator, but not with the same glory. Their rule over creation now involved frustration and pain. Language was now used to evade responsibility (Gen. 3:12–13), to aid murder (4:6), and to challenge God's sovereignty (4:23–24). Some of the effects of sin on human speech deserve special attention.

The Confusion of Tongues

The story of the Tower of Babel (Gen. 11:1–9) stands as one of the most carefully crafted pieces of narrative in the Book of Genesis.[11] The passage naturally divides into two balanced sections, the first announcing what man proposed (vv. 1–4), the second declaring what God disposed (vv. 5–9). The contrast between the two sections is heightened by mockery. In place of stone and mortar, fragile brick with tar was used by these wicked and foolish people (v. 3). Their summons, "Come, let us build" (v. 4), is echoed in God's response, "Come, let us go down" (v. 7). They desired a great name, but the name their city received—which sounds like the Hebrew word for "confusion," *babel*— was laughable. Their grand purpose was protection lest they be scattered over the earth, yet "the Lord scattered them over the face of the whole earth" (vv. 8–9). An Israelite listening to the story would have smiled with amusement from the very point where the wicked men begin to speak, since the choice of words with a high frequency of the consonants *b* and *l* (*habba nilbenah lebanim*, "Come, let's make bricks" [v. 3]) anticipates the end of their designs.

But what is the point of the story? Is this one among the similar myths in a variety of ancient cultures intended to explain the origin of linguistic diversity?[12]

When we consider how much the Book of Genesis does *not* tell us about the origin and development of civilization, it seems doubtful that this passage was written for the purpose of satisfying historical curiosity. In any case, we can demonstrate that over the course of time languages will naturally diversify (perhaps the clearest example is the development of the Romance languages, such as French and Spanish, from Latin), so this passage cannot explain every instance of language variation. It may well be that such an event as is described here could account for the origin of language *families* (such as the difference between the Indo-European family and the Afro-Asiatic family) and that a memory of the event is reflected in similar stories around the world. But the truth is that we do not have enough information to establish a clear correspondence between the event described in this passage and what we know of prehistoric language development. Moreover, we should not assume that language diversity *as such* is necessarily a bad thing or a reflection of God's curse.

Let us bear in mind that this passage serves as a backdrop to the call of Abraham. The Genesis narrative never loses sight of God's intention to save mankind (3:16). Some

---

[11]For much of what follows I am indebted to Umberto Cassuto's remarkable work, *A Commentary on the Book of Genesis,* 2 vols. (Jerusalem: Magnes, 1961–64, orig. 1944–49), 2:225–49.

[12]It is commonplace for modern commentators to refer to this passage as *etiological* in character, that is, motivated by a desire to elucidate the causes of present realities. Cf. Westermann, *Genesis 1–11*, pp. 534–35, 553–54.

have argued that even the expulsion of Adam and Eve from the Garden of Eden was intended not only as a punishment but also as a means of aiding God's redemptive purposes.[13] Certainly the Flood, colossal as it was in its retributive power, preserved mankind from the total extinction toward which it was headed through sin. Similarly, when God says in 11:6, "If as one people speaking the same language they have begun to do this, then nothing they plan to do will be impossible for them," we may infer that the judgment on the tower and its builders was not void of grace. Indeed, the scattering of people over the face of the earth restrains them from fulfilling their evil intents.[14] Henceforth God focuses his redemptive work on Abraham and his descendants, but the patriarch is told that the divine purposes are universal: ". . . and *all the peoples* on earth will be blessed through you" (12:3).

Evil Speech

The confusion resulting from the destruction of Babel implies more than our inability to understand languages foreign to us. That inability, no doubt, has often led to serious quarrels among nations and ethnic groups. But the multiplicity of languages throughout the world is perhaps only the reflection of a more fundamental discordant streak in humanity. After all, nations that speak the same language have hardly been invulnerable to the horrors of war! Without minimizing the role played by *substantive* differences of opinion among people, one must wonder how often we delude ourselves into thinking that our disputes have vital significance when in fact we have only failed to communicate clearly.[15]

It is difficult to say whether Genesis 11 alludes to this more general problem of human misunderstanding. Certainly there is nothing in the passage that appears to address the issue directly. I find it improbable, however, that a Hebrew audience, familiar with the rest of the Old Testament, would fail to link this story with the numerous scriptural warnings about the evils of the tongue.

Foremost among them are the severe commandments against harming our neighbor through deceitful words. Not only does the ninth commandment forbid giving false witness against our neighbors (Exod. 20:16); other passages in the Pentateuch also emphasize and expand on this prohibition. "Do not spread false reports. Do not help a wicked man by being a malicious witness. . . . Have nothing to do with a false charge" (23:1, 7). The code in Leviticus 19 includes the following: "Do not lie. Do not deceive

---

[13]Although it is somewhat speculative, the point is that Adam and Eve, if allowed to eat of the tree of life in their state of disobedience, would have been *confirmed* for ever in that state and thus would have placed themselves outside the possibility of salvation.

[14]Cf. Westermann, *Genesis 1–11*, p. 551: success in building the tower "must lead to the absolute autonomy of humankind. Hence the limitation which belongs to their created state would be called into question. . . . Humanity exists only in its state as creature; so its continuation is endangered by the threat of autonomy."

[15]Some decades ago, concern for the way in which the misuse of language harms human relationships led to the development of a movement known as General Semantics, made especially popular by S. I. Hayakawa et al., *Language in Thought and Action*, 4th ed. (New York: Harcourt Brace Jovanovich, 1978). Although it may be overly optimistic to think that defining our terms clearly is the key to solving many of our social and international problems, it seems undeniable that language manipulation—whether conscious or unconscious—and lack of proper communication (resulting from blindness to the other person's point of view) are prime sources of human conflict.

one another. . . . Do not curse the deaf. . . . Do not go about spreading slander among your people" (vv. 11, 14, 16). If a malicious witness is proven to have lied, "giving false testimony against his brother, then [the community must] do to him as he intended to do to his brother. You must purge the evil from among you" (Deut. 18:18–19).

Behind these strong precepts is the conviction that there is real power in speech.[16] Naïve Jack may have thought that words couldn't hurt him, but the wisdom teachers of Israel viewed slander and verbal abuse as far more damaging than sticks and stones. "With his mouth the godless destroys his neighbor"; "Reckless words pierce like a sword"; "Like a club or a sword or a sharp arrow is the man who gives false testimony against his neighbor" (Prov. 11:9; 12:18; 25:18). The Book of Psalms, which abounds with depictions of evil men, characteristically focuses on their speech. Not surprisingly, the apostle Paul supports his doctrine of the universality of sin by quoting, among others, three Psalms that condemn evil speaking: "Their throats are open graves; their tongues practice deceit"; "The poison of vipers is on their lips"; "Their mouths are full of cursing and bitterness" (Pss. 5:9; 140:3; 10:7; cited in Rom. 3:13–14).

Paul elsewhere enjoins believers not to misuse speech. Especially powerful is a series of commands in Ephesians 4:25–5:4:

> Therefore each of you must put off falsehood and speak truthfully to his neighbor. . . .
> Do not let any unwholesome talk come out of your mouths, but only what is helpful
> for building others up according to their needs. . . . Get rid of all bitterness, rage and
> anger, brawling and slander, along with every form of malice. . . . Nor should there be
> obscenity, foolish talk or coarse joking, which are out of place, but rather thanksgiving.

But the apostle is not the only New Testament writer to show deep concern over this problem. The Gospel of Matthew records these strong words of our Lord against the Pharisees who blasphemed him: "You brood of vipers, how can you who are evil say anything good? For out of the heart the mouth speaks. . . . But I tell you that men will have to give account on the day of judgment for every careless word they have spoken" (Matt. 12:34, 36). Peter commands his readers to rid themselves "of all malice and all deceit, hypocrisy, envy, and slander of every kind"; he also enjoins them not to repay insult with insult and appeals to Psalm 34:12–16: "Whoever would love life and see good days must keep his tongue from evil and his lips from deceitful speech" (1 Peter 2:1; 3:10).

No writer is more forceful, however, than James. Early in his letter he advises us to be "slow to speak" (1:19); he reminds us that keeping the royal law includes proper speaking as well as acting (2:8, 12); he specifically condemns slander (4:11); and he recalls the Lord's command that our yes must be yes and our no must be no (5:12). In addition, he devotes a central section of his letter to a discussion of the restless and almost uncontrollable evil of the tongue (3:1–12). James seems to reflect the Old Testament conviction that, since our speech is tainted with sin, the more we speak the more we are likely to sin: "When words are many, sin is not absent" (Prov. 10:19; cf. v. 14; 17:27–28). Those who teach, therefore, take on an additional risk by the influence and authority they wield.

---

[16]My use of the term *power* has nothing to do with magic or superstition. Anthony C. Thiselton has adequately dealt with this misconception in his article "The Supposed Power of Words in the Biblical Writings," *JTS* n.s. 25 (1974): 283–99. On the other hand, Thiselton's article, because of its polemical focus, is necessarily one-sided. The passages quoted below must be taken seriously.

They must learn to bridle their tongue, which controls their lives as a small rudder steers a large ship; then they will be "able to keep [their] whole body in check" (James 3:2, 4).

The verses I have cited in this section constitute but a fraction of the numerous biblical passages that emphasize the sinfulness of human speech. They are enough, however, to establish a vital truth. The Fall distorted, though it did not utterly destroy, the divine image borne by mankind. As God's image-bearers, we still speak, and our speech still has power to exercise dominion. But this power has been profaned, and sinners rule under the Prince of Darkness. Just as language is a uniquely clear reflection of the divine image, by the same token language has become a singularly blatant instrument of rebellion against the Creator.

LANGUAGE AND REDEMPTION

God's Word

The word through which God created a world that was "very good" (Gen. 1:31) must now become the instrument whereby he both judges a corrupted world and re-creates it for his glory. The word of judgment already appears in Eden, where God curses Satan and the ground and decrees pain and suffering for Adam and Eve (3:14–17). The destruction caused by the Flood is likewise attributed to God's word: "But at your rebuke the waters fled, at the sound of your thunder they took to flight" (Ps. 104:7).

The imagery of God's speaking through "natural" disasters is especially prominent in Psalm 29:

> *The voice of the LORD is over the waters;*
> *The God of glory thunders,*
> *The LORD thunders over the mighty waters. . . .*
> *The voice of the LORD strikes*
> *with flashes of lightning.*
> *The voice of the LORD shakes the desert;*
> *the LORD shakes the Desert of Kadesh.*
> *The voice of the LORD twists the oaks*
> *and strips the forests bare.*

Similarly Jeremiah, as he denounces the false prophets, compares God's word with fire and with "a hammer that breaks a rock in pieces" (Jer. 23:29). Whereas God's breath was the source of life for mankind at the creation (Gen. 2:7), it has now become a scorching wind by which the very foundations of the earth are laid bare (Exod. 15:10; 2 Sam. 22:8–16; Isa. 11:15). Indeed, God's "tongue is a consuming fire," his voice "will shatter Assyria," and his breath is "like a stream of burning sulfur" (Isa. 30:27, 31, 33). And the New Testament assures us that "by the same word the present heavens and earth are reserved for fire, being kept for the day of judgment and destruction of ungodly men" (2 Peter 3:7).

Alongside the word of judgment, however, God utters the word of salvation. It is not absent even in Eden, where God tells the serpent that the seed of the woman will crush its head (Gen. 3:15). It becomes explicit in the word of promise to Abraham (12:2–3) and in precepts that bring prosperity (Lev. 18:5; Josh. 1:7; Ps. 1:2–3). Over and over again God speaks to his people a law that "is perfect, reviving the soul"; commands that "are radiant, giving light to the eyes"; and ordinances that "are sure and altogether righteous," indeed "more precious than gold" and sweeter "than honey from the comb" (Ps. 19:7–10).

Some will object that human language, being an imperfect medium, cannot convey a perfect divine message. It may well be true that no human language can express God's truth in exhaustive and precise detail, but that is far from conceding that divine truth is incommunicable to men and women. To admit that human beings are fallible is not to imply that human beings cannot utter true sentences. The statement "John F. Kennedy was assassinated in the early 1960s," though uttered by a fallible person through the imperfect medium of the English language, does not contain error. It may indeed lack in precision, but it is reliable. Similarly, that God should choose to communicate his revelation to us through the limited resources of human speech (the only way we will understand it) hardly indicates a faulty or fallible revelation.[17]

Let us keep in mind, however, that there is more to God's word than the communication of truth. For example, the power of God's word to preserve those who belong to him is brought home to the Israelites when they are told that God fed them "with manna, which neither you nor your fathers had known, to teach you that man does not live on bread alone but on every word that comes from the mouth of the LORD" (Deut. 8:3). At first blush this statement seems odd. If God wants to teach them that they cannot live by bread alone, why does he do it by giving them bread (i.e., manna)! Clearly, the contrast being made here is not—or at least not primarily—between physical sustenance (bread) and "spiritual" instruction (word), for part of what God's word does is to give the Israelites *physical* sustenance. The contrast is rather between self-reliance and dependence on God's power, between "natural" means and "supernatural" sustenance. In other words, what is being challenged here is the presumption that we can get along reasonably well with our own efforts and schemes. God had to humble the Israelites and let them come to the end of their rope so that they would recognize how dependent they were on the power of God's word for all their needs, physical or not.

The prophet Isaiah stresses the efficacy of God's word for salvation in a well-known passage where sinners are invited to "seek the Lord while he may be found" (Isa. 55:6–11). At times it may appear that the divine revelation is impotent, but we must not fool ourselves:

> As the rain and the snow
>   come down from heaven,
> and do not return to it
>   without watering the earth
> and making it bud and flourish,
>   so that it yields seed for the sower and bread for the eater,
> so is my word that goes out from my mouth:
>   It will not return to me empty,
> but will accomplish what I desire
>   and achieve the purpose for which I sent it.

And the prophet Ezekiel prevents us from thinking that God's breath is only a destructive wind. Against the hopeless sight of a valley full of dry bones that have no life in them, the Lord commands:

---

[17]See especially John M. Frame, "God and Biblical Language: Transcendence and Immanence," in *God's Inerrant Word: An International Symposium on the Trustworthiness of Scripture,* ed. J. W. Montgomery (Minneapolis: Bethany Fellowship, 1974), pp. 159–77.

"Prophesy to the breath; prophesy, son of man, and say to it, 'This is what the Sovereign LORD says: Come from the four winds, O breath, and breathe into these slain, that they may live.'" So I prophesied as he commanded me, and breath entered them; they came to life and stood up on their feet—a vast army. (Ezek. 37:9–10)

The Lord goes on to explain that this vision refers to the spiritual restoration of his people, which will be accomplished when he puts his Spirit in them (v. 14).[18]

God's Written Word

God's word is often described as coming to people orally; with reference to Abraham, for example, we are told that "the LORD appeared to him and said . . ." (Gen. 17:1). Moreover, the prophets as God's spokesmen openly proclaimed the revelation they received. But what happens to the message after the initial proclamation? Oral transmission is usually quite unstable, as all of us have learned when seeking to communicate through more than one intermediary! Something is necessary to insure the permanence of the message among God's people, and this is where *inscripturation* comes in.

The very idea is offensive to many people today who believe that "inscripturated revelation" is a contradiction in terms and an outrage against true religion—after all, how can God be circumscribed within a book? Such a conception, they will argue, can only suffocate faith to the point of extinction. The fact is, however, that God is said to have commanded Moses to write in certain key situations. After the defeat of the Amalekites at Rephidim, for instance, the Lord instructs him: "Write this on a scroll *as something to be remembered* and make sure that Joshua hears it, because I will completely erase the memory of the Amalekites from under heaven" (Exod. 17:14, my emphasis). Moreover, at the point where the Israelites are constituted a nation, God himself is represented as writing the covenant with his own finger (Exod. 24:12; 31:18; 32:15–16; 34:1). The books of Deuteronomy and Joshua abound with references to the covenant that clearly focus attention on its written form (e.g., Deut. 28:58; 29:20; 30:10; Josh. 1:8; 8:31).[19]

The oft-heard advice, when dealing with potentially legal questions, to "put it down in writing" does not merely reflect a modern obsession. One of Isaiah's oracles includes the following: "Go now, write it on a tablet for them, inscribe it on a scroll, that for the days to come it may be an everlasting witness" (Isa. 30:8). The particular and important role played by the written word also lies behind God's explicit instructions to Jeremiah: "Write in a book all the words I have spoken to you"—a command that is linked to the Lord's promise of future redemption (Jer. 30:2–3). Similarly, Habakkuk is told: "Write down the revelation and make it plain on tablets so that a herald may run with it" (Hab. 2:2).

Very instructive in this regard is the perspective of the New Testament apostles, who saw themselves as communicating the very word of God (1 Thess. 2:13). While recognizing certain advantages in being able to speak face to face (cf. 2 John 12), they saw their writings as both useful and necessary when they themselves were absent (2 Cor. 13:10;

---

[18]In this passage, the words *Spirit, breath,* and *wind* are all renderings of the same Hebrew word, *ruaḥ*.

[19]James Barr argues that this concern with written Scripture was only a late development in the Old Testament. Then, on the basis of the fact that Jesus does not appear to have written anything (plus other similar evidence), Barr makes the remarkable, indeed baffling, comment that in the Jewish culture of the day "committal to writing was an *unworthy* mode of transmission of the profoundest truth." See his book, *Holy Scripture: Canon, Authority, Criticism* (Philadelphia: Westminster, 1983), p. 12.

1 Tim. 3:14–15; 1 John 1:4; 2:12–14; Jude 3). Naturally, their inevitable death rendered such writings essential in preserving the foundational apostolic message (2 Peter 1:12–15; 3:1–2).[20] Appropriately, the last book of the Bible is characterized by repeated instructions for John to write what he saw (Rev. 1:11, 19; 2:1 et al.; 14:13; 19:9; 21:5).

As if to anticipate the modern objection to inscripturated revelation, Paul in 2 Timothy 3:16 explicitly identifies the *written* word (*graphē*) with God's very breath (*theopneustos*, "God-breathed"). In this striking turn of expression the New Testament encapsulates the whole range of Old Testament teaching concerning the life-giving power of God's word. If fallen humanity is to be redeemed, it will be only by means of that word, which once created and must now re-create.

God's Incarnate Word

That last statement should remind us, however, that God's word is not an impersonal force. Just as God was personally present in the creation of the world, so did he become personally present in the accomplishment of redemption. It was not simply a poetic strain that led the apostle John to begin his gospel by describing Jesus as *the Word*. That Word was there at the beginning of creation with God—indeed, that Word was God himself, and all things were created by him (John 1:1–3; cf. also Col. 1:16–17; Heb. 1:2–3).[21]

Moreover, he took up residence in our midst, because as the Word he is the Revealer of divine glory (John 1:14), and as the Son only he can make the Father known (John 1:18). After all, "no one knows the Father except the Son and those to whom the Son chooses to reveal him" (Matt. 11:27). It is that status and power that give Jesus the right to extend a unique invitation: "Come to me, all you who are weary and burdened, and I will give you rest" (Matt. 11:28).

We should mark, incidentally, that to recognize the Son of God as the Word is not to minimize his *words*. It is sometimes argued that what really matters in our relationship with God is the *personal* element rather than the *propositional* and that, consequently, when Evangelicals insist that revelation conveys information—and infallible information, no less—they are not only misconstruing the nature of revelation, they are also committing "bibliolatry" by putting the Bible where God alone belongs (as it is sometimes stated, they have replaced a human pope with a paper pope!).

Now this charge of "bibliolatry," in spite of its popularity, is really quite disconcerting. Imagine a ten-year-old who, after disobeying a parental instruction and having been scolded for it, defends herself as follows:

> Why are you scolding me? I am not being disobedient or disrespectful. Quite the contrary. I hold you in the highest esteem and am fully submissive to your authority. And

---

[20] As the old Latin proverb puts it, *Verba volant, scripta manent* ("What is spoken flies away, what is written remains"). From a strictly "secular" perspective, note the comment by Gillian Brown and George Yule, *Discourse Analysis* (CTL; Cambridge: Cambridge University Press, 1983), p. 14: "The major differences between speech and writing derive from the fact that one is essentially transitory and the other is designed to be permanent. It is exactly this point which D. J. Enright makes in the observation that 'Plato may once have thought more highly of speech than of writing, but I doubt he does now!' (Review in *The Sunday Times*, 24 January 1982)." Cf. also below, chap. 3, pp. 49–50.

[21] The last two references stress the continuing providential work of Christ in preserving the world he created, and Hebrews 1:3 in particular describes that work as something that takes place through "his powerful word."

just because of that I must regard your words as having only *derived* authority. Surely you would not want me to debase my commitment to you by elevating what is merely propositional to the level of the personal, would you? Indeed, hardly anything would be more offensive to your character than such an indiscriminate subservience to mere words.

Granted, this particular child is unusually precocious. But her logic approximates that of modern theologians who tell us that we should be submissive to God *rather than* to his words. Such a dichotomy between a person's authority and the authority of what that person says is both false and meaningless. It probably would not sit very well in the armed forces, either.[22] And certainly the very John who stressed the personal character of the Word knew nothing of such a distinction, since he reports Jesus as saying: "I tell you the truth, whoever hears my word and believes him who sent me has eternal life"; "Why is my language not clear to you? Because you are unable to hear what I say [*lit.* to hear my word]" (John 5:24; 8:43; and many other passages). The psalmists, for their part, seemed quite unconcerned about the charge of bibliolatry: "In God, whose word I praise, in God I trust" (Ps. 56:4; cf. v. 10; 68:4); "You have exalted above all things your name and your word" (Ps. 138:2).

Redeemed Speech

Earlier we saw a number of biblical passages that condemn evil speech; by implication, and in certain cases quite explicitly, these passages enjoin a radical change in the speech habits of those who have been redeemed through faith in Christ, the Word. Precisely because language is powerful, it must be used to build up rather than to destroy. Contemporary psychology has recognized the strong impact that positive words can have on the emotional health of children and even adults. The Book of Proverbs anticipated that insight: "The tongue of the righteous is choice silver. . . . The lips of the righteous nourish many"; "The words of the wicked lie in wait for blood, but the speech of the upright rescues them"; "From the fruit of his lips a man is filled with good things as surely as the work of his hands rewards him"; ". . . the tongue of the wise brings healing"; "A gentle answer turns away wrath" (Prov. 10:20–21; 12:6, 14, 19; 15:1).

The emphasis of Scripture on the right use of speech would seem to have a bearing also on current concerns about the supposed decay of English (and other modern languages). As we will have occasion to see in a later chapter, some of these concerns are not founded on a proper understanding of language. Many of the alleged corruptions in contemporary English reflect natural linguistic development and are found in other languages otherwise regarded as "superior" by these same critics (e.g., double-negative constructions are common in Ancient Greek). All the same, carelessness in our use of words *is* a legitimate concern, one to which Christians in particular should pay close attention. This is not a matter of linguistic snobbery. It is one of thoughtfulness, clarity of expression, and social responsibility. Speaking clearly and to the point requires effort

---

[22]Since this dichotomy approaches absurdity, I assume that the theologians in question are bothered not so much by the principle that a person's authority is bound in the authority of his or her words but rather by the view that the words of the Bible can in fact be identified as God's words. But modern theologians are not always straightforward in identifying clearly the object of their dislike. If they were, it might become all too obvious how distant is their religious frame of reference from that of the biblical writers.

and concentration, but is that too high a cost when we remember that our speech reflects the image of our Creator and Redeemer?

Finally, we should note that the Scriptures focus on language as the object of future salvation. The curse on the builders of the Tower of Babel continues to be a reminder of the presence of sin in our world. Appropriately, the prophet Zephaniah, in describing the end-times, gives us a divine promise: "Then will I purify the lips of the peoples, that all of them may call on the name of the LORD and serve him shoulder to shoulder" (Zeph. 3:9). Also, it has often been noted that on the Day of Pentecost, when the Holy Spirit enabled the apostles to speak in other tongues so that everyone heard others speaking in his own language (Acts 2:1–21), God appears to indicate a reversal of the Babel incident. We need not infer that linguistic uniformity is a goal of redemption, but surely the ability to understand each other and thus to praise God in unanimity is very much part of his saving grace to us.

When John tells us about the sound of "a great multitude, like the roar of rushing waters and like loud peals of thunder," he is not describing the confusion and cacophony of mixed linguistic communities, but the united voice of the redeemed (Rev. 19:6–7):

> *Hallelujah!*
>   *For our Lord God Almighty reigns.*
> *Let us rejoice and be glad*
>   *and give him glory!*

three

THE SCIENTIFIC
STUDY OF
LANGUAGE

FUNDAMENTAL PRINCIPLES

As in any academic discipline, so also in linguistics controversy rages about many issues. The problem seems especially bad in linguistics, partly because of the relative newness of this field, partly because of its essentially interdisciplinary character (as we will see below, linguists argue not only among themselves, but also with students of literature, psychology, philosophy, etc.). For well over half a century, however, a set of principles has guided and given coherence to the mainstream of linguistic scholars. True, not every specialist would formulate these principles in the same way, and some respectable authorities may even wish to dissent with "the establishment" at a fundamental level. Still, we would do well to familiarize ourselves with those tenets that most clearly distinguish *modern* linguistics from previous stages in the study of language.

Synchronic Description

The label *synchronic description* covers two distinct concerns. (1) The term *description* contrasts with *prescription*: modern linguists see their task as one of discovery, analysis, and explanation of how people actually use language. It is important to note that we are dealing here with a scholar's professional goal, not with what he or she may think is valuable in a more general setting. Just because linguists do not think they should make, say, economic pronouncements as part of their profession, we should not deduce that they believe economics is bad. Similarly, individual linguists may have very strong views about certain conventions in the English language. They may insist that their children say "Yes" rather than "Yeah"; they will readily correct a student who has used the word *imply* in a term paper where *infer* was the appropriate word. While they may therefore *prescribe* language use in certain situations, they would argue that as linguists they have a different job.

To be sure, some prominent linguists, particularly in the early decades of the discipline, did not always make this distinction clear. One popular work in the 1950s, for example, seemed to argue that no one in any situation ought to prescribe language use. Ironically, the author made the point in the title of the book by issuing a rather dramatic prescription himself: *Leave Your Language Alone!*[1] And one must further acknowledge that most linguists take a rather dim view of the traditional dos and don'ts taught in the schools, though the primary reason is that many of the rules are quite arbitrary and contradict the very genius of English.[2] But we cannot allow overstatements to obscure the basic issues, and our fundamental concern here is that the scientific study of language—whatever else we may or may not decide to do with language—should consist of careful description.

(2) The other term in our label is *synchronic* (= pertaining to one well-defined chronological period), which contrasts with *diachronic* (= developmental or historical). Perhaps no principle identifies more clearly the distinctive character of linguistics in its modern dress. Prior to this century, one could have found many scholars who indeed were interested in scientific description (rather than in telling people how to speak). But these scholars harnessed most of their energies for historical purposes. How do languages develop and change? What is the historical connection between related languages? How did languages originate? These were the all-consuming questions occupying linguists from the end of the eighteenth to the beginning of the twentieth century. And at least one prominent writer at the time could not "conceive how anyone can reflect with any advantage on a language without tracing to some extent the way in which it has historically developed."[3]

Around the turn of the century, however, a Swiss linguist by the name of Ferdinand de Saussure began to suggest to his students that such an approach was misguided. Saussure himself had done significant work in comparative Indo-European grammar, and he was certainly not about to propose that historical investigations be abandoned altogether. What he did object to was the implicit notion that a language can be adequately described by analyzing its development. Speakers are not normally conscious of the way their language *has come to be*; therefore, earlier stages of that language seldom play a role in their speech.

This principle is most clearly illustrated by the vocabulary, which changes more quickly than other linguistic elements. The English word *glamour*, for example, happens to be related to *grammar*.[4] Most speakers are completely unaware of that connection, and

[1]Robert A. Hall, Jr., *Leave Your Language Alone!* (Ithaca, N.Y.: Linguistica, 1950). The second edition was wisely retitled *Linguistics and Your Language* (New York: Doubleday, 1960).

[2]For example, in his famous book, *Language: An Introduction to the Study of Speech* (New York: Harcourt, Brace & World, 1949, orig. 1921), pp. 156–63, Edward Sapir acknowledged that such a form as *Whom did you see?* could be viewed as "correct" on the analogy of I:me = he:him = who:whom. On the other hand, he gave four reasons why "there is something false about its correctness," in particular, the English rule that inflected objects must come *after* the verb. In other words, the popular tendency to say *Who did you see?* conforms to the bent of English grammar (though possibly not to that of Latin).

[3]Hermann Paul, *Principles of the History of Language* (London: Sonnenschein, 1890), p. xlvii, quoted by Roy Harris, *Reading Saussure: A Critical Commentary on the* Cours de linguistique générale (La Salle, Ill.: Open Court, 1987), p. 88. Harris, incidentally, offers a somewhat different interpretation of what the term *diachronic* implies. My comments, though in need of some nuancing, reflect a fairly standard approach that is adequate for our purposes.

[4]As early as the fifteenth century, the term *gramarye* (derived from *grammar*, "learning") was used of occult learning in particular, that is, magic. In the early eighteenth century, Scottish altered *grammar* to *glamour* and used it in a further developed sense (that of *gramarye*), "magic spell." The word *glamour* then

so the connection is quite irrelevant to their use of either term. A linguist who wishes to describe how these terms function in a community of English speakers should therefore, according to Saussurean principles, ignore this interesting historical fact and describe the terms quite independently of one another. To use one of Saussure's best-known analogies, the chess game: the *position* of the pieces after ten moves will be *described* in exactly the same terms by an observer who comes in at that point as it would be by one who has watched the previous moves. Similarly, the main goal of the linguist is to describe how a language works at a specific stage or state (*synchrony*), not how it has evolved from one state to another (*diachrony*).[5]

Language as a Structured System[6]

Continuing the chess analogy, we can illustrate another fundamental Saussurean principle. A mere annotation of where each chess piece is located does not really explain the state of a particular game. On the contrary, there is a dynamic relationship among the pieces that reveals the true "meaning" of the game. Similarly, we do not do justice to language if we treat it atomistically, analyzing its individual components without reference to their place in the linguistic system.

The value of this observation was first demonstrated in connection with the sound system. Any individual learning a foreign language will quickly identify certain sounds that are present in his or her native language and notice other sounds that may prove difficult to master. Native English speakers, for example, will sense that they are already familiar with most Spanish consonants, such as the sounds represented by the letters f, m, and s. They may notice, to be sure, that some of these familiar consonants (e.g., k, p, t) are pronounced a little differently, though not enough to create problems of communication. Only a couple of sounds, such as the distinctive pronunciation of the r, appear to lie outside the sound system of English.

In fact, these impressions are based purely on the *physical* qualities of *individual* sounds, without regard for their connections with one another. A structural approach, on the other hand, assesses the significance of a sound by the role it plays within the system. For example, the fact that the letter p is pronounced in Spanish without the accompanying expulsion of breath (*aspiration*) characteristic of English has little linguistic significance.[7]

---

passed into more general English use, meaning "magic beauty" by the nineteenth century, then further it developed the meaning of "fascinating attraction."

[5]Saussure's class lectures were posthumously published by two of his students in 1916 and later rendered into English under the title, *Course in General Linguistics* (New York: Philosophical Library, 1959, repr. McGraw-Hill, 1966); see especially pp. 88–89. Much controversy surrounds both the text and the interpretation of this seminal work. The most reliable and complete edition is by R. Engler, *Edition critique du "Cours de linguistique générale" de F. de Saussure* (Wiesbaden: Harrassowitz, 1967). Note also Tullio de Mauro's edition (Paris: Payot, 1972). For a recent, and usually negative, interpretation, see Harris, *Reading Saussure*.

[6]The term *structuralism* has been appropriated by various disciplines, sometimes without sufficient rigor. It can be argued, for example, that the use of Saussurean ideas even by the renowned anthropologist C. Lévi-Strauss and the literary scholar R. Barthes depends on a fuzzy use of those ideas, mediated by the controversial linguist L. Hjelmslev. See the important criticisms by Martin Krampen, "Ferdinand de Saussure and the Development of Semiology," in *Classics of Semiotics*, ed. M. Krampen et al. (New York and London: Plenum, 1987), pp. 59–88, especially pp. 78–83. The further extension of similar terminology in biblical studies by proponents of "structural exegesis" (a misnomer in my opinion) has very little to do with linguistics.

[7]Indeed, English speakers pronounce the p just as Spanish speakers do in certain contexts, such as in the word *speaker* (the sound represented by the preceding letter s prevents aspiration; for an interesting experiment, hold your hand in front of your mouth as you alternately say the words *pin* and *spin*).

English and Spanish possess the same trio of bilabial sounds (that is, articulated with both lips): the voiceless *p*, the voiced *b*, and the nasal *m*. Because that relationship is shared by both languages, we may say that the *p* "is the same" in both languages, that is, it plays basically the same role, has the same value.

In contrast, the letter *s* represents a sound that has the same physical characteristics in English as it does in Spanish, yet it has a different linguistic significance in each. The reason is simply that in English this voiceless sound (so-called because the vocal cords do not vibrate during its pronunciation) is paired with the voiced *z*, and such a distinction is nonexistent in Spanish.[8] Since therefore certain contrasts available in one language may not be available in another, linguists place emphasis on the concept of *opposition* as a key to the understanding of speech. This structural approach to phonology suggests that although sounds can be defined in positive terms (by the physical properties of voicing, place of articulation, etc.), their linguistic value is best defined negatively, that is, by their contrast to or difference from other sounds.[9]

Other elements of language, such as vocabulary, can be treated along similar lines. It is true, of course, that words are usually defined positively, suggesting a direct connection with their respective meanings. This possibility is especially clear with proper names: we can most easily "define" the word *Erasmus* by stating certain facts associated with the individual we refer to by that name. Other terms, however, seem to acquire their meaning by the way in which they are distinguished from other terms. Suppose that a teacher grades students by using three terms: *poor, average, good.* The area of meaning covered by *good* in this system is considerably larger than it would be if the teacher used five terms: *poor, average, good, excellent, exceptional.* More to the point, the word *good* means something quite different in each of these systems; that is, the meaning of the word seems determined by the presence or absence of related terms.

In short, the structural approach recognizes that linguistic facts are best studied, not as individual entities without relation to other facts, but as parts of a larger system. Moreover, it emphasizes that the significance of those facts is a function of their opposition or contrast to one another.

Language and Speech

A close examination of sound systems uncovers another interesting detail. The letter *l* in English represents two quite different sounds, depending on whether it is found at the beginning or the end of a syllable: contrast *leap* and *peal*. Because the difference in pronunciation is completely determined by the position of the sound, that difference cannot be used to distinguish words (as though the word *leap* could be pronounced in two different ways, each with a different meaning). As a result, most English speakers are

[8]The letter z is not distinguished at all from the s in most Spanish-speaking countries. (In Castillian Spanish, spoken throughout most of Spain, z represents the sound of English *th* in *think*.)

[9]This kind of formulation relies heavily on the so-called Prague school of phonology. I am indebted to Emilio Alarcos Llorach, *Fonología española,* 4th ed. (BRE 3:1; Madrid: Gredos, 1968), especially p. 46. For a clear description of the American structural approach, see John Lyons, *Language and Linguistics: An Introduction* (Cambridge: Cambridge University Press, 1981), chap. 3. For the more recent generative perspective, now dominant, see the survey by Hans Basbøll, "Phonological Theory," *LTCS* 1:192–215, and the textbook by Roger Lass, *Phonology: An Introduction to Basic Concepts* (CTL; Cambridge: Cambridge University Press, 1984).

not generally aware of this sound distinction, though in some other language the two sounds might be perceived as completely different.

For that matter, we should note that the "ell" sound is pronounced in a wide variety of ways: with sufficiently precise equipment, we could show that each individual (whether because of geographical "accent," physical differences in the organs of articulation, etc.) pronounces this sound in a slightly different way. Remarkably, speakers of English manage to make sense out of this phonetic mayhem and, quite unconsciously, abstract but one sound that is linguistically significant.[10]

This curious fact illustrates several features of language, but I mention it here primarily to emphasize the distinction between *langue* ("language" = a system that has the potential to become speech) and *parole* ("speech" = actual utterances). Saussure used those two French words to formulate a very important concept. According to Saussure, language [*langue*] "is a storehouse filled by the members of a given community through their active use of speaking"; it is "a grammatical system" with *potential* existence in individual brains. Moreover, "language is not complete in any speaker; it exists perfectly only within a collectivity."[11]

This distinction between *language* and *speech* is generally recognized as crucial, though linguists are not fully agreed as to which of the two is the proper object of linguistic study. Saussure himself argued for the former: he believed that the potential, but stable, system that is part of every speaker's consciousness is the appropriate field of investigation. During the past two or three decades, however, linguists have paid increasing attention to the striking amount of *variation* that characterizes actual speech. Such subjects as geographical differences, "social registers," bilingualism, and the broad category of *style* have become major fields of research. At the risk of oversimplification, we could say that most of the issues popularly associated with "grammar," insofar as they involve matters that leave little room for choice, belong in the category of language rather than speech. On the other hand, "what grammar leaves out"[12] is the area of style, where considerable variety exists among individuals, social groups, and geographical areas.

Other Principles

In addition to the matters already mentioned, most linguists work with certain assumptions that may be regarded as relatively obvious (though the word *relatively* has been known to cover a multitude of sins). For example, even a cursory acquaintance with modern linguistics reveals that its practitioners give primary, though not exclusive, attention to the spoken language. This approach reflects a "common sense" understanding

---

[10]Linguists use the term *phoneme* to describe such a significant sound; further, they enclose it within slashes to distinguish it from nonphonemic sounds, which are enclosed in square brackets. We would then say that the English letter l represents the phoneme / l /, and that this phoneme is "realized" (i.e., actually pronounced) in a variety of ways, primarily as the "clear" [l] and the "dark" or "velarized" [l].

[11]Saussure, *Course*, pp. 13–14. (Some theoreticians would regard *langue* as an abstract system, since it is possible to describe speakers as abstracting what is linguistically significant out of the specific and concrete instances of speaking. Saussure himself, however, regarded *langue* as concrete [ibid., p. 15].) Motivated by somewhat different concerns, the contemporary linguist Noam Chomsky, followed by many, has used the terms *competence* and *performance* in a way that corresponds, if only roughly, to the Saussurean distinction between *langue* and *parole*.

[12]G. W. Turner, *Stylistics* (Harmondsworth: Penguin, 1973), p. 19.

that writing is a derivative form of language. To be sure, it would be difficult to prove conclusively that human beings spoke before they ever wrote (though the opposite viewpoint would seem to contradict what little information we have on this topic). It is enough to remind ourselves, however, that while there exist many societies that possess no written literature, all known linguistic communities consist of people who speak (unless physiologically impaired). More to the point, perhaps, is the fact that even in a modern society, where the written word has become exceedingly important, children learn to speak—indeed, they master the basic structure of their language—several years before they learn to read or write.

One should not deduce that linguists consider written literature unimportant. Here again we should note a distinction between what is and what is not the specific professional focus of the researcher. An individual linguist may indeed be a passionate lover of literature—he or she may even regard it as a more significant cultural symbol than the spoken form of language. The linguist recognizes, however, that written works by themselves tell us only how a small sample of a society uses language in a restricted number of activities. Literature, in other words, provides a truncated and thus inadequate base for determining how language actually works in a society.

Some readers may wonder how the linguist's concern for the "priority" of the spoken form affects our approach to Scripture, which by definition is *written*. Note, however, that as far as any philosophical aversion to writing is concerned, such an aversion goes back at least as far as Plato[13] and therefore could not have originated from recent developments in linguistics. Although one could probably find linguists on both sides of this philosophical question, the *methodological* issue at hand is of quite a different character, since it seeks merely to define the proper object of scientific inquiry, not the relative merits or validity of these two forms of language. Moreover, we should keep in mind that, while we have no access to the spoken form of many ancient languages (including of course Old Testament Hebrew and New Testament Greek), *general* linguistics seeks to formulate principles and rules that are characteristic of human language as such, not necessarily those that belong exclusively to specific languages. Therefore, many of the results arising from modern linguistic research are applicable even to communities in the past for which a spoken form is not extant.

This brings us to our last introductory concept, namely, that modern linguists are interested in all languages alike. Prior to the twentieth century, the influence of classical

---

[13]See above, chap. 2, pp. 36–37. Cf. Paul Ricoeur, *Interpretation Theory: Discourse and the Surplus of Meaning* (Fort Worth: Texas Christian University Press, 1976), chap. 2, especially pp. 38–40. Ricoeur, who incidentally is not altogether a stranger to linguistic science, offers here an interesting, and in many (though not all) respects powerful, philosophical defense of writing. Less restrained, but still worthy of note, is Etienne Gilson, *Linguistics and Philosophy: An Essay on the Philosophical Constants of Language* (Notre Dame, Ind.: University of Notre Dame Press, 1988): "Every writer concerned with the quality of his work and aware of its nature knows that the written thought is not a simple record of the spoken thought but is another thought, conceived with a view to writing and obedient to its own laws" (p. 131); "writing is not just the husk of the spoken word, . . . for it . . . does with and for language . . . many things of which the spoken word is incapable" (p. 132); "born of the spoken language from which it remains inseparable, the written language confers upon it, nevertheless, a peculiar status, as of an empire within an empire, a permanent refuge of the works of the most true and most beautiful intelligence. It is a holy and quasi-divine domain, in the strict sense of the term, for in the written the spoken endures, and in the spoken the intellect lives, a witness in man of a power of creation superior to man" (p. 146).

culture led students to pay disproportionate attention to Greek and Latin, and it was often assumed that the particular structure of these languages ("synthetic" or "inflecting") evinced a higher order of thought. In contrast, so-called "analytical" languages (such as English, in which nominal case endings and verbal conjugations play a less important role) were thought inferior—to say nothing of "agglutinative" languages like Turkish. This prejudice was sometimes taken to curious extremes: "One celebrated American writer on culture and language delivered himself of the dictum that, estimable as the speakers of agglutinative languages might be, it was nevertheless a crime for an inflecting woman to marry an agglutinative man."[14]

The careful study of American Indian languages and other "primitive" cultures early in this century, however, had a powerful impact on this point of view. And well it should. Anyone who had previously thought that grammatical complexity was a sign of advanced culture could not help but be shocked. If the inflections of the classical languages represented sophisticated logic (each adjective, for example, must be marked for case, number, and gender), what was one to do with the Bantu languages, which mark nouns according to various classes on the basis of such contrasts as person/nonperson and countable/uncountable? And if the many conjugations of the Greek verb appeared daunting, the Basque verb could only be described as "impossible"![15]

These facts do not of course diminish the great achievements of classical culture, nor do they minimize the beauty of its literature. That greatness and beauty, however, do not inhere in the grammatical structure of Greek and Latin; rather, they are the result of great minds using those languages to their full potential. Moreover, the question that concerns us here is not whether certain languages may be more esthetically pleasing than others. Even the most committed linguist, no doubt, has personal preferences about that sort of thing. What really matters is the willingness to take seriously all the linguistic evidence, wherever it may come from, and to use it responsibly in the formulation of theories and principles.

THE INTERDISCIPLINARY OUTLOOK

Even a shallow exposure to linguistics quickly reveals that the study of language cannot be confined to the approaches used by one or two academic disciplines. Consciously or not, students of language have always had to use an interdisciplinary technique. During the past few decades, however, this feature has become so prominent that one may wonder whether it is any longer possible to think of linguistics as a specific discipline. We can best survey the landscape by using the conventional threefold division of higher education: humanities, natural sciences, and social sciences.

---

[14]Sapir, *Language*, p. 124, n. 2. In modern dress: "Some of my best friends are agglutinative...."

[15]*El imposible vencido* ("The Impossible Conquered") was in fact the title of a Spanish grammar of the Basque verb. See Otto Jespersen, *Language: Its Nature, Development, and Origin* (New York: Norton, 1964, orig. 1921), p. 427. Jespersen adds, "At Béarn they have the story that the good God, wishing to punish the devil for the temptation of Eve, sent him to the Pays Basque with the command that he should remain there till he had mastered the language. At the end of seven years God relented, finding the punishment too severe, and called the devil to him. The devil had no sooner crossed the bridge of Castelondo than he found he had forgotten all that he had so hardly learned."

The Humanities

For many of us, the study of language is primarily the province of the humanities. After all, our elementary and secondary education includes this field under the general rubric of *language arts*. And indeed, modern universities often explore the subject matter of linguistics within the curriculum of English studies and foreign languages (including classics). Moreover, and obviously, there is a close interface between the fields of literature and language, especially in the related areas of stylistics and rhetorical criticism. It should be pointed out, however, that in some English and foreign language departments the study of language is not well integrated with *modern* linguistics; indeed, the latter may be ignored altogether.

Insofar as *history* is perceived as a humanistic field (usually it is brought together with the social sciences), one can also see a close relationship between it and language study. As we will notice in the next chapter, linguistics must deal with the reality of language development even if it does not consider such a development its primary concern. The tools honed by the historical method, as well as the evidence uncovered by historical investigation, provide an essential service to linguists, some of whom fully integrate the two disciplines in their own careers.

Then there is *philosophy*. The earliest serious discussions of language known to us were carried on by ancient Greek philosophers. While their primary concerns—both then and in later centuries—were rather broad and speculative in character, they managed to make important (empirical) observations that continue to hold the interest of language students. Moreover, the technical field of logic is closely bound to the character of language. At the beginning of this century, however, philosophical thought experienced something of a revolution that came to be known as "the linguistic turn."[16] Tired of the abstract quality of the so-called idealist tradition, such brilliant British thinkers as G. E. Moore and Bertrand Russell decided that the real task of philosophy was to clarify our concepts and therefore our language. The Austrian Ludwig Wittgenstein and other prominent philosophers took up this theme and generated a new subdiscipline known as Analytic Philosophy. (The question of "God-talk," which we have broached in chapter 2, often emerges in this context and so overlaps with the concerns of *religious studies*.)

Although working independently of twentieth-century linguistic science, these philosophers developed principles and methods that were very similar indeed to what linguists were doing.[17] The isolation between linguists and philosophers has gradually given way to cooperation, and it is no longer unusual to find philosophers fully abreast of developments in linguistics or linguists who capably try their hand at philosophical investigation.[18] Nevertheless, one must be careful not to blur some important distinctions between the two disciplines. In particular, it is unhelpful and misleading to assume that

---

[16]Cf. Richard Rorty, ed., *The Linguistic Turn: Recent Essays in Philosophical Method* (Chicago: University of Chicago Press, 1967). It is important to distinguish "philosophy of language," which indicates one of the subject matters of philosophy, from "linguistic (or analytical) philosophy," which refers to a particular method of doing philosophy.

[17]The prominent linguist Stephen Ullmann, in *The Principles of Semantics*, 2d ed. (New York: Philosophical Library, 1957), p. 137, expressed surprise to find out that Wittgenstein's ideas paralleled developments in linguistics. Cf. also James Barr, *Biblical Words for Time*, 2d ed. (SBT 1/33; London: SCM, 1969), p. 197.

[18]Cf. Colin Lyas, ed., *Philosophy and Linguistics* (New York: Macmillan, 1971). For the most recent developments, see Alice ter Meulen, "Linguistics and the Philosophy of Language," *LTCS* 1:430–46.

all modern linguists share the *philosophical* commitments of analytical philosophers (except in the very general sense that a valid philosophy of language must build on an accurate understanding of human language).

In addition to the disciplines already mentioned, it may not be far-fetched to recognize some links between language study and the *fine arts*. It isn't just a matter of the commonplace that "artists are trying to communicate something." Both painting and music, along with language, may be said to be part of the broader field of *semiotics* (the science of signs): "Sounds in music work as elements of a system and acquire a value according to specific criteria of pertinence: a primitive who makes timbre pertinent instead of pitch perceives as the same melody what a European feels as two different melodies played on two different instruments."[19] But analogies of this type should not be pressed. And while phoneticians may profitably use musical notations to describe "suprasegmental" features of speech (tempo, pitch, etc.), we need not fear the development of a new hybrid known as "musicolinguists."

The Natural Sciences

At the other end of the academic spectrum stand the so-called hard sciences. Toward the end of the nineteenth century, comparative philologists who came to be known as Neogrammarians were able to demonstrate the presence of "laws" (that is, clear regularities) in sound changes. As a result, they claimed, their discipline had become a science. Is there a genuine integration between the sciences and linguistics?

The most obvious point of contact is in the field of *acoustics*. For a phonetician to be able to understand and describe speech sounds, he or she must have a strong grounding in the physics of sound. To be precise, however, phonetics is not linguistics, but rather an ancillary discipline.

Another area of interaction is that of *biology*. Both zoologists and paleontologists contribute to various aspects of linguistics, such as the debated question of language origin and the problems associated with language development in children. Of particular value is the work of researchers in the field of neurology, which is able to examine the control of the human brain over speech processes (this field is closely related to that of *psycholinguistics*; see below).[20]

The most fruitful field is *mathematics* broadly considered. Some linguists have attempted to describe language through algebraic concepts. More productive still has been the application of statistics to language study. We can predict, for example, that the fifteen most common words in any language will make up about 25 percent of the total words used in a (sufficiently long) sample text; more than half of the total words in the text will consist of the one hundred most frequently used words. It has also been demonstrated

---

[19]Umberto Eco, "The Influence of Roman Jakobson on the Development of Semiotics," in *Classics of Semiotics* (ed. Krampen et al.), pp. 109–27, quotation from p. 120. Leonard Bernstein, in one of his TV series, was daring enough to use the terminology and principles of transformational grammar to explain various features of music. Although a few of his analogies were thought-provoking, one must not think that he effected an integration of the two disciplines. See *The Unanswered Question: Six Talks at Harvard (The Charles Eliot Norton Lectures)* (Cambridge, Mass.: Harvard University Press, 1976).

[20]Cf. David Caplan, "The Biological Basis for Language," *LTCS* 3:237–55; Sheila E. Blumstein, "Neurolinguistics: An Overview of Language-Brain Relations in Aphasia," ibid., pp. 210–36.

that an inverse relationship exists between the length of a word and its frequency of use. Statistics such as these are not mere curiosities: they shed light on the way language is structured and functions.[21]

Of special importance is the contribution of *communication engineering,* in particular information theory.[22] The mathematical analysis of what is involved in the transmission of information has led to major discoveries. For example, we have become aware of the value and need for *redundancy* in language: if language were perfectly efficient, then even the slightest *noise* (a technical term referring to any type of distortion) would hamper communication. It has also become clear that *uncertainty* is a requirement for conveying information. If a unit of language is completely certain or predictable (e.g., *to* in *I want to eat* —the speaker has no choice but to use this particle if he wants to speak with acceptable grammar), it communicates no information; on the other hand, the greater the degree of choice or uncertainty, the greater the measure of information conveyed.[23]

Finally, we must note the growing significance of *computer science,* with its own "programming languages," its progress in machine translation, its use for information retrieval, and its promise of artificial intelligence. Yet for all the real contributions of the sciences, it would be difficult to maintain that these disciplines are the most appropriate context for the study of language. Language is foremost a social activity. Accordingly, linguistics is usually viewed as belonging to the behavioral sciences.

The Social Sciences

There is much to be said for the view that linguistics is primarily an *anthropological* field. Indeed, most of the progress made in the modern study of language in North America was accomplished by anthropologists who worked with various American Indian groups. This important field continues to contribute essential information about the relationship between cultural patterns and language expression.[24]

Closely related to these concerns are those of *sociology.* At this point we certainly meet a complete integration between two fields of study, so that we can accurately refer to the new discipline of *sociolinguistics.*[25] Much of the growth in this field is directly related

---

[21]The statistical study of language owes much to the writings of G. K. Zipf and G. U. Yule. For a very rigorous study, which includes a discussion of stylostatistics, see Gustav Herdan, *The Advanced Theory of Language as Choice and Chance* (Kommunikation und Kybernetik in Einzeldarstellungen 4; New York: Springer-Verlag, 1966).

[22]For a wide-ranging, lively, and provocative treatment, see Jeremy Campbell, *Grammatical Man: Information, Entropy, Language, and Life* (New York: Simon and Schuster, 1982). One need not follow Campbell's fertile imagination in every respect to appreciate the validity of many of the connections he draws in his book. Cf. especially chap. 5 on redundancy. For a more technical treatment, see Herdan, *Advanced Theory,* §§ 15–17.

[23]To be pedantically precise: "The amount of information in any signal is the logarithm to the base two of the reciprocal of the probability of that signal. That is: $I = \mathrm{Log}_2\, 1\,/\,p$." See H. A. Gleason, Jr., *An Introduction to Descriptive Linguistics,* rev. ed. (New York: Holt, Rinehart and Winston, 1961), p. 377, for an explanation!

[24]For some interesting illustrations, see Robbins Burling, *Man's Many Voices: Language in Its Cultural Context* (New York: Holt, Rinehart and Winston, 1970), especially chaps. 2–5.

[25]See the survey by Beatriz R. Lavandera, "The Study of Language in Its Socio-Cultural Context," *LTCS* 4:1–13, and the rest of the chapters in the same volume. The more narrowly focused field of *ethnolinguistics* could be viewed as a subdivision of either sociology or anthropology.

to the view that the proper object of linguistics is not *langue*, as Saussure suggested, but rather *parole*, that is, the actual utterances of people in specific contexts. Questions of social stratification, politics, sexism, verbal art, humor, bilingualism, style, and many more are seen to be essential for a proper understanding of language. This new approach has also generated interest in discourse analysis (see chap. 6).

Finally, there are some who would argue that the study of language is essentially *psycholinguistics*. One of the most influential linguists in America is Noam Chomsky, who, beginning in the 1950s, developed a view of language that challenged the behaviorism of B. F. Skinner. Impressed by the ability of children to create new sentences that they had never heard before, he argued that human beings have an innate capacity to learn and use language. In connection with this insight he developed a new method of language description, closely tied to psychological investigation, which came to be known as *transformational* (or *generative*) grammar.[26]

Psycholinguists, however, are primarily interested in such questions as the neurological role of the brain in the production of speech, the development of speech in children, the analogies between human speech and animal communication, the effects of bilingualism, the more general relationships between thought and language, and so on.[27] It is obvious that some of the challenges faced by anthropologists and sociologists (e.g., what effect culture has on language and vice-versa) cannot be adequately met without the help of psycholinguistics.

Even this important field, however, cannot claim absolute rights over the study of language. Indeed, whether we view linguistics as belonging primarily to the behavioral sciences or to the humanities, this discipline must be viewed as both an independent field of study and one that is inherently amenable to interdisciplinary research.

---

[26]Because transformational linguists depend heavily on native speakers (including themselves) to determine whether utterances are grammatical, this approach has not been vigorously applied to the study of ancient languages. For an attempt to do so, cf. Daryl Dean Schmidt, *Hellenistic Greek Grammar and Noam Chomsky: Nominalizing Transformations* (SBLDS 62; Chico, Calif.: Scholars Press, 1981).

[27]See Michael K. Tanenhaus, "Psycholinguistics: An Overview," *LTCS* 3:1–37, and the rest of the chapters in the same volume.

four

THE
HISTORICAL
DIMENSION

Although modern linguistics, as we have seen, places less emphasis on the diachronic (or historical) approach than on the synchronic, one must not conclude that historical considerations are unimportant. In particular, students of ancient literature sometimes face problems that require historical research. One obvious example is the occurrence of words referring to cultural artifacts that no longer exist. The attempt to discover information about an earlier culture is, to be sure, an *extra*-linguistic task not to be confused with the analysis of a linguistic system, but it would be artificial to draw a sharp dichotomy between language and culture.

Besides, there are other, more subtle, problems. If we are studying the Lord's Prayer, we will need to deal with the rare word *epiousios*, usually translated "daily" (Matt. 6:11; Luke 11:3). Because the word does not occur elsewhere in the New Testament, or for that matter in other Greek literature (except for later Christian writers quoting the Gospels), scholars need to consider the possible derivation of the word: Does it mean "necessary for existence" (*epi + ousia*), or "for the current day" (*epi tēn ousan hēmeran*), or "for the following day" (*hē epiousa hēmera*)? In order to come up with these and other options, one has to consider the etymology of the word—a diachronic exercise. This kind of problem, incidentally, while very unusual in the Greek New Testament, is faced with some frequency by Old Testament scholars.

We may, and should, insist that a language be described according to the way it is used at a particular chronological stage (synchronic description). But a broad knowledge of the prehistory, as well as the historical development, of the language can help the student handle certain linguistic difficulties.[1]

---

[1]Cf. the treatment of Greek phonology in chap. 5. For a wide-ranging survey, including the comparative method, structuralist and transformationalist models, and issues of language contact, see Theodora Bynon, *Historical Linguistics* (CTL; Cambridge: Cambridge University Press, 1977).

LANGUAGE FAMILIES

Among historical questions, few are more challenging than those addressed by the comparative method. This method was in effect born toward the end of the eighteenth century, when Sir William Jones, having carefully studied Sanskrit, the ancient language of India, discovered similarities between it and the classic European languages that could hardly be explained as accidental. The likelihood that Greek, Latin, and Sanskrit had all developed from one common language sparked the interest of scholars, and a tremendous amount of intellectual energy during the nineteenth century was expended on refining comparative techniques.

We can demonstrate, for example, that there is such a thing as a *Romance* family of languages—comprising French, Italian, Portuguese, Rumanian, Spanish, etc.—that has descended from Latin. Similarly, such languages as Danish, Dutch, English, German, Gothic (an ancient language no longer spoken), Norwegian, and Swedish are closely related and belong to the *Germanic* family, even though in this case the parent language (comparable to Latin for the Romance tongues) has not survived. Linguists refer to this parent language as Proto-Germanic and attempt to reconstruct it on the basis of the evidence provided by the languages that have survived.

Moreover, the Romance and Germanic families can be shown to have developed from a common "proto"-language. Thus we could speak of French and English as "cousins," for example. Indeed, English speakers can recognize many similarities between their language and French. Some of these similarities, of course, are the result of cultural contact: in earlier centuries English *borrowed* heavily from French (e.g., *closet, depart, faith, joy, president, prestige*),[2] while recently French has become influenced by English (e.g., *drugstore, sexy, weekend*). But other resemblances, such as the basic vocabulary of numbers (English *one, two, three*; French *un, deux, trois*), can only be explained on the assumption of a common descent.

Further research shows that the Romance and Germanic languages, in addition, are closely related to other families, such as *Celtic* (e.g., the Gaelic spoken in Scotland), *Balto-Slavic* (Russian, Polish, etc.), *Indo-Iranian* (Sanskrit, Hindi, Persian, etc.), and others. We can therefore subsume all of these important languages under one large category known as *Indo-European*, and some scholars devote their research to determine what Proto-Indo-European must have looked like. The evidence that certain words must indeed go back to a time before the subfamilies developed is of interest not only to linguists, but also to students of prehistorical culture. Archaeological evidence thus goes hand in hand with reconstructed linguistic data.[3] For our purposes, we need only keep in mind that Greek belongs to this Indo-European family.

Hebrew and Aramaic, on the other hand, belong to the *Semitic* family of languages.[4] This family is often subdivided into (1) an eastern branch, known as Akkadian, consisting

---

[2]Among many fine histories of English, note Albert C. Baugh and Thomas Cable, *A History of the English Language*, 3d ed. (Englewood Cliffs, N. J.: Prentice Hall, 1978).

[3]For a recent hypothesis, see A. Colin Renfrew, *Archaeology and Language: The Puzzle of Indo-European Origins* (Cambridge: Cambridge University Press, 1988). Cf. also T. V. Gamkrelidze and V. V. Ivanov, "The Early History of Indo-European Languages," *Scientific American* 262, no. 3 (March 1990): 110-16.

[4]More precisely, we should expand the family to include Egyptian and related languages. The older term used to describe this broader family, *Hamito-Semitic*, has given way to *Afro-Asiatic*; cf. Carleton T. Hodge, "Afroasiatic: An Overview," in Thomas A. Sebeok, ed., *Current Trends in Linguistics*, vol. 6 (The

of Babylonian and Assyrian dialects; (2) a southern branch, which includes Arabic, Ethiopic, and South Arabian; and (3) a northwestern branch.[5] Our main interest is in this last branch, *Northwest Semitic*, which is usually further subdivided into two main groups, *Canaanite* (consisting of Phoenician, Moabite, Hebrew, etc.) and *Aramaic* (various forms, including Jewish Palestinian Aramaic, Syriac, Mandean, etc.).

This kind of information can be very useful in our appreciation of the languages involved. For example, many students of the Bible tend to assume that Aramaic, as spoken by Jews in New Testament times, was a late and inferior (corrupt?) dialect of Hebrew. In fact, however, we may describe the relationship between Hebrew and Aramaic as analogous to that of "close cousins"—an even closer relationship than that between, say, English and German. (Aramaic, incidentally, had a long and, from a political point of view, more distinguished history than Hebrew. More on this question below.)

The sound inventory of Hebrew, for example, was basically identical to that of Aramaic,[6] but different in some important respects from the inventory of other Semitic languages, such as Arabic (which preserved several additional consonants) and Akkadian (which lost a number of consonantal distinctions). Hebrew and Aramaic also shared a large number of vocabulary items; not a few of them were pronounced a little differently ("gold" = Heb. *zahab*, Aram. *dehab*), but as a rule the similarities were quite obvious. Some of the more significant differences include the structure of the verbal system and the way in which definiteness is indicated: Hebrew, in a manner roughly comparable to English and Greek, uses a definite article attached to the front of the noun, whereas Aramaic adds something like a suffix (usually the vowel *-a* is attached to the end of the noun).

What needs to be appreciated, in any case, is that Hebrew and Aramaic, along with the other Semitic languages, differ greatly from Greek and the other Indo-European languages. With regard to the sound system, Greek does not have a series of consonants, popularly described as "gutturals" and "emphatics," that are distinctive of Semitic. But even those consonants that are found both in Greek and in Hebrew/Aramaic cannot be simply

---

Hague and Paris: Mouton, 1970), pp. 237–54. Furthermore, some scholars believe that behind the Indo-European and Afroasiatic families there lies an older common root. Even if this theory is true, most linguists doubt that we will ever have the evidence necessary to prove it. On the difficulties of defining Semitic characteristics, see the well-known article by E. Ullendorff, "What Is a Semitic Language?" *Orientalia* NS 27 (1958): 66–75, reprinted in *Is Biblical Hebrew a Language? Studies in Semitic Languages and Civilizations* (Wiesbaden: Harrassowitz, 1977), pp. 155–71.

[5]For a convenient handbook, see Sabatino Moscati et al., *An Introduction to the Comparative Grammar of Semitic Languages: Phonology and Morphology* (Porta linguarum orientalium, n.s. 6; Wiesbaden: Harrassowitz, 1964). Cf. also Edward Ullendorff, "Comparative Semitics," in *Current Trends* (ed. Sebeok) 6:261–73, and Peter T. Daniels' important translation and updating of Gotthelf Bergsträsser, *Introduction to the Semitic Languages* (Winona Lake, Ind.: Eisenbrauns, 1983; orig. 1928). The threefold division mentioned above, while convenient, oversimplifies the facts. Some linguists seem increasingly reluctant to develop neat arrangements of this sort. The discovery of Ugaritic and Eblite, in particular, has not only increased our knowledge but also created considerable debate. See, for example, the articles by I. M. Diakonoff and W. von Soden in *Studies on the Language of Ebla*, ed. Pelio Fronzaroli (Quaderni di semitistica 13; Florence: Universitá di Firenze, 1984). For a new proposal, building on the work of R. Hetzron (who argued that Arabic is not part of South Semitic but belongs with Canaanite and Aramaic), see Rainer M. Voigt, "The Classification of Central Semitic," *Journal of Semitic Studies* 32 (1987): 1–21, especially the diagram on p. 15.

[6]This comment, as well as others in the subsequent discussion, need qualification. The oldest inscriptions, for example, suggest that Aramaic, at that stage, preserved some "proto-Semitic" sounds not attested at all in Hebrew.

identified: the respective sound *structures* are quite unlike each other, and so the sounds in question "behave" differently. The phonological differences are most obvious in the case of the vowels, which are used in Semitic primarily to alter the grammatical function of words.[7] That, incidentally, is the reason Hebrew speakers can easily read a text that consists only of consonants (indeed, Hebrew and other Semitic languages were written for many centuries before a full system for indicating vowels was introduced).

The vocabulary of Greek is also vastly different from that of Hebrew. Rarely does one find a pair of corresponding words that have the same meaning in both languages and also sound somewhat alike. In some of these cases, the similarities are purely coincidental; in other instances, they reflect cultural contact rather than a genetic connection (e.g., Greek *sakkos*, "sack, coarse garment," corresponds to Hebrew *saq* because the early Greeks borrowed the word from the Phoenicians). The disparities between the two language families become even more significant when one examines the grammar. The Hebrew and Aramaic verbs are built on several different stems (each of which includes a prefixed and a suffixed conjugation),[8] while the Greek verbs follow a complicated system of moods and tenses/aspects. A Hebrew narrative is typically made up of simple sentences linked by the conjunction "and," but Greek relies on a variety of conjunctions as well as complex subordinate clauses (especially with the rich use of the participle).

Many other details could be listed to illustrate the systematic differences between Greek (as a representative of Indo-European) and Hebrew/Aramaic (as representatives of Semitic). On the other hand, one should avoid exaggerating these differences, as though they implied widely divergent worldviews that made communication impossible. One of the strengths of modern linguistics lies precisely in its universal focus. Without minimizing the peculiarities of each language, linguists seek to understand the nature of language *as such*. At the most fundamental level, Greek, Hebrew, and Aramaic share all the features that constitute them, quite simply, as human languages.

We have not yet addressed, however, the practical question: What value does the comparative method have for the *interpretation* of texts (biblical or otherwise)? In all frankness, not much. When Jeremiah or Paul spoke and wrote, they did so without knowledge of "language families"—much less would they have been aware of the specific prehistorical connections that modern scholars have established. In other words, the biblical writings have to be understood in the context of what their respective authors knew and meant to say. For example, the evidence from Sanskrit makes clear that Greek, in an earlier form no longer extant, used eight grammatical cases. This piece of information is

[7]Most Hebrew words consist of three consonants (the root), while the vowel patterns are in general the same for the different roots. The vast majority of verbs, for example, use a specific vowel pattern for the simple third masculine singular form (*katab*, "he wrote"; *'ahab*, "he loved," etc.). One thus would never find two different Hebrew verbs that had the same consonants but that could be distinguished merely by their use of different vowel patterns, something quite possible in Indo-European (cf. English *kill/call*, *bag/beg*, *arm/ram*).

[8]For example, the simple stem *zkr* means "remember," while the so-called causative stem *hzkr* means "remind" (= cause to remember). Other basic verbal concepts, such as reflexive activity, the passive voice, repetitive action, and so on, are likewise indicated by using different stems. (See the full discussion of verbal stems in Waltke and O'Connor, *Biblical Hebrew Syntax*, chap. 21.) Moreover, the first person singular (simple stem) takes the form *'ezkor* in the prefixed or imperfect conjugation (used of nonperfective aspect and often translated with a future, "I will remember"), while in the suffixed or perfect conjugation the form is *zakarti* (often translated with a past tense, "I remembered"). See also below, chap. 6, pp. 259–63.

useful for certain technical questions, but it is misleading to say, as some grammar books do, that New Testament Greek has eight cases.[9] Thus the significance of, say, the genitive case in a particular New Testament passage has to be deduced from the use of the genitive in first-century Greek; it cannot be determined by reading into the first-century writers grammatical features that existed in prehistoric times.

I do not mean to suggest, however, that comparative linguistics has no place or relevance in biblical scholarship. On the contrary. For one thing, it can prove utterly fascinating. Students of Greek often feel frustrated when they come across irregularities that seem to have no rhyme or reason. Being able to account for these irregularities will not help them learn Greek better (English speakers understand their native language quite well even though they have little idea why the past tense of *break* is not *breaked*). Often, however, it is both exciting and encouraging to discover that there is an answer for something that seemed unexplainable—much as some people feel exhilarated when they find out how a complicated machine works and are thereby stimulated to learn more.

Of greater importance, however, is the fact that we do need people who know how to repair the machine when it breaks! Not everybody is cut out for this sort of thing. Nor is it necessary for someone to know how to tune up an engine in order to go out for a drive. Similarly, a biblical interpreter can understand New Testament Greek quite well—indeed, he or she could be an expert exegete—without being able to explain why, for example, certain third-declension nouns are accented on the antepenult even though the ultima is long.[10] Behind the scenes, however, specialists are needed who can control the data and provide a coherent explanation.

In addition, there are times when we come across important texts that are fraught with obscurities, and a firm historical and comparative knowledge can provide possible answers. Because the Greek language is so richly attested, the evidence from Greek itself is almost always sufficient to clarify difficult texts in the New Testament and contemporary literature. The Hebrew Old Testament, however, contains a significant number of passages (especially in such poetic books as Job) that cannot be understood without some help from the cognate languages. Even in the case of Hebrew, the comparative approach cannot hold primacy, since contextual considerations are more relevant than what a cognate word or grammatical form may have meant in a distant language such as Arabic.[11] It would be foolhardy to deny, however, that some facility in Comparative Semitics is very important to gain expertise in Old Testament exegesis.

---

[9]Note the discussion in chap. 6, p. 254–55.

[10]I mention this example because, when I came across the problem in my first year of Greek study, it well-nigh destroyed my confidence in the rationality of the Greek language! The answer is fairly simple, once we become acquainted with the history of early Greek dialects. That history makes clear that, at the stage when this phonological rule about accents was operative, the form was different: *poleōs* (genitive case), that is, with a short ultima (and a long penult), which allows the accent to go back to the antepenult. *After* this rule ceased to operate in the living speech, however, the form in question in the Attic dialect went through a metathesis (or transposition) of vowel length, *poleōs*. By this time, however, the accent was firmly in place and thus Attic (and the related Koine) ended up with a set of irregular forms.

[11]The abuse of this method has been carefully documented by James Barr, *Comparative Philology and the Text of the Old Testament* (Oxford: Clarendon Press, 1968). Comparative work is especially useful in deciphering languages newly discovered, such as Ugaritic a couple of generations ago.

LINGUISTIC DEVELOPMENT

Apart from the comparative method, historical concerns can also prove valuable when we restrict ourselves to individual languages in their *attested* forms. (Comparative philology is primarily interested in reconstructing the prehistorical—that is, unattested—forms.) Tracing the development of a language can focus on either external or internal history. External history refers to broad cultural questions: Who spoke Aramaic and where? How widespread was its use? What factors influenced its development? What kind of literature was produced with it? What impact did it have on civilization? Internal history, on the other hand, has to do with linguistic change as such: Did Greek lose or gain specific consonantal sounds in the course of its development? Was its syntax simplified or made more complex? To what extent did the meanings of words change? These two kinds of concerns cannot always be separated from one another, but keeping the distinction in mind helps clarify some of the issues involved.

Hebrew and Aramaic

Quite possibly, Abraham, whose relatives resided in an Aramean region north of Palestine, spoke a very ancient form of Aramaic at the time he entered Canaan.[12] It is reasonable to suppose that he and his descendants adopted the closely related language spoken by their Canaanite neighbors. In the course of time, this Canaanite language would have developed into distinct forms corresponding to tribal groupings. Accordingly, Canaanite as spoken by the Hebrews became a distinct language and would have been viewed as one of many dialects spoken in Palestine and surrounding areas. And although the prestige of Hebrew would have grown significantly with the development of the Davidic and Solomonic monarchies (10th–9th centuries B.C.), it does not appear to have had much influence outside the Israelite boundaries.

In contrast, Aramaic became an international language in the Ancient Near East. The biblical narrative itself reflects this situation in the well-known story of Sennacherib's invasion of Judah. When the Assyrian king sent his field commander to threaten the people in Jerusalem, the Hebrew officials requested, "Please speak to your servants in Aramaic, since we understand it. Don't speak to us in Hebrew in the hearing of the people on the wall" (2 Kings 18:26). Subsequently, after the destruction of Jerusalem by the Babylonians, the Hebrews taken captive to Babylon adopted Aramaic (including the so-called "square script," used even today to write Hebrew) as a common means of communication. Those who returned to Palestine preserved both Hebrew and Aramaic, though Aramaic seemed to gain increasingly popular acceptance, especially among the Jews who lived in Galilee.[13]

---

[12]For a recent and capable discussion of the history of the Arameans, see Wayne T. Pitard, *Ancient Damascus: A Historical Study of the Syrian City-State from Earliest Times until Its Fall to the Assyrians in 732 B.C.E.* (Winona Lake, Ind.: Eisenbrauns, 1987). His own conclusions regarding the data from Genesis are cautiously stated: "There is no reason why there could not have been some relation between the ancestors of Israel and ancestors of the Aramaean tribes who set up the states in Syria at the end of the second millennium" (p. 87).

[13]See the thorough survey by Joseph A. Fitzmyer, *A Wandering Aramean: Collected Aramaic Essays* (SBLMS 25; Missoula, Mont.: Scholars Press, 1979), chap. 2.

After the close of the New Testament era, the Jewish state was destroyed (A.D. 135). Many Jews remained in some areas of Palestine, such as Tiberias, and continued to use Aramaic, whereas Hebrew was restricted more and more to academic contexts and writing. A similar situation obtained among the Jews in Babylon and other eastern settings. Throughout the Middle Ages and the modern period, Hebrew was not a living, spoken language. At the end of the nineteenth century, however, the language experienced an astonishing revival, and upon the emergence of the modern state of Israel in 1948, Hebrew took its place as a vital, national tongue.

The use of Aramaic continued to be much more widespread than that of Hebrew in late antiquity. Pockets of Aramaic-speaking communities in Palestine survived into modern times. So-called Eastern Aramaic had a particularly vibrant history, especially through a dialect known to modern scholars as Syriac (not to be confused with the language of the modern state of Syria, where Arabic is spoken). Christians in the environments of Antioch and in other population centers of the Near East, such as Edessa, but also as far as India, spoke this form of Aramaic and produced a very significant body of literature.[14]

Tracing the internal or linguistic changes of Hebrew and Aramaic is beset by certain complications. In the case of Aramaic, those changes are closely tied to dialectal variation. The Aramaic of the earliest inscriptions certainly shows some differences from that of the fifth-century B.C. Egyptian papyri (discovered in Elephantine), and this stage in turn must be distinguished from the later Aramaic documents discovered in Qumran. Unfortunately, however, there is no clear continuity between these various stages.

In the case of Hebrew, we do have a richer literary tradition extending for several centuries, but here too some obstacles stand in the way. In the first place, there is considerable debate concerning the date of some of the books of the Old Testament. Moreover, it appears that the text went through a linguistic updating; most likely, for example, the spelling may have been standardized toward the end of the biblical period, thus removing traces of earlier grammatical differences. Nevertheless, scholars would be in general agreement that some poetic portions of the Old Testament—notably the Song of Deborah in Judges 5—preserve archaic features going back beyond the first millennium B.C., while the Books of Chronicles represent the Hebrew spoken in postexilic Judah as late as the fourth century B.C.

Because of the technical character of this subject, only a few examples are appropriate here. The Hebrew verb distinguishes between masculine and feminine: *'azal* = "he went," but *'azelah* = "she went." The feminine ending *-ah* is standard through the Old Testament, but in Deuteronomy 32:36, a poetic passage, the expression "is gone" appears as *'azelat*, preserving the archaic ending *-at*.[15] With regard to syntax, as we will note in chapter 6, in most Old Testament books the so-called imperfect and perfect tenses of Hebrew are not used primarily to indicate the temporal distinctions of past-present-future. In Chronicles, however, this temporal indication becomes prominent. An example from the vocabulary may be especially interesting. The standard Old Testament word for "take" is

[14]Survivors of this Christian tradition in northern Iraq and Iran refer to themselves as Assyrians. Another important form of Aramaic, known as Mandean, was spoken in Persia by various groups.

[15]The subject of the verb, "strength," is feminine in Hebrew. For other examples see Eduard Y. Kutscher, *A History of the Hebrew Language*, ed. Raphael Kutscher (Jerusalem: Magnes, and Leiden: Brill, 1982), p. 39.

lqḥ, but this word underwent a semantic shift in the direction of "buy," and so the meaning "take" was appropriated by *ns'* ("carry").[16]

Greek

Our earliest historical evidence for the Greek language consists of some important tablets discovered in Mycene early in the twentieth century, though not deciphered until the 1950s.[17] The language of these documents is a form of Greek spoken at least as far back as the thirteenth century B.C., that is, about half a millennium earlier than our oldest, previously known inscriptions. Mycenean Greek has had an enormous impact on our understanding of both Aegean prehistory and post-Mycenean dialectal developments.

The reason this material is of such importance is that the Greek language in the classical period was greatly fragmented. Because of geographical distance and the isolation characteristic of the city-states, the dialect spoken by Greeks who lived on the western coast of Asia Minor (Ionia) differed significantly from that spoken in Athens (part of Attica); the differences would have been more noticeable when Ionic was contrasted with Aeolic (spoken in Thessaly and elsewhere), and even more so when contrasted with Doric (spoken in Corinth, for example). These dialects appear to have been mutually intelligible, and the Greeks were very much conscious of their common ethnic identity, but we should not minimize the degree of linguistic diversity that characterized the Greek-speaking world from the time of the earliest inscriptions in the eighth century to the period in which the New Testament was written.

For example, the Greek word for *sea* would have been pronounced *thalassa* in Ionic but *thalatta* in Attic. In both of these dialects the word for *house* was *oikias*, whereas the rest of the Greek dialects pronounced it *woikia*. Most of the Greek dialects used the ending -*men* to indicate that the subject of the verb is the first person plural (e.g., *esthiomen*, "we eat"), while the Dorians preserved the older ending -*mes* (cf. the related Latin ending, as in *amamus*, "we love"). In addition to these and many other phonological and grammatical differences, the vocabulary in each region had its own distinctives.

As is well known, Athens became the cultural center of the Greek-speaking peoples in the classical period. Naturally, the Attic dialect spoken in this city played a special role in literary work. Indeed, most authors (especially if they were writing prose) chose Attic as their primary medium. It may be worthwhile pointing out that among all the Greek dialects Attic was the most "corrupt"—at least if we use this word as many do today when they argue that the English language is being corrupted! The three examples mentioned in the previous paragraph consist of sound *changes* found in Attic but not always in the other dialects. The loss of the *w*-sound, as in *oikia*, was shared by Ionic (a closely related dialect), but not by others, while the sound -*tt*- for -*ss*- was unique to Attic. How corrupt (or dynamic, depending on one's perspective!) Attic must have sounded to other Greek

---

[16]Kutscher (ibid., p. 83) contrasts 1 Samuel 31:12–13 with 1 Chronicles 10:12, which changes two other words in addition to *lqḥ*. He also notes that the expression *laqaḥ ʾiššah* ("take a wife" = "marry") is changed to *nasaʾ ʾiššah* in Ezra 10:44.

[17]These tablets were not written using the Greek alphabet but a previously unknown script. The exciting story of its decipherment is available in John Chadwick, *The Decipherment of Linear B* (Cambridge: Cambridge University Press, 1958). For the linguistic implications of Mycenean, cf. L. R. Palmer, *The Greek Language* (Atlantic Highlands, N. J.: Humanities Press, 1980), chap. 2.

speakers is especially evident in its characteristic vowel contractions. The Ionic -*eo*- combination, for example (as in *kaleomenos*, "called") was "slurred" in Attic to the *u*-sound (*kaloumenos*).[18]

Of course, Attic was neither worse nor better than other dialects, as far as its linguistic structure was concerned. Because it was put to use by brilliant minds, however, this dialect became ideally suited, through a rich vocabulary and a broad stylistic potential, to express in written form the great intellectual flowering of the classical period. As long as we keep in mind that *any* language, spoken by these same intellectuals, would have become ideally suited for the same purpose, we may indeed celebrate the excellence of Attic Greek and its influence in Western civilization.

After the fourth century B.C., and as a result of Alexander the Great's extraordinary conquests, Attic was gradually adopted as a *lingua franca* not only by other Greek speakers but also by the populations of many diverse countries. Inevitably, the language underwent some radical changes in its process of becoming a *koinē dialektos* (the common speech). Many of these changes consisted of simplifications, as in the gradual abandonment of uncommon formations (the verb *deiknymi*, "to show," could now be conjugated as though it belonged to the more usual pattern, *deiknyō*). Following the popular tendency to intensify verbs, the Greeks formed numerous new compounds. The vocabulary was otherwise greatly enriched, often by the adoption of non-Greek words.

Not surprisingly, around New Testament times a reaction to these developments set in. It was indeed claimed by some that the Greek language had degenerated and that it must be restored to its former greatness. Books were written specifying what forms were acceptable—namely, those that could be attested in the writings of the classical period. For example, the lexicographer Phrynichus, who lived in the second century A.D., condemned the verb *eucharistō* (the common New Testament term for "give thanks," still alive and well in Modern Greek) on the grounds that "the approved ones" used the phrase *charin eidenai*.[19] This movement, which came to be known as *Atticism*, succeeded in creating a deep division in the Greek language, so that the speech of the home had to compete with an artificial form (used mainly in writing and formal speech). This infamous "language question" was a basic element in various social and political upheavals in Greece, and it has been only in the last decade or so that the country has enjoyed a measure of linguistic peace.

It is interesting that the language of the New Testament is quite free of the usual Atticizing features. Indeed, some of the books, especially the Gospel of Mark, are written in a very informal, colloquial style, but even the Epistle to the Hebrews, whose author must have had some literary pretensions, avoids the stilted expression that characterized the Atticists. The differences between the language of the New Testament and the Greek used

---

[18]To take things a step further: Greek was one of the most "corrupt" Indo-European languages. For example, the initial Indo-European sound *y*- (preserved not only in Sanskrit *yugám* and Latin *iugum* but even in English *yoke*) changed to *z*- in Greek (*zygon*); while initial *s*- became *h*, as in the pronoun *ho* (Sansk. *sá*). This last example is especially interesting to me because in many forms of Spanish (my native language) a comparable sound change, the partial loss of final -*s* (*las casas* becomes *lah casah*), is judged by some to be an ignorant corruption of Castillian. (And, incidentally, Castillian was the most progressive, or "corrupt," of all the medieval dialects in Spain!)

[19]Robert Browning, *Medieval and Modern Greek*, 2d ed. (Cambridge: Cambridge University Press, 1983), p. 47.

by pagan writers provoked much discussion throughout the history of the church. In the nineteenth century, the view that the New Testament was written in a unique language—heavily semiticized and perhaps made to order by the Holy Spirit—gained in popularity. The discovery in Egypt of thousands of Greek papyri, however, showed that most of the grammatical and lexical peculiarities of the New Testament could be paralleled in documents written by ordinary people for day-to-day purposes (family letters, commercial transactions, etc.).

Of special interest in this connection is the influence that Hebrew and Aramaic must have exerted on Palestinian Greek. This influence is most clearly seen in the vocabulary, which changes more quickly and easily than other aspects of language. The most obvious (though also the most superficial) evidence of foreign influence is the phenomenon of loanwords, as when English "borrows" the Spanish word *sombrero* to describe a particular type of hat for which there is no native English term. Several examples of this tendency are found in the Greek New Testament, perhaps the best known being *abba* (the Aramaic word for "father"; cf. Rom. 8:15).

A somewhat different phenomenon consists of so-called loan translations, that is, attempts to translate an idiom or expression by imitating the word-combination of the foreign language. For example, instead of simply borrowing the word *skyscraper*, Spanish speakers tried to reproduce it with the similar combination *rascacielos*. In the same way, the LXX translators took the Hebrew idiom *nasa' panim* ("to lift the face" = "to pay regard to a person, to be partial") and rendered it literally as *prosōpon lambanein* (cf. Gal. 2:6).

Perhaps the most important examples of foreign lexical influence are semantic loans. Instead of borrowing a whole word (a sound combination plus its meaning), speakers who recognize a partial equivalence between a certain native word and the corresponding foreign term may decide, consciously or unconsciously, to "borrow the rest" of the foreign word's meaning—that is, to "extend" the meaning of the native word so that it corresponds more fully to the foreign word. When we say, *I give you my word*, we are using the term *word* in imitation of the French *parole*, with its extended meaning "promise." Some important theological terms in the New Testament reflect a similar development. The Hebrew *kabod* ("weight, honor") is difficult to translate when used to describe a brilliant divine manifestation. Because the Greek *doxa* ("opinion") could be used in the sense of "reputation," the LXX translators chose it to render the Hebrew term and thus the Greek word took on an extra theological nuance, "glory."[20]

It is beyond dispute that most New Testament authors wrote in a style that occasionally reflects their Hebrew/Aramaic background. Moreover, the intellectual and spiritual power of the gospel message would inevitably have left an imprint on the speech of the early Christians, just as it has on the language of modern English-speaking believers. Nevertheless, there is nothing exotic or artificial about New Testament Greek. The apostles were primarily interested in communicating their message clearly and vigorously. And under God's guidance they succeeded.

---

[20]For a more detailed discussion see chap. 3 of *Biblical Words and Their Meaning: An Introduction to Lexical Semantics* in this volume. More broadly, on the question of whether New Testament Greek is a unique language, see my article, "Bilingualism and the Character of Palestinian Greek," *Biblica* 61 (1980): 198–219. For a fine study of syntactical influence from Hebrew-Aramaic, see E. C. Maloney, *Semitic Influence in Marcan Syntax* (SBLDS 51; Chico, Calif.: Scholars Press, 1981).

five

DESCRIBING
THE BIBLICAL
LANGUAGES (I)

*I*n attempting to describe and understand any language, the question soon arises: How shall we slice the pie? Traditionally, a sharp distinction has existed between (1) dictionaries or lexicons, which describe the vocabulary, and (2) grammars, where almost every other aspect of language is treated. Grammar books in turn have been divided into (a) a description of the sounds (*phonology*) and writing of the language; (b) an analysis of the rules for word formation and inflection (*morphology* or *accidence*); and (c) a more substantive section dealing with *syntax*, that is, the arrangement of words to form phrases and sentences, along with their resultant meaning.

The boundaries dividing these areas are not always clear, and inconsistencies often develop. Contemporary linguists, influenced primarily by so-called transformational grammar, add a fourth category, *semantics*. A recent textbook, for example, outlines as follows the sets of rules involved in language acquisition:

(i) a set of *syntactic* rules which specify how sentences are built up out of phrases, and phrases out of words

(ii) a set of *morphological* rules which specify how words are built up out of morphemes (i.e., grammatical units smaller than the word)

(iii) a set of *phonological* rules which specify how words, phrases, and sentences are pronounced

(iv) a set of *semantic* rules which specify how words, phrases, and sentences are interpreted (i.e., what their meaning is)[1]

---

[1]Andrew Radford, *Transformational Grammar: A First Course* (CTL; Cambridge: Cambridge University Press, 1988), pp. 18–19.

For our purposes—which do not really include the teaching of grammar—a less popular, but pedagogically more useful, classification will serve just as well.[2] Based on those units of language that are quickly recognized by all speakers, our outline will focus successively on (1) sounds = phonology, (2) words = lexicology, (3) phrases and sentences = syntax, and (4) paragraphs and larger units = discourse and genre analysis. Each of the last three items will be further subdivided into matters of form (morphology in the broad sense) and meaning (semantics).

SOUNDS

Since neither Hellenistic Greek nor the Hebrew of ancient Israel is spoken today—and since the tape recordings that were produced in the ancient world are of notoriously poor quality—modern phonologists are somewhat handicapped when they seek to analyze the sound systems of the biblical languages. Moreover, only very rarely do phonological questions have a direct bearing on the interpretation of texts. For these reasons, we need not devote much attention to the sounds of ancient Greek and Hebrew/Aramaic in this book.[3] On the other hand, it would be a mistake to ignore phonology altogether. In the first place, we do know a great deal—if not as much as we would like—about ancient sounds, and especially about the structural significance of those sounds in their respective languages. Second, there is no better way to understand what modern linguistics is all about than by seeing this discipline operate on sound systems: phonological structures are small (often thirty to forty significant sounds) and consist of relatively simple relationships, so that linguistic analysis becomes clearer and firmer than it is when dealing with the other, more complex aspects of language. In the third place, some familiarity with the phonology of Greek and Hebrew provides a base on which to build an accurate knowledge of the biblical languages as a whole; indeed, certain kinds of interpretive questions, though not directly affected by phonology, can be answered more reliably if the interpreter has a good grasp of linguistic structure (of which sounds are a part).

Probably the most elementary principle of phonology is *the need to distinguish between letters and sounds*. This distinction could be viewed as a restatement (or at least a specific example) of the principle that, in linguistic study, oral language takes precedence over its written expression. In our modern society, where the written form has such a strong cultural significance, we tend to confuse these elements. Moreover, since we cannot study Greek and Hebrew by interviewing ancient speakers, we are confined to literary remains, and that factor tends to blur distinctions even further.

The point at issue here is that alphabets are only *approximations* of sound inventories. When the alphabet was first devised—probably by Northwest Semites no later than 1500 B.C.—it presumably corresponded quite closely to the set of significant sounds used by the language in question. As that language (as well as its relatives, such as Hebrew, which used the same alphabet) developed, the written system could not easily keep up with gradual changes in the phonology. The problem was further complicated when that

[2]This approach, which has not caught on, was suggested (excluding the attention to paragraphs) many years ago by J. Ries and commended by Ullmann, *Principles,* pp. 26, 32–36 (note the diagram on p. 39).

[3]For a useful integration of modern phonology and Ancient Greek, see David A. Black, *Linguistics for Students of New Testament Greek: A Survey of Basic Concepts and Applications* (Grand Rapids: Baker, 1988), chap. 2.

alphabet was adopted by unrelated languages, such as Greek.[4] In any case, sound and writing move almost inexorably farther and farther apart. Languages that have experienced very rapid phonological changes (e.g., French and English) end up with a significant disparity between sounds and alphabet. To dramatize the problem, George Bernard Shaw once pointed out, somewhat unfairly to be sure, that in English it is possible to spell the word *fish* with the letter sequence *ghoti*.[5]

Now as we noticed in the previous chapter, Hebrew and its cognate languages depend heavily on their consonantal system and only secondarily on the vowels. Prior to the Middle Ages, in fact, all Hebrew writing was done exclusively with consonants (though a few of the consonants could serve to indicate vowel sounds in some instances of ambiguity). Jewish medieval scholars responsible for the transmission of the Hebrew Scriptures—these scribes were known as *Masoretes*, "transmitters"—developed a sophisticated system of notation to indicate not only the vowels but also almost every phonetic variation imaginable. Their purpose was not primarily linguistic: they were interested in preserving as carefully as possible, now that Hebrew was no longer a living tongue, the precise way in which the Bible was read (and cantillated—that is, chanted in the synagogue services).

As a result, modern seminarians who undertake the study of the Hebrew Bible are confronted with a bewildering number of signs. Many of these signs (especially the "accents" used for cantillation) are usually ignored, but that still leaves some complications. Textbooks, unfortunately, seldom make clear to the student that most of those notations have little linguistic significance. For example, as soon as students are introduced to the alphabet, they note that a few of the consonants can be pronounced in two different ways, depending on whether or not they have a dot (the *dagesh*) in the middle. Thus students are usually taught to pronounce the letter *dalet* like the English *d* if it has that dot (ד), but like *th* as in *them* if it does not (ד). Strictly speaking, that distinction is merely *phonetic*, not *phonemic*, because it cannot be used to distinguish between words. Speakers of ancient Hebrew were probably quite unaware of the distinction, much as modern speakers of Spanish are unaware of a similar distinction in their pronunciation of the two *d*'s in the word *soldado* ("soldier"; the last syllable is pronounced roughly like English *though*).[6]

Another example of the same class is the large number of vowel signs used by the Masoretes. How many actual *phonemes* (belonging to any given chronological stage) were represented by these signs is a matter of debate, but we may be sure that there was no one-to-one correspondence.[7] Modern seminarians, however, tend to identify all the written vowel signs as significant sounds; and while this mistake may not affect adversely the doctrinal content of their future sermons, they go through a period of unnecessary confusion

---

[4]See Joseph Naveh, *Early History of the Alphabet: An Introduction to West Semitic Epigraphy and Palaeography* (Jerusalem: Magnes, and Leiden: Brill, 1982), which includes a chapter on the Greek alphabet.

[5]Pronounce the *gh* as in *tough*, the *o* as in *women*, and the *ti* as in *nation*.

[6]I mention this item from personal experience. Though Spanish is my native language, it never occurred to me that I pronounced the *d* (as well as *b* and *g*) in two different ways—until my early twenties, when I began the study of Hebrew! The rule, for both Hebrew and Spanish, is that the consonants in question are *spirantized* (the breath is not blocked by the tongue [or lips or glottis] but allowed to flow) when they follow a vowel sound. Thus the *d* and *th* sounds are said to be *allophones* of the one *phoneme* /d/: which of the two is used is determined by the sound context, not by a desire of the speaker to distinguish meaning. Allophones therefore are found in "complementary distribution" and cannot be linguistically contrasted; they do not play a role in the phonological structure of the language.

[7]Some estimates put the number of vocalic phonemes as low as five; see Kutscher, *History*, p. 29.

that affects their perception of the language as a whole. This problem is further aggravated by the fact that most grammars seek to describe the Masoretic vowels through diachronic and comparative data.

Sound values are a little easier in the case of New Testament Greek, but here too misunderstandings are not uncommon. The problem begins as soon as students are required to attach an English sound to each Greek letter. The "classroom" pronunciation of Greek in America (and, *mutatis mutandis,* in most European countries) is quite odd and artificial: it mixes sounds from various stages in the evolution of the language and creates a couple of new ones! Our task is made harder by the fact that the New Testament was written at a time when important phonological changes were taking place— no doubt at different rates and in different ways from region to region. The differences between Classical Greek (say, in fifth-century B.C. Athens) and Medieval Greek are many. The most striking change is in the vowels. Ancient Greek had, aside from the diphthongs, a set of ten phonemes:

> long and short[8] α
>
> long and short ι
>
> long and short υ
>
> long η and short ε
>
> long ω and short ο

By the Middle Ages, however, many of these sounds had merged; indeed, all of the following are today pronounced the same way (like English *ee*): ι, η, υ, ει, οι.

The question then becomes: Where does the New Testament language belong in this process? Precision eludes us. The initial breakdown of the vowel system can be traced as far back as the fourth century B.C.,[9] but we cannot be sure how many changes had taken place by the first century. Ancient writings of an informal nature (especially graffiti) can be especially helpful to the linguist, since people often violate spelling conventions by writing as they speak. For example, the Greek word for "rod," ῥάβδος (*rhabdos*), has been attested with the spelling ραυδος as early as the New Testament period. It is therefore clear that already at that time (1) the sound represented by β had shifted from the occlusive [b], in which the air is stopped momentarily, to a sound that allowed the air to flow freely; and (2) the diphthong αυ had shifted to a sound approaching that of the English combination *av*.[10]

---

[8]The words "long" and "short" here mean exactly what they say. Unlike the English vowels often described as long, which are really diphthongs (e.g., the *a* in *cake*, where the quality of the vowel changes during its pronunciation), vowels in Ancient Greek, as well as in many other languages, could be pronounced for a duration of what we may call one unit of time or for a duration of two units (that is, twice as long), but without a change in the quality of the vowel. Such a distinction seems overly subtle to English speakers, yet in Arabic (to use the classic example) the difference between *jamāl* and *jamal* is that between "beauty" and "camel."

[9]According to the researches of Sven-Tage Teodorsson, *The Phonemic System of the Attic Dialect 400/340 B.C.* (Studia graeca et latina gathoburgensia 32; Lund: Berlingska Boytryckeriet, 1974), cf. also *The Phonology of Ptolemaic Greek* (Studia 36; 1977) and *The Phonology of Attic in the Hellenistic Period* (Studia 40; 1978).

[10]In Modern Greek β is pronounced like English *v*, while αυ and ευ are pronounced *av* and *ev* (or, before certain consonants, *af, ef*). For details see especially Peter Mackridge, *The Modern Greek Language: A Descriptive Analysis of Standard Modern Greek* (Oxford: Oxford University Press, 1985).

It is useful to keep in mind that certain features of Hellenistic Greek are remnants of previous centuries. Students learn early on in their study of Greek, for instance, that the preposition ἀπό (*apo*, "from") drops the last vowel if the next word begins with a vowel (ἀπ' ἀρχῆς). Moreover, if that next word begins with a vowel that has the rough breathing mark, a further change takes place, as in ἀφ' ὑμῶν (*aph' hymōn*, "from you"). By New Testament times the letter φ was probably already pronounced [f], and there would seem to be no reason why the sound [p] should change to [f] just because the following word begins with the sound [h]. In the classical period, however, the φ was pronounced [pʰ],[11] so one can easily understand how the sequence *ap hymōn* would lead to a spelling representing *apʰ hymōn*.

The attentive reader may have noticed that in my effort to describe the state of the sound system of Greek in the first century (synchronic linguistics), I have been compelled to take into account historical (diachronic) data. Because of our limited information, this problem is inevitable and shows that the two perspectives, while distinct, are not totally separable. Using them to supplement each other, however, is not the same as *confusing* them. The key is to avoid our tendency to explain synchrony by means of diachrony, as though one could read the linguistic realities of an earlier period into the state of the language we are concerned with.

WORDS

Form

Just as we can distinguish phonemes (linguistically meaningful sounds) from those variations (allophones) that do not affect the structure of the system, so can we distinguish *morphemes* from *allomorphs*. Like phonemes, morphemes are minimal units; unlike phonemes, which do not by themselves convey meaning, morphemes have semantic content. For example, the unit *cat* happens to be a complete word, but because it cannot be further subdivided it is also a morpheme. We can, however, add the morpheme *-s*, which has the semantic content of plurality, to form the "new" word *cats* (composed of two morphemes). The morpheme of plurality, though, can be "realized" in more than one way, leading to a variety of allomorphs: compare the different pronunciation of this morpheme in *cats, boys,* and *boxes.*

The rules for formal changes in words differ significantly among languages. Chinese, for example, is characterized by a large number of monosyllabic words that do not change in form. Turkish, on the other hand, takes a base word and adds not one but several morphemes at the end:

ev = "house"
evler = "houses"
evleri = "his houses"
evlerinden = "from his houses"[12]

---

[11]The reader should recall, from the discussion in chap. 2, that the sound represented by English *p* is in fact an aspirate very much like Ancient Greek φ; the unaspirated *p* of French and Spanish (but also of English in such words as spot) corresponds to Greek π. Thus Ancient Greek had two distinct phonemes for what in English is one phoneme (with two allophones). The situation is similar with the pairs τ/θ and κ/χ.

[12]The example is taken (in simplified form) from John Lyons, *Introduction to Theoretical Linguistics* (Cambridge: Cambridge University Press, 1969), p. 188. This feature of Turkish, shared by some other languages, is what motivated the description *agglutinative.*

In contrast to both of these types, the biblical languages are *inflecting* in character, that is, they modify a part of the word (usually the ending) to express various relationships. English in its early history was primarily inflecting, but in its modern dress it retains few inflections (the plural morpheme mentioned above, the past *-ed* ending, the possessive *-'s*, etc.). Hebrew and Aramaic have retained a larger proportion of inflecting features, and Greek even more.

For example, the only inflections allowed by most English nouns are those of plurality and possession, though the personal pronouns have also retained the so-called accusative case (*him, her, them*), indicating the object of the verb. In addition to features comparable to those three forms (each of which, incidentally, serves a variety of purposes), Greek adds a fourth, called dative, usually to indicate the indirect object of the verb, and a fifth, the vocative (more restricted in use). Hebrew and Aramaic lost the nominal inflections,[13] except those indicating plurality. Adjectives, however, can be inflected to indicate gender (as can Greek adjectives), something unknown in English: the word *tall* does not change at all, regardless of the kind of noun it modifies (contrast Spanish, *el hombre alto*, "the tall man," but *la mujer alta*, "the tall woman").[14]

The richness of Greek inflections is especially apparent in the verbal conjugations. While English has retained only one inflectional morpheme to indicate the category of person,[15] Greek and Hebrew, along with many other languages, have six: first, second, and third persons, each singular and plural. While English has only one morpheme to indicate tense (*-ed*, simple past), Greek has a variety of forms, each of which is combined with the indicator of person: .

> *pempō*, "I send"; *pempomen*, "we send"
>
> *pempsō*, "I will send"; *pempsomen*, "we will send"
>
> *epempon*, "I was sending"; *epempomen*, "we were sending"
>
> *epempsa*, "I sent"; *epempsamen*, "we sent"
>
> etc.

Although Hebrew does not have as many tenses, it goes Greek one better by including gender in its inflections:

> *malak*, "he reigned"; *malekah*, "she reigned"
>
> *yimlok*, "he will reign"; *timlok*, "she will reign"
>
> etc.

We could devote much more space to the intricacies of lexical morphology.[16] One other item, however, may be worth mentioning here, and that is the ease with which

---

[13]Proto-Semitic had three nominal inflexions, still preserved in Arabic. As we will see, there is a relationship between the presence/absence of case endings and the question of word order in a sentence.

[14]It should be noted, incidentally, that these inflectional endings, though applauded by some admirers of the classical languages, add absolutely nothing to what the speaker wants to say. One could just as easily argue that English, by wisely dropping these changes, is a model of linguistic economy and thus saves its speakers a great deal of mental energy!

[15]The ending *-s* for the third person singular in the present tense: *I come*, but *he/she/it comes*.

[16]For a clear discussion of Greek morphology, see Black, *Linguistics*, chap. 3. The morphology of biblical Hebrew is summarized in Kutscher, *History*, pp. 30–43.

Greek forms compounds. Every speaker of English is familiar with the process: we may, for example, prefix the adjective *counter* to other adjectives or nouns, such as *attack, culture, revolutionary*, etc., and thus create new words. This process is much more productive in such a language as German, whose speakers coin numerous words every day, especially by combining prepositions with nouns and verbs. Similarly, a Greek speaker could easily take the verb *dechomai* ("take, receive, await"), then prefix a preposition to form *ekdechomai* ("take from"), then further "strengthen" the verb by prefixing another preposition to form *apekdechomai* ("to await eagerly"). As a result, many Greek words are "transparent"; that is, the reader can readily identify their components and thus infer their approximate meaning. Hebrew, on the other hand, does not lend itself easily to this kind of word formation; but as we saw in the previous chapter, the Semitic languages can generate a large number of forms by means of verbal stems.

Meaning

The study of meaning encompasses a broad and bewildering range of subjects. For the moment we are concerned only with word-meaning or lexical semantics, a topic that attracts great popular interest and, partly for that very reason, is susceptible to much misunderstanding. As will become clear, separating lexical semantics from other aspects of meaning is somewhat artificial, but this procedure can provide the foundation for subsequent discussion.[17]

Etymology

Perhaps no aspect of language study proves more fascinating than tracing the development of word meanings. Who can resist the charm of finding out that the word *gossip* comes from *godsib* ("related to God"), used of godparents in the Middle Ages, and that the current meaning of the word arose from the chatter—not always edifying—typical at christenings in those days? This kind of information can shed much light on the workings of language as well as on society.[18] For some reason, however, most of us go on to infer that such a discovery gives us a better understanding of the *present* meaning of the word. And that is where our troubles begin.

The distinction between synchrony and diachrony is nowhere more relevant than in our study of lexical semantics. It should be quite apparent that the vast majority of English speakers today, being quite unaware of the history behind *gossip*, use the word without any reference to christenings, the concept of godparenting, or anything of the sort. Imagine, then, the following conversation between Harry and Mike:

> "Say, Mike, I heard some interesting gossip at the convention last week."
> "Oh, really? Who was being christened?"
> "Nobody was being christened. Why do you ask?"

---

[17]What follows summarizes most of the principles covered in my book, *Biblical Words*, to which the reader is referred for fuller documentation and detail. The recent and successful work by Peter Cotterell and Max Turner, *Linguistics and Biblical Interpretation* (Downers Grove, Ill.: InterVarsity, 1989), includes a substantive chapter on lexical semantics that I heartily recommend. Note also D. A. Cruse, *Lexical Semantics* (CTL; Cambridge: Cambridge University Press, 1986).

[18]See especially the literate discussion of the social dimensions of semantic change by Geoffrey Hughes, *Words in Time: The Social History of English Vocabulary* (New York: Blackwell, 1988).

"Come on, Harry! The basic meaning of the word *gossip* has to do with god-parenting."

"Who cares? I was just talking about the rumors I heard last week."

"That's what you think. Words preserve their core meanings, so it's impossible to understand your statement without some reference to christening."

"Take my word for it, Mike: I did not intend to say anything at all about christenings or godparents."

"But you can't just make language mean what you want it to. Seems like you would have more respect for the essence of language. I'm rather disappointed in you."

Such a conversation sounds ludicrous, and indeed none of us goes around injecting historical ideas of that sort into statements made by our friends. When it comes to literature, however, especially older literature, this method of interpretation becomes the order of the day—and, unlike Harry, the apostle Paul is not here to defend himself. As mentioned in the previous chapter, there are occasions (as in some poetic passages of the Old Testament) when we come across rare words whose meaning is unclear and for which etymological analysis can provide some help. Most words, however, are widely attested and their meaning can be clearly established from the numerous contexts in which they appear. This state of affairs is especially true of New Testament Greek, which ironically has been subjected to a great deal of (unneeded) etymologizing.

One of the reasons etymologies have become popular is that they provide interesting illustrations. A preacher, for example, may feel that his sermon is more concrete if he tells the congregation that the "basic meaning" of the Greek word for truth, *alētheia*, is "unhiddenness," or that the "real point" of sin, *hamartia*, is "missing the mark." Certainly the idea of "release upward from a binding contract" as the meaning of Greek *analysis* is much more exciting than the simple translation "departure."[19] Even more productive of sermon illustrations is what may be called "reverse etymologizing," as when we are told, on the basis of the verb *metamorphoō* ("transform," Rom. 12:2), that sanctification is like the process of change from a chrysalis to a butterfly. The use of English *metamorphosis* as a technical term to describe this process, however, is a modern peculiarity, and there is no reason to think that Paul had such a biological thought in mind when he penned those words.

Perhaps there is no harm done by using etymological information for illustrative purposes, as long as the person doing so and the audience that hears it are clear on what is happening. For exegetical purposes, however, our guiding principle ought to be, What did the author have in mind to say? And since authors cannot have in mind what they and their audiences are unaware of, etymology seldom has a role to play in the interpretation of texts. Other factors must be brought to bear, and we will consider these now.

Reference and Structure

As children grow up, they often learn the meaning of a new word by the parents' pointing to an object and pronouncing the word in question: "Look out the window, Karen; that's a *cow*." If the needed object is not readily available for pointing, the next best method—not fundamentally different from pointing—is to give a description: "A cow

---

[19]See above, chap. 1, p. 201.

is like a puppy, only much bigger, has horns, and goes 'Moooo.'" Even as adults, we partly build up our vocabulary in a similar way.

Almost inevitably, we tend to think of meaning as a one-to-one correspondence between an object in the world (the extralinguistic referent) and the word that refers to it. This way of looking at meaning seems to work much of the time, but careful reflection makes clear that, by itself, it is a rather unsatisfactory explanation. To begin with, children learn the most basic and frequent words in their language without any pointing or description. This is true not only of what we may call "function words," such as articles and prepositions (which act primarily as grammatical markers); it also applies to many verbs, abstract nouns, etc.

More to the point, both children and adults build up *most* of their vocabulary simply by hearing (or reading) words used in a variety of contexts. Much of this learning is unconscious. While reading a magazine article, we come across a word we haven't really seen before; without even noticing that it is a "new" word, we manage to infer its meaning, more or less automatically, from the whole context. This fact demonstrates that word meaning is not only—and perhaps not primarily—a matter of *reference,* of linking up words with objects outside of language.[20] To a large extent, word meaning is constituted by the relationships that exist *within language itself*.

Just as English-speaking children intuitively figure out (through gradual familiarity with phonological relations) that the [t] in *stop* and the [tʰ] in *top* are alternate sounds of the one phoneme /t/, and that this phoneme is quite a different one from the very similar /d/, so do they learn the "value" and therefore proper use of words by ascertaining their contrasts and combinations, in short, by mastering lexical *structure*. Consider this sentence: *Some tall men ate slowly*. We could say that the meaning of *some* is largely determined by its contrast with other words that can occupy the same slot in that sentence, for example, *the, few, several, many* (similarly, *tall* contrasts with *short, thin, fat*, etc.; *men* with *women, boys*; and so on).[21] Each of these words occupies a segment out of a larger field of meaning, and the presence of other words in the same field affects its value. Suppose, for example, that the word *several* were to disappear from the language without a new word taking its place; in that case, *some* or *few* (or both) would have to occupy the area vacated by *several*. In short, the range of meaning, and therefore the potential sentence use, of a word is established by its opposition to semantically neighboring words.

But "range of meaning" and "potential use" are vague concepts. What really matters is what happens when words are combined with each other in specific *contexts*. The rules of English do not allow for certain combinations, such as *Slowly men ate tall*. Words

---

[20]My comments here are not intended to prejudice the larger questions involved in evaluating "the reference theory of meaning." One may downplay the role of reference in lexical meaning without suggesting that the concept of reference as such is invalid or inappropriate. In particular, I would want to argue that the reference theory accounts satisfactorily (if not exhaustively) for *propositions,* such as those involved in historical narratives. Cotterell and Turner have an excellent, balanced discussion of this subject in *Linguistics*, pp. 82–90.

[21]These contrasting relationships are technically known as *paradigmatic*, a term used in phonology to indicate the contrast among similar phonemes, such as /b/, /v/, /p/, /f/. The term *syntagmatic* is used to describe the possible combinations into which phonemes can enter, such as /t/-/o/-/p/ in the word *top*. Note that certain combinations, such as /o/-/t/-/p/, are not permissible in English; similarly, English rules do not permit beginning a word with the sound represented by *ng* (as in *-ing*), even though that combination is common in some languages, as in the African name, (Lake) Ngami.

that are similar in meaning (synonyms) are often distinguished simply by the contexts in which they can occur: the expressions *deep thinker* and *profound thinker* are almost interchangeable, but whereas *deep water* is common enough, *profound water* is regarded as unacceptable. Accordingly, one should treat with healthy skepticism discussions of biblical synonyms that fail to indicate the specific contexts in which the supposed similarities and differences among the words occur.

We may illustrate how structural relations function in the biblical vocabulary by citing a specific application that has become well known.[22] The terms "image" and "likeness" (Hebrew *ṣelem* and *demut*) in Genesis 1:26 have caused heated debate among scholars. Much of the disagreement, however, arises out of the assumption that the terms are primarily (or exclusively) referential and that by focusing on each word we can "squeeze from it alone a decisive oracle about its meaning." Instead, Barr proposes to "look at a whole group of words and hope that meaning may be indicated by the choice of one word rather than another within this group." The results of Barr's research are that *ṣelem* was probably chosen because, though somewhat ambiguous, it was the term least likely to be misunderstood. The addition of *demut* then helped to circumscribe its meaning "by indicating that the sense intended for *ṣelem* must lie within that part of its range which overlaps with the range of *demut*."

A significant advance in biblical lexicology is the recent publication of the United Bible Societies' dictionary of New Testament Greek, prepared according to structural relations.[23] By using this tool, students can develop valuable sensitivity to the makeup of the Greek vocabulary generally, as opposed to the tunnel-vision characteristic of much word study. In this dictionary, words are not arranged alphabetically (the index is the place for that) but according to semantic fields or domains. At a glance, the user can see the various choices (that is, the lexical contrasts) available to the New Testament writers when they sought to express an idea. By focusing on groups of words rather than on isolated items, biblical interpreters can analyze the text with greater reliability.

Suppose that we are studying Paul's letter to the Philippians and become intrigued by 1:3–4: "I thank my God every time I remember you. In all my prayers for all of you, I always pray with joy." A more literal translation would read, "I thank [*eucharistō*] my God upon every remembrance of you always in every prayer [*deēsei*] of mine for all of you with joy making the prayer [*tēn deēsin poioumenos*]." Apart from some syntactical questions in this passage, we may wonder what is the precise meaning of the noun *deēsis*. If we check the index of the UBS *Lexicon*, we find that only one meaning ("plea") is assigned to this word and that it is treated in section 33 (terms dealing with communication), subsection L (general meaning "ask for, request"). This subsection, however, includes more than a dozen additional terms that belong to the same area of meaning (semantic domain); moreover, we notice that subsection M includes terms with the more specific meaning "pray."

[22]James Barr, "The Image of God in the Book of Genesis—A Study of Terminology," *BJRL* 51 (1968–69): 11–26; quotations from pp. 14–15, 24.

[23]Johannes P. Louw and Eugene A. Nida, eds., *Greek-English Lexicon of the New Testament Based on Semantic Domains*, 2 vols. (New York: United Bible Societies, 1988). Cf. my review in *WTJ* 51 (1989): 163–67.

As we compare these various terms and check them more carefully, we discover some interesting facts, such as the preference in the Gospel of John for common words that have no distinct religious nuance (e.g., *aiteō* and *erōtaō*). In some passages there seems to be a clear distinction between *proseuchē/proseuchomai* as general terms and *deēsis/deomai* as specific: ". . . always in my prayers [*proseuchēn*] asking [*deomenos*] . . ." (Rom. 1:10, literal translation). It would be misleading, however, to apply this distinction everywhere.[24] In Philippians 1:3–4, for example, Paul appears to include the giving of thanks (not only the petitions) under *deēsis*; that is, in this particular context *proseuchē* could have been substituted without any loss of meaning. Similarly, we could argue that in Philippians 4:6, where both of these terms are used, no special distinction is intended;[25] rather, Paul is probably exploiting their similarity to strengthen the stylistic force of his exhortation.

We may be sure that a greater emphasis on the vocabulary as a whole—and a corresponding downplaying of etymological study of individual words by themselves—will lead to responsible exegesis. There is, however, one additional matter that requires our attention.

Ambiguity

One often hears complaints about the supposed lack of precision in English. A preacher will say: "We use the word *love* in too many ways: we love God, we love children, we love our work, we even love chocolate. In contrast, the Greeks were very precise in their use of three distinct words for 'love.'" Comments of that sort romanticize Ancient Greek by failing to appreciate the character of language. To begin with, modern English probably has a greater number of words for "love" (both nouns and verbs) than Greek ever did: *affection, devotion, fondness, amorousness, adore, cherish, dote on*, etc., etc.

But even that consideration misses the important point that ambiguity is a valuable and even necessary aspect of all languages, since otherwise the number of words in everyone's active vocabulary would grow to unmanageable proportions. A very high percentage of words in English do double or triple duty, and it is not uncommon to find words that can be assigned half a dozen meanings. A few words even seem to be out of control: the verb *run*, for instance (even after excluding such phrasal constructions as *run against, run in*, etc.), has well over fifty "dictionary" meanings. In spite of this apparent confusion, however, we are rarely stumped by it. Can we even remember when was the last time we failed to grasp a specific use of *run*?

The reason ambiguity is seldom a problem in communication is that the context almost always excludes irrelevant meanings. The context may consist simply of the immediate word linkage: the combination *run an advertisement*, for example, instantly eliminates intransitive meanings (such as "take part in a race") as well as transitive meanings

---

[24]The principle of *neutralization* cuts across all levels of language. Cf. my *Biblical Words*, pp. 165–66. See also David Sankoff, "Sociolinguistics and Syntactic Variation," *LTCS* 4:140–61, especially p. 153: "While it is indisputable that some difference in connotation may, *upon reflection*, be postulated among so-called synonyms whether in isolation or in context, and that in the case of each one a number of competing syntactic constructions may be acceptable in somewhat different contexts, there is no reason to expect these differences to be pertinent every time one of the variant forms is used."

[25]If *proseuchē* is the general term, then it surely includes "petition" as part of its meaning; and if *deēsis* merely means "petition," the inclusion of this term would add no semantic content to the sentence. Cf. my *Philippians* (WEC; Chicago: Moody, 1988), pp. 49–50, 227.

that do not fit that combination (e.g., "accomplish," as in *run errands*; "operate," as in *run the computer*; "cause to crash," as in *run the car into the wall*). Or the context may consist of the subject matter: *He listed the names of the characters* is, in isolation, an ambiguous sentence, since the word combination here allows for a reference to either the names of letters in an alphabet or the names of persons portrayed in a play; the obscurity disappears, however, if we know the sentence was spoken by someone lecturing on Shakespeare. Again, the context may consist of the broad setting in which a sentence was spoken or written: *He brought a suit* has a simple, unequivocal meaning in a laundry shop, but quite a different one in a court of law.

Ambiguity arises more frequently when we read literature distant in time and culture from us, since we are less familiar with the whole context in which the writing originated. Scholars have debated whether Galatians 3:4 should be translated, "Did you suffer so many things in vain?" or "Did you experience so many things [= spiritual blessings] in vain?" The Greek word in question, *paschō*, usually has the negative meaning "suffer," but occasionally it may be used when describing a neutral or even positive experience. The immediate context suggests a positive reference, but if Paul was aware that the Galatians had gone through much suffering, that broader context may have determined the meaning of the verb at 3:4. It is difficult to reach a definitive conclusion.[26]

The fact that we occasionally meet such examples of unintentional ambiguity should not lead us to exaggerate the problem. In particular, we ought to resist the temptation to come up with new, but unattested, meanings that *might* fit the context. A recent article proposed that the use of the Greek words *peritomē* ("circumcision") and *akrobystia* ("uncircumcision") in the New Testament reflects an ethnic slur, that is, "epithets hurled at Gentiles and at Jews respectively by members of the opposite group in Rome and elsewhere."[27] According to this view, *peritomē* should be translated concretely, "circumcised penis" (and *akrobystia* should be translated literally, "foreskin").

All of the evidence for this view, however, is indirect in nature. Indeed, the only unambiguous evidence the author can offer is not from Greek at all but from the corresponding Hebrew word *milah*—and even that from rabbinic writings produced much later than the New Testament. Without explicit information that in fact Gentiles used to throw this kind of insult at Jews, we would need a few examples of *peritomē* where the new proposed meaning is the only one that makes sense.[28] In other words, the reality of lexical ambiguity cannot become a pretext for overworked imagination.

Quite different is the problem we face when a writer is deliberately ambiguous. We rarely come across deliberate ambiguity in normal prose writing, since authors write to be understood. For literary effect, however, authors sometimes tease their readers with double meanings, as when the Gospel of John 1:5 tells us that the darkness did not understand the light; since the Greek verb (*katalambanō*) can also mean "overcome," quite pos-

---

[26]For a more extensive discussion of this passage, see my *Biblical Words*, pp. 153–56.

[27]Joel Marcus, "The Circumcision and the Uncircumcision in Rome," *NTS* 35 (1989): 67–81, esp. p. 79.

[28]In the case of rare words or poorly attested literature, we sometimes may need to be satisfied with a less rigorous criterion. In the case of abundantly attested words, however, it is an elementary lexicographical principle that a proposed new meaning that happens to make sense in some contexts cannot be established as long as the attested meanings also make sense. One must offer examples where the alternate meanings do not work. Indeed, Marcus himself (ibid., p. 75) recognizes that there are some passages in Paul where the usual translation is the only one that is possible.

sibly John has deliberately used an ambiguous word. Before drawing such a conclusion, however, one should have fairly strong contextual reasons. In the case of the Gospel of John, the character of the book as a whole and other likely instances of ambiguity support the conclusion.[29]

More often, deliberate ambiguity arises in poetry, and there are many examples of this in the Old Testament. To be sure, we should not assume that this technique was as important to the psalmists as it seems to be to some modern poets. The evocative features of language, however, do play a significant role in Hebrew poetry. This is especially true of metaphorical language, which has a greater emotional impact on the reader than bare description has. For the psalmist to say that the Lord is his shepherd creates some ambiguity, since the reader is expected to identify the point of comparison between God and a shepherd. The psalmist does resolve the ambiguity when he adds, "I shall not want": clearly, the point of comparison is that the shepherd provides fully for the needs of his sheep. But there remains a measure of ambiguity (richness?) in that the reader can fill in the details, and the psalmist himself goes on to give some instances of the divine provision he has in mind.

Sometimes the ambiguity is more difficult to resolve. After God warns Isaiah about the spiritual callousness of Israel, the prophet asks how long that obduracy will continue. God responds: "Until the cities lie ruined and without inhabitant" (Isa. 6:11). At the end of the passage, however, we read:

> But as the terebinth and oak
>> leave stumps when they are cut down,
>> so the holy seed will be the stump in the land. (v. 13)

Clearly, the word *stump* is used figuratively for a residue of God's people, but the point of comparison is not obvious, even though the context suggests a hopeful note. By the time we get to chapter 11, however, the obscurity is removed:

> A shoot will come up from the stump of Jesse;
>> from his roots a Branch will bear fruit.
> The Spirit of the LORD will rest on him . . .
> and he will delight in the fear of the LORD. (vv. 1–3)

God will leave a holy remnant among his people, out of whom the Messiah will arise and bring salvation to them.

It is clear, then, that even in poetic passages where the author wishes to exploit the ambiguity of language, the purpose is not at all to confuse but to impress on our hearts the force of the divine message.

---

[29]A similar case can be made for the language of Ezekiel. Cf. Daniel I. Block, "The Prophet of the Spirit: The Use of *rwḥ* in the Book of Ezekiel," *JETS* 32 (1989): 27–49.

six

DESCRIBING

THE BIBLICAL

LANGUAGES (II)

SENTENCES

In the previous section I proposed to deal with words as individual items, more or less in isolation from sentences. The reader must have noticed, however, that it was impossible to carry through with that proposal. Apart from a few interjections (e.g., *Ouch!*) and simple imperatives (*Come!*), words are not normally used by themselves to communicate what we mean. Evangelicals often stress the view that biblical revelation is *propositional*, that is, it does not consist merely in a vague (and contentless) relationship between God and human beings. This concern, which involves a very important theological truth, acknowledges that the *meaning* of Scripture is to be found in its propositions, not in isolated words. Thus what really matters about the Bible is not just the fact that it contains, say, the verb *sin*, but that it communicates such statements as *All have sinned* (Rom. 3:23).

Not all word-combinations, of course, are sentences in the strict sense of the term. Some combinations are very difficult to distinguish in function from individual words. The meaning of such idioms as *a pain in the neck* cannot really be derived by adding up its parts: the whole combination stands for a simple concept comparable to that of *nuisance*. That is the reason good dictionaries do not merely give the meanings of an individual word: they go on to specify the sense of peculiar combinations in which that word may be found.

Other combinations consist of normal phrases, such as *the brown house, very likely, through the woods*, and so on. We use the term *clause* to describe word combinations that, while seemingly more "important" than phrases because they include a subject and a predicate,[1] may themselves be part of, and even dependent on, a larger utterance; for

---

[1] A *predicate* is that part of an utterance that comments on the subject. In Standard English the predicate always consists of at least a verb, but Hebrew and Greek, among other languages, frequently use verbless clauses (subject plus predicate nominative, with what appears to us an ellipsis of the verb *to be*; Gk. *ho anthrōpos kalos,* "the man [is] good"). Strictly speaking, a clause may be coextensive with a full and

example, *if they arrive in time*, or *after she ate her lunch*. Full, independent sentences can be quite short: *John arrived*. In languages (including Greek and Hebrew) that incorporate the subject in the verbal form, a single verb can constitute a complete sentence. Sentences can become extremely long and complex, however. Modern English versions may not show it, but Ephesians 1:3–11 consists of one sentence, made up of many shorter sentences and clauses.

Since we are interested in what is usually called *syntax*, this section will not be restricted to full sentences. Phrases and clauses will come under purview as well. On the other hand, we will not be concerned here with complex sentences: the linking together of sentences brings us close to the area of paragraphs and is best considered in the next section. In any case, the boundaries between the various levels of language are often fuzzy indeed.

Form

Each language has its own rules regarding phrase and sentence formation. In English, Greek, and Hebrew (but not in Aramaic), for example, the definite article must come before the noun to which it is connected: *the man = ho anthrōpos = ha- 'iš*. Both English and Greek (but not Hebrew) allow the insertion of an adjective between the article and the noun: *the good man = ho kalos anthrōpos*. Both Greek and Hebrew (but not English) allow the adjective, with its own article, to be placed after the noun: *(the man the good)*[2] *= ho anthrōpos ho kalos = ha- 'iš ha-tob*. And only Greek allows the insertion of a whole clause between article and noun: *ho erchomenos eis ton oikon anthrōpos (the coming-into-the-house man* = "the man who is/was coming into the house").

Both English and Hebrew, having lost most case endings, rely heavily on a fixed word order to indicate grammatical relationships among words. Greek, on the other hand, has few restrictions of that sort. The sentence (a) *The man loved the woman* is hardly identical in meaning to (b) *The woman loved the man*. The way we can tell in English who is doing the loving is precisely by looking at the position of the nouns. But that clue is completely useless in Greek. Sentence (a) can appear in Greek in any of these forms:

ho anthrōpos ēgapēsen tēn gynaika

ho anthrōpos tēn gynaika ēgapēsen

ēgapēsen ho anthrōpos tēn gynaika

ēgapēsen tēn gynaika ho anthrōpos

tēn gynaika ho anthrōpos ēgapēsen

tēn gynaika ēgapēsen ho anthrōpos

In order to get the meaning of sentence (b) we simply change the case of the word for "man" from nominative to accusative (*ton anthrōpon*), which marks it as the object of the verb, and "woman" from accusative to nominative (*hē gynē*), which marks it as the subject. Having done so, we can proceed to use any of the six patterns above. (Of course, some of these patterns are more common or likely than the rest, and thus a different nuance or emphasis can be achieved by choosing one over another. Note also that the position of the definite article with respect to its noun is pretty much fixed.)

---

independent (but simple) sentence. For our purposes, I will restrict the term *clause* to units that are syntactically dependent on other units.

    [2]The asterisk is commonly used to indicate linguistic forms that are unattested or grammatically unacceptable.

In the course of interpreting a biblical passage, students of Greek and Hebrew often find it necessary to consult standard grammars. Sometimes we merely need to identify an unusual form, and so we turn to the section entitled "Morphology" or "Accidence." More often than not, however, what we are really after is help in figuring out the particular force of a grammatical construction, and for that we must look under "Syntax." Rather than attempt a comprehensive and superficial survey of this field, let us consider in some detail the problems involved in interpreting nominal cases and verbal tenses. By doing so we should find it possible to formulate general principles that will prove applicable to most other syntactical problems.

Meaning: Case Relationships

As noted earlier, Hebrew (and Aramaic) do not make much use of case endings. Other means are available, however, for expressing syntactical relationships involving nouns. In particular, Hebrew makes frequent use of the so-called *construct state*, whereby two nominal forms are brought into close relationship. The resulting meanings are quite varied, and they parallel roughly the nuances conveyed by the cases (such as genitive and dative) in Greek. For example, just as the Greek genitive can be interpreted as subjective or objective, so a similar distinction is possible in Hebrew.[3] In Isaiah 9:7 (Heb. v. 6) we find the phrase *qin'at Yhwh*, "the zeal of the LORD"; in 26:11 there is the similar construction *qin'at- 'am*, "the zeal of the people." The context makes clear, however, that the relationship being intended in one is quite different from the other. The complete clause in the first passage is translated, "the zeal of the LORD Almighty will accomplish this" (subjective genitive, since the reference is to God's own zeal); in the second passage, more or less literally, "they will see zeal [for] the people" (objective genitive, because the people are the object rather than the source of the zeal; cf. NIV, "let them see your zeal for your people").

One of the first things that students of the biblical languages learn is that Greek has five distinct cases. The vocative case ending, used infrequently to indicate the person being spoken to, is fairly straightforward and does not concern us here. The nominative and the accusative, as we noticed above, are used primarily to indicate the subject and the direct object, and this distinction seldom creates exegetical problems (though certain other uses of the accusative can prove puzzling to the beginning student). Most interpretive questions arise in attempting to identify the precise relationship expressed by the dative[4] and (especially) the genitive.

Heavily influenced by the historical bias of nineteenth-century comparative linguistics, some New Testament scholars have argued, on the basis of the Sanskrit case system,

---

[3]That is, the noun in the genitive construction functions as either the subject or the object of an implied verb. The English phrase *the love of God* contains two nouns, *love* and *God*. We could say that *of God* is a genitive construction and that the phrase contains an implied verb, *to love*. If the speaker intends to refer to God's love for us, then the phrase is a subjective genitive, because *God* functions as the subject of the implied verb. If what is in view is our love for God, then it is an objective genitive, because *God* functions as the direct object. The example from Isaiah is taken from A. B. Davidson, *Hebrew Syntax*, 3d ed. (Edinburgh: T. & T. Clark, 1901), p. 31. For a detailed classification scheme and numerous examples, see Waltke and O'Connor, *Biblical Hebrew Syntax* § 9.5.

[4]A frequent and noncontroversial use of the dative is that of indicating the indirect object of the verb. "The woman [subject] gave a book [direct object] to the men [indirect object]" would be expressed, *hē gynē edōke biblion tois anthrōpois* (the *-ois* ending here is the marker for the dative plural).

that Greek originally had three other cases: the *ablative*, which had the "basic" idea of origin or separation but merged in form with the genitive; and the *instrumental* and *locative*, both of which merged with the dative. The great American grammarian A. T. Robertson adopted this approach and used it to describe the Greek cases in the New Testament.[5] This historical reconstruction is probably not too far from the truth, but even if it could be fully validated, we would have no good reason to adopt it as the proper framework with which to describe (as opposed to "explain the origins of") the cases in Hellenistic Greek. The very fact that these two extra cases cannot be distinguished from the others by their form tells us something about the speakers' linguistic consciousness. And if someone argues that the distinctive meanings if not the forms of these two cases can still be identified,[6] one must respond that such evidence would also justify creating numerous other "cases" to account for the many different meanings conveyed—such as the "temporal case" when the dative is used to indicate time, or the "caring case" when the genitive is used after such verbs as *epimeleomai* ("take care") and *pronoeomai* ("provide")!

So rule number one for interpreting the cases is to avoid being unduly influenced by historical data drawn from a previous stage of the language. A second important principle has to do with recognizing the close connection that obtains between case endings and prepositions. Both of these linguistic features function very much the same way, and in some respects they are interchangeable. Most of the syntactical relationships expressed with prepositions-plus-case can be expressed by case endings alone. For example, the instrumental idea "with the sword" occurs in Luke 22:49 as *en machairē*, but simply as *machairē* in Acts 12:2. Perhaps because prepositions are less ambiguous than cases (though not by much!), once a language begins to use prepositions, case endings become less important.[7] Prepositions have in fact taken over completely in Modern English and other languages.

It may be helpful for the English student to reflect on the parallels between English prepositions and Greek case endings. It is very difficult to describe the "meaning" of a preposition, since its force depends so heavily on the context. If we were asked, for example, what is the meaning of *with*, we would possibly first think of "association" or "companionship," as in *The American soldier spent time with his friends*. But then we might think of a quite different, almost opposite, idea, "against": *The American soldier fought with the Japanese*. Or

---

[5]A. T. Robertson, *A Grammar of the Greek New Testament in the Light of Historical Research*, 4th ed. (Nashville: Broadman, 1934), pp. 446–48. Quoting B. Green, he argued that "in every instance the true method of explanation of any particular idiom is to trace its connection to the general meaning of the original Aryan [= Indo-European] case" (p. 447). Robertson was followed, among many, by H. E. Dana and Julius R. Mantey, who wrote one of the most popular and thus influential intermediate-level textbooks in this country, *A Manual Grammar of the Greek New Testament* (New York: Macmillan, 1957); see especially pp. 65–68.

[6]As Robertson himself states, "There are indeed some instances where either of the blended cases will make sense. . . . But such occasional ambiguity is not surprising and these instances on the 'border-line' made syncretism possible. In general the context makes it perfectly clear which of the syncretistic cases is meant" (*Grammar*, p. 448).

[7]That statement is of course historical in nature. We do have evidence that in its earlier stages Greek used prepositions less frequently; in fact, comparative linguists can demonstrate that prepositions are a "late" development in the history of Greek and other languages. By medieval times, Greek case endings were much more restricted in use than they were in the Hellenistic period. In Modern Greek, all prepositions take the same case.

we are reminded of "instrument": *The American soldier struck the enemy with his rifle*. Or something close to "responsibility": *The general left the orders with the soldier*. Or "manner": *The soldier discharged his mission with grace*. We can list more than two dozen ideas, some of them quite disparate from the others, that can be expressed with this preposition!

It is interesting that English speakers are only vaguely aware of this wide flexibility. They do not have to be taught in first grade that there is a "with of companionship" and an "instrumental with," etc.; and yet they rarely fail to catch the force of the preposition. Most important, no one tries to explain what a preposition means in a particular sentence by appealing to a different use of that preposition. If we saw the phrase "with grace" and we wanted to analyze it or explain it to a foreign student, it would probably not occur to us to say, "The literal or basic meaning of *with* is 'companionship.'" A comment of that sort would be at best irrelevant and at worst confusing. Yet that is one of the most common ways in which modern writers, including some competent scholars, try to explain the use of case endings.

Labeling syntactical uses (whether of cases or tenses or whatever) is probably a pedagogical necessity: how else can adult students who are not learning Greek as a living language master the syntax? But if they do not get past the labeling, they in fact develop a very artificial understanding of how language works. A related problem is the need to learn the most common or important uses before becoming familiar with the others. For example, a student will be told that the genitive case indicates possession, "of." That is indeed a very common use of the genitive, but then the student assumes that it is the *basic* or *essential* meaning and tries to see it everywhere.

A preacher may come to Mark 11:22, where Jesus says, "Have faith in God." This preacher is serious about his study of the text, so he looks it up in the Greek and finds that the text does not have the preposition "in" and that the word for "God" is in the genitive. Come Sunday morning, the audience will almost certainly hear: "The original says literally, 'Have the faith *of* God,'" followed by various inferences (perhaps theologically sound, perhaps not) that have little or nothing to do with the text at hand. The Greek phrase is of course one instance of what we label the objective genitive: the word in the genitive ("God") acts as the object of the implied verb ("believe"). Because to English ears it sounds very strange to express that idea with the preposition "of," we tend to reject the idea or modify it. One suspects, in fact, that this problem has played a role in the opinion, adopted by some recent interpreters, that the expression *pistis Iēsou Christou* ("faith in Jesus Christ," in Gal. 2:16 et al.) should be translated "the faith [or faithfulness] of Jesus Christ."[8]

---

[8]Richard B. Hays, for example, thinks that the objective genitive interpretation does not sound natural. See his important book *The Faith of Jesus Christ: An Investigation of the Narrative Substructure of Galatians 3:1–4:11* (SBLDS 56; Chico, Calif.: Scholars Press, 1983), p. 187. Interesting, but rather fanciful, I think, is William L. Lane's suggestion that Mark 11:22 is not an exhortation but an encouraging statement, "you have the faithfulness of God" (*The Gospel According to Mark* [NICNT; Grand Rapid: Eerdmans, 1974], p. 409). Robertson (*Grammar*, p. 500) recognizes that here is an objective genitive, but misled by his historical approach, confusingly appeals "to the root-idea of the genitive as the case of genus or kind," and interprets this phrase as "the God kind of faith." C. E. B. Cranfield is closer to the truth when he says, "The suggestion that the genitive is subjective—'have the sort of faith God has'—is surely a monstrosity of exegesis" (*The Gospel According to Mark: An Introduction and Commentary* [CGTC; Cambridge: Cambridge University Press, 1974], p. 361).

But how *can* we know whether the use is objective or something else? Essentially, by the way we determine the meaning of the preposition *with* in English: by means of the context. We could point out that neither in Mark 11:22 nor in the broad context of the book does the author seem concerned about our having God's own faith as opposed to someone else's. Indeed, nowhere in the New Testament do we find even one *unambiguous* reference to our having the faith that belongs to God, whereas we come across scores of clear passages that speak about having faith *in* God or Christ.[9] For indisputable instances of *pistis* with the objective genitive, we may refer to Acts 3:16, "faith in his name" (*pistei tou onomatos autou*), and Colossians 2:12, "faith in the power of God" (*pisteōs tēs energeias tou theou*). One wonders if doubts about the objective interpretation of *pistis Iēsou Christou* could have occurred only to a modern Western speaker who had identified the Greek genitive with the meaning "of." At least, I am not aware of any ancient Greek father who even raised the possibility of understanding it as subjective.

We should note, incidentally, that the methods of transformational grammar shed some light on the expression *pistis Iēsou Christou*. One way of describing the ambiguity inherent in such a genitive is to say that it can be interpreted as the grammatical transformation of two different "kernel" constructions, (1) *Iēsous pistei*, "Jesus believes" (possibly *Iēsous pistos estin*, "Jesus is faithful"), and (2) *pisteuein eis Iēsoun,* "to believe in Jesus." Now while the second construction is found several times in Paul (and the concept behind it is central to the New Testament), the first one, in either form, is absent.[10] This kind of data is very much part of the context for the construction and should be seen as decisive for our problem.

Note, however, that our use of precise syntactical labels tends to obscure what really goes on when we speak or write. In an unpublished paper, Vern S. Poythress has clearly illustrated this issue.

> Suppose in the course of a conversation I say, "The destruction of the army appalled the political leaders." Many times my audience will automatically pick the proper sense of the "of" construction by means of context. It will never occur to them that the sentence in *isolation* is formally ambiguous.
>
> But suppose someone else overhears just this part of the conversation, and is left in the dark about its meaning. He says to me, "Do you mean that the army destroyed something else or that it was itself destroyed in a battle?" How do I answer? Do I remember the decision I made about the use of the "of" construction at the time I used it? No, I do not. It is impossible to remember a decision that I did not make, but that was, as it were, "made for me" in the act of speaking. What I do, typically, is to recall what I was speaking about, what topic I was discussing. And I report to my interlocutor the facts about that topic, namely that the army was the destroyer (or

---

[9]It may be useful to note that the objective genitive is especially common "with substantives denoting a frame of mind or an emotion." See Herbert Weir Smyth, *Greek Grammar* (Cambridge, Mass.: Harvard University Press, 1956) §1331.

[10]In response to my oral comments on this point, Richard Hays some years ago appealed to 2 Thessalonians 3:13; 2 Timothy 2:13; and 2 Corinthians 4:13. See *Conflict and Context: Hermeneutics in the Americas*, ed. M. L. Branson and C. R. Padilla (Grand Rapids: Eerdmans, 1986), pp. 276–77. No one doubts that the *concept* of Jesus' faithfulness (or even of his believing) is biblical and Pauline; my argument is based on the specific form of Paul's language. But even if those three passages used the name *Jesus*, one would still have to consider the preponderance of the evidence, especially in those contexts (Romans and Galatians) where the debate focuses.

alternatively the destroyed). My intention was *not* to "choose" a particular force of "of" from among a list of possibilities, but to communicate a certain truth concerning what happened to the army.[11]

Finally, the interpreter must be sensitive to the possibility that a biblical author, when using ambiguous syntax, has in fact produced a "vague" expression. Unfortunately, the concept of vagueness, like that of redundancy,[12] carries a negative association for most people. We must carefully distinguish between, on the one hand, vagueness in the sense of sloppiness (that is, in contexts where some precision is appropriate and expected) and, on the other, vagueness that contributes to effective communication (that is, in contexts where greater precision may mislead the reader or hearer to draw an invalid inference). The term *Siamese* is more precise than *cat*, yet there are many times when we do not wish to call attention to the specific kind of cat we happen to own but rather we simply wish to make a general statement that has broader applicability.

The classic example here is *to euangelion tou Christou*, "the gospel of Christ" (e.g., Phil. 1:27). What precisely is the relationship between the two nouns in this phrase? The gospel that belongs to Christ (genitive of possession)? The gospel that comes from Christ (genitive of source)? The gospel that Christ proclaimed (subjective genitive)? The gospel that proclaims Christ (objective genitive)? Perhaps the very asking of the question throws us off track. Countless readers of Paul's letters, without asking the question, have understood the apostle perfectly well. It would not be quite right to say that Paul meant *all* of these things at once—a suggestion that aims at stressing the richness of the apostle's idiom, but at the expense of misunderstanding the way that language normally works.[13] The point is that Paul was not thinking about any one of these possibilities in particular: he was using a general ("vague") expression that served simply to identify his message.

There is a fine line, however, between recognizing genuine linguistic ambiguity and becoming slipshod in our exegesis. For one thing, we may read a passage that comes across as ambiguous in English, but a careful look shows that the same ambiguity does not exist in the original. In an English translation of a Spanish document, the word *corner* may occur without clear indication whether the writer has in mind, say, the inside of a room or the outside of a building; the original cannot contain such an ambiguity, however, for Spanish uses *rincón* for the former and *esquina* for the latter.[14] Conversely, we could make the mistake of attributing precision to the original where it does not exist, as when Spanish uses *techo* for both "ceiling" and "roof."[15]

But even apart from that consideration, we need to remember that speakers and writers normally have a single meaning in view. In other words, we cannot allow the fact of linguistic vagueness to become an excuse for laziness in grammatical analysis or a pretense for uncontrolled interpretation. Take Galatians 1:12, where Paul insists that the

[11]Vern S. Poythress, "Is Exegesis Possible? I. A Relational Perspective on Meaning" (unpublished typescript), p. 11.

[12]See above, chap. 3, p. 227.

[13]Nigel Turner, I think, makes this mistake when he argues that "with a mind like St. Paul's, quicker than his own pen or a scribe's, it will not be unreasonable to distill every ounce of richness from the simple genitives of abstract qualities which abound in his epistles." See his work, *Grammatical Insights into the New Testament* (Edinburgh: T. & T. Clark, 1965), p. 111, and my comments in *Biblical Words*, pp. 150–51.

[14]"Isn't Spanish wonderfully precise?"

[15]"Can't Spanish speakers tell the difference between an interior and an exterior surface?!"

gospel he preaches is not a human product but that it came to him *di' apokalypseōs Iēsou Christou*. Should we take "Jesus Christ" as a subjective genitive (more specifically, of origin) and translate with the NIV, "I received it by revelation from Jesus Christ"? Or should we interpret it as an objective genitive, with the implication, "I received it when God revealed Jesus Christ to me"?

A strong argument in favor of the second interpretation is the fact that only two (Greek) sentences later, Paul uses what could be viewed as the unambiguous kernel clause: God was pleased "to reveal his Son in me" (*apokalypsai ton huion autou en emoi*, v. 16). On the other hand, the first interpretation is supported by the thrust of verse 12 itself, particularly since the phrase in question serves as the direct opposite of "from man" (*para anthrōpou*). Faced by this dilemma, the interpreter will be tempted to avoid a decision by arguing that it must be both, since the two aspects cannot be separated.

What may be conceptually or theologically true, however, is quite a different question from what a linguistic expression actually conveys. It would, I think, be legitimate to say, "We cannot reach a definitive decision on this problem, but the ambiguity does not affect significantly our understanding of Paul's point, since the two ideas are closely related and both are reflected in this very passage." On the other hand, it is probably misleading to argue that Paul intended to communicate these two distinct ideas with the one expression *di' apokalypseōs Iēsou Christou*.

At any rate, we can probably reach a decision. The other two Pauline uses of this construction (1 Cor. 1:7; 2 Thess. 1:7; both referring to the Second Coming) are unambiguously objective. Moreover, the objective interpretation does not at all contradict or even minimize Paul's emphasis on the origin of his gospel: given the fact that he received the gospel on the occasion when Jesus Christ was manifested to him, the message he preaches cannot possibly be attributed to human invention.

Meaning: Tense and Aspect

Perhaps no feature of the biblical languages is the source of more confusion and fanciful interpretation than the verbal "tenses." Beginning Greek students, upon being confronted with the term *aorist* (which is normally not used in English grammar), tend to inject quasi-mysterious associations into it. After all, they are first taught that it is roughly equivalent to the simple past tense (preterite) in English, only to find out, a few weeks later, that the Greek imperative can have an aorist as well as a present form. How can one request a person today to do something yesterday? And when the teacher informs the students that the aorist does not really indicate time, they become ripe either for experiencing total bewilderment or for developing preposterous exegesis.

And things hardly get better when they move into Hebrew class. Fairly early on they are told that Hebrew has only two tenses, "perfect" and "imperfect," as though the Israelites were unable to talk about the present and the future. And sooner or later the class is granted the ultimate oracle: merely add the Hebrew word for "and" to the verb, and lo, the perfect becomes imperfect and the imperfect becomes perfect! Fortunately or unfortunately (depending on one's point of view), this revelation is too much for most seminarians, who tend to ignore what little Hebrew they learned and return to the more fertile ground of Greek grammar.

Surely the first step out of this mire is to appreciate that there is nothing peculiar about verbs that indicate *aspect* (= how is the action presented by the speaker) rather than *time* (= when does the action take place).[16] In English, for example, the difference between *John wrote a letter* and *John was writing a letter* is not one of temporal reference: both verbal constructions could be used when referring to the *one* event that took place, say, last Monday evening. Rather, the distinction is an aspectual one: the second expression indicates progressive action (to use a traditional category), while the first one does not. Moreover, English has the lexical means to express a wide variety of aspectual distinctions: *used to write; kept on writing; started to write.*

There are indeed some differences between English and the biblical languages, and it is those differences that create confusion. Whereas English verbs, whatever else they do, always seem to indicate time reference,[17] a rather large number of languages around the world manage quite nicely, thank you, with verbs that do not by themselves have that reference. The speakers of these languages, of course, can indicate the time through lexical and other means (*yesterday, tomorrow*, the context of the utterance, etc.), but the verbal form itself gives no hint. Greek does grammaticalize temporal reference by, for example, adding the prefix *e-* (called an *augment*) to indicate past tense: the verb *krinomen*, "we judge," can become *ekrinomen*, "we were judging," or *ekrinamen*, "we judged."

In biblical Hebrew, however, the situation is different, since the two tenses mentioned above do not necessarily indicate past-present-future. That is why English translations (particularly in the poetic sections, where the context gives no explicit indication of time) vary significantly in their rendering of the tenses, as in Psalm 27:2:

> When the wicked, *even* mine enemies and my foes, came upon me to eat up my flesh, they stumbled and fell. (KJV)

> *When evildoers close in on me to devour me,*
> *   it is my enemies, my assailants,*
> *   who stumble and fall.* (NEB)

> *When evil men advance against me*
> *   to devour my flesh,*
> *when my enemies and my foes attack me,*
> *   they will stumble and fall.* (NIV)

---

[16]Strictly speaking, verbal aspect too has something to do with time, and so it would be more accurate to distinguish between *aspectual time* and *deictic time*. See John Lyons, *Semantics*, 2 vols. (Cambridge: Cambridge University Press, 1977), vol. 2, chap. 15, especially pp. 677–90; and Bernard Comrie, *Aspect: An Introduction to the Study of Verbal Aspect and Related Problems* (CTL, Cambridge: Cambridge University Press, 1976), especially pp. 1–6. For more technical and wide-ranging discussions, see Östen Dahl, *Tense and Aspect Systems* (Oxford: Blackwell, 1985), and the anthology edited by Paul J. Hopper, *Tense-Aspect: Between Semantics and Pragmatics, Containing the Contributions to a Symposium on Tense and Aspect, Held at UCLA, May 1979* (Typological Studies in Language 1; Amsterdam/Philadelphia: John Benjamins, 1982). Special note must be taken of Juan Mateos, *El aspecto verbal en el Nuevo Testamento* (Estudios de Nuevo Testamento 1; Madrid: Ediciones Cristiandad, 1977); Stanley E. Porter, *Verbal Aspect in the Greek of the New Testament: With Special Reference to Tense and Mood* (Studies in Biblical Greek 1; New York: P. Lang, 1989); and B. M. Fanning, *Verbal Aspect in New Testament Greek* (Oxford University Press, 1990). Alviero Niccacci, *The Syntax of the Verb in Classical Hebrew Prose* (JSOTSS 86; Sheffield: JSOT, 1990), makes much use of "text linguistics."

[17]I say "seem" because even in English the temporal element can be obscured. When we say that the earth *moves* around the sun, we are using what some would call a "gnomic present": the point is that the earth is so moving, not only right now, but always—past, present, and future. It has even been suggested that the English present is best described as a "nonpast."

The two main verbs in the sentence ("stumble" and "fall"—the two other verbs are infinitives) occur here in the so-called perfect tense. Because the character of the English verbal system forces the translator to indicate the temporal reference, which is nonexistent in the Hebrew, KJV translated the verbs as past, NEB as present, NIV as future. Note that in this context the tense does not alter the message of the psalmist. A translation in the past does not exclude a reference to the present or future; on the contrary, the past event would be the basis for later confidence. A translation in the future, on the other hand, could well reflect the psalmist's *previous* experience. The point, however, is that the psalmist has not explicitly indicated a time reference: the Hebrew verbal system allows him to "get away with" this ambiguity without jeopardizing (indeed, perhaps it enhances) the central message that God always protects his people.[18]

Another important difference between English and the biblical languages is that English depends heavily on the vocabulary to indicate aspect; that is, aspectual distinctions are seldom grammaticalized. Even the distinction between *John wrote* and *John was writing*, since it involves a periphrasis (adding the helping verb *was* to form the imperfect), is regarded by some linguists as more lexical than grammatical. A clearer example, already noted, is *used to write*, an idea a Greek writer can express grammatically, by using the imperfect tense. Consider also the verbs *obtain* and *have*: the former verb can be understood as expressing the incipient or ingressive aspect of an action involving "possession," while the latter verb expresses a resultative or stative aspect of the same action. Greek can achieve the same goal by merely alternating the tenses of the same verb.[19]

These differences, though important, must not obscure what is more *fundamentally common* between English and the biblical languages. The primary consideration here is that aspectual choices are usually unconscious and to a large extent dictated either by the requirements of the grammar or by the thrust of the context. Very rarely, if ever, does an English speaker or writer pause to consider whether a simple past tense or an imperfect should be used: the decision is virtually automatic. When the decision is not an obvious one, English speakers would have some difficulty distinguishing between the two. Note these two questions: (1) *How do you feel today?* (2) *How are you feeling today?* What exactly is the difference between these utterances? Even specialists in English grammar cannot agree. And we would certainly get nowhere if we asked a particular speaker what made him or her choose one of these questions over the other! We would go too far if we were to argue that a writer's decision between, say, an aorist and a present subjunctive never reflects a stylistic decision that may be of some interest to the interpreter. But we can feel confident that no reasonable writer would seek to express a major point by leaning on a subtle grammatical distinction—especially if it is a point not otherwise clear from the whole context (and if it *is* clear from the context, then the grammatical subtlety plays at best a secondary role in exegesis).

---

[18]For a very valuable survey of the debate concerning the Hebrew conjugations, see Waltke and O'Connor, *Biblical Hebrew Syntax,* chap. 29.

[19]For example, in Romans 1:13 Paul expresses his desire to "have" (*schō*, aorist subjunctive of *echō*); the nuance is clearly "to start having," "to receive." In this case, English "have" adequately conveys that idea. Notice, however, Philem. 7: "Your love has given me great joy and encouragement" (NIV). A literal translation would be, "I had [*eschen*, aorist indicative = I received, obtained] much joy and encouragement because of your love." See also J. H. Moulton, *Grammar of New Testament Greek,* vol. 1 (3d ed.; Edinburgh: T. & T. Clark, 1908), pp. 110, 145.

A second consideration in interpreting tenses is that the usual labels can prove misleading. Grammar books of New Testament Greek, for example, often use the terms *linear* and *punctiliar* to express the force of the present (or imperfect) and the aorist respectively. If very carefully defined and qualified, these labels might be of some value, but we would be much better off getting rid of them. When ancient Greek grammarians coined the term *aorist* (from *horizō*, "determine, define," plus the privative or negating alpha), they correctly perceived that this tense was "undetermined," that is, general or even vague, exactly the opposite of what most Greek students, and not a few professional exegetes, think. The aorist was normally used to refer to an action as a whole, a complete event; thus it was the tense chosen when the writer did *not* want to say something special about the action. The label *punctiliar*, however, suggests to students a momentary event (contrast Rev. 20:4, the martyrs "reigned [*ebasileusan*, aor. ind.] with Christ a thousand years"!), and that in turn leads people to think of emphasis, definitiveness, once-for-allness, and other related ideas not at all inherent in the aorist.[20] How misguided is the popular notion that the aorist can serve to emphasize the once-for-all character of Christ's death (a truth clearly expressed by the whole context of several passages, not by grammatical subtlety) may be demonstrated from the author of Hebrews, who was certainly a master of the Greek language. In 9:26 he tells us that if Christ were like other priests, he "would have had to suffer many times since the creation of the world." The adverb *pollakis* ("many times, frequently") would seem to require a present tense; in fact, it modifies the verb "suffer," *pathein*, which is the aorist infinitive of *paschō* (cf. also 2 Cor. 11:24–25).

One final, and important, consideration is that aspectual distinctions reflect the speaker's subjective perspective rather than objective reality. Suppose someone says, *When I examined the building, I was eating my lunch*. We could describe the verb *examined* as aoristic and *was eating* as imperfective; the former views the complete action of "examining" in its totality,[21] while the latter looks "internally" at the ongoing (noncomplete) event of eating. However, one might describe the *same* event as follows: *When I ate my lunch, I was examining the building*. In this case, it is the act of eating that the speaker is looking at, as it were, from the outside, while the act of examining is presented as ongoing. We can therefore see that a speaker or writer can refer to the same objective reality with different aspects, and so the aspectual decision only tells us how he or she is perceiving it and presenting it, not whether the reality is *intrinsically* progressive in character, or punctiliar, or whatever.

Even these qualifications may not be sufficient to discourage exegetes from overinterpreting aspectual distinctions. A classic example is the difficult statement in 1 John

---

[20]For examples, cf. D. A. Carson, *Exegetical Fallacies* (Grand Rapids: Baker, 1984), pp. 69–72.

[21]That is, "the whole of the situation is presented as a single unanalysable whole, with beginning, middle, and end rolled into one; no attempt is made to divide this situation up into the various individual phases that make up the action" (Comrie, *Aspect*, p. 3). However, as my colleague Vern S. Poythress has pointed out in personal conversation, the alternation of tenses in a narrative may well be primarily a function of discourse, that is, the need to relate the various actions to one another. If so, even a description of aspects that focuses on the way the speaker or writer *views* the action may turn out to be an overinterpretation. Cf. the introductory chapter in *Tense-Aspect* (ed. Hopper), where the editor proposes to view aspect "as an essentially discourse-level, rather than a semantic, sentence-level phenomenon. . . . My proposal does not, so far as I can see, conflict with the recognized achievements of recent work on aspect, but it does argue that our understanding of aspect should be rooted in the last resort in discourse" (p. 16).

3:6, which we may translate literally, "Everyone who remains in him does not sin [*ouch hamartanei*]." Is John setting forth here the doctrine of sinless perfection? A very popular solution to the problem is to focus on the present tense of the verb and argue on that basis that John must have in mind a habitual and unrepentant life of sin. Even the NIV reflects this understanding: "No one who lives in him keeps on sinning." It is perhaps possible to defend such an interpretation of the verse on broad theological grounds, but the argument based on aspectual distinction simply will not work. While Greek has an aorist/imperfect contrast in the past tenses of the indicative, no such contrast exists in the present tense. Since Greek does not have an "aoristic" form in the present tense, John had no choice but to use the present form.[22] The use of *hamartanei*, in other words, conveys a temporal piece of information (present or gnomic rather than past or future), not an aspectual perspective as such.

But what about the aorist/present distinction in the other moods, such as the imperative and the subjunctive? One often hears that the present imperatives in Matthew 7:7 indicate continuation and perseverance and that therefore we should translate, "*Keep on asking* and it will be given to you; *keep on seeking* and you will find; *keep on knocking* and the door will be opened to you." It is true that one of the functions of the present imperative is to indicate a command or request when the action in view is already in progress, while the aorist is more commonly used when the action has not begun, with the implication "Start doing." However, the distinction does not always hold up. When 1 John 5:21 commands, "Guard [aor. *phylaxate*] yourselves from idols," are we to understand, "Start guarding yourselves," as though the recipients of the letter were already guilty of idolatry? Even when the distinction holds, we need to keep in mind that the choice of the aspect is largely determined by the circumstances; that is, the choice is not made in order to accentuate the point.[23] The whole thrust of Matthew 7:7, of course, is the need for persistence in prayer. One is not surprised, therefore, to see the imperatives in the present tense; but it is quite improbable that the verbal form by itself ever conveys the notion of perseverance.

In conclusion, we may say that an interpreter is unwise to emphasize an idea that allegedly comes from the use of a tense (or some other subtle grammatical distinction) unless the context as a whole clearly sets forth that idea. Whether the use of the tense contributes to that idea or whether it is the idea that contributes to the use of the tense is perhaps debatable, but no interpretation is worth considering unless it has strong contextual support. If it doesn't, then the use of the grammatical detail becomes irrelevant; if it does, then the grammar is at best a pointer to, not the basis of, the correct interpretation.

---

[22]Of course, John might have used a paraphrastic construction, but that would have contained, if anything, an even stronger "progressive" nuance. In the following clause, John uses a present participle, *ho hamartanōn*, "the one sinning," which can be contrasted with the aorist form. The function of the aorist participle, however, is to refer to action prior to the action of the main verb. If John had used the aorist participle, the meaning would have been "he who has sinned," so the argument does not work for this clause either. In verse 9 John uses the present infinitive, *dynatai hamartanein*, which can indeed be contrasted aspectually with the aorist form. Even in moods other than the indicative, however, aspectual distinctions are not normally used to make a substantive point. See further below.

[23]Note that in the Lord's Prayer, Matthew 6:11 has the aorist *dos*, "give," which we may say is grammatically appropriate in the context of the word "today." Luke 11:3, on the other hand, has "every day," and so the form of the verb is present, *didou*. The point is that the idea of repetition or continuation is presented primarily by the explicit "every day," only secondarily and implicitly by the verbal aspect.

PARAGRAPHS AND LARGER UNITS

Traditionally, grammar books have stopped at the sentence level when describing syntax. The past two decades or so, however, have witnessed a vigorous interest in how sentences are linked with one another to form paragraphs and how paragraphs are put together to construct a whole discourse. The resulting discipline is variously called *text linguistics, discourse grammar, discourse analysis*, etc. Almost by definition, the boundaries of this discipline are rather fuzzy. One can pick up several books claiming to deal with discourse and find only partial overlapping among them. One author may view the field primarily as sociological in character, but another one as anthropological or even psychological; one author is interested in conversation and another one in the plot progression of narratives; and so on.[24]

Moreover, the discipline is rather young, characterized by gaps in research and a fluctuating terminology. Indeed, only a few years ago an important textbook acknowledged that "workers in discourse analysis have only a partial understanding of even the most-studied ingredients."[25] Rather than attempt a thorough presentation, therefore, I will only sample some of the concerns of discourse analysts. In spite of the differences among researchers, there is one theme that comes up again and again in the literature, and that is the desire to understand *what language is used for*. This "functional" or "pragmatic" approach reflects a dissatisfaction with the tendency, even in "modern" linguistics, to examine sentences more or less in isolation, that is, by deliberately removing them from the speaker's or writer's purpose in uttering those sentences. In the field(s) of discourse analysis, therefore, no concept is more crucial than that of *context*.

Form

What formal means do languages have to mark the various possible relationships among sentences? Consider the following examples:

---

[24]Two early works, both comprehensive and influential, are Teun A. Van Dijk, *Some Aspects of Text Grammars: A Study in Theoretical Linguistics and Poetics* (Janua linguarum, ser. mai. 63; The Hague/Paris: Mouton, 1972), and Joseph Grimes, *The Thread of Discourse* (Janua linguarum, ser. min. 207; The Hague/Paris: Mouton, 1975). A good textbook focusing on conversation is Malcolm Coulthard, *An Introduction to Discourse Analysis* (Applied Linguistics and Language Study; London: Longman, 1977). Wholly devoted to formulating the criteria that determine "textuality" (that is, whether a string of utterances constitutes a unified text) is Robert de Beaugrande and Wolfgang Dressler, *Introduction to Text Linguistics* (Longman Linguistics Library 26; London: Longman, 1981). I have profited greatly from the comprehensive survey by Enrique Bernárdez, *Introducción a la lingüística del texto* (Madrid: Espasa-Calpe, 1982). The sociological approach is well represented by Michael Stubbs, *Discourse Analysis: The Sociolinguistic Analysis of Natural Language* (Language in Society 4; Chicago: University of Chicago Press, 1983). An emphasis on narrative, arising out of much anthropological experience, characterizes the work of Robert E. Longacre, *The Grammar of Discourse* (New York and London: Plenum, 1983). For a strictly linguistic perspective, see especially Gillian Brown and George Yule, *Discourse Analysis* (Cambridge Textbooks in Linguistics; Cambridge: Cambridge University Press, 1983). One may gauge recent advances in this field through the anthologies (often quite technical) published in the series Research in Text Theory / Untersuchungen zur Texttheorie, under the general editorship of János S. Petöfi. Among the latest in this series is number 11, *Literary Discourse: Aspects of Cognitive and Social Psychological Approaches*, ed. L. Halász (Berlin/New York: Walter de Gruyter, 1987).

[25]Brown and Yule, *Discourse Analysis*, p. 270.

Mary fell. She broke her wrist.

Mary fell and [she] broke her wrist.

Mary broke her wrist because she fell.

These are only three out of the many different ways in which English can express the connection between the two concepts, "Mary fell" and "Mary broke her wrist." In the first example there appears to be no connector, but in fact the pronoun *she*, referring back to the subject of the previous sentence, serves effectively to link the two sentences. In the second example, the two ideas are formally but vaguely connected by means of the coordinating conjunction *and*, which by itself does not make explicit the nature of the connection. In the last example, the sentence relationship is made clearer with the subordinating conjunction *because*.

All three of these techniques are also used in the biblical languages, but even a beginning student will quickly notice a difference in frequency. Hebrew narrative, for example, is characterized by an almost endless string of *and*s. Greek story-tellers, insofar as they use conjunctions, alternate between *kai* ("and") and *de* ("but," "now"); in addition, however, they will often use such adverbs as *euthys* (characteristic of Mark), *tote* ("then," characteristic of Matthew), *oun* ("therefore"), etc. Most striking of all is the frequency with which Greek writers use participles to link clauses (rather than "independent" sentences) together. The technique is certainly available in English: *Falling down, Mary broke her wrist* (the closest that Hebrew can come to this adverbial use of the participle is by using the so-called infinitive absolute). Nevertheless, the abundance of adverbial participles, as well as their flexibility, is one of the truly distinctive features of Ancient Greek.

In addition to linking one clause (or sentence) to the next one, speakers have ways of indicating that a series of sentences belong together as part of a larger unit, which we may call the *paragraph*. Defining linguistic units is never easy—scholars have vigorously disagreed even over the proper way of determining what constitutes a word! The debate becomes much more complicated when they seek to define a paragraph.[26] Of course, we do not have in mind here an "orthographic" paragraph, that is, a chunk of text that begins with an indented line. Such a printing technique may indeed mark a shift in topic, but not always: the audience in view, for example, or even the width of the column, may dictate breaking up the text into smaller pieces.

Sometimes we are very explicit in marking a shift: *Let's move on to a related topic*, or, *To change the subject . . . .* At other times the shift is less obvious but still formally marked by such expressions as *Now, Moreover,* and *On the other hand.* Just as frequently, especially in informal conversation, we dispense with any formal markers because it is fairly obvious, from the tone or the general context, that there is some disjunction between the last string of utterances and the string that is about to begin. All of these conditions can be found in the biblical languages. A Hebrew narrative will often mark the beginning of a paragraph with *wayhi* ("And it was," reflected sometimes in the New Testament with *kai egeneto*); Paul may introduce a new section in his letters with *gnōrizō de hymin* ("Now I make known to you") or a similar clause. More sophisticated techniques can also be used,

---

[26]Cf. ibid., pp. 95–100.

such as *inclusio*, whereby a paragraph is explicitly bracketed, that is, it begins and ends with the same or similar word(s).[27]

Not infrequently, however, formal markers are absent, and we need to depend on other features to identify the paragraph boundaries. Careful students of literary texts, long before the development of discourse analysis, have appreciated the exegetical value of noticing such boundaries (usually reflected in a commentator's outline, for example). Modern linguistics cannot replace the "common sense" skills of a good interpreter— indeed, it has the potential for an exaggerated formalism that can swallow up those skills—but it can provide new perspectives and methods leading to greater consistency.

Although I need not here catalog all the formal features that contribute to the unity of a paragraph, I must mention a technique that has received increasing attention among biblical scholars. It has long been noticed that short portions of discourse (even modern conversations) sometimes take the form, A-B-B'-A', known as *chiasm*. Note Galatians 4:4–5:

A   *God sent his Son,*
B   *born of a woman, born under law,*
B' *to redeem those under law,*
A' *that we might receive the full right of sons.*[28]

Lines A and A' parallel each other (we could say they form an *inclusio*), and so do B and B'. The pattern is very common in Hebrew poetry and has been clearly detected in larger units, not only consisting of a large paragraph but even containing many paragraphs within it.

Among many interesting examples, we may note the proposal that a large chiastic structure characterizes a major section of 2 Chronicles:

A   *Solomon's wealth and wisdom (1:1–17)*
B   *Recognition by Gentiles / dealings with Hiram (2:1–16)*
C   *Temple construction / gentile labor (2:17–5:1)*
D   *Dedication of temple (5:2–7:10)*
D' *Divine response (7:11–22)*
C' *Other construction / gentile labor (8:1–16)*
B' *Recognition by Gentiles / dealings with Hiram (8:17–9:12)*
A' *Solomon's wealth and wisdom (9:13–28)*[29]

At times this approach gets out of hand, as when John Bligh "discovers" that the whole Epistle to the Galatians is one large chiasm, composed of many subchiasms and

---

[27]It has been suggested, for example, that the noun *prokopē*, "advance," in Philippians 1:12 and 25 (otherwise found only once in the New Testament: 1 Tim. 4:15) formally marks the unit that extends from verse 12 to verse 26 (vv. 25–26 constitute one sentence). For a detailed attempt to identify paragraph breaks in the epistles of Paul, see John R. Werner, "Discourse Analysis of the Greek New Testament," in *The New Testament Student and His Field* (The NT Student 5; ed. J. H. Skilton [Phillipsburg, N. J.: Presbyterian and Reformed, 1982]), pp. 213–33, which includes an analysis of 2 Thessalonians originally prepared by Robert H. Sterner.

[28]This common example was noted over a century ago by J. B. Lightfoot, *The Epistle to the Galatians* (London: Macmillan, 1865), p. 168. It is very probable that Philippians 1:15–17 was written by Paul in a chiastic form, as attested by all early manuscripts. Later copyists, however, transposed verses 16 and 17 so as to produce a more common parallel structure (A-B-A'-B', with negative motives mentioned in verse 15a and verse 16, positive in verse 15b and verse 17). This latter form, found in a majority of (late) manuscripts, is reflected in the KJV. Cf. my comments in *Philippians*, p. 74.

[29]Adapted from Raymond B. Dillard, *2 Chronicles* (WBC 15; Waco: Word, 1987), pp. 5–6.

sub-subchiasms.[30] More often than not, proposals of this sort are characterized by acknowledged irregularities, textual emendations, and source-critical surgery. It would be a mistake, however, to deny the presence of chiastic structure in many biblical passages or to ignore its value for exegesis.

Meaning

What was Paul trying to do when he used a particular conjunction or when he grouped together a specific string of sentences? Another way of phrasing the question is quite simply, What did Paul mean? The functional concern that characterizes discourse analysis is therefore inseparable from semantics. The inverse is also true: semantics is inseparable from discourse—meaning cannot be discovered apart from context. At the beginning of this chapter I noted that only occasionally can a word by itself be used to convey meaning. Normally, meaning is conveyed by whole propositions. But now we must go a step further and recognize that we do not normally convey meaning by single propositions, but by propositions that form part of a larger whole (including the situation common to speaker and hearer).

We can certainly think of partial exceptions. *Give me liberty or give me death!* is an isolated sentence that communicates a great deal of meaning, but even here we fool ourselves if we do not recognize that there is much prior information (historical knowledge, national identification, familiarity with the statement itself, etc.) that makes the utterance so meaningful. All of that information constitutes the context that provides the necessary semantic framework. The best biblical examples of propositions that seem to convey meaning in isolation are the pithy sayings in the Book of Proverbs. Yet how easy it is for readers to misuse those sayings, converting them into comfortable moralistic principles that sit quite well with pagan presuppositions. In the context of the book as a whole, with its emphasis on true wisdom as the fear of the Lord—to say nothing of the biblical and redemptive context more generally—the meaning may be quite different.

More to the point, we should note that even the smallest books of the Bible consist of whole discourses. If propositions by themselves were quite sufficient, the Scriptures might be composed of a long list of individual sayings. Instead, God has given us narratives (some quite long), hymns, letters. And these various portions are brought together in a coherent and unified whole. The principle that the Bible is its own best interpreter is not wishful thinking.[31] From one perspective, this principle is but a reflection of the nature of all communication: sentences must be understood in the light of their total context. Even if we are reading Plato, we cannot artificially wrench one proposition in the *Republic* from the philosopher's whole thought. From another perspective, however, this principle is unique to Scripture. For those who are persuaded that the Bible comes from God in a sense that is not true of other writings, its unity and coherence take on a completely new dimension. God does not fail to speak in a consistent fashion—as Plato or an

---

[30]John Bligh, *Galatians in Greek: A Structural Analysis of St. Paul's Epistle to the Galatians, with Notes on the Greek* (Detroit: University of Detroit Press, 1966). Cf. also Kenneth Bailey, Poet and Peasant: *A Literary Cultural Approach to the Parables in Luke* (Grand Rapids: Eerdmans, 1976), pp. 79–85, and my review in *WTJ* 41 (1978–79): 213–15.

[31]See *Has the Church Misread the Bible?*, pp. 71–72, in this volume.

uninspired Paul might—and thus individual propositions in Scripture do perfectly cohere with other propositions and shed light on each other.

In our effort to interpret the Bible, therefore, we should give special attention to the way sentences are joined, how they form paragraphs, and how the paragraphs combine to constitute larger units. At the simplest level, this means that we should read the Bible the way we read other literature. When we receive a letter from a friend, do we read the middle paragraph today, the last sentence next week, the introductory section two months from now? Unfortunately, many Christians use precisely that "method" in their reading of Paul's letters. The biblical books were meant to be read as wholes and that is the way we should read them.

At a more specialized level, we should make the effort to identify in some detail textual features connecting propositions to one another and to understand how those features actually function. Even this step is to a large extent accessible to the common believer. Does this sentence give the reason for the preceding one or does it merely expand on it? Does that paragraph build on the previous argument or does it move to a new topic altogether? One can come up with more than two dozen ways of expressing the linkage between any one pair of sentences.[32]

Students of Greek and Hebrew, however, can delve into these questions at greater depth and with greater profit, since English translations are often unable to represent the formal structure of sentences in the original text. Probably the most efficient method is to attempt a visual representation of the syntax, that is, to diagram the clauses and sentences making up a paragraph. One need not learn or develop a complicated method. Merely by indenting the appropriate clauses and labeling them, the student can gain a new appreciation for the flow of the argument.[33]

Consider Romans 1:16–18, first in the NIV rendering:

> I am not ashamed of the gospel, because it is the power of God for the salvation of everyone who believes: first for the Jew, then for the Gentile. For in the gospel a righteousness from God is revealed, a righteousness that is by faith from first to last, just as it is written: "The righteous will live by faith."
>
> The wrath of God is being revealed from heaven against all the godlessness and wickedness of men who suppress the truth by their wickedness. . . .

Now compare a literal rendering (that is, one that tries to represent the formal features of the Greek), accompanied by clearer visual distinctions and some tentative (interpretive) labels:

> *For* I am not ashamed of the gospel [*response* to anticipated question]
>   *for* it is the power of God [*reason* for not being ashamed]
>   *unto* salvation [*result* of God's power]

---

[32]Building on the work of such scholars as John Beekman and Robert E. Longacre, and without having to appeal to Hebrew grammar, Vern S. Poythress has illustrated this approach by applying a detailed taxonomy to Isaiah 51:9–11. See his article "Propositional Relations" in *The New Testament Student and His Field,* pp. 159–212. Cf. also Cotterell and Turner, *Linguistics,* chap. 6. For an impressive and technical application, see Robert E. Longacre, *Joseph: A Story of Divine Providence: A Text Theoretical and Textlinguistic Analysis of Genesis 37 and 39–48* (Winona Lake: Eisenbrauns, 1989).

[33]Very helpful in this connection is the set of guidelines put together by Gordon D. Fee, *New Testament Exegesis: A Handbook for Students and Pastors* (Philadelphia: Westminster, 1983), pp. 60–77.

> *to* everyone who believes [*recipients* of salvation]
>> *to* the Jew first [*expands* on recipients: priority]
>> and *to* the Greek [*expands* on recipients: universality]
> *for* the righteousness of God is revealed in it [*explanation*]
>> *out of* faith to faith [*character* of revelation]
>> *as* it is written . . . [*proof*]

For the wrath of God is revealed . . . [*contrast*: new paragraph]

If the time and effort often invested in isolated word studies were redirected toward this kind of analysis, Bible students would gain a proportionately greater understanding of what the text says. This approach forces us to ask questions that might otherwise not occur to us—and when we fail to ask these questions, we are left with only a vague impression of how the biblical author is linking together the various parts of his argument or narrative. It should be clear from Romans 1:16–18, for example, that the Greek conjunction *gar* does not always introduce a simple cause for what precedes. Paul uses it to serve a variety of transitional functions that cannot be discovered if we think only about "grammar." We can, in addition, proceed to analyze a portion of text by means of more detailed and sophisticated techniques and terminology.[34] To be sure, one always runs the risk of imposing on the text complicated connections that the biblical author conceived of in only a general way (recall the discussion of the genitive case earlier in this chapter). Nevertheless, students of the Bible tend to make the opposite mistake and pay less attention than they should to the need for determining clause relationships and paragraph units.

Finally, interpreters must give full consideration to the broader context of the passages they analyze. For example, the type of literature (i.e., its genre) can significantly affect the total meaning of a statement. Another volume in the present series has devoted attention to this matter and so we need not pursue it here.[35] Also the occasion and general purpose of a writing can become an important (sometimes definitive) clue. Even a form of address, such as *Mr. Smith*, can "mean" something positive (a courteous touch in a business letter) or something quite negative (a reproachful tone when writing to a close acquaintance). Whether Paul intended his letter to the Romans as a theological treatise more or less abstracted from historical circumstances or as a "real" letter directly provoked by those historical circumstances will substantially affect our interpretation. In the first instance, chapters 9–11 (to take but one example) may be, and often have been, perceived as something of a parenthesis; alternatively, if the letter was motivated by the struggles arising out of the Judaistic controversy, those chapters take on a much more prominent role, possibly the crowning argument in a whole series of answers to objections that had been raised against Paul's gospel.

---

[34]For an application of this method to a very elegant NT passage, see David Alan Black, "Hebrews 1:1–4: A Study in Discourse Analysis," *WTJ* 49 (1987): 175–94. A fine introduction, with helpful diagrams, is the last chapter of J. P. Louw, *Semantics of New Testament Greek* (SBLSS; Philadelphia: Fortress, and Chico, Calif.: Scholars Press, 1982).

[35]See Tremper Longman III, *Literary Approaches to Biblical Interpretation*, Foundations of Contemporary Interpretation 3 (Grand Rapids: Zondervan, 1988), esp. pp. 73–83.

seven

EPILOGUE—

PASSING IT ON

*T*hroughout this small book we have treated our subject as though we had immediate access to it, as though nothing whatever could come between us and the biblical text. It is true that at the most fundamental level Christians enjoy direct access
to God and that his Spirit directly witnesses to our spirit through the Scriptures. On the
other hand, we cannot allow this precious truth to degenerate into a sense of personal infallibility. For one thing, our own finitude and sinfulness get in the way of perfect understanding.[1] Then again, we are greatly removed in time and culture from the writings that
make up the Bible.

But there is an additional matter that needs to be considered, if only in summary
fashion, and that is the process of *transmission*. In one sense we have been dealing with
this matter all along, insofar as communication—and therefore the transmission of information, emotions, etc.—is inherent to language itself. It may prove helpful, nevertheless, to discuss briefly some other important aspects of linguistic transmission.

TEXTUAL TRANSMISSION

Every time a scribe sat down to copy one or several of the books of the Bible he
became involved in the process of transmitting the text, and therefore the language, of the
Scriptures. Of course, we have no direct access to the original manuscripts used by Luke
or Paul, but only to such later copies as were produced by scribes. We must recognize that
this process creates a certain distance between us and the text. And just as we do what

---

[1] I have discussed this important issue in *Has the Church Misread the Bible?* (see esp. pp. 68–69).

we can to bridge, for example, the *cultural* distance that separates us from the Bible by learning about archaeology, so also we must make every effort to bridge the *textual* distance, that is, to remove from the text alien elements introduced by scribes. In short, we must be prepared to do textual criticism.

All literary works go through comparable processes of transmission. Many important works from the ancient world have not survived at all, while most of those that have survived are represented by very few and often fragmented manuscripts. In contrast, manuscripts of the New Testament (in whole or in part) are very numerous, easily exceeding—both in numbers and in antiquity—the most famous classical works.[2] With regard to the Old Testament books, the numbers are not as great, but two important factors compensate for that: (1) the primary tradition, known as the Masoretic Text and reaching back into Late Antiquity (though extant manuscripts were produced during the Middle Ages), is characterized by exceptional homogeneity and accuracy; (2) supporting witnesses, primarily the Septuagint translation and the Dead Sea Scrolls, provide rich attestation prior to the Christian era.[3]

Although we may therefore have full confidence in the integrity of the biblical text, there continue to be theoretical problems as well as specific questions that require attention. This book is hardly the place to provide instruction in such a difficult and specialized discipline, but the topic is of relevance to us insofar as it overlaps with more general linguistic issues.

We may, for example, apply the concepts of *noise* and *redundancy* to the transmission of texts.[4] When a textual error is introduced by a scribe, the message is distorted: noise (in the technical sense) has affected the transmission. Because of the inherent redundancy of language (and of writing in particular), the vast majority of these errors are self-correcting and do not affect the reader's perception of the message. Suppose we read a story in the newspaper that contains the following statement: *All four woman were hurt in tne accident.* If we are reading quickly, we may not even notice at all the two instances of noise in it: (1) the typesetter keyed the letter *a* rather than *e* in *women*; (2) the top of the letter *h* in *the* did not print out and so it looks like the letter *n*.

The reason we often fail to notice errors of this sort—even after laborious proofreading!—is that the message is perfectly clear from the context. Certainly the subject of the sentence must be plural, as the modifier *all four* and the verb *were* (both instances of redundancy) establish. As for the second error, there is no such word as *tne* in English; besides, the occurrence of *the* in such a context is highly predictable. Even if we notice the errors, of course, we will only be amused (or upset): we will not be misled into attributing a meaning to the sentence different from that intended by the writer. And if

---

[2]Standard textbooks include B. M. Metzger, *The Text of the New Testament: Its Transmission, Corruption, and Restoration,* 2d ed. (New York: Oxford University Press, 1964), and Kurt Aland and Barbara Aland, *The Text of the New Testament: An Introduction to the Critical Editions and to the Theory and Practice of Modern Textual Criticism* (Grand Rapids: Eerdmans, 1987). For the latter, which is the most up-to-date and complete introduction, cf. my review in *WTJ* 50 (1988): 195–200; a second edition appeared in 1989.

[3]Cf. F. E. Deist, *Towards the Text of the Old Testament* (Pretoria: D. R. Church Booksellers, 1978); Ernst Würthwein, *The Text of the Old Testament: An Introduction to the Biblia Hebraica* (Grand Rapids: Eerdmans, 1979); E. Tov, *The Text-Critical Use of the Septuagint in Biblical Research,* Jerusalem Biblical Studies 3 (Jerusalem: Simor, 1981).

[4]See above, chap. 3, p. 227, and chap. 6, p. 258.

we happen to have pen in hand, we may be tempted to correct the errors. At that point, we are playing the role of textual critics. We are correcting "scribal errors" by means of the redundancy provided by the context.

As I have already pointed out, an exceedingly high proportion of errors in biblical (or other) manuscripts are of this kind, and so the textual scholar need not think for longer than a second to determine what is the correct reading. There are, however, errors of various types. Note especially those errors introduced by scribes when they, consciously or unconsciously, were playing the role of textual critics themselves. It is fairly easy to demonstrate that, from time to time, copyists came across passages that did not "sound right" to them. They might notice an unexpected (i.e., not highly predictable) word, or a construction that seemed to them stylistically weak, or a statement that did not clearly fit their theological understanding of the topic at hand. If they thought that their master copy was in error, naturally they would alter the text toward greater redundancy.[5] Relying on the concept of entropy, Nida deals with such textual variations as follows:

> One might describe this process as a kind of semantic leveling in which unusual, difficult and complex expressions are changed into expressions which are easier to understand and more readily anticipated by a reader because they fit the context more neatly. They are "easier readings"—easier precisely because they are less specialized or unusual, hence having a greater degree of probability or predictability in relation to their contexts than do the "harder" or more unusual readings.[6]

It turns out, then, that the scholar is faced by two opposing tendencies (among others) that are operative in the process of textual transmission: the introduction of bad readings (i.e., noise, errors) and the creation of "improved" readings (in order to eliminate what the scribes perceived as noise but wasn't). Good textual critics, in other words, appreciate the conflict between *intrinsic probability* (Which of two or more variant readings makes the best contextual sense?) and *transcriptional probability* (Which reading was created by scribes because it may have made better sense *to them*?).[7] A good understanding of the character and function of language can help students of the Bible implement these principles in a responsible way.

Finally, it should be obvious that textual changes are not purely formal but semantic as well. As such, variant readings reflect broad interpretive frameworks and specific exegetical traditions. That is to say, textual transmission and exegetical history are closely related. Except for some rare instances when, say, Latin scribes may have mechanically copied Greek manuscripts they did not understand, the process of reading and interpretation was very

---

[5] I must emphasize that these kinds of changes were not always the result of a conscious decision. A scribe may have been only vaguely aware of some unusual feature in the text; rather than taking the time to deliberate, he may have continued the writing process and semiconsciously adapted the text to a more commonplace construction. Some of the material in this section is taken from my article "Internal Evidence in the Text-Critical Use of the LXX," in *La Septuaginta en la investigación comtemporánea*, ed. N. Fernández Marcos (Madrid: C.S.I.C., 1985), pp. 151–67, esp. pp. 161–62.

[6] Eugene A. Nida, "The 'Harder Reading' in Textual Criticism: An Application of the Second Law of Thermodynamics," *BT* 32 (1981): 101–7, quotation from p. 105.

[7] For a penetrating description of this problem, see the classic statement in B. F. Westcott and F. J. A. Hort, *The New Testament in the Original Greek*, 2 vols. (Graz, Austria: Akademische Druck- und Verlagsanstalt, 1974, orig. 1881), 2:26–27.

much part of the scribes' activity. That is why even secondary readings that have no claim to represent the original text can nevertheless be of value to the interpreter.

Suppose, for example, that we notice some interesting readings introduced by the scribe of Papyrus 46 (or by the one who wrote his master copy?), such as his changing the phrase "the glory and praise of God" in Philippians 1:11 to "the glory of God and my praise"; or his adding to Philippians 3:12 the clause, "or have already been justified." We may well decide, in the process of *textual criticism*, that these variations are not original, but that is no reason to dismiss them in the process of *interpretation*.[8] Through variant readings scribes have passed on to us what they believed (rightly or wrongly) was the meaning of the text.

TRANSLATION

If scribes were involved in the difficult process of interpretation (and communicating that interpretation) when they merely transcribed the text in the *same* language, what shall we say about those poor souls who seek to reproduce the message of Scripture in a different language? It is of course impossible (or at least unhelpful!) to translate a passage from language X into language Y unless one *knows* language X and *understands* what the original text says. Translators who view their work as pure renderings rather than interpretations only delude themselves; indeed, if they could achieve some kind of noninterpretative rendering, their work would be completely useless.

The task of producing a good translation is exceedingly arduous. Students of the biblical languages do not always have a good appreciation of what is involved. They have learned to produce "literal" translations by consulting the lexicon and so the process seems rather straightforward. In fact, however, a successful translation requires (1) mastery of the source language—certainly a much more sophisticated knowledge than one can acquire over a period of four or five years; (2) superb interpretive skills and breadth of knowledge so as not to miss the nuances of the original; and (3) a very high aptitude for writing in the target language so as to express accurately both the cognitive and the affective elements of the message.

Even when one has all that equipment, frustration lurks at every turn. If we capture with some precision the propositional content of a statement, we may give up the emotional nuances that form part of the total meaning. If we have a stroke of genius and come up with a turn of phrase that conveys powerfully the message of the original, we may realize that our rendering blurs somewhat its cognitive detail. Not surprisingly, some rabbis used to complain: "He who translates a verse literally is a liar, and he who paraphrases is a blasphemer!"[9] Italians are more concise: *traduttore traditore*, "translators are traitors."

The question of faithfulness in translation has become increasingly pressing in our time because of the very large number of available English versions of the Bible. What is a lay Christian to do when these versions differ from one another? Some of the differences are merely stylistic, as when one translator prefers the word *liberty* while another one uses *freedom*; most of us can live with that. A little more difficult to handle are differences that

---

[8]Cf. my discussion in *Philippians*, pp. 63–64, 203–4; more generally, pp. 21-22.

[9]My own rendering of this saying is both literal and paraphrastic. See *The Babylonian Talmud*, Seder Nashim 8: Kiddushin, ed. I. Epstein (London: Soncino, 1936), p. 246 (= folio 49b): "R. Judah said: If one translates a verse literally, he is a liar; if he adds thereto, he is a blasphemer and a libeler."

arise because the translators have used a different text base, as in Romans 5:1, where the NIV says, "we have peace with God," but the NEB renders, "let us continue at peace with God."[10] A third problem arises from differences in interpretation: KJV translates the first verb in John 5:39 as an imperative, "Search the Scriptures," while the NIV assumes it is an indicative, "You diligently study the Scriptures."[11]

The most fundamental difference, however, is that which pertains to philosophy of translation. We often speak of translations as being "literal" or "free." More precisely, some translations aim at representing the *form* of the original as closely as possible (without, however, doing violence to English grammar) while others, especially those influenced by linguistics, do not. It has become customary to describe the first approach as *formal correspondence* and the second as *dynamic equivalence*.[12] One seeks to achieve formal correspondence primarily by the following means: (1) representing each word of the original with one word in English, as opposed to omitting or adding words; (2) establishing strict lexical equivalences, so that any given word in the original is rendered consistently with the corresponding English word throughout; and (3) retaining the word order of the original.

We may illustrate the differences with two translations produced by evangelical scholars. The NASB is the most widely used "literal" version, while the NIV adopts a moderate dynamic-equivalence approach. (1) If we read a narrative section of the Gospel of Mark in the NASB, we will notice that the word *and*, translating Greek *kai*, is used with high frequency. Because such repetition is not characteristic of written English narrative, the NIV simply omits most of these occurrences. (2) In the NASB the word *flesh* occurs quite a few times in Galatians as the standard equivalent for Greek *sarx*, whereas the NIV renders the word in the following ways:

"man" (1:16, lit. "flesh and blood")

"no one" (2:16, lit. "all flesh not")

"human effort" (3:3)

"illness" (4:13, lit. "weakness of the flesh")

"in the ordinary way" (4:23, lit. "according to the flesh")

"sinful nature" (5:13–24)

---

[10]Two textual variants are involved. The first rendering reflects the indicative *echōmen*, while the latter reflects the subjunctive echommen.

[11]In contrast to the previous example, there is no textual variation here. The manuscripts are agreed in giving the verb *eraunate*, but this form can be analyzed as either indicative or imperative.

[12]A very influential work that propounds the method of dynamic equivalence is Eugene A. Nida, *Toward a Science of Translating: With Special Reference to Principles and Procedures Involved in Bible Translating* (Leiden: Brill, 1964). For a comprehensive textbook based on the ideas of Nida, John Beekman, and others, see Mildred L. Larson, *Meaning-Based Translation: A Guide to Cross-Language Equivalence* (Lanham, Md.: University Press of America, 1984). Among various important works from the Continent, see especially Wolfram Wilss, *The Science of Translation: Problems and Methods* (Tübinger Beiträge zur Linguistik 180; Tübingen: Gunter Narr, 1982), and the extensive manual by Valentín García Yebra, *Teoría y práctica de la traducción*, 2 vols. (Biblioteca románica hispánica 3/53; Madrid: Gredos, 1982). Literary scholars are often critical of the approach taken by linguists because the latter allegedly see translation as merely the transmission of data rather than as the process of literary creation. See especially L. G. Kelly, *The True Interpreter: A History of Translation Theory and Practice in the West* (New York: St. Martin's, 1979), and Stephen Prickett, *Words and* The Word: *Language, Poetics and Biblical Interpretation* (Cambridge: Cambridge University Press, 1986). For a more explicitly theological critique of dynamic equivalence, see Jakob van Bruggen, *The Future of the Bible* (Nashville: Thomas Nelson, 1978), chap. 4.

"outwardly" (6:12, lit. "in the flesh")

"flesh" (6:13!)

Finally, (3) notice how the complex sentence structure of Hebrews 7:20–22 is followed closely by the NASB:

> And inasmuch as *it was* not without an oath (for they indeed became priests without an oath, but He with an oath through the One who said to Him,
>> "The Lord has sworn,
>> And will not change His mind,
>> 'Thou art a priest forever'");
>
> so much the more also Jesus has become the guarantee of a better covenant.

The NIV, on the other hand, renders the sentence with more idiomatic English by breaking it up into smaller ones:

> And it was not without an oath! Others became priests without any oath, but he became a priest with an oath when God said to him:
>> "The Lord has sworn
>>> and will not change his mind:
>> 'You are a priest forever.'"
>
> Because of this oath, Jesus has become the guarantee of a better covenant.

In fact, no translation is fully consistent in implementing its approach. Some years ago I was asked to review a "literal" Spanish version of Isaiah, and I did so by comparing it to another Spanish version fully committed to the principle of dynamic equivalence. It was surprising, and amusing, to notice a significant number of passages where the former version avoided a literal rendering (perhaps because the Hebrew idiom sounded strange) while the latter translated literally (perhaps because of the literary quaintness of the original)! Differences in translation philosophy have produced much debate, some of it highly emotional, and this book is not the place to solve the controversy, but readers may find it worthwhile to note the following points.

The principle of dynamic equivalence is widely favored by professional linguists, and so it has become common to denounce versions such as the NASB as linguistically naïve and inadequate. From the other side, it is just as common to hear complaints that the dynamic-equivalence approach reflects a low view of the authority of Scripture. Both of these complaints suffer from the slur factor, both are misleading, and they both tend to polarize parties unnecessarily.

We must ever keep in mind that no one translation can possibly convey fully and unambiguously the meaning of the original. Different translators, and even different philosophies of translation, contribute to express various features of the original. If we isolate some of the passages from Galatians quoted above, the NIV renderings do convey more faithfully to the English reader the point of Paul's statements than does the literal translation, "flesh." On the other hand, there is a conceptual connection among some of those uses of the Greek *sarx*; such a connection is part of the total meaning expressed by Paul, and the NASB reader is much more likely to capture it.[13]

---

[13]Cf. also Edward L. Greenstein, *Essays on Biblical Method and Translation* (BJS 92; Atlanta: Scholars Press, 1989), p. 87, who complains that the *Good News Bible,* by translating Hebrew *bayit* in 2 Samuel 7 with three different English words ("palace," "temple," "dynasty"), "completely [obliterates] the thematic connections

Moreover, recent advances in linguistics place much emphasis on the context of speech. The admirable desire to produce translations that *do not sound like translations* and are thus clearer and more accessible to the modern reader must be accompanied by the reminder that the biblical stories took place in the Middle East rather than the Western world, in ancient times rather than in the twentieth century. To the extent that "readable" translations indirectly encourage modern readers to forget such a setting, to that extent they also fail to capture part of the meaning of the text.[14] Besides, one detects a definite tendency to make modern translations much simpler than the original Greek and Hebrew. If the Corinthians had some difficulty understanding Paul's Greek, it is no disgrace when a modern English reader has to struggle through a long apostolic sentence.

It is also misleading, however, to assume that a rendering that is *formally* equivalent to the original necessarily conveys the meaning more faithfully. If I translate the Spanish sentence *Tengo frío en los pies* literally, "I have cold in the feet," rather than idiomatically, "My feet are cold," English readers will probably understand the rendering, but they will gain absolutely nothing by its literalness—indeed, they could be misled to think that there is some special nuance they are missing! Literal translations are easier to produce, and the approach can degenerate into an excuse for not doing the hard exegetical and literary work of conveying faithfully the meaning of the ancient text to the modern reader.

TEACHING

What a scribe does imperceptibly when transcribing a manuscript, and what a translator does behind the scenes when translating a biblical book—that is what a teacher does explicitly when passing on the meaning of the text to someone else. There is a long, unbroken process of linguistic transmission that reaches a climax when the gospel message is proclaimed today.

The effort we spend on interpreting the Bible cannot end with our personal enjoyment. We learn so that we may teach (cf. Heb. 5:12). We receive so that we may give. The serious study of human language helps us to understand the divine word. May we faithfully use that language to communicate to others the message of grace.

---

of the original," that is, the royal house of David, the temporary house where God dwelt, and the dynastic house that God promised to David.

[14]Prickett goes so far as to suggest that "those who see translation essentially in terms of data-transmission" (i.e., linguists) are the ones "who turn most readily to paraphrase, while those who think in interpretative terms tend to cling more faithfully to the actual words of the original text. Literal translation is a form of hermeneutics" (*Words*, p. 29). Cf. also my comments in *Has the Church Misread the Bible?* pp. 46–47.

Appendix
The Biblical Languages in Theological Education

F rom time to time a few of my Greek students, upon hearing my point of view, work up the courage to ask me what probably all of them are thinking: What then is the point of learning the biblical languages? Some readers of this book may be asking themselves the same question.

A few years ago, when our seminary was conducting one of its recruiting conferences, I was asked to address the prospective students on the value of studying Greek. Suspecting that some of these students were already looking forward to the possibility of accomplishing great feats of exegetical prestidigitation, I began by giving a list of *bad* reasons for studying the biblical languages. Unfortunately, my time was limited and I ended up with only a few minutes to expound on the good reasons. Some weeks later a colleague reported to me that one of those students had decided not to come to our seminary. Evidently I had convinced him that there was no point in attending an institution that had such hefty language requirements! I have not been asked to give my talk again.

During the past few generations, teachers of New Testament Greek—particularly in conservative American institutions—have been inclined, in the interest of encouraging their students, to overemphasize the *direct* value of Greek grammar for exegesis and theology. As a colleague in another institution has remarked, the process of "demythologizing" the value of the biblical languages has created the need for a valid justification of the traditional seminary requirement. Indeed, not a few seminaries have weakened or altogether abandoned such language requirements. While I have no intentions in this brief appendix to provide a full rationale for the study of biblical languages, readers of this book deserve at least a few comments regarding this important issue.

We should note at the outset that there are two distinct questions before us. One has a strictly personal character: Why should an *individual* preparing for ministry study the biblical languages? The second question has wider implications: Why should a *theological seminary* require the study of the biblical languages? Of course, these two issues are closely related: presumably, no seminary would require the languages if they were of no value at all to individuals. Nevertheless, the questions are distinct and may require somewhat different answers.

I do not hesitate to acknowledge that, in some situations, it may be possible for pastors, as well as others engaged in more general kinds of Christian ministry, to do their jobs without solid training in the biblical languages. Many of the early Latin fathers— notably Augustine—had only a smattering of Greek and knew virtually no Hebrew, yet they appear to have managed respectably well! But that is hardly a conclusive argument against language requirements. Augustine also had no formal training in modern counseling and other areas of practical theology, yet most of us would consider that fact somewhat irrelevant in determining curricular requirements.

Today we are far removed from the cultural and linguistic world of the Bible. It is an illusion for us to think that we can understand the biblical text while ignoring the distance—both temporal and geographic—that separates us from that text. Someone has to bridge the gap. Translations act as our primary bridges. Individual translators have done the hard work necessary to make the ancient text accessible to the modern believer. It could be said that ministers who have not studied the biblical languages enslave themselves to English translations. To be sure, this need not be an absolutely fatal relationship, but it certainly puts ministers at a serious disadvantage.

Suppose, for example, that a parishioner notices a significant difference between two New Testament translations. On what grounds will the "Greekless" pastor offer a responsible solution? Again, while we are blessed with a multitude of fine commentaries, they can prove to be almost useless if we cannot follow the linguistic arguments involved. The problem becomes critical if the pastor has a well-educated congregation—and even more so if some of the members are college students who find themselves bombarded by the arguments of unbelieving professors. Inability by the pastor to provide reasonable responses to pressing questions can prove destructive in some sensitive situations.

It may be worthwhile to keep in mind that, more often than not, grammar has a negative yet important function: grammatical knowledge may not directly result in a sensational new truth, but it may play a key role in *preventing* interpretive mistakes. Take, for instance, the doctrine of Christ's deity. It would *not* be quite accurate to say that Greek syntax directly proves this doctrine. It is certainly true, however, that it can *disprove* certain heretical ideas. For example, proponents of some cults are fond of pointing out that the last reference to God in John 1:1 does not include the definite article and so should be translated "a god" or "divine." Someone with little or no knowledge of Greek could easily be persuaded by this argument. A reasonably good understanding of predicate clauses in Greek, however, is all one needs to demonstrate that the argument has no foundation whatever (the article that accompanies the predicate noun is routinely dropped to distinguish the predicate from the subject of the clause—besides, there are numerous and indisputable references to God, as in verses 6, 13, and 18 of the same chapter, that do not include the article).

Quite possibly, however, the most significant benefit of acquiring a knowledge of the biblical languages is intangible. Most of us are conditioned to think that nothing is truly valuable that does not have an immediate and concrete payoff, but a little reflection dispels that illusion. Consider the teaching we all received from birth. Has most of it been *immediately* rewarding? We are simply not conscious of how deeply we have been molded by countless experiences that affect our perspective, our thinking, our decisions. Similarly, a measure of proficiency in the biblical languages provides the framework that promotes responsibility in the handling of the text. Continued exposure to the original text expands our horizon and furnishes us with a fresh and more authentic perspective than that which we bring from our modern, English-speaking situation.

In my own preaching during the past twenty-five years, explicit references to Greek and Hebrew have become less and less frequent. But that hardly means I have paid less attention to the languages or that they have become less significant in my work of interpretation. Quite the contrary. It's just that coming up with those rich "exegetical nuggets" is not necessarily where the real, substantial payoff lies.

There is, however, a whole different set of reasons that we ought to appeal to in favor of a strong biblical language requirement in seminary training. That is, even if we were to decide that many *individual* ministers have in fact little use for Greek and Hebrew, there are some powerful considerations that come to bear when we focus attention on the larger, *corporate* responsibilities of theological institutions. In a nutshell: Relaxing the language requirements inevitably lowers the quality of instruction and adversely affects biblical scholarship.

No doubt, it will be argued by some that as long as the languages continue to be offered as electives, students interested in the subject can be trained. But that makes about as much sense as saying that algebra and history should merely be electives in the high schools. As the argument goes: How often does the typical graduate make use of algebraic equations and historical dates in his or her day-to-day work? Among various responses to such a question, I am interested in pointing out, first, that such an elective system would necessarily weaken the intellectual character of the whole school by lowering its cultural literacy; and second, that potentially brilliant scholars in math and history might never have an opportunity to develop an interest in those subjects.

It should go without saying that if a professor in biblical studies is unable to deal with technical linguistic arguments in a class because most of the students have not taken Greek and Hebrew, the level of instruction necessarily drops. Moreover, the important education that takes place as students converse with one another also plummets several notches. The natural tendency to gravitate toward "relevancy" and pragmatism can do nothing but flourish in such an environment. And the end result is an increase in the poisonous anti-intellectualism that has already taken its toll in the evangelical church.

But I fear most of all for the future of biblical scholarship. Many are the students who have acknowledged that, if they had not been forced to take Greek and Hebrew, they would not have done so, thus missing what they now consider a foundational element in their theological education. Dropping the language requirement leads inexorably to a drain in the pool of potential scholars. Can we afford to abandon the scientific study of the Bible and leave it in the hands of those who have no regard for its authority?

These considerations have a special significance in the context of today's hermeneutical debates. We would all like to find shortcuts that may lead us to the right answers without the hard, and sometimes tedious, work of responsible biblical exegesis. But the shortcuts simply do not exist. May we be given the tenacity to do whatever needs to be done to advance the church's understanding of God's infallible Word.

For Further Reading

A complete list of works cited may be found in the index of modern authors and titles. In this section I have included only a few helpful works.

Cambridge University Press has produced numerous works in the area of linguistics. At a popular level notice especially David Crystal, *The Cambridge Encyclopedia of Language* (1987), a clear and profusely illustrated work covering virtually every field related to the study of language. The four-volume work *Linguistics: The Cambridge Survey*, ed. Frederick J. Newmeyer (1988) is an unusually successful anthology in which each contributor has sought to describe the state of the art in modern linguistics. Although this work presupposes some knowledge of the field, most of the articles avoid highly technical language and are therefore accessible to a wide range of readers. In addition, the series Cambridge Textbooks in Linguistics offers full-length, intermediate-level volumes on almost every subdiscipline, such as phonology, morphology, dialectology, historical linguistics, and the like.

On the application of linguistics to biblical studies, see the Annotated Bibliography in M. Silva, *Biblical Words and Their Meaning: An Introduction to Lexical Semantics, rev. ed.* (Grand Rapids: Zondervan, 1983), pp. 179–82. Recent publications in this field include David A. Black, *Linguistics for Students of New Testament Greek: A Survey of Basic Concepts and Applications* (Grand Rapids: Baker, 1988), and Peter Cotterell and Max Turner, *Linguistics and Biblical Interpretation* (Downers Grove, Ill.: InterVarsity, 1989); cf. my review of the latter in *WTJ* 51 (1989): 389–90. Of special significance is the forthcoming volume by J. P. Louw and E. A. Nida, *Lexical Semantics of the Greek New Testament*.

The reader should also refer to the footnotes in relevant sections of the present book, especially pages 260 (verbal aspect), 264 (discourse analysis), and 274 (translation).

THE ART
OF BIBLICAL
HISTORY
V. Philips Long

Better the end of a matter than its beginning,
Better a patient spirit than a prideful one.
—Ecclesiastes 7:8

This work is dedicated with love and gratitude
to my wife, Polly,
and our children,
Philip, Taylor, Andrea, and Duncan.

They undoubtedly share Qoheleth's sentiment about beginnings and endings, and have admirably exhibited the patience of which he speaks.

Contents

"History is the only science enjoying the ambiguous fortune of being required to be at the same time an art."

—Johann Gustav Droysen

"History is the most difficult of the belles lettres, for it must be true."

—Garrett Mattingly

". . . the appeal of history to us all is in the last analysis poetic. But the poetry of history does not consist of imagination roaming large, but of imagination pursuing the fact and fastening upon it."

—G. M. Trevelyan*

*All quoted in J. Axtell, "History as Imagination," *The Historian: A Journal of History* 49 (1987): 453.

Editor's Preface

Few distinctives of Christian theology are as foundational in character and pervasive in their consequences as the conviction that the Bible is historically trustworthy. Attempts to salvage Christianity while abandoning that conviction invariably result in a message so crippled at its very roots that one has to wonder whether it is worth preserving at all.

Understandably, much of conservative biblical scholarship has been devoted to the defense of that conviction. And so it should be. What is not so clear is whether this great effort has always contributed positively to the interpretation of Scripture. The issue is not precisely that conservatives may have expended a disproportionate amount of time on historical apologetics to the detriment of other important fields of investigation (though perhaps a strong argument could be made in support of that judgment). Rather, the question needs to be asked whether the typical focus and approach run the risk of not doing justice to the character of Scripture itself. That there are some hermeneutical weaknesses in the traditional method is hardly to be disputed, and those weaknesses, no doubt, have contributed to the tendency of mainstream scholarship to downplay the historicity of biblical narrative.

There has long been a need for capable evangelical scholars to address this issue head-on. Those who have tried their hand at it have usually hesitated to go much below the surface (so that the product is little more than a reaffirmation of the traditional viewpoint) or they have adopted mainstream positions without integrating them into basic tenets of the Christian faith (so that the term *evangelicalism* becomes progressively more diffused in application).

Each reader, of course, must decide whether Dr. Long has been successful in avoiding the Scylla of historical skepticism as well as the Charybdis of literary insensitivity. Given the controversial and emotional character of the subject, one can safely predict that at least some readers on both sides of the issue will find something to which they will object. Dr. Long's clear commitment to biblical historicity will, almost by definition, offend those who believe no one can be considered a scholar who does not find error, myth, or contradiction in the narratives of Scripture. By contrast, his very willingness to ask the hard questions—and thus inevitably to recognize the literary artistry of the narratives—may well put off readers who think there is only one kind of history-writing.

As the editor of the series, I may be suspected of prejudice in stating that Dr. Long has indeed been successful in meeting the goals set for this volume. Actually, he has far exceeded my expectations. There is not one significant issue that he has failed to take seriously. He has neither tried to camouflage his theological commitments nor sought to minimize the difficulties raised by the evidence. Within relatively short compass he has managed to cover complex subjects with both breadth and depth. And, to boot, he has accomplished it all with great clarity of writing and literary flair.

Dr. Long would be the first to recognize that many important questions are yet to be answered with definitiveness. Nonetheless, this volume is, in my opinion, the first to provide theological students with a truly solid foundation for the hermeneutics of biblical history. And they will ignore it to their peril.

Moisés Silva

Author's Preface

*I*n a brief review of the first three volumes to appear in the Foundations of Contemporary Interpretation series, Robert Morgan comments that "judgment on the series as a whole must await the volume on history, the traditional rock of offence."[1] A comment such as this is an indication of the importance and magnitude of the questions to be addressed in the present study. What is the relationship between historical inquiry and biblical interpretation? Just how important are historical questions to biblical faith?

Colin Brown describes his own study of the relationship of history and faith as a personal exploration.[2] And, indeed, any who set out to probe this topic soon find themselves explorers in a vast terrain, oft-traveled but far from tamed, studded with bibliographic mountains the tops of which few have ever seen and philosophical seas the depths of which few, if any, have plumbed.[3] In this landscape I feel myself very much a traveler, and not a very seasoned one at that. I cannot claim to have conquered all the bibliographic mountains, though I have begun the ascent on not a few. Nor can I claim to have touched bottom in the philosophical seas, though I have navigated the shallows of some of them and at least peered into their mysterious depths, which I find both alluring and foreboding—one cannot dismiss the possibility of drowning in them!

It is often said of journeys that "getting there is half the fun." This is true; and it would be a pity, as we traverse the topography of our topic, not to take time to consider significant landmarks along the way. But since most readers of this volume will be not simply sightseers but travelers desiring to discover what lies at journey's end, and since the time allotted for our journey is limited, it will be necessary to place reasonable limits on side-trips as we seek to discover a route that will lead across the terrain and to our destination. The route I have chosen is but one of several routes by which we might set out to explore the historical character of the Bible. I do not even claim that it is the best route, but I do think that it deserves more frequent travel than it has received thus far.

The title of this book was chosen for several reasons. First, echoing as it does the titles of two recent works by Robert Alter, *The Art of Biblical Narrative* and *The Art of Biblical Poetry*,[4] it expresses my conviction that advances in the literary study of the Bible, typified by such works as Alter's or by the more monumental work of Meir Sternberg, *The Poetics*

---

[1]*Expository Times* 101 (1990): 210.

[2]*History and Faith: A Personal Exploration* (Grand Rapids: Zondervan, 1987).

[3]In fact, comprehensive exploration may no longer even be possible; cf. F. R. Ankersmit's comments on the "present-day overproduction in our [the historical] discipline. We are all familiar with the fact that in any imaginable area of historiography, within any specialty, an overwhelming number of books and articles is produced annually, making a comprehensive view of them all impossible" ("Historiography and Postmodernism," *HTh* 28 [1989]: 137).

[4]New York: Basic Books, 1982 and 1985, respectively.

of Biblical Narrative,[5] have much to contribute to our understanding of the Bible not only as literature but as a source of historical information as well. As Burke Long has succinctly remarked, "Given our lack of varied sources, if one is to understand Israel's history, one must first investigate with more literary sensitivity its styles of telling history."[6] Second, the title reflects my feeling that we may learn much about *verbal representation*—which I would adopt as a provisional, working definition of history-writing—by exploring points of analogy with modes of *visual representation* such as representational painting or portraiture. Third, if we understand *art* in our title as connoting not simply craft or artistry, but also slant and perspective, then the title may serve to suggest the Bible's widely recognized trio of interests in matters theological, historical, and literary. How these three interests are coordinated in the biblical texts is, as Sternberg remarks, "a tricky question,"[7] and one that we shall want to explore.

I have structured the discussion around fundamental questions regarding the historical character of the Bible and of the Christian faith: (1) Is the Bible a history book? If it is not, as is consistently pointed out by biblical scholars and theologians of virtually all stripes, what is it? What is its essential character, its *macro-genre,* as it were? (2) What do we mean by *history* anyway? What is *history?* (3) Does the Bible need to be historical to be true? If truth can be imparted in fictional stories, such as parables, is the question of historicity at all important? (4) If biblical scholarship strives for objectivity (while recognizing that subjectivity in interpretation can never be entirely eliminated), why do biblical scholars differ so widely in their historical conclusions? (5) When we read the Bible, how do we know whether what we are reading is to be understood as history, as parable, or as fable? How can we determine which parts of the Bible convey historical information?

Since the purpose of the present volume is to offer principles of interpretation as regards both the historical character of the Bible and the character of biblical historiography (history-writing), and since the size of the volume is limited, I shall not attempt anything like a comprehensive survey of "historiographical" passages in the Bible. I shall focus, rather, on the principal questions. Most of my examples will be drawn from the narrative portions of the Bible, since among those who believe that the Bible exhibits a historiographical impulse (that is, an intent to represent and reflect on past events) it is generally agreed that this impulse is most clearly evidenced in the Bible's narratives. This is not to deny, of course, that a historical impulse is apparent also in many poetical passages, such as the Song of the Sea (Exod. 15), the Song of Deborah (Judg. 5), the "historical psalms," the prophetic writings, and so forth.

Before launching into our subject, I would like to pause to thank the many who in one way or another have helped me with this project. A number of friends, some of whom are also colleagues, have read portions of the manuscript in progress and offered helpful advice. Improvements have often resulted from their counsel, while responsibility for flaws that remain is mine alone. Thanks are due to the late Dr. Raymond L. Dillard for reading and commenting on my section on Chronicles, to Dr. Richard S. Hess for similarly treating my section dealing with archaeology, and to Dr. Tremper Longman III for

---

[5]Subtitled *Ideological Literature and the Drama of Reading* (Bloomington: Indiana University Press, 1985).

[6]"Historical narrative and the fictionalizing imagination," *VT* 35 (1985): 416.

[7]*Poetics of Biblical Narrative,* p. 41.

initially getting me interested in the project and for encouraging me along the way as regards both content and completion.

Thanks are also due to Dr. David M. Howard for his careful reading and evaluation of the work at an intermediate stage and to the students of two sessions of Trinity Evangelical Divinity School's Ph.D. seminar on biblical historiography, who graciously read and reviewed the work as it then was. I would also like to express appreciation to students at Covenant Theological Seminary, who read and commented on the work in several different drafts. Among these, special thanks go to David Wilcher for his assistance in the preparation of indices. Among my colleagues, I owe a debt of gratitude to Drs. C. John Collins, Esther L. Meek, and Robert W. Yarbrough for taking time from busy schedules to help me with the project. And I am particularly grateful to James L. Meek, who read the work in its fuller form and suggested many helpful modifications. I also want to thank the administration and the board of trustees of Covenant Theological Seminary for granting sabbatical leaves that enabled me to engage in intensive research and writing at Tyndale House in Cambridge. Tyndale House generously made its facilities available to me and my family during two short sabbatical stints and during my years of Ph.D. research; the benefits of library access and of personal contact with those working at Tyndale have been inestimable.

During my latest sabbatical leave, three individuals gave of their time not only to read the manuscript in its final draft but also to spend hours in conversation with me; thus, special thanks go to Dr. Iain W. Provan, to Dr. Phillip E. Satterthwaite, and to my former Ph.D. adviser, Dr. Robert P. Gordon. Special thanks go also to Dr. Moisés Silva, who, as general editor of the FCI series, has guided the work throughout, has read the manuscript at various stages, and has offered much good counsel and encouragement. Finally I thank my life-partner, Polly, for reading (and rereading) the work, for occasionally penning "so what?" in the margin, and for aiding me in the elimination of "zingers." We together thank our God and Father for the wonderful privilege of being about his business.

V. Philips Long

Introduction

Consider the following narrative:

The two brothers had been in the attic for nearly two hours when they came upon something that intrigued them more than all their previous discoveries. Much of what they had already found was what they had expected: old letters and photographs at once inviting and discreetly forbidding perusal; items of clothing too frayed or unfashionable to be worn but too fraught with memories to be discarded; boxes of old books decrepit with age and, in the case of the favored, with much use; odd bits of furniture with careers cut short by injury or rivalry but resting serenely in the dimly lit confidence of eventual rediscovery and rehabilitation by a future generation; stacks of sheet music that chronicled the first fifty years of the twentieth century and whose melodies were as much a part of the boys' concept of "grandmother" as was the scent of the roses that she had so lovingly cultivated; sun hats and fishing poles that brought back memories of Granddad and of the "good old days" when speckled trout and spanish mackerel were plentiful on the grass flats of the Gulf of Mexico.

These and many other discoveries were made as the boys explored the attic, but it was a small painting, carefully wrapped in brown paper, that most intrigued them. In the painting was a young girl sitting before a piano, atop which was an embroidered cloth. On the cloth lay cut roses, garden gloves, and shears. Leaning against the piano stool was a field hockey stick and at its base a basketball. The style and condition of the painting indicated considerable age. Particularly striking was the face of the girl, which, though rendered with an economy of brush strokes, suggested experience of life and wisdom unusual in a child so young. Most peculiar was the depiction of the girl's right hand, which displayed what appeared to be a second thumb!

Upon uncovering this curious painting, the boys immediately set about to discover its nature. The medium appeared to be oil paint. No signature was apparent—though, as best the boys could judge such things, the artist seemed to have been quite accomplished. The question that most interested them was whether the painting was a portrait, perhaps of a member of the family, or some other type of painting—a kind of visual parable perhaps, or just an interesting example of "art for art's sake." Their first impression was that the scene seemed somewhat artificial—pianos are hardly normal resting places for gardening tools or sports equipment. Nevertheless, the girl's appearance was more suggestive of personality and individuality than would be expected in a "young maiden" painting of the generic variety.

The tentative theory that soon emerged was that the painting must indeed be a portrait, the oddly arranged assortment of props serving to indicate not idiosyncratic house-keeping but the young girl's budding interests. Should this theory be correct, then the painting might even be of the boys' grandmother in her youth. Her interests in music and gardening were well-known and could still be corroborated by material evidence from the attic itself. Of her athletic prowess the boys knew little, though the thought that further searching in the attic might turn up a hockey stick excited them. Troubling for their theory, however, was the matter of the extra thumb, for in their experience their grandmother had never sported more than the usual complement of digits. Perhaps the extra thumb could be explained simply as a symbol of unusual precocity on the keyboard; the matter, however, bore further investigation.

Before ending their exploration of the attic, the boys turned up some evidence that tended to corroborate the portrait theory. Several other paintings were discovered in a corner, among them three more paintings of people and two landscapes. Three of the paintings were signed by the same artist, and given the similarities in style and the fact that the paintings were all found in the same attic, the boys felt it likely that all the paintings were by the one artist. Both landscapes were quite freely rendered, the artist apparently taking as much delight in the potentialities of the medium as in the subject itself.

The boys scrutinized the paintings of the people particularly closely and concluded that the positioning of the subject and the presence of a limited number of props in each painting tended to confirm their portrait theory. The artist's apparently strict adherence to the normal organization of physical features, however, left them even more undecided as to the significance of the extra thumb in the first painting. The additional paintings confirmed their common-sense judgment that in the artist's world, as in theirs, people have but one thumb per hand. Nevertheless, if the artist had felt free to include a symbolic thumb in one painting, why had no symbols been included in the others?

Determining that their investigation had been advanced as far as possible on the basis of the evidence before them, the boys exited the attic to take their inquiry farther afield. Searching out their mother at her desk, they presented her with the six paintings and mooted their theory that four of them must be portraits. This theory she was able to confirm, even to the point of giving names to the faces. The boys had been right in their assumption that the props in each of the portraits were included to give a fuller picture of the subject's character and interests and not to give information about where the items were normally kept.

On the matter of the extra thumb, while the mother granted the logic of the boys' empirical argument that its significance must be only symbolic (in all their experience with hands, they had never encountered one with six digits), she told them that in this case they must allow an exception. It seemed that their grandmother had been born with a thumblike appendage on her right hand. The slight embarrassment that this had caused her as a child had been somewhat compensated by her ability to play chords on the piano forbidden to most other mortals. As she approached age twelve, however, her parents began to reason that a suitor someday might be more attracted by physical normalcy than musical virtuosity, and they wisely decided to have the surplus appendage surgically removed.

On the matter of whether the portrait in question offered a good likeness of the boys' grandmother as a young girl, the mother was not in a position to render an opinion, except to observe that it seemed to have been the artist's intention to give a fair representation and, if the artist whose signature appeared on one of the landscapes was responsible also for the portrait in question, she had it on good authority that he had enjoyed an outstanding reputation for doing justice to his subjects. As for the two landscapes, the mother was unable to decide whether they were intended to record the artist's impression of specific vistas, were meant simply to present scenes typical of the gulf coast, or were created solely for their aesthetic appeal.

What can we learn from this strange tale? In what possible sense does it relate to the issue of biblical historiography, which is our present concern? While analogies are never perfect and should not be over-pressed, there are a number of parallels between the boys' attempts to explore the nature and significance of the artwork they discovered and the challenges that face those who would understand the Bible.

The boys' first challenge was to determine the genre (type or kind) of the painting of the young girl. They quickly recognized that the object before them was a painting and not, for example, a photograph. This perception was arrived at automatically and intuitively—though, had argument become necessary, the boys might have observed that the texture of the work's surface revealed brush strokes and not the fine-grained detail typical of photographs and that, at any rate, the apparent age of the work would place its creation in a period prior to the development of the techniques of color photography.

Having arrived at a very general genre description (i.e., *painting*), the boys sought to become more specific. The question that particularly intrigued them was whether and in what sense the painting might be referential, that is, depictive of a reality outside itself. If so, and not just art for art's sake, was it a representation of a particular person in a particular setting, perhaps even one of their ancestors, or simply a picture of what a typical young girl of the period might have looked like? Although the composition of the painting (e.g., the particular placement of some of the objects) suggested a certain intentional artificiality of arrangement, the painting overall gave a realistic impression. The rendering of the young girl's face in particular showed careful selection of detail, suggestive of a desire to capture a true likeness, and was accomplished with an economy of strokes that attested to the genius of the artist. Tentatively, the boys decided that the artwork before them was essentially representational, though the referential aspect was considerably more pronounced in some passages (e.g., the girl's face and figure) and less so in others (e.g., the props were rather loosely rendered and background objects only indicated by blocks of color).

Those who would read the Bible with understanding are similarly faced with the challenge of genre recognition. At a very general level, the Bible is literature, or, more specifically, a unified collection of literary works. Going beyond this very basic recognition, one may distinguish broadly between passages that tend to be more poetic in character and those that are in prose.[1] Further still, these basic divisions may be subdivided into subordinate categories and so on to the point of diminishing returns. Thus, genre description may take place on various levels of generality. I shall have more to say about genre criticism in chapter 1. The point that needs to be made at this juncture is simply this: The Bible is literature, but to recognize it as such does not settle the question of reference (whether it refers to realities beyond itself, real people and real events) any more than the boys' recognition of the work before them as a painting foreclosed the question of whether the painting was representational or nonrepresentational. Much of the Bible gives the impression of, and some of it explicitly presents itself as, *representational* literature—history-writing. It will be important for our consideration of biblical historiography to consider the relationship between subject matter and artistic medium. This will be the focus of chapter 2.

---

[1] See, e.g., D. J. A. Clines, "Story and Poem: The Old Testament as Literature and Scripture," *Interpretation* 34 (1980): 115–27.

Now back to the boys in the attic. We may recall that their tentative decision that the painting before them must be representational was arrived at initially through close inspection of the painting itself, that is, on the basis of *internal evidence*. Certain features were somewhat perplexing, such as the unusual arrangement of props and especially the surplus thumb. But the boys were able to overcome this difficulty by nuancing their understanding of the painting's genre. In a portrait, for example, some artificiality in the arrangement of props would be quite acceptable. Further, a portrait might well tolerate some deviation from strict literality in the interest of capturing some aspect of the subject's essence. This made room for the boys' hypothesis that the entirely unnatural thumb must be a symbol of something else.

To this stage in the investigation the boys had proceeded largely on the basis of internal evidence, though some external considerations had already begun to creep in. Without their experience of life and the world, for example, the boys would never have been able to distinguish between the normal and the abnormal. Moreover, without some understanding of the conventions of portraiture the boys would have had no basis for classifying their painting as a portrait; they might have decided that the painting was a more or less realistic depiction of a particular person, but they would not have known to call it a portrait. Discovery of comparative material (more paintings) tended to confirm their tentative genre decision. None of the figures in the three additional portraits displayed any unusual features, however. This led the boys to conclude, falsely as it turned out, that the extra thumb in the first painting must indeed be a mere symbol and not a feature to be taken literally. It was in conversation with their mother that the boys learned that their concept of the "possible" needed expanding. The "possible," they discovered, should not in every instance be limited to the "normal," for their grandmother had in fact been born with an abnormality.

Again, there seem to be parallels between the way the boys assessed the visual art before them and the way biblical interpreters should assess the literature of the Bible. In either endeavor, the proper place to begin is with a close inspection of the work itself. The focus should be on both form and content. Careful reading of biblical texts will inevitably turn up perplexing features from time to time, features that call for explanatory theories. Tentative ideas regarding the text's specific genre will begin to emerge as reading proceeds, and these will require testing and perhaps modification as the investigation continues. The wider context and comparative literature (whether biblical or extrabiblical, ancient or modern) will often shed light on the biblical text, but again the interpreter must resist the urge to allow the "normal" to delimit the field of the "possible."

When once the boys' deduction that the first painting must be a portrait of their grandmother had been confirmed by their mother, their attention turned to the question of whether or not the portrait captured a good likeness. In rendering an opinion on this matter, the mother did two things. First, she moved beyond the basic genre descriptor *portrait* to inquire after the artist's specific intentions. What style of portrait did he intend? In fact, of course, as the artist was unavailable for interview or investigation, her aim was to discern the intentionality apparent in the execution of the work itself—what might be called *embodied intention*. It was her judgment that the artist's style and detail suggested an intention to capture, to the extent allowed by the chosen medium, the essence of the visual appearance and character of the subject.

Now, the mere intention to achieve a good likeness does not in itself guarantee a good likeness, as many a mediocre portrait artist (and even a good artist on a bad day) can readily attest. Thus, before rendering an opinion on the painting in question, it was necessary for the mother to move on to a second consideration. Was the artist skilled in his craft? Strictly speaking, of course, some might wish to debate the identity of the artist—after all, the painting in question was unsigned, and even were it signed, the signature could be a forgery. The mother felt convinced, however, on what appeared to her to be reasonable grounds, that the artist was to be identified with the one whose signature appeared on several of the other paintings. Having made this identification, the mother felt herself in a position to attest to the artist's high level of competence. Her final deduction, based on these several considerations, was that the portrait was quite likely a fine representation of the boys' grandmother at a young age.

Biblical interpretation also tends to move beyond the basic question of genre to ask more specific questions. Having once identified a given text as, for example, historiography (a form of representational literature), interpreters will want to ask, What kind of historiography? If the author (or authors; the singular is used merely as a term of convenience) offers no statement of intention or, as is often the case in biblical literature, is not even identified, interpreters will focus on embodied intention, insofar as this may be inferred from the work itself on the basis of its literary strategies, compositional structure, selection of detail, and manner of expression.

At this stage the interpreter is sharpening the question of the text's *truth claim*. The genre descriptor, historiography, already implies a basic claim to referentiality; the added nuance is to ask after the level of detail and precision intended. What kind of likeness of reality is the narrator attempting to create? When once a decision on this matter is reached, the interpreter is faced with a second question, How capable is the narrator of achieving his intention? How competent is he in his craft? Here questions of biblical introduction (isogogics)—authorship, date, provenance—may become important. Here, too, the fundamental issue of the Bible's ultimate author(ity) must be considered. It is one thing to discern what a work intends (truth claim), it is quite another to decide whether it succeeds (truth value). Interpreters' opinions on the latter question are inevitably affected, at least in part, by their view of the identity and competence of the work's creator.

Shifting gears, now, we may use the story of the boys in the attic to introduce a further issue that must be considered in any discussion of biblical historiography. Our focus in this instance will not be on the genre of the painting in the story, but on the genre of the story itself. While in most contexts genre decisions are made intuitively and almost unconsciously, the reader may have experienced some difficulty in deciding just what the story of the boys in the attic is meant to be, particularly since the text's form and content are not exactly what one would expect in a book on biblical interpretation.

The reader has perhaps thought to ask whether the story is true or not. As it happens, a straightforward answer to this question cannot be offered, at least not until more thought is given to the genre of the story. The descriptors applied to the text—narrative, story, tale—are too general to get the reader very far in discovering the text's intended purpose. Even the authorship of the text may be in some doubt. The apparent significance of the fact that the story is found between the covers of a book upon which the present author's name appears, is somewhat offset by the fact that the text is formally distinguished, by its differing layout, from the main text.

Readers familiar with the convention in academic writing of citing sources for all excerpted materials might deduce from the lack of any such ascription that the little story must be the work of the author of the larger work; but, of course, literary conventions (even academic ones) may at times be modified or even disregarded by a given author. I may, for example, simply have forgotten to cite my source, or I may have chosen not to do so to make a point. Much of the biblical literature, as far as human authorship is concerned, is officially anonymous, and in many, even most, such instances, the human author may be beyond discovering.

To continue our discussion of the little story, then, let me confess to having composed it. And let us assume, very hypothetically, for the sake of discussion, that I have composed it perfectly to accomplish my intended purpose—that is to say, the truth value of each and every truth claim made by the text is assured. Even so, before I can answer the question regarding the story's truth, I must ask what you understand to be the purpose (and consequent truth claims) of the story.

We are back to the issue of genre. If you are asking, as you probably are, whether the sequence of events actually happened, the answer is no. If you are asking whether particular details in the story correspond to reality, the answers will vary. Did the painting of the young girl actually exist? No. Was someone's grandmother actually born with a surplus thumb? Yes, my own in fact. Was my grandmother a noted gardener and musician? Yes. Did my grandfather enjoy fishing and sometimes take me with him? Yes. Did my grandmother actually use her third thumb to play the piano before losing it to the surgeon's scalpel? Yes! Many of the details of the story are true, others are not, but the episode itself never took place. Does this make me a liar? I would argue that it does not, though were you to misconstrue the truth claim of the story to include factuality of the event and then learn that the event never took place, you might think me so.

To be fair, however, the truth question must be properly cast. Is the story true in terms of its intended purpose? Since the story is included in a book on biblical interpretation, the reader may well have surmised that its purpose is to illustrate some of the issues faced by those interpreting the Bible. For this purpose it is not important whether the events described actually took place or not. They may have, or they may not have; it does not matter. Even to ask if the story is "true," without qualifying the question, may seem a little out of place, since the story's purpose is to *illustrate* a point and not to *affirm* or *establish* it.

It would be more appropriate to ask if the story succeeds in accomplishing its purpose. That the story is a fiction is acceptable, since its purpose is essentially illustrative and didactic (even though this or that item of detail may refer to some aspect of reality). Were the story meant to establish a truth on the basis of the sequence of events recorded, however, then the factuality of the sequence would be a much more pressing question. We shall look more closely at these issues in chapter 3.

As we move now to take up in turn certain basic questions relating to the historical character of the Bible, we do well to recognize that the Bible contains various kinds of stories, some meant to illustrate truth and others meant to establish it. The fictional scenario above is intended to introduce some of the kinds of issues that biblical interpreters encounter when they seek to come to terms with the Bible in all its historical, theological, and literary complexity. These issues will be given closer attention in the chapters that follow.

one

HISTORY

AND THE GENRE(S)

OF THE BIBLE

Is the Bible a History Book?

T he simple answer to the question posed in the title to this chapter is *No, the Bible is not a history book*.[1] But this is just the kind of question to which a simple (simplistic?) answer should not be given, at least not without going on to say what else the Bible is not. It is also not a science book, a law book, an ethics book, a theology book, or even a book of literature or politics (the list could go on). The Bible may be of vital interest in each of these areas, but its essence cannot be reduced to any one of them. If the question means to get at the essential nature of the Bible, then *history book* is not an adequate answer. It is important to recognize the all-encompassing character of the question, however, lest one fall prey to the kinds of false dichotomies often encountered in discussions of the historical character of the Bible—namely, the Bible is not history but literature, or the Bible is not history but theology.[2] The Bible, in terms of its essence, cannot be fully and adequately described by any of the above labels.

What then is the Bible? Much of the modern problem of biblical interpretation is linked to what Robert Morgan describes as "concealed disagreements" about how the subject matter of the Bible is to be defined: "Some call the Bible superstition, others the word of God."[3] The definition likely to enjoy widest acceptance is that the Bible is a *religious*

---

[1] At least not in the sense of being a history *textbook*. This point is widely acknowledged across the theological spectrum; see Moisés Silva, "The Place of Historical Reconstruction in New Testament Criticism," in *Hermeneutics, Authority, and Canon*, ed. D. A. Carson and J. D. Woodbridge (Grand Rapids: Zondervan, 1986), p. 109.

[2] Cf., e.g., G. Garbini: The Bible is "no longer politics or religion or history—but only ideology" (*History and Ideology in Ancient Israel* [London: SCM, 1988], p. xvi; cf. pp. xiv–xv, 14, 176); cf. also T. L. Thompson, following N. P. Lemche: "In terms of genre, the biblical traditions are rather origin traditions than historiography" (*Early History of Israel: From the Written and Archaeological Sources*, Studies in the History of the Ancient Near East 4, ed. M. H. E. Weippert [Leiden: E. J. Brill, 1992], p. 168).

[3] R. Morgan, with J. Barton, *Biblical Interpretation* (Oxford: Oxford University Press, 1988), p. 19.

book. As the canonical Scriptures of two of the world's major religions, Judaism (Hebrew Bible = Old Testament) and Christianity (Old and New Testaments),[4] the Bible certainly qualifies as a religious book.

But is *religious book* an adequate definition? To some it will seem so. To secular interpreters, for example, the Bible may appear to be just one religious book among many. For confessing Christians, however, the Bible is not simply *a* religious book but *the* religious book of their community of faith (though some in this group may assume that the Bible's authority is not intrinsic but is simply accorded to it by the community of faith itself).[5] For those Christians who would take their cue from the Bible's own self-understanding, the Bible is not simply *a* religious book or even *the* religious book of a given community but, rather, *the* religious book that is above all others and quite distinct from all others—its very words being "God-breathed" (2 Tim. 3:16).[6]

THE BIBLE'S MACRO-GENRE AND THE ISSUE OF TRUTH

What view one takes on the question of the Bible's essential nature, what we might call its *macro-genre,* will have far-reaching implications for how one assesses the truth value of the text. Secular readers, the first group described above, will find it easy to assume that the Bible, as just one religious book among many, may often be lacking in truth value. Confessing Christians, the second group, will at least want to regard the Bible as true in some sense—for example, "true for me." They will ascribe to the Bible at least a relative or subjective truth value. Christians of the third group, among whom I wish to be included, will hold that the Bible is true in a much more sweeping sense and will assume, consciously or unconsciously, that the Bible's truth claims (i.e., what the Bible teaches, commands, promises, and threatens) and its truth value (i.e., the veracity and/or authority of these speech acts) coincide.[7] Having said this, I must emphasize that one's commitment to the truth value of the Bible does not automatically settle the question of the truth claim(s) of any given text. It is one thing to believe the Bible to be true; it is another to understand what it says.[8]

This point may be illustrated by imagining a situation in which you tell me that you have written something that you would like me to read. Let us assume that I believe

---

[4]M. Weinfeld ("Old Testament—The Discipline and Its Goals," in *Congress Volume Vienna 1980,* ed. J. A. Emerton, VTSup 32 [Leiden: E. J. Brill, 1981], p. 423) mentions also Islam, referring to the Old Testament as "the basis of the three great world religions and of Western culture in general."

[5]Cf. Morgan (*Biblical Interpretation,* p. 7): "Where texts are accepted as authoritative within a community it is the community's authority that is invested in them." For a critical review of Morgan's book, see A. C. Thiselton, "On Models and Methods: A Conversation with Robert Morgan," in *The Bible in Three Dimensions,* ed. D. J. A. Clines et al., JSOTS 87 (Sheffield: JSOT, 1990), pp. 337–56 (esp. pp. 353–55).

[6]See, e.g., D. A. Carson and J. D. Woodbridge, eds., *Scripture and Truth* (Grand Rapids: Zondervan, 1983); idem, *Hermeneutics, Authority, and Canon;* G. Fackre, "Evangelical Hermeneutics: Commonality and Diversity," *Interpretation* 43 (1989): 117–29.

[7]On the diversity of the Bible's truth claims, see K. J. Vanhoozer, "The Semantics of Biblical Literature: Truth and Scripture's Diverse Literary Forms," in *Hermeneutics, Authority, and Canon,* ed. Carson and Woodbridge, pp. 49–104.

[8]That this important distinction sometimes becomes blurred is illustrated by the fact that "for many believers, unfortunately, assurance that the Bible is true appears to be inseparable from assurance about traditional interpretive positions, so that if we question the latter we seem to be doubting the former" (M. Silva, "Old Princeton, Westminster, and Inerrancy," *WTJ* 50 [1988]: 78).

you to be both trustworthy and competent and thus have confidence in the truth value of what you write. Despite this confidence, if you offer no further comment, and if the circumstances surrounding our conversation offer no hint, I shall have very little idea of what it is you have written (i.e., what its genre, and thus its truth claim, is). Is it a telephone message, a list of things you would like me to do, a complaint, a poem, a joke, a riddle, a grocery list, a letter of recommendation, a contract, an essay, or what? The fact that I have confidence in your veracity and competence will, of course, influence the attitude with which I approach what you have written and the manner in which I respond, once I understand it. But my confidence in you does not guarantee that I will have an easy time comprehending what you have written.

All this is to make the point that questions of truth value and truth claim are essentially distinct. On the one hand, one's assumption regarding the likely truth value of the Bible is fundamentally affected by one's assessment of the macro-genre (or, more properly, the essential character or ontological status) of the Bible. If the Bible is a merely human document, then it may well be untrustworthy; if it is the very word of God, then the assumption will be the opposite.[9] On the other hand, one's discernment of the particular truth claims of the Bible requires that more specific genre decisions be made. Since the Bible comprises a collection of works of diverse literary genres, the truth claim(s) of this or that biblical text (what this or that text intends to convey, command, etc.) can be discovered only as each text is read on its own terms, with due recognition of its genre and due attention to its content and wider and narrower contexts.

THE BIBLE AS A FOREIGN BOOK

Something like genre recognition plays an important role in all forms of communication. People who have never experienced a foreign culture may not be very aware of this fact, since within their own culture they tend to make correct "genre decisions" automatically and even subconsciously, so that a break-down in communication seldom occurs.[10] But as soon as one enters a foreign culture the rules change. Not only is the language itself different, but even gestures may take on different significances, social expectations and rules of etiquette change, codes of friendship and hospitality may differ, and so on. "Culture shock," to a greater or lesser degree, is often the result. The following provides an extreme example of the potential for miscommunication and misunderstanding in cross-cultural situations.[11]

---

[9]To Morgan's assertion (*Biblical Interpretation,* pp. 278–79) that "a secular and pluralist culture no longer thinks of the Bible as the Word of God, and to start out with that claim would be to break off communication with the world outside," I would respond (1) that despite his reference to *pluralism,* Morgan may be assuming too monolithic an understanding of the modern world, and (2) that this may be, in any case, just the kind of question that "the world outside" should not be trusted to answer. On the matter of the Bible's trustworthiness, Vanhoozer ("Semantics of Biblical Literature") draws a helpful distinction between biblical *infallibility* (a term applicable to the full variety of Scripture's utterances) and biblical *inerrancy* (a subcategory of *infallibility* pertaining specifically to propositional statements).

[10]Cf. D. Patte's comments on the fairly reliable process by which the subconscious application of rules of intentionality within one's native culture allows the intentionality, and hence the communicative import, of a speech act to be discerned ("Speech Act Theory and Biblical Exegesis," *Semeia* 41 [1988]: 98).

[11]This is a slightly modified version of an account by missiologist M. Wilson (from a letter dated February 1986).

They were new missionaries . . . alone in a remote tribal village. These two single women had the highest of goals . . . the best of intentions . . . the purest of motives: they were to translate the Bible into this, as yet, unwritten tribal language. But after a year's worth of labor, they had no results. Oh, they had been well received . . . at first! The tribe had even built them a small house, complete with screened-in porch. It was a hot muggy climate; with only a hint of a breeze right at daybreak. So, every morning they used to sit on that porch to read their Bibles and sip lime juice, the only refreshment they could find. But it seemed that rather quickly they became outcasts, with tribal members avoiding them, and they were unable to find someone to become their language helper. Just over a year later they and the mission decided something had to be done. A veteran missionary couple was sent to replace them. It seemed that in no time flat this couple had won the confidence of the tribe and began to make progress toward a translation. As they began to probe to find out why the two women had encountered such resistance, they were astonished to learn that the women had a reputation for exhibiting blatant immorality. The wives of the tribesmen even forbade their husbands and sons to go anywhere near the women. Inquiring further, the couple listened in utter shock to the tribesmen's description of the activity that had "confirmed" the two women's guilt: "Because *they drank lime juice every morning!*" You see, limes were the only citrus that grew near the village. For centuries the women of the tribe had drunk its juice in the belief that it was a "morning-after" contraceptive. The two single women, having been observed drinking it *every morning,* were thus a scandal in the village. The tribal people assumed that they had had gentlemen visitors each night. Of course, the truth is that there were no nightly visitors. The two women had no idea of what drinking a glass of lime juice meant in that culture. They had no idea of what that simple act was communicating.

If such misunderstandings can arise in cross-cultural situations today, is it any wonder that the Bible too can in places be misunderstood even by the most well-meaning of interpreters? The Bible is, after all, a *foreign* book, and though the existence of modern translations and a general, if diminishing, cultural familiarity with at least some of the Bible's contents can tend to dull our sensitivity to the Bible's foreignness, we overlook it at our own exegetical peril. After all, as Philip Hughes has observed, "the Bible is a collection of documents belonging to a period of history now long past. The most recent of its writings, those that comprise the books of the New Testament, are nineteen hundred years removed from the age in which we live."[12] If "every culture has its own sense of values," as Tomoo Ishida remarks, then the challenge of rightly interpreting literature from such distant and different cultures as the ancient Near Eastern world of the Old Testament or the first century world of the New Testament must not be underestimated. He writes:

> I am very doubtful of the ability of western society to understand the sense of values of Oriental countries, and vice versa. If we feel difficulties in understanding foreign cultures in our modern world, how can we correctly interpret the compositions from the ancient Near East which come to us not only from different cultures but from different and distant times?[13]

---

[12]"The Truth of Scripture and the Problem of Historical Relativity," in *Scripture and Truth,* ed. Carson and Woodbridge, p. 173.

[13]"Adonijah the Son of Haggith and His Supporters: An Inquiry into Problems About History and Historiography," in *The Future of Biblical Studies,* ed. R. E. Friedman and H. G. M. Williamson (Atlanta: Scholars Press, 1987), pp. 166–67.

One may not wish to adopt quite such a pessimistic view as this,[14] but the basic point is unassailable: "a naive application of modern western logic and judgement to the interpretation of ancient Near Eastern sources, including biblical literature, has [often] led us into error."[15] John Barton makes a similar comment with regard to criticisms sometimes leveled against various biblical passages: "An exclusive acquaintance with the literary genres available within our own culture can all too easily lead us to regard as impossible or composite works which are in fact entirely unproblematic within a different literary system."[16] Unless students of the Bible are willing to sacrifice, as it were, their monolingual and monocultural integrity—that is, unless they are willing, by an effort of imagination, to enter a cultural and literary world different in many respects from their own—even a high view of the Bible's veracity is no guarantee of a right view of its interpretation.

What is called for then, if mistakes are to be avoided, is the attainment of what has been called an *ancient literary competence.* The need to expend considerable effort to attain such competence is widely recognized among secular historians. S. W. Baron, writing on historical method, contends that the would-be interpreter must seek to discover the "intrinsic meaning of the source, not from some of his own scale of values, but that of the original writer or speaker."[17] C. Behan McCullagh illustrates how this works in practice:

> There certainly is a danger that an historian who intuitively interprets the behaviour and products of people in other societies will use general knowledge appropriate to his own. This danger can be averted, however, if the historian immerses himself in the conventions of the society he is studying, learning the significance of its words and actions by studying them in different contexts. This is precisely what professional historians do, as J. H. Hexter has fully explained in his essay "The Historian and His Day" (Hexter, 1961). Hexter regularly spent nine or ten hours a day reading "things written between 1450 and 1650 or books written by historians on the basis of things written between 1450 and 1650" (p. 6). As a result he found that "instead of the passions, prejudices, assumptions and pre-possessions, the events, crises and tensions of the present dominating my view of the past, *it is the other way about*" (p. 9). . . . Professional historians avoid the danger of interpreting the past by the conventions of the present by building up a comprehensive knowledge of the conventions and preoccupations of the past.[18]

If, as G. B. Caird observes, the past "is not accessible to us by direct scrutiny, but only through the interrogation of witnesses," then perception of the past will depend in no small measure on "the historian's ability to 'speak the same language' as his source."[19]

---

[14]And, indeed, Ishida himself takes steps toward establishing, through the judicious use of the comparative method, "a set of criteria for interpretation that is free from the prejudices of our modern society" (ibid., p. 167).

[15]Ibid. (my insertion).

[16]*Reading the Old Testament: Method in Biblical Study* (London: Darton, Longman and Todd, 1984), p. 27. Barton cites the amusing example of French literary critics of the seventeenth and eighteenth centuries who, familiar only with the conventions of classical French tragedy, ridiculed Shakespeare's tragedies as "crude and barbaric in conception" or sometimes even refused to believe that they were "properly finished works at all."

[17]*The Contemporary Relevance of History: A Study of Approaches and Methods* (New York: Columbia University Press, 1986), p. 93.

[18]*Justifying Historical Descriptions* (Cambridge: Cambridge University Press, 1984), p. 72.

[19]*The Language and Imagery of the Bible* (London: Duckworth, 1980), p. 202.

Unfortunately, not a few contemporary interpreters dismiss the notion of ancient literary competence as unattainable, and instead advocate ahistorical or even antihistorical approaches to biblical interpretation.[20] Meir Sternberg's criticism of such approaches, once heard, is as obvious as it is insightful:

> From the premise that we cannot become people of the past, it does not follow that we cannot approximate to this state by imagination and training—just as we learn the rules of any other cultural game—still less that we must not or do not make the effort. Indeed the antihistorical argument never goes all the way, usually balking as early as the hurdle of language. Nobody, to the best of my knowledge, has proposed that we each invent our own biblical Hebrew. But is the language any more or less of a historical datum to be reconstructed than the artistic conventions, the reality-model, the value system?[21]

Sternberg emphasizes that if the task of becoming competent in the original languages of the Bible is as indispensable as it is demanding, then so too is the task of becoming competent in the literary conventions of the Bible and its neighboring cultures. "As with linguistic code, so with artistic code."[22] (I recognize, of course, that many readers of this book will have had no opportunity to learn either Greek, Hebrew, or Aramaic and therefore must rely on the judgments of experts as to how the various portions of the Bible are best translated. Similarly, there may be some need to rely on the aid of experts in seeking to develop an ancient literary competence.)[23]

The emphasis in the above discussion on the "foreignness" of the Bible may seem to suggest that the Bible is a closed book to all but specialists in the fields of ancient Near Eastern or Hellenistic languages and literatures. But this is not the case. Despite the many distinctives of the Bible's literary genres—its narratives, its poems, its epistles, and so forth—there is also considerable commonality between those genres and their modern-day counterparts, with which we are familiar. Were this not the case, comprehending them would be as inconceivable as comprehending a foreign language that shared no conceptual categories with our own (e.g., nouns, verbs, prepositions).[24] As Barton explains, "all literary study must assume that even quite remote cultures have *some* affinities with our own," so that, while we must "be on our guard, as biblical critics have sometimes failed to be, against thinking we know more than we do about the literary conventions of ancient Israel," we must not allow this realization to "drive us into a kind of critical nihilism according to which texts from the past are simply inscrutable."[25]

---

[20]I shall have more to say on this in chap. 4.

[21]*Poetics of Biblical Narrative,* p. 10.

[22]Ibid., p. 12.

[23]Recent books on the literature of the Bible that may prove useful to students include, in addition to the works of Alter and Sternberg already mentioned, J. Licht, *Storytelling in the Bible* (Jerusalem: Magnes, 1978); G. D. Fee and D. Stuart, *How to Read the Bible For All Its Worth,* 2d ed. (Grand Rapids: Zondervan, 1993); A. Berlin, *Poetics and Interpretation of Biblical Narrative* (Sheffield: Almond, 1983); M. A. Powell, *What Is Narrative Criticism?* (Minneapolis: Fortress, 1990); R. Alter, *The World of Biblical Literature* (New York: Basic Books, 1992); L. Ryken and T. Longman, *A Complete Literary Guide to the Bible* (Grand Rapids: Zondervan, 1993); and T. Longman III, *Literary Approaches to Biblical Interpretation,* elsewhere in this volume.

[24]Cf. R. Trigg, "Tales Artfully Spun," in *The Bible as Rhetoric: Studies in Biblical Persuasion,* ed. Martin Warner (New York: Routledge, 1990), p. 125: "The practice of history and even the possibility of the translation of ancient languages depend on the assumption that there are major points of contact between what may seem alien worlds."

[25]*Reading the Old Testament,* pp. 28–29.

Robert Alter makes much the same point, contending that responsible biblical interpretation requires the adoption of a "self-conscious sense of historical perspective" that is alert to the "stubborn and interesting differences" between the world of the Bible and the modern world, but that at the same time recognizes that there are also "elements of continuity or at least close analogy in the literary modes of disparate ages," since "the repertory of narrative devices used by different cultures and eras is hardly infinite."[26]

In addition to drawing some reassurance from the significant degree of commonality between the literary forms of the biblical world and those of our own day, students of the Bible may be encouraged by what traditional Protestant thought has called the "perspicuity" (or clarity) of Scripture.[27] In a carefully nuanced discussion of the clarity or obscurity of the Bible, Moisés Silva notes that the doctrine of perspicuity, while not exempt from challenge or misunderstanding, is nevertheless a necessary corrective to the dispiriting misconception that the Bible is a book inaccessible to all but an elite few.[28] As formulated in the Westminster Confession of Faith, for example, the doctrine of the perspicuity of Scripture offers encouragement to all students of the Bible, the "unlearned" as well as the "learned."[29] But, as Silva explains, it does not deny the value of diligent personal study, the importance of "specialists who seek to bridge the gap that separates us from the languages and cultures of the biblical writers," or the need for the illumination of the Spirit of God for the attainment of "saving understanding."[30] Nor does it deny that some readers of the Bible may become, as Paul puts it, "darkened in their understanding and separated from the life of God because of the ignorance that is in them due to the hardening of their hearts" (Eph. 4:18; cf. Rom. 1:21).[31]

In view of the degree of commonality between the literatures of various ages and cultures and in view of the Bible's clarity (perspicuity), every Bible reader (while recognizing that saving knowledge, like faith, is a gift of God) should be encouraged and challenged to know that with a good will and by the use of "ordinary means" a sufficient, if not comprehensive, understanding of biblical truth is attainable. Does this mean that the work of biblical scholars and specialists need be of little interest to ordinary readers? On the contrary, "leaning on the expertise of scholars who have specialized interest should be regarded as one more instance of using 'ordinary means' in the study of Scripture." To dismiss the work

---

[26]"How Convention Helps Us Read: The Case of the Bible's Annunciation Type-Scene," *Proof* 3 (1983): 117–18.

[27]The perspicuity of Scripture is included along with the concepts of *sola Scriptura* and the analogy of faith in Fackre's list of "standard features of traditional Protestant hermeneutics" ("Evangelical Hermeneutics," p. 123).

[28]*Has the Church Misread the Bible?* pp. 62–74 in this volume.

[29]See ibid., p. 85.

[30]Ibid., pp. 84, 89.

[31]The doctrine of the perspicuity of Scripture is similar in some respects to Sternberg's concept of the Bible's "foolproof composition," by which he means the ability of the biblical discourse to "bring home its essentials to all readers." The Bible may be "difficult to read, easy to underread and overread and even misread, but virtually impossible to, so to speak, counterread." Sternberg is alert to the fact that "ignorance, preconception, tendentiousness—all amply manifested throughout history, in the religious and other approaches—may perform wonders of distortion," but, nevertheless, "short of such extremes, the essentials of the biblical narrative are made transparent to all comers: the story line, the world order, the value system" (*Poetics of Biblical Narrative*, pp. 50–51).

of scholars as irrelevant is to forget that the vast majority of people "cannot even read the Bible without depending on the scholarly work that has made Bible translations possible."[32]

These observations are true, but it should also be stressed that scholars can and do make mistakes and sometimes argue with great conviction and erudition for erroneous theories. It is therefore incumbent on ordinary readers, wherever possible, not simply to accept on faith this or that scholarly pronouncement, nor to be cowed by scholarly erudition or reputation, but to approach the contributions of scholars critically, testing them in the light of logic and common sense, and, preeminently, in the light of Scripture. Such was the treatment accorded no less a notable than the apostle Paul himself (Acts 17:11).

GENRE CRITICISM AND BIBLICAL INTERPRETATION

We turn now to look more closely at the work being done in the genre criticism of the Bible. The first thing that a newcomer to the discipline of genre criticism is likely to notice is the complexity of the field. Even the matter of how the term *genre* should be defined has not yet been finally settled. Among the better attempts at definition would be Barton's description of genre as "any recognizable and distinguishable type of writing or speech—whether 'literary' in the complimentary sense of that word or merely utilitarian, like a business letter—which operates within certain conventions that are in principle (not necessarily in practice) stateable."[33] Briefer is Collins's definition: "By 'literary genre' we mean a group of written texts marked by distinctive recurring characteristics which constitute a recognizable and coherent type of writing."[34]

While they are helpful as far as they go, such definitions as these remain quite general, and it seems fair to say with Grant Osborne that "the concept of genre, so central to hermeneutical theory in recent years, is an elusive one."[35] Among the possible reasons for this, the two following seem particularly noteworthy.

First, the question of genre can legitimately be addressed to a particular writing on various levels of discourse. Earlier in this chapter, I rather loosely used the term *macro-genre* to refer to the essential character of the Bible as a whole, and I also used the term *genres* to refer to subunits or parts within the whole. It could be argued, of course, that a concept like genre, based as it is on the principle of a wide-ranging comparison of similar texts, is hardly applicable to the Bible.[36] There is a sense in which "the Bible by its very nature as divine revelation transcends 'all actual genres, since divine revelation could not be generic in a logical sense of the word.'"[37]

---

[32]Silva, *Has the Church Misread the Bible?* p. 69.

[33]*Reading the Old Testament*, p. 16.

[34]J. J. Collins, "Introduction: Towards the Morphology of a Genre," *Semeia* 14 (1979): 1; cf. also Longman, *Literary Approaches*, pp. 76-83.

[35]So begins Osborne's essay entitled "Genre Criticism—Sensus Literalis" (*TrinJ* 4 ns/2 [1983]: 1). Similarly, C. Blomberg (*The Historical Reliability of the Gospels* [Leicester: IVP, 1987], p. 235 n. 1) observes that while "genre has traditionally been defined as a category of literary composition characterized by a particular style, form, or content, . . . the whole question of whether or not literature can be so categorized is one of increasing debate."

[36]As E. D. Hirsch has observed: "Anything that is unique cannot, with respect to those aspects which are unique, be a type" (*Validity in Interpretation* [New Haven: Yale University Press, 1967], p. 64).

[37]Osborne, "Genre Criticism," p. 3; quoting M. Beaujour. Osborne's criticism of Beaujour's position as ignoring "the analogical nature of God-talk as well as its human accommodation" (pp. 3–4) seems more appropriate in terms of the specific genres and subgenres within the Bible than of the Bible as a whole.

But even were we to avoid the term *genre* when speaking of the Bible as a whole, the problem of multi-level genre descriptions would still persist. For example, we can describe the book of Psalms at one level as a poetical book, at another level as a hymn book or a prayer book, and at another level still as a collection containing lament psalms, songs of thanksgiving, hymns, royal psalms, wisdom psalms, and the like. The books of 1 and 2 Samuel can be described at one level as (predominantly) narrative discourse, at another perhaps as royal apology (i.e., historiographic narratives defending theologically the legitimacy of the Davidic royal house), and at still another as a composition containing stories, sayings, proverbs, poems, songs, battle reports, genealogies, prayers, and prophecies.

One way scholars have sought to minimize the confusion is by limiting the use of the term *genre* to a particular level of discourse. Longman, for example, prefers to use "*genre* . . . to refer to a work as a whole and *form* to refer to a unit within a whole text."[38] Similarly, Osborne, following J. A. Baird, distinguishes "genre, form and mode."

> Baird says that "form" is a literary device, based on the nature of the material, which is used to analyze small units of literature; "genre" takes several of these units and collects them into a single whole for the purpose of classification; and "mode" is even more diffuse, noting characteristics which (sometimes artificially) unite various forms or genres under a single rubric.[39]

Sidney Greidanus takes a similar three-tiered approach. He labels the Bible as a whole "proclamation"—this would be its *mode.* Under this general rubric he lists the following canonical *genres:* narrative, prophecy, wisdom, psalm, gospel, epistle, apocalypse. Narrowing the focus yet further, he mentions various specific *forms* that may occur in one or another of the above genres: law, dream, lament, parable, miracle, exhortation, autobiography, funeral dirge, lawsuit, pronouncement, report, royal accession, and passion.[40] Such terminological distinctions are useful but, unfortunately, have yet to become standardized.

A second feature of contemporary genre criticism that sometimes leads to confusion is the frequent application of genre labels derived from extrabiblical (and sometimes modern) literary and cultural contexts to biblical texts. While the use of extrabiblical literary terminology is to an extent unavoidable and indeed can be helpful in describing certain features in the biblical texts, it is important to bear in mind that genre categories that have been developed through the study of literatures outside the Bible may not be fully applicable to the biblical texts.[41]

Despite the above concerns regarding genre criticisms, it nevertheless remains the case that genre recognition, whether on a conscious or subconscious level, plays a vital role in all forms of successful communication. At its best, genre criticism is not a *name game*[42] but an indispensable prerequisite for comprehending the *sensus literalis* of a text.[43]

---

[38]*Literary Approaches,* p. 141 n. 3.

[39]"Genre Criticism," p. 4.

[40]*The Modern Preacher and the Ancient Text: Interpreting and Preaching Biblical Literature* (Grand Rapids: Eerdmans, 1988), pp. 20–23.

[41]Cf. W. G. Lambert, "Old Testament Mythology in Its Ancient Near Eastern Context," in *Congress Volume Jerusalem 1986,* ed. J. A. Emerton, VTSup 40 (Leiden: E. J. Brill, 1988), p. 127.

[42]Cf. G. W. Coats, ed., *Saga, Legend, Tale, Novella, Fable: Narrative Forms in Old Testament Literature,* JSOTS 35 (Sheffield: JSOT, 1985), p. 8.

[43]Cf. Osborne, "Genre Criticism," p. 5.

Blomberg writes: "To recognize what for a longer work of literature would be called its 'genre' is necessary for valid interpretation. Parables, for example, must not be interpreted like straightforward history; although they are very lifelike in many ways, Jesus may have included some details in them simply to make the stories lively and interesting."[44]

To illustrate this last point Blomberg cites the occasional misreading of "the story of the rich man and Lazarus (Luke 16:19–31)" as if it were concerned to present "a realistic depiction of life after death." In Blomberg's view, such an approach fails to recognize the true genre of the story, which he classifies as parable. To the objection that the passage is not labeled parable by the gospel writer, Blomberg points out that "approximately half the stories in the gospels which are commonly called parables are not specifically labelled as such, but they are recognized by the common form and structure which they share with passages specifically termed parables." In other words, they are recognized on the basis of *generic signals.*

Chief among the generic signals that Blomberg detects is the phrase with which the story opens, "A certain man was. . . ." He notes that the same phrase introduces "the two preceding parables of the prodigal son (15:11–32) and the unjust steward (16:1–13) and seems to correspond to the modern 'Once upon a time. . . .' Just as people today recognize such a phrase as the opening of a fairy-tale, so Jesus' audience would have been prepared by the start of a parable to recognize it as a fictitious narrative."[45]

A survey of other occurrences of the phrase "certain man" in Luke confirms Blomberg's point. It is a frequent formula in Jesus' parables, both in those that are explicitly labeled parables and in those that are not.[46] Given this *generic* (or more properly *formal*) signal, we must ask why all commentators are not agreed that the story of the rich man and Lazarus is a parable. For one thing, modern interpreters may not be as quick to recognize the signal as Jesus' first-century audience would have been; this will depend on each interpreter's level of ancient literary and cultural competence. For another, a single indicator is not usually sufficient to determine genre. We may note, for example, that the phrase "certain man" occurs also at 14:2 in a nonparabolic context.[47] Finally, and perhaps most importantly, the fact that one of the characters in the story is given a name, Lazarus, may seem to suggest an element of historical specificity normally lacking in parables. The force of this last observation is much diminished, however, when one realizes that the name Lazarus means "God helps."[48] Hence it may have been used for its semantic or symbolic effect and not because a particular, historical person is in view. As J. A. Fitzmyer observes, "it is a fitting name for the beggar in this parable, who was not helped by a fellow human being, but in his afterlife is consoled by God."[49]

---

[44]*Historical Reliability*, p. 22.

[45]Ibid., p. 23.

[46]The former include Luke 12:16 (rich fool); 13:6 (fig tree); 15:3–4 (lost sheep); 19:12 (ten minas); 20:9 (tenants); and the latter include 10:30 (good Samaritan); 14:16 (great banquet); plus the three noted by Blomberg: 15:11 (prodigal son); 16:1 (unjust steward); 16:19 (rich man and Lazarus).

[47]According to most Greek witnesses.

[48]So J. Jeremias, *The Parables of Jesus*, rev. ed. (London: SCM, 1963), pp. 183, 185. The name, as J. A. Fitzmyer notes, is "a grecized, shortened form" of the Old Testament name Eleazar (*The Gospel According to Luke X–XXIV*, AB 28a [Garden City, N.Y.: Doubleday, 1985], p. 1131).

[49]Ibid.; see also p. 1130 for an explanation of how the rich man mistakenly came to be called "Dives" in postbiblical tradition.

The above example illustrates how important the reader's linguistic and literary competence is for proper interpretation of textual discourse. This is as true for historical texts as for any other. As Michael Stanford puts it in *The Nature of Historical Knowledge*,[50] "the more we understand how a historian has done the work the better we can penetrate to what that work is about—the world of the past 'as it really was.'" That is to say, the better we pay "some attention to the glass through which we look, the better we shall understand what we are looking at." Alter makes the same point with respect to biblical interpretation when he speaks of "a complete interfusion of literary art with theological, moral, or historiographical vision, the fullest perception of the latter dependent on the fullest grasp of the former."[51] In short, as I have written elsewhere, "an increased appreciation of the literary mechanisms of a text—*how* a story is told—often becomes the avenue of greater insight into the theological, religious and even historical significance of the text—*what* the story means."[52]

As important as linguistic and literary competence is, true communication between text and reader requires also a further point of shared understanding. Wittgenstein has stated: "If language is to be a means of communication there must be agreement not only in definitions but also (queer as this may sound) in judgments."[53] Putting it another way, Stanford contends that "if people are to talk to one another they must agree not only about words but about how they see the world."[54] The compatibility (or, as the case may be, incompatibility) of the view of the world held by the interpreter and the worldview evinced by the text is a significant conditioning factor in the interpretive process. I shall have more to say on this important issue in chapters 4 and 5.

Having stressed the importance of genre criticism in broad terms, we need now to consider several important qualifications, or cautions, lest genre criticism become an interpretive straitjacket.

First, we must recognize that genre criticism is primarily a *descriptive* and not a *prescriptive* enterprise. The genre classifications proposed by scholars are not to be regarded as inviolable rules of literature any more than the generalized descriptions of language found in grammar books are to be regarded as inviolable rules of speech.[55] Native writers or speakers are free to press the limits of genre, of which they may have little *conscious* awareness in any case. Still, just as it is useful for an outsider seeking to learn a foreign language to become acquainted with as much as possible of the grammar and syntax of that language, so it is very useful for the modern reader of the Bible to learn as much as possible of the Bible's literary grammar and syntax.

Second, we must resist the nineteenth-century notion that shorter, "purer" forms are early and "mixed" or "elaborated" forms are late. Under pressure from archaeological discovery and the logic of everyday experience, this old notion has been generally

---

[50]Oxford: Basil Blackwell, 1986, p. 137.

[51]*Art of Biblical Narrative*, p. 19; cf. p. 179.

[52]V. Philips Long, *The Reign and Rejection of King Saul: A Case for Literary and Theological Coherence*, SBLDS 118 (Atlanta: Scholars Press, 1989), p. 14.

[53]*Philosophical Investigations*, part no. I, 242 (London: Basil Blackwell, 1968), p. 88; quoted by Stanford (*Nature*, p. 117).

[54]Ibid.

[55]Cf. Longman, *Literary Approaches*, pp. 141–42.

abandoned and a more fluid concept of genre has now emerged.[56] The result of this more fluid concept is the recognition "that no genre-class can have unrestricted access to any single generic trait."[57] This observation is significant when we come to ask about the historicity or historical intent of a given passage of Scripture. It is not sufficient simply to point to this or that individual trait, such as high literary style or a strong didactic intent, as signaling a nonhistoriographical genre or, conversely, to point to narrative form or elements of factual content as indicating a historiographical genre. As we shall see, such questions can only be decided on the basis of the broader context and the apparent over-all purpose of the text under consideration.

Third, while genre criticism is fundamentally based on commonality and comparisons, it is reductionistic to assume that unique texts cannot exist. Allowance must be made for the possibility (and, considering the nature of the source, even probability) that biblical texts may explode the generic categories derived from comparisons with other literature. As Coats has observed, "Some species of literature—or of any kind of object—may be genuinely unique, not readily subject to classification in a group."[58] The difficulty of finding extrabiblical literature comparable to the Gospels, for example, has led many scholars to the conclusion that "the Gospels are *sui generis* in the sense that they are 'a recombination of earlier forms and genres into novel configurations.'"[59]

One of the limitations of genre and form criticism is the fact that terms such as *saga, legend,* and even *historiography*—in fact, most of our genre labels—"have been drawn by and large from fields of literature outside the OT, indeed, from outside the period of time that produced the principal narratives." Thus, as Coats reminds us, the labels apply to the biblical literature "only with a limited degree of accuracy. . . . Giving a name to the genre is necessary but only as a convenience for the discipline."[60] Genre labels may even prove to be a liability if they prevent us from seeing that the Bible, if it is indeed the word of God, can be expected to surpass (as a whole and, we may assume, in some of its parts) the human productions of its day.[61] In this regard it may be appropriate to draw a comparison between Scripture (the written word) and Jesus (the living Word), "who as to his human nature was a descendant of David" (Rom. 1:3), but whose birth nevertheless could not be fully explained in human terms.

---

[56]The "simplicity criterion" does continue to find expression occasionally. K. Koch, for example, in his study of the form-critical method, agrees with H. Gunkel that a "concise style" indicates greater antiquity and an "elaborated style" betrays a later period (*The Growth of the Biblical Tradition: The Form-Critical Method,* trans. S. M. Cupitt [London: Adam & Charles Black, 1969], p. 126). Nevertheless, Koch elsewhere allows that earlier, elaborated forms may have been condensed at a later period (see p. 201; cf. pp. 189, 211). C. Westermann also assumes the "simplicity criterion" in his influential *Basic Forms of Prophetic Speech,* trans. H. C. White (London: Lutterworth, 1967), pp. 24, 130–31, 148. For a recent critique of form criticism, including the "simplicity criterion," see J. Muddiman, "Form Criticism," in *A Dictionary of Biblical Interpretation,* ed. R. J. Coggins and J. L. Houlden (Philadelphia: Trinity Press International, 1990), pp. 240–43.

[57]Osborne, "Genre Criticism," p. 8.

[58]G. W. Coats, *Genesis: With an Introduction to Narrative Literature* (Grand Rapids: Eerdmans, 1983), p. 10.

[59]Osborne, "Genre Criticism," pp. 25–26; citing D. E. Aune.

[60]*Genesis,* p. 4. In other words, genre labels represent *etic* (non-native) as opposed to *emic* (native) categories. On the terminology *emic* versus *etic,* see M. G. Brett, "Four or Five Things to do With Texts: A Taxonomy of Interpretative Interests," in *Bible in Three Dimensions,* ed. Clines et al., esp. p. 363. On both the necessity and the danger of employing etic as well as emic categories, see Longman, *Literary Approaches,* pp. 52–53.

[61]See, e.g., E. L. Greenstein, "On the Genesis of Biblical Narrative," *Proof* 8 (1988): 347; Osborne, "Genre Criticism," p. 26.

Fourth, since genre criticism by its very nature makes use of the comparative method, care must be taken that the comparative method does not become imperative. That is, the temptation must be avoided either to insist that only those biblical genres are possible that find analogies outside the Bible (see the preceding paragraph) or to assume that whatever genres are attested outside the Bible may without qualification find a place in the Bible. If certain speech acts, such as lying or blasphemy, would be deemed unacceptable in the mouths of God's inspired messengers, then it stands to reason that certain genres might be deemed unacceptable in the biblical corpus.[62] In his study of Sumerian literature as a background to the Bible, W. W. Hallo comes to the following conclusion:

> The parallels I have drawn may in many cases owe more to a common Ancient Near
> Eastern heritage—shared by Israel—than to any direct dependence of one body of
> literature on the other. . . . Sometimes, as in the case of casuistic law, the biblical
> authors adopted these genres with little change; at other times, as in the case of indi-
> vidual prayer and congregational laments, they adapted them to Israelite needs; occa-
> sionally, as with divination and incantation, they rejected them altogether in favor of
> new genres of their own devising (in this case, prophecy).[63]

Finally, genre criticism must resist the temptation to focus exclusively on smaller units of discourse and instead must be alert to the way in which the genre of a larger discourse unit affects every smaller discourse unit within it. One of the drawbacks of form criticism and historical criticism as traditionally practiced is that these approaches have tended to focus primarily, if not exclusively, on the smaller units, with far too little attention being given to the larger.[64]

David Clines points out that instead of treating the books of the Bible as "literary works that generate meaning through their overall shape, their structure, and their dominant tendencies, that is, through their identity as wholes," it has been customary for biblical scholarship to value them "piecemeal for their diverse contents."[65] This is an unfortunate tendency and one that runs directly counter to the fundamental principles of discourse. First among these principles, as articulated by Robert Bergen, is the fact that "language texts are composed of successively smaller organizational units of language." In other words, "language is multi-tiered."

---

[62]I am aware of course of such passages as 1 Samuel 16 and 1 Kings 22, but these do not disprove the point being made. In 1 Samuel 16 the Lord provides Samuel with a "half-truth" to tell Saul—"I have come to sacrifice to the Lord" (v. 2)—which clearly echoes Saul's own attempted deception in the preceding chapter (cf. 15:15, 21) and suggests that Saul is getting his just desserts (cf. R. P. Gordon, "Simplicity of the Highest Cunning: Narrative Art in the Old Testament," *ScotBEv* 6 [1988]: 80; for a defense of the viewpoint that Saul's "sacrificial excuse" in 1 Samuel 15 is a prevarication, see my *Reign and Rejection*, pp. 145–46, 152). In 1 Kings 22:22, the Lord in his sovereignty releases a "lying spirit" (*rûaḥ šeqer*) to enter the mouths of Ahab's prophets, but even in this instance the true prophet of the Lord, Micaiah, ultimately speaks the truth.

[63]"Sumerian Literature: Background to the Bible," *Bible Review* 4/3 (1988): 38. One would perhaps want to qualify Hallo's last statement with some mention of prophecy as attested at Mari.

[64]This complaint is at the heart of the synchronic versus diachronic debate in literary criticism; see Long, *Reign and Rejection*, pp. 7–20.

[65]*What Does Eve Do to Help? and Other Readerly Questions to the Old Testament*, JSOTS 94 (Sheffield: JSOT, 1990), p. 101.

Letters and vowel points function as the lowest echelon in the Biblical language texts. These in turn form syllables, which may be used to create words. Words may be integrated into phrase patterns, which can be arranged into clauses, which in turn may be woven together into sentences. Sentences in turn may be ordered in such a way as to create paragraphs, which may be structured so as to create episodes (narrative discourse). Higher structures of language include (among others) episode clusters, stories, story cycles, subgenre, and genres. The number of organizational levels present within a text depends upon the complexity and type of the communication task.[66]

The second of Bergen's discourse principles is that "each successively higher level of textual organization influences all of the lower levels of which it is composed. Language is organized from the top down. . . . Upper levels of text organization, such as genre, place broad constraints on all lower levels. . . ."[67] This principle is of particular relevance when we begin to explore the issue of the historicity or historical truth claims of a text. One must consider the character and truth claims (the apparent [embodied] intent) of the larger discourse unit before passing judgment on the historical value of the smaller. In this task the interpreter will find little help in the comparative method, for the simple reason that, as Porter points out,

> in the cultures surrounding Israel, . . . literary forms are found almost entirely as separate units. In this sense it would be true to say that they are the raw materials of history, rather than history proper, although many of them are genuine historiography, in so far as they present interpretations and understanding of history and an awareness of direction within it. By contrast, in the Old Testament, all these elements, as far as the Pentateuch and the Former Prophets are concerned, are embedded in a chronologically added narrative. Nowhere else in the ancient Near East is there to be found anything strictly comparable to this collecting and arranging of traditions and documents as successive elements in larger corpora and, ultimately, into a single corpus.[68]

The ancient Near East, then, offers little that can compare to the larger discourse units of the Old Testament—to say nothing of the whole Old Testament, or the whole Bible! This fact, however, does not justify a piecemeal approach to the biblical texts, as tempting as it may be to focus exclusively on smaller units where at least rough analogies in extrabiblical literature can be found. It is not wrong, of course, to study the smaller units; it is indeed useful and necessary. But final judgment on a smaller unit's import, historical or whatever, must not be passed without first considering the larger discourse of which the smaller is a part.[69]

The following may serve as a brief example of the importance of considering the larger discourse unit before rendering generic or form-critical verdicts. George Ramsey,

---

[66]"Text as a Guide to Authorial Intention: An Introduction to Discourse Criticism," *JETS* 30 (1987): 327–36.

[67]Ibid., p. 330. Cf. Vanhoozer, "Semantics of Biblical Literature," p. 80: "Recent literary studies show that literary forms serve more than classificatory purposes. The genre provides the literary context for a given sentence and, therefore, partly determines what the sentence means and how it should be taken."

[68]J. R. Porter, "Old Testament Historiography," in *Tradition and Interpretation: Essays by Members of the Society for Old Testament Study,* ed. G. W. Anderson (Oxford: Clarendon Press, 1979), pp. 130–31.

[69]This is as true for the New Testament as it is for the Old—e.g., M. Davies ("Genre," in *Dictionary of Biblical Interpretation,* ed. Coggins and Houlden, p. 258) has recently observed with respect to the New Testament epistles that "the collection into a corpus of letters, originally occasioned by individual circumstances, modifies the genre, giving to all of them a representative character."

in *The Quest for the Historical Israel,* issues the following "common sense" judgment based on the "laws of nature": "We recognize that the story told by Jotham (Judg. 9:7–15) is a fable, since trees do not talk. A similar judgment is made about the story of Balaam's ass speaking (Num. 22:28–30)" (p. 15).[70] But is this reasoning sound? Is the fact that trees do not talk sufficient reason to label Jotham's speech a fable? After all, according to the "laws of nature," bushes do not burn without being consumed, and dead people do not rise from the grave.

In the case of Jotham's speech, it is not the fabulous storyline but, rather, the larger context that makes it unmistakable that Jotham's speech is a fable. The verses that precede it introduce the historical personages and the point of tension reflected in the fable, and Jotham concludes his speech with direct references to the same: "Now if you have acted honorably and in good faith when you made Abimelech king, and if you have been fair to Jerub-Baal. . . . But if you have not, let fire come out from Abimelech and consume you, citizens of Shechem and Beth Millo, and let fire come out from you, citizens of Shechem and Beth Millo, and consume Abimelech!" (Judg 9:16, 20). The phrase "let fire come out" is a repetition of the phrase found at the end of the fable: "then let fire come out of the thornbush and consume the cedars of Lebanon" (v. 15). This is clear evidence that Jotham's final words in his speech (vv. 16–20) are an interpretation of his fable.

But what of the story of Balaam (Num. 22–24)? It too has its "fabulous" elements (e.g., the appearance of the angel and the speech of the donkey in chapter 23), but do these elements alone make it a fable? The broader context apparently offers nothing that would mark it out as such; no *interpretation,* for example, is given. What one has, rather, is a story involving certain wondrous occurrences within the larger account of the book of Numbers, with no indication that a new formal literary type has been introduced. Thus, unless one is willing to argue that the book of Numbers as a whole must be characterized as fable, there appears to be no valid literary reason to label the Balaam stories as such.

GENRE CRITICISM AND THE RISE OF BIBLICAL POETICS

Form criticism may be described as a sort of lower-level genre criticism. It focuses on the smaller textual units that, in the case of biblical literature at least, are combined so as to form larger textual entities. As noted above, one of the deficiencies of the form-critical approach is that it can tend to overlook the significance of the larger discourse unit. Nevertheless, there are hopeful signs that increasing attention is being given to the larger units.

A convenient survey of higher-level genre criticism in New Testament studies is provided by Craig Blomberg.[71] He divides his discussion under the headings *Gospels, Acts, Epistles,* and *Revelation.* Of greatest interest for our present concern with biblical historiography are the first two categories. While recognizing that debate continues, Blomberg comes to rather positive conclusions on questions of historicity. After summarizing recent debates over the genre of the Gospels, Blomberg ultimately concludes that they may be identified as "theological histories of selected events surrounding the life and death of Jesus of Nazareth" (p. 42). Moreover, "Once allowance is made for paraphrase, abbreviation, explanation, omission, rearrangement and a variety of similar editorial techniques,

---

[70]London: SCM, 1982. On the problematic status of the concept of "autonomous laws of nature," see J. C. Sharp, "Miracles and the 'Laws of Nature,'" *ScotBEv* 6 (1988): 1–19.

[71]"New Testament Genre Criticism for the 1990s," *Them* 15/2 (1990): 40–49.

one may remain confident that the gospels give trustworthy accounts of who Jesus was and what he did" (p. 41).[72]

Blomberg comes to similarly positive conclusions with respect to the book of Acts: "As with the gospels, the Acts may be compared with a known genre of Hellenistic literature while at the same time retaining features which made it *sui generis*. Theological history may be the best label for the combination" (p. 42).[73]

In Old Testament studies, some of the more useful attempts at *higher-level* genre criticism might be broadly grouped under the rubric of biblical *poetics*. As described by Adele Berlin, poetics is "an inductive science that seeks to abstract the general principles of literature from many different manifestations of those principles as they occur in actual literary texts." Poetics serves interpretation, but is distinct from it. While interpretation focuses on an individual text, poetics canvases many texts in an attempt "to find the building blocks of literature and the rules by which they are assembled. . . . Poetics is to literature as linguistics is to language. . . . Poetics strives to write a grammar, as it were, of literature." Changing the analogy, Berlin explains that "if literature is likened to a cake, then poetics gives us the recipe and interpretation tells us how it tastes."[74]

So far, poetic criticism in Old Testament studies has focused largely on the higher-level genres of poetry and narrative. With respect to the former, influential works include James Kugel's *Idea of Biblical Poetry: Parallelism and Its History*,[75] Alter's *Art of Biblical Poetry*, and Adele Berlin's *Dynamics of Biblical Parallelism*,[76] to name but a few. The dust has not yet settled, but it is already apparent that significant new gains have been achieved, particularly in the corrective that has been issued to the older view, first espoused by Robert Lowth,[77] that Hebrew poetry is characterized by three types, and only three types, of parallelism: synthetic, antithetic, and synonymous. The recent studies have highlighted the tendency of the second of the parallel (half-)lines to sharpen, intensify, and advance the thought of the first.[78]

Of greater pertinence to our concern with biblical historiography is the work being done in the area of biblical narrative discourse. The appearance of Alter's *Art of Biblical Narrative* in 1981 awakened new interest in the literary qualities of the Hebrew Bible, and a lively debate has followed. More substantial, and certainly no less controversial, is Sternberg's *Poetics of Biblical Narrative*, which first appeared in 1985.[79] These works and others like them have been less concerned with *classifying* the biblical texts than with

---

[72]For a book-length defense of this position, see Blomberg's *Historical Reliability*; cf. also R. T. France, *The Evidence for Jesus* (Downers Grove, Ill.: InterVarsity, 1986); G. N. Stanton, *The Gospels and Jesus* (Oxford: Oxford University Press, 1989).

[73]For a thorough and learned treatment of the question, see C. J. Hemer's *Book of Acts in the Setting of Hellenistic History*, Wissenschaftliche Untersuchungen zum Neuen Testament 49 (Tübingen: J. C. B. Mohr, 1989).

[74]*Poetics and Interpretation*, p. 15.

[75]New Haven: Yale University Press, 1981.

[76]Bloomington: Indiana University Press, 1985.

[77]*Lectures on the Sacred Poetry of the Hebrews*, trans. G. Gregory, new ed. with notes by C. E. Stowe (Andover: Codman Press, 1829).

[78]For a convenient presentation of recent thinking on biblical poetry, see Longman, *Literary Approaches*, chap. 6.

[79]For a selective, comparative review of these works by Alter and Sternberg, see Long, "Toward a Better Theory and Understanding of Old Testament Narrative," *Presbyterion* 13 (1987): 102–9.

exploring the specific *workings* of biblical narrative. This is a salutary emphasis, inasmuch as it aims to equip the interpreter with preunderstandings and reading strategies that are appropriate to the texts being studied. As for the impact that poetics may have on the historical study of the Bible, it is already apparent that phenomena in the biblical texts often cited by historical critics as tensions, contradictions, and the like are increasingly coming to be recognized as *narrative devices* employed by the biblical writers for communicative effect. It can only be hoped that the future will see increasing dialogue between the proponents of traditional historical criticism and those more versed in the poetics of biblical narrative. For if some of the insights of the latter are valid, then some of the historical conclusions of the former can no longer stand.[80]

Since poetics focuses on the internal workings of texts, it is an avowedly literary pursuit. This can and has seemed threatening to those more concerned with the historical and theological significance of the Bible. But as Sternberg has cogently argued, these three interests should not be set in opposition. He insists that "Biblical narrative emerges as a complex, because multifunctional, discourse. Functionally speaking, it is regulated by a set of three principles: ideological, historiographic, and aesthetic. How they *cooperate* is a tricky question."[81] It is the nature of this cooperation, especially between the historical and the aesthetic (literary) aspects, that we shall consider in the next chapter. But first, let us consider an example of how consciousness of genre is basic to proper interpretation.

AN EXAMPLE: JUDGES 4 AND 5

In broad generic terms, Judges 4 is prose and Judges 5 is poetry. Since both chapters treat the same basic episode (the defeat of Sisera and his Canaanite forces by Deborah, Barak, and especially Jael), these two chapters offer a nice example of the importance of interpreting biblical passages in the light of the genres in which they are cast. Not surprisingly, differences between the two renditions of the defeat of Sisera have elicited lively discussion and an extensive literature. For our own purposes, two recent treatments will be highlighted.

The first is Halpern's study, most recently published as chapter 4, "Sisera and Old Lace: The Case of Deborah and Yael," in his book *The First Historians: The Hebrew Bible and History.*[82] In this book Halpern defends the thesis that some biblical authors "who wrote works recognizably historical" had "authentic antiquarian intentions" in the sense that "they meant to furnish fair and accurate representations of Israelite antiquity" (p. 3). As sensible as this basic thesis is, some of the ways Halpern attempts to demonstrate its validity are open to question. With respect to Judges 4 and 5, for example, Halpern's aim is to show that the prose account of Judges 4 is a well-intended, if somewhat flawed,

[80]I shall have more to say on these matters in the pages that follow; cf. also chap. 1 of Long, *Reign and Rejection*. A disappointing feature of D. Damrosch's otherwise stimulating book, *The Narrative Covenant: Transformation of Genre in the Growth of Biblical Literature* (San Francisco: Harper & Row, 1987), is his ready acceptance of the results of conventional source and redaction criticism, with little apparent consideration of how these results are often undermined by recent studies in biblical poetics; see, e.g., R. Polzin's critique in his review article "1 Samuel: Biblical Studies and the Humanities," *Religious Studies Review* 15/4 (1989): esp. 304–5.
[81]*Poetics of Biblical Narrative*, p. 41.
[82]San Francisco: Harper & Row, 1988.

attempt to distill *history* from the poetry of Judges 5. To do this, Halpern proposes the following criterion for detecting dependence of one text on another:

> Short of secure dating, only one circumstance permits confidence as to the relationship between parallel texts: there must be substantive points of difference, preferably several, such that one text only could be derived from the other. In practice, this means that the author of the derivative version must have interpreted the source in a manner with which the modern analyst takes issue: if the two agree, no basis for arbitrating priority remains. (p. 77)

One cannot help wondering how fairly a modern interpreter who adopts this criterion will be able to approach the texts in question. Looking for grounds to take issue with the writer of Judges 4, Halpern does not take long to find them. Preeminently, he cites "two disparities between the accounts [which] have, since the nineteenth century, provoked comment" (p. 78). The first is that while the poetical account, the Song of Deborah, mentions at least six tribes as participating in the defeat of Sisera, the prose account mentions only Zebulun and Naphtali. The second "concerns the manner of Sisera's demise." In chapter 4 Jael drives a tent peg through the skull of the sleeping Sisera, while in chapter 5, on Halpern's reading, Jael "sneaks up behind him and bludgeons him, so that he collapses at her feet (5:24–27)" (p. 78).

Regarding the first difficulty, Halpern notes that Malamat and Weiser have suggested readings that, if correct, would harmonize the apparent discrepancies between the tribal references in Judges 4 and 5. He also admits that "the historian of Judges 4" may have read the pertinent verses along the same lines that Weiser suggests. Nevertheless, he continues to maintain that the differences are such as to prove the dependence of Judges 4 on Judges 5.

My intention here is not to debate the merits of either Malamat's or Weiser's harmonizations (or of others that have been suggested) but to assess briefly the merits of Halpern's own method. Space limitations do not permit a full evaluation, but it seems fair to say, as a first general observation, that Halpern approaches the song of chapter 5 with expectations respecting sequencing and chronology that are too rigid for dealing with poetry.[83]

Second, he does not appear to make adequate allowance for the imagistic character of poetry. He is of course correct that in the prose account there is "no question of [Sisera's] falling after the blow (4:17–22)," at least not in the literal sense of *falling down*—Sisera is already sleeping. It is noteworthy, however, that when the prose narrative itself recounts Jael's presentation of the slain Sisera to Barak, it describes Sisera as *nōpēl mēt,* "fallen dead"

---

[83]An example would be the argument that Halpern builds on the occurrence of Hebrew *'amz* in 5:19. In Halpern's view, "the poem situates the tribal muster all in the stage before the battle (5:9–18, and the consecutive *'amz* 'then,' in v. 19)" and thus renders impossible Malamat's theory that the poem enumerates the tribes that participated in the pursuit, though not necessarily in the battle (p. 78). But this argument, in addition to exhibiting an overly rigid chronological expectation where poetry is involved, also assumes that *'amz* necessarily carries a temporal significance in this context. In fact, however, *'amz* can be used (and in this context probably is used) as a stylistic device for indicating the emphasized portion of a sentence (cf., e.g., Josh. 22:31; Isa. 33:23; 41:1; Hab. 1:11; Ps. 96:12; Mal. 3:16; cf. also W. L. Holladay, *A Concise Hebrew and Aramaic Lexicon of the Old Testament* [Grand Rapids: Eerdmans, 1971], p. 8; L. Koehler, W. Baumgartner et al., *Hebräisches und Aramäisches Lexikon zum Alten Testament,* 3d ed., 4 vols. [Leiden: E. J. Brill, 1967–1990], 1: 26; the latter explicity cites Judges 5:19 and 22 under this usage).

(4:22). English translations tend to render this phrase "lying dead" (e.g., NRSV) or to leave the participle *nōpēl* untranslated—"dead" (so NIV), but it remains the case that the prose account uses the same verb that is used to describe Sisera's "falling" in the poetical account (5:27). This suggests that the imagery in the poem should not be pressed in too literalistic a direction.

This observation is in general agreement with the conclusions reached in the second of the studies we wish to highlight. In *"Heads! Tails! Or the Whole Coin?! Contextual Method and Intertextual Analysis: Judges 4 and 5,"*[84] Lawson Younger conducts a systematic investigation of comparative cuneiform and Egyptian texts to test the thesis, which he attributes to Athalya Brenner,[85] that Judges 4 and 5 are complementary, not contradictory. His engagement with a wide range of comparative ancient Near Eastern literature in which a single event or episode is represented in two or more texts of differing genres helps him develop the ancient literary competence necessary for approaching Judges 4 and 5 fairly. Younger concludes the first half of his essay, a survey of the ancient Near Eastern parallel texts, with these words:

> Ancient scribes could write different accounts about the same referents. But differences in purpose could determine differences in detail . . ., and in the selectivity of the events narrated. . . . If the scribes' purpose was to praise the king and/or the gods, poetry naturally offered a medium to heighten the emotions of the praise through rhetorical embellishment. Hence, divine activity and praise of the deities is encountered more often in the poetic versions. . . . But in most instances the poetic (or more rhetorical) text also added significant historical details so that the complementary nature of the accounts is manifest. (p. 127)

By taking seriously the prose-poetry distinction and, even more importantly, by allowing the "ancient Near Eastern contextual literary data" to provide "a means for evaluating and interpreting Judges 4 and 5," Younger concludes that "neither account must be dependent on the other." Rather, "both probably derive from a common source (probably the historical referent itself) and possess a complementary relationship" (p. 135).

I realize, of course, that it does an injustice to both Halpern and Younger to treat their studies so briefly and selectively, and I encourage the reader to weigh their respective arguments in their full contexts. Younger's essay, as the latter of the two, is aware of Halpern's treatment and is, overall, the more convincing. It effectively demonstrates, on the basis of actual ancient Near Eastern literature, that purpose affects selection and representation and that it is not at all uncommon for complementary (though not identical) portraits to be painted in the differing media of prose and poetry. All of this illustrates and underscores the importance of recognizing that the Bible comprises a library of various genres, and that interpretation must never lose sight of this fact.

---

[84] In *The Biblical Canon in Comparative Perspective: Scripture in Context IV*, ed. by K. Lawson Younger, Jr., William W. Hallo, and Bernard F. Batto, Ancient Near Eastern Texts and Studies (Lewiston, Me.: Edwin Mellen, 1991), pp. 109–46.

[85] "A Triangle and a Rhombus in Narrative Structure: A Proposed Integrative Reading of Judges IV and V," *VT* 40 (1990): 129–38.

CONCLUSION

We began this chapter by asking if the Bible is a history book. We are now in a position to give a more nuanced answer. As we have seen, an affirmative answer cannot be given to this question if what is in view is the essential character of the Bible. But to give a negative answer is not entirely appropriate either. The Bible is in fact, as I have just stated, a library of books of diverse literary genres, so that no single description will suffice to characterize it, other than such very general labels as *religious book* or *Word of God*. Often the specific genres represented in the Bible are not employed in pure form, but are modified or blended by the biblical narrators and poets. Furthermore, the significance of smaller-scale literary forms within a larger textual discourse is necessarily affected by the larger entity. For this reason, we argued, study of the larger discourse unit, as in biblical poetics, for example, should be a priority in deciding questions of historical intent and import.

Classifying biblical texts according to genre categories derived from other literatures of the biblical world or even the modern world is sometimes enlightening, so long as we remain alert to the danger that such externally derived categories may be anachronistic or not quite suited to the biblical text. The comparative method, as useful as it often is, must not be allowed to become imperative—that is to say, we must not allow our genre classification to prescribe what a biblical text can and cannot contain.

We saw further that a historical impulse runs throughout the Bible, which, though not in every place and not always equally evident, is nevertheless pervasive. Hence, *lower-level* genre classification (as, for example, in form criticism) should not be regarded as a shortcut for determining the historical interest and significance of a given text. Above all, false dichotomies such as "the Bible is theology not history" or "the Bible is literature not history" must be avoided. The Bible evinces an interest in all three. In the next chapter we shall explore more fully the interrelationships of theology, history, and literary artistry as we ask, *What is history?*

t w o

HISTORY
AND FICTION

What Is History?

H istory . . . is all fictionalized, and yet history."[1] It may come as a surprise to readers unfamiliar with recent debates in biblical studies to discover the frequency
with which the term *fiction* has begun to appear in discussions of biblical narrative. Alter, for example, in a provocative essay entitled "Sacred History and the Beginnings of Prose Fiction," emphasizes the vital role of fiction in biblical historiography. He
even goes so far as to claim that "prose fiction is the best general rubric for describing
biblical narrative."[2] It will be my aim in this chapter to argue that the concept of fiction,
if it can be properly defined and guarded against misunderstanding, may be fruitfully
employed in discussions of biblical historiography, but that it is in practice often applied
in inappropriate and confusing ways, perhaps not least by Alter himself.[3] I shall suggest
further that the confusion over fictionality derives in part from ambiguities within the
term *fiction* itself. To complicate matters further, the term *history* is also ambiguous, being
understood even by nonspecialists in at least two distinct senses.

Confusion over the role played by fictionality in history is apparent since some are
proclaiming fictionality as lying at the heart of history-writing, while others are declaim-
ing fiction as the very opposite of history. Blomberg insists, for example, that "a historical
narrative recounts that which actually happened; it is the opposite of fiction."[4] Similarly,

---

[1]Halpern, *First Historians*, p. 68.
[2]The essay constitutes chap. 2 of *The Art of Biblical Narrative*, and the quote is from p. 24.
[3]See Sternberg, *Poetics of Biblical Narrative*, pp. 23–30.
[4]*Historical Reliability*, p. xviii n. 2.

Colin Hemer observes that "it is no good raising the question of historicity if we are dealing with avowed fairy-tale or fiction."[5] But Alter seems to have in mind some other concept of fiction, for he insists that fictionality and historicity are not antithetical. He writes:

> In giving such weight to fictionality, I do not mean to discount the historical impulse
> that informs the Hebrew Bible. The God of Israel, as so often has been observed, is
> above all the God of history: the working out of his purposes in history is a process
> that compels the attention of the Hebrew imagination, which is thus led to the most
> vital interest in the concrete and differential character of historical events. The point
> is that fiction was the principal means which the biblical authors had at their dis-
> posal for realizing history.[6]

A first step in coming to terms with the apparent disagreement is to clarify what the
terms history and fiction can mean. History, for example, as the term is commonly
employed, can refer either to the past or to the study of the past; or, to put it another way,
history can denote both events in the past and verbal accounts of these events. Consider the following illustration provided by David Bebbington.

> A visitor to the Tower of London may well buy a copy of its history. When 'history' is
> used in this way it means something different from 'history' in the claim that history
> repeats itself. A history of the Tower of London is its written history, a record of the
> past. The history that may or may not repeat itself, on the other hand, is the past itself,
> not a record but what really took place. In the English language the word history can
> mean either what people write about time gone by, that is historiography; or else it
> can mean what people have done and suffered, that is the historical process.[7]

No doubt many disputes could be settled if the various terms of discussion were
consistently defined and applied. If, for example, as Philip Davies suggests, the term *history* were reserved for "the events of the past as a *continuum*" and the term *historiography*
for "the selective telling of those events," much confusion could be avoided.[8] But since
such terminological consistency is frequently lacking in academic discussion,[9] about all
one can do is to recognize that *history* is used in two quite distinct senses—to refer to the
past itself and to interpretive verbal accounts of the past—and to discern in each context
which is intended.[10] (It is perhaps also worth mentioning that much confusion and misunderstanding could be avoided if specialists would bear in mind that laypersons often
have little understanding of the way *history* and *historical* are used as technical terms in
professional discussions and, not surprisingly, are baffled when confronted by statements

[5]*Book of Acts*, p. 34.
[6]*Art of Biblical Narrative*, p. 32.
[7]*Patterns in History: A Christian Perspective on Historical Thought*, new ed. (Leicester: Apollos, 1990), p. 1.
[8]J. Rogerson and P. R. Davies, *The Old Testament World* (Englewood Cliffs: Prentice-Hall, 1989), p. 218.
[9]E.g., with respect to Old Testament studies, J. Van Seters (*In Search of History: Historiography in the Ancient World and the Origins of Biblical History* [New Haven: Yale University Press, 1983], p. 209) comments: "the subject of Israelite historiography has become highly diversified and the terminology increas-
ingly ambiguous and confusing, [so that] the same terms are used in quite different ways."
[10]This discussion of *history* might easily be extended to cover such terms as *historic* and *historical*,
Historie and *Geschichte*, and so forth, but what is important for our present purposes is the basic distinction between history-as-event and history-as-account. On the former pair, see Caird, *Language and Imagery*,
p. 202; on the latter, see R. N. Soulen, *Handbook of Biblical Criticism* (Atlanta: John Knox, 1976), s.v. "Historie"; F. S. Leahy, "The Gospel and History," *Reformed Theological Journal* (Nov. 1985): 52–54.

that both deny that some event is *historical* and at the same time insist that this does not mean it didn't happen.[11] To the layperson, history is what happened in the past.)

What about the term *fiction*? To the average person, who tends to regard history and fiction as virtual opposites, a statement like the one by Alter quoted above—"fiction was the principal means which the biblical authors had at their disposal for realizing history"—will seem like nonsense. But Alter explains:

> The essential and ineluctable fact is that most of the narrative portions of the Hebrew Bible are organized on literary principles, however intent the authors may have been in conveying an account of national origins and cosmic beginnings and a vision of what the Lord God requires of man. We are repeatedly confronted, that is, with shrewdly defined characters, artfully staged scenes, subtle arrangements of dialogue, artifices of significant analogy among episodes, recurrent images and motifs and other aspects of narrative that are formally identical with the means of prose fiction as a general mode of verbal art.[12]

What Alter seems to be saying, in essence, is that literary shaping and artistry play no less significant a role in biblical historiography than in fiction. Halpern puts it succinctly when he states that "history [by which he means history as account] is fictional and employs the devices of all narrative presentation."[13]

The point in all this is that the word *fiction*, like the term *history*, may be used in two senses. Unfortunately, the two senses of fiction are not always clearly distinguished in discussions of narrative historiography. Alter, for example, sometimes speaks of "historicized fiction" and other times of "fictionalized history," without ever offering a clear articulation of the rather fundamental difference between the two.[14] The crucial term in each of these expressions, however, is the last one. In "historicized fiction," the weight of emphasis falls on *fiction*, suggesting that whatever bits of factual information may be included the story itself is nonfactual (as, for example, in a historical novel). In "fictionalized history," on the other hand, the weight falls on *history*, the claim being that the story is a representation of a real event in the past, whatever fictionalizing may be involved in the crafting of the narrative.[15] Only when this double sense of the term fiction is understood—fiction as *genre*, and fiction as *artistry* or *craft*—does it become possible to agree with Blomberg that history "is the opposite of fiction" and at the same time to agree with Halpern that "all history ... is fictionalized, and yet history."[16] Blomberg's focus is on history and fiction as distinct

---

[11]Cf. J. Barr, *The Scope and Authority of the Bible,* Explorations in Theology 7 (London: SCM, 1980), p. 9: "Again, it may be argued that the view just expressed assumes that God does not act in history and does not affect it. It assumes nothing of the sort. It simply observes that we do not apply the term 'history' to a form of investigation which resorts to divine agency as a mode of explanation."

[12]"How Convention Helps," p. 116.

[13]*First Historians,* p. 269.

[14]He does show awareness of the distinction on occasion; see, e.g., *Art of Biblical Narrative,* pp. 25, 33–34, 41. But his lack of clarity on this important point still leaves him open to criticism; e.g., D. Patrick and A. Scult (*Rhetoric and Biblical Interpretation,* JSOTS 82 [Sheffield: Almond, 1990], p. 50) write: "Alter has done much to open the Bible to serious reading by a wider audience, but by limiting himself to aesthetic judgments, he still does not integrate the Bible's truth-claims, as they are spoken, into his interpretative approach. He essentially reads the text as realistic fiction."

[15]For a similar distinction, cf. F. F. Bruce ("Myth and History," in *History, Criticism and Faith,* ed. Colin Brown [Leicester: IVP, 1979], p. 84), where he favors "mythologization of history" to "historicization of myth," but prefers "theological interpretation of history" to both.

[16]Both quotations occur at the beginning of this chapter.

literary genres, whereas Halpern's point seems to be that any representation of the past, inasmuch as it is not (literally) the past, involves a "fictionalizing" aspect.[17] Halpern has in mind *form* (i.e., the way the story is told), while Blomberg is apparently thinking of *function* (i.e., for what purpose the story is told).

So long as we bear in mind this important distinction between form and function we may speak of a certain fictionality involved in all narrative discourse while still maintaining the common-sense differentiation between *historical* narratives, which "claim to tell us what really happened," and *fictional* narratives, which "portray events that of course by definition never happened, [though] they are often said to be true-to-life."[18] The point is simply that fictionality of a certain sort is as likely to be found in the historian's toolbox as in the fiction writer's.[19]

Still, given the potential for (and indeed the presence of) much confusion resulting from the use of an ambiguous (bivalent) term like *fiction*, it would be far better, at least with respect to the perceptions of the average person, to substitute a term like *artistry* to describe the historian's literary technique, and reserve the term fiction for the nonfactual genre of that name. Since this is not likely to happen, however, it will be necessary when reading this or that scholar to discover how the term *fiction* is being used.

The issues raised so far can be elucidated by comparing historiography, which might be fairly described as a kind of a verbal representational art, with a visual type of representational art such as painting.[20]

HISTORY-WRITING AS REPRESENTATIONAL ART

In his oil painting classes in Chicago, my former teacher Karl Steele would occasionally reflect on a criticism that he, as an impressionist painter, sometimes received from those more attracted by what is commonly called abstract or expressionist art. The

---

[17]Cf. Powell, *What Is Narrative Criticism?* p. 100: "The real world is never identical with the world of a story, even if that story is regarded as portraying life in the real world quite accurately."

[18]D. Carr, "Narrative and the Real World: An Argument for Continuity," *HTh* 25 (1986): 117.

[19]Sternberg (*Poetics of Biblical Narrative*, p. 28) illustrates this point well by citing an evaluation of historian Garret Mattingly's *The Defeat of the Spanish Armada* (1959) by a fellow professional historian and observing "how many of [Robert] Alter's *measures of fictionality* are invoked to define Mattingly's professional *excellence as a historian*" (insertion and italics mine).

[20]The analogy between historiography and art has a venerable history and continues to evoke interest today; see, e.g., F. R. Ankersmit, "Historical Representation," *HTh* 27 (1988): 205–28. No analogy is perfect, of course, and a criticism that could be made of this one is that a text should not be treated "as a static spatial form, like a painting, a sculpture, or a piece of architecture" (so R. M. Fowler, *Let the Reader Understand: Reader-Response Criticism and the Gospel of Mark* [Minneapolis: Fortress, 1991], p. 42), since reading is a "dynamic, concrete, temporal experience, instead of the abstract perception of a spatial form" (ibid., p. 25). I would argue, however, that the distinction between reading texts and viewing paintings should not be overpressed. While countless tourists may spend a few hours in the Louvre casting a glance this way and that to see the paintings, it can hardly be said that many of them have properly *viewed* the paintings. Time and dynamic interplay are as involved in giving a painting a "close viewing" as they are in giving a text a "close reading." If anything, the distinction between viewing a painting and reading a text is in the sequence of perception: with a painting, one generally begins with an impression of the whole, then proceeds to study individual *passages* of the painting, and finally returns to a greater appreciation of the whole in the light of its parts; with an unfamiliar narrative, one must generally begin by reading the individual passages in sequence, which leads eventually to an impression of the whole, and then finally to a greater appreciation of the parts in the light of the whole.

basic criticism was that since his paintings were *representational*, or at least *realistic*[21] (primarily landscapes and seascapes), there was less *artfulness* in his craft—he simply *copied* nature. Steele's response was to challenge his critics to inspect at very close range any two-inch square of one of his canvases. Should the critics agree to the challenge, what they would find would not be nature, or even an exact copy of the appearance of nature, but a tiny abstract painting! In other words, each of Steele's *realistic* paintings consisted of a series of abstractions, which taken together and viewed from the proper vantage point gave a convincing and indeed realistic impression of the scene depicted. In one sense, then, Steele's paintings were *fictions* and not *literal* renderings of reality. There could be no question of counting blades of grass or leaves on trees; each brush stroke was an abstraction, just paint on canvas. In another sense, however, his paintings were very much representations of reality, imparting to receptive viewers a truer sense and appreciation of the scene, as Steele perceived it, than even the best color photography could have done.

The above illustration relates to the issue of historiography in the following manner. Common sense suggests that it would be a *reductio ad absurdum* to argue that since Steele's paintings at one level make use of techniques indistinguishable from those employed by abstract or expressionist painters, they therefore cannot be representational, or make reference to a reality outside themselves. One can find, however, among the writings of those who challenge the representational capacity of narrative discourse, statements that seem similarly reductionistic. Roland Barthes, for example, in drawing attention to what he calls "the fallacy of referentiality," writes:

> Claims concerning the "realism" of narrative are therefore to be discounted. . . . The function of narrative is not to "represent," it is to constitute a spectacle. . . . Narrative does not show, does not imitate. . . . "What takes place" in a narrative is from the referential (reality) point of view literally *nothing*; "what happens" is language alone, the adventure of language, the unceasing celebration of its coming.[22]

This sounds very much like saying that "what happens" in one of Steele's paintings is *paint alone*. Barthes's statement may be true of some narratives, but surely not all. If paintings can be broadly divided into representational and nonrepresentational varieties, into those that attempt to depict some aspect of the world outside and those that simply celebrate the potentialities of paint as a medium, then is it possible that narratives can be similarly classified? Of course, even representational (referential) painters enjoy considerable freedom in terms of how they choose to depict their subject—compositional and stylisitic decisions have to be made.[23] But this does not mean that a generic distinction cannot and

---

[21] I am using the term in a general, not a technical sense, as a virtual synonym for *naturalistic*—i.e., concerned with depicting the world more or less as it appears. For a more technical description of these two terms, see, e.g., K. Reynolds with R. Seddon, *Illustrated Dictionary of Art Terms: A Handbook for the Artist and Art Lover* (London: Ebury Press, 1981), ad loc.

[22] "Introduction to the Structural Analysis of Narratives" (1966), p. 124; quoted by Hayden White ("The Question of Narrative in Contemporary Historical Theory" *HTh* 23 [1984]: 14), which see for an extended critique of Barthes's position (pp. 12–15).

[23] E. H. Gombrich ("The Mask and the Face: Perception of Physiognomic Likeness in Life and in Art," in *Art, Perception, and Reality*, ed. Maurice Mandelbaum [Baltimore: The Johns Hopkins University Press, 1972], pp. 1–46) offers an extreme example of this in his description of a portrait painted by Picasso in which the subject's head is given a perfectly oblong shape, but then, in "a balancing of compensatory moves . . . to compensate for her face not being really oblong but narrow, Picasso paints it blue—maybe

should not be made between paintings that are representational and those that are not. By the same token, I would contend that a distinction can and should be made between narratives that are essentially representational (historiographical) and those that are not.

On what basis then are narratives to be classified? Form alone is not a sufficient criterion: "there are simply no universals of historical vs. fictive form. Nothing on the surface, that is, infallibly marks off the two genres. As modes of discourse, history and fiction make *functional* categories that may remain constant under the most assorted *formal* variations and are distinguishable only by their overall sense of purpose."[24] In other words, "there are no formal features, no textual properties that identify a given text as a work of fiction,"[25] yet history and fiction can still be distinguished on the basis of their overall purpose. Aristotle, writing more than two thousand years ago, came close to saying the same thing: "The difference between a historian and a poet is not that one writes in prose and the other in verse. . . . The real difference is this, that one tells what happened and the other what might happen."[26] This general point can be illustrated by observing the chiastic structure of the last four chapters of 2 Samuel.

21:1–14	A	Famine resulting from Saul's sin is stopped
21:15–22	B	Short list of Davidic champions
22:1–51	C	Long poetic composition:
		David's song of praise
23:1–7	C'	Short poetic composition:
		David's last words
23:8–39	B'	Long list of Davidic champions
24:1–25	A'	Plague resulting from David's sin is stopped

As Sternberg points out, chiasm is now widely recognized as "one of the indisputable literary devices" found in the Old Testament, and yet the chief goal of the epilogue to 2 Samuel "remains informational and memorial." The conclusion to be drawn from this is that while "form can produce or imply an artistic function, it still cannot enthrone one regardless of context."[27]

If, then, historical literature and fictional literature are "distinguishable only by their overall sense of purpose," *context* becomes one of the primary means of discovering this purpose. We are reminded of one of the fundamental principles of discourse introduced in the preceding chapter—viz., that "each successively higher level of textual organization influences all of the lower levels of which it is composed." The question to be asked then is this: What is the apparent function of a particular narrative within its broader context? A sense of the purpose of a narrative is, as Sternberg puts it, "a matter of inference from clues planted in and around the writing."[28] Again let me illustrate with an example from the visual arts.

---

the pallor is here felt to be an equivalent to the impression of slimness" (p. 30). The interesting point is that despite the abstractions, the painting retains a referential function.

[24]Sternberg, *Poetics of Biblical Narrative*, p. 30.

[25]Vanhoozer ("Semantics of Biblical Literature," p. 68), summarizing the view of J. R. Searle, "The Logical Status of Fictional Discourse," *New Literary History* 6 (1975): 319–32.

[26]*Poetics*, Loeb Classical Library (Cambridge, Mass.: Harvard University Press, 1982), chap. 9 (1451b).

[27]*Poetics of Biblical Narrative*, pp. 40–41.

[28]Ibid., p. 30.

Imagine that we are viewing a painting of an old railroad depot. Imagine also that for the moment we are not allowed to look around to gain our bearings and to discover where the painting is hung. Without some knowledge of the painting's setting, we may be unable to decide whether the painting's primary function is a *historical* one—to be a lasting reminder of the appearance of an old landmark—or an *aesthetic* one—simply to be a pleasing work of art. Imagine that we are now allowed to look around. If we find that the painting is prominently displayed (with a bronze plaque beneath it) in the foyer of a brand new railroad terminal, we shall likely conclude that some *historical* function is being served (perhaps this was the old terminal that was demolished to make room for the new one). If, on the other hand, we find that the painting is displayed in an art gallery along with other paintings depicting various subjects, we shall be more inclined to assume that the aesthetic function is primary. Now, of course, the historical (or referential) purpose implicit in the first scenario does not exclude a concern with artistic quality. It is the greater aesthetic appeal of a painting over a photograph that will have prompted the railroad company to choose the more expensive option. The first scenario does imply, however, that the artist will have worked under some *referential constraints*. He will have been constrained by the actualities of the subject, at least to the point of making the subject recognizable. In the second scenario, though the artist may in fact fairly represent the appearance of the old depot, he will have been under no obligation to do so.[29]

What is true of visual art (paintings) is true also of verbal art (narratives). The difference between a narrative whose primary purpose is representational (or referential) and one whose primary purpose is aesthetic is the degree to which the artist is constrained by the actualities of the subject matter. As Matt Oja puts it, "historians are constrained by the need to discover and work with a set of facts which already exist and which they look upon from without. Writers of fiction are not so constrained.... A fictional narrative does not have objective reality until the author creates it."[30] In some instances external evidence—material remains, eyewitness reports—may offer clues as to a narrative's purpose and its degree of adherence to the "facts,"[31] but in all instances our quest to discover a narrative's overall sense of purpose should begin with attention to clues in and around the narrative. If both the subject matter of the narrative itself and the nature of the surrounding context suggest a representational purpose, then we may assume that the writer has been in some measure constrained by the facts. I say "in some measure," because neither representational artists nor historians simply reproduce their subjects.

HISTORY-WRITING AS A CREATIVE ENTERPRISE

I have argued that the chief difference between writers of history and writers of fiction is that the former are constrained by the facts of the past, while the latter are not. Does

---

[29]Illustrations of the continuum between referential and aesthetic interests might easily be multiplied: an architectural blueprint is referential, while an architectural rendering of the planned construction combines representational and aesthetic interests in almost equal measure; a "mug shot" is referential, while a portrait combines representational and aesthetic interests, etc.

[30]"Fictional History and Historical Fiction: Solzhenitsyn and *Kiš* as Exemplars," *HTh* 27 (1988): 120; similarly, Sternberg, *Poetics of Biblical Narrative*, p. 29.

[31]For nuanced discussions of the slippery concept of "facts," see Stanford, *Nature*, pp. 71–74; R. H. Nash, *Christian Faith and Historical Understanding* (Grand Rapids: Zondervan, 1984), pp. 93–109.

this disallow any creative input from the historian in the writing of history? Not at all, for as we have just noted, historians do not simply reproduce the past. Rather, they must contribute to the work they produce in at least a couple of ways. First, they must study all available evidence pertinent to their subject and develop their own vision of the past. Second, this vision must be encoded in a verbal medium in such a way that it can be shared with others. The first task, "the historian's construction of the past," is described by Stanford as "the pivot of historical knowledge" that stands between "history-as-event and history-as-record." The second task, the transposition of this construction into "written or spoken form," is equally important, since it "stands between the historian's mental construction and those of the audience."[32]

Few historians or philosophers would dispute the notion that writers of history make significant contributions in the ways mentioned above. What is hotly disputed, however, is the *nature* and *extent* of the historian's contribution. One of the major points of debate is whether *narrative form* as such is an aspect of reality itself or is a product solely of the historian's imagination. A narrative is characterized by having a plot, for example, with a beginning, a middle, and an end. Are such features aspects of reality itself or constructions created solely in the mind of the historian? Does the past present itself in narrative form, as a meaningful sequence, or is it a meaningless chaos, upon which the historian must impose a narrative structure?

Some historians and literary theorists today assume that "real events simply do not hang together in a narrative way, and if we treat them as if they did we are being *untrue* to life."[33] Others, however, disagree. David Carr, for example, strongly challenges the view that meaningful sequence is merely an invention of historians.[34] He sets the stage by quoting such notables as Louis Mink ("Life has no beginnings, middles and ends. . . . Narrative qualities are transferred from art to life") and Hayden White ("Does the world really present itself to perception in the form of well-made stories? Or does it present itself more in the way that the annals and chronicles suggest, either as a mere sequence without beginning or end or as sequences of beginnings that only terminate and never conclude?").[35] Carr himself maintains that "narrative is not merely a possibly successful way of describing events; its structure inheres in the events themselves."[36]

If Carr is correct, does this mean that the historian simply finds historical narratives rather than constructs them? I would contend that the answer lies somewhere in the middle, and that two extremes should be avoided: (1) that which denies the importance of the historian's vision and creative imagination and (2) that which denies to the past any inherent/coherent structure whatsoever. Historians, as verbal representational artists, find themselves in a position analogous to that of visual representational artists. The latter can paint a number of different pictures of a single subject, no two of which are alike, but this does not mean that the subject itself lacks inherent structure or that the artists are unconstrained

---

[32]*Nature,* pp. 143–44. Similarly, Axtell ("History as Imagination," p. 458) writes: "Since history at its best is shared discovery, the historian's final and most important task is to translate his vision, his 'achieved awareness' and understanding, of the past for the modern reader."

[33]Carr ("Narrative and the Real World," p. 117), who goes on to contest this view.

[34]Both in the article mentioned in the preceding note and in a book entitled *Time, Narrative, and History* (Bloomington: Indiana University Press, 1986).

[35]"Narrative and the Real World," p. 118.

[36]Ibid., p. 117.

by the facts. The production of a representational painting involves a coordination of creativity and constraint, the creativity of the artist under the constraint of the subject. The subject matter does not simply present itself to the artist as a painting waiting to be painted. The artist must make various kinds of choices. First, a subject must be chosen from among the multitude of possible subjects in the world around. Second, a vantage point must be chosen from which to view the subject. Third, compositional decisions must be made: what are to be the boundaries or limits of the painting? Do these boundaries result in an overall sense of balance? Depending on the purpose of the painting, the artist may have some freedom to arrange or rearrange elements of his subject. The portrait artist, for example, enjoys considerable freedom to rearrange objects in the setting but is rather constrained when it comes to rearranging the subject's face! Fourth, a paint medium must be chosen (oil, acrylic, watercolor, etc.), the palette of colors selected (will it include a limited or a full range of colors?), the style decided (will the painting be rendered in intricate detail with small brushes or will it be executed boldly and rapidly with a palette knife?), and so forth.

Just as the physical world does not present itself in such a way that no creative choices are required of artists who would depict some aspect of it, so the past does not present itself in such a way that historians need make no creative choices in the construction of a historical account of some aspect of it. But if the past does have some inherent structure (as I believe it does), then the first task of historians is to seek to discern that structure. Beyond this, they must also choose a point of view—the most appropriate perspective from which to depict the subject and the "best light" in which to see it. And they must make aesthetic choices—how shall the work be composed, what degree of detail shall be included, what shall be the boundaries of their "picture" of the past, and so forth.

Constraint by the subject matter, point of view, aesthetic choices—our painting analogy can help us begin to understand how the three impulses mentioned in the preceding chapter might be coordinated in the biblical literature, not only its narratives but also in other genres (such as poetry) that may include historical reference. The *historiographical* impulse implies constraint by the subject, the *theological* implies point of view, and the *literary* implies aesthetic choices. But the fruitfulness of the painting analogy does not end here. So far, the creative choices required of painter and historian alike are but preliminaries to the actual execution of the work. When it comes to the latter, there are again a number of helpful parallels between the requirements of visual and of verbal representation.

CHARACTERISTICS OF SUCCESSFUL REPRESENTATION

Of the numerous points of advice that Karl Steele would customarily offer his painting classes, several stand out as particularly important. First, he would often instruct students at work on their paintings to blur their vision occasionally by half-closing their eyes; the effect of this was to eliminate the distraction of too much detail and to facilitate perception of the major contours and tonal relationships of the subject. Second, and as a corollary to this first point of advice, he would stress the importance of standing back from the canvas, or even walking backward, in order to view the subject and the canvas from a distance. Close proximity to the canvas, he would say, does not guarantee more accurate results but quite often the opposite, since the painter sometimes gets lost among the trees and loses sight of the overall shape of the forest. Third, he would contend that the most effective paintings are those that exploit the suggestiveness of visual ambiguities—lost edges, mysterious shadows, etc. He would point out that a common mistake of beginners is to attempt to record the great mass of detail exhibited by the subject, whereas the best way to achieve a realistic representation is to be very selective, limiting the depiction of details to a suggestive few so as to allow the mind of the viewers to fill in the rest.

These procedures of the visual artist—what we might call *creative means* to *representational ends*—find ready analogues in the work of the verbal artists we call historians. Since the "Ideal Chronicler"—viz., one who records everything that happens as it happens—does not exist, it is obvious that all historians must, to some extent at least, simplify their presentations of their subjects.[37] As Peter Ackroyd rightly observes, "the recounting of what happened, even a few moments later, inevitably introduces simplifications, selections, interpretations."[38] Indeed, one of the main tasks of historians, Axtell reminds us, is to discern and represent "the larger patterns, structures and meanings behind particular events and facts which contemporaries were not able to see."[39]

How do historians accomplish this? Where data are plentiful, historians must seek to discern the major contours of the subject by, as it were, half-closing their eyes so as to perceive the big picture. Alternatively, or additionally, they may enjoy the advantage of being able to view the subject from a distance, from across the room of time. As important as empirical evidence and eye-witness testimony are, historians standing at some remove from the subject are often in a favorable position to discern the major shapes and relations of the past. We often say of prominent contemporaries (presidents or prime ministers) that "it will be interesting to see how history treats them." Again, Ackroyd makes the point well: "the historian who writes at some distance from the events may be in a better position to give a true appraisal than one who is so involved as to see only a part of what makes up the whole."[40] One reason that the historian writing some time after the event may be at an advantage is that "the significance of a historial phenomenon is often recognized by its sequences or consequences, i.e., its posthistory."[41] Finally, historians, like painters, must avoid the temptation to include too much detail in their depiction. There must be an economy to their craft; if carefully selected, only a few suggestive details may be necessary to capture their subject (Esau's hairiness, Ehud's left-handedness, Eli's heaviness, etc.). "What matters most in history . . . is 'the great outline and the significant detail; what must be avoided is [a] deadly morass of irrelevant narrative' in between."[42]

[37]For a critical evaluation of the concept of the "Ideal Chronicler," see P. A. Roth, "Narrative Explanations: The Case of History," *HTh* 27 (1988): 1–13; also L. O. Mink, "Narrative Form as a Cognitive Instrument," in *The Writing of History: Literary Form and Historical Understanding,* ed. R. H. Canary and H. Kozicki (Madison: University of Wisconsin Press, 1978), p. 140. Even if an exhaustive "Ideal Chronicler" existed, the resulting history would be so massive as to be useless.

[38]"Historians and Prophets," *Svensk Exegetisk Årsbok* 33 (1968): 21.

[39]"History as Imagination," p. 457.

[40]"Historians and Prophets," p. 21.

[41]M. Tsevat, "Israelite History and the Historical Books of the Old Testament," in *The Meaning of the Book of Job and Other Biblical Essays* (New York: Ktav, 1980), p. 181; note also Tsevat's important qualification that "the significance is not bestowed by the latter upon the former; the consequences are indicators and not generators" (ibid.).

[42]Axtell, "History as Imagination," p. 459; quoting Lewis Namier.

THE ADEQUACY AND AUTHORITY OF REPRESENTATION

Simplification, selectivity, suggestive detail—these hallmarks of effective historiography are reminiscent of the kinds of features often highlighted in discussions of the *literary* artistry of biblical narrative. I hope that by now enough has been said to make the point that literary artistry and reliable historiography should not be set in opposition. But still the challenge might be raised: "In making a case that the Bible presents us with 'representational paintings,' have you not reduced our confidence in what the Bible can tell us about the past? Wouldn't photographs serve us better?" The answer to this question is that it very much depends on the artist! Admittedly, painting often involves a greater interpretive component than does photography (though even the latter requires that creative choices be made), but this is not necessarily a bad thing. As Carl F. H. Henry asserts, "Christian faith requires not simply the redemptive historical act but its meaning or significance as well; historical research alone is impotent either to guarantee any past event or to adduce its meaning or theological import."[43]

"But I'm just interested in the bare facts," the challenge might continue. Such a statement is both wrong-headed and a bit naive. Since the past is *past* and unrepeatable, it will never be possible to recover the "bare facts" pure and simple, at least not all of them; we are inevitably dependent on witnesses and evidences. As Caird explains, "History has a factual content, but it comes to the historian not as fact but as evidence, emanating from persons with whom he must engage in conversation."[44] Even if we could return to the past and record it on videotape, this would still not guarantee us an adequate understanding of the past. In the aftermath of the Persian Gulf War, I remember hearing a commentator on National Public Radio express a frustration he had felt while the war was in progress. It went something like this: "They kept sending us videotapes, but they didn't tell us what they meant. We had the video images, but no interpretation."

It is the greater interpretive capacity of painting over photography that makes it the generally preferred medium for portraiture (visual historiography). And it is the greater interpretive (explanatory) capacity of literary narrative over bare chronicle that makes it the preferred medium of biblical historiography. These preferences are only justified, of course, to the extent that the narrators or painters are skillful and competent in their craft, and they have adequate access to their subject. No one would dispute that a portrait by an artist who is incompetent or who has no clear notion of the character and appearance of the subject will be inferior (on either artistic or referential grounds, or both) to even a simple photograph of the subject. But recent studies are increasingly demonstrating that the biblical narrators were consummate literary artists. And for those willing to accept it, their claim to have written under divine inspiration more than adequately guarantees their access to their subject.[45]

There are, of course, many in today's world who dismiss any notion of divine inspiration. In so doing, however, they find themselves in a rather perplexing position. As

---

[43]*God, Revelation and Authority* (Waco: Word, 1976), 2: 330.

[44]*Language and Imagery*, p. 202.

[45]As Henry aptly puts it (*God, Revelation and Authority*, 2: 330): "Empirical probability can indeed be combined with inner certainty when the meaning of specific happenings is transcendently vouchsafed, that is, when that meaning is objectively given by divine revelation." Cf. also Sternberg, *Poetics of Biblical Narrative*, pp. 32–35.

Mink explains in "Narrative Form as a Cognitive Instrument," many moderns continue to embrace (consciously or unconsciously) a concept of Universal History—the notion that "the ensemble of human events belongs to a single story"—but they have no notion as to "who devises or tells this story. In its original theological form, as with Augustine, Universal History was the work of divine Providence; but as the idea became secularized by the eighteenth century, God the Author retreated, leaving the idea of a story which is simply *there*, devised by no one ... but waiting to be told by someone" (pp. 136–37). Mink's proposed solution to this rather unstable state of affairs brought about by modernism's elimination of the Author but retention of the Story is, in the end, to abandon altogether the residual belief that the past contains an "untold story to which narrative histories approximate" and to assert that only "individual statements of fact" are "determinate." But since "the significance of past occurrences" cannot be grasped except insofar as they find a place within a narrative, Mink concludes that a story must yet be told, and it is *we* who must tell the story; *we* must "make the past determinate in that respect" (p. 148). Having shown "God the Author" the door, modernism is left to tell the story itself. And though Mink does not address the issue, it would seem that since "we" denotes a plurality of persons, none of whom possesses more than a relative authority, the inevitable result of Mink's "solution" will be a thoroughgoing historical relativism.

The alternative to modernism's dilemma is to embrace a concept of biblical inspiration such that the authority of the Bible's pictures of the past (whatever may be the differences between them, and however incorrectly we may at times view them) is as secure as the authority of the One who inspired them.

AN EXAMPLE: SAMUEL–KINGS AND CHRONICLES

In the preceding paragraph, mention was made of differences that sometimes exist among the Bible's pictures of the past. Indeed, even biblical accounts of the same events often differ in various ways. Some might wish that these differences did not exist, but the fact of the matter is that our having different presentations of the same subject often puts us at an advantage! Multiple presentations enable us to view the subject from different angles and under various lights, and to benefit from the narrative artists' own interpretive contributions. However brilliantly a biography may be written, or however masterfully a portrait may be painted, our knowledge of the life and visage of a given individual is surely enhanced if we have access to more than one biography or portrait. When approaching the New Testament's four gospels, for example, or the Old Testament's two histories of the monarchy (Samuel–Kings and Chronicles), we do well to keep this perspective in mind.[46]

---

[46]The real question, of course, for those who are perplexed by differences among accounts of the same event(s) is whether or not these constitute *irreconcilable* differences—that is, contradictions—that would force us to call in question the narrative artists' competence, motives, control of the subject matter, or the like. While it would be obscurantist to deny that the Bible presents vexing difficulties for which solutions are not readily forthcoming, I would maintain (1) that a properly nuanced understanding of the nature and purpose of the biblical literature greatly lessens the number of perceived difficulties and (2) that the remainder of stubborn cases should be held in abeyance or, preferably, made the object of special study by those whose technical training and theological orientation might place them in a position to find, not strained harmonizations, but true solutions.

To investigate how we might go about negotiating differences among biblical accounts purporting to cover similar historical terrain, let us look more closely at the *synoptic histories* of the Old Testament. As Roddy Braun has observed, a comparative reading of Israel's synoptic histories affords an opportunity "to learn much about both the nature of historical writing in Israel and the manner in which God used His inspired writers to speak a message to their own day."[47] Even a quick reading discovers that Samuel–Kings and Chronicles paint rather different pictures, not only in points of detail but even in terms of their overall shape. The Chronicler's history, for instance, has little or nothing to say on matters that were of great concern in the earlier history of Samuel–Kings: reference to King Saul (whose election, rejection, and decline occupy much of 1 Samuel) is limited to a brief summary of his death and its cause in 1 Chronicles 10;[48] nothing is said of the Saulide opposition to David's rise to power (though this opposition is a focus of interest in the second half of 1 Samuel and the early chapters of 2 Samuel); no mention is made of David's adultery with Bathsheba and his arranged murder of Uriah, nor of the disastrous political and domestic consequences of these actions (though 2 Samuel 11–20 are largely taken up with these matters); no mention is made of Adonijah's threat to Solomon, or of Solomon's palace, or of his apostasy (though these figure prominently in 1 Kings 1–11); no mention is made of the prophetic ministries of Elijah and Elisha that occupy center stage in 1 Kings 17–2 Kings 8, save the report of a letter of judgment from Elijah to Jehoram of Judah in 2 Chronicles 21:11–17 (which letter, curiously, is not mentioned in Kings);[49] no mention is made of the fall of the Northern Kingdom (an event of signal importance recounted in 2 Kings 17). The list could continue and be presented in much greater detail, but enough has been indicated to show that by virtue of its omissions the Chronicler's presentation of Israel's past is given a quite different shape than that of Samuel–Kings.

Not only does the Chronicler's picture omit much that is found in Samuel–Kings, it also includes much that is not found in the earlier corpus: extensive genealogical lists stretching back to Adam (1 Chron. 1–9); additional lists of David's mighty men (chap. 12); reports of David's Levitical appointments (chaps. 15–16); descriptions of his preparations for temple building and temple worship (chaps. 22–29); much additional material relating to the Kingdom of Judah (various additions in the stretch of text from 2 Chron. 11–32); and Cyrus's decree marking the end of the exile (36:22–23).

From this very general overview, we can see that the Old Testament's two histories of the monarchy present different pictures in terms of overall shape and composition. But the differences between them are not limited to such large-scale matters. The two histories often differ significantly even in the way they render the same event or in the way they portray the same person. As an example, we might compare the two accounts of God's dynastic promise to David as presented in 2 Samuel 7 and 1 Chronicles 17.[50] That

---

[47]"The Message of Chronicles: Rally 'Round the Temple," *Concordia Theological Monthly* 42 (1971): 502.

[48]For a recent discussion of the significance of the brief treatment of Saul in Chronicles, see Saul Zalewski, "The purpose of the story of the death of Saul in 1 Chronicles X," *VT* 39 (1989): 449–67; cf. also Akroyd, "The Chronicler as Exegete," *JSOT* 2 (1977): 2–32.

[49]For discussion, see R. Dillard, *2 Chronicles*, WBC (Waco: Word, 1988), pp. 167–69.

[50]Other instructive examples would include, e.g., the Chronicler's depiction of King Abijah, which is comparatively more positive than that found in Kings (cf. 2 Chron. 13 and 1 Kings 15; for discussion see D. G. Deboys, "History and Theology in the Chronicler's Portrayal of Abijah," *Biblica* 71 [1990]: 48–62);

"there is a clear literary relationship between the two" is beyond dispute.[51] But when we compare the two passages, we discover a number of differences between them. The chart on the next two pages basically follows the NIV, but with some adjustments to reflect more closely the Hebrew texts. In the chart, some (though not all) differences have been highlighted: material peculiar to one passage only is placed in italics and the location of this material is indicated by a dotted line in both texts; solid underlining identifies noticeable differences in phraseology; alternation of the divine names *God* and LORD (Yahweh) are in bold type. (See chart on pages 334–35.)

A side-by-side reading of these parallel texts discovers numerous divergences— some minor, others more major. What are we to make of them? In the present context we must limit ourselves to a few brief comments on some of the apparently more significant differences. But first a word of caution: it should not be assumed that all differences represent motivated changes by the Chronicler.[52] Some may simply reflect the Chronicler's freedom to paraphrase or generalize, as he does often in his composition.[53] Other differences seem to result from stylistic or lexical preferences.[54] In still other instances, the Chronicler may simply be repeating what he finds in his *Vorlage* (the text of Samuel with which he was familiar).[55]

There are, however, some differences between the two renditions that may require explanation on other grounds. Particularly striking are the Chronicler's omission in verse 13 of any reference to the chastisement of David's royal descendant, should he sin (contrast 2 Sam. 7:14), and his alteration of pronouns in the succeeding verse from "your house and your kingdom" to "my house and my kingdom." What are we to make of changes such as these?

Perhaps the way to begin is to recognize that the Chronicler presents a *second* painting of Israel's monarchical history, not an *over* painting of Samuel–Kings. It is now widely acknowledged that both the Chronicler and his audience were well familiar with the Samuel–Kings material, and that the Chronicler's aim was to recast and supplement, not

---

the Chronicler's presentation of David's census as compared to the Samuel account of the same episode (1 Chron. 21 and 2 Sam. 24; see Dillard, "David's Census: Perspectives on 2 Samuel 24 and 1 Chronicles 21," in *Through Christ's Word: A Festschrift for Dr. Philip E. Hughes,* ed. W. R. Godfrey and J. L. Boyd [Phillipsburg, NJ: Presbyterian and Reformed, 1985], pp. 94–107; J. H. Sailhamer, "1 Chronicles 21:1—A Study in Inter-Biblical Interpretation," TrinJ 10 [1989]: 33–48); the depiction of Josiah and his reforms in Chronicles as compared to the presentation in Kings (see, on 2 Chron. 34:4–7 and 2 Kings 23:4–14; D. L. Washburn, "Perspective and Purpose: Understanding the Josiah Story," TrinJ 12 [1991]: 59–78); and many more.

[51]So H. G. M. Williamson, "Eschatology in Chronicles," TynB 28 (1977): 134.

[52]See Dillard, "David's Census," pp. 94–96; Williamson, "History," in *It is Written: Scripture Citing Scripture. Essays in Honour of Barnabas Lindars,* ed. D. A. Carson and H. G. M. Williamson (Cambridge: Cambridge University Press, 1988), pp. 31–32.

[53]This may be all that is involved in the Chronicler's "You are not the one . . ." (v. 4) instead of 2 Samuel's "Are you the one . . ." (v. 5).

[54]An example would be the Chronicler's preference for the shorter form of the first person singular pronoun (*'anî*) over the longer form (*'ānōkî*) that is prevalent in Samuel–Kings. Whereas in Samuel–Kings the ratio of shorter to longer is something like 3 to 2, in Chronicles it is more like 25 to 1.

[55]For example, 2 Sam. 7:7 has "tribes" (*šibṭê*), while 1 Chron. 17:6 has "leaders" (*šōpṭê*). Since the latter is contextually more appropriate and is attested also in 2 Sam. 7:11, it appears that the Chronicler's *Vorlage* may preserve the better reading. On this and other matters discussed in this paragraph, see R. L. Braun, *1 Chronicles,* WBC (Waco: Word, 1986), p. 198. For speculation on the character of the Chronicler's Hebrew *Vorlage*, see Dillard, "David's Census," pp. 94–95.

repress or supplant, the earlier history.[56] Thus, the Chronicler could feel free, for example, without pang of historical conscience, to omit the warning of 2 Samuel 7:14 as of little interest to his particular purpose for writing. After all, those who had experienced the Babylonian captivity and could look back on the checkered history of the divided monarchy did not need reminding that wrongdoing leads to "floggings inflicted by men." Moreover, in keeping with his overall purpose, the Chronicler wished to highlight Solomon's obedience, not his disobedience.

What then was the Chronicler's overall purpose for writing? To answer this question adequately would require not only a thorough study of the entirety of the Chronicler's work but also a consideration of the Chronicler's intended audience. The former is, of course, out of the question here.[57] As regards the Chronicler's audience, 2 Chronicles 36:22–23 (along with the evidence of the genealogies in 1 Chron. 3) makes it clear that the Chronicler is addressing the postexilic, restoration community in Jerusalem. We must ask, then, in assessing the Chronicler's rendition of the dynastic promise, "What must have been the pressing theological concerns of those who had returned out of exile in Babylon, or their descendants?" The unthinkable had happened—Judah had fallen and God's elect people had been swept away into exile. The question as to why this calamity had befallen God's people had been answered already for the exiles by Samuel–Kings. But for those now back in the land of Israel the pressing questions must surely be not "Why the exile?" but, rather, "Is God still interested in us? Are the covenants still in force?"[58] The Chronicler's answer to these questions is affirmative: God still cares for his people and is bound to them in covenant.

In his rendering of the promise to David, the Chronicler seeks to underscore these truths by bringing into the light what could only be dimly perceived in the shadows of the earlier rendering. That is to say, the Chronicler draws forth and makes explicit what was only implicit in 2 Samuel 7.[59] Perhaps it is this practice of making the implicit *explic-*

---

[56]B. S. Childs insists that "it is a basic error of interpretation to infer . . . that the Chr's purpose lies in suppressing or replacing the earlier tradition with his own account" (*Introduction to the Old Testament as Scripture* [Philadelphia: Fortress], p. 646, which see for Childs's reasoning). Similarly, Dillard points out that "the numerous points at which he [the Chronicler] assumes the reader's familiarity with the account in Samuel/Kings shows that he is using the Deuteronomic history as a 'control' to an audience well familiar with that account" ("The Reign of Asa [2 Chronicles 14-16]: An Example of the Chronicler's Theological Method," *JETS* 23 [1980]: 214). On the Chronicler's many allusions to the earlier history, see also Ackroyd, "The Chronicler as Exegete."

[57]If we were to attempt such an investigation, we might take our initial cues from the overall structure of Chronicles. It appears, for instance, that the Chronicler wishes to stress the continuity of Yahweh's dealings with (and interest in) his chosen people, as this is most strikingly expressed in the covenant with David. The Davidic kingdom is at a fundamental level the kingdom of Yahweh. And since this is so, events pertaining to the kingdom of Judah, where Davidic descendants once reigned, take on significance for "all Israel." Moreover, since in the Chronicler's day there is no Davidic king on an earthly throne, greater emphasis falls on the temple as the locus of Yahweh's continued rule. For more adequate appraisals, see the literature; e.g., Ackroyd, "Chronicler as Exegete"; Braun, "Message of Chronicles"; J. Goldingay, "The Chronicler as Theologian," *BTB* 5 (1975): 99–126; M. A. Throntveit, *When Kings Speak: Royal Speech and Royal Prayer in Chronicles*, SBLDS 93 (Atlanta: Scholars Press, 1987), pp. 77–88; Williamson, *Israel in the Book of Chronicles* (Cambridge: Cambridge University Press, 1977).

[58]Cf. Dillard, "David's Census," pp. 99–101.

[59]This is fully in keeping with the Chronicler's general practice; so, e.g., Childs: "Often the Chronicler spelled out in detail what was already partially implied in his source" (*Introduction*, p. 652; cf. p. 648). Cf. also Dillard, "Reward and Punishment in Chronicles: the Theology of Immediate Retribution," *WTJ* 46 (1984): 164–72.

2 Samuel 7:1–17

After <u>the king</u> was settled in his palace *and the LORD had given him rest from all his enemies around him*,² <u>the king</u> said to Nathan the prophet, "Here I am, living in a palace of cedar, while the ark............ .... of **God** <u>remains</u> in a tent."³ Nathan replied to <u>the king</u>, "Whatever you have in mind, *go ahead and do it*, for the **LORD** is with you."⁴ That night the word of the **LORD** came to Nathan, saying:⁵ "Go and tell my servant David, "This is what the LORD says: 'Are you the one to build me a house to dwell in?⁶ I have not dwelt in a house from the day I brought the Israelites up *out of Egypt* to this day. I have been moving from <u>place to place with a tent as my dwelling</u>.

⁷ Wherever I have moved with all the Israelites, did I ever say to any of their <u>tribes</u> whom I commanded to shepherd my people *Israel*, "Why have you not built me a house of cedar?"' ⁸ Now then, tell my servant David, "This is what the LORD Almighty says: I took you from the pasture and from following the flock to be ruler over my people of Israel. ⁹ I have been with you wherever you have gone, and I have cut all of your enemies from before you. Now I will make your name *great*, like the names of the greatest men of the earth. ¹⁰ And I will provide a place for my people Israel and will plant them so that they can have a home of their own and no longer be disturbed. Wicked people will not <u>wipe</u> them <u>out</u> anymore, as they did at the beginning ¹¹ and have done ever since the time I appointed leaders over my people Israel. I will also <u>give you rest from</u> all your enemies. <u>The LORD</u> declares to you that the LORD will <u>establish</u> a house for you: ¹² When your days are over and you <u>rest</u> with your fathers, I will raise up your offspring to succeed you, <u>who will come from your own body</u>, and I will establish his kingdom. ¹³ He is the one who will build a house for <u>my Name</u>, and I will establish <u>the</u> throne *of his kingdom* forever. ¹⁴ I will be his father, and he will be my son. *When he does wrong, I will punish him with the rod of men, with floggings inflicted by men*. ¹⁵ But my love will never be taken away from him, as I took it away from <u>Saul</u>, *whom I removed from before you.* ¹⁶ <u>Your</u> house and <u>your</u> kingdom <u>will endure</u> forever *before me*; <u>your</u> throne will be established forever." ¹⁷ Nathan reported to David all the words of this entire revelation.

1 Chronicles 17:1–15

After <u>David</u> was settled in his palace, ...
....<u>David</u> said to Nathan the prophet, "Here I am, living in a palace of cedar, while the ark of the covenant of the **LORD** <u>is under</u> a tent." [2] Nathan replied to <u>David</u>, "Whatever you have in mind, ...do it, for **God** is with you." [3] That night the word of **God** came to Nathan, saying: [4] "Go and tell my servant David, 'This is what the LORD says: <u>You are not</u> the one to build me a house to dwell in. [5] I have not dwelt in a house from the day I brought Israel up......................to this day. I have moved from <u>one tent site to another, from one dwelling place to another</u>. [6] Wherever I have moved with all the Israelites, did I ever say to any of their <u>leaders</u> whom I commanded to shepherd my people ...., "Why have you not built me a house of cedar?" [7] Now then, tell my servant David, 'This is what the LORD Almighty says: I took you from the pasture and from following the flock to be ruler over my people Israel. [8] I have been with you wherever you have gone, and I have cut off all your enemies from before you. Now I will make your name.........like the names of the greatest men of the earth. [9] And I will provide a place for my people Israel and will plant them so that they can have a home of their own and no longer be disturbed. Wicked people will not <u>oppress</u> them anymore, as they did at the beginning [10] and have done ever since the time I appointed leaders over my people Israel. I will also <u>subdue</u> all your enemies. <u>I</u> declare to you that the LORD will <u>build</u> a house for you: [11] When your days are over and you <u>go to be</u> with your fathers, I will raise up your offspring to succeed you, <u>one of your own sons</u>, ...and I will establish his kingdom. [12] He is the one who will build a house for <u>me</u>, and I will establish <u>his</u> throne ....forever. [13] I will be his father, and he will be my son....
....
....I will never take <u>my</u> love away from him, as I took it away from <u>your predecessor</u>. ....[14] <u>I will set him over my house</u> and <u>my</u> kingdom forever................................, <u>his</u> throne will be established forever.'" [15] Nathan reported to David all the words of this entire revelation.

it that best explains the Chronicler's alteration of the pronouns in verse 14. At the time of the Chronicler's writing, there is no longer a Davidic kingdom, literally speaking, but the kingdom of God, of course, remains. Thus "your house and your kingdom will endure forever before me" of 2 Samuel 7:16 becomes "I will set him over my house and my kingdom forever." In underscoring the theocratic character of the Davidic throne, the Chronicler is simply making explicit what is already implicit in the promise of 2 Samuel 7:14: "I will be his father, and he will be my son."

In other ways as well, the Chronicler renders the dynastic promise so as to drive home its pertinence to his audience. Perhaps his replacement of "the king" with the more personal "David" in verses 1 and 2 is meant to evoke the thought that, though Israel no longer has a human king on the throne, the Davidic line has not vanished and neither has God's promise, which after all was made *personally* to David. His addition of a reference to the "covenant" in verse 1 may serve to remind his hearers that they are still bound to God in covenant. His omission of "out of Egypt" in verse 5 tends to generalize the statement and make it perhaps more immediately relevant to those who themselves have been delivered out of bondage, though in a different land. A similar dynamic may be involved in the Chronicler's replacement of "Saul" with "your predecessor" in verse 13. Even his rephrasing of the reference to God's dwelling in a tent may serve to take the focus away from the tabernacle *per se* and to suggest the more general point that God's presence is not confined to any particular locale or structure. Could it also be that the change in terminology from "who will come from your own body" (which recalls the promise to Abraham in Gen. 15:4 and seems to suggest an immediate descendant) to "one of your sons" (which allows reference to future descendants; compare 2 Kings 20:18) is meant to hearten the Chronicler's hearers with the thought that the Lord may yet raise up a Davidic scion? In context, of course, the literal referent remains Solomon (v. 12: "He is the one who will build a house for me"). But a future son of David is not thereby excluded, at least not if the significance of the "house for me" is allowed to extend beyond the physical temple of Solomon.

To the above considerations, more could be added,[60] but perhaps we had better stop and hear Williamson's caution that the Chronicler's "handling of the dynastic oracle in 1 Chronicles 17 is but one element of this larger whole [i.e., the 'larger narrative structure' of Chronicles], and rash conclusions concerning his *Tendenz* should thus not be drawn hastily from a single text without further ado."[61] For our immediate purpose, however, it does not so much matter that we discover the precise nature of the Chronicler's *Tendenz* as that we recognize that he had a *Tendenz*—a desire to present Israel's history in a certain light and for a certain purpose—and that this has influenced his depiction of the dynastic promise.

What then have we learned from this brief comparison of Israel's synoptic histories? Does the fact that 2 Samuel and 1 Chronicles present the dynastic promise to David in distinctive ways present a problem for those who wish to take seriously the historiographical character of each? If both texts are given a flat reading, as if they were verbatim transcripts of the event, then the answer would have to be yes. But as we have tried to show in this chapter, historical reportage is often more akin to painting than

---

[60]We have not discussed, e.g., the Chronicler's avoidance of the term *rest* in his parallels to 2 Sam. 7:1, 11–12; see Dillard, "The Chronicler's Solomon," *WTJ* 43 (1980): 294.
[61]"Eschatology in Chronicles," p. 136.

photography. That the Chronicler should explicitly present what is implicitly present in his source is entirely acceptable. After all, we do this sort of thing everyday. Imagine that in response to an invitation, we are told, "I'm afraid that we shall be busy that evening." If we then bring home the report, "They said they couldn't come," we will not be accused of fabrication—we have only made explicit what is implicit in the literal reply. The Chronicler's more interpretive presentation, focusing as it does on the inner significance of the promise, is all the more justified inasmuch as he seems to assume knowledge of the Samuel version on the part of his audience. In short, what the comparison of the two renderings of the dynastic promise illustrates is the extent to which historians may be creative in their presentations, while at the same time remaining constrained by the facts.

CONCLUSION

We began this chapter by asking the question *What is history?* In the opening paragraphs, we noted that the term *history* is used in at least two different senses: history-as-event and history-as-account. While never losing sight of the former, we focused primarily on the latter, which might better be termed *historiography*. Because there is so much talk nowadays of *fictionality* in narrative, it was necessary also to investigate whether and in what sense this term might legitimately be applied to historiography. The conclusion reached was that since an account of something (just like a painting of something) is not literally that something, one may legitimately describe the account or the painting as in one sense *fictional*. We noted, however, that because the term *fiction* is also used to designate a genre of literature that is not constrained by any "something" external to it (i.e., by any *referential* constraint), the term is not ideally suited to discussions of historiography and could profitably be replaced by less ambiguous terms such as *artistry or crafting*.

Having noted the analogy between historiography and representational painting, we went on to explore the place of *creativity* even in depictions whose essential purpose is referential. The analogy alerted us to some of the characteristics of successful representation such as selectivity, slant, simplification, suggestive detail, and so forth. As to the adequacy and authority of representation, we saw that these issues very much depend on the competence and credentials of the (visual or narrative) artists, as well as on their access to their subject.

Finally, we looked briefly at the synoptic histories of the Old Testament: Samuel–Kings and Chronicles. We saw that, though these cover much the same territory historically speaking, they are anything but identical. While a flat reading of the two might lead to the conclusion that they are mutually contradictory, we noted that many of the differences between them can be better explained on the basis of their distinct purposes and audiences. We noted also that the Chronicler is not only himself acquainted with Samuel–Kings but apparently assumes a similar acquaintance on the part of his audience. This frees him to present his didactic history in creative ways, sometimes making explicit what may have been only implicit in his sources.

We conclude then that historiography involves a creative, though constrained, attempt to depict and interpret significant events or sequences of events from the past. In this chapter we have considered some of what might be said in answer to the question *What is history?* In the next we shall take up the question *Is historicity important?*

three

HISTORY

AND TRUTH

Is Historicity Important?

*I*n an essay entitled "On Reading the Bible Critically and Otherwise," Alan Cooper makes the statement that "the historicity of the events described in the Bible is irrelevant; indeed, the idea that either the meaning of the Bible or its truth depends on its historical accuracy is probably the silliest manifestation of historical criticism."[1] To readers conversant with current debates over method in biblical studies, this statement may not seem all that unusual,[2] but it is certainly extraordinary when measured against the standard of classic Christianity. The traditional answer to the question whether the historicity of certain central events is necessary to the Christian faith has been a resounding *yes!* The following observation by Norman Anderson may be taken as representative:

> It seems to me inescapable . . . that anyone who chanced to read the pages of the New Testament for the first time would come away with one overwhelming impression— that here is a faith that 'does not understand itself to be the discovering and imparting of generally valid, timeless truths,' but that is firmly based on certain allegedly historical events—a faith which would be false and misleading if those events had not actually taken place, but which, if they did take place, is unique in its relevance and exclusive in its demands on our allegiance.[3]

---

[1]In *Future of Biblical Studies,* ed. Friedman and Williamson, pp. 65–66.

[2]Cf., e.g., J. J. Collins, "Is a Critical Biblical Theology Possible?" in *The Hebrew Bible and Its Interpreters,* ed. W. H. Propp, B. Halpern, and D. N. Freedman (Winona Lake, Ind.: Eisenbrauns, 1990), p. 11: the value of biblical narratives for theology "lies in their functions as myth or story rather than in their historical accuracy." See also Brown (*History and Faith,* p. 74), who observes that "the contemporary cultural and intellectual climate has encouraged numerous attempts to cut faith loose from history," and then proceeds to note several examples.

[3]*Jesus Christ: The Witness of History* (Leicester: IVP, 1985), p. 14. Cf. also Nash, *Christian Faith,* pp. 11–12.

Anderson speaks of the New Testament, but what is true for the New Testament is true also for the Old. Mattitiahu Tsevat comments that "it should be evident that if Israelite history is removed from the theological edifice of divine redemption coming at the point of man's complete failure, God becomes whimsical, toying with mankind, or even turns into a gnostic deity."[4] G. E. Wright put it plainly when he said, "In biblical faith everything depends upon whether the central events actually occurred." The "central events," according to Wright, are "that there was an Exodus, that the nation [of Israel] was established at Mount Sinai, that it did obtain the land, that it did lose it subsequently, that Jesus did live, that he did die on a cross, and that he did appear subsequently to a large number of independent witnesses."[5]

As foundational as affirmations of this sort have been in traditional Christianity, the trend in much modern theological discussion has been in the direction indicated at the start of this chapter—the disavowal of the importance of history in favor of, say, *artistic* or *philosophical* truth. Already in 1906 Geerhardus Vos lamented what he perceived as a growing tendency to depreciate the importance of biblical historicity:

> For some time past the assertion has been made, and it is being made in our own day with greater confidence and insistence than ever, that our Christian faith and historical facts have very little or nothing to do with each other. Most frequently this assertion is made with reference to some one particular event of Sacred History, which has for the time being become the subject of debate from the point of view of its historicity. Those who incline to doubt the historical truthfulness of some such narrative as, e.g., that of the supernatural birth or the resurrection of the Saviour, or at least incline to consider it an open question, are, when their skepticism awakens remonstrance from the conservative side, ever ready with the answer that Christianity is something too great and too deep, too inward, ideal and vital to be dependent in its essence on this or that single occurrence in the world of history.[6]

What Vos perceived as a developing trend in his day is even more in evidence in our own. Stephen Prickett, for example, commenting on Hans Frei's *The Eclipse of Biblical Narrative*,[7] draws attention to the current popularity of interpretative strategies that avoid asking the hard historical questions:

> Central to Frei's strategy is the notion that so far from trying to regard biblical narrative as "history" in our modern post-Rankean sense, and thinking of it as "factual" or "non-factual," we should rather think of it as, in his words, "fact-like". . . . We should not ask of it, therefore, did this actually happen to real people like this? but is this "true-to-life," is this artistically true? In the present crisis over biblical studies, this is proving a popular strategy in many quarters.[8]

---

[4]"Israelite History," p. 178.

[5]*God Who Acts: Biblical Theology as Recital* (London: SCM, 1952), pp. 126–27.

[6]"Christian Faith and the Truthfulness of Bible History," *The Princeton Theological Review* 4 (1906): 289; I am indebted to my colleague David C. Jones for drawing my attention to this essay. See also J. Greshan Machen, "History and Faith," *PTR* 13 (1915): 337–51.

[7]Subtitle: *A Study in Eighteenth and Nineteenth Century Hermeneutics* (New Haven: Yale University Press, 1974).

[8]"Status of Biblical Narrative," *Pacifica* 2 (1989): 32. For a further critique of Frei's nonreferential theory of biblical literature, see Barton, *Reading the Old Testament*, pp. 158–79.

What are we to make of this? Is the truth of the Bible somehow tied up with historical questions, or is it not? If we are convinced (by our study of truth claims) that the Bible presents certain events as having occurred, must they have *actually* occurred for the Bible to be true? Might not the essence of biblical truth lie in its "true-to-life" quality, its "artistic truth"? Or might not the Bible's truth lie simply in the ideas, the philosophical system, that it propounds? Couldn't it be that current debates over biblical historicity are nothing more than the dying gasps of a bygone era that should now be quietly buried? After all, Jesus himself often expounded theological truth through unhistorical parables. Couldn't the Bible be one big parable and still teach us truth about God?

"WHAT IS TRUTH?"

Having posed the question of truth, Pilate in John 18:38 did not wait for an answer. His "What is truth?" was intended to dismiss the issue, not to pursue it. And having dismissed it, Pilate went on to play his part (hand-washing notwithstanding) in the most infamous deed of all history. The question of truth is a serious matter. Fortunately, it is not necessary for our present purposes to tackle this question in a broad theological or philosophical sense. Because God's word comes to us in the form of Scripture, our concern, rather, is with the kinds of truth that literature, and particularly narrative literature, can convey. But even this more narrowly defined question cannot be answered adequately in the space available here. Happily, Kevin Vanhoozer has already provided a useful treatment of the issue in "The Semantics of Biblical Literature: Truth and Scripture's Diverse Literary Forms."[9] After arguing convincingly that the principles of *speech-act theory*[10] can be usefully applied also to units of discourse above the sentence level, Vanhoozer explains how these larger literary forms relate to the question of truth.

> Truth, like Reality, is in one sense One. However, Reality is so rich and multifaceted that it, like white light, can only be conveyed (verbally) by an equally rich "spectrum"—diverse literary forms. While Truth may be "about" Reality (what *is*), we only receive the full picture of Reality (*what is*) by contemplating "true" history, "true" parable, "true" song, "true" poetry. That Scripture has many literary forms is no impediment to the Truth; instead, it is the very possibility of Truth's expression. The diversity of literary forms does not imply that Scripture contains competing kinds of Truth; it shows rather that Scripture is about various kinds of *fact* (i.e., historical, metaphysical, moral, etc.). A sentence or text is true if things are as it says they are, but as Aristotle observed, "Being may be said in many ways." (p. 85)

Thus the diversity of the Bible's literary forms does not imply a hierarchy in which some forms or genres are more revelatory than others, more truly the word of God. As Vanhoozer explains, "The Bible is divine discourse act. The 'divine' qualifies the literary forms of Scripture (the 'micro-genres,' as it were) and so renders them 'revelatory' (the 'macro-genre'). Revealed truth may be said in many ways" (p. 93).

Every form of discourse makes its own *truth claims*, and the *truth value* of different discourses must be assessed in terms of the truth claims of each, that is, in terms of what

---

[9] In *Hermeneutics, Authority, and Canon,* ed. Carson and Woodbridge, pp. 49–104. Cf. also Oja, "Fictional History," esp. pp. 115–16.

[10] For brief summaries of speech-act theory, see, in addition to Vanhoozer, also Stanford, *Nature,* p. 69; M. H. Abrams, *A Glossary of Literary Terms,* 4th ed. (New York: Holt, Rinehart and Winston, 1981), pp. 181–83.

each intends to communicate or accomplish. If parables, for example, are "stories designed to teach theological truth without reference to whether or not the events depicted within them actually happened,"[11] then it is incorrect to try to mine them for historical information and unfair to fault them if they fail to yield such. Parables are not to be read as history, for they imply no historical truth claim. This is an obvious point, and one that is universally acknowledged. But by the same token (and this point is not universally acknowledged), texts that do imply a historical truth claim must not be read as if they didn't, at least not if one's purpose is exegesis. The prologue to Luke's gospel (1:1–4), for example, offers the most explicit statement of intent of all the gospels. Noting that "many have undertaken to draw up an account of the things that have been fulfilled among us," Luke states his intention to write his own "orderly account," after having "carefully investigated everything from the beginning." That a historical truth claim is being made is unmistakable.[12] One may choose to deny the truth value of Luke's account, but one is simply not free to read Luke as if no historical truth claim has been made.

To return then to the question posed earlier—"Couldn't the Bible be one big parable and still teach us truth about God?"—it would appear now that the question is moot, for the truth claims of the Bible simply do not allow us that option. In some of its parts— the so-called historical books of the Old Testament, for example, or the Gospels and the book of Acts in the New—the Bible makes fairly unmistakable historical truth claims.[13] The motive of its historiography as well as its standards of representation may differ from the political/sociological motive and minimalist approach of much modern historiography. But it can hardly be denied that it presents many of its stories—and, more particularly, the central thread of its one Story—as reflecting a real, and not simply a fictive, past. But still the question might be asked, *Is it not at least* hypothetically *possible that God could have taught us all we need to know about him without ever entering history?* After all, "Jesus' teaching in parables highlights how narrative prose can communicate theological truth by means of realistic but fictitious stories."[14] Could not biblical *faith* survive even if biblical *history* were destroyed? The answer of classic Christianity to this question is that it could not—and for good reason, as we shall see below.

THE IMPORTANCE OF HISTORY FOR CHRISTIAN FAITH

Irrespective of questions of textual truth claims, in the current climate of biblical scholarship many voices are being raised to challenge the importance of history for Christian faith, as we noted at the beginning of this chapter. We shall discover below that some of the challenges are rooted in a worldview and a way of reasoning introduced by Enlightenment thinkers of the eighteenth and nineteenth centuries. Others find their impetus in modern trends in literary criticism (to be discussed in chap. 4), while some arise from

[11]Blomberg, *Historical Reliability,* p. 238.

[12]So, e.g., T. Callan, "The Preface of Luke-Acts and Historiography," *New Testament Studies* 31 (1985): 580: "The stated purpose of Luke-Acts seems to mark it as a history . . . written to provide a true account of something." A historical truth claim is also implied in, e.g., John 20:30–31; 21:24–25.

[13]With respect to the Old Testament, see, e.g., Tsevat, "Israelite History," p. 184; Halpern, *First Historians,* pp. 97, 181; Smelik, *Converting the Past: Studies in Ancient Israelite and Moabite Historiography,* Oudtestamentische Studiën 28 (Leiden: E. J. Brill, 1992), p. 19; with respect to the New, see Trigg, "Tales artfully spun," pp. 129–30; Powell, *What Is Narrative Criticism?* p. 3; Hemer, *Book of Acts,* p. 85.

[14]Blomberg, *Historical Reliability,* p. 255.

a misapplication of valid insights into the multifaceted nature of truth, noted above. But this myriad of voices notwithstanding, history, or more precisely the historicity of certain core events recorded in the Old and New Testaments, is indispensable to the vitality and even validity of the Christian faith. This is especially true, as Vos forcefully argues, "in regard to the soteriological, or, if another more popular term be preferred, the evangelical character of Christianity."[15] One's assessment of the importance of history for faith will be a more or less direct reflection of one's understanding of the *essence* of Christianity. On this vital point, Vos's argument is worthy of quotation at some length.

> Let us suppose for a moment that our religion aimed at nothing more than the disclosure of a system of truth for the spiritual enlightenment of mankind—that there were no sins to atone and no hearts to regenerate and no world to transform. In that case its connection with historical facts would have to be regarded as a purely incidental matter, established for the sake of a more vivid presentation of the truth, and therefore separable from the essence of the truth itself. Obviously, further, it would on this supposition be of no consequence whether the historical mold into which the truth was cast consisted of a record of actual events, or of mythical and legendary lore having only a partial basis in facts, or of conscious literary fiction having no basis of facts at all. The same will apply to every view of religion which makes the action of truth consist exclusively in the moral suasion exercised by it on the human mind. It is plain, however, that both these conceptions of the function of Christianity, the intellectualistic as well as the moralizing, are tenable only from the standpoint of Pelagianism with its defective sense of sin. To the Christian Church, in the most catholic sense of the word, supernatural religion has always stood for something far more than a system of spiritual instruction or an instrument of moral suasion. The deep sense of sin, which is central in her faith, demands such a divine interposition in the course of natural development as shall work actual changes from guilt to righteousness, from sin to holiness, from life to death, in the sphere not merely of consciousness but of being. Here revelation is on principle inseparable from a background of historic facts, with which to bring man's life into vital contact is indeed the main reason for its existence. . . .
>
> If what has been said be correct, it will follow that the proposal to declare the facts inessential betrays a lamentably defective appreciation of the soteriological character of Christianity. As a matter of fact, if one carefully examines the representations of those who claim that the results of criticism leave the religious substance of the Old Testament intact, one finds in each case that the truth left intact belongs to the sphere of natural religion and has no direct bearing on the question of sin and salvation. Such truths as monotheism and the ethical nature of God may still be found in the reconstructed Old Testament; what we look for in vain is the Gospel of redemption.[16]

For those, like the present author, who share Vos's view of the essence of Christianity, he makes a strong case that the central salvific events of the Gospel must be historical for Christian faith to be valid.[17] But what of the other, less central events recorded in biblical narrative? Need they too be historical? While it may be admitted that the validity of the Christian faith is not dependent on the historicity of events peripheral to the central flow of redemptive history, this does not mean that the question of historicity can simply be dismissed out of hand. The crucial question is again what *truth claims*

---

[15]"Christian Faith," p. 299.
[16]Ibid., pp. 299–300.
[17]For a more recent defense of this basic position, see Blomberg, *Historical Reliability*, pp. 57–58.

are implied by each narrative within its broader context. Finding answers to this question is not always a simple matter, and some narratives (e.g., Gen. 1–11; the patriarchal narratives) or even whole books (e.g., Job, Jonah, Esther) will undoubtedly continue to elicit debate. But as Vos points out, the nature of God's work in Christ does create a certain presumption in favor of the historicity of other events in Scripture, even of those that by ordinary standards would seem quite fabulous: "If we can show that revealed religion is inseparably linked to a system of supernatural historical facts at its culminating epoch in Christ," then "it is certainly reasonable to assume that God will have adjusted the course of things that led up to Christ, to the fundamental character of the work of Christ—in the sense that He will have scattered over it great miraculous interpositions, to shadow forth the true nature of redemption, and, more than this, that He will have hung it not on the slender thread of legend or fiction, but on the solid chain of actual history."[18]

Again I must stress that the discernment of each text's truth claims is of primary importance, for it is no good defending a text with respect to claims that it never makes. For example, in the controversial matter of the historicity of the patriarchal narratives, George Ramsey is in principle correct that "a different form-critical analysis of the patriarchal narratives might be offered, with attendant implications for the historical reliability of the stories,"[19] and indeed Ramsey himself comes to a rather minimalist conclusion: "Figures like Abraham and Jacob became in time paradigmatic figures rather like the figures of the 'prodigal son' or the 'good Samaritan' of Jesus' parables; were they such from the beginning?"[20] But as we argued in the preceding chapter, such questions should not be decided without careful consideration of the overall purpose of the larger discourse in which the smaller plays a part. If Ramsey's last question were to be answered in the affirmative, then Abraham and Jacob would become not so much *sources* of faith as the *products* of faith. John Goldingay's consideration of the patriarchal narratives in the light of the broader sweep of the Bible leads him to the opposite conclusion—"not that faith creates Abraham, but that Abraham creates faith."[21] Like Ramsey, Goldingay sets out to discover whether the stories of the patriarchs are "more like a parable or a gospel" (p. 35). By this he means to ask whether or not the patriarchal narratives have an "implied vested interest . . . in the historicity of the events they narrate." He asks:

> Are they the kind of stories that could be completely fictional but still be coherent and carry conviction? A parable is fictional, but nevertheless carries conviction on the basis of who it is that tells it and of the validity of his world-view as it expresses it. A gospel, however, invites commitment to the person portrayed in it, and in my view this implies that it cannot be both fictional and true. The kind of response it invites demands that the events it narrates bear a reasonably close relationship to events that took place at the time. Without this it cannot be coherent and carry conviction. In the absence of reference, it cannot even really have sense. (p. 35)

---

[18]"Christian Faith," pp. 301–2. Cf. J. Goldingay, *Approaches to Old Testament Interpretation*, rev. ed. (Leicester: Apollos, 1990), p. 81.

[19]*The Quest for the Historical Israel: Reconstructing Israel's Early History* (London: SCM, 1982), p. 12.

[20]Ibid., p. 44.

[21]"The Patriarchs in Scripture and History," in *Essays on the Patriarchal Narratives*, ed. A. R. Millard and D. J. Wiseman (Leicester: IVP, 1980), p. 37.

In the course of his discussion Goldingay disputes in particular T. L. Thompson's contention, in *The Historicity of the Patriarchal Narratives*,[22] that these narratives need have no historical value whatsoever to be true. While he grants some validity to Thompson's criticism of the "Wright-Bright-Albright approach to biblical history," which in its over-stress on *event* tends to ignore "the revelation in word or in language embodied in the Bible itself," he points out that Thompson's view is equally guilty of ignoring and even deny-ing the *event aspect* of revelation. For Goldingay, "Event and word are both part of reve-lation." This truth can be most clearly seen when the patriarchal narratives are "set in a subsequent literary and historical context." Goldingay writes:

> First, Yahweh's words to the patriarchs constitute the divine undertaking fulfilled in the exodus and conquest. They constitute Israel's charter for her possession of the land of Canaan. They explain how this was Yahweh's gift rather than the Israelites' desert. They set Israel's position in the land in the context of the sweep of a divine pur-pose concerned with the destiny of the nations. If the patriarchal narrative is pure fiction (which Thompson suggests it may well be), is anything lost? Surely much is, because the exodus-conquest narrative grounds its statements of faith in these events. If the events did not take place, the grounds of faith are removed. (p. 36)

Goldingay demonstrates how biblical writers viewed present faith as resting on prior events by citing Isaiah 51:1–2 and reflecting on the significance of the prophet's exhortation.

> *Hearken to me, you who pursue deliverance,*
> *you who seek Yahweh,*
> *Look to the rock from which you were hewn,*
> *and to the quarry from which you were digged.*
> *Look to Abraham your father*
> *and to Sarah who bore you,*
> *for when he was but one I called him,*
> *and I blessed him and made him many.* (Isa. 51:1–2)

Goldingay comments: "*on Thompson's thesis it does not matter that the call, the blessing, and the increase of Abraham are imaginative creations of faith! The prophet's position seems to be the opposite.*" It is (if we may say it again) "not that faith creates Abraham, but that Abraham creates faith" (p. 37).

Is historicity important? Perhaps enough has been said, even in this very brief treat-ment, to suggest that without the historicity of the central events of the biblical story truly *biblical* faith cannot survive. Goldingay has argued this point convincingly from the Old Testament, and the same is of course true of the New. Roger Trigg concludes his essay on the centrality of historicity to the message of the New Testament with these words:

> To suggest that an account (or *logos*) can carry a meaning even if it is based on lying or mistaken witness is not in the spirit of the New Testament. We may wish to reject parts of what is written. What we cannot do is to suspend our belief in what actually happened and still be guided by the 'message' of the putative events. Keeping the mes-sage of a story while denying its truth, is to treat the accounts as *muthoi* and not *logoi*. It is like trying to hold on to the grin while the Cheshire Cat has long since departed.[23]

---

[22]Subtitle: *The Quest for the Historical Abraham* (Berlin: Walter de Gruyter, 1974).
[23]"Tales artfully spun," p. 132.

In the light of the truth claims of Scripture and the most widely agreed upon understanding of the essence of the Christian religion, it simply cannot be denied that the historicity of certain events is vitally necessary to true Christian faith. But, of course, simply to acknowledge this necessity in no way proves that the relevant events took place. Moreover, even could the bare events be conclusively demonstrated, this would still fall short of proof that they have been accurately interpreted by the biblical writers. In the end, one's acceptance of the biblical construal of events will very much depend on one's confidence in the biblical testimony, or (to use terms from the preceding chapter) on one's convictions regarding the adequacy and authority of the biblical representations.

One way to express the relationship of event and interpretation is to say that while the factuality of the core events of redemptive history is a necessary condition of the truth of the Christian faith, it is not a sufficient condition thereof.[24] This means that any faith that can properly call itself Christian can never entirely insulate itself from the findings of historical study. Faith does not require that the factuality of the biblical events be proven (such proof is, at any rate, seldom possible). On the other hand, should it be conclusively shown that the core events of redemptive history did not happen, not only would the veracity of the Bible be seriously undermined, but the fall of historicity would inevitably bring down Christian faith with it. It is imperative, then, that we consider carefully the challenges that have been issued against the historicity of the Bible's central events.

THE (POST–)ENLIGHTENMENT CHALLENGE TO THE IMPORTANCE OF HISTORY FOR FAITH

Biblical scholarship is seldom unaffected by the intellectual currents and cross-currents of its own day. As Brevard Childs remarks in his *Introduction to the Old Testament as Scripture*, "The rise of the modern historical study of the Old Testament must be seen in connection with the entire intellectual revolution which occurred during the late sixteenth and early seventeenth centuries, and which issued in a radically different understanding of God, man, and the world" (p. 34). It was in the eighteenth-century Enlightenment in Europe that these radically new understandings came to full flower. Associated with such thinkers as Reimarus (1694–1768), Kant (1724–1804), Lessing (1729–1781), and Mendelssohn (1729–1786) in Germany, Voltaire (1694–1778), Rousseau (1712–1778), and Diderot (1713–1784) in France, and Locke (1632–1704), Newton (1642–1727), and Gibbon (1737–1794) in England,[25] the Enlightenment (or Age of Reason) has been characterized as a time when "increasing scientific knowledge gave rise to the development of empiricist, naturalist, and materialist doctrines and strong opposition to clericalism."[26] It was a time when human reason, and human reason alone, was deemed worthy of trust.

"Enlightenment," according to Kant, entails "man's release from his self-incurred tutelage," a tutelage defined as "man's inability to make use of his understanding without direction from another."[27] This call to emancipate human reason from all external constraints

---

[24]Cf. Goldingay, *Approaches to Old Testament Interpretation,* p. 77.
[25]The dates are as in *The Encyclopedia of Philosophy*, ed. P. Edwards, 8 vols. (New York: Macmillan, 1967), ad loc.
[26]*A Dictionary of Philosophy*, ed. A. Flew (London: Macmillan, 1979), p.106.
[27]The quote is from Kant's "Beantwortung der Frage: Was ist Aufklärung?" ("Reply to the Question: What is Enlightenment?"), cited by Brown, *History and Faith*, p. 13, q.v. for further bibliography.

finds full expression in the writings of German-born French *philosophe* Holbach (1723–1789). Beginning with the premise that "Man is unhappy because he is ignorant of Nature," Holbach in his *Système de la nature* (1770) laid out an agenda for addressing this problem. His main ideas have been summarized as follows:

> Nature, he [Holbach] maintains, is knowable through human experience and thought, and explanations should not be sought in traditional beliefs or the alleged "revelations" of the Church. There is a fundamental continuity between man and the rest of nature, between animal and human behaviour; all natural phenomena, including mental ones, are explicable in terms of the organization and activity of matter. Religion and extranatural beliefs inculcate habits inhibiting enquiry and the acquisition of the knowledge that is necessary to achieve the fundamental aims of man: happiness and self-preservation.[28]

Though characterized as "the foremost exponent of atheistic materialism and the most intransigent polemicist against religion in the Enlightenment,"[29] Holbach's views differed from those of many of his contemporaries more in degree than in kind.[30]

D. F. STRAUSS AND THE DEMOLITION OF BIBLICAL HISTORY

Of particular interest for the history of biblical studies up to the present are two other names—one the Enlightenment thinker Reimarus (already mentioned) and the other D. F. Strauss, a nineteenth-century German theologian who was deeply influenced by Reimarus. The literary offerings and intellectual impact of both of these men are well summarized by Robert Morgan in a chapter entitled "Criticism and the Death of Scripture."[31] Reimarus was a deist. He "believed in God, but not in revelation, miracles, or other supernatural interventions." In keeping with these beliefs, Reimarus was among the first to write "a non-supernatural, historical account of Christian origins in which he anticipated many of the insights of twentieth-century 'history of traditions' research on the Gospels" (p. 53). Many of Reimarus's views were subsequently adopted by Strauss, who, after correcting and refining them, set himself the task of, as he saw it, rescuing Christianity in an age when the central tenets of historic Christianity were no longer rationally viable or intellectually responsible. In this respect his program was more positive in intent, if not in result, than that of Reimarus. As Morgan explains, "Strauss thought he was doing Christianity a favour, Reimarus had no such illusions" (p. 54).

Strauss's rescue operation was to entail two phases: a "critical destruction of the Gospel history" followed by a "theological reconstruction of Christian belief" (p. 45). It was to the former endeavor that Strauss dedicated more than seven hundred pages of his massive *The Life of Jesus Critically Examined* (first published in German in 1835),[32] while his program for theological reconstruction, which was meant to "re-establish dogmatically

---

[28]*Dictionary of Philosophy*, ed. Flew, p. 106.

[29]Aram Vartanian, "Holbach," in *Encyclopedia*, ed. P. Edwards, 4:49.

[30]To be fair, it should be noted that Holbach was one of the Enlightenment "minor thinkers" and, therefore, to be counted among the "terrible simplifiers" unworthy of the major figures of the period. Nevertheless, it was just such a simplified version of Enlightenment thinking that impressed itself on the "great audience of the enlightened"; see C. Brinton, "Enlightenment," in *Encyclopedia*, ed. Edwards, 2: 525.

[31]*Biblical Interpretation*, pp. 44–57.

[32]The standard English edition is edited, with introduction, by P. C. Hodgson (New York: Fortress, 1972).

[i.e., at the theological level] that which has been destroyed critically [i.e., at the histor-ical level],"[33] received only brief treatment in the final twenty-eight pages. Strauss's "philo-sophical theology," as distinct from the history-centered theology of traditional Chris-tianity, was to have been worked out fully in a later volume, but this was never written. Not surprisingly, then, it was Strauss's massive assault on the historicity of the Gospels that had the greatest impact on his contemporaries and on subsequent biblical scholarship.

It is worth noting at this juncture that others in addition to Reimarus influenced Strauss in ways that facilitated his attack on biblical historicity. As Morgan explains,

> His critical aim of demolishing the historicity of the Gospel records was a first step in the programme of a theologian who had learned from Kant that the historical could serve only for illustration, from Lessing that there was a 'big, ugly ditch' between the truths of history and the truths of reason, and finally from Hegel how to get theolog-ical truth from these largely unhistorical Gospel records.[34]

Thus, Strauss formulated his ideas in an atmosphere in which the importance of history for faith was already diminished. If for Kant, history was useful only as illustration, might not *parable* or, as Strauss preferred, *myth* serve just as well? Lessing also viewed history as of limited value, as is evidenced by his oft-quoted assertion: "Accidental truths of his-tory can never become the proof of necessary truths of reason." Henry Chadwick sheds light on this cryptic statement by pointing out that it

> presupposes on the one hand the epistemology of Leibniz, with its sharp distinction between necessary truths of reason (mathematically certain and known a priori) and contingent truths (known by sense perception), and on the other hand the thesis of Spinoza's *Tractatus Theologico-politicus*, that the truth of a historical narrative, how-ever certain, cannot give us the knowledge of God, which should be derived from general ideas that are themselves certain and known.[35]

For Lessing then, as Gordon Michalson explains, "authentic faith is rational and potentially universalizable, meaning that it does not hang on the acceptance of any historical facts; and historical revelations do not introduce new and indispensable religious information but sim-ply illustrate, or bring into our field of vision, what we are capable of knowing all along."[36]

Kant, Lessing, Hegel, Reimarus—against this background of influences it is appar-ent that Strauss was very much a man of his own time, a time when the underestimation of the importance of history was matched only by the overestimation of the potency and potential of autonomous human reason. Strauss differed from his predecessors not so much in theory as in the relentless energy with which he put theory to practice in the form of a frontal attack on the historicity of the Gospels and the "title-deeds" of the Christian faith. Not surprisingly, the publication of Strauss's *Life of Jesus* caused outrage in Christendom and proved very costly for Strauss's career,[37] for its "non-supernatural account of Jesus and

---

[33]Strauss, *Life of Jesus*, p. 757; cited with explanatory insertions by Morgan, Biblical Interpretation, p. 45.
[34]Ibid., p. 47.
[35]"Lessing, Gotthold Ephraim," in *Encyclopedia*, ed. Edwards, 4: 445.
[36]*Lessing's "Ugly Ditch": A Study of Theology and History* (University Park: Pennsylvania State Uni-versity Press, 1985), p. 39.
[37]Morgan (*Biblical Interpretation*, p. 44) reports that "Strauss lost his post in Tübingen, and when in 1839 a liberal government in Zurich offered him a professorship the people rebelled, the government fell, and the young offender was pensioned off before he arrived."

early Christianity was inevitably an anti-supernatural account. If the historian had no need of that hypothesis (God), why should anyone else adopt it? Modern rationalism held a dagger to the heart of Christianity."[38]

After Strauss

Despite the furor that Strauss's *Life of Jesus* evoked, it is not inaccurate to say that his approach "opened a new era in Western religious thought."[39] Does this mean that Strauss's views won the day? A twofold answer is required. Strauss's theological program failed, but his exegetical method, with its systematic undermining of confidence in the historicity of the Gospels, endured among many scholars.[40] Again, Morgan's historical survey of scholarship in *Biblical Interpretation* (chaps. 3 and 4) is helpful. Contemporary with Strauss were two other scholars whose works were to prove highly influential in the history of biblical criticism: Old Testament scholar Wilhelm Vatke (1806–1882), who was to have a profound influence on Julius Wellhausen (1844–1918), and New Testament professor Ferdinand Christian Baur (1792–1860), known as the founder of the *Tübingen school* of radical historical criticism. All three, Strauss, Baur, and Vatke, "followed Reimarus in opting for a rational, historical, i.e. non-supernatural, account of Israel and of Christian origins" (p. 68). And all three were also in one way or another influenced by Hegel to believe that theological truth was not dependent in any essential respect on historical truth. Strauss, for example, credited Hegel with freeing "him for untrammelled academic work by convincing him that 'the essence of the Christian faith is perfectly independent' of historical criticism."[41] The sad irony in all this is that the brand of Hegelian theology by which Strauss and others thought to safeguard the Christian faith soon faded, leaving only their erosion of confidence in biblical historicity as their legacy.

The history of interpretation since Strauss is marked by a variety of responses to the wedge that had been driven between history and theology. In the mid-to-late nineteenth century, Baur and Wellhausen, for example, led a "shift away from synthesizing the new historical knowledge with philosophical and theological convictions to a new historical realism that was hostile to philosophical and theological speculation."[42] In the twentieth century, Gerhard von Rad (1901–1971), following the lead of Hermann Gunkel (1862–1932), tried to swing the pendulum in the other direction by reintroducing a theological focus in biblical interpretation. This attempt, however, did not include an effort to restore confidence in biblical historicity. What mattered for von Rad was not so much what actually happened in, say, the Exodus event, but how the Exodus had been theologically construed in Israel's traditions. Von Rad cared less for the event than for the tradition that arose about the event.[43] As Goldingay has observed, von Rad ultimately found himself "retelling the history of the development of Israel's faith in God's acts in history (contrary to his overt intention), not retelling the acts of God."[44]

---

[38]Ibid., p. 54.
[39]Ibid., p. 45.
[40]Cf. ibid., p. 47.
[41]Ibid., pp. 62–63 (citing Strauss, *Life of Jesus*, p. lii).
[42]Ibid., p. 93.
[43]Cf. ibid., pp. 99–100.
[44]*Approaches to Old Testament Interpretation*, p. 72.

The difference between von Rad's brand of salvation-history—a kind of traditio-historical idealism—and the history of salvation espoused by traditional Christianity is pronounced and problematic, as Morgan notes: "Taken at face value, the Old Testament depicts the history of Israel as a history of salvation, in the straightforward sense that God himself was the agent of all the great events which the Old Testament records" (p. 101). "How," then, "can we locate 'revelation' in the process that led Israel to develop and eventually to 'canonize' traditions, when the explicit content of these traditions states that revelation is actually located somewhere else, namely, in certain things that God has said and done?" The last phrase, "said and done," is key and is suggestive of how the relationship between event and tradition can be understood. Though he does not develop the point, Morgan notes that "it is quite consistent to claim that divine Providence both directed *events* in a certain way in Israel's history and controlled the *traditions* that grew up to interpret those events in such an unerring way that they were correctly interpreted: one can, that is, consistently locate revelation in both events *and* traditions" (p. 102).

This seems to me to be the most promising approach—*divine revelation should be located in both historical events and the interpretative word which mediates these events to us.* It also seems to be the approach that is most in keeping with the biblical witness itself. Nevertheless, for some time now the hermeneutic pendulum in biblical studies has continued to swing back and forth between the two poles of *event* and *word*. One extreme position excites a reaction, which then leads to the opposite extreme, which in turn excites a counter-reaction, and on it goes. In the 1950s and 60s, for example, the Albright-Wright-Bright school, reacting to the depreciation of biblical history early in this century, laid great stress on the historical events, the "mighty acts of God" in actual history. More recently, as already noted, T. L. Thompson (among others) has launched a counter-reaction. After charging Albright and company (particularly G. E. Wright) with adopting "a deistic and positivistic historicism" that leaves "very little room for any theology of the word," Thompson has in essence tried to push the pendulum back to the other extreme, stressing the importance of the *word* irrespective of the *event*.[45] For Thompson, "salvation history did not happen," and it doesn't matter! What matters is "the reality and the truth of the human experience which transcends the historical forms in which this experience has been expressed."[46] And so the pendulum swings. Most recently the trend in some quarters has been toward ahistorical varieties of literary criticism, but I shall reserve discussion of this trend until the next chapter.

What is needed, I would argue, is to bring the pendulum to a halt in the middle, where it does not lose touch with either historical event or interpretive word. Again to invoke an analogy from painting, the question can be put this way, "What is of essential importance in a portrait by a great master, the subject itself as a historical person or the masterful interpretation of the subject?" Surely both are important. Even to ask the question in this way is to assume a false dichotomy. Art critics may tend to focus on the artistry of the rendering, while historians may be more interested in what can be learned of the historical personage portrayed, but neither should mistake their particular interest for the full significance of the painting. If historians ignore the painterly aspect (that is, if

---

[45]*Historicity,* p. 327. For a critical evaluation of the Thompson vs. Wright debate, see Goldingay, "Patriarchs," pp. 35–40.

[46]*Historicity,* pp. 328, 330.

they lack understanding and appreciation of the artistic medium), they may easily "misread" the portrait or unjustly criticize it as an inadequate representation of the subject. Or worse, if they discount the significance of the portrait simply because it is an *artistic interpretation*, they thereby cut themselves off from perhaps their only source of historical information about the subject. On the other hand, should art critics, in their appreciation of the artistic genius of the painter, lose sight of the painting's *referential character*, they would miss something of the painting's essential purpose and so prove themselves to be poor critics. A similar dynamic obtains in the study of biblical historiography. What is needed is the ability to do full justice to both the subject and the historian's (the artist's) particular interpretation. In other words, both event and interpretive word are important. This, at least, seems to be the Bible's own view of the matter. As G. B. Caird explains, after considering the Exodus and the crucifixion,

> the most important item in the framework within which the people of biblical times interpreted their history was the conviction that God was lord of history. He uttered his voice and events followed (Isa. 55:11–12). Thus the course of events was itself a quasi-linguistic system, in which God was disclosing his character and purpose. . . . The interpretation of God's history-language required the exercise of moral judgment (Jer. 15:19; cf. Heb. 5:14), and it was the task of the prophet to be the qualified interpreter. . . . The prophet thus discharged for his people the kind of responsibility which in this chapter we have been ascribing to the historian.[47]

God, the "lord of history"; the prophet, His "qualified interpreter"; the result: *authoritative testimony to event through the word*. Does this not solve the problem? Does not this combination provide a sound basis for a historically grounded Christian theology? Some biblical scholars have consistently answered this question in the affirmative. Many others, however, encounter greater difficulties. As inheritors of the legacy of Strauss, many find themselves in the uncomfortable position of accepting some of Strauss's major tenets while denying others. They agree with Strauss's historical skepticism and assume a worldview that, if not identical to Strauss's in every respect, is at least closer to his than to the worldview evidenced in the Bible. But at the same time (and this is where the problem comes in), they no longer accept Strauss's ahistorical, philosophical theology. Though still largely convinced by the radical historical criticism promoted by Strauss, they are unable to share with him the view that the Christian faith can survive quite well without a foundation in history. Morgan puts it this way:

> Christian theology is reflection on a faith in God, which centres on the incarnate, crucified, and risen Lord Jesus. This faith is nourished by the Gospel story and stories. Such a faith does not need the historical reality of Jesus to be laid bare or fully disclosed. But it does need to know that it is based on that historical reality, and that it has nothing to fear from historical research.[48]

In short, Christianity needs a grounding in history, but the Bible, for the heirs of Strauss, appears inadequate to provide such grounding.

---

[47]*Language and Imagery,* pp. 217–18. On the "rhetorical signification" of God's actions in history, see also Patrick and Scult, *Rhetoric and Biblical Interpretation,* p. 31.

[48]*Biblical Interpretation,* p. 121.

D. F. Strauss's Criteria for Detecting the Unhistorical: An Evaluation

From their first publication Strauss's ideas encountered strong opposition from some of Europe's most notable scholars. Bishop J. B. Lightfoot, for example, lauded as "the greatest English biblical scholar of the nineteenth century," voiced a sentiment that countless others from his own day to the present would echo: "I cannot pretend to be indifferent about the veracity of the records which profess to reveal him whom I believe to be not only the very Truth but the very Life."[49] Lightfoot was certainly not alone in his insistence on the importance of the historical accuracy of the Gospels. Indeed, "The outstanding critical historians of the English Church, Thirlwall, Lightfoot, and Stubbs, . . . were all," as Morgan puts it, "'pre-critical' in their attitudes to the Gospels."[50] That Morgan can speak of the English church's outstanding *critical* historians as *pre-critical* suggests something of the ambiguity that inheres in the term *critical*. When certain scholars are branded as pre-critical in their approach to Scripture, is the implication that they have not yet developed the capacity to *think critically* (a charge that would be unjustified in a great number of cases) or that they are hesitant to *find fault* (their conviction of the authority of Scripture disallowing commitment to at least some principles of post-Enlightenment rationalism)? It would further understanding if such distinctions were made whenever the pre-critical charge is made.[51]

Lighfoot's emphasis was very much in line with the import of the New Testament witness itself. Commenting on the First Epistle of John, for example, G. B. Caird stresses the importance that history held for the writers of the New Testament:

> According to John there is no Christianity apart from the solid reality of the earthly life of Jesus recorded in the apostolic tradition. . . . Eternal life remains an unsubstantial dream unless in one man's life it has become earthly reality. . . . Without the Jesus of history we know neither the Christ of faith nor the God he came to reveal.[52]

In view of the magnitude of the issues at stake, it will be worthwhile to take a closer look at Strauss's own criteria for detecting unhistorical materials in the Gospels. These he develops in the Introduction to *The Life of Jesus* in a section entitled "Criteria by which to distinguish the unhistorical in the Gospel narrative" (pp. 87–92). Strauss divides his criteria into two kinds: *negative* criteria by which one can detect what is *not history*, and *positive* criteria by which one can detect what is *fiction*, i.e., "the product of the particular mental tendency of a certain community" (p. 87). The negative criteria are basically two, the first of which relates to worldview. An account is not historical, according to Strauss, when

> the narration is irreconcilable with the known and the universal laws which govern the course of events. Now according to these laws, agreeing with all just *philosophical conceptions* and all credible *experience*, the absolute cause [God] never disturbs the chain of secondary causes by single *arbitrary acts of interposition*, but rather manifests

---

[49] Ibid., p. 46.

[50] Ibid.

[51] There is clearly a need for a *criticism* of the sort described by Thistleton ("On Models and Methods," p. 348)—viz. "critical detachment and checking [which] *follows* the immediacy of engagement" with the biblical text. We shall return to the question of *criticism* in our discussion of the historical-critical method in the next chapter.

[52] *Language and Imagery*, pp. 215–16.

itself in the production of the aggregate of finite causalities, and of their reciprocal action. When therefore we meet an account of certain phenomena or events of which it is either expressly stated or implied that they were produced immediately by God himself (divine apparitions—voices from heaven and the like), or by human beings possessed of supernatural powers (miracles, prophecies), such an account is *in so far* to be considered as not historical. (p. 88)[53]

Strauss's argument can be reduced to the following syllogism:

1. All accounts irreconcilable with the known and universal laws that govern events are unhistorical.

2. All accounts in which God disturbs the natural course of events are irreconcilable with the known and universal laws that govern events.

3. Therefore, all accounts in which God disturbs the natural course of events are unhistorical.

This syllogism is logically valid, but its conclusion is sound only if each of its premises is true. In this regard, Strauss's argument is vulnerable. But we shall postpone discussion of *divine intervention* until the next chapter.

The second of Strauss's negative criteria relates to matters of *internal consistency* and *external noncontradiction*: "An account which shall be regarded as historically valid, must neither be inconsistent with itself, nor in contradiction with other accounts" (p. 88). This twofold criterion of consistency and noncontradiction is sound, so long as proper notions of consistency and contradiction are applied. But this is precisely where disagreements arise. What constitutes a genuine inconsistency or contradiction? The challenges inherent in making such judgments are highlighted by Walter Moberly in a discussion of Old Testament source criticism. He notes that while the "reconstruction of sources is . . . entirely dependent upon unevennesses and difficulties in the present text—doublets, contradictions, anachronisms, variant linguistic usages, divergent theological emphases, etc.," the challenge "is to determine what constitutes a genuine unevenness."[54] To illustrate the possibility of divergent assessments of the same textual phenomena, Moberly compares two quite different reactions to the description of the rising of the flood waters in Genesis 7:17–20. The text reads as follows:

> For forty days the flood kept coming on the earth, and as *the waters increased* they lifted the ark high above the earth. 18 The *waters rose and increased greatly* on the earth, and the ark floated on the surface of the water. 19 The *waters rose very greatly* on the earth, and all the high mountains under the entire heavens were covered. 20 The *waters rose* and covered the mountains to a depth of more than twenty feet.[55]

---

[53]The insertion [God] and all italics, apart from the last, are mine. As subsidiary points, Strauss cites also the so-called "law of succession, in accordance with which all occurrences, not excepting the most violent convulsions and the most rapid changes, follow in a certain order of sequence of increase and decrease" and "all those psychological laws, which render it improbable that a human being should feel, think, and act in a manner directly opposed to his own habitual mode and that of men in general." These subsidiary criteria are to be "cautiously applied, and in conjunction only with other tests," since they may be less reliable when it comes of "men of genius" (p. 88).

[54]R. W. L. Moberly, *At the Mountain of God: Story and Theology in Exodus 32–34*, JSOTS 22 (Sheffield: JSOT, 1983), p. 23.

[55]The English translation generally follows the NIV, though the italics are mine and a few phrases have been changed to approximate more closely the Hebrew text and to draw attention to the repetition of key phrases.

For Richard Simon, in his *Histoire critique du Vieux Testament*, the repetitions are indicative of multiple authorship: "Is it not reasonable to suppose that if one and the same writer had been describing that event, he would have done so in far fewer words, especially in a history?" For Bernard W. Anderson, on the other hand, the repetitions constitute a dramatic literary device to convey a sense of the water's progressive ascent.[56] Thus, Simon's signal of disunity is Anderson's mark of aesthetic dexterity; one man sees composite authorship, while the other sees authorial competence. Who is right? In view of the now widely recognized use of repetition as a rhetorical device in Old Testament narrative, Anderson's interpretation seems by far the more convincing.

This simple example is indicative of the difficulties that can arise in attempting to apply the second of Strauss's negative criteria, which states that inconsistencies and contradictions prove a text unhistorical.[57] What constitutes a genuine inconsistency or contradiction is very much a matter of opinion and literary judgment. The insights being gained in the study of narrative poetics, for example, often call for reassessing negative historical judgments of the kind pioneered by Strauss. Advances in historical understanding and reconstruction will likely take place only as more readers of the Bible recognize the necessity of attaining sufficient literary competence to approach biblical texts fairly on their own terms. It may be hoped that the future will see increased dialogue taking place between those claiming to discover textual discrepancies and failures and those who see in the same phenomena narratorial dexterity and finesse.

In addition to the two negative criteria, Strauss in *The Life of Jesus* also proposes a positive criterion, namely, a text may be judged unhistorical if it exhibits characteristics of legend or fiction. According to Strauss, "The positive characters of legend and fiction are to be recognized sometimes in the form, sometimes in the substance of a narrative" (p. 89). As to form, he writes:

> If the form be poetical, if the actors converse in hymns, and in a more diffuse and elevated strain than might be expected from their training and situations, such discourses, at all events, are not to be regarded as historical. The absence of these marks of the unhistorical does not however prove the historical validity of the narration, since the mythus often wears the most simple and apparently historical form: in which case the proof lies in the substance. (p. 89)

If what was said in the preceding chapter has any validity, then our response to the criterion based on *form* can be brief. In the section entitled "History as Representational Art," we concluded, in agreement with Sternberg and many others, that "there are simply no universals of historical vs. fictive form."[58] The biblical writers of course make choices in how their accounts are formulated, whether briefly or expansively, whether in straight narrative prose or in the elevated diction of poetry, and so forth. And Bible readers will need to give heed to these formal dimensions of the texts, lest poetry, for example, be read off as straight prose, or figurative speech be misconstrued literally. Still, the question of historicity cannot be decided on the basis of the narrator's preferred literary style (the form)

[56]For bibliographical information on Simon and Anderson, see Moberly, *At the Mountain*, pp. 29–30 nn. 51–52.
[57]For a more extended example, see the discussion of 1 Samuel 15:24–29 in Long, *Reign and Rejection*, pp. 37–38.
[58]Sternberg, *Poetics of Biblical Narrative*, p. 30.

but, as we have already argued, only in the light of the *overall purpose* of the broader discourse unit.

As to the matter of *substance*, Strauss writes:

> If the contents of a narrative strikingly accord with certain ideas existing and prevailing within the circle from which the narrative proceeded, which ideas themselves seem to be the product of preconceived opinions rather than of practical experience, it is more or less probable, according to circumstances, that such a narrative is of mythical origin. The knowledge of the fact, that the Jews were fond of representing their great men as the children of parents who had long been childless, cannot but make us doubtful of the historical truth of the statement that this was the case with John the Baptist;. . . (p. 89)

This criterion based on substance is notoriously slippery and raises several questions. Who is to say, for example, that John the Baptist was given a "barren-mother birth narrative" simply because the Jews were fond of such stories? And, more importantly, whence came this fondness in the first place? If we assume that the birth narratives of the Old Testament are also only inventions reflecting the Jews' fondness for such stories, we have not answered the question of origin but have only pushed it back to an even earlier stage. If, on the other hand, we assume that at least some unusual births did actually occur in Israel's history, and these were recounted with delight, who is to say that another such birth did not mark John the Baptist's entry into the world? To be sure, there is often an element of *patterning* in the Bible's portrayal of people and events, but this does not disprove the essential historicity of those portrayals. The life of Abraham Lincoln can be recounted according to the man-of-humble-origin-makes-good pattern, but no one would cite this fact as evidence against the historicity of Lincoln's career. On the contrary, it is Lincoln's historical experience that has contributed to the fondness for such stories.[59]

Before leaving Strauss, we should note how he extends his skeptical approach to cover even texts that in and of themselves show no sign of being unhistorical.

> It may be that a narrative, standing alone, would discover but slight indications, or perhaps, might present no one distinct feature of the mythus; but it is connected with others, or proceeds from the author of other narratives which exhibit unquestionable marks of a mythical or legendary character; and consequently suspicion is reflected back from the latter, on the former. (p. 90)

So certain is Strauss that "the absolute cause never disturbs the chain of secondary causes" (p. 88) that he feels compelled not only to label as unhistorical any text that would suggest otherwise but to apply the same label to all texts that are in any way associated with the first. But for those who do not embrace Strauss's assumption regarding the impossibility of divine intervention, I would suggest that where the larger discourse unit implies a historical purpose (and in the absence of other indicators) the burden of proof rests on those who would deny the historicity of a given text within the larger unit, whatever fabulous or miraculous elements it might contain.[60]

---

[59]W. A. Bacon (*The Art of Interpretation*, 2d ed. [New York: Holt, Rinehart and Winston, 1972], p. 496) cites "the rise of the poor boy from log cabin to the White House" as a typical "stock situation in American lore."

[60]Cf. Blomberg's similar observation with respect to the Gospels: "Once one accepts that the gospels reflect attempts to write reliable history or biography, however theological or stylized its presentation may be, then one must immediately recognize an important presupposition which guides most historians in

It should be apparent from the foregoing discussion how vitally one's view of the world, religion, and reality affects one's interpretation of the Bible. But herein lies a curious inconsistency in the history of biblical scholarship. As Morgan has observed, "Strauss destroyed history to make room for his kind of theology; his proposal, too, involved a theory of religion and reality. Those who later kept his history but ignored his theory and repudiated his theology had alternative theories of religion and reality as well as new theologies of their own."[61] But if scholars have largely rejected Strauss's view of religion and reality, by what right do they continue to accept his "destroyed" history, founded as it is on the very view of religion and reality now rejected? Of course, the issue is not quite as simple as this query suggests, for in fact it is only Strauss's first negative criterion, based on "all just philosophical conceptions and all credible experience," that is directly affected. But the other criteria—inconsistency and contradiction, characteristics of fiction or legend (whether in form or substance), guilt by association—are at least indirectly affected. At any rate, as we have seen, these other criteria are less than clear-cut in application.

As influential as Strauss has been in the history of modern scholarship, he was never without opponents among the ranks of biblical scholars. It can only be hoped that those who no longer share Strauss's view of religion and reality will proceed to a rethinking of the historical method he advocated and that, when the necessary adjustments have been made, a more positive historical-critical practice may emerge. I shall have more to say about these matters in the chapters that follow.

AN EXAMPLE: "IF JERICHO WAS NOT RAZED, IS OUR FAITH IN VAIN?"

The aim of this chapter has been to explore the issue of whether questions of historicity are of significant import for Christian faith. Our deliberations have led us to answer the question in the affirmative. Far from being inconsequential, questions of history are of great importance to Christianity. Perhaps a good way to draw the chapter to a close is with a brief evaluation of a recent challenge to this view.

In his *Quest for the Historical Israel*, George Ramsey gives his final chapter the provocative title, "If Jericho Was Not Razed, Is Our Faith in Vain?" His clever play on Paul's confession, "If Christ was not raised, . . . your faith is vain" (1 Cor. 15:14), serves notice that serious issues will be at stake in his discussion of the relationship of historical study to Christian faith and makes it all the more curious that Ramsey never actually gets around to addressing the Pauline assertion directly. This raises a first question: Is it appropriate to base a discussion of the importance of history for faith on the razing of Jericho, to the neglect of the far more central and significant event to which Ramsey's phraseology so clearly alludes? In one respect, of course, Christian faith might well survive without the razing of Jericho, since it is not the razing of Jericho but the raising of Christ that saves us. But this evokes a further question. On what basis do we believe that Christ was raised? Surely an important part of the answer (in addition to, for example, the internal prompting of the Holy Spirit) is that we do so on the basis of trust in the scriptural testimony to that event.

their work. Unless there is good reason for believing otherwise one will assume that a given detail in the work of a particular historian is factual. This method places the burden of proof squarely on the person who would doubt the reliability of a given portion of the text" (*Historical Reliability*, p. 240).

[61]*Biblical Interpretation*, p. 188.

It is our confidence in the truth value (i.e., the trustworthiness) of Scripture that enables us to accept the otherwise astonishing truth claim that Christ was raised from the dead. In this light, then, the question of the razing of Jericho appears to be of greater import than Ramsey allows. Were we to be absolutely certain that the book of Joshua claims unequivocally that Jericho was razed in space-time history, and were we likewise certain that archaeological study proves just the opposite, we would have a problem. Our confidence in the general trustworthiness of Scripture would not necessarily be destroyed, but neither would it be entirely unaffected. As regards the Jericho question, however, such certainties are elusive, despite the fact that Jericho is often cited as a parade example of irresolvable conflict between the "plain sense" of the Bible and the "proven results" of archaeology. On the one hand, given the powerful co-mingling of theological, literary, and historiographical impulses in the book of Joshua, discovery of the "plain sense" may not always be a simple matter. On the other hand, many are the "proven results" of archaeology that have subsequently been "*un*proven." Indeed, the case of Jericho itself provides an instructive example. After the excavations of Garstang in the 1930s, Jericho was put forward as a prime example of the close correlation of archaeology and biblical history. But as a result of the subsequent excavations of Kenyon in the 1950s, the site has come to be viewed as a prime example of just the opposite. In fact, however, there are indications that the archaeological verdict may still not be in.[62] We shall consider the nature of archaeological data as "objective" evidence in the next chapter.

Returning to Ramsey's question, "If Jericho was not razed, is our faith in vain?", the answer would now seem to be, "Not necessarily, but possibly." "Not necessarily," because the heart of the Christian gospel requires the raising of Christ, not the razing of Jericho. But "possibly," because we would be made less sure either of the trustworthiness of the biblical witness or of our ability to discover its basic sense. And in either case, the possibility that our faith might be in vain is increased. That is, our trust might well be misplaced or misguided. What is striking in Ramsey's discussion is that he does not appear to feel the force of these concerns. This may suggest, if we take our cue from Vos's words cited earlier in this chapter, that Ramsey embraces a different notion of the essence of Christianity than we, for our part, have been assuming. Ramsey's last words in his *Quest for the Historical Israel* are these:

> If we can demonstrate, with our research tools, that parts of that tradition tell of events or persons that never were, or at least never were like the tradition describes them, this does not alter the fact that the tradition has spoken to believers for generation after generation with power and expressed things which they believed to be true. The tradition 'rang true' in their own experience and enabled them to develop a self-understanding and a lifestyle. It was the tradition as received which accomplished this, not the past-as-it-actually-was. (p. 124)

To be fair, I should point out that in the volume under discussion Ramsey nowhere explicitly articulates his understanding of the essence of Christianity. But insofar as it may be inferred from the general tenor of his book and these concluding words, it does appear

---

[62]We note, e.g., B. G. Wood's recent attempts at a reassessment of Kenyon's excavation results ("Did the Israelites Conquer Jericho? A New Look at the Archaeological Evidence," *Biblical Archaeology Review* 16/2 [1990]: 44–59) and D. N. Pinaar's call for further excavation to be conducted at Jericho ("Die stad Jerigo en die boek Josua," *Journal for Semitics* 1 [1989]: 272–86).

to betray, as Vos predicted it would, a "defective appreciation of the soteriological charac-ter of Christianity."[63] Those whose understanding of the essence of Christianity approxi-mates that implied by Ramsey's last remark may find his arguments for the inconsequen-tiality of the "past-as-it-actually-was" appealing. But Christian faith has classically stood for more than a "self-understanding and a lifestyle." For the majority of those who call themselves Christians, the historicity of the core events of redemptive history, precisely because it is *redemptive* history, can never be dismissed as insignificant considerations.

CONCLUSION

Living near the end of the fast-paced twentieth century and looking to a new mil-lennium that promises to move even faster, most of us share an aversion to endless debate. This chapter's consideration of post-Enlightenment controversy over the historicity of the Bible, though selective and abbreviated perhaps to a fault, can nevertheless give the impression of endless debate. So we ask ourselves the question: Might it not be better simply to stay out of it? Shouldn't we heed the warning of Proverbs 26:17: "Like one who seizes a dog by the ears is a passer-by who meddles in a quarrel not his own"? For those who regard the Bible as God's inspired word for us to read and obey today, is it all that important to concern ourselves with questions of the past? Can't we simply enter imag-inatively into the world that the Bible creates and let that imaginative identification mould our thoughts and actions—even if that world itself, like Tolkien's Middle Earth, should turn out to be purely imaginary?

Such questions and the pragmatic sentiments that prompt them have been around for a long time. "The present religious mind has a veritable dread of everything that is not immediately practical or experimental," wrote Vos of his own generation in the first decade of this century. "Thus the whole theoretical side of faith has fallen into neglect, and this neglect involves, besides other things, the historic basis of facts." In Vos's day, as in ours, there was even a sense that interest in questions of history was a sign of a deficient faith:

> the peculiarity of the present situation is not merely that the facts are neglected, but that in the name and for the sake of the integrity of the Christian faith itself the non-essentialness of the facts is clamorously insisted upon. It is held that where the facts play a central and necessary part in the psychological process of religious trust, that there faith must lose its purity and power.[64]

I hope that enough has already been said about the importance of history as it per-tains to both soteriology and divine disclosure to suggest the unacceptability of the above line of thinking. Few persons in the New Testament display a more practical turn of mind than the first missionary to the Gentiles, and yet Paul insists that if certain events that lie at the heart of the Gospel did not happen—specifically, "if Christ has not been raised"—then there really is no Gospel to preach, and faith itself is ultimately futile (1 Cor. 15:14–19).

---

[63]"Christian Faith," p. 300; quoted already above.
[64]"Christian Faith," pp. 294–95.

four
HISTORY
AND MODERN
SCHOLARSHIP
Why Do Scholars Disagree?

A ssuming that most scholars mean well and are seeking to be as fair and objective as possible in their assessments, why is it that they come to such widely differing opinions regarding the historicity of various portions of the Bible? As we saw in the preceding chapter, part of the answer lies in what individual scholars themselves bring to the historical task, for as Stanford has observed,

> How a historian sees the past is only a part of how he or she sees the world. The final colour and shape of a historian's construction is bestowed by his or her own *Weltanschauung* (assuming that this world-view is not merely a copy of someone else's). Dominating all technical considerations of evidence, method, interpretation and construction is the individual human being.[1]

In other words, the individual historian's basic intellectual and spiritual commitments ("how he or she sees the world") exercise an inevitable, even "dominating," influence over which historical reconstructions will appear plausible to that historian. Some historians are theists, others nontheists; some believe in an open universe, others in a closed universe; some regard material forces as the prime motors of historical change, others accord this role to personal (whether human or divine) agency. All of these basic beliefs influence how historians read the biblical texts and at least in part determine whether the Bible's accounts of the past appear plausible or not.

---

[1]*Nature*, p. 96.

A second part of the answer to the question why well-meaning scholars disagree on matters of biblical historicity is closely related to the first. Just as the historian's world-view, (or *model* of reality) influences how he or she perceives the past, so also the *model* influences his or her preference for certain *methods* of investigation and the manner in which these methods are applied. In the final analysis, the historian's *model* of reality, expressing itself through the historian's preferred *methods* of investigation, inevitably affects the historian's historical conclusions/constructions. Thus it is not so much the data in themselves—textual, artifactual, comparative, etc.—that account for the wide diversity of opinion among scholars. Most well informed scholars have access to essentially the same data. It is, rather, in the assessment of the data that differences arise.[2] Ernst Troeltsch, whose writings have been very influential in modern conceptions of historical method, seemed himself to recognize this, as Michalson reminds us: "Troeltsch appreciated that the real problem for theology was not that biblical critics emerged 'from their libraries with results disturbing to believers,' but that the historical-critical method itself was 'based on assumptions quite irreconcilable with traditional belief.'"[3]

In this chapter we shall look at some of the different methodological approaches to biblical interpretation, the models of reality that underlie them, and the ways in which each of these affects historical conclusions. Our aim will not be to discover "the correct method," for Barton is in a sense correct that "much harm has been done in biblical studies by insisting that there is, somewhere, a 'correct' method which, if only we could find it, would unlock the mysteries of the text."[4] The biblical texts are more likely to yield their fruits when approached from various angles with a diversity of questions in mind. Thus, distinctive methodological approaches should not be viewed as mutually exclusive,[5] so long as each is compatible with a consistently held worldview, or model of reality. Our aim, therefore, will be to explore some of the assumptions and affirmations that underlie prominent trends in contemporary biblical scholarship. There will be no attempt, of course, to offer an exhaustive survey of methods. We shall focus, rather, on those methodological approaches that tend to influence assessments of Scripture as a historical source and which, in turn, account for some of the scholarly disagreements on questions of biblical historicity. Specifically, we shall look at (1) anti-theological tendencies in the historical-critical method as traditionally practiced, (2) anti-literary tendencies in some of today's social-scientific and archaeological approaches to historical reconstruction, and (3) anti-historical tendencies in some forms of modern literary and reader-response criticism. If this plan sounds too negative, we might recall the words of A. E. Housman, who said, "I have spent most of my time finding faults because finding faults, if they are real

---

[2]For some telling illustrations of how "interpreters of the past reflect their underlying assumptions by what they select to serve as evidence," see Henry, *God, Revelation and Authority,* 2: 318–19.

[3]Lessing's *"Ugly Ditch,"* p. 94; citing V. A. Harvey, *The Historian and the Believer: A Confrontation Between the Modern Historian's Principles of Judgment and the Christian's Will-to-Believe* (New York: Macmillan, 1966).

[4]*Reading the Old Testament,* p. 5; cf. pp. 196–97 and *passim.* A. C. Thiselton (*New Horizons in Hermeneutics: The Theory and Practice of Transforming Biblical Reading* [Grand Rapids: Zondervan, 1992], p. 502) points out that there is a "tantalizing half-truth" in this statement by Barton. I am taking it in the "correct and healthy" sense mentioned by Thiselton, namely, that various methods "make some positive contribution to textual elucidation, and that one method should not be judged in terms of the reading-competence appropriate to another" (ibid.).

[5]See, e.g., Brett, "Four or Five Things," pp. 357–77.

and not imaginary, is the most useful sort of criticism."[6] More positively, however, it should be emphasized that the unfortunate tendencies evident in many studies are not, in fact, *necessary* aspects of the approaches themselves. As we shall see, if the various approaches are properly understood and qualified, the historically interested biblical scholar may gain useful insights from all of them.

ANTI-THEOLOGICAL TENDENCIES IN SOME HISTORICAL-CRITICAL APPROACHES

What Is the Historical-Critical Method and Who Can Use It?

It is often asserted that those who study the Bible as a source of history must, if they wish to merit the title *historian*, acknowledge and adhere to the same canons of historical research as those espoused by their secular counterparts. In principle, this assertion is valid. In practice, however, difficulties are encountered because the canons of historical research are still a matter of some debate and, at any rate, are often misunderstood and misapplied.

For example, Halpern has recently asserted that "confessional" scholars (the "faithful" as he also calls them) simply cannot be critical historians. He writes:

> The straightjacket of doctrinal conservatism . . . prohibits critical historical analysis of the Bible. . . . The confessional use of the Bible is fundamentally anti-historical. . . . Worshipers do not read the Bible with an intrinsic interest in human events. Like the prophet, or psalmist, or, in Acts, the saint, they seek behind the events a single, unifying cause that lends them meaning, and makes the historical differences among them irrelevant. In history, the *faith*ful seek the permanent, the ahistorical; in time, they quest for timelessness; in reality, in the concrete, they seek Spirit, the insubstantial.[7]

After what was said in the preceding chapter about the importance of history for faith, Halpern's "anti-historical" charge leveled at the "*faith*ful" comes as something of a surprise and raises a number of questions.[8] The validity of his basic claim, however—that confessional scholars cannot engage in historical-critical analysis—hinges on how one defines the terms *historical and critical*. Paul Achtemeier, for instance, defines *historical* as implying the "continuing necessity to recognize that the Bible is the product of another time, and that this must be taken into account whenever we attempt to use it to solve contemporary problems." *Critical* he defines as implying a "critical attitude to what *we* think a given passage means. We are not to assume that what seems obvious to us as modern people is necessarily the meaning of the passage when seen in its total historical and literary context."[9] If this were all that is involved in the historical-critical method, it would

---

[6]*Selected Prose* (Cambridge: Cambridge University Press, 1961), p. xii; cited by D. R. Hall, *The Seven Pillories of Wisdom* (Macon, GA: Mercer University Press, 1990), p. viii.

[7]*First Historians*, pp. 3–4.

[8]E.g., is not Halpern assuming false oppositions here? May not a past, *historical* event have a continuing significance for the present and the future and, in that sense, be timeless? And what is wrong with following the precedent of prophet, psalmist, and saint in seeking the unifying meaning that ties disparate events together? At least for the theist, who believes that the past constitutes more than a meaningless chaos of isolated events, this would seem to be a fair procedure. And does Halpern really mean to equate "reality" with "the concrete" and oppose these to the "Spirit," as if the latter were not only "insubstantial" but also unreal?

[9]"The Authority of the Bible: What Shall We Then Preach?" *TSF Bulletin* (November–December 1986): 21–22.

be hard to imagine why it should ever have encountered resistance from confessing schol-ars. Surely, they are as prepared as any to admit that the Bible is the "product of another time" and that "what *we* think a given passage means" is open to criticism.

But this is not, in fact, what has traditionally been understood as the historical-crit-ical method. James Barr, for example, offers a rather different description:

> 'Historical' reading of a text means a reading which aims at the reconstruction of spa-tial-temporal events in the past: it asks what was the actual sequence of the events to which the text refers, or what was the sequence of events by which the text came into existence. This constitutes the 'historical' component. Such historical reading is, I would further say, 'critical' in this sense, that it accepts the possibility that events were not in fact as they are described in the text: that things happened differently, or that the text was written at a different time, or by a different person. No operation is gen-uinely historical if it does not accept this critical component: in other words, being 'critical' is analytically involved in being historical.[10]

Whether confessing scholars can be historical critics of Barr's variety depends on what is meant by the somewhat ambiguous phrase, "accepts the possibility." When functioning strictly as historians, they may leave open the hypothetical possibility that the text may be wrong, but their tendency will be to approach the text expectantly, assuming its reliabili-ty until proven otherwise. Secular biblical critics, on the other hand, who regard the Bible as a *merely* human composition, will approach the text assuming not only the possibility but the probability (if not certainty) that the text has erred in places, since "to err is human."

Who then can make use of the historical-critical method? Until clarity of definition is achieved for the terms *historical* and *critical*, a firm answer cannot be given. As tradi-tionally practiced, at least, the historical-critical method rests on certain assumptions that the "faithful" scholar, to use Halpern's designation, will not wish to embrace. We may illustrate this point by quoting Maxwell Miller's description in *The Old Testament and the Historian* of three basic ways in which the modern "critical" historian differs from his "pre-critical" counterparts.[11]

> The contemporary historian's approach tends to differ from that of his earlier coun-terparts in three ways: (1) he generally takes a critical stance toward his sources; (2) he is inclined to disregard the supernatural or miraculous in his treatment of past events; (3) he is very much aware of his own historicity and, accordingly, of the sub-jective and tentative character of his own historical conclusions. (pp. 12–13)

Because of its second element, such an approach naturally encounters difficulties in deal-ing with the

> frequent references in the ancient texts to divine involvement in human affairs . . ., espe-cially when the involvement is depicted as direct and overt. The historian of today may not specifically deny the supernatural or miraculous. But it is obvious from the histo-ry books which he writes that he disregards overt supernatural activity as a significant cause in his history and that he is skeptical of claims regarding supposedly unique his-torical occurrences which defy normal explanation—i.e., the miraculous. (p. 17)

---

[10]*Scope and Authority of the Bible,* pp. 30–31.
[11]Philadelphia: Fortress, 1976.

Where reports of miracles or of divine involvement in human affairs do occur, the historian's first reflex, according to Miller, is to ignore them or to *re-explain* them in naturalistic terms. As an example, Miller cites the Mesha Inscription (Moabite Stone), in which it is reported that after the defeat of Moab by Omri of Israel and after some years of Israelite domination, king Mesha finally succeeded in regaining Moab's independence. The initial oppression, according to the inscription, came about because "Chemosh was angry with his land," and the deliverance was accomplished when "Chemosh drove him out before me."[12] Historians have little trouble accepting the essential political assertions of the inscription, but as Miller observes, "they ignore Mesha's insistence that these turns of events were the doings of Chemosh and seek to re-explain them without reference to the supernatural. If Chemosh enters into this 're-explanation' at all, he enters only as an element of Mesha's theology" (p. 17).

Now unless Mesha's *theological* explanation be dismissed as no more than a conventional manner of speaking, a meaningless religious overlay believed by no one even in Mesha's day, then the modern scholar must at least acknowledge that some ancient Moabites believed in a god Chemosh who involved himself in human affairs.[13] Of course, few if any modern scholars will share this belief in the existence and activity of Chemosh, and so it is understandable that they seek to re-explain the events described without reference to a god whose existence they deny. Confessing biblical historians are not likely to raise much objection to this procedure, since they are no more inclined to believe in a god called Chemosh than are their secular counterparts (though they may, in principle, be more open to the possibility of a metaphysical dimension in the story). But does it follow that "Biblical sources [should] receive essentially the same treatment" (p. 17)? For those at least who claim to believe in the reality and sovereignty of the God of the Bible, such a move would be illogical. Why should the possible activity of the God whose existence they affirm be limited to that of the false god whose existence they deny? Surely a Christian or Jewish historian is free to believe that the one true God is sovereign above history and also active in its processes, without at the same time having to allow that a god called Chemosh ever occupied such a position. Or put the other way, surely Jewish or Christian scholars may dismiss or re-explain claims about Chemosh's purported role in historical events without subjecting the God whom they confess to similar treatment.[14]

Beyond the tendency described above, there is a fundamental principle of the historical-critical method that tends to bring its results into direct conflict with the biblical testimony. As Miller describes it, this *principle of analogy* assumes that "all historical phenomena are subject to 'analogous' explanation—i.e., explanation in terms of other similar phenomena." By virtue of this methodological criterion, "the modern historian appears to be presuming in advance that there are no truly miraculous or unique occurrences in history." This presumption creates a point of tension between the modern historian and the biblical witness. Miller puts it succinctly: "The obvious conflict between the biblical claims regarding God's overt and unique actions in Israel's history on the one hand, and

---

[12]Lines 5 and 19 of the Mesha Inscription; available *inter alios* in John C. L. Gibson, *Textbook of Semitic Inscriptions. Vol. I: Hebrew and Moabite Inscriptions* (Oxford: Clarendon Press, 1971), pp. 71–83.

[13]On the issue generally, see A. R. Millard, "The Old Testament and History: Some Considerations," *Faith and Thought* 110 (1983): 34–53.

[14]On the issue generally, cf. Goldingay, *Approaches to Old Testament Interpretation*, pp. 77–79.

the presuppositions of the historical-critical method of inquiry on the other, lies at the heart of much of the present-day theological discussion" (p. 18).

Why, then, do biblical scholars disagree in their historical conclusions? In practice, the answer often depends on which side of the above conflict enjoys their greater loyalty—"the biblical claims" or "the historical-critical method" as traditionally practiced. But this raises a further question. Must the issue be cast in terms of such an opposition? Must one either discount the biblical claims or else commit the apparent *sacrificium intellectus* of rejecting the historical method? Van Harvey in his influential book *The Historian and the Believer: A Confrontation between the Modern Historian's Principles of Judgment and the Christian's Will-to-Believe*, seems to suggest as much when he sets in opposition "the morality of historical knowledge" and the traditional, orthodox "ethic of belief."[15] But is it not possible to embrace a sound historical method and still maintain that God has intervened decisively in history? In *Divine Revelation and the Limits of Historical Criticism*[16] William Abraham argues compellingly that it is. Not only does he maintain that the "theologian who would turn his back on this [the historical discipline] is a fool, however much he may feel that his work has been in bondage to a discipline whose experts threaten to swallow up the riches of faith" but, even more importantly, he contends that "the theologian need have no fears that the historian must pronounce his commitment to divine intervention as hostile to the critical canons of the historian's trade" (p. 188). In the next section we shall investigate how Abraham arrives at these convictions.

The Historical-Critical Method and the Question of Divine Intervention

Abraham sets two tasks for himself in *Divine Revelation and the Limits of Historical Criticism*. First, in chapters one to four he seeks to demonstrate that the "traditional understanding of divine revelation" necessarily entails a "commitment to divine intervention of a substantial sort." Second, in chapters five to eight he argues that "it is possible to believe in special divine revelation without any sacrifice of critical judgement in either history or science" (p. 7). A full summary of Abraham's argumentation is not possible here, but we may at least focus on the crucial issue addressed in the second half of his book.

The question, as Abraham puts it at the beginning of chapter five, is whether "the traditional claims as set forth in the first four chapters [should] be abandoned because of the character of critical historical investigation" (p. 92). To help describe what is involved in critical historical investigation, Abraham turns to the writings of German theologian, historian, and social scientist Ernst Troeltsch (1865–1923), already mentioned above. According to Troeltsch, a true historian must be committed not only to the principle of *analogy*, but to two other principles (or presuppositions)[17] as well: *criticism* and *correlation*. As Abraham explains, the principle of *criticism* means that

---

[15]See esp. his chap. 4.

[16]Oxford: Oxford University Press, 1982.

[17]For Abraham's defense of his use of the not altogether happy term *presupposition*, see *Divine Revelation*, pp. 98–99. Note well also Harvey's warning against too undifferentiated a notion of *presuppositions* (*Historian and the Believer*, esp. chap. 3). In Harvey's view, "the assertion, 'Every historian has his presuppositions' is both true and misleading," since it tends to mask the fact that presuppositions are of many different types and are operative on various levels of inquiry (p. 84).

the historian is to offer his conclusions in the form of probability judgments of a greater or lesser degree. His conclusions, that is, do not take the form of necessary truths, as in mathematics, but are contingent in character and can be ranged on a scale of truth so that some conclusions may be claimed to be more likely to be true than others. Given this, there will be differences in the inner attitude of the historian to his claims. Concerning some claims he will feel very sure, concerning others less sure, etc. Further, his conclusions will always be open to revision should fresh evidence emerge, and thus they cannot be treated as absolute or final. (p. 100)

This description of *criticism*, or what it means to be a *critical* historian, comes closer to Achtemeier's concept than to Barr's (both mentioned above). Historians' claims must remain open to criticism, that is, review and revision (so Achtemeier). But there is no insistence that source documents must, as a point of principle, be systematically doubted (Barr). Troeltsch's second principle, *analogy*, is related to the first in the following manner, as Abraham again explains:

As the historian seeks to determine what happened in the past he guides his work by his convictions about what is taking place in his own time, and uses this as a scale for judging the probability of claims about the past. 'Harmony with the normal, familiar or at least repeatedly witnessed events and conditions as we know them is the distinguishing mark of reality for the events which criticism can recognize as really having happened or leave aside.' (p. 100)

As noted earlier, this principle can seem to be assuming in advance that the unique cannot occur, that miracles do not happen, and that God never intervenes in history. Indeed, in practice this is often the way the principle of analogy is applied, with the result that the *theological* presentation of history in the Bible is rejected out of hand by "critical" historians and replaced with an *atheological*, nonmetaphysical reconstruction. When this happens, scholars are again placed in the uncomfortable position of choosing between the biblical testimony to the past and "real" history as critically reconstructed. But must the principle of analogy be applied so woodenly? Must it entail a dismissal of the unique or miraculous in history? Abraham contends that it need not, and he charts a pathway out of the impasse by refining the notion of analogy.

He begins by noting that the principle of analogy "can be understood in either a narrow or wide sense." Depending on the sense, the historian is limited to what is "normal, usual, or widely attested" in his own personal experience (the narrow sense) or in the experience of people currently living (the wide sense). The narrow sense is clearly too restrictive, for historians regularly accept the reality of events and practices that lie outside their immediate experience.[18] The wide sense is less "hyper-restrictive" but is still open to several objections: (1) "it is quite impossible to put into effect," since historians could never travel widely enough, consult enough encyclopedias of *normalcy*, etc. to ascertain what in fact is normal, usual, or widely attested; and even if they could, they would be left with little time or energy for historical research; (2) even "with respect to what is claimed to have happened in the present," historians exercise "critical judgement" that is derived in part, at least, from their knowledge of the past (thus, one might on occasion reverse the

---

[18]To underscore this point, Abraham (p. 101) cites Collingwood's telling remark: "That the Greeks and Romans exposed their new-born children in order to control the numbers of their population is no less true for being unlike anything that happens in the experience of contributors to the Cambridge Ancient History."

standard adage that "the present is the key to the past" and say that "the past is the key to the present"); (3) "in some cases historians would be prepared to allow as happening events that are not normal, usual, or widely attested"—e.g., "the climbing of Mount Everest or the first human landing on the moon" (pp. 101–103).

To illustrate how the principle of analogy may properly function in determining the historicity, or factuality, of a claim about the past, Abraham describes two imaginary scenarios. The first involves the discovery in an ancient document of a claim that Plato wrote *The Republic* when he was only two years old. The immediate reaction of historians will be to dismiss such a claim, since, as everyone knows, "children of two years of age do not write books like *The Republic*" (p. 103). The second scenario involves a primitive tribe confronted for the first time with the claim that man has landed on the moon. Again, on the principle of analogy, this claim will be immediately dismissed by the tribe. Nevertheless, a historian may succeed in convincing the tribe that a moon landing did in fact occur if he does three things: (1) bring corroborating testimony, "e.g., from fellow westerners who are trusted by the tribe," (2) "initiate the members of the tribe into the theories and concepts of natural science," especially as these relate to space flight, and (3) explain "the purposes and intentions of those who planned and carried out the moon landings." If the tribe still refuse to believe on the grounds that "this event is not normal, usual, or widely attested even in the west" (p. 104), the historian will need to bring further arguments. He might explain the infrequency or even uniqueness of the event on the basis of cost, government restrictions, safety concerns, and so forth. In the end, the tribe may be led to believe in an occurrence that finds no analogy in their own experience.

What becomes clear in all of this is that "the principle of analogy is a principle that operates within a wider context." There is "an intimate relation between analogy and its context or network of background beliefs" (p. 105). As the example of the tribe illustrates, *conclusions drawn from an application of the principle of analogy are only as sound as the background beliefs held by those drawing the conclusions.* How then do we discern the background beliefs of this or that historian or, for that matter, how do we examine our own? The key, according to Troeltsch (and Abraham), is to investigate what each of us thinks about the third basic principle of the historical-critical method, the principle of *correlation.*

The principle of correlation maintains that "events are interdependent and interrelated in intimate reciprocity" (p. 105). In other words, events do not simply happen unprompted. They are caused either by the choices and actions of personal agents or by natural forces, or by some combination of the two. As regards personal agency, the decisive question is, as Abraham puts it, whether the historian adopts a *formal* conception of correlation (which would allow both human and divine agency) or a *material* conception of correlation (which would limit causation to the terrestrial sphere and disallow divine agency).

For those like Troeltsch and so many after him who are committed to a material conception, any record of events that expresses or implies divine agency must, in that regard at least, be discounted as history. Indeed, to those steeped in Troeltschian thinking any appeal to direct divine activity in earthly affairs will appear to be the epitome of "an uncritical and even superstitious mentality" (p. 110).

But such thinking must be challenged. Abraham argues forcefully that "direct actions of God are not bolts from the blue or random events, but are related to a wider conceptual scheme that gives point and intelligibility to their occurrence" (p. 111).[19] This being the case, to admit discourse about divine intervention as an acceptable component of historical explanation is not to abandon the principle of correlation but to widen it. If one's network of background beliefs includes belief in a personal God, one may affirm that this God has acted in history—for example, that he has spoken, that he has become incarnate in Christ, that he has performed miracles—and still remain true to the principle of correlation: the belief that events do not simply happen unprompted.

At times, of course, for the sake of dialogue with those who do not share the same background beliefs, theistic historians may legitimately adopt a qualified material conception of correlation, but only as a temporary *methodological* constraint. In other words, theistic historians may choose not to talk about *all* they believe in order to talk profitably, even if on a minimalist level, with those who believe less. As Bebbington explains, "the Christian historian is not obliged to tell the whole truth as he sees it in every piece of historical writing. He can write of providence or not according to his judgment of the composition of his audience. So long as his account accords with the Christian vision of the historical process, he will be fulfilling his vocation."[20] The last sentence above is key. It recognizes that, whatever limitations may be set on the terms of discussion, Christian historians, if they are to be consistent, must take care that what they do say is compatible with their full set of background beliefs. To safeguard this compatibility, they must remain aware of two dangers that typically attend lowest-common-denominator discussions.

First, whenever talk of divine agency is methodologically excluded, there can be a real temptation to seek an exclusively *natural* explanation for each and every occurrence in the past, even for those occurrences that the Bible presents as involving direct divine action. This temptation must be resisted, for succumbing to it may lead to an endorsement of historical reconstructions at odds with the Christian historian's full set of background beliefs.[21] In contexts where explicit affirmation of divine activity would be a "conversation stopper," Christian historians should at least refrain from endorsing historical reconstructions that explicitly deny such activity, for that too is a conversation stopper, or should be. As an example of appropriate restraint, John Bright remarks regarding the events surrounding the Israelite exodus from Egypt, "If Israel saw in this the hand of God, the historian certainly has no evidence to contradict it!"[22]

A second, equally grave danger is that biblical historians may unwittingly allow the *minimalist* method, adopted for the sake of dialogue, to begin to infect their model of reality. Methodological procedure can all too easily slide into metaphysical profession. Such a shift is a logical and procedural error of the first order, for it is one's model of reality that should suggest what methods are appropriate in approaching a given subject,

---

[19]The resurrection of Jesus from the dead, for example, is not an arbitrary abrogation of the laws of nature but is "one part of a complex and sophisticated story of divine action that stretches from eternity to eternity and involves in a unique way the person of Jesus" (Abraham, *Divine Revelation*, p. 132; see also pp. 116–35 for a full discussion of this very important point).

[20]*Patterns*, pp. 187–88.

[21]As Bebbington (*Patterns*, p. 186) warns, "If a Christian historian tries to write without a thought for providence, he is likely to succumb to some alternative view or blend of views that happens to be in fashion. He will probably grow accustomed to the current assumptions of the academic world, positivist, historicist, Marxist or whatever."

[22]*A History of Israel*, 3d ed. (Philadelphia: Westminster, 1981), p. 122.

and not the reverse. I am not suggesting that one's model of reality should be immune from challenge. But the fallacy of unthinkingly allowing a chosen method to determine one's model of reality is like that of the fisherman who is convinced that his fishing hole contains no fish smaller than five centimeters in length simply because he has never caught any. When a bystander points out that the fisherman's net has a mesh too large to catch fish smaller than five centimeters, the fisherman insists, mistakenly, that what his net (method) cannot catch does not exist (model of reality).[23]

In summary, while the historical-critical method (as traditionally practiced) systematically and insistently excludes the notion of divine intervention, the method itself, if applied in the context of a theistic set of background beliefs, need not exclude talk of divine intervention. For those willing to embrace a historical-critical method of the type developed by Abraham and advocated above, Miller's "obvious conflict between the biblical claims . . . and the presuppositions of the historical-critical method"[24] disappears. The historian may believe that God is the "lord of history,"[25] sovereignly at work behind the scenes and even intervening on occasion, and still remain a competent historian. Indeed, unless theists are badly mistaken in their theism, then surely it is the denial of any place for God in the historical process that is the mark of bad history.

Why do scholars disagree on historical questions relating to the Bible? One reason, as we have seen, is the common though unnecessary tendency of the historical-critical method to exclude from the realm of history any notion of direct divine intervention. This tendency leads to an a priori dismissal of many events recorded in the Bible and, in some cases, to a general skepticism towards the biblical text as a historical source. It is perhaps this skepticism that contributes to the popularity of approaches to historical reconstruction that seek to minimize the importance of literary, or textual, evidence. Among such are the social-scientific approaches to which we now turn.

ANTI-LITERARY TENDENCIES IN SOME SOCIAL-SCIENTIFIC APPROACHES

Sociology: The New Handmaid?

As Carolyn Osiek observes in "The New Handmaid: The Bible and the Social Sciences," now that the once-dominant influence of nineteenth-century-style historical criticism is in decline, it is social study of the Bible that has staked its claim to being "the scientific investigative mode."[26] A fundamental difference between historical study,

---

[23]Cf. Hans Peter Dürr's more elaborate parable of the ichthyologist and the metaphysician, described by J. Spieß, "Die Geschichtlichkeit der Heiligen Schrift," Jahrbuch für Evangelikale Theologie 4 (1990): 117.

[24]*Old Testament and the Historian*, p. 18.

[25]So Caird, *Language and Imagery*, p. 217.

[26]*Theological Studies* 50 (1989): 260. Osiek provides a convenient historical survey of the growth of sociological approaches to the Bible, from the planting of the seeds in the last century by, e.g., J. Wellhausen and W. Robertson Smith, to their subsequent cultivation by Gunkel, Mowinckel, Pederson, Weber, and others, and finally to the current burgeoning of interest in such approaches, as evidenced by the attention given, e.g., to the writings of Norman Gottwald. For other evaluative surveys, see A. D. H. Mayes, "Sociology and the Old Testament," in *The World of Ancient Israel*, ed. R. E. Clements (Cambridge: Cambridge University Press, 1989), pp. 39–63; Morgan, *Biblical Interpretation*, chap. 5; C. S. Rodd, "Sociology and Social Anthropology," in *Dictionary*, ed. Coggins and Houlden, pp. 635–39. And for an up-to-date treatment of sociological investigations of the New Testament, see B. Holmberg, *Sociology and the New Testament: An Appraisal* (Minneapolis: Fortress, 1990).

as traditionally conceived, and sociological analysis is that while the former tends to stress the importance of the "individual and particular," the latter is more concerned with the "general and typical."[27] This is often referred to as the distinction between an *idiographic* and a *nomothetic* approach. These terms were apparently first introduced by Wilhelm Windelband, rector of the University of Strassburg, in his inaugural address in 1894 entitled "History and Natural Science."[28] Windelband's distinction between the natural sciences and the historical disciplines is summarized by McCullagh as follows:

> Natural scientists . . . proceed by quantification and abstraction to formulate, as precisely as they can, general laws of nature, true of many individual sequences of events. Historians, on the other hand, are forever seeking a particularity and uniqueness. Windelband called the natural sciences 'nomothetic' (lawgiving) and the historical disciplines 'idiographic' (describing the separate, distinct, individual).[29]

Broadly speaking, this distinction is valid. Traditional histories tend to focus on significant individuals as shapers of history, while the social sciences, insofar as they strive to be "scientific," seek to discover general "laws" about the way large-scale societal forces influence historical change. This does not mean, of course, that historians have no interest in generalizations. "If they are to describe what life was like for groups of people in the past, they must generalize." Moreover, they need to become familiar with "the conventions of a society" if they are to "understand documents relating to it." Generalizations play a big part in the historian's development of what we have earlier referred to as an ancient literary and cultural competence. "Historians must know the general significance within a society of certain words and actions if they are to make sense of the evidence they have of that society, and of the deeds to which that evidence relates."[30]

There is, then, a place for nomothetic investigation in historical study as traditionally practiced. Its chief function is to describe "the abiding institutions and patterns of culture, against which the quicker movements that catch the scholarly eye are visible."[31] Nomothetic study, in other words, seeks to present the general cultural, material, and historical background against which the specific actions of individuals and groups are to be viewed.

Some of the best sociological approaches to the history of ancient cultures acknowledge the complementarity of nomothetic and idiographic forces in the processes of history. Unfortunately, however, this is not always the case. Many (though certainly not all) social-scientific treatments of biblical issues are explicitly or implicitly Marxist in perspective, and this inevitably influences the way in which the actions of past individuals, and the texts that report them, are assessed. In Marx's view, individuals play a very minor role in history. At best, they may affect specific details of historical transformation, but they have no power, as individuals, to bring about major changes.[32] For Marx, it is not

---

[27]Morgan, *Biblical Interpretation*, p. 139.
[28]See McCullagh, *Justifying Historical Descriptions*, p. 129.
[29]Ibid., p. 129.
[30]Ibid., p. 130.
[31]So Halpern, *First Historians*, p. 122.
[32]See McCullagh (*Justifying Historical Descriptions*, pp. 225–26), who cites as counter-evidence to the Marxist perspective the impressive case that can be made in support of the view "that the Russian Revolution of 1917 would not have occurred without Lenin's leadership, and that there was no chance of anyone else bringing it about in his absence."

individuals but material/economic forces that drive history. In *A Contribution to the Critique of Political Economy* he writes: "The mode of production of material life determines the general character of the social, political and spiritual processes of life. It is not the consciousness of men that determines their being, but, on the contrary, their social being determines their consciousness." In other words, as he puts it in *The German Ideology*, it is the "process of production" that ultimately accounts for "the different theoretical productions and forms of consciousness, religion, philosophy, ethics, etc."[33]

What does all this have to do with the claim that some social-scientific approaches exhibit an anti-literary, or anti-textual, tendency? It is this. Denials of the significance of individuals, such as we have noted above, almost inevitably lead to a depreciation of texts (particularly narrative texts such as are found in the Bible) in which individuals and their actions are portrayed as vitally important in "making history." Hayden White provides a nice illustration of this point in a discussion of the place of narrative discourse in historical theory. He observes that "certain social-scientifically oriented historians, of whom the members of the French *Annales* group may be considered exemplary . . . regarded narrative historiography as a non-scientific, even *ideological representation strategy*, the extirpation of which was necessary for the transformation of historical studies into a genuine science."[34] The explicit charge brought against narrative history by the *Annalistes* was that "narrativity is inherently 'dramatizing' or 'novelizing' of its subject-matter, as if dramatic events either did not exist in history or, if they did exist, are by virtue of their dramatic nature not fit objects of historical study."[35] White maintains, however, that what actually underlies the depreciation of "narrative history" is not the supposed antithesis between the "dramatic" and the "scientific" but, rather, "a distaste for a genre of literature that puts human agents rather than impersonal processes at the center of interest and suggests that such agents have some significant control over their own destinies."[36]

The issue then is between a nomothetic view of historical change, which ascribes primary significance to impersonal processes, and an idiographic view, which allows individual personalities to exercise significant influence. Wherever the former viewpoint holds sway, narratives in general and biblical narratives in particular (in which individual persons, to say nothing of a personal God, play so large a part) will receive little respect as sources of historical information. In a recent essay addressing questions of historical method, Keith Whitelam argues that "the whole concept of the study of the history of Israel needs to be enlarged and reformulated in order to overcome the constraints and limitations, *for the historian*, of the traditions preserved in the Hebrew Bible."[37] To be sure, historians may wish to overcome the "limitations" of the biblical evidence by investigating, for example, sociological or cultural or economic or political questions that the text *does not address*. But if they insist also on escaping the "constraints" of the text on matters to which it does speak, then what is to provide the basis of historical reconstruction?

Whitelam defends his dismissal of the text with the observation that "the text is not a witness to historical reality, only to itself. It is a witness to a particular perception

---

[33]Both quoted in ibid., pp. 157–58.
[34]"Question of Narrative," p. 7.
[35]Ibid., p. 9.
[36]Ibid., p. 10.
[37]"Recreating the History of Israel," *JSOT* 35 (1986): 55; cf. Thompson, *Early History of Israel*, p. 169.

of reality."[38] But surely we are always limited to a particular perception of reality—if not the text's, then our own. Having jettisoned the former, Whitelam is left with only the latter, and this leads him to conclude that "all [historical] reconstructions [of the history of Israel] are contingent." He writes:

> As our perspective or vantage point shifts, a frequent occurrence in the present age, so our view of the history of Israel must be readjusted. This is not to suggest that what happened in the past or the reasons why it happened change, but our perspective of these two aspects of the past radically changes with adjustments in our own situation, new discoveries, or fresh perspectives on the interrelationship of various pieces of data.[39]

There is a sense in which Whitelam is correct, of course. Our own perceptions of the past do change as we gain new data and see the past in new lights. The social sciences can be useful, as we have already suggested, in pursuing questions that the text does not address, or does not address directly. But are we well advised to seek to escape the *constraints* of the text in matters that it *does* address? Should not the text at least be included among the available data?

The anti-textual, or anti-literary, error of some sociological approaches is all too easily compounded by an anachronistic error. As Charles Tilly observes in *As Sociology Meets History*,[40] sociological theory is grounded in "one piece of history: the piece their formulators are currently living. . . . The mistake is to extrapolate backwards, without attempting to place the small contemporary strip of history into the broad band of social transformation to which it belongs" (p. 214).

What is needed, it would seem, is a properly balanced perspective on both the *nomothetic* and the *idiographic* forces at work in history. Exclusively idiographic, text-based reconstructions of history may well capture the soul of past events but have little understanding of their embodiment. Exclusively nomothetic reconstructions, on the other hand, easily fall into a kind of reductionism and determinism that loses sight of the very soul of past events.[41] Morgan stresses the importance of coordinating the emphases: "Anyone wanting to understand past or present societies will use both [history and sociology]. Whether or not either can 'explain' a society, both offer partial explanations of particular features."[42]

Finding the balance between the nomothetic emphasis of the social sciences and the idiographic emphasis of the historical discipline is a desideratum. But there is a further

---

[38]"Recreating the History of Israel," p. 52.

[39]Ibid., p. 64.

[40]New York: Academic Press, 1981.

[41]Gottwald himself (*The Hebrew Bible: A Socio-Literary Introduction* [Philadelphia: Fortress, 1985], p. 33) acknowledges that "anthropological and sociological categories deal with the typical and thus provide 'average' descriptions and general tendencies which by themselves may miss the momentary oddities and exceptions of historical figures and happenings." Cf. also Holmberg, *Sociology*, p. 157. For an insightful critique of sociology's tendency toward positivism, relativism, reductionism, and determinism, see G. A. Herion "The Impact of Modern and Social Science Assumptions on the Reconstruction of Israelite History," *JSOT* 34 (1986): 3–33. To catch something of the flavor of the nomothetic vs. idiographic debate that is going on in the field of secular history, see C. Parker's review of recent writers in "Methods, Ideas and Historians" *Literature and History* 11 (1985): 288–291; cf. also F. K. Ringer, "Causal Analysis in Historical Reasoning," *HTh* 28 (1989): 154–72.

[42]*Biblical Interpretation*, p. 140.

aspect to the problem, as is perhaps suggested by Morgan's last statement above. Sociology, like the nineteenth-century-style historical criticism discussed above, is ill-equipped to treat the religious dimension in human experience without becoming reductionistic. This may not be too surprising if, as Cyril Rodd asserts, "many of the early anthropologists and sociologists were atheists."[43] The tendency of some social scientists to overbalance the equation in the direction of nomothetic forces must be resisted by historians of the Bible, since, as Stanford insists, every culture is the product not only of "human volition and adaptation, as well as of physical energies" but also of "spiritual energy." He explains: "Religious experience in many different ages and cultures seems to have borne witness to a power that rules the universe yet can be found within the individual man or woman."[44]

Even among sociological approaches that are less directly influenced by Marxist materialism, there is a tendency to downplay the significance of individuals and their religious commitments. As Bengt Holmberg observes,

> The tendency of modern sociological theory is to minimize the part played by cognitive interests in social actions, such as generating and sustaining religious commitments. The religious viewpoint of the actors is registered but not accorded any validity or effect, which is reserved for social factors (level of education, family background, relative deprivation, etc.). Thus the implicit claim of the sociologists is that they understand the basis of religious belief and action better than religious people do.[45]

Andrew Hill and Gary Herion likewise lament sociology's "innate deficiency to properly address the role of personal faith in the socio-political process." They point out that "the application of modern social science concepts to the OT often fails to disclose adequately the true nature of the relationship between politics and religion in ancient Israel. This is due in large measure to the inability of such concepts to account fully for the dynamic variable of individual faith in Yahweh."[46]

Is it any wonder then that scholars who employ methods that share this "innate deficiency" arrive at historical reconstructions radically different from those employing methods that do not? Only time will tell whether the application of social-science analysis will ultimately clarify or cloud our perception of the history and culture of the people of the Bible. Much depends on making the necessary adjustments to give not only nomothetic, but also idiographic and religious influences their due. While the social sciences have great potential for increasing our understanding, particularly of the background against which the events of biblical history played themselves out, they are inadequate to predict specific courses of events.[47] For purposes of *historical* reconstruction, the social sciences must resist the anti-literary tendency and remain in some measure dependent on written sources.

---

[43]According to Rodd ("Sociology," p. 636), "Only W. Robertson Smith, among the circle of early anthropologists, retained his firm Christian faith up to his death. . . . It is curious, therefore, that the early theories were accepted so uncritically by OT scholars."

[44]*Nature*, pp. 39–40.

[45]*Sociology*, pp. 147–48.

[46]"Functional Yahwism and Social Control in the Early Israelite Monarchy," *JETS* 29 (1986): 277.

[47]Halpern ("Biblical or Israelite History?" in *Future of Biblical Studies*, ed. Friedman and Williamson, p. 122) rightly warns that "we cannot deterministically 'predict' on this basis [i.e., knowledge of background] developments the sources do not register. But *Kulturgeschichte* and sociology can afford us what they did classical history: a means to evaluate specific reports about specific events."

Archaeology: A Discipline in Flux

The present century has witnessed a dramatic increase in archaeological knowledge of the lands of the Bible, and some of this new knowledge has proved very helpful in the interpretation of biblical texts. Yet when it comes to the matter of historical reconstruction, archaeology is subject to some of the same limitations and potential abuses as described above with respect to the social sciences. To complicate matters further, the very nature and proper function of archaeological investigation has in recent years been hotly debated. As the late D. Glenn Rose observed, not only are "archaeological method and associated methods of interpreting the data . . . in flux," but "the relationship of this changing archaeology to the Bible is . . . also in flux."[48] What for years was called *biblical archaeology* has today generally been displaced in favor of *Syro-Palestinian archaeology* or what is called the *new archaeology*, and there are signs that even these terms may fall into disfavor and be replaced by others.[49]

But what is this *new archaeology* that has enjoyed popularity in recent decades? Philip King describes it as a "model of interdisciplinary archaeology" in which "natural and social scientists and archaeologists" work side-by-side at a particular site. He attributes the early cultivation of this brand of archaeology in Palestine to the influence of G. Ernest Wright's dream of "ecological archaeology."[50] Lawrence Toombs further elucidates the nature of the new archaeology by comparing it with traditional archaeology, which embraced three principle aims: to reconstruct "cultural history," to reconstruct the "life-ways of the people who left the archaeological record," and to study "cultural process."[51] To illustrate these three aims, Toombs compares them to various aspects of the work of excavating a tell. The chronological concerns of reconstructing history he compares to the stratigraphic trench, the interest in life-ways to the "area of exposure of a single level or stratum," and the interest in cultural process to the "interstices between the levels." The primary goal of the new archaeology, according to Toombs, is the "processual" one. That is, it is most concerned with discovering "the laws of cultural change" (p. 46). In keeping with this concern, the new archaeology is "not primarily a revision of methodology but rather a profound reexamination of philosophy and theory. . . . The movement is from theory to praxis, not the reverse" (p. 42). And what is the theory? In broad terms, it is the notion that archaeology belongs to the sciences and not to the humanities. So conceived, archaeology is constrained to "develop its theories and procedures in ways congruent with those of the physical sciences" (p. 43). The result is that "archaeological knowledge" becomes limited to "confirmed generalizations" (p. 44) or purely "materialistic" explanations, to the unhappy exclusion, for purposes of historical reconstruction at least, of any proper recognition of the "role of ideology" (or theology) or of "individual creativity and imagination in producing cultural variability" (p. 48).

---

[48]"The Bible and Archaeology: The State of the Art," in *Archaeology and Biblical Interpretation,* ed. L. G. Perdue, L. E. Toombs, and G. L. Johnson (Atlanta: John Knox, 1987), p. 57.

[49]See, e.g., W. G. Dever, "Biblical Archaeology: Death and Rebirth?" in *Proceedings of the Second International Congress on Biblical Archaeology (Jerusalem, 1990),* forthcoming.

[50]"The Influence of G. Ernest Wright on the Archaeology of Palestine," in *Archaeology and Biblical Interpretation,* ed. Perdue et al., p. 22.

[51]"A Perspective on the New Archaeology," in *Archaeology and Biblical Interpretation,* ed. Perdue et al., p. 45.

As with the social sciences, these nomothetic tendencies of the new archaeology can lead to a reductionism and environmental determinism that discounts the significance of individuals in making history and thus encourages a downplaying of the historical import of the Bible's admittedly idiographical narratives. As Rose aptly puts it, because of the new archaeology's theoretical framework, in which culture is conceived as "the product of human adaptation to environmental change" rather than as the "shaping agent of that environment," the approach sometimes becomes "very deterministic as it is handled through statistics and systems theory."[52]

In view of the fact that much current archaeological practice downplays or denies the significance of textual evidence, the question that must be addressed is whether archaeology alone, independent of literary evidence, is an adequate basis for *historical* reconstruction. Several observations suggest that it is not.

First, with the exception of inscriptional evidence, most of what archaeology can discover (artifactual remains and stratigraphic sequence) speaks of life conditions in general and not of specific events. As Miller notes, "Although it is a good source for clarifying the material culture of times past, artifactual evidence is a very poor source of information about specific people and events."[53]

Second, and again with the exception of inscriptional evidence, the material remains unearthed by archaeology do not in fact *speak* at all, but *must be interpreted* on some basis. Frederic Brandfon has recently drawn attention to the fallacy of assuming that archaeological evidence, whether artifactual or stratigraphic, is somehow more *objective* than other types of evidence: "once the researcher begins the necessary task of grouping the evidence into typologies of artifacts on the one hand, or charts of comparative stratigraphy on the other, theoretical concerns begin to transform the archaeological evidence into an historical account. In this sense, archaeological evidence, despite its brute factuality, is no more objective than any other type of evidence."[54] He explains:

> I can experience a given ash layer by touching it, seeing it and even tasting it; but this immediate experience is not history until I talk about it or write about it to someone else. The minute I do that, however, I begin to interpret the facts. I have to choose the words which will describe that layer, e.g. 'destruction debris' or 'burnt debris.' This interpretation transforms the individual facts into 'general concepts' by grouping them with other facts and other ideas. This transformation is the creative process of historiography.[55]

Third, the archaeological evidence available to the historian is both partial and constantly changing. It is partial, since not all significant sites nor all sections of given sites have been excavated (to say nothing of the fact that only a small percentage of material remains from the past will have survived anyway). And it is constantly changing, since continuing archaeological investigation is regularly bringing new evidence to light.

---

[52]"Bible and Archaeology," p. 56.

[53]"Old Testament History and Archaeology," *Biblical Archaeologist* 50 (1987): 59.

[54]"The Limits of Evidence: Archaeology and Objectivity," *Maarav* 4/1 (1987): 30. Cf. Miller's assertion that archaeological investigation "involves highly subjective judgments on the part of the interpreter" ("Reflections on the Study of Israelite History," in *What Has Archaeology to Do With Faith?*, ed. J. H. Charlesworth and W. P. Weaver [Philadelphia: Trinity Press International, 1992], p. 67).

[55]"Limits of Evidence," p. 30.

All of these factors indicate that archaeology alone does not provide an adequate foundation for historical reconstruction, at least not in terms of traditional history's interest in particular events and individuals. As with the social sciences discussed earlier, archaeology's greatest potential is in the delineation of the general milieu (cultural, material, etc.) within which specific events may have taken place. Archaeological evidence may form part of a cumulative case suggesting the plausibility of a specific event, but it is hardly adequate to prove it (or, in most instances, to disprove it). As Boling and Campbell aptly state, "only rarely will archaeology settle an issue and only rarely is it of total irrelevance."[56] We do well, then, to go slowly when advised on the basis of archaeological discussion (for example, the continuing controversies over the site of Ai) to "redirect our thinking about Bible."[57] Surely, we should recall how often the assured archaeological results of one generation have been overturned in the next.[58]

If, then, archaeology alone is an inadequate basis for historical reconstruction, and if, as Brandfon has argued, "theoretical concerns" inevitably come into play whenever archaeological evidence is marshalled in the service of historical reconstruction, the crucial question becomes: what provides our theoretical grid? As Brandfon points out, "An historian may use any number of theories in order to transform evidence into history, e.g., Marxist theory, Freudian theory, or a combination; possibly literary or religious theories. Some of these theories we may judge apt or applicable and others not."[59] Certain of these theories, as we have already seen, will by virtue of their generalized, nomothetic tendencies downplay the significance of texts (especially the biblical text) in reconstructing history. But we must not forget that for many aspects of Israelite history, the Bible is our *main*—and sometimes even our *only*—source.[60] Admittedly, scholars wishing to prove the veracity of the Bible have sometimes been guilty of wittingly or unwittingly misconstruing archaeological results. But this does not mean that archaeologists are well advised to bracket out the biblical evidence entirely.[61] Where the Bible, with its particular view of reality, is excluded from the archaeologist's interpretive grid, some other theory will fill the void, with no less potential for distortion. Individual archaeologists will quite naturally be attracted to those theories whose views of reality most closely resemble their own set of background beliefs. These various considerations lead to the following conclusions with respect to the place of archaeology in the reconstruction of history.

---

[56]"Jeroboam and Rehoboam at Shechem," in *Archaeology*, ed. Perdue et al., p. 264.

[57]So J. A. Callaway, "Ai (et-Tell): Problem Site for Biblical Archaeologists," in *Archaeology*, ed. Perdue et al., p. 97.

[58]One thinks, e.g., of N. Glueck's contention, based on surface-surveys of Transjordan, that the region was lacking in settled population between the 19th and 13th centuries B.C.; more recent archaeological work in the area suggests otherwise (see R. G. Boling, *The Early Biblical Community in Transjordan* [Sheffield: Almond, 1988], pp. 11–35).

[59]"Limits of Evidence," pp. 30–31.

[60]Clines (*What Does Eve*, p. 101) notes that what he calls the "Primary History" (i.e., Genesis–2 Kings) is "for most of the period it covers . . . the only source we have for knowing anything at all about what actually happened in ancient Israel"; cf. Miller, "Reflections," pp. 65–66; Garbini, *History and Ideology*, p. 16.

[61]As D. W. J. Gill notes in a review article of Robin Lane Fox's *The Unauthorized Version: Truth and Fiction in the Bible* (London: Viking, 1991), "Just because biblical archaeologists have made some 'howlers' . . . that with hindsight look ridiculous does not mean that biblical archaeology (or the Bible) is wrong. The same straw-man arguments could be used against the classical historian Herodotus" ("Authorized or Unauthorized: A Dilemma for the Historian," *TynB* 43/1 [1992]: 194).

First, historians should recognize archaeology's innate limitations (i.e., its partial, ever changing, and generalized character). Where this is done, two results will follow: historians will be less likely to attempt to establish specific courses of events on the basis of archaeological evidence alone, and they will be more cautious about accepting without qualification what some might regard as archaeology's "proven results."

Second, since the archaeological data are neither purely objective nor self-interpreting, historians should remind themselves that as soon as they begin to talk about the data, they are doing so on the basis of an interpretive grid that they themselves bring to the task.

Thus, third, where archaeological evidence is used in building a cumulative case for the likelihood or unlikelihood of a specific historical scenario, historians should openly acknowledge, to themselves and to their audience, the extent to which their own background beliefs influence their judgments. To put the matter another way: clarity would be served if archaeologists and historians would be more self-conscious and explicit about their own belief systems, since theory plays such a large part in the interpretation of archaeology's limited, changing, and essentially mute data. Awareness of one's own presuppositions and predispositions is, of course, also the first step toward avoiding special pleading and the distortion of evidence.

Fourth, far from dismissing the literary (biblical) evidence as little more than a hindrance to historical reconstruction, historians should seek a closer coordination of archaeological and literary studies, despite the difficulties and dangers that attend such an enterprise. Admittedly, as Ephraim Stern has observed,[62] this task is made more difficult by the "information explosion" of recent decades and the consequent "narrow specialization" of scholars. The rigors of mastering the various technologies that are employed by the new archaeology have cut sharply into the time that scholars can find "to devote themselves to the literary sources, whether biblical or external." But this, as Stern rightly notes, is a "genuine loss," and one with which historical and archaeological scholarship can ill afford to rest content.

Finally, whenever scholars begin to reflect on the relationship of archaeology and the Bible, they should give some indication not only of their general attitude toward the Bible but also of their level of competence in dealing with its literature.[63] In the end, biblical archaeology is, according to Philip King, "a Biblical, not an archaeological, discipline. It is the responsibility of Biblical scholars, not archaeologists, to ferret out pertinent material evidence and apply it to the Bible." King cites the "crying need for synthesizing works that bring archaeological data to bear on the Biblical text."[64]

Where scholars are willing to proceed cautiously, with such issues as these in mind, archaeology has much to contribute to the historical study of the Bible. Indeed, as Darrell Lance maintains, "Archaeology helps to keep vital biblical scholarship as a whole. When all is said and done, few tasks in the study of the Bible can match it in excitement and importance, for it is the source of ever-new data to increase our ability to read the Bible with understanding and appreciation."[65]

So then, what can archaeology contribute to the task of historical reconstruction? It can supplement, but should not be allowed to supplant, written sources, including the

---

[62]"The Bible and Israeli Archaeology," in *Archaeology*, ed. Perdue et al., p. 37.
[63]Cf., e.g., Gill's comments in "Authorized or Unauthorized," pp. 199–200.
[64]"The *Marzeah* Amos Denounces," *Biblical Archeology Review* 14/4 (1988): 34.
[65]*The Old Testament and the Archaeologist* (Philadelphia: Fortress, 1981), p. 96.

Bible. It can suggest the plausibility, or otherwise, of specific events, but it can seldom prove or disprove them. Even where it can render probable the *occurrence* of an event, it is ill-suited to pronounce on the *interpretation* of that event. As we turn now to consider literary approaches to the Bible, we shall discover that the tendency of some of them is to err in a different direction—viz., so to stress the interpretive word as to deny, or at best disavow interest in, the occurrence of any underlying event.

ANTI-HISTORICAL TENDENCIES IN SOME LITERARY APPROACHES

Literary Approaches: A Mixed Blessing?

After well over a century of domination by *historical* criticism, biblical studies has welcomed, hesitantly at first but then more readily, the arrival of *literary* approaches to the Bible. The quickening of interest in adopting explicitly literary approaches to biblical interpretation can be attributed in part to "a sense of disappointment and disillusionment with the traditional historical-critical methods" and in part to a desire of biblical scholars to apply trends in secular literary theory to their own discipline.[66] A further motivating factor is the simple fact that the Bible is, after all, a literary work. If the Bible comprises a library of literary genres (as I argued in the first chapter of this book), then a literary approach is not a luxury, but a necessity. Even the Bible's historiography, which I described in chapter 2 as a kind of verbal representational art, requires that we seek to become as competent as possible in the conventions of ancient literature. Without some understanding and appreciation of the literary medium of the Bible, we are likely to misperceive its messages (historical, theological, or whatever).[67] Self-consciously literary approaches often shed new light on the workings of biblical texts, and this new light frequently calls for revision, or even reversal, of previously held opinions about the nature of these texts.[68] Thus, as Thiselton insists, "literary theory in biblical interpretation has nothing to do with 'icing on the cake' or with 'fluff.'"[69] It is essential.

Essential though it be, the adoption of a literary approach to biblical interpretation is not without attendant dangers. Indeed, Thiselton warns that the application of literary theory to the Bible "provides the most radical challenge to traditional hermeneutical models which has yet arisen."[70] The benefits of becoming acquainted with the literary workings of biblical texts are manifold, to be sure,[71] and this not least for Bible readers interested in historical questions. But under the general rubric *literary approach* is to be found an astonishing diversity of methods, not all of which are well suited for dealing with

---

[66]Barton, *Reading the Old Testament*, pp. 105–6. The results achieved by historical criticism were deemed by many as theologically rather sparse, if not detrimental. Even among those who did not think "that historical criticism had failed or that its goals were invalid," there was a sense that "something else should also be done" (Powell, *What Is Narrative Criticism?* p. 3).

[67]For fuller remarks, see the section "Genre Criticism and Biblical Interpretation" in chap. 1 above. Cf. also Alter, *The World of Biblical Literature*, p. 56.

[68]Cf., e.g., Hall, *Seven Pillories*, p. 110; Powell, *What Is Narrative Criticism?* pp. 86–87, 96–98; Polzin, "1 Samuel," p. 305; Long, *Reign and Rejection*, pp. 10–20.

[69]*New Horizons*, p. 473.

[70]Ibid.

[71]See, e.g., ibid., pp. 471–79; Powell, *What Is Narrative Criticism?* pp. 85–90; Longman, *Literary Approaches*, pp. 131–33; W. W. Klein, C. L. Blomberg, and R. L. Hubbard, eds., *Introduction to Biblical Interpretation* (Dallas: Word, 1993), pp. 432–38.

the Bible. "Literary theory, for good or for ill, brings into biblical studies an intimidating and complicated network of assumptions and methods which were not in origin designed to take account of the particular nature of *biblical* texts. These carry with them their own agenda of deeply philosophical questions about the status of language, the nature of texts, and relations between language, the world, and theories of knowledge."[72]

Surveys of the assumptions and methods of the various literary approaches that have enjoyed some influence in biblical studies—New Criticism, formalism, rhetorical criticism, structuralism, narrative criticism, deconstruction, and the like—are readily available, so that I need not attempt one here.[73] Of more pertinence to our present concern with the issue of why scholars disagree over historical questions is the fact that certain of the "literary approaches" tend in *ahistorical*, or even *anti-historical*, directions.[74] In some instances the anti-historical bias simply reflects philosophical assumptions—that is, some of the newer literary approaches "incorporate concepts derived from movements in secular literary criticism that repudiate the significance of historical investigation for the interpretation of texts."[75] In other instances, however, the anti-historical tendency may stem from a lack of clarity over just what the terms *literature* and *history* mean and over how the two interrelate. Recent studies have made it ever more apparent that the Bible's narratives, even those regarded as historiographical, exhibit markedly *literary* traits. Does this mean that they should no longer be considered *historical*? I think not, not only for the reasons presented earlier (especially in chap. 2) but also for those given in the next paragraph.

The assumption that literature and history constitute mutually exclusive categories is a distinctly modern one, as Lionel Gossman has argued: "For a long time the relation of history to literature was not notably problematic. History was a branch of literature. It was not until the meaning of the word *literature,* or the institution of literature itself, began to change, toward the end of the eighteenth century, that history came to appear as something distinct from literature."[76] As *literature* increasingly came to be associated with poetry and fiction, and as *history* came to be thought of in positivistic terms as needing to draw "as close as possible, epistemologically and methodologically, to the natural sciences," the gap between literature and history widened. "Finally," continues Gossman, "in our own times, the very idea that the historian's activity consists in discovering and

---

[72]Thiselton, *New Horizons*, p. 471.

[73]See, e.g., Barton, *Reading the Old Testament*; Longman, *Literary Approaches*, chap. 1; P. R. House, *Beyond Form Criticism: Essays in Old Testament Literary Criticism*, Sources for Biblical and Theological Studies 2 (Winona Lake: Eisenbrauns, 1992); Powell, *What Is Narrative Criticism?* chap. 2; Thiselton, *New Horizons*, chaps. 13–14; as well as the glossaries of literary terms and literary theory by, e.g., Abrams (*Glossary*), C. Baldick (*The Concise Oxford Dictionary of Literary Terms* [Oxford: Oxford University Press, 1990]), J. A. Cuddon (*A Dictionary of Literary Terms and Literary Theory*, 3rd ed., [Oxford: Basil Blackwell, 1991]), J. Hawthorn (*A Glossary of Contemporary Literary Theory* [London: Edward Arnold, 1992]).

[74]See Longman, *Literary Approaches*, pp. 128–31; Sternberg, *Poetics*, chap. 1; Gunn, "New Directions in the Study of Biblical Hebrew Narrative," *JSOT* 39 (1987): 73; Geller, "Through Windows and Mirrors into the Bible: History, Literature and Language in the Study of Text," in *A Sense of Text: The Art of Language in the Study of Biblical Literature* (Winona Lake: Eisenbrauns, 1983), p. 39.

[75]Powell, *What Is Narrative Criticism?* p. 7; cf. Whitelam, "Between History and Literature: The Social Production of Israel's Traditions of Origin," *JSOT* 2 (1991): 64.

[76]"History and Literature: Reproduction or Signification," in *The Writing of History: Literary Form and Historical Understanding*, ed. R. H. Canary and H. Kozicki (Madison: University of Wisconsin Press, 1978), p. 3.

reconstituting, by whatever means, a past reality conceived of as something objectively fixed, has begun to be questioned. The old common ground of history and literature— the idea of mimesis and the central importance of rhetoric—has thus been gradually vacated by both. The practicing historian is now rarely a practicing literary artist."[77]

Whatever may be the modern trend, if the line that we have been taking in this book is at all leading in the right direction, there are grounds for rebridging the gap between literature and history, at least when our concern is with *ancient* historiography.[78] Perhaps one way to accomplish this is to be more circumspect in our definition of literature. As David Robertson points out in *The Old Testament and the Literary Critic,*[79] literature can be subdivided into two general types: *pure* (imaginative, nonutilitarian) literature and *applied* (utilitarian) literature. Much in the Bible "was originally written as applied literature: as history, liturgy, laws, preaching, and the like" (p. 3). This needs to be borne in mind whenever we speak of the Bible as literature, lest we wrongly assume that it will display only the characteristics of pure literature.[80] If literature, broadly conceived, involves "an interpretive presentation of experience in an artistic form"[81] and is distinguished by "artful verbal expression and compelling ideas,"[82] then a history may qualify as literature and merit a literary interpretive approach no less than a novel or a poem.

The problem with some modern literary approaches to the Bible is that they tend to dismiss historical questions as either uninteresting or illegitimate. But to bracket out forever or to banish historical questions is to do an injustice to the biblical literature. Much of the Bible presents itself as applied literature—literature meant to serve a communicative function.[83] And literary communication, as analyzed in the now familiar diagram first developed by M. H. Abrams, involves four constituent elements, or "co-ordinates."[84] The central element in Abrams' diagram is the *work* (the text), but it is not the only element. Around it are arranged three others: the *universe* (i.e., the *subject*, which may include "people

---

[77]Ibid., pp. 5–7.

[78]It may be noted in passing that many modern historians are calling for renewed attention to the relationship between historiography and literature; see, e.g., A. Rigney, *The Rhetoric of Historical Representation: Three Narrative Histories of the French Revolution* (Cambridge: Cambridge University Press, 1990); A. Cameron, ed., *History as Text: The Writing of Ancient History* (London: Duckworth, 1989).

[79]Philadelphia: Fortress, 1977.

[80]For a fuller discussion of Robertson's own approach and his curious decision to view the Old Testament as pure or imaginative literature, see Long, *Reign and Rejection,* p. 13. On the general point that *literature* includes both referential and non-referential varieties, we may note New Criticism's adoption of T. S. Eliot's coinage *autotelic* to describe literature which has "no end or purpose beyond its own existence" and which is distinguishable from "works that involve practical reference to things outside themselves" (Baldick, *Dictionary of Literary Terms,* p. 19).

[81]L. Ryken, *The Literature of the Bible* (Grand Rapids: Zondervan, 1974), p. 13.

[82]A. Berlin, "On the Bible as Literature," *Proof* 2 (1982): 324.

[83]Cf. Thiselton, *New Horizons,* p. 502: "Many, perhaps most, of the biblical writings at one level remain 'literary'; but it is even more fundamental to their *raison d'etre* that they reflect what human beings say and do, and how, in turn, they are addressed, *in everyday life.* This is not to deny that these texts are often also literary products, which are designed to produce certain *effects,* but *it is to deny that this latter aspect provides the primary, only, or supposedly most comprehensive model of meaning.*"

[84]*The Mirror and the Lamp: Romantic Theory and the Critical Tradition* (New York: Oxford University Press, 1953), pp. 3–29. Cf. also Barton, *Reading the Old Testament,* pp. 199–203; Longman, *Literary Approaches,* p. 18.

and actions, ideas and feelings, material things and events, or supersensible essences"[85]), the *artist* (the author or authors), and the *audience* (the reader or reading community). The *text* rightfully belongs in the middle because this is where the other three elements meet in the act of literary communication, as the author presents the universe (subject matter) via the text to the reader. Historical criticism, in its preoccupation with questions of authorship and textual prehistory, frequently fails to give the "text as it stands" adequate consideration in its own right and on its own terms before moving to extratextual issues. Literary criticism seeks to redress the balance by emphasizing the text and, more recently, the reader (as we shall see below). Attentiveness to text and reader can be welcomed, *but not if it becomes excessive to the point of excluding the other coordinates of author and universe.* "Text-immanent exegesis" is of great value, as Barton has stressed, but only if "counterintuitive tendencies" (such as an "unreasonable hatred of authorial intention, referential meaning, and the possibility of paraphrase or restatement") are kept in check.[86]

If the last several decades have witnessed a shift of interest in biblical studies from historical concerns with author, historical event, and textual prehistory to a (sometimes myopic) focus on the text, the last decade or so has witnessed a shift to the last remaining co-ordinate in Abrams's diagram, the *reader*. In the next section we shall consider reader-response criticism, which, like some of its literary cousins, can (but need not necessarily) tend in an anti-historical direction.

Reader-Response Criticism: Where's the Meaning?

No less than the literary approaches discussed in the preceding section, reader-response criticism is characterized by great variety. Robert Fowler, in *Let the Reader Understand: Reader-Response Criticism and the Gospel of Mark*, comments that "the spectrum of reader-response critics is so broad that whether they can all be categorized under that one heading is questionable."[87] Fowler is nevertheless able to highlight two common features shared by "most varieties of reader-response criticism": "(1) a preeminent concern for the reader and the reading experience and (2) a critical model of the reading experience, which itself has two major aspects: (a) an understanding of reading as a dynamic, concrete, temporal experience, instead of the abstract perception of a spatial form; and (b) an emphasis on meaning as event instead of meaning as content" (p. 25).

The first feature of reader-response criticism can be cautiously welcomed. In the discussion of the "Characteristics of Successful Representation" in chapter 2, we noted the way in which representational painting achieves its goal by "limiting the depiction of details to a suggestive few so as to allow the mind of the viewers to fill in the rest." The same is true of representational narrative, so that focusing on the way in which readers are active in *filling in* or *completing the picture* on the basis of promptings embedded in the text can be illuminating.[88] That Fowler should describe concern for the reader as "preeminent,"

---

[85]Abrams, *Mirror*, p. 6.

[86]*Reading the Old Testament*, p. 191.

[87](Minneapolis: Fortress, 1991), p. 25; cf. p. 23. For a summary of the diversity among reader-response approaches, see Thiselton, *New Horizons*, p. 529.

[88]Cf. Thiselton's comments (*New Horizons*, p. 515) on Wolfgang Iser's use of "a theory of perception to establish the role of readers in *filling in or completing* a textual meaning which would otherwise remain only potential rather than actual."

however, is disquieting. It hints at what in fact turns out to be the case for many reader-response approaches: in their desire to correct the imbalance resulting from neglect of the readerly element, some reader-response theories themselves end up neglecting the other vital elements in the act of literary communication—viz., text, author, and universe (e.g., for historiographical texts, the people and events referred to).

As for the "critical model of the reading experience" described by Fowler, the most perplexing aspect is its "emphasis on meaning as event instead of meaning as content."[89] This seems to me to involve a blurring of the distinction between *meaning* and *perception of meaning* or, as speech act theory would put it, between *illocution* (what the speaker wishes to accomplish in uttering a *locution*) and *perlocution* (the effect the speech act actually has on the hearer). Fowler is not unaware of the problematic status of *meaning* in reader-response theory: "Concerning meaning, is its locus in the text or in the reader?" (p. 34). But on at least one occasion in his discussion he evidences the kind of confusion over the locus of meaning that typifies many reader-response approaches. He writes:

> The obverse of the illocutionary force set in motion by the speaker is the hearer's apprehension or uptake of that illocutionary force (see chap. 1). Both illocutionary force and its *uptake* are functions of the context of the utterance, which is to say that the meaning of an illocution in speech act theory has the nature of dynamic event rather than static content. Thus does speech act theory teach us not to seek meanings in locutions alone but in the exercise and uptake of the illocutionary force of utterances. *In brief, an utterance means what it does, not what it says.* (p. 48; my italics)   .

Fowler is quite correct to insist that the meaning of a speech act rests not only in the locution (the words themselves) but in the illocutionary force behind them (e.g., the intent to inform, persuade, threaten, console, etc.). But his inclusion of "uptake" in the definition of meaning is troubling and runs counter to common-sense and everyday experience. "Don't forget to write," John reminds Mary as she boards the airplane. "Why didn't you write me?" he chides her upon her return. "Oh," she responds, "the speech act we shared didn't mean that I should write *to you*. That's not the way I took it. Your exact words (your *locution*) were 'don't forget to write,' and I did write a few things: a shopping list, a letter to my mother, my name on the hotel register. Your utterance couldn't have meant that I should write to you, an utterance means what it does, not what it says." Is John likely to find Mary's construal of the meaning of his speech act convincing? She has wrongly (con)fused *his* illocutionary intent and *her* perlocutionary "uptake" as the standard by which the meaning of his speech act is to be measured.

Fowler's inclusion of "uptake" in his definition of "meaning" is all the more curious in the light of what he has to say in the paragraph immediately preceding the above quotation. He explains that locutions "refer just to the utterances themselves," while "*illocutions* are what a speaker intends to do by uttering a particular locution, and *perlocutions* are what the speaker actually accomplishes through uttering the locution." Further, he asserts that perlocutions can be "laid aside" as "ultimately beyond anyone's control" (pp. 47–48). Why then does he fuse "uptake" (perlocution) to the concept of illocution?

[89]I have already commented on the inadequacy of Fowler's assumption that "perception of a spatial form" is *not* "a dynamic, concrete, temporal experience" (see p. 322 n. 20).

Again, it seems to me that this illicit *fusion* typifies the *confusion* found in some reader-response theories of meaning.

I have intentionally chosen to focus on Fowler's work because his reader-response approach is on the whole insightful, moderate, and useful. Unlike some of the more radical reader-response critics, Fowler recognizes that "the text imposes powerful constraints upon the reading experience, constraints that to this point have been acknowledged only sporadically and unsystematically" (p. 15). In this moderate stance, which allows the text a vital role in constraining readers' perceptions of meaning, Fowler is joined by others such as Wolfgang Iser and Umberto Eco. But within the reader-response camp there are also those (Stanley Fish, for example, in his later writings) who divest texts (and so, of course, also authors of texts) of virtually all authority in the establishment of meaning. "The reader's response is not *to* the meaning: it *is* the meaning," writes Fish.[90]

In such extreme versions of reader-response criticism, the text becomes little more than a Rorschach ink blot; how you "read" the ink on paper, whether text or blot, may reveal much about *you* (or your interpretive community), but little indeed about anything else (thus the recent emphasis on the "ethics of ideological reading"—*you, not the text or its author, are responsible for what you read out of the text*). Where biblical texts are read in this extreme fashion, questions of authorial intent and historical reference either will never be asked or will be dismissed as inappropriate. No longer will the Bible have any power to address readers or to change them "from outside."[91] Ultimately, as Thiselton warns, Fish's brand of reader-response criticism can disintegrate "into the anarchy in which *the most militant pressure-group actually carries the day about what satisfies their pragmatic criteria of 'right' reading.*"[92] As to its consequences for Christian faith, such a "socio-pragmatic hermeneutics transposes the meaning of texts into projections which are *potentially idolatrous* as instruments of self-affirmation. *Such a model transposes a Christian theology of grace and revelation into a phenomenology of religious self-discovery.*"[93]

Equally in vogue among some contemporary biblical scholars, and similar in effect to the more radical reader-response theories in its denial that meaning resides in authorial intent as this comes to expression in texts, is the literary theory of *deconstruction*, sometimes referred to as *post-structuralism*. As "a philosophically skeptical approach to the possibility of coherent meaning in language," deconstruction quite naturally challenges "the status of the author's intention or of the external world as a source of meaning in texts."[94] Indeed, for deconstructionists, "a text does not have a meaning in the sense of something that is 'signified,' that is meant, by the configuration of the words of which

---

[90]Quoted in Thiselton, *New Horizons*, p. 474. For a full discussion of the weaknesses of Fish's approach, especially his insistence that one must choose between a formalist approach in which the text absolutely determines reader perceptions and a socio-pragmatic approach in which readers themselves (or more properly the reading community) autonomously determine what counts as "right reading," see ibid., pp. 535–50. Thiselton insists rather that *"it is not the case, as Fish suggests it is, that we must choose between the sharply-bounded crystalline purity of formalist concepts and the unstable concepts of contextual pragmatism. Concepts may function with a measure of operational stability, but with 'blurred edges.' Differences of* social context and practice may *push or pull them into relatively different shapes,* but do not necessarily change their stable *identity"* (p. 541).
[91]Ibid., pp. 503–50 *passim.*
[92]Ibid., p. 535, cf. 515.
[93]Ibid., p. 550.
[94]Baldick, *Dictionary of Literary Terms*, p. 51.

it consists." Rather, "the text is said to practice 'the infinite deferral of the signified.'"[95] Because of the ceaseless play of language, meaning is ultimately indeterminate, or undecidable. And since "the author is no longer seen as the source of meaning,. . . . deconstruction is guilty of being an accessory after the fact with regard to the death of the author."[96] Having dispatched the author (and therewith also any notion of an author's illocutionary intent), deconstruction "invites us instead to read any writing 'creatively,' as a play of systemic 'differences' which generate innumerable possibilities of meaning."[97]

Clearly, a deconstructionist approach to textual meaning will not prove fruitful for those wishing to discover what a text may have to say about times past. An historical approach requires a degree of confidence in the ability of texts to serve as a medium for communication between writer and reader. But, as Juhl points out, if the deconstructionist theory "is even roughly correct, it is clear that anything like a speech act model of literary interpretation cannot be right." The converse, however, is also true, as Juhls goes on to observe: "if there is such a thing as understanding a text and if that is essentially like understanding a person's speech act and hence necessarily involves reference to the speaker's intentions, then not much remains of the theory of the text sketched above."[98]

So, what does the future hold? The deconstructionist wave will presumably continue to play itself out on the beach of scholarly fashion, and some of its insights may leave a lasting mark. But since even the most ardent deconstructionists tend to assume a more traditional concept of meaning in their own critical practice (e.g., they expect their audiences to "get their drift"), Wright is correct that "deconstructive criticism probably will go away: it is in the nature of sudden reflex-movements of absurdist cognitive skepticism to be short-lived."[99] Reader-response criticism may enjoy a longer tenure, provided that common sense prevails and the less radical forms of reader-response theory are adopted (i.e., those that, while giving attention to the often neglected *readerly* aspect of literary communication, nevertheless also take account of *text, author,* and *universe*).[100] Modern literary approaches to the Bible, at least those that can avoid falling into a counter-intuitive, anti-historical bias, may well develop a "symbiotic relationship" with "historical approaches to the text."[101] After all, careful literary reading is a prerequisite of responsible historical reconstruction. That is to say, a conscientious, fair-minded attempt to understand a biblical text on its own terms is logically prior to any historicizing about it. Therefore, the more skilled biblical interpreters become in reading texts *literarily,* the more competent they will become in assessing them *historically*.

---

[95] P. D. Juhl, "Playing with Texts: Can Deconstruction Account for Critical Practice?" in *Criticism and Critical Theory,* ed. Jeremy Hawthorn (London: Edward Arnold, 1984), p. 59.

[96] Hawthorn, *Glossary of Contemporary Literary Theory,* p. 49.

[97] Abrams, *Glossary,* p. 150.

[98] "Playing with Texts," p. 60. For a critique of deconstruction's "anti-historical," "ultra-relativist," "reader's liberationist" hermeneutic and a qualified commendation of a dialogue model of textual communication in which texts are treated as persons who address us from outside and with whom we may agree or disagree, see I. Wright, "History, Hermeneutics, Deconstruction," in *Criticism,* ed. Hawthorn, pp. 83–98.

[99] Ibid., p. 88.

[100] An example would be Powell's approach in *What Is Narrative Criticism?*; Powell (p. 16) classifies his own method as a kind of reader-response criticism at the opposite end of the spectrum from deconstruction.

[101] Ibid., p. 98.

We may bring this section to a close by observing that, as in so many areas of life, beatitude in biblical interpretation comes in finding balance and avoiding one-sided extremes. The problem with approaches that go so far wrong is often simply that they go so far. To the extent that biblical literature comprises *communicative* texts,[102] what is needed in biblical interpretation is an integrative approach that gives due attention to all the co-ordinates of Abrams' model of literary communication—author, reader, and reference as these meet on the ground of text.

AN EXAMPLE: THE EMERGENCE OF ISRAEL IN CANAAN DEBATE

My intent in this chapter has been to address the question of why it is that biblical scholars often disagree profoundly in their historical assessments of the biblical traditions and the biblical periods. In pursuing this question, I have explored several prominent approaches to biblical interpretation and historical reconstruction (though of course I have not attempted anything like a comprehensive survey). We are now in a position to look at a specific example, and the much-debated question of the emergence of Israel in Canaan comes to mind. It is hard to think of any period in Israel's history about which opinions differ more widely and over which more ink has been spilt in recent years. To attempt a survey of the literature that has appeared on this subject even during the last decade would require far more space than I can spare here. My intent, rather, will be simply to mention some of the main lines of approach and, more particularly, to ask how the tendencies of the various criticisms discussed above might bear on the kinds of questions asked and the results achieved.

Until the modern period, the general understanding of how Israel came to be in Canaan was that it entered from the outside by means of conquest, as described particularly in the book of Joshua. In this century, however, a number of other scenarios have been proposed, such as Alt's *infiltration theory*, Mendenhall's *peasant revolt theory* (revived and modified in Gottwald's *social revolution theory*), and a variety of more recent theories in which Israel is thought to have been formed from nomadic or displaced populations already indigenous to Canaan (see the works of Fritz, Finkelstein, Callaway, Lemche, Coote and Whitelam, etc.).[103]

The preference for alternatives to the conquest model may be accounted for in several ways. One predisposing factor (which relates to our earlier discussion of the presuppositions of traditional historical criticism) is the modernist assumption that texts in which divine agency plays any part are to be considered historically suspect. By this measure, of course, both Joshua and Judges would hardly be deemed trustworthy as historical sources. But quite apart from this modern a priori, which not all will share, there is also a general sense that the conquest model simply does not square with recent archaeological findings. Specifically, archaeology has failed to provide evidence of the extensive destruction commonly associated with the conquest model. Moreover, there is the perception that Joshua and Judges present rather different, even conflicting, pictures of the conquest, and this quite naturally leads some to doubt the historical plausibility of the one or the other,

---

[102]On the "Functions of Biblical Literature," see the section by that name in Longman, *Literary Approaches*, pp. 137–39.

[103]For a convenient summary and critique of these various positions, plus a proposal of his own, see J. J. Bimson, "The origins of Israel in Canaan: an examination of recent theories," *Them* 15/1 (1989): 4–15.

or both. Finally, increased literary sensitivities and recognition of the challenge of properly discerning textual truth claims has caused some scholars to be more open to the possibility that the book of Joshua, for instance, does not even *intend* to be taken historically.

How are we to assess these considerations? Having already noted the inappropriateness of the anti-theological tendency of traditional historical criticism, we may now focus on the other concerns. Each of these, in its own way, has to do with the way the biblical texts are *read*. First, then, let us consider the apparent conflict between the biblical tradition and the archaeological data. In the popular (and, indeed, scholarly) imagination there has crystallized over the years a picture of the Israelite conquest of Canaan as an event of almost unprecedented violence and destructiveness.[104] But is this in fact the *biblical* picture? Has the *literature* been properly read before turning to archaeology? In our discussion of the anti-literary tendency of some sociological and archaeological approaches, we noted the proclivity of such approaches to bracket out or even to ban literary considerations in the assessment of material evidence. Whatever may be the pros and cons of this attempt at methodological purity, the deficit is that experts in biblical literature and indeed literary expertise in general are sometimes lacking from the archaeological team.[105] This in itself need not be so bad, provided that field archaeologists are careful always to consult with experts in the biblical literature before beginning to speculate about the import of their discoveries for questions of biblical history or, failing that, are willing simply to refrain from such speculation. But sometimes archaeologists who exercise the greatest of care and rigor in their own discipline fall into the trap of giving the biblical text a rather flat, unnuanced reading and then, on the basis of this reading, pronouncing on the "fit" or "lack of fit" between the Bible and the archaeological data.

But this brings us back to the important question: does the Bible, properly understood, depict a violent conquest involving great destruction of persons and property? The answer is yes and no. Yes, because both Joshua and Judges attest that Israel entered Canaan from outside and that this involved much loss of life to the indigenous populations, but *no*, because property damage is said to have been much more minimal. Specifically, the Book of Joshua testifies that the populations of numerous cities were placed under the ban and totally destroyed (e.g., Makkedah, Libnah, Lachish, Eglon, Hebron, and Debir [10:28–39]), but of only three sites is it explicitly said that property, too, was utterly destroyed: Jericho (6:24), Ai (8:28; 10:1), and Hazor (11:12–14). The latter instance is particularly instructive, for while the report of Joshua's defeat of Jabin's coalition (11:1–5) states that "Joshua took all these royal cities and their kings and put them to the sword. He totally destroyed them, as Moses the servant of the LORD had commanded" (v. 12), it immediately adds that "Israel did not burn any of the cities built on their mounds—except Hazor, which Joshua burned" (v. 13). Clearly, then, to "take a city," "put it to the sword," and "utterly destroy it" (that is, place it under the ban) implies the

---

[104]E.g., W. S. LaSor et al. (*Old Testament Survey* [Grand Rapids: Eerdmans, 1982], p. 214) write: "A careful reading of Joshua would give the impression that the Israelites had 'devoted' every city and destroyed every pagan altar. The story of the Conquest stresses that side."

[105]For a balanced approach that seeks to respect the individual integrity of both archaeological and literary studies while at the same time taking care to bring the two together in a "dialogical method," see J. F. Strange, "Some Implications of Archaeology for New Testament Studies," in *What Has Archaeology*, ed. Charlesworth and Weaver, pp. 23–59.

decimation (or, at least, driving out) of its population but may say nothing of property damage. The picture presented in Joshua is that destruction of property was the exception, not the rule. Indeed, 24:13 finds Israel living in "cities you did not build" (see also Deut. 6:10–11).[106]

In the light of the *literary* evidence, then, it is a mistake to look for extensive *archaeological* evidence of the conquest, as scholars across the theological spectrum have tended to do.[107] And it is a double error to assume that if archaeology fails to yield evidence of wide-spread destruction in this or that time period, then the conquest could not have taken place at that time, or did not take place at all.[108]

This is not to say, of course, that archaeology may not shed significant light on the Israelite *settlement* in Canaan. In a recent volume of the *Scandinavian Journal of the Old Testament* dedicated to the question of the emergence of Israel in Canaan, the volume's editor, Diana Edelman, points to four areas of growing consensus: (1) that beginning in the Late Bronze Age and continuing throughout the Iron I period "population shifts and displacements" were taking place in Canaan, the net result of which was "the growth of new settlements in the Cisjordanian highlands"; (2) that "the Merneptah Stele indicates the existence of some entity called Israel somewhere in Palestine in the late 13th century"; (3) that "Israel is somehow to be related to the surge in small settlements in the highlands during the end of the Late Bronze–Iron I periods," though "how this relationship is to be understood remains problematic"; (4) that "the biblical texts must be used with great caution in reconstructing the history of Israel's origins and prestate conditions."[109] The issue, of course, is how these archaeological results are to be interpreted and applied to the questions of Israel in Canaan. The predominant contemporary approach is to associate these transformations with Israel's initial *emergence* in Canaan and as a consequence to dismiss the possibility of a conquest in favor of one of the other models. But as Bimson has recently argued, the Merneptah (or Merenptah) Stele presents something of a

---

[106]The book of Judges reports the destruction of several other cities—Zephath by the men of Judah (Judg. 1:17), Shechem by Abimelech (9:45), and Laish by the Danites (18:27)—but the basic pattern is the same, populations were destroyed or displaced but cities remained.

[107]On this point, see B. K. Waltke, "Palestinian Artifactual Evidence Supporting the Early Date of the Exodus," *Bibliotheca Sacra* 129 (1972): 34–35; E. H. Merrill, "Palestinian Archaeology and the Date of the Conquest: Do Tells Tell Tales?" *Grace Theological Journal* 3 (1982): 107–21; idem, "The LB/EI Transition and the Emergence of Israel: An Assessment and Preliminary Proposal" (forthcoming).

[108]Unfortunately, this error is all too common. For instance, M. D. Coogan ("Archaeology and Biblical Studies: The Book of Joshua," in *Hebrew Bible*, ed. Propp et al., pp. 22–23), denies the "essential historicity" of the list of conquered kings in Joshua 12:9–24 on the basis of a supposed conflict between archaeology and text. Noting that the archaeological evidence suggests that the city of Lachish was destroyed "at least a century after the destruction of Late Bronze Age Hazor," Coogan concludes that this "contradicts the plain sense of the biblical narrative in Joshua, namely that the cities, or at least their populations, were destroyed within a generation." But Coogan's statement of the "plain sense" is imprecise; were the *cities* themselves destroyed or just their *citizens*? Only if it were the former could we expect to find much evidence in the archaeological record. But as we have already seen, destruction of cities was the exception, not the rule. Thus, the date of the destruction of the *city* of Lachish is irrelevant to the list of kings in question. Coogan's implicit reading of the textual witness is in fact better than his explicit statement of the "plain sense," for he recognizes that the biblical narrators did *not* in fact claim that many of the cities themselves were destroyed.

[109]*Toward a Consensus on the Emergence of Israel in Canaan*, Papers Read at the SBL/ASOR Hebrew Bible, History and Archaeology Section (New Orleans, 18th November 1990), *SJOT* 2 (1991): 4–5.

problem for this view, and it is equally possible to regard the proliferation of Iron I high-land sites as evidence of the *sedentarization* (settling down) of Israel towards the end of the Judges period.[110] Which explanation one favors will depend in part on how serious-ly one is willing to take the "biblical texts" mentioned in item 4 above and the care with which one reads them.

This brings us to the next reason that many contemporary scholars have moved away from the conquest model as an explanation of Israel's emergence in Canaan. This is their sense that Joshua and Judges mutually undermine one another's historical cred-ibility by painting conflicting pictures of the conquest—the former a hugely successful *Blitzkrieg* and the latter a much more protracted, complex affair.[111] It is quite true, of course, that the two books present different pictures, but are they in fact contradictory? While the question cannot be adequately addressed in the space available here, it may at least be observed that the sense of tension between the two books is greatly lessened when each is understood on its own terms and in the light of its own purposes. At the risk of oversimplification, it could be said that the book of Joshua stresses God's faithfulness in *giving* his people the land (i.e., in giving them the upper hand by not allowing any of their adversaries to withstand them),[112] while Judges stresses the people's failure to act faithfully in *occupying* it.[113] The introductory section of Judges (1:1–3:6), for example, describes how "after the death of Joshua" (1:1) the people of Israel gradually lost their grip on the land until, instead of having the upper hand, they found themselves living among the Canaanites, intermarrying with them and worshiping their gods (3:5–6).[114] But even the book of Joshua, amidst its stress on Joshua's success in taking the land (11:16, 23), acknowledges that the war was a protracted affair (11:18), that there was much to be done even after the land was "subdued" (18:1; see also v. 3), and that the tribes of Israel sometimes failed to occupy fully their allotted territory (e.g., 13:13; 17:12). Thus Joshua can speak in the same breath of Israel having "rest from all their enemies round about" (23:1) and yet needing still to contend with "these nations that remain among you" (23:7). In sum, it seems that the pictures presented by the books of Joshua and Judges, though different in their emphases, are ultimately compatible and complementary.

We come then to a final reason why the conquest model is sometimes rejected in favor of one of the other theories. Simply put, this has to do with the anti-historical ten-dency that characterizes some modern literary approaches to the Bible. A literary approach can, of course, be of great value in establishing the character and historical import of a book like Joshua.[115] But for those interpreters who take their cue from trends

---

[110]"Merenptah's Israel and Recent Theories of Israelite Origins," *JSOT* 49 (1991): 3–29.
[111]E.g., a flat reading of Josh. 21:43–45 in comparison with Judg. 2: 21–23 might create such an impression. For a brief summary of this view and a response, see L. K. Younger, *Ancient Conquest Accounts: A Study in Ancient Near Eastern and Biblical History Writing,* JSOTS 98 (Sheffield: JSOT, 1990), pp. 241–47.
[112]See, e.g., Josh. 21:43–45; 23:9. References to the Lord giving the land (of Canaan) to his people are at least five times as frequent in Joshua as in Judges.
[113]Younger (*Ancient Conquest Accounts*, p. 246) aptly distinguishes between *subjugation* and *occupation*.
[114]Of particular interest is the way in which the section 1:16–36 conveys a sense of progressive decline in Israel's ability to displace the Canaanites; see B. G. Webb, *The Book of Judges: An Integrated Reading,* JSOTS 46 (Sheffield: JSOT, 1987), pp. 88–101.
[115]Again, we may mention as an example Younger's ground-breaking semiotic analysis of ancient Near Eastern conquest accounts, including the accounts in Joshua and Judges (*Ancient Conquest Accounts*).

in secular literary criticism that are essentially ahistorical in orientation, historical questions can easily be seen as uninteresting and even unwelcome interruptions to the enjoyment of a *good story* such as the book of Joshua presents. Of course, if a convincing case were to be made that the book of Joshua means to present itself as nothing more than a good story, that it doesn't at all intend to make any sort of historical truth claim, then it would not only be permissible to dismiss historical considerations from the interpretive enterprise, but mandatory. But so long as an historiographical impulse is felt to be present, valid interpretation must take this into account and seek to explore the precise nature of the claims made. In the case of the book of Joshua, it is difficult to escape the conclusion that, whatever simplifications, idealizations, and hyperbole may be present, a historiographical claim is being made that military conquest played a significant role in Israel's emergence in Canaan.

CONCLUSION

In the first chapter of this book, and often thereafter, I noted that biblical literature tends to exhibit three basic impulses: theological (or ideological), historical (or referential), and literary (or aesthetic). The presence of the one or the other may be more pronounced in some biblical passages than in others, but there are relatively few places in the Bible, at least in the Bible's narratives, where one of the three is entirely absent. An example of biblical narratives lacking in the historical impulse would, of course, be parables, but even parables generally function within a larger narrative framework that itself exhibits an historical impulse.

In this chapter, I have asked why scholars so often come to very different conclusions regarding the historical import of biblical passages. The results of our exploration of this question suggest that the answer has much to do both with the models of reality held by different scholars and with their consequent preference for certain types of methods, or approaches. As this chapter now draws to a close, it is worth noting that each of the several approaches discussed above appears deficient precisely to the degree that it downplays or dismisses one of the three characteristic impulses of biblical narrative. Some historical-critical approaches methodologically exclude divine agency (the theological impulse), some social-scientific and archaeological approaches downplay the value of texts (the literary impulse), and some literary approaches systematically ignore the possibility that texts may be referential (the historical impulse). Where biblical scholars adopt one or the other of these deficient approaches in seeking to reconstruct (or deconstruct) biblical history, it is not surprising that they should come to radically differing results.

But to end on a more positive note, I would add that each of the approaches, if properly conceived and incorporated into a synthetic methodological symbiosis, can serve a very useful function. A proper literary approach helps us to read texts on their own terms and thus to come to more accurate conclusions regarding textual truth claims (historical and otherwise). The fruits of sociological and archaeological study provide much-needed flesh to the bones of biblical history. And historical criticism's three principles of criticism, analogy, and correlation, if conceived in terms appropriate to the object of study (in this instance the Bible), offer helpful guidelines for assessing evidence and drawing historical conclusions.

five

HISTORY AND

HERMENEUTICS

How Then Should We Read the Bible "Historically"?

We come now to that point in our journey when we may begin to draw some conclusions about how the traveler interested in historical questions should traverse the biblical landscape. The basic question we face is this: can we develop an approach that will help us discover the historical import of the various stages in our journey through the Bible? How can we know, for example, when reading this or that biblical narrative, whether we are to read it as historiography—viz., an account claiming to represent and interpret events of the past—or as some other literary genre? What about books like Jonah and Job? Masterful literature with unmistakably didactic intentions, these books are among the most debated with respect to their historiographical intentions and are likely to remain so.[1] Some scholars extend the uncertainty regarding historiographical intentionality to cover much, or even most, of the biblical testimony. Reflecting recently on the study of Israelite history, Maxwell Miller laments that some scholars "regard the Bible as essentially useless for the historian's purposes. It is 'a holy book that tells stories.'"[2]

While wishing to remain far from such a reductionistic approach to the biblical narratives, we must nevertheless admit that, with our present state of knowledge, there may be times in our reading of Scripture when we are simply not sure whether, or to what precise degree, a biblical story means to be taken as a historical account. This admission will seem

---

[1]The relative independence of these two books from a larger literary context may also contribute to their debated status; we have already discussed the importance of context for determining the primary *purpose* of a work of literature (chap. 2, section "History as Representational Art").

[2]"Reflections," p. 74.

as obvious as it is necessary to some students of the Bible, but it will likely make others uneasy. Silva has noted, for example, that "for some conservative Christians, certainty about historical details appears to be inseparable from a high view of Scripture." But as Silva rightly goes on to argue, "such a connection [i.e., between the historicity of a scriptural account and the veracity of scripture itself] is valid . . . only where Scripture speaks directly and unambiguously on the historical question involved."[3] In other words, only where a text's *truth claims* involve historicity does a denial of historicity become a denial of the *truth value* of the biblical text, and thus become a problem for those holding a high view of Scripture.

Understanding the matter in this way, we may freely admit to the presence of some border cases where we are uncertain whether or to what degree a text's truth claims involve historicity. It would be a grave error, however, to extend this uncertainty respecting *some* passages of Scripture to cover *all* passages of Scripture. And it would be an equally grave error to cite our occasional historical uncertainties as grounds for treating the whole Bible as if its overall truth value could somehow stand apart from historical questions.[4] If, as Halpern has recently argued at length, the writers of the Bible's historiographical portions "had authentic antiquarian intentions"—that is, if "they meant to furnish fair and accurate representations of Israelite antiquity"—then valid interpretation must recognize these intentions and the truth claims implied by them and admit that the truth value of the Bible stands or falls, in part at least, on questions of history and historicity.[5]

Having encountered the concepts of *truth claim* and *truth value* at numerous junctures in our discussion so far, we may now build on them in what follows. Part of the aim of the present chapter will be to show how these concepts provide the basis of a procedure for exploring the historical import of biblical passages as we encounter them. My aim will not be to discuss specific methods in any detail but, rather, to suggest how the various methods associated with Bible study can be fruitfully arranged under the rubrics *truth claim* and *truth value* as we seek to read the Bible historically. Before we can discuss methods, however, I must address the prior question of models. As we have already seen (particularly in the preceding chapter), there is a close correlation between one's model of reality (that is, one's worldview or fundamental set of background beliefs) and the methods of study that one deems appropriate. Since much confusion and even harm can result where methods are adopted and employed without adequate reflection on the model(s) of reality underlying them, it is to the question of models that we must first turn in preparing to explore the historical import of a biblical passage.

---

[3]"Historical Reconstruction," p. 111.

[4]The vital relationship between biblical historicity and authentic Christian faith was discussed in chap. 3 above.

[5]*First Historians*, p. 3. For a compelling case for the antiquarian intentions of, e.g., the writer of Luke–Acts, see C. Hemer, *Book of Acts*, esp. chaps. 1–3. New Testament references suggestive of the high value placed on giving an accurate account of past events could be multiplied: e.g., in addition to the prologue to Luke, also John 20:30–31; 21:24–25; Acts 4:20; 2 Peter 1:16; 2:3; 1 John 1:1.

PREPARATION: CONTEMPLATING MODELS

In an essay entitled "The Role of Theory in Biblical Criticism,"[6] E. L. Greenstein observes that "in biblical studies we often argue as though we all shared the same beliefs and principles, as though the field were all built upon a single theoretical foundation. But it is not" (p. 167). Greenstein acknowledges the link between one's model (one's "theoretical foundation") and one's methods, and he insists that "if we have different models, and then of necessity different methods—and we do—we can only understand each other in the terms of each other's theories" (p. 173). In other words, proper evaluation of a specific interpretation (one's own or someone else's) of a given biblical passage must have at least two foci—viz., the truth of the fundamental assumptions (model of reality) behind the interpretation and the appropriateness of the means (methodological steps) by which the interpretation is arrived at. Greenstein puts it this way: "I can get somewhere when I challenge the deductions you make from your fundamental assumptions. But I can get nowhere if I think I am challenging your deductions when in fact I am differing from your assumptions, your presuppositions, your premises, your beliefs" (p. 167).

The issue of fundamental assumptions, presuppositions, premises, beliefs, worldview, model of reality, and so forth (the terms are many but the concept is the same) must be approached on several levels. Not only must I, as an interpreter, seek to gain a more conscious awareness of my own worldview, but I must also seek to discover the worldview embodied in the text I am studying, the worldview undergirding the method I am applying, and the worldviews held by other interpreters whose writings I am consulting. Where there are differences at the fundamental level of worldview, tensions and disagreements on the levels of interpretation and/or application are inevitable. If the interpreter's model of reality is distinctly different from that embodied in the text, there will be tension. If a method is applied to a text whose fundamental assumptions about the world and reality run counter to the assumptions underlying the method, there will be tensions. If interpreters approaching a given text disagree fundamentally on how they view reality, they will likely also disagree on how to interpret the text, or at least on whether the text, once interpreted, is to be accepted as trustworthy and authoritative.[8]

Once we recognize that various texts and various interpreters assume a variety of worldviews, the question of validity arises. Are all worldviews equally valid? In many modern societies there is an insistence that individuals have the right to believe what they will. But this affirmation need not, and should not, slide into the kind of relativism or subjectivism that would insist that every individual's beliefs are right. Put another way, the *right to believe* and the *rightness of belief* are separate issues, the former by no means guaranteeing the latter. Common sense would tell us that if in using the phrase *model of reality* we mean *Reality* in an ultimate sense, then by definition there can be only one

---

[6]In *Proceedings of the Ninth World Congress of Jewish Studies: Jerusalem, August 4–12, 1985* (Jerusalem: World Union of Jewish Studies, 1986), pp. 167–74.

[7]"All historians work from some philosophical or theological base, whether consciously or not" (Miller, "Reflections," p. 65).

[8]This is not to suggest that an appeal to presuppositions, or fundamental assumptions, can be used as a short-cut by which to accept or reject specific interpretations of Scripture or specific historical reconstructions (see Silva, "Historical Reconstruction," pp. 123–25, 131); still, "one can hardly deny that a scholar's fundamental assumptions about God will radically affect one's handling of the biblical material" (ibid., p. 124).

completely valid worldview.[9] Only one view of the world can be in every respect true to the way things are. To be sure, no fallible human being can claim fully to have grasped this "perfect worldview." But it is still fair to say that some worldviews are better, more promising, more likely to be true than others. In his recent book entitled *Faith and Reason: Searching for a Rational Faith*, Ronald Nash explores such questions as what a worldview is, what constitutes a Christian worldview, and even how to choose a worldview.[10] Nash's treatment is generally helpful but cannot be discussed further here.

For our present purposes, it is only necessary to stress the vital importance, as a first step in the historical interpretation of the Bible, of examining worldviews—our own, that embodied in the text, that implied by the method, and those embraced by other interpreters. As already noted, where worldviews differ interpretive tensions will surely arise. A further observation can now be made. The manner in which interpreters go about arbitrating the points of tension is a sure indication of where their fundamental commitments lie. Where is the final test of truth to be found? In the Bible? In the interpretive community of faith? In the academic community? Or in the individual interpreter as a sentient and rational being? Of course, all of these are in some measure involved. But the question is who or what, in the final analysis, represents the locus of ultimate authority for the interpreter.

Some interpreters seek to accord the Bible itself this status, in keeping with the reformation principle of *sola Scriptura*. Indeed, the Bible appears to demand as much, for it teaches, as Royce Gruenler reminds us, "a definite hierarchy of authority by which God's Word takes precedence over his revelation in nature and self, requiring a rebirthing of heart and mind."[11] Thus, while not denying the light of nature or of personal experience, interpreters who take this approach will allow the biblical testimony to play the primary role in shaping their view of the world and of reality. If convinced for example that Scripture, rightly understood, claims to report instances in which God has directly intervened in the course of history, these interpreters will make room in their worldview for the occurrence of miracles, specifically those reported in the Bible, though they may well disagree over whether such miracles continue to occur today.

For other interpreters, the locus of final authority may lie elsewhere than in the biblical text—sometimes in the private sphere of their own deliberations and preferences, sometimes in the accepted standards of their community of faith, or of their academic community, sometimes simply in the cultural or intellectual *Zeitgeist* (spirit of the age). These interpreters may esteem the Bible as in some sense important, but they are hesitant to allow it *the* decisive role in determining how they view and talk about the world, religion, and reality. Consider, for example, the very fundamental question of the existence of God. Whatever ambiguities may inhere in talk about "the" worldview of the Bible,[12] it can hardly be doubted that among its most central tenets is the assertion that there is one true God, and that this God is deserving of the trust and allegiance of his

---

[9]For the kind of realism I have in mind here, see M. A. Noll, *Between Faith and Criticism: Evangelicals, Scholarship, and the Bible in America* (San Francisco: Harper & Row, 1986), p. 146.

[10](Grand Rapids: Zondervan, 1988), esp. chaps. 2–4. Cf. also Nash's *Worldviews in Conflict: Choosing Christianity in a World of Ideas* (Grand Rapids: Zondervan, 1992).

[11]*Meaning and Understanding: The Philosophical Framework for Biblical Interpretation*, FCI 2 (Grand Rapids: Zondervan, 1991), p. xii.

[12]There is a measure of diversity exhibited within the unity that is the Bible, but I believe it is still valid to speak, in general terms, of "the worldview of the Bible."

human creatures. And yet many modern interpreters feel a tension in allowing this fundamental theistic truth to come to expression in their scholarly work. Robert Morgan, for example, begins with the assumption that "scholarship is bound to respect the rational norms of the day" and concludes from this that "if these do not speak of God, the result is a biblical scholarship which does not speak directly of God in a believing way either." He recognizes that this approach is "bound to seem alien to those who use the Bible religiously." But he recognizes further that "the methods themselves are only a symptom of the conflict between religious assumptions and much modern thought."[13] We see, then, that where religious (or biblical) assumptions conflict with modern thought, some scholars feel compelled to side with the latter, while others feel a greater loyalty to the former. John Stott puts the matter succinctly, but profoundly, in David Edwards' recent *Evangelical Essentials: A Liberal-Evangelical Dialogue*:[14] "Perhaps the crucial question between us, then, is whether culture is to judge Scripture, or Scripture culture" (p. 168).

Having stressed the importance of reflecting on one's own fundamental understanding of the world and reality and of divulging one's background beliefs to one's audience, it is time to state explicitly what is surely implicit in the preceding pages. While this is not the place to offer a full "statement of faith," it seems appropriate to highlight at least those tenets of belief that have a bearing on the issues under consideration in this volume. The worldview and basic assumptions embraced by the present writer are founded on the belief that there is one true God who not only acts in history (through both primary and secondary causes) but also speaks (through both the Incarnate Word and the written word, the Bible; cf. Heb. 12:25). The Bible, as the word of God written—and in keeping with the very character of God—is assumed to present truth and to be authoritative. This means, to put the matter plainly, that whatever the Bible—*rightly interpreted and applied*—affirms or enjoins is to be believed and obeyed.

Stating one's position as boldly as this raises an important question. Does clarity regarding our own assumptions cut us off from all discussion with those who do not share these same assumptions? Not at all, or at least not necessarily. As the recurring phrase "rightly interpreted" suggests, there is plenty of room for debate and discussion as to a text's truth claims, whatever one's stance regarding the text's truth value. Scholars of diverse persuasions may work fruitfully together in seeking to discover what a text is saying (i.e., what its "speech acts" are), while nevertheless recognizing that there may be a parting of the ways when it comes to the question of how these speech acts are to be received.[15] Peter Craigie suggests as much in his comparison of the secular historian with the Jewish or Christian reader:

> While a secular historian will be interested in the manner in which the ancient writer has expressed history in theological terms, his own understanding will remain strictly secular. On the other hand, a Jewish or Christian reader, while sharing the interests

---

[13] *Biblical Interpretation*, p. 271.
[14] Downers Grove: InterVarsity Press, 1988.
[15] I recognize that other, less theological (or metaphysical) assumptions may still inhibit fruitful interchange—disagreements over the sufficiency of language, the determinacy of meaning, the legitimacy of such notions as embodied intention, and the like. But, then, it is a curious inconsistency that those who hold a low view of any or all of the above nevertheless in their writings frequently exhibit an *intention* to engage in *meaningful verbal* communication.

of the secular historian, may also share the faith of the ancient writer. That is, religious readers may accept the ancient theological understanding of events as much as the historical data themselves.[16]

Having considered the importance of reality models and the significance of background beliefs, we may now turn to questions of method.

PROCEDURE: COORDINATING METHODS

While individual interpreters can commit themselves to only one model of reality, they may employ a variety of methods to get at the meaning of a text. There is, however, one qualification: each of the methods adopted must be appropriate to the model of reality embraced by the interpreter. My aim in this section is not to discuss specific methods *per se*, but rather to set forth some basic procedural steps for first discovering and then testing the historical claims of biblical texts. This procedure arranges itself around the twin issues of truth claim and truth value, of which much has already been said. The proposed procedure, then, has two basic steps. The first is to *listen* to the text in an effort to discover what, if any, historical truth claims it makes. The second is to *test* the truth value of these truth claims by subjecting them to internal and external checks.

Listen: Seek to Determine the Truth Claim

Like the importance of "location, location, location" in considering a real estate purchase, the importance of *listening* in biblical interpretation can hardly be overestimated. "The task of the theologian-exegete," writes Martin Woudstra, "is a humble yet a significant one. It begins with listening; it continues and ends with listening."[17] Good listening implies, of course, asking many questions of the text—thus the need for the various exegetical disciplines such as textual criticism, linguistic analysis, literary criticism, structural analysis, and so forth. Each of these probes and explores the text in different ways and enables the interpreter to "hear" it more clearly.

Moreover, since the Bible is a "foreign book" coming to us in languages other than our own and from cultures far removed from our own both in time and place, *trained* listeners are often in a better position to "hear clearly" than are the untrained.[18] I say "often," because a measure of good faith towards one's source is also a prerequisite of good listening. This suggests a first principle of listening.

Good Listening Requires an Open Attitude

Despite Harvey's approval of the dictum that "the beginning of wisdom in history is doubt"[19] and Ramsey's insistence that in assessing sources "the first requirement of a good

---

[16]*The Old Testament: Its Background, Growth, and Content* (Nashville: Abingdon, 1986), pp. 256–57.

[17]*The Book of Joshua*, New International Commentary on the Old Testament (Grand Rapids: Eerdmans, 1981), p. 29.

[18]But see chap. 1 on the perspicuity of Scripture.

[19]*Historian and the Believer*, p. 111, citing Allan Nevins. To be sure, Harvey is correct in calling for a "certain toughness of mind" in those who would interpret the Bible responsibly (p. 111), but is he justified in rejecting the "old morality [that] celebrated faith and belief" and advocating a "new morality [that] celebrates methodological scepticism" and equates "integrity . . . with loyalty to the methodological procedures of the intellectual community" (p. 103)? Surely, this latter equation tends to beg the question of truth and to overlook the diversity and often shifting consensus within the "intellectual community" itself. More

historian is a healthy streak of skepticism,"[20] I would contend that this very much depends on the character of the sources. Gerhard Maier insists that "systematic doubt is . . . the most inappropriate procedure imaginable for dealing with the Bible."[21] Credulity (i.e., the tendency to believe on the basis of only slight evidence) is, of course, to be avoided, and carefulness and caution are to be encouraged. But overly skeptical listeners tend to make poor listeners. Assuming the worst of their sources, they sometimes fail to expend the energy necessary to discover the sense of what the sources say.

When it comes to the Bible, the energy necessary to "hear clearly" may be considerable, especially given the Bible's "remove" from the listener's own language, literary traditions, and culture. Thus, an important characteristic of the good listener or, in the case of texts, the good reader is an open, expectant attitude in approaching the text. As Jan Fokkelman has argued, "the good reader . . . has the experience that the significance of an encounter varies with the attitude he assumes during the establishment of contact. He realizes that the contact can be deepened and enriched if he goes into it with a positive attitude. Loving attention and the trust that the other partner is worth the trouble are essential conditions for a genuine dialogue." By contrast, "the attitude of treating a narrative from the very outset as a barrel full of problems creates a negative climate and runs the risk of acting as a self-fulfilling prophecy."[22]

Whether one views the Bible as deserving of initial skepticism or of trust (or of something in between) is in part a reflection of one's general belief about the Bible's macro-genre[23] and in part a result of one's specific encounters with the biblical text. Certainly, no one who has seriously studied the Bible will claim that such study is without difficulties, but again Fokkelman lends a helpful perspective.

> With this I do not want to deny that Old Testament studies have their real problems. What I am pleading for, however, is that from text to text we remain aware that they are not intended to be problematical cases, and that we understand about the problems that they are *our* problems which are in part genuine inasmuch as they correspond with the great difference in time and environment between us and the Bible, but which, in part, arise from our own scholastic habits of making things difficult. I am convinced that Old Testament studies will be a Jezreel for us more often than a Negeb if we practise asking the proper questions.[24]

The ability to ask the proper questions presupposes that we come to the text with the proper expectations, and this in turn presupposes that we make an effort to bridge the spatio-temporal gap by developing, as best we can, an ancient linguistic-literary-cultural competence. Just as an understanding of the conventional workings of, say, impressionist art is very useful for rightly interpreting an impressionist painting, so too some

---

over, when Harvey condemns the "falsifying influence of the demand for belief" (p. 111), he seems to overlook the fact that unbelief can have a similarly distorting effect, constraining the historian always to come to conclusions that are compatible with this unbelief.

[20]*Quest*, p. 7.

[21]*Biblische Hermeneutik* (Wuppertal: R. Brockhaus, 1990), p. 14 (English translation here is from Robert W. Yarbrough's forthcoming translation of this work).

[22]*King David (II Sam 9–20 and 1 Kings 1–2)* (Assen: Van Gorcum, 1981), p. 4.

[23]On which, see chap. 1.

[24]*King David*, pp. 4–5.

understanding of the conventional workings of biblical narrative is a great help in "getting the picture" that individual biblical narratives wish to convey.

But even after we "get the picture" (i.e., understand the story), we may still not be sure if the *story* should be taken as *history*. We have already seen that one can no more distinguish fictional story from factual history on the basis of *formal* characteristics than one can distinguish nonreferential from referential paintings on the basis of *brush strokes*. Nor is content alone an adequate indicator; just as a work of art may be realistic and yet not specifically representational, so a narrative may be realistic and yet not historiographical. How then is one to distinguish representational/historiographical narrative from realistic but nonhistoriographical narrative? The key, as we saw already in chapter 2, is to discern the narrative's *overall sense of purpose*. But how are we to discover this sense of purpose? If not by form alone, nor even by content, then the answer has to be context. Again, as I suggested in chapters 1 and 2, the way to begin is by observing the narrative's placement within its larger narrative continuum. This brings us to a second characteristic of good listening.

Good Listening Requires Attention to Context

The principle that I am suggesting runs parallel to Strauss's positive criterion for distinguishing between historical and unhistorical narratives, but in the reverse direction. As I noted in chapter 3, Strauss promoted a sort of guilt-by-association approach whereby one begins by asking whether any narrative units within a larger textual continuum "exhibit unquestionable marks of a mythical or legendary character." If such are found, then the historicity of any texts connected to these, or even proceeding from the same author, is suspect.[25] Thus Strauss extrapolates from a determination about smaller textual units to a judgment about the larger unit of which these are a part. But if the principles of discourse articulated in chapter 1 are correct (especially the principle that "upper levels of text organization, such as genre, place broad constraints on all lower levels"[26]), then the extrapolation should be reversed—viz., from the larger to the smaller. If the larger narrative complex exhibits a historiographical intent, then, barring indications to the contrary, smaller units within the complex should be assumed to share in the historical impulse.

To grasp what is at stake here, we need only consider what goes on in everyday conversation. When talking with someone, we intuitively gauge the import of individual sentences in the light of the overall tenor and direction of the conversation. A sentence like "That will be the day!" means one thing if spoken in answer to a flirtatious and insincere "Will you marry me?" and quite another if in answer to a prospective partner's serious inquiry "How about setting December 18th as our wedding day?" Now, a form critic might easily collect numerous examples of actual verbal exchanges in which "That will be the day!" is a sarcastic rejoinder, but, as our second scenario makes clear, to ignore the larger communicative context and simply label the clause in question as a "sarcastic rejoinder formula" would be to miss the point badly.

How does this principle apply to issues of biblical historicity? Perhaps a specific example will help. Let us take a brief look at one of the more perplexing stretches of text

[25]*Life of Jesus,* p. 90.
[26]Bergen, "Text as a Guide," p. 330.

in the books of Kings. The section comprising 1 Kings 17–2 Kings 8 recounts the prophetic activities of Elijah and Elisha. These chapters display a striking concentration of miracle stories, including even one in which Elisha throws a stick into water and causes an axhead to float to the surface (2 Kings 6:1–7). As Richard Nelson points out, this story is "something of an embarrassment for modern readers. The miracle seems both trivial and pointless."[27] Nelson has more to say on the subject, and I shall return to him later. But for the moment, the question that faces us is this: what are we to make of this fantastic story, and indeed of the whole collection of fantastic stories that comes in the midst of the books of Kings? In keeping with the significance of *context*, argued above, it would seem appropriate to begin by reflecting on the apparent purpose(s) of the books of Kings.

It is generally recognized that 1 and 2 Kings exhibit a historiographical impulse. Simon DeVries, for example, in his Word Biblical Commentary on 1 Kings,[28] observes with respect to the so-called Deuteronomistic history, of which 1 and 2 Kings are a part, that "we are blind if we cannot see that it is meaningful *historical event* that Dtr is recording and interpreting" (p. xxxiv). More specifically he writes, "1 Kgs—and the other sections of the historiographic collection—was written by men who wished to bear testimony to Yahweh's self-revelation in historical event" (p. xxxv).

And yet when DeVries comes to consider the Elijah/Elisha narratives, he describes them not as historiography but as "prophet legend," which he immediately amends to "prophet story," reasoning that "'legend' can be popularly misconstrued as meaning fanciful or unreal" (p. xxxvii). In principle, if we follow Burke Long's definition of a prophet legend as "a story which chiefly portrays a wondrous deed or ideal virtue of an exemplary holy man,"[29] then historicity is not necessarily ruled out, at least for those who are willing to allow a place for the "wondrous" in history (see my discussion of the historical-critical method in chap. 4). In practice, however, DeVries finds little room for historicity when it comes to the Elijah/Elisha stories, preferring rather to contrast these "pious stories" with the "historiography" of the rest of Kings. Why does he come to this position? According to his own profession, it is not because of any anti-supernaturalist bias on his part. Indeed, he warns of "two errors, opposite to each other," of which we must beware in approaching the Elijah and Elisha stories: "(1) to reject them because they clash with the naturalism of the modern mind, or (2) to interpret them only literally while insisting that the biblical God always works in this way" (p. xxxvi).

Both these warnings are apt. But what is it, if not the miraculous elements in the Elijah/Elisha stories, that leads DeVries to conclude that "the aim of these stories is less to record what God *has done* (historically, at one particular time and place), than to declare what God *can do* (throughout history, in every time and place)" (p. xxxvii)? Why does he insist that "their intent is not to record what *has* happened, but what happens and can happen"? Having expressed himself so strongly on the historiographical purpose of 1 Kings, on what grounds does he exempt these prophet stories, so intertwined as they are in the careers of kings? Perhaps it is the miraculous element, after all, that gives him pause, for he later speaks of "the exaggerated supernatural element in some of them" that

---

[27]*First and Second Kings*, Interpretation (Louisville: John Knox, 1987), p. 184.

[28]Waco: Word Books, 1985.

[29]*1 Kings with an Introduction to Historical Literature*, The Forms of the Old Testament Literature (Grand Rapids: Eerdmans, 1984), p. 80.

functions as "a metaphor for God's power and the power of God-filled men" (p. 206). But this is not the reason that he explicitly gives. Rather, beginning with the valid observation that it is not necessary that "everything narrated in the Bible . . . be taken literally," DeVries moves quickly to a comparison of the Elijah and Elisha stories with the *parables* of Jesus, which are lacking in "historicity," though they are rich in "historicality"—viz., "self-awareness in historical existence" (pp. xxxvi–xxxvii).

But is this comparison apposite? By DeVries' own admission, the prophet stories' emphasis on "the wondrous and the supernatural" distinguishes them from Jesus' parables, which have no such emphasis (p. xxxvii). This being the case, surely the more appropriate comparison would be with the *miracle stories* of Jesus. Elijah's raising of the widow of Zarephath's son (1 Kings 17:17–24) might be compared with Jesus' raising of the widow of Nain's son (Luke 7:11–17); the story of Elisha's feeding of one hundred (2 Kings 4:42–44) with Jesus' feeding of the multitude (e.g., Matt. 14:16–20); Elisha's healing of Naaman's leprosy (2 Kings 5) with Jesus' healings of lepers (e.g., Luke 5:12–16); and the list could be continued. In Luke 4:25–27 Jesus himself draws a comparison between his own wonder-working ministry and the ministries of Elijah and Elisha.[30]

What, then, are we to conclude from all this? First, if the discourse principle of larger influencing smaller is correct, then the apparent historiographical impulse of the books of Kings should be taken into consideration in our reading of the Elijah/Elisha narratives.[31] We may still decide that the latter are devoid of historical value, but the burden of proof will be on us to give reasons for that judgment. For scholars who continue in the spirit of Strauss, the miraculous features of these stories may seem reason enough, but as argued in chapter 4, a naturalist presupposition should not be deemed the *sine qua non* of historical study. Second, attention should be given to the degree of integration of the smaller units into the broader context and to the presence or absence of indicators that distinctive literary forms (parables, fables, or the like) are being introduced.[32] Where such indicators are present, the specific truth claims of the smaller units may well differ from the overall truth claims of the larger narratives. But where such indicators are absent, the discourse principle of larger influencing smaller continues in force. Third, when attempting to argue from analogous genres, or literary forms, we must take care that the most appropriate analogies are adduced. In the case before us, the accounts of Jesus' *miracles*, not his *parables*, provide the appropriate comparison. Thus, our view of the historical import of Jesus' miracle stories may play a part in our assessment of the miracle stories of Elijah/Elisha.

Returning to the specific case of the floating axhead (2 Kings 6:1–7), I would make one further observation: our first impression of an incident may reflect the limitations of our own cultural context and thus should not be implicitly trusted. As Nelson remarks, our sense that the axhead miracle is "trivial and pointless" is in part at least "caused by our inability to empathize with a poor man's consternation over an expensive borrowed tool. Iron was not cheap in those days."[33] More importantly, this incident, along with others that follow, is by no means "trivial and pointless," inasmuch as it serves to "emphasize the power of the prophet" and of the God he represents. "God's power invades the world of

---

[30]Cf. Nelson, *First and Second Kings,* p. 114, which see for fuller discussion; cf. also ibid., pp. 175–76.

[31]In practice, of course, there will be something of a spiraling back and forth between close examination of the smaller units and one's understanding of the overall sense of purpose of the larger.

[32]See my discussion of Jotham's fable in the section "Genre Criticism and Biblical Interpretation" in chap. 1.

[33]*First and Second Kings,* p. 184.

the ordinary to effect strange reversals. The lowly are raised to places of honor (Luke 1:51–53). The unrighteous are justified (Luke 18:9–14). The lost are found (Luke 15:3–10). The dead are raised. These are as much incredible reversals as is iron that floats."[34]

Test: Seek to Determine the Truth Value

So far in this chapter we have discussed two important elements in any responsible attempt to discover what historical information the Bible may contain. The first is to reflect on the importance of worldviews, or models of reality (one's own, the text's, other interpreters'). This provides the opportunity to modify, if necessary, the reality model with which one implicitly operates, or at least to become more self-consciously aware of one's own fundamental assumptions and the assumptions of others. The second is to listen as carefully and competently as possible to the biblical witness, to use every available means to discover its truth claims by approaching the text as fairly as possible on its own terms and in view of its context.

We now come to a third crucial step in the historical exploration of the Bible. Once we believe that we have some sense of what historical truth claims the biblical witness is making, our next step is to test the reliability of these claims by subjecting them to two checks. First, is the testimony internally consistent? And secondly, do its claims square with what other sources and evidences lead us to believe is true? Since our focus is on biblical testimony, some investigators will, of course, be predisposed to trust the witness while others will not. In either case, by testing our witness for internal and external consistency, we may be able to confirm or disconfirm our initial judgments.

When we find ourselves using words such as *testimony*, *witness*, and *evidence*, we are reminded of the analogy that is often drawn between the historical discipline and the law court.[35] This analogy is helpful in several respects. It reminds us that both historical study and the law court are interested in discovering what has happened in the past. It reminds us that both are *field-encompassing fields*, that is, both proceed by examining various kinds of evidence, derived from a variety of fields. It reminds us that both depend heavily on verbal testimony (e.g., written documents, depositions, the cross-examination of witnesses) and not just on the discovery and inspection of material evidence, though the latter may still play an important role. It reminds us that both are only required to establish that a particular view of the past is true *beyond any reasonable doubt* and are seldom in a position to offer anything approaching *scientific proof*. It reminds us that both are required to give reasons for the judgments they reach, though these reasons may be of many different sorts. And finally, it reminds us that for testimony to be credible it must pass the two tests of internal and external consistency. We turn now to the first of these two tests.

Internal Consistency of Testimony

In a court of law, an attorney can discredit a witness—even without conflicting testimony or material evidence—simply by demonstrating that the witness's testimony

---

[34]Ibid., p. 185.

[35]Simply put, "historical knowledge is based upon evidence in just the way the deliberations of a jury are" (Halpern, *First Historians*, p. 13); see also, e.g., Harvey, *Historian and the Believer*, pp. 58–59; Parker, "Methods," p. 289; Ramsey, *Quest*, pp. 22–23; Trigg, "Tales artfully spun," pp. 130–32.

is internally inconsistent (i.e., self-contradictory or incoherent). It may be that the witness is lying, or perhaps simply confused, but in any case he/she is not to be trusted. The same is true of biblical testimony. If a biblical narrative is incoherent or self-contradictory, if it doesn't make sense as a *story*, then it is hardly likely to be true as *history* (though it might still contain isolated historical reminiscences).

The place to begin, then, in testing the truth value of biblical testimony that appears to make historical truth claims is with a careful literary reading of the text with an eye to internal consistency. As Ramsey remarks, when exploring the historical import of biblical texts, "the careful scrutiny of the 'internal evidence,' meaning literary study of the biblical text, should be attended to first."[36]

A word of caution is warranted here. In this first-stage scrutiny of the literary deposit with an eye to coherence or lack thereof, it is vitally important that appropriate standards of coherence and consistency be applied—viz., standards appropriate to the ancient genre under inspection.[37] In seeking to establish these standards, a judicious use of comparative literature may prove useful. This point has recently been articulated and illustrated by Lawson Younger in an essay entitled "The Figurative Aspect and the Contextual Method in the Evaluation of the Solomonic Empire (1 Kings 1–11)." He writes:

> As biblical historians continue to formulate and to debate their methodology for writing histories of Israel, it is becoming more and more apparent that one of the greatest needs in establishing a method is the realization that a literary reading of the biblical text must precede any historical reconstruction. It is clear that such a reading is advantaged by anchoring the reading in the literary environment from which the text is derived.[38]

In addition to the cautious use of comparative literature, another source of guidance in assessing the coherence of biblical narrative is provided by literary approaches to the Bible such as biblical poetics, narrative criticism, discourse analysis and the like. As we have noted before, the heightened awareness of narrative conventions and literary strategies that these approaches yield sometimes calls for a reassessment of earlier judgments regarding a text's sense and coherence.

In addition to the examples presented elsewhere in this book,[39] the story of the encounter between Saul and Samuel described in 1 Samuel 9 nicely illustrates this point. The standard critical approach to this chapter has been to see in it a conflation of two originally distinct traditions, the one involving an encounter between Saul and an obscure village seer and the other involving the famous Samuel. The basis of this view is the fact that the "man of God" or "seer" remains anonymous until verse 14, where it is revealed

---

[36]*Quest*, p. 99.

[37]See, e.g., Hemer's "guidelines to what seem to be the reasonable expectations of historicity in a writing like Acts" (*Book of Acts*, pp. 46–49). He remarks, *inter alia*, that "narratives are embodied in natural, phenomenological language, which is not to be judged by over-literal criteria. Though independent sources for the same incidents are not commonly available for Acts, it will not necessarily matter for historicity if such cases exhibit varying details and perspectives, provided the differences are not radically contradictory. Indeed, we should be concerned to force neither harmonization nor contradiction, if only because we stand in too distant an external position to possess a completeness of context on which such decisions are likely to depend. There may be places where we have enough information to attempt a positive fit. Otherwise we are wise to be cautious" (p. 47).

[38]In *Bible in Three Dimensions*, ed. Clines et al., p. 157.

[39]E.g., in chap. 3 (an evaluation of Strauss, pp. 352–53). The final chapter of this book will provide a more extended example on the basis of the narratives in 1 Samuel recounting Saul's ascent to the throne of Israel.

to the reader, though not to Saul, that this "seer" is in fact Samuel! Why is Samuel not named earlier? Diachronic scholarship has sought to answer the question by assuming, two sources—an "anonymous seer" source and a "Samuel source"—which originally existed independently but at some point were conflated. Contrary to this standard approach, however, scholars such as Langlamet, Birch, McCarter, and others have argued that the masking of the identity of the seer in the early verses is not an evidence of a composite text but, rather, is a literary strategy intended to allow the reader to share in Saul's process of discovery.[40] It is "one of the dramatic highlights of the story."[41] As a slight modification of this synchronic explanation, it can be argued that the real point of the literary treatment is not so much to allow the reader to share in Saul's discovery as to highlight Saul's slowness in coming to understand what the reader has undoubtedly deduced much earlier.[42] In any case, the former consensus that 1 Samuel 9 is a conflation of two distinct sources and thus lacking in the consistency and unity to be expected of a reliable historical source has now been undercut by the literary reading that sees a unified and coherent, even sophisticated, narrative.

Does this more positive assessment of the self-consistency and coherence of 1 Samuel 9 prove its historicity? Of course not, or at least not entirely, for while internal consistency is a *necessary* condition of historicity, it is surely not a *sufficient* one. In other words, while demonstrating internal contradictions within an account would tell against its historicity, internal coherence is no guarantee of historicity. A lying witness, a clever one at least, might tell a tale that is perfectly self-consistent and yet utterly out of accord with what actually happened. Further considerations must be brought to bear: the general character and trustworthiness of the witness, the over-arching sense of purpose of the larger context within which the testimony is given, and the consistency of the testimony with external evidence. We have already had something to say on the character and context questions, so we turn now to the test of external consistency.

External Consistency of Testimony

This test presupposes, at least provisionally, that the interpreter has rightly understood the witness to be making historical truth claims.[43] The purpose of the external consistency test, as the name implies, is to check the truth value of these claims against whatever *external* evidences can be adduced. These evidences might include other verbal testimony—portions of the Bible or extrabiblical writings that in some way speak to the same events described by the first witness—as well as purely material remains, whether architectural, artifactual, biological, or such like.

---

[40]F. Langlamet, "Les récits de l'institution de la royauté (I Sam, VII–XII). De Wellhausen aux travaux récents," *Revue biblique* 77 (1970): 173; B. C. Birch, *The Rise of the Israelite Monarchy: The Growth and Development of 1 Samuel 7–15*, SBLDS 27 (Missoula: Scholars Press, 1976), pp. 34–35; cf. 135; P. K. McCarter, *I Samuel: A New Translation with Introduction, Notes and Commentary*, AB 8 (Garden City: Doubleday, 1980), p. 185.

[41]N. Na'aman, "The Pre-Deuteronomistic Story of King Saul and Its Historical Significance," *CBQ* 54 (1992): 640.

[42]For a fuller discussion, see Long, *Reign and Rejection*, pp. 196–99; cf. also R. P. Gordon, *I and II Samuel: A Commentary*, Library of Biblical Interpretation (Grand Rapids: Zondervan, 1986), pp. 32–33.

[43]If, on the other hand, it has been determined that the witness's testimony is hopelessly muddled or that no historical truth claims are being made, then it might not be necessary to proceed to the external test. But even in such cases, the safest approach would be to investigate the testimony of other witnesses and to inspect whatever material evidence might be at hand, since this would allow investigators either

In some instances, of course, there may be little or no external evidence that can be brought to bear on the biblical text under consideration. In these instances we are in a situation comparable to that of judge or jury who must render a verdict based on the testimony of only one witness. With neither other witnesses nor pertinent material evidence, about all judge or jury will have to go on is the character of the single witness and the coherence of the witness's story. In the same way, some purportedly historical events are recounted in only one place in the Bible and, so far as archaeology has been able to discover, are without supporting material evidence. In such instances, biblical historians have little more to consider in reaching a verdict regarding historicity than their view of the character of the (biblical) witness and the coherence of the testimony.

In many instances, however, external checks on the biblical account can be made on the basis of other biblical literature, extrabiblical literature, material remains, or some combination of these three. We must make these external checks with great caution. With respect to written evidence, for example, whether biblical or extrabiblical, we must bear in mind that these sources themselves, no less than the text in question, require interpretation and testing. Moreover, we must recognize that it is almost inevitable that different sources will yield differing perspectives on historical events, and we must remind ourselves that "different" does not necessarily mean "conflicting." When due allowance is made for the genre and purpose of the literature we are reading, many assumed discrepancies turn out to be more apparent than real. As for material evidence, we must bear in mind the point made earlier that archaeological remains are neither self-interpreting nor more objective than other kinds of evidence. The minute we begin to talk about material evidence, we are interpreting it. So we dare not forget what we ourselves, or the archaeologists we read, bring to the task of assessment.

In view of such considerations as these, it should be evident that the proper application of the external consistency test, as important as it is, is no simple matter. What is more, the results that can fairly be expected from the study of external, especially material, evidence are limited. As noted in the preceding chapter, material evidence is best suited to provide information of a generalized, background nature—mode and standard of living, diet, customs, population growth and migration, and so forth. Material evidence is seldom able to confirm even that a specific event has taken place, much less to provide guidance as to the significance, or interpretation, of that event. For interpretation, we are ultimately dependent on written sources, biblical or extrabiblical, or our own theories.

About all we can hope for, then, in terms of external confirmation of an apparently historical account is that there will be a general coherence, or compatibility, between the written account and whatever can be learned from external evidences. As is often remarked, archaeological evidence will not be in a position to prove a biblical account true in any absolute sense, for even if it could confirm every aspect of an event by yielding a corresponding piece of material evidence, it would still fall short of confirming the interpretive component of all history-writing.

Excursus: The occurrence of the terms *coherence* and *correspondence* in the preceding paragraph brings to mind the two dominant *theories of truth* that are often debated in

---

(1) to confirm their impression that the witness is not to be trusted by amassing contradictory evidences or (2) to discover that they have misunderstood the witness and need to reevaluate their initial judgments.

discussions of historical method. This is not the place to attempt a full treatment of the complex issues involved in these discussions, but a few comments may be useful. While a survey of the literature suggests that scholars do not always agree on what precisely is meant by the correspondence theory and the coherence theory, the general (if somewhat simplistic) understanding seems to be the following. The correspondence theory defines truth in terms of correspondence to the "facts," correspondence to "the way things are."[44] The coherence theory, by contrast, "defines truth not as the relationship of statements to facts but as the relationship of statements to each other."[45] Statements that are *coherent* with all other statements within a system of thought are regarded as true. The former theory, with its definition of truth "in terms of the correspondence between a proposition and a state of affairs,"[46] is often referred to as the "common-sense theory of truth,"[47] while the latter, with its definition of truth "in terms of the unified nature of a system of thought," has its roots in idealism and finds its most devoted adherents among idealists.[48]

Not surprisingly, both theories have been subjected to criticism as regards their applicability to historical study.[49] The correspondence theory is criticized by Nash, for example, "for the simple reason that the past to which our historical propositions are supposed to correspond no longer exists."[50] The coherence theory, on the other hand, is criticized on the basis that coherence alone is no guarantee of truth. A. R. White puts it this way: "it is an objection to coherence as the meaning of 'truth' or as the only criterion of truth that it is logically possible to have two different but equally comprehensive sets of coherent statements between which there would be, in the coherence theory, no way to decide which was the set of true statements."[51] When faced with this sort of criticism, "objective idealist" proponents of the coherence theory counter by insisting that "the coherence of which they speak attaches only to a concrete system, of which human experiences form a part; it does not attach to abstract systems of mathematics or logic, where several mutually incompatible systems are possible."[52]

In the final analysis, it is probably best to make a place for both notions, correspondence and coherence, in our thinking about historical truth. Perhaps one way to attempt a synthesis is to distinguish between a *theory* of truth and a *criterion* of truth. As a *theory* of historical truth, the "common-sense" *correspondence* theory is attractive, but as a criterion, or test, of truth, it is useful only to a limited degree, since the past is unrepeatable. The *coherence* theory (in all but the most qualified formulations, perhaps) is inadequate as a theory of truth, but it offers a useful *criterion* of truth, if by it we mean, as Nash suggests, that "a proposition is true when it coheres with, fits in with, everything else that we know." Nash explains: "A police investigator who is forced to solve a crime on the basis of circumstantial evidence must use the coherence standard of truth. So must the historian in his study of history."[53]

---

[44]Cf. Brandfon, "Limits of Evidence," p. 31; Nash, *Christian Faith*, p. 108.

[45]Brandfon, "Limits of Evidence," p. 35.

[46]A. F. Holmes, "Christian Philosophy," in *The New Encyclopedia Brittanica*, ed. Mortimer J. Adler et al., 15th ed. (1977), Macropaedia 4: 561.

[47]*Dictionary of Philosophy*, ed. Flew, p. 355.

[48]Holmes, "Christian Philosophy," p. 561.

[49]For convenient summaries, see A. R. White, "Coherence Theory of Truth," in *Encyclopedia*, ed. Edwards, 2: 130–33; A. N. Prior, "Correspondence Theory of Truth," in ibid., 2: 223–32.

[50]Nash, *Christian Faith*, p. 108.

[51]"Coherence Theory," 131, q.v. for further criticisms.

[52]*Dictionary of Philosophy*, ed. Flew, p. 66.

[53]*Christian Faith*, pp. 108–9. Unfortunately, as White ("Coherence Theory," p. 133) points out, sometimes advocates of the coherence theory confuse "the reasons, or criteria, for calling a statement true or false with the meaning of 'truth' or 'falsity.'"

In the light of all this, we might say that historical reconstructions that are *coherent* with all that we now know about a subject may be deemed reliable guides to the past, and may be assumed (barring discovery of conflicting evidence) to *correspond* to the past in a manner similar to the way in which a representational painting corresponds to its subject.[54] The criterion of *coherence* in the preceding statement encompasses both of my suggested tests of truth value—viz., internal consistency and external consistency. The concept of *correspondence*, on the other hand, represents an ontological affirmation of the sense in which written history represents the historical past—it "corresponds" to its subject as much as, but no more than, a representational painting does to its subject.

To sum up our discussion to this point, we may again observe that the approach to reading the Bible historically suggested in this chapter runs parallel to Strauss's tests of historicity, briefly outlined and evaluated in chapter 3. Of Strauss's several criteria for determining whether a text is to be understood as historical or unhistorical, I addressed his first negative criterion related to worldview in the section on examining models; there I differed with his opinion that "all just philosophical conceptions" mandate an anti-supernaturalist presupposition. His positive criterion that determinations regarding the historicity of smaller units may be extended to implicate the larger units of which they are a part was discussed in the section on the importance of context; there I in effect reversed Strauss's position to argue that the apparent purpose of larger discourse units places the burden of proof on those who believe that smaller units do not partake in this overarching sense of purpose. Finally, the discussion of internal and external tests of the truth value of historical truth claims parallels Strauss's second negative criterion—viz., that reliable testimony must be consistent with itself and with other reliable witnesses or evidence; there my main concern was that interpreters take care to develop a proper sense of what constitutes "consistency" in an ancient document.

As we move now to the final stage in our deliberations over how we should read the Bible historically, I shall again build on the legal analogy. A lawyer's task entails more than ascertaining what a witness is saying (truth claim) and even more than coming to a personal opinion as to the veracity (truth value) of the witness's testimony. The lawyer has not done his job until he has put the various pieces of evidence together and built a case designed to convince others, the jury or the judge, that a particular understanding of "what happened in the past" is to be accepted. Similarly, the task of biblical historians is not only to come to informed opinions regarding the truth claims of biblical texts and to personal convictions regarding the truth value of these claims. They must also seek to put the pieces together within a plausible historical reconstruction designed to convince others that a particular understanding of "what happened in the past" is worthy of acceptance.

The manner in which lawyers and historians present their summations (their reconstructions of what actually happened) will vary, depending on their sense of how the jury is leaning, but in general they will need to do three things. First, they must briefly rehearse the testimony—recall what truth claims have been made. Second, they must evaluate the testimony—remind their hearers of which truth claims were found to be deserving of trust (e.g., by virtue of their coming from reliable witnesses whose character is well attested and whose testimony is internally consistent and also consonant with

---

[54]For an insightful discussion of coherence, correspondence, and reliability in historical study, see McCullagh, *Justifying Historical Descriptions*, pp. 1–8.

whatever external evidence is available). Finally, they must convince their hearers that their proposed reconstruction of "what actually happened," their *argument* as it were, has been arrived at logically, or at least does not rest on any logical fallacies. It is to this question of argumentation that we now turn.

PRESENTATION: CONSTRUCTING ARGUMENTS

In his book entitled *The Uses of Argument*, Stephen Toulmin develops a system for analyzing the structure of arguments (especially of the sort employed in jurisprudence) that has proved particularly attractive to historians and philosophers of history, as well as to theologians and others.[55] The essence of Toulmin's approach is to identify the various components of an argument, such as data, warrants, and backing, and to chart the argument in a candid fashion so that the function of each component in the overall argument becomes clear. The benefits of Toulmin's approach are several. It demonstrates that arguments are complex, not simple, affairs. It also affords a clear view of how an argument is put together, what data it cites, what assumptions it involves, what warrants must be true for the argument to hold, what rebuttals are conceivable that could overturn the argument, and how logically the conclusion is derived from the data. Where historians disagree in their historical reconstructions, the straightforward analysis of arguments afforded by Toulmin's scheme makes it possible to retrace the (logical) pathways by which the differing conclusions were reached and to identify specific points of strength or weakness, agreement or disagreement.

Toulmin's scheme is presented rather fully by Harvey, Kelsey, and Cameron,[56] so it will be presented only briefly here, and then exemplified. The type of argument employed in historical studies typically involves the following components in the following relation: this datum/these data (**D**) exist(s), so, with this *qualification* (**Q**; e.g., necessarily, presumably, possibly), since this *warrant* (**W**) holds, on account of this *backing* (**B**), this *conclusion* (**C**) follows, unless a *rebuttal* (**R**) of one or more aspects of the argument is forthcoming. In chart form, the structure of such an argument looks like this.[57]

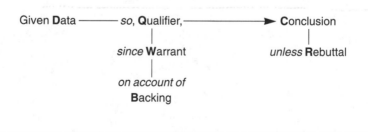

[55]Cambridge: Cambridge University Press, 1958 (see esp. pp. 94–145). Those who have built on Toulmin's approach, to name a few, include Harvey, *Historian and the Believer,* pp. 43–64 (and through him many others; e.g., Abraham, *Divine Revelation,* esp. chap. 6); D. H. Kelsey, *The Uses of Scripture in Recent Theology* (London: SCM, 1975), pp. 122–38 (whose focus is on arguments for theological positions); N. M. de S. Cameron, *Biblical Higher Criticism and the Defense of Infallibilism in 19th Century Britain* (Lewiston: Edwin Mellen, 1987), pp. 276–89; Brown, *History and Faith,* pp. 38–40.

[56]See the preceding note.

[57]This chart is essentially the same as Toulmin's, with the slight difference that I have shifted the "*so*, Qualifier" component to the left to stand over the warrant and backing, as this, it seems to me, allows the argument to be read more naturally in columns from left to right.

To offer a concrete example, we may chart the fairly simple argument that was tentatively suggested above with respect to how the Elijah/Elisha narratives in 1 and 2 Kings should be read. It would look something like this.

Given **D** ——— *so,* **Q** presumably, ——————▶ **C**
that the   the Elijah/Elisha narratives
Elijah/   *since* **W**   should be read as sharing in
Elisha   every lower level   the historical impulse,
narratives   of discourse is
are well   influenced by every   *unless* **R**
integrated   higher,   1)there are indications in
into the   the text that the prophet
books of   *on account of* **B**   stories are to be treated
Kings,   the principles of   differently from the rest,
whose   discourse,   2) the historical impulse of
historical   the books of Kings be
impulse is   denied,
recognized,   or
                                            3)sufficient contrary
                                            evidence emerges to
                                            discredit warrant and/or
                                                    backing.

The argument could be presented, using precisely the same words, in one rather long sentence, but the advantage of Toulmin's chart is that it makes the overall structure of the argument and the function of its various components more immediately apparent.

In this particular argument, as the chart indicates, at least three rebuttals can be envisaged that would undercut the argument. The first two relate to the two-part statement of the data, while the third relates to warrant and backing. The first two rebuttals would require demonstration on exegetical grounds—namely, an identification of clues *in the text* that the prophet stories are to be treated differently than the surrounding context, or an exegetical reassessment of the overall sense of purpose and the supposed historical impulse of the books of Kings. The third rebuttal might involve a questioning of the warrant that "every lower level of discourse is influenced by every higher." In answer to such a challenge, we would need to construct a second argument, in which the former backing would become the data, the former warrant would become the conclusion, and a new warrant, with its own backing, would need to be introduced to justify the move from data to conclusion.[58] The second argument might look something like this.

---

[58]Cf. Kelsey, *Uses of Scripture,* p. 127.

Given **D** ——— *so,* **Q** presumably, ————————→ **C**
the   every lower level of
principles of   *since* **W**   discourse is influenced by
discourse,   these principles   every higher,
                       appear to be valid,
                                                            unless **R**
                       on account of **B**   1)the principles of discourse
                       confirmation not   have been misunderstood,
                       only from the   or
                       academic discipline   2) it can be shown that the
                       of discourse   principles of discourse are
                       analysis but also   faulty or do not hold in the
                       from common   particular case under
                       sense, everyday   discussion.
                       conversation, etc.,

Should some aspect of this argument be challenged, then a further argument would need to be constructed, and so on. Virtually any argument (historical, theological, legal, etc.) can be analyzed in terms of Toulmin's structure, and it is very useful to make a habit of subjecting one's own and others' arguments to such analysis. Often it will be discovered that warrants or backing are left unstated (or are lacking), possible rebuttals are not considered, and so forth. An added benefit is that one will constantly be reminded that history is a field-encompassing field and that historical argumentation is complex, often involving many steps (or sub-arguments) and making use of various kinds of authorizations, deductions, and evidence. In his discussion of "theological macro-arguments," Kelsey observes that "several logically different kinds of statement may all serve to help authorize a given conclusion, although in different senses of 'authorize.'"[59] This observation about theological arguments applies equally well to historical ones. Similarly applicable are his comments on theological method and reasoning.

> There is no one distinctively "theological method," if that means a single character-
> istically theological structure of argument. So too, there is no special theological "way"
> to argue or "think," if that is taken to imply a peculiarly theological structure to argu-
> ment. Accordingly, analysis and criticism of theological "systems" are not likely to be
> illuminating if undertaken on the tacit assumption that they may be measured by an

---

[59]Ibid., p. 135.

ideal or standard mode of "theological thinking," "theological method," or "theological way of arguing." Arguments in theology have the same pattern as arguments actually used in connection with any other subject matter, but belong in several different fields of argument.[60]

In the above quotation, it would not be inaccurate to substitute *history/historical* for each occurrence of *theology/theological*. There simply is no ideal or standard mode of historical thinking, historical method, or historical way of arguing, but rather, as Ramsey rightly observes, "The historian, like the lawyer in court, must employ arguments of the most diverse sorts. . . . *The element which is common to all the arguments of the lawyer or the historian (or anyone else) is the obligation to give reasons for his conclusions.*"[61]

CONCLUSION

The present chapter began with the question, *How then should we read the Bible "historically"?* The "then" was meant to recall what had been discussed in the preceding four chapters. The specific aim of this chapter has been to move toward an answer to that question by exploring foundational issues and procedural steps, which, when further developed and refined, might yield something of a program, or hermeneutic, for approaching the Bible historically.

We considered first the importance, as preparation for any historical reading of the Bible, of gaining some awareness of the reality models, or background beliefs, that we and others bring to our reading. We are unlikely ever to understand ourselves, others, or our Bibles, unless we have some sense of where each of us, as it were, "is coming from." Having addressed the foundational issues, we then moved to a consideration of a simple, two-part procedure for exploring the historical import of the Bible. The basis of the procedure is the twofold need to *listen* carefully and competently to the biblical texts so as to detect their truth claims and to *test* the truth value of whatever historical claims are made. The procedure itself does not constitute an exegetical method but, rather, provides a framework around which the various exegetical and related disciplines might be arranged. As to the first part of the procedure, stress was laid on two requirements of good listening—viz., an open, expectant attitude and careful attention to context. As to the second part, we noted that testimony should pass two tests in order to qualify as reliable—the *internal consistency* test that requires the testimony to be coherent and self-consistent, and the *external consistency* test that requires the testimony to be compatible with whatever external evidence, rightly interpreted, might be available.

Finally, we turned to the matter of historical reconstruction and argumentation. This is where the historian seeks to assemble all the evidence that has been tested and found reliable into a convincing historical reconstruction. We likened the historian's reconstruction to a lawyer's summation at the end of a trial where witnesses have been heard and cross-examined. In this regard we explored the value of Toulmin's *anatomy of*

---

[60]Ibid., pp. 134–35.
[61]*Quest*, p. 22 (emphasis Ramsey's).

an argument as an aid to assessing the validity and cogency of historical, and other types, of argumentation.

While there is a certain logical sequencing to the discussion in this chapter, in practice there will be more of a hermeneutical spiral, since later discoveries will often call for reassessing earlier conclusions. In the next chapter we shall consider a historically much-disputed stretch of text (the *rise of Saul* in 1 Sam. 9–11) as a testing-ground for the programmatic approach presented in this chapter.

AN EXTENDED
EXAMPLE

The Rise of Saul

*I*n discussions of biblical historiography, the Saul narratives in 1 Samuel have elicited much attention and interest.[1] Despite the high level of interest, however, historical study of the Saul narratives seems to have yielded rather disappointing results.[2] On the archaeological side, little has been learned to date that is of direct assistance in reconstructing the rise of Israel's first king. And this is not surprising, for as Amihai Mazar has recently pointed out, "the archaeological evidence for the period of the United Monarchy is sparse" and "often controversial."[3] In particular, "the time of Saul hardly finds any

---

[1]See, e.g., J. Licht, "Biblical Historicism" in *History, Historiography and Interpretation: Historiography in the Ancient World and the Origins of Biblical History,* ed. H. Tadmor and M. Weinfeld (New Haven and London: Yale University Press, 1983), p. 247; H. Donner, "Basic Elements of Old Testament Historiography Illustrated By the Saul Traditions," *Die Ou-Testamentiese Werkgemeenskap in Suid-Afrika* 24 (1981): 40–54; G. von Rad, *Old Testament Theology,* trans. D. M. G. Stalker (New York: Harper & Row, 1962) 1:48–49; *idem,* "The Beginnings of Historical Writing in Ancient Israel," *The Problem of the Hexateuch and Other Essays,* trans. E. W. Trueman Dicken (Edinburgh: Oliver & Boyd, 1966), pp. 166–204; W. E. Evans, "An Historical Reconstruction of the Emergence of Israelite Kingship and the Reign of Saul," *Scripture in Context II: More Essays on the Comparative Method,* eds. W. W. Hallo, J. C. Moyer and L. G. Perdue (Winona Lake, Ind.: Eisenbrauns, 1983), p. 61; Van Seters, *In Search of History,* p. 247.

[2]A shorter version of this chapter appears in *Faith, Tradition, and History,* ed. D. W. Baker, J. K. Hoffmeier, and A. R. Millard (Winona Lake, Ind.: Eisenbrauns, 1994).

[3]*Archaeology of the Land of the Bible: 10,000–586 B.C.E.* (New York: Doubleday, 1990), p. 371.

expression in the archaeological record."[4] Social-scientific and ethno-archaeological studies are in the process of providing general background information, but specific information
about Israel's first kings must still be derived almost exclusively from the literary deposit
in Scripture. And here we encounter a problem. A majority of scholars finds the biblical
account of Saul's rise to the throne to be, as Jacob Licht puts it, "rather unconvincing as
a statement of fact."[5] Indeed, most would still subscribe to the verdict rendered back in
1932 by W. W. Cannon that "the events by which he [Saul] came to the throne are and
will remain a mystery."[6]

This rather unhopeful verdict may derive from one or more of several basic lines
of reasoning. I noted already in chapter 3 (pp. 112ff.) the Enlightenment dictum that no
narrative that includes God or the gods among the active participants in the events
described can qualify as a historical account.[7] When this dictum is applied to the biblical account of Saul's rise, the resulting argument looks something like this (employing the
chart described in the preceding chapter).

| *Given* **D** —— *so,* **Q** presumably, —————▶ **C** |
that the		the biblical account cannot
biblical	*since* **W**	be historical,
account of	divine agency can	
Saul's rise	never play a part in	*unless* **R**
involves	historical accounts,	warrant or backing is
God as an		fallacious.
agent in	*on account of* **B**	
the action	"all just	
(1 Sam	philosophical	
9:15–16;	conceptions" as	
10:6, 9, 22;	defined by the	
11:6, etc.),	Enlightenment,	

Some, no doubt, dismiss the potential historicity of the Saul narratives on a basis such
as this, but for those who do not share the exclusively naturalistic worldview of Strauss and
his philosophical descendents, and particularly for those who regard the Bible as a distinctive book describing distinctive events, such an argument will carry no weight.

---

[4]Ibid. The one potential exception to this generalization—viz., the Iron I tower foundation at Tell
el-Ful thought by Albright to represent the "Citadel of Saul"—is now regarded as far less certain evidence
of Saulide construction than scholars had previously believed; see, most recently, P. M. Arnold, *Gibeah: The
Search for a Biblical City,* JSOTS 79 (Sheffield: JSOT, 1990), pp. 51–52.
[5]"Biblical Historicism," p. 107.
[6]"The Reign of Saul," *Theology* 25 (1932): 326.
[7]For a corrective to this view, see, e.g., A. R. Millard, "Old Testament and History," pp. 39–40.

Others, such as Klaas Smelik, have argued that the Saul narratives cannot be historical because the ancient Near East provides too few "inspiring examples" ("inspirerende voorbeelden") of history writing from around the time of David or Solomon to justify any expectation that Israel might have had a historiographical tradition stemming from that time.[8] This is not the place to attempt a full critique of Smelik's contention, but a few brief comments may be in order: (1) Smelik's is an argument from silence; (2) it seems to underplay the significance of, for example, the royal apology literature attested from the chancelleries of the ancient Near East;[9] and (3) it rests, at any rate, on the questionable assumption that a truly new literary form can never arise spontaneously but only by means of an evolutionary development from earlier forms.[10]

Neither of the above reasons for doubting the historicity of the Saul narratives is very compelling, and indeed neither is very often cited. By far the *most frequently cited reason* for the historical agnosticism regarding Saul's kingship is the belief that the biblical narratives recounting Saul's rise simply *do not make sense as a story.* That is to say, they do not constitute a coherent, sequential narrative. Tomoo Ishida speaks for a majority of scholars when he asserts that "it is futile from the outset to attempt reconstruction of a harmonious history from all the narratives."[11] Even the (by contemporary standards) rather conservative John Bright insists that "in view of these varying accounts, we cannot undertake to reconstruct the sequence of events" by which Saul became king.[12]

In what follows, we shall focus on this last and most pervasive line of reasoning believed by the vast majority of scholars to discredit any attempt to reconstruct the historical rise of Saul from the narratives of 1 Samuel, or at least from all of them taken together. In chart form, the argument representative of the current consensus would look something like the chart on the top of the next page.

---

[8]*Saul: de voorstelling van Israëls eerste koning in de Masoretische tekst van het Oude Testament* (Amsterdam: drukkerij en Uitgeverij P. E. T., 1977), p. 76.

[9]In this regard it seems fairer to say, with R. K. Gnuse ("Holy History in the Hebrew Scriptures and the Ancient World: Beyond the Present Debate," *BTB* 17 [1987]: 131), that "Israelite thought was different, not unique; it moved beyond the ancient world in certain respects, but it was not diametrically opposed to the predecessor cultures."

[10]Patrick and Scult (*Rhetoric*, p. 36) seem to be closer to the mark in their observation that "the Biblical narrative was an innovative form of prose art not seen before in the ancient Near East," a form developed by the biblical writers apparently "because they found the already existing literary forms available to them, namely the chronicle and the epic, so inadequate to their purposes."

[11]*The Royal Dynasties in Ancient Israel: A Study on the Formation and Development of Royal-Dynastic Ideology* (Berlin: Walter de Gruyter, 1977), p. 42.

[12]*History of Israel*, p. 188.

Given **D** —— *so,* **Q** presumably, ——————▶ **C**

Given **D**	*so,* **Q** presumably,	**C**
that the		the biblical account cannot
Bible fails	*since* **W**	be viewed as an accurate
to present	internal	historical account
an	consistency is a	
internally	necessary	*unless* **R**
coherent,	condition of	1) the data statement is
unifed	accurate historical	incorrect (i.e., the Bible does
account of	accounts,	present a coherent, unifed
how Saul		reading of the biblical
became	*on account of* **B**	account of Saul's rise),
king,	the self-consistent	or
	character of reality,	2) sufficient contrary
		evidence emerges to
		discredit warrant or backing.

Properly understood, the warrant and backing seem unassailable, so that the second rebuttal above is essentially out of the question. The first rebuttal, however, may be possible, so this is where the investigation should concentrate. The goal, then, is to *listen* once more, as carefully and competently as possible, to the biblical testimony. Despite the weight of a consensus, we must guard against presupposing in advance that the narratives will not make sense, for in so doing we are likely to foreclose any real opportunity of discovering otherwise. Rather, as we have argued in the preceding chapter, if we would be good listeners, we must approach the text with an open (though not naive or credulous) attitude.

PURPORTED OBSTACLES TO A COHERENT LITERARY READING OF SAUL'S RISE

Perhaps the place to begin is with a review of the literary, or logical, difficulties thought to stand in the way of a straightforward reading of the rise of Saul. These are basically three. First, since Wellhausen it has been customary in discussions of the rise of the monarchy as recorded in 1 Samuel 8–12 to distinguish at least two originally independent narratives detectable on the basis of discrepant attitudes to kingship. Bright explains:

> The account of Saul's election comes to us in two (probably originally three) parallel narratives, one tacitly favorable to the monarchy, and the other bitterly hostile. The first (I Sam. 9:1 to 10:16) tells how Saul was privately anointed by Samuel in Ramah; it is continued in 13:3b, 4b–15. Woven with this narrative is the originally separate account (ch. 11) of Saul's victory over Ammon and his subsequent acclamation by the people at Gilgal. The other strand (chs. 8; 10:17–27; 12) has Samuel, having yielded with angry protests to popular demand, presiding over Saul's election at Mizpah.[13]

---

[13]Ibid., pp. 187–88.

This quotation from Bright, highlighting the apparently contradictory promonarchical and antimonarchical sentiments of the assumed sources, touches also upon the second of the most frequently cited difficulties in the biblical account of Saul's rise. This is the fact that Saul appears to come to power by too many different routes. Did he come to power by distinguishing himself in battle against the Ammonites (as many historical critics believe), or as a result of his anointing followed by battle (as the combined promonarchical source would have it), or by lot-casting (as the antimonarchical source would have it)? The consensus of scholarly opinion is well summarized by Herbert Donner when he says of the various accounts, "they contradict each other: Saul could not have become king in so many ways."[14] Even restricting himself to a consideration of the so-called promonarchical source, William Irwin insists that "we are embarrassed by our very wealth! Either account [i.e., the anointing episode or the Ammonite victory] would suffice as an explanation of this revolutionary change in Hebrew history, to be given both baffles credence."[15]

To these two apparent difficulties—the differing attitudes towards the monarchy and the multiple accession accounts—must be added a third. The account of Saul's anointing in 1 Samuel 10 contains a longstanding *crux interpretum,* which comes in verse 8. In this verse Samuel instructs Saul to go down to Gilgal and wait for him, so that he may come and offer sacrifices and tell Saul what he is to do. The problem is that this instruction comes on the heels of verse 7, in which Samuel tells Saul to "do what your hand finds to do." Assuming the verse 7 directive to be an unqualified authorization for Saul to act in kingly fashion whenever the need should arise, scholars have felt that verse 8 constitutes a blatant contradiction.[16] What verse 7 seems to authorize, "Do what your hand finds to do," verse 8 seems to take away, "go down to Gilgal" and "wait." To make matters worse, the fulfillment of the injunction in verse 8 does not come until chapter 13, all of which contributes to the impression that verse 8 must not be original to its present context in chapter 10, but must be a later insertion, perhaps a sort of "theological correction" inserted by a later prophetic circle unhappy with the apparently free hand being given Saul by Samuel in verse 7.[17] As a corollary to the assumption that verse 8 is secondary to chapter 10, scholars have customarily assumed that the Gilgal episode in chapter 13 (vv. 4b, 7b–15a) must also be secondary.[18]

[14]"Old Testament Historiography," p. 43.
[15]"Samuel and the Rise of the Monarchy," *American Journal of Semitic Languages and Literatures* 58 (1941): 117.
[16]See, e.g., J. Wellhausen, *Prolegomena zur Geschichte Israel,* 3rd ed. (Berlin: Georg Reimer, 1886), p. 268; K. D. Budde, *Die Bücher Samuel,* Kurzer Hand-Commentar zum Alten Testament 8 (Tübingen: J. C. B. Mohr, 1902), p. 69; R. J. Thompson, *Penitence and Sacrifice in Early Israel outside the Levitical Law* (Leiden: E. J. Brill, 1963), p. 106; H. J. Stoebe, *Das erste Buch Samuelis,* Kommentar zum Alten Testament 8/1 (Gütersloh: Gert Mohn, 1973), p. 210.
[17]Cf. J. Kegler's characterization of 10:8 as a "theologische Korrektur" in *Politisches Geschehen und theologisches Verstehen: Zum Geschichtsverständnis in der frühen israelitischen Königszeit,* Calwer Theologische Monographien 8 (Stuttgart: Calwer, 1977), p. 264.
[18]This statement by T. Veijola (*Die Ewige Dynastie: David und die Entstehung seiner Dynastie nach der deuteronomistischen Darstellung,* Annales academiae scientiarum Fennicae, Series B, 193 [Helsinki: Suomalainen Tiedeakatemia, 1975], p. 55) is typical: "That the entire Gilgal episode in 1 Sam. 13:7b–15a (which falls outside its present context) is a secondary insertion (along with its similarly isolated anticipation in 1 Sam. 10:8), is no longer in need of demonstration" (my translation). In addition to the literature cited by Veijola, cf. also Stoebe, *Das erste Buch Samuelis,* p. 207; McCarter, *I Samuel,* p. 228.

How are we to evaluate these three arguments to the effect that the biblical account of the rise of Saul is at points contradictory and incoherent, and thus an unreliable source of historical information? I would contend that the data are now available to enable solutions to all three problems. The first two I shall consider only briefly, since the relevant insights necessary to their resolution have already been published by others.

In chart form, the first argument, based on the apparently differing attitudes towards monarchy, looks like this.

Given **D** ——— *so,* **Q** presumably, ————————▶ **C**		
that the		the story of Saul's rise
various	*since* **W**	cannot be viewed as a
episoded in	consistency of	unified, self-consistent
the biblical	perpective is	historical account
account of	expected in unified	
Saul's rise	histories,	*unless* **R**
exhibit		1) the apparent differences
differing	*on account of* **B**	can be explained on
attitudes	the controlling	grounds other than
towards	perspective of	authorial inconsistency,
the	competent	2) the data statement can be
monarchy,	historians,	faulted for lack of precision
		(e.g., a distincition should be
		made between attitudes
		towards monarchy in
		general and towards Saul in
		particular),
		or
		3) sufficient contrary
		evidence emerges to
		discredit warrant or backing.

Those who espouse the argument from differing monarchical attitudes often fail to consider possible rebuttals such as are listed above. But, in fact, recent studies confirm the validity of at least the first two. Tsevat, McCarthy, Childs, and others have pointed out, for example, that the more antimonarchical statements are made in the episodes involving assemblies (natural contexts for expression of strong opinions) and not so much in the action reports. Eslinger has stressed that monarchical attitudes expressed are not always those of the narrator; in each instance we must ask "the simple question of who says what to whom." Others have emphasized the important distinction between attitudes that are antimonarchical *per se* and those that are merely anti-Saul.[19] When we begin

---

[19]For bibliography and discussion pertaining to all of the above, see my *Reign and Rejection*, pp. 173–83.

to look at the problem of differing attitudes to the monarchy through these corrective lenses, we discover that our sharpened vision reveals not a more clearly defined problem but the absence of any problem at all. In other words, the above argument fails, because adequate rebuttals are forthcoming.

The second challenge to the literary coherence (and thus *potential* historicity) of the biblical account of Saul's rise relates to the fact that Saul appears to have come to power via several distinct pathways. The basic argument, with potential rebuttals, may be laid out like this.

Given **D** ——	so, **Q** presumably,	——————►**C**
that the various episodes in the biblical account of Saul's rise present multiple (and apparently mutually exclusive) accounts of how Saul came to power,	*since* **W** reliable historiography excludes contradictory, mutually exclusive renditions of how a particular historical circumstance came to be, *on account of* **B** the self-consistent character of reality,	the biblical account of Saul's rise cannot be trusted as historiography, *unless* **R** 1) the data statement is incorrect and it can be shown that the episodes are not in fact mutually exclusive (e.g., that each is but a stage in a larger process), or 2) sufficient contrary evidence emerges to discredit warrant or backing.

The raw material for confirming the first rebuttal has been provided in recent work by Baruch Halpern[20] and has been further fashioned by Dianna Edelman.[21] Halpern has argued on the basis of both biblical and extrabiblical evidence that the process by which leaders in early Israel came to power quite likely entailed three stages, which we might describe simply as designation, demonstration, and confirmation.[22] The process would

---

[20]The *Constitution of the Monarchy in Israel*, Harvard Semitic Monographs 25 (Chico, CA: Scholars, 1981); "The Uneasy Compromise: Israel between League and Monarchy," *Traditions in Transformation: Turning Points in Biblical Faith*, Cross Festschrift; ed. B. Halpern and J. D. Levenson (Winona Lake: Eisenbrauns, 1981), pp. 59–96.

[21]"Saul's Rescue of Jabesh-Gilead (1 Sam. 11:1–11): Sorting Story from History," *Zeitschrift für die alttestamentliche Wissenschaft* 96 (1984): 195–209.

[22]While Halpern sometimes explicitly names only two stages—viz., *designation* and *confirmation* (cf. *Constitution*, pp. 125ff., 173–74)—it is clear that he presupposes a middle *demonstration* stage consisting of a real or ritual victory of some sort (cf. "Uneasy Compromise," p. 72; *Constitution*, pp. 95, 173–74). On the validity of distinguishing three stages, see also Edelman, "Saul's Rescue," p. 198 n. 9.

go something like this. An individual is first *designated* in some way as God's chosen instrument. The new appointee is then expected to *demonstrate* his special status and suitability for leadership by a feat of arms or military victory, whether real or merely ritual. Having thus distinguished himself publicly, he is in a position to be confirmed publicly as leader.

Both Halpern and Edelman attempt to elucidate the biblical account of Saul's rise on the basis of this tripartite pattern. Halpern isolates what he believes to be two complete exemplars of the accession pattern in the stretch of text from 1 Samuel 9 to 14.[23] The impetus for this discovery, however, appears to come more from Halpern's commitment to a theory of sources and doublets[24] than from the texts themselves.[25] Edelman improves on Halpern's analysis by discerning but one instance of the accession pattern in 1 Samuel 9–11. In her view, the divine designation is represented by Saul's anointing in the section 9:1–10:16, the demonstration by his defeat of the Ammonites in 11:1–11, and the confirmation by the "renewal" of the kingdom in 11:14–15.[26]

Edelman's scheme is plausible so far as it goes, but it leaves some unanswered questions. For example, it provides little explanation of the lot-casting episode in 10:17–27, which comes between the anointing and the Ammonite victory.[27] A further and more significant tension in Edelman's scheme has to do with Samuel's charge to Saul in 10:7 to "do what your hand finds to do." Edelman rightly recognizes that this charge implies some kind of military engagement, and she assumes that this must be none other than Saul's Ammonite victory. But she also recognizes—and herein lies the problem—that the real focus of 10:7 in context is not the Ammonites but the Philistines, and particularly the Philistine presence in Gibeah (which is to become the object of Jonathan's aggression in chapter 13). To come to terms with this awkward situation, some scholars postulate that the events of chapter 13 must have followed more closely on 10:7 in some hypothetical earlier stage of development.[28] In other words, they assume that episodes originally joined have now been redactionally put asunder.

This suggestion of textual dislocation brings us to the third and final challenge to the literary coherence of the rise of Saul as recounted in 1 Samuel. In what follows I shall attempt to demonstrate that this perceived difficulty actually offers the key to a rather straightforward synchronic reading of the narrative of Saul's rise.

---

[23]"Uneasy Compromise," p. 70.

[24]He writes, "The first step in investigating Saul's election is, as the histories recognize, a division of the sources in 1 Samuel 8ff." (ibid., p. 63).

[25]For a critical evaluation of Halpern's two-source theory, see my *Reign and Rejection*, pp. 191–93.

[26]"Saul's Rescue," pp. 197–99.

[27]Edelman (ibid., pp. 200–202) notes only that this episode "appears to augment the discussion of the first stage of the process of installing a king" and to look forward to the public coronation that will eventually occur in 11:14–15; for Edelman's most recent thoughts on the issue, see her *King Saul in the Historiography of Judah*, JSOTS 121 (Sheffield: JSOT, 1991), pp. 51–58, 76–82.

[28]Ibid., p. 200. Those who seek to explain the apparent relationship between chaps. 10 and 13 in traditio-historical terms include H. J. Stoebe, "Zur Topographie und Überlieferung der Schlact von Mikmas, 1 Sam. 13 und 14," *Theologische Zeitschrift* 21 (1965): 277–80; J. M. Miller, "Saul's Rise to Power: Some Observations Concerning 1 Sam 9:1–10:16; 10:26–11:15 and 13:2–14:46," *CBQ* 36 (1974): 162; T. N. D. Mettinger, *King and Messiah: The Civil and Sacral Legitimation of the Israelite Kings*, Coniectanea Biblica: Old Testament Series 8 (Lund: CWK Gleerup, 1976), p. 97; and most recently P. J. Arnold, *Gibeah*, pp. 89–90.

SAUL'S FIRST CHARGE AS A TWO-STAGE AFFAIR

As mentioned earlier, the impression of textual dislocation derives from two felt tensions in the text: first, the apparently contradictory commands given to Saul by Samuel in consecutive verses in chapter 10 ("do what your hand finds to do" [v.7] and "go down ahead of me to Gilgal [and] wait ... until I come to you and tell you what you are to do" [v.8]) and, second, the fact that the trip to Gilgal is not made until chapter 13. We shall take these up in order.

As regards the commands of 10:7–8, it is my contention that they should be viewed not as contradictory but as complementary instructions, the execution of the second being contingent upon the fulfillment of the first. This view seems to be quite in keeping with the larger narrative context, which runs as follows. After a divinely orchestrated meeting between the two principals in chapter 9, Samuel anoints Saul in 10:1 as the Lord's designate to lead his people. Samuel then describes three signs that will confirm Saul in his new station (vv. 2–6). The third sign is to take place at Gibeah of God, where, as Samuel points out, there is a Philistine outpost (v. 5). This reference to a Philistine outpost is regarded by many scholars as at best superfluous, if not indeed out of place. No better justification is given for this opinion than that these scholars fail to see any reason why the biblical narrator should mention a Philistine installation at this particular juncture in the narrative.[29] When we recall, however, that Saul was appointed especially to deal with the Philistine menace (cf. the Lord's instructions to Samuel in 9:16), and when we notice that it is as soon as the three signs have come to pass that Saul is to do what his hand finds to do (10:7), then the mention of a Philistine presence at the site of the third and final sign takes on special significance. There is much to commend the view that Samuel's mention of the Philistines in 10:5 represents a fairly obvious hint to Saul of what, in fact, his hand should find to do.[30]

Against this background, and recalling the tripartite accession process worked out by Halpern and Edelman, we are prompted to ask what could possibly serve as a more appropriate *demonstration,* after Saul's divine *designation,* than that he should "throw down the gauntlet" to the Philistines by attacking one of their installations? Samuel, of course, realizes that such an act of provocation will signal only the beginning and not the end of trouble, and so he issues a *second* instruction to Saul in verse 8: "Go down ahead of me to Gilgal. I will surely come down to you to sacrifice burnt offerings and fellowship offerings, but you must wait seven days until I come to you and tell you what you are to do." In other words, as soon as Saul has done what his hand finds to do, thereby provoking

---

[29]P. K. McCarter (*I Samuel,* p. 182), for example, remarks simply that "this notice is immaterial at this point and probably secondary, having been added along with the instructions in v 8 as preparation for c 13."

[30]This understanding of the significance of 10:5 is attested already in the writings of grammarian and biblical commentator David Kimchi (1160–1235), who sees in Samuel's reference to the "officers of the Philistines" (Kimchi's apparent understanding of the Philistine presence) a hint that Saul "should remove them from there and save Israel out of their hands" (my translation of Kimchi's commentary to 1 Sam. 10:5 found in standard editions of the rabbinic Hebrew Bible). Other commentators who have sensed something of the significance of 10:5 include R. Kittel, *Geschichte des Volkes Israel,* 7th ed. (Gotha: Leopold Klotz, 1925), 2: 82; A. Lods, *Israel from its Beginnings to the Middle of the Eighth Century,* trans. S. H. Hooke (London: Kegan Paul, Trench, Trubner, 1932), p. 353: C. J. Goslinga, *Het eerste boek Samuël,* Commentaar op het Oude Testament (Kampen: J. H. Kok, 1968), p. 223; Smelik, *Saul: de voorstelling van Israëls eerste koning,* p. 107.

the Philistines, he is to repair to Gilgal, where Samuel will join him in order to consecrate the ensuing battle with sacrifices and to give him further instructions.[31]

In this way, then, the two injunctions of 10:7–8 appear to be not contradictory but complementary and sequentially contingent. We still have a problem, however, since the prescribed trip to Gilgal does not take place until chapter 13. The wording of 13:8, which speaks of Saul waiting "seven days, the time set by Samuel," leaves no room for doubt that the allusion is to 10:8—on this point there is universal agreement. What is often overlooked, however, is that a similar relationship exists between the notice in 13:3 that Jonathan has attacked the Philistine outpost at Geba and Saul's first charge in 10:7. In other words, in 13:3 we see Jonathan doing what Saul was instructed to do back in 10:7. As Stoebe succinctly puts it, "the deed that is here [13:3] ascribed to Jonathan is what one awaits as the continuation of Saul's Spirit-endowment in Gibeah and of the charge 'Do what your hand finds to do' (10:7)" (my translation).[32] It is noteworthy that Jonathan's provocative act in 13:3 is immediately followed by Saul's going down to Gilgal to wait for Samuel (13:4). Thus, we see the procedure envisaged in chapter 10 (i.e., provocation of the Philistines followed by convocation in Gilgal) actually followed in chapter 13. While this double attestation of the provocation-followed-by-convocation pattern does not constitute a proof of the genuineness and originality of the pattern in either context, it would at least seem to shift the burden of proof to those who would wish to assert the contrary.

In view of the obvious relationship between chapters 10 and 13, we are faced then with a final, very crucial question. How are we to explain the rather large gap, in both narrative time and real time, between Samuel's two-part instruction to Saul in 10:7–8 and its evident fulfillment three chapters and several episodes later? Must we assume traditio-historical or redactional dislocation of originally sequential episodes, or might we not consider the possibility that Saul simply falters in his first assignment, that he simply doesn't do what his hand finds to do, thus delaying indefinitely the execution of his second instruction—viz., the trip to Gilgal? The latter alternative seems to offer a rather promising possibility for explaining the gap between the issuance of Saul's first charge and its eventual fulfillment through the agency of Jonathan. The objection might be raised, however, that if Saul falters at the start, why does the text not explicitly say so or condemn Saul for his inaction? In addressing this objection, it will be helpful to contemplate a different kind of gap or gapping.

"GAPPING" AS LITERARY DEVICE AND THE GAP BETWEEN 1 SAMUEL 10 AND 13

In his *Poetics of Biblical Narrative* (pp. 186–88), Meir Sternberg points out that all literary works establish "a system of gaps that must be filled in" by the reader in the process of reading. Every literary work raises a number of questions in the mind of the reader, but it only provides explicit answers to a few of these. The remaining questions, the "gaps" as Sternberg calls them, are to be answered or filled in by the reader on the basis of clues in the text itself. Sternberg illustrates what he means by citing the following Hebrew nursery rhyme.

[31]For a discussion of the prophet's role in pre-battle consecration and instruction, see my *Reign and Rejection*, pp. 61–63.
[32]*Das erste Buch Samuelis*, p. 247; cf. p. 207. More recently, Halpern (*Constitution*, pp. 155–56) has also drawn attention to the command/fulfillment relationship between 10:7 and 13:3.

Every day, that's the way
Jonathan goes out to play.
Climbed a tree. What did he see?
Birdies: one, two, three!
Naughty boy! What have we seen?
There's a hole in your new jeans!

How did Jonathan tear his jeans? In the tree, of course. Even a child can draw this conclusion quite readily from the information given in the rhyme, though the point is never explicitly made. Of course, gap-filling may not always be as simple as this, especially in narratives as artful and sophisticated as the Samuel narratives. Sternberg writes, "gap-filling ranges from simple linkages of elements, which the reader performs automatically, to intricate networks that are figured out consciously, laboriously, hesitantly, and with constant modifications in the light of additional information disclosed in later stages of reading."

It seems fair to say that the *literary* gap created by the *literal* gap between Saul's first charge and its eventual fulfillment is of the more difficult sort described above. That it should take conscious effort to fill it should not surprise us, for as Sternberg remarks, "in works of greater complexity, the filling-in of gaps becomes much more difficult and therefore more conscious and anything but automatic." The test of any attempt at gap-filling is, of course, whether the hypothesis is "legitimated by the text."

One way to formulate an argument against the coherence of the Saul story on the basis of the datum that there is a gap between the charge of 1 Samuel 10:7–8 and its apparent fulfillment in chapter 13 would be the following.

Given **D** ──	*so,* **Q** *presumably,* ──────▶	**C**
that the		either there is no intent to
fulfillment	*since* **W**	convey a coherent,
of the	proper sequencing	sequential account, or the
charge	is a usual aspect of	texts must have suffered
given in	storytelling (unless	some dislocation,
1 Sam	there are specific	
10:7–8	indications of	*unless* **R**
does not	flashback,	1) it can be shown that,
come until	prolepsis, etc.),	despite appearances,
1 Sam 13,		proper sequencing has in
after	*on account of* **B**	fact been preserved,
several	the importance of	or
intervening	establishing cause-	2) sufficient contrary
episodes,	effect relationships	evidence emerges to
	in coherent	undermine warrant or
	narratives,	backing.

Even leaving aside the possible rebuttals for the moment, we can see that the above argument is not a very tight one, for it tacitly assumes that "proper sequence" inevitably means that fulfillment follows *immediately* after charge. But everyday experience belies such an assumption; as every parent knows, the charge, "Clean your room!" is often followed by many intervening episodes before the fulfillment finally comes. Thus, even were we to grant absolute status to the warrant, the conclusion would not necessarily follow from the data.

Moreover, and perhaps more importantly, we have seen that greater sensitivity to the literary device of *gapping* establishes the first rebuttal listed above as a distinct possibility. In what follows we shall take a necessarily cursory look at how my theory that Saul "faltered in the starting gate" might help to explain the entire narrative sequence of his rise to power.

MAKING SENSE OF SAUL'S RISE

Immediately following the anointing episode, the text recounts a rather enigmatic conversation between Saul and his uncle (10:14–16), the significance of which has largely eluded scholars. In this conversation, Saul is reasonably loquacious on the topic of his search for his father's lost donkeys and even as regards his "chance" meeting with Samuel, but he is absolutely silent, as our narrator informs us, on the matter of the kingship. Saul's silence regarding the "big news" of the day has baffled most commentators. But might this not simply be the behavior of a man who is shrinking back from a fearful first duty as the "Lord's anointed" and who would just as soon not talk about it, at least not with one of such militant leanings as Uncle Abner (if that is who is in view)?

Moving on to the next episode (10:17–27), I would argue that Saul's failure to carry out his first charge also helps to explain why it is necessary for Samuel to convene an assembly in Mizpah and why there is a certain negative tone to the proceedings there. Saul's inaction after his designation means that he has done nothing to gain public attention or to demonstrate his fitness as a leader. This means, of course, that the normal accession process, whereby designation was to be followed by demonstration that would then lead to confirmation, has stalled. The Mizpah assembly may be viewed as Samuel's attempt to bring Saul to public attention by a different route than that originally envisaged and to show by the lot-casting that Saul is the leader given by God in response to the people's request for a king (chap. 8). If this reading of the episode is basically correct, it becomes increasingly difficult to interpret Saul's hiding behind the baggage at the time of his selection as evidence of laudable humility. One senses, rather, a timidity and even fearfulness in Saul, the crouching "giant" (cf. 9:2), that will express itself again in Saul, the cringing "giant" of chapter 17, who shrinks back in fear and dismay before the Philistines' own giant (17:11). Moreover, if my theory is correct that there has yet been no demonstration of Saul's valor or fitness in battle, then it is not too surprising that some troublemakers protest, when Saul is dragged from behind the baggage, "How can this one save us?" (10:27).

In chapter 11 Saul's rescue of Jabesh-gilead from the Ammonite threat provides the long-awaited *demonstration,* and the kingship is "renewed" (v. 14), that is, the accession process, derailed by Saul's initial faltering, is set back on track. The defeat of the Ammonites serves, then, as a sort of substitute for the demonstration originally envisaged by Samuel in 10:7, which was to have been a provocation of the Philistines. After Saul's Ammonite victory, all the people are delighted with their new king (11:12–15). Only Samuel seems to remain cautious, issuing in the next chapter rebuke and warning that kingship can yet fail. Samuel's tone in chapter 12 suggests that the experiment of kingship, and in particular Israel's new king, must yet stand a test. It is my contention that this test relates directly to Saul's first charge. It is no mere coincidence, then, that the very next chapter recounts

Jonathan's attack upon the Philistine outpost in Geba (13:3), phase one of Saul's first charge (cf. 10:7), followed by Saul's immediate retreat to Gilgal to await Samuel's arrival (13:4), in accordance with phase two of his first charge (10:8). Lamentably, Saul fails in the execution of phase two, and receives a stinging rebuke from the belated Samuel (13:8–14). Although Samuel's reaction to Saul's failure has often been interpreted as excessively harsh, this assessment no longer seems justified once we recognize the link between Saul's failure in chapter 13 and his all-important first charge in 10:7–8.

Space limitations do not allow a full exploration of the significance of Saul's first charge, but one may at least observe that it seems designed to create an authority structure whereby human kingship can be accommodated within what remains essentially theocratic rule. In the new order established by Samuel in his first charge to Saul, the king is to become the military agent, but the prophet is to remain the recipient and mediator of the divine initiative.[33] If the king will but obey the word of the Lord as mediated by the prophet, then the experiment of kingship can succeed (see 12:13–15, 24–25). Saul does not obey, however, either in chapter 13 or subsequently in chapter 15, and so proves himself unfit to remain on the throne of Israel.

GOOD STORY, BUT IS IT HISTORY?

If the foregoing study of the Saul traditions is moving in the right direction, it seems more likely than has generally been assumed that the Bible does present an internally coherent account of Saul's rise to power. The *story* makes sense. But does this mean that we should understand the story as *history*? Not necessarily, for as noted in the preceding chapter, the consistency of a story is no guarantee of its truth, including historical truth. Moreover, so far we have focused exclusively on the chapters recounting Saul's rise and have yet to look to the broader context and overall sense of purpose of the books of Samuel. To this point, we are only able to suggest that the account of Saul's rise is "possibly" to be read as a historical account. This is how my argument would look.

Given **D** ——— *so,* **Q** possibly, ————————▶ **C**		
that the Bible presents an internally coherent, unified account of how Saul became king,	*since* **W** internal consistency is a necessary (but not a sufficient) condition of accurate historical accounts, *on account of* **B** the self-consistent character of reality,	the biblical account could be viewed as a historical account, *unless* **R** 1)the data statement is shown to be incorrect after all, or 2)sufficient contrary evidence emerges to discredit warrant or backing.

---

[33]On the mediatorial role of prophets in the monarchical period, see my *Reign and Rejection of King Saul,* pp. 60–65.

    All we know to this point is that the account of Saul's rise could possibly be a historical account. In order to discover whether it probably should be understood in this way, we must broaden our investigation to consider the larger context of which the Saul narratives are a part. If these display a historiographical character, and if the Saul narratives are lacking in textual indications that they should be treated differently from their context, then the presumption will be in favor of reading the Saul narratives historically. The important question of the overall sense of purpose of the books of Samuel is deserving of at least a chapter, if not an entire book, so it cannot be treated adequately in the short compass of the present volume. Perhaps the best we can do in the space available is to recall what was said at the beginning of this chapter about the central place the books of Samuel have enjoyed in discussions on ancient Israelite historiography and to note that, despite a minority opinion to the contrary, most scholars are agreed that a historical impulse is evident in these books. As sophisticated as is the literary art of 1 and 2 Samuel, and as prominent as is the ideological/theological impulse, the historiographical character of the stories is still felt. A majority of scholars would concur that the same can be said of the larger literary context of which the books of Samuel are a part (i.e., the so-called Deuteronomistic History, or the Former Prophets). Taking the larger context into consideration, then, we may construct the following argument. We are still focusing on truth claim, not truth value, and the effect of the argument is to shift the *qualifier* from *possibly* to *probably*.

Given **D** ————	*so,* **Q** probably, ————————▶	**C**
that the Bible presents an internally coherent, unified account of how Saul became king, which could qualify as historiography,	*since* **W** the story is presented in a larger context in which a historical impulse is evident, *on account of* **B** the apparent historiographical intentions of the so-called Deuteronomistic History (or Former Prophets) of which the books of Samuel are a part,	the biblical account of Saul's rise should be read as making historical truth claims, *unless* **R** 1) the written data have been misinterpreted, 2) conflicting external evidences indicate otherwise or 3) sufficient contrary evidence emerges to discredit warrant or backing.

To assert that the biblical account of Saul's rise probably should be *read* as historiography (i.e., to recognize that the text makes historical truth claims) is not the same as saying that the account must be *accepted* as history. What one decides on the latter issue may depend in part on how the text's truth claims square with external evidences (which in the present instance are minimal, as noted earlier). How one weighs up the various evidences, however, will be affected by one's fundamental assumptions about the Bible's *macro-genre*. On the one hand, for those who regard the Bible as an ancient document of *merely* human origin, there may be little reason to assume the truth value of the Bible's truth claims, and it may take very little conflicting evidence to cast these claims into doubt. Moreover, no quantity of positive correlations will by themselves be likely to bring about a rethinking of the Bible's origins. On the other hand, for those who accept the Bible's self-testimony to its divine as well as human origin, there will be warrant for accepting the testimony as reliable, and there will be a profound reluctance to overturn this confidence on the basis of apparently negative correlations.

In the argument below, the backing is admittedly a dogmatic one, but it is presented without apology, for I am convinced that, as Soggin has said, "no historian starts from an ideological void."[34] And what is ideology if not, at its most basic level, dogma? It is inevitable, it seems to me, that as arguments are pushed deeper and deeper to the level of basic warrants and backing, they all will be found to rest ultimately on some fundamental set of beliefs about God, self, the world, the Bible, and so forth—in other words, on dogmatically held positions.

My final argument looks like this.

Given **D** ——— *so,* **Q** presumably, ————————▶ **C**
that the   the historical Saul became
Bible   king basically as described,
presents an   *since* **W**
internally   the Bible speaks
coherent,   truth,   *unless* **R**
unified   1) the data statement is
account of   *on account of* **B**   incorrect—i.e., written data
how Saul   its status as the   have been misinterpreted
became   word of God,   or
king that   2) sufficient contrary
(probably)   evidence emerges to
should be   discredit warrant or backing.
viewed as a
historical
account,

---

[34]J. Alberto Soggin, *Introduction to the Old Testament,* 3d ed., trans. John Bowden, Old Testament Library (Louisville: John Knox, 1989), p. 182.

What is interesting about this argument is that even with its dogmatic backing the conclusion is only "probably" true. This is so because the degree of certainty of the conclusion is limited by the degree of certainty of the data (truth claim) as established in the earlier arguments. This means that one may affirm the total trustworthiness of the Bible and still hold only a qualified assurance that Saul became king in a certain way.

CONCLUSION

The aim of this chapter has been to offer a more extended example than was possible in the earlier chapters of how one might approach a biblical narrative with historical questions in mind. Our consideration of the narratives in 1 Samuel having to do with Saul's rise to power has illustrated how intertwined literary reading and historical reconstruction often are. It has also illustrated some of the ways in which interpreters' background beliefs and fundamental assumptions influence (to a limited degree) assessments of a text's truth claims and (to a large degree) assessments of a text's truth value.

Proceeding along lines suggested in the preceding chapter, we sought to listen afresh to the story of Saul's rise to power. And with the aid of some of the newer insights of modern literary study, we discovered a more coherent storyline than has previously been recognized by most scholars. The coherence of a story is not, of course, a guarantee of its historicity. As already noted, coherence is a necessary but not a sufficient condition of historicity. But discovering a sensible, sequential story in 1 Samuel 9–13 does at least remove the most common reason for assuming that the events surrounding Saul's rise to power must forever remain a mystery.

Anything approaching "scientific proof" is, of course, impossible in matters of history, since the object of study—the past—no longer exists and is certainly not susceptible to repeated experimentation and observation. But this does not mean that a cumulative case cannot be built for the *probability* that a given narrative fairly represents its historical subject . . . in the same way that a portrait fairly represents its subject. But even if the biblical narratives prove to be sensible, how are we to choose between the "pictures" of the past they present and the sometimes widely divergent "pictures" presented by some modern scholars? Abraham Malamat puts it very simply: "We could all do well to give heed to Wellhausen's dictum, astounding for him: 'If it [the Israelite tradition] is at all feasible, it would be utter folly (*Torheit*) to give preference to any other feasibility.'"[35]

---

[35]"The Proto-History of Israel: A Study in Method," in *The Word of the Lord Shall Go Forth: Essays in Honor of David Noel Freedman in Celebration of His Sixtieth Birthday,* ed. Carol L. Meyers and M. O'Connor (Winona Lake: Eisenbrauns, 1983), p. 309. The quotation is from Wellhausen's *Die Composition des Hexateuchs und der historischen Bücher des Alten Testaments,* 3d ed. (Berlin: Reimer, 1899), p. 347, and is, as Malamat notes, "limited in context."

Epilogue

ollowing a precedent set by several other volumes in this series, I have decided to bring this book to a close with an epilogue rather than a conclusion. This seems fitting, as the journey of exploration that we began at the start of this volume has not yet reached its conclusion—at least not its final conclusion. At this juncture in the writing process I feel much the same as I did several years ago when making my first climb in England's Lake District. From the base of the small mountain, called Barrow, the climb to the top looked achievable within the allotted amount of time, even if not particularly easy. As it turned out, Barrow has several "false peaks." I can well remember the mixture of satisfaction and deflation I felt, as a first-time climber unaware of this feature, upon reaching what I thought was the top of the mountain, only to discover that it was a false peak and that the trail, after running level for a short stretch, continued sharply upward to another peak, and even another after that!

Still, there is value in attaining a peak, even if not the final one. Even from lesser heights, one can get a view of the surrounding terrain. One can see more clearly where one has been. And one can see other paths that might have been taken and can at least imagine the kinds of things that would have been seen along the other routes. Perhaps most importantly, it is only upon reaching the false peak that the climb still ahead can be seen.

This is where we are—at a point where we can look back over the ground we have covered and recall what we have seen. At an early stage in our journey we discovered that the Bible, though not a history book *per se*, is a book deeply concerned with history. Amidst the library of literary genres that constitutes the Bible, there are those—particularly (but not exclusively) its narratives—that evidence a historiographical impulse, albeit not of the modern, secular variety. The Bible's narratives concern themselves not merely with the human actors on the stage of history but with the Lord of history himself and with his perspective on and participation in the unfolding drama. The story is, as the well-worn phrase puts it, *His* story. And it is masterfully told. Thus, with the historical impulse are combined two others: the theological and the literary.

Respecting the latter, we discovered in the second stage of our journey that literary artistry plays as important a role in (narrative) historiography as does visual artistry in portraiture. We even explored the idea that a good way to view ancient historiography is as a kind of *verbal representational art*, with all that this implies about the interplay of creativity and constraint in the depiction.

At the third stage of our journey, we looked at the fundamental question of the importance of history for faith. We discovered that how one answers this question is often a reflection of one's understanding of the essence of Christianity. We noted that for classic Christianity the gospel of redemption from sin and of new life in Christ has depended for its validity on redemptive history, not redemptive fiction.

At the fourth stage of our journey we halted to have a look round at our fellow travelers and to ask why it is that there is so often radical disagreement on historical questions. We observed that several of the more prominent approaches to biblical interpretation have, in addition to their strengths, also some weaknesses that prevent them from doing full justice to the biblical testimony.

We then resumed our journey and in its fifth stage began to develop a basic hermeneutical strategy for approaching biblical texts with historical questions in mind. After considering the importance of contemplating fundamental assumptions—ours, others' and the texts'—we stressed the need for first seeking to discover the truth claims of biblical texts by *listening* to them as carefully and competently as possible, and then thoughtfully *testing* these claims on the basis of both internal and external considerations. We also explored a method of analyzing, constructing, and presenting historical arguments. Finally, having sketched out a basic approach, we tried it out on a specific example.

This, in brief, is the ground we have covered. We can now turn and look at the climb still ahead. Several areas come into view that invite further exploration. The concept of historiography as representational art and the implications of this view invite further discussion, as does the question of how literary theory may impinge on some of the specific historical-critical conclusions reached by earlier scholars. The related disciplines of narrative theory and biblical poetics are still relatively new, and it can be hoped that the future will see further developments and refinements in these approaches. The exploration of comparative literatures from the ancient Near Eastern and Hellenistic worlds represents an ongoing task. And perhaps most importantly, one would like to see in the future further reflection on the Bible's own *theology of history*.

So it appears that the journey must continue (though not within the confines of this small volume). In the preface, I commented with respect to journeys that "getting there is half the fun." At this stage, looking back but also looking forward, perhaps all I can hope for is that some of my fellow travelers will agree and will be encouraged to continue to explore the historical dimension of the Bible.

For Further Reading

A complete list of works cited in this volume may be found in the index of authors and titles. In this section I have selected contributions in English that should prove helpful for those wishing to research further some of the topics discussed in the preceding pages. Since I am convinced that a proper historical assessment of biblical texts is dependent, in the first instance, on a proper literary reading of them, I shall begin by mentioning works that offer guidance in reading biblical literature more competently. Beginning students might well want to start with Robert Alter's stimulating book *The Art of Biblical Narrative* (New York: Basic Books, 1981). For the study of poetry, James Kugel's *The Idea of Biblical Poetry: Parallelism and Its History* (New Haven: Yale University Press, 1981) offers seminal insights, which are further developed by Alter in *The Art of Biblical Poetry* (New York: Basic Books, 1985). Tremper Longman III's *Literary Approaches to Biblical Interpretation* in this volume is a useful, brief introduction to both prose and poetry in the Bible, and it includes example readings. Alter's *World of Biblical Literature* (New York: Basic Books, 1992) also treats both prose and poetry as well as a number of general issues arising from the study of the Bible as literature. Literary critic Leland Ryken has contributed a number of studies on the Bible as literature, including *How to Read the Bible as Literature* (Grand Rapids: Zondervan, 1984) and *Words of Delight: A Literary Introduction to the Bible* (Grand Rapids; Baker, 1987).

Influential treatments of the narrative poetics of the Hebrew Bible include Shimon Bar-Efrat's *Narrative Art in the Bible*, JSOTS 70 (Sheffield: Almond Press, 1989 [Hebrew orig. 1979, 2d ed. 1984]), Adele Berlin's *Poetics and Biblical Interpretation* (Sheffield: Almond Press, 1983), Jacob Licht's *Storytelling in the Bible* (Jerusalem: Magnes Press, 1978), and, of course, Meir Sternberg's magisterial *Poetics of Biblical Narrative: Ideological Literature and the Drama of Reading* (Bloomington: Indiana University Press, 1985). A strength of Sternberg's tome is its stress on the complementarity of literary, historical, and theological study; a weakness, with respect to beginning students, is its length and high literary style, which beginners will find challenging. A perspective on biblical narrative that differs philosophically from Sternberg's is offered by David M. Gunn and Danna Nolan Fewell in *Narrative in the Hebrew Bible*, Oxford Bible Series, ed. P. R. Ackroyd and G. N. Stanton (Oxford: Oxford University Press, 1993). Mark Allan Powell's *What Is Narrative Criticism?* (Minneapolis: Fortress, 1990) is a well-written introduction to the study of New Testament narrative. The best "literary commentary" on the entire Bible is entitled *A Complete Literary Guide to the Bible*, ed. Leland Ryken and Tremper Longman III (Grand Rapids: Zondervan, 1993). Also useful is *The Literary Guide to the Bible*, ed. Robert Alter and Frank Kermode (Cambridge, Mass.: Belknap Press of Harvard University Press, 1987). The list of works in the burgeoning field of modern literary criticism of the Bible could easily be continued, but perhaps this is enough to give students a start. For more, see Mark Allan Powell, *The Bible and Modern Literary Criticism: A Critical Assessment and Annotated Bibliography* (New York: Greenwood Press, 1991).

The historical study of the Bible is deeply enmeshed in issues of general hermeneutics. This is made particularly evident by Robert Morgan (with John Barton) in *Biblical Interpretation*, Oxford Bible Series, ed. P. R. Ackroyd and G. N. Stanton (Oxford: Oxford University Press, 1988). Morgan helpfully traces the development of modern, liberal critical study of the Bible and exposes many of the philosophical/ hermeneutical influences that have led to the current crisis among biblical scholars wishing to embrace the rational methods of secularism without jeopardizing religious convictions. For an evangelical perspective on the history of biblical interpretation, Moisés Silva's *Has the Church Misread the Bible?* is recommended. Recent full-length, evangelical introductions to biblical hermeneutics include Grant R. Osborne's *Hermeneutical Spiral: A Comprehensive Introduction to Biblical Interpretation* (Downers Grove: InterVarsity Press, 1991) and Anthony C. Thiselton's monumental *New Horizons in Hermeneutics: The Theory and Practice of Transforming Biblical Reading* (Grand Rapids: Zondervan, 1992). Also worthy of note is Gerhard Maier's *Biblische Hermeneutik* (Wuppertal: R. Brockhaus, 1990), now available in English translation by Robert W. Yarbrough under the title *Biblical Hermeneutics* (Wheaton: Crossway, 1994). Summaries of current mainline thinking on a broad range of topics are conveniently accessible in *A Dictionary of Biblical Interpretation*, ed. R. J. Coggins and J. L. Houlden (Philadelphia: Trinity Press International, 1990).

Among general discussions of historical knowledge and historical method, I have found to be most useful Michael Stanford's *Nature of Historical Knowledge* (Oxford: Basil Blackwell, 1986), C. Behan McCullagh's *Justifying Historical Descriptions* (Cambridge: Cambridge University Press, 1984), and David Carr's *Time, Narrative, and History* (Bloomington: Indiana University Press, 1986). For a brief description of traditional historical-critical interpretation of the Bible, see J. Maxwell Miller's *Old Testament and the Historian* (Philadelphia: Fortress, 1976). And for an insightful analysis of the historical-critical method as applied to the Bible, I know of nothing better than William J. Abraham's *Divine Revelation and the Limits of Historical Criticism* (Oxford: Oxford University Press, 1982).

A number of works treat special topics that fall under the general heading of biblical historiography. As regards the historiography of the Old Testament, for example, some scholars argue that it should be dated very late (e.g., John Van Seters, *In Search of History: Historiography in the Ancient World and the Origins of Biblical History* [New Haven: Yale University Press, 1983]; *idem, Prologue to History: The Yahwist as Historian in Genesis* [New Haven: Yale University Press, 1992]), while others argue that the Old Testament texts for the most part do not intend to be taken as historiography in the first place (e.g., Thomas L. Thompson, *Early History of Israel: From the Written and Archaeological Sources*, Studies in the History of the Ancient Near East 4, ed. M. H. E. Weippert [Leiden: E. J. Brill, 1992]). While often rich in individual insights, such works, it seems to me, are unable to sustain their major theses. I find more of value in Baruch Halpern's *First Historians: The Hebrew Bible and History* (San Francisco: Harper & Row, 1988). As regards historical study of the New Testament, Craig L. Blomberg's *Historical Reliability of the Gospels* (Leicester: Inter-Varsity, 1987) and Colin J. Hemer's *Book of Acts in the Setting of Hellenistic History*, Wissenschaftliche Untersuchungen zum Neuen Testament 49 (Tübingen: J. C. B. Mohr, 1989), merit special mention.

On the relationship between historical study and Christian faith, students may benefit from reading David Bebbington, *Patterns in History: A Christian Perspective on Historical Thought* (Grand Rapids: Baker, 1990); Colin Brown, *History and Faith: A Personal Exploration* (Grand Rapids: Zondervan, 1987); *idem*, ed., *History, Criticism and Faith* (Leicester: Inter-Varsity Press, 1976); Ronald H. Nash, *Christian Faith and Historical Understanding* (Grand Rapids: Zondervan, 1984).

Those wishing to explore the homiletical potential of Scripture's diverse literary genres, including its historiographical portions, might wish to consult Sidney Greidanus, *The Modern Preacher and the Ancient Text: Interpreting and Preaching Biblical Literature* (Grand Rapids: Eerdmans, 1988), and the relevant essays in Michael Duduit, ed., *Handbook of Contemporary Preaching* (Nashville: Broadman, 1992).

SCIENCE AND HERMENEUTICS

Implications of Scientific Method for Biblical Interpretation

Vern S. Poythress

To my wife Diane

Contents

Editor's Preface

Many years ago, upon reading Thomas S. Kuhn's work *The Structure of Scientific Revolutions*, I was taken aback by the obvious parallels between the subject of that book and the field of biblical exegesis. It seemed strange then—and more so now after all these years—that no one had sought to draw out the implications of Kuhn's ideas for better understanding the conflicts that frequently arise over the interpretation of Scripture.

It would be difficult to find someone better suited to tackle this issue than Vern Poythress. After earning a Ph.D. in mathematics at Harvard University, Poythress developed concurrent interests in the fields of linguistics and theology. Though he later specialized in New Testament studies, receiving a Th.D. in Pauline theology from the University of Stellenbosch, he has continued to pursue his interests in the relationship between science and theology. Indeed, this concern plays a significant role in his teaching of doctoral-level courses in biblical hermeneutics at Westminster Theological Seminary.

The author does not assume any prior knowledge of the field on the part of the reader, but novices and experts alike will surely be fascinated by the clear and perceptive account to be found in this work. A thoughtful reading of Poythress's analysis will help students of the Bible appreciate the origin and nature of interpretive disputes. It will also aid them in developing their own exegetical skills without too quickly dismissing the views of those with whom they disagree.

Moisés Silva

one

HOW SHOULD WE INTERPRET THE BIBLE?

S cience has proved remarkably successful as a technique for enhancing our knowledge of the natural world. Can we also learn something from science about how to
enhance our knowledge of the Bible?

SHOULD BIBLICAL INTERPRETATION BECOME SCIENTIFIC?

One way of following science is to try to make our study of the Bible "scientific."
Would such an approach mean simply that we study the Bible more intensively, more
painstakingly? Would it mean that we supply ourselves with all the aids and all the information about the Bible that we can gather? Such steps are obviously useful. They are
what we might do with respect to any subject about which we were intensely interested.
But such steps by themselves would make us scientific only in a very loose sense. What
else might we do? Should we study the Bible "objectively," without ever asking how it
affects our own lives personally? But such study would disastrously ignore the Bible's
concern to be a means for our spiritual communion with God. If the Bible is God's Word,
can it ever be subject to scientific investigation in quite the same way as we would investigate an animal or a plant?

These questions are obviously important, but we cannot explore them all. Questions about whether theology should be scientific will be covered in more detail in
another volume in this series on hermeneutics. In this volume, we will explore whether
the growth of knowledge in science can tell us something about how knowledge grows
in biblical interpretation and in theology.

What is scientific method? Does it guarantee a cumulative growth of knowledge?
Until recently, people commonly thought that scientific knowledge increased by the

smooth addition of one fact to another, the smooth refinement of an existing theory, or the smooth extension of a theory to cover new data. By analogy, ought we to expect knowledge of the Bible to progress by accumulation? Can we devise a method that will provide such progress? Or is such progress illusory even in science? Are we to expect occasional "revolutions" in biblical interpretation analogous to the revolutions in scientific theory that are investigated in some of the recent trends in the history and philosophy of science?[1] What part do underlying hermeneutical or philosophical frameworks play in influencing the results of biblical interpretation?

To answer these questions, we will have to look in some detail at theories concerned with the nature and history of scientific knowledge (chaps. 2 and 3). But first, let us start with an actual example of biblical interpretation, namely, the interpretation of Romans 7. Because this passage has proved to be a difficult and controversial passage, it effectively illustrates some of the problems.

AN EXAMPLE: INTERPRETING ROMANS 7

How do we understand Romans 7, a passage that many have found some difficulty in grasping? What kind of experience is being described in verses 7–13 and above all in verses 14–25? And who is the "I" about whom the passage speaks? Is Paul describing his own experience or an experience typical of a whole class of people?

Through most of church history there have been disagreements over Romans 7.[2] Most interpreters have thought that Paul was describing his own experience. The use of the pronoun "I" naturally suggests this. But interpreters have also sensed that Paul's discussion here has a broader bearing. Paul would not have written at such length if he had not thought that, in some respects, his experience was typical. It was intended to illustrate something relevant for the Roman Christians' understanding of themselves, of sin, of the law, and so on.

We cannot hope to survey all the options for interpretation that have been suggested. For the purpose of illustration, it is enough for us to concentrate on the interpretations that see Romans 7:14–25 as an example of a general pattern applicable to a whole class of people. Perhaps these verses derived from Paul's personal experience, but it is not essential for us that they did. The crucial question is, What is this passage an example of? What class of people does it apply to? Does the "I" in Romans 7:14–25 stand for a believer or an unbeliever, a regenerate person or one who is unregenerate? Augustine and his followers, including Calvin, Luther, and most of the Protestant Reformation, thought that Paul was describing the conflict with sin that characterizes the life of a regenerate person, a true believer. Pelagius and some Arminians thought that this passage depicts a typical unregenerate person, or unbeliever.

---

[1]The key idea of revolution was introduced into the discussion by Thomas S. Kuhn, *The Structure of Scientific Revolutions,* 2d ed. (Chicago: University of Chicago Press, 1970). I comment extensively below on Kuhn's work.

[2]For an introduction to the major options in the interpretation of Romans 7, see Heinrich A. W. Meyer, *Critical and Exegetical Hand-Book to the Epistle to the Romans* (New York: Funk & Wagnalls, 1884); and C. E. B. Cranfield, *A Critical and Exegetical Commentary on the Epistle to the Romans,* 2 vols. (Edinburgh: T. & T. Clark, 1975–79), 1:342–47. Note also the important contribution of Werner G. Kümmel, *Römer 7 und die Bekehrung des Paulus* (Leipzig: J. C. Heinrichs, 1929).

A third alternative is available. Some people have seen in this passage a description of people who are regenerate but not mature, people who have not yet come into a position of triumph and victory over sin. This interpretation often goes together with a "second blessing" theology, according to which sanctification, or "victory over sin," comes as a separate work of the Holy Spirit, brought about by a second step of faith. There are two kinds of Christians—those who are in the state of full sanctification and victory over sin and those who are not. Christians who do not have this victory over sin are a kind of third category intermediate between unregenerate people and ideal Christians.

How do we decide a conflict in interpretation like this one? At first glance, it might seem that we decide simply by looking at the passage and seeing which interpretation actually fits. Which interpretation is consistent with all the facts of the passage? All three interpretations above, however, *claim* to be consistent with the passage; all three claim to account for all the words and sentences in the passage.

As a next step, then, we might begin to weigh strengths and weaknesses of the three interpretations. The view that Paul is describing the experience not of an unbeliever but of a typical believer has in its favor the fact that the description of the "inner man" and the "mind" in verses 22–23, 25 appears to harmonize with Paul's statements elsewhere about Christians (e.g., Rom. 8:6; 1 Cor. 2:10), but not with his statements about non-Christians (e.g., Rom. 8:7; Eph. 4:17–18). These same facts are a problem, however, for the second interpretation.

But there are some facts on the other side. The view that the passage refers to unregenerate persons has in its favor the correspondence between Romans 7:14–15 and Paul's descriptions elsewhere of non-Christians as slaves of sin (e.g., 6:20). Romans 7:14–15 does not match Paul's descriptions of Christian freedom (e.g., 6:22; 8:4). These facts are difficult for the first interpretation to explain.

The third interpretation, that is, the "second blessing" interpretation, might therefore seem to be the best of both worlds. This interpretation creates a third category, intermediate between an unregenerate person and an ideal (sanctified) regenerate Christian, namely, an immature (unsanctified) regenerate person. By using a third category, this view avoids some of the difficulties in harmonizing the passage with statements elsewhere in Paul. But it has weaknesses of its own. Romans 7 seems to provide no clues to the reader that Paul has some third category in view. Moreover, chapter 6 seems to be talking about all Christians who have come to union with Christ, as the appeal to baptism suggests (v. 3). If so, no third category is available in the context of Romans 7. Moreover, the competing interpretations argue that no distinctive second-blessing theology is to be found in Paul or in Scripture generally. If so, the third interpretation is not viable for Romans 7 in particular.

USING CONTEXT IN INTERPRETATION

Now let us stand back for a bit and ask how we have proceeded in our analysis of Romans 7:14–25. We have looked at particular verses within the passage (vv. 22–23 and 14–15) and have seen how well the competing interpretations are able to deal with them. But in doing so, we have also had to go outside Romans 7 and look at other statements of Paul about Christians and non-Christians, slavery and freedom. These other statements need to be weighed in their own contexts to see whether they really harmonize with or contradict the chosen interpretation of Romans 7. Whether an interpretation of this chapter is viable depends on whether it is harmonizable with Paul's views as a whole.

In addition, we should not oversimplify the process of judging when an interpretation generates a contradiction or an insuperable difficulty. Each of the three interpretations has a difficulty at one point or another. If we were harsh, we would say that each generates a contradiction. But they are not necessarily all false. In fact, some people continue to advocate each of these lines of interpretation even though they are well aware of the difficulties. But they think that the difficulties are greater with competing interpretations than with their own. Hence they still endeavor to give a coherent interpretation of the difficult texts within their own viewpoint.

For example, the so-called regenerate interpretation explains that Romans 7:14–15, though similar in language to 6:20, is not saying quite the same thing. The former verses describe the real hold that the remnants of sin still have on the regenerate person until the time of glorification. In comparison with perfection, our own state might still be described as "sold under sin." This is a necessary qualification of the apparently absolute language of Romans 6. Romans 7:14–25 as a whole depicts a situation of struggle against sin, unlike the "slavery" in 6:20.

Similarly, the unregenerate interpretation endeavors to explain that the language of Romans 7:22–23, 25, though not usually applied to unbelievers by Paul, can nevertheless be used for unbelievers. Even unbelievers, it could be noted, cannot escape the knowledge of the law of God (1:32; 2:14–15).

Hence we can see that a text like Romans 7:14–15 or 7:22–23 does not just display its meaning on its sleeve, so to speak. It is not just a brute datum, about which no one can dispute. A particular verse or passage might conceivably mean something slightly different from what we think it means at first. Making sure of its meaning involves assessing context as well. What might initially appear to be a contradiction, and thus rule out one line of interpretation, might on further investigation have an explanation.

THE INFLUENCE OF OVERALL THEOLOGICAL SYSTEM AND PERSONAL EXPERIENCE

Next, we should note that people's overall theological system influences their interpretation of Romans 7. In the past, most Calvinists have advocated the regenerate interpretation; most Arminians have advocated the unregenerate interpretation. Many, if not most, adherents to second-blessing theology have advocated the second-blessing interpretation. Other combinations are possible in principle. But one can see why these influences exist.

Calvinists, for example, have a low view of the spiritual abilities of fallen, sinful, unregenerate people. Calvinists emphasize that such people are spiritually unable to turn to God and to love God unless the Holy Spirit performs a special work of regeneration to change their hearts. Calvinists are therefore reluctant to accept the positive statements of Romans 7:14–25 as descriptions of an unregenerate person.

Conversely, Arminians have a higher view of the spiritual abilities of fallen, unregenerate people. Such people have "free will." Spiritual decisions that these people make when they hear the gospel are decisive in whether they become believers. Hence Arminians are not so uneasy about attributing the positive statements in Romans 7 to unregenerate people.

Next, we should not discount the role of personal experience in influencing people's decisions about the interpretation of this passage. Some Christians are more often and more acutely aware of their failings and remaining sins. Such people can identify readily with much of the language of Romans 7:14–25 and therefore find it easy to believe that the passage describes the state of a Christian. Other Christians are more frequently aware of their joy in victory over sin. They more readily think of the contrast of their present life with their previous unbelief. They seldom dwell on the remaining areas of sin and inconsistency in their present life. Such people identify more readily with the language of Romans 6 and 8. Because 7:14–25 presents such notable contrasts with chapters 6 and 8, they are disposed to believe that it describes an unregenerate person.

Individual experience also has a role in people's attitude toward second-blessing theology. Some people have experienced a sharp transition from defeat to victory over some of their prominent sins. They may find that second-blessing theology seems to match their experience, particularly if they have undergone a radical change under the influence of hearing the teaching of second-blessing theology.

On the other hand, other people have experienced very gradual growth in their spiritual life. They have come to understand and appropriate Romans 6 and 8 gradually. But they have continued to be aware that subtle tendencies to sin still lurk in them. To them second-blessing theology seems not to match their experience. All this background of experience will influence whether a particular person finds it plausible to claim that Romans 7:14–25 describes the first-blessing stage or immature stage in a second-blessing theology.

SCIENTIFIC METHOD AND OBJECTIVITY

The interpretation of Romans 7 has been disputed for centuries. Augustine and Pelagius in the late fourth and fifth centuries were early representatives of the regenerate and unregenerate interpretations. The second-blessing interpretation arose later. But no one of the three interpretations has been able permanently to "win the day." When we look at some of the factors that go into the decision, we can begin to understand why. Differences in theological systems and in personal experience and temperament are involved.

Is there any way out of this impasse? Can the triumphs of science and the way in which science proceeds be of any value? The analogy with science might suggest to many people that the way out is through objectivity. Science, it is said, consists in a dispassionate, objective analysis of the data. The problem with the interpretation of Romans 7 is that it gets mixed up with the doctrinal commitments and personal experiences of the people doing the interpretation. The process of interpretation needs to be freed from such doctrinal commitments and personal experiences.

The historical-critical method, as developed in the eighteenth and nineteenth centuries, represented an attempt to free the study of the Bible from doctrinal commitments and to become scientific in its study. The claim to scientific objectivity was attractive, but illusory. Scholarship never takes place in a vacuum. In particular, historical research cannot be undertaken without presuppositions; the researcher must presuppose some idea of history, of what is historically probable, and of what standards to use in weighing the claims of ancient texts. Hence there is not one way of investigating history, but many, corresponding to many philosophical possibilities for one's view of history and of the possibility or actuality of God's providential control of history.

As Ernst Troeltsch incisively argued, historical research in the context of Enlightenment thought presupposed three fundamental principles.[3] According to the *principle of criticism,* no documents of the past can be accepted as authoritative; all claims about the past must be weighed by the modern critic. At most, we can arrive at a greater or lesser probability concerning the past, never a certainty. According to the *principle of analogy,* the present is the key to the past. Events of the past must all be analogous to what is possible today. According to the *principle of causality,* history is a closed continuum of events, in which every event has an antecedent immanent cause and there is no divine intervention (miracle) in history. Troeltsch saw that since the assumptions of the method already denied traditional Christianity, the results would necessarily confirm this denial.

By "historical-critical method," then, we mean historical research on the Bible, proceeding on the basis of these Enlightenment assumptions. Historical-critical method aspired to scientific objectivity, but in the nature of the case it could not succeed. In freeing biblical study from commitments to denominational doctrine, it made study subject to the philosophical commitments of rationalistic, antisupernaturalistic historiography and metaphysics and to the ethical commitments of contemporary humanism. It did not give people pristine, absolute objectivity. Furthermore, the historical-critical method did not result in any more agreement over the meaning of biblical passages. It resulted most often in more diversity and disagreement than before. It simply multiplied the number of assumptions, philosophies, and background commitments that could now exert their influence on interpretation.[4]

Is science a suitable guide, then, for biblical interpretation? Science itself, it turns out, is not purely objective and neutral. That is, science is not unaffected by commitments, assumptions, and philosophies. Until recently, most people have thought that science presented a totally objective analysis of the facts. But recent examination of the history of science has cast doubt on this assumption. In fact, it has revealed within the realm of natural science some disputes that look curiously like the disputes over the interpretation of Romans 7. It has revealed, in a word, how people's understanding of a particular datum (e.g., Rom. 7:14–25) is influenced by a whole cluster of interpretations, assumptions, and experiences, which provide the matrix for understanding in the field as a whole. The problems with interpreting Romans 7 appear not to be such an oddity or perversity when compared with those that occur in science. Understanding this state of affairs, and learning how to deal with it, may be part of the way to a solution.

First of all, however, we must take a step backward and see what people have thought about the nature of science, scientific method, and scientific objectivity.

---

[3]Ernst Troeltsch, "Ueber historische und dogmatische Methode in der Theologie," in *Gesammelte Schriften, vol. 2, Zur religiösen Lage, Religionsphilosophie, und Ethik,* 2d ed. (Aalen: Scientia, 1962), pp. 729–953.

[4]For a further discussion of historical-critical method, see the section "The Historical-Critical Method as a Revolution," in chapter 4.

THE INFLUENCE OF NATURAL SCIENCE ON BIBLICAL INTERPRETATION

Modern science did not suddenly spring into existence, nor, once it had established itself, did it suddenly revolutionize people's thinking about the world. Yet in the long run, Western culture has been revolutionized by the impact of science. In fact, in some respects we are still embedded in a continuing process of cultural revolution. How then do we understand what science is, and how do we assess its bearing on the way that we interpret the Bible?

We should first ask whether science ought to have any influence at all on how we interpret the Bible. Biblical interpretation went on its own way, and prospered, even before modern science was in existence. Could not biblical interpretation simply continue without interaction with science?

But people cannot help making comparisons between science and biblical interpretation. The triumphs of science have proved impressive, whereas the history of biblical interpretation does not look so impressive by comparison. Physical sciences succeed in making accurate predictions. They provide integrated explanations of diverse phenomena on the basis of powerful but "simple" general principles or laws. They provide a framework for producing a continuous stream of new machines and technological innovations, increasingly useful and powerful.

The success of science and technology, even by the late eighteenth century, made intellectuals pay attention. Not only did science provide knowledge about the world; it was generating an ever-increasing amount of knowledge. By contrast, medieval and Reformational theological debates seemed to go on and on, without ever reaching a definitive conclusion. But science moved forward irreversibly. It had become not merely a body of knowledge but an engine for manufacturing more knowledge, deeper knowledge, and

knowledge but an engine for manufacturing more knowledge, deeper knowledge, and more solidly verified knowledge.

It is no wonder, then, that people tried to learn lessons from science. They looked especially to the physical sciences (physics, astronomy, chemistry; later, geology and biology), where the triumphs took place the earliest and have been the most thorough.[1] At least three different kinds of lessons were drawn from nineteenth-century science. The lessons differed depending on what people looked at.

USING SPECIFIC THEORIES TO TEST THE TRUTH OF THE BIBLE

First of all, some people compared specific scientific theories with views that theology had derived from the Bible, a procedure we may call evaluation using specific theories. The debates over Darwin's theory of evolution were the most notable case. Earlier, thinkers had debated whether the biblical descriptions of the sun's motion were compatible with the sun-centered astronomy of Copernicus.

Debates over specific questions of fact are certainly important in their own right. But it is not our purpose to take up such matters in this book. We should only note briefly that people responded in a variety of ways. Some (e.g., agnostics, atheists, and some deists) decided that cases of apparent conflict between the Bible and modern science were irresolvable. Since such people viewed science as the wave of the future, they repudiated biblical religion. Orthodox antievolutionists, however, decided that the scientific theory in question was dubious and poorly supported. Theological liberals, for their part, decided that the Bible was scientifically primitive and needed to be updated theologically. Finally, conservative theistic evolutionists thought that they could reexegete crucial biblical passages and show that the Bible did not intend to teach anything in conflict with the new theories.[2]

How do we assess this use of science? How and when do we need to use the content of a specific scientific theory as a guide for our lives? The specific theories of physical science represent impressive intellectual triumphs and provide valuable insight into the workings of the world. But they concern us more broadly only when they touch on a specific question of human values. Average people are interested in enjoying the results of technology, but few are interested in the underlying scientific theories for their own sake. They are interested in a scientific theory only if it appears to suggest answers to the meaning of their lives. Likewise, people are interested in whether the Bible is true, because such a question affects their lives vitally. Hence they ask whether science confirms or disproves the truthfulness of the Bible.

Not much within the physical sciences, however, could conceivably either contradict or confirm the Bible. Even when there is some apparent contradiction it is often easy to show that a better interpretation of the scientific theory or a better interpretation of the Bible obviates the problem. The scientific theory holds only if things continue as they ordinarily are, that is, if we exclude exceptional cases of God's dealing with the world, such as miracles. On the other side, the Bible's description of the sun's rising and of the creation

---

[1] In this book, the word *science* generally refers to natural sciences, not social sciences. The natural sciences have the most widespread agreement among practitioners, and so they have naturally become the model. In fact, the desire of social sciences to attain the prestige of natural sciences influences the history of their development.

[2] See Bernard Ramm, *The Christian View of Science and Scripture* (Grand Rapids: Eerdmans, 1964).

of the world can be shown to be ordinary language, the language of appearances, rather than technical scientific description.

Specific scientific theories do affect biblical interpretation at least to the extent that they become the occasion for reassessing the interpretation of a few passages (Gen. 1–2; 6–8). In the light of scientific claims we return to the passages to reassess whether they implied all the scientific conclusions that we have drawn from them. Likewise, biblical interpretation affects science at the very least by leading us to reassess whether all the conclusions drawn from a scientific theory are warranted, or in some cases to ask whether the theory as a whole is suspect.

Such observations do not solve all the difficulties. But they considerably narrow the scope of those that are left. The remaining difficulties must be dealt with on a technical level, by refining our scientific knowledge and refining our understanding of the Bible until we can see that they agree.[3]

BUILDING A WORLDVIEW ON THE BASIS OF SCIENTIFIC RESULTS

Besides comparing specific scientific theories with specific passages of the Bible, people drew lessons from science in a second way. They produced whole worldviews by extrapolating from the picture presented by physical science. Let us call this process the procedure of building a worldview.

People extrapolated worldviews from science because physical science seemed to offer the beginnings of a whole worldview, an explanation of how the whole world fit together and of the role of human beings in it. If scientific knowledge was superior to theological knowledge in its accuracy and indisputability, perhaps it was also superior in providing a platform for a total explanation. Newtonian science, in particular, offered us a world consisting of massive particles interacting with one another by means of forces calculable from physical measurements of distance, orientation, velocity, and the like. Some people did not hesitate to draw the conclusion: the world was a mechanistic world of particles and forces, nothing more. There was no room for God's intervention, for chance, or for human free will. Newton's theory was thereby converted into a worldview, namely, the view that the world was a mechanistic, deterministic collection of particles in motion.[4]

Though Darwin's theory of evolution has already been considered as a case of using a specific scientific theory, it was also used as the platform for a worldview. "Social Darwinism" extrapolated Darwin's claims about survival, fitness, and evolution into the area of human social interaction.[5] Even those who did not go all the way into social Darwinism often saw Darwin's theory as a complete explanation of life—an explanation that eliminated God. Of

---

[3]As I have already observed, some people may resolve the tensions by simply abandoning belief in the Bible or abandoning belief in modern science. But it is best to exercise more patience in working through the difficulties. Sometimes, as finite human beings, we may not have enough information to resolve a difficulty within our lifetime.

[4]It should be noted that early scientists like Newton and Boyle operated within a Christian worldview and did not think that their theories undermined the reality of God's rule over the world. See John Dillenberger, *Protestant Thought and Natural Science: A Historical Interpretation* (Westport, Conn.: Greenwood, 1977); and Francis Oakley, *Omnipotence, Covenant, and Order: An Excursion in the History of Ideas from Abelard to Leibniz* (Ithaca: Cornell University Press, 1984).

[5]Richard Hofstadter, *Social Darwinism in American Thought, 1860–1915* (Philadelphia: University of Pennsylvania Press, 1945); Thomas H. Huxley, *Evolution and Ethics, and Other Essays* (New York: Appleton, 1898).

course, Darwin's theory could be narrowly construed as a technical scientific hypothesis for explaining the fossil record and the existing distribution of species. But the cultural atmosphere made it convenient to invoke the theory in support of much broader conclusions. Many people, for religious, philosophical, and ethical reasons, wanted to legitimize a naturalistic view of the world. Darwin, by eliminating the need for miracles in the origin of life, gave crucial support to these philosophical longings.[6]

How do we evaluate these efforts? Do physical sciences provide us with a worldview? Does this worldview agree with the worldview offered in the Bible? To a certain extent, one might say that science and the Bible both provide us with only pieces of a worldview. The Bible here and there provides information touching on scientific questions, but it does not answer all our questions about the way in which the physical world functions. Conversely, physical science, understood soberly and modestly, does not answer questions about human values and destiny, nor does it give information on supernatural acts that may be an exception to God's normal government of the world.[7]

But many people did not remain content with these limitations. They boldly extrapolated from physical science to comprehensive worldviews, deriving mechanistic determinism from Newton and the naturalistic world of evolutionism from Darwin. Such worldviews, because they pretended to offer a total explanation, competed with the Bible's claims. They did not simply contradict a single passage of the Bible, as a specific scientific theory might. Rather, they contradicted the Bible globally, by offering an alternative worldview, an alternative set of values, and an alternative explanation of origins and destiny.[8]

This second use of science (as a platform for a worldview) is thus even more significant theologically than the first. It offers deeper challenges and potentially more destructive conclusions because it can threaten biblical religion as a whole. Nevertheless, it is not our purpose to pursue this difficulty. The most adequate answers are to be found in writings on Christian approaches to science. A number of Evangelicals have put forward ways of integrating the scientific task as a whole into a biblical worldview.[9]

---

[6]Loren Eiseley, *Darwin's Century: Evolution and the Men Who Discovered It* (Garden City, N.Y.: Doubleday, 1961).

[7]See Charles Hummel, *The Galileo Connection: Resolving Conflicts Between Science and the Bible* (Downers Grove, Ill.: InterVarsity, 1986); Del Ratzsch, *Philosophy of Science* (Downers Grove, Ill.: InterVarsity, 1986).

[8]The feeling that modern science contradicts the biblical view of the world is far from dead. Rudolf Bultmann claims, "It is impossible to use electric light and the wireless and to avail ourselves of modern medical and surgical discoveries, and at the same time to believe in the New Testament world of spirits and miracles" ("New Testament and Mythology," in *Kerygma and Myth*, ed. Hans Werner Bartsch [New York: Harper & Row, 1961], p. 5).

[9]See Hummel, *Galileo Connection*; Robert Ream, *Science Teaching: A Christian Approach* (Philadelphia: Presbyterian & Reformed, 1972); Russell Maatman, *The Bible, Natural Science, and Evolution* (Grand Rapids: Baker, 1970); Ratzsch, *Philosophy of Science*; Vern S. Poythress, *Philosophy, Science and the Sovereignty of God* (Nutley, N.J.: Presbyterian & Reformed, 1976); idem, "Science as Allegory," *Journal of the American Scientific Affiliation* 35 (1983):65–71; Herman Dooyeweerd, *A New Critique of Theoretical Thought*, 2 vols. (Philadelphia: Presbyterian & Reformed, 1969); idem, *The Secularization of Science* (Memphis: Christian Studies Center, 1979); Hendrik van Riessen, *Wijsbegeerte* (Kampen: Kok, 1970); Stanley Jaki, *The Road of Science and the Ways of God* (Chicago: University of Chicago Press, 1980).

BUILDING AN EPISTEMOLOGY ON THE BASIS OF SCIENTIFIC METHOD: THE EXAMPLE OF KANT

Finally, science was used in a third way, namely, as a source of insight about the nature of knowledge itself. Let us call this the procedure of building an epistemology, or a philosophical theory of knowledge.

This third way is in many respects the most promising. As we observed, the procedure of using specific scientific theories is useful only when a specific theory happens to touch on issues of human concern. Most of the time it does not. The procedure of building a worldview is questionable, since one must extrapolate science beyond what has been verified. On the other hand, the procedure of building an epistemology relies on the undoubted success of science as a means for producing knowledge. Even if science does not include all knowledge, its success surely contains lessons that apply to all knowledge.

The classic example of using science as a platform for epistemology is to be found in Immanuel Kant.[10] Kant at an early point in his life followed the rationalistic, deductive approach of Leibniz. In opposition to this rationalism, Hume defended an empiricism that started with pure events and did not assume that they were connected, merely that they sometimes occurred together. As Kant testified, Hume "awakened him from his dogmatic slumber." Kant then rejected rationalism. He was convinced that there was no guarantee that phenomena would turn out to be connected in the way that a rationalist supposed. And yet, Hume's own empiricist solution was also inadequate. Hume's world contained no intrinsic connection between individual events. Hence Hume could not account for the reliability of scientific knowledge. The rationalistic approach of Leibniz did not lead to fruitful science either.

Kant therefore endeavored to provide an epistemology that was adequate to science and that also preserved room for religion. Kant accepted the obvious fact that science did provide knowledge. Kant's task was then to provide an epistemology that accounted for the success of science. Science arose from a combination of empirical data (Hume's concern) and rational inference (Leibniz's concern). An adequate epistemology would do justice to both these elements.

Kant's solution was to say that, whatever we observed empirically, we observed necessarily in terms of categories presupposed by the human mind. Inner experience (experience even within one's mind, without looking at the world) was necessarily experience against the background of time. Outer experience was necessarily experience in a framework of both time and space. To these categories of time and space one could also add the categories of quantity and causality, which are basic to physics. The empirical element in science was accounted for, since human experience was experience of a world outside that was not always predictable. On the other hand, the rational element in science was accounted for, since human experience necessarily conformed to the preestablished categories of the mind. The world of phenomena was not pure confusion, as Hume had it. Rather, it was necessarily a world of time, space, and causality, and this was the foundation for sure knowledge.

---

[10]For further discussion of Kant, see Royce G. Gruenler, *Meaning and Understanding: The Philosophical Framework for Biblical Interpretation,* FCI 2 (Grand Rapids: Zondervan, 1991).

On the surface, Kant's solution seems attractive. In fact, however, a closer examination shows that it provides both too little and too much for the needs of physical science.[11] On the one hand, it provides too little. Suppose we agree that it shows the necessity of conceiving the world in terms of the categories of time, space, causality, and
quantity. This result still does not constitute scientific knowledge, nor is it an adequate
basis for guaranteeing that we can obtain scientific knowledge.

After all, any particular physical theory, such as Newton's laws, Boyle's law, and
Dalton's law, furnishes predictions to the effect that the world will behave in one way, not
another, within the general framework of time, space, and causality. To say that there are
causal connections (Kant) is not yet to say what kind of causal connections there are
(Newton). To say that everything has a cause (Kant) is a long way from saying that all
bodies attract one another with a force given by the formula $F = GmM/r^2$ (Newton). Kant's
epistemology guarantees only that there is necessarily a cause for any event. It does not
allow anyone to say that the cause must necessarily be what Newton says it is. In fact, in
Kant's scheme the particular way that the world is, within the conceptual framework of
causality, is ultimately not predictable. It is contingent. The phenomena presuppose
things in themselves that cannot be predicted beforehand. A tightly formulated general
law, like Newton's, predicts something that Kant says cannot be predicted. Hence Kant
still is unable to explain why a simple formula like $F = GmM/r^2$ should hold true all the
time, while other formulas do not.

Second, Kant's epistemology provides too much for the needs of science. Namely,
it dictates to science assumptions that may not turn out to be factually correct. Kant's categories of time, space, and causality are most naturally understood as actually implying
a particular theory of physical time, space, and causality. In Kant's environment, these
categories seemed to imply a linear absolute time scale, Euclidean space, and determinism in the realm of physical causes. These things were virtually part of people's intuitions
about space, time, and causality. In turn, these intuitions or views were compatible with
Newton's theory of gravitation, so people were content with them at the time.

In the light of better scientific knowledge, however, physicists today are not willing to agree with Kant. Physicists now realize that the ideas of absolute time, Euclidean
space, and determinism were all assumptions about the world that might be either true
or false, not presuppositions that were necessarily true. Kant did not take into account
two facts. First, the psychic experience of time, space, and causality by the ordinary person is not the same as the time, space, and causality that may be most suitable to physical theory. Intuitions derived from psychic experiences may or may not be immediately
useful in physical theory. Second, intuitions themselves can be reformed. In Kant's time,
"space" meant Euclidean space. Given a line and a point not on the line, one and only one
line could be drawn through the point, parallel to the first line. But modern physicists,
confronted with coherent alternatives to this scheme, have had their intuitions changed.
For them it is not obvious (in fact, it is false) that physical space is Euclidean.

Kant's solution, then, did not really correspond well with the nature of science. It did
not even fit the specifics of Newtonian science. And it fit even less well the developments
of the twentieth century that were destined to supersede Newton. But Kant's philosophy

---

[11]See especially Jaki, *Road of Science,* pp. 112–27.

had enormous impact nonetheless. It was accepted because of its promise in the field of philosophy rather than because of its accuracy in the realm of science.

For Kant, in fact, epistemology became the basis for philosophy as a whole. By means of his reflection on the categories of the human mind, Kant specified what could and could not be the object of knowledge. And this pronouncement virtually determined what could and could not be part of the world. From Kant until the twentieth century, epistemology has been the key to philosophy as a whole. Hence Kant's work was not just an epistemology. It was a full-blown philosophy. It provided its own worldview.

In Kant, then, epistemology leads to a worldview. Hence we cannot rigidly separate the third use of science (building an epistemology) from the second use (building a worldview). Epistemology is a part of a worldview, and in post-Kantian philosophy often it is the principal part. Nevertheless, a rough-and-ready distinction between these two ways of using science is useful. The second use wants to read off a worldview directly from the picture of the physical world presented in current scientific theory. The third use, the more philosophical use followed by Kant, wishes to reflect primarily on *how* scientists know what they know, rather than on *what* they know. From this reflection it derives general conclusions about the nature of human knowledge, and from there it derives further conclusions about what there is to know. (See figure 1 on the next page.)

Kant provides us with a cautionary lesson here. When we seek to derive from science an epistemology or a worldview, we may produce a worldview that in fact does not really match science but that may be heavily motivated by philosophical and religious needs.

BACONIAN AND POSITIVISTIC UNDERSTANDING OF SCIENCE

Not everyone followed Kant, however. The scientists, perhaps, followed him least of all. Alongside Kant and his followers there continued a longstanding empirical tradition going back to Sir Francis Bacon (1561–1626). Bacon and scientists after him assumed that science studied the real world. Science did not just study "phenomena" in a Kantian sense; it did not just observe a world whose order derived from the categories of the human mind already read into it in the act of perception. The world was "out there," and scientists had the task of discovering its laws.

Scientists also assumed that the world was regular and had its laws. Hume's philosophical skepticism made him doubt whether there were real laws. But practicing scientists ignored Hume's theoretical problem. The laws were there. People could discover them by a series of steps laid out by Bacon. The steps came to be known as the scientific method.

1. Gather data.
2. Formulate a general rule (hypothesis) accounting for the data.
3. Derive predictions from the hypothesis.
4. Check the predictions by making experiments.
5. If the predictions prove true, give the hypothesis the status of a (tentative) law. Laws are always subject to further testing.
6. If a prediction proves false, return to step 1 and attempt to derive another hypothesis.[12]

---

[12]This conception of scientific method was further formulated, refined, and set in the context of a comprehensive philosophical viewpoint by the school of logical positivism, beginning in the early twentieth century. See Ratzsch, *Philosophy of Science*, pp. 21–39. For our purposes, we may ignore the variations in conception and concentrate on the common features.

Figure 1. Deriving Broader Conclusions from Science

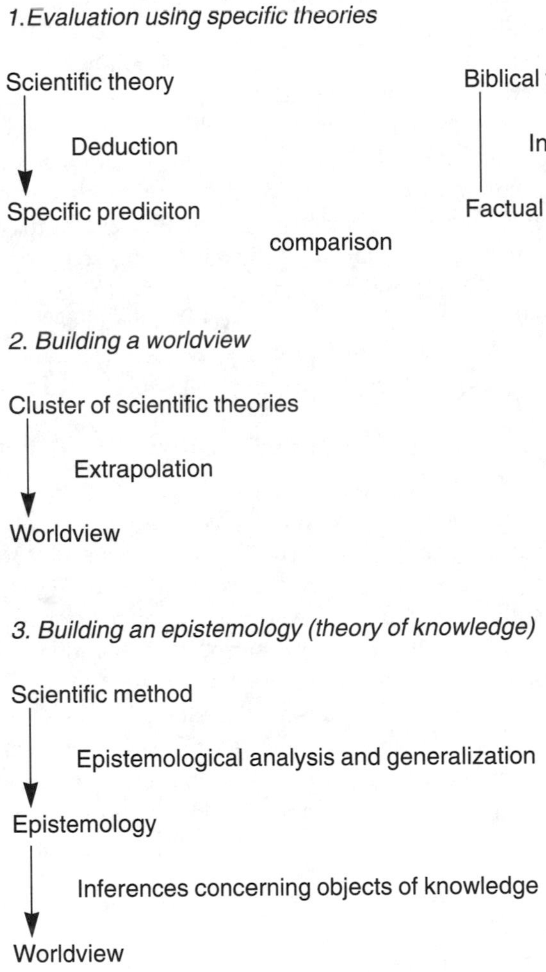

1. Evaluation using specific theories

Scientific theory   Biblical texts

    ↓   Deduction   Interpretation

Specific prediciton   Factual claim

                comparison

2. Building a worldview

Cluster of scientific theories

    ↓   Extrapolation

Worldview

3. Building an epistemology (theory of knowledge)

Scientific method

    ↓   Epistemological analysis and generalization

Epistemology

    ↓   Inferences concerning objects of knowledge

Worldview

As we shall see in the next chapter, these steps are not an adequate representation of how scientists actually proceed. The six steps are only an idealization. They leave out some crucial aspects of scientific research. But until about 1962, most scientists and philosophers of science thought that scientific progress occurred in this manner. And in reality, the above six steps are close enough to the truth to enable people to ignore the discrepancies for a long time. For the sake of clarity, we will call the six steps the Baconian scientific method.

Baconian scientific method, then, does not match what scientists actually do. But until recently it did match what nearly everyone, scientists and nonscientists, *thought* that the scientists were doing (or ought to be doing). Moreover, there was no doubt that science produced impressive results. Hence the conclusion was not far behind: Baconian scientific method was the preferred instrument for producing impressive results.

It was attractive to try to assimilate the practice of biblical interpretation to the practice (or supposed practice) of science. One important area of this assimilation was historical reconstruction.[13] Biblical interpretation involves a lot of historical work. Accurate grammatical-historical interpretation involves assessing the historical environment in which biblical books were written, determining the human authors and original readers of each book, understanding relevant cultural and geographical information, and so on. Historical reconstruction cannot be an exact science, but it can benefit from some of the methodological care exercised in the natural sciences. Hence Baconian scientific method was applied.

Some adjustments were clearly necessary. Historical reconstruction is concerned with single events in the past rather than a general law (see step 2). But one can still formulate hypotheses about a past event. One cannot perform experiments on history in the same way that one can perform experiments on frogs. But checking one's hypothesis for consistency with data not originally included could serve as a substitute for experimental confirmation in step 4.

The application of Baconian method to historical investigation seemed reasonable. But the development of the historical-critical method showed that it was not always innocent. The historical-critical method assumed, just as scientists supposedly assumed, that the same laws governed the past, present, and future and that tight causal laws governed the sequence of events.[14] Historical research conducted on this basis already assumed that the miraculous was impossible. At this point, something out of the mechanism of post-Newtonian science, or out of the rationalistic worldview of the Enlightenment, slipped into the very methods of research in biblical study. And having slipped into the methods, it naturally dictated the conclusions.

One qualification to this picture is necessary. The historical-critical method took its clue not so much directly from natural science as from the general intellectual developments of the Enlightenment and the refinement of standards for intellectual research of all kinds. But these general intellectual developments were in turn influenced by the example of science. In one way or another the natural sciences influenced biblical studies.

Of course, the historical-critical method, with its naturalistic assumptions, was not the only way to do historical research. Orthodox theologians and biblical scholars continued

---

[13]For a more thorough discussion of the role of historical investigation in biblical interpretation, see the section *The Art of Biblical History* by V. Philips Long elsewhere in this volume.

[14]Troeltsch, "Ueber historische und dogmatische Methode."

to believe in the supernatural. They believed that the world was governed by God for rational purposes. This belief provided a basis for historical research just as much as did belief that the world was governed by rational laws untouched by God.

In addition to the controversy over the canons of historical research, the Baconian ideal had an influence on biblical interpretation and on theology. Biblical scholars were interested in making their own work more rigorous. It was easy to say that theology had to become scientific, and it did so by following the Baconian scientific method. Charles Hodge, for example, lays out what he considers to be proper method in theology by explicitly invoking the analogy of scientific method.[15] The individual texts of the Bible are the data, which the theologian/"scientist" uses inductively to formulate principles in the form of general doctrinal truths. The principles are to be checked for their consistency with the whole Bible.

Baconian scientific method had its effect even on people who did not consciously endeavor to assimilate their work to the methods and standards of science. The method presupposed a certain relation between data, hypotheses, scientific laws, and the sciences that codified the laws into coherent wholes. Underlying the Baconian method were the following assumptions:

1. Data are hard facts, about which there is and can be no dispute.
2. Hypotheses arise from seeing a pattern in the data and making an inductive generalization. The generalization says simply that all cases fit the observed pattern. Seeing a pattern is an act of insight that cannot be perfectly controlled, but once a pattern is seen, the generalization follows.
3. Predictions from a hypothesis are derived by simple deduction from the hypothesis itself.
4. Discarding or retaining a hypothesis is a relatively simple matter, depending merely on whether the additional experimental data support it.
5. Confirmed hypotheses are added to the existing list of general laws. Progress in science consists in piecemeal additions to the list of known laws.

These assumptions summarize the heart of an inductive, positivist view of scientific knowledge. According to this view, knowledge has two parts—individual *bits of hard data,* which are the indisputable basis for knowledge, and *general laws,* which are its superstructure. Each law summarizes a pattern found inductively in the data. The laws group together the data that they generalize. But except for the grouping of data under laws, all of knowledge is fundamentally atomistic. Each bit of data stands on its own feet, and each law in the existing list of laws stands on its own feet over against other laws.

Moreover, it could also be said that scientific method has two parts. In the inductive part, one gathers data and generalizes to hypotheses. In the deductive part, one derives predictions and discards disconfirmed hypotheses. The production of hypotheses cannot be completely mechanized, but all the other steps are in principle purely objective.

The above assumptions represent only a simplified summary, but do express an important tendency in thinking about science. And this tendency has also infected exegesis and theology. In exegesis, this view of knowledge says that the individual words and morphemes

---

[15]Charles Hodge, *Systematic Theology,* 3 vols. (Grand Rapids: Eerdmans, 1970), 1:9–17.

are the hard data. The statements about the meaning of paragraphs and discourses are the laws. Hypotheses about meaning are discarded when they do not agree with some of the data (i.e., when they do not account for some word, phrase, or sentence). Progress in exegesis means adding to the store of correct interpretations of individual passages.

In systematic theology, individual passages of the Bible are the data, and the laws are general theological truths. Theological hypotheses are discarded when some passage contradicts them. Progress in theology means adding to the store of general truths derived from the Bible.

Both in natural science and in biblical interpretation, this inductive view of knowledge is inadequate. Worse, it leads to distortions and hindrances in the progress of knowledge. To see why, we will first look at the revisions that have taken place in the understanding of scientific method (chap. 3). We will then ask what implications we can draw for biblical interpretation (chaps. 4–11).

three

THOMAS KUHN AND CONTEMPORARY DISCUSSIONS OF SCIENTIFIC DISCOVERY

A t the end of the nineteenth century, scientists had reason to be confident about their achievements. Newton's theory of gravitation had proved successful. It not only gave accurate predictions of the movements of planets but did so with an aesthetically pleasing, mathematically elegant set of equations. More important, it furnished a fundamental framework in which all further scientific investigation could be integrated. To be sure, scientists had still not thoroughly explored and mastered every potential area of investigation in physics, let alone every area of biology. But they could confidently expect that those yet-to-be-explored areas would harmonize with Newton's framework.

THE SCIENTIFIC REVOLUTIONS OF THE TWENTIETH CENTURY

The twentieth century rudely shattered this complacency. Within a period of thirty years, two revolutions in physics overturned Newton's universe in a way that a nineteenth-century physicist would have said was impossible. In 1905, Albert Einstein published his first paper on the special theory of relativity. This theory contradicted the fundamental assumption of Newton that measurements of length in space, length in time, and mass of particles are independent of the person's situation who does the measuring. Since space, time, and mass were fundamental to Newton's entire theory, the whole view of the physical universe had to be rethought.

The second revolution, the quantum revolution, began with Max Planck's papers on radiation in 1900.[1] Planck postulated that light was emitted in fixed quantities of energy,

---

[1]See Sir Edmund Whittaker, *A History of the Theories of Aether and Electricity,* rev. ed. (New York: Harper, 1960), 2:81; George Gamow, *Thirty Years That Shook Physics: The Story of Quantum Theory* (New York: Dover, 1966).

rather than being emitted in a simple continuous stream. Planck's idea remained an oddity in physics for more than twenty years. The corpuscular character of light that Planck's theory implied could not be fully reconciled with many other phenomena showing the interference patterns of waves. But to this oddity were gradually added other oddities showing a similar pattern. Neils Bohr in 1913 succeeded in explaining atomic spectra on the basis of quantum ideas, but this account was in one respect still odd: there was no framework capable of thoroughly reconciling particle and wave aspects of the behavior. Finally, in 1925 and 1926, Werner Heisenberg and Erwin Schrödinger produced formulations accurately predicting atomic-energy levels. Schrödinger's formulation ("wave mechanics") depended on representing atomic electrons by waves corresponding to fixed quantities of energy, that is, quantized levels of energy. The universe that Newton had assumed to have continuous levels of energy was found to be discrete. Worse, this universe, at an atomic level, behaved not like a particle, not like a wave, but in a way showing features of both. Causality itself seemed to function oddly at an atomic level. In order for the equations of quantum mechanics to hold, it was argued, some events must be innately unpredictable or indeterminate.

Both special relativity and quantum theory invalidated Newton's equations. Furthermore, they showed that the basic intuitions behind Newton's universe were invalid. They produced a picture of the universe that went contrary to intuition. According to special relativity, events at high speed deviate in strange ways from what we are accustomed to in our everyday world. According to quantum theory, events on a very small scale deviate in strange ways. The quantum revolution proved, if possible, even more unsettling because it was impossible to picture the underlying realities. They could be accurately described only in terms of equations that provided no good intuitive picture of the world. Relativity and quantum theory both spawned further developments that were nearly revolutions in their own right and moved the world of physical theory even further away from the old world of Newton.

First, as a development of relativity, Einstein published in 1915 his "General Theory of Relativity." In this theory he expanded the theory of special relativity to include an account of gravitation. In the new theory mass and energy corresponded to curvature in the very structure of space and time. Newton's view of the universe, by contrast, had assumed that space and time were flat. And it had assumed that gravitation was a "real" force, not something that could be equated with the structure of space and time itself.

Second, in the area of quantum theory, Max Born and Werner Heisenberg introduced an alternative to Schrödinger's formulation, called matrix mechanics. The details of this proposal are not important for our purposes. At a deep level it was, in fact, mathematically equivalent to Schrödinger's formulation. But Heisenberg for the first time explicitly formulated the uncertainty relations of quantum mechanics, namely, mathematical statements implying that one cannot measure a particle's position and momentum simultaneously.

Reflection on the uncertainty relations and on the phenomena of wave/particle duality spawned a philosophical interpretation of quantum theory, namely, the "Copenhagen interpretation." This school said that, in many atomic situations, key quantities like position and velocity were not fully defined in a classical sense until an experiment was performed measuring them. The measurements in the experiment in effect "forced" a particle to take a determinate position or velocity. This view was more radical than several alternatives. For instance, one could have said merely that we as observers did not know what the actual value was (as a Newtonian might have said). Or one could say that we could never in principle know the actual values of all the variables, because measurement of one value inevitably disturbed the others (this conclusion was a result of quantum theory, not of Newton, but it was still fairly safe). But the Copenhagen interpretation said that talk about definite actual values, independent of measuring them, was virtually meaningless.[2]

After Heisenberg and Schrödinger, refinements in quantum theory have continued to appear. These refinements have made the nature of quantum description ever more esoteric. Heisenberg's and Schrödinger's work has now been surpassed in turn by Dirac's relativistic quantum mechanics, quantized field theory, quantum electrodynamics, and quantum chromodynamics. One does not know what theories will appear in the future on the border of knowledge.

After these two revolutions, one could still claim in retrospect that Newton's theory worked as a first approximation. Relativity was a refinement of Newton in the domain of high velocities. Quantum theory was a refinement in the domain of very small physical systems. This qualification helped people to preserve the idea that scientific advance consists simply in adding to the body of known truths.[3]

But it was difficult to deny that some other things were going on as well. Both relativity and quantum theory challenged not primarily some poorly established hypothesis or some theory just beginning to be established, but the very best and most firmly established physical theory (Newton's). And they offered the challenge at the very basis of the theory, by disputing the very ideas of measurement and reality interwoven with every single experiment.

Hence the existence of these revolutions raises questions about the naïve inductive view of scientific research discussed in the previous chapter. Are scientific data and scientific laws atomistic? Does scientific progress consist simply in adding more data and adding more laws to the list of approved laws? Or if such a picture is not quite right, is it enough to add a footnote to the effect that occasional pruning of old laws may replace them with more accurate versions of the same? The revolutions produced by the theory of relativity and quantum theory, however, included changes in the shape of physical theory of a most radical nature.

THOMAS KUHN AND THE REVOLUTION IN HISTORY AND PHILOSOPHY OF SCIENCE

The watershed in thinking about scientific progress occurred in 1962. In that year Thomas S. Kuhn published *The Structure of Scientific Revolutions,* in which he rejected the classic view of science, the view associated with Baconian scientific method. Kuhn argued that science did *not* advance merely by a step-by-step inductive method.[4] Research on specific problems always took place against the background of assumptions and convictions produced by previously existing science. In mature science, this background took

---

[2] See, for example, Norwood Russell Hanson, "Quantum Mechanics, Philosophical Implications of," in *The Encyclopedia of Philosophy,* ed. Paul Edwards (New York: Macmillan, 1967), 7:41–49. For a nonmathematical explanation of quantum theory, see John Gribbin, *In Search of Schrödinger's Cat: Quantum Physics and Reality* (New York: Bantam, 1984). Slightly more advanced is J. C. Polkinghorne, *The Quantum World* (Princeton: Princeton University Press, 1984). A thorough exploration of the issues is to be found in the more technical book by Max Jammer, *The Philosophy of Quantum Mechanics: The Interpretation of Quantum Mechanics in Historical Perspective* (New York: Wiley, 1974).

[3] See Kuhn, *Structure of Scientific Revolutions,* pp. 98–102.

[4] Ibid., pp. 1–4.

the form of "paradigms," a cluster of beliefs, theories, values, standards for research, and exemplary research results that provided a framework for scientific advance within a whole field. Since the word *paradigm* has come to be used in several different senses, we will instead use the phrase *disciplinary matrix*.[5] Newton's fundamental work, *Philosophiae Naturalis Principia Mathematica,* generated just such a disciplinary matrix within the field of natural science in general and physics in particular. Newton's work was an exemplar, a concrete research result that suggested a way of problem-solving for a large number of unsolved problems. At the same time, as people reflected on the implications of Newton's work, they obtained from it not only a prime example of a successful theory but a framework that suggested further questions, experiments, and generalizations building on and within the overall theory. Newton's theory evolved, then, into a disciplinary matrix for subsequent research.

In chapter 2, we analyzed Baconian scientific method as involving six fundamental assumptions. Over against these assumptions, we may summarize Kuhn's view in a series of counterassumptions:

1. Data are never "hard facts," completely independent of any theory. What counts as data depends on the disciplinary matrix, or framework of assumptions, that scientists use. All data is "theory-laden." It already presupposes, in its very status as data for a given experiment or a given theory, that the universe is organized in a way compatible with the assumptions of the science as a whole. The current disciplinary matrix affects how scientists make observations, what they think the observations actually measure, and what kinds of data or experiments are relevant to the outstanding open questions in their field.

2. Hypotheses do not arise from making a generalization in a vacuum. Rather, they arise from the combined influence of the overall disciplinary matrix in the field, detailed experimental results, the structure of theories in related areas that may suggest analogous solutions in the area currently under scrutiny, and expectations generated by the ruling disciplinary matrix as to what types of theory are most likely to be successful.

3. One cannot simply deduce a prediction from an isolated hypothesis. Predictions from a hypothesis depend not only on the hypothesis itself but on a surrounding body of theory specifying how the hypothesis is related to any particular experimental setup. One must also include here "observation theories," theories about any specialized apparatus used in measurements and the meaning of those measurements.

4. Discarding or retaining a hypothesis is almost never easy. Experiments can go wrong for a large number of reasons. Some unforeseen interference may not have been excluded from the experiment. Any one of a group of hypotheses or laws helping to relate the given hypothesis to the experiment may be invalid. One of these may have to be discarded, but a single experiment, or frequently even a whole series of

---

[5] In the first edition of Kuhn's work, he failed to distinguish two main senses of his use of the word *paradigm*. In the first sense, it designates "the entire constellation of beliefs, values, techniques, and so on shared by the members of a given community" (p. 175). In the second sense it designates "concrete puzzle-solutions" that provide models for further research (ibid.). It is usually not too hard to disentangle these two senses within Kuhn's book. In the discussion below I use *disciplinary matrix* for the first sense, *exemplar* for the second sense. Kuhn himself has now recommended this terminology (pp. 182, 187).

experiments, does not indicate which of a series of connected, mutually dependent hypotheses is incorrect.

5. Most important, science does not advance merely by adding confirmed hypotheses to an existing atomistic list of laws. The laws of a given field of science are related to one another in a coherent way. Additions and subtractions affect the whole. Moreover, there can be times of "revolution" when the whole body of knowledge is recast.

Kuhn is particularly stimulating on the subject of this fifth point, the question of scientific progress. In this area, Kuhn distinguishes between at least three kinds of situations in the development of a particular scientific field. The first is "immature" science. In this situation, the field of investigation for the science is poorly defined. Different workers in the field dispute the kinds of data that are relevant to their field, the purpose of the investigation, the shape a finished theory will have, and the kind of tests that confirm or disconfirm the theory. Investigators are casting about for a fundamental insight that will bring order into a disparate field. In immature sciences, it is not clear how one measures progress. People do experiments and gather data, but because of the unsettled character of the field, it is seldom clear whether their work will make a lasting contribution. Kuhn thinks that the social sciences, for the most part, may still be in this state.

The second kind of situation is that of normal "mature" science. A particular science becomes mature when some investigator or group of investigators advances a fundamental theory, including supporting data, that proves clearly superior. This theory becomes an exemplar, a key research result that largely determines the whole disciplinary matrix for subsequent research. It suggests a whole line of experiments, a "research program."[6] The theory explains and organizes a significant body of data. In addition, it confirms its promise by engendering a whole line of experiments that refine, extend, and confirm the theory and that link it with other existing theories. The success of the new disciplinary matrix inaugurates a period of "normal science," devoted to "puzzle-solving."[7] Most of the scientists working in the field devote themselves to small puzzles, the remaining areas of investigation where the overall disciplinary matrix already suggests lines of questioning and the forms of hypotheses that might solve the puzzle.[8]

As long as the scientists in a field continue to solve the puzzles that they find for themselves, they go forward in a way that superficially resembles the Baconian inductive ideal. They add small bits of generalization to the existing body of generalizations. There are always some remaining anomalies, or areas where explanations have not been produced. Here and there are some potentially embarrassing data that do not seem to be compatible with the existing disciplinary matrix. Nevertheless, as long as people are making progress in the puzzle-solving, they assume that incremental advances in the field

---

[6]Imre Lakatos, not Thomas Kuhn, introduced the phrase *research program* (see Lakatos, *The Methodology of Scientific Research Programmes*, ed. John Worrall and Gregory Currie [Cambridge: Cambridge University Press, 1978]). This phrase expresses insights similar to Kuhn's.

[7]See Kuhn, *Structure of Scientific Revolutions*, pp. 35–42. Kuhn also calls this activity "mop up work" (p. 24).

[8]Kuhn subclassifies the puzzle-solving into three types (pp. 25–30). The first type works at a more accurate and more comprehensive determination of quantities that "the paradigm [disciplinary matrix and exemplar together] has shown to be particularly revealing of the nature of things" (p. 25). A second type works on those areas where the most direct, definitive experimental checks on the theory can be performed. A third type consists in work attempting to extend or articulate further the disciplinary matrix. All of these types of investigation are closely regulated by the disciplinary matrix.

(or in some neighboring field) will eventually enable them to see the compatibility of the anomalies with the disciplinary matrix.

The third situation is that of "extraordinary" science, leading to scientific revolution. Revolution occurs when an existing disciplinary matrix is replaced by a new one incompatible with the original. A revolutionary situation first arises when anomalies in a particular field cannot easily be ignored. The anomalies begin to fall into patterns that show an order of their own. More and more tinkering with the disciplinary matrix is necessary in order to produce any kind of rational summary of the anomalies. Inelegant, complex, unmotivated hypotheses arise to account for the anomalies. As more and more energy is devoted to working on the anomalies, tinkering with the reigning disciplinary matrix leads people to produce different versions of the disciplinary matrix. The disciplinary matrix itself no longer looks so unified as it once did.[9]

In this situation people are willing to search about more broadly, looking for better solutions. In the process they are willing even to challenge ideas traditionally associated with the existing disciplinary matrix. Eventually they stumble upon an alternative approach, inexact at first, but appearing to offer some possibility of dealing with the anomalies. This approach is refined, enhanced, and reformed in order to increase its accuracy and the scope of data accounted for. If the process continues, this new approach generates a disciplinary matrix of its own. A fight then ensues between adherents to the old disciplinary matrix and those holding the new as to which matrix is to be used in the future development of science. In this period, it is difficult for adherents of the two disciplinary matrices even to communicate well with one another, because they may have different standards for what counts as data and different standards as to what sorts of explanation have the most promise.[10]

Kuhn also notes that, if no satisfactory solution arises, even after prolonged effort and radical attempts to generate alternative explanations, people may fall back on the existing disciplinary matrix and treat the anomalies as an intractable area reserved for future generations. In this case, the period of extraordinary science has not generated a revolution but has collapsed back into normal science, working with essentially the same disciplinary matrix as before.

A SPECIFIC ILLUSTRATION OF KUHN'S THEORY

The study of electricity provides an example of the process of change in science. According to Kuhn, in the first half of the eighteenth century there was no standard theory of electricity. There was no clear exemplar to bring coherence to the progress of research. Instead, "there were almost as many views about the nature of electricity as there were important electrical experimenters, men like Hauksbee, Gray, Desaguliers, Du Fay, Nollett, Watson, Franklin, and others."[11] In such a stage of immature science, there is as yet no standard disciplinary matrix in the field. Some of the theories of electricity of the time regarded "attraction and frictional generation as the fundamental electrical phenomena." Others regarded attraction and repulsion as equally fundamental. A third group

---

[9]See, for example, ibid., p. 83.
[10]See, for example, ibid., pp. 109–110, 198–204.
[11]Ibid., pp. 13–14.

regarded electricity as a fluid that ran through conductors. In each case the idea of which phenomena were fundamental directed the concentration and goal of the research.

The preparadigm stage came to an end with Franklin's work *Electricity,* which became the exemplar for future research. It proved its superior promise by encompassing all the phenomena within its scope.[12]

Subsequent to Franklin's time, the field of electrical research represented a field of normal science. Franklin's theory was elaborated, refined, enhanced, and extended. Scientists no longer debated about the fundamental nature of electricity or the fundamental directions that research should take. They could therefore concentrate more on esoteric phenomena; they could study in great detail the phenomena that the theory indicated were of greatest significance. No individual scientist needed to return and reconstruct the whole field from its foundations up. The resulting specialization made the literature on electricity less accessible to the general public but meant efficiency in making progress within the specialization.

The theory of electricity has since been normal science. However, according to Kuhn, normal science may at times be interrupted by revolutions in theory. These revolutions may take place within a small specialty (such as studies of diamagnetism) or within a broader field. Kuhn is not explicit, but inspection of the history of electricity subsequent to Franklin suggests a series of mini-revolutions in small areas. Kuhn does mention explicitly a revolution introduced by James Clerk Maxwell in the second half of the nineteenth century.[13] Maxwell's electromagnetic theory introduced "displacement current" and other ideas difficult for his contemporaries to digest. The triumph of his theory therefore took time, during which some adherents to older views were converted and some were displaced by a younger generation.[14]

---

[12]Franklin provided a theory that "could account with something like equal facility for very nearly all these effects and that therefore could and did provide . . . a common paradigm [exemplar]" (ibid., p. 15).

[13]Ibid., pp. 107–8.

[14]See Whittaker, *History of the Theories,* 1:254: "It was inevitable that a theory so novel and so capricious as that of Maxwell should involve conceptions which his contemporaries understood with difficulty and accepted with reluctance."

four

IMPLICATIONS
OF KUHN'S THEORY
FOR BIBLICAL
INTERPRETATION

W hat do we make of Kuhn's theory of scientific revolutions? Kuhn's book has had mixed reception by philosophers and historians of science.[1] Such a reception is just what we might expect. Kuhn claims that his book is part of a revolutionary change in the historiography of science.[2] A revolutionary change will meet resistance at the beginning.

PRELIMINARY EVALUATION OF KUHN

My own opinion is that Kuhn is on the right track, that he does bring to light many aspects in the development of science concealed by the reigning philosophy of science and by textbook remarks about the history of science.[3] Moreover, there are reasons for thinking that much of what Kuhn says is applicable to scholarly communities of any kind, not just to science. Hence his ideas should be applicable to biblical interpretation. But not everything that is true of science is true of biblical interpretation. Kuhn himself is just as concerned with the uniqueness of science as he is with its similarities to scholarly research of other kinds.[4]

---

[1]See Gary Gutting, ed., *Paradigms and Revolutions: Appraisals and Applications of Thomas Kuhn's Philosophy of Science* (Notre Dame: University of Notre Dame Press, 1980); Imre Lakatos and Alan Musgrave, eds., *Criticism and the Growth of Knowledge* (Cambridge: Cambridge University Press, 1970); Ian Hacking, ed., *Scientific Revolutions* (Oxford: Oxford University Press, 1981).

[2]Kuhn, *Structure of Scientific Revolutions*, pp. 1–3.

[3]On the role of textbooks in concealing revolutions, see ibid., pp. 136–43.

[4]Ibid., pp. 208–9.

What relevance, then, does the activity of science have for biblical interpretation? More particularly, what relevance might Kuhn's ideas have? To answer this question, we must determine to what extent biblical interpretation does or does not have analogues to the processes that Kuhn describes in science. Whether or not Kuhn is right about science is somewhat secondary. Even if he is right, the same patterns and principles might not hold in biblical interpretation. Even if he is wrong about science, he may be right when we apply his claims to biblical interpretation.

ROMANS 7 COMPARED WITH IMMATURE SCIENCE

Let us, then, look at a particular example: the interpretation of Romans 7. Recall from chapter 1 the conflict between three different interpretations of this passage. This conflict looks vaguely like the situation that Kuhn describes in immature science, when a scientific field has not produced a single unified paradigm or disciplinary matrix based on a successful exemplar.

The most striking similarity between the two cases lies in the unresolved disputes between schools. In immature science the investigators may be grouped into a number of competing schools. Each school has a different idea about the fundamental nature of the field and about the lines of explanation along which understanding will come. Similarly, in the interpretation of Romans 7 there are two schools, what I have called the regenerate school of interpretation and the unregenerate school. Later in history, these two were eventually joined by the second-blessing school. Just as in immature science, progress is possible in a sense within a school.[5] Members of the regenerate school can refine the understanding of individual verses, draw out the implications of these verses, expand on the connections that the verses have with other parts of the Bible, and so on. But there are two hindrances to progress, just as there are in immature science. First, if the existing school turns out to be wrong, all its work will later be judged as just a false trail, and not progress at all. Second, the existence of competing schools means that a good deal of the energy of any one school is spent in reexamining its own foundations and trying to show that its foundations are superior to those of competing schools. Only when everyone in the field agrees on the foundations can there be concentration on the details and progress on those details.

We should not be surprised at these similarities between immature science and the situation in interpreting Romans 7. The similarities arise largely because schools are composed of human beings aiming to understand some subject. In this situation people inevitably behave in ways that they think will most enhance understanding. Enhancing understanding involves interacting with their peers and with competing schools along the lines that we have just laid out—the same lines that scientific schools follow, according to Kuhn.

But there are also certain important differences between the schools of thought concerning Romans 7 and the schools in immature sciences. The former do not really have social cohesiveness, for we have simply classified people into schools for convenience in classifying the different interpretations. By contrast, the schools in immature science, the schools that Kuhn has in mind, have inner social cohesiveness. They form natural subgroups within a community of investigators. The community is bound together, first of all, by

---

common interests in the subject matter. Because of the common interests, letters and articles will be sent back and forth, and there may be some degree of personal acquaintance. Each subgroup will, of course, be more intensely united because of the similarity of their views of the subject they are investigating.

The analogue of scientific schools within biblical interpretation would seem to be not the different schools of thought on Romans 7 but the schools of theology, such as Calvinists, Arminians, and advocates of second-blessing theology. These schools are schools within a larger community, consisting of all biblical scholars and theologians. These schools and the broader community in which they exist both have demonstrable social cohesiveness. The schools are social groups with communication back and forth; they have common goals and some common standards of evaluation.

The problem of interpreting Romans 7 is one research problem on which the community works. The preferred approach to dealing with the problem varies from school to school, just as it might in an immature science.

There is one more difference between interpretation of Romans 7 and immature science. Typically, in immature science, there may not even be agreement as to which phenomena are part of the field of investigation or which phenomena are most revealing of the nature of things. Different investigators concentrate their research on different areas. The effect may be reminiscent of the story of blind men investigating an elephant; one described the trunk, one the side, one a leg, one the tail, and one an ear. As long as no one has a clue to the true extent of the phenomena that may be amenable to explanation by a unified theory, and as long as no theory has succeeded in dominating the field, the boundaries of the field itself are understandably uncertain.

In biblical interpretation and theology, however, the field of investigation is fixed. The schools in theology—Calvinists, Arminians, and second-blessing theologians—can pretty much agree on their subject matter. All study Romans 7, all take into account the same lexical and grammatical information, and all use the same standard lexicons and grammars. All agree on the relevance not only of Romans 7 but of other passages of Romans, the rest of Paul's epistles, and ultimately the rest of biblical teaching as a whole.

But here we can begin to see that this measure of agreement is not always achievable. Roman Catholics include in their list of canonical books some books and additions not included in the Protestant list. Traditional Roman Catholics also allow a role for church tradition and for papal teaching such as Protestants would not allow. Some critical scholars want to have a canon within the canon, perhaps Paul's epistles or Paul's teaching on justification, in terms of which they think it possible to judge other teachings of other parts of the Bible as substandard. Cultic groups like the Mormons and Christian Scientists have their own holy books supplementing the Bible. Clearly these different groups do not have the same standards or the same field of investigation.

Even if we concentrate on evangelical Protestantism, which accepts the Bible as its standard, there are some differences. Confessional churches also give a role to their confessions. The confessions are "secondary standards," while the Bible is the primary standard. The confessions are in theory fallible and correctable, whereas the Bible is not. But confessional theologians are committed to paying attention to their confession. They respect it because it embodies the collective wisdom of their denomination and of past generations, as these generations have been illumined by the Holy Spirit. Confessional theologians will not lightly conclude that the Bible contradicts their particular confession.

The advantage of this stance is that it restrains arbitrary and facile innovation. It protects biblical interpreters from reinventing old heresies—that is, old schools of investigation that have been found to be dead ends. Its disadvantage is that it may keep investigators from acknowledging new truth that they find in the Bible. Moreover, to the degree that a confession actively functions as a standard for judging an interpretation of the Bible, it produces a difference of atmosphere in interpretation for the school that holds it. Thus there may be an attenuated sense in which the Calvinists, the Arminians, and the second-blessing theologians, or at least those who are bound to a doctrinal statement, do not completely agree on the very field of investigation or the methods by which to do the investigation.

THE POSSIBILITY OF REVOLUTION IN BIBLICAL INTERPRETATION

According to Kuhn's scheme immature sciences become normal, mature sciences when they develop a single, stable disciplinary matrix. The unified disciplinary matrix includes a key exemplar, a research result in the form of a theory with supporting experimental evidences. By its aesthetic appeal, its superiority in explanatory power, and its fruitfulness as a basis for further research, this exemplar wins more and more adherents. Eventually it dominates the field. Some older scholars in the field never accept the new theory. They have too much confidence and too much investment in the old. But eventually they die or are effectively excluded from the research community. If they do research, they do it using other ground rules, and the main portion of the community simply pays no attention to their results.

It is natural to ask whether we might find something similar in biblical interpretation. As long as theology is divided into schools of Calvinists, Arminians, Roman Catholics, and so on, it is like immature science. Can a revolution bring unity into this field, similar to the unity in a mature science? If so, how do we set such a revolution in motion?

Some people have already tried to apply Kuhn in a similar way to social sciences. For instance, the science of psychology presently includes a number of competing schools that maintain different principles and fundamental frameworks for research. Behaviorism, Freudianism, Marxism, and humanism each offers itself as a base for psychological research. This situation is immature science. Hence people point to Kuhn and argue that psychology must become mature. To do so, psychology must first decide on a unified approach. And then people offer their own approach as the basis.

But this response is a misunderstanding of Kuhn. Kuhn does not think that one can have a revolution any time one wants. Immaturity is precisely the state in which no one disciplinary matrix, no one theory, is able to win everyone's allegiance. One cannot simply impose allegiance but must wait for the arrival of a theory with clear superiority or at least a promise of superiority. The progress of time, and the refinement of the theory, then makes its superiority more and more evident and irresistible. Or perhaps the progress of time makes things no better: attempts at refining the theory succeed well in some cases but not so well in other cases, and the new theory may not uncover order in new sets of phenomena in any more promising ways than the old ones did. A revolution that one hopes will take place on the basis of a new theory may not take place.

When we look more closely at the history of biblical interpretation, we can see some patterns of revolutionary breaks, followed by periods of stability and consolidation. Western theology after Augustine largely built on Augustine and the ancient creeds. These sources, in a sense, formed the exemplars for biblical and theological scholarship through most of the medieval period. Something of a crisis was provoked by the absorption of Aristotelian philosophy in the late medieval period. More and more anomalies were found through the efforts to assimilate and harmonize the new philosophical influences with the Augustinian framework. The work of Thomas Aquinas was an answer to this problem. Thomas's continuities with Augustine make it unclear whether he essentially refined Augustine or whether he produced a revolutionary triumph. (And one must not forget that Thomas never won over the allegiance of the whole Western theological community to the extent that Augustine did.)

The Reformation period confronts us with a theological revolution in a sense. Humanistic interpretation introduced a new disciplinary matrix for the study of the Greek classics and the Bible. This framework produced more and more anomalies in the relation between the meaning of the Bible and the teaching and practice of the church. In addition, the late medieval synthesis in theology broke down as philosophical reflection found more and more anomalies in theological reasoning itself. The increasing number of anomalies, the finding of anomalies in areas of importance, and the finding of patterns in the anomalies all showed more and more the unsatisfactory character of piecemeal tinkering within the framework of dominant late-medieval synthesis. The time was ripe for theological revolution, which, in the broad sense, did come. People abandoned the old disciplinary matrix for theology. But no one new disciplinary matrix won everyone's allegiance, and so theology divided into multiple schools.

To describe the medieval and Reformation periods in this way is undoubtedly a vast oversimplification. And yet there seems to be an insight here. As we already observed, it appears that human beings in communities, interested in understanding a subject and solving its problems, are bound to proceed in similar ways in both science and theology.

THE HISTORICAL-CRITICAL METHOD AS A REVOLUTION

A second revolution in biblical interpretation took place with the growth of the historical-critical method. This revolution was again provoked by the increasing prominence of anomalies in theology of two main kinds. First, the doctrinal differences within the Reformation and the theological schools associated with them did not disappear. Each school refined its arguments. Each position maintained that it was right, that its arguments were fully persuasive, and that it had adequately refuted the competing positions. Over time, people could not help wondering whether each position was maintained partly by prejudice. The anomaly here was the inability of the schools to deal with prejudice. Moreover, the differences between theologies were all the more painful because they were one factor in wars. Overcoming the differences seemed to be critically important. At the same time, it was impossible to solve the differences using existing modes of argumentation.

Second, developing interest in study of human nature and culture gave people awareness of religious differences between cultures. It was easy to ask whether human reason could be used to sort through religious differences and perhaps to adjudicate between theological schools. Philosophical reason, used by sinful people, wished to dictate what God was like and what divine revelation was like. Deism arose and was at odds with what the Bible claimed. For those attracted to deism, the conflict represented an anomaly.

The historical-critical method arose within this framework as an attempt to produce a scientific exegesis and an objective historical study of the biblical documents. The same standards were to apply to the Bible as applied to any secular historical document. The theological commitment of the practitioner was not to intervene. By this means one eliminated the "prejudice" contained in the interpreter's background within one of the theological schools or a church associated with a fixed theological school.

The historical-critical method did represent a revolutionary challenge in the Kuhnian sense. It altered, sometimes subtly, sometimes radically, the entire framework in which exegesis had been carried on. Under the old framework, or disciplinary matrix, exegesis took place by comparing a passage with other passages and trying to arrive at an interpretation that harmonized them all. Now, exegesis found tensions and contradictions wherever it could, seeing these as clues to the different sources behind the final text.

The old framework required that the exegete inquire concerning the meaning of the text in its final context within the canon. Now, the exegete inquired into the history behind the text, the history of story telling, composition, combination, deletion, and editing that led to the final text. In the old framework, the exegete found guidance from the church's confession and doctrinal commitments. Now, the exegete was systematically to ignore such guidance. In the old framework, the exegete accepted the supernatural claims of the Bible at face value. Now, the exegete sifted such claims in the same way as the claims of any other historical document were evaluated. This position typically meant that the exegete rejected supernatural claims out of hand, because a scientific historian assumed that the history was composed of natural causes.

The contrast between old and new frameworks shows the potentially revolutionary character of the historical-critical method. It was a method capable of altering a person's perspective and method of attack on *all* of the subject. To a certain degree, one might even say that it changed the boundaries of the subject. The canon was no longer separated from other religious writings. Christianity in the first century rather than the New Testament might be the primary focus of research.

The contrast also shows that, even though the post-Reformation theologies were divided, they shared to some degree a common hermeneutical framework. That unified framework, the old framework, still provided something of a disciplinary matrix for coherent research communities. The historical-critical method introduced an alternative disciplinary matrix.

The historical-critical method triumphed within academic circles. It won over enough adherents to make possible a new unified basis for proceeding with future research. As in the case of scientific revolutions, the people who were not willing to conform to the new standards of research were gradually excluded from participation in the scholarly community.

Of course, the historical-critical method never triumphed so completely as did the Newtonian revolution or the Einsteinian revolution in physics. Some orthodox, supernaturalistic theologians and biblical scholars remained, and some held academic positions in major universities. The results differed from country to country. Roman Catholic countries were for a long time little affected by historical-critical innovations. Germany was more thoroughly antisupernatural than England, England more than the United States.

Kuhn's comments about the later stages of a scientific revolution to some extent also characterize the historical-critical revolution. A revolution creates a divide between people who accept it and those who do not. The two groups have different conceptions of the important problems, standards, and goals of research; they make different assumptions about the truths that are "assured results" and the kinds of evidence that are relevant. Once some people are sure that the revolution has triumphed, they waste little time debating with other people who are still not convinced. Those who are convinced find that it is a waste of time to continue debating the foundations of the field. It is time to go on with research on detailed problems, because the disciplinary matrix provides agreed-upon foundations for the field.

After the historical-critical method had gained sufficient adherents, new faculty hired in university departments of theology were therefore bound to be those who showed their promise partly by adherence to the method. Hence after a time, people not adhering to critical method would effectively disappear from academic positions. To some extent, students had to conform to the method to pass courses and receive degrees. The same is still true today in some cases. Evangelical students have sometimes been told frankly by a scholar in the historical-critical tradition, "You don't belong in the doctoral program here. You can't be a scholar unless you are willing to study the Bible critically." Such a comment sounds harsh. But it is no more harsh than a physicist's telling students that they do not belong in a doctoral program as long as they do not accept the special theory of relativity.[6]

The practice of exclusion also takes place in scholarly publication. Articles are accepted in scholarly journals of biblical interpretation only if they conform to the standard of the method. Today evangelical scholars often write articles for publication in academic journals that move within the historical-critical tradition. For the article to be accepted, however, they must write about a subject in which sufficient methodological agreement is possible. Some of the topics most important to Evangelicals, such as the authority of Scripture, the resurrection of Christ, and the deity of Christ, are difficult to write about because in most cases the Evangelical finds it important to appeal to a high view of biblical authority, which is just what the historical-critical method denies in principle, at its very foundation.

Finally, the practice of exclusion takes place in the publication and reading of scholarly books. Individual adherents to the historical-critical method often think that reading evangelical books would be a waste of time. Often it is a waste of time, at least under the assumption that the historical-critical method is right. Some books by Evangelicals on some topics use methods sufficiently close to historical-critical standards to be of interest. But a good many do not. When a book uses different standards, its results will be less interesting. The situation seems parallel to the situation in science. Scientists will never see the point of reading works of a previous (uninformed) generation or contemporary works of what they consider pseudoscience.

The effect holds also for whole seminaries and university departments of theology. If a seminary or department is committed to the historical-critical tradition, it will in all probability have few, if any, books by Evangelicals on its reading lists. For this tradition, those books are a waste of time for the students as well as the professors. Evangelical works, it is said, are less "scholarly." But of course most such books are bound to be less scholarly because they are judged by the historical-critical standard. The result is that

---

[6]Although I think that special relativity is basically right and the historical-critical method is basically wrong, the issue here is not whether some disciplinary matrix is right or wrong in an absolute sense. The issue is whether the existing community of scholars has, for one reason or another, valid or invalid, come to be assured that its position is so clearly right as to need no further discussion. Such people characteristically think that only obtuseness or intellectual failure could prevent someone from working in their framework.

the next generation of students is mostly unaware that there is a reasoned alternative to the historical-critical tradition. Even those who for personal religious reasons would like to be Evangelicals think that this position is intellectually untenable.

To some extent, however, Evangelicals have been less scholarly by any standard. Evangelicals, because of their views on the spiritual and eternal importance of biblical knowledge, have a natural concern to produce suitable popular and semipopular literature. In addition, the triumph of the historical-critical revolution has meant that few Evangelicals were *allowed* to be scholars in the first place. Churches who still wished to hold to orthodox doctrine could and did react to this situation with anger and withdrawal, which often produced anti-intellectualism. Such an attitude in the church discourages the next generation from doing scholarship. And so the unhappy situation continues. Today, fortunately, we see a resurgence of evangelical scholarship of high caliber in the United States, Britain, and South Africa.[7]

In summary, the history of the historical-critical method shows that there are many striking similarities between the social structure of knowledge in biblical interpretation and in science. Comparable elements include the structure of an immense discipline with many schools, the problems of debating the foundations and boundaries of a field, the transition to a single dominant disciplinary matrix in a mature discipline, the effects of social exclusion on people who do not share this matrix, and the ability of the dominant framework to enable research to progress to details.

Evangelicals have repeatedly refused to accept some of the crucial assumptions of the historical-critical method. They have done so even though this method has become the dominant disciplinary matrix in biblical interpretation. Is this refusal really as obtuse as a refusal to accept special relativity?

---

[7]See Mark A. Noll, *Between Faith and Criticism: Evangelicals, Scholarship, and the Bible in America* (San Francisco: Harper & Row, 1986).

five
DIFFERENCES
BETWEEN BIBLICAL
INTERPRETATION
AND SCIENCE

T he similarities between the historical-critical revolution and revolutions in natural science might make us wonder whether sheer obtuseness has prevented Evangelicals from accepting the whole historical-critical package. It is important, however, that a significant number of people reject the historical-critical method. There is a reason for this rejection, however illogical and irrational it may appear to people who adhere to the reigning method.

WHAT COUNTS AS SUPERIOR BIBLICAL INTERPRETATION?

We may assess what makes a particular disciplinary matrix superior by following the logic of Kuhn's analysis of scientific revolutions. Kuhn does not merely assert that a revolution happens when a new disciplinary matrix displaces an old one. He shows why and how this revolution takes place in a community of scientists. First, a growing number of anomalies arise that are seen as important, and a growing number of researchers devote their energies to solving the anomalies within the existing disciplinary matrix. As attention is concentrated on anomalies, more and more are discovered. If repeated attempts to deal with the anomalies produce solutions that are less than satisfactory, some researchers begin to explore more radical alternatives. Variants of the disciplinary matrix arise. Then some researcher, typically one new to the field, finds a fundamentally new way of looking at some of the anomalies. Even though this new way is incompatible with parts of the reigning disciplinary matrix, it seems to have some promise. As it is developed into a full-blown theory, it eventually proves superior in explaining the anomalies, is able to explain most of the phenomena explained by the old theory, and above all suggests a whole pattern of research that shows promise of uncovering and explaining large bodies of additional phenomena that the old theory could not handle. When the new theory begins to show itself superior in this way, more and more scientists in the field get on the bandwagon.

However, Kuhn notes that, in the earlier stages of the revolution, the new theory may not allow quantitative explanation any better than the old one did. Copernicus's sun-centered astronomy did not at first provide quantitative predictions any more accurate than Ptolemy's. At the beginning it is not easy to decide which approach is superior, because people are trying to guess how well the alternative approaches will solve problems in the future. Typically there is no one point in time when one can say that now, and not before, the new theory is decisively proved and the old one refuted.[1]

Now let us take this approach to the revolution introduced by the historical-critical method. Was this method, as a disciplinary matrix, superior to the older approach of reading the Bible as a harmonious source of doctrine? In what way is it superior? What problems did it promise to solve better?

The proponents of the historical-critical method might have listed the following benefits:

1. It offered the promise of superseding the old doctrinal disputes by providing an objective standard for interpretation.
2. It abandoned belief in the supernatural, which was an embarrassment in the age of reason.
3. It promised to explain, rather than gloss over, differences, tensions, and "contradictions" between parallel passages.
4. It promised to give insight into the history of each text's origin.

The last point is particularly important, because the cultural atmosphere was moving toward the view that, in human affairs, historical explanation was the correct, satisfying type of explanation to seek.[2]

Point (2) and, in part, point (4) touch on philosophical and cultural influences that did not affect all biblical interpreters equally. Similar philosophical influences can be found during scientific revolutions. In times of extraordinary science, people's evaluations of anomalies and alternative theories are often influenced by philosophy and other cultural forces.

From the standpoint of theologians who were firmly committed to the supernatural, point (2) made the historical-critical method inferior, not superior. But why were some people firmly committed to the supernatural, and why should this commitment be any different than firm commitments that some scientists have to elements within the old, prerevolutionary disciplinary matrix?

Here we touch on at least one important difference between natural science and biblical interpretation. Biblical interpretation has things to say more directly about human life and about the life of the individual practicing interpreter as a whole person. Religious commitments are some of the deepest commitments that people have. People have emotional investments in their religion that often exceed the investments they have

---

[1]See the similar observations in Lakatos, *Methodology of Scientific Research Programmes.*
[2]See James Barr, "The Interpretation of Scripture, II. Revelation Through History in the Old Testament and in Modern Theology," *Interpretation* 17 (1963): 193–205.

in a vocational interest such as doing research or doing science. Hence they more vigorously resist giving up these commitments.

How, then, do we rate the relative potentials of various approaches to studying the Bible? Evidently one factor in our evaluation should be a requirement that biblical interpretation say something about what we should believe and not merely do research on the Bible and on ancient religion. The historical-critical method, within the twentieth century, has now come under criticism from within for its failure to produce from its researches anything preachable. Many opponents as well as a few proponents of the historical-critical revolution saw this problem from the beginning.[3]

The requirement, then, that research on the Bible eventually relate to the needs of the church was unlike the requirements within a discipline of natural science. Not surprisingly, more radical representatives of the historical-critical method called for a complete separation from the church in order to achieve scientific status. But too many biblical scholars were interested in the Bible partly because of its personal, existential value. The pure separation may have been an ideal for the historical-critical method, but it was never achieved.

THE EXPERIENCE OF GOD: A FUNDAMENTAL DIFFERENCE BETWEEN BIBLICAL INTERPRETATION AND SCIENCE

But we have still not penetrated quite to the heart of the matter. The Bible claims to be what God says.[4] Within the precritical disciplinary matrix, people heard God speaking to them as they read the Bible. All of the Bible testified that what God said could be trusted and that it ought to be trusted, even in situations that seemed to throw doubts on it. God was the Lord. Obedience to Him, including trusting what He said, was a supreme religious duty. Whenever conflicts arose, the apostles' priority was clear: "We must obey God rather than men" (Acts 5:29). This commitment ruled out sifting, criticizing, doubting, or contradicting any part of what the Bible said. Moreover, it ruled out rejecting miracles or the supernatural aspects of the world, to which the Bible clearly testified. In a word, it ruled out the historical-critical method from the beginning. Conversely, the historical-critical method ruled out true biblical religion from its beginning.

Two things must be noticed about this process. First, the Bible made supreme claims about its own authority. People adhering to biblical religion had religious and emotional investments in it in ways formally similar to the emotional investments of non-Christians in non-Christian religions or the investments of Enlightenment secularists in humanism or rationalism. But biblical religion (and ultimately non-Christian religions and secularist idolatries as well) requires supreme loyalty and supreme emotional commitment. Hence the refusal to give up one's religion, seen from the outside as stubbornness in the face of facts, is, from the inside, loyalty in the face of temptation to treason.

---

[3]Opponents of the historical-critical method were, of course, well aware of the antisupernatural bias of the method and saw that it would leave us without a supernatural gospel. But even some proponents like Troeltsch saw the implications: the method guaranteed the dissolution of orthodox doctrinal Christianity as it had existed up to that time (see Troeltsch, "Ueber historische und dogmatische Methode").

[4]This claim is, of course, disputed by many adherents to the historical-critical method. Occasionally, however, one can find critics admitting that some parts of the Bible do have similar claims. The critics, on their part, simply disagree with the claims. See F. C. Grant, *Introduction to New Testament Thought* (Nashville: Abingdon, 1950), p. 75; Benjamin B. Warfield, *The Inspiration and Authority of the Bible* (Philadelphia: Presbyterian & Reformed, 1948), pp. 115, 175–77, 423–24.

By their very nature, supreme loyalties or basic commitments are supreme. They do not tolerate rivals.[5] The Bible requires adherents to biblical religion, if necessary, not merely to suffer intellectual puzzlement and dissatisfaction at not having key answers, scorn for being unscholarly, or loss of vocation by being ostracized, but to submit even to torture and death for the sake of being loyal to God. In short, the commitments to biblical religion are more serious than any scientific commitment could be.

Second, people really did hear God speaking in the Bible. Or (as a skeptic would say) they thought that they did. The historical-critical method ignored from the outset the heart of the Bible, because it ignored, and in effect denied, this experience. But not everyone who read the Bible had this same experience. Different people, looking at the same Bible, heard different things. Naturally this discrepancy produced a division within scholarship. Scholars who heard God refused to follow the historical-critical method. Whatever its other advantages, the historical-critical method had a crucial disadvantage: it falsified the whole nature of the field to be investigated. Scholars who did not hear God embraced the historical-critical method because, whatever its current unsolved problems, it approached the Bible at last without the old dogmatic commitments.

Of course, things were a bit more complex. Some people who once thought that the Bible was God's Word and that they heard God speaking to them in its words later came, under the influence of the debate, to reinterpret their experience. Some people who once did not hear God in the Bible, under the same influences, later came to realize that He was speaking those words.

What do we make of this situation? I agree with the explanation found in the Bible itself. Two forces, two persuasive powers, are at war with one another in human hearts.[6] Sometimes the forces exert themselves in the clamor of popular debate, sometimes in the cultural atmosphere and worldview of a society, sometimes in the careful arguments of scholars, sometimes in the appeals of orators, and sometimes in the quietness of individuals alone, weighing their own desires and hunches. God the Holy Spirit is one force, testifying to the truth. The sinful human heart is the other force, desiring to be like God, to reach its conclusions independent of all other authority. And this sinfulness is the platform for the seductions of Satan and his preternatural assistant demons.

Some people, but not all, come to new birth by the Holy Spirit. When their hearts are enlightened, they see and hear in a way that other people, bound in sin, do not see and hear. In principle, this change may affect all of life, because all of life belongs to God. But obviously some areas and aspects of life touch more closely on people's obedience to God or to Satan. Studies of humanity are, on the average, closer to the issues of the heart than are studies of subhuman nature. Studies of the Bible, the Word of God, are typically closer to the heart of the matter than studies of economics or sociology.

---

[5]For elaboration, see John M. Frame, "God and Biblical Language: Transcendence and Immanence," in *God's Inerrant Word,* ed. John W. Montgomery (Minneapolis: Bethany Fellowship, 1974), pp. 159–77.

[6]Christians and non-Christians participate in spiritual war in fundamentally different ways, since they belong to opposite kingdoms (1 John 5:19). But neither Christians nor non-Christians are consistently loyal to their own side. Christians give in to sin and Satanic temptation, while non-Christians do not escape the knowledge of God and of good (Rom. 1:20, 32).

KUHN'S RELEVANCE IN THE MIDST OF THE DIFFERENCES

It would seem, then, that biblical interpretation is different from natural sciences. Some of its differences it shares with social sciences, or with any kind of research that studies some aspect of human experience. Other differences arise because it touches on basic commitments and on the heart of the spiritual conflict in this world.

In spite of such differences, Kuhn uncannily describes the situation in a scientific revolution in a way reminiscent of religious conversion. Revolutions are "changes of worldview ," which "cause scientists to see the world of their research-engagement differently."[7] To demonstrate this claim, Kuhn finds it useful to distinguish between "stimuli," the physical forces impinging on the human body, and "sensations," the items we are actually aware of. The stimuli are the same, but the sensations are the same only for people who have had the same upbringing and education. Changes in worldview affect the manner in which we interpret the stimuli. To this observation I might add that most people, myself included, do not experience sensations either, if this word connotes in a narrow way bits of experience associated each with a single sensory apparatus, cleanly isolated from everything else. Only people influenced by an empiricist worldview learn to isolate sense bits from a holistic human experience of wholes. Others with a different worldview know that we experience a unified world. We experience God as well, since created things testify to Him (Rom. 1:21; Ps. 19:1–6).

Whatever one might say about worldviews in general (and it is worth reflecting on Kuhn's views on this subject), Kuhn's observations fit the situation introduced with the rise of the historical-critical method. Practitioners of the method and opponents of the method did not see the same thing when they examined the Bible. One saw a human product of the social evolution of religious ideas. The other saw God speaking. Their methods of investigation were correspondingly different.

Actually, in the history of interpretation there are not merely two interpretive positions, one a thoroughgoing historical-critical method and the other a thoroughgoing belief in all the Bible's claims because of its divine authority. Many people struggled to find intermediate positions that accepted the historical-critical method as one means of attaining a more accurate knowledge of a uniquely "inspired" but fallible biblical message. Others claimed to follow the historical-critical method wholeheartedly but introduced extra religious or philosophical assumptions of their own. Others in the fundamentalist camp maintained the full authority of the Bible but denied the profitability of scholarly reflection. In a sense the anomalies generated by the Enlightenment crisis of Christian faith and autonomous reason generated not two disciplinary matrices but a whole spectrum.

---

[7]Kuhn, *Structure of Scientific Revolutions*, p. 111. See further pp. 111–35, 191–207.

six

DISCIPLINARY
MATRICES
IN BIBLICAL
INTERPRETATION

*I*t is time now to take stock of what we have observed about biblical interpretation as
an academic discipline.

THE DYNAMICS OF INTELLECTUAL DEVELOPMENT
IN BIBLICAL INTERPRETATION

I note first that there are communities and subcommunities of people engaged in
intensive intellectual reflection concerning biblical interpretation. I am not thinking here
of the community of all members of a church or a denomination, whose concerns and
interests are usually different from those interested in solving intellectual problems in
biblical interpretation. I focus on communities consisting of scholars working on some
common concerns and communicating with one another. A disciplinary matrix in biblical interpretation consists of the "constellation of group commitments" of such a community.[1] Unity within interpretive communities depends on just such a disciplinary
matrix, a network of shared assumptions, methods, standards, and sources. Sometimes
a particularly outstanding work in theology may set the pace for the future of theological reflection. Augustine's theology became the exemplar for the medieval period, and
Calvin's theology became the exemplar for one post-Reformation school (Calvinism). At
some times and places in the history of the church, a great deal of unity has existed; at

---

[1]Kuhn, *Structure of Scientific Revolutions,* p. 181.

other times, a number of competing schools have vied for dominance, each offering a somewhat different version of a preferred disciplinary matrix.

Over time, it is possible for one disciplinary matrix to be replaced by another. Such an event might be labeled an interpretive revolution or a theological revolution. The Reformation and the rise of the historical-critical method are examples of revolutions. The description of such revolutions can to a great extent follow the lines of Kuhn's description of scientific revolutions. In fact, Kuhn indicates that his own idea of revolution is originally borrowed from the history of other fields:

> Historians of literature, of music, of the arts, of political development, and of many other human activities have long described their subjects in the same way. Periodization in terms of revolutionary breaks in style, taste, and institutional structure have been among their standard tools. If I have been original with respect to concepts like these, it has mainly been by applying them to the sciences, fields which had been widely thought to develop in a different way.[2]

We might expect this commonality simply because human communities interested in giving explanations in a field and solving the problems of the field are bound to behave in similar ways, whatever the field. If one line of explanation (one exemplar) seems promising, they stick with this line of explanation until they start having problems with it. Anomalies multiply. Then some more adventuresome souls tinker with the existing disciplinary matrix. If a resolution is not found, more radical alternatives are tried. If one of these seems to promise success, more and more people convert to the new alternative. A revolution thus begins. We have applied this analysis to both science and biblical interpretation.

I note, however, that revolutions in biblical interpretation never seem to be as successful as those in science. A generation after Einstein's work, it is impossible to find a pure Newtonian. But it is still possible to find Augustinians, Thomists, and people who reject the historical-critical method.

TYPES OF DISCIPLINARY MATRICES IN BIBLICAL INTERPRETATION

Revolutions in biblical interpretation, or changes in disciplinary matrix, can be more or less major, or radical, in character. Changing from medieval theology to Calvinism, or from Calvinism to Arminianism, represents a major change. But through the change some things remain similar. All three theologies agree that the Bible is God's Word. What the Bible says, God says. The historical-critical revolution, in challenging the common assumption of all three of these theologies, represented a more radical revolution than a change from one to another of the three. Since the Bible was the primary source for theology, changing the status of the Bible and the way that it was investigated would radically change theology as a whole.

Moreover, the disciplinary matrix of a theological community includes a network of many different kinds of assumptions and values. We have summaries of theological truths in confessions and doctrinal statements. We have assumptions about the source of theological authority, whether authority is ascribed to the Bible, to experience, to doctrinal standards, to church tradition, or to some combination of these. We have assumptions

---

[2]Ibid., p. 208.

about the methods to be used in interpreting the Bible, the relation of human authors to God, the relation of the Old and New Testaments, and so on. We have standards for the kinds of argumentative procedures to be used, such as the *Sic et Non* of Abelard, the syllogisms of Aristotle, or the logic of Petrus Ramus. We have assumptions about the responsibility of biblical interpreters to the church. We have assumptions about human nature and its ability to penetrate theological truth.

Conceivably, a mini-revolution in biblical interpretation might touch one of these areas more than the others. Thus we might distinguish between hermeneutical revolutions, doctrinal revolutions, and revolutions in authority. But since many revolutions in practice have touched to some degree on several of these areas at once, any classification is likely to be artificial.

It might be more fruitful to think of the size of the community that is revolutionized by a particular change. Today we can distinguish, at least in a rough and ready way, the subcommunities of Old Testament scholars, New Testament scholars, systematic theologians, church historians, homileticians, specialists in Christian education, specialists in counseling, missiologists, and the church at large. A change that was revolutionary within a given field might cause minor changes, but not revolution, in sister fields. Kuhn notes that the same is true in natural science.[3] Finally, we must remember that the change of a single individual from one disciplinary matrix to another is a kind of revolution for that person. For example, a Calvinist might become an Arminian, or an adherent of orthodox theology might turn to the historical-critical method. Kuhn calls this kind of personal revolution a conversion.[4] Obviously this type of conversion does have some epistemological similarity to religious conversion in the ordinary sense. But for the sake of clarity I will call this type of personal revolution an alternation.[5]

A religious conversion to Christianity is the most radical possible change. Such conversion affects one's whole worldview. Even from a sociological or anthropological point of view, the change is more radical than changes of theology within the Christian faith. Moreover, we must say that the change is not merely intellectual, or even primarily intellectual. It involves a new set of beliefs, but it also involves a new life. Theologically speaking, we are dealing here with the religious root of human existence. Is a person for God or against Him? Is a person reconciled to God or still alienated? This question points to roots deeper even than a change of worldview, since changes of worldview can take place in a conversion from one non-Christian religion to another, or a transition (by either a non-Christian or a Christian) from tribal to modern Western culture.

The next most radical change is a change in worldview. By *worldview* I mean the network of assumptions, values, customs, and ways of coping with the world that are common to one's culture or subculture, held largely unconsciously. The final qualification here is important, for a worldview is not simply a self-consciously adopted philosophy or theory of the world. It is what one assumes without realizing that one is even assuming it. A change from the supernatural worldview of medieval society or the worldview of a tribal society to the naturalistic, mechanistic worldview of the modern West is such

---

[3]Ibid., p. 181.
[4]Ibid., p. 204.
[5]The term is from Peter L. Berger and Thomas Luckmann, *The Social Construction of Reality: A Treatise in the Society of Knowledge* (New York: Doubleday, 1967), pp. 157–61.

a change. It involves changes in self-consciously held beliefs, to be sure. But it involves changes also in things that one thought were impossible to change.

Less radical than changes in worldview are changes of theological systems. Changes in theology from Roman Catholic to Protestant or from Arminian to Calvinist are examples. Such changes represent revolutions for a systematic theologian. For specialists in exegesis, changes in one's view of the historical setting or one's view of the author's genre and purpose would often have a sweeping effect analogous to a systematic theologian's change of dogmatic system. Changes in hermeneutical method might result in revolutions in either systematic theology or exegesis or both. In my opinion, exegesis and systematic theology belong together, in one large-scale project of understanding the Bible better. But in current scholarly practice, the two disciplines have their own distinctive subcultures, so that an analysis of patterns of development and revolution must to some extent treat the disciplines separately.

After changes in theological systems come changes in views on individual points—for example, changes in points of doctrine if one is a systematic theologian, or changes in interpretations of individual texts if one is an exegete. Many of these changes will not seem revolutionary. But many do still involve a kind of change of perspective, in which all the parts get rearranged and are seen in a new way. For instance, consider someone who changes from interpreting the subject of Romans 7:14–25 as a regenerate person to interpreting it as someone who is unregenerate. Such a change involves a simultaneous alternation in one's understanding of nearly all the verses, of the verses' relations to one another, and of the relation of the passage to neighboring passages.

A similar kind of classification has already been suggested in the philosophy of science. After the appearance of the first edition of Kuhn's *Structure of Scientific Revolutions*, Margaret Masterman endeavored to clarify Kuhn's multiple uses of the word *paradigm*.[6] Masterman distinguishes not less than twenty-one different senses. They all refer to clusters of beliefs of one kind or another, but she observes that they fall into three main categories.

In the first, broadest category are "metaphysical paradigms." These are the unquestioned presuppositions about the nature of the world. They are analogous to what we have called worldviews. A second, narrower category consists in "sociological paradigms," roughly what Kuhn later called disciplinary matrices. These are the specific assumptions and values in the background of a specific discipline. They are analogous to theological systems in systematic theology or hermeneutical systems in exegetical disciplines.

Third, there are "artifact" or "construct" paradigms, what Kuhn later calls exemplars. These are the specific scientific achievements, embodied in crucial theoretical advances and crucial experimental results supporting the theories. This third category is in some ways the most important for Kuhn, and it is also the one that tends to distinguish science from other academic disciplines. Exemplars that have been accepted as models by an entire community of scientists have a key role in the puzzle-solving process that characterizes normal science.

---

[6]Margaret Masterman, "The Nature of a Paradigm," in *Criticism and the Growth of Knowledge,* ed. Imre Lakatos and Alan Musgrave (Cambridge: Cambridge University Press, 1970), pp. 59–90. See also the reflections in Douglas Lee Eckberg and Lester Hill, Jr., "The Paradigm Concept and Sociology: A Critical Review," in *Paradigms and Revolutions: Appraisals and Applications of Thomas Kuhn's Philosophy of Science,* ed. Gary Gutting (Notre Dame: University of Notre Dame Press, 1980), pp. 117–36.

Biblical interpretation has no exact analogy. Standard theological answers in specific areas of doctrine (such as the ancient creeds provided) and standard exegetical answers on specific texts are similar to exemplars in at least some ways. They are results to which people often refer back. However, they do not usually serve as a model for future research. The creedal formulations with respect to the doctrine of God have for the most part functioned as decisive formulations of a given point of doctrine, not as models of how theology is to be done in other areas. Each area of doctrine needs its own solution, and it is not clear how the solution in one area could serve as a model.

In a very few cases, however, one may find examples that come closer to being exemplars in a Kuhnian sense. Within the historical-critical method, the classic four-document hypothesis about the sources of the Pentateuch became something of an exemplar for how source criticism ought to be done on any book of the Bible. Scholarly work on the Pentateuch was expected to make advances by solving puzzles about particular texts on the basis of the overall framework provided by the four-document hypothesis. The work of Evangelicals was virtually excluded from this scholarly community of historical-critical scholarship in the Old Testament because Evangelicals would not work on the basis of this paradigm. Within the twentieth century, of course, we have seen the paradigm begin to break up under the weight of anomalies.

KNOWLEDGE AS CONTEXTUALLY COLORED

Do all the types of changes considered above really have anything special about them? Why not just talk about changes in people and in their views? Kuhn would not have had anything original to say if he claimed only that science changes with time and that the views of scientists change. What makes Kuhn so interesting, and potentially fruitful, is his claim that knowledge does not always change by piecemeal additions and subtractions. Human knowledge is not to be viewed as so many bits, added to the total sum of knowledge like so many marbles to a pile. Rather, what we know is colored by the framework in which we have our knowledge. This framework includes assumptions, values, procedures, standards, and so on, in the particular field of knowledge.[7]

Even what we see, or what seem to be the most elementary steps in knowledge or data that provide a basis for knowledge, are things seen and already to an extent organized in a way conditioned by our education, background, and experience. Kuhn discusses at some length a psychological experiment with anomalously marked playing cards (e.g., a black seven of hearts or a red three of spades).[8] When allowed to look at a card only for a short time, subjects saw what they thought were normal cards. When longer exposures were used, subjects often became emotionally upset or uneasy without becoming aware of the actual source of their unease. Another experiment with special glasses that inverted the visual field showed that, after a time of adjustment, subjects saw the world normally once again (even though their retinal images were the reverse of normal). Such experiments suggest a much more general principle, already anticipated in Gestalt psychology: understanding a part is

[7]Kuhn is aware of the potentially radical character of his viewpoint; he speaks of anomalies within the "epistemological viewpoint that has most often guided Western philosophy for three centuries" (Kuhn, *Structure of Scientific Revolutions*, p. 126).
[8]Ibid., pp. 62–64.

influenced by understanding the whole. The influence may be subtle or radical. Knowledge is contextually conditioned.

This contextual conditioning easily explains why it is so notoriously difficult to argue someone into an alternation of the type considered in the previous section. For instance, as is well known, arguments aiming at religious conversion often do not succeed. Failures occur not merely because potential converts have deep emotional investments in religious views that they already hold but because they have difficulty integrating any particular argument offered them into their own full-fledged framework of knowledge, assumptions, standards, values, and the like. Judged by *their* standards, or by what they suppose that they know, the argument does not seem plausible.

For instance, to the modern materialist, as to the ancient Greek, claims about a resurrection from the dead are ludicrous (Acts 17:32). To the pantheist or animist, claims that the natural world reveals its Creator are missing the point. I do not say that no communication is possible, only that substantive communication takes discipline and patience.[9] One must make explicit the hidden assumptions behind the rejection of the Christian message.

Similarly, arguments between Arminians and Calvinists may easily become ineffective. To someone with an Arminian framework, the Calvinist claim that God decrees all things sounds like fatalism. Passages that appear to teach or imply God's decretal control must be interpreted otherwise, in view of the clear passages about human choice and responsibility on which Arminianism feels itself to be solidly based. Conversely, Arminian appeals to the passages on human responsibility do not move the Calvinist. Since clear passages on divine sovereignty have confirmed the Calvinist position, the passages on human responsibility must be understood as speaking of such responsibility within the framework of divine control. If we cannot resolve the relation of the two in our own mind, it does not mean that such a resolution is impossible for God.

As theological debaters have found out, appeal to a proof text does not always persuade the opponent. From the advocate's point of view, the implications of the proof text seem to be clear. But the opposing position, *as an entire framework for analysis and synthesis,* provides standard resources for handling problem texts.

SEEING PATTERNS

We can illustrate some influences of contextual knowledge even at the level of interpreting an individual text. Let us return again to Romans 7:14–25. Historically, a large part of the debate has centered on two alternatives, the regenerate interpretation and the unregenerate interpretation. Behind this debate lurked an assumption commonly made by both sides, namely, that these two interpretations are the only alternatives. Such an assumption seems natural. Every person is either regenerate or not; hence, the passage must be speaking about one or the other. This assumption, then, functioned as part of the disciplinary matrix for reflection on the meaning of Romans 7:14–25. It was part of the context of knowledge informing the discussion of any details of the passage. Hence to establish one's own alternative, one had only to refute the other alternatives. One can see this pattern in commentaries up to this day. John Murray, for

[9]See analogous remarks in ibid., pp. 200–204.

example, lists five main points in favor of the regenerate interpretation.[10] Four out of the five points include a remark to the effect that a given aspect of Romans 7:14–15 is impossible for an unregenerate person. These four points in effect presuppose the assumption that, if Romans 7:14–25 is inconsistent with an unregenerate person, it must be dealing with one who is regenerate.

Consider now the effect of introducing the second-blessing interpretation. This interpretation introduces a third option, and suddenly it is no longer so easy to establish one's own alternative. The alternatives that appeared to cover the field now no longer do. To say that a regenerate person is in view in Romans 7:14–25 is no longer enough. Murray, in fact, notes the existence of a third alternative, but then does not address the possibility that it may be correct.[11] Technically, the third alternative agrees with Murray that the passage considers one who is regenerate. But instead of being the regenerate person in general, it is more specifically a regenerate person who has lapsed from an ideal that is possible in this life. Hence, an argument that beforehand appeared to establish a solid case now reveals some crucial holes.

We can make the situation still more complicated by introducing still another view. According to D. Martin Lloyd-Jones, the person of Romans 7:14–25 is "neither unregenerate nor regenerate."[12] Lloyd-Jones's claim sounds contradictory, but what he actually has in view is perfectly sensible. He refers to "awakened sinners," people who, under the influence of preaching, Bible reading, or other forms of contact with the Christian faith, have come to realize that they are guilty before a holy God. But these people have not yet understood the work of Christ and have not come to an assurance of forgiveness and death to sin. In theory, of course, such people would still be either regenerate or unregenerate in an absolute sense. But when we meet such people, we may not be able to tell which is the case. Moreover, such people do not match what we know of the typical unregenerate or the typical regenerate person.

Now suppose that one returns to Murray's commentary after hearing Lloyd-Jones's position. Murray's arguments, which before appeared solid, now seem dubious. Murray's interpretation may still be right in the end. But his whole argument is going to have to be rethought, because it apparently does not anticipate the possibility of Lloyd-Jones's interpretation. Murray's argument in effect assumes that Romans 7:14–25 cannot be describing personal characteristics intermediate between typical regenerate and typical unregenerate cases.

The alternative interpretations produced by second-blessing theology and by Lloyd-Jones are interesting because of the way in which they break up a previously established pattern of looking at the passage. People using this old pattern could not see that any other alternative was possible.

The second-blessing alternative presents, in a sense, a relatively mild challenge to the pattern. It says, "There indeed are regenerate and unregenerate people. The person spoken of in Romans 7:14–25 must be one or the other. But there may be further subdivisions within these basic types." The arguments will then no longer proceed the same way in detail. A tension between Romans 7:14–25 and Romans 8, for example, has more

[10]John Murray, *The Epistle to the Romans* (Grand Rapids: Eerdmans, 1959), 1:257–59.
[11]Ibid., 1:257 n. 19.
[12]D. Martin Lloyd-Jones, *Romans* (Grand Rapids: Zondervan, 1973), 4:256.

than one solution if the former may be describing one type of regenerate person, and Romans 8, another type.

Lloyd-Jones's approach is more radical, because it partly denies the relevance of the regenerate/unregenerate contrast itself. According to Lloyd-Jones, Paul is not asking himself whether the person in question is regenerate or unregenerate. Paul is describing a psychological and spiritual state that cuts across the old categories. Its symptoms are intermediate between the symptoms usually characterizing regenerate people and those characterizing unregenerate people. Lloyd-Jones, one might say, is asking us to focus on a different question altogether. We should not ask, "Are they regenerate or unregenerate?" but, "What spiritual symptoms do they show in response to the law?" Lloyd-Jones has changed the debate by focusing on a cluster of spiritual symptoms rather than on the root of the process, namely whether or not the Holy Spirit has worked regeneration.

For a theologian, it seems so natural to go to the root of the matter immediately and ask about regeneration. Regeneration is the theologically important watershed, and so surely it must be the right question to ask here. To construe theological texts against the background of regeneration is, or was, part of the disciplinary matrix of doing theology.

But Lloyd-Jones did not take this step. Why not? One might wonder whether Lloyd-Jones discovered an alternative partly because of his previous experience in medicine. In medicine, the distinction between symptom and cause is common. Did Lloyd-Jones, then, find it natural to apply this distinction in a new field?[13] Kuhn points out that people coming from another discipline are more likely to make innovative steps.[14] They are not fully assimilated to the reigning disciplinary matrix.

Despite Lloyd-Jones's paradoxical language ("neither unregenerate nor regenerate"), his distinction is not really a third category alongside regenerate and unregenerate. Rather, it superimposes another plane of discussion, the plane of spiritual symptoms in response to the law. This tack subtly alters the entire nature of the discussion and the use of Romans 7. Romans is not first of all a theological treatise or a classification; it is a kind of handbook for pastoral care.

People usually do not realize that this kind of shift of viewpoint is possible until they are shown. The whole history of interpretation may miss an important alternative interpretation simply because it includes a framework of assumptions in which some questions are asked (regenerate or unregenerate) and others are not (which symptoms does the spiritual patient show?).

The experience of interpreters of Romans 7 is indeed reminiscent of the psychological experiments with human vision to which Kuhn refers. To some extent, people see what their past experience has trained them to expect to see. The subjects in the psychological experiments, having been trained by experience to see red hearts and black spades, typically do not notice that a different category, a red spade, is before their eyes. They may even become emotionally upset over seeing a red spade. Similarly, interpreters of Romans 7 think only of the categories of regenerate and unregenerate even when other categories are possible in principle. And possibly, like the subjects in the psychological experiments, they become emotionally upset over the controversies that ensue in interpretation.

---

[13]Lloyd-Jones's book, *Spiritual Depression: Its Causes and Cure* (Grand Rapids: Eerdmans, 1966), shows signs of the author's medical background.

[14]Kuhn, *Structure of Scientific Revolutions,* p. 90.

Some puzzles and riddles also offer suggestive analogies. In one riddle, people are told that Jim's father died in a car accident in which Jim was seriously injured. When Jim arrived at the hospital, the surgeon looked at him and said, "I cannot operate on him, because he is my son." People do not solve the riddle until they question the underlying assumption, based perhaps on generalization from their past experience, that the surgeon is a man, not a woman.

In another puzzle, a gardener is given the assignment of planting four trees so that each tree is equidistant from each of the other three trees.[15] People do not solve the problem unless they question the assumption that the trees are planted on level ground. The problem can be solved by planting three trees on level ground at the vertices of an equilateral triangle and the fourth tree on a hill in the middle of the triangle.

As a final example, try to connect all nine dots of figure 2 by placing a pencil on one dot, and then drawing four straight lines without once raising the pencil from the paper. People solve the puzzle only when they question the natural (but unjustified) assumption that the line segments are not allowed to extend beyond the outermost dots.

Figure 2. Drawing Puzzle

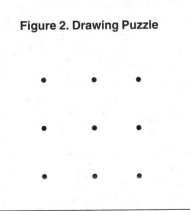

In general, we may not see a possible solution to a riddle or a puzzle until we abandon a way of thinking that has become a rut. Likewise, in Bible study we may not see a possible interpretive alternative until we abandon familiar ways of thinking.

We are still not through with Romans 7:14–25. Herman Ridderbos advocates still a fifth approach to interpreting the passage.[16] According to Ridderbos, the basic contrast here is not regenerate versus unregenerate, neither is it a contrast of symptoms of spiritual patients (for example, unawakened vs. awakened vs. at-home-with-Christ). It is the contrast of two ages, pre-Pentecost and post-Pentecost. Prior to the resurrection of Christ and the sending of the Holy Spirit in Pentecostal power and presence, the people of God

---

[15]This and the following example are taken from Edward de Bono, *Lateral Thinking: Creativity Step by Step* (New York: Harper & Row, 1970), pp. 94–95.

[16]Herman Ridderbos, *Aan de Romeinen* (Kampen: Kok, 1959).

were bound under the law of Moses. Now they are "released from the law so that [they] serve in the new way of the Spirit, and not in the old way of the written code" (Rom. 7:6).

Paul is not talking here merely about the general fact that God in his holiness passes judgment against everyone who sins, and that in this sense they are under his standards (or "law"). The law is concretely a "written code" (*grammatos,* Rom. 7:6)—the law of Moses. It is the law in its full particularity, including food laws and ceremonial sacrifices. Historically only the Jews, as God's people in special covenant with Him, were under its provisions. And now those who have died with Christ have been released.

Ridderbos introduces another dimension to reading Romans 7. All of the previous interpretations shared a common assumption: that Paul was making statements about the common condition of all people, irrespective of the historical circumstances. All were sinners, all fell short of the glory of God, all were condemned by God's righteous standards, all who were saved were saved by faith in Christ, all were justified by faith and so freed from the curse of God's condemnation, and so on. The preceding set of assumptions is nothing less than the common disciplinary framework of assumptions about Paul, Romans, and the New Testament.

Ridderbos does not disagree with any of the doctrines of this theology as such. But he maintains that here Paul was focusing not just on the biography of individuals standing before God but on the history of the race and of the Jews as the people of God uniquely set apart from all other peoples. Paul was writing about *historia redemptionis* (history of redemption), not simply or primarily about *ordo salutis* (steps in the salvation of an individual).[17]

The categories that Ridderbos uses cut across the conventional categories unregenerate and regenerate. Ridderbos is saying that Paul focuses not on the spiritual state of the individual in abstract terms (unregenerate vs. regenerate), nor on the symptoms of response to the law (unawakened vs. awakened), but on the systematic differences in life created by the objective transition between two orders of existence (under the law of Moses vs. under the realm of union with the resurrected Christ).

It is interesting that people within the same doctrinal tradition can advocate different interpretations of this chapter. Calvin, Lloyd-Jones, and Ridderbos, all adherents of Reformed theology, advocate respectively the regenerate interpretation, the awakened-sinner interpretation, and the pre-Pentecost interpretation of Romans 7:14–25. The differences between them must accordingly be viewed not as differences between systems of theology but as differences affecting only the interpretation of a single passage.

But we should note that the differences are capable of becoming differences of theological style of an extensive kind. Followers of Calvin have traditionally made it a point to read many other passages with the regenerate/unregenerate distinction in mind. Followers of Lloyd-Jones might also read many other passages in terms of the questions of spiritual symptoms. Followers of Ridderbos might make it a policy to read many other passages in terms of the transition of ages between the Old Testament and the New Testament. In fact, Ridderbos participates in the redemptive-historical tradition within New Testament biblical theology that has adopted precisely this emphasis. This tradition claims consistently to arrive at more accurate interpretations of texts within the redemptive-historical framework.

---

[17]See also the discussion in Douglas J. Moo, "Israel and Paul in Romans 7:7–12," *New Testament Studies* 32 (1986): 122–35.

The transition to this framework from a preceding framework of reading passages in terms of justification and *ordo salutis* might possibly be analyzed in terms of the categories of revolution.

WHY LIMITED VISION DOES NOT IMPLY RELATIVISM

Some readers may ask whether my analysis above leads to relativism. Does it mean that a text such as Romans 7:14–25 has no fixed meaning but that the meaning depends on the framework (disciplinary matrix) that one uses to look at the text? Does it mean that systems of theology (e.g., Roman Catholicism, Calvinism, or Arminianism) are neither right nor wrong, but all are right depending on the disciplinary matrix one uses in systematic theology? Similar questions were addressed to Kuhn in the wake of his book on revolutions in science.[18]

Kuhn's answer is complex. He is not a nihilist or a relativist in the sense of believing that the choice between systems is irrational. Theists, however, are bound to be dissatisfied with Kuhn's answer, because they do not believe that human beings are the only standard for truth. The proper standard for truth is not found in human beings corporately or individually but in God who is the source of all truth.[19]

Accordingly one must say that there is a right and wrong in the interpretation of Romans 7, and a right and wrong in a theological system. However, it is not necessarily easy for human beings to arrive at what is right. Larger frameworks or disciplinary matrices have an influence. In part, the influence is a good one. An effective, fruitful disciplinary matrix regularly steers researchers toward fruitful ways of looking at a passage and fruitful ways of analyzing and solving theological difficulties. But any disciplinary matrix, by suggesting solutions primarily in one direction, can make people almost blind to the possibility of solutions in another direction. Such, surely, is one of the lessons to draw from the history of interpretation of Romans 7.

---

[18]Kuhn, *Structure of Scientific Revolutions,* pp. 205–7.
[19]On this question, see further my discussion in Vern S. Poythress, *Symphonic Theology: The Validity of Multiple Perspectives in Theology* (Grand Rapids: Zondervan, 1987).

seven

MODELS
IN SCIENCE
AND IN BIBLICAL
INTERPRETATION

We need now to look at one major factor in the disciplinary matrices of natural sciences, namely, the use of models. It is important to consider models because of their influence on what investigators see or fail to see. Models are detailed analogies between one subject and another. The subject needing explanation or visualization is called the "principal" subject, while the one used to do the explaining is called the "subsidiary" subject.[1] In the billiard-ball model of a gas, for example, a gas is represented as a large number of billiard balls moving in all directions through an enclosed space. The gas itself is the principal subject, while the moving billiard balls are the subsidiary subject.

As a second example, consider Newton's theory of gravitation. Newton's equation $F = GmM/r^2$, along with Newton's laws linking force and motion, is a mathematical model for motion in a gravitational field. The mathematical equations are the subsidiary subject, while the moving physical objects are the principal subject.

Models can be of many kinds, depending on the type of subsidiary subject chosen and the relations between the subsidiary subject and the principal subject. Thus we may speak of mathematical models, mechanical models, electrical models, scale models, and so on.

---

[1]The terminology is taken from Max Black, *Models and Metaphors: Studies in Language and Philosophy* (Ithaca: Cornell University Press, 1962), p. 44. Black's book forms one of the principal backgrounds for our discussion.

INFLUENCE OF MODELS IN SCIENCE

In science, models play the role of illustrating theories already considered established. A scale model of the solar system makes the astronomical theory of the solar system clearer to the neophyte. More important, models play an important role in the discovery and improvement of new scientific theories. The billiard-ball model of a gas was crucial to the development of the kinetic theory of gases and its predictions about gas pressure, temperature, and the like. Similarly, James Clerk Maxwell developed his theory of electricity and magnetism by creative use of analogy between electricity (principal subject) and an ideal incompressible fluid (subsidiary subject). Today physicists would be likely to say that Maxwell's equations are the real model (a mathematical model) and that we can dispense with the fluid. But in Maxwell's own day people were still thinking in terms of an ether that was a real physical object and that might have properties analogous to a fluid.[2]

A properly chosen analogy thus suggests questions to be asked, lines of research, or possible general laws. Mathematical equations known to hold for the subsidiary subject can be carried over to the principal subject, albeit sometimes with slight modifications. The analogy needs to be used flexibly, because the principal subject is usually not analogous to the subsidiary subject in all respects.[3]

Everyone agrees that models have a decisive role in *discovery*. But what happens after the theory is drawn up? Philosophy of science in the positivist tradition would like to say that models are dispensable when it comes to assessing the justification of theories and their truth content. Others, Max Black included, think that some models are an integral, indissoluble part of the finished theory.[4] Even a mathematical model consists not merely in a mathematical formula but also in rules of thumb for relating the mathematics to the phenomena. These rules of thumb cannot be completely formalized without losing some of the potential of the model to suggest extensions to other phenomena. Thomas Kuhn does not address directly this question about models in *The Structure of Scientific Revolutions*. But from what he says about the role of exemplars and disciplinary matrices in directing further lines of research, one can infer that he agrees with Black about the indispensability of models.

Is biblical interpretation analogous to science in its use of models? To be sure, some models are to be found within the Bible itself. Adam, for example, is a model for Christ with respect to his role in representing humanity (Rom. 5:12–21). But analogies in biblical interpretation seldom have the detailed, quantitative character of mathematical models or physical models in science. Perhaps we had better talk about analogies rather than models.[5]

Now let us ask whether models (analogies) are dispensable in biblical interpretation. Even if we granted that in theory they were dispensable in natural science, it would be dif-

---

[2]Ibid., pp. 226–28.

[3]See Maxwell's discussion, quoted in ibid., p. 226.

[4]See ibid., pp. 219–43.

[5]For a further exploration of the use of models, analogies, and metaphors, see Ian Barbour, *Myths, Models, and Paradigms: A Comparative Study in Science and Religion* (New York: Harper & Row, 1974); and Sallie McFague TeSelle, *Speaking in Parables: A Study in Metaphor and Theology* (Philadelphia: Fortress, 1975). Barbour and TeSelle presuppose a non-evangelical view of biblical authority. Evangelicals will find in their works a combination of stimulating insights and the effort to displace biblical teaching by analogically projecting biblical language into the framework of modern culture.

ficult to present an analogous argument for biblical interpretation. The less-than-exact character of models in biblical interpretation means that they are most often not dispensable.

As an example, take again Romans 5:12–21. Can we eliminate the comparison with Adam and still retain the theological substance of the passage? We could, to be sure, paraphrase a good deal of the main points in order to eliminate specific reference to Adam. But even if we studied such a paraphrase for a long time, we would miss something. Romans 5:12–21 has a suggestiveness about it that is characteristic of metaphor.[6] It invites us to think of many ways in which Adam and Christ are analogous (and dissimilar). Once we eliminate completely any reference to Adam, we thereby eliminate the possibility of exploring just how far these analogies extend.

ANALOGY IN ROMANS 7

Do analogies really make a difference in interpretive controversies? Sometimes, at least, they do. Ridderbos, for example, argues that Romans 7 has in view primarily the contrast between two ages, before and after the resurrection of Christ and the day of Pentecost. Romans 7:14–25, we might say, is analogous to the statements elsewhere in Scripture about the resurrection of Christ, the coming of the kingdom of God, and the fulfillment of the ages. The model that Ridderbos assumes is the model of two ages and a redemptive transition between them. By contrast, the model that the regenerate and the unregenerate interpretations assume is the model of the individual soul and its life. Using such a model, Romans 7:14–25 is viewed as analogous to the statements about individual experiences of being saved.

These two models are not tight-knit and mathematically describable structures like models in natural science. They are more like generalizations or clusters of patterns derived from a loose collection of biblical texts. Ridderbos shows us common patterns linking much of what Paul (and other New Testament writers) say about the death of Christ, the resurrection of Christ, the coming of the Spirit, the reconciliation of Jews and Gentiles, and events representing a global transition of redemptive epochs. Against this background he invites us to see Romans 7:14–25 as an embodiment of the pattern. Likewise the regenerate interpretation collects verses describing the situation of individuals who are Christian and who are not Christian and invites us to see the same passage as embodying a pattern corresponding to the passages that describe Christians.

Both of these models do not so much exploit a particular analogy (say, with the resurrection of Christ or with the conversion of Cornelius) as they use generalized patterns. They are less like a metaphor than like a generalization. Moreover, to a large extent these models describe what we may bring to any text whatsoever when we study it.

But we may also ask whether a particular text introduces its own analogies. For example, Romans 7:2–4 clearly invokes an analogy using marriage as the subsidiary subject, in order to elucidate a principal subject, namely, our responsibilities toward the law and toward Christ. What analogies, then, are operative in verses 7–25? It is difficult to decide whether there is any dominant analogy. But when interpreters come to the passage, they may have an analogical framework in which they understand biblical descriptions of

---

[6]See Black, *Models and Metaphors*, pp. 38–47.

sin. In the Bible as a whole there are a number of basic analogies or metaphors for explaining, illustrating, and driving home to readers the power of sin.

First, sin is viewed as a sickness. Using this analogy, one can emphasize the power of sin by arguing that this sickness has infected every part of the body (e.g., Isa. 1:5–6; James 3:8). Second, sin is like darkness. One can stress sin's power by pointing out that every part of people is dark (e.g., Eph. 4:18; Luke 11:33–36). Third, sin is like fire. One points out the power of sin by affirming that it is unstoppable (James 3:6). Finally, sin is like the relationship of a master to a slave. In this analogy, one points out the power of sin by showing that, however the slave may struggle to become free, the master will subdue him. Romans 6 uses this analogy in describing the situation before having died with Christ.

Which analogies are operating in Romans 7:14–25? If we have the analogy with sickness or darkness, we expect to find affirmations about the pervasiveness of sickness or darkness in the unregenerate. What is actually said in the passage appears to be inconsistent with such a pervasive sickness. Hence the regenerate interpretation appears to be more attractive. On the other hand, if the analogy is with master and slave (as it appears to be in v. 14), the struggles of the enslaved person to become free may have been introduced to make the point about sin's power more effectively. Hence the mention of the struggles of the "mind" in verse 23 might still be compatible with the unregenerate interpretation. When we use this perspective the unregenerate interpretation appears more attractive, inasmuch as similar points about sin's mastery over the unregenerate are made in Romans 6. One's preference for the regenerate or unregenerate interpretation (or still some other interpretation) may therefore be influenced by what one sees as the governing analogy here.

Perhaps, however, the problem is still deeper. Do we come to Scripture expecting to find a single, uniform theory of sin, accompanied by a single, fixed, precise vocabulary to designate the various states of sin and righteousness? If so, we are predisposed to see difficulties in harmonizing Romans 7:22–23 with statements elsewhere about unregenerate people. Hence the regenerate interpretation wins our allegiance.

Suppose, however, that we approach Scripture expecting to find a number of analogies making complementary points. Since each analogy is partial, the various analogies may sometimes superficially appear to be at odds with one another. For example, the analogy with slavery may appear to be at odds with the analogy of sickness. In the slavery analogy, the slave may attempt rebellion only to illustrate how inescapable is the master's dominion. But the slave's rebellious activity appears to contradict what the sickness analogy says about the pervasive penetration of the disease. We reconcile the two only by recognizing that each is a partial analogy about the nature of sin. Using this approach, we are then able to harmonize the unregenerate interpretation of Romans 7:22–23, which uses a slave analogy, with the texts elsewhere in Paul using the analogy of sickness or darkness.

We may extend our example in another direction. Our reading of Romans 7:14–25 depends on the kind of exposition of sin that we expect. Do we anticipate a colorful, imaginative, dramatic characterization? Then sin can be personified as the master, the individual as the slave, and the subsequent imaginary confrontation traced out. Or do we expect a careful, scientific exposition analyzing the ontological relations of the various human faculties, as these are touched by sin? In the latter case we are predisposed to find verses 22–23 consistent only with what is said of the regenerate mind, because words like *mind* and *flesh* must always designate the same fixed aspects of human beings. In the former case, we are predisposed to allow that these two verses might simply be making a different point by dramatization. Hence even if these verses referred to an unregenerate person, it would not contradict the point made elsewhere when the unregenerate are characterized as dead and unresponsive to God.

A ROLE FOR ANALOGY IN THEOLOGICAL CONTROVERSIES

What difference does it make that biblical interpretation employs analogies? First, some people could say that this leads to the conclusion that biblical interpretation and, with its resulting theology, is "mere" analogy, hence not really true to the facts, and that knowing objective truth is impossible.

But such a conclusion misunderstands the power of analogy. Analogies at their best • are aids to the truth rather than hindrances. Remember that sciences use analogies in the form of models, and the Bible itself uses analogies. We need to say that, when we read a passage of the Bible, the analogies or models that we have in mind influence what we see and influence our judgments about which competing interpretations are plausible. Becoming aware of some of the analogies that we are using and some of the alternatives that might be possible may help us to understand the Bible better.

For example, in interpreting Romans 7, is it better to be aware of the several alternative approaches? Knowing that there are several alternatives could wrongly make us think, "There is no right answer. Any answer is okay, because any answer can be achieved if we start with the right analogy."

But I would disagree. One answer is right. Of course, there can be overlapping partial answers, more than one of which could be right as far as it goes. But the major alternatives in interpreting Romans 7 are mutually exclusive, unless we claim that Paul was intentionally ambiguous (which is not plausible here). Hence one of the alternatives is right. But we can properly judge the relative claims of the alternatives only when we view each one of them in its strongest form and compare it with the others. As long as we are unaware of the possibility of using an alternate analogy (one that Paul himself may have had in mind in writing), we are not in as good a position to make an accurate judgment.

The same holds true when we consider theological doctrines or theological systems rather than individual passages of the Bible. Consider, for example, the doctrinal dispute between creationism and traducianism. Creationism says that God, by an immediate act, creates the soul of each new human being who comes into the world. On the other hand, according to traducianism, the soul of the child derives by providential processes from the soul of the parents.

Each of these two views appeals to various biblical passages. Each passage must be studied and weighed in its own right. We can never eliminate this step in theology. But we should also be aware that each view is made plausible partly by the use of a governing analogy. For traducianism, the key analogy is between generation of the soul and generation of the body. After the initial direct creation of Adam in Genesis 1–2, the propagation of the race takes place by providence. The bodies of children are formed providentially from substance deriving from their parents. The traducianist claims that the generation of the soul is analogous. In addition, a realist view of human nature sometimes enters into traducianism, and such realism rests on an analogy between human souls and parts of a whole. The souls are related to human nature as parts are to a whole.

For creationism, on the other hand, the principal analogy is between the generation of the soul and the creative acts of God in Genesis, which create new beings. Both of these acts of making new things contrast with the later providential acts of God, in which he sustains what he has already made.

Being aware of these analogies does not by itself tell us which of these two positions is right. (Or perhaps some combination of the two or a third alternative could be right.) But such awareness can alert us to some of the reasons why both positions are attractive and why both have had their advocates.

Next, consider classic dispensationalism and classic covenant theology as examples of theological systems. Each system gives an important role to a certain key concept. For covenant theology, that concept is the covenant of grace; for dispensationalism, it is the dispensations, that is, epochs marked by distinctive arrangements in God's government of human beings. Covenant theology naturally leads to a concentration on the salvific purposes of God. Such purposes are embodied in the covenant of grace and form a main strand to which other purposes of God are linked. Dispensationalism, on the other hand, has classically been interested in the purpose that the dispensations serve by showing success or failure of human beings under different governmental arrangements. Salvation of individuals runs alongside this purpose.

Dispensationalism and covenant theology are both complex systems. They cannot simply be reduced to some one analogy. And yet analogy has an important role. In covenant theology, the covenant of grace is understood as embodied in (and therefore analogous to) the concrete covenants mentioned in the Bible, which in turn are analogous to treaties or contracts made between human beings (except that God sovereignly lays down the conditions). In dispensationalism, the governing analogy in understanding dispensations is the analogy between God the great King and a human ruler who inaugurates a new form of government.

TYPES OF ANALOGIES

We have already uncovered a considerable diversity of analogies used in biblical interpretation, many of which occur in the Bible itself. Here we may distinguish six distinct uses of analogy.

First, a one-line comparison, a small-scale analogy, in the form of a simple metaphor or simile. For example, Psalm 23:5, "You prepare a table before me in the presence of my enemies," compares God's provision with that of a host.

Second, an extended analogy, constituting a controlling force in a whole passage. Most of the parables of Jesus (the parable of the lost sheep, the parable of the great banquet, the parable of the mustard seed, the parable of the wheat and the tares, and so on) use an analogy in this way. But analogies can also be used in direct exposition of theological truths. For example, analogies with dying and slavery control the extended discussion in Romans 6. The analogy between Adam and Christ controls Romans 5:12–21. Sometimes the use of an analogy may be more subtle than in these instances. For example, the interpretation of Romans 7:14–25 partly turns on the question of whether Paul is here using a sort of dramatic, theatrical analogy between sin and a human being, on the one hand, and two personal opponents striving with one another for mastery, on the other. Because Paul does not say, in so many words, "Now let us compare one thing to another," it is more difficult to assess what he is doing.

Third, an analogy used repeatedly in different passages in the Bible, so that it constitutes a biblical theme. For example, comparisons of God with a king or a father frequently form a biblical theme, as do comparisons between God's relations to human beings and agreements, or covenants, between human beings.

Fourth, an analogy used to help interpret a passage, even though it is not the governing analogy for the passage itself. For example, in discussing Romans 7, if we wanted to defend a dramatic understanding of what Paul is doing, we might appeal not only to an analogy with drama in general but also to an analogy with other passages of the Bible that present moral conflict in more dramatic terms: for example, the personifications of wisdom and folly in Proverbs 7–9. Neither drama in general nor Proverbs 7–9 in particular is a governing force in the actual structure of Romans 7. Both of these analogies, however, might make it easier for someone to see that Paul perhaps is speaking in a more dramatically colored, semipersonified way about sin in its relation to human beings.

Fifth, an analogy used in formulating a particular doctrine. For example, the analogy between generation of the soul and generation of the body is used by traducianism.

Sixth, an analogy used as a key element in a theological or hermeneutical system. For example, the covenant of grace, analogous to covenants between human beings, is a key element in classic covenant theology.

To a certain extent, these different types of analogies are related to the different types of disciplinary matrices that were discussed in chapter 6. Just as in science, so also in biblical interpretation, a disciplinary matrix within a given field is likely to make use of some controlling analogy. Some analogies function as master analogies and thus control a larger field. The idea of covenant, for example, analogous to human treaties or agreements, influences the whole system of covenant theology. Other analogies function as useful analogies only within the smaller area of a single doctrine or of the interpretation of a single text.

We should note, however, a certain uniqueness to the largest disciplinary matrix or context for biblical interpretation. As I argued in chapter 6, the deepest factor influencing biblical interpretation is the work of the Holy Spirit in regeneration. Without this work of the Spirit, a person cannot understand what the Spirit teaches in Scripture (1 Cor. 2:6–16). This work of the Spirit affects the heart and mind of people in the deepest and fullest way. We cannot fully describe the Spirit's work by saying, for instance, that regeneration is merely making available to a person in an intellectual way some new analogy. Doubtless the Holy Spirit enables the person involved to see the relevance of certain relations and analogies, not only analogies in the Bible itself, but relations between the biblical teaching and the person's own life and experience. But it would be false to say that the work of the Holy Spirit is exhausted in making clear any one analogy. Nor could we say that an unregenerate person would in principle be unable to use a particular analogy. The use of particular analogies is a salient characteristic of less comprehensive disciplinary matrices, but regeneration has a more comprehensive character.

eight

ANALOGIES

AS PERSPECTIVES

A t any one point in our study of the Bible, must we use only one analogy or one type of analogy? To answer this question, let us first look at the situation in natural sciences.

ANALOGIES AS COMPLEMENTARY

In science we are accustomed to seeing one model used as the key element in a particular theory. Other proposed models are discarded when one model gains dominance. For example, the Ptolemaic model, with the earth at the center of the solar system, was discarded after the Copernican model, with the sun at the center, gained dominance. If biblical interpretation is analogous to science at this point, we should expect that the currently favored interpretation would supersede all previous interpretations and would invoke one dominant model.

To some extent, the use of a single dominant model has indeed characterized some theological controversies. The historical-critical method, for example, used as its main analogy the example of historical investigation of secular history. The Bible had to be treated like any other book from the ancient past. This model virtually defined the historical-critical method and gradually gained dominance in academic circles. In these circles the older "dogmatic" methods of interpretation ceased to be practiced.

Consider further the controversy between traducianism and creationism. One of the issues at stake here is the dominance of an analogy. What is the best analogy for understanding the origin of individual souls—the analogy with the generation and growth of the bodies of children or the analogy with the original creation of new beings in Genesis

1? Once one decides which analogy is correct, the other analogy is seen to be invalid and is therefore discarded.

However, this second example gives us pause. On an issue like traducianism and creationism, it seems that the debate is difficult to decide, even when we have basic agreement on the authority of the Bible. Could it be that neither position is wholly right? Could more than one analogy sometimes apply (at least up to a point)? At the same time, perhaps no one analogy captures with superior clarity all the features of biblical teaching on the subject. The origin of human souls might be like an original creation in some respects and like the generation of human bodies in other respects. Then each side would be able to appeal to verses that appear to validate its position.

In many cases of interpretive controversy, only one position can be right. In understanding Romans 7, the two major interpretations, regenerate and unregenerate, cannot both be right. Perhaps one of the two is right; or perhaps neither is right, and some third position, like Lloyd-Jones's "awakened sinner" interpretation, is correct. In the interpretation of 1 Thessalonians 4:4, "one's own vessel" must mean either "one's own body" or "one's own wife," not both. Likewise, with respect to the historical-critical revolution, it was either right or wrong to practice historical reconstruction with antisupernaturalist assumptions built into the use of historical analogy.[1]

In other cases, however, the use of multiple analogies may be permissible. Certainly, the Bible itself uses multiple analogies in its teaching about the church. The church is the temple of God, the body of Christ, and the assembly of God's people (analogous to the assembly of Israelites at Mount Sinai or Mount Zion). These affirmations about the church are complementary rather than contradictory. Similarly, God is a king, a father, and a husband, three analogies expressing complementary truths.

Likewise, we might say that the four Gospels present us with complementary pictures of the earthly life of Christ. Of course, the Gospels do have much in common. The differences among them can easily be exaggerated. Yet, differences of a subtle kind do exist. Such differences are complex and difficult to summarize adequately. Some of the differences of emphasis among the Gospels can indeed be related to differences of perspective on the idea of messiahship. Matthew, for example, strongly emphasizes Christ's Davidic kingship. The Gospel of Matthew begins with a genealogy that includes a list of Davidic kings. John, on the other hand, emphasizes Christ's role as the Son of God. Christ as Son exists in close relation to the Father and reveals the Father in his work. Likewise Mark and Luke have some distinctive emphases.

Christ's messiahship and his work of redemption are so rich in significance that they might be viewed from many angles and in the light of many connections with Old Testament promises and institutions. No one of these approaches by itself would capture everything. Surely the idea of Christ as Davidic King (Matthew) and the idea of Christ as

---

[1]The choice between the historical-critical method and alternative methods is not always as clear-cut as it may seem. Acknowledgment of the supernatural can be used as a platform for denying God's involvement with the ordinary, or for presupposing that God could not use ordinary means in writing Scripture (such as Luke's research, alluded to in Luke 1:3), or as an excuse to ignore the human authors and circumstances that God has used in bringing the books of the Bible into being. The historical-critical method, in spite of its bad presuppositions, has sometimes been instrumental in causing reluctant supernaturalists to look at the Bible from angles other than those they would most comfortably adopt on their own initiative.

Son revealing the Father (John) are both true. But it would be unfortunate if we used only one of these approaches.

The two ways of explaining Christ and his work invite us to relate his life to two different sets of Old Testament texts. If we say that Christ is Davidic King, we link up our thinking right away with the history of Old Testament kingship, with its successes and failures and with the promises made to David, which never find a final fulfillment within the pages of the Old Testament. If we say that Christ is the Son of God, we make some contact with the texts that speak of Israel as son in a subordinate sense (e.g., Exod. 4:22–23; Deut. 8:5). Christ was obedient to God, whereas Israel failed. We also relate to the Old Testament theme of revelation, both in creation (John 1:1–5) and in redemption (vv. 14, 17).

Furthermore, the two ways of understanding Christ have different purposes apologetically. The emphasis on Davidic kingship corresponds to the interest of Jews in expecting a Davidic Messiah. The emphasis on revelation of the Father proclaims the universal relevance of Christ's work and answers questions about knowing God.

USING MULTIPLE ANALOGIES

We can now generalize this pattern of multiple analogies. In many areas of studying the Bible, it is illuminating and profitable to approach the same text or the same topic from a number of different perspectives, each of which will use a somewhat different analogy or controlling concept.[2] As our test case, let us use 1 Corinthians 3:10–17.

It might seem at first that, in studying this passage, we are confined to using the analogy between believers and a temple. After all, this analogy is the one that Paul himself uses! Anyone who neglects this analogy and substitutes another is just going to ignore or distort what the Bible is saying at this point. Certainly the use of multiple analogies must never overrun or obscure the fact that a single passage often uses a single dominant analogy.

But even in a passage with a clearly dominant analogy, something may be learned from using other analogies. By using other analogies, we obtain illumination, not so much about the passage in itself, but about the relation of the passage to larger concerns in the Bible.

For example, consider the analogy between God and a judge. When this alternate analogy is invoked in the Bible, it teaches at least some of the same things that 1 Corinthians 3:10–17 teaches in its analogy with a temple. For instance, Paul brings in the theme of judgment, particularly in verses 13–15. Consistent with the temple analogy, he speaks of a fire's coming to destroy everything in the building that is made out of poor material. This fire results in a kind of judgment on the building.

The analogy of a judge makes a similar point. God is the Judge, and we as human beings come before him to have our deeds evaluated. God rewards patience (James 5:7–11) and good labor (2 Cor. 5:10) and punishes evil.

So far, we see that the same things can be said using either analogy. But in addition, the analogy with judging helps to illuminate 1 Corinthians 3:13–15. If we just had verses 10–17 in isolation, we might wonder why there should be a fire at all. Why does it come? Does it have to come? Why should the whole building be encompassed (rather than some people's parts of the building escaping completely)? Observing fires and buildings on earth does not really help us answer these questions. On the other hand, the analogy

---

[2]For further discussion, see my book *Symphonic Theology*.

involving judges clears things up immediately. The fire is there to accomplish the negative judgment on what is inadequate.

Moreover, the analogy with judging also helps us with the question, What is the standard for success or failure? In 1 Corinthians 3:10–17, Paul says that those who build with gold, silver, and precious stones succeed, while those who build with wood, hay, and straw ultimately fail. But what sort of contrast is Paul making? What do gold, silver, and precious stones stand for? That is, what are they analogous to? The mere fact of analogy between temple and group of believers does not make it clear. Paul gives some of the answer in verse 11, where he indicates what the right foundation is. We might guess that the gold, silver, and precious stones represent any activity based on Christ's work. But then verse 12 seems to envision that one might build on this (correct) foundation, but still with the wrong materials. One might guess that using the wrong materials amounts to building in a way inconsistent doctrinally or practically with the foundation, namely, the core of Christianity, the doctrines of Christ. But how would this error differ from not building on the right foundation at all?

To some questions of this kind, Paul may not have given us full answers. The context of discussion about Apollos (1 Cor. 3:4–9) and Peter (1:12) does make it clear that Paul is concerned that teachers should build up unity and that those who follow them should guard that unity. But beyond these conclusions it is hard to be specific.

The analogy with judging can help here. If God is Judge, the standards for judgment will be God's standards. These standards include the concerns for church unity and consistency with the doctrine of Christ (and other things besides). These standards help us to draw out the broader implications of the picture offered in 1 Corinthians 3:10–17. It has a lesson about good workmanship in the church. The lesson certainly applies most immediately to the circumstances of disunity at Corinth. But it will also apply quite broadly to whatever work we do, as measured by all the standards of God's Word.

On the other hand, we must not claim that the analogy with judging is so good that it ought to replace the analogy with the temple. The analogy with a temple is very effective in certain respects. In particular, it shows that defective work in the context of the church receives a reward that is really fitting for it ("If you are foolish enough to build with inferior stuff, anybody can see that you will lose, because the inferior stuff will perish"). This point is less obvious if we use the analogy with judging. Human judges may or may not have good standards of judgment. There may or may not be a connection between the intrinsic quality of one's work and the reward that one gets from the judge. God, of course, is a just judge, so it is different with Him. But an analogy with the temple can help to demonstrate precisely that point.

Now let us use still another analogy, the one between the church and a human body with its members. This analogy is used overtly in 1 Corinthians 12 and Romans 12:4–5. But can we apply this analogy to 1 Corinthians 3:10–17?

Once again, we find a basic harmony. Using the analogy with the temple, 1 Corinthians 3:10–17 makes some of the same basic theological points as those that come out in 1 Corinthians 12 and Romans 12:4–5, which use the analogy with a human body. All three passages are concerned with Christian unity. First Corinthians 3:10–17 makes the point by stressing that all the building must take place on the one foundation. The other two passages make the point by showing that each person in the church has a need for the gifts and contributions of all the other people. Only by working together as many members can there be a healthy, well-functioning body.

But there are also some differences of focus between the passages. First Corinthians 3:10–17, by using an analogy with a fixed structure, helps us to focus on the significance of the once-for-all unity founded in the work of Jesus Christ. Everything that we do in the church must rest on that finished achievement. First Corinthians 12 and Romans 12, on the other hand, focus more on the practical, working, functional unity of the church. It is fitting for them to use the analogy with the human body, since the organs of the body show their unity by practically functioning together toward harmonious goals.

The analogy with the human body can now help to reveal something that otherwise might be mysterious or overlooked in 1 Corinthians 3:10–17. Paul wants the principles of unity and sound growth to be applied not only to the area of teaching content but also to the practical manner in which believers relate to one another (with jealousy, pride, or party spirit, or with humility and gentleness). We might make the mistake of interpreting the fixed, stony character of the pieces of the building in this passage to mean that only doctrinal issues or issues of individual morality were at stake. In view of the rest of 1 Corinthians, such a conclusion would be a mistake.

When we transform 1 Corinthians 3:10–17 into the alternative analogy with the body, we help to make the implications clear. For example, unity on one foundation corresponds to unity in being a member of the body—not just any body, but the body of Christ. Building on the foundation corresponds to functioning as a member of the body. The type of building material corresponds to the type of activity of the member, helpful or unhelpful to the health and goals of the body as a whole. At this point we find the strength of the analogy with the human body. When we use the analogy of the body, we make clear the dependence of each member on the others.

The testing of the building with fire corresponds to the testing on the basis of the history of healthfulness and helpfulness of each member of the body. Here the analogy with the body does not serve us as well as the analogy of judge or some other analogy.

What do we conclude from our analysis of 1 Corinthians 3:10–17? The principles of multiple analogies that we have applied here can be useful with many other texts. When a passage of the Bible is dominated by a single analogy, it is important to take this feature into account and not to pretend that all analogies are equal. But even in such a situation, some details of the passage, or more often aspects of the relation of the passage to its larger context, can be illuminated when we use alternate analogies. The alternate analogies may not be absolutely necessary, but they help to draw our attention to aspects of the passage that might otherwise be neglected.

The same lesson holds on a higher level. Consider the general issue of organizing a biblical theology of one or both Testaments. There has been considerable controversy over what is the best organizing theme or center when writing a theology of the Old Testament or of the New Testament. Biblical theology desires to have a center that will capture the inner structure of the biblical material itself, not simply organize the teaching of the Bible in terms of traditional topics (God, human beings, Christ, salvation, last things, etc.).

More than one center has been advocated for the Old Testament: the covenant, the kingdom of God, Israel's confession, and promise.[3] Similarly, for the New Testament there has been debate over two major centers: justification and redemptive history. Should the

---

[3]Gerhard F. Hasel, *Old Testament Theology: Basic Issues in the Current Debate*, rev. ed. (Grand Rapids: Eerdmans, 1972), pp. 77–103.

primary center be the nature of humanity as lost and saved, particularly the work of justification? Or should we have as a center the theme of redemptive history and the transition between epochs of redemption (two ages) achieved in the work of Christ, especially his resurrection?[4]

These issues are complex, and it would be impossible for us to analyze them in detail here. But our argument thus far suggests at least two implications. First, the kind of organizing center chosen does make a difference. It functions as an exemplar, an important element in the disciplinary framework for studying the Bible. To shift from one such center to another may involve a major, even a traumatic, change.

Second, no single organizing center is uniquely the right one. Gerhard F. Hasel, in his books surveying biblical theology of the two Testaments, suggests as much.[5] He wonders whether the Bible is so rich that no one center will succeed in capturing all its aspects equally. In our own framework, we might say that, even if one or more than one center could achieve such a result, there would still be need on a practical level for a variety of analogies and perspectives on the Bible. The Bible itself offers us a variety of analogies in various areas of doctrine. When we attempt to synthesize biblical teaching as a whole, we are bound to try to relate these analogies to one another. The best results would be achieved if these analogies could all illuminate one another. We would then notice aspects of biblical teaching that we might overlook using a single perspective, however correct it might be.

CAN AN ANALOGY REPRESENT TRUTH?

For many modern people, the word *analogy* or *metaphor* tends to suggest something unreal or untrue, a mere rhetorical trick. Hence it seems to depreciate the seriousness of biblical revelation when we say that the Bible uses many analogies and metaphors and that we should do so too.

However, we must not underestimate the power of metaphors to express truth. Well-chosen metaphors assert the existence of analogies that God has placed in the world, not merely analogies that we impose on an unformed or chaotic world. Thus metaphors assert truth about an analogical structure in the world, and by invoking such analogical structures, they also assert truth about their principal subject. For example, when Paul says, "You yourselves are God's temple" (1 Cor. 3:16), he implies that God himself has ordained that there would be revealing analogies between temples of stone and the structure of the New Testament community. Both are dwelling places of God, both are holy and involve penalties on those who defile them (v. 17), both have foundations that function to establish a unified plan for the whole, and both are constructed with good or bad workmanship, as the case may be. In implying these things, Paul thereby also implies some true assertions about the nature of his principal subject, the Corinthian church.

Similarly, much of the Bible's language about God Himself is metaphoric in character (so-called anthropomorphic language), but not less true for that reason. The Bible's use of metaphor is both true and useful and functions rightly when we freely recognize such use.

[4]Gerhard F. Hasel, *New Testament Theology: Basic Issues in the Current Debate* (Grand Rapids: Eerdmans, 1978), pp. 140–70; Herman Ridderbos, *Paul: An Outline of His Theology* (Grand Rapids: Eerdmans, 1975), pp. 13–43.
[5]Hasel, *New Testament Theology*, p. 164; idem, *Old Testament Theology*, p. 141.

In addition, when biblical metaphors touch on the deepest realities, they often surpass what we would casually expect from a superficial analogy. We can illustrate this principle from 1 Corinthians 3:16. A metaphor invokes an analogy between a principal subject (in this case, the church) and a subsidiary subject (temples). Here the temple is the known original thing, and the church is compared to it. Thus we might say that the temple is the original, while the church is only a copy analogous to this original.[6]

But what is a temple? A temple of stone is more than just an architectural object. It symbolically represents religious truth. It is a dwelling place for God (or in the pagan case, for a false god). In fact, temples in the ancient Near East were built somewhat like royal residences. In their architectural arrangements temples themselves exploit a further analogy between God (or gods) and human kings. Whether we look at the temple as a dwelling for God or a residence of a king, the fundamental religious ideas do not depend on there being a stone structure. Something else might serve as a temple as well, for instance, a human body.

In fact, the final temple of God is Christ's body (John 2:20–21). The tabernacle and the temple in the Old Testament were constructed according to God's plan to display beforehand some of the things that would be realized in full only when Christ came (Heb. 8–10). The design of the temple looked forward to Christ, though this fact was not perfectly understood until New Testament times.

It appears, then, that the Old Testament temple was built after analogy with the "real" temple, Christ's human body. Believers in Christ become human temples, not merely temples of stone. In this respect, they are better or more perfect temples than the Old Testament temple of stone and wood. Earlier, at a more superficial level, we said that the stone temple was the original and the church was the copy. Now at a deeper level we find that the church is closer to the original and the stone temple is the copy.

From these observations we may conclude that the church is indeed analogous to the Old Testament temple of stone. Such a statement expresses truth, not illusion. Moreover, the analogy is not an accident. In this case and in many others in the Bible, the analogy reveals a depth dimension that transcends merely superficial comparisons. We find here multiple relationships based on the profound unity of God's wisdom for creation and redemption. The symbolic structures and institutions of the Old Testament, which seem to be the starting point for forming analogies, are themselves always based on an original in heaven, in the plan of God.

Another example may help make this point clear. When the Bible says that God is king, it uses an analogy between God and human, earthly kings. We would be tempted to say, therefore, that the earthly kings are real kings, whereas God is king only in a secondary, analogical, metaphorical sense. But where do earthly kings come from? God created human beings with power to govern, and God providentially appoints some to be in positions of authority (Ps. 75:6–7; Dan. 2:21; Rom. 13:1–7). In such positions these

---

[6]In 1 Corinthians 3:10–17, did Paul have in mind a pagan temple or the Jewish temple as his model? Since his metaphor applies to either kind of temple, perhaps the question is unnecessary. If we are forced to decide, the Jewish temple is clearly more appropriate to verse 16. There was a vast difference between a pagan temple, which falsely claimed to be a dwelling place of a god, and the Jewish temple, which really was a dwelling place for the true God. Paul says that believers are a real temple for the real God, not a pseudotemple for a pseudogod.

people are representatives of God and God's authority. Hence human kingship and rule ultimately derive from the fact that God created human beings in his image and that he delegates his kingly power in a limited form to governmental authorities. The earthly kings are not the "real" ones but are kings only in a secondary sense by analogy with the real King, God himself. Rather than saying that God is described anthropomorphically, we might better say that human beings are described theomorphically, after analogy with God the Original.[7]

In sum, when we identify a biblical saying as an analogy or a metaphor, we should remember that, far from being rhetorical tricks, biblical analogies express profound truths.

FOUNDATIONS FOR MULTIPLICITY IN BIBLICAL INTERPRETATION

One disturbing aspect of using multiple themes or multiple analogies in studying the Bible is that this procedure does not agree with the practice in natural sciences. Once a scientific field has reached a certain stage of maturity, according to Kuhn, it will normally operate in terms of one dominant disciplinary framework. Included in this framework will normally be some specific theories using models. Only in times of revolution, when the existing framework does not seem to be solving problems satisfactorily, will there be some degree of multiplication of analogies or models, as people cast about for some better way of coping. Should biblical interpretation try to imitate science at this point and use only one dominant model or analogy?

There are at least three possible responses to this difficulty. First, we may say that, in biblical interpretation as well as science, the use of multiple analogies or perspectives to describe the same subject is an imperfection that ought to be overcome by the development and consistent use of a single more comprehensive model. Second, we may agree that using multiple perspectives is appropriate in biblical interpretation, but only because biblical interpretation is not really analogous to science. The third response is to say that even within science, it may be too rigid to require a single dominant model.

Let us examine each of these alternatives. First, should biblical interpretation strive ideally to use only a single dominant model? Scientific practice shows us that scientists usually pursue their goal using only a single dominant analogy or model. But this practice seems unduly rigid in biblical interpretation, particularly because the Bible itself sometimes authorizes multiple analogies. We have already seen that the doctrine of the church and the presentation of Christ's messiahship in the Gospels involve more than one dominant motif. We could not rigidly exclude the use of such analogies without implying a criticism of the Bible itself. That course is not acceptable to anyone who believes that the Bible is really the Word of God.

Second, we might argue that biblical interpretation and theology are not analogous to science. This position is, I think, closer to the point. But what kind of biblical interpretation are we talking about? Biblical interpretation of a very practical, down-to-earth kind is continually practiced in the church, by people with and without formal training. Though such interpretation is hardly scientific, as a human activity it does still have some distant relation to science. Some generalities apply pretty well to all activities of human

---

[7]In using this language, I am indebted to an unpublished comment by J. I. Packer.

groups and all activities that share human knowledge.[8] But the distant analogy between science and human activity in general does not permit us to impose scientific practice on all of life. Interpretation in a broad sense will continue to make use of the full range of analogies in the Bible and other analogies from modern life as well.

Are different conclusions warranted when we consider the study of the Bible in an intellectually rigorous way? Rigor in biblical interpretation will have greater similarities to the intellectual rigor demanded in scientific activity. But the subject matter of biblical interpretation is different from that of natural science. We are dealing with the Bible and with its teaching, hence with God, humanity, salvation, sin, and many other complex topics. By contrast, the physical aspects of the world are the natural focal topics within natural science. Even the physical aspects of the world are complex and marvelous enough. But a different order of complexity may emerge in the direct study of phenomena involving persons. If human phenomena are innately more complex, it may not be possible to capture them adequately using only one model or analogy.

Of course, some people do try to understand all of human nature from a single starting point, whether that be the economic aspect (Marx), the biological or sexual (Freud), the political, or the aesthetic. Such people sometimes achieve useful insights. But over all, they always misrepresent humanity by reducing and flattening humanity to one dimension.[9]

From a theological point of view, we should not be surprised that human phenomena are difficult to capture through only one dimension. Human beings are made in the image of God. To understand them one must simultaneously understand something of God.[10] And how does one understand God? Through his revelation of himself. But of course the Bible uses many analogies in speaking of God. He is the great King, the Father of his people, the Maker of heaven and earth, the Judge, the Holy One of Israel (an analogy by way of the holiness code and the holiness of the tabernacle and the priests). He speaks, plans, thinks, loves, hates, blesses, and so on. All these actions are analogous to the actions of human beings. Human beings as the image of God present, in a striking way, many analogies to what God does. But even the other created things speak in a general way of God's everlasting power and deity (Rom. 1:20–21). No one thing in creation is a uniquely suitable standpoint from which and through which to understand God. These verses imply that everything could in some sense be a starting point.

Thus it would appear that, because of the very nature of God and the nature of his relations to creation, there is no one analogy that could claim uniquely to be an adequate starting point for forming a model of God or a theory of God. God is revealed in everything, and yet as the Creator he is unique, unlike anything in creation. We are forbidden to think that we could capture him with a model. All that the Bible reveals about God and all the ways that it has of speaking, using many analogies, are relevant and profitable. We are to use them all.

It follows, then, that the Bible itself, and the nature of God himself, keeps us from reducing things to a single model or analogy. This restriction holds true, certainly, in our

---

[8]See, for example, Peter L. Berger and Thomas Luckmann, *Social Construction of Reality* (New York: Doubleday, 1966).

[9]On the theme of reductionism, see Dooyeweerd, *New Critique*; and Poythress, *Philosophy, Science, and Sovereignty*.

[10]John Calvin, *Institutes of the Christian Religion* 1.1.1.

study of God. But, by analogy, it will be true in a subordinate sense in our study of human- ity. Since human beings are made in the image of God, some similar problems present them- selves in a study of human beings, particularly as we focus on the all-important question of their relation to God.

In sum, then, there are good reasons for thinking that the subject matter of bibli- cal interpretation presents us with new demands. These demands are not necessarily the same as the demands in natural science. Science may satisfy itself with a single dominant model, but biblical interpretation cannot.

Moreover, one can understand this conclusion also on the practical level. Kuhn identifies some of the social reasons motivating scientists to gravitate toward a single dominant model. If the model appears to be promising and begins to be fruitful in sug- gesting avenues of research and extensions of its own theory, it is more efficient to follow the one model than to multiply models. Many of the alternatives will prove to be dead ends. The model tends to suggest detailed tests and extensions. In following these, people notice facts that would otherwise escape the most careful observer working without a fixed model. Moreover, when the community of scientists can agree on the overall shape of their field and the ways of making advance, they can go on to treat in great detail the problems that are left. Experience shows that most profit comes from dealing with the remaining problems and by carrying on more and more detailed and extended lines of questioning. By this route, any real long-range inadequacies of the theory will eventual- ly be uncovered. They will not be uncovered by simply casting about wildly in the indef- initely large space of alternate models.

In biblical interpretation, to some extent, analogous observations could be made. The person who has a particular narrow point of view (say, economic or sociological) will often notice things that escape others. The person who analyzes the Bible, attending only to what it says on a single issue (e.g., about God's knowledge), will discover much that might be overlooked by other readers. Therein lies the attractiveness of using a single dominant analogy. The recent stream of theologies illustrates this approach: we have seen theology of the Word, theology of love, theology of hope, theology of liberation, each seizing on a single theme through which to see the whole of theology. But in the long run this approach must be complemented by others, lest the theologian overlook the other analogies that the Bible itself endorses. No one analogy will ever be so uniquely effective in every respect that it has exclusive claim to our attention. By contrast, a scientific model, during periods of normal science, is able to make this claim. The difference in subject mat- ter between science and biblical interpretation therefore explains why the use of a single model is appropriate in one area but not in the other.

The third alternative mentioned above holds that multiple analogies ought to be used within natural science itself. On a certain level, this practice already occurs. In teaching and in illustration, a scientist may invoke a multiplicity of analogies in explaining theo- ries to an outsider. The quantum theory of light may be introduced by comparing light both to a wave (water wave, sound wave in air, vibration of a string) and to a stream of particles (marbles, water droplets, molecules). But the theory itself, in its inner structure, still has an internal coherence on the basis of extended analogy between certain mathe- matical equations and the physical world. This state of affairs would thus not seem to get us beyond the use of a single dominant model within the inner core of the theory. (Note, however, that the wave and particle views of light and of elementary particles seemed in the early days of quantum mechanics to be irreconcilable.)

We can still say that the essence of the unity of scientific disciplines is to be found not in the use of a single dominant model but in the unity of a disciplinary matrix. This disciplinary matrix includes models, of course. But it includes standards for judging research success, ideas about what sorts of research are promising, a general framework of assumptions about what the universe is like, concrete exemplars in the form of past definitive results, and so on. Both biblical interpretation as a whole and various subdisciplines could have a coherent disciplinary matrix without sticking to only one analogy in each case.

In fact, we have been arguing here that in many circumstances it is profitable to use first one, then another, analogy in order to learn all that one can about a particular passage or a particular topic in the Bible. The use of multiple analogies could itself become a rule of thumb that would be one element in the disciplinary matrix. In that case, it would serve to unite interpretive method in much the same way that science is united by some rules of thumb about research directions.

Our original question was whether biblical interpretation could justify the use of multiple analogies in contrast to the practice of science. The answer, I believe, is yes. The reasons arise from the differences in subject matter between biblical interpretation and natural science. Of course, the value of using several analogies still does not guarantee that all analogies whatsoever will be fruitful. And we must remember that, if an analogy means introducing false assumptions about God and his world, it can lead us astray. The historical-critical method is the prime example. For similar reasons the recent theologies of hope and of liberation appear to have destructive elements. The Bible has been made to fit into an alien worldview by seizing on a theme and reinterpreting it against the background of that worldview.

n i n e

LESSONS TO BE
LEARNED FROM
THE CONTEXTUAL
CHARACTER OF
KNOWLEDGE

*I*t is time now to take stock of what we have learned. Our concern so far has been primarily to look at natural science and biblical interpretation to understand what is involved in research and theory formation, using Kuhn's work as a stimulus. The main conclusion is that the context of one's assumptions and past knowledge has a profound effect on what one learns in any area of scientific study. Such a context or background includes assumptions about the world, past successes within the discipline (exemplars), tacit guidelines for fruitful areas of future research, and assumptions about the kinds of data that are relevant and valuable.

But should things be going the way they are? Can we improve on the way that biblical interpretation is done? In preceding chapters, I have hinted at some of the answers that I would give. Here we must draw together these evaluations and examine directly the question of how biblical interpretation ought to learn from Kuhn and others who are doing work in the history and philosophy of science.

LEARNING ABOUT BASIC COMMITMENTS OR PRESUPPOSITIONS

First, it is valuable for an exegete or a theologian to be aware of the role of basic commitments or presuppositions in the formation of knowledge. Kuhn and others alert us to the fact that such basic commitments or presuppositions do exist.[1] Exegesis and theological reflection always take place against the background of fundamental assumptions about the nature of the world. They are always motivated by the personal values of the

---

[1]Presuppositional apologetics, as represented by the work of Cornelius Van Til, has long insisted on the importance of basic commitments (see, e.g., Van Til, *The Defense of the Faith*, 2d ed. [Philadelphia:

biblical interpreter. Both methods and results are evaluated in terms of standards and epistemological values already presupposed by the interpreter.

At this level, there can be no neutrality. No one evaluates methods or results without standards of evaluation, whether these be explicit or implicit. And not everyone cherishes the same values or the same standards! Often, indeed, there is some overlap in different people's standards. But there are very often subtle differences as well. For example, compare (1) historical standards used by advocates of the historical-critical method and (2) historical standards used by scholarly Evangelicals who view history as the domain of God's providential and occasionally miraculous action. People in both groups are alert to the importance of weighing human testimony and not being credulous. To a degree, both would agree about the psychological and social likelihood of certain kinds of human behavior in certain circumstances. But they differ about what kind of evidence makes miracles credible, because their views of the limits of the world and the prerogatives of historical method differ. Behind this difference, their beliefs differ concerning what allegiance to God requires of someone engaged in intellectual reflection.

Some people use the idea of basic commitments as an excuse for complacency. They think that, since everyone is committed to something, they have as much right to their commitments as anyone else. But precisely because basic commitments are basic, it is important that people have the right ones. These commitments will affect everything that they do. And though, by common grace, they may do some helpful things in spite of bad basic commitments, their actions will be tainted by these same commitments.

Even we who have Christian commitments must not be complacent. We know that our motives are contaminated by sin. Sometimes we are aware of sinful motivations and assumptions, but other times, even when we are missing the mark, we may easily deceive ourselves into thinking that our basic commitments are fully biblical and in accord with God's standards.

We must remember that, though the Bible is infallible, our own understanding of the Bible is not. Hence some practice of critical self-doubt, in the light of the Bible's searchlight, is in order. As long as this doubting criticizes ourselves, rather than doubting God or doubting the Bible as God's Word, we are acting in conformity with Christian standards.

Moreover, we cannot be complacent about persuading others to adopt our basic commitments. Unfortunately, sometimes people do become complacent. They argue that, since each person evaluates evidence in the light of their basic commitments, it is useless to argue with anyone. Others will just use their own standards. They will not accept any argument given on the basis of Christian standards.

Basic commitments are indeed at stake here. Arguments with non-Christians are frequently not easy. We are sometimes tempted to give up or to compromise by adopting standards based on alien basic commitments. How, then, do we remain persuasive while not compromising? Although whole books are needed to deal with these issues, we can

---

Presbyterian & Reformed, 1963]). Van Til argues that whether a person is regenerate or unregenerate profoundly influences every aspect of thought and behavior. Believers presuppose that God exists, rules the world, and governs all facts; that human beings are abnormal since the Fall; that human beings must find their standards for criticism, evaluation, and truth in God. Unbelievers presuppose the opposite. But believers are inconsistent because of their remaining sinfulness, while unbelievers are inconsistent because they must carry on in God's world, in which order and standards so clearly exist but do not derive from finite humanity or finite idols. These basic presuppositions affect people's interaction with every fact of experience, every human attitude, and every proposed criterion for evaluation.

note here a few simple elements in the solution.[2] Everyone lives in God's world, and no one can escape that world or the knowledge of God that impresses itself on creatures in God's image (Rom. 1:18–22). Argument is not futile, because the facts are on our side, the standards that are truly legitimate are on our side, and—most importantly—the Holy Spirit works to break down people's resistance to the truth.

Moreover, people can also be challenged concerning the idolatrous character of their basic commitments. Whenever people have basic commitments to anything other than God and His Word, they are practicing a subtle form of idolatry. They are often attempting to escape responsibility for submitting to God. Christ died in order to free us from these sins as well as others. We may command people to repent of these sins, just as the apostles commanded people to repent.

But awareness of basic commitments has relevance for more than just carrying on argument. The fundamental value of this awareness is that it enables us to evaluate our own work and the work of others on more than one level. We can evaluate people's work both in terms of the basic commitments that motivate it and in terms of the value of its individual parts and details. Sometimes both the basic commitments and the details are good. Sometimes both are bad. But sometimes sloppy work comes from people with good commitments, or high-quality work from people with bad commitments. Sometimes there is a complex mixture of good and bad in several areas.

Awareness of the influence of basic commitments makes us better able to discern the effects that good or bad commitments have had on scholarly work, and so to make adjustments. We will not be swept off our feet by a highly insightful work showing effects of bad commitments. We will be able to learn from the insights, while noticing places where the bad commitments have infected the product. Conversely, we will not be impressed by mediocre work from those with good commitments. We will be able to honor the good commitments that a person has, while not ignoring the faults of the resulting ideas.

Finally, awareness of the importance of basic commitments and their resistance to refutation should make us all the more aware of our finiteness and of our need for divine verbal revelation from the Bible. We never rise above our basic commitments. They control us and our interpretation more than we control them. In particular, human beings determined to escape from God's authority and to be their own gods can generate basic commitments, but they do so merely by projecting their own finite guesses into the infinite. They make idols that subsequently enslave them. To reform and purify our basic commitments from our sin and idolatry, we need a clear word from God expressing the content of the standards, a divine power of the Spirit transforming us, and a divine Savior from God cleansing us. In other words, we need just the richness of salvation that the message of Scripture promises and bestows.

LEARNING THAT FACTS ARE THEORY-LADEN

Another area from which we can learn is Kuhn's discussion of the role of facts in natural science. All facts, according to Kuhn, are theory-laden. That is, the facts are not strictly objective, the same for everyone, regardless of their disciplinary framework.

---

[2]For a clear introduction to the problem, see Frame, "God and Biblical Language," pp. 159–77. For an extended exposition, see John M. Frame, *The Doctrine of the Knowledge of God* (Phillipsburg, N.J.: Presbyterian and Reformed, 1987).

Rather, the facts are subtly different depending on who is looking at them. The relative importance of a fact, its relevance and even whether it counts as a fact at all, depends on the view of the world and the standards contained in a disciplinary framework.

To be sure, not everyone within the history and philosophy of science agrees with Kuhn. Opponents of Kuhn are uneasy with the provocative language that he uses. They would disagree with some of his formulations and prefer to stress the ways in which the history of science shows considerable common ground between differing disciplinary matrices with respect to some kinds of facts.[3]

But Kuhn does not mean that competing disciplinary frameworks have no way of talking to one another. Usually there will be many facts on which they agree. But the difference in framework may result in subtle differences in how those facts are seen. There is no perfect separation between fact and interpretation; facts always exist against a background view of the world. People in different frameworks therefore frequently use key words in different ways. Communication between two different disciplinary frameworks may resemble a work of translation.

Moreover, one cannot single out beforehand a special domain of pure facts that must be accepted and accounted for by any scientific theory whatsoever. In science, the typical facts are the results of instrumental measurements and presuppose at least a theory of the instruments. In addition, anomalies (i.e., phenomena that do not fit into the framework of existing theory) are frequently ignored until for some reason—controlled by the disciplinary framework—they draw the attention of scientists.

Even if Kuhn is not entirely right about science, there is something here for biblical interpreters to learn. Biblical interpretation deals first of all with the concrete tests of Scripture. In addition, all interpretation in one way or another interacts with the modern world. In some cases the facts of the modern world can be left in the background. Interpretation that is interacting with questions of application will, however, be directly concerned with the facts about the modern world.

Such facts are typically about churches, human beliefs, philosophy, and economic, social, and political structures. But how does one gather facts? Does one rely on individual personal spiritual experience, personal contacts, statistical surveys, social critics, or Marxist class analysis? Clearly, gathering facts is influenced by one's worldview and what sorts of facts one counts as important. The supposed fact of a person's membership in a particular socioeconomic class is a fact only if one first accepts such classes as an objective reality rather than merely a theoretical construct.

Even when we come to the study of the biblical text, we are not free from these difficulties. Careful study of the Bible requires some attention to the historical and cultural environments in which particular books of the Bible were written (at least if our framework of assumptions tells us that the original historical setting is relevant to interpretation!). Getting facts about these environments is again conditioned by one's methods and disciplinary framework. Practitioners of the historical-critical method have sometimes inferred whole social movements, schools, and literary sources on the basis of scant evidence. When the evidence is scant, the role of overall assumptions is even greater than usual.

---

[3]See, for example, Dudley Shapere, "Meaning and Scientific Change," in *Scientific Revolutions,* ed. Ian Hacking (Oxford: Oxford University Press, 1981), pp. 28–59.

When we come to the text of Scripture itself, it might be thought that everyone agrees on the facts. Everyone agrees that certain Hebrew and Greek letters occur in a certain order in the received text (ignoring textual criticism). But it is easy to show that, beyond a very elementary level, the same phenomena are interpreted very differently within different disciplinary frameworks. For example, traditional historical-critical method uses the facts of aporias (apparent tensions or contradictions) and sudden transitions ("seams") in the biblical text as evidence for different sources. Traditional inerrantist method uses these same facts as a starting point for an investigation of harmonization. Newer literary approaches use the same facts as key clues to the techniques of literary artistry and subtlety.

Moreover, the text itself is not an object of study in the same way within different disciplinary frameworks. Traditional historical-critical method treats the text as merely one layer in a tradition. According to this method, the text has earlier sources and traditions as well as later evolutions. No particular special status is to be assigned to the text itself, except that by historical accident it, rather than its sources or its later evolutions, has survived.

On the other hand, traditional inerrantist method treats the text as part of a whole canon, all of which is the Word of God and in principle harmonizable. Some texts may have sources (e.g., Luke may have used Mark), but even then the sources are irrelevant to the meaning and authority of the final product.

Newer literary approaches sometimes abstract the text from its environment. They may ignore the sources and later uses valued by the historical-critical method. They may choose equally to ignore the references to historical events valued by Evangelicals. They treat the material simply as a product of literary artistry, ignoring its straightforward truth claims in favor of finding a kind of artistic or aesthetic truth in its manner of expression.[4]

In sum, the facts receive vastly different treatment, depending on which disciplinary frameworks they fall under. And we have looked only at disciplinary frameworks that are in current widespread use. We have not talked about the medieval framework for exegesis or theology, or a framework that might be generated by Buddhism or Islam.

In one respect, the influence of basic commitments is being recapitulated here. Basic commitments are bound to influence the development of any disciplinary framework, including methods of approach to the biblical text and to modern facts. Historically speaking, basic commitments certainly did influence the development of the historical-critical method, traditional inerrantist method, newer literary methods, theology of liberation, and so on. But the influence sometimes goes the other way as well. A disciplinary framework can influence the basic commitments of those involved with it.

A disciplinary framework has a momentum of its own, a record of success, that sometimes appeals to people with different basic commitments. People adopt the framework because of its successes, without studying whether the framework itself assumes or encourages a certain set of basic commitments. Then, as they immerse themselves in the framework, they find that their basic commitments themselves undergo subtle (or violent) change under the influence of hidden assumptions that they begin to adopt consciously or unconsciously.

Moreover, what counts as a fact has a subtle influence. If one is immersed in an environment where a single disciplinary framework is being used, one is constantly

---

[4]See the section *Literary Approaches to Biblical Interpretation* by Tremper Longman III elsewhere in this volume.

confronted with the facts that the framework considers especially revealing. One is made to feel that such facts do reveal something. To deny what they reveal is to "ignore the facts." Hence people are swept along into conformity with the framework, usually without ever adequately examining how a competing framework might treat the same "facts."

This kind of influence of disciplinary frameworks is not merely hypothetical. Students at a seminary operating exclusively under the framework of the historical-critical method are often exposed only to the critical historical reconstructions of Israelite history, the supposed contradictions in the Bible showing its historically limited character, and theologies of revelation that have adjusted themselves to these viewpoints. Conversely, students at a conservative Evangelical seminary may be exposed only to historical explanations and theology of revelation compatible with verbal inspiration. Some seminaries, of course, make an effort at wider exposure, but the professors will naturally spend by far the most time on those points of view that they themselves think have some positive contribution or some hope of being right.

What lesson can we learn here? One must not, indeed, "ignore the facts." But every research framework is confronted with anomalies that are difficult to explain. Every research framework tends to talk about its successes and to concentrate on problems that the method has some hope of solving, rather than on what is most intractable. If one is trying to choose between disciplinary frameworks or is trying to modify an existing framework, one must avoid being intimidated by people who appeal to "the facts." Such people are most often thinking of those facts that (they think) prove their case. Other facts, less easily explained, are not mentioned.

EVALUATING COMPETING RESEARCH PROGRAMS
IN BIBLICAL INTERPRETATION

We can also learn some lessons about the possibility of evaluating competing schools in biblical interpretation and research. Does Kuhn's idea of scientific progress through revolutions help us? How do we judge whether one of two competing schools is the more fruitful?

From Kuhn we learn that evaluation is not easy. Kuhn points out that, when a new exemplar appears, it appears as a theory in the process of development, not as a finished product. It may explain only experimental results in a tiny field but be unable to explain the great body of facts covered by a theory already in existence. Only time can tell whether a fresh idea can be developed far enough and fruitfully enough to supersede a theory already dominating the field.

Hence Kuhn does not think that his analysis provides any basis for prejudging the success of new ideas or theories. For evaluating new ideas, the practitioners in the field are the best judges.[5] Often people are presented with a choice between two disciplinary frameworks, both of which have some strengths and some weaknesses. The difficulty in making a choice is not surprising. If only one framework had strengths, only it would have a significant number of adherents, and we would not be thinking about how to choose between two frameworks.

---

[5]Kuhn, *Structure of Scientific Revolutions*, p. 200.

Suppose two disciplinary frameworks vie for our attention and allegiance. One disciplinary framework has a long record of success. But it is now struggling with growing areas of anomalies that so far have been integrated into the framework only with difficulty or not at all. Nevertheless, because of its record of past success, it is rational to hope that continued effort might succeed in explaining the anomalies.

The second framework, by contrast, is new. It is a modification of the old one, and so hopes to build on the successes of the old framework. But it has not yet succeeded in explaining the whole field that the old framework covered so well. It has no long track record. However, it shows promise because it has done better in accounting for some of the anomalies that have come to trouble the old framework. It is rational, then, to hope that continued effort might enable people to succeed in using the new approach to explain everything explained by the old framework, and the anomalies as well.

While tension between frameworks takes place within science, one can see something resembling this dynamic process in biblical interpretation as well. When the historical-critical method first began to arise, it was an inchoate framework in comparison with the established dogmatic, supernaturalistic frameworks. The initial developers of the historical-critical method did not explain all the details of the Bible with nearly the thoroughness attained by later practitioners. They were followed because of hopes that the evolutionary and naturalistic assumptions that gave a certain coherent picture of the modern world and of certain aspects of biblical religion would in the end provide a more satisfactory picture of everything.

The historical-critical method is one case of successful development of a new disciplinary framework—successful in the sense that it gradually came to be a dominating framework in scholarly circles. Arianism, in contrast, is an example of a failure. It was eventually rejected by the mainstream of the church, although at one time it gained many adherents and continues to have periodic revivals in liberalism and cults.

We may also note that scientific theories thought to be outmoded may experience revival later on. The corpuscular theory of light gained dominance from Newton's time onward. It was superseded by the wave theory in the nineteenth century, and then corpuscular aspects of light were reintroduced in the twentieth century in connection with the development of quantum theory. From this instance one can see that the historical eclipse of a point of view does not guarantee its long-range invalidity.

One suspects that similar changes may occur even more often in biblical interpretation and in the humanities than in science. In biblical interpretation and humanities basic commitments about the nature of human beings have had more direct influence on the nature of theory building and disciplinary frameworks. Alterations in basic commitments over the centuries may result in the dominance of first one, then another, interpretive school, without proving the superiority of the later results over the earlier. Moreover, because of the multifaceted character of human beings, as people made in God's image, more than one type of explanation can account for a large number of facts. For example, there can be economic, sociological, psychological, political, and religious explanations. Such explanations have actually been offered for the events of the Reformation, and all of the explanations have some plausibility.

Even the domination of a single disciplinary framework for a long time may show mainly the dominant attraction of an ideology, a philosophy, or a worldview more than the inherent superiority of the framework. Marxism dominates scholarly analysis of religion in the communist world partly because of its appeal as a worldview and its importance in supporting the present political structures. Likewise, one may suggest, the historical-critical method has dominated Christian scholarship for so long, partly because it supports the ideology of naturalism, which has dominated Western thought since the Enlightenment.

One cannot, of course, prove scientifically that an inerrantist approach to Scripture is superior to the mainstream historical-critical approach. Showing in detail how an inerrantist approach makes sense of the data is important. But the differences between these two frameworks touch on one's deepest religious commitments. In evaluation, one must appeal to those commitments. And one must appeal to the hope for future success as well, since the present successes of a framework may not fully reveal its future potential. Evangelicals know that the future ultimately leads to the second coming of Christ. The Second Coming will be the ultimate place for revealing success or failure of disciplinary frameworks investigating Scripture. Because we base our hopes on God's promises, it is rational to think that at that point an Evangelical framework will be seen to be superior.

I have used examples from biblical interpretation that represent rather deep-seated cleavages. But something can also be said about differences that are less serious. Consider only Evangelical interpretation. Among Evangelicals there is a good measure of agreement on the basic teachings of the Bible and on hermeneutical principles. Hence there are also standards to which we may appeal in evaluating theological innovations and competitions between different schools. Even with such a measure of agreement, however, we confront some complexities.

For example, suppose that we are evaluating a new interpretation of Romans 7. A new idea, one that is just getting off the ground, may have greater promise, both because it has not been worked on yet and because it has apparently shed light on some difficulty in the Bible. In this case, the new interpretation claims to shed light on the difficulty of dealing with the language of Romans 7. But it is likely to be only weakly integrated with dominant theological systems. If it cannot succeed in integrating the insights of older theology, it may just spawn error or even heresy. In the particular case of Romans 7, Lloyd-Jones's interpretation might lead to the idea that there was, ontologically, a third category of people distinct from regenerate or unregenerate. (This is not what Lloyd-Jones means, but one can see how someone else might further develop his approach.)

A new idea always has to compete with the older approaches. The strength of the older approaches is that they have thoroughly worked through the details of biblical passages and that they are more thoroughly integrated with whole theological systems. People might prefer an older explanation because of this very thoroughness.

In such situations there is no easy answer. Whenever new ideas or new approaches arise, we must evaluate them. Evaluation takes into account their potential for future development, not just their present adequacy (or deficiency). But we must also take into account the fact that an older approach offers actual explanations at some points where a new approach may remain only a potential hope. Even when people have similar standards (as the community of Evangelicals does), they may reasonably disagree about the relative merits of two approaches to a difficulty. This disagreement in turn will lead to differences in judgment about whether it is more worthwhile to spend time in developing a new approach or to reinforce and enhance an old one.

t e n
USING
PERSPECTIVES

*L*et us now examine whether differences in disciplinary frameworks must always lead to a competition between different schools and the eventual triumph of one school. Can we sometimes incorporate insights from different points of view into a richer whole?

DEALING WITH DIFFERING POINTS OF VIEW

Recall first, that, according to Kuhn, sciences begin their history in a preparadigm, or immature, stage. In this situation a number of schools compete for dominance, and no particular way of formulating the problems or of moving toward solutions is so superior to its rivals that it effectively drives them from the field. According to Kuhn, this stage cannot be eliminated. One cannot simply choose one school and ignore the others, because one does not know which school will produce the most effective advance in science in the long run. The immature stage comes to an end only when a superior theory or exemplar arises within one school or when features from several schools are combined. One cannot hasten this process. One cannot simply decree that a superior theory will arise now rather than later.

One might liken biblical interpretation to an immature science. In systematic theology, even if some theological system is dominant for a time, it does not permanently banish its rivals. The history of millennial theories illustrates this fact. One can see the same thing even in the history of christological controversies. In a sense the Nicene Creed and the Chalcedonian creed set forth exemplars that obtain dominance and form the basis for subsequent reflection. One might thus argue that these creeds represent turning points toward mature christology and mature Trinitarianism.

But forms of Arianism have cropped up again and again through the ages, up until modern times. They are never permanently eradicated by orthodoxy. In this case, I would say that non-Arian orthodoxy is correct, but Arianism is never permanently eliminated because it appeals to sinful tendencies in human nature that would subject God to tight, over-simplified rationalistic categories. The Trinity and the Incarnation are permanent offenses to such autonomous human reasoning.

The example of Arianism shows that sometimes we cannot hope to combine rival schools. To try to synthesize Trinitarian theology with Arianism is to try to combine truth and error. Of course, a revival of Arianism might conceivably arise in reaction to one-sided orthodoxy. If orthodox theologians in emphasizing the deity of Christ lose sight of his humanity, they will eventually provoke a reaction by people who rediscover Christ's humanity. This rediscovery may overreact by eliminating Christ's deity. If we lived through such a situation, it would behoove us to note the problems on both sides. Sometimes the side that is in the wrong may yet be grasping at a fragment of truth ignored by the side that is basically in the right.

In the area of hermeneutics, similarly, we might argue that one interpretive system has never obtained absolute dominance and completely superseded all others. The historical-critical method has dominated biblical exegesis for at least a century, but it never completely eliminated inerrantist approaches and traditional Roman Catholic approaches. The Reformers championed grammatical-historical interpretation over against medieval allegorical interpretation, but allegorical interpretation never completely disappeared from the churches that derived from the Reformation.[1]

MULTIPLE APPROACHES TO TRUTH

Must we say that all differences in biblical interpretation and in theology are differences between truth and error? Are they all like the difference between Arianism and Trinitarianism? No. Sometimes the differences are like the difference between viewing the church as the temple of God and viewing it as the body of Christ. Clearly we have to do here with complementary truths rather than opposition between truth and error. The difference here is a difference between two perspectives on the same truths.

In such a situation, each perspective is better at seeing and emphasizing certain truths of Scripture. Hence it would seem advisable to use a multiplicity of perspectives. As we have seen, this use of multiple perspectives can be valuable even when we are dealing with a passage such as 1 Corinthians 3:10–15, where one analogy dominates in the text. After determining what analogy, if any, is indeed dominant in a given passage of Scripture, we should not hesitate to see how other biblical analogies illumine the same passage. Such a procedure may alert us to neglected features of the passage. (For example, the role of fire in 1 Cor. 3:10–15 is illuminated when we use the biblical picture of God as Judge rather than confining ourselves simply to the analogy between church and temple.) Use of some other analogy will almost certainly make us more aware of connections between the passage that we are studying and the many other passages of the Bible that use the analogy that we have chosen.

---

[1]See the section *Has the Church Misread the Bible?* by Moisés Silva elsewhere in this volume.

We can extend these observations still further. As I have argued at length in another place,[2] there is value not only in using a variety of analogies but in trying to extend the analogies, to enrich them, until they are huge theories or explanations that can cover all facts of Scripture. We start with a single biblical analogy or motif like the temple or the judge. Then we view all of the Bible through the spectacles of this one motif. In the process, we try to enrich the motif itself so as to include and explain things that were originally not thought to be related to it. It is as if we pretended that we were going to form our own theological school and that this school would put forth a scientific theory of theology based on a single coherent model that was in turn some form of our starting analogy or a modification or enrichment of it.

This procedure is really not so dissimilar to the way a scientific theory originates. Scientists work with suggestive analogies or models that they tinker with and modify as they go. For example, Maxwell invokes a model in reflecting on his researches leading to the famous equations of electromagnetic theory:

> By referring everything to the purely geometrical idea of the motion of an imaginary fluid, I hope to attain generality and precision, and to avoid the dangers arising from a premature theory professing to explain the cause of the phenomena. . . . The substance here treated of . . . is not even a hypothetical fluid which is introduced to explain actual phenomena. It is merely a collection of imaginary properties which may be employed for establishing certain theorems in pure mathematics in a way more intelligible to many minds and more applicable to physical problems than that in which algebraic symbols alone are used.[3]

Maxwell thus begins using the model of a fluid in order to suggest a series of connections between mathematical equations and the physical object (electromagnetism). The analogy suggests certain lines of development mathematically. Such development would not have been easy if one were dealing only with the results of previous investigation without simplifying or organizing them.[4]

In the case of biblical research, one may argue that there are even stronger reasons for utilizing analogies. For one thing, the analogies that I consider here are presented in one form or another within the Bible itself. We know that these are good analogies, albeit of a limited character. Physical scientists, by contrast, must cast about on their own for analogies from the physical world. They have not been told directly by God which analogies will work.

One relatively successful example of just this procedure is the history of covenant theology. Covenant theology in its mature form is capable of viewing all of God's relations with human beings, and even the redemptive counsel between the Father and the Son, in terms of analogies with the concrete covenants of the Bible. At the start of the process, theologians observe that the Hebrew and Greek equivalents of the word *covenant* are used in the Bible to draw an analogy between relations of God and human beings and treaties between human beings. This analogy is then stretched and generalized, and the

---

[2]Poythress, *Symphonic Theology.*
[3]James Clerk Maxwell, *The Scientific Papers of James Clerk Maxwell* (Cambridge: Cambridge University Press, 1890), pp. 159–60.
[4]Ibid., pp. 155–56.

word *covenant* becomes a technical term filled with all the ideas developed by comparing a large number of passages that speak about God's relation to human beings.[5]

Covenant theology in fact succeeds in integrating, explaining, and organizing into a coherent whole the vast sweep of biblical revelation. But it does so partly by enriching the idea of covenant. The word *covenant* within theological vocabulary is now related by a rich series of connotations to the entire complex of biblical revelation about the relation of God to human beings through history.

People who are used to thinking in terms of covenant theology may not think that there are really alternatives. In a sense, if covenant theology is right, there are no other alternatives. That is, no system contradicting covenant theology can possibly be right. But a contradictory system is not the only alternative—there could also be complementary ways of expounding the *same* truths. If we chose to do it another way, there would be differences of emphasis or differences in organization, but no contradiction.

For example, we could develop the whole theological system in terms of the theme of God's family, and the relation of God as Father to his people as children. Surely the theme of fatherhood and family is an important theme in Scripture, and surely it touches on the heart of God's purposes and his intentions as much as does covenant theology.

One might reply that covenant theology has already achieved this result. To talk about God's fatherly relation to his people is simply to talk about his covenant with his people, no more and no less. Both sides are talking about the same thing, no doubt. But there are still different ways of talking, and the different ways bring to the fore different aspects of biblical teaching. The idea of covenant within covenant theology has definite legal associations, while the idea of family suggests first of all social, emotional, and personal relations. If we use only one of these types of vocabulary, we will have to be careful somewhere along the line to alert people to complementary truths. For example, if we used *covenant* to include everything, we would have to say that the word is intended (unlike its use outside of God-human relationships) to connote all the familial ideas. Or vice versa, if we used the idea of family as our central organizational idea, we would have to say that the idea of family is intended to include a legal side of adoption, whereby according to God's standards we who were castaways have been given the legal rights of family members.

Because covenant theology has a long history of development, it may seem more natural to view the family ideas in the Bible as a metaphorical or analogical expression of one aspect of covenant. According to this viewpoint, God's covenant is the basic underlying reality. Expressions using family ideas bring out one aspect of the covenant. But let us ask ourselves what might have happened if the history of theology had been different. What if the idea of familial theology had been developed with great thoroughness? What if someone now made the bizarre suggestion that we should redo the whole of the theological enterprise using covenant (a comparatively lesser-used theme in theology) as the center point?

---

[5]See Meredith G. Kline, *The Structure of Biblical Authority* (Grand Rapids: Eerdmans, 1972); *idem, Treaty of the Great King: The Covenant Structure of Deuteronomy* (Grand Rapids: Eerdmans, 1963); *idem, Kingdom Prologue*, 2 vols. (South Hamilton, Mass.: Meredith G. Kline, 1981–83); John Murray, "Covenant Theology," in *The Encyclopedia of Christianity,* ed. Philip E. Hughes (Marshallton, Del.: National Foundation for Christian Education, 1972), 3:199–219.

I anticipate that we would find some die-hard advocates of familial theology who would resist the idea that covenant could ever have the centrality that the idea of God's family clearly had. They would say something like this:

> The familial relation between God as Father and the people of God as his children is the underlying reality. This relation is nothing less than a reflection on the creature-ly level of the Trinitarian relation between the Father and the Son. What could be deeper than that? Covenants in the Bible are used as analogical or metaphorical expressions for one aspect of this family relation, namely the aspect of legal privilege, fatherly requirements, and obedience expected of children. Familial theology already includes these aspects. We do not ignore the covenants. Clearly familial theology has already done the job that this newfangled covenant theology proposes to do. Familial theology has already uncovered the real nature of the relation of God to human beings. The proposed covenant theology shifts things away from this center. Hence it will have a subtly incorrect emphasis. At the same time, it will achieve nothing new, since familial theology already includes an account of covenants.

Do we need to choose between covenant theology and familial theology? Is one of these superior in every respect? Or are they equivalent? It would seem that they are closer to being equivalent. Each has a natural tendency to a different emphasis (legal vs. social/personal), but there is no disharmony. A good theologian working with either of these starting points will eventually notice in Scripture all the aspects of God's relation to human beings.

Unfortunately, we are not all good theologians. Or at least we do not always find it so easy to notice everything that the Bible says. Some people sitting under the teaching of covenant theology have understood God's covenant in a merely legal, one might say legalistic, way. They have missed the personal dimension of relationship to God. They have not really been affected by the fact that God is our Father. This overlooking of the personal dimension is contrary to the intentions and express teaching of the great covenant theologians. But it sometimes happens anyway. Conversely, one might imagine that, if familial theology dominated history, some people would not realize that God had rules—yes, laws. They would misconstrue the familial relation as lawless, in spite of the intentions of the greatest familial theologians.

Hence I conclude that, since we do not always observe everything and see all the angles, it is perhaps better not to put all our eggs in one basket. That is to say, it is better not to use only one analogy or theme as the route by which we approach biblical interpretation. If we do, we may miss something. The situation in theology is vaguely analogous to the situation with the wave and particle theories of light. Within quantum theory the two approaches achieve a reconciliation in principle. But some particular phenomena concerning light show more prominently one aspect rather than the other, and one viewpoint is frequently more useful than another for making a particular analysis. Similarly, in the Bible there is harmony between viewing God's relation to human beings as a covenant and viewing it as a relation between father and son. But some particular passages of the Bible show one aspect more prominently, and one viewpoint may be more useful for making a particular point or noticing particular features of a text.

The use of multiple perspectives must itself be qualified as one approach among many. Within the body of Christ, different people have different gifts. Perhaps, because of our natural disposition or the background that God has given to us, we will use only one theme ourselves. We perhaps understand one approach better, and we are more familiar with it. But we must be ready to listen to other people in the body of Christ whom God has gifted in other ways. Men have to listen to women and women to men; scholars to non-scholars and vice versa; Americans to Latinos and vice versa.

We therefore must listen to other people with other perspectives. Listening to people does not mean that we must tolerate whatever we hear or whatever someone else does; we are not to be complacent about sin or error. But neither are we to be quick to brand something as sin or error, before listening enough to find out whether a complementary perspective may be involved. The earlier example of Arianism shows that we must sometimes draw a clear line. But the example of covenant theology versus familial theology shows equally that we must not have a hair-trigger intolerance. Only growth in discernment, love, and knowledge of God's Word will enable us to succeed more and more effectively in building up the body of Christ in the truth (Eph. 4:15–16; cf. Phil. 1:9–11).

eleven

BIBLICAL INTERPRETATION REORGANIZED USING DIFFERENT PERSPECTIVES

*I*n practice, how can we reorganize the entire system of biblical interpretation in terms of a new perspective? What happens when we deliberately set about to use a new analogy? It is difficult to work out an example thoroughly within a short space. Such a reorganization might easily involve writing one or more whole books of systematic theology or biblical theology.

THEMATIC REORGANIZATION

Among non-evangelical theologies one can find examples of work that has nearly attempted reorganizing biblical interpretation in terms of a new theme. We can find numerous theologies that are organized in terms of a single theme chosen as the dominant one: theology of liberation, theology of hope (Moltmann), theology of the future, theology of human existence (Bultmann). The fact that most of these theologies are gross distortions might seem to argue strongly against the wisdom or legitimacy of doing "thematic" theology. The grave danger, however, lies not in the mere fact of organizing theology around a theme. It lies in the fact that, if one understands the theme itself in an unbiblical way, this unbiblical understanding can then easily penetrate the whole texture of the theology rather than being confined to one part.

But one might also see an advantage here. For all their distortions, non-evangelical thematic theologies sometimes include bits of insight and truth, sometimes uncovering logical and thematic linkages in the Bible that are really there. They are often close enough to the truth to seem plausible and to capture followers.

Naturally, part of the solution to the problem of distorted thematic theologies lies in critical observations to the effect that the central theme of the theology is itself understood

517

in a distorted and unbiblical way. Such critical observations are useful and necessary. But there is room also for reworking the whole theology the right way, by starting with the same theme understood now in a genuinely biblical way.

LIBERATION AS A THEME

Thus, for example, in imitation of liberation theology one can indeed argue that the whole of the biblical record can be understood as a record of God's liberating deeds. But in the Bible the deepest liberation is liberation from sin and the kingdom of Satan. Changes in political and social structures, though significant, are secondary to this most basic liberation. In this light, the present-day theologies of liberation, insofar as they reduce liberation to a purely horizontal and human level, not only truncate the richness of biblical liberation but are in danger of reversing it.[1] However much it may appeal to religious language, the "liberation" set in motion by political education and action will be tainted with autosoterism. The folly that thinks that people (conceived now as social human beings rather than individual beings) must save themselves is itself the beginning of bondage, not true liberation.

By reorganizing theology under the theme of liberation, we might show, for example, that the Marxist-oriented theologies of liberation are not the only way in which one might plausibly appeal to an important biblical theme. But we might also learn something that our earlier interpretation of the Bible had neglected, namely, that God's liberation of his people does include a corporate social and political dimension, not merely the salvation of individual souls. We would have enriched and reformed not only the theology of liberation but also our own previous practice of interpretation.

MONEY AS A THEME

Second, let us take the theme of money as a dominant theme around which to organize the whole of biblical interpretation. At first glance such a reorganization might seem difficult or impossible. Money is a prominent theme in the Gospels, but most of the remarks about it seem to be negative! How could one make these negative comments the starting point of a positive theology?

I have in mind here using money as a perspective on the *whole* of biblical interpretation, not simply picking out from the whole of theology whatever tidbits have implications in the area of economics. We are looking for a kind of "monetary theology" corresponding to theology of liberation or theology of hope.

When we start with what seems to be an unpromising theme one of the first helpful things to do is to expand or enrich the starting theme. That is, we redefine it or enlarge it so that the enlargement suggests an increasing number of connections with many passages and themes of the Bible. In the case of money, we are dealing with some means of exchange for wealth and for valuable things. Typically this means of exchange has been

---

[1] I recognize that the situation in theology of liberation is complex and that I cannot claim to offer a thoroughgoing critique in this context. Not all the work under the banner of theology of liberation is merely horizontal in character. But to the degree that Marxist social and economic analysis dominates, reductionistic horizontalizing tendencies are inevitable. Marx assumed that society can be scientifically analyzed without reference to God.

socially and politically agreed upon. In short, money is not just a piece of paper or a round piece of metal. Its meaning is closely connected with its use in facilitating the exchange of valuable materials. It is a symbolic means for designating and exchanging wealth and valuables.

Hence we can make the step of expanding or enriching the theme of money by redefining it as the theme of means for exchange of wealth and value. From there it is only a short step to seeing the potential for a God-centered approach to money. In the beginning God has all wealth and all value. When he creates the world, he produces wealth and value from his own fullness and bounty. The world belongs to him. He owns it. All wealth, all value, is therefore in a fundamental sense God's. God's creation and providence are thus the point of origin for all of our understanding of money.

God has created the world for his own glory. That purpose involves also the multiplication of wealth within the world, including wealth given to his creatures and in particular to human beings made in God's image. The money of human beings is a product of their abilities given by God to subdue the world and fill it with his wealth. Certain created substances, such as silver and gold, are suited from the beginning for such use. The human ability to produce fresh meanings and significance leads to their agreeing to establish a precise economic significance for particular manufactured objects like coins.

These abilities and actions on the part of human beings are reflections on a creaturely level of abilities of God. God is the original Creator of wealth, value, silver, gold, and the symbolic significance of each thing. Human beings are derivatively creative, as imitators of God. The original wealth is the fullness of God's own all-sufficiency and bounty. The original from which human money derives is the symbolic significance that God gives to his wealth: it signifies God himself.

Moreover, we have observed that human money is a symbolic means for facilitating exchange of value. God himself is the originator of all means. In fact, the whole creation is a means for producing the exchange of his glory (i.e., wealth!) with human beings. The history of the world is nothing less than the history of "money," in this tremendously expanded sense of the word.

Starting from our newly expanded concept of money, we can more easily see how a whole approach to biblical interpretation and theology could be built up around the theme of money. God himself is source of both wealth and money in the extended sense. God's law is the money (i.e., the means of facilitating exchange of wealth) for regulating the conduct of human beings. God's redemption is his paying the price of the life of his own Son in exchange (a monetary transaction) for the lives of sinful people. The purpose of human life is to accumulate wealth (namely, the inheritance of God Himself and God's kingdom; see Matt. 6:33). They store up "treasure in heaven" (Luke 12:33–34). At the same time they are to do all for the glory of God, that is, for the increase of his praise (a form of wealth or value). All their service is means (money) toward these goals. Money in the narrow sense is simply one means among many. Within this framework we may then proceed to translate various passages of the Bible into the terminology of our monetary theology.

What use is it to interpret the Bible in this way? For one thing, it may help us to see that the use of money in the narrow sense is not an isolated issue. Nor are the commandments arbitrary that God gives concerning the use of money. The use of money is related to the totality of God's purposes for the world and for human beings in the world.

A second possible use would be in connection with people whose ideas about money are not fully biblical. In the United States in certain quarters, a theology of wealth has taken hold, a popularized theology that tells people that God wants them to be rich. This pseudotheology does not speak of the Atonement or of the necessity of criticism of worldly standards, but only of a Jesus who wants them to be happy and of how they can promote their happiness and wealth by believing in him.

We might choose to attack this perverse theology in many ways. But one way that most orthodox evangelicals would not immediately think of would be to "steal the thunder" of theology of wealth by emphasizing their own theme of wealth. Does this capitulate to their perversion? Not if we enrich our idea of wealth in the way that I have sketched out above. Then we may say,

> Indeed Jesus wants us to be wealthy! But what is wealth? Are the most valuable things always those that are manufactured in American society? Who is the most wealthy person of all? God himself. What does he say about wealth? His wealth is first of all in his character. He undertakes to spread his wealth abroad by reproducing his character in us. The law of God is a recipe for imitating God and, in so doing, being transformed into a wealthy person. But initially we have too much poverty to keep God's law. It takes money to make money. So God sent his own Son, who became poor for our sake, in order that we might become rich. Riches now mean investing in character conforming to Christ, including sharing in his suffering, so that we may enjoy our full inheritance in the future.

It is possible that, by the working of God's Spirit through such an approach, some people addicted to the theology of wealth might be jarred loose and have their values transformed into conformity with biblical values.

REORGANIZING THE STUDY OF A BIBLICAL PASSAGE

The same principles can be applied in the study of particular passages. We try to make new sense of the passage by looking at it from the viewpoint of a new theme or analogy. Taking a new view does not mean that we ignore or deny the internal themes of the passage. It means simply that we try to see whether we can notice something else about the passage by looking at it in a noncustomary way.

As an example, let us return one final time to Romans 7:14–25. Like any other passage, Romans 7 has an internal thematic organization and its own prominent themes. Because of the difficulty in interpreting this passage and the disputes over it, there is also some measure of disagreement over its internal themes. But it is not hard to see that the conflict over willing and doing good and evil is a major theme of verses 14–25. Moreover, the conflict is expressed in dramatic, almost psychologistic fashion. It is understandable that many people have adopted an interpretation along primarily psychological lines.

But suppose that, rather than using dramatic or psychologistic analogies as our main way of understanding the passage, we use as analogy any prominent theme within Paul's writings—for example, justification, union with Christ, or the hope for Christ's return. None of these starting points is guaranteed to reveal anything interesting. But in using one of them, we might turn up some connections that we would otherwise overlook. For instance, in looking at the passage in terms of union with Christ, we would naturally ask whether Paul is describing what he is in himself (apart from his union with Christ) in Romans 7:14–25 and what he is in Christ in chapter 8. Such a contrast still needs greater definition. But one can see that it is not necessarily quite the same as the contrast between regenerate and unregenerate and so might open the way to a new view.

In fact, not only Pauline themes but any prominent theme of the Bible can potentially be used as a perspective or window to look at Romans 7:14–25 in a new way. For the sake of illustration, let us use a rather unpromising theme: money. Once again, the theme must be expanded in order to be useful. If we expand it to include the whole complex concerning ownership, wealth, and exchange, we may begin to see at least some potential relevance to the passage. In verse 14, Paul specifically uses monetary language: he is "sold as a slave to sin." There is admittedly little other reference to money, but now we are only playing with a perspective or analogy to see whether it might throw light on the passage.

Let us go a step further. In Romans 7:23, Paul mentions "the members of my body." Paul is clearly the owner of his members. And yet, perversely and paradoxically, those members are apparently not under his control. We can construe this as a case of disputed ownership and disputed control. If Paul is "sold as a slave to sin," he is clearly owned by sin as master. He tries to assert his own ownership, by his desire for good, but finds that control is being exerted from other directions. It is still true that, from creation, he is owned by God.

Now we can already suggest one reason why Romans 7:14–25 is so hard to interpret. *Both* regenerate and unregenerate people experience some kind of contested ownership. Unregenerate people are owned by sin and Satan. And yet they can never escape the fact that they are creatures, that they owe everything to God, and that God has power to dispose of them as he wills. On a psychological level God's ownership is acknowledged in the cries of guilty consciences. But the dispute between God and Satan is broader and deeper than just their consciences.

By contrast, regenerate people are owned by God and by righteousness. And yet, as long as they are in this life, sin and Satan still try to capture them and bring them under their ownership. The "flesh" still belongs to this realm (see, e.g., Gal. 5:16–18). This situation is manifested in psychological conflicts—but not only there.

Hence the presence of conflict does not by itself tell us who is being talked about in Romans 7:14–25. Moreover, it is clear that disputes about ownership exist on more than one level. On the one hand, there are legal facts to be established about who has the *right* of ownership. This issue is analogous to justification. On the other hand, there are facts about possession, that is, facts about current control over what one legally owns or does not own. The thief controls stolen goods but does not own them. The question of control (in particular, control over one's own actions) is analogous to sanctification.

On still another level, we can have a contrast between the situation of slavery under the Old Testament law and the situation of freedom since Christ has come (Gal. 4:1–7). In this sense even regenerate people in the Old Testament were owned by "the basic principles of the world" (v. 3). They were "bought" (redeemed) by Christ (v. 5). Hence conceivably the apparent contrast between Romans 7:14–25 and Romans 8 may be a contrast between pre-Pentecost slavery and post-Pentecost freedom (ownership of oneself).

What do we conclude from this analysis? We should retain our original judgment about prominent themes. Dramatic and psychological pictures, not ownership, are the primary vehicles of expression in Romans 7:14–25. But we may still have learned something. These dramatic and psychological pictures may be just that: pictures, vehicles of expression for realities that are not purely dramatic or psychological. Paul's primary purpose in using such language may be to impress on the reader the pathos and helplessness of the situation, not to produce an exact psychological theory. The realities to which he points include legal facts, ownership facts, facts about control, and facts characteristic of two kingdoms at war with each other. These facts are not exhausted by their psychic manifestations.

Our little exploration of money and ownership in Romans 7:14–25 has not solved all our problems. But it alerts us to the fact that there may be more than just two possible interpretations of this passage. When we are dealing with a difficult passage, anything that can move us away from a deadlock is worth looking at.

STUDYING THE THEMATIC RELATIONS OF BIBLICAL PASSAGES

One of the values of using a new analogy is that it may help us to relate one passage of the Bible to others. Sometimes the traditional way of interpreting a certain passage may so govern our thoughts that we do not notice potentially relevant parallels. Consider, for example, John 3:1–15, verses that have been widely taken as a classic passage about being "born again," about regeneration, about being saved by God after a previous life of sin and alienation from him. The passage indeed is relevant to our understanding of regeneration. But does it say anything more? Let us see what happens with an altered disciplinary framework.

The traditional disciplinary framework for understanding John 3 is the framework of the theology of regeneration. But if we look at John 3 using the theme of fulfillment of the Old Testament or the theme of eschatology, we may notice what we did not notice before. In the Gospels a historical period of time is associated with "the kingdom of God" (vv. 3, 5). The phrase is not merely a designation for God's rule over the world from all eternity. Nor does it simply designate God's rule over human hearts. Rather, it is the exercise of God's rule in Christ's earthly life to save his people in a definite way. It is God's saving activity, to which the whole Old Testament looked forward. It is the fulfillment of Old Testament promises of God's salvation and the inauguration of the last days (i.e., eschatology in a broad sense).

Now in John 3, being "born anew" is closely related to being able to "see the kingdom of God." Being born anew may thus uniquely characterize the time of fulfillment. It is something that was prophesied would take place later, not something that occurred within the bounds of the Old Testament. Of course, regeneration, as systematic theology understands it, took place in the Old Testament. But John is discussing not regeneration as such but rather the fulfilled form that regeneration is to have now that Christ has come.

Jesus mentions the key role of the Spirit in being born anew (John 3:5–8). These comments agree with what he says to the Samaritan woman in John 4. Jesus himself provides the "living water," the water of the Spirit, and does so *after* his glorification (7:37–39; chap. 16). As Jesus says in 4:23, "A time is coming and has now come [*not* has always been] when the true worshipers will worship the Father in spirit and truth." In verse 21, he contrasts this time with the time when people worshiped at fixed locations (correctly at Jerusalem, incorrectly at Gerazim). When we link John 4 with John 16, we see that the Gospel of John must be talking about the depth of communion with God that is possible only after Pentecost.

Looking at John 3 from a new perspective has thus led us to a deeper and more accurate interpretation, primarily because it has enabled us to link it and other passages in John and elsewhere with the theme of fulfillment and eschatology. The chapter still has some implications for our doctrine of regeneration. But if we think that John 3 is directly discussing regeneration, with no focus on an eschatological coming of the Holy Spirit, we miss some of John's meaning.

As a second example, consider Psalm 23. All Christians are familiar with the practical use of this psalm with its meaning of the comfort, care, and protection of God. God undertakes to care for Christians just as he cared for Old Testament saints.

Many Christians have also gone a step further. They have noted that, in John 10, Jesus calls himself the Good Shepherd. They also know the New Testament teaching concerning Christ's deity. When we put all these passages together, we see that Psalm 23 is a passage not only about the care of God the Father but about the care of Christ. Christ is our Shepherd and says to us the words of Psalm 23.

Thus we have a twofold use of this passage. It applies to the relation of God the Father to Christians, and to the relation of the Lord Jesus Christ to Christians. This twofold use has become something of a traditional disciplinary framework for the practical and devotional interpretation of Psalm 23.

I agree with this traditional twofold use. But I would suggest that something else is visible when we move outside the traditional disciplinary framework. We know that Christ is fully God. Hence it is legitimate to apply the words "the *Lord* is my shepherd" to Him. But what happens when we take a nontraditional look at the same words through the "window" of Christ's humanity?

The Psalms give inspired expression to the experience of the people of Israel in communion with God. Especially they are expressions related to the king of Israel, because the king was the representative of the people. Many of the psalms were in fact written by David or with David in view. David and godly descendants after him experienced the care of God their Shepherd.

Now the line of David's descendants led forward to Christ. Christ was the ultimate and climactic Son of David. As a human being, a descendant of David, he experienced the care of God during his earthly life. When he was confronted with difficulties and with enemies, he doubtless applied this psalm and others to himself for sustenance. Psalm 23, for example, says that "even though I walk through the valley of the shadow of death, I will fear no evil" (v. 4). It speaks of rescue either from literal death or from a metaphorical analogy of death in the form of great distress, and life with God afterward (v. 6). Christ confronted not merely "the shadow of death" but real death. He was also rescued, not before he died but afterward, in his resurrection. And he now sits at God's right hand, having life with God forever. Because we are united with Christ in his life, death, resurrection, and rule, the psalm applies to us also.

Thus we see that Psalm 23 applies not only to the Father's relation to us and to Christ's relation to us but also to God the Father's relation to Christ. The use of a new perspective, outside of the traditional disciplinary framework, has alerted us to a new relationship between texts of the Bible.

Finally, let us consider David's fight with Goliath, narrated in 1 Samuel 17. Traditionally, Sunday schools have used the passage to give a moral lesson: Just as David had faith in God, stood up for God's name, and showed bravery for God's cause, so we should do today. Such a use expresses one valid perspective on the passage, since Old Testament passages are in many cases intended as examples for us (James 5:16–19; 1 Cor. 10:6–13).

Using a second perspective, we may note that the historical-critical tradition typically understands the passage as functioning to vindicate David's rise to kingship and to show that he is the man qualified by Yahweh to fill the role. This perspective also is valid.[2] In view of the interest of Samuel-Kings in the history of the kingship and in the contrast between Saul and David, we are invited to reflect on the politico-religious implications of this battle for Israel's understanding of its relation to the king chosen by God. Thus a perspective focusing on the corporate political implications of the passage within its immediate historical context is useful.

We may also use a perspective focusing on God and God's activity. We then note the faithfulness of God to David and God's power to turn events in the direction that he chooses, so that the outcome is contrary to human reckoning.

We may also use a perspective that asks about the role of mediators in the passage. When we ask that question, we realize that David, as the one anointed to become king, is a mediatorial representative of all the people in his combat. As the anointed one, he fore-shadows Christ and Christ's kingship. Christ as the representative single-handedly triumphs over Satan in a decisive battle at the cross (Col. 2:15). David is thus emblematic of Christ's victory, and we enjoy the fruits of Christ's victory in a manner similar to the Israelite army's despoiling the Philistines (1 Sam. 17:51–53). Since the Old Testament kings and David in particular point forward to Christ (2 Sam. 7:13–14; Acts 13:22–23, 33–35), the parallel that we have drawn between David and Christ is not farfetched.

In sum, when we are studying a single passage like Psalm 23 or 1 Samuel 17, it is useful to adopt several different perspectives in order that we may notice several types of points being made and several types of possible connections with the message of the Bible as a whole. In particular, it is useful to ask (1) whether the human beings in a passage are analogous to us (e.g., David is an example for us of faith and bravery); (2) whether the passage reveals something of God's character that remains the same for us (e.g., God who is faithful to vindicate David will be faithful to us); (3) whether a mediatorial figure in a passage functions in a way illumining Christ's final mediatorship (e.g., David is a type of Christ); and (4) whether themes of a whole book of the Bible illumine the purpose of the passage (the theme of God's establishment of the kingly line and its destiny in 1 Samuel). In addition, we view the passage from the perspective of various prominent biblical themes: covenant, promise and fulfillment, judgment, temple, theophany, kingdom, eschatology, creation/re-creation, and so on.[3]

---

[2] In this case I agree with the *results* of the historical-critical tradition, not its presuppositions. Here, as elsewhere, I repudiate the antisupernaturalism and low view of Scripture inherent in the total framework.

[3] The fourfold medieval allegorical approach to interpretation, though subject to excess, might be seen as a confused and poorly formulated attempt to see passages from a multiplicity of perspectives. In particular, we may ask whether passages are related to immediate propositional truth ("literal" meaning), to moral applications ("psychical" or "moral" meaning), to fulfillment in Christ and the church ("spiritual" meaning), or to the promise of the heavenly Jerusalem to which our history is progressing ("anagogical" meaning). In fact, many passages will to some degree manifest all four of these dimensions and other dimensions as well, when we see them in the context of the total canon of Scripture. The allegorical approach could not have survived as long as it did if it had not had a grain of truth.

twelve

PROSPECTS FOR DEEPENING OUR UNDERSTANDING OF THE BIBLE

The common thread through all our discussion has been the theme that worldviews, frameworks, and overall contexts influence knowledge and discovery in all areas. Knowledge is always qualified by its context. People know what they know against a background of other knowledge. This background includes both closely related knowledge in closely related fields and knowledge of a whole worldview, some of which is tacit rather than known explicitly. In fact, all of us know many things that we do not realize that we know. If we are Americans, we know that we are supposed to knock at other people's front door to announce our presence. But in some cultures people cough instead of knocking. Such tacit knowledge is valuable, but it can also be dangerous. We can make assumptions that block out access to discovery (such as when we assume that everyone in other cultures has to knock at other people's doors).

Our background of knowledge colors any particular bit of knowledge and colors our expectations about what we will discover when we look at something new or when we look at something old for a second or third time. Because background knowledge is limited and differs from person to person, no one has a pristine neutral standpoint from which to acquire more knowledge. Such a situation is part of what it means to be a creature, to be finite. Hence it holds true for biblical interpretation and scientific investigation alike. Kuhn's work in the history and philosophy of science, by revising our idea of scientific method, makes more noticeable the parallels in this respect between science and biblical interpretation. Kuhn draws out attention to the contextualized character of knowledge in both fields.

The implications for biblical interpretation are multifarious. On the deepest level, we are challenged to become more aware of our dependence on God and of the significant role of the Holy Spirit and of our Christian commitment in influencing the acquisition of knowledge in general and biblical interpretation in particular (see chap. 9). Also, we become more aware of the contaminations of sin in the intellectual realm. We must train ourselves to detect alien, antibiblical presuppositions underlying the disciplinary frameworks for interpretation influenced by the Enlightenment. At the same time, none of us escapes the influence of our own sin or the sinful biases of the surrounding culture. Hence, we must be self-critical as well as critical of others.

Second, by becoming more aware of the influence of theological systems on interpretation, we are in a better position to conduct dialogue with those adhering to other systems.

Third, as the surrounding culture changes, we may be called upon to undertake a reorganization of our theological system or our interpretive practices in order, without compromising the biblical message, to communicate it more effectively to the people inhabiting the culture. Traditional Western theology has long been structured largely in terms of answering the question of guilt: How may I, a guilty sinner, escape condemnation before the holy and perfect Judge of the universe? But modern secularists find such questions less intelligible and less relevant than questions about the meaning of their life in a lonely, seemingly impersonal universe. A familial theology organized more prominently around the deeply personal categories of sonship and adoption may perhaps address secularists more effectively than a covenant theology organized more prominently around the question of legal guilt. Both types of organization and both types of question are legitimate in principle, but one may be more useful as a point of contact.

Or again, in many Third World tribal cultures the prominent existential question is how to escape the power of evil spirits. Most of Western theology is far less equipped than is the Bible itself to address such a question.

Fourth, our observations about perspectives challenge us to look at old passages of the Bible in new ways. Sometimes a new perspective may open up for us new interpretive possibilities for difficult passages like Romans 7. Other times we will discover new truths about relatively uncontroversial passages like Psalm 23, or new relationships that passages like 1 Samuel 17 sustain to major themes of the Bible. In all this process, we will discover anew that the wisdom of God is unsearchably deep (Rom. 11:33–36).

Appendix
Interpretive Method and Other Fields of Research

I n the course of our discussion we have here and there noticed points of contact between methods in biblical interpretation and methodological discussions in several different areas. I summarize here the points of contact with a larger body of literature, focusing particularly on the theme that larger contexts influence and qualify knowledge. Readers must remember that the people who write books and who have these ideas operate with their own presuppositions, which color what they know and what they write. We must therefore sift what is said in the light of our own presuppositions.

The Philosophy of Science

The philosophy of science has been vigorously discussing the contextual character of knowledge ever since the appearance of Thomas Kuhn's book. Various edited collections of articles interacting with Kuhn provide an introduction to the literature and the state of the discussion. One should note Gary Gutting, ed., *Paradigms and Revolutions* (Notre Dame: University of Notre Dame Press, 1980); Ian Hacking, ed., *Scientific Revolutions* (Oxford: Oxford University Press, 1981); Imre Lakatos and Alan Musgrave, eds., *Criticism and the Growth of Knowledge* (Cambridge: Cambridge University Press, 1970).

Predecessors of Kuhn also shared some of his interests in the contextual conditioning of scientific research. In his preface, Kuhn acknowledges the influence of Alexandre Koyré, *Etudes Galiléennes,* 3 vols. (Paris: Hermann, 1939); Emile Meyerson, *Identity and Reality* (New York: Macmillan, 1930); Hélène Metzger, *Les doctrines chimiques en France, du début du XVIIe :KSà la fin du XVIIIe :KSsiècle* (Paris: Presses universitaires de France, 1923); idem, *Newton, Stahl, Boerhaave et la doctrine chimique* (Paris: Alcan, 1930); and Anneliese Maier, *Die Vorläufer Galileis im 14. Jahrhundert* (Rome: Edizioni di storia e letteratura, 1949). See also Michael Polanyi, *Personal Knowledge: Towards a Post-Critical Philosophy* (Chicago: University of Chicago Press, 1958); idem, *Science, Faith, and Society* (Chicago: University of Chicago Press, 1964); idem, *The Tacit Dimension* (London: Routledge & Kegan Paul, 1967); Jean Piaget, *The Child's Conception of Physical Causality* (London: Routledge & Kegan Paul, 1930); idem, *Les notions de mouvement et de vitesse chez l'enfant* (Paris: Presses universitaires de France, 1946).

Other developments react in important ways to Kuhn. Some critics have simply misunderstood Kuhn, but there are also some significant positive developments. On the left of Kuhn, taking a more relativist, even anarchist, position, is Paul Feyerabend, *Against Method* (London: Verso, 1978). On the right of Kuhn, but endeavoring to take account of his insights, is Imre Lakatos, *The Methodology of Scientific Research Programmes* (Cambridge: Cambridge University Press, 1978). A significant extension of Kuhn in the direction of embedding scientific explanation in historical explanation is Alasdaire MacIntyre, "Epistemological Crises, Dramatic Narrative, and the Philosophy of Science," in *Paradigms and Revolutions,* ed. Gary Gutting (Notre Dame: University of Notre Dame Press, 1980), pp. 54–74.

Presuppositional Apologetics

Presuppositional apologetics as developed by Cornelius Van Til has emphasized the key role of presuppositions in theological and apologetic discussions. Presuppositions include not only consciously held philosophical assumptions but unconsciously assumed elements of one's worldview. They are one's basic commitments.[1] Van Til has repeatedly emphasized the all-important question of religious roots, asking his reader in effect, Are you for God or against him? Do you bow before God as your Lord, or do you wish to be your own god and lord? Do you endeavor to obey God, or do you obey your own autonomous ideas and standards? The antithesis between Christian and non-Christian life and thinking affects everything that we do. See Cornelius Van Til, *The Defense of the Faith,* 2d ed. (Philadelphia: Presbyterian & Reformed, 1963); idem, *An Introduction to Systematic Theology* (Phillipsburg, N.J.: Presbyterian & Reformed, 1974); idem, *A Christian Theory of Knowledge* (Philadelphia: Presbyterian and Reformed, 1969); idem, *Christian-Theistic Evidences* (Nutley, N.J.: Presbyterian and Reformed, 1976); Thom Notaro, *Van Til and the Use of Evidence* (Phillipsburg, N.J.: Presbyterian and Reformed, 1980); John M. Frame, *The Doctrine of the Knowledge of God* (Phillipsburg, N.J.: Presbyterian and Reformed, 1987). For an elementary introduction, see Richard L. Pratt, *Every Thought Captive: A Study Manual for the Defense of Christian Truth* (Phillipsburg, N.J.: Presbyterian and Reformed, 1979). Though some think that there are significant differences between Van Til and Francis Schaeffer, the latter's works also belong in this category. See especially Francis A. Schaeffer, *Escape from Reason* (Downers Grove, Ill.: InterVarsity, 1968); idem, *The God Who Is There* (Chicago: InterVarsity, 1968); idem, *He Is There and He Is Not Silent* (Wheaton, Ill.: Tyndale, 1972).

Ideas similar to Van Til's have also been articulated by the Christian philosophers in the tradition of cosmonomic philosophy. See Herman Dooyeweerd, *A New Critique of Theoretical Thought* (Philadelphia: Presbyterian and Reformed, 1969); Hendrik van Riessen, *Wijsbegeerte* (Kampen: Kok, 1970); Hendrik G. Stoker, *Beginsels en metodes in die wetenskap* (Potchefstroom: Pro Rege-Pers, 1961); Daniël F. M. Strauss, *Wysbegeerte en vakwetenskap* (Bloemfontein: Sacum, 1973). See also Nicholas Wolterstorff, *Reason Within the Bounds of Religion* (Grand Rapids: Eerdmans, 1976).

Van Til concentrated almost wholly on the question of religious basic commitments. The cultural outworkings of those commitments are less explored, although Francis Scha-

---

[1]See Frame, "God and Biblical Language."

effer and those associated with him have done important ground-breaking work in exploring the cultural effects. See, for example, Os Guinness, *The Dust of Death* (Downers Grove, Ill.: InterVarsity, 1973); Hendrik R. Rookmaaker, *Modern Art and the Death of a Culture* (London: InterVarsity, 1970). Moreover, the general idea that one needs to inspect the philosophical presuppositions of theological and scientific work has become fairly widespread in evangelical circles. See, for example, John S. Feinberg, "Truth: Relationship of Theories of Truth to Hermeneutics"; Winfried Corduan, "Philosophical Presuppositions Affecting Biblical Hermeneutics"; and Millard J. Erickson, "Presuppositions of Non-Evangelical Hermeneutics"; all in *Hermeneutics, Inerrancy, and the Bible,* ed. Earl D. Radmacher and Robert D. Preus (Grand Rapids: Zondervan, 1984).

Relativistic Philosophy

Various forms of relativism and pragmatism have enjoyed a rapid growth of attention and interest because they focus on the relativity of pieces of knowledge to a whole framework or conceptual system. See, for example, the works of Nicholas Rescher, *Methodological Pragmatism* (New York: New York University Press, 1977); Richard Rorty, *Philosophy and the Mirror of Nature* (Princeton: Princeton University Press, 1979); Fredrick Christopher Swoyer, "Conceptual Relativism" (Ph.D. diss., University of Minnesota, 1976); Jack W. Meiland and Michael Krausz, eds., *Relativism, Cognitive and Moral* (Notre Dame: University of Notre Dame Press, 1982).

These philosophies may be called relativistic because they do not see any supposed knowledge as foundational. No area is immune to criticism for all time, no area is in principle so certain that we can say it is not subject to revision, no matter what may come. We may be confronted with facts or alternative interpretations that lead us to revise our worldview. These philosophies, however, usually believe in truth of some kind, although they do not allow that we can achieve an absolute philosophical certainty about that truth. Hence they cannot be dismissed simply by using the typical antirelativist argument to the effect that, if all knowledge is relative, the statement "all knowledge is relative" is itself relative and therefore refuted.

Evangelical Christians, of course, know of a source of knowledge outside of the limitations of human finiteness. We can never adopt a full-fledged relativism. But we ought not for that reason to ignore the revival in relativistic philosophy. Non-Christians can still have insights about the implications of human finiteness.

Philosophical Hermeneutics

The phenomenological/existentialist tradition in philosophical hermeneutics has long been interested in the conditioned character of human understanding. In this tradition, human understanding always takes place against the background of assumptions and realities of human existence in history, existence as a person in society, existence as a person immersed in language as a pre- and supraindividual reality, and existence "unto death." The key figures are Heidegger and Gadamer. See Martin Heidegger, *Unterwegs zur Sprache* (Frankfurt am Main: Klostermann, 1985); Hans-Georg Gadamer, *Truth and Method* (New York: Seabury, 1975). One may also add the "hermeneutics of suspicion," practiced by people with interest in economic and political conditioning of ideologies and propaganda. See Jürgen Habermas, *Knowledge and Human Interests* (Boston: Beacon, 1972); idem, *Theorie und Praxis,* 3d ed. (Neuwied: Luchterhand, 1969). For a combined approach, see Paul Ricoeur, *Interpretation Theory* (Fort Worth: Texas Christian University Press, 1976); idem, *The Rule of Metaphor* (Toronto: University of Toronto Press, 1977).

Sociology of Knowledge

The sociology of knowledge has long dealt with ways in which the information and beliefs that a society counts as knowledge are passed along, maintained, legitimated, and supplemented by social processes and institutions. The sociology of knowledge makes clear the great dependence that knowledge has on a social setting for its maintenance. Kuhn's work might be understood as nothing more than the application of sociology of knowledge to the field of science. Sociology of knowledge is in fact interested in the social context for knowledge in any academic discipline, including biblical interpretation. It is also interested in the social context of the more informal and tacit knowledge of ordinary practitioners of religion. Many of the similarities that we have observed between biblical interpretation and Kuhn's view of science are similarities rooted in the general characteristics of the social context of all human knowledge.

Sociology of knowledge has roots even in the previous century, but it received a kind of formal inauguration with Karl Mannheim, *Ideology and Utopia: An Introduction to the Sociology of Knowledge* (New York: Harcourt, Brace & World, 1968; orig. ed., 1929). One may find more up-to-date discussion in Peter L. Berger and Thomas Luckmann, *The Social Construction of Reality: A Treatise in the Sociology of Knowledge* (Garden City, N.Y.: Doubleday, 1966); Irving L. Horowitz, *Philosophy, Science, and the Sociology of Knowledge* (Westport, Conn.: Greenwood, 1976); Michael Mulkay, *Science and the Sociology of Knowledge* (London: Allen & Unwin, 1979); K. J. Regelous, ed., *The Sociology of Knowledge* (New York: State Mutual, 1980); Gunter W. Remmling, ed., *Towards the Sociology of Knowledge: Origin and Development of a Sociological Thought Style* (Atlantic Highlands, N.J.: Humanities, 1974); Nico Stehr and Volker Meja, eds., *Society and Knowledge: Contemporary Perspectives on the Sociology of Knowledge* (New Brunswick, N.J.: Transaction, 1984); Susan J. Hekman, *Hermeneutics and the Sociology of Knowledge* (Notre Dame: Notre Dame University Press, 1983).

Anthropology

The field of cultural anthropology includes numerous studies of the influence of worldviews and the influence of culture on knowledge. Here I refer readers only to evangelical discussions of the implications of anthropology. See especially Harvie M. Conn, *Eternal Word and Changing Worlds: Theology, Anthropology, and Mission in Trialogue* (Grand Rapids: Zondervan, 1984); Paul G. Hiebert, *Cultural Anthropology*, 2d ed. (Grand Rapids: Baker, 1983); Charles H. Kraft, *Christianity in Culture: A Study in Dynamic Biblical Theologizing in Cross-Cultural Perspective* (Maryknoll, N.Y.: Orbis, 1979).

Theological Method

Some discussions are also taking place concerning the implications of contexts for our methods of biblical interpretation. Liberation theology and contextualization (as the term is used in missions theory) both study the influence of culture on the shape of our theological questions and answers. They involve strenuous reexamination of traditional interpretive method. The radicals in these areas are advocating something like a Kuhnian revolution in method.[2]

---

[2]See the section *The Study of Theology* by Richard A. Muller elsewhere in this volume.

More to the point are discussions of the implications of modern science for biblical interpretation. As we noted at the beginning of this book, many discussions have considered the relation of science and theology. But there have been fewer discussions on scientific *method* in comparison with theological *method*.[3] Still less has recent work taken into account Kuhn's move away from the idea that science presents us with a purely objective, disinterested account of the way the world is. The most notable exception is Ian G. Barbour, *Myths, Models, and Pardigms: A Comparative Study in Science and Religion* (New York: Harper & Row, 1974).[4] Barbour's book is a very important work in this area because it stands almost alone in being a post-Kuhnian attempt to spell out some of the connections between science and religion on a methodological level.

But Barbour's book does not do all that one might wish. In the first place, Barbour is interested mostly in the comparison of science and *religion*, not science and Christianity or science and theology. He is most concerned with philosophical issues concerning the viability of religious language in general. On this philosophical level, Barbour's book contains many useful ideas. But he says too little about the implications for hermeneutical method and the academic subdisciplines of biblical interpretation. What he does say shows that he is uncomfortable with the exclusive claims of Christianity, the claims of propositional revelation, and the orthodox doctrine of God.[5] In particular, when Barbour provides us with examples of alternative models for Christ and for God, the newer alternatives are heterodox. Though Barbour is interested in worldviews, he is not willing to challenge in a radical way the dominant Western dream of human autonomy in thought. Hence Evangelicals will find here a mixture of good and bad. If we wish to find a book that reforms biblical interpretation on the basis of a biblical worldview, we will have to look elsewhere.

My own book *Symphonic Theology: The Validity of Multiple Perspectives in Theology* (Grand Rapids: Zondervan, 1987) works out the methodological problems related to the practice of single-perspective versus multiple-perspective approaches to theological problems. Many of its concerns are similar to those I discuss in this book. But *Symphonic Theology* interacts primarily not with Kuhn but with internal developments within theology and linguistics and should be seen as complementary to the discussions in this book.

---

[3]Despite expressed concerns for theological method, Thomas F. Torrance's work should be classified with others that explore the general topic of science and theology. His procedure is more like that of a philosopher building a worldview or an epistemology than it is like Kuhn's sociological approach. See Torrance's works, *Christian Theology and Scientific Culture* (New York: Oxford University Press, 1981), *Divine and Contingent Order* (Oxford: Oxford University Press, 1981), *Reality and Evangelical Theology* (Philadelphia: Westminster, 1982), and *Transformation and Convergence in the Frame of Knowledge* (Grand Rapids: Eerdmans, 1984). In *Transformation and Convergence*, Torrance mentions Kuhn (p. 243) and notes the conditioning character of worldviews and the social backgrounds of knowledge, especially the philosophical dualisms of modern Western thought (e.g., pp. x–xiii). Nevertheless, Kuhn has not substantially influenced Torrance. A closer analysis shows that Torrance selects from modern physics and from philosophical epistemology just those features that he finds convenient for analogically illustrating his Barthian theology. His presuppositions greatly influence what he selects and how he describes it. Torrance's work is thus more an illustration of Kuhn's observations about the role of frameworks and presuppositions than a continuation or supplement to Kuhn's work.

[4]Note also a related book by Barbour, *Issues in Science and Relgion* (New York: Harper & Row, 1971). Some very sweeping appeals to paradigm shifts appear in James P. Martin, "Toward a Post-Critical Paradigm," *New Testament Studies* 33 (1987): 370–85.

[5]Barbour, *Myths, Models, and Paradigms*, pp. 8, 176–77; pp. 18, 134, 138; idem, *Issues in Science and Religion*.

THE STUDY
OF THEOLOGY

*From Biblical Interpretation
to Contemporary Formulation*

Richard A. Muller

Contents

Editor's Preface

Interpretation does not end with exegesis" (see below, p. 541). With that understatement, Dr. Muller alerts us to the great breadth of theological perspective that should inform our reading of Scripture.

As I sought to point out in the first volume in this series, much biblical scholarship has overreacted to the danger—a real danger to be sure—of allowing theological commitments to impose a predetermined meaning on the text (see *Has the Church Misread the Bible?* elsewhere in this volume). This overreaction has led many interpreters to ignore the intimate connection that exists between exegesis and the other theological disciplines. In his defense of the classical fourfold model (the biblical, historical, systematic, and practical disciplines), Dr. Muller broadens the reader's horizons and brings in a much-needed corrective.

What also comes through in his exposition, however, is that (in a somewhat different sense) interpretation does not *begin* with exegesis either. Biblical scholars who downplay the significance of theology for exegesis only fool themselves if they think they can approach the text without theological predispositions. And the best antidote for the *unconscious*, and often detrimental, intrusion of such assumptions is to develop a coherent understanding of the way theology functions in the hermeneutical process.

Dr. Muller proves himself a capable guide for doing just that. He is one of those rare scholars who have managed to combine deep specialization in a chosen field with breadth of erudition. A recognized authority in the area of post-Reformation dogmatics, he has however also written on a wide variety of theological topics. Accordingly, he demands some effort and concentration on the part of the reader. Biblical students with little prior interest in theology may be tempted to balk. They will be the poorer if they give in to that temptation. Cutting corners seldom works in hermeneutics.

The author acknowledges the controversial character of many of the issues he discusses. His primary aim, however, is not to persuade us about a particular way of solving the problems, but to understand the nature of those problems. Whether we agree or disagree with him, he wants us to do so consciously and intelligently. I commend this volume as a signal contribution to the all-important task of integrating hermeneutics into the whole theological enterprise.

Moisés Silva

Introduction

A middle-aged and much-experienced minister stood before the graduating class, faculty, and guests at the commencement exercises of a well-known American seminary. He had been called upon to speak as a representative new graduate of one of the more popular degree programs, the Doctor of Ministry. Dressed in his new robe and elegant doctoral hood, he mounted the podium with words of praise for the seminary, words that, by his own admission, were as much a surprise to himself as to anyone else. He had always frowned on seminaries and seminary education. He had warned dozens of young people about the "ivory tower" of academic study and its irrelevance to the "real work" of ministry. He had mocked processes of accreditation that only resulted in making seminaries more academic and more isolated from reality. He had scorned the theological speculations that led away from and undermined the faith. Why, then, was he graduating from a seminary? He was there because of the practical, "how-to" approach of the Doctor of Ministry degree. He was there because this degree was different—it demanded no theological speculation, no academic, ivory-tower critical thinking, no retreat from the nitty-gritty reality of daily ministry. In fact, the ivory-tower courses—courses dealing with critical exegesis, the history of Christian doctrine, and philosophical and systematic theology—had not been a part of his program of education. He had studied only useful, relevant subjects.

The speaker didn't see me wince. Nor did he see me shake my head somewhat sadly over what appeared to me to be his failure to see the crucial interrelationship of the task of ministry and the work of theology. He couldn't see me because I was behind him on the platform sitting quietly with the other benighted residents of the ivory tower. This new graduate, dressed in the splendid new robes of his new degree, I noted to myself, was taking nothing home with him but his diploma and his hood. He had come and gone and remained inwardly unchanged. He was quite pleased with himself and quite representative not only of a certain constituency in any graduating class of almost any seminary but also of a deep problem in the study of theology in America. Theology made no sense to him. He was intent on practicing ministry without it. Where had he gone wrong? Where had *we* gone wrong?

Perhaps what was most disturbing to me was that my own teaching career in seminary had been preceded by seven years of parish ministry, three as an assistant in a fairly large urban church and four as the sole minister in a small rural church, and I had come to the task of teaching with a firm conviction that everything I had learned both in seminary and in graduate school had been of use to me in my ministry. I firmly believed and still do believe that the year-long sequence that I teach on the history of Christian doctrine does relate directly to the concerns of ministry. When I taught systematic theology, I operated under the same conviction. And I hold a similar conviction for the courses in Old and New Testament—including the courses that deal with critical, textual problems— taught by my colleagues in those fields. On the one hand, I was somewhat relieved that our new Doctor of Ministry had taken no courses in historical, systematic, or biblical theology at our seminary: at least his remarks had been made in ignorance of our course offerings in those areas. On the other hand, I was filled with deep worries over the nature of his studies and over his failure to recognize the importance not merely of theological study but also of thinking theologically.

What is the connection between the interpretive study of Scripture and the other fields of study emphasized in seminary training and in Christian ministry? How do the results of our exegesis of Scripture impinge on our reading and understanding of the history of the church and its doctrines, on our study and use of systematic theology, on our apologetics or defense of the faith, and on the widely varied areas of ministerial practice and Christian life? From one point of view, the answers to these questions ought to be self-evident. If the Reformation battle cry of *sola Scriptura* still echoes at the heart of Protestantism, then the interpretation of Scripture must be the foundation of our evaluation and use of the materials of historical and systematic theology and the firm basis of all preaching, counseling, and Christian living. We should not even need to ask the questions.

The questions, however, do press upon us constantly and consistently, particularly because the interpretive problems recognized by most contemporary theologians and felt, albeit uncomprehendingly, by our graduation speaker render the movement from biblical text to doctrinal formulation considerably more difficult today than in the sixteenth century. The traditional forms of theology and preaching frequently fail the tests of exegesis and contemporary theologizing—while, at the same time, much contemporary theology and exegesis fails to address directly the needs of the church.

How often do we hear quaint moralizing or amateurish psychologizing instead of biblical, exegetical, or expository preaching? Even the best of preachers experience at times the feeling that direct address of contemporary problems sometimes calls for a less-than-traditional sermon, and that such sermons move away from the time-honored exegetical and expository forms. How often do we hear the complaint (or experience it ourselves) that a particular doctrine or confession or system, whether it be the doctrine of the divine attributes or of the Trinity or of penal substitutionary atonement, does not easily fit into the modern practice of Christianity—perhaps because it is difficult to document directly from any single text of Scripture properly interpreted according to modern critical standards or perhaps because it seems impossible to correlate with any experience of life in our world? The most confessionally orthodox of teachers and preachers experience such worries, and those less content with the traditional forms of theology often find themselves at odds with the confessions of their church and divorced from the biblical message in its ancient context.

The problems illustrated by the speech at a seminary graduation cannot be dismissed as an individual aberration. They reach much deeper. They are the result of severance of theory from practice and practice from theory that has made many theological theoreticians question the intellectual and spiritual future of the church at large and the academic future of their disciplines—and that has led many ministerial practitioners to doubt the value of all things theological. But there ought to be no theology divorced from the practice of religion and no practice of religion without some theological consciousness of the meaning of its activity and work. Theological training as a whole—biblical, historical, and systematic, as well as "practical" or ministerial—ought to reflect the life of the church and be of value to the life of the church. Theological training, in short, ought to cohere. The basic, churchly meditation on Scripture ought, as it has in the past, to issue in a theology relevant to Christian life and practice.

There is, in other words, an intellectual and spiritual short circuit or, more accurately, a series of short circuits, that occur at some point between the study of Scripture and of the various other foundational disciplines in theology and the practice of preaching, teaching or counseling, the churchly work that ought to move forward on the basis of the church's theology. We have evidence of these short circuits in the remarks of the graduate, but we also have evidence of them in the frequently heard complaints that critical, historical exegesis does not lead to preaching, that theological system fails to address even indirectly either the problems identified by a critical exegesis of the text or by a life of ministry in the church, that the historical study of Christianity functions more as a display of museum-pieces than as a discovery of materials useful to us in our present. The graduating student had a problem, but he was not alone in it. The problem stands at the heart of theological study in the present day.

This book has grown out of a reflection on the needs and problems confronting theology in our time. Theology suffers from a lack of direction and a loss of unity among its subdisciplines. Exegesis and theological system, in particular, do not seem to function as part of a larger interpretive unity. This is, moreover, a problem that is not confined to students. The problem exists also among professionals, trained in the disciplines and charged with the task of teaching theology. We teach at a high level of sophistication, frequently with little or no concern for the way in which our subject contributes to the work of our colleagues or how the work of the entire theological faculty fits together into a greater whole for the service of Christian ministry. Several authors have come forward to demand the wholesale reappraisal of theological curriculum. There is a widespread doubt concerning the continued viability of the classical "fourfold" curriculum. And colleagues criticize what they call the "university model" of seminary education based on departmental units representing the four "classical" divisions of theological study.

I do not claim to find a definitive answer to these problems for all sectors of the theological community. I hope only to discuss the interpretive or hermeneutical implications of the fourfold curriculum—biblical, historical, systematic, and practical theology—to present a case for its structure, and to argue the essential unity of the disciplines in their service to the church. My hope, in other words, is to show that the biblical, historical, systematic, practical model is an interpretive structure that leads from the exegetical disciplines to theological formulation. There is, and there must be, a hermeneutical enterprise that is larger than the interpretive ventures of each of the various theological disciplines. Interpretation does not end with exegesis. The point of interpretation is not simply to show where an author is "coming from" but where the teachings of the author point. If, moreover, the teachings of biblical authors point authoritatively into our present, then our interpretive task leads far beyond the fundamental exegetical inquiry into the meaning of a text in its original context. Our interpretive task extends from the text, via the various disciplines that show the path of the text and its meaning into the present, to contemporary formulation.

The seeming dual emphasis of the present volume, therefore, is really a single emphasis, approached by way of two descriptions of its form. The emphasis falls on interpretation, specifically on patterns of interpretation larger than the initial address to a text. Formally, that emphasis can be described in terms of hermeneutics and "hermeneutical circles" (chap. 4) and in terms of the structure of biblical, historical, systematic, and practical study that should generate both the interest in interpretation and the proper context for address both to the authoritative text of Scripture and to the needs of the present-day community of faith.

My hope implies a rather ambitious venture. Were it not for the need, one might be tempted to consider it impossible and pass on to a highly specialized and therefore less troublesome exercise. My own attempt to teach what has been traditionally termed theological encyclopedia has only confirmed the difficulty of dealing, theoretically and schematically, with an entire curriculum. I am also impressed by the necessity of the task. If seminary study is to have any coherence and if it is to issue forth in coherent ministry, theology must make sense as a whole.

The contemporary critique of the fourfold curriculum, particularly as represented by the work of Edward Farley, contains some very important criticisms and insights, and any discussion of the study of theology and of the unity of "biblical, historical, systematic, and practical theology" must take them into consideration together with the works on theological study and formulation by Ebeling and Pannenberg. The second, related issue—the complaint against the "university model"—also needs to be discussed, albeit more briefly. The educational model found in our seminaries is not and never was a pure university model but rather a churchly model developed in recognition of the need of clergy to engage not simply in ministry but in *educated ministry*. The content and methods of the biblical, historical, and systematic disciplines, as traditionally taught in our seminaries, have rested on an assumption of a solid liberal arts education and have built on the liberal arts model, of course in a churchly direction. The complaint against the university model is, sadly, a complaint not unlike the complaint mounted against the classical liberal arts and social science curricula of our universities by the "forward looking" and incredibly mistaken educators of the mid-sixties and early seventies, who held that courses on Western Civilization and the Great Books could be replaced by "relevant" and "practical" courses.

Our situation is doubly sad, inasmuch as the seminary-based critics of the classical model have not learned from the disaster caused by their fellow-educators in the university. We have, in fact, encountered in our seminaries a problem identical to that examined in E. D. Hirsch's *Cultural Literacy* and Allan Bloom's *Closing of the American Mind*.[1] By looking away not only from the fourfold model for the study of theology but also from the traditional *content* of the fourfold model—instead of engaging in the admittedly difficult task of making the fourfold model work—seminaries have been guilty of creating several generations of clergy and teachers who are fundamentally ignorant of the materials of the theological task and prepared to argue (in their own defense) the irrelevance of classical study to the practical operation of ministry. The sad result has been the loss, in many places, of the central, cultural function of the church in the West and the replacement of a culturally and intellectually rich clergy with a group of practitioners and operations-directors who can do almost anything except make sense of the church's theological message in the contemporary context.

---

[1]E. D. Hirsch, Jr., *Cultural Literacy: What Every American Needs to Know* (New York: Houghton Mifflin, 1987); Allan Bloom, *The Closing of the American Mind: How Higher Education Has Failed Democracy and Impoverished the Souls of Today's Students* (New York: Simon & Schuster, 1987).

Making sense of the church's theological message in the contemporary context is really little more than the decisively Christian version of the great educational quest of the old liberal arts curriculum on which theology has rested since the foundation of the universities in the twelfth and thirteenth centuries. The issue has always been to understand and to be able to express our understanding of the world-order and of our place in it as human beings. The success of the great philosophers in addressing that issue is what makes Plato and Aristotle still worth reading. And the success of such theologians as Aquinas, Luther, Calvin, and Schleiermacher in pressing the very same issue from the point of view of a theological or religious construction of reality is what makes their works crucial to the study of theology as it leads toward contemporary theological statement and to the task of ministry.

Beyond this fundamentally intellectual issue of the coherence of the message and of the ability of theology to address the deep concerns of world and culture, lies another, more subtle problem. As Hirsch and Bloom have recognized in their critiques of secular education,[2] the classical curricula did not only instill great ideas into young minds, they also instilled values along with the ideas. At a rather profound level, classical study built character. And as one colleague of mine has pointed out, the classical seminary education of the nineteenth and early twentieth centuries, like the classical university curriculum, was also profoundly concerned with building character.[3] It is a sad by-product of the loss of the older academic curricula that we also lie in danger of losing something not always noted in connection with intellectual growth: spiritual and moral fiber.

In my own experience in ministry, whether in a relatively large urban church or in a rural congregation, I was consistently impressed by the direct application to life, the immediate relevance, of my seminary training, particularly my training in the so-called classical disciplines, and even of my later graduate training in theology. I came from parish ministry to seminary teaching with the conviction, resting on the experience of day-to-day ministry, that biblical exegesis, church history, history of Christian doctrine, philosophy of religion, and doctrinal or dogmatic theology provided crucial resources for the everyday life of the believing community. Beyond this, the longer I worked in ministry, the stronger became my conviction that all of my studies, despite their diversity (whether diversity of subject or diversity of approach as dictated by particular professors) functioned as an interpretive unity—and that theological thinking and Christian living were profoundly interrelated. To make the point in a somewhat different way: the theology I learned from my teachers in both the theoretical and the practical fields and the Christianity I both taught to and learned from the members of my two congregations are one and the same.

Finally, a word about the character and tone of this book: the themes and discussions I present are unabashedly theological and unabashedly systematizing. This does not mean that I intend for the study of theology or of any particular theological discipline to be conducted without any objectivity or without any examination of presuppositions. On the contrary, theological study is distinct from the generalized exercise of piety precisely because it is a self-conscious exercise that knows and examines its presuppositions, follows sound principles of analysis and interpretation, and consistently attempts to let its materials speak in terms of their own presuppositions and contents (particularly when

[2]Cf. Hirsch, *Cultural Literacy,* pp. 82–92, 98–102; Bloom, *Closing,* e.g., pp. 136–37.
[3]James E. Bradley, now engaged in work on the relationship of the building of character to seminary education in the United States under an ATS grant.[1]

some of those presuppositions and contents stand critically juxtaposed with the cherished assumptions of the present). Nonetheless the basic principles of analysis and interpretation recognize a fundamental connection between exegete and text, between the Christian and the Christian tradition, between the student of theology and all of his materials. Objectivity in analysis and commitment in faith need not be mutually exclusive.

All of the preceding considerations point to the fact that the theological pluralism of the present age is a barrier—perhaps an insurmountable one—to the creation of a single paradigm for the unified understanding and study of theology. No particular paradigm will be universally received. Granting this premise, the paradigm presented here has a certain specificity and restriction. I am unwilling, however, to adopt such classifications as "liberal" or "conservative," "rationalist" or "fideist" as characterizations either of what my position is or what it is not. Not only are these labels divisive, they are also misleading: when I read the theology of a "liberal" theologian of the early twentieth century, such as William Adams Brown or William Newton Clarke or even the somewhat notorious Charles Augustus Briggs, I come away with the distinct impression that none of these writers can easily be classified as "liberal" in terms of our present-day theological spectrum. I much prefer terms like "contemporary" or "contemporizing," "traditional," "historical perspective," "critically orthodox," or even a term like Oden's "post-modern orthodoxy"—although each of these is also far from perfect.

My underlying hope in writing this book is to present a view of theology that respects and preserves the truths and insights of the Christian tradition but that also points toward a way of understanding and stating those truths and insights in the contemporary context. In other words, the model proposed here for the study of theology attempts to be traditional but not locked into the past; orthodox in proposing a churchly "right teaching" but without attempting to repristinate a particular historical form of orthodoxy; historical and critical in its recognition of the character of our tradition and the tools necessary to its correct examination but not to the extent either of tearing down the edifice of the tradition or of turning it into a museum incapable of present-day relevance. In addition, the model is intended to be broadly and generally useful, granting that it provides a pattern for understanding the working of theology and the productive movement of study through the disciplines rather than a discussion of a particular theological system or the relationship of the various parts of theological study to such a system.

Since, moreover, this book is about the interpretive unity of the studies that spring historically and functionally from the biblical foundations of Christian faith, it is written at all points with a view toward that unity. Thus, the sections on biblical and historical study will contain references to the systematic and practical disciplines. Whereas I hope to stand firmly against the tendency to prejudge the biblical materials on the basis of the history of doctrine or contemporary dogmatics or contemporary praxis, I find myself totally incapable of considering any one aspect of theological study or any one of the basic theological disciplines apart from its relationship to the others. It is precisely the development of a viable picture of those relationships that is the subject of this book.

I undertake this synthesizing approach fully aware that my own academic specialization stands in the way of the task and that the problem of the fragmentation of theology into isolated subdisciplines is a problem in which I participate and, to the extent that I teach in my own area of specialization to the exclusion of other areas, a problem of my own making. This book is a prospectus for overcoming the problem and the perception of fragmentation in the study of theology. I come to it as a historian of doctrine who also works in the area of systematic theology—so that I have a sense of the historically conceived unity of theological thinking and some hope for present-day synthesis. My weaknesses, apart from those inherent in my own specialized work, will surely lie in the other areas touched on by this volume. I especially ask the forgiveness of colleagues in the fields of Old and New Testament study, where I am a dabbler at best—but I also hope that my attempt here at forming an overarching prospectus for unified study and interpretation of theology will provide both help and stimulation to teachers and students, to concerned clergy and laity who feel the need for such an effort as strongly as I do.

one

THE STUDY

OF THEOLOGY

Issues and Problems

PRELIMINARY ASSUMPTIONS

The study of theology has never been an easy task. Writers in past ages of the church—from the age of the fathers, to the high scholastic era of the thirteenth and fourteenth centuries, to the era of Reformation and post-Reformation Protestantism—have declared with a notable uniformity that the study of theology calls for a complete devotion on the part of the student. They were convinced that it demands a mastery of tools and sources, a grasp of language and philosophy, and an openness to, indeed, a desire for inward, spiritual formation and development. Christian thinkers have always recognized, moreover, the difficulty of moving from the text of Scripture into the church's present with a doctrine and a preaching relevant to the concerns of Christian congregations and Christian missions. Nevertheless, despite these difficulties, the church in past ages was remarkably successful in its work. Methods of interpretation, credal formulations, overarching systematic expressions of the faith, and architectonic consideration of the interrelationship of the several disciplines and subdisciplines in theology have, in these past ages, proved capable of opening the text of Scripture and bringing the Word to bear doctrinally and practically on the life of the church.[1]

When we survey the contemporary state of theology, however, a different picture emerges. We see profound debate over methods of interpretation focused on the seemingly negative effects of the higher criticism on the doctrinal and practical work of Christian

---

[1]Cf. the section *Has the Church Misread the Bible?* by Moisés Silva elsewhere in this volume, especially chaps. 2 and 3.

theology. We see a decay of interest in and commitment to old creeds and confessions without any corresponding interest in or commitment to the production of new creeds and confessions of a comparable biblical and doctrinal quality to those being quietly set aside. We detect no dearth of theological systems, but even a cursory examination of most of these productions reveals a failure to reflect concerns of the contemporary church and a certain intellectual and spiritual distance between dogmatic system and Christian piety or the Christian pulpit. Finally, we encounter a degree of curricular uncertainty among many Christian educators concerning the possibility of creating a cohesive model for the integration and churchly use of the disciplines and subdisciplines in the theological "encyclopedia."

Of course, not all of these problems are present everywhere in the life of church and seminary, nor are they felt with equal intensity. Some denominations still maintain a strong commitment to their creeds and confessions, and there are surely some seminaries and some individual theologians who are reasonably successful in overcoming the separation frequently noted between theological system and Christian life. The theological curriculum, moreover, ought to function as an organized body of teaching that is production-oriented. When we ask the question of the relationship of biblical studies to contemporary theological statement, we are in fact asking the question of theological study, a question that ought to be answered at a general and theoretical level by the theological curriculum in order that it can also be answered at a specific and concrete level by the individual practitioner whether teacher, clergy, or laity.

Much of the discussion about contemporary theology and theological education has focused on the standard division of theology into the biblical, historical, systematic, and practical fields, as inherited by our schools and seminaries from the teachers of the nineteenth century. The fourfold model appears to be a fairly objective description of the structure of theology until one examines the subdisciplines that fit rather uncomfortably at times under the rubrics of biblical, historical, systematic, and practical theology. These subdisciplines, at least as they are typically presented in the present day, exist as more or less isolated subject areas rather than as individual aspects of a larger whole cohering harmoniously in dialogue with one another. The problem is illustrated by a survey of the various topics in the curriculum and the problems encountered as we study these topics or subject areas.

The beginning theological student and the parish minister in our highly pluralistic society are both faced with a profound educational, spiritual, and intellectual problem, considerably greater and graver in scope and implication than that faced by theological students and clergy in past ages. That problem may be addressed, at least in part, from the point of view of the many and varied sources and perspectives that must be addressed by theology today. The modern era has brought about a proliferation of theological disciplines and subdisciplines. Theology today does not build, simply, as it did in the eleventh and twelfth centuries, on two clearly defined bodies of knowledge—Scripture and tradition. Nor can we, today, pronounce the solution of the Reformation—*sola Scriptura*, Scripture alone—with the simplicity and ease of the sixteenth century. We now face, not one tradition, but many traditions: denominational theologies, independent academic theologies, infinite numbers of "isms," and a growing number of restricted topical theologies, products of the religious version of the "political action committee" or private-interest lobby. This plethora of traditions and types of theology clouds the *sola Scriptura* of the Reformers, because any number of these separate theologies—particularly the denominational and private-interest theologies—lay exclusive claim to biblical truth. If one comes to theological study with a fairly open mind, the problem of affiliation, alignment, and basic perspective will be enormous.

For example, in studying systematic theology, you will quickly come to realize that you are not studying systematic theology as such but one of many variations of it. It will be Reformed or Lutheran or Arminian or Roman Catholic systematic theology—or perhaps "evangelical" systematic theology, although that label does not really identify the contents of a system very closely. Or it might be an existentialist system like Macquarrie's *Principles of Theology* or a "liberation" theology like that of Gutiérrez or Segundo. In looking to biblical studies, students will find a variety of approaches to the interpretation of Scripture, ranging from a strict application of Hirsch's belief that a text means essentially one thing, to a loose reading of a theory like Gadamer's that would have a text mean different things and point in several directions, all of them quite correctly! Historical events and the progress of ideas are subject to a variety of interpretations—and any honest historian will point out that one always deals with interpretation and never simple fact. As for the practical field, students and ministers will find not only a wide array of topics but also an entire spectrum of relationships to the other fields of study, including the rather extreme opinion that identifies biblical, systematic, and historical studies as essentially theoretical and then demands that theory take its point of departure from practice.

The diversification of theological curriculum presents a similar problem. Whereas the theological student of earlier times—from the rise of the cathedral schools in the eleventh century down to the period of Protestant orthodoxy in the seventeenth century—learned essentially a single discipline of traditional exegetical-dogmatic theology, the modern theological student is called upon to study such diverse subjects as exegesis; hermeneutics; systematic, philosophical, and apologetic theology; ethics; church history; history of doctrine; homiletics; liturgics; counseling; marriage and family ministry; and Christian formation. It is quite true that all of these topics were covered by the older theology—only then the package was neater and more unified. Since there was virtually only one pattern of biblical interpretation prior to the sixteenth century, and in the sixteenth century essentially two opposing models, hermeneutics or the science of interpretation was simply a presuppositional element in exegesis, the interpretation itself. And since the assumption was held by virtually all theologians of these earlier times that the interpretation of Scripture led directly to the doctrine of the church, with no underlying problematic disturbing the transition, exegesis and dogmatics (or systematic theology) were quite easily conjoined.

As for the other subdisciplines, it was formerly assumed that all systems of doctrine would have a certain philosophical component—philosophy being the humble handmaid of theology—and that ethics sprang directly from the biblical command with an occasional nod to Aristotle. Since the Ten Commandments could be virtually equated with natural law, the divergences between Scripture and Aristotle could be dealt with easily. The so-called practical or ministerial disciplines were not taught: homilies were simply popular elaborations on scriptural texts that were done, not taught; liturgics was the repetition of a tradition of great antiquity; counseling ministries and personal formation were essentially taken for granted as the necessary by-products of the exegetical and doctrinal study. Church history and history of doctrine were, until the late seventeenth century, simply the sense of tradition and of the chronology of debate that underlay doctrinal formulation—again, not separate disciplines.

Today, by way of contrast, these subjects do not fit together so neatly, and they have all become the discrete specialty areas of scholars. The vast body of literature in each area has made it impossible for anyone to be a truly competent generalist in theological study or to be a recognized specialist in more than one particular area. On the positive side, of course, specialization can mean the considerable refinement of any given subject area and a better grasp of its materials. But few theological students will even train to be specialists: ministry is by its very nature the work of a generalist who can understand Scripture and church, preach sermons, make sense out of Christian doctrine in discussion with laity, counsel with individuals, and function as an interpreter of reality in an increasingly pluralistic world.

All of this can be a bit daunting to students and to clergy, particularly when it has been spelled out in stark detail. The difficulty is enormous, particularly for anyone who hopes to find a coherent whole in seminary education today. But it is not insurmountable. Our fear of the problem ought not to deter us from the study—any more than Christian's increasing knowledge of the dangers on his pilgrim way ought to have ended his progress before he reached the goal of Mount Zion. We do need, more than ever in history, to meditate on our theological curriculum as we encounter it (rather than in retrospect) and to discover the relationships between its various elements—for the sake of consistent and unified Christian ministry and witness. We need, in short, to understand, to map out the territory of theological study.

That is precisely the purpose of the subject traditionally called theological encyclopedia. *Encyclopedia* is a term that has fallen on bad times. It is used, typically, to refer to works like the *Encyclopedia of Philosophy*, the *Schaff-Herzog Encyclopedia of Religious Knowledge*, the *World Book Encyclopedia* or *Columbia Desk Encyclopedia*. Etymologically, however, the word offers a broader meaning. It contains three Greek components: *en-cyclo-paideia*. *Paideia* means teaching and, thus, "encyclopedia" means a complete circle or circuit of teaching. "Theological Encyclopedia" indicates the complete circle of theological knowing, organized not alphabetically but in terms of the interrelationships of the several subject areas of theology.[2]

Thus Old and New Testament studies, whether historical, exegetical, or theological can be grouped together as "biblical theology." The history of the church, as distinct from the history of God's people within the canon of Scripture, encompasses institutional and doctrinal histories plus such subdivisions as the history of piety or spirituality. In the realm of contemporary theological endeavor, we can distinguish, more or less precisely, between disciplines that relate principally to knowing, the "systematic," and disciplines that relate principally to doing, the "practical." Systematic thinking includes doctrinal theology (sometimes called "systematic theology"), philosophical theology, apologetics, and ethics—all of which attempt to provide coherent structures of knowledge based on a given set of problems or ideas. The "practical" field encompasses those areas that relate directly to churchly practice or "doing"—homiletics; liturgics, or worship; counseling; ministry; and the practice of personal and corporate piety, which can be called Christian formation.

This broadly defined clustering of disciplines into four basic categories—biblical, historical, systematic, and practical—is not simply a convenient pattern for study. It is also a pattern that was developed in the light of interpretive considerations and with a view toward the "organic" unity of the various forms of theological study, primarily by a

---

[2]Cf. the discussion in Abraham Kuyper, *Principles of Sacred Theology*, trans. De Vries (New York: Scribner, 1898; repr. Grand Rapids: Baker, 1980), pp. 1–23.

group of teachers and scholars in the nineteenth century.[3] Granting the historical origins of the model, it is certainly a mistake to view it as precritical or uncritical—and an even graver mistake to ignore its hermeneutical significance and its implications not merely for the path of study but also for the path to theological formulation. There is clear evidence in the works of several nineteenth-century formulators of the fourfold model of theological study that they viewed it as a model for the integration, not so much of a myriad of diverse disciplines, but of distinct but nonetheless related patterns of theological understanding into a framework for the contemporary interpretation of Christian doctrine.[4] Rightly understood, the traditional encyclopedic approach to theology can provide a larger hermeneutical or interpretive structure for the movement from exegesis to contemporary formulation.

TOWARD A UNIFIED STUDY OF THEOLOGY

Virtually all of the writers who have examined the study of theology in recent times—most notably Gerhard Ebeling, Edward Farley, and Wolfhart Pannenberg[5]—have remarked on the diversity and general disarray of the subject. And virtually all have recognized that this diversity and disarray both undermine the credibility of theology in our time and render exceedingly difficult if not impossible the task of reintegrating the theological disciplines in such a way that they support a cohesive and cogent ministry of the gospel. Ebeling, Farley, and Pannenberg not only agree on this rather negative point, they also agree that this disunity and dispersion of theology arises from a crisis of understanding concerning theology that has its roots in the age of Enlightenment and the nineteenth century. Earlier periods in the history of Christian thought were capable of devising a more unified approach to theology. Farley and Pannenberg acknowledge, moreover, that the history of the concept of theology and its problems offers some hope for a solution to the present impasse. Farley finds the solution on the subjective and formational side of the problem, while Pannenberg locates it on the objective, scientific side.

Ebeling does not offer a specific solution to the problem. He does, however, indicate a direction. Ebeling looks toward a "fundamental theology" that is essentially hermeneutical or interpretive as the key to unity. Within the larger interpretive structure identified by this "fundamental theology," the various disparate disciplines would maintain their integrity and their distinct methodologies, but each would assume the interpretive task of identifying the truth toward which it points. Ebeling's fundamental theology, with its concentration on this question of truth, would draw the disciplines toward a union that lies beyond their individual competency but also arises out of the basic intention

---

[3] Cf. Kuyper, *Principles*, pp. 17–20; and see Edward Farley, *Theologia: The Fragmentation and Unity of Theological Education* (Philadelphia: Fortress, 1983), for a recent survey and analysis of the problems confronting the study of theology. For extended discussion of the history of theological study, see Charles Augustus Briggs, *History of the Study of Theology*, 2 vols. (London: Duckworth, 1916); George R. Crooks and John F. Hurst, *Theological Encyclopedia and Methodology, on the Basis of Hagenbach*, new ed., rev. (New York: Hunt & Eaton, 1894); Yves Congar, *A History of Theology*, trans. Guthrie (Garden City: Doubleday, 1968); recent, but rather poorly conceived, is Gillian R. Evans, Alister McGrath, and Allan D. Galloway, *The Science of Theology* (Grand Rapids: Eerdmans, 1987); cf. my review in *Consensus: A Canadian Lutheran Journal of Theology*, 13,1 (Spring 1987), pp. 114–15.

[4] Cf., further, below, chap. 4.

[5] See below, appendix to chap. 1.

552 The Study of Theology

and direction of each discipline. Although there are major differences between Ebeling and Pannenberg, both point toward an objective unity of the various disciplines into a single theology or study of theology.

The proliferation of subdisciplines does not necessarily destroy the unity of such a paradigm, just as the proliferation of techniques necessary to the accomplishment of a large task does not destroy the possibility of a cohesive outcome. This diversity may simply mean that there has been an inward diversification of specializations under the larger fourfold curricular model. The model may need some explanation and interpretation, but it may still serve as a pattern for organizing the various subdisciplines. Indeed, it may offer a pattern for an overarching interpretive "fundamental theology."

In his discussion of the historicity and temporal relativity of theologies, Ebeling also introduces a major problem that does not seem to have troubled either Farley or Pannenberg. Theologies supercede one another historically and stand alongside one another in opposition and even mutual contradiction today. In striving for their own theological understanding of the unity of theology, both Farley and Pannenberg implicitly fall under Ebeling's warning: they address only a segment, never the whole of the theological community. The problems of historicity and relativity are not, however, in and of themselves, dangers or insurmountable barriers to theological understanding in the present. On the one hand, a superceded theology does not necessarily lose all relevance to the future simply by being superceded. A theological cul-de-sac like Arianism is superceded by Nicene orthodoxy largely because, considered as a perspective on God, Christ, and redemption, it does not work: it was not simply superceded in time, it was set aside with good reason. The post-Nicene theology of the Cappadocian fathers was, however, simply superceded—particularly in the Latin West. It was appropriated in the fourth century by writers like Victorinus, Hilary, and Ambrose and superceded in the fifth century by Augustine's grand Trinitarian vision. Nonetheless, the Cappadocian theology remains a useful resource, a point for critique of Trinitarianism in the present.[6]

On the other hand, mutually exclusive theologies are—or at least ought to be—capable of enlightening one another. I know, for example, that "Death of God" theology is and must be quite unacceptable to evangelical Christians. Evangelical theology rests on the certainty that the God of the Bible and the church cannot die and cannot cease to be of significance. Nonetheless, when we look at the incredible secularization of American culture and see how little place secular culture allows for the divine and also just how many churches and congregations participate in that secularization and by their fundamental accommodation to the culture effectively rule God out of large segments of human life, then the particular construction given to the phrase "Death of God" by Gabriel Vahanian becomes particularly significant. We may not like what we read in Vahanian's book—but we have to recognize the accuracy of the indictment even now, some twenty years later.

The diversity itself, then, inasmuch as it is neither a barrier to learning nor a hindrance to theological formulation, does not stand in the way of a unified theological understanding. It merely makes us aware that the diversity or pluralism of the modern world must somehow be dealt with in the search for unity. Another way to make this point is simply to recognize that a unity of perspective ought not to be gained by

---

[6]Cf. Robert Jenson, *The Triune Identity: God According to the Gospel* (Philadelphia: Fortress, 1982).

a sectarian procedure of narrowing the theological focus until our picture contains only those views that we find congenial.

Farley's critique pinpoints a general problem in the contemporary American perception of theology. Although the problem is not evidenced uniformly throughout the country, it is certainly true that American seminaries and churches have tended to externalize the unity of theology by emphasizing the practice of ministry and, further, by defining practice in terms of the techniques of ministry. Again, it is not a universal problem uniformly evidenced, but the teachers of ministerial practice have been notoriously unable to deal with theological issues drawn from biblical, historical, or dogmatic theology and to apply these issues to contemporary situations. (There is also considerable irony in the frequently heard claim that the teachers of the so-called theoretical disciplines ought to make their courses more practical when the teachers of practice have difficulty working with theological categories.) Farley is correct, too, when he notes that the denominational and clerical emphasis on technique has become, retroactively, a barrier to the merger of nominally theoretical and nominally practical concerns in theological education. All too often it seems that the theoretical subjects are necessary for obtaining the degree, but not necessary for carrying on subsequent ministry. The result is that both education and ministry suffer.

Even so, Farley points to a genuine need in theological education and in subsequent engagement in the theological tasks of ministry when he focuses on *paideia* defined, in a classical sense, as an understanding related to the cultivation of character and culture. Theological understanding, defined as an inward, interpretive theological disposition, must be a goal of theological training. I differ with Farley, however, on his location of the unity of theology primarily on the subjective side of the study in the cultivation of theological understanding.

The greatest problem that a more classical approach to theology will have with Farley's argument stems from his willingness to set aside the objective foundation of the older concept of *theologia*. He no longer views as possible the derivation of the unity of the discipline from the unity of its object. Instead, the unity of the discipline is to be defined functionally, inasmuch as the *theologia* that Farley recovers is "salvation viewed as a self-conscious interpretive activity." From a classical perspective, the unity of interpretive activity must arise out of the unity of the discipline itself, not out of the singularity of the interpreter.

In his discussion of the shift of theology "from unitary discipline to aggregate of specialties," Farley argues that, prior to the Enlightenment, "the norms for theology" or *prin cipia* of theology were the articles of faith, the "doctrines of church tradition." With the rise of critical methodologies in the Enlightenment and the application of critical historical, philological, and hermeneutical methods to Scripture, now viewed as a body of data, Scripture became the object of various diverse "sciences" or disciplines, and each theological activity, exegetical, historical, dogmatic, became a specialized science in its own right.[7] On the one hand, Farley is quite correct in recognizing the critical methods of the Enlightenment as bringing about a separation of disciplines. Most notable is the rise of biblical theology as a historical description of the religion of Israel or of the New Testament church. On the other hand, Farley is somewhat mistaken in his identification of *principia* and therefore in his view of the pre-Enlightenment unity of the discipline.

[7]Farley, *Theologia*, pp. 40–42.

Although late medieval writers who spoke of foundations or *principia* did identify them as the articles of faith, the Protestant orthodox, both Lutheran and Reformed, adapted the term to the *sola Scriptura* of the Reformation and to a more philosophically adequate identification of *principia* with *archai*. The *archai*, the ultimate or truly foundational principles available to theology were God, the principle of being or essential foundation, and Scripture, the principle of knowing or cognitive foundation.[8] This view of the Protestant language gives us quite a different perception of the unity of theology in the pre-Enlightenment phase of Protestantism from that given by Farley's analysis. The methods, tools, and approaches used in theology could be quite diverse; theology could be practical and theoretical in its emphases; and the ability to understand "divine things" could vary from subject to subject—but theological knowledge as such could still be regarded as a unity because of the singleness of its cognitive foundation, its *principium cognoscendi*. And resting on that unity, theology could further identify the unity of its subject matter, its "substance" or its "object" of study.

In other words, there is an unnecessary dichotomy underlying Farley's arguments. In contrasting the pre-Enlightenment with the post-Enlightenment view of theology he writes:

> Insofar as theology is a *habitus* of practical wisdom which attends salvation, it has no additional end since the existential, saving knowledge of God is itself the end for which the human being is created. In that way of thinking, theology itself is the end (telos) of the study of theology. On the other hand, when theology names an objective referent, doctrinal truths, and when it is a generic term for a faculty of disciplines, then it does need an end beyond itself, and the training of clergy is an obvious solution to that problem.[9]

In the first place, the older view of theology as "a *habitus* of practical wisdom" did not at all place the end of theology within theology itself. Rather, the identification of theology as practical was intended to indicate specifically that the discipline was oriented toward a goal beyond itself! This same theology also defined theology as theoretical or contemplative, indicating that theological knowledge was capable of being an end in itself. Indeed, the older theology debated at length the question of how theology could be theoretical or practical or a combination of *theoria* and *praxis*.[10] Theology is an objective knowledge, valuable in itself (theory) that has as its goal (praxis) the union of the believer with God, the highest good.

In the second place, the language of *theoria* and *praxis* typical of this older theology, whether medieval or orthodox Protestant, did not in any way alter the fact that theology was understood both as an objective discipline composed of various subdisciplines and ancillary competencies and as a subjective disposition to know a certain body of knowledge. As a matter of fact, traditional theology assumed that a balance of objectivity and subjectivity needed to be maintained in the discussion of theology and the study of theology. The unity of the discipline of theology in the older Protestantism did not arise out of an absence of subdisciplines. Nor did it arise, as Ebeling's arguments seem to indicate, out of an absence of diverse methodologies. There were, after all, distinctions

---

[8] See Richard A. Muller, *Post-Reformation Reformed Dogmatics,* vol. 1: Prolegomena (Grand Rapids: Baker, 1987), pp. 295–311.

[9] Farley, *Theologia*, p. 82.

[10] Cf. Muller, *Post-Reformation Reformed Dogmatics* , chap. 6, section 3.

made in sixteenth- and seventeenth-century Protestantism between the study of Old and New Testament, the study of "positive" or didactic theology, the study of polemical theology, and the study of ancillary disciplines such as language, logic, and philosophy. In the seventeenth century, practical theology and Christian rhetoric or homiletics took shape as disciplines. Nonetheless, theology was recognized as a unity according to its substance or object—God and God's works. Farley does recognize that the older theology differentiated between what we now call separate disciplines in terms of the way a theologian's cognitive disposition was directed toward its object, but what he does not fully acknowledge is that the unity of theology was considered to be objective, not subjective, arising out of the unity of *principium* and of substance, not out of the theologian's or pastor's cognitive powers.[11]

The fact that we can trace the origins of the fourfold model through the seventeenth and eighteenth centuries and the fact that the nineteenth-century framers of the modern "theological encyclopedia" either misunderstood or, as is more likely, altered the underlying rationale for the encyclopedia do not in and of themselves discredit the model. As we have seen in Pannenberg's argument for an objective unity of the disciplines into a single science, a historical analysis of the theological reasons for the separate disciplines can in fact reinforce the structure of the encyclopedia and, in addition, indicate its unity. Beyond this, Farley's assumption that neither the authority of Scripture nor salvation history are viable concepts does not carry weight in all parts of the theological world! In addition, because the canon of Scripture exists as a historically and theologically defined document distinct from the church-historical documents of the Christian community and functions in the church as no other document functions, it has its distinct theological function apart from, indeed, despite modern doubts concerning its authority, and even for those who express the doubts.

If Farley's rejection of "the way of authority," of a canon of Scripture, of a concept of salvation history, and of an identifiable divine revelation is unacceptable, there are nonetheless a series of insights in his study that are of major importance to us. He is entirely correct in identifying the central issue confronting theological study as the unification of that study around a *paideia*, a cultivation of theological understanding. He is also correct in seeing contemporary emphasis on ministerial technique as problematic. If technique governs theology, the whole enterprise is stood on its head and the actions that ought to be guided by a theological understanding of reality become the determinant of understanding. The result of this topsy-turvy approach to theology is stultifying.

The fourfold model, initially conceived with a view toward the organic unity of the disciplines, of itself does not necessarily result in a fragmentation of disciplines and a loss of the earlier unity of the theological disciplines. Whereas it is true, as Farley points out, that some of the nineteenth-century encyclopedists assumed that the four areas of the model were four neatly defined disciplinary areas, it is also true that several of the major encyclopedists, like Luthardt and Räbiger, recognized that the biblical, historical, systematic, and practical areas simply identify broad types or categories of study that relate to one another in the life of the church. Right use of the basic fourfold pattern ought not necessarily to exclude any disciplines useful to the church, nor should it cause "the question of faith and science" to be "isolated as a subquestion" dealt with occasionally in one

---

[11]Cf. Farley, *Theologia*, p. 40.

or another of the various and sundry subdisciplines.[12] Much of the burden of this book is to take seriously Farley's critique of the fourfold model as it has often been represented and used, but also to argue the usefulness of the model when it is understood as an interpretive tool that unifies the various biblical, historical, systematic, and practical disciplines in and for the work of theological formulation, with theology itself being understood as the "science of the Christian religion."[13]

Much more telling is Farley's perception of the alteration of the practical aspect of theology from a sense of goal-directedness to a category training in ministerial practice. The danger of the shift from a view of all theology as involved in a praxis to a part of theology identified as practice lies in the tendency of this separated—and internally fragmented—practice to cause us to lose sight of its theological underpinnings and of its relation to the other subdisciplines in the curriculum, particularly the so-called theoretical ones. "Theory," too, has shifted in meaning—instead of indicating the character of theology as worth knowing in and for itself, it has come to indicate a nonpractical intellectual superstructure, somehow bracketing and guiding the practice of ministry. Here, too, the unity of theological study and the clear line of movement from biblical interpretation to contemporary faith-statement and ministry are obscured by the potential fragmentation of disciplines.

I am convinced that there is considerably less irony than Farley notes in the conservative adoption of the fourfold encyclopedia, inasmuch as certain nineteenth-century encyclopedists—notably Luthardt, Hagenbach, Schaff, and Kuyper—were already moving toward the reconstruction or reevaluation of the fourfold model in terms of their historical grasp of older theological perspectives. In addition, and perhaps more importantly, the fourfold model, as developed in the wake of Gabler and Schleiermacher, embodies the recognition, even among the more conservative theological educators, that a major change had taken place in the study of theology during the eighteenth and early nineteenth centuries and that even a more traditionalistic model than that proposed by Schleiermacher had to bear those changes in mind.

Of considerably greater impact on the study of theology than the nineteenth-century attempt to gather the various theological disciplines into a three- or fourfold encyclopedia was the rise of the historical-critical method and the development of new approaches in hermeneutics. What presently stands in the way of a unified approach to theological study, far more than the gathering of the disciplines into four groups, is the critical approach to the text of Scripture. Inasmuch as modern critical methods focus primarily on the meaning of the text in its ancient historical situation, they can create barriers to the closure of the "hermeneutical circle"—barriers to the attempt of hermeneutics to draw text and interpreter together and to bring the ancient meaning to bear, with contemporary significance, on the present situation.[14] These barriers continue to exist, at least in part, because the study of theology as a whole has not kept pace with the hermeneutical developments of the last

---

[12]Ibid., p. 134.

[13]It is worth noting that Farley recognizes this nineteenth-century option (ibid., p. 138) but has not worked out its transmission into the twentieth century at the hands of Pannenberg.

[14]Some of the difficulties brought on by changes in hermeneutics, together with insights into the value of older exegetical methods, are presented in chapter 4 of the section *Has the Church Misread the Bible?* by Moisés Silva elsewhere in this book.

several centuries. We cannot move from Scripture to systematic theology and ministry in the way the medieval doctors or the seventeenth-century Protestant orthodox did because the alteration of approach to the text of Scripture demands a wholly different approach not only to the other disciplines but also and more importantly to their interrelationship.

We have already observed, with Farley, the importance of an altered view of theory and praxis to the reconstruction of theological study. The resources for this aspect of the reconstruction come from the older, precritical theology. A second resource or set of resources come directly from the critical developments of the eighteenth and nineteenth centuries. In addition to the rise of practical theology, these centuries witnessed the rise of historical theology. The eighteenth century began with a group of writers—most notably Mosheim and Walch—who attempted to replace the chronologically arranged polemics of the older theology with an objective discussion of history. The result of their labors was the rise of the modern discipline of historical theology and, as a by-product in the hands of Semler and others, the historical-critical method together with its attendant hermeneutical insights. If critical, textual, and historical methods have caused some disruption of traditional theology, they have also brought a clearer sense of the meaning of Scripture while the historical discipline itself has provided theology with a far more accurate sense of its own roots and of its resources for formulation. Indeed, the consciousness of history provides an insight into the character of the entire theological task that, together with a recovery of the concepts of theory and praxis and with a use of modern hermeneutical insights, can lead to a unification of theological study.

It is also true that part of the problem of theological education is the separation of the university-based study of religion from the seminary-based study of theology. The university has retained a sense of the personally formative character of education while the seminary has retained materials of theology without a sense of their intrinsically formative character. Farley recognizes this curious impasse but, after rejecting traditional patterns of authority, does not offer a clear way past the problem. He does not provide a definition of the way in which the "truth" and the "reality" toward which the various materials of theology point can be identified and grasped. Although Farley would probably object to this criticism of his conclusions as tending to reduce "theological understanding" to a particular form of study, the proper solution to this problem of university-seminary split and of curricular disunity seems to be the development not only of an attitude toward study but also of a material unity of the curriculum resting on a legitimation of the theological disciplines as together constituting a unified science and possessing, in their unity, a single object of knowledge. This criticism points us clearly in the direction indicated both by pre-Enlightenment orthodoxy and, in our own time, by Pannenberg.

It is regrettable that the university model, with its drive toward uncommitted objectivity, retains an interest in *paideia* and the cultivation of understanding while the seminary-model with its sense of commitment has lost much of its interest in *paideia* and the cultivation of understanding. It is also unfortunate that there is a bifurcation of commitment and objectivity—particularly because these categories are not mutually exclusive. Again, Pannenberg provides a useful insight even if we do not adopt his model in all of its detail: theology can and ought to be constructed and studied with a view toward objectivity and toward the proper use of historical, critical, and hermeneutical tools. If the basic character of religion in general and of Christianity in particular is historical, the right use of critical and hermeneutical tools, grounded as they are in historical understanding, cannot ultimately be a problem. Commitment to the historical faith does not rule out, indeed, can be enhanced by, historical objectivity in method.

Over against the inherent subjectivism of Farley's approach we can place Pannenberg's insistence on the objective character of theology, even if the object of theological science can only be presented and analyzed indirectly as a problem to be solved or a hypothesis to be proved. Pannenberg's approach has not only an affinity for the more traditional view of theology (at least on this particular point), but it also has the virtue of presenting theology as a genuine academic discipline capable of maintaining its place among the disciplines. We must question only the second part of the proposal, that God is a problem to be solved or a hypothesis to be proven. This approach has merit in a purely academic context, but the churchly perspective of the seminary and the normative character of theology as studied and used in ministry demand something more—in short, both seminary and parish demand faith in the existence of God, as testified in Scripture and tradition, as the beginning point of study and of proclamation.

The seemingly insurmountable barrier standing in the way of an American attempt to realize Pannenberg's schema for a theological curriculum is the opposition, typical of American education, between the history-of-religions approach usually associated with college and university-based, secular study and the churchly, theological and ministerial approach associated with seminary-based study, whether liberal or conservative. Farley recognizes this problem but offers no real solution other than the inclusion of the study of non-Christian religions or of comparative religion in the seminary curriculum. He provides no model comparable to that of Pannenberg for discerning the objective or scientific unity of this study of religion with the rest of the curriculum. To find such a unity in and for the churchly purposes of the seminary would probably demand a return to and a successful completion of the quest, indicated by Ernst Troeltsch in the first quarter of this century, for a definition of the "absoluteness of Christianity" in the context of world religion.[15] Troeltsch's insight, long neglected in many parts of the theological world because of neoorthodoxy's myopic rejection of the concepts of religion as a merely human phenomenon and of natural revelation as universally accessible, has come of age in the global community of the late twentieth century. The question that Troeltsch raises, of course, is how to maintain the absoluteness or ultimacy of the Christian message once it is acknowledged for the sake of objectivity in study that Christianity is a religion among the religions. Neoorthodoxy ignored the question and claimed, without clear warrant, the absoluteness of Christianity.

The great danger here is that, because of the possible pitfalls of the approach, we ignore the mandate to study Christianity historically, as a historical religion in the context of world history. Each of the views of the study of theology has, in its own way, underlined the importance of the historical and of the investigation of Christianity as a religion in history. Without arguing for a fundamental unity of theologia out of which to construct a unified pattern of study and thought, Ebeling does emphasize the universal scope of church history as a bridge from biblical study and the general study of religion to the

[15]Cf. Ernst Troeltsch, *The Absoluteness of Christianity and the History of Religion*, trans. David Reid (Richmond: John Knox, 1971), and note that Pannenberg's theological project points in this very direction; see his *Theology and the Philosophy of Science*, trans. Francis McDonagh (Philadelphia: Westminster, 1976), esp. pp. 301–45, 358–71, and his essay "Toward a Theology of the History of Religions," in *Basic Questions in Theology*, trans. George Kehm, 2 vols. (Philadelphia: Westminster, 1983), 2:65–118.

various ancillary disciplines (the humanities and the sciences, natural and social) and to the standard contemporizing disciplines—practical theology, dogmatics, ethics, and fundamental theology. Farley clearly sees the study of history—particularly the history of the concept of theology and of the organized study of theology—as the key to our present-day recovery of unified and meaningful theological study. For Pannenberg, the concept of history and the history of religion take on a fundamental theological significance.

Each of these perceptions can be carried over into our approach to the study of theology. Church history and the history of doctrine do establish a broad perspective for the study of Christianity and do have the effect of bridging the gap between biblical study and the various contemporizing disciplines. They do this both by providing a historical link connecting the past of the religious community with its present and by revealing the way in which the church has developed disciplines like dogmatics, ethics, and practical theology in the past and has folded materials from literature, philosophy, and the sciences into its teaching. Knowledge of this historical path provides both positive and negative models for the present—the recovery of useful concepts and tools from the past, the identification of the origins and reasons for ongoing problems, and the clarification not only of the ideas and teachings we presently hold but also of ways in which useful and valid ideas and teachings are constructed within the community of faith and brought to bear on its present. Finally, the historical and religious trajectory of Christianity has its own theological significance when it is understood as the fundamental reality of the life of the community of faith and as the key to our own grasp of the ongoing significance of the biblical and churchly materials that remain, today, the primary statements of the faith of Christians.

How, then, can a unified approach to theological study be constructed? If my presentation and critique of Ebeling, Farley, and Pannenberg *are* correct, a unified approach to the study of theology must begin with a clear understanding of the sources of theology and their mutual interrelation. This interrelation must be understood, moreover, both historically and, with a view toward the fundamental historical reality of the faith, with a methodological and interpretive consistency. Method and interpretation must, in turn, reflect the needs of theology as a discipline or "science" that stands objectively on its foundations and materials and also functions subjectively in the context of human understanding. The human understanding cultivated in theology must involve a construction and analysis of reality, of God, the world, and our place before God in the world. This consideration points, finally, to a balance in theology of theory and praxis, of knowledge known in and for itself and of knowledge known for the sake of attaining a goal—that mirrors the balance of the objective and subjective aspects of the study.

This balance of the subjective and the objective, of the theoretical and the practical depends on the clear identification of Christianity, not only in our definition of its reality but also in our approach to the study of theology, as both a religion with its own history and a revelation given and understood historically in a particular religion. The historical character of the religion and its revelation provides a basis in Christianity itself for the positive use of contemporary hermeneutics. Indeed, it yields a promise that the historical approach to Scripture dictated by modern hermeneutics will have a positive result in the construction of a model for the study of the whole of Christianity and for the formulation of contemporary definitions of Christian faith, whether in theological system or in the contextualization of the church's message in preaching and witness. The religious character of Christianity, moreover, provides a basis in Christianity itself for the positive relationship of theory and practice. It holds a promise that the ongoing life and worship of the community—its religion and spirituality—point both toward the possibility of an objectively grounded statement of the meaning of Christianity on a theoretical level and toward the possibility of a well-defined practice directly related to and drawing guidance from the theoretical statement.

APPENDIX: CONTEMPORARY PROBLEMS AND INSIGHTS: THREE APPROACHES

Ebeling's *Study of Theology*

Gerhard Ebeling's eminent introduction to theological study begins with the statement "The study of theology is beset by a crisis in orientation."[16] Ebeling speaks of a disruption of "access to the unity and totality that constitutes the subject matter of theology"; and the fact that, in the absence of this unity, "the domain of the subject matter and tasks" of theology has not only diversified but "broken apart and crumbled" into isolated disciplines and subdisciplines. In addition, Ebeling argues that this absence of "inner unity" is reflected by the erosion of the relationship between theology and the "totality of the experience of reality."[17] These problems are not entirely new—they have identifiable historical roots—but they have been intensified in the twentieth century.

The study of theology, Ebeling continues, is fraught with tensions. Theology is an ecclesial discipline that experiences a built-in tension between scholarship and vocation. On the one hand, the necessity of being a generalist concerned with the life of congregations and churches can become a barrier to ongoing meditation on theological problems, and "academic study appears to be more of a hindrance than a preparation"; once a student has received the basic theological degree, there is little incentive to continue studying the materials of theology. On the other hand, study can become an island unto itself, detached from vocation. The reason that these two opposite tendencies represent a tension and not simply a congenial separation of interests and specializations is that "what is called the study of theology in the technical sense is only the introduction to the continuous study of theology in a person's vocation."[18] At least this is the purpose of technical study and the ideal tendency of vocation!

Theology, no matter how scholarly its exercise, always "involves something that does not seem compatible with scholarship": it deals with revelation of and faith in God, neither of which can be subservient to the techniques and methods of scholarship. When theology has a "scholarly character," therefore, it has that character only in the context of vocation and faith. Theology, according to Ebeling, cannot be justified as a discipline among other disciplines, as a "science" among other "sciences," according to generalized scholarly criteria. Without denying the need and the place for theological scholarship, it must also be recognized that the scholarship itself is finally responsible to the faith and that faith, the life, the vocation, is not lessened in importance because it fails to maintain contact with a mass of scholarly literature.

---

[16]Gerhard Ebeling, *The Study of Theology,* trans. Duane Priebe (Philadelphia: Fortress, 1978), p. 1.
[17]Ibid.
[18]Ibid., p. 3.

In addition to this basic tension between study and vocation, Ebeling notes three basic problems that arise out of "the historicity of theology": first, theologies "supercede one another historically"; second, theologies can and do "substantively exclude each other"; and third, within theology "there are disciplines that compete methodologically."[19] In each case, the historical diversity of theologies stands in the way of a unity of approach in theology. The first of these problems can be defined by the fact that "theologies cannot be conserved or repristinated." Theology does not move from lesser to greater or from worse to better—frequently the reverse seems to be closer to the truth, but the old cannot be retained inasmuch as theology must be rooted in its historical context and therefore must move forward in time, although not necessarily toward a higher or better form of expression. If a unity can be detected in this succession of theologies, that unity must arise out of the subject matter of theology as it is reflected under different conditions and in different circumstances.

The second problem is equally serious: theologies do not merely succeed one another, they also frequently stand alongside one another in opposition and contradiction. Not only are there the traditional opposition of heresy and orthodoxy and of one confessional "orthodoxy" to another, there are also the theologies, typical of the present age, that do not fit precisely into any of these traditional categories. Confessional theologies no longer seem to be "definitive," Ebeling notes, and "the decisive theological fronts appear to cut across them."[20] The unity of theology, identified by the subject matter, is not a unity that carries over into the articulation of that subject matter. Theological agreement is difficult to achieve in our century—and any unity that we find must be able to deal with multiplicity of forms and diversity of statements.

Whereas the first and second problems tend to stand in the way of any single analysis of the study of theology becoming normative throughout the Christian community, the third problem noted by Ebeling stands in the way of any unified analysis of the study of theology, even one that is limited in its address to a particular and fairly homogeneous segment of the larger Christian community. There are a host of theological disciplines and subdisciplines that, in Ebeling's words, "compete methodologically." By this Ebeling means that the organization and unity of the disciplines is not achieved as a simple movement from the biblical materials through the history of the church and its doctrines into our own time in systematic and practical theology. Although the materials certainly line up chronologically in this way, the question of the methodology to be followed in contemporary system and practice forces us to recognize that the issue is complex. Tracing out the history of a problem does not automatically provide a solution in the present: Is dogmatic theology to follow an exegetical or a "systematic" method? How does biblical theology relate to dogmatics now that it is an independent discipline rather than a part of the dogmatic enterprise? There are, as Ebeling notes, "competing claims" of the historical and the systematizing disciplines.[21]

Ebeling's recognition of this host of problems leads him to conclude that there is an unresolvable tension underlying theological study in the present day and that his own essay on the study of theology can only be a "reflection about the individual disciplines,"

---

[19]Ibid., pp. 5–8.
[20]Ibid., p. 6.
[21]Ibid., pp. 7–8.

each in its own methodological integrity. He is unable to develop a "systematic deduction of the disciplines from the nature of theology" or to present a unitive schema that includes all of the theological disciplines. Nonetheless Ebeling does wish to draw out connections and relationships in the hope that a clearer view of the "whole of theology" will emerge from his discussion. He thus begins with the New Testament as foundational to Christianity; proceeds via the Old Testament and the study of religion and philosophy to the "most universal theological discipline," church history; and from that universal basis looks out on the ancillary disciplines in order, finally, to draw the whole together in practical theology, dogmatics, ethics, and "fundamental" or interpretive, hermeneutical theology. When he has done so, then at last the question of unity can again be raised at the level of the foundational truth embodied in the subject-matter of the several disciplines.[22]

Ebeling's work raises a series of issues that cannot be ignored. They must be settled or in some way set aside if the study of theology is ever to be conceived or undertaken as a unified whole. In the first place, the problem of tension between scholarship and vocation can hardly be done away with, inasmuch as the sacrifice of either side of the problem spells death to the whole theological enterprise. This problem will have to be incorporated into study as a basic fact of theological existence. In the second place, some decision will have to be made concerning the relationship of the disciplines and subdisciplines of theology to one another, and this decision will have to involve historical and methodological choices. Such choices will create as well as solve problems: to the extent that Ebeling feels he cannot make those choices and must sacrifice the larger unity of the discipline, he fails to solve the basic problem that he poses—but to the extent that we move beyond the impasse noted by Ebeling, we will also exclude options that his approach left open.

Farley's *Theologia*

One of the more important attempts to come to terms on a theoretical level with the study of theology and its problems is Edward Farley's *Theologia: The Fragmentation and Unity of Theological Education* (1983). Farley's work is important because its arguments rest on an extensive evaluation of the history of the study of theology and because it addresses, quite specifically, the American scene. Farley begins his argument with a historical overview of the study of theology in which he points out that theology, as studied in the Middle Ages and in the Reformation and post-Reformation eras, was regarded as a knowledge (*scientia*) or a wisdom (*sapientia*) directed toward salvation. This view of theology was not only cognitive, it was also grounded on doctrinal governing-principles and controlled methodologically as a unified academic discipline in its own right. With the rise of pietism and the dawn of the Enlightenment, this view of theology was challenged and, Farley argues, brought to an end. The unity of theological education has been lost and this loss is "responsible more than anything else for the problematic character of that education as a course of study."[23] Unlike Ebeling, however, Farley hopes to find a unified approach to the study of theology.

In order to isolate the problem and pose a solution, Farley presses quickly beyond the older patterns of the Middle Ages, the Reformation, and the post-Reformation era

---

[22]Ibid., pp. 8–11; cf. 156–58.
[23]Farley, *Theologia*, p. ix.

and concentrates the historical portion of his study on the development of "theological encyclopedia" during the Enlightenment and in the nineteenth century. Before the Enlightenment, the various disciplines and subdisciplines of theology were studied reverently for the purpose of "forming" in the mind "that sapiential knowledge called theologia." This knowledge was, in turn, the proper foundation for the exercise of ministry. The Enlightenment marks a major change in attitude toward both the disciplines and the rationale for studying them. Farley points to Mosheim and Semler as inaugurators of this change: for Mosheim, theological study is not the cultivation of a disposition to know a particular unified wisdom or knowledge so much as training in a set of disciplines useful to leaders in the church; for Semler, similarly, theological study is training in skills for the sake of cultivating the "dexterity proper to teachers of the Christian religion." In other words, study is no longer unified by a sense of a single object of knowing but by a sense of the practical application of the diverse theological disciplines.[24]

Similarly, the rationalism of the eighteenth century conjoined to historical method wreaked havoc on traditional theology. Farley goes so far as to call this alliance a "hermeneutics of destruction" that led to the identification of "discrete efforts of inquiry and scholarship, each applying rational and historical principles." The theology that had once been drawn together as a unity and maintained in a unified form by Protestants in particular under the theme of an authoritative Scripture, was no longer an academic possibility.[25]

The development of "theological encyclopedia," beginning around 1760 and extending through the nineteenth century, takes for granted these basic shifts in emphasis and definition accomplished in the first half of the eighteenth century. The various so-called theological encyclopedias all attempt to define the disciplines that belong to the study of theology and to identify the pattern and unity of those disciplines. By the end of the eighteenth century there had emerged the basic fourfold pattern of three "theoretical" disciplines (biblical, historical, and systematic) and the practical field. This fourfold pattern marks the emergence of church history from polemical theology as a positive discipline aiding in the formulation of doctrine and in the present-day formation of personal piety. It also marks the redefinition of "practical" theology as the application of the truths of the theoretical disciplines by the clergy in preaching, catechesis, and the care of souls.[26]

The disciplines gathered together in the theological encyclopedias do reflect the categories of theological literature set forth in guide-books of the orthodox era, but virtually none of these essays in encyclopedia reflects an orthodox understanding of theology as "divinely imparted knowledge" resting on God's archetypal self-knowledge. Scripture is retained as the foundation of theologizing, but Scripture itself is now viewed historically and critically. As Farley points out, the encyclopedia itself, for all its "orthodox" appearance, is a postorthodox phenomenon, reflecting a postorthodox conceptuality. The encyclopedia itself is rooted in the separation of disciplines and subdisciplines—of history from polemical theology, of practical theology from the application of biblical and systematic study, of biblical theology both from exegesis strictly defined and from dogmatic or systematic theology. The disciplines as we understand them today were defined for us by the nineteenth century in the wake of Schleiermacher.[27]

---

[24]Ibid., pp. 62–63.
[25]Ibid., p. 65.
[26]Ibid., pp. 78–80.
[27]Ibid. p. 81.

These historical considerations point toward a problem inherent in the encyclopedia itself. On the one hand, the unified study of theology as a theoretical-practical, biblical-historical discipline was possible in the context of "the confessional churches of Protestantism." In theological terms, Farley argues, "the great Reformed and Lutheran dogmatic structures functioning within the Protestant 'way of authority' is the foundation of the initial Protestant encyclopedia." Since theology was considered, in these dogmatic systems, as "a single thing, the knowledge of God and divine things as it is given in the written form of revelation, the inspired Scriptures," the study of theology could also be "one thing."[28] On the other hand, the postorthodox, Enlightenment construction of the fourfold encyclopedia meant that the various disciplines came to be viewed as methodologically independent areas of study. Theology, as defined in this fourfold curriculum, was "no longer one thing but an umbrella term for a number of different enterprises." Their unity was derived not from a cognitive, objective unity of *theologia* but from a "clerical paradigm" focused on the minister and the competencies needs "for ministry."[29] The victory of the "clerical paradigm" has meant the loss of an internal, intellectual, and spiritual motive and goal for theology. The loss of this sense of a single unified theological wisdom, Farley quite convincingly argues, has resulted in the dispersion of the encyclopedia into a series of unrelated specializations—subdisciplines that do not interrelate and do not cooperate to produce a single knowledge called theology. The subdisciplines have distinguished themselves independently as academic exercises but they no longer function together to produce a *paideia*, a unified teaching that can be directed toward the goal of ministry.

The American scene is, as Farley's essay recognizes, quite different from the European. The tension seen by Ebeling between scholarship and vocation appears, in the American context, as a total separation of concerns. In the same vein Farley writes, "The present ethos of the Protestant churches is such that a theologically oriented approach to the preparation of ministers is not only irrelevant but counterproductive." Theology is studied in seminary but not practiced in the parish. "At its very best, a theological education is only the beginning of career-long discipline, and it is just this continuing 'study of theology' which does not occur."[30] The point is stated radically, but it is substantially correct. It is also, as Farley argues, ironic inasmuch as the study of theology, for most of the history of the church, did in fact nourish ministry.

When theology is reduced to "a pedagogy for ministerial education," it may be justified by "practice," but at the same time, Farley recognizes, "practice in its widest and most significant sense is systematically eliminated from the structure of theological study." When theology was defined as a mental or spiritual disposition, practice was an integral part of theology as a whole inasmuch as all theological study, whether nominally biblical or historical or dogmatic, was directed toward personal formation. When theological study is restrictively directed toward the techniques of ministry, practice is made "external to theology" and the three "theoretical" areas of the encyclopedia are set over against the ministerial field. Part of the problem, Farley notes, is seen in the "exclusion of 'theology' from the university"—so that "theology," although taught as an academic specialty, is attached

[28]Edward Farley, "The Reform of Theological Education," in *Theological Education* 17, no. 2 (Spring 1981): 96.
[29]Ibid., p. 98.
[30]Farley, *Theologia*, p. 4.

to the clerical paradigm and forced out of the broader realm of education. Theology functions neither in relation to the ministerial skills that dominate the seminary nor in relation to the larger issues of religious understanding assumed by the university to belong to the common property of human beings—i.e., to the laity![31]

Farley proposes a total reevaluation of the theological curriculum focused on the "recovery" of "*theologia* or theological understanding."[32] If *theologia* is to be recovered for theological education, there must be a revision not simply of the various subject-areas of theology in and for themselves but a new understanding of the entire theological enterprise. "Theological understanding" is not a subject-matter for study; as an example, Farley notes a course on the origins of Christianity in the first and second centuries. The issue is to teach this subject-matter in such a way that it contributes to theological understanding. "Theology" is a matter of personal formation. In order to achieve this recovery of theology, moreover, the "clerical paradigm" must be discarded: training cannot focus on "the exercise of clerical activities," but rather it must emphasize a "general paideia" or "culturing" of human beings, a "shaping of human beings "under an ideal.""[33]

This reform of theological education, Farley recognizes, cannot be accomplished purely at the graduate level: the interpretive skills necessary to study the materials of the church and its history, to understand the "origin, history, tradition, mythos and contemporary form" of the ecclesial representation of truth and reality, can only be learned over a lengthy "process of education."[34] "The life of encyclopedia is a dialectic of interpretation impelled by faith and its mythos occurring in and toward life's settings."[35] What Farley proposes, therefore, is not a curriculum but an approach to study. If something resembling the fourfold pattern is retained, it will be altered attitudinally and find its unity somewhere other than in ministerial practice—if a freer, more open-ended curriculum is adopted, the assumption is the same: its unity will be attitudinal and interpretive rather than based on an externalized goal of technique.

Pannenberg's *Theology and the Philosophy of Science*

The major study, in our time, of theology as a discipline is surely Wolfhart Pannenberg's *Theology and the Philosophy of Science*. The concern underlying Pannenberg's study is very different from that underlying Farley's. Although both writers perceive a threat to the integrity and unity of theology, Farley's analysis is geared to an intellectual community in which a deep split has long been recognized and, in some quarters, cherished, between the "academic study of religion" in the university and the ministerial or churchly study of theology in the seminary, whereas Pannenberg's analysis is addressed to an intellectual community long accustomed both to church involvement in the university and to the acceptance of theology as a discipline alongside the other academic disciplines in the university curriculum. Farley's work, at least in part because of this divided mind of American religious studies, stresses the problem of viewing the study of theology as a "science." Pannenberg's, however, is directed precisely toward that end: the

---

[31]Cf. ibid., pp. 133–34.
[32]Ibid., p. 151.
[33]Ibid., pp. 152–53, 179–81.
[34]Ibid., p. 183.
[35]Ibid., p. 185.

correct understanding of Christian theology as a "science" in the context of the other academic disciplines.

What is significant from the outset of Pannenberg's essay is his assumption that theology need not sacrifice either its traditional, churchly rootage and function or its academic, scientific integrity. He argues that theology "can be adequately understood only as a science of God." He disputes the view that theology must rest its integrity on either "a unity of method" or "the unity of a connection with practical activity" that is "external to its objects."[36] This concept of a unity resting on "practical activity" was the fruit of Schleiermacher's labors and an ultimate source of difficulty for theology—on the one hand, it could (and did) reduce theology to a historical and antiquarian discipline, while on the other it could (and did) generate a "positivistic" view of theology that placed theology outside the bounds of science and grounded it in a priori decision.[37]

In Pannenberg's view, we cannot escape the meaning of the term *theology* as determined by its history and embedded by that history in the discipline itself. Nor would it be desirable to escape: "God is the true object of theology," and theology is the study of the "divine economy" of "saving history, from creation to the eschatological fulfillment." Theology, then, recognizes God as its object and studies all things in their relation to God. Granting the reality of this relation, theology surmounts the problem of subjectivity and enters the realm of objective discipline, of science.[38] In the contemporary situation, however, "God" is "under suspicion of being no more than a concept of faith." In other words, theology stands in danger of being reduced to a fideistic positivism, of losing its object. In order to find a solution to this problem and to retain the scientific objectivity necessary to a rightly conceived theology, Pannenberg proposes that theologians recognize the "openness . . . of the question of God" and approach God as the fundamental problem of the science of theology rather than as a dogma.[39]

This proposal, of course, raises another problem, inasmuch as it may reduce God to the status of a hypothesis and collapse theology into other disciplines, like "philosophical anthropology, psychology or sociology." Pannenberg sums up the issue:

> It is part of the finite nature of theological knowledge that even in theology the idea of God remains hypothetical and gives way to man's knowledge of the world and himself, by which it must be substantiated. On the other hand, as the theme of theology, God by definition includes the empirical reality by which the idea of God must be tested, and so defines the object of theology.[40]

The problem is, in a sense, circular. "The way in which God is to be understood as the object of theology therefore corresponds exactly to the problematic position of the idea of God in our experience."[41] God is known, Pannenberg argues, as a reality "co-given to experience in other objects" and known as the "all-determining reality" only by anticipation and hypothesis.

[36]Pennenberg, *Theology and the Philosophy of Science,* p. 297.
[37]Ibid., pp. 297–98.
[38]Ibid., p. 298.
[39]Ibid., p. 299.
[40]Ibid., p. 300.
[41]Ibid.

> The reality of God is always present only in subjective anticipations of the totality of reality in models of the totality of meaning presupposed in all particular experience. These models, however, are historic, which means that they are subject to confirmation or refutation by subsequent experience.[42]

Since reality as we know and experience it is not a finished whole but is part of a cosmic process, this view of religion as anticipatory places it into the realm of science. Granting, moreover, the connection between religion and theology, theology is, in fact, the science of religion. Pannenberg denies that theology is the science of religion in general—rather, he says, it is the science of "historic religions." Christian theology must, therefore, be defined as the "study of the Christian religion, the science of Christianity . . . in so far as it is the science of God."[43] Theology, as a science, examines historical religion with a view to determining how adequately religion deals with the experience of reality and, as a consequence, how adequately it identifies God as "the all-determining reality." "The traditional claims of a religion may therefore be regarded as hypotheses to be tested by the full range of currently accessible experience."[44] The further implication of this argument—which Pannenberg fully accepts—is that Christian theology must be regarded as a "specialized branch of theology in general," justified by the historical limits of Christianity and not by the personal faith of the theologian.[45]

This view of theological science leads Pannenberg directly to a descriptive statement of the organization of theological study. As a preparation for his presentation of the actual disciplines in the "theological encyclopedia," Pannenberg discusses "the relationship of the systematic and historical tasks in theology" and the "science of religion as theology of religion."[46] Theology is the science of God or the science that takes God as its object—but it approaches that object of "subject-matter only indirectly, through the study of religions."[47]

This indirect approach is necessitated by the nature of theological knowing and points directly toward the historical as well as systematic approach characteristic of the study of theology. Theology is necessarily historical since it is a reflection on historical religion and specifically on historically located interpretations of God and world. Nonetheless, "theology cannot be just historical, because it is concerned not just with religious experiences, convictions and institutions of former ages, but also with deciding about their truth, deciding, that is to say, about the reality of God."[48]

The systematic side of theology arises precisely because the historical tradition of the religion mediates a religious meaning, a theological content, that must be investigated and assessed for the truth that is reflected in it. Historical knowledge, therefore, is the basis of systematic or constructive theology in the present. Pannenberg insists on this basic polarity of theology—materials that are necessarily addressed historically, particularly in view of the historical datum, the life and work of Christ, that lies at the heart of

---

[42]Ibid.
[43]Ibid., pp. 314–15.
[44]Ibid., p. 315.
[45]Ibid., pp. 321–22.
[46]Ibid., pp. 346–71.
[47]Ibid., p. 346.
[48]Ibid., p. 347.

Christianity, but are also necessarily addressed systematically for the sake of a present-day statement of the content of faith and present-day assessment of its truth-claims. The various specialized fields of investigation—Old Testament and New Testament, church history, philology, and so forth—are an integral part of the theological task of discerning "the extent to which the particular historical data under investigation represents a self-communication of the all-determining divine reality."[49]

Pannenberg notes that any discussion of this theological task will manifest the difficulty of dividing the task into separate disciplines: the specializations are, of course, distinguishable, but this distinction is merely "pragmatic," inasmuch as the examination of the history of the religion for the sake of present-day systematization requires the concerted and cooperative effort of all disciplinary areas. One cannot systematize theology directly on the basis of reading the text of Scripture; such "theological exegesis," particularly as practiced by dialectical theology on the assumption of a "direct application" of biblical sayings to the present, lacks the requisite "historical accuracy."[50] Nonetheless, theological interpretation, with reference to the present course of intellectual history and to contemporary philosophical problems, is necessary to the task of moving from the historical text to contemporary systematic presentation. In reality, therefore, the task is a single, united effort that transcends its division into disciplines and subdisciplines.

When the organization of theology into various disciplines and subdisciplines is examined, Pannenberg quickly adds, this organization is clearly more than merely pragmatic. The creation of each independent discipline, when understood historically, was a matter of theological and theoretical evaluation. Pannenberg insists that these historical and theological grounds must be understood and the unity as well as the distinction of the disciplines constructed for the present on the basis of a clear historical understanding. It is self-defeating to assume the validity of the present structure of theology and to justify it after the fact, as was frequently done in the theological encyclopedias of the last century.[51]

A primary distinction between biblical interpretation and systematic theology can be discerned in the Middle Ages, but it did not solidify into separate disciplinary areas until the eighteenth century. The other disciplinary distinctions are more recent.[52] It was the Protestant "rehabilitation" of scholastic theology alongside biblical exegesis that created the disciplinary distinction between the biblical and systematic fields for Protestantism. In the eighteenth century this distinction, understood both in the light of pietist and rationalist or historicist critique, became a distinction between biblical theology conceived as a historical investigation and dogmatic theology understood as a present-day formulation resting on the historical materials.[53] Church history was separately studied for the first time at the end of the sixteenth century and became a standardized area of study in the seventeenth, understood as part of the preparation for both polemical and dogmatic theology. Although lectures on pastoral theology were given from the Reformation onward, the separate discipline of

[49]Ibid., p. 348.
[50]Ibid., pp. 348–49.
[51]Cf. ibid., p. 350.
[52]Ibid., p. 351.
[53]Ibid., pp. 355–56.

practical theology arose only at the end of the eighteenth century, with its chief justification being provided in the nineteenth by Schleiermacher.[54]

The last discipline to be identified and given distinct academic status is the "science of religion"—which Pannenberg characterizes also as the "theology of religion." This discipline arose only at the very end of the nineteenth century and then only in profound debate. Many theologians, including Harnack, were so convinced of the "absoluteness" of Christianity that they took the study of Christianity as paradigmatic for the study of religion. The independence of the "science of religion" from dogmatic Christianity is recognized today, Pannenberg notes, in England, America, and Scandinavia—but not in Germany, at least not to the extent that Pannenberg believes is necessary. Christian theology, Pannenberg argues, can be correctly understood only "within the framework of a history of world religions."[55] Against the opposing view (which has all of the characteristics of neoorthodoxy) he remarks, "Only a dogmatic view of Christianity, which separates faith as knowledge of revelation from the world of religions, could treat religions as a phenomenon so external to Christianity as not to require consideration until missionary work makes Christianity look outwards."[56] In direct contradiction to this positivistic approach, Pannenberg declares that the spectrum of theological disciplines and subdisciplines can be rightly understood only in the context of the "science of religion."

This argument for a "science of religion" understood as a "theology of religion" provides the key to Pannenberg's vision of a unified study of theology that maintains for the most part the typical divisions of the discipline that have arisen during its history. Indeed, inasmuch as the science of religion is an essentially historical investigation and inasmuch as history is the vehicle or means by which we receive and understand divine reality, the historical forms of that understanding have a lasting value and are not easily set aside; instead, they ought to be modified for use in the present. In this model, the foundational exercise would be the anthropologically grounded construction of a philosophy of religion in which the concept of religion could be defined "in connection with the objects of human experience of meaning, that is, so as to take account of the totality of meaning implicit in all experience of meaning, a totality which implies the existence of an all determining reality as its unifying unity."[57] This concept of religion in general would in turn lead to the development of a rightly constructed history of religions within which, in turn, "the religion of Israel and Christianity" could be correctly understood. Finally, within that understanding of Christianity, the various theological disciplines could be meaningfully presented.[58]

When he passes on to examine the particular disciplines belonging to Christian theology, Pannenberg draws together the subjects of biblical exegesis and church history as essentially historical in character. Nonetheless, the study of the history of theology must recognize the differences between biblical and church-historical study that led to their distinction as separate disciplines and must raise the question of the status of church history. Is church history a purely ancillary discipline as the Protestant orthodox of the

---

[54]Ibid., pp. 356–57.
[55]Ibid., p. 361.
[56]Ibid., pp. 361–62.
[57]Ibid., p. 368.
[58]Ibid., p. 369.

seventeenth century and the neoorthodox of the twentieth, particularly Karl Barth, have argued?[59] Pannenberg resolves the question, at least tentatively, into one of canon: the distinction of biblical and churchly history rests on a dogmatic identification of the canon—the grouping of both disciplines into "historical theology" runs the risk of relegating the canon to a place of "secondary importance."[60]

While retaining the distinctive realms of the specialists, Pannenberg finds his overarching solution to this question in the history-of-religions model: "The history of religion in Israel, Judaism and primitive Christianity must be treated as a single process of tradition in which the spread of Christianity into the world of hellenism appears as only the last phase of a chain of receptions of non-Israelite religious traditions with Israel's religious consciousness."[61] The documents that are identified as canonical arose out of this history—and the goal of analyzing this literature in its proper literary, cultural, and historical context is the presentation of the religious tradition and its transmission from the era of ancient Israel to the period of primitive Christianity.

This study of the religious tradition of Israel and earliest Christianity is linked to the study of church history not only by the historical character of the investigation and the continuity of the history of earliest Christianity with the history of the church but also by the fact that church history is a discipline that "embraces the whole of theology."[62] Biblical exegesis is required, as a discipline, to restrict itself to the historical-critical task, whereas church history reaches out into biblical studies in its search for origins and presses forward, systematically and practically, in the present in its quest for explanation. It was the great mistake of Barthian theology to lower the status of history by severing church history from the apostolic age and by suppressing the historical questions raised by post-Reformation theology "in an attempt to make direct contact with the Reformation." As this mistake has become more and more obvious to theologians, church history has appeared more and more in the unifying discipline that connects the present of the church to its origins. The proper study of history will both clarify the problems of the present and manifest as yet untapped resources for theological formulation.[63]

Pannenberg can now point out that there is good reason to describe dogmatics also as historical theology. Inasmuch as dogmatic or systematic theology is "the present formulation of the Christian doctrinal tradition," it is an essentially historical enterprise that must pass to a large extent under the critical judgment of church history. It is also the case that only the modes of presentation differ; the substance of systematic and historical theology is virtually identical. Granting, then, the rise of historical consciousness that made church history into an independent discipline, is there any reason to separate systematic theology from history as a discipline in its own right?[64] Pannenberg finds the identification of systematic theology as an organized study of the truths of Christianity in which their mutual interrelation is set forth and explained as fruitful in this regard: systematic theology can never be a field independent from historical theology, much less from historically adequate biblical exegesis, but its separate

---

[59]Ibid., p. 372.
[60]Ibid., p. 375.
[61]Ibid., p. 387.
[62]Ibid., p. 392.
[63]Ibid., pp. 392, 393.
[64]Ibid., pp. 392, 405.

existence is justified precisely by its systematic character. Polemics and apologetics appear as natural subdivisions of the systematic task.

Christian ethics, which was historically considered a branch of the systematic exercise and did not become separated until the eighteenth and nineteenth centuries, can be viewed as the link connecting systematic with "practical" theology insofar as practical theology can be defined in "the ethics of action in the church."[65] Although practical theology has been typically defined as a separate discipline on the moral or ethical side of the curriculum, it is clearly also indicative of "the character of theology as a whole."[66] As a solution to the problems raised by attempts to ground practical theology in either dogmatics or ethics—or to view it as an instruction in church management—Pannenberg suggests "making the history of Christianity and the church the common basis of dogmatics, ethics, and practical theology" not in the sense of making it an antiquarian discipline, but in the sense as already indicated in his discussion of dogmatics, of viewing present practice as arising out of the richness of the ongoing tradition of the church in the encounter with the present.[67]

From these three theologians we receive both a sense of the difficulty of the task that confronts the study of theology in the present and of the vast resources available to the church in the accomplishment of that task. Clearly, the study of theology in our time cannot simply be conducted according to older patterns of understanding. We are confronted by a differentiation and specialization of fields of study such that our theology cannot well serve the church unless a unifying perspective is also provided. Whereas Ebeling only hints at a hermeneutical or interpretive unity, Farley and Pannenberg point to this unity directly, with Pannenberg offering the more objective solution to the problem. The proposal offered in the present volume attempts to deal constructively with these three paradigms of study and to offer an approach to theology that does justice both to the need for an objective, historically and "scientifically" organized study of theology and to the equally important need for the recognition of the subjective aspect, both personal and corporate, of theological formulation in the present.

[65]Ibid., p. 423.
[66]Ibid., p. 424.
[67]Ibid., p. 435.

two

THE THEOLOGICAL DISCIPLINES

Biblical and Historical Foundations

*I*t should be clear by now that the standard division of theological studies into the biblical, historical, systematic, and practical fields cannot rest either on the purely academic separation of four basic specializations or on the frequently made distinctions between theoretical and practical fields, classical and ministerial studies, or academic and spiritual or formational disciplines. The purely academic separation is a false separation inasmuch as all four fields are intimately related and, particularly in the cases of the systematic and practical fields, consistently use materials that belong to one or another of their collateral disciplines. The distinction between theoretical and practical is impossible to maintain because, on the one hand, it misunderstands the meanings in and for theology of *theoria* and *praxis* and, on the other, whatever definitions of these terms is accepted, the so-called theoretical disciplines are eminently practical while the practical disciplines are taught in the light of theoretical considerations. In the same way, the classical and academic disciplines belong to the life of ministry and spiritual formation while ministry and spiritual formation have been taken up into the disciplines of the academy.

Rather, as Pannenberg's arguments tend to confirm, the fourfold division of theological disciplines stands on a clear historical and functional basis that both makes necessary their distinction and, at the same time, renders impossible their separation. The paradigm that is offered in this chapter and the next maintains the four basic subject areas but also attempts to discuss them in a unitive and interpretive manner, so that the four areas are drawn into an argumentatively conjoined three-part model of biblical-historical foundations plus two forms of contemporary application. The discussion that follows is intended to provide, not a traditional "theological encyclopedia," but a fundamentally historical interpretive path *through* the biblical and historical disciplines toward contemporary formulation. The genius of theology in the Judeo-Christian tradition has always been the fact that the tradition set in the context of a living community of belief provides the clearest and surest trajectory into the future.

HISTORY, CANON, AND CRITICISM

Christian faith begins both historically and functionally or existentially in the Bible and meditation on it. As Dietrich Ritschl has recently noted, theology, in the technical sense, "is unnecessary for the existence of belief grounded in the Bible" but necessary "in practice ... because of the complications of our history."[1] The interpretive study of theology properly begins in Scripture and moves forward through these "complications of our history" in order to understand the way in which Scripture addresses us and is interpreted today.

The study of Scripture, Old Testament and New Testament, can be divided fairly neatly into linguistic, historical-exegetical, and theological elements. The basic issues and basic methods belong to both fields—and, indeed, to the historical study of Christianity in its development after the era of the New Testament. What I argue here for the use of Hebrew and Greek, for the application of historical method, and for the examination of theological issues will apply also to the discussion of church history and its place in the contemporary study of theology: the methods are the same, only the languages differ.

By linguistic study I do not mean the rather perfunctory exercise of working through a grammar book. That, of course, is presupposed. Rather, by linguistic studies I mean the essentially interpretive task, based on grammatical study, of using the biblical languages as tools, as means of entry into the thought-world of the text. This very basic linguistic exercise is, moreover, both a hermeneutical task and, in the context of seminary and church, an element of spiritual formation. On the one hand, acquaintance with the way in which a language constructs its world and conveys its meaning is necessary to understanding the biblical view of God. The Old Testament conception of God as transcendent and immanent, trans-historical but historically active, other than worldly yet personally involved cannot be grasped unless our contemporary God-language is challenged and superceded, in exegesis, by an understanding not just of words and phrases taken over from the Old Testament and placed into our own language but of the way in which the reality of the divine is expressed in the language of the Old Testament itself. On the other hand, this new understanding of the language of the Old Testament in and for itself in its original context becomes an avenue for the development and formulation of our own understanding of the divine—specifically in and through the recognition that our own linguistic forms can be transcended and our conception of God enriched and expanded.

These comments on language must not be construed as an advocacy of the claim that we are, today, victims of a Greek or Latin view of God that has somehow replaced the Hebraic conception simply because of the conceptual framework inherent in these languages. In other words, nothing metaphysical or theological is inherent in a language that either demands or precludes certain forms of understanding. "Hebraic thinking" does not yield up a dynamic, concrete, personally related notion of God because of inherent linguistic necessities any more than "Greek" or "Latin thinking" yields up a static

---

[1]Dietrich Ritschl, *The Logic of Theology: A Brief Account of the Relationship Between Basic Concepts in Theology* (Philadelphia: Fortress, 1986), p. 298.

abstract, uninvolved notion of a divine Prime Mover. In addition, we need to recognize that the absence of certain ideas from the Hebrew mind as we know it from the Bible does not falsify those ideas. If this were so, biblical study would not enrich and expand our understanding; it would only replace our modern patterns of understanding conditioned as they are by the course of Western civilization, Hebraic, Hellenistic, and Latinate forms of expression, philosophies that use and transcend these linguistic forms, social perceptions and scientific achievements, and so forth, with an ancient pattern of understanding out of sympathy with, and perhaps unable to communicate with, our present cultural context. Linguistic study ought to open doors, not close them.[2]

Specifically, linguistic study includes the vocabulary, grammar, and syntax of a language, with attention given to the way in which words function as signifiers or signs, as place-holders that bear meaning and are capable of sustaining a range of meaning; to the way in which phrases and figures of speech point toward meaning beyond the wooden, literal implication of words set in a particular order; and to the way in which the grammatical structure of a language, the tense-structure of its verbs, the declension of its nouns and adjectives and so forth, facilitates or does not facilitate the conveyance of meaning. We can understand these issues in terms of the sensitivities of a translator whose task is the transfer of meaning from one language to another. In moving from Greek or Latin into modern English, perhaps the greatest difficulty lying in wait for the translator is the elaborate structure of declensions in the classical languages—nouns, pronouns, verbs, and adjectives all receive their forms from their role in the grammar of a sentence. This structure is not difficult to learn, but it is difficult to represent in English, which retains little evidence of declension and in which word order determines the role of words in a sentence. Beyond this problem lies the fact that there is virtually never a perfect equivalence between a word in one language and the word used to translate it in another language.

Since virtually all of our theological concepts have a multilingual history—moving from Hebrew to Greek, from Greek to Latin, and from Latin to one or more modern languages, sometimes from one modern language to another—some acquaintance with the original languages of the Bible and of our theology is necessary if only for the sake of recognizing how ideas may shift in emphasis and in meaning when they cross linguistic frontiers and how the transmission and retention of a theological idea, as Christianity moves from one language and culture to another, is a delicate and difficult process. Study of the biblical languages, then, is itself a theological exercise that not only enables one to understand the Scriptures more fully but also clarifies and enriches one's understanding of theology.

By way of example, even a beginning knowledge of Hebrew will enable a person to see that Hebrew has no exact equivalents of the terms of Greek and Latin philosophical and theological anthropology—body, soul, and spirit. Indeed, the language of the Old Testament points us toward the recognition that the problem of dichotomistic (body-soul) and trichotomistic (body-soul-spirit) anthropologies is that they turn aspects or functions of the human being into "parts" standing over against one another. Thus, the word typically translated "soul," *nephesh*, more accurately is rendered "living being": it does not indicate a spiritual over against a corporeal reality, but a whole person, an organic

---

[2]On the subject of linguistics and interpretation, see the section *God, Language and Scripture* by Moisés Silva elsewhere in this book.

unity. *Nephesh* can even, albeit rarely, refer to a corpse (cf. Lev. 21:11; Num. 6:6). At the very least, it cannot be understood as "soul" in a philosophical sense.

Linguistic foundations, however, no matter how much insight they provide, are only a preparation for historical and exegetical study. History provides the background for exegesis, and exegesis functions, at least in part, to uncover the history. If we have learned nothing other than this from the frequently jarring history of the critical study of the Bible since the Enlightenment, the result was well worth the travail. The exegesis of the patristic and medieval periods, and even of the Reformation period, was frequently determined by then-contemporary theological confession rather than by a clear sense of the original historical setting of the text. Thus, although it would be unwise to discard the Niceno-Constantinopolitan language of the Trinity on the basis of the most recent critical commentary on the Johannine prologue, it would also be utterly foolhardy to examine the Johannine prologue with the preconceived assumption that the *monogenēs* of John 1:14, 18 stands as a direct reference to the eternal intra-Trinitarian relations of the first and second persons of the Trinity rather than to the unique filial relation of Jesus, understood by John as the Logos made flesh, to the fatherly God of Israel and the church. From a strictly historical and linguistic point of view, the author of the gospel of John could not have known the language of Nicea and Constantinople, and the fathers who sat at those councils were dealing with words and terms that had developed in their meaning and significance since the time of John.

Even more problematic than such a reading of the New Testament is the Christological exegesis of the Old Testament: there can be no access to the meaning of "image of God" in Genesis 1:27 if the phrase is read out in terms of New Testament and church usage—where "image of God" refers either to Christ or to certain spiritual virtues in human beings. One major exegetical and linguistic study relates the word "image" (*tselem*) to the use of a royal seal or boundary marker to set forth the delegated power of a viceroy: thus the image according to which male and female are made is a mark of dominion over the earth, a sign of custodianship that correlates with the rest of the language of the verse.[3] Similarly, the reading of a text like Psalm 2:7, "You are my son; today I have begotten you," (RSV) in terms of an intra-Trinitarian begetting or even in terms of the New Testament application of the text to Christ (Heb. 1:5), if done as a primary level of interpretation, can only obscure the relationship between God and the king of Israel described in this psalm of enthronement.

Historical and exegetical study of the materials in both testaments cannot simply follow an analytical or "critical" pattern of "divide and conquer." It is both to the credit and to the condemnation of much biblical scholarship that it has focused on the basic forms and pericopes of the text—to its credit because this procedure has enabled us to learn so much more about the context, the culture, and the history of the ancient world and about the text itself in the discrete elements that together contribute to its meaning, and to its condemnation insofar as this procedure has banished consideration of the whole of the literature in its final forms as the vehicle of greater and more enduring meaning than

---

[3]David Clines, "The Image of God in Man," in *Tyndale Bulletin* 19 (1968): 53–103; cf. Walther Eichrodt, *Theology of the Old Testament,* 2 vols. (Philadelphia: Westminster, 1967), 2:122–31, where Eichrodt emphasizes the "special character" of the human being in relation to God as the central implication of the text.

any particular pericope. Exegetical and historical study, as recent advocates of canonical criticism have argued, is incomplete until it has asked the larger questions. A similar point has been made by advocates of rhetorical criticism.[4]

Once the form, source, redaction, and textual critical work has been done, the final form of the text—the canonical form—in its literary and rhetorical unity must be considered. It is, for example, one thing to examine the text of Genesis and, as Jewish and Christian exegetes down through the centuries have done, to ponder the differences between the creation account that runs from Genesis 1:1 to 2:4a and the creation account that runs from Genesis 2:4b to 2:25, and quite another thing to leave one's readers or hearers with the impression that the two accounts pose an insoluble problem for the modern reader—as if the differences were obvious to us and not to the writer of Genesis. However one explains the juxtaposition of the two accounts, one is also bound to explain their presence in the canonical form of the Book of Genesis. These two tasks, moreover, are not at all mutually exclusive. Once critical reading has pointed to the juxtaposition of different accounts, the theological task must begin. That task includes determining not only the theological meaning of each account but also, as canonical and rhetorical criticism demand, the theological significance of the juxtaposition itself and of the larger view of creation in relation to the narrative of beginnings in the first eleven chapters of Genesis.

The purpose of this critical and historical approach to Scripture is to place us as readers of the text into the milieu of the authors. We need to learn to read the text from its own point of view if we are ever to bring it to bear on our own context. After all, apart from what we may conclude from our doctrine of inspiration about the perpetual and perennial importance of the text, the biblical authors did not write with the later history of the Christian church in mind. They wrote in order to address the religious needs of particular communities at particular points in time. The critical and historical method ought to serve us by opening up the meaning of the text to us.

As G. B. Caird has pointed out, "It is a common modern fallacy that the development of scientific knowledge"—and, I add, critical method—has "made Christianity harder to accept." From the very first, as the apostle Paul wrote, Christianity was "a stumbling block to Jews and foolishness to Gentiles" (1 Cor. 1:23). "Only if," writes Caird, "we have the skill and the patience to discover why the gospel was a shock to man of the first century, shall we be able to use it to shatter the complacency and lift the vision of our own generation."[5]

As a final point in this section, we address the problem of canon. If, as I have argued from the outset of this study, the understanding of Christianity made possible through a cohesive and constructive study of theology and the development, out of this understanding, of adequate theological formulations are both religious and historical issues, then the broader issues raised by the history of the Judeo-Christian religious community come to bear on the critical discussion of Scripture most clearly and pointedly when

---

[4]On these issues and for a discussion of various kinds of criticism, see the section *Literary Approaches to Biblical Interpretation* by Tremper Longman III elsewhere in this book; see also Edgar Krentz, *The Historical-Critical Method* (Philadelphia: Fortress, 1975).

[5]G. B. Caird, "The New Testament," in *The Scope of Theology*, ed. Daniel T. Jenkins (Cleveland: World, 1965), p. 54.

we address the question of the canon of Scripture. The canon as we use it today is a dogmatically constituted document that was written and subsequently collected and defined over the course of the centuries. It neither represents the entire religious experience of ancient Israel and the earliest church nor expresses in its existence as canon the intentions of the biblical authors for the future use of their writings. There were quite a few documents produced by Jews and Christians during the canonical periods of their history that are not included in the canon, and the authors of the books presently in our canon did not produce those writings for the sake of their inclusion in the canon of Scripture! The canon was identified through the efforts of later generations to codify and regularize the religious traditions of the community.[6]

Although we do not have a body of ancient Israelite religious literature that stands outside of—either prior to or alongside—the Old Testament canon, there are references in the canon itself to books used as sources, like the Book of Jashar or the Book of the Wars of Yahweh, and there are also references to religious pronouncements that did not become canonical, like the prophecies of Hananiah and Shemiah. More importantly, the close of the Old Testament canon represents, in large part, a linguistic decision associated rather vaguely with the experienced end of prophecy. The writings that belong to the Apocryphal or Deuterocanonical scriptures are not in classical Hebrew or even in the Aramaic that appears in portions of Daniel, but in Greek. These writings represent, in part, a shift from prophecy to apocalyptic, but they also represent a continuation of the historical narrative of the Jewish people and of the wisdom tradition. The final, doctrinal exclusion of these books from the canon occurred only with the beginnings of Protestantism in the sixteenth century, and the decision to exclude the Apocrypha was not at all so easily made as the decision to exclude the second-century Gnostic witness to Jesus.

There are, moreover, noncanonical writings of the New Testament era that do stand in close relation not only to the New Testament but also to themes and doctrines resident in the Christian tradition. Writings such as the Similitudes of Enoch and IV Ezra, the Shepherd of Hermas, the Didache, and the Apocalypse of Peter left their mark on later Christianity—perhaps most noteworthy here is the enormous importance of the Apocalypse of Peter for the patristic and medieval pictures of what may be called "the geography of hell." There are also works, like the so-called Epistle of Paul to the Laodiceans, that faded in and out of the canon throughout the Middle Ages.

Since the identification of the canon of Scripture was not a historical-critical but a traditio-normative activity accomplished from within the community of belief, we can make a firm distinction between our historical and critical use of noncanonical documents for the better understanding of documents within the canon and our own theologically constructive use of only those documents that are in the canon. In other words, the historically blurred edges of the canon—like the historically blurred edges of the community—cannot become the basis for adopting a new and wider set of doctrinal norms than those established by the believing community with increasing precision during its long history. We cannot undo the early church's decision to exclude the Gnostic scriptures nor, as Protestants, can we undo the Reformers' decision to exclude the Deuterocanonical books

---

[6]A significant approach to this problem of the creation of canon is found in H. N. Ridderbos, *Redemptive History and the New Testament Scriptures* (Phillipsburg, N.J.: Presbyterian and Reformed, 1988).

from the Old Testament. All that has been preserved can be edifying, but only the canon can be doctrinally normative.

I say this so pointedly because of the recent tendency among some writers to have recourse to the Gnostic scriptures as an alternative trajectory for Christian doctrine and as a basis for developing a theological critique of the fathers of the first five centuries. Whereas the thought of the fathers must be understood in the context of such alternative trajectories, it remains true that contemporary Christianity rests on the thought of the fathers and their successors rather than on the alternative doctrinal perspective. The canon of Scripture, as the church now possesses it, partakes of the necessary particularity—indeed, of what some have called "the scandal of particularity"—of our religion. It is not within our ability to alter the past or to remove from our religion those characteristics that make it uniquely what it is. (I will make much the same point when we come to the issue of comparative religion and the history of religions.)

THE OLD TESTAMENT

Biblical study must provide the foundation for Christian theology, and Old Testament study is foundational to the understanding of the Bible. Separate study of the Old Testament apart from prior considerations grounded either in the New Testament or in the history and doctrine of the church is a relatively new phenomenon—newer even than Gabler's identification of a separate biblical theology. Of course, the Christian community regarded what we now call the Old Testament as Scripture before there was a New Testament, and the Old Testament has remained a primary source for Christian doctrines—the primary source for doctrines not directly bound to the order of salvation established in Christ and of doctrines, like covenant, that provide a context for understanding the offer of redemption in Christ. Historical understanding, particularly the historical understanding of the way in which teachings of the religious community (whether Israel or the church) arise and develop, however, demands that the chronological priority of the Old Testament be taken seriously as a foundation and ground-point of interpretation. For a right understanding of the religion of ancient Israel, the Old Testament must be studied separately—what is more, the separation is necessary for the right understanding of the New Testament as well.

The first and the most profound issue that we must address on our way from study of the Old Testament to the formulation of contemporary theology, then, concerns the relationship of the Old Testament to Christianity and the character of the Christian right to the theological traditions of ancient Israel that belong to the Old Testament. Very much as we propose to answer the larger question of the unity of the disciplines and of the character of theological formulation, and in fact as a part of that larger problem, we can look for a resolution of this issue along historical lines. The New Testament itself and its theological center, the work of Jesus of Nazareth, can hardly be understood in isolation from the history and religion of Israel and, specifically, from the history of the Jewish people in the centuries immediately preceding the time of Jesus. As many writers have pointed out, the history of the Jewish people, as recounted in the Old Testament and the intertestamental literature, is a theological and a theologized history. The work of God in and through the history of Israel provides the foundation for understanding the New Testament's approach to the work of God for Israel and for the nations in Jesus Christ.

This is not to say that the Old Testament is simply a background to the New. It is the normative account of the religion of Israel—and, therefore, of the religion of Jesus. It is a major error of interpretation to claim that the Old Testament is law without gospel and the New Testament gospel without law. The message of obedience to God flows through the whole of Scripture and cannot be understood in the church apart from the Old Testament statement of the law and the prophetic meditation on it. The message of salvation, similarly, belongs to the whole of Scripture and can hardly be grasped apart from the Old Testament meditation on the promise given to Israel. Indeed, without the Old Testament, the corporate character of religion, of obedience, and of grace, would be greatly obscured. This has occurred in churches that deemphasize the Old Testament, view it as background, separate the history of the church from the history of Israel, and believe that the Old Testament adds little to the New Testament message of repentance, faith, justification, and sanctification.

By making the point in this way, I intend to disagree with Ebeling's ordering of the disciplines—New Testament before Old Testament—and with his initial claim that "the pathway through the theological disciplines begins with the study of the New Testament."[7] While it is obviously true that Christianity itself exists because of the events recorded and the revelation proclaimed in the New Testament, it is also true, though perhaps not so obviously, that it is dangerous to read the Old Testament as if it stands interpretatively subordinate in all its statements to the New Testament. It is equally dangerous to read the New Testament apart from the theological foundation provided in the earlier meditations of God's people, principally the writings contained in the canonical Old Testament. If we look forward to the discussion of systematic theology, we ought to be prepared to recognize that the great body of "Christian doctrine," like the New Testament itself, however much it is illuminated by the revelation of God in Christ, is drawn from the Old Testament. This foundational character of the Old Testament is evident in the doctrines of God, creation, providence, human nature, the fall, sin, and the covenant, that is, the doctrines placed traditionally at the beginning or in the first half of a theological system, doctrines that set the stage and provide the interpretative foundation, both theological and anthropological, of all that follows.

These introductory comments indicate a sharp rejection of the virtually Marcionite position of modern Christianity that refuses to consider the Old Testament as a proper text for preaching and theology and gravitates toward certain New Testament texts as a "canon within the canon." They indicate also an equally sharp rebuttal of the essentially allegorical method of reading the Old Testament that passes for theology under the term "Christocentrism." The Old Testament can speak to theology only if it is permitted to speak on its own terms as a foundational element of the theological curriculum and as a field of study in its own right. The Old Testament can be of genuine service to Christianity only if it is studied critically as a pre-Christian and, therefore, to a certain extent non-Christian body of literature.

It is not only a disservice to Old Testament exegesis but also a disservice to the history of Christian doctrine and to contemporary theology both systematic and practical to include Trinitarian considerations in the basic interpretation of Genesis chapter 1 or Christological considerations in the primary exegetical reading of the "Servant Songs" in

---

[7]Gerhard Ebeling, *The Study of Theology,* trans. Duane Priebe (Philadelphia: Fortress, 1978), p. 13.

Isaiah. On the one hand such a procedure would render the meaning of the text inaccessible to the text's own author and prejudice the modern interpreter against the original and basic meaning of the text. On the other hand the procedure conceals the interpretive efforts of succeeding generations—some of them following the close of the canon—to draw the text forward, in view of its original meaning, into the framework of meaning then characteristic of the community of belief.

From an initial, historical point of view, the Old Testament is the remaining literature of ancient Israel that surveys the history and religion of the Jewish people. In its variety, the Old Testament offers historical narratives, religious and ethical codes, preaching and prophecy, prayers, liturgies, and ancestral traditions, all of which existed in oral form prior to the writing of the text as we have it today. Beginning in the eighteenth century with Jean Astruc's *Conjectures on the Reminiscences which Moses Appears to Have Used in Composing the Book of Genesis* (1753), scholars have recognized that older sources underlay the final form of the books of the Old Testament, but it wasn't until 1835 with the appearance of Wilhelm Vatke's *Religion of the Old Testament* that these perceptions of earlier sources were united with a historical, developmental insight into a view of the historical course of the religion of the Old Testament. Although Vatke's views on the chronology and development of Old Testament religion have been greatly modified, his emphasis on a historical and developmental model for the study of the Old Testament remains with us. This is true of "conservative" as well as "liberal" discussion of the religion of the Old Testament—of Geerhardus Vos as well as Gerhard von Rad. The historical study of the Old Testament demands an openness to the past reality of Israelite religion and permits, in the second place, a more surefooted use of the Old Testament, as better understood, in the contemporary teaching of the church.

It is one of the great demerits of much modern Christianity, both nominally "conservative" and nominally "liberal," that it tends to ignore the Old Testament in its preaching and in its daily life, except for the occasional reference to the Decalogue and the Psalms. We need to be reminded continually that the greater part of the body of Christian doctrine rests on the Old Testament—and that the doctrine taught by Jesus had the Old Testament as its primary point of reference. As the Protestant theologians of the sixteenth and seventeenth centuries well recognized, the Old Testament records the life of the people of God and offers counsel and example to the church for all seasons.

The historical and theological understanding of the Old Testament has, in the last century, been enhanced by archaeological, literary, and linguistic study of the ancient Near East. Each of these areas of study is so specialized that theological students, ministers, and theologians cannot be expected to have a grasp of current scholarship or of all known documents—even documents in translation. Nonetheless, a general knowledge of these fields is so crucial to an understanding of Scripture that anyone attempting to formulate theology today must have an appreciation of the results of archaeology and of the literary and cultural study not only of Israel but also of her neighbors.

We cannot, for example, continue to make simplistic comments about the dynamic, concrete view of the world held by Israel and the Semitic nations over against the static, abstract approach of the Greeks or about the uniqueness of Israel's view of God acting in a linear history over against the presumed cyclic approach to history found in the thought of Israel's neighbors. Not only have the typical Hebrew/Greek dichotomies been shown, by linguists like James Barr, to be lacking in any foundation in the biblical languages themselves,[8] but also a very important essay by Bertil Albrektson has demonstrated that "the Old Testament idea of historical events as divine revelation must be counted among the similarities, not among the distinctive traits: it is part of the common theology of the ancient Near East."[9]

We can, however, learn about the distinctive character of Old Testament theology on a considerably more detailed and significant level through the careful use of such cultural comparisons. Thus the biblical and the Babylonian creation narratives, despite their enormous differences, share several significant features. It is not at all accidental that the primal chaos, the *tehom*, of Genesis 1:2 is divided by God and held back by a firmament and that the chaos deity, *Tiamat*, of the Babylonian narrative is divided by the victorious Marduk and formed into earth, sea, and heavenly vault. The worldviews, indeed, the religious worldviews of Israel and her neighbors were similar. From these similarities, but also from the differences between the narratives, we learn how the fundamental monotheism of Israel interpreted and, in effect, demythologized the world-order. In Israel's account there is no cosmic battle between gods, and the primal chaos is not some divine being set in contrast to the one true God of heaven and earth. In its ancient Near Eastern context, Genesis 1:1–2:4a becomes more than just a statement concerning the origins of the world-order—a profound monotheistic manifesto against all forms of polytheism or dualism, uttered in the face of opposing religious beliefs. We find, in such a passage and in our critical perception of its meaning, an important element in and for the contextualization of Christianity today—not only in view of cults in the Western world but also in view of the polytheism and virtual polytheism that surrounds Christianity in Third World cultures.

We are also in a far better position to understand both the dangers and pressures of religious syncretism and the prophetic attack on the inroads of Canaanite religion when we have some access to the common elements between Yahwism and Baalism as well as to the differences. The cyclic character of worship associated with the agricultural life of Canaan was not foreign to Israelite worship and, indeed, the covenantal offering of first-fruits became in Canaan an integral part of Israelite worship. The Canaanite word *Baal*, moreover, was the equivalent of one of Israel's most cherished names for God, *Adonai*: both mean "Lord." It is not at all difficult to see how Israelites might be tempted to adopt some of the features of Canaanite religion, particularly in view of their adoption of agriculture when they settled in Canaan. Here again, the issue is not the direct use of materials but the application of principle: what we learn from the study of the text in its historical and cultural context becomes a basis for understanding the religious mind of the present as Christianity in America confronts other religions in the conduct of daily life.

One final comment: in addressing the Old Testament theologically as one element in the larger work of theological formulation in the present, we must never allow our present-day concerns to overrule the need to interpret the Old Testament on its own terms, but equally so, we must never allow our recognition of the necessity of interpreting the Old Testament on its own terms to negate our commitment to drawing it into our theological present. In fact, these two concerns ought not to stand against each other in

---

[8]James Barr, *The Semantics of Biblical Language* (London: Oxford University Press, 1961).
[9]Bertil Albrektson, *History and the Gods: An Essay on the Idea of Historical Events as Divine Manifestations in the Ancient Near East and in Israel* (Lund: Gleerup, 1967), p. 114.

conflict. I have tried to argue throughout this chapter, and throughout this entire volume, that historical understanding is the foundation for theological understanding. The Old Testament, we must always remember, presents to us a past reality. Scripture presents us, not, as Barth commented, with a "strange new world," but with a strange *old* world, a world that is mediated to us and given its present significance by a historical tradition of use and a historical pattern of interpretation.[10]

Inasmuch, moreover, as the Old Testament is the representation of the religious life of ancient Israel, not of ancient Christianity, our historical and theological approach to its literature needs to consider not only the meaning of the great transition from Old Testament to New Testament and the early church but also the ongoing life of Israel itself. I began this section by stating the priority of the Old Testament over the New Testament even in the Christian context and by insisting on the need to interpret the Old Testament without doctrinal preconditions dictated by the New Testament or by the early church. I close it by noting the need of Christian exegetes to respect and reckon with the work of Jewish exegetes and the need of Christian theologians to recognize both the common right of the two religious communities to the same literature and the shared exegetical and hermeneutical tradition that did not cease with the close of the canon. In moving, legitimately, from the Old Testament to the New Testament, the primary theological issue that we address is the way in which our tradition, the Christian tradition, has taken up these materials into its ongoing history and has reinterpreted them and imparted new significance in the light of successive stages in the life of our community. The existence of another community of faith, grounded in the same literature, does not challenge the present existence of our community of faith, but it does provide an important limit to our interpretation of that literature.

The historical model for theological formulation establishes the religious unity of the disciplines by recognizing that religion is a historical phenomenon and that therefore the interpretation of religion is a forward-moving historical process. Doctrinal statements that are legitimate readings of the past in the present life of the community cannot be pressed into the past as if they had arisen in that past historical context. Old Testament exegesis and Old Testament theology are rooted in the history of the religion of ancient Israel, not in the history of Christian doctrine or in systematic theology. Such an understanding of the task is crucial, moreover, not only to the integrity of the study of the Old Testament but also to the study—and the unified use in contemporary theological formulation—of the other disciplines.

THE NEW TESTAMENT

New Testament studies lie at the heart if not exactly at the beginning of the theological enterprise. It is therefore crucial that these studies be constructed and directed with a clear definition of their focus and boundaries. As we have already seen, "New Testament" identifies a body of literature that is historically vague but doctrinally or dogmatically precise. The New Testament does not stand in a vacuum nor can it be understood as the second of two books that God once wrote. The New Testament is a theologically and canonically defined body of literature that is preceded historically by an unbroken stream of writings

---

[10]Cf. Karl Barth, *The Word of God and the Word of Man*, trans., with a new foreword by Douglas Horton (New York: Harper & Row, 1957), pp. 28–50.

extending from the Old Testament through the so-called intertestamental period, and followed historically by an unbroken stream of writings extending from the last book of the New Testament down to the present. In addition, this stream of writings from the Old Testament through the intertestamental, New Testament, patristic, medieval, Reformation, and modern periods, contains "trajectories" of ideas and writings that pass through the New Testament period without contributing to the New Testament: the Mishnah and the Talmud contain the living Jewish tradition that links the Old Testament canon to the present day for Judaism.

Crucial, therefore, to an exegetical and theological understanding of the New Testament is the continuance of the historical model introduced in our discussion of the Old Testament. The way in which biblical religion moves through the New Testament is nearly as important to Christian self-understanding as the unique language and teaching of the New Testament. Not only is it true that all documents must be understood in relation to their background and context, it is also true that the meaning of the New Testament witness belongs to the religion of an ongoing religious community that has existed both before and after the New Testament itself. The New Testament is both a contributor to the religious tradition of the community of belief and a bearer of it. Study of the New Testament, thus, must be guided by a sense of history, particularly by a sense of the history of the community of belief and of the role of the New Testament in that history.

The earliest Christian community existed within the bounds of Judaism and, together with other religious groups within Judaism—Pharisees, Sadducees, Essenes—shared the great tradition of the Old Testament and the intertestamental literature while also interpreting that tradition in its own way, in the light of the revelation of God in and through Jesus of Nazareth. Our theological approach to the writings of the New Testament must, therefore, be aware of the continuities and discontinuities of belief between the various religious groups. It is significant, for example, to our understanding of Jesus' conflict with the Pharisees that he stood closer to them than to the Sadducees: Jesus and the New Testament authors shared with the Pharisees a doctrine of the final glorious resurrection of the dead, a doctrine denied by the Sadducees on the ground of a strict reading of the Torah.

Similarly, our theological understanding and our theological use of the New Testament ought to be guided by a recognition of the broader context of the New Testament in the emerging Christian religion and, more generally, in the Graeco-Roman world. The early Christian community, as is easily seen in the Pauline epistles, included groups and teachers whose doctrines would not become normative and would receive only a negative reference in the New Testament. Gnostic and docetic beliefs seem to have been held in Corinth and, somewhat later (as testified by 2 Corinthians), a Judaizing tendency manifested itself in the same place, perhaps similar to, though not identical with, the Judaizing tendency in Galatia. The Gnostic tendency represents a contact between Christianity and a religious phenomenon broader than Judaism, whereas the so-called Judaizing tendency represents the original context of the Christian message in conflict with emerging Christianity, in the persons of some of the earliest converts. All of these variant readings belong to earliest Christianity, to its attempt to identify and interpret the significance of Jesus of Nazareth and his work—and all are important to our understanding of the meaning of the gospel and of the way it was formulated by Paul over against these various alternatives.

Outside of the Christian community, moreover, stood other religious traditions and practices that also colored the way in which the New Testament states its teachings and conditioned the way in which the gospel was received by the pagan population of the empire. Thus our theological understanding of the New Testament must include some acquaintance with the mystery religions of the ancient world with their blood-baptisms into life eternal and their foundational myths of a dying and rising god. Whereas teachings about baptism and resurrection were rejected in certain quarters of the Jewish community, such teachings were in fact welcomed by many pagans who could be attracted to Christianity on the basis both of this seeming common ground and of the ethical superiority of Christianity to these other religious options. In other words, we can begin to understand the success of the gentile mission in part on the grounds of the ability of the gentile world to grasp, albeit at a superficial level, some of the basic teachings of the church. The New Testament was, particularly in its Pauline expression, capable of cross-cultural transmission and contextualization.

These historical issues and the problems they raise for interpretation stand in a constant tension with the doctrinally and dogmatically precise canon of the New Testament in which we have the closest and clearest witness to Jesus Christ as Savior and Redeemer, which is to say, the genuine apostolic witness. This statement is, of course, a theological judgment reflecting the judgment of the early church. It must, in fact, be a theological judgment inasmuch as the materials being considered are, in their very substance, theological. Any contrary judgment, such as, for example, the contemporary claim that there is a genuine Jesus-tradition in Gnostic sources of the second century,[11] is also a theological judgment. The objective and critical study of the New Testament in its first- and second-century context does not escape the realm of theological judgment—but the objective historical and theological consideration of the canon as we have it can and does clearly justify both the identification of the canon as apostolic and of the noncanonical witness to Jesus as belonging, as one scholar has commented, to a category of "the bizarre" in which "fantastic symbols, beautifully intricate myths, weird heavenly denizens, and extraordinary poetry" indicate both a certain element of common ground with ancient Judaism and Christianity and a vast divergence.[12]

Historical understanding, then, does not give us the canon of the New Testament, but it does offer a basis for grasping first historically and then theologically the significance of the canon. The canon of the New Testament, which provides us with the theological materials central to our Christian faith, is a highly selective set of documents that established the doctrinal bounds of Christianity and set in motion the central trajectory of the church's faith long before the church produced the full number of its creeds and dogmas. The documents within the canon, moreover, notwithstanding their profound agreement about the identity and meaning of Jesus Christ over against the views expressed in the noncanonical documents, do evidence considerable diversity.

The Synoptic Gospels are quite different in organization and somewhat different in content from one another. The gospel of John bears little resemblance to the synoptics. The Pauline writings speak differently of Jesus than do the Petrine and Johannine writings and the Epistle to the Hebrews. The chronology of the Pauline mission indicated by

---

[11]See James M. Robinson and Helmut Koester, *Trajectories Through Early Christianity* (Philadelphia: Fortress, 1971).

[12]Bentley Layton, *The Gnostic Scriptures,* a new translation with annotations and introductions (Garden City: Doubleday, 1987), pp. xviii–xix.

the Epistles is difficult (though not impossible) to reconcile with the book of Acts. The full significance of these writings in their diversity can be grasped only through a careful interpretation of their contents and context. (Without historical and critical under-standing, the tendency to overlook the differences of approach and to find a theological common denominator—typical of later orthodox dogmatics—becomes all too easily the norm for interpretation, and the New Testament can no longer critique our theology.)

In the Pauline and Johannine literature we find, with the sole exception of the Epis-tle to the Hebrews, the most highly developed theologies of the New Testament, the for-mer representing an early stage of the Christian witness, predating the final form of the Synoptic Gospels, the latter representing a late first-century preaching, probably the lat-est theological testament in the canon. In the movement from exegesis and interpretation to theology, not only these differences—including both the differences in forms of speech arising from different cultural or social contexts and the differences arising from the devel-opment of Christian teaching—have to be considered but also the ways in which those differences express or address theological problems. And all of this has, as well as possi-ble, to be drawn into the contemporary situation. By way of example: contemporary dis-cussions of Christology need to ask how the various and rather distinct ways of present-ing the divinity of Christ, from Pauline preexistence language to the statements in Colossians that Jesus Christ is "the firstborn over all creation" and that the "fullness" of the Godhead dwelt in him (Col. 1:15, 19), to the Logos language of the Johannine pro-logue and the Son language in the larger part of the gospel of John, not to mention the various titles provided by the Synoptic Gospels, point toward ways in which the church's proclamation can be made to speak more directly to various cultures in the world today. We live in an age when the traditional "person" and "nature" language of the church has become increasingly difficult to use, particularly because of the shift in the meaning of the term *person* since the sixteenth century. Both theological system and Christian procla-mation need to take up the challenge and reinvestigate the problem—not for the sake of saying anything against the tradition that has served us so well on this matter, but for the sake of doing as much justice to the New Testament preaching of Christ in our time as the church did in the first five centuries of its existence.

Similarly, the Synoptic Gospels, once viewed as a form of biography, have yielded up to historical and critical study a wealth of theology. As the medieval church easily rec-ognized for the gospel of John, the differences in arrangement of materials in the gospels indicate, not a disagreement over the strict chronology of Jesus' life, but differences of theological perspective. This theological richness has been recovered for us by analysis of the materials in the gospels with a view to their form and to the historical situation that produced them. At the very least, the Jewish Christian background of Matthew and probably of Mark can be contrasted theologically as well as stylistically with the Hel-lenistic perspective of Luke, with significant results. Matthew's Christology rests on the preaching of Christ as the new or second Moses, the One who fulfills and delivers the law of the new Israel. There may even be a parallel between the five major discourses in Matthew (chaps. 5–7; 10; 13; 18; 23–25) and the five books of the Law. Luke, howev-er, as befits his Hellenistic context, takes a broader perspective and understands Christ as the center of salvation history. In both cases we are presented with theological per-spectives that, like those noted above for Paul and John, can and ought to be developed in contemporary theology, both systematic and practical, as ways of moving the church of the present day forward into its own cultures with a message that is better adapted to the patterns and forms of expression characteristic of our times.

It is worth noting that Oscar Cullmann,[13] Johannes Munck,[14] Jürgen Moltmann,[15] and Wolfhart Pannenberg,[16] whose works many of us have found so engrossing theologically, precisely because they pressed us to reconsider the ways in which the biblical message could and ought to be stated in the present and precisely because their options for theological reconstruction seemed to speak so directly to the twentieth century, have all listened carefully to the ways in which the New Testament text, in its variety of forms, expressed the identity of Jesus of Nazareth and his role in the history of salvation. Cullmann and Pannenberg in particular have directed our attention toward the historical as a fundamental biblical and theological category capable of being used in the present, granting that Western culture at least is gripped by its own historicity and that the category of history provides one way of understanding the interrelatedness of humanity throughout our world.

BIBLICAL THEOLOGY

Biblical interpretation is incomplete until it has addressed the history of Israel and its religion, the history of earliest Christianity and the development of its understanding of Jesus Christ, and the question of the theology of the Old and New Testaments. In other words, biblical study involves questions of the unity and larger implication as well as the diversity of the message, of the trajectory of biblical religion as well as the minute forms of the text. If this is the most difficult step in the process of biblical interpretation, it is also the most important one for the determination of the theological implications of the biblical message. It is, in other words, the theological link that joins biblical study to the other theological disciplines, just as historical consciousness is the broad methodological link.

It is worth noting here, if only for the purpose of setting aside the statement as useless, that all Christian theology is in some sense "biblical." Frequently systematic or dogmatic theologies will make the claim that they are writing or teaching "biblical theology." Their work is biblical because, in the spirit of traditional Protestantism, they look to Scripture as their primary norm for the statement of Christian doctrine. All well and good. But then these systems go on to discuss the divine essence and attributes by dividing the discussion into such categories as *attributa incommunicabilia* and *attributa communicabilia* or to derive the attributes by the *via negativa, via eminentiae,* and *via causalitatis*. They go on to structure their systems around such concepts as the *pactum salutis,* the *foedus gratiae,* the *foedus operum,* and the *ordo salutis*. At this point the "gentle reader" may well begin to wonder which Bible this systematic theologian has been reading.[17] I make the point with no intention of impugning the value of the terms but only to point out that the technical

---

[13]Oscar Cullmann, *Salvation in History,* trans. Sowers, et al. (London: SCM, 1967).

[14]Johannes Munck, *Paul and the Salvation of Mankind* (London: SCM/Atlanta: John Knox, 1977).

[15]Jürgen Moltmann, *Theology of Hope: On the Ground and Implications of a Christian Eschatology* (New York: Harper & Row, 1965).

[16]Wolfhart Pannenberg, *Jesus—God and Man,* trans. L. Wilkins and D. Priebe, rev. ed. (Philadelphia: Westminster, 1968).

[17]And since my purpose was to note a problem for theology, I have no intention of offering definitions for these terms here. Anyone desiring a definition may consult Richard A. Muller, *Dictionary of Latin and Greek Theological Terms, Drawn Principally from Protestant Scholastic Theology* (Grand Rapids: Baker, 1985).

language of the divine attributes arose during the Middle Ages, while the various terms for covenant (*pactum* and *foedus*) did not appear in these forms before the sixteenth and seventeenth centuries, and the much-valued dogmatic term for "order of salvation" originated in the early eighteenth century.

How biblical is a "biblical theology" that takes its most important terms and its major doctrinal topics from somewhere other than the Bible? Even more importantly, how can we formulate a theology that is at once cognizant of its biblical roots and norms and capable of dealing with the doctrinal categories that the church has developed over the course of many centuries of meditation on its faith? A first step toward the solution to these problems is to distinguish carefully between biblical and systematic theology— to allow biblical theology to address the religion of the Bible on its own terms and to allow systematic theology to incorporate biblical materials into a larger structure that acknowledges its biblical foundation but also uses the tools provided by the church.

Biblical theology represents a crucial step in the interpretive enterprise that reaches from exegesis toward the contemporary theoretical and practical use of the materials of theology. In order to understand just how crucial this step is, we must take a brief look at the origins and the implications of this subdiscipline. Biblical theology did not exist as a distinct genre, in the modern sense of the term, in the patristic, medieval, Reformation, or post-Reformation eras. Christian thinkers simply assumed that their theology was "biblical" in the broadest sense and that the step from exegesis to doctrinal statement or to preaching was short and direct. This assumption was justified, in large part, by exegetical and hermeneutical assumptions held in the so-called precritical eras of the church's history. The beginnings of historical consciousness and of textual, critical study of Scripture in the sixteenth and seventeenth centuries led to a shift away from the allegorical exegesis of the Middle Ages to a more literal, grammatical, and historical emphasis. At the same time, beginning in the seventeenth century, Protestant theologians like Hermann à Diest and Sebastian Schmid recognized, in a rudimentary way, the need for a step between exegesis and system, a gathering of texts related to particular doctrinal concerns into a compendium of biblical doctrine. These compendia they called "biblical" theologies.

In the eighteenth century, under the impact of historical method and the rising sense of the historicity of knowledge itself, biblical scholars and theologians developed the category of "biblical theology" into a discipline in its own right—so that it was no longer a mere gathering of texts in support of and governed by the topics and methods of dogmatic theology, but instead a study of the theology of Scripture itself, governed by a historical understanding of the biblical materials themselves. Although several Bible scholars had produced critiques of the older biblical theologies and had attempted to write strictly textual expositions of the doctrines of the Bible without recourse to the historical expression of the church's doctrines prior to Johann Philipp Gabler's effort, his address "On the Proper Distinction between Biblical and Dogmatic Theology" (1787) marks the beginning of a conscious methodological distinction between the theological examination of biblical concepts in their own historical setting and development and the construction of a churchly dogmatics.

The theological encyclopedists of the nineteenth century recognized the methodological problem of dealing with this new discipline of "biblical theology." Schleiermacher, who valued exegetical theology highly, doubted the usefulness of a separate discipline of "biblical dogmatics" as developed in his day and placed it, together with church polity and symbolics, under the larger category of "historical knowledge of the present condition of Christianity," as a kind of adjunct to dogmatic theology proper.[18] (Note that Schleiermacher viewed exegetical theology, church history, and dogmatics together as forms of "historical theology.") Hagenbach, who presented theology in a strict fourfold model, followed Gabler's definition and included "biblical dogmatics" under the rubric "historical theology," while Schaff, recognizing on the one hand that the Bible itself is not a theological system and on the other that "biblical theology" is a systematization of exegetically gathered materials, placed it into the field of "systematic theology" and defined it as "the first and fundamental form of Didactic Theology, on which ecclesiastical and philosophical dogmatic and Ethic must rest throughout."[19]

This older problem of the methodological placement of the discipline is reflected today in the debate over the shape and method of biblical theology. It is generally recognized that such a theology must deal either with the Old Testament or with the New Testament and certainly not with a synthesis of the materials of the two testaments. The historical differences between the individual books of the Bible together with the historical development of the teaching of both the Old Testament and the New Testament as distinct disciplines stands in the way of a synthetically arranged theology of the whole Bible or a dogmatically organized theology of either testament. In addition, it is clear that the topics of a modern dogmatic system cannot be legitimately imposed on the text of Scripture (just as they cannot be legitimately imposed on the theological materials of the patristic period). Thus the older dogmatic models for biblical theology, like A. B. Davidson's *Theology of the Old Testament* or Van Oosterzee's *Theology of the New Testament*, no matter how insightful their comments on individual texts or on larger points of biblical teaching, are viewed—and rightly so—as methodologically unacceptable. These strictures apply even to Vriezen's brilliant *Outline of Old Testament Theology*. Despite problems in establishing the date of books of the Bible, the historical method manifest in Eichrodt's and Von Rad's Old Testament theologies, Ringgren's *History of the Religion of Israel,* or Goppelt's *New Testament Theology* is preferable.

As even a cursory examination of these latter volumes will reveal, the historical concern that unites them also allows for considerable diversity and even disagreement in approach to the materials and the literature of biblical theology. Eichrodt's work, for example, holds in tension the methodological assertion that Old Testament theology is a historical and descriptive discipline with a thematic organization that maintains some points of resemblance to the older topical theological models of Old Testament theology and with a highly kerygmatic style of exposition that attempts to do justice to the revelatory character of Israelite religion. Von Rad, by way of contrast, totally avoids the thematic or topical approach and, in profound disagreement with Eichrodt, moves away from an attempt at theological synthesis to an examination of the historical lines of development of the different traditions within the Old Testament. Both, however, understand their quest for a central characteristic of the Old Testament—whether as in Eichrodt's case its theological, structural unity or in Von Rad's its traditionary tendencies—as the

---

[18]Friedrich Schleiermacher, *Brief Outline on the Study of Theology* (Atlanta: John Knox, 1966), pp. 86–87.

[19]Cf. Crooks and Hurst, *Theological Encyclopedia,* pp. 310–11 with Philip Schaff, *Theological Propaedeutic: A General Introduction to the Study of Theology, Exegetical, Historical, Systematic, and Practical* (New York: Scribner, 1894), pp. 316–17.

basis for pointing to what Eichrodt has called "the essential coherence" of the Old Testament with the New Testament.[20]

Another way of posing the issue of biblical theology is to note that although it is much easier to adapt to present-day use a "theology of the Old Testament" organized on doctrinal principles, it may be more useful to the understanding of the beliefs of the Old Testament to follow out a "history of the religion of Israel." Despite all the problems entailed upon the dating of the books of the Old Testament, the meaning, for example, of the words of the prophets on various provisions in the law, or of the many different accounts of the divine work of creation, can be more clearly and surely understood through a historically aware analysis of the purpose and setting of documents and parts of documents than through a theological harmonization. For example, Ezekiel's vision of the valley of dry bones (37:1–14) makes little sense apart from the knowledge that Ezekiel is an exilic prophet and that the bones of the slain represent the slain nation of Israel, then in captivity, but soon, like the dry bones, to be restored to life and health. Lacking a clear knowledge of or interest in the history of Israel, not a few past theologies have misread the passage as a prophecy of the final resurrection and have entirely lost the relationship between Ezekiel's preaching and the rest of the prophetic witness. The historical/theological point is, moreover, not simply a curiosity to be locked away in an erudite book: it has direct bearing on how the text of Ezekiel 37 can be used in the pulpit—and how it ought not to be used.

Another methodological issue should be noted: the history of religion model would have more interest in nonbiblical materials, the religions of surrounding peoples, and those teachings rejected by the canonical tradition of Israelite religion than would a theology of the Old Testament. This means that a history of the religion of Israel would tend to be more descriptive, whereas an Old Testament theology would tend to set forth a more normative presentation of the religious thought of ancient Israel. Eichrodt, for example, described the fundamental task of his theology as providing a topical cross-section of the thought of the Old Testament.[21] Nonetheless, as virtually all modern writers on the subject have acknowledged—largely because of the impact and importance of the study of the history of Israelite religion—these topics must reflect the faith of Israel, not the faith of the Christian church. The topics must be drawn from the religious life of Israel itself. This means, in turn, that the normative character of Old Testament theology (considered as a genre of theological writing) is a normative statement in and for the context of ancient Israel, recognized as normative in its ability to address the national religious experience of ancient Israel.

Significantly, this history of the religion of Israel (together with a historically constructed theology of the New Testament) follows out a pattern and a method not unlike the history of Christian doctrine and, like the history of Christian doctrine, remains distinct from systematic theology. Understood in this way, the theology of the books of the Old Testament and the historically conceived theology of the Old Testament as a whole will have a cohesion and a clarity of meaning that can contribute to contemporary theology far more constructively than a dogmatically presented Old Testament theology. For one thing, the historical and methodological separation between biblical and systematic

---

[20]Eichrodt, *Theology of the Old Testament*, 1:31.
[21]Ibid., p. 28.

theology enables us to find a point for critiquing or developing our own theology that, without the separation, would have been unavailable. What is more, properly used, the historical insight can provide clues to what we will later discuss under the rubric of "contextualization."

The point is somewhat more difficult to make concerning New Testament theology, granting the place of the New Testament witness to Jesus Christ in Christian theology and the traditional Protestant sense of the immediate relationship between Christ and faith. This makes the point all the more important, however, with reference to the New Testament. Instead, for example, of approaching the New Testament with a strict definition of the order of salvation lined out neatly from election and calling to glorification, Christians ought to be in a position to allow the New Testament itself to govern directly the concept of an order of salvation, even to the point of asking whether such a concept can be constructed on the basis of the New Testament, out of an understanding of the meaning of the New Testament materials in their original context.

Of course, a historical approach to the theology of the New Testament must be profoundly compressed and far more attendant to minutiae than a similar approach to the Old Testament—and still more so than the historical study of the church's doctrines from the second century to the present. Periodization becomes exceedingly difficult, but clarity concerning the broad outlines of the religious and cultural milieu becomes easier to discern. It is also easier to organize a theology of the New Testament along historical lines than it is to organize a theology of the Old Testament. There is a general agreement about the order of composition of the gospels. Pauline chronology, although troublesome in some of its particulars, is clear in its general outlines: no one doubts that 1 Thessalonians is early Paul and Colossians is late—and this chronology has significant theological implications, as, for example, for the relationship of eschatology and ethics. The Johannine and Petrine literature separates out easily into distinct units, as does the Epistle to the Hebrews. Once these basic divisions are made, then such theological questions as the development of Christological formulae and the movement from Jesus' preaching of the kingdom to the earliest community's postresurrection preaching about Jesus as Christ and Lord can be opened for discussion and clarification.

Without appearing naïve about a hope for consensus among New Testament scholars on questions of date, authorship, and patterns of development, we can still look with some confidence to New Testament theology for a discussion of the meaning of Jesus of Nazareth to the earliest Christian community that is free from the encumbrances of later dogmatic language. And because it is free from these encumbrances, it is capable of becoming a basis for critiquing and formulating Christology meaningfully in the present. It is precisely because New Testament theology is not a discipline directed primarily toward a normative churchly statement of doctrine in the present that it can be a point of critique and a ground for new insight into contemporary theology.

Before we conclude this section, it is worth observing that the theological study of the New Testament shares the debate between a strict history of religion approach and a theological approach that we have noted previously with reference to Old Testament theology. The broad spectrum of approach is well evidenced in the recent works of Koester, Goppelt, and Schelkle. All feel it is important to understand the materials of the New Testament historically and all are aware of the religious environment of earliest Christianity and of the ways it impacted on the thought of the New Testament authors. Koester's *Introduction to the New Testament*, not strictly a theology, offers a foundational survey of earliest Christianity in its cultural context.[22] The entire first volume presents non-Christian materials: Greek and Roman religion, the oriental mystery religions, and later Judaism. When Koester approaches earliest Christianity in volume 2, he consciously avoids an exclusive emphasis on the canonical materials and includes the New Testament apocrypha and Gnostic sources in his analysis. The earliest Christian theology that Koester presents, therefore, is discussed entirely from the perspective of the history of religion, without any separation of canonical from noncanonical, "orthodox" from "heterodox" materials. The value of this approach is precisely that it manifests the early Christian experience as it might have appeared to its Hellenistic and Roman environment, where no neat distinction could be made between Christian orthodoxy and Christian heresy and where any distinction between canonical and noncanonical writings could be only anachronistically applied.

With Goppelt's eminent *Theology of the New Testament* , we enter a more traditional form of the discipline in which the historical perspective is applied to the discussion of the canonical New Testament. Goppelt states from the very outset of his first volume that "the New Testament is our only source of reliable traditions about the ministry of Jesus and the founding of the church and its proclamation."[23] Goppelt orients his work toward the views of the individual canonical writers with close attention to exegetical and historical issues, moving from a discussion of background and sources to the teaching of Jesus and on to Pauline and post-Pauline teaching. His approach is historical and essentially descriptive.

Schelkle's *Theology of the New Testament* adds a significant dimension to our discussion because it breaks with the trend in New Testament studies and follows an unabashedly systematic model. It begins with creation (world, time and history, and man), moves on to salvation history and revelation (including Schelkle's Christology and doctrine of God), obedience, sin, grace, and the virtues of Christian life gathered under the topic of "morality," and concludes with a volume on church and eschatology. Schelkle follows, nonetheless, a historical and descriptive method that is concerned with the chronology of earliest Christianity and, under each doctrinal topic, with the movement of thought from the Old Testament and the Hellenistic Jewish background, through the canonical writings of the New Testament toward the writings of the postapostolic period.[24] Schelkle is saved from most of the problems of the older, dogmatic approach to New Testament theology by his historical approach and by the fact that his broad doctrinal categories are grounded and arranged, for the most part, on the basis of his reading of the text rather than on the basis of churchly dogmatics.

Although biblical theology defined and developed in this independent, historical form has proved somewhat disconcerting to the dogmatic enterprise of some not merely conservative but distinctly "old fashioned" modern-day theologians, this newer view of the theology of Scripture ultimately proves to be a positive development not only in the field of biblical study but also in the construction of the other theological disciplines,

---

[22]Helmut Koester, *Introduction to the New Testament,* 2 vols. (New York and Berlin: DeGruyter, 1982).

[23]Leonhard Goppelt, *Theology of the New Testament,* trans. John Alsup, 2 vols. (Grand Rapids: Eerdmans, 1981–82), 1:xxv.

[24]Karl Hermann Schelkle, *Theology of the New Testament,* trans. William Jurgens, 4 vols. (Collegeville, Minn.: Liturgical Press, 1971–78).

indeed, of the whole fourfold model for the study of theology. When biblical theology is placed firmly into the biblical field (and not into either the historical or the systematic fields), it appears as the final exegetical task, conceived within the limits of exegetical method but designed to draw biblical study together by making sense of the whole. Biblical theology ought to be the distillate of the exegete's labors—and, as such, it can point directly toward the history of Christian doctrine, with which it shares its historical-doctrinal method and outlook. Moreover, together with the history of Christian doctrine, it ought also to point critically and constructively toward contemporary systematic and practical theology *precisely because* it is constructed biblically and historically without reference to the structures of churchly dogmatics.

Adolf Schlatter underlined this point in his epochal essay "The Theology of the New Testament and Dogmatics" (1909).[25] On the one hand, he declared that "the justification for a New Testament theology conceived as history is that the independent development of historical science gives a measure of protection, admittedly not infallible, against arbitrary reconstructions of its object." Schlatter was particularly concerned to avoid an intermixture of Scripture, churchly dogma, and personal theological opinion that would prevent both Scripture and dogma—not to mention personal opinion—from being "correctly grasped and fruitfully applied." "Conversely," Schlatter concluded, "the good conscience of the Christian dogmatician, and his ability to mediate effectively what the New Testament presents us with both to himself and the church, is partly dependent on the faithfulness and success with which we do our historical work on the New Testament."[26]

All of the historical and critical approaches—whether Koester's, Goppelt's, or Schelkle's—ought to have, therefore, an attractiveness to those who are presently involved in the study and formulation of Christian theology. Koester's history-of-religions approach, like the strict history-of-religions approach to the Old Testament, offers more religious materials from the first and second centuries than would probably find their way into a systematic or practical theological statement, even negatively as examples of paths that Christianity did not take. Nonetheless, the noncanonical and, by patristic standards, heterodox views of Jesus and of early Christian proclamation provided in the materials surveyed by Koester, manifest in clear relief the nature of the choices made by the early church in its identification of the genuine apostolic preaching. In the Gnostic *Acts of John*, for example, we encounter an argument for docetism against the views of the canonical New Testament: here Jesus is portrayed as being human only in appearance, indeed, as changing his appearance at will—at times appearing as a child, at other times as a young man or as an old man with a beard, at times having a "hard," material body, at other times being "soft and immaterial and leaving no footprints."[27] The early church, by means of its identification of canonical writings and its application of an apostolic "rule of faith" not unlike our present-day Apostle's Creed, set aside this view and taught, as we see in the Synoptic Gospels, a fully human Jesus whose genuine humanity was necessary to the work of salvation. This point, manifest in extreme clarity by the contrast between the canonical and noncanonical writings, ought not to be lost on contemporary

[25]In *The Nature of New Testament Theology: The Contribution of William Wrede and Adolf Schlatter,* ed. and trans. with an intro. by Robert Morgan (Naperville, Ill.: Allenson; London: SCM, 1973), pp. 117–66.
[26]Ibid., p. 128.
[27]Koester, *Introduction,* 2:197–98.

theological formulation. This is particularly true insofar as docetism, the claim that Jesus' humanity was mere appearance, remains a danger to the church's proclamation in our own times.

The other two approaches, whether the canonical, historical approach of Goppelt or the systematic approach of Schelkle, have a more direct impact on contemporary formulation, as does an Old Testament theology presented in the manner of Eichrodt's. In both cases, the trajectories of canonical teaching that are analyzed historically for their theological implications offer insight into the character and rationale of later churchly formulations and provide a foundation for the analysis and critique of systematic formulations and practical approaches in use today. From the point of view of present-day formulation, these theologies of the New Testament codify and present the results of exegesis to nonspecialists who are laity, clergy, and, potentially, specialists in other fields, such as the history of doctrine, systematic theology, or homiletics.

CHURCH HISTORY AND THE HISTORY OF DOCTRINE

Once we recognize the problem of the canon of Scripture and the problem (or question!) of our own relation to that canon as a single and rather momentous hermeneutical question that cannot be answered solely from the side of the canon (inasmuch as we as church are responsible for the identification of the canon) or solely from the side of our own present (inasmuch as our present, understood theologically or religiously, has been constructed in the light of the canon and its previous interpretation)—then we are in a position to understand the relevance of church history and the history of doctrine both objectively and subjectively, hermeneutically and spiritually, to the study of theology. Church history and the history of doctrine provide the connecting link between us and the text. They belong to the hermeneutical circle in which the text is carried forward, interpreted, and shown to be significant in the present.

The separation of the biblical and the church historical disciplines, moreover, is a natural and necessary result of the church's self-understanding and of the way in which the various documents have affected and influenced the life of the community of belief. Farley's questioning of the fourfold curriculum and, by implication, of a particular way of doing theology on the basis of Scripture but in the light of an ongoing albeit less-normative tradition falls short of the mark. We do not have to invoke classic orthodox doctrines like the inspiration, infallibility, and divine authority of Scripture at this point: in the context of the question, such doctrines do not amount to proofs in any case. Instead, it is quite enough that we register the fact that the dogmatically defined canon of Scripture, even granting the different identifications of canon in the several great Christian communions, has had a qualitatively different effect and continues to have a qualitatively different effect on the consciousness of the community of belief than does the body of noncanonical documents. When we enter the realm of church history, we enter a portion of the Judeo-Christian tradition that functions differently in theology and in worship than the portion that belongs to the canon.

The danger presently confronting the study of church history and historical theology, as for the several biblical disciplines, is that they become fragmented into specialties defined by narrow areas of scholarly research rather than pointing, in their own way, toward the unity of theology as a whole. Here again, the importance of the survey—what in my own teaching I tend to characterize as "theology from Ignatius of Antioch to Pannenberg et al."—

cannot be underestimated. No specialist can afford to forget that even the minutiae of research into the events of a few years in the twelfth century stand in relation to and, in fact, are illuminated by a broad knowledge of the larger whole of the life of the church in its history. This is not a matter of attempting to continue a biblical salvation history out into the life of the church or of making tradition a coequal norm with Scripture. Rather, it is a matter of recognizing the place of the larger flow of the history of the church and its teachings in the hermeneutical circle that links and binds us in the present to any and all other moments in that history—whether technically "biblical" or churchly—and conveys their significance to the present.

Some definition of the two disciplines is in order. It was typical of the nineteenth-century idealist approach to historical study to focus on the history of ideas as the focus of historical meaning. From that approach comes the still frequently heard definition of church history as the history of the institution of the church, including its doctrines, as it existed in relation to the culture of the world around it—and of the history of doctrine as the inward or interior history of the teachings of the church in their organic development. This definition does have the advantage of clearly showing church history to be the larger category that contains with it, among other things, the history of doctrine. It carries, however, the disadvantage and grave defect of severing events from ideas and giving the impression that "external history" is a husk ultimately discarded in the quest for inner, ideational reality. The opposite, however, is the case. Just as church history is the larger disciplinary category, so also is it the context within which the history of doctrine must be understood. Ideas do influence events, but the ideas themselves must be understood within their proper cultural, social, political, and intellectual setting inasmuch as the setting gives rise to and shapes the ideas.

Church history, then, is the larger investigation of the corporate body of believers in its cultural, social, political, geographical, and intellectual context and in the development of its institutions, worship, mission, and intellectual and spiritual life. This investigation, moreover, must be undertaken critically, with the understanding that the history even of spiritual things is a history that is analyzed and explained in terms of the usual criteria of historical investigation. For example, it is doctrinally arguable to attribute the accurate preservation of the text of Scripture to divine providence inasmuch as Scripture contains the foundation of the church's preaching of salvation. Historical investigation cannot, however, rest content with the doctrinal explanation but must look to the process of the transmission of the text and examine the procedures and techniques of the Masoretes, the monastic calligraphers of the church, and the scholarly editors of later centuries, and find in the actual practice of these people the historical grounds for arguing whether or not the text has been accurately preserved. It also ought to be clear that, at least in our times, the historical investigation must precede the doctrinal statement and in fact supply the information from which the doctrinal statement takes its shape and on which it rests.

History of doctrine is the examination of the theological teachings of the church in their historical setting and their development. Like church history, the history of doctrine is an essentially analytical and descriptive discipline. Thus, in examining the teachings of Arius and the movement of doctrine toward Nicea, it is not the task of the historian of doctrine to evaluate in any ultimate sense the rightness or wrongness of Arius' views or of the response to Arius and Arianism made by the Council of Nicea and its defenders. Rather, the historian is committed to the precise exposition of Arius' theology, including the way in which it arose from and contributed to its cultural and intellectual context. Rightly or wrongly, Arianism had considerable power and appeal: it is the task of the historian to examine this appeal. The orthodoxy of Nicea must also be examined in its cultural and intellectual context—so that the forms of its doctrinal expression and their adequacy to the needs of fourth-century Trinitarianism can be fully understood. A dogmatic reading of the materials that assumes the rightness of Nicea on the basis of some contemporary orthodoxy will entirely miss the full significance of the council.

Church history, therefore, can hardly be studied without attention to the history of doctrine—inasmuch as the history of doctrine is an integral part of the social, cultural, institutional, and intellectual history of the church. And whether or not the whole is greater than the sum of its parts, it cannot be understood if one of the parts is omitted from the equation. History of doctrine, on the other hand, cannot be rightly studied in isolation from the larger history of the church. Its teachings—even at their most abstract—still reflect the churchly context out of which they arise. As we noted in the previous discussion of biblical theology, the method and organization of these disciplines arise out of historical and contextual concerns: like biblical theology, the history of doctrine cannot be constructed on systematic models drawn from the present. This was the great problem with the nineteenth-century histories of doctrine, such as those of Neander, Hagenbach, and Shedd. They all place a primary emphasis on doctrinal theology, Scripture, God, Creation, sin, and so forth—and they press each age of the church into a predetermined pattern. If we really wish to understand the past on its own terms and utilize our understanding in a critique of the present, the discussion of any period in history must rest on thought-categories drawn from that period. Only then, for example, can we see that the typical model of theological system did not begin to appear in the West until the twelfth century; whatever its validity, it does not arise directly out of the teaching either of Scripture or of the early church.

History of doctrine and church history both draw on churchly, confessional understandings and on general, methodological concepts held in common by ecclesiastical and secular historians. Church history and history of doctrine very naturally gravitate toward emphases and even periodizations of history that carry with them theological assumptions and judgments. Rather than view history as merely chronology—a list of "one thing after another" with no interpretive statement of relationship or importance of events—historians engage in constructive interpretation. And herein lies both a danger to understanding and a great help to understanding. It is dangerous to confuse interpretation with "fact" or with "truth," but it is also necessary to the larger, suprahistorical task of corporate and individual self-interpretation that the interpretive exercise be undertaken.

Thus the first great historian of the church, Eusebius of Caesarea, can hardly be faulted for interpreting the history of the church theologically, in the light both of God's biblical promises and of his own situation, in addition to preserving materials and data from the past history of the church. Eusebius had, after all, lived through the last great persecutions under the emperors Galerius and Maximin Daza; he had seen the rise of young Constantine, the coming of toleration, and the Constantinian patronage of the church; and he had participated in the almost unbelievable event of three hundred bishops meeting safely in one place, under imperial auspices, to debate the future of Christian doctrine. He had participated, he believed, in the dawning of the great age of the church: he could chart a history, in which the church, the body of Christ continuing the work of the Incarnation in this world, had prevailed against the gates of hell and had reached what seemed to be an eschatological vindication after a great tribulation. His history marks the central place of the church in the divinely guaranteed march of history toward the eschaton.

Eusebius' view of history made conceptually possible the Augustinian interpretation of the course of the entirety of world history from the creation onward. Augustine saw the church as the City of God seeking its foundations, with its Lord, outside of the gate of the earthly city, in the heavenly Jerusalem. Just as Eusebius' view of history provided Christians in the fourth and fifth centuries with a sense of the meaning of their place in the community of faith, so did Augustine's view provide Christians throughout the Middle Ages with a sense of their purpose and destiny. Among other things, it was Augustine's picture of the church "in via, on its way toward its heavenly and redemptive goal," that gave the writers of the Middle Ages a sense of the purpose of theology itself and gave, also, the common life of the Middle Ages its pilgrim character, from the practice of pilgrimage to shrines to the creation of the great mendicant orders.

The Reformation, too, brought with it a sense of history. Building upon the late medieval sense of newness or "modernity" and the Renaissance sense of a new grasp of insight by a renewed recourse to the classical and biblical sources of knowledge, the Reformation identified itself as the retrieved and repristinated church after centuries of Babylonian captivity. At the same time, the historians of the Reformation, like the famous Flacius Illyricus, the guiding force of the great project known as the Magdeburg Centuries, who wrote of the "forerunners" of the Reformation, saw the need of stressing the catholicity of the Reformers and the theological rootage of the Reformation in the heritage of Christian truth preserved by the church in all ages. Protestants, ever since, have expressed both a distaste for and a fascination with things medieval as well as a great and positive interest in the theology of the fathers of the first five centuries, before the reputed fall of the church into medieval darkness.

Quite in contrast to these corporately and individually significant but also incredibly theologically biased interpretations and assessments of the history of the church, the study of the church and its teachings also draws on the standard, critical methodology of the historical disciplines. On a very basic level, critical methodology enables us to see that Eusebius had not entered the eschaton and that the success of Christianity in the empire had social and cultural causes. It enables us to see that the institutional church is somewhat less of an image of the "city of God" than some of the medieval writers suggested, while at the same time the Middle Ages cannot be dismissed as a dark, Babylonian Captivity, or the Reformation construed as a radical break with the medieval past. Historical study, from the vantage point of its critical methodology, examines and interprets not only discrete pieces of data but also the broader course of historical events and the theories previously used to make those events meaningful. Thus today Protestants can learn the value of the medieval heritage to Protestantism and its theology without losing sight of the importance of the Reformation.

Church history and the history of doctrine today maintain some of the basic periodizations handed down by the old theological histories, although, of course, recognizing problems with these periodizations in particular and with the division of an essentially seamless history into periods in general. The needs of both academic specialization and cohesive and coherent understanding have led to the division of the historical examination of the church into patristic, medieval, Reformation and post-Reformation, and modern history. Some historians make a stronger distinction between the Reformation and post-Reformation eras, and others speak of a postmodern era in which we presently live. Even if the lines between these periods cannot be rigidly drawn, there are identifiable characteristics of, for example, patristic theology that are not duplicated in the other periods of the history of the church. The Reformation did bring about major changes in the life of the church, indeed, in the whole of Western culture, that still have their impact on us today. And the perspectives on God, man, and the world that dominated the West through the Middle Ages and the Reformation and post-Reformation eras were altered profoundly in the Enlightenment of the eighteenth century, marking the dawn of the "modern" era.

Understanding both the flow of this history and the different characteristics of and issues raised by each of these great periods (not to mention the further subdivision of the periods themselves into shorter segments, each with its own distinctive historical patterns) serves as a guide in interpreting the ideas, cultural monuments, social structures, and institutional developments of our history, many of which continue to have an impact on us. Inasmuch as all ideas and institutions take their form from the culture or society in which they arise—and inasmuch as cultural monuments and social structures frequently outlast the age of their formation and sometimes live on without obvious explanation or warrant into subsequent eras—knowledge of origins and development is crucial to the critical examination of the cultural and doctrinal patterns of the present.

Beyond this mutual interrelationship and enlightenment of the two subdisciplines, there are larger objective and subjective theological reasons for the study of church history and history of doctrine. Objectively the history of the church and its teachings provides crucial clarification of our present situation in relation both to the biblical foundations of Christianity and to the practices and teachings of the present day. It is certainly a truism, but equally certainly a truism worth repeating, that we cannot understand the present apart from a clear vision of its rootage in the past. The church today, for example, manifests a wide variety of divergent and even conflicting forms of governance: some denominations are governed by bishops who oversee the life of many congregations gathered into a diocese; other denominations identify the minister of each congregation as bishop and presbyter and see to the governance of the whole church through the deliberative work of gatherings of presbyters or presbyteries; and other groups still refuse the notion of denominational oversight, adopting a purely congregational form of government.

When these differences are argued on exegetical grounds alone—and here I realize I will be offending someone—the arguments fall short of cogency. They fail to convince. There are several reasons for this. On the one hand there seem to be at least two church orders in the New Testament—a more "charismatic" order in Paul's congregational epistles (cf. 1 Cor. 12:27ff.) and a more "institutional" order in the Pastoral Epistles. In addition, it is not entirely clear whether or not an "order" for church governance is being suggested in either place. What is clear is that virtually all of the present-day orders of church governance take the names for the various church officers from the New Testament and construct an order out of those names. On the other hand, the history of the church not only manifests the growth and development of several different forms of church governance (particularly in the modern period), it also manifests the social, cultural, and contextual reasons why one order thrives in a given situation and not in another and why certain orders have arisen at particular times. The democratic representative structure of Presbyterianism owes at least as much to the politics of the Swiss cantons as it does to New Testament exegesis. The quasi-episcopal supervisory model found in Lutheranism arose out of the political conditions of sixteenth- and seventeenth-century

Germany. Both models can be guided by Scripture, but neither can be explained apart from the history of the church.

The history of the church, therefore, provides a foundation for understanding the forms of church government and the way in which nominally scriptural patterns have been used by Christians throughout the centuries to inform their church governance. This history also offers a salutary lesson in the problems of applying New Testament order to social situations that are radically different from that of the New Testament church. It also shows why, after centuries of meditation on such questions, many church bodies have been willing to place such issues as church governance into the category of adiaphora, "things indifferent," that are not specifically ordained in and by Scripture.

Doctrinal examples of the importance of history to the understanding of issues can be given equally easily. One example will suffice. The orthodox Protestant doctrine of penal substitutionary atonement is firmly rooted in Scripture. That cannot be denied. But it is very difficult to argue purely on the basis of the text of Scripture, without examination of centuries of churchly meditation on Christ's saving work, why this particular formulation, rather than some other, equally biblical statement, has become the doctrinal or systematic centerpiece of orthodox Protestant teaching on the work of Christ. There is biblical language about Christ's work as a ransom from bondage to the powers of the world and ample collateral warrant for such a view in the Pauline contrast of flesh and spirit. There is also biblical language regarding the free gift of reconciling love through the loving example of Christ. The question is not, "Why penal substitutionary atonement?" Scripture clearly speaks of Christ standing in our place as a substitute and bearing for us the divine punishment for sin. The question is, rather, "Why this doctrine as our primary doctrinal position?"

The answer to this latter question is not at all a simple one, and if it is exegetical, it is exegetical in the sense of a churchly exegesis of a whole series of interrelated doctrinal issues over the course of centuries. The early church did not select any particular view of the atonement as primary, but tended to use all of the biblical statements concerning the meaning of Christ's death with equal authority. There was, in short, no systematizing effort made by the early church on the doctrine of Christ's work, no codification of a dogma on this issue. Only in the late twelfth century, in the work of Anselm of Canterbury do we find a concerted attempt to show the logic of the doctrine of the atonement and why the payment made in sacrifice of Christ must be a payment to God rather than to the Devil. In Anselm's *Cur Deus Homo (Why the God-Man?)*, then, the satisfaction theory comes to the fore. After several centuries of debate and massive critique and modification at the hands of Aquinas, Scotus, and others, the satisfaction theory passed into the hands of the Reformers. Calvin in particular was responsible for giving it a central place, for couching the language of satisfaction in substitutionary terms, and for replacing the Anselmic notions of satisfaction made to the wronged honor of God with concept of the satisfaction of divine justice.[28]

In the following century, in the theological works of the Protestant orthodox, the doctrine of penal substitutionary atonement reached its final form. An examination of the Protestant orthodox systems, particularly of the way in which they follow the systematic

---

[28]Cf. Reinhold Seeberg, *Text-book of the History of Doctrines*, trans. Charles Hay, 2 vols. (repr. Grand Rapids: Baker, 1983), 2:68-74, 110–13, 156–58, 399–400.

pattern established by Calvin and others of moving from the work of Christ not to the sacraments as the medieval systems did but instead to the application of Christ's work through faith in justification by grace alone, makes clear the fundamental reason for the dominance of penal substitutionary atonement as the basic explanation of Christ's work. Not only does the doctrine have powerful exegetical warrant on its own terms but, in addition, its view of Christ's work as the acceptance by the sinless Christ of the punishment of our sins revealed the objective ground of a salvation offered apart from human works of satisfaction. It is, in other words, the perfect corollary of the doctrine of justification through faith alone. The doctrine of penal substitutionary atonement comes to the fore in the light of the larger exegetical and systematizing work of the Reformers and their successors.

The objective use and importance of history that we have just now illustrated from church polity and church doctrine point directly to their subjective importance. How is a person to be trained as a Christian in the present? How is the study of theology to provide not merely an objective body of data but also a subjective character, a Christian mind and spirituality? The answers to these questions are certainly not provided in the increasingly secular, non-Christian cultural context of the church in America. Instead, the answers to these questions arise in the context of the self-understanding of the Christian community itself, particularly insofar as that communal self-understanding becomes the basis for individual self-understanding. The study of the history of the church and its teachings is not only an objective, external discipline, it is also a subjective, internal exercise by which and through which the life and mind of the church become an integral part of the life and mind of the individual Christian.

Study of the history of the church and its teaching serves to identify for the individual Christian his or her place in relation to the life and teaching of the church in the present. Some years ago, the television mini-series "Roots" made a great impression on the American public—in fact it assured, among other things, the future of television mini-series! The reason it made such a great impression is that the story itself, like the historical novel on which it was based, charted the quest of one individual, a black American, for his own personal identity. That identity was not given to him either fully or positively by a society that has long oppressed its black members and that, as one of the forms of its oppression, has tended to obscure and to exclude from the societal and cultural history the past of black Americans. Alex Haley's personal quest was a quest for meaning, for identity, for the solidification of his positive place in the present-day life of America in and through the affirmation of his heritage.

The parallel between Alex Haley's search for his roots and the personal, subjective, and spiritual appropriation of church history ought to be clear. There is no overt oppression of Christians in this culture, and in this country we never had to struggle to gain recognition of the importance and rightful place of Christianity in our culture. We did, of course, need to guarantee the freedom of expression of various forms of religion—but that is another issue. Christians in America are not overtly oppressed simply because they are Christian. Nonetheless, as our society and its values grow less and less Christian and therefore less and less supportive of and even hospitable to the Christian way of life and belief, our identity as Christians and the Christian heritage of our past became obscured. Only by engagement in a quest for our Christian "roots" can this heritage be known, its cultural values understood and maintained, and our own personal identity as Christians in Christian community be affirmed and perpetuated. Recognition of this personal, existential need for roots is hardly new: it was Cicero who said, "Not to know the events that happened before one was born is to remain always a child"; and the identity of the children of Israel was passed on from generation to generation in the confessional recitation of the history of the people, "My father was a wandering Aramean . . ." (Deut. 26:5ff.).

THE UNITY OF BIBLICAL AND HISTORICAL STUDIES

Biblical and church historical studies are closely related to each other and ought to be studied with a consistent recognition of their interdependence. A historical, developmental perspective presents us with an essentially seamless flow of events from the era of the Old Testament, through the so-called intertestamental period and the era of earliest Christianity in the New Testament, on into the patristic, medieval, Reformation, post-Reformation, and modern eras. Not only can we speak of a continuous development or trajectory of Judeo-Christian religion, we can also speak of a continuous cultural and social development around and with the Judeo-Christian trajectory that places it into the ongoing history of civilization and of religions. Separation of the canon of Scripture from the culture and the history around it is thus doctrinally justifiable but interpretatively problematic. The culture of the ancient Near East and of the Roman world must be brought to bear on the interpretation of Scripture.

Far from creating a problem for church and theology, these historical continuities point toward a continuity in the development of the Christian community and its message that not only informs the study of theology but, in a profound and fundamental way, makes that study possible. The biblical message is not a message from the past that sits, as a self-contained and isolated canon, on a bookshelf waiting for the proper moment to speak and then, having spoken, returning to its shelf until such time as it may again prove useful. If that were the case, the Bible would be a normative reference book, comparable in function to the *Encyclopedia Britannica* or *Webster's Unabridged Dictionary*. Instead, the biblical message is and has always been a message situated in the present life of the religious community, a message heard as normative in the context of other messages, some based on it and some not, each with its own degree of authority and usefulness. The ongoing life of the religious community—the history of the church—modeled in faith and in practice upon an interpretation of the biblical message in relation to the social and cultural situation of the times, carries forward the message, not as a dead letter but as a living Word into our present.

From a methodological point of view the disciplines also form a basic unity. The same, essentially historical, textual, grammatical, contextual, and critical method is used by Bible scholars, church historians, historians of doctrine, and secular historians. This is not to deny the fact that Bible scholars and historians of church and doctrine frequently hold theological presuppositions concerning the truth of the message contained in the documents they analyze, presuppositions of a somewhat different order than a secular historian's presumption of the truthful intention of the sources he analyzes. The point needs to be made, nonetheless, that the basic methods of analysis are the same and that the basic rules of hermeneutics observed are identical. Historical method is historical method. Differences in method concerning the presence or absence of a distinction between "fact" and "interpretation" or concerning the kind of "meaning" to be found in history (i.e., moral conclusions, self-understanding, and so forth) are shared alike by historical investigators of Scripture, church, and the Second World War. The issue is one of the competence of method and the potential scope of its conclusions. In any case, one methodology, replete as it is with its own internal disputes, is used by biblical scholars, by historians of church and doctrine, and by secular historians.

A concrete indication of this unity of perspective and method is seen in that the works on "earliest Christianity," whether on the general history of the New Testament church and its mission or on the theology of the New Testament, at the same time that they respect the canon of the New Testament in theological terms, tend to argue the meaning of the New Testament in terms of its general cultural context, its roots in the Old Testament and the intertestamental literature, and, quite strikingly, its implications as seen in the writing of the apostolic fathers of the early second century. Ignatius' language concerning the Incarnation illuminates discussion of the purpose of the infancy narratives in the gospels. The docetistic attempt to rationalize away the problem of Christ's humanity and to remove the difficulty of teaching the union of the divine with a finite and fleshly body by denying the reality of Christ's humanity is countered directly by Ignatius with reference to the Davidic lineage and human birth of Jesus. If indeed the priority of Mark and the later addition of the infancy narratives to the gospel accounts are accepted on the basis of historical and textual analysis, the arguments presented by Ignatius point toward the theological significance of the addition.

The early church, beginning in the first century during the time of the preparation of our canonical New Testament, not only saw the danger to Christian teaching of a failure to deal with the true humanity of Jesus of Nazareth, it also moved toward a doctrinal solution to that problem by concentrating on the question of the divine and human identity of Jesus. In this sense, the infancy narratives, like the prologue to the gospel of John, taken together with the arguments of Ignatius and, after him, the second-century apologists, lie on a doctrinal trajectory that leads to the consideration of the "person" of Christ in the third, fourth, and fifth centuries. The development of the language of one person of Christ in two natures by Tertullian and other writers of the early church can be understood, valued, and used by us only if we recognize what it attempted to say about the apostolic witness to Christ.

Another instance of early patristic testimony adding a new dimension to the interpretation of the biblical materials is the statement found in 1 Clement concerning the ministry of the apostle Paul. Clement testifies to seven imprisonments of Paul and to Paul's mission to the "whole world" as far as "the limit of the West."[29] In the light of Paul's stated desire to journey to Spain after his ministry in Rome (Rom. 15:28) and the rather buoyant conclusion of Acts (28:30–31) Clement's early testimony (ca. A.D. 100) to a mission to Spain and the way in which it opens up the Pauline chronology ought to be taken seriously. At the very least, historical study must inquire carefully whether or not Clement's words are merely an elaboration of Romans 15:28 or a glimpse into a history otherwise lost to us.

In addition to these and many other instances of the interpretative relationships that exist between the writings of the canonical New Testament and the documents of the early church, the continuity between the one body of literature and the other must be recognized in the shape and contents of the canon of the New Testament itself. In A.D. 117 the terminus ad quem of the episcopate of Ignatius of Antioch, the canon of the New Testament

---

[29]1 Clement, 5, in ANF, 1:6.

had not yet been defined by the church. The strict identification of the canon of the New Testament took place over the next two centuries as Christian communities around the Mediterranean basin shared the apostolic writings over against writings that claimed to be apostolic but contained doctrines unacceptable to the faith of the church. Thus, between the beginning of the second and the beginning of the fourth century, the gospel of Mark, a document probably of Roman origin; the gospel of Matthew, a document probably of Syrian provenance; the epistles of Paul to the Corinthians, which were originally in possession of the Corinthian church, and so forth, became the common property of Christians everywhere. During the same period, the heretical Marcion proposed a purified canon of exclusively Pauline materials plus the gospel of Luke, purged of references to the Old Testament, and the Gnostics offered a wide variety of gospels and epistles written under the names of the apostles.

Inasmuch as the apostles themselves had not created a canonical witness to Christ limited to their own literary productions, the church of the second and third centuries was pressed to perform the task itself. Since, moreover, many theologically unacceptable writings were put forth under the names of the apostles—like the Gospel and Acts of Thomas—and since several theologically important documents were known to have been written not by the apostles themselves but by followers of the apostles—like the Gospel of Mark and Luke–Acts—the church needed to identify a standard of canonicity in some sense external to the books themselves yet firmly grounded in the apostolic preaching itself. In the so-called Rule of Faith found in slightly different forms in the writings of Irenaeus, Hippolytus, and Tertullian, the church found that standard. The Rule of Faith was a distillate of the apostolic preaching very much like the Apostle's Creed in form and content. As R. B. Rackham argued, all of the articles of the Rule can be identified in the apostolic preaching of the Book of Acts.[30] In addition, confession of the Rule excluded both the Gnostic distinction between the good high God and the deficient creator and the Gnostic denial of the reality of Christ's bodily existence and death; applied to purportedly apostolic documents, the rule excluded those of a Gnostic and Marcionite theology. This canonical principle, together with the assumption of apostolic authorship or close proximity to direct apostolic witness, made possible the creation of the canon.

Granting this historical and churchly creation of the canon itself, it becomes impossible to sever New Testament study from the study of the history of the church and its doctrines. The identification of the New Testament belongs to the history of the church, and therefore in a very real sense the study of church history contains the completion of the historical study of the New Testament. The Protestant *sola Scriptura* is, therefore, as much a mandate to the study of the history of the church as is the Roman Catholic emphasis on tradition. In fact, Protestant theology in general needs to be more conscious, in a functional and constructive sense, of the importance of the tradition in mediating both Scripture and fundamental understanding of Scripture to the present. Thus, Pannenberg has recently argued:

> Church history is not just a particular discipline, as biblical theology can be said to be. It embraces the whole of theology, whereas biblical theology as a discipline can

---

[30]Richard B. Rackham, *The Acts of the Apostles: An Exposition* (London: Methuen, 1901; 14th ed., 1951), pp. lxix–lxxi.

only *per nefas* [lit., going beyond proper jurisdiction], and the individual exegete only by exercising considerable courage, transcend the limits of their own discipline in order to consider its contribution to theology as a whole. The matter cannot be the concern uniquely of historical-critical biblical science. In contrast it is the field of church history as church history which stretches beyond its formal boundaries into biblical theology on the one side and dogmatics and practical theology on the other.[31]

Pannenberg's comments are echoed, moreover, in Ebeling's citation of the maxim that church history can be understood "as a history of the exegesis of the New Testament Scripture" and by Schaff's statement that

> Church History is the connecting link between Exegetical and Systematic theology. It embraces all that is of permanent interest in the past fortunes of Christendom. But in a wider sense it covers also the whole extent of exegesis and runs parallel with it. . . . [Church history] is by far the most extensive and copious part of sacred learning, and supplies material to all other departments. If exegesis is the root, church history is the main trunk. We are connected with the Bible through the intervening links of the past and all its educational influences, and cannot safely disregard the wisdom and experience of ages.[32]

The statement that "church history is the history of exegesis" contains only some hyperbole: it is more accurate, strictly speaking, to say with Schaff that church history "covers" or contains "the whole of exegesis." And, beyond Schaff, we must recognize that church history not only "supplies materials" but also provides a heuristic key to unlocking their meaning. The study of history not only presents us with the doctrinal, ethical, and practical or ministerial materials of past generations of Christians, it also presents us with the context for understanding why those materials appear in their particular forms and with their own specific ways of expressing and addressing issues. All of these considerations point us toward the conclusion that the study of history is both a hermeneutical and a spiritually formative task.

More important than any number of examples we can offer is the cultivation of an approach to historical study that is fundamentally exegetical and interpretive, that continues into these other areas of study the hermeneutical emphasis necessary to the study of Scripture. The history of Christian doctrine, in other words, ought not to be reduced to a list of formulae to be memorized for the sake of avoiding heresy. The issue in studying the formulae is to understand their interpretive relationship to the Christian message and the way in which they have served in particular historical contexts to convey that message and, in addition, to preserve it into the future. Historical formulations, such as the Nicene doctrine of the Trinity and the Chalcedonian doctrine of the person of Christ, become elements of our doctrinal perspective today, not as contemporary results of New Testament exegesis, but as interpretive tools marking out the history of the ongoing significance of the gospel—on its way to becoming the gospel for us.

---

[31]Pannenberg, *Theology and the Philosophy of Science,* p. 392.
[32]Schaff, *Theological Propaedeutic,* pp. 234–35; cf. Ebeling, *The Study of Theology,* p. 77.

COMPARATIVE RELIGION AND HISTORY OF RELIGIONS

I have already, at several points, indicated the importance of a larger cultural, historical, religious, and intellectual context to the understanding of the documents in the Bible and in the history of the church and to the theological task in the present. This larger context is surveyed and interpreted through the study of comparative religion and the history of religions. Christian theologians and the organizers of seminary curricula have been slow to acknowledge the importance of these subjects to the study of theology and, as noted in my analysis of Pannenberg, have thereby become responsible at least in part for the unproductive severance between the university study of religion and the seminary study of theology typical of American academia. They have also become responsible for an isolation of theology from the world around it and, as a result, for the frequently felt inability of contemporary theology to address the world and the culture in terms that actually speak to the contemporary situation.

There are several reasons for this separation of the study of comparative religion and history of religions from the traditional study of theology, none of them negligible. In the first place, there is the issue of the necessary particularity of a religion and its message of salvation. From a religious and theological point of view, whereas value is the necessary presupposition of the churchly study of Christianity, there is no value in the generalized study of religion. Christians, Jews, and Muslims can, at very least, agree that religion in general is not what delivers human beings from the spiritual problems of life in this world. What delivers human beings from the spiritual problems of life in this world is a particular religion with a particular message of salvation. If we set aside our particularity, we set aside the very thing that makes possible our message of salvation. From the purely religious viewpoint of the Christian community, the study of contemporary Judaism, Islam, Buddhism, Hinduism, or Taoism is not useful to the salvation of individuals. As Cyprian of Carthage said in the third century A.D.: "Outside of the church, there is no salvation." Why study religions comparatively when we understand salvation in a strictly Christian sense?

In the second place, courses in comparative religion and history of religions have tended to relativize religion and set aside precisely what particular religions value the most: their particularity. The study of religion in general has tended to seek out broad themes, large-scale mythic constructions—such as teachings of heavenly redeemers and life beyond death—and to point toward common human aspirations and hopes underlying all religion. The effect of this investigation, whether intended or not, has been in many cases to evacuate these generalized symbols of salvation and eternal reality of genuine meaning and, in the name of objectivity, to sever the language and claims of religion from the real world of daily human existence.

Third, Christian theology and the history of religions method have a history of negative interaction: one need only mention Richard Reitzenstein's work *The Hellenistic Mystery Religions* and Wilhelm Bousset's *Kyrios Christos* to make the point. Reitzenstein examined, among other features of the Hellenistic mystery religions, their emphasis on myths of a dying and rising god, while Bousset concentrated on the transplanting of Christianity from its original Palestinian and Jewish context into "the soil of Hellenistic mysticism." The result, in both cases, was a placement of Christianity into a broad, ancient history of religions and, from the point of view of Christian theology, a rather disconcerting association of the main teachings of the church concerning the divinity and the resurrection of Christ with Hellenistic religion rather than with Judaism or with the teachings of Jesus.

All of these factors have contributed to the separation of Christian theology from the study of comparative religion and the history of religions. Nonetheless, the separation has not been total and the relationship, when pursued, not entirely negative. Indeed, the use of history of religions and the comparative study of religions in biblical studies has generally proved very fruitful and, as I will try to argue, ought to prove as fruitful in the study of theology. There can be no doubt that the historical study of ancient Egyptian, Mesopotamian, and Canaanite religion has proved highly significant to the understanding of the development of Israelite monotheism, of the way in which Israel saw the working of God in history, and of the confrontation between the Yahwism of the prophets and the Baalism of the Canaanites, and of those Israelites swayed by the agrarian culture and religion of the Promised Land.

Despite the uproar once caused by Reitzenstein and Bousset, history of religions and the comparative study of religions can also prove useful to our theological understanding of the New Testament and of the early church, particularly in view of the success of Christianity in moving from a Palestinian, Jewish context to a broader Mediterranean, Graeco-Roman context. The success of this cross-cultural transmission of Christianity offers a way of assessing the religious and theological significance of Christianity over against its religious competitors: it is not a useful explanation of the success of Christianity simply to claim that it is true. Truth is not, after all, always appealing to the human mind and heart. It is useful, however, both historically and theologically to see that Christianity, with its teaching about death and resurrection, was religiously understandable to a population schooled in the similar beliefs of the mystery religions, but that Christianity added a historical focus on Jesus of Nazareth, a high ethical content, and a philosophically significant monotheism to the message of death and resurrection, issues and themes that the mysteries could not match. Christianity gave to the culture something that it desired deeply: it answered the ethical, religious, and philosophical questionings of the Graeco-Roman culture. We learn this not so much by reading the New Testament and the writings of the fathers but by comparing those churchly texts with the religious and philosophical movements of the first and second centuries.

Christianity also gained from the culture an ability to address religious and ethical problems on a high philosophical plane—something that it had not received directly from Judaism. There was, of course, the precedent of the Platonic theology of Philo of Alexandria, but this was hardly a model accepted generally by the Judaism of the time or, for that matter, by the disciples of Jesus. When, however, the early church moved definitively across the cultural divide into the Hellenistic world, it rapidly recognized the ability of the Christian message to supercede the popular religion of the day and to address the higher ethical questions and the monotheistic tendencies of Graeco-Roman philosophy. By recognizing the elements of truth known to these philosophies and by acknowledging the one divine source of truth, the early church was able to discern in Graeco-Roman philosophy and ethics an old covenant given to the Gentiles more vague and less revelatory of divine truth but nonetheless parallel to the old covenant given to the Jews. This theological understanding of Gentile tradition allowed the early church to draw on the great philosophies and create a Christian amalgam that was, in Paul's words, "neither Jew nor Greek," but that drew on the best of both traditions and set aside what was unusable in both.

In fact, it is the historical and comparative study of religion that makes possible an understanding of the character and the success of the cross-cultural transmission of Christianity throughout its history. Although some recent writers have tended to view Christianity as a "Western" and even monocultural phenomenon apart from its recent extension into the Third World, this is far from being a historically accurate approach to the Christian faith. Historically, Christianity represents an initially Palestinian, Jewish religious movement, introduced first into a Hellenistic Greek context, next into a Latin cultural and linguistic context and then into various Celtic, Germanic, and Slavic contexts. There has hardly been an era in the history of the church in which the gospel and the attendant doctrines of the believing community have not been addressed to a new cultural and religious context—and, therefore, explained in terms understandable to cultural and (non-Christian) religious groups very different in their language and worldview from the earliest Christians. Just as historical and comparative study of religion is essential to our understanding of the biblical message, so also is it crucial to our understanding of the historical message of the church.

As an antidote to the tendency of many contemporary "theologians" of comparative religion or religion in general to find the lowest or most banal common denominator as the ground for a synthesis of world religions, traditional, conservative Christianity needs to listen to the words of Ernst Troeltsch about the place of Christianity among the world religions and about the importance of history of religions to the method of theology. There is a need to guide our study between the extremes of a generalized religiosity that follows no religion and a Barthian rejection of religion on the claim that Christianity is something else. Christianity is a religion that claims ultimacy for itself in a world of religions. Troeltsch could argue, on the basis of perspectives drawn from history of religions methodology, that

> what is to be expected from the few great breakthroughs of the religious principle . . . is not the aimless vagary of a multiplicity of revelations but the victory of the purest and most profound idea of God. As the history of religions shows, this idea of God is not to be sought in some kind of scientistic religion or in a general principle of religion that abstracts only what the various religions hold in common and for that reason overlooks their important differences. It is to be sought, rather, among the positive, historical, religious orientations and revelations.[33]

Nor did Troeltsch accept the argument that historical method demands the kind of neutrality that bars the way to a declaration of the superiority of the Christian faith. "History," according to Troeltsch, "is the sphere of knowledge because it is the sphere of the individual and nonrecurrent" with which, nonetheless, is found "something universally valid—or something connected with the universally valid."[34] Within the relative and conditioned we see an "indication of the unconditional." This coincidence or intersection of the relative and the absolute, the particular and the universal, not only permits Troeltsch to argue the existence of higher religions, it also provides him with a religious index, within history, of the achievement of Christianity, with an indication that, on historical grounds, Christianity offers "the highest religious truth that has relevance to us."[35] Christianity is, arguably, "the strongest and most concentrated revelation of personalistic religious apprehension." It alone among the

[33]Ernst Troeltsch, *The Absoluteness of Christianity*, trans. David Reid (Richmond: John Knox, 1971), p. 103.
[34]Ibid., p. 106.
[35]Ibid., pp. 106–7.

higher religions "takes empirical reality as actually given and experienced, builds upon it, transforms it, and at length raises it up to a new level."[36]

Thus the study of the history of religions and of comparative religion belongs to theological study and to theological formulation inasmuch as it provides us with a sense of the larger world context within which Christianity exists and from which Christianity must learn issues and problems that it must address. Such a study, however, must not cause a relativization of the Christian message or a loss of its particularity. From its very beginnings, the Judeo-Christian tradition encountered and responded to its religious context in the larger world—first Canaanite, Egyptian, and Mesopotamian and later Greek and Roman religion. Our understanding of this tradition rests in no small measure on our theological assessment of these encounters. We saw this point illustrated in our brief discussion of the Old Testament and the broadening of Israelite monotheism during the exilic period. Similar examples appear in the discussions of the New Testament and of church history.

When we extend this model to contemporary theological understanding, it becomes apparent that Christianity stands today in much the same relation to the great religions of the world—Buddhism, Hinduism, Taoism, and so forth—as it once stood to the religions of the ancient Mediterranean world. Not only must we understand these religions in order to grasp the very real impact they have had and are having on segments of our own culture and society, but we must also understand them in order that a Christian theology can address the world around it in a cogent and convincing way. And, if our past is any index to our present, we may engage in this part of our study in the hope that our Christianity will be strengthened and our Christian message both broadened and made more relevant to the needs of our world.

---

[36]Ibid., p. 112.

three

THE THEOLOGICAL
DISCIPLINES

Contemporary
Statement and Practice

The historical sweep of the Judeo-Christian tradition, from the call of Abraham to the present-day expression of faith in God, has always had a doctrinal and a practical dimension. What has become, in our study and practice of theology, a disciplinary division into systematic and practical fields has always existed in some form and exists today for the church whether one looks at a seminary curriculum or at a pastor's weekly work. The study of theology, as it moves through its biblical and historical roots toward the expression of present-day concerns, ought to find itself immersed in profound questions concerning the impact of the biblical and historical materials on the ways in which people think and act. The division between "systematic" and "practical" is nothing more or less than a statement that the life of the Christian community can be distinguished into categories of faith and obedience, of what is believed and what is done. It should also be clear that this distinction of aspects of the religious life or of elements of a theological curriculum does not permit a radical separation of fields of study or aspects of church practice: what is believed not only ought to relate to what is done, it ought also to govern and guide it; what is done or, better, what is learned from what has been done, ought, likewise, to draw consistently on and, occasionally, modify the expression of belief, though not the substance. Thus the study of the historical disciplines—of the biblical and the churchly materials—offers a foundation for the formation and encouragement of individuals, for the development of intellectual, spiritual, and moral character.

Since the systematic and the practical disciplines are really no more than the formalization, for the purpose of study and analysis, of the church's beliefs and practices, grown naturally out of and built on the historical experience of the Christian community, their existence does not at all depend on seminary study or on the creation of a particular kind of theological encyclopedia during the nineteenth century. In other words, "systematic" and "practical" theology are the formal expressions, in an academic context, of the faith and obedience that have always been a part of the life of the believing community. In our own time, the formal elements of these disciplines—including a maze of subdisciplines—have tended to obscure the fact that systematic and practical theology are nothing more than the studied presentation of what the church believes and how the church lives and behaves. In the following discussion, granting the historical rootage of these two major divisions of theological study, we will attempt to outline an approach to systematics and to praxis—or, as the title of the chapter indicates, to contemporary statement and contemporary practice.

Systematic theology is a much used and a much abused term, but it remains the broadest usage for the contemporary task of gathering together the elements of our faith into a coherent whole. In making this statement, I have already, in a sense, defined the field and a fundamental approach to it. Just as the entirety of biblical and church historical study can be gathered under the larger methodological rubric of "historical theology," so can all of the contemporizing, constructive disciplines be gathered together under the rubric of "systematic theology." This broad usage is not always observed, and "systematic theology" is frequently taken to be a synonym for "dogmatics" or "doctrinal theology"—but it is both arguable and highly instructive to focus on the broad usage as part of the methodological question of the unity of theological study and as, in fact, the proper meaning of the term.

Whereas "dogmatic" or "doctrinal theology" necessarily indicates a restrictive focus on the examination and exposition of the dogmas of the church—of the doctrines of the Trinity and the person of Christ, of human nature, sin and grace, of the church and the last things, the standard *loci* of classical dogmatics—"systematic theology" implies a discussion of those and of other topics that moves beyond exposition of churchly doctrine to philosophical questioning, presuppositional statement, argumentative defense, and cohesive analysis in the present context. It is very clear, for example, that Barth entitled his theology *Church Dogmatics* for the purpose of excluding from the outset of discussion all reference to philosophical categories and apologetic interests. And although his dogmatics has a certain cohesion when considered on its own terms and with a view to its own internal logic, it has very little reference to or application in the present context.[1]

Gerhard Ebeling well says:

> While [dogmatics] is used in a limited way of the coherent presentation of religious doctrine, thus predominantly being set off against ethics . . . the expression "systematic theology" has the tendency to embrace everything in theology methodologically oriented to the question of contemporary validity and to the testing of the claim to truth.[2]

To make the point in another way: just as the ethical life of Christians must be lived in the world and in a particular social context that is not "Christian" but that, nonetheless, shares certain beliefs and practices with the Christian community, so also does the intellectual and spiritual life of Christians take place in a larger social context. Systematic theology must be "oriented to the question of contemporary validity" and must consider philosophical and apologetic issues if only because the believing community cannot exist

---

[1] Cf. the pointed critique in Heinz Zahrnt, *The Question of God*, trans R. A. Wilson (London: Collins, 1969), p. 117.

[2] Gerhard Ebeling, *The Study of Theology*, trans. Duane Priebe (Philadelphia: Fortress, 1978), p. 126.

for long in dialogue only with itself and in ignorance of the issues being addressed or demanding to be addressed in the world around it.

Once it is recognized that systematic theology, simply by being genuinely "systematic," must ask the larger question of coherence in the contemporary context, the concept of a "systematic theology" can become the second focus of our discussion of the unity of theological discourse. Just as the history of doctrine is a unifying discipline that must be responsive to the entire trajectory of the Judeo-Christian tradition in its cultural and historical context and to the way in which that trajectory points toward the present, so also is systematic theology a unitive discipline that must be responsive to the findings and claims of the other theological disciplines: the historical model seeks chronological and developmental cohesion while the systematic model seeks constructive, relational, and conceptual cohesion in the present. The very nature of this constructive and cohesive task demands the use of historical and critical, doctrinal or dogmatic, philosophical and apologetic categories. Systematic theology is, then, correctly understood in terms of its methodological comprehension of the whole gamut of contemporizing and constructive disciplines. The attempt to identify systematics with a limited set of these disciplines undermines its proper method and negates its basic task. Pannenberg sums up the task of systematics in terms of the universality of the theological task. Systematic theology, he points out, is concerned with the "faithfulness" both of "theology itself and . . . of the Christian church" to the "revelation of God in Jesus Christ," but precisely because this special focus of theology on Christ leads to speech about God, the theological task must be open to "all truth whatever." The universality of the subject leads to the universal outlook of the task.[3]

Systematic theology, then, must consider all of the constructive topics in theology—dogmatics, apologetics, philosophical theology, philosophy and phenomenology of religion, ethics—and draw them out in the light of the materials provided in the historical analyses of biblical study and church history. In an academically extended or expanded model such as that proposed by Pannenberg—and we might add, suitable to the constructive discussion of the Christian message in the larger world context of the twentieth century—the "history of religions" and "philosophy of religion," as objective disciplines distinct from apologetics in its missiological application, would also fall under the category of systematics. The constructive as well as the critical impact of social and humane sciences like anthropology, sociology, and psychology would also be felt in systematic theology. Thus part of the systematic task today is the establishment of principles and procedures for the theological use of the results of these disciplines, a task analogous to the discussion, begun in the Middle Ages and still going on in the present, concerning the use of philosophical categories in theology.[4]

---

[3]Wolfhart Pannenberg, *Basic Questions in Theology: Collected Essays*, trans. George H. Kehm, 2 vols. (repr. Philadelphia: Westminster, 1983), 1:1.

[4]Cf. my "Giving Direction to Theology: the Scholastic Dimension," *Journal of the Evangelical Theological Society* 28,2 (June 1985): 183–93.

DOGMATIC OR DOCTRINAL THEOLOGY

Doctrinal or dogmatic theology, simply defined, is the contemporary exposition of the greater doctrines of the church. The two parts of this definition must be balanced evenly: dogmatics cannot just be the recitation of the doctrinal statements of the church in a topical rather than a historical order nor can it be just the contemporary exposition of someone's theological ideas, no matter how brilliant they might be. The doctrines must be churchly, and the exposition, also churchly in its basic attitude and approach, must be contemporary in its expression. If the contemporary aspect of the definition is lost, the exposition lapses into a reconstructive, historically defined approach that can at best produce for present-day examination a doctrinal overview from a bygone era. This kind of theology is no better than the attempt to take a particular document from a past era— even a document as valuable as Calvin's *Institutes* or Aquinas' *Summa Theologiae*—and use it as a textbook in theology. The past must be consulted, but not copied without regard to the new historical and cultural situation in which we find ourselves. If, on the other hand, the great doctrines of the church are not addressed, the exposition lapses into subjectivity and personal or even idiosyncratic statement. The value of such theologies is obviously limited—and limited to a nonchurchly constituency!

There is, therefore, in dogmatic or doctrinal theology a clear relationship between contemporary faith-statement and the normative doctrinal constructs known as dogmas. The question for dogmatic theology is precisely how these dogmas relate to the biblical witness on which they have been founded, to the larger body of doctrines that belongs to theology but that has not been as closely defined as the so-called dogmas, and to the ability of the contemporary theologian or minister to proclaim the significance of the biblical witness for the present. The historical element in the method of systematic theology enters at this point, inasmuch as the reconstruction of the meaning both of Scripture and of churchly dogmas and doctrines is the necessary basis for the identification of their contemporary significance.

Dogmas, then, are not the sole content of dogmatics. Dogmatics presents the whole body of Christian doctrine—but it does so "dogmatically," that is, with a view toward the regulatory character of dogmas and, by extension, with a view toward the regulatory character of the language of doctrine in general. This latter statement demands some explanation. The term *dogma* derives from the Greek *dokein*, to think or believe, and it indicates a fundamental tenet of thought or belief. The derivation is not modern: the word "dogma" appears in classical Greek, indicating either a propositional truth of philosophy or an authoritative decree in law. The early church took over the term and used it as a characterization of divine truths, although virtually always in statements distinguishing between specifically divine or revealed dogmas and human dogmas having no authority in the church. In the Renaissance and Reformation the term was used particularly with reference to human decrees belonging to the church as distinct from the teachings of biblical revelation. This is the sense of the term adopted by Adolf von Harnack in his *History of Dogma*.[5]

By way of contrast, largely because of later usage both Catholic and Protestant, dogma has come to indicate the churchly determination of doctrine by ecumenical consensus,

---

[5]Adolf von Harnack, *History of Dogma*, trans. Neil Buchanan, 7 vols. (New York: Dover, 1961); cf. Ebeling, *The Study of Theology*, pp. 128–29.

specifically the dogmas of the Trinity and the person of Christ. Here, of course, the connotation of the term is positive.

Granting this historical use of the term *dogma*, it is not at all surprising that doctrinal theology was not referred to as "dogmatics" until the seventeenth century and that the use of "dogmatic theology" as a title for the exposition of a body of Christian doctrine did not become common until the eighteenth. In addition, inasmuch as the doctrines that can be identified as ecclesiastical dogmas in the strictest sense are relatively few in number (i.e., Trinity and the person of Christ), the adoption of the term *dogmatics* for doctrinal theology is primarily a reference to the regulative or normative character of the way in which all doctrines are set forth rather than a reference to concentration on particular doctrines. As Ebeling argues, "dogmatic theology" intends to produce assertions of truth—it is an assertoric as opposed to a problematic form of discourse.[6]

This assertive character of dogmatics arises only in the context of the whole of a theological study in which dogmatic declaration is one of the final steps. Doctrinal theology, given its dogmatic character, cannot arise prior to biblical and historical theology and cannot impose itself as a methodological rule on biblical or historical study: it is a result, not a premise of the other disciplines. Nonetheless, this regulatory function does stand in a fundamental relationship to the other primary theological disciplines. In the churchly hermeneutical circle identified previously as moving from the text of Scripture to the tradition that has carried forward the meaning of the text into the present, and as including the exegete, minister, theologian, or student of theology, the dogmatic conclusion marks the closure of the circle. The result of the theological task is a theologically regulative conclusion that not only expresses the faith of the believing community in the present but also returns, via the tradition, to the text and provides a set of theological boundary-concepts for the continuing work of theology.

The mistaken self-exaltation of which doctrinal or dogmatic theology is all too easily capable can, moreover, be described and avoided in terms of this hermeneutical model. If a theologian exalts any particular doctrinal construction and insists that it become the key to interpreting the entirety of Scripture and to organizing the entirety of theological system, the scriptural Word becomes stifled by a human a priori, by what is perhaps a brilliant but nonetheless false contrivance of a particular theological ego. It is an error for a systematic theologian to assume that any particular systematization of a biblical idea or group of biblical ideas can become the basis for the interpretation of texts in which those ideas or doctrines do not appear.

This would appear, on the surface, to be a very simple rule—a rule that no right-minded theologian would violate. When, however, we cite particular examples, the frequency with which the rule has been violated becomes obvious. The so-called predestinarian system advocated by a few, mostly modern, Reformed theologians is one example; the radical Christocentrism (or Christomonism) of several nineteenth-century theologians and of neoorthodoxy is another; the use of justification and reconciliation as central dogmas by Albrecht Ritschl, yet another; and the emphasis on God as love to the exclusion of other attributes, typical of Ritschlianism and of American "Christocentric liberalism," still another.

---

[6]Ibid., p. 131.

Each of these "centrisms"—with, presumably, the best of theological intentions—ignores the variety of the biblical witness and the variety of the church's tradition of interpretation and forgets that the unity of the proclamation and the unity of any system of doctrine arises out of the biblical witness rather than being imposed on it. The proper hermeneutical approach within theological system is one that arises out of biblical and historical exegesis—that arises out of exegesis not only via the commentary but also via the disciplines of biblical theology and history of doctrine. Whereas the history of Christian doctrine provides systematic theology with a preliminary collation and interpretation of the biblical materials that precede any contemporary system in time and supply a churchly precedent for theological formulation in the present, biblical theology, insofar as it is a contemporary theological exercise and not an account of its own past, provides a preliminary collation and interpretation of the Scriptures that precede contemporary theological system not temporally but logically, in view of the proper principles and priorities of system itself.

The method and organization of doctrinal theology, its principles and its priorities, rest on two foundations, the biblical and the historical. In the spirit of the Reformation, Protestant theology accepts the canonical Scriptures as its primary norm and the history of the church's faith, particularly as it is expressed in the great ecumenical creeds and the great churchly confessions of the Reformation, as a secondary guide in matters of doctrine and interpretation. In other words, the canon of Scripture functions as a point of division of the larger tradition. As indicated previously, the canon is historically vague but doctrinally precise.

The biblical norm provides doctrinal theology with its primary topics, while the historical norm provides theology with an ongoing meditation on and interpretive elaboration of the contents of Scripture in the light of the historical experience of the believing community. The philosophical materials, both historical and contemporary, will provide critical and collateral standards for formulation—frequently taking the form of checks on the language and reasonability of our formulations. The way in which these materials are appropriated and used in doctrinal theology can and ought to evidence the unity of theological study as a whole and ought to contribute, both theoretically and practically, to the ongoing life of the Christian community.

Biblical theology, as discussed in the preceding chapter, is a theological discipline intended specifically to provide an overview of the religion and theology of the Old Testament and the New Testament in their own historical contexts. As such, it offers systematic theology an interpretive bridge to the overarching meaning of the biblical witness and its many theologies and themes. Inasmuch, moreover, as this interpretive bridge is methodologically and intentionally distinct from the bridge created by the history of doctrine, it serves not only as another point of contact between ourselves and the biblical text but also as a check on our potential exaltation of the tradition, as given by the history of doctrine, over the text. In other words, biblical theology has the potential of reopening the text of Scripture for systematic use on issues and topics where traditional interpretations have either been mistaken or have led to omissions of insights of themes from our theological systems.

By way of example, few systems of doctrinal theology deal with the issue of anthropomorphism and anthropopathism in God-language except to note it as a problem to be overcome on the way to a clear presentation of the doctrine of God. Yet biblical theology, particularly the theology of the Old Testament, helps us to recognize that the description of God with language drawn from the human form and from the human emotions is intrinsic to the biblical message and, in fact, provides the foundation for our identification of God as "personal." In this case, the results of biblical theology demand a reshaping of the systematic theological discussion of the doctrine of God and a fuller use of the category of anthropomorphisms and anthropopathisms in our theology.[7]

Another, perhaps more serious example is the traditional use of the terms "Son of Man" and "Son of God" as a point of reference to the humanity and divinity of Jesus, respectively. This usage is not only typical of the early church and of the church of the medieval and Reformation periods, it remains typical of systems of theology (usually—and unfortunately—"conservative" systems) even in our own day.[8] The early church brought the Palestinian, Jewish terminology of Son of Man and Son of God into a Hellenistic setting and very rapidly lost sight of the apocalyptic content of the former term and of the biblical, radically monotheistic context of the latter. The terms eventually were fastened to the two-nature language of the church's Christological formulae, and their original meaning was lost. Whereas Son of Man—particularly in the texts concerning the coming of the Son of Man on clouds of glory—indicates a heavenly figure of the end-times (and hardly a human "nature" like ours!), Son of God and "Son" used in relation to the divine Father most frequently indicate the close, filial relationship between Jesus and God, the relationship identified by Jesus' address to God as *"Abba,"* and the establishment of God's kingdom in and through Jesus, not a "divine nature" in Jesus. Jesus' divinity can better be inferred from other portions of the New Testament, like the *logos* language of John or the preexistence language of Paul.[9]

If doctrinal theology fails to pay attention to these results of exegesis and to their place in the Christological expositions of recent theologies of the New Testament, it will become guilty of perpetuating an exegetical error. We can no longer divine our dogmatic discussions of the person of Christ into sections dealing with Christ as Son of Man and as Son of God, as if those sections are sufficient and exhaustive presentations of his humanity and divinity. Nor can we easily press the traditional language of "person" and "natures" on to the biblical language as it is presently understood.

Indeed, doctrinal theology can learn from biblical theology to reorganize its discussion of Christology in terms of the New Testament "Jesus sayings" and the various names and titles of Christ, understood exegetically and historically. As a result it will have a firmer basis in the New Testament and will also provide a more substantial as well as more ecclesially useful foundation for the proclamation of Christ's humanity and divinity. In other words, a revision of the dogmatic *locus* of the person of Christ in terms of the results of New Testament theology does not set aside churchly teaching. Rather, it allows us to understand the church's dogmas in a new and, surely, clearer light.

---

[7]Cf. the discussions of anthropomorphisms and anthropopathisms in Gustav Friedrich Oehler, *Old Testament Theology*, trans. George Day (Edinburgh: T. & T. Clark, 1873), pp. 111–12; Hermann Schultz, *Old Testament Theology*, trans. J. A. Paterson, 2d ed., 2 vols. (Edinburgh: T. & T. Clark, 1898), 2:103–11; and Ludwig Köhler, *Theology of the Old Testament*, trans. A. S. Todd (Philadelphia: Westminster, 1957), pp. 22–25.

[8]Cf. J. Rodman Williams, *Renewal Theology*, 3 vols. (Grand Rapids: Zondervan, 1988–92), 1:306, 328, 342.

[9]Cf. Oscar Cullmann, *Christology of the New Testament*, trans. Shirley Guthrie and Charles Hall (Philadelphia: Westminster, 1959), pp. 265–69, 270, 293–94.

We return to the fact that the construction and exposition of doctrinal or systematic theology is a hermeneutical task: the results of contemporary exegesis of Christological language like "Son of Man" and "Son of God," although different from the traditional usage, do not so much falsify the tradition as add another dimension to it by returning to the documents from which the tradition itself arose and by finding there a meaning that had been forgotten. Our contemporary restructuring of Christology retains both the fundamental issue of the humanity and divinity of Christ and the religious and theological value of past testimony to that issue, albeit in and through a use of biblical language different from our own. We must continue to refer to the tradition inasmuch as the tradition is the bearer of the gospel as a significant message to us.

Our doctrinal theology, then, cannot simply replace one usage with another. It must rather present and analyze the various usages, identifying with care why and how a contemporary exegetical result demands the reinterpretation of traditional language, but at the same time eliciting from the traditional language its underlying doctrinal and religious intention as of continuing significance in the community of belief. In other words, the patristic understanding of the New Testament language of "Son of Man" and "Son of God" may no longer be exegetically acceptable, but the religious and theological significance of that language, gained through the use of an exegetical method considerably different from our own, still bears scrutiny as a significant approach to the Christological problem, an approach from which we can learn in the present.

In addition, from a somewhat negative methodological perspective, it remains true that those who do not learn from history will simply repeat its mistakes. Much as a critical, historical exegetical method permits us to encounter a text or idea with a surer sense of its original meaning, so also does a critical approach to the historical materials of Christianity enable us to understand why we formulate our theology in particular ways—especially when those ways are different from the results of present-day exegesis. We live, in other words, not only with the results of our own exegesis, but with the results of the exegesis of the past. When those past results are held unexamined as doctrinal tenets, they can stand in the way of exegesis as easily as they can support it.

A perfect example of the function of historical materials in providing a secondary norm for doctrinal theology as well as an excellent example of the problem of past exegetical results impinging on contemporary exegesis is the doctrine of the Trinity. It was Bishop Gore who commented, toward the end of the last century, that the doctrine of the Trinity "is not so much heard as overheard" in the New Testament. Not only can we understand why the early church developed such a doctrine as the way of dealing with the problem of monotheism in the context of the affirmations of the divinity of Christ and of the Holy Spirit, we can also grasp the problem of the modern exegete who sees in the New Testament no language of divine essence and persons and who finds that virtually all of the texts referring to God as Father are not Trinitarian in character but rather intend simply to identify God in a close relationship with his creatures. Similarly, many of the texts that identify Jesus as the "Son" refer to Jesus in his humanity as one who stood in a close, "filial" relationship with God.

On the one hand, we must not allow our postbiblical Trinitarian terms to hide from us the meaning of the text. On the other hand, we ought not permit the difficulties brought to theology by modern exegesis to deprive us of a view of God—the doctrine of the Trinity—that provides a solution to the theological difficulties in such texts as the prologue to John or the various Pauline texts indicating Christ's heavenly preexistence and divinity. In its function as a secondary norm for Christian teaching, the doctrine of the Trinity supplies us with a cogent meditation on the essential relatedness of God and of the ability of God to relate in creation and redemption to the created order. The genius of the doctrine is that it presses on us the theological point that the agent of redemption is fully divine—not a secondary being who cannot ultimately draw humanity into relation with God. The doctrine has stood for so long because its fundamental intention is profoundly biblical and profoundly monotheistic; and in this sense it remains a guide to our exegesis. We are not required to press the Nicene doctrine into every nook and cranny of the text of the New Testament, but we ought to be very careful to maintain, in all of our exegesis, the recognition that Scripture, echoed in the church's doctrine, speaks to us of one God who is Creator and Redeemer.

Historical materials also provide paradigms and principles of organization for theology. A brief examination of modern theological systems bears this out. Very few systems of theology are original in their basic organization—nor is there any necessity that they should be, as long as the traditional patterns of organization continue to serve the biblical and historical materials of theology and the needs of the present-day community of faith. (It has been, moreover, a standard practice in systems of theology and studies of "theological encyclopedia" written in a classical or traditional teaching style to incorporate short histories of the discipline in their prolegomena—so that basic information about the historical development of theological system is readily available and can easily be incorporated into contemporary study.)[10]

By way of example, the basic paradigm followed by such diverse thinkers as Thomas Aquinas, John Calvin, Johann Gerhard, Francis Turretin, Karl Barth, J. T. Mueller, Louis Berkhof, and Carl Braaten moves from an initial declaration of the grounds of theology to a doctrine of God and creation, to a discussion of the human predicament and the work of redemption in Christ, to a presentation of such topics as church, sacraments, and the last things. Order may vary from system to system, but the basic pattern of four groupings of topics—prolegomena, theology, anthropology and soteriology, ecclesiology and eschatology—is present in all of the theological systems mentioned. We can trace the pattern back to the *Sentences* of Peter Lombard (d. 1160) and from there to the treatise *On the Orthodox Faith* of John of Damascus (d. 754).

The question confronting contemporary systematic theology, of course, is whether or not the traditional form still serves adequately the presentation of the body of Christian doctrine—whether, in fact, the preliminary examination of the character, sources, and methods of theology that ought to precede any system of theology now demands the alteration not only of detail but also of basic patterns of organization. In the nineteenth century, the Kantian interpretation of religion as grounded on ethics led to the ethical interpretation of the Christian hope, with the result that a radical eschatology is lacking

---

[10]In, e.g., Louis Berkhof, *Introduction to Systematic Theology* (Grand Rapids: Eerdmans, 1932; repr. Grand Rapids: Baker, 1979); George R. Crooks and John F. Hurst, *Theological Encyclopaedia and Methodology*, new ed., rev. (New York: Hunt & Eaton, 1894). Christoph Luthardt, *Kompen dium der Dogmatik*, 11th posthumous ed. (Leipzig: Dörfling & Franke, 1914); Philip Schaff, *Theological Propaedeutic: a General Introduction to the Study of Theology, Exegetical, Historical, Systematic, and Practical* (New York: Scribner, 1894); Otto Weber, *Foundations of Dogmatics*, trans. Darrell Guder, 2 vols. (Grand Rapids: Eerdmans, 1981–82); Revere Franklin Weidner, *Introduction to Dogmatic Theology, Based on Luthardt* (Rock Island, Ill.: Augustana Book Concern, 1888).

from Albrecht Ritschl's theology. In addition, the assumption of many nineteenth-century thinkers that theology could and ought to be focused on certain fundamental or principial doctrines led to the structural revision of systems: Alexander Schweizer centered his theology on the divine causality and our dependence on it; Gottfried Thomasius focused his entire system on the doctrine of the person and work of Christ; Albrecht Ritschl produced an entire theology under the rubric of "justification and reconciliation." Should we today, for example, follow the realization that the New Testament preaching of Jesus is guided by a thoroughly eschatological perspective to a new form of theology centered on "the last things"?[11] Or should we, granting the difficulty of confronting God-language in the twentieth century, find some beginning point for a theological system other than discussions of revelation, Scripture, and God—perhaps a phenomenology of religion in general, or a philosophical discussion of the grounds of religion.

PHILOSOPHICAL APPROACHES AND THE STUDY OF RELIGION

If the problems and directions of theological system in our day point in the direction of philosophical and phenomenological approaches to religion, it is also true that philosophical theology and the closely related disciplines of the philosophy and phenomenology of religion are subjects that strain at the bounds of the traditional fourfold encyclopedia and which, in fact, belong in part to theological study and in part to secular academic study. These subjects straddle the fence, so to speak, between the sacred and the secular. Without implying a pejorative view of either subject and while affirming the necessity of both to the contemporary formulation of theology, both may be said to view the sacred from a generalized point of view that stands within the bounds of no particular theological or religious community. In so doing, both philosophical theology and philosophy of religion stand in a position over against doctrinal theology that is at once propaedeutic and critical.

Philosophical theology can be defined as the philosophical discussion of topics held in common by theology and philosophy. This means that philosophical theology would discuss the existence, essence, and attributes of God but not the doctrine of the Trinity; it would discuss the problem of evil but not the doctrines of sin and grace. Whereas the topics of this discipline come from both theology and philosophy and mark out the common subject of both, the methodology comes from philosophy and focuses on questions of knowledge and being—epistemology and ontology. As over against theology, or more specifically, "Christian" or "revealed" theology, philosophical theology, in order to be true to itself, must not utilize Scripture or churchly standards of truth: it rests on the truths of logic and reason—and occupies the ground of what has typically been called "natural theology." In this sense, philosophical theology provides a logical and rational check on dogmatic formulation. Philosophy of religion, by way of contrast, considers the nature of religion itself a focus that it shares with the phenomenology of religion.

From a propaedeutic or "preparatory" perspective, both philosophical theology and philosophy of religion stand as points of transition between purely philosophical study and the study of theology. In order to think theologically with any precision, one

---

[11]Cf. Thomas N. Finger, *Christian Theology: An Eschatological Approach*, 2 vols. (Scottsdale, Pa.: Herald, 1985-89).

needs to be able to deal with basic categories of philosophy as they come to bear on the questions of knowing and of being. Thus philosophical theology has an interest in the broad questions of knowledge of God, including the traditional proofs of God's existence; in issues concerning the nature of language about God; in the discussion of human nature and human destiny; in the relation of God and world; and in the problem of evil. Philosophical theology is the discipline of basic questions—so that here also we take up, as a philosophical question, the feasibility of theology as an academic discipline, as examined in Pannenberg's *Theology and the Philosophy of Science*.[12]

There is also, and equally importantly, a critically constructive function of philosophical theology and philosophy of religion within the framework of systematics. These two subject areas belong to the study of theology and to the theological curriculum precisely because they ask the broad, foundational questions necessary to the existence of theology as a discipline. There are also two basic locations for these subject areas within the larger historical/constructive pattern of theology: both philosophical theology and philosophy of religion can be treated historically and both can be treated synthetically or constructively. In the former case, they parallel the biblical and church historical studies as ancillary fields devoted to the creation of a proper context for understanding the historical progress of the Judeo-Christian religion and its theology. In the latter case they provide a conceptual framework for dealing with the religious and the philosophical elements that belong to the contemporary expression of Christianity. Both of these locations are legitimate. What is more, they are mutually enlightening and ought to be held simultaneously in view as one of the grounds of the interpretive unity of theology.

The term *philosophical theology* denotes a more intimate relationship between philosophy and theology than obtains in the other subdisciplines and, what is more important to the definition, the determination of the topics and contents of theology by another set of interest and competencies, the philosophical. For philosophical theology clearly cannot deal with issues that are incapable of philosophical treatment. This fact makes philosophical theology unique among the "systematic" disciplines: it is the only one of the subdisciplines grouped together as "systematic theology" the structure of which is determined by a nontheological discipline, a discipline external to the circle of the theological encyclopedia.

The very name "philosophical theology" implies something negative about the relationship of philosophy and theology: it implies that not all theology is philosophical, that the relationship is not a necessary one, and, by extension, that some forms of theology may find an element of their identity and reason for being in the fact that they are not at all philosophical. We have already encountered one of those forms in the discipline or subdiscipline "biblical theology" and its divisions "Old Testament theology" and "New Testament theology." Even when biblical theology implies no particular antagonism for other theological disciplines, like philosophical or doctrinal theology, it does imply an exclusion of purely philosophical (or doctrinal) categories from its presuppositions and essential structures or definitions for the sake of an exclusive reliance on the theological categories provided by the text of Scripture. Biblical theology can, however, be juxtaposed with both philosophical and doctrinal theology as a genre unaffected by categories extraneous and therefore inimical to the biblical revelation.

---

[12]Wolfhart Pannenberg, *Theology and the Philosophy of Science*, trans. Francis McDonagh (Philadelphia: Westminster, 1976).

Philosophical theology is distinct from philosophy of religion. There is, of course, considerable common ground: both disciplines deal with the concepts of God, good and evil, human nature, and human destiny. The difference between the disciplines, even in this area of common interest, is the more purely phenomenological perspective of the philosophy of religion: here the philosophical concern predominates to the point that all religion becomes the phenomenon under investigation and the Christian perspective, if present, will need to be justified phenomenologically. Philosophical theology, however, so long as it stands within the circle of the theological encyclopedia, must be a Christian discipline, no matter how philosophically determined its contents. Topics proper to philosophy of religion, such as primitive religion and the origin of religious belief, magic, and ritual, cannot properly belong to philosophical theology. Philosophy of religion has a profound interest in comparative religion—whereas philosophical theology does not.

This typology, no more than any other, falls short of perfection when we move from theory to actuality. There are quite a few words the titles of which blur the lines we have drawn between philosophical theology and philosophy of religion. One work in particular that comes to mind is Fairbairn's *Philosophy of the Christian Religion*.[13] This work, one of the major theoretical expositions of Christianity from the early part of this century, contains a fully developed comparative philosophy of religion within the structure of a Christian philosophical theology—it is interested both in the comparison of religions and in the philosophical examination of Christianity as the highest and the true religion. There can, in short, be such a thing as a Christian philosophy of religion, just as there can be a non-Christian philosophical theology. But the basic typology holds insofar as philosophy of religion must encompass the whole phenomenon of religion and encounter beliefs other than the Christian, while philosophical theology, when written from a Christian perspective will not be an essay in comparative religion.

Philosophy of religion is a broader topic than philosophical theology, just as "religion" is a broader category than "theology." Here religion in general is the subject and, in addition to the purely philosophical issues of epistemology and ontology, the methodology of comparative religion or "history of religions" must be brought to bear. John Caird, the British idealist, commented in his *Introduction to the Philosophy of Religion*:

> There is no province of human experience, there is nothing in the whole realm of reality, which lies beyond the domain of philosophy, or to which philosophical investigation does not extend. Religion, so far from forming an exception to the all-embracing sphere of philosophy, is rather just that province which lies nearest to it, for, in one point of view religion and philosophy have common objects and a common content.[14]

In the spirit of grasping "the whole realm of reality," philosophy examines religion and finds that it cannot be confined to the Christian religion but must examine the phenomenon of human religiosity.

By placing philosophy of religion into the context of the constructive or systematizing effort, we in no way mean to de-emphasize its historical and critical importance. The study of religion, in the first place, has become in our times a crucial adjunct to exegesis. As Ebeling comments,

---

[13]Andrew M. Fairbairn, *The Philosophy of the Christian Religion* (New York: Macmillan, 1902).
[14]John Caird, *An Introduction to the Philosophy of Religion* (New York: Macmillan, 1881), p. 3.

We meet a multitude of foreign religions within the Old and New Testaments, such as, for example, the Canaanite cults vis-à-vis Israel or the Hellenistic cults as counterparts of primitive Christianity. The worship of the true God necessarily conflicts with the worship of false gods, and the gospel with any other message of salvation. Biblical, Christian faith cannot be expressed apart from polemical contact with the world of the religions. It is also apparent in the biblical texts that faith in Yahweh as well as in Christ is susceptible to foreign influences.[15]

In other words, the study of religions provides the context for understanding both the formation and the contextualization of Israelite and Christian religion. Without some grasp of this context there can be little understanding, for example, of how the originally Palestinian phenomenon of Christianity was able to adapt its expression of the gospel to the thought-forms of the Graeco-Roman world and become over the course of time the world religion that it is today.

In addition, without this contextualized understanding of the forms of the Christian message, we can easily fall into the trap of moving from the thought-world of the first century to the thought-world of the twentieth as if a process of interpretation and recontextualization were unnecessary. When that incredibly erudite exponent of late nineteenth-century German liberalism, Adolf von Harnack, endeavored to explain "the essence of Christianity"[16]—having first dispensed with the historical Hellenization of doctrine and, indeed, the entire history of dogma—he brought on himself the stinging critique of having ignored history and having found his own theology in the New Testament rather than the teaching of the New Testament itself. In George Tyrrell's words, Harnack had looked down the well of history and had seen a liberal Postestant face reflected back at him.[17]

In the light of these considerations, we must differ with Ebeling's pronouncement that "through religious studies theology is neither increased by a further discipline nor supplemented by a discipline outside of theology, but is rather placed in question as such."[18] On the one hand, religious studies that take as their subject the phenomenon of religion in general do in fact constitute a disciplinary augmentation of theology as it has traditionally been understood. On the other hand, such general studies of the phenomenon cannot—and in a methodological sense *ought* not—call in question the normative expression of any particular religion. (It is one of the curious features of American academic life that Buddhism and Hinduism are permitted to be taught as value-systems from which truth can be learned and self-understanding gained, while the similar teaching of Christianity in the university or secular college context is deemed a violation of canons of objectivity or denial of the salutary separation of "church" and "state"!)

The study of religions can provide the proper phenomenological context for the understanding of a normative Christianity. It is one of the negative elements of the heritage of neoorthodoxy that religion and revelation are severed and Christianity is cut off from religion in general. Such thinking, while seemingly affirmative of the absoluteness and uniqueness of the Christian message, actually serves to cut the ground out from

---

[15]Ebeling, *The Study of Theology*, p. 39.

[16]Adolf von Harnack, *What Is Christianity*, trans. Thomas Saunders, intro. by Rudolf Bultmann (New York: Harper & Row, 1957).

[17]George Tyrrell, *Christianity at the Cross-Roads* (London: Longmans, Green, 1910), p. 44.

[18]Ebeling, *The Study of Theology*, p. 40.

under Christianity. By defining Christianity alone as based on revelation and by viewing human religiosity, generally and phenomenologically conceived, as either simply error or as having nothing to do with the way in which we understand our Christianity or frame our theology, neoorthodoxy left Christianity open to the standard rationalistic critiques of revelation and of theological language. At the same time it removes the broad justification of Christianity as one of the higher forms (arguably the highest!) of the general and genuine human apprehension of the divine as the ultimate and necessary element in a coherent construction of reality. In the final analysis, the neoorthodox approach to religion and revelation reduces to an obscurantist ploy that avoids a series of difficult phenomenological and historical questions rather than trying to answer them.

ETHICS AND APOLOGETICS

In addressing the movement of theological formulation from its biblical, historical, and philosophical roots toward ethics and apologetics, we are in fact anticipating the next two sections of our discussion—the relation of statement to practice and the work of formulation in the present. Both ethics and apologetics function as theological disciplines on the boundary between theory and practice, each having a theoretical pole consisting in formal statement and a practical or active pole consisting in an address to the present situation that demands active result. This boundary-character of the disciplines has led, in various of the older "encyclopedias," to their discussion either as practical or systematic disciplines, and either as component parts of or as adjuncts to dogmatic theology— manifesting, if nothing else, the problem of the "diversified encyclopedia" in the organization and study of theology.

This problem of the relationship of ethics and apologetics to the other disciplines indicates also a problem of formulation in the disciplines of ethics and apologetics themselves: Do they function independently? do they rest directly on Scripture? or do they draw their principles and materials from other disciplines, and if so which ones? In the case of ethics, this is a fairly old debate, extending back at least to the sixteenth century, when the question arose whether or not there ought to be Christian ethics, distinct from the philosophical ethics based on Aristotle. Quite a few Reformed theologians understood dogmatics and ethics—faith and works, or obedience—to constitute the basic divisions of doctrinal theology. The renewed study of Aristotle and, to a certain extent, the strict division between teachings concerning the faith and teachings concerning obedience led to the eventual separation of the disciplines of dogmatics and ethics. This separation was strengthened at the close of the eighteenth century by Kant's derivation of religion from ethics—making ethics a foundational discipline, not controlled by principles drawn from religion and not to be fashioned on the basis of a system of dogmatic theology, itself derived from ethics by way of religion.

Several American theologians of the last century attempted to overcome this separation by identifying ethics as a subdivision of doctrinal theology: the Methodist theologian Miner Raymond presented an entire ethical system within his *Systematic Theology*.[19] Charles Hodge and Robert Dabney attempted, somewhat less successfully, to deal with ethics under the rubric of the Ten Commandments, within a somewhat catechetically

---

[19]Miner Raymond, *Systematic Theology,* 2 vols. (New York: Eaton & Mains, 1892–94).

ordered system of theology.[20] For the most part, however, theologians of the nineteenth and twentieth centuries have allowed the separation of the disciplines, leaving us with the question of their relationship with each other and with the other disciplines within the larger study of theology.

In the first place, it should be clear that ethics does not simply deal with "things to be done," in the highly useful and instructive language of scholasticism, the *agenda*, but also and in some sense prior to the agenda, with "things to be believed" or *credenda*. It should also be clear—inasmuch as it is historically and phenomenologically correct—that the basic principles known to Judeo-Christian ethics by the investigation of the biblical revelation are also known to Western philosophy, to the "higher" religions, and to "natural reason." There is, in other words, a kinship between the principles of a purely "biblical" ethics based on the Decalogue, a philosophical ethics drawn from "natural reason," and a religious ethics learned from Buddhism, Hinduism, or Confucianism. (This point reinforces the point made previously about the importance of the study not only of philosophy but also of the history and phenomenology of religion as disciplines collateral to theology.)

We must, however, disagree with Ebeling's argument that ethics "treats what is purely human because it deals with the behavior and actions of people on their own responsibility, cast upon themselves as though there were no God."[21] The general acceptance and multiple sources of ethical principles and the utterly concrete address and application of ethics ought not to be understood as making ethics any less a theological discipline. Christian ethics—indeed, a religious ethics generally understood—must stand in contrast to those few systems of philosophical ethics that rule the divine out of consideration. Theological ethics arises in the context and is built on the terms set by our creatureliness. (This context and foundation leads, in the formulation of ethics, to the same kind of biblical, historical, philosophical, and phenomenological richness that we found to obtain in the formulation of doctrinal theology and provides, as well, a theological basis for the inclusion of the results of philosophical, phenomenological, and history-of-religions investigation in our ethical formulations.)

The ethical task is nothing less than the translation of the materials of Christian teaching—whether biblical, historical, doctrinal, or philosophical—into the contemporary life situation of the community of belief, first as principles and then as enactments. This task demands, as in the case of doctrinal theology, close attention to interpretive questions concerning the relationship between the situation in which the original ethical statement or principle was operative and the contemporary situation—together with close attention to the question of whether a particular standard is *apodictic*, expressing a necessary truth, or *casuistic*, expressing a prudent solution to a particular issue.

By way of example, certain of the mandates in the Levitical Code have long been recognized by the church as belonging legitimately to the life of ancient Israel but equally as not transferable to the contemporary situation. Not only can we recognize that the sacrificial aspects of the Code have been superceded in and for the church by Christ's work of atonement, but also we are forced, historically, to note the absence of a temple at which to sacrifice. Our theological and historical situation does not require observance:

---

[20]Cf. the comments in Berkhof, *Introduction*, pp. 50–51.
[21]Ebeling, *The Study of Theology*, p. 139.

these commands must be regarded as casuistic. A somewhat different issue confronts us in the case of commands such as the death penalty by stoning in cases of adultery. Whereas we can understand—particularly with the aid of social anthropology—the need of smaller societies to have more stringent forms of social control, and we can also understand, in the case of ancient Israel, the confluence of religious with social controls in an essentially theocratic state, yielding a basic equation of religious ethic with civil law, we must also recognize the rather different situation of our own society. In our contemporary social situation, the religious and the civil are separate, agreeing in some points but not in others. Religious authorities no longer have the power of life and death, and religiously grounded ethical codes do not directly demand civil action. The difference between our contemporary context and the Old Testament context demonstrates that this particular aspect of the law, also, cannot be counted as apodictic. Nonetheless, the law against adultery itself—apart from the question of penalties—remains within the context of the apodictic law, granting that the moral and personal impact of the breakdown of marriage is not limited to a particular historical context. Ethics, thus, must be a practical but not an utterly pragmatic discipline: it points toward enactment or praxis, but it maintains at the same time certain absolute standards in and through its response to all situations.

As has frequently been observed, apologetics is the oldest kind of formally conceived Christian theology, dating from the works of the so-called Greek apologists of the mid-second century. From that point onward, it has been a discipline that has argued both the philosophical and the ethical excellence of Christianity both in terms of the teachings of Scripture and the church and in terms of the standards set, external to Christianity, both by philosophy and by other religions.

The questions that we noted concerning the relationship of ethics to the other disciplines thus also obtain in the discussion of apologetics. "Apologetics," of course, indicates a defense of the faith and not at all a case of second thoughts—being "sorry" for one's beliefs. The discipline of apologetic theology represents the logical and rational defense of the principles and truths of the Christian religion. The topics of apologetics, therefore, relate directly to the contents both of philosophical and of doctrinal theology, with the intention of manifesting those contents to be believable and even compelling in the face of skepticism or disbelief.

This task is, in a sense, precisely the opposite of the task of philosophical theology considered as a propaedeutic and critical discipline. Whereas philosophical theology brings to bear critical faculties on theology by moving from the secular to the sacred, apologetic theology brings critical faculties to bear on unbelief by moving—with the prior development of philosophical and doctrinal theology well in hand—from the sacred to the secular. Because of the logical and critical approach necessary to this discipline, it has frequently been developed, particularly in more empirically oriented works, as a study in the "evidences of Christianity."[22]

The question of the place of apologetics in theological study arises out of the nature of apologetics in relation to doctrinal theology: Is it a prolegomenon to or a result of dogmatics? Does the defensive discipline precede and make a case for the viability of the declarative discipline, or does it follow, and on the basis of a prior declaration of faith, argue

---

[22]See, for example, George P. Fisher, *The Grounds of Theistic and Christian Belief* (New York: Scribner, 1883) and *idem, Christian Evidences* (New York: Macmillan, 1882).

the truth of the essential articles of Christian doctrine? The answer to these questions determines not only the scope of apologetics but also the patterns of argument and interpretation belonging to the discipline itself. The issue has been one of the most pointed addressed internally by Reformed theology during the last two centuries. Philip Schaff, the two Hodges, and Benjamin B. Warfield placed apologetics first as a prolegomenon or propaedeutic and limited its function to the general "proof" of the perfection or rectitude of Christianity, excluding both doctrinal discussion and "denominational differences" from apologetics correctly so called.[23] Defense of specific doctrinal points, according to these theologians, would belong to "polemics," which is seldom taught as a discipline in the twentieth century. This view of apologetics stands in continuity with the function given to the discipline in Schleiermacher's *Brief Outline*, where it is identified as a fundamental form of philosophical theology, prior in function to the historical-exegetical disciplines.[24] However, the Dutch Reformed school—Kuyper and Bavinck and, in America, Berkhof and Van Til—insisted that apologetics follow dogmatics even as reason, when used in theology, must take its point of departure from faith. And since, in their view, dogmatics itself rested on the biblical and historical disciplines, apologetics would naturally come at the very conclusion of the work of theological formulation or of theological study—and would absorb the task of polemics.

A partial answer to the question of placement and significance, not altogether satisfying to either of these groups, can be gathered from the interpretive context of the apologetic task and from the use to which apologetic treatises have been put in particular ages of the church. In the second century, the age of the first and arguably the greatest apologetic effort of the Christian church, a series of treatises that argued the ethical purity of the Christian religion and the philosophical superiority of its monotheism were addressed by a series of philosophically trained converts to the Roman emperors Hadrian, Antoninus Pius, and Marcus Aurelius. The documents, on the surface, were designed as pleas to these judicious and philosophically minded emperors to hear the case of the persecuted Christians and to deal justly with their situation: the rectitude of their lives and the high philosophical monotheism advocated by the Christians deserved tolerance, not persecution. Here is a fundamental, preliminary apologetic.

Yet, as one major patristic scholar has pointed out, the address to the emperor may only be a literary device, and the documents may have been used primarily as missionary documents directed to near-converts at the edge of the community or to newly converted Christians in doubt about the substance of the new religion. Here we cross over from preliminary apologetic into the realm of the defense of the faith, replete with the lengthy, often highly developed examination of Christian beliefs. The same documents functioned, potentially, in two different ways. Beyond this, as anyone who has studied the history of Christian doctrine knows, whatever the intention of the authors of these documents, their doctrinal arguments contributed to the development of early Trinitarianism and to the rise of *logos* Christology.

In the interpretive history of the Christian community, apologetics rises out of theological conviction and passes back into theology, influencing its formulation. As in the

---

[23]Cf. Schaff, *Theological Propaedeutic,* p. 311.
[24]Friedrich Schleiermacher, *A Brief Outline of the Study of Theology* (Atlanta: John Knox, 1966), pp. 32–35.

case of the broader history of doctrine—the forward temporal motion, as it were, of doctrinal theology—so also in the case of apologetics does the present formulation arise out of the biblical-churchly tradition, drawing on the basic assumptions of the original proclamation of the gospel as interpreted in and through the ongoing religious life of the believing community. What is defended, however unchanged its central focus on the Christ-event, constantly changes in response to the language, the needs, and the problems of new historical contexts.

The form and use of apologetics, therefore, draws both on the biblical and historical tradition of teaching and on the contemporary situation. Apologetics rests on the presupposition of faith or belief and never stands entirely outside of the other disciplines—i.e., it cannot be presuppositionless and absolutely preparatory or foundational—but its actual content must be dictated as much by the circumstances of the argument as by the content of the message. Thus the apologetic task may involve the defense of foundational issues such as the existence of God, or it may involve the discussion of the exegesis of biblical texts or even the appropriateness of various methods of interpretation to the task of exegesis. In each case, the apologetic task is an essentially interpretive function of the believing community in the present as the community interacts with its situation in the world.

Ethics and apologetics, taken together, are in fact the place where the success or failure of our biblical, historical, and systematic study of theology becomes most obvious. If all we have done in our study is absorb a large amount of discrete and unrelated data, then the end result of our intellectual and spiritual pilgrimage will not be a religious or theological construction of reality—and it will not make sense ethically or apologetically of the world-order around us or of our place in it.

Ethics, after all, is not simply about abstract values. Ethics is about the correlation between values understood on the level of absolutes with the positive and constructive effect of the application of those values to concrete situations. A decisively Christian ethic will agree with classical philosophical ethics that value must be located in or identified as the absolute good—but it will add, as some but not all philosophical ethicists have argued, that this absolute good is God. If this identification is provided by doctrinal and philosophical theology, it is certainly put into its practical framework by ethics, where it becomes a practical guide for the identification of human beings as moral agents capable of responsible action.

At the level of making practical sense out of our world, it is the task of ethics to deal with such problems as the frequent absence of any immediate correlation between good conduct and good fortune in this life. The great problem, here, which Kant rightly identified, is not merely the problem of a simplistic ethical hedonism, in which good is identified as that which brings happiness. More than this, it is the problem of the correlation of the internal moral order with the external world-order. As Kant rightly saw, ethics must rest on religion, and God is a necessary postulate of the ethical. What a Christian ethics must do is inculcate value not only as a series of demands but as part of a religious construction of reality that identifies the good with God and, derivatively, with God's work.

On a very practical level, this identification manifests ecology and ecologically positive behavior as central issues for Christian ethics today. If the world as created is itself a value, our ethical conduct must involve the conservation of the natural order and the cultivation of the proper place of humanity in our world—not only in terms of empirically demonstrable goals that, however convincingly stated, will always be debated or abated out of various economic or corporate interests, but also and primarily in terms of the non–empirically verifiable identification of God and the divine purpose as the ultimate good.

We can note here the correlation of the results of contemporary exegesis both with theological formulation and with practical ethical need. Both against those critics of Christianity who have rightly noted the tendency of Western Christians to think that the gift of dominion (Gen. 1:28) was a gift of license, but who have wrongly seen this as the genuine meaning of the text, and against those Christians who have used the text as a ground for abusing nature, we can point to a fundamentally different implication of the words of Scripture. The gift of dominion in verse 28 clearly parallels and is defined by the creation of human beings in the image of God in verse 27. We know from archaeological and linguistic study that the bestowing of the image of a lord or ruler was a typical sign, in the concrete political life of the ancient world, of the bestowing of the powers of a viceroy and of the identification not of an abdication but of an extension of the power of the ruler. The viceroy bears the power but also the responsibility of conserving the ruler's property. The dominion of Genesis 1 relates very closely to the imagery of Genesis 2, where the newly created Adam is placed into the role of gardener-caretaker in the earthly paradise of Eden. The ethical implication of the exegesis is clear.

Apologetics similarly stands in a concrete and directly relevant relationship to the Christian task of making sense of life in this world. When apologetics, for instance, argues the cogency of religious language and the validity of the fundamental religious experience of the existence of God, it is not merely engaging in a philosophical task. True, much of the formal argumentation comes from philosophical theology, but, unlike philosophical theology, apologetics is arguing not only a theory but also and primarily a view of the world in which all things stand under and are responsible to a knowing Ultimate. If apologetics does indeed presuppose a body of belief, then its defensive argumentation takes on a highly existential significance: what is at stake in the apologetical discussion of the existence of God is the foundational truth concerning the higher reality on which all existence, all value, and all hope depend, and in terms of which all that we do ultimately makes sense.

If, as I have indicated from the outset of this book, theology is the "science of the Christian religion," the formal discipline that clarifies and codifies the meaning offered by the religion, then the ethical and apologetical tasks mark the point at which the interpretive argument comes full circle and the abstractive, discursive work of drawing meanings out of the documents and the life of the religion and working toward formulation of their contemporary significance returns to the religion with positive result. Ethics and apologetics, as disciplines at the boundary of theory and practice, take the results of the other theological disciplines and return them to the concrete life of the believing community.

THE RELATION OF STATEMENT TO PRACTICE

The effective relation of theological statement or formulation to churchly practice stands as one of the great problems of the church today. It is not at all untypical for expert "practitioners" of ministry—like the individual mentioned in the preface to this book—to have virtually no use for theology in the classical sense; and for expert "theologians" to have either very little contact with churchly practice or, when they do have the contact, very little liking for the style and substance of the practice. That there ought to be a positive relationship between statement and practice ought to be obvious. A Christianity that operates on a "do as I say, don't do as I do" or a "do as I do, ignore what I say" basis has not long to live. Our conception of God and God's work ought to make sense in terms of our practice—and our practice ought to support what we think about God and God's work.

One of the great maxims of the theological tradition, forgotten or set aside in the contemporary failure of theological study, is *lex orandi, lex credendi*: "The rule of praying [is] the rule of believing." Our prayers, our worship services, our counseling, and our personal development as Christians all ought to fall into a theological pattern following the same fundamental rule as our doctrinal statements. Much of the problem experienced in the church arises, as Farley recognized, from the mistaken or partial identification of the practical; specifically, I would add, from the assumption that the classical or "theoretical" and "academic" theological disciplines are not "practical" or directly related to such theologically ill-defined contemporary goals as "equipping for ministry," "leadership training," and "church growth"—as if one can be properly equipped, trained as a leader, or pastor a church that is large for the right reasons without any knowledge of the substance of the faith or the disciplines designed to help interpret that substance!

Practical theology today is such a diverse field, with so many subdisciplines, so many partially identified areas of study seeking disciplinary status, and so many specialized ministerial tasks, that it echoes the general problem of the "diversified encyclopedia" within its own smaller compass. In addition to the traditional disciplines of worship or liturgy, homiletics, and counseling, we can also count spirituality or personal formation, various kinds of teaching and group study, youth ministry, marriage and family ministry, geriatric ministry, and so forth. All of these specializations and more would have to be enumerated if the point of our discussion were to outline specialized techniques—but our purpose is precisely the opposite. The task that confronts us is the analysis of practical theology in its widest sense, in relation to the study of theology and the unity of theological knowing. Specifically, the task before us is the relation of the so-called theoretical disciplines to practice as biblical, historical, and systematic theology are brought to bear on the life of the church.

The argument put forth previously that all theology is both theoretical and practical also applies to the field of "practical theology." Inasmuch as practical theology is *theology* and a category for the gathering together of several theological subdisciplines, it brings with it both the theoretical considerations characteristic of its separate disciplines and the theological *praxis*, the orientation toward the goal of salvation that is characteristic of all the theological disciplines, including the so-called theoretical ones. The point is important, granting the frequently made mistake of identifying ministerial or pastoral theology with practice and historical or systematic theology with theory—as if the former were never theoretical and the latter never practical.

Ebeling reflects on the contemporary bias toward the "practical" in his comment, "It is characteristic of modern times that theory is valid only in relationship to practice."[25] The point is well taken, if rightly understood. And it relates directly to the emphasis on history and religion present throughout our discussion. The church's "theory," its theological formulation, has never arisen, except in very recent times, apart from the religious life of the believing community. This is not only a fundamental fact of church history, it is also a fundamental fact of the biblical witness. The process of corporate reflection that brought together the canon of Scripture was in no small part a verification of the message

[25]Ebeling, *The Study of Theology*, p. 116.

of the prophets and the apostles in and through the religious life, the practice of the community. A similar point can very easily be made concerning the church's worship: except for the usually less-than-successful attempts of modern denominational worship committees to produce "new liturgy," the practice of the church has been to develop forms of worship in and through the practice of worship. Prayers, creeds, and hymns become set forms only after long development and use. Theological formulae, particularly in the early church, ultimately became normative only when they were understood as constructive or supportive of the teaching of salvation as offered in worship. It is widely recognized that the defeat of Arianism in the fourth century had virtually as much to do with the church's adherence to a Trinitarian reading of the baptismal formula (Matt. 28:19) as it did with detailed theological discussion.

No one would claim, either historically or presently, that theory absolutely precedes practice. It is true, however, that theory typically precedes coherent practice—and that knowledge of biblical, historical, and systematic theology precedes coherent ministry in and for the church. The several practical disciplines teach this point as clearly as do any of the theoretical disciplines. Homiletics has, perhaps longer than any of the other divisions of practical theology, had a clear method of approach. Whether one is taught to develop "three-point" sermons, or to argue in an expository fashion directly on the text of Scripture, or to work out, in a manner similar to the Puritan preachers of the seventeenth century, a carefully conceived doctrinal or moral treatise resting, with the proper balance of emphases, on Scripture and reason, the coherence of what is preached clearly rests on a method of moving from the text through interpretation, to the point of delivery. And, as experience demonstrates to anyone who has attempted to preach, coherent practice does rest on some grasp of the theory, not only of exegesis, interpretation, and theological formulation, but also of the task of preaching.

A similar example can be drawn from the somewhat newer discipline of pastoral counseling. The counseling work of the Christian minister—the care and cure of souls—has always been a part of the ministerial task, but only in this century has it become a fully developed discipline. The rise of the discipline of pastoral counseling has to do in large measure with the rise of psychology and the increased understanding provided by psychology of the inner problems faced by individuals, of the meaning and dynamics of personal existence in relation to other persons, and of various ways of analyzing personal problems, counseling persons through their difficulties, of initiating therapeutic interventions with persons, and, indeed, of modifying behavior.

As Seward Hiltner well argued in several of his ground-breaking essays, clinical pastoral training and pastoral psychology have rightly "stressed their connection with and indebtedness to psychotherapy, and the other life sciences and technologies."[26] Hiltner went on to argue for the further development of a genuine pastoral *theology* that would have much the same content as pastoral psychology but would have "a different frame of reference" and would see its "content in a different context."[27]

As in the case of ethics, so also in pastoral counseling, the Christian context implies a theological framework of meaning in which the individual is understood as standing

---

[26]Seward Hiltner, "Pastoral Theology and Psychology," in Arnold S. Nash, ed., *Protestant Thought in the Twentieth Century: Whence and Whither* (New York: Macmillan, 1951), p. 196.
[27]Ibid., pp. 196–97.

within God's world—but here, not so much in terms of right relationship to the world order as in terms of right relationship with other persons and right construction of patterns of behavior. What is distinctively Christian here is the conviction concerning values and norms and the assumption that these values and norms arise not as projections of self, but as truths about the self and its relationships given by God and belonging, therefore, to the fabric of the world order.

If placed into the context of modern psychology, pastoral counseling will have as much of a problem with the soul as most psychological theory does. Psychology, despite the etymology of its name, has little use for the concept of soul and of ultimate values associated with the traditional theological and philosophical meditations on the soul. Typically, psychology, of its very nature, studies the phenomenal order and looks either toward measurable evidence, such as patterns of brain waves, or toward quantifiable data, such as the behavior of certain types of persons. The categories of psychological analysis and counseling are drawn, therefore, out of the phenomenal order and relate directly to practice. There is a profound—and necessary—pragmatism in much of the work of psychology.

This means, however, that such techniques as transactional analysis or behavior modification are not designed to raise philosophical questions, particularly questions concerning reality and value. Transactional analysis, for example, understands individuals in terms of the "child," the "adult," and the "parent" that are "in" the individual—because these categories *work* in analysis and counseling. As far as I know, however, this approach never asks the question of the nature of these categories: Are they really or only formally or rationally distinct—i.e., should they be viewed as mutually exclusive "things" or are they merely functions? If they do not have the status of "thing," of *what* are they functions? Or, are there other possible categories—such as "sibling," "adolescent," "aunt/uncle"—and if not, why not? And finally, is there any moral value assignable to any of these categories or related to their functions as aspects of a larger "psychical" (i.e., soulish or spiritual) reality in and of the individual? Similarly, behavior modification refrains from asking the questions of value and seeks, simply, to alter the patterns of a person's behavior by means of a therapy involving positive and negative inducements or stimuli.

When pastoral counseling draws on these various psychological perspectives and uses their techniques in ministry, it must also ask the theological and philosophical questions that do not and cannot belong to psychological science as it is presently constituted. Ministry, of its very nature, deals with values, absolutes, and ultimates as identified by and in Christianity. Far from being merely a speculative or philosophical question, the question of the soul marks the point at which the consideration of values and absolutes comes into view—because it identifies an orientation of the person that rises above the animal, the visceral, and the sexual and that lodges value on a "higher" plane than individual or social self-interest. Discussion of "soul," unlike discussion of behavior and its modification, raises questions concerning the identification of the good and the true—and it presses standards of behavior toward the ultimate.[28] Pastoral counseling, because of its rootage beyond itself in the biblical, historical, and systematic theological disciplines must rest on such concepts.

---

[28]This problem is not merely a churchly or theological problem; it is clearly described from the purely secular academic and societal point of view by Allan Bloom, *The Closing of the American Mind* (New York: Simon & Shuster, 1987), pp. 42–43, 58–67, 74–78, 118–21, 136–37, passim.

What remains for the practical disciplines, therefore, once they have mastered their own internal theories—whether of the preparation and delivery of sermons or of the psychology of counseling—is to draw those theories back into the structure of the theological disciplines. Otherwise, homiletics lies in danger of becoming identical with secular rhetoric, and ministerial counseling with the psychiatrist's couch. The uniqueness of ministry, recently and very pointedly identified by John Leith as "what the church has to say that no one else can say,"[29] lies in the religious wholeness and theological unity of the task—where preaching is not merely speechmaking, and counseling offers something distinct from psychoanalysis—and in the answerability of our practice to the biblical, historical, and systematic identity of Christianity in the contemporary interpretation of its doctrines.

The unity of theological study via the examination of the biblical, historical, and systematic disciplines *as they relate* to the life of the believing community is not, therefore, a purely academic, curricular, or theoretical issue. It is an issue involving the most fundamental values in and of the practice of Christianity. The contemporary emphasis on technique and operations in ministry, like the various techniques in psychological counseling, is not problematic to the church in and of itself—it only becomes problematic when it moves toward the exclusion of biblical, historical, and systematic categories from practice, because then it has ceased to be distinctively Christian and to be the means of the communication of the values held by the church in its rich tradition.

THE WORK OF FORMULATION

All of the areas of study discussed in this chapter belong to the work of contemporary formulation and draw, whether directly or indirectly, on the materials presented in the discussion of "biblical and historical foundations" in chapter 2. This formulation consists both in word and in act—in other words, it is both systematic and practical, both theory and praxis. It is crucial to the work of contemporary formulation—and to the unity of theology in its biblical, historical, systematic, and practical model—that we not only address the contemporary issue of theory and practice but that we enlighten and enrich our approach to this issue through some recovery of the historical understanding of the theoretical and the practical balance of theology.

Practical theology must not be left out in the cold, so to speak, understood as an activity only remotely related to the "theoretical disciplines" or as an "application" of theory without a clear mechanism by which that application can take place. For instance, we need to overcome what one of my professors called "the black box" approach to homiletical application. His point was that exegetical method typically concludes with the meaning of a text in its original historical context while homiletics typically requires, as a foundational step, some statement of the significance of the text in the present. Neither exegesis nor homiletics offers a method of moving from original meaning to contemporary significance. What is left to the exegetically responsible preacher is "the black box": the results of exegesis are thrown into one door of the box and the application of the text to the present is taken out of another door on the opposite side. One has the impression of a somewhat mysterious and arbitrary passage, of a magical act, rather than

---

[29]Cf. John H. Leith, *The Reformed Imperative: What the Church Has to Say That No One Else Can Say* (Philadelphia: Westminster, 1988).

of an organic relationship between original meaning and application. What went on inside the box remains a secret, and the arbitrariness of the procedure is obscured from view by a few well-placed anecdotes.

We do not want to set aside the modern insight into practical theology as requiring an activity in the world: our praxis does not consist simply in the contemplation of a goal, however much the goal ought to be the primary focus of all Christian activity. Nonetheless, Farley is quite correct in seeing the quandary of modern theological education as arising in large part from the reduction of theology to training in "something that clergy need in order to be leaders of the church community" rather than in a particular kind of knowing "attendant on Christian existence."[30] If there is a solution to this problem, it must arise out of a recognition of the churchly or communal character of both the words and the acts belonging to theology and, therefore, out of a recognition of the biblical-historical tradition in which those words and acts have been and continue to be generated. All words and acts belonging to the tradition, whether in its past or in its present forms, ought to be understood in the light of the redemptive goal of the church's preaching—and that goal both identifies the practical aspect of all theology (in the older sense of "practical") and demonstrates the substantial relationship of the disciplines now identified as "practical" or "ministerial" theology to the classical areas of study, the biblical, historical, and systematic disciplines.

When systematic theology in the larger sense—the contemporary discipline of theological statement—fails to take seriously the foundational materials provided by biblical and historical study, it not only brings down on itself the charge of methodological ineptitude and of failure to recognize its own historical conditionedness, it also gives itself over to increasingly arbitrary and rootless speculations. In other words, systematic theology cannot either simply repeat the doctrinal, philosophical, and phenomenological results of previous generations or argue its own case, whether doctrinally, philosophically, or phenomenologically, in the present, without reference to the foundational disciplines.

On the other hand, systematic theology cannot afford to be merely the repetition of the results of biblical theology and the history of doctrine. A systematic theology that duplicates the materials of either one of these essentially historical disciplines will fail to address the present and will appear like a relic of the past taken from a museum. Thus, works like Ringgren's *History of the Religion of Israel* or Eichrodt's *Theology of the Old Testament* are fine works on the beliefs of ancient Israel that could be consulted with profit by anyone hoping to formulate a biblically based theology in the present. If used, however, without alteration or adaptation as the basis of a contemporary dogmatics, they would produce a terrible failure—not only because they lack the New Testament materials essential to any presentation of Christian teaching, but also and *primarily* because they survey the religion of an era now dead, for the sake of an accurate presentation of the beliefs of that era. Precisely because they are admirable studies of the religion and theology of ancient Israel, they cannot also supply the form for a study of the religion or theology of the present.

The problem of using an Old Testament theology or a history of Israelite religion as a contemporary dogmatics ought to be incredibly obvious—but the same problem,

[30]Farley, *Theologia*, p. 130.

phrased in terms of the use of a sixteenth- or seventeenth-century, or even a nineteenth-century theological system as a contemporary dogmatics has not been nearly as obvious to ministers and to teachers of theology. Neither Schleiermacher's *Christian Faith*, nor Turretin's *Institutio theologiae elencticae* (*Instituti on of Polemical Theology*), nor Calvin's *Institutes of the Christian Religion*, however highly one might estimate their contribution to the history of doctrine, can serve adequately as a contemporary dogmatics or as a textbook in a class on systematic theology! The problems with which Schleiermacher wrestles are not identical with the problems of the present. The adversaries with whom Turretin and Calvin debate—like Conrad Vorstius (many readers ought to be muttering, "Who?") or Fausto Socinus, Michael Servetus, and Andreas Osiander—are no longer of any pressing importance. And some of Calvin's "adversaries," like Peter Lombard and Thomas Aquinas, have come to be viewed as allies—even of the cause of Protestant dogmatics—or at least as such close neighbors to our own teaching that they ought to be consulted rather than attacked. From the realm of historical theology, Calvin, Turretin, and Schleiermacher can provide us with important lessons in theological formulation, useful and sometimes even archetypal patterns for the formulation or refutation of a particular point; in the realm of contemporary formulation, however, we must say something beyond what they have said.

How then do we formulate systematic theology in the present? How else but as the statement of Christian doctrine written in the light of the biblical and historical materials, in consultation with collateral disciplines belonging to our contemporary "science of the Christian religion," but on the day after the end of the "history of doctrine." The issue is to use, but not duplicate an earlier formulation, to assess earlier formulations—their meaning, significance, applicability, and the comprehensibility of their language—in the light of what we know biblically, historically, philosophically, and phenomenologically about our Christianity and its context both in this culture and among the religions of the world. The point, certainly, is *not* that every minister, teacher, and missionary must become a specialist in each and every one of a rather forbidding list of religious and theological subdisciplines, but rather that each formulator of Christian teachings needs to recognize, via an introductory acquaintance with the diversified elements within the fourfold interpretive pattern of theology, what are the issues facing the contemporary formulation of her or his Christian doctrine.

Those who become dissatisfied with the credal, confessional, and systematic formulations offered by the church, on the ground that these formulations do not coincide with the results of a restrictive exegetical enterprise, must come to terms with the historical and cultural movement of the community of belief and recognize that the text of Scripture itself and the forms of doctrinal expression are mediated by and retain their significance within the ongoing community. If it is not the role of historical or contemporary systematic and practical formulations to govern the basic task of exegesis, it surely is their role to offer an interpretive context within which exegesis can speak to the present-day church. Both the interpretation of Scripture and the interpretation of the church's tradition of doctrine are necessary to contemporary formulation—the latter, if only to make clear why we state particular issues in particular ways and how we must redirect and reformulate our theological language in the present.

The study of systematic and practical theology, therefore, like the study of history, must take on an increasingly interpretive character. The exegetical and hermeneutical approach that we have learned to apply to the text of Scripture and, hopefully, to the materials of the history of the church, must also be applied to the contemporary work of formulation. Formulation in the present must, in other words, consider the movement of history, culture, and ideas between the original context of a doctrinal formulation and the present context in which that formulation must be restated or reformulated.

The formulation, today, of a doctrine of revelation cannot simply observe the standard or classical Protestant (and, from one point of view, very useful) distinctions between "natural" and "supernatural," "general" and "special" revelation. Both distinctions must be modified in the light of the increased knowledge of religion available to us since the sixteenth- and seventeenth- and eighteenth-century adoption and development of these distinctions by Protestantism, and in the light of conceptual problems caused within Christian theology since the rise of Deism and of modern science.

In addition, any formulation of the concept of revelation must come to grips with the fact that, although Scripture certainly contains a record of the revelation given to ancient Israel and to the early Christian church, it does not have *a doctrine* of revelation in the same way that it may be said to have a doctrine of God, of creation, or of redemption in Christ. Scripture, in other words, does not discuss the character of "revelation" as such. The doctrine of revelation is a product of churchly meditation on the problem of the knowledge of God, and it has, therefore, taken on many of the assumptions of fairly recent times in our history. Distinctions that we make between different kinds of revelation reflect the shifting dogmatic meditations of the church through various eras in its history, under the influence of various philosophical and scientific perspectives.

The distinction commonly made between the natural and the supernatural assumes that some events are governed entirely within the sphere of the finite by an order of law embedded within the world-order, while other events are governed primarily by divine power exerted upon nature "from above" or from without by an intelligent Other. The former events are related to the human race as part of its environment, but they are not viewed as intentional acts directed by an intelligence (or by a will) toward human beings; the latter events are also a part of the environment of human life, but they are understood as arising out of a transcendent divine intention to act, through the things of the finite order, upon human life, for good or for ill. It is clear that this distinction is historically and culturally conditioned and does not obtain at all times or at all stages in the history of religions. Prehistoric, "primitive," and prescientific cultures make no such distinction, but rather assume all of nature to be alive, sentient, and active. All "natural" events, in this view, are filled with intentionality, and no event can be conceived of as implying a divine presence that is not somehow implied in other events. The gradual increase of human control over the natural environment has led both to the rise of science and to the contraction of religion, so that, with the rise of civilization, the distinction between the natural and the supernatural also arises.

The varieties of religion from animism to polytheism and henotheism and, finally, to various forms of monotheism (including pantheism) indicate differences in the perception of the natural order over against the supernatural. Whereas animism clearly stands in the way of the distinction between natural and supernatural by understanding all things to be infused with life and spirit, polytheism fosters the distinction between natural and supernatural by identifying a finite number of finite gods who at will (i.e., not always) act upon certain parts of the environment. The eventual ordering and arrangement of the pantheon according to speculative, cosmological concerns and the consequent emergence of the idea of a high god who is the creator of the temporal order also places considerable strain on our modern distinction between the natural and the supernatural, especially insofar as the creator is not conceived to be absent from his world after the act of creation.

Thus the tradition of Judeo-Christian monotheism, with its assumption of a creation *ex nihilo* by a transcendent divine power, together with the continuing temporal involvement of that power (providence), actually militates as much against the distinction between the natural and the supernatural, as initially defined, as do the animistic and the polytheistic models just noted. Indeed, the only forms of Western theology actually conducive to the distinction are Deism, with its view of a now-absent creator who fashioned the world in such a way that it might operate according to ordained laws in his absence, and process theology, with its conception of a finite god who does not entirely control the universal natural order.

Judeo-Christian monotheism, on the grounds of its doctrines of creation, providence, and the providential *concursus* that maintains the contingent order of creation in its created being, together with the various religious and philosophical forms of pantheism and panentheism (Hinduism, Spinozism, Absolute Idealism), must, accordingly, recognize that all phenomena are at the same time natural events and divine acts. In other words, the distinction between natural and supernatural rests on an assumption, untenable in the higher religions, of an intermittent divine presence and/or divine intervention. The distinction between natural and supernatural theology, at least to the extent that it assumes the former to be a rational construction formulated apart from the divine and the latter to be a revelational construction formulated in isolation from "natural reason," must also, therefore, be rejected as untenable in a genuinely monotheistic context.

This train of thought, incidentally, shows quite clearly the problem inherent in the neoorthodox rejection of natural theology and the *analogia entis* or "analogy of being," as somehow un-Christian and out of place in the Christian attempt to formulate theology. The analogy of being, which hypothesizes a likeness in the divine handiwork to the divine Creator and allows, therefore, a discussion of God based on the natural order, does not, as alleged by neoorthodoxy, represent a prideful and mistaken human effort to ascend toward the divine. It represents an examination of the revelation of God, brought about by divine act, in the natural order—indeed, it assumes the overcoming of an absolute dichotomy between nature and so-called supernature.

The distinction between natural and supernatural theology also is untenable and, I think, fundamentally damaging to Christianity in the modern scientific context. As science more and more completely explains the phenomena of the universe, the so-called supernatural is relegated to a smaller and smaller sphere: when a thunderstorm arose in the ancient world, it might have been credited to Yahweh by Israel or to Zeus by the Greeks; when lightning struck near Erfurt in 1505, a young Luther understood it as a sign from God and cried out to St. Anne for help; when the same phenomena are experienced today in the United States, people either commend or criticize the local television station's meteorologist—with no reference at all to the divine. Typically, we pray for help with the weather only in moments of extreme difficulty when the meteorologist forecasts no relief in sight. The theological issue here is that the loss of the sense of direct "supernatural" involvement or initiative not be allowed to become a loss of the divine relationship to the "natural" order.

Theology encountered a similar problem in the seventeenth and early eighteenth century as the Ptolemaic, geocentric view of the universe was definitively replaced by the Copernican, heliocentric conception of the solar system and, ultimately, by a conception of an infinite universe. The notion, typical of (but hardly necessary to) traditional theology, of a God and a "heaven" somewhere "out there" had to be modified by a rather different notion of divine presence. If, on the one hand, by our theology and piety we maintain, unconsciously, the notion of God "out there" at the edge of the solar system while, on the other hand, we assume, again virtually unconsciously, that the supernatural is to be understood only as a rare intervention in the natural order, we will end up with a sense of the absence of God. The theory of an infinite universe demands, among other things, a stronger emphasis on divine immanence—what I would call a presence so ultimate that it could be identified as a transcendent immanence, transcending, that is, the usual understanding of immanence. Once again, the radical, Deistic distinction between natural and supernatural and, therefore, between natural and supernatural revelation, must be abandoned.

The language of natural and supernatural, general and special revelation can be maintained only when it is understood as distinguishing between an original, generalized revelation of the divine, grounded in the divine presence in and through all things, and a subsequent, special and gracious revelation of the divine, specific to a single religion, distinguishing it from all others, and understood as the completion and fulfillment of the original revelation, in and for a particular community of belief. Thus our view of revelation must take into consideration the phenomenon identified in the early part of this century by Fr. Wilhelm Schmidt as "primitive monotheism": there is a general belief in the one God or, at least, in an ultimate "high god" or creator god, held throughout the world by peoples usually identified as "primitive." Often, as in the case of the Australian Bushman, this monotheism is associated closely with a highly developed ethic not unlike the Decalogue. Such data, gathered by students of the history and phenomenology of religion, prevent us from claiming either that Christianity is just revelation and not also a religion or that the religions of the world do not have revelation. In addition, the concept of a "general revelation" ought not to be understood as defining a "natural" as opposed to a "supernatural" revelation or as indicating a revelation of truths about God so accessible to unaided reason as to be useless or inconsequential. Rather, the concept indicates a body of beliefs held in common across a large spectrum of world religion, as distinct from those beliefs held within each religion. Our theology must recognize the breadth and generality of revelation, the common elements of many religions, as well as identifying clearly the particularity of our own Christian message of salvation and the "special" or specialized revelation, held and respected within the Christian community, on which that message is founded.

These considerations of the problem of theological formulation point us back to our original question, the question of the unity of theology, of theological study, and, ultimately, of theological discourse. We ought to be prepared, however, to return to the topic on another, hopefully higher, level and to raise issues of interpretation arising out of our meditation on the historical character of Christian theology in its developing systematic and practical aspects. We ought also to be able to hold more clearly in view the issue of the relationship of patterns of study and formulation to the issue of the cultivation of the spiritual and moral values conveyed by the materials of theology, specifically with a view to understanding how the interpretation of the tradition of belief is also an exercise in the inculcation and activation of those values.

four
THE UNITY
OF THEOLOGICAL
DISCOURSE

The entire argument of this book has tended toward the identification of a modified fourfold encyclopedia of theology as a useful model not only for the study
and general understanding but also for the formulation of theology in the present
day. The traditional breakdown of theology into the biblical, historical, systematic, and
practical fields remains a useful tool, particularly when these four "fields" are recognized
as parts of a historical/hermeneutical model rather than as a group of rigidly defined and
easily controllable subject areas for short-term study. The "diversified encyclopedia" identified by Farley is a fact of contemporary theological life and the specialization of the various subdisciplines will not disappear. Nonetheless, a case can be made for the competent grasp at an introductory level of all or at least most of the various subdisciplines.
And, more importantly, a hermeneutically unified model for understanding these subdisciplines both in their relationships to one another and in their relationship to contemporary theological formulation can be constructed.

This hermeneutical unity, moreover, was embedded in the initial construction of the
fourfold model by at least some of the encyclopedists of the nineteenth century. Christoph
Luthardt, writing in the mid-nineteenth century could argue that, rightly understood,

> the usual division into biblical, historical, systematic and practical theology is justi-
> fied by the nature of the subject, inasmuch as Christianity, of which theology is the
> science, rests on revelation as it was handed down originally in the Holy Scripture;
> has a history in the church, which is the home of Christianity; gains expression in a
> body of doctrine, which forms a system; while the church, by means of the practical
> life, is carried on into the future.[1]

---

[1]Christoph Luthardt, *Kompendium der Dogmatik*, 11th posthumous ed. (Leipzig: Dörffling & Franke,
1914), §4.1.

To state the case even more theologically, the scriptural principle of the Reformation requires an initial distinction between biblical and historical theology, while the biblical commands to believe and to obey create the distinction between the disciplines of thought and action, system and practice.

The first theological point—the scriptural principle—establishes the fourfold encyclopedia as an interpretive model over against the threefold division of study into philosophical, historical, and practical theology advocated by Schleiermacher. Schleiermacher's very compelling model was based on a series of methodological considerations that remain a part of our theological efforts in the present. According to his model, philosophy or system deals with the descriptive science of religious feeling, practical theology deals with religious doing or action, while historical theology occupies a methodological center between the present-day descriptive science of feeling and the praxis of doing by analyzing the historical course of the church's feeling and doing—and by critiquing or justifying contemporary forms by means of its analysis. This historical center consists of the study of Scripture and of the historical church, inasmuch as the historical method applies to both areas of study.

Emphasis on the scriptural principle maintains a theological distinction between Scripture and the tradition of the historical church, between the prior biblical norm of Christian teaching and the secondary, pedagogical, and interpretive norm of the church's tradition. It also places the study of Scripture and, in a certain sense, the study of the tradition, prior to the formulation of theological system in the present. From a methodological and hermeneutical point of view, the historical approach characteristic of both biblical and church-historical studies becomes the rule for understanding the fundamental issues at stake in doctrinal theology. The second theological point drawn from Luthardt—the distinction between systematic and practical—accords with the rest of Schleiermacher's argument.

The logic of the fourfold definition of theology can also be stated in a more philosophical form, as evidenced by the arguments in Julius Räbiger's *Encyclopedia of Theology* (1879). Räbiger's work manifests the influences of idealist philosophy and assumes, in Hegelian fashion, that Christianity is the absolute religion and, as such, the highest manifestation of the phenomenon of religion. The objection to the fourfold model of the study of theology, that it follows the pattern of a historical development and is therefore accidental and unnecessary, he argues, fails to consider the integral relationship between the historical reality of Christianity and the historical character of the study of Christianity. "If theology has the task of attaining to a knowledge of Christianity, viewed in its connection with the historical religions, according to its historical reality, . . . [theology] must also ground its principle of arrangement upon the historical course of Christianity."[2]

We must regard Christ, Räbiger continues, as the founder of Christianity and, consequently, the truth revealed in Christ as the underlying truth that makes possible the life of the church. The church is, therefore, the "organ" that gives historical expression to the truth of Christ. This relationship between Christ and the church points toward four stages in the development of Christianity and four basic divisions of the task of study: the "origin," the "historical development," the "Christian spirit . . . becoming the subject of ideal treatment," and the movement toward "practical application."[3]

---

[2]Julius F. Räbiger, *Encyclopaedia of Theology*, trans. John Macpherson, 2 vols. (Edinburgh: T. & T. Clark, 1884), 1:297.
[3]Ibid., p. 299.

Without accepting the philosophy underlying Räbiger's remarks about the spiritual necessity of the development of religion toward the absolute, it is quite possible to see in his analysis, as in Luthardt's, a proper grasp of the historical character of the science of religion and an equally accurate view of the interpretive structure given to Christianity by its history and, therefore, capable of analysis in a contemporary interpretive science of the Christian religion. The unity of theological study is an interpretive unity resting on a historical trajectory of belief and a historical approach to the materials of belief as they reflect the thought and the action of the believing community. This unity, moreover, can be described in terms of the objective discipline of study and analysis as well as the subjective involvement of the individual in the life of the community. The task of this final chapter is to present an overview of this unity.

OBJECTIVITY AND SUBJECTIVITY

Theology has never been a purely academic discipline. The phenomenon of an academic study of religion and of teachers of theology who are responsible only (or at least primarily) to educational institutions is a comparatively recent one. The fathers of the church and the theologians of the early Middle Ages were all churchmen—bishops, priests, monks—involved in the preaching of the gospel and in the daily work of organizing and administering the life of the church. Their writings are, for the most part, occasional: Augustine did not write on baptism, the church, and predestination simply for the sake of producing up-to-date theological formulae; rather, his treatises on these subjects arose directly out of debate over the nature and content of the church's teaching. Even Augustine's great treatise *On the Trinity* arose out of religious need, in part out of a churchly desire to clarify an important issue for the faithful, in part our of a desire to provide a definitive treatise against the continuing Arian threat in the West, and in part out of a personal spiritual concern to meditate on this most profound of theological topics. Similarly, Gregory the Great's *Pastoral Rule* arose directly out of the writer's own experience of governance in the church and was intended as a guide to others who followed the same path as Gregory toward the office of bishop.

This daily involvement of theologians in the life of the church did not cease with the rise of the monastic schools and universities in the twelfth century. We might be led to expect that the creation of schools and of academic specialists, professors of theology, to teach in the universities would lead to a separation of theological study from churchly concerns and from personal piety, but such was not the case. One of the most philosophically significant essays of the early scholastic era, Anselm's *Proslogion*, found its point of origin in the spiritual life of the monastery and took the form of a prayer. Its author lived out his life as an active abbot and an archbishop involved in the debates over the extent of royal power to invest bishops. Major systematizers of theology such as Bonaventure, Albert the Great, and Thomas Aquinas served as vicars of their orders, bishops, and defenders of the faith who saw their theology as an integral part of the religious life. In the eras of the Reformation and post-Reformation orthodoxy the theologians who did not also occupy pulpits were the exceptions, not the rule.

The study of theology, then, throughout the greater part of the Christian tradition, was a study of materials relevant to the life of the church and to the spirituality of the individual. More than this, meditation on the materials of theology was a spiritual as well as an academic discipline. The discipline of theology—indeed, the discipline of studying theology—ought to create in the mind of the student a series of patterns of ideas and interpretations that can frame and influence both mind and will, thought and action. Thus the unity of theological study and of theological curriculum or theological formulation must not be a unity only of objectively stated ideas that cohere in a systematic form, but also a unity, subjectively experienced, of thought and action. The creation of a cohesive systematization of Christian doctrine will not be sufficient by itself to the creation of a unified and fruitful pattern of study. Nor, on the other hand, will the cultivation of piety or spirituality be successful apart from a well-conceived program of study in the so-called theoretical or academic subdisciplines of theology. Theological study, in order to maintain, or shall we say, regain, the crucial role that it has played throughout the earlier history of the church, will have to balance once again the theoretical and the practical, the objective and the subjective elements of the religious life.

Another clue to the unity of the discipline can be found in the patristic practice of citing Scripture. Beginning students of patristics are frequently surprised and a bit befuddled by the mixture of precise and seemingly imprecise citations of Scripture with what appear to be allusions or even virtual quotations that appear without citation in the text. Are the church fathers guilty of a form of sloppy referencing that would be unacceptable today in a student paper? No, not at all. On the one hand, it is certainly true that the modern style of precise documentation has been in use for only a few hundred years. On the other hand, and far more importantly, the church fathers were less interested in citing Scripture than in thinking biblically and traditionally. Their patterns of citation and of interpretation were quite like the patterns found in Scripture itself, granting, however, that they had a sense of the distinction between their own writings and those of either the Old Testament or the apostolic authors.

There were, of course, no quotation marks in the original writings of the fathers. Modern editors have identified the quotations and have given them the chapter and verse references that exist only in modern (post–fifteenth-century) editions of Scripture. The fathers themselves evidence an approach to the text of Scripture that ranges across a spectrum of usage from precise quotation to less precise referencing, to paraphrase, to increasingly vague allusion—probably in most cases resting on memory rather than on a codex of the Old Testament or New Testament immediately at hand. Again, their purpose was not precise quotation but rather biblical or biblical-traditional thinking and speaking: the words of the text become their words, the thoughts expressed or implied by the text their thoughts, with the result that the patristic writings offer a theological tapestry through which threads from Scripture, threads from the tradition, and threads from the mind of the author are woven into a more or less harmonious whole.

What the writers of the patristic period manifest so clearly, then, is a unity of theological thinking—and of Christian living—that arises out of a total immersion of an author in Scripture, in tradition, and in the church's life of the present. Scripture has meaning in the writer's present because he is immersed in a tradition of reading and understanding the text that mediates the text to him and that ratifies its meaning and usefulness to the present. What is more, this sense of the meaning and usefulness of the biblical witness moves on both the doctrinal and the practical levels. The patristic writers do not separate doctrine from spirituality and spirituality from the daily life of the Christian community.

Several other clues to the success of writers of past ages in their efforts to integrate theological study in and with the life of the church can be found in the basic definitions of theology that come to us from the classic formulations of both the Catholic and Protestant traditions. I refer to the great theological syntheses of the medieval doctors and the Protestant orthodox theologians. These churchly teachers recognized that theology must indicate, objectively, a recognizable body of teaching and, subjectively, an inward disposition to know it.

Theology, objectively considered, is an academic discipline. It claims a distinct body of knowledge as its own or, when aspects or elements of that body of knowledge also belong to other disciplines, it claims a distinct approach and rationale for dealing with that knowledge. In the language of past centuries, theology is called a *scientia* or "science." Both the term *scientia* and the understanding of the theological task have, as we have seen, altered substantially since theology was first called a science by Alain of Lille and his contemporaries in the late twelfth century. The term, however, is still applied to theology and, more importantly, is capable, when rightly interpreted, of providing theological study with a sense of method and direction. It is, after all, one thing to call theology an academic discipline and quite another to call it a science, particularly granting the connotations of present-day English usage. The former description is rather loose and could be applied to virtually any subject that is taught in schools, colleges, universities, and seminaries. Since theology has a history, has documents and materials drawn from that history, and has contemporary expositors, it most certainly can be taught—if only from the point of view of history. But the fact that it can be turned into an academic discipline and taught does not demonstrate anything concerning the character and quality of its materials and claims. Heresies can be taught; the materials and theories of discredited philosophies can be gathered and examined in a classroom; the most arbitrary and outrageous theosophy can be the object of academic investigation as long as it is documented; and outmoded worldviews can be examined out of historical interest. The academic investigation may be legitimate while the subject-matter being investigated may be fraudulent or worthless, or simply inapplicable to the concerns of the present.

The latter description, the identification of theology as a science, however, implies that theology is a cogent discipline, a legitimate subject for study in its own right. Both in the twelfth century and in the twentieth, the description of theology as a science forces the discipline of theology to examine not only its materials but also the character and quality of its materials and of their claims. When theology was first called a science, the term *scientia* meant a distinct body of knowledge that contained its own self-evident first principles together with the conclusions that could be drawn from them—in other words, an independent, self-sustaining intellectual discipline resting on legitimate presuppositions and possessing its own internal logic and coherence.

This identification of theology as a unified *scientia* was considerably easier to maintain prior to the eighteenth century than it is today. The problem of the "diversified encyclopedia" and of the specialization of the academic practitioners of each subdiscipline give one the impression that if theology can be called a "science" in any sense, it ought to be defined as a grouping of more or less related sciences than as a single science. In addition, the critique of rational metaphysics leveled by Kant at the end of the eighteenth century and the reconstruction of theology proposed by Schleiermacher at the beginning of the nineteenth have led many theologians away from all definitions of theology that focus on it as a form of knowledge: it is either an ethical system (a ground for doing) or an experiential system (a description of profound feeling). In either case, it cannot be a *scientia* in any sense of the term.

Beyond this, it has been precisely the more "scientific" or critical aspects of modern theological reflection that have typically been seen as barriers or even threats to the large-scale systematization of theology—or even to the establishment of a unifying structure for understanding the theology of the Old Testament or of the New. Post-Enlightenment exegesis has forced theology to ask critical scientific and textual questions that frequently render the path to traditional theological formulation difficult if not impossible. Inasmuch as most of the formulae and doctrinal expositions of the older dogmatics draw on a tradition of exegesis that is no longer directly accessible to us—particularly in view of its typological and allegorical aspects and its tendency to move away from rather than toward the grammatical meaning of a text in its original life-situation. The hermeneutical gap between the text and the dogmas and between the dogmas and the contemporary situation calls into question our ability to construct a "science of theology" out of these very diverse and divergent materials.

Finally, the contemporary mind discerns such differences in approach between disciplines commonly called sciences—chemistry, physics, and biology, or, granting the presence of social sciences, anthropology and sociology—and theology that the name "science" appears hardly to fit the theological disciplines. The intensity of the problem can be seen in a theological work like Charles Hodge's famous *Systematic Theology*. There we see an effort to understand theology as a science in the context of the highly empirical mood of late nineteenth-century chemistry, physics, and geology. Hodge argues that Scripture, like the earth, provides raw data in an unordered manner—and that theology, like geology, performs an inductive analysis of the data that discerns the order and draws sound conclusions leading to a systematic presentation. The fundamental flaw in heterodox theologies, Hodge argued, was an imperfect induction from the basic evidence.[4]

The impossibility of maintaining such a perspective ought to be obvious. The claim of physics that, at a constant temperature, the volume of a given quantity of gas is inversely proportionate to the pressure—Boyle's law—has a rather different cognitive status than the claim of theology that "God so loved the world that he gave his one and only Son, that whoever believes in him shall not perish but have eternal life" (John 3:16). The grammar used in physical and spiritual propositions may well be structurally equivalent, but the subject-matter is so vastly different that the two sets of truths belong to qualitatively different realms of discourse: the constancy of temperature, the quantity of gas, and the degree of pressure are all measurable, verifiable terms—God's love, the divine sonship of Jesus of Nazareth, perdition, and everlasting life are neither measurable nor verifiable, at least not according to the same criteria. All of the terms of Boyle's law represent physically demonstrable and repeatable data, whereas none of the terms in John 3:16 are physical, demonstrable, or in any way repeatable. Also, the logic of Hodge's argument, if pressed to its own conclusions, would make systematic theology, as written by Hodge, a more desirable and perhaps superior form of knowledge than Scripture itself (granting that geology and physics are superior to unorganized perceptions of the natural order)—a conclusion that Hodge himself would surely have wished to avoid. If theology is a science, it will have to be defined as one neither in terms of the old scholastic definition nor in terms like those adopted by Hodge from the physical sciences.

---

[4]Charles Hodge, *Systematic Theology*, 3 vols. (1871–73; repr. Grand Rapids: Eerdmans, 1975), 1:1–2.

Significantly, Hodge disagreed with his textbook and model, Francis Turretin's *Institutio theologiae* on this point: Turretin had argued explicitly that theology is not a science because it is not based on rational evidence but rather on teachings to be accepted by faith.[5] What Turretin recognized—and, indeed, what most of the older dogmaticians, including those who did define theology as a science also understood—was that the materials offered in Scripture were fundamentally different from those offered by nature for inductive analysis or, for that matter, by reason alone for purely deductive construction. From the vantage point of the present, we can clearly see that Hodge's approach to theology as a science analogous to geology falls into the same predicament as the so-called biblical-theology movement of this century did in its language of "the God who acts in history": the religious "data" presented by Scripture is, already in the form it takes in the text itself, the subject of theological interpretation. A "mighty act of God," like the Israelite crossing of the Red Sea, was not interpreted as such by the Egyptians and, if it could be re-viewed by a neutral "scientific" observer—a meteorologist, for example—of the twentieth century, it could just as easily be explained on purely natural grounds. The point is not that the religious explanation needs to be set aside but only that it represents, in itself, a step beyond mere "data" and that its use in theology places theology outside of the realm of empirical science.[6]

The problem here is not merely one of nomenclature. Theology claims to deal, both objectively and subjectively, with a distinct body of knowledge and with knowledge generally from a distinct perspective. Even if the definition of theology as a science, used here as a convenient starting point for discussion, is set aside, the problem remains. In the twentieth century there are major barriers to the identification of theology as a methodologically unified discipline dealing with a cohesive body of knowledge. These barriers need to be surmounted if theology is to remain—or, some might say, become again—both a substantive and a useful study.

Somewhat more difficult to argue is the objective character of theological formulation over against the Kantian and Schleiermacherian critiques and in the light of postcritical exegesis. Kant argued that our categories of perception and understanding are categories of mind that interpret and frame our experience of phenomena. By extension of this argument, "things-in-themselves," or noumena, that lie behind the phenomena of our experience are not the source of the interpretive categories—such as quantity, quality, space, time, and cause. Kant's conclusion was that reason could not reach these things-in-themselves and that rational metaphysics, which assumed that space, time, and cause were in things and could be used in arguments for the existence of God, was a fallacy. According to Kant, the content of religion was not rational knowledge of a divine noumenon but rather an ethics based on subjectively rooted moral values and directed toward the divine as the guarantor of those values. In this Kantian perspective, the objective basis for dogmas is lost.[7]

---

[5]Francis Turretin, *Institutio theologiae elencticae,* 3 vols. (Geneva, 1677–89; reissued, Edinburgh and New York, 1847), I.vi.5.

[6]Cf. Vern S. Poythress, *Symphonic Theology* (Grand Rapids: Zondervan, 1987), p. 49, for a theological perspective on the inseparability of event and interpretation.

[7]Cf. Royce G. Gruenler, *Meaning and Understanding: The Philosophical Framework for Biblical Interpretation,* FCI 2 (Grand Rapids: Zondervan, 1991), for a review of the history of philosophy as it bears on epistemological issues.

Schleiermacher's explanation of the contents of dogmatics as a series of objectifications of the feeling of absolute or utter dependence was an attempt to reconstruct theology following the Kantian critique of rational knowing. If indeed God is an unknowable noumenon, then even our theology cannot "know" God, but we can encounter the divine reality at a deeper level, the level of "feeling," or, as Schleiermacher's term might be translated, with greater justice, "immediate apprehension." Thus Schleiermacher endeavored to set theology on a different foundation, a foundation not subject to the Kantian critique of rational metaphysics. Theologians in the nineteenth century soon realized, however, that this deobjectification of the ground of theology was not entirely satisfactory: if all dogmas are but reflections on a single kind of consciousness, the question remains concerning the correlation between these objectifications and the identity of the being on whom we are absolutely dependent. In other words, if dogmas are objectifications of feeling, and if this feeling arises out of an encounter with and a consciousness or immediate apprehension of a reality noumenal or otherwise, then the dogmas must have some reference to that reality. The question of objectivity returns and demands an answer. Ludwig Feuerbach, in a sense, stood Schleiermacher on his head by arguing that the language of theology was only a projection of the subjective hopes and desires of human beings. The so-called Mediating School moved theology in the other direction, retaining some of Schleiermacher's emphasis on consciousness, particularly on the self-consciousness of Jesus, and sought to find, in the historical Jesus, a basis for objective theological statement: we are thrown back, even after Kant, on the sense of theology as a discipline with an objective content, but also with a subjective or personal reference.

If not entirely satisfactory as a statement of the objectivity of theology, Schleiermacher's theology did serve to direct attention both theologically and hermeneutically to the subjective aspects of theology—both to the individual and to the corporate experience of belief. His work is particularly important, even to the more conservative side of Christianity, because he recognized so clearly that the personal, subjective basis of theology is mediated in and through the community of belief and that doctrines and practices become important to individuals and the conduct of individuals is modified by structures of belief in and through the life of the corporate community of faith.

Granting this insight, we are able to argue that the subjective side of theology, defined by the older orthodoxy as a habit or disposition of knowing (*habitus sciendi*), arises in an individual in community and that the ongoing historical life of the community is necessary to the mediation of objective statements of doctrine, as significant statements, to individuals. In other words, we recognize the interrelationship, in theology and religion, of the objective and objectivizing statement of doctrine with the individual formulator and of both the doctrine itself and the formulator with the ongoing life of the community of faith. Theology arises and becomes significant in this corporate context of belief and interpretation.

The subjectivity of belief and interpretation, whether considered as thought or as action, is not the subjectivity of the isolated ego. Piety and spirituality are developed in and through the interaction of believers with one another in the context of an ongoing, living tradition of faith and obedience. Insofar as the formal study of theology takes place within this ongoing community of belief, moreover, the objectivity sought under the rubric of theology as "science" and the subjectivity identified under the rubric of theology as "disposition" complement one another.

Indeed, what goes on at a spiritual level in the study of theology very closely resembles the contemplative exercise described by Tilden Edwards as "re-membering"—an escape from the isolation of our own limited temporality through the use of memory in meditation. Memory, he notes, "affects all the other dimensions" of our lives "through the imprints of experience it carries into the present." Even so, it is through the opening of memory to the religious dimension that self-healing can take place and, in the presence of the larger reality, "God, self, and world are re-membered."[8] Theological study should serve to open the individual spirit to the spiritual life of the community in such a way that the many-faceted spirituality of the tradition enriches the spirituality of the individual, drawing and developing it beyond its own limited resources. The corporate memory of the community becomes the possession of the individual memory—not totally, of course, but in such measure that the corporate testimony enriches and interprets the individual's language of faith.

This necessary interrelationship of the objective and the subjective ought not to stand in the way of theology, rightly understood as the "science of the Christian religion." Scientific theory, in the "exact sciences" as well as in the human and social sciences, has long since set aside the illusion of "detached objectivity" in scientific inquiry. The scientist is not a neutral observer who has no involvement with her work. Not only must a scientist have an initial reason for doing the work and a commitment to the completion of the investigation arising out of interest, but also the observer's or investigator's own patterns and categories of knowing belong both to the work of observation and to the work of interpretation. In other words, the scientist is and must be involved in the identification of data, in the selection of significant data, and in the interpretation of the data and its significance. In fact, there is arguably a prejudgment concerning significance in the initial identification and selection of data.

A similar point can be made concerning historical study. Historians recognize that there is no such thing as a "brute fact." "Facts" or, as they are better termed, "data" or "traces," are preserved, are selected, and are interpreted because someone or some group has identified them as significant either by creating traces of such a nature that they will remain intact or by selecting certain data rather than other data for interpretation. Even the collection and publication of documents without comment or analysis is an act of interpretation, granting that some selection and some judgment concerning significance has been made. Involvement with and commitment to the materials of history does not in itself indicate loss of the objective or scientific nature of the inquiry.

By extension, and in view of the historical methods used in the investigation, involvement in the religious does not bar an individual from the scientific study of religion.[9] In fact, some level of involvement is necessary in the initial selection of the study of religion as opposed to some other study.

---

[8]Tilden Edwards, *Living in the Presence: Disciplines for the Spiritual Heart* (San Francisco: Harper & Row, 1987), pp. 77, 85, 96.

[9]On the nature of historical objectivity, see Marc Bloch, *The Historian's Craft* (New York: Vintage 1953); E. H. Carr, *What Is History?* (New York: Vintage, 1963); G. J. Renier, *History: Its Purpose and Method* (New York: Harper & Row, 1950), and Trygve Tholfsen, *Historical Thinking: An Introduction* (New York Harper & Row, 1967). On the problem of objectivity in the application of historical materials to theological formulation, see further, Richard A. Muller, "The Role of Church History in the Study of Systematic Theology," in *Doing Theology in Today's World*, ed. Thomas McComiskey and John Woodbridge (Grand Rapids: Zondervan, 1990), chap. 4.

HERMENEUTICAL CIRCLES

The unity of the theological task—in fact, the ability to engage productively in the theological task—rests on the intimate and meaningful relationship of the tradition found within the canon of Scripture and the tradition of interpretation, theology, and spirituality, to the believing community of the present and to the individual interpreter as part of that community. Standing in the way of such a relationship is the relative isolation of a dogmatically defined and exposited canon of Scripture from the history of Christian theology and spirituality, from the patterns and practices of contemporary critical exegesis, and of both of these ingredients of theology from the present-day life of the church.

The reason that Scripture is authoritative—apart from our traditional doctrinal statements concerning its divine inspiration and its authority as a doctrinal norm—is that its contents are mirrored in the life of the church and that, in this historical process of reflection, the believing community has gradually identified as canon the books that rightly guide and reflect its faith while setting aside those books that fail to reflect its faith adequately. The history of Christian theology and spirituality has not only carried this canon forward and delivered it to the present day; it has also provided an ongoing meditation on the contents of the canon in relation to the life of the church. This meditation, in turn, has assured contemporary recognition of the continuing relevance of the biblical message to the believing community. There is, in other words, a necessary interrelationship between all questions of theological formulation and the ongoing interpretive life of the church. The movement from the authoritative text to the formulation of doctrine as accomplished in the life of the believing community is necessarily circular.

At the heart of the enormous churchly, curricular, and systematic problem that presently confronts theology is the issue of hermeneutics. Of all of the issues noted in the preceding chapters, the issue of hermeneutics is arguably the most pressing, because it is the most fundamental. And its settlement is arguably the only basis for a convincing solution to the other problems. Establishment of a formal and functional unity to theology in its several disciplines cannot be a matter of artificial or external construction. Rather, it must be a theological task internal to the disciplines themselves in their relationships, a task that is essentially interpretive in nature.

One way to approach this hermeneutical or interpretive task is to ask the question of how and why a text—any text, whether biblical, church historical, or contemporary—comes to us with an identifiable meaning that is grounded in its original intentions and original historical, cultural, religious, and social milieu, how and why that meaning can be known by us, how and why that meaning, as preserved through a long history or mediated by contemporary events, yields up a significance for us in our own situation. The answer to such questions is often given in terms of the construction or identification of a "hermeneutical circle."

The concept of a "hermeneutical circle" comes to us from the nineteenth century, most probably from the work of Friedrich Ast (1778-1841), one of the first writers to sketch out the foundations for the modern science of interpretation or hermeneutics. The idea was subsequently developed at length by Friedrich Schleiermacher (1768-1834) and has since become the common property of virtually all students of interpretation and of the theory of interpretation.[10] The basic idea of the hermeneutical circle arises from

---

[10]Cf. Richard E. Palmer, *Hermeneutics: Interpretation Theory in Schleiermacher, Dilthey, Heidegger, and Gadamer* (Evanston: Northwestern University Press, 1969), pp. 76–81, 87–88.

the recognition that there is more to understanding a text than the parsing of its various clauses or phrases. The meaning of the parts belongs to the whole—and the whole, the larger frame of reference of the text, is larger than the text itself. The hermeneutical circle indicates the whole and its parts, the understanding of the parts with reference to the whole and of the whole with reference to its parts—and, specifically, the understanding of a single part with reference to the other parts and to the whole to which it belongs.

What is most important about this idea of a hermeneutical circle is that it recognizes the intimate involvement of the interpreter with the work of interpretation. The circle has, of course, an objective rootage in the verbal meaning of a text (the part) and in the larger significance (the whole) of the document as placed into its proper intellectual, cultural, and religious context—but the circle is, primarily, a description of the way in which the mind of the interpreter ought to approach the document, i.e., with a view to understanding the part in relation to the whole and the whole in relation to the part. As a preliminary inquiry we must, therefore, ask about the nature of the circle: How can the legitimate circle arise—i.e., what is the nature of the relationship of the interpreter to the text that gives rise to a legitimate and truly fruitful circle of understanding, that knows the part and the whole in relation to one another—and what or *where*, precisely, is this mysterious "whole" that guides our interpretation of the textual part? Hirsch notes, importantly, that this whole can be identified, at least in a preliminary manner, in terms of questions concerning the genre of the document.[11]

Identification of genre is a fundamental interpretive step in all disciplines. In theology, we tend to identify such questions with biblical exegesis—particularly with so-called form criticism. But the question is of much broader application. It belongs not only to biblical studies but also to historical and systematic theology, and it even has an application in the practical or ministerial field. In historical studies, as in biblical, the identification of genre consists, typically, in the initial characterization of a document as to kind and in the subsequent recognition of the limitation placed on its scope and contents by its basic intentionality or purpose. More than simply an identification of the "kind" of document, the answer to the question of genre provides an opening into the mind of the author and the function of the document for the interpreter—it is, in a sense, the point of entry into the hermeneutical circle or, from the vantage of the interpreter, the moment of the preliminary and tentative creation of the circle.

In the systematic and practical fields, this basic question is also present, but not always or even primarily with reference to a historical document. There are, of course, moments of study in which students, pastors, and teachers take up a document written in the field of systematic or practical theology and—if they wish to enter the thought-world of its author and learn from the document—ask the question of genre. One does not approach a book on pastoral counseling as a first level of preparation for a sermon or a system of theology for help in pastoral counseling. On a far deeper level, the level of individual formulation and preparation, however, the hermeneutical question of genre presents itself in systematic and practical theology in the form of an identification of task. As I will argue further, below, this identification of task, understood as a hermeneutical venture, takes on meaning and depth in relation to the individual interpreter's ability to

---

[11]E. D. Hirsch, *Validity in Interpretation* (New Haven: Yale University Press, 1967), pp. 76–77.

enter into and draw on the historical life of the believing community in the creation of a living "hermeneutical circle" in contemporary formulation.

To return to our three basic questions concerning the nature and character of the circle: How can the legitimate circle arise—i.e., what is the nature of the relationship of the interpreter to the text that gives rise to a legitimate and truly fruitful circle of understanding, that knows the part and the whole in relation to one another—and what or *where*, precisely, is this mysterious "whole" that guides our interpretation of the textual part?

Everything I have just said about the hermeneutical circle assumes the text (or the task) and the exegete/interpreter or theologian. I do not want to leave the impression, as is sometimes done in contemporary manuals of hermeneutics and biblical interpretation, that interpretation occurs between the text and the exegete in a manner exclusive of any other parties to the exchange or task: the exegete, armed with a set of lexical and grammatical tools, aided perhaps by a commentary or two and by a broad acquaintance with the history and culture of the age in which the text was written, engineers a frontal assault on the text. Out of the literal, verbal, grammatical meaning of the words, granting their place in the whole of the book or treatise in which they occur, the implications of the text are derived. As a part of this task, the interpreter infers from the text the context or life-situation of the writer of the text, inferring problems, adversaries, or even dialogue partners implied by the text. The text and, we may hope, the document of which it is a part, can then be understood in terms of the historical, social, and cultural background of the text in which it originally spoke and found its purpose.

The "whole" that gives meaning to the part has already been identified, in these basic hermeneutical and exegetical procedures, as being larger than the document in which the text appears: it is the whole historical, cultural, and social context of the document with particular reference to the issues that gave rise to the document. The circularity as well as the importance of the procedure is obvious—if not the entirety of the historical, cultural, and social context, surely the issues that gave rise to the document have been identified by critical examination of the document itself. The larger context, however, governs the identification of issues within the purview of the document and its author: no matter how much we would like to do so, we are prevented by a right (even if necessarily incomplete) identification of the context of a document from imposing our own views on it. We are prevented, for example, by our knowledge of the larger context of the gospel of Matthew from identifying the *ecclesia* that Christ founds upon the Petrine rock as—either in the mind of Christ or in the mind of the author of the Gospel—consisting in an elaborate hierarchy of deacons, priests, bishops, and pope or, alternatively, of deacons, elders (ruling and teaching), sessions, presbyteries, synods, and general assemblies! The *ecclesia* that Matthew had in mind simply did not look like the twentieth-century church.

Our ability to identify this Matthean *ecclesia*, then, rests on two basic sets of data. On the one hand, we rely on the text of the Matthew's gospel itself and, on the other, we rely on other documents from the same period of time, particularly documents from the early church that offer somewhat different perceptions of the identity of the *ecclesia*. If all we possessed were our own wits and the gospel of Matthew, we would have very little chance of developing a picture of the particular community out of which the gospel of Matthew arose, of the larger context of earliest Christianity in its cultural setting, and therefore of the limits of meaning placed by these several contexts on the term *ecclesia*. The naked hermeneutical circle of the individual exegete and the text is a hopeless circle inasmuch as neither the text nor the exegete can supply a clear picture of the larger whole of which the text is a part—not only of the pericope, but also of the entire document.

We must readily admit, then, that the hermeneutical circle is larger than the mental world of the lonely exegete confronting the isolated text. To describe the circle in this way is to threaten its legitimacy by placing it under a set of restrictions that stand in the way of interpretation. This is not merely a technical problem: such barriers are ultimately more threatening to the exegetical work of the nonspecialist, who may not fully understand the problem and who may assume—as the evidence of all too many textual or "expository" sermons indicates—that the individual and the text are all that is needed for a valid and theologically productive reading of Scripture.

Context is more than what we can infer from a text or document. The interpreter of a text must rely on broader historical, cultural, and social study and must be illuminated by archaeological discoveries and by the study of the folkways of Israel's and the church's neighbors in the ancient world. This compares with the work of the interpreter of a text from Luther's writings who ought not simply to infer the context from a particular document but ought rather to deal with the text out of an awareness of the movement of Western thought through the later Middle Ages into the sixteenth century, of the cultural and political situation in Europe and in Saxony, and of the issues raised by the juxtaposition of the Augustinianism of Luther's monastic order with the Semi-Pelagianism of Luther's nominalist teachers at Erfurt.

In both of the cases just noted, examination of the larger context begins to answer not only the question of the "whole" and, specifically, of the genre of the document, but also the question of the significance that looms behind the deciphering of the verbal meaning of the passage. The difficulty of mastering all of these materials and of relating the materials to the text, together with the difficulty of understanding precisely what kind of approach is required by a particular document, raises for us the issue of critical method. By what right and according to what warrants do we address a text or a document and elicit meaning from it?

Surely we address any text or any document by right of our own existence, together with its existence within our present and within the admittedly vast realm of human consciousness. I believe that Aristotle was utterly correct—granting a few notable exceptions among the students I have encountered—when he announced as a basic rationale for his *Metaphysics* that "all people, by nature, desire to know." When we encounter an unknown standing in some vague relation to us, we cannot be content with calling it an "unknown." Immediately it becomes a puzzle to be solved. We see precisely this issue at stake in the problem of the "UFO," the "Unidentified Flying Object": the problem is not that there are UFOs—the problem is that these unknowns immediately become puzzles and that people persist in *identifying* them, almost invariably with bizarre results.

Just as the meaning of a particular text is hedged about and defined by the larger context out of which the text arises, so is the role of any interpreter is hedged about and defined by a context of rules and methods of interpretation. The misidentification of UFOs arises out of a certain lack of restraint on the part of the interpreter of the evidence. In fact, it arises out of a methodological error that permits the placement of real evidence into a context created by the highly imaginative authors of science fiction. In order for any legitimate interpretation to occur, there must not only be a document or some sort of evidence to be placed into a context of meaning, and an interpreter ready to perform the exegetical exercise—there must also be a set of constraints placed on the interpreter.

There is a hermeneutical circle, in other words, that arises out of the interaction of the individual exegete with a text in and through the use of critical, historical method.

On the most basic level, the interpreter must have linguistic control, characterized both by a knowledge of the language in which the text is written and by a knowledge of semantics, of the way in which language works to convey meaning. Not only grammar and syntax but also figures of speech must be understood, and, in addition, an interpreter must be sensitive to the range of meaning of words and how usage governs which portion of a given range of meaning belongs to a word in a particular instance. For example, just because the Hebrew word *emet*, usually translated "truth," includes in its root the connotation of "faithfulness" or even "faithfulness in relationship" and carries that root meaning with it into certain usages, we cannot assume that "faithfulness" is part of its meaning in all contexts. Nor, when Jewish authors of the Greek New Testament use the word *aletheia*, truth, are we permitted to assume that their Jewish or Hebraic background implies *emet* under the *aletheia* and, therefore, a "Hebrew" notion of "faithfulness" somehow now attached to a Greek word that never before had such a connotation and that cannot, from its use in the Greek New Testament, be directly inferred to have that connotation.[12]

When applied theologically, this "root fallacy" can have far-reaching and highly problematic results. In the case of the relationship of *aletheia* to *emet*, the conclusion has frequently been drawn that a "Greek" notion of truth as clarification of an idea or datum, often understood in a propositional sense as the right statement of a case, could not be found in Scripture. Even in the Greek text of the New Testament, it was asserted, the Greek word *aletheia* ought to be interpreted as *emet* and *emet* interpreted as a relational faithfulness, indeed, as "encounter" with a "person" rather than as the statement of a propositional truth. The problem here is that even in the Old Testament, where we are dealing with *emet*, we find a large number of cases, such as those occurring in the book of Proverbs, in which the word is used to indicate right correspondence, clear and accurate statement, and so forth. In the Greek of the New Testament as well, the meaning of the word is determined by its linguistic context and use, not by theorizations about roots. There is no linguistic reason on earth to claim that Christ's statement to the Father "Your word is truth" (John 17:17) ought to be interpreted as "Your word is a personal encounter." Right interpretation, in this instance, has enormous implications for the theological task—for the identification of what theology is and of what theology is capable of saying about God and God's work.

The older grammatical-historical criticism and the more recent methodological tools of source, form, redaction, rhetorical, and canon criticism also provide necessary limits and restraints for interpretation. Each of these critical approaches supplements the others and provides some checks on them, hedging and defining the interpretive task and providing the interpreter with patterns and methods that can open a text. The critical tools provide a certain degree of objectivity and distance, enabling the exegete to ask questions of the text that might not normally be asked apart from the application of a clearly defined method. Thus the question of form—the genre question on a small scale—can be applied to a psalm: Is it an imprecatory psalm or a psalm of praise? The answer to the question both reveals and limits the way in which the text can be interpreted.

---

[12]Cf. James Barr, *The Semantics of Biblical Language* (Oxford: Oxford University Press, 1961).

The value of source and redaction criticism, together with the breadth of their application to documents throughout the history of theology, can easily be seen in the case of the *Didache* or *Teaching of the Twelve Apostles*, a document of the early church recovered in 1873. The original of the document is in Greek, and the document appears to consist of two parts, an initial catechetical section describing the "two ways"—the way of good and the way of evil—and demanding that the choice for the good be made in and through Christ, and a subsequent liturgical section describing early Christian practice, including our earliest extant description of the modes of baptism. The document is of utmost importance to our understanding of the early church not only because of its late first- or early second-century date but also because of its detail concerning the kinds of ministry in at least one community and geographical area. The discussion of baptism is particularly significant inasmuch as it allows either immersion or infusion—casting some doubt on the usefulness of modern debate.

We also have in our possession a Latin version of part of the treatise, dating from a later period, and a vast elaboration of the treatise in the third-century liturgical document known as the *Constitutions of the Twelve Apostles*. These other documents allow us to look at the *Didache* as part of a developing liturgical tradition and to examine that tradition in terms of both source and redaction criticism. The two parts of the *Didache* itself give a reader the impression of two documents that have been edited into a single piece—a short catechetical document and a stylistically different liturgical document. In the mind of the editor or redactor, we might hypothesize, the catechesis of the "two ways" led religiously to the practices of the early church. This inference is supported by the Latin text from a later period, which translates only the document concerning the "two ways" and which leads toward the conclusion that the catechetical document did in fact exist in an independent form at some date prior to its diffusion from the Greek-speaking, eastern Mediterranean world to the Western, Latin-speaking lands. The later liturgical document, the *Constitutions*, can now also be recognized definitively as a product of redaction—granting the almost total inclusion of the *Didache* in it, augmented by other materials. By studying this redaction, we are able to assess the way in which liturgical and ministerial traditions develop over the course of time, by a process of modification and augmentation. The three related documents, taken together, present a picture of the developing life of the Christian church in its earliest centuries and, when interpreted in the context of other catechetical and liturgical documents from the same period, offer a picture of the variety of practices in the early church, together with some sense of their geographical specificity.

This hermeneutical circle of the critically armed interpreter, the text or document in question, and the context as learned from other sources contemporary with it, although fundamental to right interpretation, does not yet provide us with the whole picture or, more importantly, with a hermeneutical circle of which we as interpreters are genuinely, existentially, a part. On the one hand, this personal or existential dimension of interpretation ought to be viewed as somewhat perilous, while on the other, it must be recognized as absolutely necessary. Personal involvement with a text and its potential meaning may easily become a barrier to interpretation. We may be easily induced to import our own meanings, or meanings given to us by the community in which we belong, to a text or document. Nonetheless, without some existential involvement, the interpreter must ultimately be unable to perceive the significance of the text in its present-day location. In other words, there will be no reason for the interpretive exercise to take place, and no reason for the meaning of the text to be understood as relating either directly or indirectly to the present.

It is a simple fact of the world of writing and publishing that there are far more commentaries on the book of Isaiah than on the *Code of Hammurabi*, far more minds bent to the task of deciphering the prologue to the gospel of John than have worried through the discussion of the Demiurge in Plato's *Timaeus*. It is also obvious why this is the case. We take away nothing from the intrinsic worth of the *Code of Hammurabi* or of the *Timaeus* when we recognize that they play less of a role in the fashioning of the intellectual and spiritual identity of the contemporary Western or worldwide Christian community than do Isaiah and the gospel of John. Nor do we detract from the worth of Isaiah or the gospel of John if we note that the reverse was most certainly the case in ancient Mesopotamia and in the first and second centuries A.D.

It should be clear that neither the limited circle of the text and the exegete nor the somewhat expanded circle governed by the use of critical-historical tools and by a set of methodological criteria fully represents the work of the interpreter or provides the interpreter with the key to unlocking the present significance of the text. The work of the interpreter, whether biblical or church-historical, whether in a technically specialized field or in the larger, generalized, field of the communication of theology in ministry to the church, finally reaches out toward issues of present-day meaning, of the "application" or "significance" of a given text or document to the contemporary life-situation of the interpreter and his intended audience.

The term *significance* is probably preferable to the frequently heard "application" insofar as "application" bears the connotation of a somewhat artificial and necessarily adjunctive procedure accomplished in isolation from the basic work of interpretation, whereas "significance" connotes the discovery of a real relationship between the text and its context—including the new context provided by the work of the contemporary interpreter and the community of belief within which the text continues to have its normative function.

The necessary inclusion of the interpreter himself and of the community of belief in the hermeneutical circle once the issue of significance is raised points us toward a far larger circle—in fact, it points us toward the hermeneutical circle marked out by the fourfold curriculum of theology and its implication for the concrete task of doing theology in the contemporary church. The fourfold division of theology into biblical, historical, systematic, and practical theology identifies the larger hermeneutical circle within which Christian exegesis and theology operate and offers, in addition, a structure for understanding the norms of theology and their interrelationship. Once the critical task has been accomplished, a given text must be identified in terms of its place in the tradition as a whole—i.e., in its place as either a biblical, a church historical, or a contemporary systematic or practical statement. This whole, in turn, is the larger "whole" of which the text not only is a part, but is a part in relation to us in our present.

We not only identify the significance of texts differently, depending on whether they are biblical, church historical, or contemporary, we also understand texts differently, depending on the relationship between their context of understanding and our own. Modern hermeneutics recognized the role played in the work of interpretation by the self-understanding of the interpreter. The hermeneutical circle does not consist of a text or doctrine that stands in a particular context of meaning and an interpreter who exists without presuppositions, preunderstandings, or some inchoate relationship to the text chosen for interpretation.

The basic point has been made especially well by Anthony Thiselton in his discussion of the "two horizons" of interpretation.[13] Thiselton points out that older hermeneutics recognized the need of the interpreter to understand the historical and cultural context of the text or document but that it was only in the nineteenth century and, specifically, with Schleiermacher's approach to hermeneutics, that the historical and cultural context of the interpreter played a role in the understanding of a text. Or, as Thistleton states the issue:

> Understanding takes place when two sets of horizons are brought into relation to each other, namely those of the text and those of the interpreter. On this basis understanding presupposes a shared area of common perspectives, concepts or even judgments. . . . Since understanding new subject-matter still depends on a positive relation to the interpreter's own horizons, "lack of understanding is never totally removed." It constitutes a progressive experience or process, not simply an act that can be definitively completed.[14]

In the interpretive process, the horizon of the text and the horizon of the interpreter interact, and the horizon of the interpreter is broadened as the meaning of the text comes to light and as it becomes significant in the present. The unreachable goal of the process is a "fusion of horizons"—unreachable because the context of the document being interpreted and the context of the interpreter can never become identical, no matter how clearly the former is understood by the latter.

In the contemporary formulation of theology, based as it must be on the findings of the past, the ongoing community of belief occupies a crucial place in the hermeneutical circle. It is precisely this historical community that provides a commonality of context and a concrete historical link between text and interpreter. In and through the historical community of belief, the horizon of the text maintains some existential relationship to the horizon of the interpreter, insofar as the text is interpreted anew from generation to generation and its ongoing significance in the tradition preserves elements of the original meaning. The historical record of faith and obedience, of theory and praxis, drawn out through the Old Testament, the New Testament, and the history of the church issues forth interpretively in contemporary theory and praxis—systematic and practical theology. The contemporary disciplines, in turn, look back interpretively into their biblical and historical roots, with the centuries of tradition intervening between the interpreter and a given text offering guidance concerning its meaning and its significance for the present.

The larger interpretive task, therefore, includes not only the initial work of exegesis that identifies the meaning of the text in its original context and the implications of that particular theological context for the somewhat larger structure of biblical theology. It also includes the movement through the theological and spiritual heritage of the community of belief into the present and, then, back again into the text. The theological hermeneutic that goes on following the initial work of exegesis continually asks the question of how a particular point in biblical theology continues to lay claim, by means of the historical path of theory and praxis, to the church's present. The historical creeds and confessions of the church not only offer crucial indications of the way in which the text

---

[13]Anthony C. Thiselton, *The Two Horizons: New Testament Hermeneutics and Philosophical Description* (Grand Rapids: Eerdmans, 1980).

[14]Ibid., pp. 103–4, citing Schleiermacher, *Hermeneutik*, p. 141.

lays claim on the life and thought of the community, they also provide pathways back into the text from the present. By asking, in a final contemporizing step of interpretation, how the text has led the community of belief to particular credal and confessional conclusions, we open the text on a different level to our own theological concerns.

At a previous point in this study, we noted that the Johannine prologue does not easily yield up language of essence, person, and intra-Trinitarian relationships. Indeed, it would be a terrible mistake for exegesis to assume the Nicene language as a presupposition to interpretation. Nonetheless, once the exegesis has been done and we have understood as best we can the first-century implications of logos-language, we must ask the further question of why this text rather than other New Testament texts is drawn to our attention as a focus for theological formulation. Not the least among the reasons for this attention is that logos-language was crucial to the contextualization of the gospel in the second century, when the apologists recognized the significance of logos to the surrounding culture and made the Johannine prologue central to the church's work of communicating the gospel.

Once we have recognized this issue, we then can move forward toward an understanding of the church's endeavor to hold fast to its monotheistic faith while at the same time doing justice to the ideal of an immanent divine Logos sent forth into the world. The church not only fastened on to the Johannine term *monogenēs*, "unique," or as traditionally rendered, "only-begotten," but also used this term in order to maintain the full divinity of the Logos. The adaptation idea of "begetting" to the discussion of the inner workings of the Godhead, helpful in identifying a distinction between God as such and the Logos sent forth into the world, also caused a certain difficulty for monotheism. The church needed to make clear that this begetting did not mirror human begetting and did not result in the generation of a quasi-divine being separate from God. Following the third century, the idea of an "eternal begetting"—of an internal, eternal, distinction of logos from the divine essence as such—arose as a way of resolving the dilemma of the language.

In our own theological efforts this element of traditional churchly Trinitarianism, although not a direct exegetical result of the text, becomes an important element in the subsequent interpretive work of understanding the text in our present context—particularly granting the continuing importance of the fundamental confession of the presence of God in Christ reconciling the world to himself. The church's Trinitarian creeds and confessions enter the hermeneutical circle, following exegesis, as an essential element in the appropriation of the text in and for our confessing present. This remains the case inasmuch as the basic exegesis of the text, prior to the investigation of the creeds and confessions, will raise questions about the relation of logos-language and of incarnation to our monotheism not at all unlike the questions already encountered by the early church. The church's previous meditation on these issues—in view of its doctrinal intentions, even more than because of its specific terminological results—is crucial to our understanding of the function of the text in our own faith today.

CONTEXTUALIZATION AND THE INTERPRETIVE TASK

The term *contextualization* is a relatively new addition to the theological vocabulary. It points toward a new sensitivity to the problem of bringing the message of Christianity to bear on faith and life in the present. The message of the gospel arose in one cultural, social, historical, and linguistic context, and we live in another. Those to whom the church attempts to bring the message of the gospel live in yet another cultural, social, historical, and linguistic context: for, even as our histories converge in this "global village" and become intertwined, the variety of the past continues to affect our future, as do the divergent cultures and languages of the world.

In order for the gospel to become meaningful to us in our own present life-situation and to others in different places and different cultures in their distinctive life-situations, it must be brought into the diverse contexts of the modern world. It must be contextualized. It ought to be made clear that the work of contextualization has been a part of the interpretive task of the church throughout the ages: contextualization occurred—with incredible success—when the essentially Palestinian phenomenon of earliest Christianity moved out into the gentile mission and became the faith first of the Greek-speaking world of the ancient Mediterranean basin and then of the Latin world of the western Mediterranean. It occurred again as Christianity was brought to the barbarian kingdoms beyond the bounds of the Roman Empire, and to the barbarian rulers who became the lords of Rome—and it has occurred again with enormous diversity of expression in the spread of Christianity to sub-Saharan Africa and to Asia. In other words, contextualization is one of the basic elements of the life, spread, and survival of Christianity.

The newness of the term *contextualization*, however, points us to the fact that this age-old interpretive exercise has been recognized, analyzed, and *consciously* attempted only recently. There are at least three basic reasons for this fact. First, the process of contextualization has gone on so long and so successfully in the West, at least until recently, that it has tended to become culturally invisible. Christianity, as interpreted by the early, medieval, and Reformation church, is so imbedded in our culture that the cultural differences between the ancient culture presented in Scripture and the civilization of the West are at times difficult to discern. And those differences that do appear are easily explained as belonging to the development of culture from its ancient origins toward the modern, scientific world. Contextualization, as a cultural problem, becomes readily visible only when the gospel is interpreted in different terms by divergent cultures that are also in dialogue with one another.

Second, the modern missionary efforts of Western churches, from their sixteenth-century beginnings onward, were just as imperialistic as the expansion and colonization efforts that brought the missions. The underlying assumption of mission work during most of its history has been that Western Christianity needed to be superimposed on other cultures and the Christianity of native populations conformed to Western standards. Any deviation from the Western model—even if undertaken in the name of the gospel—was viewed as a declension from the truth. Granting the historical difficulty of recognizing one's own faith as a contextualization and recognizing the historical presence, noted previously, of Christianity at the heart of the development of Western culture, this imperialistic approach, if not ultimately justifiable, is surely understandable. Christianization was confused with westernization. Only recently have we become sensitive to the possibility of different formulations of the gospel grounded in different cultural contexts.

This new cultural awareness leads us to the third point: the development of Western hermeneutics has led, in the last century and a half, to an understanding of patterns of interpretation that recognizes the fact of contextualization and the relationship of contextualization to a larger frame of reference. The significance of a document or concept in a new context arises out of the relationship already existing between the interpreter's self-understanding and the framework of understanding lodged in the document or concept. By way of example, a text from the Bible attains significance in the present far more surely and certainly than an ancient Babylonian religious text because the Western, Christian interpreter, before any work of interpretation, stands in a cultural and historical relationship to the biblical text. We are able to contextualize or re-contextualize the biblical message because, at a fundamental level, that message has had a long-term impact on our culture.

In accordance not only with this view of contextualization but also with the approach to theology that we have been developing throughout this study, contemporary Christians must find a way to affirm their theologies—including their theological systems—that does justice both to the absoluteness of the divine object of theology and the relativity of its contemporary forms. Christians tend, all too much like the missionaries of preceding centuries, to view their own confessional or theological system as an absolute, that is, as the only possible form that can be taken by the biblical message. The point is not that there is a problem with the systematic presentation of theology and not that, within a given culture or society, this presentation ought to strive for diversity of expression (as if diversity in and of itself were a virtue). Nor is it the point that, within a particular culture, no single systematic presentation may be arguably better than another. Systematic presentation itself is valuable, perhaps even necessary; and it is clearly possible that, within a given culture or society, one systematic presentation will best express the biblical message at the heart of Christianity.

A problem arises when a particular system or a particular grouping of systematic presentations is so identified with the biblical message that the transmission of the message either to another culture or society or to another phase or era of the same culture or society becomes extremely difficult if not impossible. In other words, one way of stating the message can become absolutized, usually because it has been a highly effective and successful formulation, with the result that a culturally conditioned theological statement is transmitted to and forced upon a cultural situation in which it cannot function. The historical course of Western Christianity in its chronological length, intellectual breadth, and conceptual depth offers us a multitude of examples of the problem and of its solution. Rather than view the history of Western Christianity as the gradual and progressive construction of the ultimate theological system, we ought to view it as a laboratory of successful contextualization, indeed, of a series of such contextualizations.

Thus understood, the work of contextualization is little more than the self-conscious exercise of a form of historical method for the sake of the present-day statement of the faith. The result of an effective contextualization of the Christian message is no more and no less than the adaptation of the substance of Christian teaching to a new linguistic and cultural life situation. The result of a successful exercise in historical criticism is no more and no less than the understanding of the meaning of Christian teaching in a past linguistic and cultural life situation. It should be clear that the present-day effort to contextualize a historical faith rests on an ability to grasp the meaning of the faith in its basic forms by means of historical method. Contextualization, therefore, when it becomes a conscious exercise, is part of a historically controlled exercise in hermeneutics.

Atonement theory provides an excellent series of examples for discussion. The New Testament provides not one but several ways of describing the atoning work of Christ: it is a ransom paid for sin, a sacrificial expiation of sin, a substitutionary act that puts Christ in our place under the divine punishment for sin; it is the victory of Christ over the powers of evil; it is the redemptive manifestation of divine love; it is the act of the second man or new Adam becoming the head of redeemed humanity in Adam's place. All of these approaches to atonement can be found in the New Testament and all, most probably, can be linked exegetically to the demand of particular life-situations on the preaching and interpretation of the gospel. They are, thus, not to be viewed as mutually exclusive, nor are they to be viewed as easily harmonizable into a single theory. Throughout the history of the church, theologians and churchmen have drawn selectively on these models of atonement and have brought the gospel to bear on various situations and contexts in which, perhaps, not all of the various models would have been readily understood.

In a culture that well recognized the corporate character of human identity and responsibility and the representative character of monarchs and heads of households—and that universally accepted a more or less allegorical and typological reading of sacred texts—Irenaeus of Lyons looked at the various ways in which the New Testament had defined Christ's work and selected, not the language of sacrifice or ransom, but rather the language of "first" and "second man," the "old" and the "new Adam," as the foundation of his preaching of salvation. His so-called Recapitulation Theory is literally a theory of new headship (*anakephaliosis*; re-capitu-lation) or repetition in one individual, of the corporate development of the race.

Against the Gnostics, Irenaeus could argue that the human predicament is not the result of a cosmic dualism, of a good and an evil ultimate engaged in battle, of the entrapment of elements of the good—souls—in the evil realm of matter, but rather the result of an all-too-human catastrophe, the sinful disobedience of the first head of the human race. Redemption is made possible by the creation of a new corporate humanity gathered under a new head—the second man, the new Adam, Jesus Christ. In order to argue this model for Christ's atoning and reconciling work, Irenaeus looked at the stories of Adam's defeat and Christ's victory and, allegorically and typologically, demonstrated that the story of Christ undoes, in a recapitulatory mirror-image repetition, the story of Adam. Adam brought the race into sin at the instance of the virgin Eve; Christ brought the race into salvation through the instrumentality of the virgin Mary. Adam sinned in taking fruit from a tree; Christ brought redemption nailed to a tree. As we all fell in Adam, so do we all rise in Christ. The basic paradigm is Pauline—the elaboration is Irenaean and capable of speaking to the social and corporate understanding of the late second century.

Other writers of Irenaeus' day and throughout the patristic era selected other New Testament themes, such as our bondage to "the god of this age" (2 Cor. 4:4) or the similar theme of Christ's victory over the powers (cf. Rom. 8:37–39; Col. 2:8, 14–15)—again, not because these themes necessarily appeared to them to be the central themes of the New Testament in its own right, but because this particular New Testament way of understanding Christ's work spoke directly to their own cultural and historical context. In the Christian apologetic tradition, from the mid–second century onward, the early church had to confront a polytheistic world with a monotheistic message of salvation. In doing so, the fathers did not deny the existence of the pagan gods; instead, much like the Old Testament, they demoted the gods of the pagan nations and interpreted them as lesser beings—indeed, as demons, principalities and powers of the spiritual world. The New Testament message of Christ's victory over the powers, over the "god of this age," was easily adapted to the cultural situation as a message of the divine agency in Christ offering victory over the many and often capricious deities of the pagan world.

As well as these two models of atonement theory served the early church, they did not seem adequate to communicate the gospel to the altered social and cultural situation of the Middle Ages. The problem of polytheism still existed on the edges of Christianity, but, in contrast to the culture of the ancient world, the culture of the Middle Ages was officially Christian and monotheistic. In a general sense at least, granting that polytheism was no longer a recognized cultural option by the end of the eleventh century, that evil spiritual powers could be dealt with by other means than atonement theory, and that the corporate understanding of the social order and of the place of human beings in it had changed considerably, the language of Christ's work was in need of a new model, a model capable of communicating the gospel in a different context.

The great treatise of Anselm of Canterbury on the logic of incarnation and atonement, the *Cur Deus Homo* (*Why the God-Man?*), argued the inadequacy of the patristic theories of atonement and pressed the question not simply of the meaning of atonement but of the way in which Christ's identity as Mediator points toward the underlying logic of salvation. Anselm attacked the notion that Christ's death was a payment made to Satan, the god of this world: why, after all, should payment be made to one to whom nothing is rightly owed? Satan does indeed exercise power over human beings, but that power is wrongly gained and unjustly exercised. No payment, therefore, is necessary to break his power. Nonetheless, Christ's work does have the character of a transaction, and the human disobedience for which Christ atones does stand as a debt that must be paid. The debt is a debt of obedience—indeed, argues Anselm, it is the obedience originally and perpetually owed by human beings to God. Our plight is that we, locked in our sinfulness and disobedience, are unable to pay God what we owe.

Apart from Christ we stand before God as debtors. We owe an obedience that we cannot pay. Nor can God simply overlook the problem: by failing to pay obedient homage to God we have in fact dishonored God's name. The debt must be paid and God's honor restored before the human race can enjoy renewed fellowship with God. It was clear to Anselm that only a human being could repay the debt: it would hardly be fitting for a human debt to be paid by an angelic being! It was equally clear that no sinful human being is capable of making such a payment both because no individual debtor, himself in jeopardy, is capable of paying the debt of others, and because the enormity of sin is such that no human being is capable of satisfying the debt. Satisfaction must, therefore, be made by a member of the human race who is somehow free from its sinfulness and who somehow transcends its limitations. Such a person is the God-man, Jesus Christ—born sinless of the virgin Mary and incarnate God in union with human nature. The divine-human person of Christ is, thus, suitable to the task of atonement or, as Anselm would say, satisfaction.

Such, in a nutshell, was Anselm's theory. We recognize in it many of the elements of the standard orthodox Protestant penal substitution theory, but we note also substantial differences in language. Rather than a language of vicarious substitution for punishment, Anselm offers a language of satisfaction made to the divine honor. Theologians have often observed, usually in order to discredit Anselm's theory, that the logic of his argument is not so much biblical as medieval and that the picture of sinners having failed to pay a debt of honor is very much like the picture of a medieval vassal who has fallen short of the obligation he owes to his feudal lord. The satisfaction exacted either from the disobedient vassal (eternal punishment in the case of God's human "vassals") or from a substitute, a champion, is a legal model drawn from medieval feudal practice. Anselm's theological critics, together with the critics of the Anselmian elements that remain in the penal substitution theory, typically argue against its excessive legalism and its "medieval" character.

Far from being a problem for atonement theory or for theology in general, however, Anselm's use of feudal legal imagery is a perfect example of successful contextualization. The atoning work of Christ, which none of the gospel writers and none of the fathers of the church could have conceived of in precisely this manner, has been beautifully presented in the language and the logic of the late eleventh century. Earlier centuries—and later ones—may have little contact with Anselm's language of honor and satisfaction, with its hints of lords and vassals, but Anselm's century and the centuries immediately following found in this terminology the basis of a suitable way of making the work of Christ intelligible, a point of departure for an adequate contextualization of the message, capable of establishing in a language suitable to its time, the objective achievement of Christ on the cross.

Modern-day critics of Anselm's feudal metaphors have not undermined Anselm's achievement at all. What they have done is to recognize that it no longer represents Christ's atonement to us in terms that partake of the very fabric of our lives and our cultural context, and that a new and altered language of atonement is needed. Critics of the Anselmian view also seem to forget that it did not enter the stream of developing Christian doctrine without challenge and modification and that both the challenge (from Abelard) and the modification (at the hands of Lombard, Aquinas, and others) tell us something about the way in which Christian doctrine can be successfully contextualized. It must be debated through the eyes of individuals and groups immersed in the culture of the time.

Anselm's atonement theory also points us toward a crucial issue in our understanding of theological language. Theological language is not a special, exalted language delivered by God and preserved somehow from involvement in the world. Theological language is ordinary language, and it follows the rules of ordinary language. Theology can be intelligible only when it speaks the linguistic coin of the realm. Using Augustine's or Anselm's or Calvin's or Wesley's language in an era unaccustomed to their usage is like trying to buy lunch in Chicago with a handful of German marks. The coinage is valuable, but not useful in Chicago. What Anselm did for atonement theory was to express it in the linguistic currency of the eleventh and early twelfth centuries. As in all theological usage, he took terms and concepts that had, previously, only a secular and a legal meaning, and he shifted their focus, enlarging their range of meaning to include a religious dimension.

Any time that theology crosses a cultural boundary, whether historical or geographical, new terms and new metaphors must be drawn out of the spiritual, intellectual, and linguistic storehouse of the culture and adapted for use in Christian theology. There is, of course, no ready-made formula, no standard blueprint, for making this crosscultural transition and bringing about a successful contextualization of the message. History has demonstrated, especially in the history of the early church, that the enormously difficult passage from one linguistically identified cultural form to another is fraught with problems—indeed, with heresies—and is successfully traversed primarily by bilingual thinkers whose life-experience has given them a close acquaintance with both cultures. We see such transmitters and translators in the apostle Paul, Tertullian, and Hilary of Poitiers, each of whom, particularly Paul and Tertullian, was responsible for a language of theology fundamental to our Western form of Christianity, so fundamental that we can hardly conceive of Christianity apart from their vocabulary. From Paul we have, among other things, our language of grace, faith, and justification; from Tertullian we receive the Trinitarian/Christological terminology of person and nature.

The contextualization of theology is both an objective and a subjective, both a corporate and an individual exercise. On one level, it is an exercise performed by Christians every day. When a Christian family prays at mealtime, particularly if the prayer is not one of the standard blessings typically repeated on such occasions but is an extemporaneous prayer that reflects the present moment and its concerns, the contextualization of the Christian message has occurred. The same can be said of an effective sermon, a visitation of the sick, a counseling session, and a rudimentary application of the Christian moral principles in everyday life. In each of these exercises, two basic functions of theological thinking and living have taken place. On the one hand, some basic truth or principle held by the larger, historical and contemporary community of faith has been interpreted in relation to a new and highly particularized context or life-situation. On the other hand, the interpretive work is paralleled by and, in fact, completed in an inward appropriation of the message—the truth, the principle—through which the believer is enabled to understand her context religiously. Daily religious activities, in other words, are predicated on a hermeneutical and spiritual exercise.

Everything that we said about the study of language, about the interpretive and self-interpretive encounter via language with different worlds of thought, and about the necessity of grappling with the extracanonical or larger cultural context of a theology applies directly to the work of contextualization in the present. Contextualization is nothing other than the "presentizing" conclusion of the hermeneutical task, the completion of the hermeneutical circle in our own persons and in the context of present-day existence. The more successful the exercise in addressing both the meaning of the original text or doctrine and drawing it forward toward a contemporary significance that respects the intention of the original formulator but also serves the religious needs of the present, the more the hermeneutical circle has led to a broadening of the interpreter's religious and spiritual horizon in and through the "fusion" of her horizon with that of the text or doctrine.

From the point of view of the hermeneutical procedure, then, contextualization means the widening of the present horizon, the addition of yet another interpretive context or life-situation to the historical pattern of interpretation. In other words, contextualization is also the "cutting edge" of the tradition of the believing community as it moves into and engages with the present situation. The original biblical or churchly meaning does not change, but the text, the document, the doctrine, the idea or principle in question attains a significance in a new context and, therefore, to a certain extent, attains a new significance related to the old and, at the same time, broadens the horizon of the believing community in the present.

The limitations of interpretation that we recognized earlier now come into play. The hermeneutical circle of interpreter and text created anew by a new address to a doctrinal issue in a new context of belief must be legitimized—it must be a churchly circle linking the interpreter to the text in and through the historical path that has linked the text to the interpreter. It must be a circle that establishes the boundaries of significance without preventing the reception of the text into the life of the present community. The "new" significance, therefore, cannot ever be entirely new: rather it is a dimension of interpretation, arising from a particular context, that draws on the original meaning of the text but also on its tradition of meaning and that, without negating the past, draws that rich realm of interpretation into a new present.

The point is simply that the present significance of the text or doctrine must not only be rooted in its original meaning, but that its rootage can be guaranteed in only one place—in the ongoing life of the historical community in which the text or doctrine first came into being. A text or doctrine that does *not* belong to the ongoing life of the historical community of belief of which the interpreter is a part cannot easily be drawn significantly into the present situation. By way of example, the following passage from "The

Surangama Sutra" makes very little religious sense to the Western Christian mind and spirit and, even with lengthy interpretation, has little chance of attaining the significance of Psalm 23 or the prologue to the gospel of John:

> Ananda replied:—You are now asking me about the existence of my mind. To answer that question I must use my thinking and reasoning faculty to search and find an answer. Yes, now I understand. This thinking and reasoning being is what is meant as "my mind."
>
> The Lord Buddha rebuked Ananda sharply and said:—surely that is nonsense, to assert that your being is your mind. . . . [This] is simply one of the false conceptions that arises from reflecting about the relations of yourself and outside objects, which obscures your true and essential Mind. It is because, since from beginningless time down to the present life, you have been constantly misunderstanding your true and essential Mind. It is like treating a petty thief as your own son. By so doing you have lost consciousness of your original and permanent mind and because of it have been forced to undergo the sufferings of successive deaths and rebirths.[15]

The editor of the volume from which this quotation is taken, Lin Yutang, characterizes "The Surangama Sutra" as "a kind of *Essay on Human Understanding* and *Gospel of St. John* combined, with the intellectual force of the one and the religious spirit of the other."[16]

The Western Christian interpreter—without passing any judgment whatsoever on the religious and philosophical teachings present in the above text—would not have much success in attempting to draw out of "The Surangama Sutra" a significance for himself for his community of belief. Granting that the horizon of the interpreter is determined by the somewhat broader horizon of the community in which he lives and believes, and that the horizon of the community is determined by its own historical and cultural trajectory, this text from another community with its own utterly distinct historical and cultural trajectory simply does not speak in the new, Western context, certainly not with the power and significance with which it speaks in its own Eastern context.

From a hermeneutical and contextual perspective, therefore, there is no question that the "presuppositional" approach to theology carries the day against a purely "evidential" approach. As we noted briefly in the discussion of apologetics in the previous chapter, there is always a sense in which explanation and defense of a theological point must follow the doctrinal declaration of the point. This is not to say that our beliefs need not be rational or that they ought not to be supported by sound evidences, but only that the rational proofs and the historical or empirical evidences are seldom if ever the reason for belief. They are, however, to paraphrase Anselm, the foundation of subsequent understanding. We come to a text or a doctrine with predispositions, rooted in our community of belief and formed by a particular cultural context and historical situation.

The presence of the tradition also makes possible a pattern of mutual enlightenment between different cultural and historical expressions of the Christian message. Interpretation of the gospel in a Latin American or Asian or African context, insofar as it remains true to the basic intention of the church in its preaching and insofar as it has arisen out of the tradition that bears the text and brings it into each new situation, can be significant no

---

[15]From "The Surangama Sutra," in *The Wisdom of China and India,* ed. Lin Yutang (New York: Random House, 1942), p. 512.
[16]Ibid., p. 491.

only to the life of the culture into which the gospel has been newly brought but also to the tradition as a whole. Just as present-day exegesis and application draw on an understanding of two historical and cultural moments—that of the text and that of the modern-day interpreter—so also can the encounter of two acculturated or contextualized interpretations shed light on both and on the meaning of the text as well.

EPILOGUE: THE STUDY OF THEOLOGY AS AN EXERCISE IN CHRISTIAN CULTURE

Much of what has already been said in this and the preceding chapters has tended not only toward the thesis that hermeneutics and spirituality are closely linked but also toward its corollary, the realization that spirituality is a characteristic of the entire study of theology and not simply a subject that can be studied or an exercise in "Christian personal formation" that can be tacked on to a curriculum or on to the individual, personal study of theology. One of the great virtues of Farley's *Theologia* is that it draws attention to the older model of theology as consisting in part of a "disposition" or *habitus* for theological knowing.[17] In this model, as both the medieval and the post-Reformation Protestant treatments of the method or *ratio* for the study of theology invariably indicate, theology involved not only the examination of ideas and documents but also the cultivation of the spiritual, attitudinal life of the individual. Johann Heinrich Alsted, writing in the early seventeenth century, even argued the necessary relation between a healthy mind and a healthy body and prescribed good physical care for students of theology—a point, we note, that has been profoundly neglected in modern theological study.

The assumption of the older study of theology was that the exegetical study of Scripture in the original languages, the meditation on classic works of theology by thinkers like Athanasius, Augustine, Anselm, Aquinas, Luther, and Calvin, and the careful contemplation of the technical language of dogmatics could and ought to be a spiritually uplifting experience—inasmuch as the student would be trained by such study in a regimen of meditation on the "things of God," that is, on God and God's works of creation and redemption. It was also assumed, not only in the study of theology, but in education in general, certainly through the nineteenth century, that the exercise of the mind in worthy subjects brought with it the upbuilding of character. History and philosophy were to be studied, not only because they were important for the intellectual background of the "educated person" but also because they inculcated wisdom concerning human nature, its heights and its depths. Equally so, and, indeed, even more, ought the study of the "things of God"—of the history and thought of the community of belief—be experienced as the inculcation of a spiritually enlightening wisdom, of a way of life as well as a pattern of thought.

This sense of the confluence of theological formulation and personal formation in the rightly ordered study of theology is hardly an academic pipedream. It is a foundational principle of spirituality recognized in our times by a writer as well known in the realm of piety and spirituality as A. W. Tozer. Tozer began one of his best-loved works with the lament that "the Church has surrendered her once lofty concept of God" and that with

---

[17]Cf. Edward Farley, *Theologia: The Fragmentation and Unity of Theological Education* (Philadelphia: Fortress, 1983), pp. 31–39.

this "loss of the sense of majesty has come the further loss of religious awe and consciousness of the divine Presence."[18] Tozer notes with irony the "dramatic gains" in wealth and size of churches—external gains that are paralleled by "internal losses" in the "quality of our religion." He offers his book as pointing toward a solution to the problem and then adds, "Were Christians today reading such works as those of Augustine and Anselm a book like this would have no reason for being."[19]

When Tozer looked to the wellsprings of his own spirituality and to the basis of a solution to the church's spiritual dilemma, he looked to the giants of the history of theology, to thinkers who gave not only to the church but also to Western culture both substance and inspiration. In Augustine and Anselm, Tozer found two writers in whom theology and spirituality were one and the same, who identified theological study both as the search for truth and as the identification of the good and the approach to God. In the thought of these and other theologians of the past, God, Being, the good, and truth were assumed to be identical—so that the study of theology was also an examination of foundational principles of the natural order, of ethics, and of philosophy.

In other words, the study of theology, in the classical sense, is a study of values or, more precisely, of a fairly well-defined body of materials that, in their primary intention, communicate values—values to be believed and values to be acted upon. If, on the one hand, the historical method of examining and analyzing the biblical and church historical materials serves to locate their grammatical meaning and original cultural significance within a particular historical, cultural, social, and religious context (and, to a certain extent, relativize the documents), our membership, on the other hand, in the ongoing community of belief that locates its identity in the tradition of these materials places us in a position to receive the truths and the values expressed in the materials as our own. The historical relativity of the form of expression does not in any way detract from the ultimacy of the values toward which the particular form of expression points.

Study of the materials of the church—the various historical forms in which the community has expressed its beliefs and formulated its ethical standards—becomes an exercise in the expression of one's own beliefs and the formulation of one's own standards. The cultural and social relativity of the documents serves, moreover, in the exercise, to press us toward our own statement of these corporately held values, insofar as we recognize both the limitation of the particular cultural form and the ultimacy of the values expressed under it.

Although no one should dispute that any of the theological disciplines—whether biblical, historical, systematic, or practical—represents an intellectual and a spiritual effort, conducted with attention to a theoretical as well as to a practical dimension, for the sake of developing a clearer understanding of the nature and the subject of the discipline, it is historical theology and systematic theology that suffer the greatest pressures in our time from the anti-intellectualist spirit. How often do we hear, in many different forms and phrases, the complaint that such "theoretical" disciplines are divorced from the spiritual life of Christianity and place barriers in the way of piety? How often do we hear that emphasis on abstract formulae is a "Greek" way of thinking that ought not to be

    [18]A. W. Tozer, *The Knowledge of the Holy: The Attributes of God: Their Meaning in Christian Life* (San Francisco: Harper & Row, 1961), p. vii.
    [19]Ibid., pp. vii–viii.

imposed on the "Hebraic" faith of the gospel? How often have we heard that mind, the intellect, the "head," ought not to displace the "heart"—as if the heart (with profuse apologies to William Harvey!) were actually the seat of the emotions? We hear these complaints so frequently and some of their presuppositions are so ingrained into the contemporary religious psyche, that the simple mention of them has the force of argument in some quarters—and any argument against them will be faced with considerable opposition from the outset. Yet the argument must be mounted if the faith is to survive and if our theology and spirituality are to be understood and appreciated for what they actually are.

The discussion of hermeneutics and contextualization points toward what may well be the basic question that needs to be addressed in the study of theology as it moves from the historically defined biblical foundations of Christianity toward contemporary formulation: Does the theological result of any individual effort at formulation both address and inform the culture within which that formulation has taken place? Granting the long history of the Judeo-Christian tradition, any statement of the contemporary significance of our basic beliefs and values will be an experiment in the crosscultural transmission of theology and in the contextualization or, indeed, recontextualization of particular teachings of the believing community. The success of Christianity and its great gift to the world cannot simply be defined in the standard theological language of the salvation of the individual; they must also be defined in terms of the formation of Western culture.

Our culture is, of course, not entirely Christian or Judeo-Christian. It is also profoundly Greek and Roman, Anglo-Saxon and Germanic—and in the twentieth century increasingly influenced by the thoughts, tastes, and sounds of the Far East. But Christianity has not merely been one component of this larger cultural experience. It has also been the preserver, mediator, and interpreter of the other ancient elements of Western culture. We do not, in other words, experience a cultural tradition internally at odds with itself, consisting in many unrelated streams or trajectories, but instead a cultural tradition that has tended to draw the wealth of past ages together into the service of its present. Much of this work has been the work of Christianity.

What the Christianity of the past has done, time and time again, has been to give to Western culture a sense of historical and moral direction, a structure of values, an identification of the ultimate good, and a coherent view of reality. There have, of course, been moments of grave difficulty. The rediscovery of the physical and metaphysical works of Aristotle in the early thirteenth century created a problem of the first order: here was what seemed to be an alternative worldview. Similarly, the discoveries of Copernicus, Kepler, and Galileo appeared to fracture the Christian worldview. But in both cases, theology was able to adapt: the so-called Thomistic synthesis of Aristotelian philosophy and Christian theology remains a monument to formulation in both fields of inquiry. And as for the heliocentric solar system, it was integrated quite easily into a fairly traditional view of the relationship of God and world, finally proving to be not at all the monster it once seemed to be.

In both cases, and in numerous others, we can see both the resilience of the core of Christian theology and piety and the ability of the church's fundamental teachings to address a changing society. Whatever our differences or disagreements with the exegetical methods and doctrinal formulations of past ages, it remains true that the church in other times was capable both of recognizing the needs and addressing the issues of the contemporary cultural situation—and capable, also, of recognizing the fundamental intention of its doctrinal formulations as, sometimes, distinct from the language in which they had been stated. Exegetes and theologians of the past, as illustrated in this volume, were able, by means of the methods of interpretation available to them in their time, to draw together the whole of theology—the biblical and historical materials, contemporary statement and practice—into forms capable of addressing the needs of individuals, of the community of belief, and of the larger culture around it.

The great difficulty of theological formulation today, and the great difficulty of the relevance of theological formulation to the present life of Western culture stems in no small part from a failure of intellectual and spiritual nerve in the church in the twentieth century. The clergyman of my introductory chapter, however expert a technician or operations manager he may be, is not a bearer of culture. He may be able to organize a group in the present and he may be able to offer many of its members all of the emotional solace they need, but he will leave their children spiritually impoverished. The theology that he set aside in the name of practice is nothing more or less than the cultural heritage of the church, the tools for a Christian construction not just of a congregational body but of a view of God and world, of ultimate reality, of our universe and the place of human beings in it.

The task of theological formulation in the present day is to draw together into an interpretive unity the various elements of theology and to produce, from within the community of faith, a contemporary science of the Christian religion that recognizes as its proper object the construction of a view of reality suitable to the perpetuation of Christian culture. This is a very tall order. It calls not only for a general mastery, on the part of clergy and teachers, of the various elements of the "diversified encyclopedia," it also calls for an attentiveness to the way in which these elements fit together, for a responsibility both to the larger faith of the ongoing Christian community and to the needs of objective or "scientific" study. In addition, it calls for a willingness to use the materials of doctrine, the biblical and historical sources, not as gatherings of right statements that need only to be repeated but as foundations for contemporary formulation in contemporary language and in response to a contemporary situation.

For Further Reading

A complete list of works cited may be found in the index of authors and titles. In the following bibliographical discussion I have noted works that will be particularly significant and helpful in the task of understanding the pattern and organization of theological study.

The theological disciplines are analyzed and surveyed in such classic works on "encyclopedia" as J. F. Räbiger, *Encyclopaedia of Theology*, 2 vols., trans. J. Macpherson (Edinburgh: T & T Clark, 1884–1885), a work valuable for its critical analysis of other "encyclopedias" of its day; Philip Schaff, *Theological Propaedeutic: A General Introduction to the Study of Theology, Exegetical, Historical, Systematic, and Practical* (New York: Scribner, 1894), a classic study, still valuable for its survey of the fields and their relationships (as with many of the nineteenth-century efforts, its greatest weakness is on the "practical" side); George R. Crooks and John F. Hurst, *Theological Encyclopaedia and Methodology, on the basis of Hagenbach*, new ed., rev. (New York: Hunt & Eaton, 1894), perhaps the best of the nineteenth-century encyclopedias; Alfred Cave, *An Introduction to Theology: Its Principles, Its Branches, Its Results and Its Literature* (Edinburgh: T. & T. Clark, 1886); Gerald Birney Smith, ed., *A Guide to the Study of the Christian Religion* (Chicago: University of Chicago Press, 1916), a classic "liberal" introduction to the theological encyclopedia from the point of view of the study of religion, written by some of the outstanding scholars of its time; Kenneth E. Kirk, *The Study of Theology* (London: Hodder & Stoughton, 1939), and Daniel T. Jenkins, ed., *The Scope of Theology* (Cleveland and New York: World, 1965), multi-authored works that offer sound essays on most of the fields of theology; and Gerhard Ebeling, *The Study of Theology*, trans. Duane Priebe (Philadelphia: Fortress, 1978), the best modern survey of the various fields.

The seminal contemporary studies of theology, its various disciplines and the problem of the unity of theological study are Edward Farley, *Theologia: The Fragmentation and Unity of Theological Education* (Philadelphia: Fortress, 1983) and Wolfhart Pannenberg, *Theology and the Philosophy of Science*, trans. Francis McDonagh (Philadelphia: Westminster, 1976), both discussed at length in the appendix to chapter 1, above. A useful introduction to Pannenberg's theology is his *Basic Questions in Theology: Collected Essays*, trans. George H. Kehm, 2 vols. (Philadelphia: Fortress, 1970–1971; repr. Philadelphia: Westminster, 1983).

The histories of the various theological disciplines and of the ideas of theology and its encyclopedia are discussed, in addition to the presentations in Crooks and Hurst, *Encyclopedia*, and Schaff, *Theological Propaedeutic*, in Charles Augustus Briggs, *History of the Study of Theology*, 2 vols. (London: Duckworth, 1916); Yves M.-J. Congar, *A History of Theology*, trans. Hunter Guthrie (Garden City: Doubleday, 1968), a valuable survey of the history of the idea of theology, especially useful as a survey of the meaning and implications of "theology" in the patristic and medieval periods; John H. Hayes and Frederick Prussner, *Old Testament Theology: Its History and Development* (Atlanta: John Knox, 1985), and Werner Georg Kümmel, *The New Testament: The History of the Investigation of Its Problems*, trans. S. McLean Gilmour and Howard C. Kee (Nashville and New York: Abingdon, 1972), highly useful studies of the character and development of biblical theology; Louis Berkhof, *Introduction to Systematic Theology* (Grand Rapids: Eerdmans, 1932; repr. Baker, 1979), and Revere Franklin Weidner, *Introduction to Dogmatic Theology. Based on Luthardt* (Rock Island, Ill.: Augustana Book Concern, 1888), surveys of the history and method of theology, serving as prolegomena to dogmatics. Noteworthy among the histories of the practical disciplines are Edwin Charles Dargan, *A History of Preaching*, vol. 1, *From the Apostolic Fathers to the Great Reformers*, A.D. *70–1572*; vol. 2, *From the Close of the Reformation to the End of the Nineteenth Century, 1572–1900*, 2 vols. in one (repr. Grand Rapids: Baker, 1954); Bernard Cooke, *Ministry to Word and Sacraments: History and Theology* (Philadelphia: Fortress, 1976); William A. Clebsch and Charles B. Jaekle, *Pastoral Care in Historical Perspective* (New York: Harper & Row, 1967); and John T. McNeill, *A History of the Cure of Souls* (New York: Harper & Brothers, 1951).

In addition to the above noted studies, various issues and aspects of theological method are discussed in Abraham Kuyper, *Principles of Sacred Theology*, trans. De Vries, with an intro. by Benjamin B. Warfield (Grand Rapids: Baker, 1980), a classic Reformed study of the meaning of theology and the method of dogmatics; Paul Avis, *The Methods of Modern Theology* (Basingstoke: Marshall Pickering, 1986) a work containing useful discussions of Schleiermacher, Barth, Tillich, and other "makers of modern theology"; Carl E. Braaten, *History and Hermeneutics* (Philadelphia: Westminster, 1966); Van A. Harvey, *The Historian and the Believer* (New York: Macmillan, 1969), a good introduction to the problems of historical method used in the context of exegesis and belief; Edwin A. Burtt, "The Problem of Theological Method," in *The Journal of Religion*, 27/1 (January 1947), pp. 1–15, a companion essay to Tillich, "The Problem of Theological Method," in ibid., pp. 16–26, which includes a penetrating discussion of Tillich's differences with neoorthodoxy.

Among the more recent discussions of the theological task are George A. Lindbeck, *The Nature of Doctrine: Religion and Theology in a Postliberal Age* (Philadelphia: Westminster, 1984), an important modern study emphasizing the function of doctrinal statements and their necessary cultural relatedness; Robin Gill, *Theology and Social Structure* (London: Mowbrays, 1977); Charles A. M. Hall, *The Common Quest: Theology and the Search for Truth* (Philadelphia: Westminster, 1965); Walter Kasper, *The Methods of Dogmatic Theology* (New York: Paulist Press, 1969); F. G. Healey, ed., *What Theologians Do* (Grand Rapids: Eerdmans, 1971); René Latourelle and Gerald O'Collins, eds., *Problems and Perspectives of Fundamental Theology*, trans. Matthew J. O'Connell (New York: Paulist Press, 1982), a significant Roman Catholic work that deals both with the contemporary emphasis on Christology as a fundamental issue and with the foundational character of hermeneutics.

Index of Biblical Passages

Index of Modern Authors and Titles

(Full bibliographical information may be found in the first reference to individual works. Most of the page references are to the footnotes. For authors prior to the nineteenth century, see the subject index.)

Index of Subjects

English, 218–19, 220–21, 225, 231, 233, 238, 241, 244–45, 246, 247, 249, 253, 255–57, 258, 259–61, 265
Enlightenment, the, 34, 47, 83, 341, 345–46, 351, 357, 410, 442, 451, 471, 473, 510, 526, 553, 563, 575, 597, 641
epiousios (Gk.), 229
Epistemology, 447–49, 476, 504, 531; building an, 447–49, 450, 531
Erasmus, Desiderius, 64–66
erotaō (Gk.), 249
Errors, textual, 271–72
Eschatology, 33, 77–80
Essenes, 583
Ethics, 82, 558, 570, 610, 621–26
Ethiopic, 231
Etic/emic approaches, 127, 128
Etiology, 209
Etymology, 245–46, 249
eucharistoō (Gk.), 237
Eusebius of Caesarea, 57, 80a, 595–96
euthys (Gk.), 265
Evangelical(s), 18–19, 22, 26–27, 446, 463, 467–68, 469, 478, 504, 507, 508, 510, 517, 520, 529, 530, 531
Eve, 207, 208, 209, 210, 212, 656
Event and interpretation, 343–45, 348–49, 376, 401–2
Evidence: external, 398, 400–404, 407, 423; internal, 296, 398–400, 407; material, 400–401. *See also* Testimony; Archaeology
Evolution, 444, 445–46, 473, 507, 509
Exegesis, 220, 540, 541, 568, 570, 575–76, 579, 582, 587, 593, 597, 603, 613, 625, 641, 646, 651; grammatico-historical, 35, 59, 60; historical development, 33–34, 47–50; relation to theology, 29–30; priority of, 76, 78, 82
Exemplar, 457, 458, 459–60, 464, 474, 477–78, 486, 497, 502, 503, 508, 511
Exodus, book of, 18, 77
Experience, 438–39, 440–41, 442, 447–48, 472–73, 476, 478, 481

Fable, Jotham's, 313, 397
Fact and interpretation, 644
Facts: bare, 329, 345; concept of, 325
"Fallacy of referentiality," 323
Family, 514–15, 526
Feminism, 119
Feuerbach, Ludwig, 643
Fiction(al), 321–22, 353–54, 395, 425; its role in history-writing, 319–37 *passim*; senses of the word, 321–22; what it can accomplish, 298
Figurative/literal, 38, 52–53, 57–61, 62–63; definition, 45; prophecy, 79. *See also* Origen
First Clement, 601
Flacius Illyricus, Matthias, 25, 596
Flood, the, 210, 212
Folktale, 116

Form criticism, 70, 105, 109, 110, 141, 183, 311, 312
Formal correspondence, 274–76
Formalism, 377, 381
Fourfold curriculum, 541–42, 550–51, 555, 556, 563, 572, 592, 593, 632, 636–37, 651
Framework. *See* Disciplinary matrix
Franklin, Benamin, 459–60
Freedom, personal, 38, 74
French, 230
Freudianism, 464, 500
Function of biblical literature: aesthetic, 138, apologetic, 166; didactic, 138, 159, 166; doxological, 138; entertainment, 139; historical, 137, 138; history, 159, 166; theological, 138, 166
Fundamentalism, 473
Fundamental theology, 551
"Fusion of horizons," 652

Gabler, Johann Philip, 556, 578, 587–88
Galileo, 663
Gapping, literary device, 418–20
gar (Gk.), 269
General semantics, 210
Generative grammar, 228
Genitive case, 254, 255–58
Genre(s), 98, 105, 127, 137, 141, 142, 143, 144, 159, 165–66, 299–318 *passim*, 321; analysis: generalizing tendency, 145; categories, 304, 310, 313, 318; commonality of, 304–5, 310; decision, 296, 297, 301; definitions of, 306–7; diversity of in Bible, 301, 304, 318, 425; identification, 98, 141, 143, 646; labels, 310; levels of, 295, 307; macro-genre of the Bible, 290, 300–301, 306, 340; recognition of, 295–97, 301, 306–8, 318; restrictions on in Bible, 310; signals, 308
Genre criticism, 306–15; descriptive, not prescriptive, 309; simplicity criterion, 310
Gerhard, Johann, 616
German(ic), 230
Gestalt psychology, 478
Gibbon, Edward, 345
Gnosticism, 577–78, 583, 584, 592, 602, 656
God, 552, 554–55, 558, 559, 560, 566–67, 578, 579, 595, 613–14, 615–16, 617–18, 625–26, 641
Gospel of Thomas, 602
Gottwald's theory, 383
Grace, 210, 217
Grammatical-historical criticism, 649
Grammatical-historical interpretation. *See* Exegesis: grammatical-historical; Interpretation: grammatical-historical
Greek. *See* relevant grammatical topics
Gregory the Great, 53, 638

hamartia (Gk.), 246

Hamito-Semitic, 230
Hammurabi, Code of, 651
Harmonization, 59
Hebrew. *See* relevant grammatical topics.
Hegel, George W. F., 347, 348
Hermeneutical circle, 29, 84, 556, 645–53
Hermeneutics, 381, 388–408 *passim*, 426, 556–57, 563, 587, 603, 613, 632, 636, 641, 645–53, 654, 659–60; general, 20. *See also* Interpretation
"Hermeneutics of destruction," 563
Herodotus, 374
Hexapla, 40
Hilary of Poitiers, 552, 658
Hillel, 35
Hinduism, 634
Historical artifice, 130, 131
Historical criticism, 311, 315, 383, 387. *See also* Historical-critical method
Historical method, 303. *See also* Critical method; Exegesis: grammatico-historical
Historical research, 350–51; canons of, 360; law court analogy, 303, 400–401, 403–4, 407–8
Historical theology. *See* History of Christian doctrine
Historical-critical method, 108, 351, 360–67, 441–42, 451, 465–68, 470, 472, 473, 475, 493, 502, 504, 506–08, 509, 512, 523, 524; definition, 360–61
Historical-grammatical approach, 110. *See also* Exegesis: grammatico-historical
Historicity / historical perspective, 552, 567–68, 573–78, 585–86, 606–7, 613–16
Historicity: importance of for Christianity, 289, 358–87 *passim*, 341–45, 347–48, 351, 355–57, 425–26; of Acts, 314, 341; of the books of Kings, 396–97; of the Gospels, 313, 346–48, 351–55; purported irrelevance of, 338–40, 341–45, 347–49, 357; criteria for determining. *See* Criteria for determining historicity
Historiography, 295, 297, 307, 309, 310, 312, 313, 314, 322, 323, 329, 423, 442, 451–52, 461. *See also* History
History, 23, 25–27, 38, 85–86, 225, 441–42, 451–52, 461, 470, 503, 506, 525; and fiction, 319–37 *passim*; and interpretation, 329; as account, 320–21; as past events, 320–21; definition of, 290, 319–20; importance of, 289, 388–408 *passim*; 341–45; senses of the word, 320–21. *See also* Bible, as history; Dehistoricizing; Redemptive history; Universal history

Metaphor, 44, 121, 122, 175, 180, 251
Meter, 176–178, 180
Methods and models, 359, 366–67, 390, 393. *See also* Worldview
Middle Ages / medieval, 34, 55, 62, 562, 568, 596, 610, 614, 638, 656; study of literal meaning during, 35–37, 48–49, 51–52
Midrash, 77
Midrash Tehillim, 205
Mighty acts of God, 348, 350, 365
milah (Heb.), 250
Millennium, 511
Mimesis, 378
Minimalist method, 366–67
Ministry, 539–40, 543, 550, 553, 564, 626–30
Miracles/miraculous, 307, 343, 352, 354, 361, 362, 364–66, 391, 442, 444, 446, 471, 504; parallels in, 397. *See also* Supernaturalism
Mishnah, 583
Model, 485–91, 492, 498, 499–502, 513, 531
Model of reality. *See* Worldview
Modernism, 329–30
Money, 518–20
Monotheism, 656–57
Morpheme, 243, 244
Morphology, 239–40, 244, 254
Moses, 214
Mosheim, Johann Lorenz von, 557, 563
Music, 226
Mycene, 236
Myth, 321, 338, 347, 353–54

Nacherleben, 85
Narrative, 100, 123, 137, 140, 141; Hebrew, 312
Narrative criticism, 376–77, 399. *See also* Poetics
Narrative form, 329; structure of reality or authorial construct? 326
Narrator, 160, 162, 163, 167; and narratee, 146–47; omniscience, 147
nasa' (Heb.), 236
nasa' panim (Heb.), 238
Natural / supernatural, 633–35
Natural theology, 558
Naturalism, 71, 86, 446, 451, 476, 509, 510
"Nature" language, 585
Neander, August, 595
Neoorthodoxy, 558, 569, 570, 621, 634
Neutralization, 249
"New Adam," 655–56
New Criticism, 107, 111, 112, 136, 377, 378; denial of author, 111; primary tenet, 111; text as artifact, 111
New Testament, 553, 555, 562, 568, 573, 577, 578, 579, 588–93, 597–98, 601–2, 605, 607, 613–15, 631, 639, 641, 652–53, 655
Newton, Sir Isaac, 345, 445, 448, 451, 454–56, 457, 466, 475, 485; *Principia,* 457

Nicea / Nicene theology, 552, 594–95, 603
Noise, 227, 271–72
Nomothetic (focus on general and typical), 367–71, 372–73, 374
Northwest Semitic, 231
Numbers, book of, 313

Objectivity, 437, 441–42, 452, 465, 470, 483
Objectivity and subjectivity in theology, 543, 555, 557, 584, 642–44, 658
oikias (Gk.), 236
Old Testament, 34, 77–79, 553, 555, 562, 568, 573, 577, 578–82, 583, 586, 588–91, 593, 601, 607, 613, 622–23, 631, 639, 641, 652, 656
Omission, 154
Opposition, 221
Oral Law, 77
Origen, 33, 36, 45–47, 64, 65; criteria for allegory, 57–61; divine inspiration, 39–40; literal interpretation, 48, 50–51; significance of, 37–38; unity of Scripture, 71–72; usefulness of Scripture, 54
Orthodoxy, Protestant. *See* Protestant orthodoxy
Osiander, Andreas, 632
oun (Gk.), 265
Overinterpretation, 200, 262

Paideia, 553, 555, 557
Painting, 322–25
Pantheist, 479
Papyri, 70, 235, 238
Parables, 38, 59, 206, 308, 340–41, 343, 347, 397, 490; rich man and Lazarus, 308
Paradigm, 18–19, 457, 477–78
Paradigmatic analysis, 113, 116, 247
Paradigm shift in biblical studies, 99
Paragraph, 264–66, 268–69
Parallelism, 97, 105, 127, 170–72, 181–89
Parole. See langue.
Participle, 265
paschō (Gk.), 250
Past, unrepeatable, 329, 424
Pastoral counseling, 628–30
Pastoral Epistles, 597
Patriarchal narratives, 342–44
Patristic interpretation, 103
Patristic theology, 577, 583, 594–96, 601–2, 639, 653, 656–57
Patterning, 353
Paul / Pauline theology, 598, 658
Peasant revolt theory, 383
Pelagius, 438, 441
Pentecost, 217, 482
Performance. *See* Competence
peritomē (Gk.), 250
"Person" language, 585
Perspectives, 493, 497, 499, 512, 515–16, 517, 518, 521, 522, 523–24, 526, 531. *See also* Analogy
Perspicuity. *See* Bible, clarity
Pesher/pishro, 77

Peter Lombard, 616, 632, 658
Peter the Chanter, 47, 49
Pharisees, 77, 583
Philo, 33, 36, 54, 58, 60, 605
Philosophy, 20–21, 59, 71, 83–84, 225, 438, 441–42, 446 ,447–49, 455, 456–59, 465, 470, 476, 506, 509, 562, 605
Philosophy of religion, 569, 610, 617–21
Philosophy of science. *See* Science: philosophy of
Phoneme, 222, 241, 242, 243, 247
Phonetics, 226
Phonocentrism, 121
Phonology, 221, 232, 236, 239–42, 247
Phrynichus, 237
Piety, 548, 550, 563, 568, 643, 661–62. *See also* Spirituality
Pindar, 46
Plato, 121, 223, 267, 543, 651
Plot, 150, 152, 157, 159, 164–65
Poetic devices, 104, 127
Poetics, 313–17, 399, 426; definition, 313–14
Poetry, 102, 103, 127, 140, 251; character of, 316–17, 353; definition, 169; Hebrew, 314
Point of view, 147–48, 167
Polyglot, 202
Polytheism, 656–57
Portraiture, 293–94, 296–97, 329, 349–50, 424, 425
Positivism, 449, 452, 486
Posthistory, 328
Power, God's, 205, 213, 215
Practice. *See* Praxis
Praxis / practice, 543, 554, 557, 559, 572, 621, 626–30, 631, 652, 663–64
Pre-critical appraoch, 351
Preaching, 55–56
Predestination, 69, 612
Predicate, 252
Prehistory, 229, 232, 233, 234, 236
Preparadigm. *See* Science: immature
Prepositions, 256
Presuppositions/preunderstanding, 20–21, 31, 38, 75, 86, 88, 374, 390; Schleiermacher on, 84–85; theological, 28–30. *See also* Commitments, basic; Worldview
Principal subject, 498–98
Principia, 553–55
Principle: of analogy, 442; of causality, 442; of criticism, 442
Probability, 272
Prophecy, 51–52, 58, 78–80
Prophetic contest story, 159–60
Prophets as historians, 350
prosōpon lambanein (Gk.), 238
Prose, 102, 141, 169, 170
proseuchē (Gk.), 249
Protestant orthodoxy / scholasticism, 34, 35, 549, 554–55, 557, 568, 569, 598, 638
Protestantism, 540, 547, 555, 568, 577, 590, 596
Providence, 330, 349, 366

diction), 352, 403; negative criterion (philosophical), 351, 397, 403; positive criterion (form), 353–54; positive criterion (substance), 354

Structuralism, 23, 112, 114, 377; and biblical studies, 117; and prose, 115; and parable of the Good Samaritan, 117, 118

Structure, 220–21, 224, 227, 246–49. *See also* Narrative form

Style, 153–56, 222

Subject, subsidiary, 485, 498

Supernaturalism: anti-, 348, 361, 396, 403, 410. *See also* Divine intervention

Surangama Sutra, 659–60

Synchronic analysis, 109, 110, 141

Synchronic vs. diachronic reading, 311, 315, 352–53, 399–400

Synchrony, 218–20, 229, 243, 245, 248, 249

Synoptic Gospels, 584–85, 592

Synoptic histories of the Old Testament, 330–37

Syntagmatic analysis, 113, 247

Syntax, 231, 239–40, 253–54, 258

Talmud, 35, 273, 583

Technology, 443, 445, 446

Tendenz 110

Tense, 232, 235, 259,–63

Terseness, 170

Tertullian, 33, 36, 658

Testimony/witness, 329, 350, 355–56; external consistency of, 398–99, 400–404, 407, 426; internal consistency of, 398–400, 404, 407, 426; listening to, 393–98. *See also* Evidence

Testing the text, 398–401, 403–4, 426

Text, 136; as artifact, 111

Text linguistics, 264

thalassa (Gk.), 236

Theism, 484

Theodore of Mopsuestia, 33–34, 48, 52, 58, 79

Theodoret of Cyrrhus, 45, 48, 52, 73

Theological curriculum, 548, 549–50. *See also* Fourfold curriculum

Theological encyclopedia, 28–29, 548, 550–51, 553, 563–65, 567, 572, 587–88, 609, 616, 621, 636–37, 640

Theological knowing, 566–67

Theological norm. *See Principia*

Theology, 28–31, 39, 437, 440–04, 444, 446, 452–53, 462–68, 475, 477–81, 483, 492, 495, 499–500, 501, 503, 507, 508, 510, 511–12, 513, 515, 517, 518, 519, 522, 526, 530–31; biblical, 448, 496, 497, 517; covenant, 489, 513–15, 516, 526; history-centered, 347

Theology, biblical, 562, 563, 568, 578, 586–93, 595, 613–14, 618, 629, 631, 662

Theology, doctrinal, 550, 562, 609–17, 622

Theology, dogmatic, 586, 587–88, 609–10, 611–17. *See also* Theology, doctrinal

Theology, historical. *See* History of Christian doctrine

Theology, philosophical, 347, 539, 617–19

Theology, practical / ministerial, 550–51, 559, 568, 608–9, 626–30, 631, 646, 652, 662. *See also* Ministry

Theology, systematic, 539, 548, 549, 550, 563, 567, 571, 586, 589, 593, 595, 608–10, 629, 631, 632, 646, 652, 655. *See also* Theology, doctrinal

Theology as a "science," 559, 560, 562, 566–67, 569, 640–44

Theoretical relativity, 122, 124

Theoria / theory, 58, 78, 79–80, 554, 556, 559, 572, 627, 629–30, 652, 662

Theories, use of specific, 444–45, 447–49, 450

Thirlwall, Connop, 351

Thomasius, Gottfried, 617

Thomism, 475. *See also* Aquinas, Thomas

Thought, 208

Total interpretation, 111

tote (Gk.), 265

Tradition, 72–74, 558, 594

Traditional criticism, 99, 110; difference from literary theory, 109

Traditional literary criticism, 107

Traducianism, 489, 492

Transcendental signified, 121, 122

Transformational grammar, 226, 228, 239, 257

Translation, 201, 273–76

Transmission, textual, 270–73, 276

Trinitarianism, 511–12

Trinity, 540, 575, 579, 595, 612, 615–16, 617, 624, 628, 653

Truth, 31, 297–98, 340–41; coherence theory of, 401–3; establishment of, 298; illustration of, 298, 347; veiling of, 53, 68–69. *See also* Truth claim; Truth value

Truth claim, 297–98, 300–301, 312, 321, 339–40, 342–43, 387, 389, 393–99, 400, 403, 407, 422–24, 426

Truth value, 297, 300–301, 340, 356, 389, 393–94, 398–404, 407, 422–23

Tübingen school, 348

Turkish, 224, 243

Turretin, Francis, 52, 616, 632, 642

Typology, 44, 55, 58

Ugaritic, 231, 233

Uncertainty, 227

Unigenitus, 62

Universal History, 330

"University model," 542

Vagueness, 258

Verbs, 231, 232, 235, 236, 237

Victorinus, 552

Vorstius, Conrad, 632

Vowels, 231, 232, 237

Walch, Johann Georg, 557

wayhi (Heb.), 265

Wesley, John, 658

Westminster Confession of Faith, 67, 69, 71

Witness. *See* Testimony

Word, God's, 205, 212–16

World Council of Churches, 42–43

Worldview/background beliefs, 309, 341, 351, 355, 358–59, 365–67, 374, 389, 390–93, 398, 407, 423–24, 425, 445–46, 449–51, 472, 473, 476–77, 502, 506, 509, 525, 528, 529, 530, 531; building a, 445–46, 449–51, 531

Worship, 550, 594, 626, 628

zahab (Heb.), 231

Zeitgeist, 391

zygon (Gk.), 237